THE PILLAR NEW TESTAMENT COMMENTARY

General Editor

D. A. CARSON

# *The First Letter to the* CORINTHIANS

Roy E. Ciampa
*and*
Brian S. Rosner

William B. Eerdmans Publishing Company
Grand Rapids, Michigan

APOLLOS
NOTTINGHAM, ENGLAND

Wm. B. Eerdmans Publishing Co.
4035 Park East Court SE, Grand Rapids, Michigan 49546
www.eerdmans.com


Published 2010
Printed in the United States of America

and in the United Kingdom by
APOLLOS
Norton Street, Nottingham,
England NG7 3HR

27 26 25 7 8 9 10 11

**Library of Congress Cataloging-in-Publication Data**

Ciampa, Roy E., 1958-
The first letter to the Corinthians / Roy E. Ciampa and Brian S. Rosner.

p. cm. — (The Pillar New Testament commentary)
Includes bibliographical references.
ISBN 978-0-8028-3732-5 (cloth: alk. paper)
1. Bible. N.T. Corinthians — Commentaries.
I. Rosner, Brian S. II. Title.

BS2675.53.C53 2010
227′.207 — dc22

2010034444

**British Library Cataloguing in Publication Data**

A catalogue record for this book is available from the British Library.
Apollos ISBN 978-1-84474-484-8

# *Contents*

## COMMENTARY ON 1 CORINTHIANS

## INDEXES

# *Editor's Preface*

Commentaries have specific aims, and this series is no exception. Designed for serious pastors and teachers of the Bible, the Pillar commentaries seek above all to make clear the text of Scripture as we have it. The scholars writing these volumes interact with the most important informed contemporary debate, but avoid getting mired in undue technical detail. Their ideal is a blend of rigorous exegesis and exposition, with an eye alert both to biblical theology and the contemporary relevance of the Bible, without confusing the commentary and the sermon.

The rationale for this approach is that the vision of "objective scholarship" (a vain chimera) may actually be profane. God stands over against us; we do not stand in judgment of him. When God speaks to us through his Word, those who profess to know him must respond in an appropriate way, and that is certainly different from a stance in which the scholar projects an image of autonomous distance. Yet this is no surreptitious appeal for uncontrolled subjectivity. The writers of this series aim for an even-handed openness to the text that is the best kind of "objectivity" of all.

If the text is God's Word, it is appropriate that we respond with reverence, a certain fear, a holy joy, a questing obedience. These values should be reflected in the way Christians write. With these values in place, the Pillar commentaries will be warmly welcomed not only by pastors, teachers, and students, but by general readers as well.

* * *

First Corinthians touches on an astonishingly wide swath of important and sensitive topics. Few if any New Testament documents directly address so many issues, theological and pastoral, that have urgent resonances in twenty-first-century church life. The claims of unity and truth, the challenges of a party spirit, speaking in tongues, the doctrine of the resurrection, church discipline, sexual matters, marriage and divorce, "strong" and "weak" consciences, the Lord's Supper, the relationships between men and women, the nature of love, the call to preach the gospel powerfully without manipulation, the nature of Christian leadership lived under the cross—they are all here. Roy Ciampa and Brian Rosner have been thinking their way through these chapters for many years. Their work is careful, sometimes innovative, always eager to listen carefully to the text, and written with the clarity that readers long for. They pay enough attention to the historical context to root this letter in first-century Corinth, yet they are careful not to domesticate the text by appealing to arbitrarily chosen "parallels." At the same time they include brief but penetrating theological reflection that reminds readers that Scripture still speaks with authority today. Those with the responsibility to preach and teach 1 Corinthians will be grateful for this commentary for a long time, while more advanced students of the New Testament will learn some new things and be challenged to think through this epistle with fresh eyes. It is a pleasure to commend this work.

D. A. Carson

# Authors' Preface

Co-authorship, if not common, is not unheard of in commentary writing. We can't speak for anyone else who has done it, but in our case it has been a great blessing from start to finish. With a friendship that goes back seventeen years, to the University of Aberdeen, we shared a simultaneous study leave in 2004 to begin writing in earnest. It took several years to complete, with a couple of dry runs along the way (see bibliography for two other co-authored works). We can only hope readers feel as enriched by their study of 1 Corinthians by reading the commentary as we feel having written it.

Ironically, multiple authorship has resulted in a more unified view of the letter. Often regarded as Paul's makeshift response to random problems in the Corinthian church, we believe that a more coherent reading of the letter emerges by taking full account of its Old Testament and Jewish roots, along with paying careful attention to the Corinthian historical context.

The task was not undertaken in shared isolation. We are, to use a Pauline phrase, overflowing with thanksgiving for those who have lent a hand. The following deserve our thanks: student research assistants Lionel Windsor, Anthony Douglas, Nijay Gupta, Mark Jennings, Randy Lee, Matthew Ogden, Haley Goranson; Cameron Moran, who compiled the indexes; PNTC General Editor Don Carson; Gordon Conwell Theological Seminary and Moore Theological College; our respective churches, Grace Chapel in Lexington, Massachusetts, and Macquarie Anglican Churches in Sydney; various Eerdmans staff, especially Milt Essenburg; our beloved children, Tim and Christina; Elizabeth, and her husband Phil, Emily, William and Toby. We dedicate this book with heartfelt thanks to our much-loved wives, Marcelle and Natalie.

Our prayer is that God's name will be great among the nations, from where the sun rises to where it sets, and that in every place incense and pure offerings will be brought to him.

Roy E. Ciampa *and* Brian S. Rosner

# *Chief Abbreviations*

## I. MODERN WORKS

| | |
|---|---|
| *ABD* | D. N. Freedman (ed.), *Anchor Bible Dictionary* |
| *ABR* | *Australian Biblical Review* |
| AGJU | Arbeiten zur Geschichte des antiken Judentums und des Urchristentums |
| AnBib | Analecta Biblica |
| ANF | Ante-Nicene Fathers |
| ATANT | Abhandlungen zur Theologie des Alten und Neuen Testaments |
| AV | Authorized Version (= KJV) |
| *BA* | *Biblical Archaeologist* |
| BAGD | W. Bauer, W. F. Arndt, F. W. Gingrich, and F. W. Danker, *Greek-English Lexicon of the New Testament* (2d ed.) |
| *BAR* | *Biblical Archaeology Review* |
| *BBR* | *Bulletin for Biblical Research* |
| BDAG | W. Bauer, F. W. Danker, W. F. Arndt, and F. W. Gingrich, *Greek-English Lexicon of the New Testament and Other Early Christian Literature* (3d ed.) |
| BDF | F. Blass, A. Debrunner, and R. W. Funk, *A Greek Grammar of the New Testament and Other Early Christian Literature* |
| BECNT | Baker Exegetical Commentary on the New Testament |
| *BETL* | *Bibliotheca ephemeridum theologicarum lovaniensium* |
| *BGU* | *Aegyptische Urkunden aus den Königlichen Staatlichen Museen zu Berlin, Griechische Urkunden* |
| BHT | Beiträge zur historischen Theologie |
| *Bib* | *Biblica* |
| BiPa | Biblia Patristica: Index des citations et allusions bibliques dans la littérature. Paris, 1975 |
| *BJRL* | *Bulletin of the John Rylands University Library of Manchester* |
| *BSac* | *Bibliotheca Sacra* |
| *BTB* | *Biblical Theology Bulletin* |
| *BZNW* | *Beihefte zur Zeitschrift für die neutestamentliche Wissenschaft* |

| | |
|---|---|
| *CBQ* | *Catholic Biblical Quarterly* |
| *CD* | Karl Barth, *Church Dogmatics* |
| *CIG* | A. Boeckh (ed.), *Corpus Inscriptionum Graecarum* |
| CRINT | Compendia Rerum Iudaicarum ad Novum Testamentum |
| CSB | Holman Christian Standard Bible |
| *CTR* | *Criswell Theological Review* |
| *DGE* | Francisco Rodríguez Adrados and Elvira Gangutia Elícegui (eds.), *Diccionario Griego-Español* |
| *DJD* | *Discoveries in the Judaean Desert* |
| *DNTB* | Craig A. Evans and Stanley E. Porter, *Dictionary of New Testament Background* |
| *DPL* | G. F. Hawthorne, R. P. Martin, and D. G. Reid (eds.), *Dictionary of Paul and His Letters* |
| *EDNT* | H. Balz and G. Schneider (eds.), *Exegetical Dictionary of the New Testament* |
| ERV | English Revised Version |
| ESV | English Standard Version |
| *ETR* | *Etudes théologiques et religieuses* |
| *EvQ* | *Evangelical Quarterly* |
| *ExpTim* | *Expository Times* |
| Gk. | Greek |
| *HALOT* | L. Koehler, W. Baumgartner, and J. J. Stamm, *The Hebrew and Aramaic Lexicon of the Old Testament* |
| *HAR* | *Hebrew Annual Review* |
| *HBT* | *Horizons in Biblical Theology* |
| *HTR* | *Harvard Theological Review* |
| *HUT* | *Hermeneutische Untersuchungen zur Theologie* |
| *IBS* | *Irish Biblical Studies* |
| *IDBSup* | K. Crim (ed.), *Interpreter's Dictionary of the Bible: Supplementary Volume* |
| *Int* | *Interpretation* |
| *JAAR* | *Journal of the American Academy of Religion* |
| *JAC* | *Jahrbuch für Antike und Christentum* |
| JB | Jerusalem Bible |
| *JBL* | *Journal of Biblical Literature* |
| *JCE* | *Journal of Christian Education* |
| *JETS* | *Journal of the Evangelical Theological Society* |
| *JOTT* | *Journal of Translation and Textlinguistics* |
| *JSNT* | *Journal for the Study of the New Testament* |
| JSNTSup | Journal for the Study of the New Testament: Supplement Series |
| JSPSup | Journal for the Study of the Pseudepigrapha: Supplement Series |
| *JTS* | *Journal of Theological Studies* |
| KJV | King James Version (= AV) |
| L&N | J. P. Louw and E. A. Nida (eds.), *Greek-English Lexicon of the New Testament: Based on Semantic Domains* (2d ed.) |
| LCL | Loeb Classical Library |

| | |
|---|---|
| LEH | J. Lust, Erik Eynikel, K. Hauspie, and G. Chamberlain, *A Greek-English Lexicon of the Septuagint* |
| LSJ | H. G. Liddell, R. Scott, with R. S. Jones, *Greek-English Lexicon* (9th ed.) |
| LXX | Septuagint |
| MM | J. H. Moulton and G. Milligan, *The Vocabulary of the Greek New Testament* |
| MS(S) | manuscript(s) |
| MT | Masoretic Text |
| NA[27] | Nestle-Aland Greek New Testament (27th ed.) |
| NAB | New American Bible |
| NAC | New American Commentary |
| NASB | New American Standard Bible |
| NCBC | New Century Bible Commentary |
| *NDBT* | T. Desmond and Brian S. Rosner (eds.), *New Dictionary of Biblical Theology.* |
| NEB | New English Bible |
| NET | New English Translation |
| *NETR* | *Near East School of Theology Theological Review* |
| *NewDocs* | G. H. R. Horsley and S. Llewelyn (eds.), *New Documents Illustrating Early Christianity* |
| NIBCOT | New International Biblical Commentary on the Old Testament |
| NICNT | New International Commentary on the New Testament |
| NICOT | New International Commentary on the Old Testament |
| *NIDNTT* | C. Brown (ed.), *New International Dictionary of New Testament Theology* |
| NIGTC | New International Greek Testament Commentary |
| NIV | New International Version |
| NJB | New Jerusalem Bible |
| NKJV | New King James Version |
| NLB | New Living Bible |
| NLT | New Living Translation |
| *NovT* | *Novum Testamentum* |
| NovTSup | Supplements to Novum Testamentum |
| NPNF[1] | Nicene and Post-Nicene Fathers, Series 1 |
| NPNF[2] | Nicene and Post-Nicene Fathers, Series 2 |
| NRSV | New Revised Standard Version |
| *NTAbh* | *Neutestamentliche Abhandlungen* |
| *NTS* | *New Testament Studies* |
| OBT | Overtures to Biblical Theology |
| *OCD* | S. Hornblower and A. Spawforth (eds.), *Oxford Classical Dictionary* (3d ed.) |
| OTL | Old Testament Library |
| *OTP* | J. H. Charlesworth (ed.), *Old Testament Pseudepigrapha* |
| PG | Patrologia Graeca |
| PL | Patrologia Latina |
| *RB* | *Revue biblique* |

| | |
|---|---|
| REB | Revised English Bible |
| *RevExp* | *Review and Expositor* |
| RSV | Revised Standard Version |
| RV | Revised Version |
| SBB | Stuttgarter Biblische Beiträge |
| SBLDS | Society of Biblical Literature Dissertation Series |
| SBLSymS | Society of Biblical Literature Symposium Series |
| *SEÅ* | *Svensk exegetisk årsbok* |
| *SJLA* | *Studies in Judaism in Late Antiquity* |
| *SJT* | *Scottish Journal of Theology* |
| SNTSMS | Society for New Testament Studies Monograph Series |
| *TAPA* | *Transactions of the American Philological Association* |
| *TCNT* | *Twentieth-Century New Testament* |
| *TDNT* | G. Kittel and G. Friedrich (eds.), *Theological Dictionary of the New Testament* |
| TEV | Today's English Version |
| *Them* | *Themelios* |
| *TLG* | L. Berkowitz and K. A. Squitier (eds.), *Thesaurus Linguae Graecae: Canon of Greek Authors and Works* (3d ed.) |
| *TLNT* | C. Spicq, *Theological Lexicon of the New Testament* |
| TNIV | Today's New International Version |
| TNTC | Tyndale New Testament Commentaries |
| *TrinJ* | *Trinity Journal* |
| *TWOT* | R. Laird Harris, Gleason L. Archer, and Bruce K. Waltke (eds.), *Theological Wordbook of the Old Testament* |
| *TynBul* | *Tyndale Bulletin* |
| UBS | United Bible Societies Greek New Testament (4th ed.) |
| *VT* | *Vetus Testamentum* |
| WBC | Word Biblical Commentary |
| *WTJ* | *Westminster Theological Journal* |
| WUNT | Wissenschaftliche Untersuchungen zum Neuen Testament |
| *ZNW* | *Zeitschrift für die neutestamentliche Wissenschaft und die Kunde der älteren Kirche* |
| ZTK | *Zeitschrift für Theologie und Kirche* |

## II. GENERAL ABBREVIATIONS

| | |
|---|---|
| A.D. | *anno Domini*, in the year of our Lord |
| B.C. | before Christ |
| cf. | *confer*, compare |
| ch(s). | chapter(s) |
| ed(s). | editor(s), edited by, edition |
| e.g. | *exempli gratia*, for example |
| esp. | especially |
| etc. | *et cetera*, and so forth |
| fr. | fragment |
| Gk. | Greek |
| Heb. | Hebrew |

| | |
|---|---|
| i.e. | *id est*, that is |
| MS (MSS) | manuscript(s) |
| n. | footnote |
| pt. | part |
| rpt. | reprint |
| sect. | section |
| trans. | translated by |
| v. (vv.) | verse(s) |
| viz. | *videlicet*, namely |
| vol. | volume |

# *Select Bibliography*

Throughout this work we have referred to commentaries on 1 Corinthians simply by author surname and page number.

## I. COMMENTARIES ON 1 CORINTHIANS

Allo, E. B., *Saint Paul: Première Épitre aux Corinthiens* (Paris: Gabalda, 1956).
Bachmann, P., *Der erste Brief des Paulus an die Korinther* (Leipzig: Deichertsche Verlagsbuchhandlung, 1936).
Barclay, W., *The Letters to the Corinthians* (Philadelphia: Westminster, 1975).
Barnett, P., *1 Corinthians* (Fearn, Ross-shire: Christian Focus, 2000).
Barrett, C. K., *A Commentary on the First Epistle to the Corinthians* (London: A & C Black, 1971).
Baumann, R., *Mitte und Norm des Christlichen: Eine Auslegung von 1 Korinther 1, 1-3, 4* (Münster: Aschendorff, 1968).
Blomberg, C., *1 Corinthians* (Grand Rapids: Zondervan, 1994).
Bray, G. (ed.), *1-2 Corinthians* (Downers Grove: InterVarsity Press, 1999).
Bruce, F. F., *1 and 2 Corinthians* (London: Marshall, Morgan and Scott, 1971).
Calvin, J. *The First Epistle of Paul the Apostle to the Corinthians,* trans. John W. Fraser (Grand Rapids: Eerdmans, 1996). Unless otherwise indicated, this is the translation of Calvin that we cite.
Collins, R. F., *First Corinthians* (Collegeville, MN: Liturgical Press, 1999).
Conzelmann, H., *1 Corinthians* (Philadelphia: Fortress, 1975).
Edwards, T. C., *A Commentary on the First Epistle to the Corinthians* (Minneapolis: Klock & Klock, 1979).
Ellicott, C. J., *St. Paul's First Epistle to the Corinthians: With a Critical and Grammatical Commentary* (London: Longmans, Green, 1887).
Ellingworth, P., and H. Hatton., *A Translator's Handbook on Paul's First Letter to the Corinthians* (London: United Bible Societies, 1985).
Fee, G. D., *The First Epistle to the Corinthians* (Grand Rapids: Eerdmans, 1987).

Findlay, G. G., "St Paul's First Epistle to the Corinthians," in *The Expositor's Greek Testament*, ed. W. R. Nicoll (Grand Rapids: Eerdmans, 1961), 2:727-953.

Garland, D. E., *1 Corinthians* (Grand Rapids: Baker, 2003).

Godet, F. L., *Commentary on St Paul's First Epistle to the Corinthians*, 2 vols. (Edinburgh: T&T Clark, 1886-87).

Grosheide, F. W., *Commentary on the First Epistle to the Corinthians* (Grand Rapids: Eerdmans, 1953).

Hays, R. B., *First Corinthians* (Louisville: John Knox, 1997).

Heinrici, C. F. G., *Das erste Sendschreiben des Apostel Paulus an die Korinther* (Berlin: Hertz, 1880); and/or 8th ed., *Der erste Brief an die Korinther* (Göttingen: Vandenhoeck & Ruprecht, 1896).

Héring, J., *The First Epistle of St Paul to the Corinthians* (London: Epworth, 1962).

Hodge, C., *An Exposition of the First Epistle to the Corinthians* (Grand Rapids: Eerdmans, 1976).

Horsley, R. A., *1 Corinthians* (Nashville: Abingdon, 1998).

Kistemaker, S., *Exposition of the First Epistle to the Corinthians* (Grand Rapids: Baker, 1993).

Lang, F., *Die Briefe an die Korinther* (Göttingen: Vandenhoeck & Ruprecht, 1986).

Lietzmann, H., *An die Korinther 1/2* (Tübingen: Mohr, 1949).

Lightfoot, J. B., *Notes on the Epistles of St. Paul* (Grand Rapids: Zondervan, 1957).

Lindemann, A., *Der Erste Korintherbrief* (Tübingen: Mohr Siebeck, 2000).

Lockwood, G. J., *1 Corinthians* (St. Louis: Concordia, 2000).

Mare, W. H., "1 Corinthians," in *The Expositor's Bible Commentary*, ed. F. E. Gaebelein (Grand Rapids: Zondervan, 1976), 173-297.

Merklein, H., *Der erste Brief an die Korinther Kapitel 1-4* (Gütersloh: Güterloher Verlaghaus, 1992).

Meyer, H. A. W., *Critical and Exegetical Handbook to the Epistles to the Corinthians* (Winona Lake: Alpha, 1979).

Moffatt, J., *The First Epistle of Paul to the Corinthians* (London: Hodder & Stoughton, 1938).

Morris, L., *The First Epistle of Paul to the Corinthians* (London: Tyndale, 1958).

Murphy-O'Connor, J., *1 Corinthians* (New York: Doubleday, 1998).

Orr, W. F., and J. A. Walther, *I Corinthians: A New Translation* (Garden City, NY: Doubleday, 1976).

Oster, R., *1 Corinthians* (Joplin: College Press, 1995).

Parry, R. S. J., *The First Epistle of Paul the Apostle to the Corinthians* (Cambridge: Cambridge University Press, 1937).

Prior, D., *The Message of 1 Corinthians: Life in the Local Church* (Leicester: InterVarsity Press, 1985).

Robertson, A., and A. Plummer, *A Critical and Exegetical Commentary on the First Epistle of St. Paul to the Corinthians* (Edinburgh: T&T Clark, 1911).

Ruef, J., *Paul's First Letter to Corinth* (Baltimore: Penguin, 1971).
Sampley, P., "1 Corinthians," in *The New Interpreter's Bible*, vol. 10 (Nashville: Abingdon, 2001), 771-1003.
Schrage, W., *Der erste Brief an die Korinther*, 4 vols. (Zurich: Benziger, 1991-2001).
Senft, C., *La Première Épitre de Saint Paul aux Corinthiens* (Geneva: Labor et Fides, 1990).
Snyder, G. F., *First Corinthians: A Faith Community Commentary* (Macon, GA: Mercer University Press, 1992).
Strobel, A., *Der erste Brief an die Korinther* (Zürich: Theologischer Verlag, 1989).
Talbert, C. H., *Reading Corinthians: A Literary and Theological Commentary on 1 and 2 Corinthians* (New York: Crossroads, 1987).
Theodoret of Cyrus. *Commentary on the Letters of St. Paul*, trans. Robert Charles Hill, vol. 1 (Brookline, MA: Holy Cross Orthodox Press, 2001).
Thiselton, A. C., *The First Epistle to the Corinthians: A Commentary on the Greek Text* (Grand Rapids: Eerdmans, 2000).
Thrall, M. E., *The First and Second Letters of Paul to the Corinthians* (Cambridge: Cambridge University Press, 1965).
Weiss, J., *Der erste Korintherbrief* (Göttingen: Vandenhoeck & Ruprecht, 1910).
Wilckens, U., *Weisheit und Torheit: Eine exegetisch-religionsgeschichtliche Untersuchung zu 1 Kor 1 und 2* (Tübingen: J. C. B. Mohr [Paul Siebeck], 1959).
Witherington, B., *Conflict and Community in Corinth: A Socio-Rhetorical Commentary on 1 and 2 Corinthians* (Grand Rapids: Eerdmans, 1995).
Wolff, C., *Der erste Brief des Paulus an die Korinther* (Leipzig: Evangelische Verlagsanstalt, 1996).

## II. OTHER WORKS

Aasgaard, R., "'Role Ethics' in Paul: The Significance of the Sibling Role for Paul's Ethical Thinking," *NTS* 48 (2002), 513-30.
Achelis, H., *Virgines subintroductae: Ein Beitrag zum VII. Kapitel des 1. Korintherbriefs* (Leipzig, 1902).
Alexander, L. A., "'Better to Marry than to Burn': St. Paul and the Greek Novel," in *Ancient Fiction and Early Christian Narrative*, ed. R. F. Hock et al. (Atlanta: Scholars Press, 1998), 235-56.
Alexander, T. D., and B. S. Rosner, eds., *New Dictionary of Biblical Theology* (Leicester: InterVarsity Press, 2000).
Allen, L. C., *Psalms 101–150*, vol. 21 (Nashville: Thomas Nelson, 2002).
Asher, J. R., *Polarity and Change in 1 Corinthians 15: A Study of Metaphysics, Rhetoric, and Resurrection* (Tübingen: Mohr, 2000).
Ashley, T. R., *The Book of Numbers* (Grand Rapids: Eerdmans, 1993).
Aune, D. E., *The New Testament in Its Literary Environment* (Philadelphia: Westminster, 1987).

———. *Prophecy in Early Christianity and the Ancient Mediterranean World* (Grand Rapids: Eerdmans, 1983).

Bailey, Kenneth E., "Paul's Theological Foundation for Human Sexuality: I Corinthians 6:9-20 in the Light of Rhetorical Criticism," *NETR* 3 (1980), 27-41.

Baker, D. L., "The Interpretation of 1 Corinthians 12–14," *EvQ* 46 (1974), 224-34.

Banks, R., *Paul's Idea of Community* (Peabody, MA: Hendrickson, 1994).

Barclay, J. M. G., "Mirror-Reading a Polemical Letter: Galatians as a Test Case," *JSNT* 31 (1987), 73-93.

———. J. M. G., "Paul, Philemon and the Dilemma of Christian Slave-Ownership," *NTS* 37 (1991), 161-86.

Barrett, C. K., *Essays on Paul* (London: SPCK, 1982).

Barrett, David B., George Thomas Kurian, and Todd M. Johnson, eds., *World Christian Encyclopedia: A Comparative Survey of Churches and Religions in the Modern World* (2d ed.; Oxford: Oxford University Press, 2001).

Barrett, David B., Todd M. Johnson, Christopher R. Guidry, and Peter F. Crossing, eds., *World Christian Trends,* AD *30*-AD *2200: Interpreting the Annual Christian Megacensus* (Pasadena, CA: William Carey Library, 2001).

Bartchy, S. S., *Μᾶλλον Χρῆσαι: First-Century Slavery and the Interpretation of 1 Corinthians 7:21* (Missoula, MT: Society of Biblical Literature, 1973).

Barth, K., *Dogmatics in Outline* (New York: Harper & Row, 1959).

———, *The Resurrection of the Dead* (London: Hodder and Stoughton, 1933).

Barth, M., and H. Blanke, *The Letter to Philemon: A New Translation with Notes and Commentary* (Grand Rapids: Eerdmans, 2000).

Barton, S. C., and G. H. R. Horsley, "A Hellenistic Cult Group and the New Testament Churches," *JAC* 24 (1981), 7-41.

Bauckham, R. J., *The Fate of the Dead: Studies on the Jewish and Christian Apocalypses* (Boston: Brill, 1998).

———, *Jude, 2 Peter* (Dallas: Word, 1983).

Baumert, N., *Ehelosigkeit und Ehe in Herrn: Eine Neuinterpretation von 1 Kor 7* (Wurzburg: Echter, 1984).

Beale, G. K., *The Temple and the Church's Mission: A Biblical Theology of the Dwelling Place of God* (Downers Grove, IL: InterVarsity Press, 2004).

———, and D. A. Carson, eds., *Commentary on the New Testament Use of the Old Testament* (Grand Rapids: Baker, 2007).

Bedale, S., "The Meaning of *Kephalē* in the Pauline Epistles," *JTS* 5 (1954), 211-15.

BeDuhn, J. D., "'Because of the Angels': Unveiling Paul's Anthropology in 1 Corinthians 11," *JBL* 118 (1999), 295-320.

Benko, S., "The Kiss," in his *Pagan Rome and the Early Christians* (Bloomington: Indiana University Press, 1984), 79-102.

Bennema, C., *The Power of Saving Wisdom: An Investigation of Spirit and Wisdom in Relation to the Soteriology of the Fourth Gospel* (Tübingen: Mohr Siebeck, 2002).

———, "The Strands of Wisdom Tradition in Intertestamental Judaism: Origins, Developments and Characteristics," *TynBul* 52 (2001), 61-82.

Berger, K., *Paulus* (Munich: Beck, 2002).

Best, E., "1 Corinthians 7:14 and Children in the Church," *IBS* 12 (1990), 158-66.

Betz, H. D., *Galatians: A Commentary on Paul's Letter to the Churches in Galatia* (Philadelphia: Fortress, 1979).

———, and M. Mitchell, "First Epistle to the Corinthians," in *ABD*, ed. D. N. Freedman, vol. 1 (New York: Doubleday, 1992), 1139-54.

Bilezekian, G., *Beyond Sex Roles* (Grand Rapids: Baker, 1985).

Bittlinger, A., *Gifts and Graces: A Commentary on 1 Corinthians 12–14* (London: Hodder & Stoughton, 1967).

Bjerkelund, C. J., *Parakalo: Form, Funktion und Sinn der parakalo-Sätze in den paulinischen Briefe* (Oslo: Universitetsforlaget, 1967).

Black, Matthew, "The Maranatha Invocation and Jude 14, 15 (1 Enoch 1:9)," in *Christ and Spirit in the New Testament: Studies in Honour of Charles Francis Digby Moule*, ed. B. Lindars and S. S. Smalley (Cambridge: Cambridge University Press, 1973), 189-98.

Blattenberger, D. E., *Rethinking 1 Corinthians 11:2-16 through Archaeological and Moral-Rhetorical Analysis* (Lewiston, NY: Mellen, 1997).

Blidstein, G. J., "Atimia: A Greek Parallel to Ezra X.8 and to Post-Biblical Exclusion from the Community," *VT* 24/3 (1974), 357-60.

Blomberg, C., "Degrees of Reward in the Kingdom of Heaven?" *JETS* 35 (1992), 159-72.

Blue, B. B., "The House Church at Corinth and the Lord's Supper: Famine, Food Supply and the Present Distress," *CTR* 5 (1991), 221-39.

Bockmuehl, M. N. A., *Revelation and Mystery in Ancient Judaism and Pauline Christianity* (Tübingen: J. C. B. Mohr [Paul Siebeck], 1990).

Bolt, P. G., "Life, Death and the Afterlife in the Greco-Roman World," in *Life in the Face of Death*, ed. R. N. Longenecker (Grand Rapids: Eerdmans, 1998), 51-79.

Bonhoeffer, D., *Letters and Papers from Prison* (London: SCM, 1953).

———, *Life Together* (Minneapolis: Fortress, 1996).

Bonneau, N., "The Logic of Paul's Argument on the Resurrection Body in 1 Corinthians 15:35-44a," *Science et esprit* 45 (1993), 79-92.

Borgen, P., *Early Christianity and Hellenistic Judaism* (Edinburgh: T&T Clark, 1998).

Boring, M. E., "Prophecy (Early Christian)," in *ABD*, ed. D. N. Freedman, vol. 5 (New York: Doubleday, 1992), 495-502.

———, "What Are We Looking For? Toward a Definition of the Term 'Christian Prophet,'" *SBL Seminar Papers* (Missoula, MT: Society of Biblical Literature, 1973), 135-54.

Bornkamm, G., *Early Christian Experience* (London: SCM, 1969).

Boswell, J., *Christianity, Social Tolerance, and Homosexuality: Gay People in West-*

*ern Europe from the Beginning of the Christian Era to the Fourteenth Century* (Chicago: University of Chicago Press, 1980).

Bradley, K. R., *Slaves and Masters in the Roman Empire: A Study in Social Control* (Oxford: Oxford University Press, 1987).

———, *Slavery and Society at Rome* (Cambridge: Cambridge University Press, 1994).

Branick, V. P., "Source and Redaction Analysis of 1 Corinthians 1–3," *JBL* 101 (1982), 251-69.

Braxton, B. R., *The Tyranny of Resolution: 1 Corinthians 7.17-24* (Atlanta: Society of Biblical Literature, 2000).

Broneer, O., "The Apostle Paul and the Isthmian Games," *BA* 25 (1962), 1-31.

Broyles, C. C., *Psalms* (Peabody, MA: Hendrickson, 1999).

Bruce, F. F., *Paul, Apostle of the Heart Set Free* (Grand Rapids: Eerdmans, 1977).

Brueggemann, W., *Theology of the Old Testament: Testimony, Dispute, Advocacy* (Minneapolis: Fortress, 2005).

Bultmann, R., *Primitive Christianity in Its Contemporary Setting* (Cleveland/New York: World/Meridian, 1956).

Burnett, R. E., *Karl Barth's Theological Exegesis: The Hermeneutical Principles of the Römerbrief Period* (Tübingen: Mohr Siebeck, 2001).

Buss, M. J., "The Distinction between Civil and Criminal Law in Ancient Israel," in *Proceedings of the Sixth World Congress of Jewish Studies*, ed. A. Shinan (Jerusalem: World Union of Jewish Studies, 1977), 51-62.

Byron, J., "Paul and the Background of Slavery: The *Status Quaestionis* in New Testament Scholarship," *Currents in Biblical Research* 3 (2004), 116-39.

———, *Slavery Metaphors in Early Judaism and Pauline Christianity: A Traditio-Historical and Exegetical Examination* (Tübingen: Mohr Siebeck, 2003).

Callan, T., "Prophecy and Ecstasy in Greco-Roman Religion and in 1 Corinthians," *NovT* 27 (1985), 125-40.

Callow, K., "Patterns of Thematic Development in 1 Corinthians," in *Linguistics and New Testament Interpretation*, ed. by D. A. Black (Nashville: Broadman, 1992), 194-206.

Campbell, C. R., *Basics of Verbal Aspect in Biblical Greek* (Grand Rapids: Zondervan, 2008).

———, "The Stinger of Death," *The Briefing* 357 (2008), 14-15.

———, *Verbal Aspect, the Indicative Mood, and Narrative: Soundings in the Greek of the New Testament*, Studies in Biblical Greek 13 (New York: Peter Lang, 2007).

———, *Verbal Aspect and Non-Indicative Verbs: Further Soundings in the Greek of the New Testament*, Studies in Biblical Greek 15 (New York: Peter Lang, 2009).

Campbell, J. B., "Stipendium," in *OCD*, ed. S. Hornblower and A. Spawforth (Oxford: Oxford University Press, 1996), 1444.

Caragounis, C. C., *The Development of Greek and the New Testament: Morphology, Syntax, Phonology, and Textual Transmission* (Grand Rapids: Baker Academic, 2006).

———, "Ὀψώνιον: A Reconsideration of Its Meaning," *NovT* 16 (1974), 35-57.

———, "'To boast' or 'to be burned': The Crux of 1 Cor 13:3," *SEÅ* 60 (1995), 115-27.

Carmichael, C. M., *The Laws of Deuteronomy* (Ithaca, NY: Cornell University Press, 1974).

Carson, D. A., *The Cross and Christian Ministry: An Exposition of Passages from 1 Corinthians* (Grand Rapids: Baker, 1993).

———, "Pauline Inconsistency: Reflections on I Corinthians 9.19-23 and Galatians 2.11-14," *The Churchman* 100 (1986), 6-45.

———, *Showing the Spirit: A Theological Exposition of 1 Corinthians 12–14* (Grand Rapids: Baker, 1987).

Castelli, E. A., *Imitating Paul: A Discourse of Power* (Louisville: Westminster/John Knox, 1991).

Cervin, R. S., "Does *Kephalē* Mean "Source" or "Authority" in Greek Literature? A Rebuttal," *TrinJ* 10 (1989), 85-112.

Chester, S. J., *Conversion at Corinth: Perspectives on Conversion in Paul's Theology and the Corinthian Church* (Edinburgh: T&T Clark, 2003).

Cheung, A. T., *Idol Food in Corinth: Jewish Background and Pauline Legacy* (Sheffield: Sheffield Academic Press, 1999).

Childs, B. S., *The Book of Exodus: A Critical, Theological Commentary* (Philadelphia: Westminster, 1974).

Chow, J. K., *Patronage and Power: A Study of Social Networks in Corinth* (Sheffield: JSOT Press, 1992).

Chrysostom, John, *Homilies on the Epistles of Paul to the Corinthians* (1-44 on 1 Corinthians) Greek, in J.-P. Migne (ed.), *PG*, vol. 61, cols. 9-382; English, also NPNF, ed. P. Schaff (Edinburgh: T&T Clark, 1887-94; vol. 12, rpt. Grand Rapids: Eerdmans, 1989), 1-269.

Ciampa, R. E., "'Examined the Scriptures'? The Meaning of ἀνακρίνοντες τὰς γραφάς in Acts 17:11," *JBL* 130 (2011) (forthcoming).

———, "The History of Redemption," in *Central Themes in Biblical Theology: Mapping Unity in Diversity,* ed. S. Hafemann and P. House (Grand Rapids/Leicester, England: Baker/Inter-Varsity, 2007), 254-308.

———, *The Presence and Function of Scripture in Galatians 1 and 2* (Tübingen: Mohr Siebeck, 1998).

———, "Revisiting the Euphemism in 1 Corinthians 7.1," *JSNT* 31 (2009), 325-38.

———, "Scriptural Language and Ideas," in *As It Is Written: Studying Paul's Use of Scripture,* ed. S. N. Porter and C. D. Stanley (Atlanta: SBL, 2008), 41-57.

———, and B. S. Rosner, "1 Corinthians," in *Commentary on the New Testament Use of the Old Testament,* ed. D. A. Carson and G. K. Beale (Grand Rapids: Baker, 2007), 695-752.

———, and B. S. Rosner, "The Structure and Argument of 1 Corinthians: A Biblical/Jewish Approach," *NTS* 52 (2006), 205-18.

Clarke, A. D., "'Be Imitators of Me': Paul's Model of Leadership," *TynBul* 49 (1998), 329-60.

———, "'Refresh the Hearts of the Saints': A Unique Pauline Context?" *TynBul* 47 (1996), 277-300.

———, *Secular and Christian Leadership in Corinth: A Socio-Historical and Exegetical Study of 1 Corinthians 1–6* (Leiden: Brill, 1993).

———, *Serve the Community of the Church: Christians as Leaders and Ministers* (Grand Rapids: Eerdmans, 2000).

Clarke, J. R., *Looking at Lovemaking: Constructions of Sexuality in Roman Art, 100 B.C.–A.D. 250* (Berkeley: University of California Press, 2001).

Cole, R. D., *Numbers* (Nashville: Broadman & Holman, 2001).

Collier, G. D., "'That We Might Not Crave Evil': The Structure and Argument of 1 Corinthians 10:1-13," *JSNT* 55 (1994), 55-75.

Collins, A. Y., "The Function of 'Excommunication' in Paul," *HTR* 73 (1980), 251-63.

Collins, J. J., "Chiasmus, the 'ABA' Pattern and the Text of Paul," in *Studiorum Paulinorum Congressus Internationalis Catholicus, 1961* (Rome: E Pontificio Instituto biblico, 1963), 575-83.

———, "Sibylline Oracles," in *OTP*, ed. J. H. Charlesworth, vol. 1 (New York: Doubleday, 1983), 317-472.

Combes, I. A. H., *The Metaphor of Slavery in the Writings of the Early Church: From the New Testament to the Beginning of the Fifth Century* (Sheffield: Sheffield Academic Press, 1998).

Cotterell, P., and M. Turner, *Linguistics and Biblical Interpretation* (Downers Grove: InterVarsity, 1989).

Cousland, J. R. C., "Prophets and Prophecy," in *DNTB*, ed. C. A. Evans and S. E. Porter (Downers Grove: InterVarsity Press, 2000), 830-35.

Craigie, P. C., *The Book of Deuteronomy* (Grand Rapids: Eerdmans, 1976).

———, *Psalms 1–50* (Waco, TX: Word, 1983).

Cullmann, O., *Christ and Time* (London: SCM, 1951).

Dahl, M. E., *The Resurrection of the Body* (London: SCM, 1962).

D'Angelo, M. R., "The Garden: Once and Not Again: Traditional Interpretations of Genesis 1:26-27 in 1 Corinthians 11:7-12," in *Genesis 1–3 in the History of Exegesis: Intrigue in the Garden*, ed. G. A. Robbins (Lewiston, NY: Edwin Mellen, 1988), 7-21.

Danylak, Barry N. "Tiberius Claudius Dinippus and the Food Shortages in Corinth," *TynBul* 59 (2008), 231-70.

Daube, D., *The Exodus Pattern in the Bible* (London: Faber and Faber, 1963).

———, "κερδαίνω as a Missionary Term," *HTR* 40 (1947), 109-20.

Davidson, R. M., *Typology in Scripture: A Study of Hermeneutical* τύπος *Structures* (Berrien Springs, MI: Andrews University Press, 1981).

Dawes, G. W., *The Body in Question: Metaphor and Meaning in the Interpretation of Ephesians 5:21-33* (Leiden: Brill, 1998).

———, "'But If You Can Gain Your Freedom' (1 Corinthians 7:17-24)," *CBQ* 52 (1990), 681-97.

de Boer, M. C., *The Defeat of Death: Apocalyptic Eschatology in 1 Corinthians 15 and Romans 5* (Sheffield: JSOT Press, 1988).

Delcor, M., "The Courts of the Church of Corinth and the Courts of Qumran," in *Paul and Qumran,* ed. J. Murphy-O'Connor (London: Chapman, 1968), 69-84.

Deluz, G., *A Companion to 1 Corinthians* (London: Darton, Longman & Todd, 1963).

DeMaris, R. E., "Corinthian Religion and Baptism for the Dead (1 Cor 15:29): Insights from Archaeology and Anthropology," *JBL* 114 (1995), 661-82.

Deming, W., "A Diatribe Pattern in 1 Cor 7:21-22: A New Perspective on Paul's Direction to Slaves," *NovT* 37 (1995), 130-37.

———, *Paul on Marriage and Celibacy: The Hellenistic Background of 1 Corinthians 7* (Cambridge: Cambridge University Press, 1995).

———, "The Unity of 1 Corinthians 5–6," *JBL* 115/2 (1996): 289-312.

DeSilva, D. A., *Honor, Patronage, Kinship and Purity: Unlocking New Testament Culture* (Downers Grove: InterVarsity Press, 2000).

De Young, J. B., "A Critique of Prohomosexual Interpretations of the Old Testament Apocrypha and Pseudepigrapha," *BSac* 147 (1990), 437-54.

Dickson, J. P., *Mission-Commitment in Ancient Judaism and in the Pauline Communities: The Shame, Extent and Background of Early Christian Mission* (Tübingen: Mohr Siebeck, 2003).

Dillard, R. B., *2 Chronicles* (Waco, TX: Word, 1987).

Dionysius, *The Roman Antiquities of Dionysius of Halicarnassus,* 7 vols., trans. E. Cary from E. Spelman (Cambridge, MA/London: Harvard University Press/W. Heinemann, 1937-1950).

Dixon, S., *The Roman Family* (Baltimore: Johns Hopkins University Press, 1992).

Dodd, C. H., *According to the Scriptures: The Sub-Structure of New Testament Theology* (London: Fontana, 1952).

Downs, David J. *The Offering of the Gentiles* (Tübingen: Mohr Siebeck, 2008).

Dungan, D. L. *The Sayings of Jesus in the Churches of Paul* (Philadelphia: Fortress, 1971).

Dunn, J. D. G., *Baptism in the Holy Spirit: A Re-examination of the New Testament Teaching on the Gift of the Spirit in Relation to Pentecostalism Today* (Philadelphia: Westminster, 1970).

———, *Christology in the Making: A New Testament Inquiry into the Origins of the Doctrine of the Incarnation* (Grand Rapids: Eerdmans, 1996).

———, *1 Corinthians* (Sheffield: Sheffield Academic Press, 1995).

———, *Jesus and the Spirit: A Study of the Religious and Charismatic Experience of Jesus and the First Christians as Reflected in the New Testament* (Grand Rapids: Eerdmans, 1997).

———, "Reconstructions of Corinthian Christianity and the Interpretation of 1 Corinthians," in *Christianity at Corinth: The Quest for the Pauline Church,* ed. D. G. Horrell and E. Adams (Louisville: Westminster John Knox, 2004), 295-310.

———, *Romans 9–16* (Dallas: Word, 2002).

Dupont, D. J., *Gnosis* (Louvain: E. Nauwelaerts, 1949).

Elliot, J. H., *What Is Social-Scientific Criticism?* (Minneapolis: Fortress, 1993).

Elliott, J. K., "In Favour of καυθήσομαι at 1 Corinthians 13:3," *ZNW* 62 (1971), 297-98.

Elliott, M., *Faithful Feelings: Emotion in the New Testament* (Leicester: Inter-Varsity Press, 2005).

Ellis, E. E., "Note on 1 Corinthians 10:4," in *Prophecy and Hermeneutic in Early Christianity: New Testament Essays* (Grand Rapids: Eerdmans, 1978), 209-13.

———, *Prophecy and Hermeneutic in Early Christianity: New Testament Essays* (Grand Rapids: Eerdmans, 1978).

———, "The Silenced Wives of Corinth (1 Cor 14:34-35)," in *NT Textual Criticism and Its Significance for Exegesis: In Honour of Bruce Metzger,* ed. E. J. Epp and G. D. Fee (Oxford: Clarendon, 1981), 213-20.

Engels, D. W., *Roman Corinth: An Alternative Model for the Classical City* (Chicago: University of Chicago Press, 1990).

Enns, P. E., "The 'Moveable Well' in 1 Corinthians 10:4: An Extra-Biblical Tradition in an Apostolic Text," *BBR* 6 (1996), 23-38.

Epstein, L. M., *Sex Laws and Customs in Judaism* (New York: Ktav, 1967).

Evans, O. E., "New Wine in Old Skins: xiii. The Saints," *ExpTim* 86 (1975), 196-200.

Falk, Z. W., *Introduction to Jewish Law of the Second Commonwealth,* pt. 2 (Leiden: Brill, 1978).

Fanning, B. M., *Verbal Aspect in New Testament Greek* (Oxford: Clarendon, 1990).

Fape, M. O., *Paul's Concept of Baptism and Its Present Implications for Believers: Walking in the Newness of Life* (Lewiston, NY: Mellen, 1999).

Fee, G. D., "Christology and Pneumatology in Romans 8:9-11 — and Elsewhere: Some Reflections on Paul as a Trinitarian," in *Jesus of Nazareth: Lord and Christ,* ed. J. B. Green and M. Turner (Grand Rapids: Eerdmans, 1994), 312-31.

———, "Εἰδωλόθυτα Once Again: An Interpretation of 1 Corinthians 8–10," *Bib* 61 (1980), 172-97.

———, "1 Corinthians 7:1 in the *NIV,*" *JETS* 23/4 (1980), 307-14.

———, "1 Corinthians 7:1-7 Revisited," in *Paul and the Corinthians: Studies on a Community in Conflict: Essays in Honour of Margaret Thrall,* ed. T. J. Burke and J. K. Elliott (Leiden: Brill, 2003), 197-213.

———, *God's Empowering Presence: The Holy Spirit in the Letters of Paul* (Peabody, MA: Hendrickson, 1994).

Fergusson, D., "Barth's 'Resurrection of the Dead': Further Reflections," *SJT* 56 (2003), 65-72.

Fishbane, M. A., *Biblical Interpretation in Ancient Israel* (Oxford: Clarendon, 1985).

———, "The 'Exodus' Motif/The Paradigm of Historical Renewal," in *Text and Texture: Close Readings of Selected Biblical Texts* (New York: Schocken, 1979), 121-40.

———, "Through the Looking Glass: Reflections on Ezek. 43:3, Num. 12:8, and 1 Cor. 13:8 [*sic* 13:12]," *HAR* 10 (1986), 63-75.

Fisk, B. N., "Eating Meat Offered to Idols: Corinthian Behavior and Pauline Response in 1 Corinthians 8–10 (A Response to Gordon Fee)," *TrinJ* 10 (1989), 49-70.

Fitzer, G., *Das Weib schweige in der Gemeinde: Über den unpaulinischen Charakter der Mulier-taceat-Verse in 1. Korinther 14* (Munich: Chr. Kaiser, 1963).

Fitzgerald, J. T., *Cracks in an Earthen Vessel: An Examination of the Catalogues of Hardships in the Corinthian Correspondence* (Atlanta: Scholars Press, 1988).

Fitzmyer, J. A., "Another Look at ΚΕΦΑΛΗ in 1 Corinthians 11:3," *NTS* 35 (1989), 503-11.

———, "Introduction to the New Testament Epistles," in *The New Jerome Biblical Commentary,* ed. R. E. Brown, J. A. Fitzmyer, and R. D. Murphy (London: Geoffrey Chapman, 1989), 768-71.

———, *Paul and His Theology: A Brief Sketch* (Englewood Cliffs, NJ: Prentice Hall, 1989).

Flanagan, N. M., "Did Paul Put Down Women in 1 Cor. 14:34-36?" *BTB* 11 (1981), 10-12.

Forbes, C., *Prophecy and Inspired Speech in Early Christianity and Its Hellenistic Environment* (Tübingen: J. C. B. Mohr [Paul Siebeck], 1995).

Ford, D., "Jesus Christ, The Wisdom of God," in *Reading Texts, Seeking Wisdom: Scripture and Theology,* ed. D. F. Ford and G. Stanton (London: SCM, 2003), 4-21.

Foschini, B. M., "'Those Who Are Baptized for the Dead,' I Cor. 15:29, An Exegetical Historical Dissertation," *CBQ* 12 (1950), 260-76, 379-88; 13 (1951), 46-78, 172-98, 276-83.

Fotopoulos, J., *Food Offered to Idols in Roman Corinth: A Social-Rhetorical Reconsideration of 1 Corinthians 8:1–11:1* (Tübingen: J. C. B. Mohr [Paul Siebeck], 2003).

Fuller, R. M., "Rewards," in *DPL,* ed. G. F. Hawthorne and R. P. Martin (Downers Grove: InterVarsity Press, 1993), 819-20.

Furnish, V. P., *The Moral Teaching of Paul* (Nashville: Abingdon, 1979).

———, *The Theology of the First Letter to the Corinthians* (Cambridge: Cambridge University Press, 1999).

Gagnon, R. A. J., "A Comprehensive and Critical Review Essay of *Homosexuality, Science, and the 'Plain Sense' of Scripture,*" pt. 2, *HBT* 25 (2003), 230-32.

Gardner, P. D., *The Gifts of God and the Authentication of a Christian: An Exegetical Study of 1 Corinthians 8–11:1* (Lanham, MD: University Press of America, 1994).

Garnsey, P., *Famine and Food Supply in the Graeco-Roman World: Responses to Risk and Crisis* (Cambridge: Cambridge University Press, 1988).

———, *Social Status and Legal Privilege in the Roman Empire* (Oxford: Clarendon, 1970).

Georgi, Dieter, *Remembering the Poor: The History of Paul's Collection for Jerusalem* (Nashville: Abingdon, 1992).

Gereboff, J., *Rabbi Tarfon: The Tradition, the Man, and Early Rabbinic Judaism* (Missoula, MT: Scholars Press, 1979).

Gill, David W. J., and Conrad H. Gempf, eds., *The Book of Acts in Its Graeco-Roman Setting,* The Book of Acts in Its First-Century Setting, vol. 2 (Grand Rapids: Eerdmans, 1994), 397-417.

Gillespie, T. W., *The First Theologians: A Study in Early Christian Prophecy* (Grand Rapids: Eerdmans, 1994).

Gillihan, Y. M., "Jewish Laws on Illicit Marriage, the Defilement of Offspring, and the Holiness of the Temple: A New Halakic Interpretation of 1 Corinthians 7:14," *JBL* 121 (2002), 711-44.

Gillman, F. M., "Erastus (Person)," in *ABD*, ed. D. N. Freedman, vol. 2 (New York: Doubleday, 1992), 571.

Glancy, J. A., "Obstacles to Slaves' Participation in the Corinthian Church," *JBL* 117 (1998), 481-501.

———, *Slavery in Early Christianity* (Minneapolis: Fortress, 2006).

Gleason, Maud W., "Greek Cities under Roman Rule," in *A Companion to the Roman Empire,* ed. D. S. Potter; Blackwell Companions to the Ancient World (Malden, MA: Blackwell, 2006), 228-49.

Gooch, P. D., *Dangerous Food: 1 Corinthians 8–10 in Its Context* (Waterloo, ON: Published for the Canadian Corp. for Studies in Religion by Wilfrid Laurier University Press, 1993).

Gooch, P. W., *Partial Knowledge: Philosophical Studies in Paul* (Notre Dame: University of Notre Dame Press, 1987).

Goppelt, L., *Typos: The Typological Interpretation of the Old Testament in the New* (Grand Rapids: Eerdmans, 1982), 17-20.

Gorman, M. J., *Apostle of the Crucified Lord: A Theological Introduction to Paul and His Letters* (Grand Rapids: Eerdmans, 2004).

———, *Cruciformity: Paul's Narrative Spirituality of the Cross* (Grand Rapids: Eerdmans, 2001).

Gowers, E., *The Loaded Table: Representations of Food in Roman Literature* (Oxford: Oxford University Press, 1993).

Gräbe, P. J., "Die verhouding tussen indikatief en imperatief in die pauliniese etiek: Enkele aksente uit diskussie sedert 1924," *Scriptura* 32 (1990), 54-66.

Grant, R. M., *Paul in the Roman World: The Conflict at Corinth* (Louisville: Westminster John Knox, 2001).

Grayson, A. K., *Assyrian Rules of the Early First Millennium* B.C. (Toronto: University of Toronto Press, 1996).

Greenbury, J., "1 Corinthians 14:34-35: Evaluation of Prophecy Revisited," *JETS* 51 (2008), 721-31.

Grieb, A. K., "Last Things First: Karl Barth's Theological Exegesis of 1 Corinthians in *The Resurrection of the Dead*," *SJT* 56 (2003), 49-64.

Grubbs, J. E., "'Marriage More Shameful than Adultery': Slave-Mistress Relationships, 'Mixed Marriages,' and Late Roman Law," *Phoenix* 47 (1993), 125-54.

———, *Women and the Law in the Roman Empire: A Sourcebook on Marriage, Divorce and Widowhood* (London/New York: Routledge, 2002).

Grudem, W. A., "Does *kephalē* ('Head') Mean 'Source' or 'Authority Over' in Greek Literature? A Survey of 2,336 Examples," *TrinJ* 6 (1985), 38-59.

———, "1 Corinthians 14:20-25: Prophecy and Tongues as Signs of God's Attitude," *WTJ* 41 (1979), 381-96.

———, *The Gift of Prophecy in 1 Corinthians* (Washington, DC: University Press of America, 1982).

———, "The Meaning of *Kephalē* ('Head'): A Response to Recent Studies," *TrinJ* 11 (1990), 3-72.

Gundry-Volf, J., "Controlling the Bodies: A Theological Profile of the Corinthian Sexual Ascetics (1 Cor 7)," in *The Corinthian Correspondence*, ed. R. Bieringer (Leuven: Leuven University Press, 1996), 519-41.

———, "Gender and Creation in 1 Corinthians 11:2-16: A Study in Paul's Theological Method," in *Evangelium, Schriftauslegung, Kirche: Festschrift für Peter Stuhlmacher zum 65 Geburtstag*, ed. J. Ådna et al. (Göttingen: Vandenhoeck & Ruprecht, 1997), 151-71.

———, "Male and Female in Creation and New Creation: Interpretations of Galatians 3:28 in 1 Corinthians 7," in *To Tell the Mystery: Essays on New Testament Eschatology in Honor of Robert H. Gundry*, ed. T. E. Schmidt and M. Silva (Sheffield: JSOT Press, 1994), 95-121.

Hafemann, S. J., *The God of Promise and the Life of Faith: Understanding the Heart of the Bible* (Wheaton: Crossway, 2001).

———, *Paul, Moses, and the History of Israel: The Letter/Spirit Contrast and the Argument from Scripture in 2 Corinthians 3* (Tübingen: J. C. B. Mohr [Paul Siebeck], 1995).

———, "The Role of Suffering in the Mission of Paul," in *The Mission of the Early Church to Jews and Gentiles*, ed. J. Ådna and H. Kvalbein (Tübingen: J. C. B. Mohr [Paul Siebeck], 2000), 165-84.

———, *Suffering and the Spirit: An Exegetical Study of II Corinthians 2:14–3:3 within the Context of the Corinthian Correspondence* (Tübingen: J. C. B. Mohr [Paul Siebeck], 1986).

Halperin, D. M., "Homosexuality," in *OCD*, ed. S. Hornblower and A. Spawforth (Oxford: Oxford University Press, 1996), 720-23.

Hanson, A. T., *Jesus Christ in the Old Testament* (London: SPCK, 1965).

———, *Studies in Paul's Technique and Theology* (Grand Rapids: Eerdmans, 1974).

Harink, D. K., *Paul among the Postliberals: Pauline Theology beyond Christendom and Modernity* (Grand Rapids: Brazos, 2003).

Harrill, J. A., *The Manumission of Slaves in Early Christianity* (Tübingen: J. C. B. Mohr [Paul Siebeck], 1995).

Harrington, D. J., "Second Testament Exegesis and the Social Sciences: A Bibliography," *BTB* 18 (1988), 77-85.

———, "Sociological Concepts and the Early Church: A Decade of Research," *Theological Studies* 41 (1980), 181-90.

Harris, G., "The Beginnings of Church Discipline: 1 Corinthians 5," *NTS* 37 (1991), 1-21.

Harris, M. J., *Raised Immortal: Resurrection and Immortality in the New Testament* (Grand Rapids: Eerdmans, 1985).

———, *The Second Epistle to the Corinthians: A Commentary on the Greek Text* (Grand Rapids: Eerdmans, 2005).

Harris, W., "Echoing Bronze," *Journal of the Acoustical Society of America* 70 (1981), 1184-85.

———, "'Sounding Brass' and Hellenistic Technology," *BAR* 8 (1982), 38-41.

Hartman, L., "Some Remarks on I Cor 2:1-5," *SEÅ* 39 (1974), 109-20.

Hawthorne, S. C., "The Story of His Glory," in *Perspectives on the World Christian Movement: A Reader*, ed. R. D. Winter and S. C. Hawthorne (Carlisle: Paternoster, 1999), 34-48.

Hayes, C. E., *Gentile Impurities and Jewish Identities: Intermarriage and Conversion from the Bible to the Talmud* (Oxford: Oxford University Press, 2002).

Hays, R. B., *The Conversion of the Imagination: Paul as Interpreter of Israel's Scripture* (Grand Rapids: Eerdmans, 2005).

———, *Echoes of Scripture in the Letters of Paul* (New Haven: Yale University Press, 1989).

———, *The Moral Vision of the New Testament: Community, Cross, New Creation* (San Francisco: HarperSanFrancisco, 1996).

Head, P., "An Extended Review of G. D. Fee, *God's Empowering Presence*," *Churchman* 111 (1997), 62-73.

Heil, J. P., *The Rhetorical Role of Scripture in 1 Corinthians* (Atlanta: Society of Biblical Literature, 2005).

Heinrici, C. F. G., *Das erste Sendschreiben des Apostel Paulus an die Korinther* (Berlin: Hertz, 1880).

Hengel, M., *Crucifixion in the Ancient World and the Folly of the Message of the Cross* (Philadelphia: Fortress, 1977).

———, *The Pre-Christian Paul* (London/Philadelphia: SCM/TPI, 1991).

———, *The Son of God: The Origin of Christology and the History of Jewish-Hellenistic Religion* (London: SCM, 1976).

Heschel, A. J., *The Prophets* (New York: Harper & Row, 1962).

Hill, A. E., *Malachi: A New Translation with Introduction and Commentary* (New York: Doubleday, 1998).

Hill, D., *New Testament Prophecy* (London: Marshall, Morgan & Scott, 1979).

Hillyer, N., "1 Corinthians," in *The New Bible Commentary Revised*, ed. D. Guthrie and J. A. Motyer (London: InterVarsity Press, 1970), 1052-74.

Hock, R. F., *The Social Context of Paul's Ministry* (Philadelphia: Fortress, 1980).

Hodges, Z. C., "Symposium on the Tongues Movement: The Purpose of Tongues," *BSac* 120 (1963), 226-33.

Hoehner, H. W., "Reward," in *NDBT*, ed. T. D. Alexander and B. S. Rosner (Leicester: Inter-Varsity Press, 2000), 738-40.

Holladay, C. R., "1 Cor 13: Paul as Apostolic Paradigm," in *Greeks, Romans and Christians — In Honor of A. J. Malherbe*, ed. D. L. Balch, E. Ferguson, and W. A. Meeks (Minneapolis: Fortress, 1990), 80-98.

Holleman, J., *Resurrection and Parousia: A Traditio-Historical Study of Paul's Eschatology in I Corinthians 15* (Leiden: Brill, 1996).

Holmberg, B., "Paul and Commensality," in *Texts and Contexts: Biblical Texts in Their Textual and Situational Contexts: Essays in Honor of Lars Hartman*, ed. T. Fornberg and D. Hellholm (Oslo: Scandinavian University Press, 1995), 767-80.

———, *Sociology and the New Testament* (Minneapolis: Fortress, 1990).

Hooker, M. D., "Authority on Her Head: An Examination of 1 Cor. 11:10," *NTS* 10 (1964), 410-16.

———, "'Beyond the Things Which Are Written': An Examination of 1 Cor IV.6," *NTS* 10 (1963-64), 127-32.

———, "A Partner in the Gospel: Paul's Understanding of Ministry," in *Theology and Ethics in Paul and His Interpreters: Essays in Honor of Victor Paul Furnish*, ed. E. H. Lovering Jr. and J. L. Sumney (Nashville: Abingdon, 1996), 83-100.

———, "Paul — Apostle to the Gentiles," *Epworth Review* 18 (1991), 79-89.

Horbury, W., "Extirpation and Excommunication," *VT* 35 (1985), 13-38.

———, "New Wine in Old Wine Skins: ix. The Temple," *ExpTim* 86 (1974), 36-42.

Horrell, D. G., "The Development of Theological Ideology in Pauline Christianity," in *Modelling Early Christianity: Social-Scientific Studies of the New Testament in Its Context*, ed. P. F. Esler (New York: Routledge, 1995), 224-38.

———, "Other-Regard and Christ as Moral Paradigm," in *Solidarity and Difference: A Contemporary Reading of Paul's Ethics* (London: T&T Clark, 2005), 204-45.

———, *The Social Ethos of the Corinthian Correspondence: Interest and Ideology from 1 Corinthians to 1 Clement* (Edinburgh: T&T Clark, 1996).

———, *Solidarity and Difference: A Contemporary Reading of Paul's Ethics* (London: T&T Clark, 2005).

———, and E. Adams, eds., *Christianity at Corinth: The Quest for the Pauline Church* (Louisville: Westminster John Knox, 2004).

Horsley, G. H. R., "Review of John T. Fitzgerald, *Cracks in an Earthen Vessel*," *ABR* 37 (1989), 83-84.

———, and S. Llewelyn, eds., *New Documents Illustrating Early Christianity* (North Ryde, N.S.W., Australia/Grand Rapids: Macquarie University/Eerdmans, 1981-2002).

Horsley, R. A., "Gnosis in Corinth: 1 Corinthians 8:1-6," *NTS* 27 (1980), 37-39.

Houlden, J. L., "Commentary (NT)," in *A Dictionary of Biblical Interpretation,* ed. R. J. Coggins and J. L. Houlden (London/Philadelphia: SCM/Trinity Press International, 1990), 129-32.

Howard, J. K., "Christ Our Passover: A Study of the Passover-Exodus Theme in 1 Corinthians," *EvQ* 41 (1969), 97-108.

Hübner, H., *Die Theologie des Paulus und ihre neutestamentliche Wirkungsgeschichte* (Göttingen: Vandenhoeck & Ruprecht, 1993).

———, *Vetus Testamentum in Novo* (Göttingen: Vandenhoeck & Ruprecht, 1997).

Hugenberger, G., *Marriage as a Covenant: Biblical Law and Ethics as Developed from Malachi* (Grand Rapids: Baker, 1998).

Hull, M. F., *Baptism on Account of the Dead (1 Cor 15:29): An Act of Faith in the Resurrection* (Atlanta: Society of Biblical Literature, 2005).

Hurd, J. C., *The Origin of 1 Corinthians* (London: SPCK, 1965).

Hurley, J. B., *Man and Woman in Biblical Perspective* (Grand Rapids: Zondervan, 1981).

Hunter, A. M., *Paul and His Predecessors* (London: SCM, 1961).

Hutson, Christopher R., "Was Timothy Timid? On the Rhetoric of Fearlessness (1 Cor. 16:10-11) and Cowardice (2 Tim 1:7)," *Biblical Research* 42 (1997), 58-73.

Iber, G., "Zum Verständnis von 1 Cor. 12:31," *ZNW* 54 (1963), 43-53.

Instone, S. J., "Athletics," in *OCD*, ed. S. Hornblower and A. Spawforth (Oxford: Oxford University Press, 1996), 206-7.

Instone-Brewer, D., *Divorce and Remarriage in the Bible: The Social and Literary Context* (Grand Rapids: Eerdmans, 2002).

———, "1 Corinthians 7 in the Light of the Graeco-Roman Marriage and Divorce Papyri," *TynBul* 52 (2001), 225-43.

———, D., "1 Corinthians 9:9-11: A Literal Interpretation of 'Do Not Muzzle the Ox,'" *NTS* 38 (1992), 554-65.

Jeffers, J. S., *The Greco-Roman World of the New Testament: Exploring the Background of Early Christianity* (Downers Grove: InterVarsity Press, 1999).

Jeremias, J., *The Eucharistic Words of Jesus* (London: SCM, 1987).

———, "War Paulus Witwer?" *ZNW* 25 (1926), 310-12.

Jervis, L. A., "'But I Want You to Know . . .': Paul's Midrashic Intertextual Response to the Corinthian Worshipers (1 Cor 11:2-16)," *JBL* 112 (1993), 231-46.

Jewett, R., *Paul's Anthropological Terms: A Study of Their Use in Conflict Settings* (Leiden: Brill, 1971).

Johanson, B. C., "Tongues, a Sign for Unbelievers?: A Structural and Exegetical Study of I Corinthians XIV.20-25," *NTS* 25 (1979), 180-203.

Johnson, L. T., "Tongues, Gift of," in *ABD*, ed. D. N. Freedman, vol. 6 (New York: Doubleday, 1992), 597.

Jones, J. W., *The Law and Legal Theory of the Greeks* (Oxford: Oxford University Press, 1956).

Jongkind, D., "Corinth in the First Century AD: The Search for Another Class," *TynBul* 52 (2001), 139-48.

Judge, E. A., "Antike und Christentum: Towards a Definition of the Field: A Bibliographic Survey," in *Aufstieg und Niedergang der römischen Welt*, ed. H. Temporini and W. Haase (Berlin: Walter de Gruyter, 1979), 3-58.

———, "Gesellschaft: Neues Testament," in *Theologische Realenzyklopädie*, vol. 12 (Berlin and New York: Walter de Gruyter, 1984), 769-73.

———, "Gesellschaft und Christentum: Alte Kirche," in *Theologische Realenzyklopädie*, vol. 12 (Berlin and New York: Walter de Gruyter, 1984), 764-69.

———, "The Reaction against Classical Education in the New Testament," *JCE* 77 (1983), 7-14.

———, "St. Paul and Classical Society," *JAC* 15 (1972), 19-36.

———, "The Social Identity of the First Christians: A Question of Method in Religious History," *Journal of Religious History* (1980), 201-17.

Jüngel, E., *Paulus und Jesus: Eine Untersuchung zur Präzisierung der Frage nach dem Ursprung der Christologie* (Tübingen: J. C. B. Mohr [Paul Siebeck], 1972).

Kaiser, W. C., Jr., "The Current Crisis in Exegesis and the Apostolic Use of Deuteronomy 25:4 in 1 Corinthians 9:8-10," *JETS* 21 (1978), 3-18.

———, "Paul, Women, and the Church," *Worldwide Challenge* 3 (1976), 9-12.

Käsemann, E., "The Cry for Liberty in the Church's Worship," in *Perspectives on Paul* (London: SCM, 1971), 122-37.

———, *New Testament Questions of Today* (Philadelphia: Fortress, 1969).

Kee, H. C., *Knowing the Truth: A Sociological Approach to New Testament Interpretation* (Minneapolis: Fortress, 1989).

Keener, C. S., *The IVP Bible Background Commentary: New Testament* (Downers Grove: InterVarsity Press, 1993).

———, *Paul, Women, and Wives: Marriage and Women's Ministry in the Letters of Paul* (Peabody, MA: Hendrickson, 1992).

Keesmaat, S. C., "Exodus and the Intertextual Transformation of Tradition in Romans 8.14-30," *JSNT* 54 (1994), 29-56.

Kennedy, G. A., *New Testament Interpretation through Rhetorical Criticism* (Chapel Hill: University of North Carolina Press, 1984).

Kerényi, K., *Dionysos: Archetypal Image of Indestructible Life* (Princeton: Princeton University Press, 1996).

Kern, P. H., *Rhetoric and Galatians: Assessing an Approach to Paul's Epistle* (Cambridge: Cambridge University Press, 1998).

Kim, J. H., *The Significance of Clothing Imagery in the Pauline Corpus* (London: T&T Clark, 2004).

Kim, S., *The Origin of Paul's Gospel* (Tübingen: J. C. B. Mohr [Paul Siebeck], 1984).

———, *Paul and the New Perspective: Second Thoughts on the Origin of Paul's Gospel* (Grand Rapids: Eerdmans, 2001).

Kittay, E. F., *Metaphor: Its Cognitive Force and Linguistic Structure* (Oxford: Oxford University Press, 1987).

Klein, W. W., "Noisy Gong or Acoustic Vase? A Note on 1 Corinthians 13:1," *NTS* 32 (1986), 286-89.

Kleinknecht, K. T., *Der Leidende Gerechtfertigte* (Tübingen: J. C. B. Mohr [Paul Siebeck], 1984).

Knight, G. A. F., *Psalms,* The Daily Study Bible, vol. 2 (Louisville: Westminster John Knox, 1982).

Koch, D., *Die Schrift als Zeuge des Evangeliums: Untersuchungen zur Verwendung und zum Verständnis der Schrift bei Paulus* (Tübingen: J. C. B. Mohr [Paul Siebeck], 1986).

Koch, K., *The Prophets,* vol. 2, *The Babylonian and Persian Periods* (London: SCM, 1983).

Koet, B. J., "The Old Testament Background to 1 Cor. 10:7-8," in *The Corinthian Correspondence,* ed. R. Bieringer (Leuven: Leuven University Press, 1996), 607-15.

Kovacs, J., *1 Corinthians: Interpreted by Early Christian Commentators* (Grand Rapids: Eerdmans, 2005).

Kraftchick, S. J., "A Necessary Detour: Paul's Metaphorical Understanding of the Philippian Hymn," *HBT* 15/1 (1993), 1-37.

Kraus, H. J., *Psalms: A Continental Commentary* (Minneapolis: Fortress, 1993).

Kroeger, C. C., "The Classical Concept of *Head* as 'Source,'" in *Equal to Serve,* ed. G. G. Hull (London: Scripture Union, 1987), 267-83.

———, "Head," in *DPL,* ed. G. F. Hawthorne and R. P. Martin (Downers Grove: InterVarsity Press, 1993), 375-77.

Kuck, D. W., *Judgment and Community Conflict: Paul's Use of Apocalyptic Judgment Language in 1 Corinthians 3:5–4:5* (Leiden: Brill, 1992).

Kümmel, W. G., "Verlobung und Heirat bei Paulus (1 Cor 7, 36-38)," in *Neutestamentliche Studien für Rudolf Bultmann zu seinem siebzigsten Geburtstag,* ed. W. Eltester (Berlin: Töpelmann, 1954), 275-95.

Kwon, D. L., "Obfuscation and Restoration: Paul's Use of Isaiah in 1 Corinthians 14:20-25" (unpublished Th.M. thesis, Gordon-Conwell Theological Seminary, 2004).

La Follette, L., "The Costume of the Roman Bride," in *The World of Roman Costume,* ed. J. L. Sebesta and L. Bonfante (Madison: University of Wisconsin Press, 2001), 54-64.

Lakoff, G., and M. Johnson, *Metaphors We Live By* (Chicago: University of Chicago Press, 2003).

Lampe, G. W. H., "Church Discipline and the Interpretation of the Epistles to the Corinthians," in *Christian History and Interpretation: Studies Presented to John Knox,* ed. W. R. Farmer, C. F. D. Moule, and R. R. Niebuhr (Cambridge: Cambridge University Press, 1967), 337-61.

Lampe, P., "Theological Wisdom and the 'Word of the Cross': The Rhetorical Scheme in 1 Corinthians 1–4," *Int* 44 (1990), 117-31.

Lane, W. L., "Covenant: the Key to Paul's Conflict with Corinth," *TynBul* 33 (1982), 3-29.

Laney, J. C., "The Biblical Practice of Church Discipline," *BSac* 143 (1986), 353-64.

———, "Paul and the Permanence of Marriage in 1 Corinthians 7," *JETS* 25 (1982), 283-94.

Langkammer, P. H., "Literarische und theologische Einzelstücke in 1 Kor VIII:6," *NTS* 17 (1970-71), 193-97.

Lanier, D. E., "With Stammering Lips and Another Tongue: 1 Cor. 14:20-22 and Isa. 28:11-12," *CTR* 5 (1991), 259-86.

Lefkowitz, M. R., and M. B. Fant, eds., *Women's Life in Greece and Rome: A Source Book in Translation* (Baltimore: The Johns Hopkins University Press, 1992).

Levinsohn, S., *Discourse Features of New Testament Greek* (Dallas: SIL International, 2000).

Liddell, H. G., *A Lexicon Abridged from Liddell and Scott's Greek-English Lexicon* (Oxford: Clarendon, 1994).

———, and R. Scott, *A Greek-English Lexicon* (Oxford, UK: Clarendon, 1968).

Lieu, J. M., *Christian Identity in the Jewish and Graeco-Roman World* (New York: Oxford University Press, 2004).

Lieu, J. M., "'Grace to you and peace': The Apostolic Greeting," *BJRL* 68 (1985), 161-78.

Lindsay, D. R., *Josephus and Faith: Pistis and Pisteuein as Faith Terminology in the Writings of Flavius Josephus and in the New Testament* (Leiden: Brill, 1993).

Litfin, D., *St Paul's Theology of Proclamation: 1 Corinthians 1–4 and Greco-Roman Rhetoric* (Cambridge: Cambridge University Press, 1994).

Llewelyn, S. R., "The Use of Sunday for Meetings," *NovT* 43 (2001), 205-23.

Loader, W., *Enoch, Levi, and Jubilees on Sexuality: Attitudes towards Sexuality in the Early Enoch Literature, the Aramaic Levi Document, and the Book of Jubilees* (Grand Rapids: Eerdmans, 2007).

———, *The Septuagint, Sexuality, and the New Testament: Case Studies on the Impact of the LXX in Philo and the New Testament* (Grand Rapids: Eerdmans, 2004).

———, *Sexuality and the Jesus Tradition* (Grand Rapids: Eerdmans, 2005).

Lopez, D., Review of Jorunn Økland, *Women in Their Place: Paul and the Corinthian Discourse of Gender and Sanctuary Space, Review of Biblical Literature* [http://www.bookreviews.org] (2005).

Luther, M., *Lectures on Deuteronomy*, vol. 9, ed. J. Pelikan (St. Louis: Concordia, 1960).

Lyall, F., *Slaves, Citizens, and Sons: Legal Metaphors in the Epistles* (Grand Rapids: Zondervan, 1984).

Lye, J., "Some Issues in Postcolonial Theory" (http://www.brocku.ca/english/courses/4F70/postcol.php, accessed August 6, 2008).

Lyons, J., *Linguistic Semantics: An Introduction* (Cambridge: Cambridge University Press, 1995).

MacDonald, M. Y., "Was Celsus Right? The Role of Women in the Expansion of Early Christianity," in *Early Christian Families in Context: An Interdisciplinary Dialogue,* ed. D. L. Balch and C. Osiek (Grand Rapids: Eerdmans, 2003), 157-84.

———, "Slavery, Sexuality and House Churches: A Reassessment of Colossians 3.18–4.1 in Light of New Research on the Roman Family," *NTS* 53 (2007), 94-113.

Mack, B. L., *Rhetoric and the New Testament* (Minneapolis: Fortress, 1990).

MacMullen, R., *Christianizing the Roman Empire, A.D. 100-400* (New Haven, CT: Yale University Press, 1984).

———, *Roman Social Relations, 50 B.C. to A.D. 284* (New Haven, CT: Yale University Press, 1974).

———, "Women in Public in the Roman Empire," *Historia* 29 (1980), 208-18.

Malherbe, A. J., *Paul and the Popular Philosophers* (Philadelphia: Fortress, 1989).

———, *Paul and the Thessalonians* (Philadelphia: Fortress, 1987).

———, *Social Aspects of Early Christianity* (Baton Rouge: Louisiana State University Press, 1977).

Malina, B. J., *The Gospel of John in Sociolinguistic Perspective: Protocol of the Forty-eighth Colloquy, 11 March 1984* (Berkeley, CA: Center for Hermeneutical Studies in Hellenistic and Modern Culture, 1985).

Marchal, J., Review of Jorunn Økland, *Women in Their Place: Paul and the Corinthian Discourse of Gender and Sanctuary Space, Review of Biblical Literature* [http://www.bookreviews.org] (2005).

Marshall, I. H., "Church and Temple in the New Testament," *TynBul* 40 (1989), 203-22.

———, *Jesus the Saviour* (London: SPCK, 1990).

———, *Last Supper and Lord's Supper* (Grand Rapids: Eerdmans, 1981).

Marshall, P., *Enmity in Corinth: Social Conventions in Paul's Relations with the Corinthians* (Tübingen: J. C. B. Mohr [Paul Siebeck], 1987).

Martin, D. B., *The Corinthian Body* (New Haven, CT: Yale University Press, 1995).

———, "Slave Families and Slaves in Families," in *Early Christian Families in Context: An Interdisciplinary Dialogue,* ed. D. L. Balch and C. Osiek (Grand Rapids: Eerdmans, 2003), 207-30.

———, *Slavery as Salvation: The Metaphor of Slavery in Pauline Christianity* (New Haven, CT: Yale University Press, 1990).

———, "Tongues of Angels and Other Status Indicators," *JAAR* 59 (1991), 547-89.

Martin, R. P., *The Spirit and the Congregation: Studies in 1 Corinthians 12–15* (Grand Rapids: Eerdmans, 1984).

———, *Worship in the Early Church* (Grand Rapids: Eerdmans, 1974).

Martin, T., "Paul's Argument from Nature for the Veil in 1 Corinthians 11:13-15: A Testicle instead of a Head Covering," *JBL* 123 (2004), 75-84.

Matthews, V. H., M. W. Chavalas, and J. H. Walton, *The IVP Bible Background*

*Commentary: Old Testament* (Downers Grove, IL: InterVarsity Press, 2000).

May, A. S., *The Body for the Lord: Sex and Identity in 1st Corinthians 5–7* (London: T&T Clark, 2004).

McDonough, S. M., "Competent to Judge: The Old Testament Connection between 1 Corinthians 5 and 6," *JTS* 56 (2005), 99-102.

McGrath, A. E., *Luther's Theology of the Cross* (Oxford and Cambridge, MA: Blackwell, 1990).

McKay, K. L., *A New Syntax of the Verb in New Testament Greek: An Aspectual Approach,* Studies in Biblical Greek 5 (New York: Peter Lang, 1994).

McNamara, M., *Targum and Testament: Aramaic Paraphrases of the Hebrew Bible, a Light on the New Testament* (Grand Rapids: Eerdmans, 1972).

Meeks, W. A., "'And Rose Up to Play': Midrash and Paraenesis in 1 Corinthians 10:22," *JSNT* 16 (1982), 64-78.

———, *The First Urban Christians: The Social World of the Apostle Paul* (New Haven, CT: Yale University Press, 2003).

———, *The Moral World of the First Christians* (Philadelphia: Westminster Press, 1986).

———, "Social Functions of Apocalyptic Language in Pauline Christianity," in *Apocalypticism in the Mediterranean World and the Near East: Proceedings of the International Colloquium on Apocalypticism, Uppsala, August 12-17, 1979,* ed. D. Hellholm (Tübingen: J. C. B. Mohr [Paul Siebeck], 1983), 687-705.

———, "Understanding Early Christian Ethics," *JBL* 105 (1986), 3-11.

Meggitt, J. J., *Paul, Poverty and Survival* (Edinburgh: T&T Clark, 1998).

Meier, J. P., *A Marginal Jew: Rethinking the Historical Jesus,* vol. 1, *The Roots of the Problem and the Person* (New York: Doubleday, 1991).

Merklein, H., "Die Einheitlichkeit des ersten Korintherbriefes," *ZNW* 75 (1984), 153-83.

Metzger, B. M., *A Textual Commentary on the Greek New Testament* (Stuttgart: Deutsche Bibelgesellschaft, 1994).

Meurer, S., *Das Recht im Dienst der Versöhnung und des Friedens: Studie zur Frage des Rechts nach dem Neuen Testaments* (Zürich: Theologischer Verlag, 1972).

Meyers, E. M., "Ancient Synagogues: An Archaeological Introduction," in *Sacred Realm: The Emergence of the Synagogue in the Ancient World,* ed. S. Fine (New York: Oxford University Press, 1996), 3-20.

Mickelsen, A., and B. Mickelsen, "What Does *Kephalē* Mean in the New Testament?" in *Women, Authority and the Bible,* ed. A. Mickelsen (Downers Grove, IL: InterVarsity Press, 1986), 97-110.

Millar, J. G., "Deuteronomy," in *NDBT,* ed. T. D. Alexander and B. S. Rosner (Leicester: Inter-Varsity Press, 2000), 159-65.

———, *Now Choose Life: Theology and Ethics in Deuteronomy* (Leicester: Inter-Varsity Press, 1998).

Millard, A. R., "Covenant and Communion in First Corinthians," in *Apostolic*

*History and the Gospel: Biblical and Historical Essays Presented to F. F. Bruce on His 60th Birthday*, ed. W. W. Gasque and R. P. Martin (Exeter: Paternoster, 1970), 242-48.

Minear, P. S., "Christ and the Congregation: 1 Corinthians 5–6," *RevExp* 80 (1983), 341-50.

Mitchell, A. C., "Rich and Poor in the Courts of Corinth: Litigiousness and Status in 1 Corinthians 6.1-11," *NTS* 39 (1993), 562-86.

Mitchell, M., "Concerning περὶ δέ in 1 Corinthians," *NovT* 31 (1989), 229-56.

———, *Paul and the Rhetoric of Reconciliation: An Exegetical Investigation of the Language and Composition of 1 Corinthians* (Louisville: Westminster/John Knox, 1993).

Mitton, C. L., "New Wine in Old Wine Skins: IV. Leaven," *ExpTim* 84 (1973), 339-43.

Moberly, R. W. L., *The Old Testament of the Old Testament: Patriarchal Narratives and Mosaic Yahwism* (Minneapolis: Fortress, 1992).

Moltmann, J., "The Knowing of the Other and the Community of the Different," in *God for a Secular Society* (London: SCM, 1999), 135-52.

———, *The Spirit of Life: A Universal Affirmation* (Minneapolis: Fortress, 1992).

Moo, D. J., *The Epistle to the Romans* (Grand Rapids: Eerdmans, 1996).

Moore, A. L., *The Parousia in the New Testament* (Leiden: Brill, 1966).

Moores, J. D., *Wrestling with Rationality in Paul: Romans 1–8 in a New Perspective* (Cambridge: Cambridge University Press, 1995).

Moulton, J. H., W. F. Howard, and N. Turner, *A Grammar of New Testament Greek* (Edinburgh: T&T Clark, 1906).

Mullins, T. Y., "Disclosure: A Literary Form in the New Testament," *NovT* 7 (1964), 44-50.

Murphy-O'Connor, J., "'Baptized for the Dead' (I Cor., XV, 29): A Corinthian Slogan," *RB* 88 (1981), 532-43.

———, "Corinthian Bronze," *RB* 90 (1983), 80-93.

———, "1 Corinthians 11:2-16 Once Again," *CBQ* 50 (1988), 265-74.

———, "Interpolations in 1 Corinthians," *CBQ* 48 (1986), 81-94.

———, *Paul: A Critical Life* (Oxford: Clarendon, 1996).

———, *Paul the Letter Writer: His World, His Options, His Skills* (Collegeville, Minn.: Liturgical Press, 1995).

———, "Review of Winter, *Philo and Paul among the Sophists*," *RB* 110 (2003), 428-33.

Nadeau, D. J., "La problème des femmes en 1 Cor 14:33b-35," *ETR* 69 (1994), 63-65.

Nasuti, H. P., "The Woes of the Prophets and the Rights of the Apostle: The Internal Dynamics of 1 Corinthians 9," *CBQ* 50 (1988), 246-464.

Neusner, J., *The Idea of Purity in Ancient Judaism* (Leiden: Brill, 1973).

Newton, M., *The Concept of Purity at Qumran and in the Letters of Paul* (Cambridge: Cambridge University Press, 1985).

Neyrey, J. H., "Body Language in 1 Corinthians: The Use of Anthropological

Models for Understanding Paul and His Opponents," *Semeia* 35 (1986), 129-70.

———, "What's Wrong with this Picture? John 4, Cultural Stereotypes of Women, and Public and Private Space," *BTB* 24 (1994), 77-91.

Niccum, C., "The Voice of the Manuscripts on the Silence of Women: The External Evidence for 1 Cor. 14:34-35," *NTS* 43 (1997), 242-55.

Nickle, Keith F., *The Collection: A Study in Paul's Strategy,* Studies in Biblical Theology 48 (London: SCM, 1966).

Niebuhr, K. W., *Gesetz und Paränese: Katechismusartige Weisungsreihen in der frühjüdischen Literatur* (Tübingen: J. C. B. Mohr [Paul Siebeck], 1987).

O'Brien, P. T., *Consumed by Passion: Paul and the Dynamic of the Gospel* (Homebush West, Australia: Lancer, 1993).

———, *Introductory Thanksgivings in the Letters of Paul* (Leiden: Brill, 1977).

O'Donovan, O., *Resurrection and Moral Order: An Outline for Evangelical Ethics* (Grand Rapids: Eerdmans, 1986).

Økland, J., *Women in Their Place: Paul and the Corinthian Discourse of Gender and Sanctuary Space* (London and New York: T&T Clark, 2004).

Olsen, M. B., *A Semantic and Pragmatic Model of Lexical and Grammatical Aspect* (New York: Garland, 1997).

Olson, K., "*Matrona* and Whore: Clothing and Definition in Roman Antiquity," in *Prostitutes and Courtesans in the Ancient World,* ed. C. A. Faraone and L. McClure (Madison: University of Wisconsin Press, 2006), 186-204.

———, "*Matrona* and Whore: The Clothing of Women in Roman Antiquity," *Fashion Theory* 6 (2002), 387-420.

O'Neill, J. C., "1 Corinthians 15.29," *ExpTim* (1980), 310-11.

Oropeza, B. J., "Echoes of Isaiah in the Rhetoric of Paul: New Exodus, Wisdom and the Humility of the Cross in Utopian-Apocalyptic Expectations," in *The Intertexture of Apocalyptic Discourse in the New Testament,* ed. D. F. Watson (Atlanta: Society of Biblical Literature, 2002), 87-112.

Osiek, C., "Female Slaves, *Porneia,* and the Limits of Obedience," in *Early Christian Families in Context: An Interdisciplinary Dialogue,* ed. D. L. Balch and C. Osiek (Grand Rapids: Eerdmans, 2003), 255-76.

———, and D. L. Balch, *Families in the New Testament World: Households and House Churches* (Louisville: Westminster/John Knox, 1997).

———, and M. Y. MacDonald, with J. H. Tulloch, *A Women's Place: House Churches in Earliest Christianity* (Minneapolis: Augsburg Fortress, 2006).

Oster, R. E., Jr., "When Men Wore Veils to Worship: The Historical Context of 1 Corinthians 11:4," *NTS* 34 (1988), 481-505.

Paige, T., "1 Corinthians 12:2: A Pagan *Pompe?*" *JSNT* 44 (1991), 57-65.

Pangle, T. L., *The Laws of Plato: Translated, with Notes and an Interpretive Essay* (Chicago, University of Chicago Press, 1980).

Pannenberg, W., *Jesus — God and Man* (Philadelphia/London: Westminster/SCM, 1968).

Parkin, V., "Some Comments on the Pauline Prescripts," *IBS* 8 (1986), 92-99.

Parsons, M., "Being Precedes Act: Indicative and Imperative in Paul's Writing," *EvQ* (1988), 99-127.

Patrick, J. E., "Living Rewards for Dead Apostles: 'Baptized for the Dead' in 1 Corinthians 15.29," *NTS* 52 (2006), 71-85.

Patterson, O., *Slavery and Social Death: A Comparative Study* (Cambridge, MA: Harvard University Press, 1982).

Pearson, B. A., *The Pneumatikos-Psychikos Terminology in 1 Corinthians: A Study in the Theology of the Corinthian Opponents of Paul and Its Relation to Gnosticism* (Missoula, MT: Scholars Press, 1973).

Perriman, A. C., "The Head of a Woman: The Meaning of κεφαλή in 1 Cor 11:3," *JTS* 45 (1994), 602-22.

———, "'His Body, Which Is the Church . . .': Coming to Terms with Metaphor," *EvQ* 62 (1990), 123-42.

Petersen, W. L., "Can Ἀρσενοκοῖται Be Translated by 'Homosexuals'? (1 Cor 6.9; 1 Tim 1:10)," *Vigiliae Christianae* 40 (1986), 187-91.

Peterson, D., *Possessed by God* (Leicester: Apollos, 1995).

Petzer, J. H., "Contextual Evidence in Favour of ΚΑΥΧΗΣΩΜΑΙ in 1 Corinthians 13:3," *NTS* 35 (1989), 229-53.

Pfitzner, V. C., *Paul and the Agon Motif: Traditional Athletic Imagery in the Pauline Literature* (Leiden: Brill, 1967).

———, "Purified Community — Purified Sinner: Expulsion from the Community according to Matthew 18:15-18 and 1 Corinthians 5:1-5," *ABR* 30 (1982), 34-55.

Phillips, A., *Ancient Israel's Criminal Law: A New Approach to the Decalogue* (Oxford: Blackwell, 1970).

Plato, *Plato in Twelve Volumes*, vols. 10-11 (Cambridge, MA/London: Harvard University Press/William Heinemann, 1967/1968).

Plummer, R. L., "Imitation of Paul and the Church's Missionary Role in 1 Corinthians," *JETS* 44 (2001), 219-35.

Pogoloff, S. M., *Logos and Sophia: The Rhetorical Situation of 1 Corinthians* (Atlanta: Scholars Press, 1992).

Polhill, J. B., "The Wisdom of God and Factionalism," *RevExp* 80 (1983), 325-39.

Pomeroy, S. B., *Plutarch's Advice to the Bride and Groom, and A Consolation to His Wife: English Translations, Commentary, Interpretive Essays, and Bibliography* (New York: Oxford University Press, 1999).

Porter, S. E., *Idioms of the Greek New Testament* (Sheffield: JSOT Press, 1992).

———, "The Theoretical Justification for Application of Rhetorical Categories to Pauline Literature," in *Rhetoric and the New Testament: Essays from the 1992 Heidelberg Conference*, ed. S. E. Porter and T. H. Olbricht (Sheffield: Sheffield Academic Press, 1993), 100-122.

———, *Verbal Aspect in the Greek of the New Testament, with Reference to Tense and Mood*, Studies in Biblical Greek 1 (New York: Peter Lang, 1989).

———, and D. A. Carson, eds., *Biblical Greek Language and Linguistics: Open*

*Questions in Current Research,* JSNTSup 80 (Sheffield: Sheffield Academic Press, 1993).

Portier-Young, A., "Tongues and Cymbals: Contextualizing 1 Corinthians 13:1," *BTB* 35 (2005), 99.

Proctor, J., "Fire in God's House: Influence of Malachi 3 in the NT," *JETS* 36 (1993), 9-14.

Rapske, B. M., "Acts, Travel and Shipwrecks," in *The Book of Acts in Its Graeco-Roman Setting,* vol. 2, ed. D. W. J. Gill (Grand Rapids: Eerdmans, 1994), 1-47.

Ratzinger, J., *Introduction to Christianity,* translated by J. R. Foster (New York: Herder and Herder, 1970).

Rawson, B., "Adult-Child Relationships in Roman Society," in *Marriage, Divorce, and Children in Ancient Rome,* ed. B. Rawson (Canberra: Humanities Research Centre, 1991), 7-30.

Reasoner, M., "Paul's Redemptive Inversions of Jeremiah in Romans 9–11" (paper presented at the Society of Biblical Literature, Toronto, 2002).

———, *The Strong and the Weak: Romans 14:1–15.13 in Context* (Cambridge: Cambridge University Press, 1999).

Reid, D. G., "Sacrifice and Temple Service," in *DNTB,* ed. C. A. Evans and S. E. Porter (Downers Grove, IL: InterVarsity Press, 2000), 1038-44.

Rendtorff, R., *The Canonical Hebrew Bible: A Theology of the Old Testament* (Leiden: Deo, 2005).

Richards, E. R., *Paul and First-Century Letter Writing: Secretaries, Composition and Collection* (Downers Grove, IL: InterVarsity Press, 2004).

———, *The Secretary in the Letters of Paul,* WUNT 2.42 (Tübingen: J. C. B. Mohr, 1991).

Richardson, N., *Paul's Language about God* (Sheffield: Sheffield Academic Press, 1994).

Richardson, P., "Judgment in Sexual Matters in 1 Corinthians 6:1-11," *NovT* 255 (1983), 37-58.

Riesner, R., *Paul's Early Period: Chronology, Mission Strategy, Theology,* from *Die Frühzeit des Apostels Paulus,* trans. D. Stott (Tübingen/Grand Rapids: J. C. B. Mohr [Paul Siebeck]/Eerdmans, 1994/1998).

Riggans, W., "The Parousia: Getting Our Terms Right," *Themelios* 21 (1995), 14-16.

Robertson, A. T., *A Grammar of the Greek New Testament in the Light of Historical Research* (New York: Hodder & Stoughton, 1919).

Robertson, O. P., "Tongues: Sign of Covenantal Curse and Blessing," *WTJ* 38 (1975), 43-53.

Roetzel, C. J., "The Judgment Form in Paul's Letters," *JBL* 88 (1969), 305-12.

———, *Judgment in the Community: A Study in the Relationship between Eschatology and Ecclesiology in Paul* (Leiden: Brill, 1972).

Rosner, B. S., "Known by God: The Meaning and Value of a Neglected Theme," *TynBul* 59 (2008), 207-30.

———, *Paul and the Law,* New Studies in Biblical Theology (Downers Grove, IL: Apollos/InterVarsity, forthcoming).
———, "Paul and Moses Appointing Judges: An Antecedent to 1 Cor 6.1-6?" *ZNW* 82 (1991), 275-78.
———, *Paul, Scripture and Ethics: A Study of 1 Corinthians 5–7* (Grand Rapids: Baker, 1999).
———, "Paul's Ethics," in *The Cambridge Companion to St. Paul,* ed. J. D. G. Dunn (Cambridge: Cambridge University Press, 2003), 212-23.
———, "'Stronger than He?': The Strength of 1 Corinthians 10:22b," *TynBul* 43 (1992), 171-79.
———, *Understanding Paul's Ethics: Twentieth-Century Approaches* (Grand Rapids: Eerdmans, 1995).
———, "'With What Kind of Body Do They Come?' (1 Corinthians 15:35b): Paul's Conception of Resurrection Bodies," in *The New Testament in Its First-Century Setting: Essays on Context and Background in Honour of B. W. Winter on His 65th Birthday,* ed. P. J. Williams et al. (Grand Rapids: Eerdmans, 2004), 190-205.
———, "'Written for us': Paul's View of Scripture," in *A Pathway into the Holy Scripture,* ed. D. Wright and P. Satterthwaite (Grand Rapids: Eerdmans, 1994), 81-105.
Routledge, R., "Passover and the Last Supper," *TynBul* 53 (2002), 203-21.
Sailhamer, J., *Introduction to Old Testament Theology: A Canonical Approach* (Grand Rapids: Zondervan, 1995).
Sallares, J. R., "Meals," in *OCD,* ed. S. Hornblower and A. Spawforth (Oxford: Oxford University Press, 1996), 942.
Saller, R., "Women, Slaves, and the Economy of the Roman Household," in *Early Christian Families in Context: An Interdisciplinary Dialogue,* ed. D. L. Balch and C. Osiek (Grand Rapids: Eerdmans, 2003), 185-204.
Samarin, W. J., "The Linguisticality of Glossolalia," *Hartford Quarterly* 8 (1968), 49-75.
Sanders, E. P., *Paul* (Oxford: Oxford University Press, 1991).
———, *Paul, the Law and the Jewish People* (Philadelphia: Fortress Press, 1983).
Sanders, J. T., "The Transition from Opening Epistolary Thanksgiving to Body in the Letters of the Pauline Corpus," *JBL* 81 (1962), 348-62.
Sanders, T. K., "A New Approach to 1 Corinthians 13:1," *NTS* 36 (1990), 614-18.
Sandnes, K. O., *Paul — One of the Prophets? A Contribution to the Apostle's Self-Understanding* (Tübingen: J. C. B. Mohr [Paul Siebeck], 1991).
———,"Prophecy — A Sign for Believers," *Bib* 77 (1996), 1-15.
Satlow, M. L., *Jewish Marriage in Antiquity* (Princeton: Princeton University Press, 2001).
Savage, T. B., *Power through Weakness: Paul's Understanding of the Christian Ministry in 2 Corinthians* (New York: Cambridge University Press, 1995).
Scheid, J., "The Religious Roles of Roman Women," in *A History of Women in*

*the West*, vol. 1, *From Ancient Goddesses to Christian Saints*, ed. P. S. Pantel (Cambridge, MA: Belknap, 1992), 377-408.
Schiefer, F. M., *Die Sprache des Leids in den paulinischen Peristasenkatalogen* (Stuttgart: Katholisches Bibelwerk, 1991).
Schmidt, T. E., *Straight or Narrow: Compassion and Clarity in the Homosexuality Debate* (Downers Grove: InterVarsity Press, 1995).
Schrage, W., *The Ethics of the New Testament* (Philadelphia: Fortress, 1988).
———, "Die Stellung zur Welt bei Paulus, Epiktet und in der Apokalyptik," *ZTK* 61 (1964), 125-54.
Schreiner, T. R., *Romans* (Grand Rapids: Baker, 1998).
Schubert, P., *Form and Function of the Pauline Thanksgivings* (Berlin: Töpelmann, 1939).
Schürer, E., *The History of the Jewish People in the Age of Jesus Christ*, ed. G. Vermes, F. Millar, and M. Black, 3 vols. (Edinburgh: T&T Clark, 1973-87).
Schüssler, F. E., *In Memory of Her: A Feminist Theological Reconstruction of Christian Origins* (New York: Crossroad, 1984).
Schweitzer, A., *The Mysticism of Paul the Apostle* (Baltimore: Johns Hopkins University Press, 1998).
Schweizer, E., *Church Order in the New Testament* (London: SCM, 1961).
———, *The Good News according to Mark* (Richmond: John Knox, 1970).
Scott, J. M., *Adoption as Sons of God: An Exegetical Investigation into the Background of ΥΙΟΘΕΣΙΑ in the Pauline Corpus* (Tübingen: J. C. B. Mohr [Paul Siebeck], 1992).
———, *Paul and the Nations: The Old Testament and Jewish Background of Paul's Mission to the Nations with Special Reference to the Destination of Galatians* (Tübingen: J. C. B. Mohr [Paul Siebeck], 1995).
Scroggs, R., *The New Testament and Homosexuality: Contextual Background for Contemporary Debate* (Philadelphia: Fortress, 1983).
———, "Paul: σοφὸς καὶ πνευματικός," *NTS* 14 (1967-68), 33-55.
Sebesta, J. L., "Symbolism in the Costume of the Roman Woman," in *The World of Roman Costume*, ed. J. L. Sebesta and L. Bonfante (Madison: University of Wisconsin Press, 2001), 46-53.
Seneca, L. A., *Moral Epistles* (Cambridge, MA: Harvard University Press, 1917-25).
Shelton, J. A., *As the Romans Did: A Sourcebook in Roman Social History* (New York: Oxford University Press, 1998).
Sigountos, J. G., "The Genre of 1 Corinthians," *NTS* 40 (1994), 246-60.
Silva, M., *Biblical Words and Their Meaning: An Introduction to Lexical Semantics* (Grand Rapids: Zondervan, 1983).
———, *Interpreting Galatians: Explorations in Exegetical Method* (Grand Rapids: Baker, 2001).
———, "A Response to Fanning and Porter on Verbal Aspect," in *Biblical Greek Language and Linguistics: Open Questions in Current Research*, ed.

S. E. Porter and D. A. Carson (Sheffield: Sheffield Academic Press, 1993), 74-82.

Smit, J. F. M., "Argument and Genre of 1 Corinthians 12–14," in *Rhetoric and the New Testament: Essays from the 1992 Heidelberg Conference*, ed. S. E. Porter and T. H. Olbricht (Sheffield: Sheffield Academic Press, 1993).

———, "Tongues and Prophecy: Deciphering 1 Cor. 14:22," *Bib* 75 (1994), 175-90.

———, "Two Puzzles: I Corinthians 12:31 and 13:3: A Rhetorical Solution," *NTS* 39 (1993), 246-64.

———, "'What Is Apollos? What Is Paul?' In Search for the Coherence of First Corinthians 1:10–4:21," *NovT* 44 (2002), 231-51.

Smith, D. E., *From Symposium to Eucharist: The Banquet in the Early Christian World* (Minneapolis: Fortress, 2003).

Söding, T., *Das Liebesgebot bei Paulus: Die Mahnung zur Agape im Rahmen der paulinischen Ethik* (Munster: Aschendorff, 1995).

Soskice, J. M., *Metaphor and Religious Language* (Oxford: Clarendon, 1985).

South, J. T., "A Critique of the 'Curse/Death' Interpretation of 1 Corinthians 5.1-8," *NTS* 39 (1993), 539-61.

Spicq, C., *Agape in the New Testament*, vol. 2 (St. Louis and London: Herder, 1965).

Staab, K., *Pauluskommentare aus der griechischen Kirche* (Münster: Aschendorff, 1933).

Stanley, C. D., *Paul and the Language of Scripture: Citation Technique in the Pauline Epistles and Contemporary Literature* (Cambridge: Cambridge University Press, 1992).

Stein, A., "Wo trugen die korinthischen Christen ihre Rechtshändel aus?" *ZNW* 59 (1968), 86-90.

Stühlmacher, P., "The Hermeneutical Significance of 1 Cor 2:6-16," in *Tradition and Interpretation in the New Testament: Essays in Honor of E. Earle Ellis for His 60th Birthday*, ed. G. F. Hawthorne and O. Betz (Grand Rapids/Tübingen: Eerdmans/J. C. B. Mohr [Paul Siebeck], 1987), 328-47.

———, "The Pauline Gospel," in *The Gospel and the Gospels*, ed. P. Stühlmacher (Grand Rapids: Eerdmans, 1991), 149-72.

Sumney, J. L., Review of J. A. D. Weima, *Neglected Endings: The Significance of the Pauline Letter Closings*, *JBL* 115 (1996), 557-59.

Sweet, J. P. M., "Sign for Unbelievers: Paul's Attitude to Glossolalia," *NTS* 13 (1967), 240-57.

Terry, R. B., *A Discourse Analysis of First Corinthians*, Summer Institute of Linguistics and the University of Texas at Arlington Publications in Linguistics 120 (Dallas: Summer Institute of Linguistics and the University of Texas at Arlington, 1995).

———, "Patterns of Discourse Structure in 1 Corinthians," *JOTT* 7/4 (1996), 1-32.

Theissen, G., *Psychological Aspects of Pauline Theology* (Edinburgh: T&T Clark, 1987).

———, *The Social Setting of Pauline Christianity: Essays on Corinth* (Edinburgh: T&T Clark, 1982).

Thielicke, H., *Theological Ethics* (Philadelphia: Fortress, 1966).

Thielman, F., "The Coherence of Paul's View of the Law: The Evidence of First Corinthians," *NTS* 38 (1992), 235-53.

Thiselton, A. C., "The 'Interpretation' of Tongues? A New Suggestion in the Light of Greek Usage in Philo and Josephus," *JTS?* 30 (1979), 15-36.

———, "The Meaning of *SARX* in 1 Corinthians 5.5: A Fresh Approach in the Light of Logical and Semantic Factors," *SJT* 26 (1973), 204-28.

———, "Realized Eschatology at Corinth," *NTS* 24 (1977-78), 510-26.

Thornton, L. S., *The Common Life in the Body of Christ* (London: Dacre, 1950).

Tomson, P. J., *Paul and the Jewish Law: Halakha in the Letters of the Apostle to the Gentiles* (Assen/Maastricht: Van Gorcum, 1990).

Toussaint, S. D., "First Corinthians Thirteen and the Tongues Question," *BSac* 120 (1963), 311-16.

Towner, P. H., "The Pastoral Epistles," in *NDBT*, ed. T. D. Alexander and B. S. Rosner (Leicester: Inter-Varsity Press, 2000), 330-36.

Treggiari, S., "Divorce Roman Style: How Easy and How Frequent Was It?" in *Marriage, Divorce, and Children in Ancient Rome*, ed. B. Rawson (Oxford: Oxford University Press, 1991), 31-46.

———, "Marriage and Family in Roman Society," in *Marriage and Family in the Biblical World*, ed. Ken M. Campbell (Downers Grove: InterVarsity Press, 2003), 132-82.

———, *Roman Freedmen during the Late Republic* (Oxford: Clarendon Press, 1969).

———, *Roman Marriage: Iusti Coniuges from the Time of Cicero to the Time of Ulpian* (Oxford: Oxford University Press, 1991).

Tucker, C. W., "Women in the Manumission Inscriptions at Delphi," *TAPA* 112 (1982), 225-36.

van Unnik, W. C., "The Meaning of 1 Corinthians 12:31," *NovT* 35 (1993), 142-59.

———, "Reisepläne und Amen-Sagen, Zusammenhang und Gedankenfolge in 2 Korinther 1:15-24," in *Studia Paulina in Honorem Johannis de Zwaan Septuagenarii* (Haarlem: Erven Bohn, 1953), 215-34.

———, "Die Rücksicht auf die Reaktion der Nicht-Christen als Motiv in der altchristlichen Paränese," in *Judentum, Urchristentum, Kirche: Festschrift für Joachim Jeremias*, ed. Walther Eltester (Berlin: Töpelmann, 1960), 221-34.

———, "With All Those Who Call on the Name of the Lord," in *The New Testament Age: Essays in Honor of Bo Reicke*, ed. W. C. Weinrich (Macon, GA: Mercer University Press, 1984), 2:533-51.

Vander Broek, L. D., *Breaking Barriers: The Possibilities of Christian Community in a Lonely World* (Grand Rapids: Brazos, 2002).

Vanhoozer, K. J., *Is There a Meaning in This Text?: The Bible, the Reader, and the Morality of Literary Knowledge* (Grand Rapids: Zondervan, 1998).
Vaux, R. de., *Ancient Israel: Its Life and Institutions* (Grand Rapids: Eerdmans, 1997).
Vielhauer, P., *Oikodome: Aufsatze zum Neuen Testament* (Munchen: C. Kaiser, 1979).
Vischer, L., *Die Auslegungsgeschichte von I Kor. 6:1-11: Rechtsverzicht und Senlichtung* (Tübingen: J. C. B. Mohr [Paul Siebeck], 1955).
Viviano, B., *Study as Worship: Aboth and the New Testament* (Leiden: Brill, 1978).
Vlachos, C. A., *The Law and the Knowledge of Good and Evil: The Edenic Background of the Catalytic Operation of the Law in Paul* (Eugene, OR: Pickwick, 2009).
Vlachos, C. A., "Law, Sin, and Death, An Edenic Nexus? An Examination with Reference to 1 Corinthians 15:56," *JETS* 47 (2003), 277-98.
Wagner, J. R., "'Not beyond the Things Which Are Written': A Call to Boast Only in the Lord (1 Cor. 4:6)," *NTS* 44 (1998), 279-87.
Wallace, D. B., *Greek Grammar beyond the Basics: An Exegetical Syntax of the New Testament* (Grand Rapids: Zondervan, 1996).
Waltke, B. K., *An Old Testament Theology: An Exegetical, Canonical and Thematic Approach* (Grand Rapids: Zondervan, 2006).
Walton, S., "What Has Aristotle to Do with Paul? Rhetorical Criticism and 1 Thessalonians," *TynBul* 46 (1995), 229-50.
Ward, R. B., "Musonius and Paul on Marriage," *NTS* 36 (1990), 281-89.
Warren, R., *The Purpose Driven Life* (Grand Rapids: Zondervan, 2002).
Watson, F., *Agape, Eros, Gender: Towards a Pauline Sexual Ethic* (Cambridge: Cambridge University Press, 2000).
———, *Paul and the Hermeneutics of Faith* (London: T&T Clark, 2006).
———, *Text, Church and World: Biblical Interpretation in Theological Perspective* (Grand Rapids: Eerdmans, 1994).
Watson, G. R., *The Roman Soldier* (Ithaca, NY: Cornell University Press, 1969).
Weaver, P. R. C., "Children of Freedmen (and Freedwomen)," in *Marriage, Divorce, and Children in Ancient Rome*, ed. B. Rawson (Oxford: Oxford University Press, 1991), 166-90.
Webb, B. G., *The Message of Isaiah* (Leicester: Inter-Varsity, 1996).
Weber, H. R., *The Cross: Tradition and Interpretation* (Grand Rapids: Eerdmans, 1979).
Weima, J. A. D., *Neglected Endings: The Significance of the Pauline Letter Closings*, JSNTSup 101 (Sheffield: JSOT Press, 1994).
Weinfeld, M., "Covenant, Davidic," *IDBSup* (1976), 190-92.
———, "Judge and Officer in Ancient Israel and in the Ancient Near East," *Israel Oriental Studies* 7 (1977), 65-88.
Welborn, L. L., *Politics and Rhetoric in the Corinthian Epistles* (Macon, GA: Mercer University Press, 1997).

Wengst, K., *Pax Romana and the Peace of Jesus Christ* (Philadelphia: Fortress, 1987).

Wenham, D., *Paul: Follower of Jesus or Founder of Christianity?* (Grand Rapids: Eerdmans, 1995).

Wenham, G. J., *The Book of Leviticus* (Grand Rapids: Eerdmans, 1979).

———, "The Old Testament Attitude to Homosexuality," *ExpTim* 102 (1990-91), 359-63.

Westerholm, S., *Israel's Law and the Church's Faith: Paul and His Recent Interpreters* (Grand Rapids: Eerdmans, 1988).

White, J. R., "'Baptized on Account of the Dead': The Meaning of 1 Corinthians 15:29 in Its Context," *JBL* 116 (1997), 487-99.

———, *Die Erstlingsgabe im Neuen Testament* (Tübingen: Francke, 2007).

Wiedemann, T., *Greek and Roman Slavery* (London: Routledge, 1981).

Williams, C. A., *Roman Homosexuality* (Oxford: Oxford University Press, 2010).

Williams, D. J., *Paul's Metaphors: Their Context and Character* (Peabody, MA: Hendrickson, 1999).

Williams, H. H. D., "The Psalms in 1 and 2 Corinthians," in *The Psalms in the New Testament*, ed. S. Moyise and M. J. J. Menken (Edinburgh: T&T Clark, 2004), 163-80.

———, *The Wisdom of the Wise: The Presence and Function of Scripture within 1 Corinthians 1:18–3:23* (Leiden: Brill, 2001).

Williamson, H. G. M., *1 and 2 Chronicles* (Grand Rapids: Eerdmans, 1982).

Willis, W. L., *Idol Meat in Corinth: The Pauline Argument in 1 Corinthians 8 and 10* (Chico, CA: Scholars Press, 1985).

Wilson, M. R., *Our Father Abraham: Jewish Roots of the Christian Faith* (Grand Rapids: Eerdmans, 1989).

Wimbush, V. L., *Paul the Worldly Ascetic: Response to the World and Self-Understanding in 1 Corinthians 7* (Macon, GA: Mercer University Press, 1987).

Winter, B. W., *After Paul Left Corinth: The Influence of Secular Ethics and Social Change* (Grand Rapids: Eerdmans, 2001).

———, "Civil Litigation in Secular Corinth and the Church: The Forensic Background to 1 Corinthians 6.1-8," *NTS* 37 (1991), 559-72.

———, "1 Corinthians 7:6-7: A Caveat and a Framework for 'The Sayings' in 7:8-24," *TynBul* 48 (1997), 57-65.

———, *Philo and Paul among the Sophists: Alexandrian and Corinthian Responses to a Julio-Claudian Movement* (Grand Rapids: Eerdmans, 2002).

———, "Puberty or Passion? The Meaning of ὑπέρακμος in 1 Corinthians 7:36," *TynBul* 49 (1998), 71-89.

———, *Roman Wives, Roman Widows: The Appearance of New Women and the Pauline Communities* (Grand Rapids: Eerdmans, 2003).

———, "Secular and Christian Responses to Corinthian Famines," *TynBul* 40 (1989), 86-106.

———, *Seek the Welfare of the City: Christians as Benefactors and Citizens* (Grand Rapids: Eerdmans, 1994).

Wire, A. C., *The Corinthian Women Prophets: A Reconstruction through Paul's Rhetoric* (Minneapolis: Fortress, 1990).

Wischmeyer, O., *Der höchste Weg: Das 13 Kapitel des 1 Korintherbriefes* (Gütersloh: Mohn, 1981).

Wise, M. O., M. G. Abegg, and E. M. Cook, *The Dead Sea Scrolls: A New Translation* (San Francisco: HarperSanFrancisco, 1996).

Witherington, B., *Jesus, Paul, and the End of the World* (Carlisle: Paternoster, 1992).

Witmer, S. E., "θεοδίδακτοι in 1 Thessalonians 4.9: A Pauline Neologism," *NTS* 52 (2006), 239-50.

Wolterstorff, N., *Divine Discourse: Philosophical Reflections on the Claim That God Speaks* (Cambridge: Cambridge University Press, 1995).

Wright, C. J. H., "The Ethical Authority of the Old Testament: A Survey of Approaches: Part I," *TynBul* 43 (1992), 101-20.

———, "The Ethical Authority of the Old Testament: A Survey of Approaches: Part II," *TynBul* 43 (1992), 203-31.

———, *An Eye for an Eye: The Place of Old Testament Ethics Today* (Downers Grove: InterVarsity Press, 1983).

Wright, D. F., "Homosexuality: The Relevance of the Bible," *EvQ* 61 (1989), 291-300.

———, "Homosexuals or Prostitutes? The Meaning of ἀρσενοκοῖται (1 Cor. 6:9; 1 Tim. 1:10)," *Vigiliae Christianae* 38 (1984), 125-53.

———, "Translating Ἀρσενοκοῖται (1 Cor 6:9; 1 Tim 1:10)," *Vigiliae Christianae* 41 (1987), 396-98.

Wright, J. R., "Boswell on Homosexuality: A Case Undemonstrated," *Anglican Theological Review Supplement* 66 (1984), 79-94.

Wright, N. T., *The Epistles of Paul to the Colossians and Philemon* (Leicester: Inter-Varsity Press, 1986).

———, "Monotheism, Christology, and Ethics: 1 Cor. 8," in *The Climax of the Covenant: Christ and the Law in Pauline Theology* (Minneapolis: Fortress, 1992), 120-36.

———, *Paul: Fresh Perspectives* (London: SPCK, 2006).

———, *The Resurrection of the Son of God* (Minneapolis: Fortress, 2003).

———, *Simply Christian: Why Christianity Makes Sense* (New York: HarperOne, 2006).

———, *What Saint Paul Really Said: Was Paul of Tarsus the Real Founder of Christianity?* (Grand Rapids: Eerdmans, 1997).

Wuellner, W., "Greek Rhetoric and Pauline Argumentation," in *Early Christian Literature and the Classical Intellectual Tradition: In Honorem Robert M. Grant*, ed. W. R. Schoedel and R. L. Wilken (Berkeley: University of California Press, 1979), 177-88.

Yarbrough, O. L., *Not Like the Gentiles: Marriage Rules in the Letters of Paul* (Atlanta: Scholars Press, 1986).

Yarbrough, R. W., "Paul and Salvation History," in *Justification and Variegated Nomism*, vol. 2, *The Paradoxes of Paul*, ed. D. A. Carson, P. T. O'Brien, and M. A. Seifrid (Tübingen/Grand Rapids: J. C. B. Mohr [Paul Siebeck]/ Baker Academic, 2004), 297-342.

Yeo, K. K., *Rhetorical Interaction in I Corinthians 8 and 10: A Formal Analysis with Preliminary Suggestions for a Chinese, Cross-Cultural Hermeneutic* (Leiden: Brill, 1995).

Youngman, S., "Stratificational Analysis of a Hortatory Text: I Corinthians 8:1–11:1" (M.A. thesis, University of Texas at Arlington, 1987).

Zaas, P. S., "Catalogues and Context: 1 Corinthians 5 and 6," *NTS* 34 (1988), 622-29.

Zakovitch, Y., *"And You Shall Tell Your Son . . .": The Concept of the Exodus in the Bible* (Jerusalem: Magnes, 1991).

Zerbe, G., *Non-Retaliation in Early Jewish and New Testament Texts* (Sheffield: Sheffield Academic Press, 1993).

Zerwick, M., *Biblical Greek; Illustrated by Examples* (Rome: Biblical Institute Press, 1963).

———, and M. Grosvenor, *A Grammatical Analysis of the Greek New Testament* (Rome: Biblical Institute Press, 1974-79).

Zuntz, G., *The Text of the Epistles: A Disquisition upon the Corpus Paulinum* (London: Oxford University Press, 1953).

# *Introduction*

1 Corinthians has much to say to the modern world. No book in the New Testament, even Paul's letter to the Romans, does more to explain the grace of God, the lordship of Christ, and the work of the Holy Spirit. The contribution of the letter to the practical knowledge of God is immense. Not only is its ethics searching and rigorous, but its theology, especially of the cross, announces the end of the world as we know it. In addition to supplying concrete answers to many problems which have comparable manifestations today, on subjects as diverse as leadership, preaching, pluralism, sexuality, and worship, 1 Corinthians models how to approach the complexity of Christian living with the resources of the Old Testament and the example and teaching of Jesus. Above all, it shows the importance of asking, How does the gospel of the death and resurrection of Jesus Christ, which envelop the letter in chapters 1 and 15, teach us to live?

Nonetheless, John Calvin was right to describe 1 Corinthians as "no less difficult than valuable."[1] It is, in fact, one of Paul's most difficult letters. Many factors weigh against a confident and appropriate reading of this ancient text. It is far removed from our world in terms of language, geography, economics, social customs, and religious practice. It talks with little or no explanation of human wisdom, law courts, prostitution, meat markets, and pagan worship, not to mention head coverings and baptism for the dead. It apparently treats an assortment of topics in no particular order. It carries forward a conversation, but what the other parties were saying is no longer available. To make matters worse, far from arriving at a consensus, modern biblical scholarship throws up rival interpretations of the letter, and an arsenal of critical methods each boasts of its superior potency.

To read the letter for all its worth we need to answer three questions, which in turn make up the main sections of the introduction to this com-

1. Calvin, 1. Cf. the translation by John Pringle (Grand Rapids: Baker, 1981 rpt.), 29: "not less obscure than useful."

mentary: (1) What were Corinth and the church of God in Corinth like? (2) Who was Paul and what were his aims in writing to the Corinthians? And (3) how then should we read 1 Corinthians?

## I. THE CHURCH IN CORINTH

Virtually every modern commentary on 1 Corinthians agrees with James D. G. Dunn that "an ancient text like 1 Corinthians cannot be properly understood unless it is read against the background of its historical context and as part of a dialogue with the Corinthian church itself."[2] The following two sections address the nature of ancient Corinth and the character of its troubled church. Neither treatment aims to be exhaustive. The commentary is the best place to discuss the myriad of details involved in these issues in direct contact with relevant texts in the letter. The aim here is briefly to set the general parameters within which reliable and helpful answers may be constructed in the course of the commentary.

### A. Roman Corinth

At the foot of the impressive Acrocorinth, a rugged limestone summit (1,886 feet/574 meters high), Greek Corinth had existed for some several hundred years before it was destroyed by Rome in 146 B.C. The city was refounded by Julius Caesar in 44 B.C. and quickly rose to prominence again, becoming one of the most important cities of the Roman Empire. Corinth was the capital of the province of Achaia and the seat of the governor. The ancient geographer Strabo attributed the city's economic success to its strategic location.[3] It was situated on a narrow neck of land that connected the Peloponnese to the south with the rest of Greece to the north. To the east and west respectively were the Sardonic and Corinthian gulfs of the Aegean and Ionian seas, the distance between the two bodies of water being only nine kilometers, or less than six miles. A paved road, the *diolkos*, enabled boats to be dragged this short distance in order to avoid making the treacherous sea voyage around Cape Malea at the tip of the Peloponnesus. A number of leaders, as far back as Periander in 602 B.C., proposed the digging of a canal across the Isthmus. Finally, in 1923 the project came to fruition, and it is used by shipping to this day.

Archaeological excavations of ancient Corinth began in the nineteenth century, with the first report published in 1886. With information

2. James D. G. Dunn, "Reconstructions of Corinthian Christianity and the Interpretation of 1 Corinthians," in *Christianity at Corinth: The Quest for the Pauline Church* (ed. David G. Horrell and Edward Adams; Louisville: Westminster John Knox, 2004), 308-9.

3. Strabo, *Geography* 8.6.19-20a.

drawn from archaeological, epigraphic, numismatic, and ancient literary sources scholars have assembled a remarkably sharp profile of the city in Paul's day.[4]

Roman Corinth was prosperous, cosmopolitan, and religiously pluralistic, accustomed to visits by impressive, traveling public speakers and obsessed with status, self-promotion, and personal rights. From a Jewish or Christian viewpoint, as with any pagan city, its inhabitants were marked by the worship of idols, sexual immorality, and greed. Other historical information of interest about the city includes Roman law, culture, and religion, a Jewish presence, Paul's labors as a tentmaker, the nearby bi-annual Isthmian games (second only to the Olympic games), Corinth's social makeup, its social, political, and economic culture, and so on. An understanding of these and many other characteristics of the city will prove invaluable in the course of understanding the letter. This material is reviewed at appropriate points in the commentary.

## B. The Church "Belonging to God"

Paul laid the foundation for "the church of God in Corinth" (1 Cor. 1:2) on his second missionary journey and spent eighteen months there building it up (Acts 18:1-18). Most of its members were former Gentiles (cf. 1 Cor. 12:2: "when you were pagans . . .") and had turned to God from idols. Sent from Ephesus (see 1 Cor. 16:8) on his third missionary journey a few years later, in the spring of 54 or 55 A.D.,[5] 1 Corinthians mentions a previous letter (1 Cor. 5:9-11) of Paul to the Corinthians. In it he had warned them not to associate with those who were guilty of serious sins, such as sexual immorality, greed, and idolatry. Since these were the typical faults of the Gentiles, Paul was effectively exhorting them not to be "conformed to the world" (Rom. 12:2). Unfortunately, some in the church mistook Paul to be saying they should shun not just fellow believers who behaved in such ways, but their non-Christian neighbors as well. What we call 1 Corinthians is in part Paul's attempt to correct this misunderstanding and provide clearer guidance regarding problems the church was facing due to sexual immorality, greed and idolatry.

Paul was prompted to write 1 Corinthians in response to disturbing news from the church. This included both oral reports, from Chloe's people (1:11) and Stephanas, Fortunatus, and Achaicus (16:17), and a letter from the church that Paul mentions in 7:1 consisting of a series of questions

4. Jerome Murphy-O'Connor's 1983 *St. Paul's Corinth* (Collegeville, MN: Liturgical Press) was an early example, now in its third edition, with other studies continuing into the present. Later in this introduction we point to the place of such work in the study of the letter (III.D.2. — "Greco-Roman Foreground").

5. On dating the letter, which revolves largely around the date of Gallio, the proconsul of Asia (cf. Acts 18:12), see Thiselton, 29-32.

posed by the congregation. As far as we can reconstruct the situation, after Paul left Corinth, Apollos, and possibly Peter, visited, and this caused unintended problems as well as bringing various benefits. The congregation was now divided based on loyalty to their favorite Christian leader (1:12). Further, Paul learned that they were in considerable disarray, with some members engaging each other in civil litigation (6:1-11), cases of sexual immorality (5:1-13; 6:12-20), marriage problems (7:1-40), and questions concerning food offered to idols (chs. 8–10) and spiritual gifts (chs. 12–14).

The precise cause and nature of the problems in the church in Corinth have been matters of intense dispute in New Testament scholarship for half a century. Numerous religious and philosophical parallels with the putative behavior and beliefs of the church there (inferred from a mirror reading of 1 and 2 Corinthians) have been adduced, including material from Gnosticism, Hellenistic Judaism, Stoicism, Cynicism, and Epicureanism.[6] Some have attributed the problems in Corinth to a misunderstanding of one aspect of Paul's own theology, resulting in a so-called "over-realized eschatology."[7] However, in recent years a rough consensus has begun to emerge in which scholars agree that the problems Paul addresses in 1 Corinthians reflect the infiltration of Corinthian social values into the church.

Hans Conzelmann's question in 1969 was on target: "We have here to do with people [the Corinthians] who have only recently become Christians; what were the ideas they brought with them into the community?"[8] Many of their faults can be traced to their uncritical acceptance of the attitudes, values, and behaviors of the society in which they lived. The glorification of wisdom, the eating of food sacrificed to idols, the denial of bodily resurrection, and the light assessment of sexual immorality, drunkenness, greed, and vexatious litigation were all common features of their society. A sample of commentators who concur with this basic conclusion includes:

- Bruce W. Winter: "[T]he problems which arose subsequent to Paul's departure [from Corinth] did so partly because the Christians were 'cosmopolitans', i.e., citizens of this world and, in particular, citizens or residents of Roman Corinth," and thus "the primary influences on the responses of the Christians were derived principally from *Romanitas*."[9]
- Richard B. Hays: "they [the Corinthian Christians] are uncritically

6. For a survey see David G. Horrell and Edward Adams (eds.), *Christianity at Corinth: The Quest for the Pauline Church* (Louisville: Westminster John Knox, 2004), 16-23.

7. See Anthony C. Thiselton, "Realized Eschatology at Corinth," *NTS* 24 (1977-78), 510-26 and Fee, 12 and passim. According to this view, the Corinthians' problems stemmed from thinking that they were already experiencing all that Christ had won for them through the resurrection. See our comments on 1 Cor. 4:8 for an evaluation.

8. Conzelmann, 15.

9. B. W. Winter, *After Paul Left Corinth: The Influence of Secular Ethics and Social Change* (Grand Rapids: Eerdmans, 2001), 27-28.

perpetuating the norms and values of the pagan culture around them."[10]

- Wolfgang Schrage, in discussing the various influences on the Corinthians, concludes that "after their conversion they [the Corinthian Christians] remained in contact with their heathen environment, by way of mixed marriages (7:12-16), in the workplace (cf. 4:12), at the marketplace (10:25), through invitations (cf. 10:27) and elsewhere, and were influenced in these settings socially, religiously, ideologically, and in other ways."[11]
- Anthony Thiselton makes much of "the impact of the culture of Corinth upon the developing faith of newly converted believers."[12]
- R. B. Terry argues that "most, if not all, of the problems which Paul discusses in 1 Corinthians can be attributed to the influence of the Corinthian cultural setting on the Christians there."[13]
- David E. Garland rejects other suggested influences, arguing that "the influences on them [the Corinthian believers] were more amorphous and their behavior was swayed by culturally ingrained habits from their pagan past and by values instilled by a popularized secular ethics."[14]

Lyle D. Vander Broek offers a pithy summary: "Each of the community problems Paul needed to address grew out of the Corinthians' inability to let the gospel message fully reshape their gentile, Greco-Roman lives, whether because they misunderstood that message or because they rejected it outright. They were Hellenists through and through, and this eschatological, cross-centered, body-affirming Jewish sect called Christianity demanded that they enter another theological and ethical world. It is no surprise that these residents of Corinth would seek rhetorical wisdom, be unconcerned with immorality and the preservation of the body, be infatuated with asceticism and spiritual empowerment, and preserve the distinctions between rich and poor. The Corinthians were simply trying to be Christians with a minimal amount of social and theological disturbance."[15]

While other scholars have recognized that the Corinthian problems are mainly due to the influence of dominant Roman/Corinthian culture and values (rather than overrealized eschatology, Gnosticism, or some other exotic influence), we maintain that view more consistently. This is especially apparent in our interpretation of chapter 7, where other scholars

10. Hays, 71.

11. Schrage, 1:42. The translation is our own.

12. Thiselton, xviii.

13. R. B. Terry, *A Discourse Analysis of First Corinthians* (Dallas: Summer Institute of Linguistics, 1995), 57.

14. Garland, 13.

15. Lyle D. Vander Broek, *Breaking Barriers: The Possibilities of Christian Community in a Lonely World* (Grand Rapids: Brazos, 2002), 27-28.

continue to suggest that some Corinthians were advocating celibacy both outside and within marriage. That would be a rather exotic position, not in keeping with the dominant Greco-Roman culture. Our own view understands the text in light of more dominant views of sex in the Roman world (which tended to be divided over whether sex was to be engaged in for pleasure or only for procreation, and, if both, if sex for pleasure should be sought outside the marital relationship). Our interpretation assumes that here also the problem the Corinthians are dealing with is a reflection of dominant perspectives in the Roman and Corinthian context. In short, the Corinthians were "worldly," "acting like mere human beings" (1 Cor. 3:3). In this sense the letter is a timeless challenge to Christians of all generations and in all places not to be conformed to the world (Rom. 12:2).

The main problem for the Corinthian Christians is actually signaled in the opening verses of Paul's letter. He writes in 1 Corinthians 1:2 to "the church of God in Corinth, to those sanctified, called to be holy." That the church in Corinth is God's church is repeated three times. Yet the Corinthians were still behaving as if they belonged to their city! Paul's aim in writing is to urge them to adopt a way of life more in accord with their true ownership.

## II. THE IDENTITY AND AIMS OF THE APOSTLE PAUL

When one is reading other people's mail, it is helpful to know something not only about the recipients, but also about the author. Knowing his or her background and experience of life helps in the task of listening in to their correspondence. 1 Corinthians is a case in point. Knowing Paul facilitates a more accurate and satisfying reading of the letter.

Paul's story is well known. By trade he was a "tentmaker"[16] (Acts 18:3). At an early age he was sent to Jerusalem to study for the purpose of becoming a Pharisaic teacher. Brought up a Hebrew of Hebrews and a Pharisee, he violently persecuted the early church and was turned about on the road to Damascus by a blinding vision of the risen Jesus in about A.D. 34 (Acts 9:1-19; 22:3-21; 26:4-18; Gal. 1:13-16). In Damascus he regained his sight and was baptized (Acts 9:3-19). Immediately he began to preach Jesus as messiah in the synagogues. Ironically, the persecutor then became the object of persecution (Acts 9:19-25; cf. 1 Thess. 2:14-16).

As a Jew who became the apostle to the Gentiles, Paul stood between the Jewish and pagan worlds. There is good evidence that Paul was ideally suited to take the message of the long-awaited Jewish Messiah to both Jews and Gentiles across the Roman Empire in that he was well acquainted with both cultural contexts. His aims and agenda in writing 1 Corinthians are

16. Gk. σκηνοποιός.

best understood in relation to the various facets of his identity. The significance of Paul as the apostle to the Gentiles can be fully grasped only when four other descriptions are taken into account: Paul the Jew, the Roman citizen, the follower of Jesus, and the eschatological herald.

## A. Paul the Jew

Paul was a Jew (Gal. 1:13-14; Phil. 3:4-6; 2 Cor. 11:22) from the tribe of Benjamin who was born a Roman citizen in Tarsus of Cilicia, a prosperous and cultured city and a center of Hellenistic culture. Paul was probably his Roman name, Saul being his Hebrew name.

What was Paul's place in Judaism? Rather than needing to limit Paul's background to one corner or another of first-century Judaism, we have good reasons to believe that his exposure was broad indeed. The information about his pre-Christian career in Acts connects him with both Jerusalem and the Diaspora. According to the sole surviving witness to Paul's education, Acts 22:3, Paul was educated at the feet of the honored rabbi Gamaliel (possibly the grandson of Hillel). Though trained in Palestine, he maintained a living connection with Tarsus, his hometown (see Acts 9:30; 11:25), wrote his letters in Greek, and used the Greek Bible. Indeed, in Acts 21:37-40, Paul is depicted as able to speak both Greek and Aramaic. These indications of double linguistic and geographical spread are closely paralleled by what we know of the Jewish historian Josephus, who, although born in Jerusalem, later lived in the Diaspora and composed his writings in both Greek and Aramaic (see the opening of *The Jewish War*). Paul's standard greeting to the churches to which he writes, "grace and peace" (see 1 Cor. 1:3a), illustrates this combination of Greek and Hebrew influences; the phrase, as Zerwick and Grosvenor note, "combines and Christianizes" the traditional Greek and Hebrew greetings.[17]

The fact that Paul is "Jewish to the roots"[18] should alert us to the importance of the Jewish Scriptures, the Old Testament, for understanding his letters, among which 1 Corinthians is a prime example. The normal first-century Jewish experience included considerable instruction in the Scriptures in the context of both home and synagogue (cf. Josephus, *Against Apion* 2.178, 204). Philo wrote that the Jews "consider their laws to be divine revelation and are instructed in them from their youth" (*Embassy to Gaius* 210; cf. 115). According to *m. 'Abot* 5:21, "at five years old one is fit for the Scripture." 4 Maccabees 18:10 intimates that the model Jewish father gave much instruction in the Scriptures to his sons. The educational character of the synagogue service is stressed by Josephus (*Against Apion* 2.175): Jews "gather together to

17. Max Zerwick and Mary Grosvenor, *A Grammatical Analysis of the Greek New Testament* (Rome: Biblical Institute Press, 1974-79), 458.

18. Morna D. Hooker, "Paul — Apostle to the Gentiles," *Epworth Review* 18.2 (1991), 85.

listen to the law and learn it accurately." Paul confesses on no fewer than five occasions in 1 Corinthians that the Scriptures are critical for understanding the source of his teaching: 4:6; 9:10; 10:6, 11; 14:34. According to Paul, the Scriptures were "written for our instruction" (10:11; cf. Rom. 15:4).

That the audience of 1 Corinthians was familiar with the synagogue culture and that the Scriptures formed a large part of Paul's face-to-face instruction in Corinth are suggested by Acts 18, where the synagogue ruler and "his entire household believed in the Lord," and are confirmed by a variety of indications in the letter. 1 Corinthians assumes a good deal of Old Testament knowledge, which Paul presumably imparted to the Corinthian believers in person. For example, understanding 5:6-8 requires some knowledge of the feasts of Passover and Unleavened Bread, comprehending 15:20 requires a familiarity with the concept of "firstfruits" (Exod. 23:16, 19a; Lev. 23:10-14; Num. 18:8-13; Deut. 18:4; 26:2, 10; 2 Chr. 31:5; Neh. 10:37), and an acquaintance with Jewish apocalyptic/wisdom traditions is necessary to grasp properly some terms in 2:6-9. Furthermore, 16:2 mentions the Sabbath and 16:8 Pentecost, both without explanation. It appears that Paul assumed that his readers shared his culture and so recognized something of the Jewish nature of his teaching and its biblical background. It is worth remembering that Gentile adherence to Judaism in the first century was reasonably widespread, the "god-fearers" phenomenon probably being only the tip of the iceberg.[19]

## B. Paul the Roman Citizen

That Paul was familiar with the larger world of Greco-Roman culture is given striking testimony in 1 Corinthians 15:33, where he alludes to the Greek poet Menander. We should take Paul's Roman citizenship no less seriously than his Jewish identity when reading his letters. To have been born a Roman citizen was an exceptional distinction. On all his journeys throughout the Roman Empire Paul enjoyed the attendant rights and privileges of such a station, including fair public trial and exemption from some forms of punishment (cf. Acts 16:37; 22:26-29; 25:10-12). Paul was also a citizen of Tarsus in Cilicia, which was "no mean city" (Acts 21:37-39). Tarsus was indeed "a major Hellenistic city famed for its high culture."[20] Both Acts and Paul's own letters indicate that he had a broader exposure to different parts of the Roman Empire than most of its citizens, since he traveled back and forth between Jerusalem and Greece (passing through Syria, Cilicia, Galatia, etc.) and had lived for extended periods in Tarsus, Jerusalem, Antioch, Corinth, and Ephesus. The conversational style of some of his let-

19. Cf. Acts 15:21.

20. Martin Hengel, *The Pre-Christian Paul* (London: SCM, 1991), 1. For a thorough and convincing defense of the veracity of Paul's claims to being a citizen of Rome and Tarsus, see Hengel, *The Pre-Christian Paul*, 4-15.

ters, especially Romans and 1 Corinthians 9, has often been compared to the Cynic-Stoic mode of argumentation known as *diatribe.* He alludes to Greek games (1 Cor. 9:24-27) and Hellenistic slave trade (1 Cor. 7:22) and employs Hellenistic vocabulary such as "conscience" and "freedom."[21] No doubt he had intimate knowledge of the institutions and ideas of the predominantly Gentile world into which he sent this letter.

## C. Paul the Follower of Jesus

To understand the author of 1 Corinthians it is not sufficient to consider Paul's fine Jewish pedigree and his wide experience of the world in his day. Above and beyond being a Jew and a Roman citizen, Paul was a Christian, a follower of Jesus, with extensive knowledge of the life and teaching of Jesus. He learned about Jesus from Hellenistic Christians like Stephen, whom he opposed so vehemently at first (Acts 6:9; 8:1, 3; 9:29), and through contact with believers in Damascus (including Ananias; Acts 9:10-23) and in Jerusalem (including Peter; Gal. 1:18). That Paul consciously drew on Jesus' teaching as he instructed the early churches and wrote his letters is clear from 1 Corinthians 7:10-11; 9:14; 11:23 (and from 1 Thess. 4:15 and Rom. 14:14). Paul's commitment to Christ is reflected in the catalogs listing the things he had willingly suffered on his behalf in 1 Corinthians 4:9-13; 15:30-32 (cf. Gal. 6:17; 2 Cor. 11:23-29; 12:10). As Christ's own ministry focused on his crucifixion and resurrection (Mark 8:31-33; 9:31; 10:32-34; Matt. 16:21-23; 17:22-23; 20:17-19 Luke 9:22; 18:31-33), so also Paul's message focuses on the cross and resurrection, which serve as a frame for this letter (1:17–2:4; ch. 15).

## D. Paul the Eschatological Herald

Paul's allegiance to Jesus, however, was not simply a matter of following a powerful religious figure or persuasive Jewish prophet. When he says in 1 Corinthians 1:17, "Christ sent me . . . to *preach the gospel,*" he is indebted in his choice of words to Isaiah 40:9, 52:7, and 61:1, where, as Dickson points out, "'secular' messenger language had been transposed to a higher, eschatological level, depicting the end-time herald(s) commissioned by Israel's God to announce his salvific reign."[22] Paul's gospel heralding is an eschato-

21. See further Joseph A. Fitzmyer, *Paul and His Theology: A Brief Sketch* (Englewood Cliffs: Prentice Hall, 1989), 29-30. Cf. Abraham J. Malherbe, *Paul and the Popular Philosophers* (Philadelphia: Fortress, 1989), 68: "There can no longer be any doubt that Paul was thoroughly familiar with the teaching, methods of operation and style of argumentation of the philosophers of the period."

22. John P. Dickson, *Mission-Commitment in Ancient Judaism and in the Pauline Communities: The Shape, Extent and Background of Early Christian Mission* (WUNT 2.159; Tübingen: Mohr Siebeck, 2003), 176.

logical, divinely commissioned activity.[23] Although Paul the eschatological herald is less well known than other ways of describing his identity, it turns out to be a key ingredient in understanding his agenda and is worth exploring at length.

For Paul, the life, death, and resurrection of Jesus were the decisive events in the history of Israel and even the world. Galatians, for example, "reflects a salvation-historical perspective in which the coming of Christ is seen to be the climactic fulfillment towards which the whole history of Israel has been leading."[24] The promises to the Jewish forefather Abraham (Gal. 3:7-8, 16-17, 29; 4:22-23), the giving of the law (Gal. 3:17, 19; 4:24-25), the execution of the curse of the law in Israel's exile (Gal. 3:10, 13; 4:24-25), and the prophetic promise regarding the future salvation and restoration of God's people (Gal. 1:6-9) are all parts of a unified historical drama which climaxes in the coming of Jesus, his death for sins, and his resurrection from the dead. Yet Paul does not regard this "fulfillment" simply as the inevitable outworking of secular historical processes in Israel's history; it is, rather, an "apocalyptic" fulfillment, "the dramatic and climactic inbreaking of the eschatological age of salvation."[25] In Jesus Christ, God has pierced the barrier between the divine and human (Gal. 1:12), heaven and earth (Gal. 4:25-26), Spirit and flesh (Gal. 5:16-17), new and old creation (Gal. 6:15). A new age has dawned in which God the Father deals with humanity as sons, not slaves (Gal. 4:3-5); where humans relate to God not by law, but by faith working through love (Gal. 3:23, 25; 5:6).

The salvation-historical and apocalyptic perspectives are not, for Paul, two irreconcilable outlooks standing in unresolved tension. Instead, the two perspectives converge in Paul's thought such that he regards the history of the particular nation of Israel as finding its fulfillment, through Jesus Christ, in salvation for the entire world. The convergence of salvation-historical and apocalyptic motifs is nowhere more apparent than in the two "bookends" to Romans: 1:1-5 and 16:25-27. The gospel of Jesus Christ, descended from David according to the flesh yet declared to be the Son of God in power according to the Spirit of holiness by his resurrection from the dead, has cosmic significance. This "mystery" was kept secret for long ages but has now been disclosed and *through the prophetic writings* (i.e., the historical Scriptures of Israel) has been made known to all nations, and must be proclaimed to the world and its authorities. It is the eschatological "power of God for salvation" (Rom. 1:16). Paul the Jew regards himself as a herald who has been commissioned by Jesus to perform this task. Paul has been sent, through a special revelation of God's Son, to preach Christ to the Gentiles (Gal. 1:11, 16). He is one of two "point men" in God's eschatologi-

23. Peter Stuhlmacher, "The Pauline Gospel," in *The Gospel and the Gospels* (ed. Peter Stuhlmacher; Grand Rapids: Eerdmans, 1991), 156-65.

24. Roy E. Ciampa, "Galatians," in *NDBT* 311.

25. Ciampa, "Galatians," in *NDBT* 311.

cal mission, having been entrusted with the gospel to the Gentiles just as Peter was entrusted with the gospel to the Jews (Gal. 2:7).

Paul's role as eschatological herald is tightly bound up with the message he proclaims. Scott Hafemann has drawn attention to the role of Paul's suffering in his mission.[26] Hafemann argues compellingly that Paul's weakness was the *ground* and *cause* of his preaching (Gal. 4:13), not merely the circumstances.[27] Paul's personal appeal in Galatians 4:12-20 ties his suffering and his message together — Paul, in his suffering, was accepted *as Christ Jesus* and so should continue to be accepted (Gal. 4:14-16).[28] Both Christ and Paul suffer for the sake of others — Christ as an atoning sacrifice (Gal. 3:10-13), Paul as the messenger of God (Gal. 4:14; cf. v. 19). The "thesis-like affirmations" of 1 Cor. 4:9, 2 Cor. 4:11, and 2 Cor. 2:14 clearly express Paul's portrayal of "his apostolic suffering as the revelatory vehicle through which the knowledge of God as made manifest in the cross of Christ and in the power of the Spirit is being disclosed."[29] Paul's suffering is no accident: it is the appropriate vehicle for proclaiming the message of Christ crucified (1 Cor. 4:9). This, of course, makes sense only when one realizes that suffering is the very means by which God has brought about his eschatological glory, primarily for Christ (Phil. 2:6-11) and consequently for Christ's apostle (2 Cor. 2:14-16) and his people (e.g., Gal. 4:12).[30] This pattern is reflected in various ways throughout Paul's letters (e.g., 2 Cor. 1:5-7; 1 Thess. 3:4; Phil. 1:29-30; Eph. 3:13; Col. 1:24-29; 2 Tim. 1:11-12; 2:8-10).

This same pattern is evident in the description of Paul's suffering in the book of Acts. In Acts, the Lord himself announces that Paul is "a chosen instrument of mine to carry my name before the Gentiles and kings and the children of Israel" by way of great suffering (Acts 9:15-16; cf. Isa. 49:7), proclaiming that "I have made you a light for the Gentiles, that you may bring salvation to the ends of the earth" (Acts 13:47; cf. Isa. 49:6). The role of Paul as the eschatological herald of God's apocalyptic power overcoming the powers of this present evil age may explain the presence of "kings" in the list of the three groups who will be presented with God's glorious name, alongside the Gentiles and the children of Israel (Acts 9:15). Furthermore, it may explain the disproportionately large amount of space in Acts given over to descriptions of Paul's preaching on trial before human authorities. In Acts 20–28, Paul appears to be reliving the Lucan account of Jesus' passion. Both set out resolutely for Jerusalem (Luke 9:51, Acts 19:21), send disciples ahead (Luke 9:52, Acts 19:22), predict their suffering (Luke 9:22, Acts 20:22-24), prepare their followers for their "departure" (Luke 21:5-36, Acts

26. Scott Hafemann, "The Role of Suffering in the Mission of Paul," in *The Mission of the Early Church to Jews and Gentiles* (ed. Jostein Ådna and Hans Kvalbein; WUNT 127; Tübingen: Mohr, 2000), 165-84.

27. Hafemann, "The Role of Suffering in the Mission of Paul," 169-74.

28. Hafemann, "The Role of Suffering in the Mission of Paul," 174.

29. Hafemann, "The Role of Suffering in the Mission of Paul," 174.

30. Hafemann, "The Role of Suffering in the Mission of Paul," 177-78.

20:13-38), come in front of the crowds in Jerusalem (Luke 22:47–23:25, Acts 21:27–22:29), are accused of leading a rebellion (Luke 22:52, Acts 21:38), are seized by the crowd (Luke 22:54, Acts 21:30), are flogged (Luke 22:63, Acts 22:24), and are falsely accused (Luke 23:2, Acts 21:28). In both cases, Jews stir the crowds (Luke 23:5, Acts 21:28), there is mob rule (Luke 23:18, Acts 22:22), they shout for the accused to die (Luke 23:20, Acts 22:22), and the secular ruler is powerless (Luke 23:24, Acts 22:29). There are trials before the Sanhedrin (Luke 22:66-71, Acts 22:30–23:11), the governor (Luke 23:1-7, Acts 24:1–25:12), and the king (Luke 23:8-12, Acts 25:13–26:32). However, there are also important differences between the two accounts. Jesus, when face to face with earthly rulers, says nothing to defend himself and so goes to his sacrificial death (Luke 22:66-71; 23:3). Paul, however, takes the opportunity afforded by his arrest and trial to defend himself at great length against charges of Jewish apostasy and Roman insurrection (e.g., Acts 25:8; 28:17-18). The real issue, however, is the resurrection of Christ (23:6; 24:15; 24:21), and in his trials Paul soundly proclaims Jesus' resurrection and its corollaries to the worldly rulers — the Roman governors (24:24), the king (Acts 26:27), and indeed all the leaders of the city (25:23). Furthermore, in line with God's promise in 23:11, Paul goes to Rome and has the opportunity to testify before Caesar himself. In this way, Acts paints Paul as the Lord's Isaianic Servant, who, through suffering, trials, and rejection by his own people, testifies to the name of the Lord and his Christ before "kings" (Isa. 49:7). Paul in his own person takes on the prophetic role of Israel — he is the light to the nations, the bringer of salvation.

Paul's task of proclamation, therefore, is not the mere rehearsal of past facts. God is bringing to pass, through Paul, the eschatological fulfillment of salvation history. Just as the new eschatological age has already dawned with the death and resurrection of Jesus Christ, so it is currently breaking in to the old age through the preaching of Jesus Christ. Paul's message is not idle chatter or some good ideas; it is apocalyptic power (1 Cor. 4:20). As Paul proclaims and lives out "Christ crucified," all the structures of human existence are transformed, human pride is judged, and salvation comes to those who believe (1 Cor. 1:17-25; cf. 1 Thess. 1:5). Paul's gospel brings the obedience of faith for the sake of Jesus Christ among the nations (Rom. 1:5; 16:26). So Paul sees himself as not only proclaiming, but also actively bringing about, the new age of God's direct rule over the cosmos in both judgment and salvation. It is accomplished "by the power of signs and wonders, by the power of the Spirit of God" (Rom. 15:19).[31] Similar themes emerge in 1 Corinthians 2:6-11, which draws on apocalyptic motifs in Daniel (see esp. Dan. 2:19-23 LXX).[32]

31. P. T. O'Brien, *Consumed by Passion: Paul and the Dynamic of the Gospel* (Homebush West, Australia: Lancer, 1993), 35-36.

32. H. H. Drake Williams, *The Wisdom of the Wise: The Presence and Function of Scripture within 1 Cor. 1:18–3:23* (Leiden: Brill, 2001), 157-208.

## E. Paul the Apostle to the Gentiles

What is the overall goal of Paul's apostolic activity? Paul sees the final end of the mighty salvation-historical drama in which he is caught up to be *the glory of God.* While much modern biblical scholarship has marginalized both salvation history and the concept of God's glory in Paul's thought, it is clear that both themes are frequently present and often linked.[33] Paul ascribes glory to God for his gracious election and blessing of certain people and family groups in the history of Israel, for his bestowal upon the covenant people of Israel of certain key redemptive advantages (Rom. 3:2; 9:3-5; cf. Eph. 2:12), for his revelation of truth through Israel's Scriptures (2 Cor. 1:20; Rom. 11:33-36), and for his grace extended even to Paul and to Gentile Christians (Rom. 15:7; Gal. 1:3-5, 24). This emphasis on the glory of God is also not merely a quirk of Paul's personality; on the contrary, he is appropriating a theme that, in the Old Testament Scriptures, is ubiquitous, tied firmly to historical events, and theologically rich.[34] The glory of God is also of fundamental importance for Paul's mission in relation to the Gentiles.

Steven C. Hawthorne points out that the concepts of glory, God's name, and worship are closely tied together in the Scriptures.[35] "To glorify someone is to recognize their intrinsic worth and beauty, and to speak of that feature in a public way. To glorify God is to praise or to speak of Him openly and truthfully."[36] God is glorified as his name, or worthy reputation based on his great deeds, is proclaimed throughout the world (e.g., Ps. 96:2-4), and consequently recognized by all people (Ps. 96:7-9). This recognition of the greatness of God's name in both word and deed is true *worship.* Such worship is the goal of salvation (Exod. 8:1, 20; 9:1, 13; 10:3). It is not only a recognition of God's supremacy, but a heartfelt response of love to the God who has acted in love to save a people for himself (cf. Rev. 5:1-14). As people worship God, proclaiming the glory of his name, so they are brought into the highest honor by God and glorified, for worship is the fulfillment of God's love: "God *reveals* his glory *to* all peoples so that he may *receive* glory *from* all creation."[37] This is a key theme in the scriptural account of God's dealings with humanity, from Abraham through to Christ (e.g., Num. 14:17-21).

The establishment of God's glory necessarily involves the removal of all false worship. The salvation of the Exodus required judgment against the false gods of Egypt (Exod. 12:12). The taking of the Promised Land required

33. Robert W. Yarbrough, "Paul and Salvation History," in *Justification and Variegated Nomism*, vol. 2, *The Paradoxes of Paul* (ed. D. A. Carson, Peter T. O'Brien, and Mark A. Seifrid; Tübingen: Mohr Siebeck and Grand Rapids: Baker Academic, 2004), 297-342 (here 322-39).

34. Yarbrough, "Paul and Salvation History," 336-39.

35. Steven C. Hawthorne, "The Story of His Glory," in *Perspectives on the World Christian Movement: A Reader* (ed. Ralph D. Winter and Steven C. Hawthorne; Carlisle: Paternoster, 1999), 34-48.

36. Hawthorne, "The Story of His Glory," 34-35.

37. Hawthorne, "The Story of His Glory," 37.

demolition of the false idolatrous worship taking place in Canaan (Deut. 4:15-24; Josh. 23:7). A specially chosen place set apart for the worship of God's glory and name is required because of the existence of other shrines dedicated to the worship of false deities by the nations (Deut. 12:2-14). The temple, therefore, stands as the place where all the nations are beckoned to come alongside Israel and worship God (1 Chr. 16:23-33; cf. Ps. 96) — abandoning their own idolatrous practices. Yet paradoxically, the history of Israel herself is "a prolonged up-and-down struggle with idolatry."[38] The exile, along with the destruction of the temple, was the appalling conclusion to this struggle. Yet it was not simply a blow for the nation of Israel; more significantly, it was a terrible indictment of God's name and glory (Dan. 9:15-19; Ezek. 36:22-23). Nevertheless, the prophets and psalmists continued to speak of "the history and the destiny of Israel in terms of the nations being drawn to God by name, and worshiping Him with diverse, lavish glory" (Pss. 66:1-4; 138:4-5; Hab. 2:14; Zeph. 3:9-10; Mal. 1:11).[39]

In connection with Paul's appropriation of this theme, Richard B. Hays observes that "Isaiah offers the clearest expression in the Old Testament of a universalistic, eschatological vision in which the restoration of Israel in Zion is accompanied by an ingathering of Gentiles to worship the Lord; that is why the book is both statistically and substantively the most important scriptural source for Paul."[40] The extensive use of Isaiah in 1 Corinthians is widely recognized (see further below, Section III.C.1., "Two Key Old Testament Texts, [b]. Isaiah"). A striking and significant vision of the eschatological glory of God appears in the final verses of Isaiah (66:18-24):

> 18"And I, because of what they have planned and done, am about to come and gather the people of all nations and languages, and they will come and see my glory. 19 I will set a sign among them, and I will send some of those who survive to the nations — to Tarshish, to the Libyans and Lydians (famous as archers), to Tubal and Greece, and to the distant islands that have not heard of my fame or seen my glory. They will proclaim my glory among the nations. 20And they will bring all your people, from all the nations, to my holy mountain in Jerusalem as an offering to the LORD — on horses, in chariots and wagons, and on mules and camels," says the LORD. "They will bring them, as the Israelites bring their grain offerings, to the temple of the LORD in ceremonially clean vessels. 21And I will select some of them also to be priests and Levites," says the LORD.
>
> 22"As the new heavens and the new earth that I make will endure be-

38. Hawthorne, "The Story of His Glory," 42.
39. Hawthorne, "The Story of His Glory," 43.
40. Richard B. Hays, *Echoes of Scripture in the Letters of Paul* (New Haven: Yale University Press, 1989), 162, cited in James M. Scott, *Paul and the Nations: The Old Testament and Jewish Background of Paul's Mission to the Nations with Special Reference to the Destination of Galatians* (WUNT 84; Tübingen: Mohr, 1995), 146-47.

fore me," declares the LORD, "so will your name and descendants endure. [23]From one New Moon to another and from one Sabbath to another, all people will come and bow down before me," says the LORD.

[24]"And they will go out and look on the dead bodies of those who rebelled against me; their worm will not die, nor will their fire be quenched, and they will be loathsome to the whole human race."

Here, God's ultimate glory is described in terms of the involvement of the Gentiles in temple worship. There is both an "outward" and an "inward" dynamic to God's glorification: God's glory will be declared to the nations by missionaries (v. 19), and the nations will come and glorify God in temple worship (vv. 18, 23). The eschatological remnant will act as priests in God's temple in Jerusalem (v. 20), bringing those scattered among the nations as an offering to the Lord.

The geographical references to the nations in Isaiah 66:19 are of particular interest. James M. Scott has argued that the Table of Nations of Genesis 10 (cf. 1 Chr. 1:1–2:2) represents an ethnographic and geographic tradition that pervades the Old Testament and Jewish tradition.[41] It is a verbal "map"; a detailed geographical worldview that effectively places Israel in the center of the world (cf. Ezek. 5:5, chs. 38–39).[42] This "map" is also applicable to Old Testament eschatology. Isaiah 66:18-20, in many of its details, reflects the Table of Nations tradition as it announces a positive eschatological expectation for the nations.[43] In Isaiah 66:19, each of the three sons of Noah is represented: Shem (Lydians), Ham (Libyans), and Japheth (Tarshish, Tubal, Greece). The focus of the eschatological expectation is, of course, Jerusalem, situated in the center of the world.

According to Scott, the Table of Nations is at the forefront of Paul's mind when he describes his own eschatological mission to the nations in geographical terms (Rom 15:19).[44] Paul has "fully proclaimed the gospel of Christ . . . from Jerusalem all the way around to Illyricum." That is, Paul's mission to the nations is viewed from the perspective of Jerusalem as the center of a circle embracing the whole inhabited world (cf. Ezek. 5:5). Riesner makes the connection with Isaiah 66:18-21 even more explicit.[45] For Riesner, "Paul read this text as being fulfilled in his own activity, and traces of this exegesis stand behind Rom. 15:16-24."[46] The striking use of cultic

41. Scott, *Paul and the Nations*, 5-56.

42. Scott, *Paul and the Nations*, 5-10.

43. Scott, *Paul and the Nations*, 13-14.

44. Scott, *Paul and the Nations*, 135-49.

45. Rainer Riesner, *Paul's Early Period: Chronology, Mission Strategy, Theology* (trans. Doug Stott from the German *Die Frühzeit des Apostels Paulus;* Tübingen, Mohr, 1994; Grand Rapids: Eerdmans, 1998), 245-53. Scott, *Paul and the Nations*, 145-47, criticizes Riesner for relying too much on this one text. Scott claims that Paul has in mind the whole Table of Nations tradition, which in turn informs the Isaiah text. But Riesner has found numerous parallels with Isa. 66:18-21 in Rom. 15:16-28, beyond the geographical references of v. 19.

46. Riesner, *Paul's Early Period*, 246.

terminology in Romans 15:16 to describe Gentile evangelization suggests an Old Testament background. Isaiah 66:18-21, with its unique juxtaposition of Gentile mission and temple-related descriptions of Gentile worship, is the strongest contender. Riesner presents an impressive array of further parallels between these two passages.[47] For Paul, the nature of the eschatological temple and the glory that God is to receive through worldwide worship are understood in the light of the kingdom God has established through his Son, the universal Lord.

Paul's aim, then, is to bring about true worship and obedience among the Gentiles, to the glory of God (cf. Rom. 12:1-2; Acts 18:13). How did Paul envisage this happening? An examination of certain key texts shows that he followed a fairly consistent pattern. His expositions of the dynamics of pagan sin, the nature of Gentile conversion, and his own missionary agenda are consonant with the themes and structure of 1 Corinthians, as we shall see below.

### *1. The Dynamics of Pagan Sin — Romans 1*

According to Romans 1:21-28, the typical Gentile vices of idolatry and sexual immorality are rooted in the futility of Gentile thinking and the senselessness of Gentile hearts (v. 21): "Although they claimed to be wise, they became fools" (v. 22). It was their lack of true wisdom (despite their claim to possess it) that led them to "exchange the glory of the immortal God for images" of human or other creatures (v. 23), and as a result "God gave them over in the sinful desires of their hearts to sexual impurity," especially homosexual behavior (vv. 24-28). Thus it is the lack of true wisdom that ultimately led to idolatry and sexual immorality. Presumably, true wisdom (1:22) would have led Gentiles to avoid idolatry and sexual immorality (1:23-28). To Paul's way of thinking, true wisdom (1 Corinthians 1–4; cf. Rom. 1:22) will keep the Corinthians from sexual immorality (1 Cor. 4:18–7:40; cf. Rom. 1:24) and idolatry (1 Corinthians 8–14; cf. Rom. 1:23).

According to Romans 1:21-28, this is all tied to the glory of God. The foolishness of the Gentiles is related to the fact that they "neither glorified [God] as God nor gave thanks to him" (v. 21), and, as indicated above, their idolatry is described as an act of exchanging "the glory of the immortal God for images" (v. 23). The proper glorification of God, which should have been expected, was replaced by idolatry and sexual immorality. Paul's imperatives to glorify God in concluding the sections on sexual immorality and idolatry in 1 Corinthians (6:18; 10:14) reflect a similar pattern of thought (see our discussion of the letter's structure, below).

47. For example, the emissaries of Isa. 66:19 are sent to those "who have not yet heard my name," and Paul in Rom. 15:20 evangelizes "where the name Christ has not yet been named" (248-49).

### 2. Gentile Conversion — 1 Thessalonians 1:9-10

In 1 Thessalonians, Paul describes the conversion of Thessalonian pagans in terms consonant with this understanding of Gentile sin. Paul says that they "turned to God from idols to serve the living and true God and to wait for his Son from heaven, whom he raised from the dead" (1 Thess. 1:9-10). Here Gentile conversion is understood to entail the rejection of idolatry in favor of the service of the true and living God and his resurrected Son. Christine Elizabeth Hayes points out that in 1 Thessalonians 4:3-8 "peoples who do not know God are described as sexually immoral and impure. By contrast, those called by God must be sanctified, by avoiding the sexual immorality *(porneia)* and impurity of such peoples."[48] Thus, according to 1 Thessalonians, those who convert to the God of Israel and of Jesus Christ must turn away from both idols (1:9-10) and sexual immorality (4:3-8) to worship him. The notion of hope expressed by the short phrase "wait for his Son from heaven" (1:10) is expanded in 4:13-18, where future bodily resurrection is promised to all those who are "in Christ" when Jesus "descends from heaven."

### 3. Paul's Missionary Agenda — Romans 15

Romans 15 is, as we have already hinted, an important chapter for our understanding of Paul's missionary agenda. "At this important turning point, the conclusion of his missionary endeavors in the east, Paul provides significant insights into what he had been doing and what were his hopes for the future. He thus throws light on essential features of his ministry, including its goals and motivating power, its content and extraordinary results."[49] Particularly significant is verse 16, which contains an uncommon concentration of Old Testament cultic terminology.[50] Consistent with the eschatological vision of Isaiah 66:18-21,[51] Paul's *raison d'être* is explained using temple imagery: as "a minister of Christ Jesus to the Gentiles," Paul is to discharge his "priestly duty of proclaiming the gospel of God, so that the Gentiles might become an offering acceptable to God, sanctified by the Holy Spirit" (15:16; cf. Isa. 66:20).[52] In this way, Paul demonstrates his continuity with Israel's salvation history, while at the same

48. C. E. Hayes, *Gentile Impurities and Jewish Identities: Intermarriage and Conversion from the Bible to the Talmud* (Oxford: Oxford University Press, 2002), 93.

49. O'Brien, *Consumed by Passion*, 27.

50. O'Brien, *Consumed by Passion*, 30-32.

51. See Riesner's analysis (above).

52. Dunn, *Romans 9–16* (WBC 38B; Dallas: Word, 2002), 860-61, observes that Paul's eschatological vision is even more radical than that of Isaiah. In Isa. 66:20 it is the Diaspora Jews who form the "offering" in the temple. In Rom. 15:16 it is the Gentiles themselves who either form or perform (or both) the offering.

time presenting a radical eschatological vision where cultic language is transformed into the noncultic activity of gospel preaching.[53] "Paul's purpose seems to be to underline the eschatologically new fact that within God's redefined people ('set apart by the Holy Spirit') all ministry on behalf of others is priestly ministry (as in Phil. 2:25), and that cultic sacrifice has been replaced by the sacrifice of committed day-to-day living in personal relationships (12:1)."[54]

In other words (but with the same cluster of Old Testament ideas in mind), Paul states that his purpose is for the Gentiles to *glorify* God (15:6, 7, 9; cf. Isa. 66:18, 23). Romans 15:7 makes it clear that this will be achieved, not by cultic activity on the part of the Gentiles, but by ethical behavior. "Accept one another, as Christ has accepted you, in order to bring glory to God." This verse, along with the verses immediately preceding this section (15:1-4), indicates that the solution to these ethical problems is grounded in the vicarious servant-hearted suffering of Jesus Christ for his people.[55] Four Old Testament quotations reiterate the goal of the Gentiles praising God along "with his people" (Rom. 15:9-12). The final quotation returns to the notion of hope introduced in 15:4, which Paul expands into a prayer in 15:13. Hence Romans 15:5-13 may be seen as a fuller description of "the obedience of faith" (Rom. 1:5; 16:26; cf. 15:18) — that is, the constancy of Christian conduct arising from the Gentiles' believing reception of the message of the life, death, and resurrection of the Lord Jesus Christ.[56]

Paul's aims and agenda for his Gentile converts, then, can be summarized as follows. The Gentiles fail to glorify God, chiefly through idolatry and sexual immorality (which reflect their lack of true wisdom). The proclamation of the death and resurrection of the Lord Jesus Christ is a call to enter the new eschatological age established in and by him. It demands that all people submit in unity to Christ, living out the true wisdom of the other-person-centered lifestyle of the cross. They must abandon sexual immorality and idolatry and instead worship the one true God. The goal of all of this is the glory of God. The Gentiles' lives will be characterized by expectant hope for the final consummation of God's glory (and so their own glorification) in the future bodily resurrection. When we come to 1 Corinthians, much is gained by reading Paul's letter with this in mind.

53. O'Brien, *Consumed by Passion*, 30-32.

54. Dunn, *Romans 9–16*, 868.

55. This is confirmed by the quotation of Isa. 52:15 in Rom. 15:21: Paul's whole international missionary agenda has been shaped by the Suffering Servant song of Isa. 52:13–53:12. The servant who suffers vicariously for the sins of his people must be proclaimed to nations and kings.

56. O'Brien, *Consumed by Passion*, 33-34.

## III. THE INTERPRETATION OF 1 CORINTHIANS

The main task of an introduction to a commentary is to provide some orientation to the text as a whole, to its overall structure and argument; the commentary proper fills in the details. When it comes to 1 Corinthians, the arrangement and integrity of the letter have been the subject of long debate.[57] The apparent diversity of issues that it treats has led to equally diverse approaches to understanding its essential nature. Some scholars have argued that the letter is actually a composite document.[58] Such theories grow out of a conviction that 1 Corinthians is not only unusually long, but also lacks a discernible global structure. Although Jerome Murphy-O'Conner rejects such partition theories, he finds them understandable in that, in his view, "[t]he salient feature of I Corinthians is the absence of any detectable logic in the arrangement of its contents."[59]

For many the only logic of the letter's arrangement is that Paul deals with oral reports in chapters 1–6 before addressing matters raised in the Corinthian letter to him in chapters 7–16 (7:1: "Now concerning the matters about which you wrote").[60] Murphy-O'Connor exemplifies those scholars who argue for the integrity of the epistle as we have it but find great difficulty in discerning an overall structure. David Garland believes that the letter "may be summed up as a warning against various perils,"[61] and his outline of the letter entails a listing of topics under twelve Roman numerals.[62] However, Mitchell and others have raised doubts over whether the order of material in 1 Corinthians is actually dictated by the sequence in which the issues are raised in the oral and written reports that Paul received.[63] Mitchell's work represents an important step forward in that she pursues a more significant underlying unity to the letter.[64] Many commentators follow her

57. Shorter versions of the next two sections appeared as R. E. Ciampa and B. S. Rosner, "The Structure and Argument of 1 Corinthians," *NTS* 52 (2006), 205-18.

58. Thiselton, 36-37, mentions the partition theories of J. Weiss (who believed that there were two or three underlying letters), W. Schmithals (three), K.-K. Yeo (four), and R. Jewett (five). See H. Merklein, "Die Einheitlichkeit des ersten Korintherbriefes," *ZNW* 75 (1984), 153-83; and M. M. Mitchell, *Paul and the Rhetoric of Reconciliation: An Exegetical Investigation of the Language and Composition of 1 Corinthians* (Louisville: Westminster/John Knox, 1991), for effective responses to such partition theories. For a brief discussion see Lang, 6-7.

59. J. Murphy-O'Connor, *Paul: A Critical Life* (Oxford and New York: Oxford University Press, 1996), 253.

60. Cf. περὶ δέ, repeated in 7:25; 8:1; 12:1; 16:1, 12.

61. Garland, 21.

62. Garland, 22-23. Witherington, vi-viii, 76, similarly breaks the main body (the *probatio*, in his understanding) of Paul's letter (1:18–16:12) into nine distinct "arguments."

63. M. M. Mitchell, "Concerning περὶ δέ in 1 Corinthians," *NovT* 31 (1989), 229-56, disputes the assumption that περὶ δέ in 1 Corinthians always signals a reference to the letter Paul received from the Corinthians (see also Thiselton, 34-35). A number of other commentators notice that in chs. 7–16 Paul deals with oral reports in 11:2-34 and 15:1-58.

64. Karl Barth may be considered a significant precursor. In his view, "[t]he haphazard character of the series of subjects dealt with in I Cor. i.-xiv. is not to be disputed," but

in affirming that Paul's main purpose in writing 1 Corinthians is to unify the congregation.

Rhetorical and other approaches have also been used to analyze the structure of this letter.[65] Many see the letter as an example of deliberative rhetoric, a series of arguments Paul musters to persuade the audience to heed his appeal to unity in 1:10. Hence 1:10 is thought to be the theme statement for the entire letter. Among those who support this view are W. H. Wuellner,[66] G. A. Kennedy,[67] and, most fully, M. Mitchell, whose book, *Paul and the Rhetoric of Reconciliation,* is in effect an examination of 1 Corinthians in the light of the thesis that Paul wrote with one overriding aim, that is, to persuade the Corinthian Christians to become unified. She claims that this was the understanding of some of the earliest readers of the letter, including 1 Clement, Ignatius of Antioch, the Muratorian Canon, and the early Greek commentators. Even Richard Hays, whose commentary is so sensitive to the influence of the Old Testament on 1 Corinthians, calls it "the fundamental theme of the letter."[68] In 1:18–4:21 Paul opposes disunity in the church in general; in chapters 5–16 he takes on the issues that must be dealt with before genuine unity can be achieved. 1 Corinthians, then, is Paul's attempt to urge the Corinthians to come together in unity.

While it is true that disunity is a major theme of the letter, extending beyond chapters 1–4,[69] to give it primacy obscures other equally important concerns. Our contention is that rather than reading 1 Corinthians with Greco-Roman rhetorical categories in mind, it is better to take Old Testament and Jewish frames of reference as the primary lens that clarifies our understanding of both the form and contents of the letter.[70] In this light, disunity is one of several behaviors that characterize the Corinthians as

---

"whether Paul's reflections upon the subjects dealt with in I Cor. i.-xiv. are as disparate as these subjects themselves, or rather whether a thread cannot be discovered which binds them internally into a whole" (Barth, *The Resurrection of the Dead* [London: Hodder and Stoughton, 1933], 12, cf. 102-3).

65. See, e.g., M. M. Mitchell, *Paul and the Rhetoric of Reconciliation;* H. D. Betz and M. M. Mitchell, "First Epistle to the Corinthians," *ABD* 1:1139-54; Witherington, vi-viii, 76.

66. W. H. Wuellner, "Greek Rhetoric and Pauline Argumentation," in *Early Christian Literature and the Classical Intellectual Tradition* (ed. W. R. Schoedel and R. L. Wilken; Paris: Beauchesne, 1979), 177-88: "[1:10] expresses the main theme of the whole of 1 Cor[inthians]" (182-83).

67. G. A. Kennedy, *New Testament Interpretation through Rhetorical Criticism* (Chapel Hill, NC: University of North Carolina Press, 1984), 24: "He follows this [1:4-9] with the proposition of the entire letter, summarized in a single sentence."

68. Hays, 21.

69. The letter contains not only explicit references to Corinthian factionalism but also many terms, appeals, and themes that deal with divisions in the church. See M. M. Mitchell, *Paul and the Rhetoric of Reconciliation,* 68-80, 180-83.

70. On the use of the Old Testament in 1 Corinthians see B. S. Rosner and R. E. Ciampa, "1 Corinthians," in the *Commentary on the New Testament Use of the Old Testament* (ed. D. A. Carson and G. K. Beale; Grand Rapids: Baker, 2007).

"worldly," as "acting like mere human beings" (3:3). Paul's goal is bigger than merely having them live harmoniously.

## A. The Structure of 1 Corinthians

As noted above, in "The Church 'Belonging to God'" (Section I.B.), there is good evidence that in 1 Corinthians Paul basically opposes the infiltration of Corinthian social values into that city's church. Our contention is that Paul's attempt to sort out the serious problems within the largely Gentile church in Corinth consists primarily of a confrontation with the church over purity concerns in general and two vices in particular.

It is widely recognized that in early Jewish and Christian thinking Gentiles were consistently characterized by two particularly abhorrent vices: sexual immorality and idolatry. Furnish writes: "For the apostle as for the Jews, rejecting idolatry and abstaining from sexual immorality . . . are key identity markers of the faithful community."[71] For example, in relation to New Testament evidence, Peder Borgen notes that the vice lists of Galatians 5:19-21 and 1 Corinthians 6:9-11, which in context contrast pagan and Christian lifestyles, have only these two sins in common. They also occur in Colossians 3:5; Ephesians 5:5; Acts 15:20, 29; 21:25; Revelation 22:15. Borgen concludes that "[t]hese two vices are central in Jewish characterising of the pagan way of life."[72] A clear example from early Jewish writings is the *Sibylline Oracles,* for, as J. J. Collins observes, "[t]he sins in which the Sibyl expresses most interest are idolatry and sexual offenses."[73] Of particular interest for 1 Corinthians is *Sibylline Oracles* 3, "[t]he main message of [which] . . . would seem to lie in the denunciation of idolatry and sexual abuses and then the advocacy of the Temple."[74] That the emphasis on these two vices in early Jewish and Christian thought is based on scriptural interpretation can be seen in William Loader's observation that much Jewish and Christian interpretation of the Decalogue elevates the prohibition of adultery above murder such that idolatry heads the first table and sexual immorality the second.[75]

Paul's focus on the issues of sexual immorality and idolatry (see below) suggests that purity issues are of greater concern to him than the issue

71. V. P. Furnish, *The Theology of the First Letter to the Corinthians* (Cambridge: Cambridge University Press, 1999), 51.

72. P. Borgen, *Early Christianity and Hellenistic Judaism* (Edinburgh: T&T Clark, 1998), 240, 245.

73. J. J. Collins, "Sibylline Oracles," *OTP* 1:317-472; here 323.

74. J. J. Collins, "Sibylline Oracles," 1:357.

75. W. Loader, *The Septuagint, Sexuality and the New Testament* (Grand Rapids: Eerdmans, 2004), 7; "The effect is to make it [adultery] the first of the second table, thus to elevate its significance for hearers who sense this bipartite division of the decalogue, suggested to hearers by the two tablets of stone (Exod 31:18) and by the changed focus of the content in the second half. Adultery receives, in that sense, greater prominence."

of communal harmony. Concern about purity issues is to be expected in a situation where the infiltration of outside influences is believed to have deleterious effects on the health of the worshiping community.[76] As David deSilva argues, the gospel had a significant transforming effect on Christian thinking about purity issues, but "[h]oliness and purity both still require boundaries to be drawn and maintained between the surrounding culture and the Christian group."[77]

In 1 Corinthians purity issues are reflected most specifically in the identification of the readers as the temple of God (3:17) and the discussion of the moral implications of that understanding. The command to "clean out the old leaven" (5:7) and to "purge the evil person" from among them (5:11-13) reflects the language of purity concerns, and Paul's command to avoid prostitutes is based on the radical impurity that would bring to their Spirit-indwelt temple (6:16-19). Purity concerns are also reflected in the issue of the children's uncleanness or holiness based on the status of the unbelieving husband (7:14) and in the concern not to provoke the Lord by drinking from both his cup and those of demons (10:21-22). "Much of Paul's use of purity terminology," Michael Newton points out, "centres upon his view that the believers constitute the Temple of God and as such enjoy the presence of God in their midst"; if that presence is to remain with them, they must maintain the purity of the community.[78] The broader issue of the influence of Corinthian cultural values and behaviors within the church of that city is to be understood as a fundamental concern for the purity of the worshiping community. Jacob Neusner highlights the place of idolatry and sexual relations in the biblical texts that deal with the question of impurity,[79] while Hayes points to a number of Pauline passages that "suggest that the impurity of unbelievers, arising from deeds of sexual immorality and idolatry in particular, defiles the holiness of believers."[80] Judith Lieu speaks of "[t]he pervasive rejection of the ways of the Gentiles, epitomized by idolatry and by a range of other 'vices' of sexual and intemperate behaviour" as boundary markers found in much "early Christian" literature.[81] She also sees sexual immorality and eating food offered to idols as "scripturally hallowed models of the dissolution of identity."[82]

76. As pointed out by J. M. Lieu, *Christian Identity in the Jewish and Graeco-Roman World* (New York: Oxford University Press, 2004), 104, "The need to observe sacred boundaries, variously articulated, but in Judaism particularly through food and purity laws and the structuring of the Temple, correlates with the importance laid on well-defined and well-protected social boundaries."

77. D. A. deSilva, *Honor, Patronage, Kinship and Purity: Unlocking New Testament Culture* (Downers Grove, IL: InterVarsity Press, 2000), 294.

78. M. Newton, The *Concept of Purity at Qumran and in the Letters of Paul* (SNTSMS 53; Cambridge: Cambridge University, 1985), 52.

79. J. Neusner, *The Idea of Purity in Ancient Judaism* (Leiden: E. J. Brill, 1973), 13-15.

80. C. E. Hayes, *Gentile Impurities and Jewish Identities*, 93.

81. Lieu, *Christian Identity*, 133.

82. Lieu, *Christian Identity*, 137 and n. 110.

In our view, in 4:18–7:40[83] Paul deals primarily with issues related to sexual immorality, first in a negative treatment of its manifestations in the church in Corinth (4:18–6:20) and then in a positive treatment of marriage and sexual relationships[84] (ch. 7; note how the chapter is introduced in v. 2 with a reference to *porneia*). And chapters 8–14 deal with the issue of idolatry, beginning, again, with a negative treatment of its manifestations in Corinth (8:1–11:1) and then moving to a more positive treatment of the proper worship of the one true God (chs. 11–14; note how 12:2 relates the following material back to the issue of idolatry). Paul explicitly ties these two vices to their Old Testament background in his discussion of Israel's failures in 1 Corinthians 10:7-8, and their inclusion in the vice list of 5:11 is based on their inclusion in a list of sins associated with a Deuteronomic expulsion formula.[85]

Toward the end of each negative section (4:18–6:20 and 8:1–11:1) Paul provides both negative and positive imperatives using the same language relating to the broader theme. In concluding the negative section on sexual immorality, Paul exhorts the Corinthians to "flee sexual immorality" (6:18) and to "glorify God" with their bodies (6:20). In concluding the negative section on idolatry, Paul exhorts them to "flee idolatry" (10:14) and to do everything "to the glory of God" (10:31).[86] Thus 4:18–7:40 and 8:1–14:40 can be seen as discreet units dealing with issues of sexuality and worship respectively.

Almost all commentators see chapters 1–4 and 15 as unified sections. Chapters 1–4 urge the Corinthians to be united in the proclamation and service-oriented lifestyle of the cross, for they have entered the new eschatological age of salvation. There is a negative treatment of the wisdom of the world, which looks to human powers and authorities (1:10–2:5), followed by a positive section that proclaims the Christ-centered wisdom of the cross (2:6–3:5) and an application to Christian ministers (3:6–4:17). Paul treats various antisocial vices in the unit, such as divisions (1:10, 13), quarreling (1:11; 3:3), jealousy (3:3), boasting about human leaders (3:21), and pride and arrogance (4:18-19).[87] Negative and positive summary imperatives also occur here. The Corinthians are told: "no more boasting about

83. See the commentary for a defense of the demarcation of the various units.

84. This arrangement of ethical material is reminiscent of Hellenistic Jewish parenesis (reported by K.-W. Niebuhr, *Gesetz und Paränese: Katechismusartige Weisungsreihen in der frühjüdischen Literatur* [WUNT 2.28; Tübingen: Mohr Siebeck, 1987], 232), which discusses sexual deviations, such as incest and homosexual behavior, and sexual relations in marriage in close proximity.

85. B. S. Rosner, *Paul, Scripture, and Ethics: A Study of 1 Corinthians 5–7* (Grand Rapids: Baker, 1999), 69; cf. Hays, 86. 2 Corinthians carries forward this stress on the dangers of idolatry (2 Cor. 6:16–7:1) and sexual immorality (2 Cor. 12:19-21).

86. Once these comparable commands are recognized, it is also worth noticing that these are also the same two passages in which Paul cites the Corinthian slogan that "all things are lawful," reinforcing the idea that they are parallel.

87. Cf. "slanderers" in 1 Cor. 5:11 and 6:10.

human leaders!" (3:21), and the positive injunction, "let those who boast, boast in the Lord" (1:31).[88]

1 Corinthians comes to a climax in chapter 15 with Paul's discussion of the resurrection as it relates to the ultimate triumph of Christ over all adversaries and the final transformation of our corruptible humanity into humanity that fully reflects God's glory.

The main sections of the letter may thus be outlined as follows:

I. Letter Opening (1:1-9)
II. True and False Wisdom and Corinthian Factionalism (1:10–4:17)
   A. Factions in the Community (1:10-17)
   B. Negative Treatment: "No More Boasting about Human Leaders" (1:18–2:5)
   C. Positive Treatment: "Let Those Who Boast Boast in the Lord" (2:6–3:4)
   D. Application to the Church, Ministers, and Ministry (3:5–4:17)
III. "Flee Sexual Immorality" and "Glorify God with Your Bodies" (4:18–7:40)
   A. Negative Treatment: "Flee Sexual Immorality" (and Greed) (4:18–6:20)
   B. Positive Treatment: "Glorify God with Your Bodies" (7:1-40)
IV. "Flee Idolatry" and "Glorify God" in Your Worship (8:1–14:40)
   A. Negative Treatment: "Flee Idolatry" (Food Offered to Idols) (8:1–11:1)
   B. Positive Treatment: "Glorify God" in Your Worship (11:2–14:40)
V. The Resurrection and Consummation (15:1-58)
VI. Letter Closing (16:1-24)

The main exception to this outline of the letter is 6:1-11, which seems to have nothing to do with sexual immorality. Interestingly, the only other specific vice to "flee" in the New Testament, apart from sexual immorality (1 Corinthians 6) and idolatry (1 Corinthians 10), is greed (1 Tim. 6:11; in context, literally, "the love of money"; 6:10). Typically Jews and Christians added greed as a third member of the unholy triad of vices that rightly condemns the heathen. Polycarp, *To the Philippians* 11.2, makes explicit the presupposition of this material, that greed was a typical sin of the Gentiles: "If a man does not avoid love of money, . . . *he will be judged as one of the Gentiles.*" Cf. Philo, *On the Virtues* 180–82, which states that the conversion

88. The observation of this last sentence is drawn from Andrew Williamson's unpublished Ph.D. thesis, University of Western Sydney/Moore Theological College, on the influence of the murder commandment on Paul's ethics. The two commands are not placed as strategically as their counterparts in chs. 5–7 and 8–10. They do nonetheless serve as excellent summaries of the negative and positive panels in chs. 1–4, and they maintain a focus on true worship in the fullest sense, "to boast" being a synonym of "to glorify."

of pagans from idolatry entails a new lifestyle, which is, among other things, "superior to the desire for money." In 1 Corinthians"greed"[89] is mentioned alongside sexual immorality and idolatry in each of this letter's three vice lists (5:10, 11; 6:10), and it is likely that greed was a primary motivation for the lawsuit in 6:1-11.

The assertion that 1 Corinthians may be summarized as Paul's attempt to rid the Corinthians of the sins of sexual immorality, greed, and idolatry is given remarkable support in 1 Corinthians 5:9-10. In these verses Paul recalls having already written a letter to the Corinthians, and he summarizes this "previous letter" in strikingly similar terms: the Corinthian church is not to be characterized by sexual immorality, greed, theft (a synonym of greed), and idolatry.[90] Apparently Paul's first two letters to the Corinthians had a similar thrust. Paul clarifies in 1 Corinthians that his primary concern is not so much with the presence of these vices in the world at large (as the Corinthians had thought), but with their presence within the Corinthian church (5:9-13).

It should also not escape our notice that the two extant letters Paul likely wrote to churches from Corinth, namely, Romans and 1 Thessalonians, also support our view of the thrust of 1 Corinthians. As we will see below, in both cases the letters contain similar patterns of thought to 1 Corinthians. 1 Thessalonians, in particular, overlaps with 1 Corinthians in terms of its content. Robert M. Grant also thinks it significant that Paul wrote 1 Thessalonians from Corinth and summarizes the four main points of the letter as touching idolatry (1:9-10), avoiding sexual immorality (4:3-6), the necessity of work (a topic not unrelated to greed; 4:11-12), and the impending return of Jesus (4:15-17).[91] If, as seems likely, Paul's letter writing while in Corinth reflected his preaching and teaching in that city, and vice versa, it would seem that the apostle to the Gentiles' opposition to the typically pagan sins of sexual immorality and idolatry was a consistent mark of his work in that city.

## B. The Argument of 1 Corinthians

Having observed that the four main elements of 1 Corinthians are (in order) wisdom, sexuality, worship, and resurrection/consummation, it is noteworthy that similar patterns of thought appear elsewhere in Paul's letters in shorter compass. Taken together, they shed light on the argument of

89. Gk. πλεονέκτης.

90. CD iv 15-17 confirms the Jewishness of this triad of sins: "Belial's three nets . . . the first is fornication; the second, wealth; the third, defilement of the temple."

91. Robert M. Grant, *Paul in the Roman World: The Conflict at Corinth* (Louisville: Westminster John Knox, 2001), 1: "These points do not reflect the semiphilosophical concerns found in the letters to the Corinthians, but they offer insights into Paul's ideas when he was writing."

1 Corinthians. The three texts which we considered above in relation to the aims of Paul as apostle to the Gentiles (Section II.E.), Romans 1:21-28, 1 Thessalonians 1:9-10, and Romans 15:5-16, reveal a pattern that helps explain the order and coherence of material in 1 Corinthians.

The following chart displays the patterns found in the three texts and their relevance to the argument of 1 Corinthians.

| | **Romans 1:21-28** | **1 Thessalonians 1:9-10** | **Romans 15:5-16** |
|---|---|---|---|
| **1. 1 Cor. 1:10–4:17** | Lack of wisdom [and failure to glorify God] | | Paul calls for unity |
| **2. 1 Cor. 4:18–7:40** | leads to sexual immorality | | in order that ethical problems can be resolved so that the Gentile believers will glorify God |
| **3a. 1 Cor. 8:1–11:1** | and idolatry | Gentile converts go from idolatry | |
| **3b. 1 Cor. 11:2–14:40** | | to worship of the one true God | |
| **4. 1 Cor. 15:1-58** | | and wait for their resurrected Lord | and hope in his Son |

This "shape" to Paul's teaching is evident across the breadth of his corpus. To put the pattern in point form, with the overall goal of the glory of God, we find:

1. The proclamation of the death and resurrection of the Lord Jesus Christ is a call to enter the new eschatological age established in and by him. It demands that all people submit in unity to Christ, living out the wisdom of the other-person-centered lifestyle of the cross.
2. They must abandon the Gentile vice of sexual immorality (to the glory of God).
3. They must abandon the Gentile vice of idolatry, and give proper worship to the one true God (to the glory of God).
4. The Gentiles' lives will be characterized by expectant hope for the final consummation of God's glory (and so their own glorification) in the future bodily resurrection.

The same pattern, with some flexibility, is also evident in Ephesians (twice), Colossians, and Titus. In *Ephesians 4:1-30,* after a doxology ascribing glory to God in the church and in Christ (Eph. 3:21):

1. Paul, the suffering apostle (Eph. 4:1), calls his readers to live in humility, gentleness, patience, and love (Eph. 4:2), maintaining the unity to which they have been called in Christ by the Spirit (Eph. 4:4-16).
3. They must not live in the foolishness of the idolatrous Gentiles (Eph. 4:17-18),

2. who are sexually immoral (Eph. 4:19).
4. Instead, they should live now in expectation of the day of redemption to come (Eph. 4:20-30).

The pattern is then repeated in *Ephesians 4:30–5:17:*

1. As God in Christ forgave them, so they are to live lives of kind, tenderhearted forgiveness (Eph. 4:30-31), which is the lifestyle of the cross (Eph. 5:1-2).
2. Sexual immorality and
3. greed (which is idolatry) are singled out as sins that must be put to death (Eph. 5:3-5) because of the coming wrath of God (Eph. 5:6).
4. This is true eschatological wisdom (Eph. 5:7-17, esp. 15-17; cf. 6:12).

*Colossians 3:1-17* presents the same logic, but in reverse order:

4. The eschatological age of salvation has come in Christ; but it is still hidden, awaiting the final appearance of Christ and his people in glory (Col. 3:1-4).
3. Therefore the Colossians must put to death Gentile vices, beginning with sexual immorality and
2. greed, which is idolatry (Col. 3:5-10). They should worship in word and deed for the sake of Christ's name and the praise of God (Col. 3:16-17).
1. This is because of the unity in Christ (Col. 3:11), which shows itself in the cross-centered lifestyle of compassion, kindness, humility, meekness, patience, and forgiveness (Col. 3:12-15).

Three of the four elements of the pattern are prominent in *Titus 1–2:*

1. The new age manifested by God's word through Paul's preaching (Titus 1:1-3; cf. 2:11)
2. calls believers to be the husband of one wife, self-controlled, and pure (Titus 1:6; 2:2, 5-6), renouncing ungodliness and worldly passions (Titus 2:12)
4. as they wait for the blessed hope, the appearing of Jesus Christ (Titus 2:13).

That these outlines have affinities with Jewish moral teaching contemporary with Paul which stand in a biblical tradition can be seen from three examples from the *Testaments of the Twelve Patriarchs*[92] and the *Sibylline Ora-*

92. In the *Testament of Judah 18–19,* (2) the readers are exhorted to abstain from sexual immorality, for it blinds the soul (*T. Jud.* 18:2, 6), from lewdness and harlotry (*T. Jud.* 18:2; 23:1-2), and (3) from idols and idolatries (*T. Jud.* 19:1; 23:1), (4) in view of the resurrection unto life of the patriarchs and martyrs, when all the people shall glorify the Lord forever

*cles.*[93] The order of the elements is not the same as (most of) the Pauline examples, and temple worship is probably meant more literally. Also, reference to the cross is obviously not present, being by definition a Christian motivation. Nonetheless, they add further support to our contention that Paul's ethics in general and 1 Corinthians in particular are best read as in line with biblical and Jewish moral teaching.

## C. The Biblical-Theological Framework of 1 Corinthians

Having detected the main elements of the logic and structure of 1 Corinthians in relation to Paul's thought elsewhere in his letters, and even in a few case studies from Second Temple Jewish literature, it is useful to sketch the biblical-theological framework that informs his argument. This can be done in two ways. First, we offer a global comparison of two key Old Testament books with 1 Corinthians to confirm the origin not only of many of the specifics but also of the general shape of Paul's response to the problems in Corinth. Secondly, we outline the main features of the biblical-theological framework that together give the letter its unity of purpose.

### *1. Two Key Old Testament Texts*

Although Paul draws on a wide range of Old Testament material in writing 1 Corinthians, he seems to have taken his cue for his work in Corinth from two Old Testament books in particular: Deuteronomy and Isaiah. A third key book, Malachi, to which Paul alludes in 1 Corinthians 1:2, is treated in the next section. At this point a general comparison of Deuteronomy and Isaiah with 1 Corinthians reveals the extent to which 1 Corinthians may be described as "a hermeneutical event,"[94] as a text best read in its inextricable and manifold relationship to the Scriptures of Israel.

---

(*T. Jud.* 25:1-5). In the *Testament of Dan* 5, (1) the readers are exhorted to speak truth with their neighbors and to live in peace, united to one another with a true heart (*T. Dan* 5:2-3), (2) in order not to fall into lust and to be on guard against all the spirits of fornication (*T. Dan* 5:5-6), (3) and to return to the Lord and be brought into his sanctuary (*T. Dan* 5:9) (4) in anticipation of the salvation and victory of the Lord, when the saints shall rest in Eden and the righteous shall rejoice in the new Jerusalem, which shall be unto the glory of God forever and ever (*T. Dan* 5:10-13).

93. In the *Sibylline Oracles, Book 3,* (3) idolatry is denounced (*Sib. Or.* 3:35-39, 46, 741-43, 762; 4:34-35) for the sake of true temple worship (*Sib. Or.* 3:726-33, 746) and the great glory of God (*Sib. Or.* 4:37-38, 760-61), (2) as are adultery (*Sib. Or.* 3:46, 751), immoral widows (*Sib. Or.* 3:53-55), and homosexual behavior (*Sib. Or.* 3:764), (1) in the context of the promise of a renewed holy race that fully honors the temple of God (*Sib. Or.* 3:573-600).

94. Cf. Hays, *Echoes of Scripture in the Letters of Paul*, 35.

### *a. Deuteronomy and 1 Corinthians*

An accurate assessment of the role of Deuteronomy in 1 Corinthians cannot be formed simply by noticing quotations and even allusions. We need to consider how the books compare in global terms and to ascertain where they are situated in the context of the salvation history presented in the Bible.

In the context of the Pentateuch, the book of Deuteronomy is Moses' attempt to spell out for God's people the theological and ethical consequences of the exodus deliverance. Put another way, Deuteronomy explains the nature of an obedient response to God's grace. The collections of laws in chapters 5 and 12–26 stipulate that the Lord is to be worshiped at the place and in the way that he chooses (cf., e.g., ch. 12) and insist that nothing is to be done to defile the land, which is the place where God is encountered (cf. 12:7). In particular, God's people are to shun the idolatry (e.g., 12:1-6) and sexual immorality (e.g., 22:21; 23:2, 17-18; cf. 31:16) of the original inhabitants of the land, and they are to maintain justice and right relationships with each other. To this end, Moses appoints judges (ch. 1), calls on the people to listen to his teaching (4:1 and especially the Shema in 6:1-18), marks their redemption from slavery in Egypt with the Passover commemoration (ch. 16), also celebrating it in song (ch. 32), and finally inaugurates a new covenant at Moab (29:1).

Curiously, various elements strike a pessimistic note and point beyond the book to the need for the future decisive action of God. That little can be expected from God's people is signaled in chapter 2, where they are unfavorably compared to the Moabites and Ammonites. It is also expressed throughout chapters 5–11, where repeated calls to obey or remember (e.g., 5:1, 31-33; 6:1-14; 7:12-15) suggest a negative expectation. Israel's spiritual incapacity is repeatedly underscored (e.g., 29:4). Nothing less than circumcision of the heart is required, which only God can perform (30:6; cf. 10:16). Moses predicts Israel's apostasy (31:16-18; 32:19-21, 26), and he himself dies outside the land (ch. 34), suggesting that there is little hope for the nation. Moses' song ends with the one reference to atonement in the entire book (32:43). The new covenant teaching of Jeremiah and Ezekiel, in which the problem of the human heart is resolved, is thus anticipated in Deuteronomy.[95]

In many ways the theological or canonical setting of 1 Corinthians is analogous to that of Deuteronomy, with some major twists. Paul, like Mo-

95. We owe much of this reading of Deuteronomy to J. G. Millar, *Now Choose Life: Theology and Ethics in Deuteronomy* (Leicester: Inter-Varsity Press, 1998); for a summary see Millar, "Deuteronomy," *NDBT,* 159-65. Cf. J. Sailhamer, *Introduction to Old Testament Theology: A Canonical Approach* (Grand Rapids: Zondervan, 1995), who argues that the Pentateuch as a whole presents the way of Abraham, who lived by faith before the law, as better than that of Moses, who failed to keep the law once it was given. Cf. R. W. L. Moberly, *The Old Testament of the Old Testament: Patriarchal Narratives and Mosiac Yahwism* (OBT; Minneapolis: Fortress, 1992).

ses, seeks to spell out for the new people of God the theological and ethical consequences of the act of salvation that is an exodus. He too wishes to explain the nature of an obedient response to God's grace. The apostle stops short of calling himself a second Moses, but he does compare and contrast his role as a "minister of the new covenant" with that of Moses in 2 Corinthians 3. He follows the pattern of Moses' appointing judges in Deuteronomy 1 (and Exodus 18) in 1 Corinthians 6:1-6 when he tells the Corinthians to appoint wise and righteous laity to decide lesser civil cases of law between their brothers.[96] Also like Moses, Paul uses Exodus/Passover/Unleavened Bread imagery as a basis for his moral exhortation (e.g., 1 Cor. 5:6-8; 11:17-24). If in Deuteronomy repeated reference is made to *"the place* which the Lord your God will choose to have people call upon his name" (cf. LXX Deut. 12:11, 21, 26; 14:23-24; 16:2, 6, 11; 17:8, 10; 26:2) rather than to refer to that place, Paul says that the Corinthians are among those who call on the name of our Lord "in every place" (1 Cor. 1:2).

As pointed out above ("The Structure of 1 Corinthians"), two of Paul's main moral emphases in 1 Corinthians are, like Deuteronomy, the shunning of the sexual immorality and idolatry of the nations/Gentiles. As noted earlier, Paul's opposition to these two vices structures the central section of the letter, where most of the links with Deuteronomy are to be found.

In one sense, it is not only the Corinthian epistles that look back to Deuteronomy, but Deuteronomy that anticipates 1 (and 2) Corinthians. The "later days," to which Deuteronomy 4:30 refers, "when you will return to the LORD your God and obey him," of which the Hebrew prophets also speak,[97] is the time in which Paul locates the church of God in Corinth: the Corinthian believers are those "on whom the fulfillment of the ages has come" (1 Cor. 10:11). Paul writes as a minister of the new covenant, a covenant that Deuteronomy does not name but ultimately points forward to.

Especially in chapters 5–14, where Paul is primarily concerned with ethics and matters of conduct, four quotations of Deuteronomy and numerous clusters of allusions accord the book a major role in the composition of 1 Corinthians.[98] The main material of Deuteronomy, namely its laws, and the most famous texts, including the Shema and the Song of Moses, are strongly represented. Paul found in Deuteronomy and Moses a typological model and sympathetic ally. Both were concerned to explain to God's people an obedient response to God's grace in the light of the (new) exodus and (new) Passover. Both have the basic goal of securing the holiness and purity of that people in distinction from the nations and to promote the glory of God in "the land," in the case of Deuteronomy, or "in every place" (1 Cor. 1:2), as with 1 Corinthians.

96. See Rosner, *Paul, Scripture, and Ethics,* ch. 4.

97. Cf. Jer. 23:20; 30:24; 48:47; 49:39; Ezek. 38:16; Dan. 2:28; 10:14; Hos. 3:5.

98. Sean M. McDonough's recent study likewise points to the importance of Deuteronomy for the composition of 1 Corinthians: "Competent to Judge: The Old Testament Connection between 1 Corinthians 5 and 6," *JTS* 56 (2005), 99-102.

### *b. Isaiah and 1 Corinthians*

The references to the book of Isaiah in the opening chapters of 1 Corinthians inform Paul's self-understanding as the prophetic herald of God's eschatological age (see Section II.D. above), and Isaiah's vision of the eschatological glory of God (66:18-24) gave Paul the map for his work as apostle to the Gentiles (see Section II.E.). Along with these connections, it is worth observing that Isaiah has a discernible "trajectory" that takes place across the book as a whole and within its individual sections.[99] This trajectory takes us from the existing world order (with its ruling powers: Israel, Assyria, and Babylon) to a new world order established by God. This happens via demolition and reconstruction, judgment and salvation, in that order. Its crucial transformative event is the justification that comes through the discipline of a Suffering Servant, and it climaxes in God's Spirit-empowered servants being sent out (e.g., Isa. 61:1) to preach the same two-edged message which divides the world into two groups: the judged and the saved.[100]

In Isaiah, as in 1 Corinthians 1–4, there are therefore two types of wisdom: human and divine. Both types of wisdom are ultimately attempts at salvation.[101] There is the human "wisdom" of the nations (cf. 1 Cor. 1:23): their rulers (Isa. 10:12-14; 19:11; cf. 1 Cor. 2:6), and their advisers ("the wise," Isa. 19:11-12), which will be brought to nothing (cf. 1 Cor. 1:20). There is also the human "wisdom" of those within Israel who recommend trust in foreign rulers, advisers ("the wise" and "the intelligent," Isa. 29:14; cf. 1 Cor. 1:19), and scribes (Isa. 33:18);[102] this, too, will be brought to nothing (1 Cor. 1:19-20), for they are, in fact, oppressive enemies of the Messiah and God's people.[103] The "wisdom" that trusts in foreign powers is wisdom that trusts in salvation by foreign gods — foolish idolatrous worship goes hand in hand with reliance upon Egypt, Assyria, and Babylon (Isa. 10:10-14; 44:17-20).

Divine wisdom, however, ultimately triumphs in Isaiah. There is a messianic figure introduced in 11:1, a "shoot from the stump of Jesse," who is introduced with wisdom terminology: the Spirit of wisdom, understanding, counsel, and might will rest upon him (cf. 1 Cor. 2:10).[104] Even though the "wise" in Israel were blind and deaf (Isa. 28:7, 12; 29:9-14; 30:9-11; 33:18), when Israel is restored and her righteous king reappears, the blind and deaf will see and hear again (Isa. 29:18; 30:20-22; 32:1-5; 33:17-22).[105]

99. Barry Webb, *The Message of Isaiah* (The Bible Speaks Today; Leicester: Inter-Varsity Press, 1996), 30-31.

100. Webb, *Isaiah*, 30-33.

101. H. H. D. Williams, *The Wisdom of the Wise*, 88-100.

102. B. J. Oropeza, "Echoes of Isaiah in the Rhetoric of Paul: New Exodus, Wisdom and the Humility of the Cross in Utopian-Apocalyptic Expectations," in *The Intertexture of Apocalyptic Discourse in the New Testament* (ed. Duane F. Watson; Atlanta: Society of Biblical Literature, 2002), 97-98.

103. H. H. D. Williams, *The Wisdom of the Wise*, 88-100.

104. Oropeza, "Echoes of Isaiah," 98.

105. Oropeza, "Echoes of Isaiah," 98.

This king will put into effect God's plan of salvation, which is independent of human wisdom (Isa. 40:13-14, quoted in 1 Cor. 2:16). But, significantly, this salvific plan will come about in a strange and marvelous way. A Suffering Servant will come, and will suffer vicariously as a sacrifice for the sins of the people. The Servant Song of Isaiah 53 abounds in "wisdom" terminology, which is entirely consonant with the prominence of the wisdom motif throughout the whole of Isaiah. This servant shall be wise (Isa. 52:13), and by his knowledge he will justify many (Isa. 53:11). In this way, he will silence and amaze the rulers of the nations (Isa. 52:15, alluded to in 1 Cor. 2:9). So the eschatological judgment, salvation, and vindication of those who wait patiently for God is an amazing, unheard-of, unimaginable act of God's wisdom (Isa. 64:4; cf. 1 Cor. 2:9) — salvation through suffering. All are called, including Gentiles, to come under the rule of King David, where they will find repentance and forgiveness of sins (Isa. 55:3-7) through God's remarkable, transcendent wisdom: "For my thoughts are not your thoughts, neither are your ways my ways, declares the LORD" (Isa. 55:8). At this time, God's dwelling will be with the one who, like the Suffering Servant, is poor and broken in spirit and who trembles at his word (Isa. 66:1-2; cf. 53:4).

The ultimate outcome of God's salvation-historical plan in Isaiah is the *glorification of God by the Gentiles through worship in a new temple,* with the corresponding judgment of those who refuse to submit to God (Isa. 56:6-7; 60; 62:2; 66:18-24). As we have seen above, Isaiah 66:18-21 is a key text for Paul's description of his own Gentile mission. Similarly, Tobit 14:5-7 looks forward to the mass conversion of the Gentiles accompanied by a clear rejection of idolatry on their part: "All the nations of the world shall be converted and shall offer God true worship; all shall abandon their idols." This would be the time when the Lord's name would be glorified in all the earth (Pss. 57:11; 86:9; Isa. 24:15; 42:10, 12; 66:18-19; Ezek. 39:21; 43:2-5; Mic. 5:4; Hab. 2:14).

Paul's astonishing message is that the Suffering Servant and the Davidic Messiah King, who could be mistaken for two different figures in Isaiah, have both arrived in the same person: "We proclaim Christ crucified, a scandal for Jews and foolishness for Gentiles, but to those who are called, both Jews and Greeks, Christ the power of God and the wisdom of God" (1:22-24). All the eschatological expectations of the prophets have come to fulfillment in this one man — in the suffering and exaltation of Christ, God's glory is fully revealed (cf. 2 Cor. 1:20).

### 2. *Four Key Themes*

Four themes arise from the biblical-theological basis of Paul's identity, aims, and agenda in his relations with the church in Corinth. These can be seen as driving his instruction throughout 1 Corinthians, and they give the letter its essential unity. They are the lordship of Christ, worldwide worship, the eschatological temple, and the glory of God.

If the Corinthians' problems can be attributed to their cultural background, Paul's various responses may be ascribed to his understanding of the crucified Christ and his lordship over against all human and spiritual powers; in almost every case Paul pits Christ against the prevailing culture.[106] He appeals for unity in the name of Christ (1:10), who is the power and wisdom of God (2:23-24) and the foundation of the church (3:11). The church must be cleansed of the incestuous man because of Christ's sacrifice (5:7). To have relations with a prostitute is to violate Christ (6:15). Eating food sacrificed to idols must be avoided for the sake of one for whom Christ died (8:11) and in imitation of Christ (11:1). With respect to head coverings, he notes that Christ is the head of every man (11:3). The Lord's Supper must be celebrated by discerning "the body" of Christ (11:29). Spiritual gifts are to be exercised in order to build up the body of Christ (12:27). The resurrection of believers is grounded in the resurrection of Christ (15:3-23). Finally, all of history is about the subjection of all things under Christ's feet and his presentation of the fully redeemed kingdom/creation to God the Father (15:24-28). Throughout the letter "Christ" appears 64 times, "Lord" 66 times, and "Jesus" 26 times.[107]

Thus the nature of the eschatological temple and the glory that God is to receive through worldwide worship are understood in the light of the kingdom God has established through his Son, the universal Lord. The expectation that universal glory and worship would be given to God is at the heart of the significance of the lordship of Jesus Christ, whose post-crucifixion exaltation is understood by Paul and other New Testament authors to inaugurate the long-awaited time of the universal and eternal kingdom of God which would result in every knee bowing and every tongue confessing that "Jesus Christ is Lord, *to the glory of God the Father*" (Phil. 2:11; cf. Rev. 15:3-4). 1 Corinthians comes to a climax in chapter 15 with Paul's discussion of the resurrection as it relates to the ultimate triumph of Christ over all adversaries and the final transformation of our corruptible humanity into humanity that fully reflects God's glory. It is no surprise that Paul offers the resurrection as the decisive basis for his ethical instruction,[108] especially given the relationship between Christ's resurrection, Christ's reign, and God's ultimate glory (15:24-28).

In 1 Corinthians 1:2 Paul refers to the Corinthians as those "who have been sanctified in Christ Jesus, called to be saints along with all those who

106. In a similar vein, K. Barth, *The Resurrection of the Dead*, 103-4, argues that "what is at stake in Christianity is the rule of God and nothing else. That is the Either-Or with which he confronts the Corinthian Church all along the line."

107. R. B. Terry, "Patterns of Discourse Structure in I Corinthians," *JOTT* 7.4 (1996), 1-32, also draws attention to the centrality of Christ in 1 Corinthians.

108. See O. O'Donovan, *Resurrection and Moral Order: An Outline for Evangelical Ethics* (Grand Rapids: Eerdmans, 1986).

call on the name of our Lord Jesus Christ in every place — their Lord and ours." Paul's statement that the Corinthians are united with all those who call on the name of the Lord "in every place" evokes a significant scriptural tradition going back to a key theme in Deuteronomy, namely, the Lord's selection of one particular place where people would call on his name (understood to refer to Jerusalem). Repeated reference is made to "the place which the Lord your God will choose to have people call upon his name" (cf. LXX Deut. 12:11, 21, 26; 14:23-24; 16:2, 6, 11; 17:8, 10; 26:2). Rather than refer to that place, however, Paul says that the Corinthians join those who call on the name of our Lord "in every place."[109] The expression is found only in the Pauline corpus (1 Cor. 1:2; 2 Cor. 2:14; 1 Thess. 1:8; 1 Tim. 2:8) and he uses it to refer to the worship of God that is spreading around the world through his ministry to the Gentiles.[110]

The expression echoes Malachi 1:11 LXX,[111] which (in a context of frustration over the way the Lord is being worshiped in Jerusalem) prophesies a future time when God would be worshiped by Gentiles "in every place": "From the rising of the sun until its setting my name will be *glorified* among the Gentiles, and *in every place* incense is offered to my name and a pure offering, for my name is great among the Gentiles, says the Lord Almighty."[112] Similarly, Haggai 2:7 anticipates a time when the Gentiles will glorify God in his temple: "all nations will come in, and I will fill this house with glory, says the LORD of hosts." The echo of Malachi 1:11 in 1 Corinthians 1:2 suggests that the Corinthians are part of the fulfillment of God's plan to be worshiped among all the Gentiles and that it is Paul's ultimate purpose in writing to them to see them play their part in fulfilling this world-wide eschatological vision by glorifying God (see 6:20b and 10:31b).

If Malachi's purpose and message were intended to help his audience come "to terms, mentally, spiritually and ethically, with the non-appearance of the new eschatological beginning"[113] which had been expected with the return from exile, Paul's goal in 1 Corinthians is to get the Corinthians to come to terms, mentally, spiritually, and ethically, with its appearance.

109. Gk. ἐν παντὶ τόπῳ.

110. Significantly, in context all four texts evince one or more of the following temple motifs: offerings, worship, the Spirit, holiness, and prayer.

111. The influence of the text on the New Testament is suggested by the UBS[4] references to it in 2 Thess. 1:12 and Rev. 15:4 (note "all nations") as also alluding to Mal. 1:11, picking up "the glorifying of God's name" language. That Paul knew and appreciated Malachi is clear from his description of the fiery judgment of God's temple in 1 Corinthians 3, which alludes to Malachi 3.

112. P. Towner, "The Pastoral Epistles," *NDBT*, 330-36; here 333. As A. E. Hill notes (*Malachi: A New Translation with Introduction and Commentary* [Anchor Bible; New York: Doubleday, 1998], 188), this perspective of Malachi is not an isolated thought: "Like his earlier contemporaries Haggai (2:7) and Zechariah (8:22), Malachi calls upon his audience to recognize that the worship of Yahweh extends universally to the nations."

113. K. Koch, *The Prophets: The Babylonian and Persian Periods* (trans. M. Kohl; Philadelphia: Fortress, 1984), 179 (mentioned in A. E. Hill, *Malachi*, 45 n. 4).

Indeed, Paul's understanding that God would be glorified through Christ and his church — which includes people of all nations — is evident across the Pauline corpus and is one of the apostle's key pastoral and missiological motivations. His mission purpose is summarized in Romans 1:5: "to bring about the obedience of faith *for the sake of his name* among all the nations." He prays for the Thessalonian Christians, that "the name of our Lord Jesus may be glorified in you, and you in him" (2 Thess. 1:12), and for the Philippians, that they might be loving, knowledgeable, discerning, pure, blameless, and fruitful "to the glory and praise of God" (Phil. 1:9-11). The doxology of Galatians 1:5 ("to whom be glory forever and ever") indicates that God's role in providing redemption in Christ should result in eternal glory for him. The doxology in Ephesians 3:20-21 accords God "glory in the church and in Christ Jesus throughout all generations, forever and ever." According to 2 Thessalonians 1:10, the purpose of the Lord's return is "to be glorified in his holy people."

Such universal worship also required a reconceptualizing of the nature and role of the temple, one which was already developing in Second Temple Judaism[114] and which is reflected in the rest of the New Testament as well.[115] Paul's understanding of the church as both the body of Christ (12:27: "you are the body of Christ"; cf. 12:12-27) and the temple of the Spirit (3:16: "you are the God's temple and God's Spirit dwells in you"; cf. 3:17; 6:19) is central to the ecclesiology of 1 Corinthians. Since they are the temples of God, Paul finds it imperative that the Corinthians glorify God. After all, "[t]he purpose of the OT temple . . . was to house and show forth God's glory,"[116] and all four Old Testament "temples" are filled with God's glory.[117]

## D. 1 Corinthians in Recent Research

The serious study of the New Testament has always been an interdisciplinary undertaking. The New Testament documents were not let down from heaven on a string but were written by human authors in space and time such that, like any other book, they have a setting that has historical, geographical, linguistic, political, cultural, and social dimensions. In order to interpret them accurately, New Testament scholars look to a host of other disciplines for help. Progress in the study of 1 Corinthians in the last two

114. Cf. 1QS viii 5-10; ix 4-6.

115. Matt. 26:61; 27:40; Mark 14:58; 15:29; John 2:19, 21; 1 Pet. 2:5.

116. G. K. Beale, *The Temple and the Church's Mission: A Biblical Theology of the Dwelling Place of God* (Downers Grove, IL: InterVarsity Press, 2004), 252.

117. Cf. the tabernacle (Exod. 40:34-35; Num. 14:10; 16:42; cf. Exod. 20:24; 1 Sam. 4:21-22), Solomon's temple (2 Chr. 7:1-3 [3x]), the rebuilt temple (Ezra 7:27; 8:36; cf. 1 Macc. 15:9; 2 Macc. 3:2; 1 Esdr. 8:25), and the eschatological temple in Ezekiel (43:4-5). Likewise, the consummated temple in Revelation is associated with glory (Rev. 15:8; 21:11, 23, 26).

decades has arisen from studying the letter with aid from five such areas: (1) the study of ancient Judaism and the Jewish Scriptures; (2) ancient history and classics; (3) the social sciences; (4) classical rhetoric; and (5) theology and homiletics. We shall take these in order, setting out our view of their place in the study of 1 Corinthians.

### 1. *Biblical and Jewish Background*

Recognizing the main influences on a certain writer is generally accepted to be a crucial step in interpretation. This is just as true of Paul as it is of Karl Marx, C. S. Lewis, or Winston Churchill. It is also true in the study of music and art. Attempts to trace the origin of Paul's thought basically fall into two groups. One group emphasizes Paul's context, often appealing to the influence of Hellenism and other factors external to his letters. A second stresses Paul's personal experience and religious heritage, especially his Jewish training and indebtedness to the Scriptures and early Jewish moral teaching which built upon and elaborated their teaching on how to walk or conduct oneself.[118]

While the debate continues, increasingly there are those who argue that the Scriptures continue to exercise both theological and pragmatic/practical/halakic authority for Paul the Christian apostle. When Paul says hard things about the law of Moses, he does not discount its continuing ethical value.[119] The Old Testament and Jewish sources are the proper place to look for the origin of Paul's instructions in 1 Corinthians. The influence of early Jewish moral teaching, with which Paul would have had sympathetic acquaintance through, among other channels, the exposition of the Scriptures in the synagogue, was often the lens through which Paul perceived the relevance of Scripture to the problems with which he wrestled in 1 Corinthians. It is not that he regarded this material as inspired, as he did the Jewish Bible.[120] But it is by historical necessity an interpreted-Scripture that Paul read, and the extant Jewish writings are the best place to discover these interpretations. Of course he did not always subscribe to those prior or traditional exegeses with which he was familiar, often offering his own distinctive interpretations of biblical texts, especially on matters like Christology and ecclesiology. Nonetheless, in Jewish moral teaching certain biblical passages become prominent, certain biblical moral scruples are emphasized, certain biblical concerns are connected, certain biblical forms of parenesis

118. On the history of this debate see B. S. Rosner, *Understanding Paul's Ethics: Twentieth-Century Approaches* (Grand Rapids: Eerdmans, 1985), 5-10, and the chapters by Adolf von Harnack and Traugott Holtz.

119. See the remarks on Paul and the law in the commentary on 7:19.

120. See B. S. Rosner, "'Written for Us': Paul's View of Scripture," in *A Pathway into the Holy Scripture* (ed. David Wright and Philip Satterthwaite; Grand Rapids: Eerdmans, 1994), 81-105.

are popularized, certain biblical themes undergo development, and certain biblical exegeses and expositions are promulgated.[121] It is against this background that Paul's own use of Scripture is best understood.

## 2. *Greco-Roman Foreground*

Just as an awareness of his biblical/Jewish background is vital to understanding Paul, so also an acquaintance with his Greco-Roman foreground is indispensable to understand the situations into which Paul directed his instructions. So we move from the derivation to the direction of Paul's teaching, from where Paul was coming from to what Paul was looking at, from background to foreground. This is not to suggest that in numerous cases the opposite realities may also be observed, namely that Paul's thinking has been significantly influenced by his Greco-Roman context, or that the issues he addresses in his churches were generated out of Jewish influences and alternative interpretations of Scripture. In Paul's writings in general, however, and in 1 Corinthians in particular, Old Testament and Jewish backgrounds provide the primary sources for Paul's thought and teaching, while the Greco-Roman world provides the context for their application.

Here we must distinguish between the social history approach, our concern in this section, and the sociological approach (see the next section) to the study of early Christianity. There is some overlap between these concerns. They are both interested in the question, "What are the social facts of life characteristic of the world to which the New Testament belongs?"[122] They are both committed to the study of Paul's letters not just as a history of ideas, but as "a history of communities."[123] To risk a generalization, the former involves historical-descriptive work using the insights of the ancient historian and the classicist; the latter consists of analytical study, utilizing sociological models and tools.[124]

Work which places Paul, his letters, and their readers in their literary, cultural, and social environment is a growing industry.[125] Edwin Judge, a

121. On the subject of "Scriptural Influence through Jewish Moral Teaching" see Rosner, *Paul, Scripture, and Ethics,* ch. 2.

122. E. A. Judge, "The Social Identity of the First Christians: A Question of Method in Religious History," *Journal of Religious History* (1980), 210.

123. The latter expression is from Wayne A. Meeks, "Understanding Early Christian Ethics," *JBL* 105.1 (1986), 3.

124. On these distinctions see Andrew D. Clarke, *Secular and Christian Leadership in Corinth: A Socio-Historical and Exegetical Study of 1 Corinthians* 1–6 (AGAJU 18; Leiden: Brill, 1993), 3-7.

125. For surveys of such work, see E. A. Judge, "St. Paul and Classical Society," *JAC* 15 (1972), 19-36; idem, "Antike und Christentum: Towards a Definition of the Field: A Bibliographic Survey," in *Aufstieg und Niedergang der römischen Welt,* vol. 2, 23.1 (ed. H. Temporini and W. Haase [Berlin: de Gruyter, 1979]), 3-58; idem, "Gesellschaft und Christentum: Alte Kirche," in *Theologische Realenzyklopädie* (Berlin and New York: de Gruyter, 1984), 12:764-69;

pioneer of this approach, argues correctly that New Testament scholars ought not to "incestuously concentrate all their time on their few texts, when there is a magnificent array of contextual material all around their texts, increasing rapidly every year."[126] When we read of law courts, brothels, and meat markets, or conventions of friendship and enmity, or styles of secular leadership in 1 Corinthians, for example, it is vital that we do not assume that the same institutions or social conditions that exist in our culture appear in first-century Corinth. An understanding of these is critical to seeing what Paul was looking at when he wrote 1 Corinthians.

### 3. *The Social Sciences*

As Malherbe has correctly observed about Paul's missionary practice: "Rather than simply organize a church, Paul founded, shaped and nurtured a community."[127] That social factors are important to understanding Paul's letters goes without question. 1 Corinthians is not written to individuals but to a group. What it means to be a member of that group, the group boundaries, and the question of how to relate to outsiders are questions that are central to the situation that gave rise to the letter and to Paul's instructions. The increasing recognition that the New Testament is set within a social matrix and that the New Testament documents have a social dimension has led to the use of the social sciences in their study. Social scientific criticism "studies the text as both a reflection of and a response to the social and cultural settings in which the text was produced."[128]

Some sociological studies of the New Testament get carried away. The challenge for the sociological approach is to avoid uncontrolled and overly speculative projections, take careful note of clues to the answers to their questions that the epistles themselves contain, try not to explain too much in terms of social factors (the New Testament documents are first and foremost religious/theological documents), somehow be aware of the dangers of imposing social models which were developed to explain cultures far removed from the first-century Greco-Roman world, and to build upon the hard work of historical description (see the previous section: Greco-Roman Foreground). When seen as complementing rather than substituting the historical, exegetical, and theological methods, the socio-

---

and idem, "Gesellschaft: Neues Testament," in *Theologische Realenzyklopädie*, 12:769-73. Cf. also A. J. Malherbe, *Social Aspects of Early Christianity* (Baton Rouge: Louisiana State University Press, 1977), 1-59.

126. A comment published in B. J. Malina, *The Gospel of John in Sociolinguistic Perspective: Protocol of the Forty-eighth Colloquy, 11 March 1984* (Berkeley, CA: Center for Hermeneutical Studies in Hellenistic and Modern Culture, 1985), 51 (cited in Clarke, *Secular and Christian Leadership in Corinth*, 5-6).

127. A. J. Malherbe, *Paul and the Thessalonians* (Philadelphia: Fortress, 1987), 1.

128. John H. Elliot, *What Is Social-Scientific Criticism?* (Minneapolis: Fortress, 1993), 8.

logical approach has a definite contribution to make to a study of 1 Corinthians.[129] At the very least the questions they pose are often valid and insightful. Such studies occasionally inform our study of the letter but are not a primary focus.

### *4. Classical Rhetoric*

Whereas rhetoric may refer to the art of persuasion in general, by classical rhetoric we mean the categories reflected in the classical orators and in the ancient handbooks on rhetoric. The application of these categories to exegesis of parts of the New Testament, including 1 Corinthians, is a growing industry. Ben Witherington states the key assumption of this approach: "Paul chose to cast his letters in rhetorical forms, that is, he shaped them in accordance with formal oral speech, using rhetorical elements recognizable as such by his addressees."[130] In Paul's day rhetoric was the primary discipline in Roman higher education, and towns like Tarsus, Corinth, and even Jerusalem would have been exposed to rhetors on a regular basis. Since reading was done aloud, it is argued that it would not be surprising if letters of educated individuals like Paul showed some points of contact with the conventions of rhetoric, which, strictly speaking, pertained to oral speech. The argument goes that although Paul distances himself from "eloquence or human wisdom" (1 Cor. 2:1) as a means of preaching the gospel, perhaps referring to sophistic rhetoric which stressed style over substance, he nonetheless used a good deal of rhetoric to arouse the emotions and change the mind and behavior of the Corinthian church.

There were three main types of rhetoric in the first century: (1) deliberative rhetoric, which grew up in the democratic assemblies of the cities and was future oriented, was the art of persuasion or dissuasion; (2) forensic rhetoric, which came from the law courts, focused on the past and was concerned with accusations and defense; and (3) epideictic rhetoric, often used in funeral oratory or public speeches and usually focused on the present, was taken up with giving praise or blame to secure agreement with or rejection of some value.

According to Witherington, 1 Corinthians is deliberative rhetoric with a semiforensic aside in chapter 9 and an epideictic character to chapter

129. For discussion and evaluation of the method from a practitioner's viewpoint see Bengt Holmberg, *Sociology and the New Testament* (Minneapolis: Fortress, 1990), or Howard Clark Kee, *Knowing the Truth: A Sociological Approach to New Testament Interpretation* (Minneapolis: Fortress, 1989). Daniel J. Harrington has provided a helpful bibliography covering approximately twenty years of books and articles in "Sociological Concepts and the Early Church: A Decade of Research," *Theological Studies* 41 (1980), 181-90; and "Second Testament Exegesis and the Social Sciences: A Bibliography," *BTB* 18 (1988), 77-85. With reference to 1 Corinthians, see the bibliography in Witherington, 61-65.

130. Witherington, 39. In the following description of rhetoric I am indebted to Witherington's discussion, 39-48.

13.[131] Another attempt at rhetorical analysis of 1 Corinthians is Margaret M. Mitchell, *Paul and the Rhetoric of Reconciliation*.[132] Mitchell believes that in the light of the Greco-Roman rhetorical tradition 1 Corinthians turns out to be not parenesis, which she defines as general moral exhortation, but deliberative rhetoric, containing advice about specific matters and incidents. The thesis of her book is that 1 Corinthians is a single letter, not a combination of fragments, the overriding aim of which was to persuade the Corinthian Christians to become unified.

The key question in assessing such studies is, Was 1 Corinthians written in conformity with Greco-Roman rhetoric? What has Aristotle to do with Paul?[133] Three points qualify a positive reply to this question and warn against too rigid an application of the categories. First, the ancient rhetorical handbooks are not concerned with letters, except with respect to stylistic matters.[134] Secondly, and more importantly, the language appropriate to rhetoric in the ancient world is by and large not to be found in 1 Corinthians. Whereas scholars disagree as to how to characterize the Greek of the New Testament, both options, that it is heavily influenced by Semitisms and the Septuagint and that it resembles the common Greek of the papyri, remove it from the realm of oratory.[135] A third and related point is that from the church fathers to the Reformation, Christian teachers as diverse as Origen and Melanchthon, some of whom were accomplished rhetors, found Paul's style to be forceful but not artistic. They did not find in his letters the evidence of an advanced classical education. These writers often refer to 1 Corinthians 1–2 as indicating that Paul did not see himself as writing literature in the sense of rhetoric. Arguing against Celsus, the Fathers concede the point that Paul's letters do not follow the recognized means of public discourse.[136]

Thus, methodological difficulties in defining rhetoric in relation to letters, the language Paul used, and the judgment of early interpreters who knew classical rhetoric weigh against the hypothesis that 1 Corinthians is rhetoric in the formal sense.[137] We shall not adopt classical rhetoric as the interpretive strategy of this commentary. Nonetheless, such studies can still

131. Witherington, 46. 2 Corinthians is seen as forensic rhetoric, Paul's defense of his ministry, with a major deliberative digression in 6:14–7:1. 2 Corinthians 8–9 has a deliberative form within the larger forensic purpose of the letter.

132. M. M. Mitchell, *Paul and the Rhetoric of Reconciliation.* The book is a revised doctoral dissertation under the supervision of Hans Dieter Betz at the University of Chicago.

133. Cf. the title of Steve Walton, "What Has Aristotle to Do with Paul? Rhetorical Criticism and 1 Thessalonians," *TynBul* 46.2 (1995), 229-50.

134. Stanley E. Porter, "Rhetorical Categories in Pauline Literature," in Stanley E. Porter and Thoman H. Olbricht, *Rhetoric and the New Testament: Essays from the 1992 Heidelberg Conference* (Sheffield: JSOT Press, 1993), 122.

135. See Philip H. Kern, *Rhetoric and Galatians: Assessing an Approach to Paul's Epistle* (SNTSMS 101; Cambridge: Cambridge University Press, 1999), ch. 6.

136. See Kern, *Rhetoric and Galatians*, ch. 5.

137. Obviously 1 Corinthians is rhetoric if rhetoric is defined as the universal phenomenon of persuasive communication.

be read with profit for their insights into how 1 Corinthians achieves its purposes and for the structure of the letter.[138]

### 5. *Theology and Exposition*

One of the purposes of a Pillar commentary is to ask not just what the text meant in the first century, but what it means today. To many readers this may seem to be so obviously the task of the Christian commentator that it need not be said. Unfortunately, this is not the case. Since the Enlightenment, commentators on books of the Bible have seen their primary, if not their sole, responsibility to be understanding the text in its original historical setting. This also has tended to be true for evangelical commentators. However, biblical scholars are increasingly seeing the need to go beyond historical exegesis toward a theological understanding of the text, both in its original context and in the contemporary scene. Furthermore, coming from the other side, some expositions have appeared that are based on thorough exegesis and have much to offer in regard to apprehending the contemporary significance of the text.

Seeing the contemporary significance of the text as lying within the remit of the biblical commentator is now more widely accepted. Indeed, J. L. Houlden argues that Paul Ricoeur's hermeneutical work recommends "an approach which abandons the uncommitted neutrality of the historian and reintroduces faith into the process of apprehending the text."[139] Houlden goes on to say: "The Christian interpreter is foolish to come to the New Testament as if with one hand tied behind his back."[140] With this freedom in mind we have endeavored to write a commentary that has an interest both in history and in the usefulness, power, and authority of the text as God's word. However, this goal does not find expression in separate sections on preaching or application. Instead we aim throughout to offer a Christian theological interpretation of the letter that at the same time takes its historical and literary dimensions seriously.

## E. Some Features of This Commentary

A brief orientation to the commentary itself will assist in reading it, and the letter, with profit. Here we will deal with four features: (1) the use of Greek and the question of verbal aspect; (2) the general format of major sections; (3) the value of 1 Corinthians as Christian Scripture in the twenty-first cen-

138. For an annotated bibliography up to 1992 see Witherington, 55-61.

139. J. L. Houlden, "Commentary (NT)," in R. J. Coggins and J. L. Houlden (eds.), *A Dictionary of Biblical Interpretation* (London: SCM/Philadelphia: Trinity Press International, 1990), 131.

140. Houlden, "Commentary (NT)," 131.

tury; and (4) what we believe to be our distinctive contribution to the study of the letter.

## 1. *The Use of Greek and the Question of Verbal Aspect*

The past few decades have seen a revolution in the development of linguistic sophistication in the understanding of Hellenistic Greek. Such developments are still in progress, and many issues are more highly debated today than ever before. One of the main results of all these studies is that many of the assertions that were previously made regarding the significance of the usage of a particular tense are now considered highly suspect or completely unfounded (especially with subjunctives, imperatives, and infinitives, but also, to a lesser degree, with indicative verbs).[141]

It used to be common for New Testament scholars to make strong assertions about aorist verbs being "punctiliar," present tense verbs being "continuous," and perfect tense verbs communicating both a punctiliar past event and a continuous present consequence or outcome from that event. All of these ideas have been discredited to one degree or another by more recent careful linguistic analysis. Scholars also used to easily assert that a particular verb was iterative, gnomic, conative, ingressive, and so on, often giving the impression that such things were to be simply (and authoritatively) intuited, or chosen according to the needs of one's preferred interpretation. The impression was often given that the tenses themselves communicated these various kinds of meaning. Recent linguistic analysis has led to much more nuanced understandings of how verbs and verb phrases (verbs in conjunction with adverbs, prepositions, objects, etc.) function as well as more distinct consideration of the information that is communicated by a verb's tense form versus its lexical form and context.

Con Campbell has recently published an accessible introduction to verbal aspect in biblical Greek with a helpful approach to understanding the interactions between verbal and lexical aspect which relates perfective and imperfective verbal aspect to lexical aspect as marked especially by the

141. See Stanley E. Porter, *Verbal Aspect in the Greek of the New Testament, with Reference to Tense and Mood* (Studies in Biblical Greek 1; New York: Peter Lang, 1989); Buist M. Fanning, *Verbal Aspect in New Testament Greek* (Oxford: Clarendon, 1990); Stanley E. Porter and D. A. Carson, eds., *Biblical Greek Language and Linguistics: Open Questions in Current Research* (JSNTSup 80; Sheffield: Sheffield Academic Press, 1993); K. L. McKay, *A New Syntax of the Verb in New Testament Greek: An Aspectual Approach* (Studies in Biblical Greek 5; New York: Peter Lang, 1994); Mari Broman Olsen, *A Semantic and Pragmatic Model of Lexical and Grammatical Aspect* (New York: Garland, 1997); Constantine R. Campbell, *Verbal Aspect, the Indicative Mood, and Narrative: Soundings in the Greek of the New Testament* (Studies in Biblical Greek 13; New York: Peter Lang, 2007); idem, *Verbal Aspect and Non-Indicative Verbs: Further Soundings in the Greek of the New Testament* (New York: P. Lang, 2009). For a very clear and accessible introduction to the subject see Constantine R. Campbell, *Basics of Verbal Aspect in Biblical Greek* (Grand Rapids: Zondervan, 2008).

issues of durativity (he calls verbs that lack durativity "punctiliar" and those that do not "stative") and transitivity (the difference between transitive verbs which take objects and intransitive verbs which do not). Campbell elegantly depicts the elements that inform *Aktionsart*, or the various kinds of action portrayed through Greek verbs, with the following chart:[142]

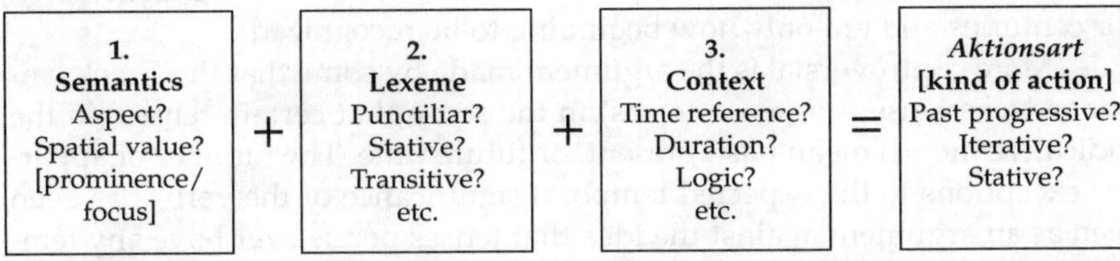


For example, an imperfective verb form/tense (e.g., present or imperfect) used in conjunction with a lexeme that is not punctiliar (e.g., an activity or accomplishment verb), in a context that refers to a specific ongoing case or situation (or that "allows progression"), suggests progressive *Aktionsart* (kind of action), for example, Galatians 1:14 — "I was advancing in Judaism."[143] On the other hand, an imperfective verb form/tense (e.g., present or imperfect) used in conjunction with a lexeme that is punctiliar (e.g., an achievement verb), in a context that allows for or requires repetition, suggests iterative (repetitive) *Aktionsart* (kind of action), for example, Matthew 17:15 "he often falls into the fire."[144] For just one more example, a perfective verb form/tense (e.g., aorist) used in conjunction with a lexeme that is punctiliar (e.g., an achievement verb), in a context that allows for or requires punctiliarity, suggests punctiliar ([near] instantaneous) *Aktionsart* (kind of action), for example, Mark 5:27: a woman "touched his robe."[145]

Scholars have not been wrong to see punctiliar, continuous, iterative, gnomic, conative, or ingressive ideas in their texts.[146] They have been wrong to think that the verbal tenses themselves express such distinct ideas. These particular kinds of actions (referred to as "*Aktionsart*") are not expressed by the verbal tenses themselves but through a combination of verbal aspect (imperfective, perfective, or perhaps stative), lexical aspect (a particular verb is stative or punctiliar, telic or atelic, transitive or intransitive), and other contextual features (adverbs, prepositional or other modifiers, etc.). Certain verb tenses (verbal aspects) combine naturally with the meanings of particular verbs (lexical aspect and meaning) to express certain kinds of ac-

142. Campbell, *Basics of Verbal Aspect*, 67. See how he relates this to the various tense-forms on pp. 67-132.

143. Campbell, *Basics of Verbal Aspect*, 68.

144. Campbell, *Basics of Verbal Aspect*, 69.

145. Campbell, *Basics of Verbal Aspect*, 99.

146. For clear and helpful discussions of these and other categories of tense usage see Daniel B. Wallace, *Greek Grammar beyond the Basics: An Exegetical Syntax of the New Testament* (Grand Rapids: Zondervan, 1996), 495-586.

tion. Perfective and imperfective aspects (not to mention the possible category of stative aspect) interact differently with states, activities, achievements, and accomplishments (that is, with different combinations of the presence or lack of durativity and telicity) and with various temporal or circumstantial contexts in ways which were presumably felt to be intuitive and natural to ancient Greeks but which have eluded nonnative readers of Greek for centuries and are only now beginning to be recognized.

More controversial is the argument made by some that the Greek language lacks tense (not tense forms) in the sense that certain tenses (in the indicative mood) mean past, present, or future time. The number of apparent exceptions to the expected temporal significance of the verbs has been seen as an argument against the idea that tenses per se ever have any temporal significance. If time were of the essence of the tense forms, temporal significance would not be cancelable (it would always be present), but that is clearly not the case. It has been suggested that temporal relationships are not communicated by verb tenses but through other deictic (contextual) indicators, such as adverbs and other temporal references in the context. Still it is usually admitted that although time may not be the essence of any of the tenses (except perhaps the future tense), a default temporal understanding is assumed except where it is clearly cancelled by some contextual indicators. It is probably in light of these default temporal significances that both ancient and modern Greeks have unanimously affirmed that temporal significance is normally communicated by Greek verbs.[147]

As we have written this commentary, we have kept in mind readers who lack any significant knowledge of Greek and have kept any significant discussion of Greek to the footnotes. We spend significant time on lexicography (careful examination of word meanings) and address issues of grammar and syntax in occasional footnotes. With respect to grammar we have followed recent developments in Greek verbal aspect and have sought to avoid the naïve comments about tense and aspect that can be found in many previous commentaries on 1 Corinthians (as well as other letters). If the commentary has fewer comments on the significance of the tense of a particular Greek verb, it is not due to unfamiliarity with the latest discussions but rather due to our commitment to avoid making exegetical choices dependent upon questionable linguistic grounds.[148]

For example, we try to avoid making unsupported exegetical distinc-

147. Ancient Greek authors who commented on the temporal significance of Greek verbs include Plato, *Parmenides* 141d-e; Aristotle, *Poetics* 1457a; *On Interpretation* 16b.6-9, 16-18; 19b.13-14 (cf. 18b.10-15); Chrysippus, *Fragmenta Logica et Physica* 165.2-4; scholia attributed to Stephanos, *Scholia Vaticana* 250.26-31; 251.9-14; Dionysius Thrax, *Ars Grammatica* 1.1.46.4-5; 1.1.53.1-3; Plutarch, *De Communibus Notitiis adversus Stoicos* 1082.A-D. See also the discussion in C. C. Caragounis, *The Development of Greek and the New Testament* (Grand Rapids: Baker Academic, 2006), 316-36.

148. Even some of the most recent commentaries make some comments about aspect that are now thought to be suspect.

tions between present and aorist subjunctive or imperative verbs. Of the ninety-nine imperatives in 1 Corinthians all but fourteen are present imperatives (the fourteen aorist imperatives may be found in 3:18; 5:7, 13; 6:20; 7:9, 11, 21; 10:15; 11:6, 13; 15:34; 16:1, 11, 20). In his recent study of the verbal aspect of nonindicative verbs Con Campbell points out that while aorist imperatives are usually used for "specific instruction, which is instruction that is relevant to a specific situation," and present imperatives are used for "general instruction, or instruction that is relevant to situations in general,"[149] we sometimes find summary aorist imperatives where we would expect a present imperative and it is difficult to demonstrate "any meaningful difference" between them.[150] Most of Paul's uses of the aorist imperative in 1 Corinthians may be explained on the assumption that he has a particular case or situation in mind (5:7, 13; 10:15; 11:13; 15:34; 16:1, 11, 20) or that he hypothesizes about a potential specific case or situation (perhaps in 3:18; 7:9, 21; 11:6), but we would not claim that these explanations are certain, and they do not seem to cover all of the examples (see 6:20 and 7:11; in the latter case we have a present imperative and an aorist imperative side by side).

Scholars have not been able to agree on how the perfect tense fits within the system of verbal aspect in Hellenistic Greek.[151] Stanley Porter and K. L. McKay have argued that the perfect and pluperfect tense forms represent a third aspect (besides the perfective and imperfective aspects), namely stative aspect, which presents not an action but a state of affairs. Since a distinction between perfective and imperfective aspect is common to many languages but stative aspect is not, this last category, and the significance of the perfect tense in general, has proven controversial. Buist Fanning has argued the perfect tense expresses perfective aspect, present temporal reference, and stative *Aktionsart*. Mari Broman Olsen has argued that the Greek perfect tense expresses present tense with perfective aspect. Her analysis comes very close to the traditional understanding of the perfect tense, as pointing to a past event which has continuing results or present relevance, although along with other recent studies on Greek verbal aspect she emphasizes that the perfect tense stresses the present situation.[152] Con Campbell argues that the perfect tense expresses imperfective aspect and "heightened proximity," which corresponds to heightened prominence.[153] Studies of the perfect tense forms are complicated by the fact that the perfect tense began to be used as the equivalent to the aorist.[154] Whether the perfect tense points to a present state due to belonging to a stative aspectual category (as argued by Porter and McKay) or by way of expressing

149. Campbell, *Verbal Aspect and Non-Indicative Verbs*, 100.

150. Campbell, *Verbal Aspect and Non-Indicative Verbs*, 88 (see 81-88).

151. We will not discuss the pluperfect tense since it does not appear in 1 Corinthians.

152. M. D. Olsen, *A Semantic and Pragmatic Model of Lexical and Grammatical Aspect*, 232-34.

153. Campbell, *Basics of Verbal Aspect*, 51-53.

154. Cf. Caragounis, *The Development of Greek and the New Testament*, 110-12.

a particular kind of action (*Aktionsart*) often implicated by that tense (and whether it is a reflection of an imperfective aspect [as Campbell argues] or perfective aspect and present tense [as argued by Olsen]), it most often stresses a present state of affairs. We will give a bit more attention to some of the perfect tense verbs in the commentary than others because we think there is often a greater (and previously misunderstood) exegetical significance to them than to some of the other aspectual distinctions.

### 2. *The Format of Major Sections*

While the commentary seeks to address major exegetical problems in the letter, such as the meaning of "baptism for the dead" (15:29), we have not written it as a work of reference in which to "dip" at will. As much as in any of Paul's letters, in 1 Corinthians the meaning of individual verses can only be grasped in terms of their place in larger units of thought. To use a metaphor, you need both a map and orientation before setting out on any journey of discovery. To this end we have given detailed outlines for this commentary (see the Contents, pp. v-xiii, as well as the headings themselves), and we open each section with an introduction that sets the stage for a compelling reading of the verses that follow.

The introductory paragraphs to larger units follow a general pattern. These each concern some level of context, whether historical, theological, or literary, and generally cover some aspects of: (1) the situation in Corinth, along with tentative reconstruction of what Paul heard or read of the Corinthians; (2) the biblical and Jewish foundations of Paul's response; (3) main problems of interpretation to be solved; (4) the passage's value to theology and ethics; and (5) its argument and structure.

Reading Paul's letters is like listening to one end of a telephone conversation; unfortunately we are left to guess what the party on the other end of the line is saying. The strategy of "mirror reading" is especially pertinent to the interpretation of 1 Corinthians. In each section attentive readers gain from Paul's responses some sense of what had been said and was going on in Corinth. Read this way, the letter is far from dry moral and religious discourse; on the contrary, it is a vibrant conversation. It is possible to speculate too much about the situation in Corinth,[155] but the English versions give a starting point by indicating where Paul is likely quoting the Corinthians, as in 1:12, "I follow Apollos"; 6:12, "I have the right to do anything"; 7:1, "It is good for a man not to have sexual relations with a woman"; and 8:1, "We all possess knowledge." Our own understanding of the other side of the conversation, that is, what the Corinthians were doing,

155. See John M. G. Barclay, "Mirror-Reading a Polemical Letter: Galatians as a Test Case," *JSNT* 31 (1987), 73-93, on the necessary cautions to avoid an uncontrolled mirror reading of an ancient document like 1 Corinthians.

thinking, and saying, is offered at the very beginning of each unit (see 1 in the previous paragraph).

As already indicated, we are convinced that 1 Corinthians is best read in the context of the Testament that precedes it. It is no accident that the two parts of Scripture are usually bound together in one "Holy Bible." We agree with Dietrich Bonhoeffer when he wrote: "It is not Christian to want to take our thoughts and feelings too quickly and too directly from the New Testament. . . . One cannot and must not speak the ultimate word before the penultimate."[156] Paul's scriptural and Jewish inheritance is the foundation upon which his teaching is usually built, and it serves our interpretation to make some general comments concerning this foundation before proceeding to inspect what Paul has built upon it (see 2 above).

We have sought in the commentary not to allow the difficulties of exegesis to obscure a positive exposition. Nonetheless, it is useful to offer some guidance as to the bigger questions that need to be answered in this regard, an orientation that may be of assistance to those using the commentary as a textbook in a setting of formal instruction (see 3 above). This material would form a good resource for student assignments and class discussions, whether or not the instructor agrees entirely with our solutions. Likewise, some preview of the passage's argument and structure will encourage a reading that places it in its proper literary context (see 5 above).

Finally, a desire to read 1 Corinthians as Christian Scripture is acknowledged in a few comments on the usefulness of the passage in question to Christian theology, preaching, and ethics (see 4 above). It is our conviction that much more can be done than is possible in a commentary format. Hopefully, our biblical-theological approach will help point the way.

### 3. *The Value of 1 Corinthians*

Two distinctive benefits of the letter to the contemporary church may be highlighted. Along with its considerable and widely acknowledged contributions to biblical theology in the doctrines of God, Christology, eschatology, salvation history, and so on, 1 Corinthians has much to offer to *Christian ethics* and to a Christian response to *postmodernity*. Even if the commentary can only "scratch the surface" in developing these two areas, both have great promise and potential for anyone reading the letter and commentary with them in mind.

Whereas much of the ethical reflection in the New Testament is piecemeal and incidental, 1 Corinthians showcases wide-ranging treatments of moral issues that are rigorous and reflective. In the first place, the letter

156. Dietrich Bonhoeffer, *Letters and Papers from Prison* (London: SCM, 1953), 157. The example he gives is that "It is only when one knows the unutterability of the name of God that one can utter the name of Jesus Christ."

provides a much needed remedy to a simplistic "divine command theory" of ethics (deontology), the view that Christian practices are mere arbitrary impositions forced upon us by the power of God's will without any connection to the structures of God's world or the impact of his salvation. In 1 Corinthians, to use a metaphor, whereas Paul does take "the high moral ground" on some issues (e.g., incest in ch. 5) and issues uncompromising directives, on others he acknowledges "the valleys" of personal preference (e.g., frequency of sex in marriage) and "the slopes" where Christians may legitimately differ from each other (e.g., on some aspects of eating food sacrificed to idols dealt with in chs. 8–10). Readers do well to notice not just the content of Paul's instructions but the way he arrives at moral decisions and the level of freedom he allows to the conscience of the individual.

Paul's letter also exemplifies the implications for ethics of not just what it is to speak, but also what it is to act. If Thiselton's commentary draws attention to "speech-acts" in 1 Corinthians, we wish to note too the prevalence of what might be called "act-speeches." As Nicholas Wolterstorff observes, "[t]he media we use for saying things extend far beyond words. . . . One doesn't need words to say things."[157] Paul is well aware of this, and explains to the Corinthians in 2 Corinthians that "you yourselves are our letter, . . . known and read by everyone. . . . a letter from Christ" (2 Cor. 3:2-3). 1 Corinthians is replete with act-speeches, both human and divine. Paul chastises the Corinthians for behavior that slanders the reputation of God and sums up God's salvation in terms of what the death of Jesus says to and about the world. When the Corinthians eat and drink the Lord's Supper, they "proclaim the Lord's death" (11:26). Corinthian boasting denies God's grace, their insensitivity to each other's needs contradicts the fact that they are one body, and so on. In response, Paul points out that the cross, God's action in choosing the weak in Corinth, and Paul's own humble demeanor announce something about such matters as human wisdom and strength. The letter underscores the profound unity of words and behavior in divine and human action.

1 Corinthians also models a Christian ethics that is fully integrated with Christian theology, specifically an apocalyptic theology of the cross that proclaims the end of the world as we know it. If Paul's role is that of an end-time herald (1:17), his proclamation declares the end of the world's puny power (1:18-25), arrogant boasting (1:26-31), fancy talk (2:1-5), and shallow wisdom (2:6-16), and of human pride (4:1-7) and meaningless suffering (4:8-17). He affirms that the Corinthian Christians belong to a new world (3:1-9, 16-23) in which there is accountability instead of autonomy (4:18–5:13), righteous suffering instead of self-assertion (6:1-11), sexual purity instead of self-indulgence (6:12-20), mutual love instead of selfishness (7:1-7), reconciliation instead of strife (7:8-16), being known instead of knowing (8:1-6), gospel re-

157. Nicholas Wolterstorff, *Divine Discourse: Philosophical Reflections on the Claim That God Speaks* (Cambridge: Cambridge University Press, 1995), 38.

sponsibilities instead of personal rights (8:7–9:23), restraint instead of self-destruction (9:24–11:1), promotion of honor rather than shame (11:2-34), unifying interdependence instead of divisions and alienation (12:1-31), the supremacy of love instead of the love of supremacy (13:1-13), and more. Without climbing the "ladder of abstraction" very far, and without leaving the theology of 1 Corinthians behind, we can see the whole letter as a direct contribution to a positive and practical Christian ethics and worldview.

Although 1 Corinthians is a letter from the first century, there are significant parallels between the situation Paul confronted there and challenges of postmodernity in our world today such that this letter may contribute to a Christian response to postmodernity.[158] Anthony Thiselton has described the Corinthians' "ever-ready move away from shared tradition and a tendency to elevate the self-constructed perceptions of peer groups above more rational reflection as anticipating a 'postmodern' mood":

> Although premodern Corinth never passed through "modernity," Paul's respect for classical, rational argument alongside his acute awareness of the molding power of the cross and the Holy Spirit stood in contrast to the seductions of more fragmented peer-group pressures experienced by many at Corinth. To them Paul re-proclaims the noncompetitive gift of grace, the humbling "reversals" of the cross, and respect for the otherness of "the other" within a dialectic of ordered difference and unity. In so doing, he speaks powerfully to the world of today, emphasizing as well the christological criteria of "spirituality," love for the other in building the whole, and the transformative promise of the resurrection of the whole person when giftedness by the Holy Spirit will become unhindered, transparent, and complete.[159]

Although postmodernism recognizes the role of narratives as hermeneutical frameworks, it rejects the possibility of a meta-narrative, an overarching, universally valid, global story or schema which serves to explain or organize human knowledge and experience. Rather, innumerable local narratives (which are not likely to be reconcilable), developed within and sustained by each community or society, are thought to provide the basis for the social construction of individual and group identities and the hermeneutical reference point for the interpretation of texts and experiences.[160] Thiselton highlights the relevant parallel: "To the degree to which Corinthian Christians imbibed secular Corinthian culture with an emphasis on peer groups and *local* value systems, the church had indeed become embroiled in what we have termed a *postmodern pragmatism of the market*

158. Cf. Thiselton, 14: "Corinthian culture has much in common with the social constructivism, competitive pragmatism, and radical pluralism which characterizes so-called postmodernity as a popular mood."

159. Thiselton, xviii.

160. Thiselton, 16, refers to "celebrations over the demise of a transcontextual rationality in favor of 'local,' social constructions of truth" (emphasis removed).

with its related *devaluation of truth, tradition, rationality, and universals.*"[161] He refers to a "postmodern mood" in Corinth which "entailed the priority of the local over traditions of more universal currency; obsession with pragmatic success at the expense of devaluing truth; social recognition and manipulation by persuasion over against argument and rationality."[162]

In 1 Corinthians Paul strongly rejects any suggestion that the Corinthians have a true understanding of personal identity based on their place within the local culture and its distinctions (especially between free and slave, elite and non-elite, Gentile and Jew, male and female, etc.; cf. 1 Cor. 7:17-19). Their identity is given to them by God and is established in light of the gospel of Jesus Christ. The Corinthian Christians are "known by God" (8:3), an emphasis that appears more often in 1 Corinthians than in any other book in the Bible (cf. 13:12; 14:38).[163] They are brothers and sisters in Christ (1:10, etc.), called by God to be his holy people (1:2), saints. They are God's eschatological temple (3:16; 6:19), children of the fathers of Israel (10:1), and much more. A significant part of the purpose of this letter is to help the Corinthians gain a better grasp of their true identity and reflect it in their behavior inside and outside the church.

This is not the outworking of just one more local narrative, but reflects what must be understood as the (imperfectly understood, but sufficiently revealed) meta-narrative composed by God himself which will reach its final climax when all of creation has been fully redeemed and restored through Christ and presented back to God the Father, who will be "all in all" once and for all (15:28). This meta-narrative rejects the idea of the ultimate autonomy of the individual (typical of modernism) as well as the hermeneutical autonomy of the community (typical of postmodernism). The God who created heaven and earth, and raised Christ from the dead, serves as the fundamental point of reference for our understanding of ourselves and of our world and our roles within it, and all of life is received and lived at his pleasure. Paul draws out some of the radical implications. It entails "placing the community as a whole under the criterion and identity of the cross of Christ," where "a reversal of value systems occurs (cf. 1:26-31), and as recipients of the sheer gift of divine grace through the cross, all stand on the same footing (cf. 4:7)."[164]

Paul's several references to "the churches" in 1 Corinthians all reinforce

161. Thiselton, 33 (his emphasis). "With today's 'postmodern' mood we may compare the self-sufficient, self-congratulatory culture of Corinth coupled with an obsession about peer-group prestige, success in competition, their devaluing of tradition and universals, and near contempt for those without standing in some chosen value system. All this provides an embarrassingly close model of a postmodern context for the gospel in our own times, even given the huge historical differences and distances in so many other respects" (16-17, emphasis removed).

162. Thiselton, 41.

163. See Rosner, "Known by God: The Meaning and Value of a Neglected Theme," *TynBul* 59 (2008): 207-30.

164. Thiselton, 33-34 (emphasis removed).

the fact that the Corinthians must not think of themselves as a local Christian community free to construct its own identity through some eclectic mix of elements of Pauline and Corinthian origin. In 1:17 he refers to "the rule I lay down in all the churches." In 11:16 he points out that "the churches of God" have no other practice than the one Paul has established in Corinth as well. The experience and practice of the other churches ground Paul's directives for Corinth again in 14:33, and in 16:1 the Corinthians are told to follow the example of the churches of Galatia. These are foundational for the concept of the catholicity of the church, which is to glorify God "in every place" (1 Cor. 1:2; Mal. 1:11). As Thiselton points out, "Whether a given local group genuinely reflects Christ and the apostolic gospel is not left to be determined by *criteria internal to the group in question,* but also relates to translocal counterchecks such as the *apostles,* Paul's *fellow workers,* and creeds, practices, and traditions followed *in all the churches.*" This, as he points out, "brings us to the heart of the global debate about so-called *postmodernity.*"[165]

The other-focused wisdom and love based in the cross of Christ also serve as the appropriate foundation for a proper hermeneutic and for healthy human relationships. As Kevin Vanhoozer argues, "The Golden Rule, for hermeneutics and ethics alike, is to treat significant others — texts, persons, God — with love and respect."[166] Thiselton grants some truth to the perception of postmodern philosophers (which he sees also in Paul) "that virtually every action and stance bears some relationship to the power interests of the self, or to one's peer group." However, only genuine love, such as that expounded by Paul in 1 Corinthians 13, "decenters the power 'interests' of the self and of its peer group, and in recentering them in the Other (primarily in God, but also in the other person) disengages from self-interest." Only in such a context "can truth emerge as disengaged from a power agenda. . . . True disinterested integrity is free to seek truth, without anxiety about what it helps or hinders in one's personal agenda."[167]

Paul's application of the gospel message to the problems of the Corinthian church provides us with considerable assets for appropriating the resources and responding to the challenges of postmodern perspectives and concerns today. It provides insight into the actual source of our true identity and role in the divinely revealed meta-narrative that leads to glory for us as well as for Christ and God the Father (2:7; 15:25-28, 43). In the cross, and the love which it demonstrates and models for us, the letter reveals a different approach to the use of power, one that leads to the sacrifice of one's own desires and preferences out of a commitment to the well-being of others. This radical and upside-down use of power speaks powerfully to postmodern concerns (as it does to those of any other culture or philosophy).

165. Thiselton, 75 (his emphases).

166. Kevin J. Vanhoozer, *Is There a Meaning in This Text? The Bible, the Reader, and the Morality of Literary Knowledge* (Grand Rapids: Zondervan, 1998), 32.

167. Thiselton, 1055 (emphases removed). See also the comments on the relevance of 1 Corinthians for a Christian response to postmodernity in Thiselton, 548, 773.

### 4. A Biblical/Jewish Approach to the Letter

What does the approach advocated in the introduction to this commentary contribute to the study of 1 Corinthians? We believe that it helps at both the "big picture" level and at the micro-level of exegesis. Major themes of Paul's theology in the letter have already been treated in earlier sections of this introduction (see esp. II.D., II.E., II.B., II.C.). Rather than attempt to summarize the theology of the letter any further, we shall draw attention to a few ways in which we believe our approach affects the interpretation of Paul and his letter.

As we have tried to show in this introduction, a biblical/Jewish approach provides a solid basis for appreciating the structure and coherence of Paul's response to Corinthian problems and also does greater justice to the fundamentally Jewish character of Paul's response to the Corinthians. The letter is not an *ad hoc* reply to a series of distinct problems treated randomly or even in the order in which they had come to Paul's attention. The order is most likely Paul's own, one to which he is drawn, perhaps instinctively, as the similar thought patterns evident in Romans 1:21-28, 15:5-16 and 1 Thessalonians 1:9-10 attest. 1 Corinthians is effectively an early Christian reformulation of the traditional Jewish approach to dealing with sexual immorality and idolatry along with expectations associated with the eschatological conversion of Gentiles. And while unity is clearly a significant issue, Paul's most fundamental concern is not with unity itself, but with the glory of God, that is, that the church in Corinth might reflect the ultimate goal, "that God may be all in all" (15:28).

The "Paul" that emerges from reading the letter turns out not to be random and inconsistent, as is often thought. Instead, he is a man focused on an impossible mission, to proclaim the message of the lordship of Christ to the glory of God throughout the entire world. He acts out of a secure and noble identity, intent on fulfilling his priestly duty to ensure the purity of God's temple, which is the new humanity that is being transformed and renewed by God.

How then should we read 1 Corinthians? Rather than settle for seeing the letter merely as Paul's response to oral and written reports of problems in the Corinthian church such as disunity, incest, lawsuits, and prostitution, we are convinced that an approach that takes full account of its biblical and Jewish roots is preferable. In this light, 1 Corinthians is:

> *Paul's attempt to tell the church of God in Corinth that they are part of the fulfillment of the Old Testament expectation of worldwide worship of the God of Israel, and as God's eschatological temple they must act in a manner appropriate to their pure and holy status by becoming unified, shunning pagan vices, and glorifying God in obedience to the lordship of Jesus Christ.*

# Commentary

## I. LETTER OPENING, 1:1-9

The opening verses of 1 Corinthians contain formal elements that are not unexpected in an ancient letter. However, these features should not be written off as merely perfunctory. Both the salutation (1:1-3) and the thanksgiving (1:4-9) are distinctive in the Pauline corpus, and together they set the stage for Paul's instructions in the ensuing sixteen chapters. Two tasks are key to discerning their function as an introduction to the rest of the letter: (1) a comparison with the openings of Paul's other letters highlights their distinctiveness; and (2) paying close attention to biblical echoes and allusions supplies clues to the biblical-theological framework that Paul is seeking to construct in his response to problems in the church in Corinth.

### A. Salutation, 1:1-3

> [1]*Paul, called to be an apostle of Christ Jesus by the will of God, and our brother Sosthenes,*
>
> [2]*To the church of God in Corinth, to those sanctified in Christ Jesus and called to be his holy people, together with all those everywhere who call on the name of our Lord Jesus Christ — their Lord and ours:*
>
> [3]*Grace and peace to you from God our Father and the Lord Jesus Christ.*

#### *1. The Sender(s): Paul, Apostle of Jesus Christ (and Sosthenes), 1:1*

**1:1** Like most letters in Paul's day 1 Corinthians begins with a salutation consisting of the form: A (v. 1) to B (v. 2), greetings (v. 3).[1] In identify-

1. To B from A, greetings were also not uncommon; see Vincent Parkin, "Some Comments on the Pauline Prescripts," *IBS* 8 (1986), 92-99.

ing himself Paul draws attention to the fact that he is an *apostle,* an agent or messenger of *Christ Jesus.* This assertion appears in all of Paul's epistolary prescripts with the exception of 1 and 2 Thessalonians, Philippians, and Philemon. In 1 Corinthians, as in Galatians, it functions to bolster his standing in a community where at least some were questioning his authority.

Paul stresses the divine origin of his apostleship in two ways: he was *called* to be an apostle of Christ Jesus,[2] probably an allusion to his experience on the Damascus road; and his apostleship is *by the will of God.* It was not of his own choosing (cf. 15:5-7 and 10: "By the grace of God I am what I am"). This conviction produced in Paul a rare combination of genuine humility and supreme confidence, a profound sense of both privilege and obligation. Paul's reference to his own apostleship, if understated here, is more fully developed later in the letter. In 9:1-2 he reminds the Corinthians that their own favorable standing before God is a result of his "work in the Lord" and that they are "the seal of [his] apostleship," thus highlighting the direct relevance of Paul's status and stature for the Corinthians' ongoing spiritual life. Further, in 4:14-16 he admonishes them as their "father," another way of referring to his role as the apostolic founder of the church. And in 15:1-2 Paul explicitly reminds them that their salvation came about when Paul preached the gospel to them.

On eight occasions Paul cites others in the address of his letters, in this case *our brother Sosthenes.* Sosthenes is not mentioned elsewhere in Paul's letters. The bare reference to him here suggests that he was known to the Corinthians. It is quite possible that he is the "Sosthenes, the ruler of the synagogue," mentioned in Acts 18:17, who was treated roughly by the bystanders at Gallio's tribunal. Perhaps he later became a Christian and traveled to Ephesus with Paul. Why does Paul refer to Sosthenes here? It is not that he is a co-author; most of the verbs and pronouns in the letter are in the first-person singular. 1 Corinthians 16:21 implies that Paul did not write out the letter, but dictated it to someone, which was a common practice in his day.[3] Since greetings from those with Paul in Asia (Minor) are left until 16:19-20, Sosthenes may be Paul's amanuensis or personal secretary, although we cannot be certain.[4]

2. The MSS are divided over whether to read "Christ Jesus" or "Jesus Christ" (cf. KJV). The sequence varies in the MSS of many of Paul's opening salutations. Whereas the order in the formula "the (our) Lord Jesus Christ" is fixed, as in vv. 2, 3, 7, and 8, the order varies in references to the Lord by name. Even when Paul refers to the exalted Lord, as here, both sequences are found (contra Fee, 27; for "Jesus Christ" see Gal. 1:1 and many MSS of Rom. 1:1). It is a difficult textual problem to judge, but the weight of external evidence slightly favors "Christ Jesus" here. The variants draw attention to the ubiquitous presence of our Lord in the opening nine verses of the letter (no fewer than ten references in a variety of different forms).

3. See E. Randolph Richards, *Paul and First-Century Letter Writing: Secretaries, Composition and Collection* (Downers Grove, IL: InterVarsity Press, 2004), 60-64.

4. If Sosthenes exerted any influence on the composition of the letter, it would likely have reinforced Paul's biblical/Jewish take on the problems plaguing the Corinthian church.

### 2. *The Addressees: The Church in Corinth as God's Holy People under the Universal Lordship of Christ, 1:2*

**1:2** Paul writes *to the church of God in Corinth.* Since there were probably several house churches in Corinth, "[t]he singular [church][5] indicates already Paul's intention to call them to unity — they are one church, God's church."[6] They belong to God, not to any of their teachers or leaders (cf. 3:21-23). The term *church* referred to Israel as the gathered people of God in the LXX and to the public political assembly in a Greek city. Paul uses it to mean the local community of believers. The addition of "of God" to "church" is unique to 1 and 2 Corinthians in Paul's epistolary prescripts. The words are echoed in 3:9 in further descriptions of the church in Corinth ("the field *of God,* the building *of God*") and recall the origin of Paul's apostleship (v. 1), which is also (by the will) *of God.* In apocalyptic Judaism, the equivalent Hebrew expression for *church of God* is used to refer to God's eschatological people. Roloff suggests that the term was used by Paul "because it corresponded with the eschatological self-understanding of the Church, which understood itself to be the company elect by God and determined by him to be the center and crystallization-point of the eschatological Israel now being called into existence by him."[7] Thus, when Paul designates the Corinthians *the church of God,* he is not comparing them to any other club or society in town but evokes their place in God's cosmic plan.

Paul gives a more elaborate description of the church to which he is writing than in any of his other letters. The church in Corinth consists of *those sanctified in Christ Jesus.* They are set apart for God's special purpose and use, just as the utensils in the Temple, the priests, and so on. They are holy, that is, a peculiar and distinctive group in Corinth. *Sanctified* here is a perfect passive participle, which, according to recent studies of verbal aspect, stresses the present state of affairs.[8] Thanks to Christ's work on the cross, believers find themselves in a state of sanctification (are now sanctified), made acceptable to God (Rom. 15:16) and able to enter into and enjoy his presence." The phrase *in Christ Jesus* refers to "their faith-union with Christ, through which they share his risen life" (cf. Acts 26:18).[9] Sanctification in the New Testament generally does not refer primarily to growth in

5. Gk. ἐκκλησία.

6. Margaret M. Mitchell, *Paul and the Rhetoric of Reconciliation: An Exegetical Investigation of the Language and Composition of 1 Corinthians* (HUT 28; Tübingen: Mohr, 1991), 192-93.

7. J. Roloff, "ἐκκλησία," *EDNT* 1:412; cf. Roy E. Ciampa, *The Presence and Function of Scripture in Galatians 1 and 2* (WUNT 2.102; Tübingen: Mohr Siebeck, 1998), 47.

8. Constantine Campbell's recent work on the perfect tense would suggest that a perfect participle such as this one would be marked by greater prominence or intensity (Campbell, *Verbal Aspect and Non-Indicative Verbs* (New York: Peter Lang, 2009), 28-29. Whether or not Campbell's analysis of the perfect tense is accepted, the Corinthians' sanctified status is certainly prominent in the letter opening, given various references to them as "saints" (or "holy ones") and those who belong to God, as well as this participle.

9. Bruce, 30.

holiness but to God's taking possession of believers.[10] However, those *sanctified in Christ Jesus* are intended to serve the purposes of God and his glory. Because God has sanctified them, they should worship him in holiness. In Romans 15:16, Paul describes his own apostolic ministry as "the priestly duty of proclaiming the gospel of God so that the Gentiles might become an offering acceptable to God, *sanctified* by the Holy Spirit." It is ironic that the Corinthian Christians are thus described since in so many ways they are behaving no differently from other people in Corinth. They act as though they belong to the world rather than to God. They use secular courts, mimic the styles of secular leaders, and dine in pagan temples; to act "like mere human beings" (3:3) is to deny their sanctification.

So important is their consecrated condition that Paul states that they are *called to be his holy people. Hagios* in this phrase is regularly translated "holy" (cf. 16:1, "God's people"), and is one of Paul's favorite designations for all Christians (cf. 2 Cor. 1:1; Rom. 1:7; 8:27; Eph. 1:1; Phil. 1:1; Col. 1:2). The term derives from Exodus 19:5-6, where Israel is called "a holy nation" set apart by God for himself through the events of the exodus (cf. Deut. 7:6; 26:19; Jer. 2:3). In later writings it was used more narrowly to refer to the elect within Israel who were destined to share in the blessings of the messianic kingdom (Dan. 7:18-27; *Psalms of Solomon* 17; many Qumran texts).[11] That they are *sanctified in Christ Jesus* is further explained in the statement that their calling is to be God's holy people. Sainthood in Paul's letters is not some elevated status reserved for a few extraordinary individuals, as regrettably in much modern usage. It refers to the sanctity of all true believers who are saints by virtue of God's call to salvation and are expected to bring him glory.

It is significant that Paul identifies the church as a singular body *(the church of God)* and then twice as a composite of individuals (*to those sanctified* and *called*). By referring first to the church as a whole and then collectively Paul excludes any form of individualism and one-upmanship. Although Mitchell overstates the importance of the theme of unity in the letter, it is an important theme, and as she points out, "the attempt to unite diverse individuals into a cohesive community — is thus alluded to already in the prescript."[12] As Paul will go on to say in 12:27, "you are the body of Christ and individually members of it."

Paul's description of the Corinthians in v. 2 mirrors elements of his self-description in v. 1. He is an *apostle* by *calling;* they are *holy people* by *calling.* He is an apostle *of Christ Jesus;* they are sanctified *in Christ Jesus.* He is an apostle *by the will of God;* they are *the church of God.* If Paul claims for himself a high station in v. 1, v. 2 accords with the Corinthians' considerable

10. Cf. David Peterson, *Possessed by God* (New Studies in Biblical Theology; Leicester: Apollos, 1995).

11. Cf. Fee, 32-33; Owen E. Evans, "New Wine in Old Skins: xiii. The Saints," *ExpTim* 86 (1975), 196-200.

12. M. M. Mitchell, *Paul and the Rhetoric of Reconciliation*, 193.

dignity and confirms his generally high opinion of them in spite of their many failings.

It is not just the Corinthian believers who are called to be saints, but they *together with all those everywhere who call on the name of our Lord Jesus Christ* (cf. 2 Cor. 1:1; Phil. 1:1). Paul gives them a gentle reminder that the holy people who belong to God extend far beyond their local congregation. Unity in one locality is to reflect the inherent unity of God's people everywhere. This unity is based on their common relation to the "Lord Jesus Christ," not primarily on a common creed or experience. A church that is aware of its connection to the church universal is less likely to be absorbed in its own problems.

Those who *call on the name of our Lord,* like "holy people," is another way of referring to all Christians (Acts 9:14, 21; 22:16; 2 Tim. 2:22). Those who thus call on the name of the Lord have already come to acknowledge him as the only true God, the one worthy of their worship and the source of all true hope. The Corinthian believers called upon the Lord when they believed and were saved (cf. Rom. 10:12-14), and they continue to address him in prayer and worship[13] and acclaim him in their meetings.[14]

Paul mentions that the Corinthians are united with all those who call on the name of the Lord, literally, "in every place."[15] A key theme in Deuteronomy is the Lord's selection of one particular place where people would call on his name (understood to refer to Jerusalem). Repeated reference is made to "the place which the LORD your God will choose to have his name called upon" (cf. Deut. 12:11, 21, 26; 14:23-24; 16:2, 6, 11; 17:8, 10; 26:2). Rather than refer to that place, however, Paul says that the Corinthians join those who call on the name of our Lord "in every place." He is the only New Testament author to use the expression (1 Cor. 1:2; 2 Cor. 2:14; 1 Thess. 1:8; 1 Tim. 2:8), and he uses it to refer to the worship of God which is spreading around the world through his ministry to the Gentiles.

The expression echoes Malachi 1:11 LXX,[16] which (in a context of frustration over the way the Lord is being worshiped in Jerusalem) prophesies a future time when God would be worshiped by Gentiles "in every place": "From the rising of the sun until its setting my name will be glorified[17] among the Gentiles, and in every place[18] incense is offered to my name and

13. Cf. Barrett, 33.

14. Cf. Conzelmann, 23.

15. Gk. ἐν παντὶ τόπῳ.

16. The influence of the text on the New Testament is suggested by the UBS[4] references to it in 2 Thess. 1:12 and Rev. 15:4 (note "all nations") as also alluding to Mal. 1:11, picking up "the glorifying of God's name" language. That Paul knew and appreciated Malachi is clear from his description of the fiery judgment of God's temple in 1 Corinthians 3, which alludes to Malachi 3.

17. Gk. τὸ ὄνομά μου δεδόξασται.

18. Gk. ἐν παντὶ τόπω.

a pure offering, for my name is great among the Gentiles, says the Lord Almighty."[19] Similarly, Haggai 2:7 anticipates a time when the Gentiles will glorify God in his Temple: "all nations will come in, and I will fill this house with glory, says the LORD of hosts."

The echo of Malachi 1:11 in 1 Corinthians 1:2 suggests that the Corinthians are part of the fulfillment of God's plan to be worshiped among all the Gentiles and that it is Paul's ultimate purpose in writing to them to see them play their part in fulfilling this worldwide eschatological vision by glorifying God (see 6:20b and 10:31b). If Malachi's purpose and message was intended to help his audience "come to terms, mentally, spiritually and ethically, with the non-appearance of the new eschatological beginning"[20] which had been expected with the return from exile, Paul's goal in 1 Corinthians is to get the Corinthians to come to terms, mentally, spiritually and ethically, with its appearance. It is this vision of God's eschatological plan, and the Corinthians' failure to act in a way that coheres with it, that governs Paul's response to them in this letter.

The final words of v. 2, literally *theirs and ours,* could modify *everywhere* (literally, "in every place"),[21] which immediately precedes in the Greek, or *our Lord Jesus Christ,* as in the TNIV: *their Lord and ours.* The latter is preferable. Lightfoot explains the need for the words in connection with Paul's reference to *our Lord* earlier in v. 2 and their significance: "'Our Lord, did I say — their Lord and ours alike.' There is a covert allusion to the divisions in the Corinthian Church, and an implied exhortation to unity."[22] The Lord belongs to all those who call upon his name, not just to Paul and the Corinthians. Later references to "our Lord" in 1:10; 6:11; 8:6; 12:3 recall this fundamental point. *Their Lord* refers to the Lord of all those who call on his name in every place, thus suggesting the universal nature of Christ's lordship. The expectation that universal glory and worship would be given to God is at the heart of the significance of the lordship of Jesus Christ. His postcrucifixion exaltation is understood by Paul and other New Testament authors to inaugurate the long-awaited time of the universal and eternal kingdom of God which would result in every knee bowing and every tongue confessing that "Jesus Christ is Lord, *to the glory of God the Father*" (Phil. 2:11; cf. Rev. 15:3-4).

19. Philip H. Towner, "The Pastoral Epistles," *NDBT* 333. As Andrew E. Hill, *Malachi: A New Translation with Introduction and Commentary* (Anchor Bible 25D; New York: Doubleday, 1998), 188, notes, this perspective of Malachi is not an isolated thought: "Like his earlier contemporaries Haggai (2:7) and Zechariah (8:22), Malachi calls upon his audience to recognize that the worship of Yahweh extends universally to the nations."

20. Klaus Koch, *The Prophets,* vol. 2, *The Babylonian and Persian Periods* (trans. Margaret Kohl; London: SCM, 1983; Philadelphia: Fortress, 1984), 179.

21. For example, Conzelmann, 23; Witherington, 80.

22. J. B. Lightfoot, *Notes on the Epistles of St. Paul* (Grand Rapids: Zondervan, 1957; rpt., London: Macmillan, 1895), 146. Cf. Eph. 4:3, 5, "maintain the unity of the Spirit, . . . [for] there is one Lord."

### 3. The Greeting: Divine Eschatological Blessing, 1:3

**1:3** Paul offers his characteristic greeting, *grace and peace.*[23] The standard Greek greeting literally meant "to rejoice,"[24] but in salutations came to mean "greetings," as in the letter of Acts 15:23-29 and James 1:1. The most common word in Semitic formulas of greeting and farewell was *shalom,* "peace." However, Greek papyrus letters written by Jews in Egypt and the two Greek letters from the Bar Kokhba Revolt use the Greek greeting. Paul's greeting must have sounded very distinctive in the first century. Some Jewish letters in Aramaic added "mercy" to "peace,"[25] the Greek equivalent of which is a more common word in the LXX than "grace" (cf. Gal. 6:16 and 2 John 3: "grace, mercy and peace"). Paul's *grace and peace* is probably his own creation.[26] The two words sum up beautifully Paul's gospel, drawing attention to God's beneficence and bounty, *grace,* the cause of salvation, and the well-being and welfare of those who are saved, *peace,* the outcome of salvation. As Fee observes, "the one flows out of the other."[27] "When one Christian wishes grace and peace to another he prays that he may apprehend more fully the grace of God in which he already stands, and the peace he already enjoys."[28] *Grace and peace* are Paul's shorthand for the eschatological benefits that we have received in Christ.

Reinforcing the eschatological context for this greeting is the fact that both *grace and peace* come from *God our Father and the Lord Jesus Christ.* The three titles used for God and Jesus here ("Father," "Lord," and "Christ") are all informed by biblical and Jewish eschatological thought. In relation to Jesus, "Lord" and "Christ" draw from messianic expectation, together pointing to the universal lordship of the Davidic king and Son of God. Although not often recognized, the fatherhood of God is frequently associated with the exodus and the second exodus (eschatological redemption) in the Old Testament (Exod. 4:22; Deut. 32:5-20; Isa. 63:16; 64:8; Jer. 3:19; 31:9; Hos. 11:1-11).[29] This eschatological association becomes even clearer in intertestamental Jewish writings. For example, *Jubilees* 1:24-25, in speaking of the eschatological redemption of Israel, cites God as promising: "I shall be a father to them, and they will be sons to me. And they will all be called 'sons of the living God.' And every an-

23. Gk. χάρις καὶ εἰρήνη.

24. Gk. χαίρειν.

25. Gk. εἰρήνη.

26. See Judith M. Lieu, "'Grace to you and peace': The Apostolic Greeting," *BJRL* 68 (1985), 161-78, on its background and influence.

27. Fee, 35.

28. Barrett, 35.

29. See Ciampa, *The Presence and Function of Scripture,* 39-44; cf. James M. Scott, *Adoption as Sons of God: An Exegetical Investigation into the Background of ΥΙΟΘΕΣΙΑ in the Pauline Corpus* (WUNT 2.48; Tübingen: Mohr, 1992), 96-117.

gel and spirit will know and acknowledge that they are my sons, and I am their father."[30]

Both God the Father and the Lord Jesus Christ cooperate in securing salvation and making it effective. Christ and the Father are thus both accorded divine functions. The centrality of Jesus Christ in these opening verses is difficult to miss. In this salutation he is mentioned four times, and in the following thanksgiving he appears in every verse.

## B. Thanksgiving, 1:4-9

> [4]*I always thank my God for you because of his grace given you in Christ Jesus.* [5]*For in him you have been enriched in every way — with all kinds of speech and with all knowledge —* [6]*God thus confirming our testimony about Christ among you.* [7]*Therefore you do not lack any spiritual gift as you eagerly wait for our Lord Jesus Christ to be revealed.* [8]*He will also keep you firm to the end, so that you will be blameless on the day of our Lord Jesus Christ.* [9]*God is faithful, who has called you into fellowship with his Son, Jesus Christ our Lord.*

Whereas the structure of Paul's introductory thanksgivings is Hellenistic, the contents stand in the tradition of biblical and Jewish thought. As Joseph A. Fitzmyer observes, "Though it [Paul's thanksgiving] resembles the Greco-Roman thanksgiving, the sentiments expressed are often phrased in characteristic Jewish 'eucharistic' formulas, sometimes recalling even the Qumran [songs of praise]."[31]

Praise and thanksgiving are interrelated in the Old Testament. In fact, the Old Testament has no independent concept of thanks. The Hebrew word for "to confess" is used of confessing sins and of confessing or declaring God's goodness. In both the Old Testament and the Apocrypha the object of thanks is always God. The thank offering (Lev. 7:12-18), a type of peace offering, was the Israelites' opportunity to say thanks to God, perhaps for some specific provision or deliverance. The Psalms include both general praise of God for his greatness and grace and specific thanksgiving in descriptive and declarative praise psalms respectively. The verb to *thank*[32] in 1:4 is not found in the LXX (Old Testament), but it does appear in the Apocrypha. The Essene *Hodayot* (songs of praise) found in the caves at Qumran, which represent a development of the Old Testament Psalms, are not unlike Paul's thanksgivings. They stress God's deliverance (usually of

30. Cf. *Psalms of Solomon* 17:27; *Testament of Judah* 24:3; 3 Macc. 6:3, 8; Tob. 13:4; 1QH ix 33-36.

31. Joseph A. Fitzmyer, "Introduction to the New Testament Epistles," in *The New Jerome Biblical Commentary* (ed. R. E. Brown, J. A. Fitzmyer, and R. D. Murphy; London: Geoffrey Chapman, 1989), 770.

32. Gk. εὐχαριστέω. The LXX typically uses ἐξομολογέω.

the "Teacher of Righteousness"), the hopelessness of the human predicament without God's intervention, sanctification from impurity, and the certainty of participating in eschatological salvation.

In Hellenistic letters a wish for the health of the recipients usually followed the salutation. 3 John 2 is quite close to this convention: "I pray that you may enjoy good health and that all may go well with you." Paul's introductory thanksgivings are more elaborate and serve several purposes. They are loosely comparable to the *exordium* of ancient rhetoric, the function of which was to use praise to secure the favorable attention of the listeners and to preview the main themes of the speech or letter.[33] In Paul's case the praise is without irony or flattery since the thanks is directed to God, and to do so in any way other than sincerely would be to mock him.

Most critical for understanding 1 Corinthians 1:4-9 is its study in comparison to Paul's other introductory thanksgivings, which appear in all of his letters directed to churches except Galatians, where he was not in a grateful mood.[34] Paul's thanksgivings in fact serve more functions than the traditional *exordium* did, and 1:4-9 is a case in point. Its purpose is fourfold.[35] It has a *didactic* function, reminding the Corinthians of teaching Paul had already given them, especially the divine source of their spiritual endowments and the second advent of Christ. A *paraenetic* or hortatory function is also evident. Although this aspect is more marked in Paul's thanksgivings which include intercessory prayer, it can be seen implicitly in the references to waiting for Christ's return and the related need to be fit for that day. The stress on the fact that their gifts (in the broadest sense) come from God might also have encouraged the Corinthians to see them as existing for the "common good" (12:7; 14:5) and not for personal aggrandizement. The positive and confident sentiments in the thanksgiving, which are so startling in a letter that deals with so many serious faults in the congregation, serve a *pastoral* purpose, communicating Paul's genuine concern and care for the church. Finally, 1:4-9 has an *epistolary* function, introducing the main themes of the letter.[36]

What Paul does not say in 1:4-9 is also significant. The achievements of God, not those of the Corinthians, are rehearsed. There is no talk of their

33. See D. E. Aune, *The New Testament in Its Literary Environment* (Philadelphia: Westminster, 1987), 186; with particular reference to 1 Cor. 1:4-9 see M. M. Mitchell, *The Rhetoric of Reconciliation*, 194-97 and Witherington, 87-90.

34. See P. T. O'Brien, *Introductory Thanksgivings in the Letters of Paul* (NovTSup 49; Leiden: Brill, 1977), esp. 107-37.

35. See O'Brien, *Introductory Thanksgivings*, 134-37.

36. It is possible to exaggerate this function, which is most clear in the Colossian parallel. Witherington, for example, suggests that Paul ends in 1:7-9 with eschatological pronouncements in anticipation of the closing of the letter in ch. 15. However, since the Pauline thanksgivings typically refer to the Second Advent, it is more likely that 1:4-9 anticipates the appearance of subjects later in the letter than their sequence. Paul's purpose in foregrounding eschatology in the thanksgiving suggests that he expects his readers to understand the whole letter within an eschatological framework.

faith, hope, and love (cf. 13:13) as in Paul's other thanksgivings, nor of their work (cf. 15:58). Paul's words are genuine and designed to build up, but they are not warm or intimate, as, say, in the introductory thanksgiving in Philippians.

Nonetheless, it is striking that Paul thanks God for the very things that are causing the church problems. He commends the presence of gifts, however, not the use to which they were being put in Corinth. In contrast to Corinthian boasting in their leaders and about themselves, Paul opens the letter by boasting about what God has done through Christ Jesus (cf. 1:31). The frequent passive verbs, all of which have God as the implied subject, stress this further: grace was given to them by God (v. 4); they had been made rich by God (v. 5); the testimony about Christ was confirmed among them by God (v. 6); they were called into fellowship with Jesus Christ by God (v. 9). In this way 1:4-9 looks forward to 4:7: "What do you have that you did not receive?"

In terms of structure Paul's introductory thanksgivings follow the following pattern: he (1) gives thanks (2) to God (3) always (4) for the recipients, (5) for certain reasons, which are then elaborated.[37] In 1:4-9 Paul gives thanks for the riches of God's grace given to them at their conversion. The riches they possess in the present include a full allowance of spiritual gifts and a certain hope of a glorious future.

The paragraph supplies several definitions of what it means to be a Christian. A Christian is someone who has been given God's grace (v. 4), who has been enriched with spiritual endowments (vv. 5-7), who eagerly awaits the Lord Jesus Christ to be revealed (v. 7), who will stand shameless on that day (v. 8), and who is in fellowship with God's Son, Jesus Christ. A more impressive list of benefits would be difficult to compose. Little wonder that they are framed in a thanksgiving.

### 1. *For the Grace of God Already Received in Christ, 1:4-6*

**1:4** Of Barnabas in Acts 11:23, who visited the church of Antioch, Luke reports: "When he came and saw the grace of God, he was glad." Likewise Paul gives thanks for the grace of God given to the church in Corinth. The verb "to give thanks" controls the whole of 1:4-9 (vv. 4-8 are in fact one sentence). After declaring that he gives thanks for them "always," in vv. 5-9 he supplies the ground for his thanksgiving. Paul habitually gives thanks to God[38] for his converts and for all Christians (cf. Rom. 1:8; 1 Thess.

37. Cf. P. Schubert, *Form and Function of the Pauline Thanksgivings* (Berlin: Töpelmann, 1939).

38. Does Paul thank "God" (TNIV), "my God," or "our God"? The MSS evidence is strongest for "my God." Against it is the possibility that copyists added the personal pronoun to conform the wording to Rom. 1:8, Phil. 1:3, and Phlm. 4. However, it is more likely that "my" was omitted accidentally. "Our God," which is found in only one minuscule

1:2; 2:13; 2 Thess. 1:3; 2:13; Col. 1:3; Phil. 1:3; Phlm. 4). It is not that Paul had done nothing toward their salvation. Quite the contrary (see 9:1-2; 15:1-2, 10: "I worked harder than all [the apostles]")! Rather, out of humility he gives the credit entirely to God.

Just as Paul can lay personal claim to the gospel, here he gives thanks to *my God.* Even though he disagreed with the Corinthians on many counts and disapproved of much of their behavior, Paul recognized that God had begun a good work in them at their conversion.

The basis for Paul's thanks is the *grace* of God which he had shown toward them. In other introductory thanksgivings Paul gives thanks for God's activity in the gospel (e.g., Phil. 1:6; Col. 1:4ff.), but nowhere else is grace such a focus. Grace here is not God's loving favor, a motive for God's acting on behalf of the helpless, but the specific effect or concrete expression of God's mercy in making the Corinthians new creatures in Christ. In Titus 2:11-13, the grace of God "teaches us to say 'No' to ungodliness and worldly passions and to live self-controlled, upright and godly lives in this present age, while we wait for the blessed hope — the appearing of the glory of our great God and Savior, Jesus Christ" (cf. 1 Thess. 1:9-10). While Paul is sincerely thankful for the grace the Corinthians have received, much of this letter will focus on helping the Corinthians learn the lessons that grace would teach them (especially that of saying "No" to immorality and idolatry and "Yes" to purity in life and worship).

Verses 5 and 7 focus in particular on their spiritual gifts as manifestations of God's grace. In v. 4 the cause for thanks is more general and broad in scope. When Paul thinks of the grace of God given to someone, he usually has in mind his apostolic ministry to Gentiles, as, for example, in 3:10: "By the grace God has given me, I laid a foundation" (Rom. 12:3; 15:15-21; Gal. 2:9; cf. 2 Cor. 6:1). Paul also uses "grace" to characterize himself as the preacher of a universal gospel, available to both Jews and Gentiles (Rom. 1:5; 15:15; Gal. 1:15-24; 2:7-9). The epitome of grace for Paul was the admission of Gentiles, people without God and without hope, like many of the Corinthians, to the glorious privileges which had been exclusive to Israel.[39]

**1:5** Paul explains further the meaning of *his grace given you in Christ Jesus,* focusing upon a specific manifestation. To be given grace is to be *enriched in every way.* Paul regularly speaks of the liberality and generosity of God in his thanksgivings, using terms like "fullness" and "abundance." Here, and throughout the Corinthian correspondence, he prefers the imagery of wealth.[40] Whereas in Romans, Colossians, Ephesians, and Philippians God is said to have riches with respect to grace, kindness, glory, and the like, in 1 and 2 Corinthians believers are made rich. This is unique in

(491), might have been influenced by "our" in vv. 2 and 3 or may be a deliberate change to carry on the thought from v. 3 that God and the Lord belong to all believers.

39. Cf. O'Brien, *Introductory Thanksgivings,* 110-11.

40. Gk. πλουτίζω and cognates.

the Pauline corpus outside of 1 Timothy 6:17-18. Quite possibly the Corinthians had used this language of themselves (cf. 4:8), which may explain its appearance here. Either way Paul uses it without reservation. Whether or not the Corinthians said it first, it is true: believers in Christ are rich. The believers in Corinth had become rich at great cost, through the poverty of Christ (2 Cor. 8:9) and of Paul himself (4:8-13; 2 Cor. 6:10).

In what sense are they rich? Paul supplies a specific example which does not so much limit the words *in every way,* but narrows the focus and picks up something they themselves valued highly: *with all kinds of speech and with all knowledge.* As O'Brien notes: "The kinds of wealth mentioned were those which made the strongest appeal to the Corinthians."[41] *Speech and knowledge* is literally "word and knowledge,"[42] and might be better translated, "utterance and knowledge." These two terms occur many more times in this letter than in Paul's other letters. Their appearance in the thanksgiving obviously anticipates later discussions in the book. Both words occur as gifts of the Spirit in chapters 12–14 (see esp. 12:8: "word of knowledge"). And in 1:18–4:17 and 8:1-13 they are used in a negative way (see 1:17-18; 2:1-4; 8:1-3, 10-11). What do they signify in 1:5? A general reference to two of "the spiritual graces which make up the Christian character"[43] is in view, no doubt alluding to certain spiritual gifts but not confined to them.

**1:6** The relationship between v. 6 and v. 5 depends on how the conjunction is understood.[44] Either the testimony being confirmed in them is the reason for the Corinthians becoming rich, and the word should be translated "since" or "because" (as in NIV), or the Corinthians' becoming rich is the evidence of the testimony being confirmed in them, and it should be translated "just as" or "even as" (as in KJV, RSV) or "thus" (as in TNIV). Although both options are acceptable grammatically, the latter is preferable in the light of 1 Thessalonians 1:5, which has an analogous use of the ambiguous conjunction, which clearly favors the comparative sense.[45] In other words, inasmuch as the Corinthians were enriched God confirmed Paul's testimony about Christ in their midst. This validation of Paul's preaching by God functions rhetorically to strengthen Paul's status in the eyes of the Corinthians.

"The testimony of Christ," to translate literally, is another way of talking about the "gospel," which is frequently found in Paul's other introductory thanksgivings. In view of this the TNIV is right to take "Christ" as the object of the phrase; the testimony is *about Christ.* Paul says that God *confirmed* this testimony *among you* or in your midst. The whole verse draws on imagery from commercial law. When Paul preached about Christ to the Corinthians, God guaranteed his testimony by enriching them with spiritual

41. O'Brien, *Introductory Thanksgivings,* 118.
42. Gk. λόγῳ καὶ γνώσει.
43. Lightfoot, 148.
44. Gk. καθώς.
45. Lightfoot, 148.

graces and gifts.[46] It is significant that Paul puts so much emphasis on their conversion, which comes to the fore again in 2:1-4 and 15:1-3. They received gifts when God confirmed the gospel among them, not at some later point in their experience. This is in effect what v. 7 goes on to say.

### 2. *For the Gifts of Grace Which Sustain Us Until Our Anticipated Approval by God on the Day of the Lord Jesus, 1:7-9*

**1:7** As a result of God's confirming Paul's testimony and the Corinthians' being enriched, they *do not lack any spiritual gift.* The word *charisma,* gift of grace, could refer exclusively to the specific spiritual gifts discussed in chapters 12–14. However, Paul is also able to use it more broadly for the gracious gifts of redemption in general, as in Romans 5:15-16 and 6:23, and for other gifts which do not fit the description of spiritual gifts.[47] Since 1:7 is the first reference to *charismata* in the letter, it need not be limited to the sense of spiritual gifts. Like "utterance and knowledge" in v. 5, it nonetheless looks forward to Paul's discussion of that subject.[48]

Paul says that the Corinthians do not fall short in any gift of grace, as they *eagerly wait for our Lord Jesus Christ to be revealed.* Paul's introductory thanksgivings regularly refer to the return of Christ (Romans and Philippians are the only exceptions). Believers *eagerly wait* for their final adoption (Rom. 8:23), the hope of righteousness (Gal. 5:5), and their revelation as the sons of God (Rom. 8:19). Here the revelation refers to the same momentous event, but it focuses on its central feature, the revelation of Jesus Christ.

Paul uses several terms for the final and dramatic manifestation of our Lord. It will be a "coming" (15:23; 16:17),[49] the Latin equivalent of which is "advent." It will also be an "appearing" (e.g., Titus 2:13),[50] the word used in the LXX for theophanies of the Lord, occasions when he came to redeem his people (e.g., Gen. 35:7; Deut. 33:2; Jer. 29:14), and for the coming "day of the Lord" (Joel 2:11; Mal. 4:5). In v. 8 he refers to it as *the day of our Lord Jesus Christ.* In v. 7 it is a revelation, a disclosing or uncovering of something (or someone) that (or who) had been hidden.[51] In the LXX the word is used for a variety of disclosures to leaders such as Balaam (Num. 22:31; 24:4, 16), Samuel (1 Sam. 3:7, 21), David (2 Sam. 7:27), and the prophets generally (e.g., Amos 3:7).[52] For Paul the gospel is a *"rev-*

46. Fee, 40-41.

47. For example, the gift of contentment in matters sexual in 1 Cor. 7:7.

48. Cf. esp. 1 Cor. 13:8-13, which spell out what 1:7 implies, that spiritual gifts are only for the present age and will cease when Christ returns.

49. Gk. παρουσία.

50. Gk. ἐπιφάνεια.

51. Gk. ἀποκάλυψις.

52. For a handy summary see Walter Riggans, "The Parousia: Getting Our Terms Right," *Them* 21.1 (1995), 14-16.

*elation* of the mystery hidden for long ages past" (Rom. 16:25; cf. Eph. 3:3). To speak of the Lord Jesus Christ being revealed in the future implies that we do not perceive him as he really is at present. The book of Revelation, the first word of which is *apocalypse,* confirms this. When John sees Jesus clearly, he falls at his feet (Rev. 1:17). The Transfiguration was a similar glimpse of the glory of Jesus to be revealed at his advent. At his revelation, heaven's opinion of Jesus (cf. Revelation 4–5) will be shared by those on earth.

With reference to the return of Jesus the revelation of our Lord will be associated with both judgment and vindication, arousing fear for some and joy for others. On "the day of God's wrath, his righteous judgment will be *revealed*" (Rom. 2:5; cf. 1 Cor. 3:13), when "the Lord Jesus is *revealed* from heaven with blazing fire with his powerful angels" (2 Thess. 1:7). Paul is also convinced that "our present sufferings are not worth comparing with the glory that will be *revealed* in us" (Rom. 8:18). A double purpose of wrath and glory is taught throughout the New Testament with respect to the coming of Christ.

Describing the church in Corinth as those who are eagerly waiting is generous on Paul's part, in view of the fact that some clearly did not fit this description (see on 4:8 and 15:12). Clearly Paul must deal with the subject at length (3:13; 4:3; 5:5; 7:29; 11:26; and ch. 15, esp. 15:23, 47, 52), and his mention of it here intended to affirm this fundamental orientation for all believers. Verses 7 and 8 look forward to this material and form a basis for subsequent teaching and admonitions.

**1:8** Paul's thanksgiving moves through three phases. In *the past* the Corinthians were given God's grace (v. 4), were enriched in every way (v. 5), and had the gospel confirmed among them (v. 6). In *the present* they are amply supplied with the gifts of grace, and they live in eager expectation of the revelation of the Lord Jesus Christ (v. 7). In *the future* they will be kept blameless on the day of Christ (v. 8).[53] As in the introductory thanksgiving of Philippians, active participation in the gospel is evidence that God is at work (and what God starts he finishes; see Phil. 1:3, 5).

*He will also keep you firm* is literally, "who will also confirm you." The verb is the same as in v. 6. Just as the testimony about Christ was "confirmed" among them by God, so also the Corinthians will be "confirmed" by God.[54] Instead of speaking of God's strengthening or establishing them (as he does of believers in 1 Thess. 3:2, 13; 2 Thess. 2:17; 3:3; Rom. 1:11; 16:25), Paul carries on the legal metaphor from v. 6. The Corinthians will be confirmed in the sense of being pronounced not guilty (cf. Col. 1:22), *blame-*

53. Cf. O'Brien, *Introductory Thanksgivings,* 126-27.

54. Some take the subject to be "our Lord Jesus Christ," the nearest antecedent of the relative pronoun, rather than God. However, God is the subject of the other passive verbs in 1:4-9 and of the prior occurrence of the same verb in v. 6. Furthermore, v. 9 implies that the faithful God is ultimately responsible for all of the blessings enumerated in the thanksgiving.

*less,* when they appear before God at the last judgment, that is, at "the End," the winding up of all of history. The word has also a moral sense that complements its legal flavor: BDAG defines it as "blameless, irreproachable." That the Corinthians would be blameless at the Great Assize suggests that they would not be found guilty of having major faults such as sexual immorality, greed, or idolatry, the errors that Paul is intent on correcting throughout the letter. Paul stresses that the day of the Lord Jesus will be a day of reckoning, a theme he develops in 3:13-15 and 4:5. "The Day will bring [all things] to light" (3:13).

The phrase *to the end* could mean "completely" or simply refer to "the End." Perhaps it has a double sense here: the Corinthians will be acquitted entirely on the last day.[55] In referring to *the day of the Lord* Paul employs a common Old Testament phrase with fearful associations for those who will not be *blameless,* which described the Day of Judgment: "Woe to you who desire the day of the LORD," writes Amos. "That day will be darkness, not light" (Amos 5:18; cf. Joel 2:31). To be *blameless* on that day, and to wait for it calmly and joyfully, is a wonderful thing. It forms a fitting climax to the thanksgiving. Paul is at pains to stress to the Corinthians that their pardon will be due to God's grace alone (1:4): "*He* will confirm you." There will be no room for Corinthian boasting on that day (cf. 5:2; etc.), except in God (1:31).

**1:9** The Corinthians can be confident as they eagerly wait for the day of the Lord because, as the first three words of v. 9 in the Greek state, *God is faithful.* The Old Testament and early Judaism stress unequivocally the trustworthiness and reliability of God. God can be trusted to come good on all his promises and to deliver on all his undertakings (cf., e.g., Deut. 7:9; Ps. 144:13; Isa. 49:7). Paul's words are reminiscent of one of the benedictions given after the *Haftarah* in the synagogue, which speaks of "the faithful God who speaks and acts."[56] The specific way in which God will demonstrate his faithfulness to them is indicated in the previous verse, namely, he will "establish" them as "blameless." The character of God is the solid basis of their certain hope.

The faithful God *called* the Corinthians. The divine call opened the letter, 1:1-2, and is taken up again in 1:26 and 7:17-24.[57] For Paul, the call to salvation, which occurs at conversion, is a summons which is irresistible; it is not like the gangster's "offer you cannot refuse," but like the wooing by a lover of his beloved. The call is the historical outworking of election, as in 1:26-27, where "choose" and "call" are used synonymously. In Romans 8:28-30 the apostle insists that the ones God calls are those upon whom he set his love (foreknew); the same group that he predestined to be con-

55. Cf. Barrett, 39; O'Brien, *Introductory Thanksgivings,* 129.

56. W. C. van Unnik, "Reisepläne und Amen-Sagen, Zusammenhang und Gedankenfolge in 2 Korinther 1:15-24," in *Studia Paulina in Honorem Johannis de Zwaan septuagenarii* (Haarlem: Erven Bohn, 1953), 221.

57. On Old Testament background to "call" see L. Coenen, *NIDNTT* 1:272-73.

formed to the likeness of his Son are justified and glorified. The identical logic is present here. If God calls, he will also confirm as blameless at the Day of Judgment those whom he has called.

The call is to *fellowship with his Son, Jesus Christ our Lord.* It is no accident that in a letter in which Paul insists that he preaches only Jesus Christ to the Corinthians (2:2), he opens with ten references to Christ in nine verses. Whereas Christian existence can be defined according to what has happened or will happen to the believer, the most comprehensive definition focuses upon the intimate relation between believers and Christ. The Corinthians have a communion and fellowship with Christ that "exists now and extends to eternity."[58] Verses 8-9 demonstrate that for Paul the judicial and participationist ways of looking at salvation are not exclusive alternatives, as sometimes thought. He moves effortlessly from speaking of forgiveness on the day of Christ to fellowship with Christ in the present.

The title *Son* (of God) is frequently used by Paul in contexts where he stresses the close relation between the Son and the Father in the work of salvation (2 Cor. 1:18; Rom. 1:9; 8:29). It appears again in 15:28 in similar fashion.[59] Like the titles "Lord" and "Christ," the title "Son," especially in relationship with God the Father, also has covenantal and eschatological associations (2 Sam. 7:14; Pss. 2:7; 110:1).[60] Jesus is both the eternal Son of God and the promised Son of God who is David's son, the king and head of the new covenant people of God, who reigns eternally over all creation.

## II. TRUE AND FALSE WISDOM AND CORINTHIAN FACTIONALISM, 1:10–4:17

1 Corinthians 1:10–4:17 is marked off as a major unit by the repetition of "I appeal to you" in 1:10 and 4:16. Following a request for unity in 1:10, Paul mounts a long and complex argument against divisions in the church. The Corinthian church, like Corinthian society in general, was keenly conscious of social status. Caught up in rivalries, they boasted about their own possession of wisdom and rhetorical eloquence or that of their favorite leaders. A point of contention with Paul was his failure to display this status-enhancing rhetoric expected of a "wise" and cultured person worthy of their allegiance.

Bruce Winter provides a comprehensive picture of first-century soph-

58. Robertson and Plummer, 8.

59. Cf. M. Hengel, *The Son of God: The Origin of Christology and the History of Jewish-Hellenistic Religion* (trans. John Bowden; London: SCM, 1976), 8: "for Paul the *soteriological* rather than the speculative significance of the term stands in the foreground."

60. See M. Weinfeld, "Covenant, Davidic," *IDBSup* 190-92, on the covenantal background of the father-son imagery and its messianic interpretation.

istry that may help explain the behavior of the believers in Corinth with respect to their leaders.[1] It is possible that Apollos's own use of rhetoric at Corinth had incited sophist-style factionalism.[2] Winter argues that Paul's discussion of wisdom in chapters 1–4 is in fact a point-by-point refutation of aspects of sophistic behavior. When sophists came into a city, they broadcast their own repute, extemporized in impressive oral displays, and used persuasive rhetoric with great flair.[3] The "spin doctors" of their day, the sophists tried to inspire a particular commitment and zeal for themselves among their disciples.[4] What Paul accuses the Corinthian Christians of, namely "quarrels" and "jealousy" (1:11, 3:3), were actually terms for sophistic discipleship.[5]

According to Winter, Paul turns all the sophistic and rhetorical terminology on its head.[6] He needed no topic upon which to extemporize and so prove his rhetorical superiority (2:1); he already had a message to proclaim (2:2). He had no renown, but used oratory characterized by weakness and fear (2:3). He inspired confidence, or "faith" (2:5), not by the "power" (2:5) of "persuasion" (2:4) or rhetorical skill, but by the "clear proof" of the work of the Spirit in his audience (2:4). Paul reverses the pattern of sophistic boasting (3:18-23)[7] and urges the Corinthians to "imitate" him and "boast" in him (as the sophists did in their leaders), not in impressive and powerful wisdom, but in sufferings and afflictions, in the way of the cross (4:6-21).[8] He warns that rhetoric would empty the cross of its power (1:17) because sophistic methods would overshadow the message itself.[9]

Some scholars have expressed doubts about Winter's reconstruction. Murphy-O'Connor, for instance, is not convinced that the sophists were a major force in first-century Corinth.[10] While he agrees that there are good grounds for their presence in Alexandria, the evidence for Achaia and Corinth is lacking. Further, terms like "jealousy" and "strife" were in everyday use, and rhetorical terms, such as we find in 1 Corinthians 2:1-5, were the vernacular of lawyers and administrators in places like Corinth. Much of Winter's contribution, however, does not depend on the specific identification of the influence of the sophistic movement on the Corinthian Christians. The sophistic movement was on the rise in Alexandria at least, a very influential city, and key cities in the empire were porous when it came to

1. Bruce W. Winter, *Philo and Paul among the Sophists: Alexandrian and Corinthian Responses to a Julio-Claudian Movement* (2d ed.; Grand Rapids: Eerdmans, 2002).

2. Winter, *Philo and Paul among the Sophists,* 177-78.

3. Winter, *Philo and Paul among the Sophists,* 144-47.

4. Winter, *Philo and Paul among the Sophists,* 185-87.

5. Winter, *Philo and Paul among the Sophists,* 175-76.

6. Winter, *Philo and Paul among the Sophists,* 149-50.

7. Winter, *Philo and Paul among the Sophists,* 195-96.

8. Winter, *Philo and Paul among the Sophists,* 195-202.

9. Winter, *Philo and Paul among the Sophists,* 188.

10. See J. Murphy-O'Connor, "Review of Winter, Philo and Paul among the Sophists," *RB* 110 (2003), 428-33.

the movement of people and ideas.[11] But whether or not the sophists were the culprits is less the point than simply that the church in Corinth was clearly in the thrall of human rhetoric, with its elevation of human brilliance and its tendency to feed competition and pride.

Either way, the apostle Paul is not just dissociating himself from a sophistic valuing of form over content.[12] Rather, Paul is arguing against the whole worldview ("wisdom") expressed by the speech pattern ("word") of sophistry, a worldview that exalts human power in both form and content. The cross as the power of salvation appears as weakness, and a speech pattern in keeping with the cross therefore takes a cruciform shape.[13] In order to nullify any human attempt at self-salvation, God "chose a means of revelation actually contradictory to [human] wisdom — the foolish proclamation of a crucified Savior (1:21b)."[14] Instead of explaining human reason and logic by human means, in 2:13 he explains spiritual things by spiritual means. Therefore, the truth of the cross "cannot be achieved through the best of human intellect and strength but must be received as a gift in the humble submission of faith and trust."[15] The truth is that Paul's own writing is highly persuasive, but its rhetoric subverts sophistic speech and therefore sophistic wisdom.[16]

The Corinthians were saying that they belonged to their favorite leaders and boasted about their wisdom and power and Paul's deficiencies in these areas. To heal their divisions, Paul says four main things in response: (1) the message of the cross spells the end of human wisdom and power; (2) the cross redefines wisdom and folly, power and weakness; (3) instead of boasting in their leaders' wisdom and power they should boast in the wisdom and power of God in the gospel which gives them a favorable and secure status before God; and (4) the Corinthians do not belong to their leaders but rather their leaders belong to them, and, above all, they all belong to Christ!

Along with profound treatments of topics such as wisdom, preaching, the Spirit, the church, and Christian leadership, the unit is undergirded by an apocalyptic eschatology of the cross and a consistent emphasis on the free and surprising grace of God. Numerous words supply an eschatologi-

11. All historians of the early church are involved in some conjecture. Winter's case must not be judged simply on external grounds. Murphy-O'Connor is convinced of sophists in Alexandria because of Philo's testimony from that city. We do well to remember the incomplete state of so much evidence from the ancient world. Were it not for Philo, he would presumably not grant the presence of sophists even there. The fact that Philo's testimony survives is remarkable and is taken as significant because it is probably the "tip of the iceberg," much of which is no longer extant.

12. *Pace* Winter, *Philo and Paul among the Sophists*, 188.

13. Thiselton, 157.

14. John B. Polhill, "The Wisdom of God and Factionalism," *RevExp* 80/3 (1983), 329.

15. Polhill, "Factionalism," 330.

16. Joop F. M. Smit, "'What Is Apollos? What Is Paul?': In Search for the Coherence of First Corinthians 1:10–4:21," *NovTest* 44.3 (2002), 247.

cal flavor (shame, nullify, mystery, etc.), and six Old Testament quotations (1:19; 1:31; 2:9; 2:16; 3:19; 3:20) announce the end-time judgment of human wisdom that the cross represents. According to 1 Corinthians 1–4, the cross signals the end of the world's puny power, arrogant boasting, fancy talk, shallow wisdom, and the like. The following chapters announce the beginning of a new world marked by such things as sexual purity, mutual love, reconciliation, self-restraint, and unity. Paul's apocalyptic thinking was made up of five elements,[17] all of which are evident in 1 Corinthians 1–4 with reference to the cross: (1) God's conflict with enslaving powers (2) involves a decisive/invasive action in Christ, (3) which issues forth in a judgment that is (4) final and (5) cosmic/universal in scope.

The grace of God also suffuses the opening chapters of the letter, and comes again to prominence in chapter 15. It was Corinthian pride that led to the divisions in the church, and it is Christian humility, the lowering of yourself before others of equal or lower social status, that is the solution. Thus it is not surprising that Paul repeatedly champions the undeserved favor and kindness of God to deflate their pride, climaxing in two piercing questions: "What do you have that you did not receive? And if you did receive it, why do you boast as if you did not?" (4:7).

If scholars such as Klaus Berger believe that Paul did not consider the cross in terms of atonement, sacrifice, or reconciliation, but rather as a symbol of the radical reversal of values of the gospel,[18] evangelicals are in danger of making the opposite mistake. As Carson observes, the Corinthians' "love of pomp, prestige, rhetoric, social approval, publicly lauded 'wisdom' . . . demonstrated that they had not reflected very deeply on the entailments of the gospel of the crucified Messiah."[19] In Thiselton's words, the cross "has transformative and epistemological implications as well as social and ethical consequences."[20]

Ellis (and others) claim to have found a standard Jewish form of biblical exegesis in the opening chapters of the letter, the proem midrash, which was used in the synagogue as a kind of homily or sermon.[21] He finds two examples in 1 Corinthians 1–2 which have a three-part structure. The first example is 1 Corinthians 1:18-31. It can be divided into (i) 1:18-20 — theme and initial texts: Isaiah 29:14 and 19:11-12; cf. 33:18; (ii) 1:20-30 — exposition linked to the initial and final texts by the catchwords "wise" (26-27), "wisdom" (21-22, 30), "foolish" (25, 27), "foolishness" (21, 23), and "boast" (29); and (iii) 1:31 — final text: Jeremiah 9:22-23. The second one is

17. See Douglas K. Harink, *Paul among the Postliberals: Pauline Theology beyond Christendom and Modernity* (Grand Rapids: Brazos, 2003), 68-69.

18. Klaus Berger, *Paulus* (Munich: Beck, 2002).

19. Donald A. Carson, *The Cross and Christian Ministry: An Exposition of Passages from 1 Corinthians* (Grand Rapids: Baker, 1993), 70.

20. Thiselton, 175.

21. E. Earle Ellis, *Prophecy and Hermeneutic in Early Christianity* (Grand Rapids: Baker, 1993), 151-59.

1 Corinthians 2:6-16. It can be subdivided into (i) 2:6-9 — theme and initial texts: Isaiah 64:4; 65:16 (LXX); (ii) 2:10-15 — exposition linked to the initial and final texts by the catchwords "man" (11, 14, cf. 13), "see" (11-12), and "know" (11, 14); and (iii) 2:16 — final text and application: Isaiah 40:13. However, three reservations caution against detecting these structures in 1 Corinthians. The Jewish form in question opened with Pentateuchal texts, not texts from Isaiah. The final texts in the above examples are not clearly linked to the initial texts. And the Jewish examples are much longer (as, e.g., in Philo). Nevertheless, Ellis's work alerts us to the crucial role of Old Testament texts at every level in these passages.

Hays's summary of the role of Scripture in the section is accurate: "The backbone of the discussion in 1.18–3.23 is a series of six OT quotations (1.19; 1.31; 2.9; 2.16; 3.19; 3.20) all taken from passages that depict God as one who acts to judge and save his people in ways that defy human imagination."[22] Paul's point is that God's wisdom is beyond the grasp of human wisdom. The citations, allusions, and echoes of Scripture are not illustrations or occasional exclamation points but rather the substance of Paul's argument.

## A. Request for Unity (1:10-17)

> [10]*I appeal to you, brothers and sisters, in the name of our Lord Jesus Christ, that all of you agree with one another in what you say and that there be no divisions among you, but that you be perfectly united in mind and thought.*
>
> [11]*My brothers and sisters, some from Chloe's household have informed me that there are quarrels among you.* [12]*What I mean is this: One of you says, "I follow Paul"; another, "I follow Apollos"; another, "I follow Cephas"; still another, "I follow Christ."*
>
> [13]*Is Christ divided? Was Paul crucified for you? Were you baptized into the name of Paul?* [14]*I thank God that I did not baptize any of you except Crispus and Gaius,* [15]*so no one can say that you were baptized into my name.* [16]*(Yes, I also baptized the household of Stephanas; beyond that, I don't remember if I baptized anyone else.)* [17]*For Christ did not send me to baptize, but to preach the gospel — not with wisdom and eloquence, lest the cross of Christ be emptied of its power.*

### 1. *Initial Request, 1:10*

**1:10** This pivotal verse marks a transition from the opening of the letter to the main body.[23] The initial words are regularly translated as *I ap-*

22. R. B. Hays, *The Conversion of the Imagination* (Grand Rapids: Eerdmans, 2005), 402-3.
23. On such transitions see J. T. Sanders, "The Transition from Opening Epistolary

*peal to you* (TNIV, REB, ESV), or "I beseech you" (KJV), or "I beg you" (Moffatt, Barrett).[24] Accordingly, those who find rhetorical patterns in Paul's letters, such as Mitchell and Witherington, regard the words as introducing deliberative rhetoric, a series of arguments Paul musters to persuade the audience to heed his appeal. In this case 1:10 is the theme statement for the entire letter.[25] In 1:18–4:21 Paul opposes disunity in the church in general; in chapters 5–16 he takes on the issues that must be dealt with before genuine unity can be achieved. 1 Corinthians, then, is Paul's attempt to urge the Corinthians to come together in unity.

However, the most thorough study of the verb in question, by Bjerkelund, contends that its occurrences in 1 Corinthians 1:10, 4:16, and 16:15 all reflect the nonrhetorical use found consistently in papyri, inscriptions, royal documents, and early Christian literature.[26] The words *I appeal to you* were a common request formula in ancient letters. Paul uses them regularly to introduce a point that he wishes to underscore (see 4:16; 16:15; 1 Thess. 4:1, 10; 5:14). A better translation in 1:10 would simply be "I ask you" (Thiselton). Rather than being "the *propositio* . . . for the entire discourse,"[27] it is a request made on the basis of Paul's special relation to the Corinthians: Paul is a member of their family *(brothers and sisters)*, and one who speaks as Christ's commissioned agent *(in the name of our Lord Jesus Christ)*, that is, as "an apostle of Christ Jesus" (1 Cor. 1:1).

While it is true that disunity is a major theme of the letter, extending beyond chapters 1–4,[28] to give it primacy obscures other equally important concerns. As argued in the introduction to the commentary, rather than reading 1 Corinthians with Greco-Roman categories such as rhetoric in mind, it is better to take Old Testament and Jewish frames of reference as the primary lens and to notice both the form and content of the letter. In this light, disunity is one of several behaviors that characterize the Corinthians as "worldly," as "acting like mere human beings" (3:3). Paul's goal is bigger than merely having them live harmoniously.

---

Thanksgiving to Body in the Letters of the Pauline Corpus," *JBL* 81(1962), 348-62 and Carl J. Bjerkelund, *Parakalo: Form, Funktion und Sinn der Parakalo-Sätze in den Paulinischen Briefen* (Oslo: Universitetsforlaget, 1967).

24. Gk. παρακαλῶ.

25. Among those who support this view are Wilhelm Wuellner, "Greek Rhetoric and Pauline Argumentation," in *Early Christian Literature and the Classical Intellectual Tradition: In Honorem Robert M. Grant* (ed. William R. Schoedel and Robert L. Wilken; Theologie Historique 54; Berkeley: University of California Press, 1979), 182-83: "[1:10] expresses the main theme of the whole of 1 Cor."; George A. Kennedy, *New Testament Interpretation through Rhetorical Criticism* (Chapel Hill, NC: University of North Carolina Press, 1984), 24; and most fully M. M. Mitchell, *Paul and the Rhetoric of Reconciliation.*

26. Cf. Thiselton, 109-14.

27. Witherington, 69.

28. The letter contains not only explicit references to Corinthian factionalism but also many terms, appeals, and themes that deal with divisions in the church. See M. M. Mitchell, *Paul and the Rhetoric of Reconciliation*, 68-80, 180-83.

As the allusion to Malachi 1:11 in 1 Corinthians 1:2 indicates, Paul's purpose in writing is anything but mundane, but rather is driven by an eschatological vision of Jews and Gentiles together as the sanctified people of God worshiping him "in every place." Paul's *raison d'etre* in v. 17, to "preach the gospel," is itself an eschatological, divinely commissioned activity modeled after the Isaianic herald (see below on 1:17). His use of the Old Testament in 1:10–4:17 also shows that Paul is seeking to redefine the Corinthians' identity within an apocalyptic framework.[29] To achieve this goal of "glorifying God's name among the nations" (Mal. 1:11), Paul must seek not only to unify the Corinthians Christians but, just as importantly, to rid them of pagan influences other than disunity, in particular sexual immorality (cf. 6:18), idolatry (cf. 10:14), and greed. Paul's task is to seek the Corinthians' transformation by the renewing of their mind, so that they might live lives that are holy (1 Cor. 1:2) and pleasing to God (Rom. 12:2; cf. Titus 2:11-13).

As already noted, Paul's request draws its force from the intimate family bond he shares with the Corinthians: he addresses them as *brothers and sisters.*[30] Given that the Corinthians and Paul do not share the same parents, this nonliteral use would have seemed odd to a Roman,[31] though Jews regularly addressed each other as siblings. Paul's reasoning was that all Christians have been adopted into God's family (Gal. 4:4-6). Interestingly, the language of kinship appears more often in 1 Corinthians than anywhere else in his letters, comprising almost a third of its occurrences.[32] The same language is repeated in the next verse. To address the Corinthians as siblings is appropriate to a call to unity, since brothers and sisters, though prone to squabbling, have a compelling basis for getting along. It also evokes Paul's affection and equal regard for them.[33] As Schrage notes, apostolic exhortation can be both brotherly and fatherly (cf. 4:14-17).[34]

Paul also makes his request *in the name of our Lord Jesus Christ.* As in 2 Thessalonians 3:6, where he appeals to Christian brothers and sisters and speaks in the name of the Lord, the authority of the Lord himself stands behind the entreaty. In biblical thought generally, name and person are interchangeable. The exhortation to concord, then, is not Paul's personal preference to be weighed and considered, but made as *an apostle of Christ Jesus by the will of God* (1:1). Paul speaks here as the Lord's representative (as in 1 Cor. 5:3). In view of the fact that the Corinthians' Christian

29. Ciampa and Rosner, "1 Corinthians" and Hays, *The Conversion of the Imagination.*

30. Gk. ἀδελφοί, a gender-inclusive term.

31. Bruce W. Winter, *After Paul Left Corinth: The Influence of Secular Ethics and Social Change* (Grand Rapids: Eerdmans, 2001), 70.

32. Garland's statistics: 39 out of 133 uses in the Pauline corpus.

33. On the other hand, as Plutarch, *Moralia* 481 B-E, points out, "while brotherly love in family life is a huge support, enmity within the family is especially painful" (reported by Thiselton, 116).

34. Schrage, 1:137.

identity is so bound up with the Lord Jesus, as Paul taught in vv. 4-9, and given that the Corinthians were baptized into Christ's name (1:13-15), it is entirely appropriate that his name be invoked when the subject of unity is broached. Unity in a local church cannot be based on race, class, or social or economic circumstances. The only common factor in otherwise diverse Christian congregations such as Corinth is every member's relation to Christ.

Paul expresses the content of his request for unity both positively (*agree with one another* and *be united*) and negatively (let *there be no divisions*), using stock phrases for political order and peace.[35] *That all of you agree with one another in what you say* is literally "that you all say the same thing." Is it that Paul, to use an English idiom, wants the Corinthians to speak with one voice, or is he literally wanting them all to say something specific as opposed to them all saying different things? If the latter, what might that something be?

Terminology having to do with speaking is common in 1:10–2:16, a unit devoted to true and false wisdom and preaching. Though none of the main commentaries suggests it, "the same thing" he expects them to say may be "the message of the cross" (1:18), the "message of wisdom" that Paul "speaks . . . among the mature" (2:6). If they did this, it would solve their problems of division, as the following chapters demonstrate, for the cross levels everyone, excluding boasting in human leaders, and then elevates everyone to a point of legitimate boasting in God. This interpretation fits with the NJB: "That you all be in agreement in what you profess."

However, Paul's use of the particular verb in question suggests a more specific answer to the question, What is "the same thing" they are all supposed "to say"? Apart from in 1:10, "to say"[36] appears only four more times in the unit: twice in 1:12 and once each in 1:15 and 3:4. In the two cases of the Corinthians' "saying" something, it is the different "party slogans'" that they say: "One of you *says*, 'I follow Paul'; another, 'I follow Apollos'; another, 'I follow Cephas'" (1:12);[37] "For when one *says*, 'I follow Paul,' and another, 'I follow Apollos,' . . ." (3:4).[38] Plainly, the different things the Corinthians are "saying" concern their inappropriate allegiances to human leaders. Paul wants them to stop saying these different things and instead to "say the same thing." Thus Moffatt's translation (of "that you all say the same thing"), "drop those party cries," though interpretive, can be validated exegetically. Depending on how the fourth slogan in 1:12

35. See M. M. Mitchell, *Paul and the Rhetoric of Reconciliation*, 68-80, and Fee, 52-54.

36. Gk. λέγω.

37. 1 Cor. 1:12 also has the verb for what Paul says to them, and 1:15 has someone saying something to the Corinthians.

38. When the elided forms are included, the verb appears twice as an explicit reference to the different things the Corinthians are "saying," and another three or four times implicitly. The number depends on whether "I follow Christ" in 1:12 is Pauline irony — see the comments on 1:12.

is understood, "the same thing" Paul wants them to "say" may well be "I follow Christ." In 3:23 he says as much: "you [plural] are of Christ."[39]

Either way, the *divisions* Paul opposes are caused by the rivalries he addresses in v. 12. The Greek word in question is similar to the English "schism,"[40] which is sometimes used in translations but can be misleading. As Mitchell explains, "schisms" "need not mean 'parties' with fixed membership, ideologies and structures, as in the modern sense of the term."[41] We discuss the nature of the *divisions* in the comments on v. 12. Whatever that might be, Paul insists that *there be no divisions among you.* As Thiselton translates the injunction, he wants them to "take the same side."

A further repetition of the same request appears at the end of the verse: *that you be perfectly united*[42] *in mind and thought.* To be "united" or "restored"[43] was a surgical term for setting bones and was aptly used as a metaphor for "resetting" broken relationships and reconciling factions.[44] Paul had occasion to use the word again in a similar context with the Corinthians in 2 Corinthians 13:11: "*Strive for full restoration,* encourage one another, be of one mind, live in peace."

The last two phrases in the verse are variously translated. Both *mind* and *thought* have wide semantic ranges: "mind and judgment" (KJV); "mind and purpose" (NRSV); "beliefs and judgments" (NJB); "mind-set and consent" (Thiselton).[45] The force of the two terms shifts according to context. Whereas "mind" in 1 Corinthians 2:16, "we have the mind of Christ," means "outlook" or "attitude," the same term in 1 Corinthians 14:14, "my mind is unfruitful," has the sense of rational reflection. Thiselton's "mind-set" in the present context "draws out the meaning of outlook, stance, orientation, or attitude, without entirely losing the dimension of rational judgment which is nearly always implicit."[46] Paul wants the Corinthians to adopt "the Chris-

39. Paul's use of λέγω elsewhere in the unit suggests that taking the words as political idioms (e.g., Lightfoot, *Notes,* 151: "We have here a strictly classical expression. It is used of political communities which are free from factions"; cf. NIV: "that all of you agree"; NRSV: "that all of you be in agreement"), while helpful in locating their usual setting, might be missing something in their context in 1 Corinthians. Paul literally wants them "all to say the same thing." The context makes it clear that his goal is to get them to be in agreement in a single-minded loyalty to Christ rather than to other leaders in a way that would be consistent with all of them saying that they follow Christ. Paul's ultimate concern, of course, is not the adoption of a common mantra, as if that by itself would solve their problem. Either way, it is the change of direction and behavior that belonging to Christ represents that is Paul's main concern.

40. Gk. σχίσματα.

41. M. M. Mitchell, *Paul and the Rhetoric of Reconciliation,* 71.

42. Here *be perfectly united* reflects a perfect subjunctive periphrasis (ἦτε κατηρτισμένοι) which, like the synthetic perfect form, typically intimates an ongoing state of affairs, suggesting Paul's desire for the church to experience a state of unity and harmony rather than continuing in its current divided state.

43. Gk. καταρτίζω.

44. M. M. Mitchell, *Paul and the Rhetoric of Reconciliation,* 74-75.

45. Gk. νοῦς and γνώμη.

46. Thiselton, 119.

tian attitude or way of thinking."[47] He also wants them to be perfectly united in *thought*, which here refers not so much to cognitive uniformity but to a voluntary willingness to act for the good of everyone (cf. 8:1–9:27). The term is translated "consent" in Philemon 14.

### 2. Report of Factionalism, 1:11-12

**1:11** The reason Paul knows of their "divisions" is that he has been reliably *informed*.[48] It is not that he has merely been told something which may or may not be true. The same verb is used in 1 Corinthians 3:13 with the sense of something being "revealed" or "made clear." The report has come from *Chloe's household*. Literally, "those of Chloe" may refer to members of her *household* (including family members, servants, slaves, and clients), as in TNIV, or even more broadly to "Chloe's people" (NRSV), meaning her business associates and agents. The reference is probably to her slaves, employees, or partners traveling between Ephesus and Corinth on her behalf. Chloe may have been a widow, since, as Theissen notes, members of a family were normally identified through the name of the father rather than the mother.[49] That Paul uses her name suggests that she and her relatives or associates belong to the church in Ephesus and have regular links with Corinth. Both cities were vibrant centers for trade.

The disturbing report they bring is of *quarrels*[50] in the church in Corinth. A frequent term in Paul's vice lists (Rom. 1:29; 13:13; Gal. 5:20; 1 Tim. 6:4; Titus 3:9), *quarrels* refers to "hot dispute, the emotional flame that ignites whenever rivalry becomes intolerable."[51] TNIV usually translates the word in the singular as "strife." "Dissension," "rivalry," or "wrangling" are other ways of translating the word here. Obviously the report consisted of more than one word. 2 Corinthians 12:20, which includes the word, gives some indication of the sort of problems which Paul may have heard were plaguing the church in Corinth: "For I am afraid that when I come I may not find you as I want you to be. . . . I fear that there may be *quarreling*, jealousy, outbursts of anger, factions, slander, gossip, arrogance and disorder."

**1:12** Paul explains something more of the nature of the reported "divisions" and "quarrels." The Corinthians were divided, rallying around particular figures whom they held to be superior to the others. Such a personality-focused approach to leadership, with its emphasis on the high rank of the leader and the status conferred on the follower, betrays the in-

47. BAGD, 163.

48. Gk. δηλόω.

49. Gerd Theissen, *The Social Setting of Pauline Christianity: Essays on Corinth* (trans. John H. Schutz; Edinburgh: T&T Clark, 1982), 57.

50. Gk. ἔρις.

51. L. L. Welborn, *Politics and Rhetoric in the Corinthian Epistles* (Macon, GA: Mercer University Press, 1997), 3.

fluence of Corinthian society.[52] The Corinthians made too much of specific leaders and specific styles of leadership. The language of sloganeering is clearly political in nature, but, as Thiselton observes, "while he uses political language for the nature of the splits, Paul draws on Christology and theology for their cure."[53]

How Paul, Apollos, Cephas, and Christ factor into the situation is difficult to tell. Was Apollos or Cephas partly to blame for the divisions? Are there theological differences between the parties? Was there really a Christ group? What happened after Paul left Corinth? The paucity of clues in the text has led to an avalanche of speculative suggestions.[54] And as Hurd laments, unfortunately the answers provided by scholars are often "determined more by what each has brought to 1 Corinthians than by what he has learned from the letter."[55] While not wanting to be buried beneath the scholarly discussion or to tie our exegesis of 1 Corinthians 1–4 too closely to any particular reconstruction of the background, it must be admitted that these questions are legitimate for any reader to ask. If we proceed cautiously, some anchor points for a secure interpretation may be recognized from the way Paul responds to the lamentable situation and from our knowledge of ancient Corinth.

That *Paul* might have some in Corinth who were loyal to him is not surprising given that he spent eighteen months there, baptized some of the first members of the church, and, by his own description, was the father, planter, and builder of the community. Two things about Paul's behavior there may have led some to oppose him or at least to prefer Apollos or Peter to him. Paul's unimpressive style of speaking apparently had some looking down on him. Additionally, his refusal to accept financial support from the Corinthians, preferring instead to ply his trade (see 9:1-27), would probably have offended some of the wealthier and more influential members of the congregation. Patronage, the giving of financial and other privileges to clients by leading figures in society, was an important feature of Greco-Roman social life. Respected teachers received such support. Paul took no part in this, and his refusal might have been construed as a rejection of friendship.[56] (See the comments on ch. 9 for his reasons.)

After Paul left Corinth, *Apollos* came to water the plants Paul had sown (1 Cor. 3:6). According to Acts 18:24-25, Apollos "had a thorough knowledge of the Scriptures" and "spoke with great fervor and taught about Jesus accurately." Acts describes Apollos as having spoken in Corinth "boldly" and "vigorously" (Acts 18:26-28). To some of the Corinthians,

52. Andrew D. Clarke, *Secular and Christian Leadership in Corinth: A Socio-Historical and Exegetical Study of 1 Corinthians 1–6* (AGJU 18; Leiden: Brill, 1993), 93.

53. Thiselton, 118.

54. See Thiselton, 123-33, for a summary of the history of research.

55. John C. Hurd, *The Origin of 1 Corinthians* (London: SPCK, 1965), 107.

56. Peter Marshall, *Enmity in Corinth: Social Conventions in Paul's Relations with the Corinthians* (WUNT 2.23; Tübingen: Mohr, 1987), 1-34, 133-64, 165-258.

this would have formed a stark contrast to Paul, who by his own admission spoke "with great fear and trembling" (1 Cor. 2:3). As a learned Alexandrian Jew, Apollos may have taught a form of Jewish wisdom which may well have had considerable appeal in Corinth. Perhaps some of those whom he had influenced also disparaged Paul on the grounds that, unlike Apollos, Paul had not taught them in this manner.[57] As Weiss argues, the group which used Apollos's name may have espoused the wisdom theology which Paul calls into question.[58] The appearance of Apollos's name six times in 1:10–4:17 suggests that in Paul's view the Apollos party lay at the heart of the divisions in Corinth. However, as Barrett observes, "Paul never suggests any difference between Apollos and himself, but rather goes out of his way to represent Apollos as his colleague (3:6-9)."[59] Any difference between Paul and Apollos was a matter of style rather than substance.[60] In fact, Paul encouraged Apollos to visit Corinth again: "Now about our brother Apollos: I strongly urged him to go to you" (16:12).[61]

As for *Cephas*, Peter's name in Aramaic, although we cannot be certain, it is likely that he had also visited Corinth after Paul's departure. Barrett argues for this on the basis of the four references in 1 Corinthians in which Paul mentions Peter.[62] Taken together, these make more sense if Peter had visited the city. In 1 Corinthians 1:12, Barrett contends that the genitive case of the names signifies agencies of conversion, with vv. 13-17 referring to the baptism of converts by those persons named in v. 12 (obviously excluding Christ): "converts tended to align themselves with the evangelist under whom they had been won to the faith."[63] Secondly, Paul, Apollos, and Cephas may be listed in 3:22 as teachers from whom the community had directly benefited. Thirdly, 9:5 may hint that Peter had visited Corinth with his wife, both of whom enjoyed their hospitality. And in 15:5 Paul may single out Cephas as someone with whom the Corinthians were personally familiar. If Peter had been to Corinth, and some Corinthians had used his name as a rallying point, Paul's silence in regard to him in his response to Corinthian factionalism, except in 3:22, indicates that the Peter group was not as much a problem as the Apollos party. If Peter himself had somehow been at fault in the Corinthian situation facing Paul, we would have expected a direct and robust response from Paul, as in his disagreement with Peter reported in Galatians 2.

57. Cf. 2:6: "We do, however, speak a message of wisdom among the mature."

58. J. Weiss, *Der erste Korintherbrief* (2d ed.; Göttingen: Vandenhoeck & Ruprecht, 1910), xxx-xxxiv.

59. Barrett, 43.

60. Schrage, 1:144.

61. For a reconstruction of what Apollos did in Corinth see Jerome Murphy-O'Connor, *Paul: A Critical Life* (Oxford: Clarendon, 1996), 274-76.

62. Barrett, "Cephas and Corinth," in his *Essays on Paul* (London: SPCK, 1982), 37.

63. Barrett, "Cephas and Corinth," 29. While conceivable, this argument is not certain, given that in such a case the church under Paul would have consisted of only two men and a household, namely, those he remembers baptizing.

The *Christ* group is without question the most puzzling of all. Thiselton lists six different explanations. The main alternatives are that some in Corinth saw no need to adhere to a particular human leader and recognized no authority save the risen Christ and that the words *I follow Christ* are an ironic touch added by Paul himself rather than a statement about the specific situation in Corinth. The latter position is supported by Chrysostom[64] and Tertullian among the church fathers[65] and is becoming increasingly popular among modern commentators.[66] The later references in 1 Corinthians to the so-called parties, which do not mention Christ and allude back to 1:12, support the view that there was in fact no Christ party in Corinth: 1 Corinthians 3:4-5 mentions Paul and Apollos; 3:22 — Paul, Apollos, and Cephas; and 4:6 — Paul and Apollos. In 1:12, to quote Garland's paraphrase of Chrysostom, Paul is in effect saying, "All this 'I am for this apostle or that' is rubbish: I am for Christ!"[67] It is Paul's way of underscoring the fact that such allegiances are ludicrous. The tone is no different from that of Paul's absurd questions in v. 13, "Was Paul crucified for you? Were you baptized into the name of Paul?" In this sense 3:21-23 comes as no surprise, for there Paul turns the tables and says, in effect, "not only don't you belong to human leaders; they in fact belong to you, *but you* [plural] *belong to Christ*" (cf. 6:19-20). Garland explains further the place of 1:12 in the argument of 1:10–4:17: "The declaration 'I belong to Christ' is Paul's and prepares for his assertions that he knew only a crucified Christ when he preached in Corinth (2:2), that he has the mind of Christ (2:16), that he is to be thought of as the servant of Christ (4:10)."[68]

The main objection to taking *I follow Christ* as an ironic twist is the symmetry of the grammatical construction in which the four so-called slogans appear. Nothing signals a break between the third and the fourth slogans, such as a strongly adversative "but," which would have made it clear that the final words in the verse were of a different order.[69] The TNIV's *One of you says . . . another . . . another . . . still another* is an accurate translation.[70] However, this is not decisive, for if the Corinthians knew of some basis to the slogans of attachment to the three human leaders, then *I follow Christ* would have been understood immediately as Paul's own ironic dig.[71] Christ has been named ten times in the previous eleven verses. The Corin-

64. Chrysostom, *Homiliae in Epistulam i ad Corinthios* 3:5: Paul added "I belong to Christ" "of himself, wishing to make the accusation more grievous."

65. Thiselton, 132.

66. Garland, 49, lists Hurd, Baumann, M. M. Mitchell, and D. G. Horsley. We may add Schrage, Thiselton, and Vincent P. Branick, "Source and Redaction Analysis of 1 Corinthians 1–3," *JBL* 101 (1982), 260, who labels the words Pauline sarcasm.

67. Garland, 49 (cf. Chrysostom, *Homiliae in Epistulam i ad Corinthios* 3:5).

68. Garland, 49.

69. For example, Gk. ἀλλά.

70. Gk. μέν, δέ, δέ, δέ.

71. Contra Vincent P. Branick, "Source and Redaction Analysis of 1 Corinthians 1–3," who thinks Paul's sarcasm in 1:12 becomes clear only in 3:23.

thians are not to boast in human leaders (3:21), but they are told to boast in Christ (1:29-31). Paul's point is that as much as the Corinthians do not belong to Paul, Apollos, or Peter, they do belong to Christ.

The four slogans are genitive constructions amenable to a number of translations. Whereas genitive of possession (e.g., "I belong to Paul"; NJB, NRSV) would be unusual for the first three attachments, it does seem appropriate for the fourth: "I belong to Christ."[72] The "I follow" construction in the TNIV is an adequate description of how the Corinthians are relating to their human leaders. However, Thiselton offers an excellent translation that shows both the flexibility of the genitives and the contrastive particles: "I mean this, that each of you says, 'I for one, am one of Paul's people'; 'I, for my part, am for Apollos'; 'I am a Peter person'; 'As for me, I belong to Christ.'"

The exact nature of the factions is difficult to pin down. The rivalries do not seem to be doctrinal in nature, somehow comparable to Christians today who might say, I follow Calvin, Luther, Arminius, or Barth. Nothing Paul says points in that direction. Elsewhere in his letters, when the opposition teaches something contradictory to the gospel Paul actually encourages factions (Gal. 1:6-9; 2:11; 5:10-12; 6:12-13; 2 Cor. 11:4, 13-15).[73] The "message of the cross" is the cure for what ails the Corinthians, but it is not that various denials or aberrations of the gospel are dividing them. Paul's point is that they are not living in accordance with the gospel. They have not seen its relevance to how they should behave. As Pogoloff quips, "the smoke of division does not necessarily imply the fire of doctrine."[74]

Rather, the Corinthians are divided according to social stratification or class,[75] or corresponding to adherence to patrons in the congregation, or in terms analogous to philosopher/student loyalty, or along with the leaders who had baptized them, or in allegiance to their respective house groups.[76] Winter's general explanation is the most historically plausible. In his view, the factions stemmed from mimicking the secular elitist educational model of the sophists, which promoted a competitive spirit and an attachment to individual teachers. Such orators were of a high social status and attracted large public followings, including wealthy families, which would laud one teacher over another and cause bitter rivalries. This would be comparable to Christians today aligning themselves with Christian

72. Cf. Phil. 1:1: "servant of Christ Jesus" = servant belonging to Christ Jesus.

73. Stephen M. Pogoloff, *Logos and Sophia: The Rhetorical Situation of 1 Corinthians* (SBLDS 134; Atlanta: Scholars Press, 1992), 99-100.

74. Pogoloff, *Logos and Sophia,* 100. Cf. Collins, 75, who contends that the fourfold repetition of "I" in v. 12 points to radical individuality as the main problem in Corinth rather than theological differences.

75. This is P. Marshall's view, *Enmity in Corinth.* In his favor is the fact that the only other divisions Paul specifically mentions, civil litigation (6:1-11) and the Lord's Supper (11:18), both suggest tensions between the rich and the poor in the church.

76. Cf. Garland, 42.

leaders whose reputation has been won through their particular style of preaching, whether experienced in person or through other media (books, radio, television, etc.). While we should be grateful for our ability to be exposed to gifted Christian teachers around the world in various ways, it also brings great potential for inappropriate allegiances to form. Apparently the Corinthian Christians picked up on this secular style of relating to their leaders with disastrous results.[77]

### 3. *Reminder of Believer's Identity in Christ, 1:13-17*

**1:13** Paul unfurls three questions further to underscore the lunacy of the Corinthians attaching themselves to human leaders when in reality they belong to Christ (1:12), have been called into fellowship with God's Son (1:9), and are in union with him (6:15).

The expected answer to the first question, *Is Christ divided?*[78] is disputed. Most commentators assume the answer is "no,"[79] as for the two questions which follow. With respect to the first question, the Greek gives no clues.[80] But the answer may well be "yes." Christ, here an allusion to the body of Christ,[81] has been "torn to pieces,"[82] by the divided loyalties in Corinth. Lightfoot defends this interpretation: "Has Christ been divided? This is only too true."[83] The question is effectively a castigation of the partisan spirit in Corinth. Their behavior has led to the unthinkable! Paul uses the same shock tactics using questions in 6:15 ("Shall I then take the members of Christ and unite them with a prostitute?") and 11:22 ("Do you despise

77. Winter, *Paul and Philo among the Sophists*, 180-202; idem *After Paul Left Corinth*, 31-43 (cf. Clarke, *Secular and Christian Leadership in Corinth*). Winter appeals to a wide range of ancient sources, including Dio Chrysostom, Favorinus, Herodes Atticus, Plutarch, and Epictetus, and argues that Philo in Alexandria along with Paul in Corinth had to contend with the rise of the sophistic movement.

78. The verb here (μεμέρισται) is a perfect indicative, emphasizing the present state in which Christ might be found. The translation *is Christ divided* is consistent with this understanding of the perfect tense.

79. This interpretation begins with the textual variant in 𝔓[46], Syriac, and Coptic MSS, which have the negative particle μή (signaling a question). Its inclusion is likely a conforming of the clause to the following two questions. The majority of early MSS omit the μή, which leaves the sentence ambiguous as to whether it is a statement or a question, and if the latter, whether the answer is yes or no. Metzger, *Textual Commentary*, 479, is right to regard the shorter reading as "virtually certain."

80. In fact, Ambrosiaster takes the sentence to be a statement ("Christ is divided") rather than a question. The original text would have lacked punctuation.

81. So Schrage, 1:152. The definite article with "Christ," a rarity in Paul's letters, links the passage with 1 Cor. 12:12, which shares the same construction: "Just as a body has many parts, . . . so it is with Christ."

82. Calvin, 28. If the text is taken as a statement rather than a question, the result would be the same.

83. Lightfoot, *Notes*, 154.

the church of God by humiliating those who have nothing?"). The verb "to divide"[84] is the same one used to describe the ill effects of disunity in Matthew 12:25: "Every kingdom *divided* against itself will be ruined" (cf. Mark 3:24).

The answer to the second and third questions is emphatically "no": *Was Paul crucified for you? Were you baptized into the name of Paul?* "Surely Paul was not crucified for you, was he?" captures the tone of Paul's disbelief and scorn. Both questions are introduced in a way that indicates that a negative answer is expected.[85] An emphasis on the centrality and sufficiency of their relation to Christ is obviously implicit in both: "Christ died for our sins" (15:3; cf. 11:24); "All of us were baptized into Christ Jesus" (Rom 6:3). Paul will go on to talk about the "message of the cross" as his central response to their factions. The subtle reference here prepares for the exposition in 1:18-25 and also for his putting leaders in their place in 3:5–4:17 (3:5a: "What, after all, is Apollos? And what is Paul?").

The reference to baptism may indicate that baptism was a factor in the Corinthians' attachment to certain leaders. As Barrett suggested, the baptized may have felt some connection to the one who baptized them. Wilckens and others point out that in pagan religion the convert remained devoted to the mystagogue who performed the rites of initiation.[86]

Paul's wording is of incidental interest to a theology of baptism. The phrase *into the name of,* which is repeated in v. 15, entails "entrance into fellowship and allegiance."[87] To be *baptized into the name of* Christ Jesus implies a unique and exclusive relationship with him. It is typical of Paul to point out the relevance of baptism to Christian ethics and living.[88] He reminds believers of their baptism to strengthen their faith, to exhort them to live lives worthy of the gospel (Rom. 6:4; Col. 2:12), and, so here, to call them to unity (cf. Eph. 4:5; Gal. 3:27). Baptism publicly declares a person to be a member of the body of Christ, a theme Paul develops in chapter 12 (see 12:12-13, 27).

**1:14-15** Some in Corinth may have thought it personally advantageous to be associated with Paul, Apollos, or Peter via the administration of baptism. This type of thinking was rife in Corinth, where personality-centered politics and status-seeking "hangers-on" were the norm in secular society.[89] If so, Paul's comments in these verses would have given such Co-

84. Gk. μερίζω.

85. Both begin with the Greek particle μή.

86. Ulrich Wilckens, *Weisheit und Torheit: Eine exegetisch-religionsgeschichtliche Untersuchung zu 1 Kor. 1 und 2* (BHT 26; Tübingen: Mohr, 1959), 16-17; cf. Fee, 61.

87. Robertson and Plummer, 13. The Greek preposition εἰς (Matt. 28:19; Acts 8:16; 19:5) is stronger than ἐπί (Acts 2:38) or ἐν (Acts 10:48). Only the first connotes movement into and not simply location.

88. M. Olusina Fape, *Paul's Concept of Baptism and Its Present Implications for Believers: Walking in Newness of Life* (Lewiston, NY: Mellen, 1999).

89. A. D. Clarke, *Secular and Christian Leadership*, 92-93.

rinthian Christians no encouragement. In what must be the greatest disappointment in Paul's otherwise impressive history of giving thanks, the apostle is grateful that he performed so few baptisms in Corinth! He wants no part in petty rivalries, even if indirectly, and is happy not to have unwittingly played into anyone's hands. In the context of his arguments in the unit, not having baptized many of the Corinthians contributes to Paul's depiction of the nature of Christian ministry as a "shared partnership."[90]

The only two Paul does admit to baptizing, at least initially (see v. 16), are *Crispus* and *Gaius*, presumably early converts in the city. *Crispus* is probably the synagogue ruler mentioned in Acts 18:8. Murphy O'Connor notes inscriptional evidence that this honorific title was bestowed on wealthy patrons who had donated something substantial to the synagogue, like part of a building, a mosaic floor, or other accoutrements.[91] *Gaius* may be the Gaius of Romans 16:23, whose "hospitality" Paul, along with "the whole church," enjoyed in Corinth. Since Gaius was a common name (cf. Acts 19:29; 20:4; 3 John 1; *Martyrdom of Polycarp* 22:2), this identification is not certain.

Since Paul had labored eighteen months in Corinth, one might have expected him to have administered more than two baptisms. Evidence for the size of the church from 1 Corinthians and Acts 18 suggests that these were not his only converts. However, speculation as to why Paul baptized, or mentions baptizing, only these two goes beyond the available evidence.[92] What can be safely concluded is that Paul did not regard baptism to be a sacrament that required the administration of "apostolic hands."[93] Ironically, the next verse adds to the impression that the question of who does the baptizing matters little; Paul finds this aspect of baptism rather forgettable.

**1:16** The parentheses around this verse indicate that it is something of a postscript. Either Paul himself has had second thoughts about the number of those he had baptized, or, as Lightfoot and Findlay suggest, his secretary tactfully jogged his memory as he dictated the letter.[94] Another exquisite possibility is that Stephanas, who may have been one of the first readers of the letter, perhaps in draft form, spotted the inaccuracy and asked Paul to correct it; 1 Corinthians 16:17 indicates that Stephanas was with Paul at the time of writing. In any case, Paul's "come to think of it," or

90. Thiselton, 140.

91. Murphy-O'Connor, *Paul: A Critical Life*, 267.

92. Murphy-O'Connor, *Paul: A Critical Life*, 268, puts forward the view that Paul concentrated on these two because, being wealthy, they had "initiative, leisure, and education [and] could function as effective assistants in the spread of the gospel." Garland, 54, thinks that Crispus and Gaius are mentioned because they were "at the root of the controversy as leaders of house churches." The simple explanation that Paul mentions them because they were the only converts he could at that moment recall baptizing must stand.

93. Hays, 24.

94. Reported by Thiselton, 141.

"on second thoughts," is a delightful demonstration of the candid and uncontrived nature of Scripture, which, though lofty and inspired, communicates its message in a fully human way. Instead of being put off by it, the "messiness" of God's word is to be celebrated.

Some commentators doubt Paul's sincerity in this lapse of memory. For example, Garland writes: "since Paul mentions the household of Stephanas again in 16:15 as the firstfruits of Achaia, he hardly could have forgotten them."[95] It has been suggested that the purpose of the ploy of deliberate underestimation is to emphasize the two particular figures in 1:14 or to stress the unimportance of the baptizer in the rite of baptism. However, the simpler explanation is preferable. Paul did not forget Stephanas altogether, but only temporarily. 1 Corinthians 16:15-17 would be a problem for believing Paul's genuineness only if he had written it before 1:14. He forgot about him, recalled him, and then wrote of him again. Further, 16:15 shows that Paul is more interested in the conversion of Stephanas than in (the details of) his baptism. The final words of this verse, *beyond that, I don't remember*[96] *if I baptized anyone else,* intimate that Paul is being open and honest throughout, and that he regrets (rather than planned) the oversight.

Paul confesses that, in addition to Crispus and Gaius, he *also baptized the household of Stephanas,* "the first converts in Achaia" (1 Cor. 16:15). The size and membership of such a *household* are impossible to determine.[97] It could have been multigenerational and may have included children, servants, slaves, clients, and even lodgers. However, this verse does not provide support for baptizing infants, for "we cannot be certain that infants were included in it."[98] In fact, even if it did include infants, it would not be decisive, for Paul does not say he baptized every member of the household; if baptizing only believers was the practice of the early church, to "baptize a household" could have meant baptizing those who (were of a sufficient age to) believe.[99]

**1:17** For Paul, not baptism but the apostolic work of the ministry of

95. Garland, 54; cf. Hays, 23.

96. *I don't remember* reflects the Greek verb οἶδα, which is a perfect tense but, consistent with the emphasis of the perfect tense, functions like a present tense stative verb like the English "to know." It does not have in mind the dynamic sense of "coming to know/understand/perceive" but, in this case, being in a state of awareness of something.

97. On "households" in the New Testament see Robert Banks, *Paul's Idea of Community* (Surry Hills, NSW: Anzea, 1979; rpt., Peabody, MA: Hendrickson, 1994), 26-36; Theissen, *Social Setting,* 83-87.

98. Thiselton, 142.

99. To say that Paul baptized "a household" may be the equivalent of saying that someone "circumcised the household of Stephanas," meaning only the males, or an army "raped the household of Stephanas," meaning only the females. The only unambiguous case of household baptism in the New Testament is that of the Philippian jailor: "he and his whole household were baptized, . . . [for] he had come to believe in God — he and his whole household" (Acts 16:33-34).

the word is all-important: God sent him *to preach the gospel.*[100] Paul restricts his usage of this term in his letters to the activity of duly authorized proclaimers (even in Philippians 1). Key to understanding his perspective is Isaiah 40–65. As John Dickson has shown, "Paul's usage of gospel-terminology [esp. *to preach the gospel*] was heavily influenced by the particular significations contained in the messenger traditions arising from Isaiah 40:9, 52:7 and 61:1, wherein 'secular' messenger language had been transposed to a higher, eschatological level, depicting the end-time herald(s) commissioned by Israel's God to announce his salvific reign."[101] Many texts in Palestinian Judaism adopt this interpretation of the word. *Targum Isaiah,* for instance, draws out from the Old Testament the notion that the herald stands for Zion's prophets: "Get you up to a high mountain, prophets who *herald* tidings to Zion" (*Tg. Isa.* 40:9); "A spirit of prophecy before the Lord God is upon me, because the Lord has exalted me *to announce good tidings* to the poor" (*Tg. Isa.* 61:1). Paul's use of Isaiah 52:7 in Romans 10:15 offers explicit support for making these connections and for taking *to preach the gospel* to refer to Paul's heralding of the gospel as an eschatological, divinely commissioned activity.[102]

The effectiveness of Paul's evangelism is not bound to a special style of delivery or in wisdom recognizable by the world's standards. The appropriate response is to the message of the cross and its content, not to the aesthetic form of the delivery of the message. Paul evangelized *not with wisdom and eloquence,* literally, "wisdom of word" or "speech." On the contrary, Paul came to Corinth with an antisophistic strategy. He eschewed the neatly packaged eloquence and wit of the orator, who sought glory from the crowds. Dio Chrysostom reported that when he visited a place like Corinth, he was "escorted with much enthusiasm and respect, the recipients of my visits being grateful for my presence and begging me to address them and advise them and flocking around my door from early dawn."[103] Such speakers put more stock in winning arguments and impressing an audience than in actually saying something of consequence. Paul distanced himself from this model of public speaking, the adoption of which in relation to Christian leaders was in part to blame for the factions in the Corinthian church.

This is the first reference to *wisdom* in the letter.[104] It introduces Paul's negative treatment of the wisdom of this world in 1:18–2:5, which he will then counterbalance with a positive treatment of the wisdom of the cross and the Spirit in 2:6–3:4. This material does not address divisions in the

100. Gk. εὐαγγελίζεσθαι.

101. J. P. Dickson, *Mission-Commitment in Ancient Judaism and in the Pauline Communities* (Tübingen: Mohr Siebeck, 2003), 176.

102. Peter Stuhlmacher, "The Pauline Gospel," 156-65.

103. Reported in Witherington, 100. See also Winter, *Philo and Paul among the Sophists,* 182-94, who emphasizes the confessions of loyalty which the sophists expected and received from their followers.

104. Gk. σοφία.

church directly, but rather "the values which lie behind them."[105] A mirror reading would imply that Paul has been criticized, or unfavorably compared with leaders like Apollos, on the score that he does not speak with the impressive wisdom of sophisticated eloquence.

*Wisdom* in these chapters has a wide semantic range. Barrett explains helpfully that Paul uses the term in two bad senses and two good senses: (1) the skilled marshaling of human arguments with a view to convincing the hearer; (2) the measure of truth, both theological and ethical, by human standards and reasoning (which judges the cross to be foolishness); (3) God's plan of redeeming the world through a crucified Messiah; and (4) the actual substance of salvation itself. The latter two positive uses find a parallel in "righteousness" as a description of the way in which God acts and the gift that he bestows upon us via those saving actions.[106] These four senses of "wisdom" develop roughly in this sequence as the unit proceeds.

Paul insists that to *preach the gospel* with *wisdom and eloquence,* in the first sense of sophisticated, impressive rhetoric,[107] would be to *empty the cross of Christ of its power. The cross of Christ* here does not just refer to the crucifixion of Christ but is Paul's shorthand for all that the death of Jesus accomplishes. The context of 1:24b, 30-31 and 2:2 shows that the reference is to more than a mere historical event. Likewise in Ephesians 2:16, "the cross" effects reconciliation, in Colossians 1:20, "the cross" makes peace, and in Colossians 2:24, "the cross" nullified the decrees against us, resulting in the forgiveness of our sins.

How does preaching the gospel in a way that draws attention to the speaker, in an eye-catching way, potentially *empty the cross* of its *power* to save?[108] The following verses, 1:18–2:5, answer this question, with 1 Corinthians 2:4-5 making the same assertion and hence rounding off the section. In between Paul will explain that *the cross of Christ* cannot be presented with human wisdom, and is not a form of human wisdom, for the message concerns a crucified Christ (1:18-25), the recipients at Corinth are not wise (1:26-31), and Paul's own preaching in Corinth was not in words of wisdom (2:1-5).

In short, the problem of preaching the gospel with *wisdom and eloquence* is that it represents a complete mismatch between message and medium.[109] The message consists of a despairing of self, a "nullifying of the things that are" (1:28b), a comprehensive exclusion of boasting in humans

105. Pogoloff, *Logos and Sophia,* 119.

106. Barrett, 67-68.

107. Aristotle defines rhetoric as "the faculty of discovering the possible means of persuasion in reference to any subject whatsoever" (*Rhetoric* 1.1.1); cited in Duane Litfin, *St Paul's Theology of Proclamation: 1 Corinthians 1–4 and Greco-Roman Rhetoric* (SNTSMS 79; Cambridge: Cambridge University Press, 1994), 191.

108. Gk. κενόω, "to cause to be without result or effect" (BDAG).

109. This raises the question of whether there are some forms of communication today that are inappropriate for presenting the content of the gospel. For example, some entertainment media may unavoidably trivialize or relativize the message they convey.

(1:29b), and a turning instead to Jesus Christ and to God (1:30-31). The medium of "wise and persuasive words" (2:4), on the other hand, exalts human brilliance and achievement. If the content of the message is not of human wisdom, neither is its presentation. Instead of responding to God himself with "deep conviction" (1 Thess. 1:5), the hearers are in danger of superficially assenting to the persuasive power of the speaker's *eloquence* (cf. 2:5).[110] It is not that Paul does not appreciate clear and engaging communication. Rather, Paul's point is that the values surrounding manipulative rhetoric contradict the message of a crucified Messiah. As Judge notes, sophisticated rhetoric "enshrined the beautiful and the strong in a position of social power," standards which, as Paul will go on to show, the gospel of the cross of Christ by definition opposes.[111]

## B. Condemnation of False Wisdom: The Wisdom of This World, 1:18–2:5

Not unlike the pagans in Corinth, many of whom acclaimed the wisdom and power of their beloved orators, the factions in the church of God in Corinth adored their favorite Christian teachers. Paul's attack on this false wisdom is marked off by the repetition of the phrase "the power of God" in 1:17b and 2:5. Marshall points out that the word "power" was commonly associated with rhetoric and eloquence, for orators could expect to win fame and glory.[1] Similarly today it is possible to describe someone as a "powerful" speaker.

Paul sets out in 1:18–4:17 to dismantle the party spirit that resulted from this adulation. To show that the gospel is the antithesis of human wisdom and power, Paul considers first those who reject the message (1:18-25), then the social standing of those who accept it (1:26-31) and, finally, the conduct of the messenger (2:1-5).

### *1. Denunciation of Human Wisdom: The Message of a Crucified Christ, 1:18-25*

> [18]*For the message of the cross is foolishness to those who are perishing, but to us who are being saved it is the power of God.* [19]*For it is written:*
>
> *"I will destroy the wisdom of the wise;*
> *the intelligence of the intelligent I will frustrate."*

110. Cf. Thiselton, 156: "A merely rhetorical or psychological exercise in communicating some belief system remains empty if it fails to engage with the cross precisely as a saving proclamation."

111. Edwin A. Judge, "The Reaction against Classical Education in the New Testament," *JCE* 77 (1983), 14.

1. P. Marshall, *Enmity in Corinth* (Tübingen: J. C. B. Mohr, 1987), 387.

*[20]Where are the wise? Where is the teacher of the law? Where is the philosopher of this age? Has not God made foolish the wisdom of the world? [21]For since in the wisdom of God the world through its wisdom did not know him, God was pleased through the foolishness of what was preached to save those who believe. [22]Jews demand signs and Greeks look for wisdom, [23]but we preach Christ crucified: a stumbling block to Jews and foolishness to Gentiles, [24]but to those whom God has called, both Jews and Greeks, Christ the power of God and the wisdom of God. [25]For the foolishness of God is wiser than human wisdom, and the weakness of God is stronger than human strength.*

As Paul pits God's wisdom against the world's wisdom in 1:18-25, his main point is not just that humans cannot grasp God's wisdom through their own wisdom, but that human wisdom is under God's eschatological judgment. Paul learns of this verdict from Scripture. Along with announcing the main theme of the paragraph by quoting Isaiah 29:14 in 1 Corinthians 1:19,[2] God's annihilation of human wisdom, Paul also echoes Isaiah 33:18 in 1:20 and Isaiah 28:16 in 1:21-24.[3] All three texts are drawn from the woe oracles of Isaiah 28–33.

By itself, 1:18-25 seems less directly relevant to Corinthian misbehavior than the rest of Paul's argument in chapters 1–4. Given its rhythmic constructions and repetition of key terms, several scholars reason that 1:18-25 existed prior to Paul's using it in 1 Corinthians. For example, Cerfaux thinks the material was originally a scriptural *testimonium,* Peterson, a homily for the Day of Atonement, and Wuellner, an exegetical sermon.[4] However, these approaches fail properly to discern the function of the paragraph in Paul's overall argument. Once grasped, hypotheses of a prehistory for the verses become needless. While it is true that Paul's derision of Jewish and Greek wisdom may well have met with some approval in the church, Lampe explains that this is quite deliberate on Paul's part. The apostle opens this major section with a kind of covert speech that forces the audience to puzzle over its relevance to the subject at hand. Rather than potentially causing an affront so early in his letter, Paul takes his time to build a case by giving some general thoughts to which the Corinthians would largely give assent. The explicit application does come eventually, but not until 3:18-23: "Do not deceive yourselves. If any of you think you are wise by the standards of this age. . . ."[5]

2. Dietrich-Alex Koch, *Die Schrift als Zeuge des Evangeliums: Untersuchungen zur Verwendung und zum Verständnis der Schrift bei Paulus* (BHT 69; Tübingen: J. C. B. Mohr [Paul Siebeck], 1986), 273-75.

3. H. H. D. Williams, *The Wisdom of the Wise: The Presence and Function of Scripture within 1 Corinthians 1:18–3:23* (AGJU 49; Leiden: Brill, 2001), 47-102.

4. Garland, 71.

5. Peter Lampe, "Theological Wisdom and the 'Word of the Cross': The Rhetorical Scheme in 1 Corinthians 1–4," *Int* 44 (1990), 117-31. Lampe compares Paul's strategy with

The implications of what Paul says in 1:18-25 are nonetheless there for the more discerning, or we might say suspicious, Corinthians. Paul's hidden agenda is that praising the apostles and other Christian teachers is out of the question. If the wisdom of the apostles is a human quality, it is bound to perish. If it is from God, then only God deserves the credit. In place of impressive displays of wisdom, Paul points to the decidedly dishonorable event of crucifixion: "we preach Christ crucified" (1:23). In terms of tracing the argument, v. 25 ties the paragraph together: "power" recalls v. 18; "wisdom" and "foolishness" look back to vv. 20-21, for which vv. 22-25 are the explanation.

*a. The Cross Divides the Human Race Absolutely, 1:18-21*

**1:18** Having rehearsed the situation that gave rise to the letter in 1:10-17, Paul sets about the strenuous task of dismantling the high towers of Corinthian pretension and in its place constructing a gospel worldview founded on the Scriptures. His first move is to give the reason[6] he refuses to preach in "wisdom and eloquence" (v. 17): because the cross signals the end of human wisdom. Paul sets up a contrast between "wisdom of word" (1:17) and "the word of the cross." TNIV translates the latter as *the message of the cross.* The phrase in question suggests both the content of the communication and the act of proclamation, just as "word" in English can mean both what is said and the act of speaking; "proclamation of the cross" captures the two dimensions.

How does Paul's preaching differ from the public speaking of the sophists? Is it just that he shuns the use of clever rhetoric as an end in itself? Litfin argues that while most orators focused on persuading their audiences of their point of view, Paul focused on the issue of comprehension, leaving persuasion to the Spirit.[7] But Paul's stress seems to fall on the unconventional and value-inverting nature of the gospel message. It is not that he does not try to persuade, but he trusts in God's power working through him and his message rather than trusting in his own powers of persuasion, knowing that *the message of the cross,* despite seeming foolish, has divine power that other messages lack.

Paul asserts that *the message of the cross* divides the race: it constitutes *foolishness* to some, but *power* to others.[8] The ancient world was familiar with a number of radical polarities: people were either Roman or barbar-

---

the rhetorical mode of speech known as the *schema.* It also has biblical precedent, for instance, in the oracles against the nations in Amos 1–2 which precede and gain a hearing for the condemnation of God's people (cf. Romans 1–3 and the way Paul condemns pagans before moving on to the Jews).

6. Note explanatory γάρ, "for."

7. Litfin, *St Paul's Theology of Proclamation,* 261. Similarly, Winter, *Philo and Paul among the Sophists,* 186-94.

8. Though untranslated, this is signaled in the Greek by the μὲν . . . δέ construction.

ian, Jew or Gentile, slave or free, male or female. Society was anything but equal and classless. However, *the cross* renders all of these divisions redundant and obsolete. The only separation that counts is between those who are *perishing* and those who are *being saved. Perishing,* a powerful word meaning "to be ruined or destroyed,"[9] is a temporal reference ("those in the process of perishing") rather than being determinative ("those who will perish ultimately").[10] The present tense represents the activity as in process.[11] In other words, *perishing* refers to the present road those who reject *the message* are on and not necessarily to their final destiny. As Paul explains to the Corinthians in 2 Corinthians 4:6-7, only God's intervention can change the state of *those who are perishing:* "this all-surpassing power is from God and not from us."

On the other hand, *us who are being saved,* like Paul's thanksgiving in 1:4-9, is a positive take on the Corinthians. In spite of their numerous faults, Paul can affirm that God is at work in delivering them. In New Testament theology generally the three tenses of salvation are each essential and true. Christ and the cross have saved us, are saving us, and will save us. Here Paul chooses the present tense, *being saved* as the best way of expressing the antithesis with *perishing.*[12] The tragedy of the two groups is that while one recognizes its true standing, the other is unaware. What distinguishes them is their response to *the message of the cross.*

The first group is defined by its negative assessment of *the message of the cross* as *foolishness.*[13] The first of five significant uses (1:21, 23; 2:14; 3:19), this term sums up the evaluation the world gives *the message of the cross.* Acts 17:16-34 illustrates this response, with some "sneering" (but others "became followers of Paul and believed"). Here, as in 1:21, not only the content of the message of the cross but also the form of delivery evokes a negative response. Both fail to make a positive impression.

The cross is nonsense to some because it represents such a repugnant worldview. It is an assault on the values of power, glory, honor, and success, so dear to Corinthian and many other societies. Paul's argument suggests that it is possible, although in reality highly inconsistent (and theologically and morally offensive), to embrace the message of the cross as the basis of one's relationship with God in Christ while continuing to live in a way that rejects its lifestyle implications as foolishness, preferring to live according to the standards of human wisdom (as the Corinthians were guilty of doing). Throughout chapters 1–4 the cross is presented as both the

9. Gk. ἀπόλλυμι.

10. See the use of the term in 2 Cor. 2:15-16; 4:3; 2 Thess. 2:10.

11. Buist M. Fanning, *Verbal Aspect in New Testament Greek* (Oxford: Clarendon, 1990), 103.

12. Garland's assertion, 64, that Paul "feels the need to remind the Corinthians that those who are being saved are still on the way and cannot afford to be self-congratulatory" reads too much into the tense.

13. Gk. μωρία.

way of salvation and a way of life. As unpalatable as it sounds, in Romans 8:17 and Philippians 3:10 Paul makes it clear that followers of Jesus must share his sufferings. The climax to the unit in 4:9-13 applies this paradigm of self-giving for the sake of others to the very apostles the Corinthians adulate. It is Paul's contention throughout the section that those whose perspective is centered on the cross find the ultimate solution to factionalism.

If the first group regards the cross as foolishness, the second knows it to be *the power of God.* The cross was a shocking image in the ancient world — of evil, shame, rejection, and punishment.[14] Carson thinks that an equivalent image today might be a Hiroshima cloud or an Auschwitz gas chamber.[15] Thus for a cross to be a positive or significant thing is deeply ironic, even paradoxical. For Paul to equate it with *the power of God* would have seemed strange indeed. The power of God is the effective action of God, the exercise of his authority, with regard to something or someone for a specific purpose. To be "powerful" in this sense is to have special competence in performing some function, to carry it off successfully. Hence Apollos is "*powerful* in the Scriptures" (Acts 18:24), meaning that he is competent in his use of them. As Thiselton notes, the phrase here indicates that "[t]he cross constitutes the point at which, and/or the means through which, God's presence and promise become operative as that which actualizes and transforms."[16] Significantly, in the Old Testament God's word is closely tied to his power (e.g., Jer. 29:23; cf. Wis. 18:14-16).[17] His powerful acts of creation and redemption regularly involve his word. In v. 18 the word of the cross is the *power of God* in the sense that God's intention to defeat evil, to make himself known, and to save those who believe will certainly be brought to completion. In other words, he is able to deliver on his promise that is the gospel.

**1:19** In announcing God's sentence of judgment on human wisdom, Paul cites Isaiah 29:14 to show that there is implacable opposition between human wisdom and the "message of the cross."[18] The quotation in question helps establish that this observation is linked to the Old Testament narrative of judgment and grace and shows that the paradox of the

14. Martin Hengel, *Crucifixion in the Ancient World and the Folly of the Message of the Cross* (Philadelphia: Fortress, 1977).

15. Carson, *The Cross and Christian Ministry,* 12.

16. Thiselton, 156.

17. Garland, 62.

18. The text is quoted verbatim except that the final word has been changed from κρύψω, "hide," in the LXX to ἀθετήσω, "frustrate," in 1 Cor. 1:19. As Christopher D. Stanley, *Paul and the Language of Scripture: Citation Technique in the Pauline Epistles and Contemporary Literature* (SNTSMS 74; Cambridge: Cambridge University Press, 1992), 186, notes, the latter term serves Paul's purposes better: "Paul's point in 1 Cor 1.18-29 is not that God has simply 'hidden' understanding from the 'wise,' but rather that he has done a work in the death of Jesus that defies all purely rational understanding. By substituting the stronger ἀθετήσω, Paul creates a chiastic parallel with the preceding ἀπολῶ [destroy] that serves to drive home his point to his readers."

cross, foolishness to some but in reality power for salvation, is in accord with Scripture.[19]

Several features of Isaiah 29:14 and its surrounding verses suggest its attractiveness to Paul and its aptness in relation to his argument. Part of a woe oracle condemning various human practices (cf. 29:1, 3), the previous verse associates wisdom with "lip service," "people drawing near [to God, only] with their mouths." The first part of v. 14 indicates that the judgment of the "wisdom of the wise" will occur when God will do "shocking and amazing" things. The threefold appearance of the Hebrew root for "wonder" in this verse may imply messianic involvement. The first name of the messianic figure in Isaiah 9:6 is "wonderful" (cf. 25:1), and in 28:29 the Lord who announces the plan of salvation is said to be "wonderful in counsel." Furthermore, that the Messiah should be associated with the judgment of human wisdom is suggested by Cyrus, who is a type of the Messiah and is involved in the reversal of wisdom in 44:25.

A wide range of Jewish texts, all of which have affinities with Isaiah 29:14, treat the theme of the absence and judgment of human wisdom (Bar. 3:9-14; 2 *Baruch* 48:31-37; 70:3-6; 4 *Ezra* 5:9-13; 13:29-32; *1 Enoch* 39:8; 42; 1Q27 1 i 1-9; 1QH iii 12-17; 3 Macc. 6:19-29; *Targum Isaiah* 29:13-14).[20] In these texts the absence of wisdom occurs in situations where strife and division are plaguing a community. Under such circumstances, God's people are enjoined to appreciate the future intervention of God in order to help sort out their present difficulties. In particular, a dearth of wisdom is seen as part of a great judgment or as a sign pointing to the final, universal judgment. The absence of wisdom and its ultimate judgment are associated with the work of the coming Messiah.

Isaiah 29:14 seems to have exerted an influence on Paul's language and thought at various points in the surrounding verses. "Those who are being destroyed" in v. 18 anticipates the "destruction" in v. 19.[21] A purely verbal show of piety, the very thing Paul faults the Corinthians for in chapters 1–4, recalls the superficial "lip service" of Isaiah 29:13. Most significantly, the "wonderful" and yet "shocking" things (29:13-14) the prophet foretells, with messianic overtones, are what Paul declares have now transpired through Christ crucified.

Paul uses Isaiah 29:14 to announce that God's eschatological judgment and salvation are taking place among the Corinthians. As Hays puts it, "God has already put the wise to shame through the foolishness of the cross, the apocalyptic event that has shattered the old order of human wis-

19. This is the first time in the letter that Paul uses the introductory formula *it is written* to introduce a quotation from Scripture. The formula uses a perfect indicative verb (γέγραπται). This verb is always translated to reflect the idea of a present stative concept ("it is written") in keeping with the focus of the perfect tense. The use of the formula also tends to highlight the importance and authority of the quoted text.

20. H. H. D. Williams, *The Wisdom of the Wise,* 61-73.

21. Gk. ἀπολῶ.

dom."[22] The Corinthians who still value *"the wisdom of the wise"* have failed to notice God's apocalyptic judgment on such wisdom through the crucified Messiah, or the inherent contradiction between that version of wisdom and the one to which they owe their redemption in Christ. The fact that in 1:18 people are still in the process of being saved (or destroyed) indicates that the unfolding of the drama of salvation is not yet complete. Thus Isaiah's words are for Paul not just a judgment on ancient Judean leaders, but also "an indictment of the rhetorical affectations of the Corinthians."[23]

**1:20** The four questions of this verse confirm the teaching of the Old Testament in v. 19. Not surprisingly, then, they also betray the influence of Scripture. Robertson and Plummer label the presence of Isaiah 33:18 in v. 20 "a very free citation from the general sense."[24] Although commentators have suggested the influence of other texts, from both the Old Testament and postbiblical sources, the proposal that v. 20 echoes the Isaiah text is the most plausible. Both Isaiah 33:18 and 1 Corinthians 1:20 contain three questions beginning with the word "where,"[25] the only two places where this structure appears in the LXX and New Testament. Both texts refer to the ineffectiveness of individuals who oppose God's people. Finally, both contain rhetorical questions expecting the response, "nowhere."

Isaiah 33:18 concerns the whereabouts of the chief officer, the one who weighed the tribute and the one who counted the towers, a composite reference to the oppressors of God's people. It announces the end of their ascendancy and dominance. The surrounding context refers to an ideal king, probably the messiah, who will overthrow the oppressors (33:17, 21-22). In related early Jewish texts the oppressors disappear following a great judgment.[26] In fact, the End Time is characterized by their absence and by the presence of a messianic ruler. Intriguingly, the absence of the oppressors coincides with the failure of human plans and the disappearance of wisdom. In this light, the echo of Isaiah 33:18 in 1 Corinthians 1:20 recalls the overthrow by the Messiah of all those who oppose God and his people in the End Time, reinforcing both the passage's Christology and eschatology.

Consonant with this background, the first three questions in v. 20 are more derisive than taunting in tone. They are not invitations for "all comers" to enter the fray, but cries of the victor after the battle has been fought and won. The *wise, the teacher of the law,* and *the philosopher of this age* are nowhere to be found, for their wisdom has been destroyed and their intelligence frustrated (1:19). They have been outsmarted and upstaged. They have nothing more to offer. They have slunk away in defeat.

But precisely who is intended by each of the three categories of persons is less clear. Many commentators argue that the terms are parallel and

22. Hays, *Conversion of the Imagination*, 403-4.
23. Hays, *Conversion of the Imagination*, 404.
24. Robertson and Plummer, 19.
25. Gk. ποῦ.
26. See H. H. D. Williams, *The Wisdom of the Wise*, 73-80.

comprehensive, each referring to all people. Ellicott takes the first as a general reference to all, then the next two as specific references to Jews and Greeks. Lightfoot and Fee understand Paul to be referring to the Greek philosopher, the Jewish scribe, and a third comprehensive category. Wilckens sees Paul's targets as the Greek sage, Jewish theology, and Greek philosophy respectively.[27] An identification of the first two with Greeks and Jews is supported by the reference to Greeks who look for wisdom and Jews who seek miraculous signs in 1:22. The third may then be best understood as a general reference to both in the light of its being the longest of the three. In all sorts of literature the third part is climactic in lists comprising three elements. Alternatively, Judge sees the third as honing in on the specific Corinthian infatuation; the three groups are types of tertiary scholars: the rationalistic scholar, the Jewish legal expert, and the rhetorician.[28] Paul's language reminds us that Christian members of the cultural elite (counselors, lawyers, philosophers, and the like) must be vigilant concerning the danger of unthinkingly adopting the dominant paradigms for their work (in terms of why they do what they do, what ends it might serve, etc.). The wisdom of the cross judges the values of the world, and Christians in all walks of life must live in ways that are consistent with it.

In any case, the three groups would have been regarded as the experts in their fields of learning. The temptation to pride, to look down on others less learned, in such individuals is easy to understand. In this sense 1:19-20 gives the first hint that, in Paul's view, the Corinthians have a problem with pride, which becomes clear in chapters 3–4 and then later in the letter. Ignatius, *To the Ephesians* 18:1, follows up an allusion to 1 Corinthians 1:20 with another question: "Where is the boasting of the so-called shrewd?" As Garland points out, Paul's three questions parallel Jesus' thanksgiving to God for hiding "these things" from the wise and learned and revealing them to "babes" (Matt. 11:25).[29] Ironically, those who think they are "in the know" may miss out on the truth in matters theological and ethical, where knowing is less a matter of intellect than of a humble character and pure motives.[30]

Paul's fourth question is framed so as to expect to be answered in the affirmative:[31] God has indeed *made foolish the wisdom of the world*.[32] The

27. Wilckens, *Weisheit und Torheit*, 28.

28. Judge, "Reaction against Classical Education," 11.

29. Garland, 65.

30. Many scholars have tried to identify the specific form of wisdom that Paul is critiquing. Proposals include the Jewish wisdom tradition, Hellenistic Jewish wisdom traditions reflected in Philo, and early forms of Gnosticism. Such specific identifications are, however, unwarranted. Paul's critical assessment of wisdom is not limited to one manifestation (cf. Collins, 97).

31. It is introduced by Gk. οὐχί.

32. A minor textual problem attaches to the final phrase. The Textus Receptus, upon the which the KJV is based, and some later witnesses have "wisdom of *this* world." A few early versions also have the longer reading. Scribes may have been influenced by "philoso-

*world* here refers to the world order opposed to God, which is driven by lust, greed, and pride (1 John 2:16). The third question's philosopher *of this age* makes the same qualification. *This age* stands in contrast to the next age ("the age to come" in Jewish parlance), the age of God's final redemption, to which believers belong and are headed. This adds another apocalyptic note that underscores the ephemeral quality of human wisdom, for "the world in its present form is passing away" (1 Cor. 7:31). Both phrases confirm that Paul is not attacking reason in and of itself, but rather reason "flawed by 'epistemic vices' of instrumental manipulation and self-deception,"[33] reason blinded by pride. God has made a fool of such wisdom, exposing it as self-serving and illusory.

**1:21** Opening with the conjunctions *for since,* this verse explains the way in which God has made a fool of "the wisdom of the world" (v. 20b).[34] Paul attributes the failure of *the world,* here, as in the previous verse, meaning "humanity in its fallen, depraved state," a world order opposed to God, to come to *know*[35] God through its wisdom to God's own wisdom. Seemingly, then, it is God's own design to prevent the wise from knowing him! At first blush this may appear arbitrary and even cavalier on God's part. Why would God intentionally frustrate those intent on knowing him? It is a step further than saying what Paul said in Lystra in Acts 14:16: "In the past, he [God] let all nations go their own way." Here he deliberately blocks their way to him.

Yet there is wisdom in not allowing human wisdom to be the key to knowing God. "In the cross, God puts both Jew and Greek, wise and foolish, trained and untrained, on the same level, canceling out all human enlightenment on the subject of salvation or redemption."[36] Those who know God are not to be congratulated for their astute insight and perceptive understanding. In finding God they were no wiser than anyone else. In looking for God's action in the world the wise have no advantage since what God does to make himself known, especially at the cross, is so unexpected and enigmatic. It is strange, to say the least, that the all-powerful creator would choose a shameful execution to redeem the world. 1 Corinthians 1:21a is thus equivalent to Paul's insistence in Romans that God shows no

---

pher of *this* age" earlier in the verse. Alternatively, it may be a deliberate change to underscore that Paul does not oppose all rationality, but only that characteristic of the present world order. This may be the reason why REB has "wisdom of this world," which may not be a preference for the longer textual reading.

33. Thiselton, 166.

34. Gk. ἐπειδὴ γάρ.

35. *Did not know him* reflects an aorist indicative verb (Gk. ἔγνω). The verb γινώσκω can have a dynamic sense (as in "arrive at a knowledge of" or "acquire information" [BDAG]) or a stative sense (as in "be aware of"). The perfective verbal aspect of the aorist tense-form often combines with stative verbs to express the entrance into a state. An inceptive idea is likely here even if the dynamic lexical idea is in mind. Either way the idea would be that "the world did not come to know God through wisdom." Fee also labels it inceptive.

36. Garland, 67.

partiality.[37] Romans 11:32 puts the matter even more firmly than 1 Corinthians 1:21a: "For God has bound everyone over to disobedience so that he may have mercy on them all." As Paul will explain in v. 21b, when it comes to knowing God, the nub of the issue is trust, not wisdom.

Having removed any advantage the wise may have thought they had in knowing God, *God was pleased* to provide a different way of knowing him. The verb "to be well pleased"[38] is used in other parts of the New Testament to refer to stupendous things that God does against all expectation. Significantly, they are all in connection with his Son. God was pleased with his Son at his baptism (Mark 1:11; Matt. 17:5; 2 Pet. 1:17). He was pleased to give the kingdom of his Son to "the little flock" (Luke 12:32). He was pleased to reveal his Son in Paul so that the apostle might preach to the Gentiles (Gal. 1:15-16). He was pleased to have all his fullness dwell in the Son (Col. 1:19). He was pleased to predestine the elect for adoption to sonship through Jesus Christ (Eph. 1:5). He was pleased to make known the mystery of his will which he purposed in Christ (Eph. 1:9). And here in 1 Corinthians 1:21, *God was pleased through the foolishness of what was preached to save those who believe* in his Son.[39] Far from his being reluctant or indifferent, it gives God the greatest pleasure to redeem us.

That knowing God *through* preaching is the solution to the problem of not knowing God *through* the wisdom of the world is signaled by the use of the same preposition in both clauses.[40] One means of enjoying that relationship replaces another means, which had failed. Once again Paul's choice of words to describe the gospel task is significant. In 1:17 his use of "preach the gospel" recalled Isaianic herald traditions. Here "preaching" is a related term that likewise marks his public speaking off from the Corinthian orators who used the skills of rhetoric. Litfin explains that the main terms Paul uses for Christian communication are decidedly nonrhetorical:[41] "no self-respecting orator could have used such verbs to describe his own *modus operandi.*" For the role of the herald or preacher was not "to discover the persuasive probabilities inherent in his subject, . . . much less to package the whole so that the message will be irresistible. The herald's task is not to create a persuasive message at all, but to convey effectively the already articulated message of another."[42]

The Greek for *what was preached* could refer to the content of the preaching and/or to its form of delivery. If the previous context favors the

37. Cf. Merklein, 182, who states that the best commentary on 1 Cor. 1:21a is Rom. 1:18–3:20.

38. Gk. εὐδόκησεν.

39. This account of usage favors the more affective sense of "pleased" over "decided" (NRSV) or "determined" (Barrett) as a translation of εὐδόκησεν.

40. Gk. διά with the genitive.

41. This includes not only εὐαγγελίζω ("preach the gospel") and κηρύσσω ("preach"), but also καταγγέλλω ("announce") and μαρτυρέω ("testify").

42. Litfin, *Paul's Theology of Proclamation,* 195.

latter sense, the following context supports the former. Both are probably intended, with Paul moving on from his criticism of preaching with "wisdom and eloquence" (1:17) to the message of "Christ crucified" (1:22), itself "a message of wisdom" (2:6). Form and content belong together. In this case both are unimpressive nonsense to the world, except, that is, to *those who believe,* Paul's favorite term for a positive response to the gospel (cf. 2:5; 3:5; 15:1-2). "Belief" here means "to entrust oneself . . . in complete confidence" with the "implication of total commitment to the one who is trusted."[43]

A number of Old Testament texts claiming that God possesses all wisdom and power are relevant to vv. 21-24 on a thematic level (e.g., Job 12:13; Jer. 10:12; Dan. 2:23; cf. 1 Macc. 2:59; Bar. 3:9–4:4).[44] A more specific connection to another Isaiah text is of particular interest, a prominent text in early Jewish and Christian circles, namely, Isaiah 28:16, which concerns "the cornerstone, a sure foundation." Paul uses the text in Romans 9:33–10:14 (cf. 1 Pet. 2:6), where the themes of dualistic predestination and stern warning are developed: perdition or salvation is the consequence of a person's response to the stone (cf. 1 Cor. 1:23-24). Along with developing these same themes, 1 Corinthians 1:21-24 has some terms that overlap with the Isaiah text: it shares the participial form of the verb "to believe" in 1:21 (in both texts God saves "those who believe"). The use of the word "stumbling block"[45] in 1:23 may also have been picked up from the broader associated "stone" tradition (which emerges in 1 Cor. 3:10-15); the word appears in Romans 9:33 in connection with Isaiah 28:16 and 8:14.

### *b. The Cross Outsmarts Human Wisdom and Overpowers Human Strength (1:22-25)*

**1:22** This verse, which opens with the same conjunction as v. 21, "since," has a logical connection to what follows in v. 23. Several English versions, including TNIV, leave the conjunction untranslated, perhaps due to difficulty discerning its significance. However, Robertson and Plummer offer an adequate explanation as to how the two verses are connected with the following paraphrase: "'Since — while Jews and Gentiles alike demand something which suits their unsympathetic limitations — we, on the other hand, preach,' etc."[46] As in Galatians 3:28, the two groups, *Jews* and *Greeks,*

43. BDAG, "πιστεύω," 2.

44. Hans Hübner, *Die Theologie des Paulus und ihre neutestamentliche Wirkungsgeschichte* (Biblische Theologie des Neuen Testaments 2; Göttingen: Vandenhoeck & Ruprecht, 1993), 114-16.

45. Gk. σκάνδαλον.

46. The structure of the Greek of v. 22 is ἐπειδὴ καὶ . . . καί. "The repeated καί brackets the typical Greek with the typical Jew, as leading examples, in the world in which St Paul's readers lived, of the ones who are perishing, the world and its wisdom" (Robertson and Plummer, 21-22).

are part of an inclusive way of looking at the world. Both *Greeks* and "Gentiles," in v. 23, are synonyms for non-Jews. Perhaps Paul uses *Greeks* here instead of "Gentiles" as the best example of a specific culture that searches for wisdom. Alternatively, or in addition, Paul may have used *Greeks* here because it was a Romanized Greek culture that exercised such a formative influence on the prevailing culture in Corinth.

Yet Paul is not commending this search. Verse 23 sets up a contrast to v. 22; Paul says "*but* we preach," not "*so* we preach." *Wisdom* at this point in the letter is a pejorative term for human rational inquiry enlisted in the pursuit of success and superiority. The goal for those in search of it is not so much genuine enlightenment as influence, honor, and power. The proclamation of the cross bursts these human pretensions. As in v. 21, it fails to impress the wise in both its substance and presentation. Likewise, when *Jews demand*[47] *signs*, or "miracles for proof" (TEV), that God is at work, this is not a legitimate, open-minded plea, but an obstinate insistence on a powerful confirmation of God's deliverance that renders faith unnecessary. Ironically, the cross is in fact a genuine sign and true wisdom from God (v. 24b).

**1:23** To those hoping for something impressive and irrefutable, Paul preaches the altogether odd and unexpected: *Christ crucified*.[48] This is akin to proclaiming as good news that the victor has been vanquished, the market has collapsed, or the holiday has been cancelled. It is only our familiarity that dulls the strangeness of Paul's message for us. In the most general sense, the "Christ" is the king destined to rule.[49] To announce his ignominious demise is to brand him an utter failure and would hardly seem to constitute a "gospel." Robertson and Plummer explain the understandable disappointment for both Jews and Greeks at such preaching: "The Jews demanded a victorious Christ, heralded by signs, who would restore the glories of the kingdom of David and Solomon. . . . Christ was not preached

47. Throughout this section, a string of present indicatives is employed to describe the parties involved. These present indicatives should not slavishly be interpreted as expressing ongoing actions in process. Rather, the imperfective aspect of these verbs is being used to portray gnomic (or possibly customary) descriptions, in which a general state of affairs (or a general tendency of a given group) is affirmed: "Jews ask for a sign," "Greeks seek wisdom" (v. 22); "we preach Christ crucified" (v. 23); "God's foolishness is wiser than human wisdom" (v. 25).

48. The perfect participle ἐσταυρωμένον is employed to describe Christ as crucified, which is the content of Paul's message. The perfect is used to describe Christ in his present (even resurrected) state as one who has undergone crucifixion (cf. John 20:25-27). Paul stresses the crucified nature of his subject. It is Christ *crucified* that Paul preaches. "Christ" is anarthrous in the Greek and can be translated "a Christ crucified" (RV margin) or, better, "a crucified Christ" (NJB). In 1 Cor. 15:11-12 Paul declares Christ raised from the dead to be the object of his proclamation. Obviously "Christ" is what Paul preaches, but here in ch. 1 he emphasizes that central element of his message most opposed to "the wisdom of the world."

49. For example, in Psalm 2, "the LORD's anointed" asserts his authority over the (other) "kings of the earth."

as a conqueror to please the one, nor as a philosopher to please the other. . . . Both had to learn the divine character of humility."[50] As Philippians 2:1-11 indicates, this aspect of the work of Christ has ethical implications. If Christ "humbled himself . . . even to death on a cross," then being "like-minded" and "doing nothing out of selfish ambition or vain conceit" follow as imperatives for his people. These qualities are the very things the Corinthians are lacking.

As already stated in vv. 18 and 21, *Gentiles*, non-Jews, in general find Paul's message of the crucified Christ to be *foolishness*. Jews typically also found Paul's message hard to swallow. In the second century, in Justin Martyr's *Dialogue with Trypho* 31–32, Justin attempts to convince Rabbi Trypho that Jesus is the Messiah with reference to Daniel 7, and Trypho responds: "Sir, these and such-like passages of scripture compel us to await One who is great and glorious, and takes the everlasting Kingdom from the Ancient of Days as Son of Man. But this your so-called Christ is without honor and glory, so that he has even fallen into the uttermost curse that is in the Law of God, for he was crucified" (cf. Deut 21:23).[51] To Jews, Paul's message was *a stumbling block*,[52] something which causes them to trip and fall. Although the word appears only here in 1 Corinthians, Paul uses it in a similar context in Romans 9:33 and 11:11-12. In both cases an Old Testament citation identifies Christ as *a stumbling block* for Israel (Isa. 8:14 and Ps. 69:23-24 respectively). Isaiah 8:14 in particular gives the flavor of the term with various synonyms: "He will become a stone of offense and *a stumbling block* to both houses of Israel, a trap and a snare to the inhabitants of Jerusalem." Together these texts suggest that *a stumbling block* is more serious than simply an insulting affront;[53] it also leads to disastrous consequences.[54]

**1:24** If both Jews and non-Jews reject the message, the group which responds positively is equally inclusive and universal. *Those whom God has called*, another way of referring to "those who believe" (v. 21), are made up of *both Jews and Greeks*. The gospel is for everyone without distinction (cf. Rom. 1:16). Verse 24 recalls the same contrast that Paul drew back in v. 18, between "those who are perishing" and "those who are being saved." This is the fourth reference to "calling" in the letter: Paul is called to be an apostle (1:1), and the Corinthian believers are called to be saints (1:2) and into fellowship with Jesus Christ (1:9). In 1:26-27 being called by God is synonymous with election, being chosen by him for salvation. Paul's distinct emphasis on "calling" in this opening chapter of the letter is another way in which he seeks to deflate Corinthian pride. "Calling" views the entry point of salvation from the divine perspective and consequently underscores its

50. Robertson and Plummer, 22.

51. Cited by Garland, 70.

52. Gk. σκάνδαλον.

53. Cf. "scandal" (Barrett and Fee), "affront" (Thiselton), and "what is offensive" (TEV) as translations of σκάνδαλον.

54. See the comments on the related verb form (σκανδαλίζω) in 8:13.

free and gracious character, further undermining any sense of pride or achievement in those who are saved; *those whom God has called,* though better off, have no grounds for considering themselves better than anyone else.

If some give "Christ crucified" a negative evaluation, the *called* are distinguished by coming to an entirely different conclusion: at the cross they experience *Christ* as *the power of God* (recalling v. 18b) *and the wisdom of God.* Their response echoes Daniel's prayer when God revealed to him the meaning of Nebuchadnezzar's dream: "Blessed be the name of God forever and ever, to whom belong wisdom and power . . . he gives wisdom to the wise and knowledge to those who have understanding; he reveals deep and hidden things; . . . you have given me wisdom and power" (Dan. 2:20-22).

Believers may recognize Christ as *the power of God* in connection with his being raised from the dead "in power" (Rom. 1:4; cf. Phil. 3:10).[55] However, it is more likely that it is Christ as "the power of God that brings salvation" (Rom. 1:16) that Paul has in mind. The explicit identification of Christ as *the wisdom of God* is unique in Paul's letters, though the thought is hardly surprising. It represents the first positive use of "wisdom" in the letter, which, along with the echo of or faint allusion to Daniel's prayer,[56] anticipates Paul's positive treatment of the wisdom of the cross and the Spirit in 2:6–3:4.

**1:25** This verse ties the paragraph together, restating its main assertions in memorable fashion. For this very reason its precise connection to what precedes is not easy to pin down. The explanatory conjunction *for*[57] links it to one of three prior verses: Either (1) v. 21 — God was pleased through the foolishness of preaching to save because the foolishness of God is wiser . . . ; or (2) v. 23 — we preach Christ crucified because the foolishness of God is wiser . . . ; or (3) v. 24b — Christ is the power of God and the wisdom of God because the foolishness of God is wiser. . . .[58] The distance separating vv. 21 and 25 renders the first view unlikely. The third view has a possible conceptual chiasm in vv. 24-25 in its favor: power, wisdom, wiser, weakness. However, the second view is probably best in that it takes the connection as reinforcing what v. 25 is affirming, namely, that God at his worst is better than humans at their best. Paul closes the paragraph by insisting that the gospel he heralds confounds the wise and overcomes the strong. The power and wisdom of the Corinthian orators pale by comparison. Remembering that human pride is at the root of the divisions in Corinth, we note once again that these assertions are designed to inject a note

55. Cf. Collins, 108.

56. As in Dan. 2:20, 23, recognition of God's wisdom and power should lead his people to praise and honor him. Those who recognize in Christ God's true wisdom and power naturally turn from false gods to honor and worship him alone.

57. Gk. ὅτι.

58. A matter of nuance largely ignored in the commentaries, the three views are supported by Findlay, Barrett, and Ellicott respectively.

of humility, as kindred thoughts later in the letter make clear. *Human wisdom* carries the danger of pride, for, as Paul states bluntly in 8:3, "knowledge puffs up." Likewise, *human strength* is no excuse for, arrogance, for as Paul asks rhetorically in 10:22b, "are we stronger than he?"

### 2. *Reminder of God's Unexpected Choice of the Lowly in Corinth: Worldly Wisdom in the Light of Divine Election, 1:26-31*

> 26*Brothers and sisters, think of what you were when you were called. Not*
> *many of you were wise by human standards; not many were influential; not*
> *many were of noble birth.* 27*But God chose the foolish things of the world to*
> *shame the wise; God chose the weak things of the world to shame the strong.*
> 28*God chose the lowly things of this world and the despised things — and the*
> *things that are not — to nullify the things that are,* 29*so that no one may*
> *boast before him.* 30*It is because of him that you are in Christ Jesus, who has*
> *become for us wisdom from God — that is, our righteousness, holiness and*
> *redemption.* 31*Therefore, as it is written: "Let those who boast boast in the*
> *Lord."*

If 1:18-25 considers those who reject the message of the cross, 1:26-31 shifts the focus to those who accept. In his critique of human wisdom Paul uses the Corinthians themselves as an illustration of the pattern of eschatological reversal that characterizes the work of Christ. The low social status of most of the Corinthians itself points to the cross, which was, humanly speaking, anything but impressive, and radically overturned expectations.

Paul uses Jeremiah 9:24 and 1 Samuel 2:10 LXX to support his contention that through the cross God has turned the world's values upside down. As Wagner concludes, "[f]ar from being an irrelevant reminder, Paul's reference to the Scriptural command, 'Let the one who boasts, boast in the Lord,' undergirds and advances his censure of the Corinthians' behavior."[59] The paradoxical nature of salvation in Christ turns out, no less than his death and resurrection, to be "according to the Scriptures." Paul's disparagement of human wisdom, power, and privilege are rooted in the Old Testament.

In terms of the overall argument, Paul's point in 1:26-31 is that since the recipients of the gospel in Corinth are not wise, its proclamation cannot be a form of human wisdom. Writing to a city and church obsessed with reputation and honor,[60] Paul risked seriously offending the Corinthians in this insulting reminder of the majority of the Corinthian Christians' humble roots and social status: he tells the Corinthians, "most of you are nobod-

59. J. Ross Wagner, "'Not beyond the Things Which Are Written': A Call to Boast Only in the Lord (1 Cor. 4:6)," *NTS* 44 (1998), 287.

60. Ramsay MacMullen, *Roman Social Relations, 50 B.C. TO A.D. 284* (New Haven: Yale University Press, 1974), 125, points to love of status and honor as a defining feature of Greco-Roman society.

ies."[61] However, several features of the text lessen the potential offense this may have caused. Paul initially addresses them as *brothers and sisters*, underlining his friendly intentions, and includes himself in the status God confers on believers with the words, *Christ has become for us* [not just for you], *wisdom from God.* Whereas normally the Corinthians may have expected an assault on their honor to be followed by self-promotion, Paul's rejoinder is the humble confession of his own weakness in their presence (2:1-5), and in 15:8-9 he describes himself unflatteringly as "one abnormally born," "the least of the apostles," labels not dissimilar to "weak" and "lowly" which he attaches to most of the Corinthians in 1:27-28.

**1:26** Paul cites his second of three arguments to prove that the proclamation of the gospel is not a form of human wisdom: not only is the message singularly unimpressive in the world's estimation (1:18-25), so are the majority of the members of the church of God in Corinth (1:26-31)![62] The apostle urges the Corinthians to reflect for a moment[63] on their own worth *by human standards.*[64] Only a few of them amount to anything "according to the flesh," to translate the Greek literally. In this sense 1:26-31 explains how the experience of their converting call to salvation confirms the way God acts in the proclamation of the cross described in 1:18-25; in both cases God repudiates what the world counts as clever or potent.[65]

The word "to call" was commonly used to refer to an invitation to a meal or party, as in 1 Corinthians 10:27. The "call" Paul has in mind here is the summons to salvation, which is also a vocational call. The Septuagint uses the concept of calling to refer to the granting of roles or tasks by God: for example, to Abraham to be the father of a nation, to Cyrus of Persia to

61. Even if the labels in v. 26 are neutral by themselves, seeing they fit the majority of those in Corinth, their unflattering nature is confirmed by those ("foolish" and "weak") in the following two verses.

62. The beginnings of the second and third arguments are signaled by the words "brothers and sisters" (1:26; 2:1).

63. Βλέπω, which normally means "to see," followed by an accusative can mean "think about" or "consider" (cf. 1 Cor. 10:18; 2 Cor. 10:7; Phil. 3:2; Col. 4:17). BDAG suggests the definition "to process information by giving thought" with "direct one's attention to someth[ing], consider, note" as possible glosses (emphases removed).

64. Gk. κατὰ σάρκα, literally, "according to the flesh."

65. An explanatory γάρ, "for," at the beginning of v. 26, though not translated by the TNIV and several other versions, makes this clear. It either explains v. 25 (their calling demonstrates God's wisdom — the composition of the church reflects God's ways [Robertson and Plummer]), or confirms the statement of v. 27 (God elected the foolish things of the world, for consider your calling [Ellicott]), or explains vv. 18-25 (the experience of their call confirms the way God acts as described above [Findlay, Godet]). The third view is preferred in the light of the mention of peoples in vv. 26-27, the wise and the strong, which looks back to ideas expressed in vv. 20-21 concerning the absence of the wise before God. Thus, the social makeup of the Corinthian community reflects that God has not chosen the way of the wise of the world. Thiselton's position, 179, that the γάρ "is not primarily explanatory here but serves as a signal to introduce a fresh stage of argument" should be adopted only if no logical connection to what precedes can be discerned, which is not the case.

be an agent of providence, and to Israel to be a light to the Gentiles. Accordingly, Paul conceives of his call to apostleship as granting him a specific task (cf. 1 Cor. 1:1). Throughout the letter, the Corinthians' calling, in keeping with their new identity as God's holy people, is that of all holy/sanctified people (or things), namely, to preserve and project God's holiness and glory. The theme of holiness and righteousness is not far from Paul's mind, appearing in v. 30 and v. 31. It suggests that God's people are to "boast in" (i.e., glorify) God (cf. the Introduction, 23-24, 33-35). The use of "call" in Isaiah to effect the restoration of God's people is roughly analogous.

The concept of calling obviously implies the need to respond in obedience. However, Paul does not use the language of response in contexts where he refers to God's converting call, leaving the impression that this calling of individuals to salvation is a decisive act of God.[66] Indeed, the action of calling is synonymous in vv. 27-28 with God choosing the weak, the despised, and the lowly. In other words, in Paul's parlance, calling is a synonym for divine election, even if the latter is logically prior. Significantly, in the present context, the calling of the Corinthians takes precedence over their ethnicity (1:24) and social status (1:26-28) in defining their identity. As Chester's study of the term concludes, "[i]rrespective of who or what they have been, those called to be saints are separated from their own pasts, but included in a new future; separated from those who do not share their calling, but joined to those who do."[67] In Paul's hands, the concept of calling becomes a call to humility and unity.

In the world's eyes, the church of God in Corinth was made up primarily of the plebeians as opposed to the elite and those of influence in society, a fact that confirms that the proclamation of the gospel is not a form of human wisdom. If the gospel were wise, its outcome would surely produce a more impressive response in Corinthian society. For *not many* of the Corinthian Christians were *wise* (well educated), *influential* (literally, "powerful," in the sense of having political clout), or *of noble birth* (having social standing through breeding). If you were looking for cleverness, power, or pedigree in Corinth, you would not start at any of the house churches. As noted below on v. 31, Paul's choice of these three terms recalls Jeremiah 9:22-23/1 Samuel 2:10 LXX, which include the injunctions: "Do not let the wise boast in their wisdom. Do not let the mighty boast in their might. Do not let the wealthy boast in their wealth."[68] In the Corinthian context, the three terms were used in connection with the status-

66. Thus ὑμῶν is an objective genitive — "the calling given to you." The use of "call" in the Gospels, where the term is general and inclusive, forms a contrast to Pauline usage; cf. "many are called but few are chosen" (Matt. 22:14).

67. Stephen J. Chester, *Conversion at Corinth: Perspectives on Conversion in Paul's Theology and the Corinthian Church* (Edinburgh: T&T Clark, 2003), 112. Chapter 3 is a good summary of the data on "God's Converting Call."

68. The σοφοί *(wise)* and δυνατοί *(influential)* appear in the LXX of Jer. 9:22 and 1 Sam. 2:10 respectively.

seeking public speakers the church wanted their leaders to emulate. As Winter explains, the *wise* may have been the sophists, whose parents were typically *influential* and *of noble birth.*[69] Paul observes that such categories do not belong in the church and have effectively been replaced by terms like "righteousness," "holiness," and "redemption" (1:30). In Christ Jesus our identity and status are inverted and radically redefined. If only a few are impressive *by human standards,* everyone has the same enviable status before God.

This verse is a rare gem in the New Testament in that it addresses directly the question of the composition of the early church. Unfortunately, exactly what it tells us is disputed. Whereas Deissmann deduced from 1 Corinthians 1:26-31 (and Matt. 11:25-29) that the early Christians were of a uniformly lowly social status, others have argued for social diversity and the presence of some Christians of considerable standing in society (notably Judge, Theissen, Clarke, and Winter).[70] The point is that *not many* is indefinite and does not necessarily mean "not any." In fact, evidence points to the presence of some Christians in Corinth with means or influence. These include (1) officeholders — Crispus (1:14; cf. Acts 18:8) and Erastus (Rom. 16:23); (2) heads of significant households — Crispus, Stephanas (1:16; 16:15), and Chloe (1:11); (3) those capable of "service" to Paul or others which presupposed a measure of wealth — Gaius (1:14; cf. Rom. 16:23) and Titius Justus (Acts 18:17); and (4) those who traveled for business purposes or as merchants — Aquila and Priscilla (16:19; cf. Rom. 16:3; Acts 18:2, 26), Phoebe (Rom. 16:1-2), Erastus, Stephanas, and possibly Chloe's people (1:11).[71] In the light of this, Witherington's conclusion is judicious: "The social level of the Corinthian Christians apparently varied from quite poor to rather well off . . . a fair cross section of urban society."[72]

However, we cannot be certain which of these eight to ten individuals in Corinth would have been considered wise, influential, or noble; being materially well off does not guarantee social standing, which is the focus of Paul's pointed reminder of the church's modest rank in society.[73] Paul's point is not that none of them amounted to anything, but that, as v. 27 indicates, they are "weak" and "foolish" as far as the world counts power and wisdom. The Corinthian Christians are themselves proof that God's categories of wisdom and power are not the world's.

**1:27-28** On the contrary, as emphatically as he can say it, Paul insists that God has repudiated the world's wisdom in choosing people like the

69. Winter, *Philo and Paul,* 189.

70. Justin J. Meggitt, *Paul, Poverty and Survival* (Edinburgh: T&T Clark, 1998), contends that the vast majority of people in the ancient world lived at the very margins of survival, with many near destitution.

71. Theissen, *The Social Setting of Pauline Christianity,* 95; cf. Thiselton, 181-82.

72. Witherington, *Conflict and Community,* 23.

73. It may be significant that the only member of the triad from Jer. 9:23/1 Sam. 2:10 LXX that Paul does not echo is "Do not let the wealthy boast in their wealth."

Corinthians out of all the inhabitants of the world.[74] Verses 27-28 open with a strong adversative conjunction, *but,* and contain a threefold repetition of the purpose clause *God chose* . . . [in order] *to.*[75] Yet the three things God did are not strictly parallel. Whereas the first two have an equivalent structure *(foolish . . . shame the wise; weak . . . shame the strong),* the third in v. 28 is longer and more comprehensive and uses a stronger verb ("nullify" instead of "shame").[76]

The two verses together leave the unmistakable impression of the deliberate, sovereign action of God in assembling, or "calling," his people in Corinth contrary to all expectations. God's choice of the humble nation Israel was likewise surprising and unanticipated: "The LORD your God chose you to be a people for his treasured possession, out of all the peoples who are on the face of the earth. It was not because you were more numerous than any other people" (Deut. 7:7). This is a stable pattern in salvation history. From Genesis onward, where he consistently bypasses the firstborn, God chooses the most unlikely figures, a model he followed in Corinth.

In short, the Corinthians are God's people not because of themselves, but "because of him" (1 Cor. 1:30). This emphasis on the free and magnanimous grace of God is also a constant theme in the teaching of Jesus, whose parables about invitations to a great banquet, for instance, "turned on the primacy of grace over religious and social degrees of status and achievement."[77] Jesus' prayer in Matthew 11:25 strikes the same note as 1 Corinthians 1:26-31: "I praise you, Father, Lord of heaven and earth, because you have hidden these things from the wise and learned, and revealed them to little children."

The individuals God chose in Corinth are the very antithesis of the wise, strong, and noble (those normally chosen for important roles). He did this quite deliberately for a specific purpose: in order *to shame the wise* and *the strong.* Ironically, honor was the very thing the Corinthians wanted to leach from their powerful and wise leaders. Yet God acts to shame those whom the world regards as impressive. But it is not just a matter of losing

74. Gk. τοῦ κόσμου is a partitive genitive, referring to the larger group to which the foolish (who were chosen) belong and of which they are a subset.

75. TNIV finds the threefold repetition of "God chose" too cumbersome in English, translating the third instance in v. 28 with the words, "He chose."

76. Some think that Paul's use of the neuter for *the foolish things, the weak things, the lowly things,* and *the despised things* refers to each of them as an impersonal class. As Godet puts it, they are "so little valued that they do not count as individuals." It may be a derogatory expression similar to those in English referring to "the help," "the hired hands," or "the body count" (Garland, 76). However, Jesus uses the neuter to refer to himself as "something greater than Solomon/the temple" in the Gospels (e.g., Matt. 12:6). Barrett's view, 58, is preferable: Paul generalizes "to spare the Corinthians too blunt a description of themselves, and because he knows that in the next verse he is going to speak of 'things that do not exist.'"

77. Thiselton, 184. Cf. Eberhard Jüngel, *Paulus und Jesus: Eine Untersuchung zur Präzisierung der Frage nach dem Ursprung der Christologie* (HUT 2; Tübingen: Mohr Siebeck, 1972), 31.

face or reputation, as serious as this may have been in Greco-Roman society. Rather, the "shaming" must be understood in the sense of being condemned by God in judgment. The Prophets and Psalms regularly attest to God's determination to vindicate the righteous and bring the unrighteous to a shameful end (Isa. 41:11; Jer. 2:26; Pss. 6:10; 31:17; 35:4, 26-27; 40:15). Speaking of the enemies of God's people, Psalm 83:16-18 intones: "Fill their faces with *shame,* that they may seek your name, O LORD. Let them be put to *shame* and dismayed forever; let them perish in disgrace, that they may know that you alone, whose name is the LORD, are the Most High over all the earth." Note that the shaming of God's arrogant enemies is in order that God's honor and glory might be properly recognized. That Paul intends the verb to have an eschatological flavor is confirmed by his choice of another verb, "to nullify," in v. 28. As Fee puts it, "[i]n choosing the Corinthians God has already begun the final vindication over his enemies."[78]

With God choosing *the lowly things of this world,* Paul completes the reversal of the triad he introduced in v. 26: (1) God chose the foolish over the wise; (2) the weak over the influential; and now (3) the lowly over those of noble birth. The following expression, *the despised things,* is the same group as *the lowly,* and is an appropriate climax to the dramatic turnaround. The low born, as opposed to the well born, were regarded with disdain, being on the bottom rung of the social hierarchy. They are, in the world's eyes, *the things that are not,* as opposed to *the things that are.* But God, against all human wisdom, has chosen the former over the latter. He preferred the nobodies over the somebodies. Thus, the cross turns the world's values upside down and effects the most radical of revolutions. This transformation is nothing less than the end of the world. Indeed, God's activity of "nullifying," which could be translated "bring to nothing" (ESV, Thiselton), is a term Paul uses throughout the letter to signal final destruction (2:6; 6:13; 13:8, 10; 15:24, 26; cf. 2 Cor. 3:11), as in 15:26: "The last enemy to be *destroyed* is death." As Lampe concludes: "When the cross is proclaimed and through this act a community is founded, human wisdom and strength do not contribute anything to it. God rejects them as legitimate tools."[79]

**1:29** God's ultimate aim in his activity of choosing, shaming, and nullifying is to preclude all human boasting. The critical purpose of God's action of exalting the foolish and lowering the proud is that no one can sing his or her own praises in the presence of God. By definition, "the things that are not" (v. 28) have no wisdom or power of their own to speak of. And "the things that are" (v. 28) have been disgraced or brought to nothing. Thus, the way is clear for everyone either to remain silent or to praise God. Hays rightly points to parallel thoughts in Hannah's prayer (1 Sam. 2:1-10) and Mary's Song (Luke 1:46-55; cf. Psalm 113), which praise God who

78. Fee, 83.

79. Lampe, "Theological Wisdom," 127.

"raises up the poor from the dust" and "has brought down the powerful from their thrones and lifted up the lowly."[80]

**1:30** Paul insists that all praise is to be reserved for God, for *it is because of him that you are in Christ Jesus.* Sometimes a brief remark carries more weight than a longer and more elaborate explanation. This is the case in point, with the first two words of the verse, literally "of him," offering a pithy summary of the conclusion of the argument in 1:31 to boast only in the Lord. The point is that if it is "of him" that the Corinthians have their standing with God, it is presumably not "of yourselves." It is hard to conceive of a more emphatic way of underscoring God's grace in such short space.[81]

Paul summarizes the blessings of salvation in similarly succinct fashion (before going on to elaborate with four further key terms); to be saved is to be *in Christ Jesus.* Pregnant with meaning, not surprisingly, this phrase has been variously interpreted.[82] If Deissmann stressed the mystical and experiential sense of the phrase, a religious energy in the soul of the believer, Weiss and Schweitzer underscored the eschatological status of being-in-Christ as the mode of existence of God's new creation (cf. 2 Cor. 5:17: "if anyone is in Christ, there is a new creation"). Charting a middle course, Davies, Wikenhauser, and Tannehill argue that the emphases on state and status both have some validity, for Christian experience derives from the objective standing of being in Christ. But this happy position is not to be construed privately or individually. In one sense, Paul will expound being in Christ in 12:12-27 with the metaphor of the body of Christ in which all believers are members. As the following four terms in v. 30 suggest, to be in Christ is to enjoy both a secure and objective status before God and a new mode of eschatological existence in solidarity with other believers.[83]

The Christ to whom the Corinthians are united brings certain benefits to the members of his body. In listing these Paul goes from speaking of what is true of the Corinthians to include himself and all other believers,

80. Hays, 77. The conjunction which opens the verse, *so that,* "introduces the ultimate end" of God's activity reported in the paragraph, just as the three purpose clauses in vv. 27-28 using "in order to" introduce subsidiary purposes or steps along the way. *No one* is literally "all flesh," a Hebraism and an inclusive expression for every human being without exception.

81. Should the phrase be understood as a genitive of origin ("from him") or causally (TNIV)? Weiss and Schrage point to Rom. 11:36 as support for the former ("from him . . . are all things" [TNIV]). Nothing is at stake, since a genitive of origin in this context carries a causal nuance. Perhaps NJB is most apt: "by him." God is both the source and cause of their union with Christ.

82. See Thiselton, 189-90, for a summary of the history of research.

83. The construction "in Christ" or "in the Lord" can also be used less absolutely as part of broader sentence constructions, e.g., with the verb "to boast" (1 Cor. 1:31; 2 Cor. 10:17) or "to hope" (Phil. 2:19), or where it carries the instrumental force of "by" (1 Thess. 4:1; Rom. 15:30). Uses comparable to 1 Cor. 1:30 include 2 Cor. 5:17 (cited above), 1 Thess. 3:8, and Phil. 4:1, 13.

switching from the second-person plural to the first-person plural: *you are in Christ Jesus, who has become for us.*[84] The syntax of the four terms to follow indicates that they are not coordinate (contra NIV, RSV, ESV), but rather, as in the TNIV, the three nouns *righteousness, holiness,* and *redemption* explicate God's *wisdom.*[85] Although all four qualities both characterize Christ and are imparted by Christ, the emphasis is on the fact that believers have them by virtue of being in union with Christ.

Wisdom, with which the Corinthians are so enamored, and which Paul has taken such pains to debunk, is now redefined through the cross as a virtual synonym of salvation.[86] This will be explained further in 2:6-16, where Paul expounds the wisdom of the cross and the Spirit (2:6: "We do, however, speak a message of wisdom among the mature"). To follow the logic of Paul's argument, to find wisdom, you must first renounce your own wisdom and become a fool.

The three terms following in apposition used to describe *wisdom* are difficult to pin down due to lack of context. Bruce suggests a three-step sequence on the analogy of Romans 8:17-39, with blessings running from the past *(righteousness)* to the present *(holiness)* and onto the future *(redemption).* However, the terms are each too broad in their usage to support this attractive scheme. They cannot be confined so neatly to the three respective tenses of salvation. Holiness or sanctification, for instance, can refer to the beginning of the Christian life,[87] and righteousness can be used of ongoing renewal or to the future verdict on believers at the Last Judgment. Instead, all three offer different perspectives on the wisdom of God, which is salvation in Christ, drawing on different metaphors. *Righteousness* recalls the law court and speaks of vindication and acquittal, *holiness* brings to mind the temple and being set apart for God, and *redemption* evokes the slave market and emancipation on the analogy of Israel's deliverance in the exodus.

David Ford's definition of wisdom properly locates its meaning across both what we traditionally call theology and what we term ethics: wisdom "asks not only about meaning, interpretation and truth but also, inextricably, about living life before God now and about how lives and communities are shaped in line with who God is and with God's purposes for the future. In short, it is about lived meaning directed towards the kingdom of God."[88] This is a good definition of what Paul is aiming at throughout 1 Corinthians.

84. A dative of advantage.

85. Note again the relationship between wisdom (or its lack) and righteousness (or its lack). While a lack of wisdom results in immorality and idolatry (Rom. 1:21-25; cf. our outline for this letter), Christ, our wisdom, is also our *righteousness, holiness and redemption.*

86. Cf. Conzelmann, 51-52; Fee, 85.

87. See Peterson, *Possessed by God.*

88. David Ford, "Jesus Christ, The Wisdom of God," in *Reading Texts, Seeking Wisdom: Scripture and Theology* (ed. David F. Ford and Graham Stanton; London: SCM, 2003), 4-5.

**1:31** As the introductory formula, *as it is written*, indicates,[89] Paul cites Scripture in v. 31 to end with a positive exhortation.[90] The apostle's solution to spiritual pride and divisions in Corinth is to focus on something worth celebrating, namely, God and his salvation in Christ, rather than on individual groups and their supposed superiority over other groups.

There are two equally likely sources for the scriptural warning in question; the wording of Jeremiah 9:24 and 1 Samuel 2:10 LXX is virtually identical, and both provide rich subtexts for Paul's argument. We are not forced to choose, for, as Hays observes, "significant writing often mingles the echoes of multiple precursors."[91] Paul cites Jeremiah 9:23/1 Samuel 2:10 LXX in 1:31 and alludes to both texts in their surrounding contexts in 1:26-29. Both texts support his contention that the Corinthians should not evaluate themselves by human criteria before God; God called them by different standards. They should consider themselves in the light of the salvation plan of God in Christ. Both the allusions and the hybrid quotation can be dealt with together, but in reverse order, since the latter provides the clue to the recognition of the former. Further echoes of both Old Testament texts may be heard in 1 Corinthians 4:6-13, which refers back to 1:31.[92]

The warning in Jeremiah is part of a series of judgment oracles. God's judgment is coming on those people guilty of a variety of sins (lies, iniquity, oppression, and idolatry [specifically, Baal worship]; 8:3–9:26). Those who claim to be wise will suffer judgment (e.g., 8:9: "The wise shall be put to shame, . . . since they have rejected the word of the Lord, what wisdom is in them?"). The climax of the section is Jeremiah 9:23-24, which warns against all boasting save in God. The verb "to boast" occurs five times in vv. 23-24 in negative and positive senses, the improper "boasts" being human wisdom,

89. See our comments on the perfect tense "it is written (γέγραπται) in 1:19.

90. Daniel B. Wallace, *Greek Grammar beyond the Basics: An Exegetical Syntax of the New Testament* (Grand Rapids: Zondervan, 1996), 576, observes that this introductory formula, using the perfect tense of γράφω, stresses Scripture's present and binding authority, whereas the use of the present tense of the verb "to say" (e.g., 1 Cor. 9:8, 10; cf. 2 Cor. 6:2) as a way of introducing an Old Testament quotation emphasizes the immediate applicability of the word.

91. Hays, *Conversion of the Imagination*, 404. 1 Sam. 2:10 LXX contains material not found in the MT. With respect to textual matters, Stanley, *Paul and the Language of Scripture*, 188, who considers only the Jeremiah text, labels Paul's use "a generalized appropriation of an attractive phrase from Jer. 9.23 LXX by Paul himself." The small differences between the precursor text and Paul's rendition number three: (1) Paul omits the initial conjunction; (2) he advances "let the one who boasts" to the beginning of the sentence; and (3) he changes the object of the boasting from τούτῳ ("this" — namely, "that he or she understands and knows me, that I am the Lord who . . .") to ἐν κυρίῳ ("in the Lord"). None of the changes are substantial. The third does not change the meaning of the verse, "but it does create a concise and generalized expression that could be adapted to a variety of contexts (cf. 2 Cor. 10.17)" (Stanley, 188). The phrase ἐν κυρίῳ, "in the Lord," appears frequently in Paul's letters. 1 Sam. 2:10 LXX is identical to Jer. 9:23 LXX except that the object of boasting is briefer and in fact closer to Paul's citation: συνίειν καὶ γινώσκειν τὸν κύριον, "that he or she understands and *knows the Lord*."

92. Wagner, "'Not beyond the Things Which Are Written': A Call to Boast Only in the Lord (1 Cor. 4:6)," 279-87.

strength, and riches. 1 Samuel 2:10 LXX concludes Hannah's song of praise, in which God is exalted for reversing the fortunes of the poor and the downtrodden. A celebration of God's gracious blessing, its accent is on this startling reversal rather than on eschatological judgment as in Jeremiah.

A number of Jewish texts cite or take up themes from the two LXX texts, especially Jeremiah 9. Consonant with Paul's use, these place the warning about improper boasting in the context of future universal judgment. They also discourage boasting in human attainments and instead promote trust in the plans of God and imply a call to glorify him.[93]

As noted in Beale and Carson, "The texts in question and their surrounding contexts have influenced the vocabulary, structure, and main theme of [1 Corinthians 1:26-31]. The culminating pithy maxim in 1:31 is only the tip of the iceberg of scriptural dependence. Jeremiah provides the pattern for Paul's threefold dismissal of the wise, the powerful, and the well born." 1 Corinthians 1:26-28 echoes Jeremiah 9:23: "Do not let the wise boast in their wisdom, do not let the strong boast in their strength, do not let the wealthy boast in their wealth." Beale and Carson continue, "Further, the reference to Christ in [v. 30] as becoming 'righteousness' echoes the last part of Jeremiah 9:24 ('I act with mercy, justice and righteousness').

"The connection to [1 Samuel 2:10 LXX] and the Song of Hannah underscores the reversal of status, a theme that Paul discusses in terms of wisdom and folly and strength and weakness throughout 1:18-31. The first reference to boasting in [1 Samuel] 2:1-10 is negative and appears in [v. 3]. It resonates powerfully with Paul's critique of the Corinthians' obsession with rhetoric and could just as easily have been quoted (along with [v. 10]): 'Do not boast . . . , and do not speak lofty things; do not let grandiloquence[94] . . . come out of your mouth, because the Lord is a God of knowledge, and God prepares his own designs.' The allusions and citations in context supply the ideas of shame and role reversal in 1:26-29, help Paul move from past to future judgment in 1:27-29, and indicate how a personified boast in a wise God could emerge in 1:30."[95] Only he ought to be glorified.

### 3. *Reminder of Paul's Ministry Strategy: Worldly Wisdom in the Light of Paul's Unimpressive Preaching in Corinth, 2:1-5*

*1And so it was with me, brothers and sisters. When I came to you, I did not come with eloquence or human wisdom as I proclaimed to you the testi-*

93. H. H. D. Williams, *The Wisdom of the Wise*, 113-24.

94. Hays's translation, 405.

95. B. K. Beale and D. A. Carson, eds., *Commentary of the New Testament Use of the Old Testament* (Grand Rapids: Baker, 2007). The referent of *the Lord* in 1:31 is not entirely clear. It may refer to Jesus (Findlay, Fee), which would be consistent with Paul's usage elsewhere; "Lord" is often used as a title for Christ (e.g., 1 Cor. 1:3, 7, 8, 9, 10 — cf. 2 Corinthians 10). Most take it here as a reference to God (the Father), noticing that the emphasis in context is on what

*mony about God. [2]For I resolved to know nothing while I was with you except Jesus Christ and him crucified. [3]I came to you in weakness with great fear and trembling. [4]My message and my preaching were not with wise and persuasive words, but with a demonstration of the Spirit's power, [5]so that your faith might not rest on human wisdom, but on God's power.*

In the ancient world a public speaker's initial visit to a city was critical to establishing their reputation. Orators would compete for applause and offer entertainment to diners in between courses at the best banquets. Competitive showmanship was the order of the day. Winter contends that 1 Corinthians 2:1-5 "reveals a distinct constellation of rhetorical terms and allusions," especially in connection with words such as "persuasive" and "demonstration" in v. 4. In contrast to the orators who wowed the citizens of Corinth, "Paul repudiated the sophistic method of 'presenting himself' when he came to Corinth." In short, he was concerned not with "projecting an image of himself," but rather of Jesus Christ.[96]

Williams has detected an echo of Zechariah 4:6 ("Not by might, nor by power, but by my Spirit, says the LORD of hosts") in 1 Corinthians 2:3-5 which helps establish the character of Paul's preaching and some of the details of interpretation: "Paul's fear and trembling as a weak human being emphasize his cornerstone message of God's power and presence. Therefore, the Corinthians should not despise the day of 'small things' (Zech 4:10)."[97] The texts resonate at a number of points. Intriguingly, Paul and Zechariah are both layers of foundation of a new temple (Zech. 4:6-10; 1 Cor. 3:10-11; cf. the Corinthians as a temple — 1 Cor. 3:16-17; 2 Cor. 6:16-18; and Paul as a temple worker — 1 Cor. 9:13-14). Combined with some shared terms (viz., spirit, wisdom, and power) and the importance of the text elsewhere in the New Testament, especially in Revelation, an echo of Zechariah 4:6 in this section of 1 Corinthians reinforces Paul's emphasis on his founding work among the Corinthians being in weakness and yet exhibiting divine power.

1 Corinthians 2:1-5 caps off Paul's argument in the unit of thought, underscoring again points made in the previous two paragraphs: 2:1 recalls 1:17; 2:2 recalls 1:18-25; 2:3 recalls 1:26-31; and 2:4-5 recall the main assertions in 1:17-18. Furthermore, the word "wisdom" occurs three times (in vv. 1, 4, and 5), all in the negative sense. The wisdom of the world that is opposed to God, introduced in 1:18, is thus brought to an impressive climax.

---

God has done in Christ Jesus (see esp. v. 30) and the nearest antecedent, "wisdom from God," in v. 30.

96. Winter, *Philo and Paul among the Sophists*, 147-48. Murphy-O'Connor's rebuttal, "Review of Winter," 430, that "it is ludicrous to imagine that he [Paul] was offered a civic reception, which he turned down" when he came to Corinth, misses the point. Paul is not saying that he necessarily could have "come with eloquence or human wisdom," but merely that he came in another manner, and that it was a good thing that he did.

97. H. H. D. Williams, *The Wisdom of the Wise*, 156.

### a. Paul's Humble Demeanor Suited His Message, 2:1-3

**2:1** As the opening words of this verse ("as for me"[98]) indicate, Paul's third argument, that the proclamation of the gospel cannot be a form of human wisdom, is from personal experience. The last point at which he wrote in the first-person singular was in 1:17, where he likewise spoke of his work in "preaching the gospel." Hence 2:1-5 takes up where 1:17 left off.[99] Paul's point here is that the manner of his preaching to the Corinthians when he first came to them was not according to human wisdom. Rather, the man and his way of conducting himself matched his message; weakness and foolishness characterized them both. Paul was no more impressive than his proclamation of a failed Messiah. Emphatically, then, Paul *did not come with eloquence or human wisdom.* This is borne out elsewhere in his letters: some Corinthians said of Paul, "in person he is unimpressive and his speaking amounts to nothing" (2 Cor. 10:10), and his initial preaching in Galatia was accompanied by "illness" (Gal. 4:14). Paul's modesty is no rhetorical exaggeration. His activity of proclaiming the gospel was often attended by difficult circumstances and factors that would have prevented him were it not for his sense of obligation: "I am compelled to preach" (9:16).

The Greek word for *eloquence* in the phrase "eloquence of word" appears rarely in the New Testament, and its precise meaning is disputed.[100] It contains a probable metaphorical reference to height or excess.[101] Hence, RSV/NRSV renders it as "lofty words," Thiselton, "high-sounding rhetoric," and TEV, "big words." Unlike the sophists who paraded their cleverness in self-display, Paul did not speak of himself but focused on someone else, namely, Jesus Christ (as v. 2 makes clear). Paul's public speaking,[102] whether in the synagogue, in private homes, or in more public settings, came without pomp and elicited no applause, nor was it meant to. His role as herald (see on 1:17) was simply to be a proclaimer, the faithful bearer of a message.

The content of Paul's proclamation is *the testimony,* or "mystery," *about God.* Whether or not "mystery" is a better reading here,[103] both terms,

98. Gk. κἀγώ.

99. Cf. Pogoloff, *Logos and Sophia,* 130.

100. Gk. ὑπεροχή. Cf. NIV: "*brilliance* of oratory." Pertinent to the Corinthian context, Pogoloff, *Logos and Sophia,* 132, cites examples of the word used to mean "rhetorical prestige." For example, a woman named Sosipatra made her sophist husband Eustathius seem inferior by her "surprising wisdom" (ὑπεροχὴ σοφίας).

101. Its appearance in 1 Tim. 2:2 and (the cognate verb) in Rom. 13:1, where it refers to the governing authorities *over* us, supports this.

102. Even though Christian "proclamation" can be broader than verbal communication, as in 11:26 where the Lord's Supper "proclaims the Lord's death," Paul intends the narrow sense here (contra Thiselton, 209, and Litfin, *St Paul's Theology of Proclamation,* 204-9).

103. An extremely difficult textual problem appears at this point, such that several commentators and some translations prefer the alternative reading of "mystery" to "testimony" (e.g., TEV, NJB, NRSV; $NA^{25}$ has "testimony"; $NA^{26}$, "mystery"). The two Greek words are easily confused. The editors of UBS (both third and fourth editions) regard the external evidence to be evenly balanced; there are more manuscripts with "testimony," but

as Thiselton notes, "emphasize that what is conveyed in Christian proclamation is truth revealed by God, not human opinions."[104] A "mystery" in the New Testament is a gift of divine revelation, and a "testimony" refers to the content of what is witnessed to. In neither case can the speaker lay any claim to any personal insight. Paul's use of either word here instead of "gospel" suits his argument.

**2:2** Paul explains further why his preaching in Corinth was not in words of human wisdom: his message focused on a crucified Messiah.[105] He *resolved to know*[106] *nothing . . . except Jesus Christ and him crucified.*[107] This assertion recalls 1:18-25. The close association in Paul's mind of the Messiah with his death can scarcely be overstated. As noted earlier, to speak enthusiastically of an executed deliverer-king was an oxymoron. Nonetheless, such preaching was Paul's regular pattern throughout his ministry. Recalling his preaching to the Galatians, he writes: "Before your very eyes Jesus Christ was portrayed as crucified" (3:1).

Again in contrast to "the wise" in Corinth and in the church, who could expatiate endlessly on all sorts of subjects, all Paul wanted to talk about was "the cross of Christ" (1:17). On first blush this may seem rather narrow and limited. After all, Paul spent eighteen months in Corinth and would have engaged in pastoral work alongside evangelism. However, as 1 Corinthians 1:10–4:17 itself demonstrates, for Paul even the most practical ills, such as divisions and problems of leadership in the church, are remedied by focusing on the cross. For Paul, *Christ crucified* is more than just the means of forgiveness and salvation; rather, it informs his total vision of the Christian life and ministry.[108]

**2:3** Paul's humble demeanor in first encountering the Corinthians could be seen not only in his words but also in his actions: he *came . . . in weakness with great fear and trembling.* This was the very opposite of the self-confident assertion expected of a cultured orator.[109] It is also very different from how some "arrogant people are talking" in the church in Corinth (4:19).

---

there is "limited but early support" for "mystery." They take the former as a scribal assimilation to 1:6 and the latter as Paul's preparation for his exposition of "God's wisdom, a mystery" in 2:7-10. While certainty is unattainable, "mystery" is preferable in 2:1 on the grounds that it seems more likely that a scribe would make a change based on what he has recently transcribed (1:6) than based on what he will transcribe a few verses later (2:7).

104. Thiselton, 208.

105. Note explanatory γάρ.

106. On the use of the perfect tense of this verb (εἰδέναι is a perfect infinitive from οἶδα), see our comments on 1:16.

107. Regarding the perfect tense verb ἐσταυρωμένον see our comments on 1:23.

108. The opening words of the verse are literally, "I did not decide to know anything . . . except," meaning, "I decided to know nothing . . . except." They should not be taken too literally. In Jewish idiom, such absolute denials can function as a way of saying, "I put my emphasis here rather than somewhere else." A clear example is Matt. 6:19-20: "Do not store up treasure on earth, . . . but store up for yourselves treasure in heaven."

109. Pogoloff, *Logos and Sophia*, 135; cf. Winter, *Philo and Paul among the Sophists*, 147-61.

Just as the message was weak (1:25), so the messenger came in *weakness.* It is difficult to know with certainty what Paul is referring to at this point. A number of commentators follow Albert Schweitzer in suggesting that Paul has some humiliating illness in mind.[110] As Collins puts it, "Paul's description of his weakness may reflect his real situation."[111] In Galatians 4:13-14 Paul says that he preached the gospel, literally, in "weakness of the flesh," which the TNIV uncontroversially translates as "an illness." And in 1 Corinthians 11:30 the adjective is used of some Corinthians' being "*weak* and sick." While a reference to a physical ailment is not out of the question, Paul's *weakness* in 2:3 could be a number of things, such as a general sense of inadequacy for the task of evangelizing the city (cf. 2 Cor. 2:16; 3:5). His weakness could also be his menial trade, his relative impoverishment, his vulnerability to persecution, or his unimpressive presence.[112]

In any case, *weakness* suits the echo of Zechariah 4:6 mentioned above. In his laying of the foundation of the new temple in Corinth, Paul's work is "not by might, nor by power."[113] That such weakness marks an apostle will be touched on again in 4:9-13, a passage which demonstrates the range of possible meanings of the term: "we are weak, . . . we are hungry and thirsty, we are in rags, we are brutally treated, we are homeless, we work hard with our own hands, . . . we are persecuted" (4:10). As Weber notes, "it is in the nature of the cross that it cannot be preached elegantly and brilliantly, but only in weakness."[114] The weak Paul shares the sufferings and death of Christ in order to bring life to the Corinthians and glory to God.

The precise referent of *great fear and trembling* is also difficult to pin down with certainty. Was Paul afraid (1) of a new setting with large crowds (Robertson and Plummer), without the support of his co-workers Silas and Timothy (according to Acts 17:15; 18:5); (2) of the magnitude of the task ahead of him (Fee; cf. Acts 18:9-11); (3) because of his personal inadequacy (Lightfoot, Bruce, Witherington); or (4) for his personal safety (Calvin, Barrett; cf. Acts 18:9; Ps. 55:5)?

Savage offers a fifth view based on the use of the phrase in the LXX, where it often depicts a humble response to the awe-inspiring majesty of God.[115] Hence, he paraphrases: Paul came to Corinth "in profound humil-

110. Albert Schweitzer, *The Mysticism of Paul the Apostle* (trans. William Montgomery; Baltimore: Johns Hopkins University Press, 1998; rpt., New York: Holt, 1931), 152-55.

111. Collins, 116.

112. Cf. Garland, 85.

113. Given its relevance to the rest of the paragraph, the influence of Zechariah 4:6 is more likely than that of Jeremiah 9:22-23 (suggested by L. Hartman, "Some Remarks on I Cor 2:1-5," *SEÅ* 39 [1974]: 109-20).

114. Hans R. Weber, *The Cross: Tradition and Interpretation* (Grand Rapids: Eerdmans, 1979), 73.

115. Gk. φόβος καὶ τρόμος. Elsewhere in the New Testament, "fear and trembling" refers to the fear of God (Phil. 2:12-13; Heb. 12:20-21) or to the attitude of an obedient slave (Eph. 6:5).

ity and trepidation."[116] But this humility was as much before God as before his fellows. Given Paul's prolific use of Scripture in the letter, taking *fear and trembling* as a biblical phrase pointing to his reverence before the majesty of God in the task of preaching the gospel is a strong possibility. Paul's clearest reference to "the fear of God" is in 2 Corinthians 7:1, which follows directly after a catena of Old Testament quotations in 6:16-18. In this case, Paul's *weakness* would refer to his posture toward the Corinthians and his *fear and trembling* toward God. Such vulnerability denuded Paul of self-importance, pride, and a competitive spirit, "qualities" so characteristic of the Corinthian sophists to whom he was being unfavorably compared. It stripped him of self-reliance and left him with no alternative but to trust in God.[117] If Savage's interpretation is right, along with "faith" in v. 5, Paul's *fear and trembling* is itself an expression of this trust.

### b. *Paul's Plain Speech Suited His Message, 2:4*

**2:4** Not only was Paul's manner uninspiring when he came to preach the gospel in Corinth, so too was his presentation: *my message and my preaching were not with wise and persuasive words.*[118] The repetition of the personal pronouns suggests that Paul distinguished between his *message* (literally, "word") and his *preaching.*[119] Commentators have suggested the first refers to form and the second to content, the how and what of proclamation, or the first to private and the second to public discourse. However,

116. Timothy B. Savage, *Power through Weakness: Paul's Understanding of the Christian Ministry in 2 Corinthians* (SNTSMS 86; New York: Cambridge University Press, 1995), 73. Garland's objection, 85, that in the LXX "fear and trembling usually fall upon the enemy because of something God has done" simply shows the flexibility of the notion of the fear of God. Exodus 20:20 has both senses, negative and positive: frightened dread and respectful awe. Likewise, Thiselton's observation, 215, that Paul claims to have been delivered from a spirit of fear, ignores positive uses of the fear of God in the New Testament (e.g., 2 Cor. 7:1).

117. Fee, 96.

118. Eleven different variant readings mark this textual problem as one of the best known in 1 Corinthians. However, the decision makes little difference to the meaning of the verse. Some MSS have "*human* wisdom" (including ἀνθρωπίνης before or after σοφίας). These seem to be the result of copyists' attempting to clarify the kind of wisdom Paul eschews, in anticipation of v. 5, a practice attested by a number of English versions which translate σοφία as "human wisdom" at different points in 1 Corinthians 1–4. The most likely variants are "by persuasive words of wisdom" or "by persuasion of wisdom." While the external evidence is not decisive, the nub of the issue concerns the adjective "persuasive" (πειθοῖς). The word appears in no other Greek literature (Barrett suggests that Paul coined the word himself), which marks it as the more difficult reading. Schrage, 1:231-32, points out that "by persuasion of wisdom" represents a better correspondence with the second half of the verse ("persuasion" and "demonstration" are both nouns). This also makes the variant with the adjective more difficult. On the other hand, the reading could easily have been a scribal mistake (the following word begins with a *sigma*). The editors of UBS[4] "hedge their bets," putting the *sigma* in brackets, but ultimately decide for retaining the reading with the adjective, which TNIV translates.

119. Gk. λόγος and κήρυγμα respectively.

usage does not support such distinctions; the words are interchangeable. Together they encompass all of Paul's speaking as an apostle.[120] Why then the redundancy? Information theory suggests a number of reasons for such repetition, including emphasis, clarification, assurance of attention, and filling in gaps for rhythmic balance.[121] In this case, it may be stylistic, to have *message and preaching* repeat the rhythm of "fear and trembling" from the previous verse so as to emphasize the comprehensive nature of Paul's singularly unimpressive first impression in Corinth. Nonetheless, Paul was in good company: Moses claimed lack of eloquence (Exod. 4:10), Isaiah had unclean lips (Isa. 6:5), and Jeremiah did "not know how to speak," for he was "only a youth" (Jer. 1:6). God regularly chooses to work through human weakness.

His failure to speak with *wise and persuasive words* turns the contrast between Paul and the sophists up to full volume. As Witherington plausibly infers, "[t]he Corinthians felt that they had the right to judge Paul and his message and were evaluating him by the same criteria by which popular orators and teachers were judged."[122] Paul's speaking generated no applause. As noted above (see on v. 18), the sophist's goal was persuasion by the manipulation of arguments and skillful rhetoric. Paul's goal was the manifestation of God's power in people's lives.

Instead of "enticing, clever words" (Thiselton) to win his audience, what accompanied Paul's preaching was *a demonstration of the Spirit's power.* "A demonstration of the Spirit and of power" (NRSV, NASB), to translate literally, has been understood by the TNIV as a hendiadys, a figure of speech in which two words connected by "and" express a single idea. An example in current English is the phrase, "nice and warm."[123] Fee supplies the validation for taking "Spirit" and "power" together here: "for Paul the terms 'Spirit' and 'power' are at times nearly interchangeable; to speak of the Spirit is to speak of power."[124] Tellingly, *demonstration,* a hapax in the New Testament, is a technical term in rhetoric for proof given in a compelling speech.[125] "The convincing proof" (TEV) that Paul's speaking supplies is not what the Corinthians might have expected. Paul uses the term polemically. The Corinthians wanted a *demonstration* of rhetorical gifts; Paul offers instead proof that is based on the fact that God's Spirit is powerfully at work.[126]

120. Schrage, 1:231.

121. Thiselton, 218.

122. Witherington, 47.

123. Paul Ellingworth and Howard Hatton, *A Translator's Handbook on Paul's First Letter to the Corinthians* (London: United Bible Societies, 1985), 47.

124. Fee, 92.

125. Garland, 87.

126. The phrase could also be understood as "proof *of the fact* that God's Spirit was powerfully at work." The issue in context, however, is that Paul's message was proved to be true by *the Spirit's power.*

In what, then, did *the Spirit's power* consist? Does the collocation of "Spirit" and "power" imply Spirit-empowered miracles? Is Paul talking here about "deeds of power"[127] (1 Cor. 12:28), translated "miracles" in the TNIV? In other words, did "signs and wonders" (Rom. 15:19; 2 Cor. 12:12) accompany Paul's preaching in Corinth? Fee rightly notes that the "demonstration of the Spirit and power" here cannot be taken as a reference to miracles since in the context of 1 Corinthians this is the very triumphalist assumption Paul is arguing against. In contrast to Jewish requests for signs and the Greek desire for wisdom, Paul preaches Christ crucified (cf. 1:22-23). It would thus be a little odd, as Fee notes, if Paul were to appeal to powerful signs and wonders that persuaded hearers! In the context of his own personal weakness, the demonstration of the Spirit's power is seen in the Corinthians' conversion, as the Spirit applies the word of the gospel, Christ and him crucified, to their hearts: "the evidence lies with the Corinthians themselves and their own experience of the Spirit as they responded to the message of the gospel."[128] The plural of *power* would have been a more unambiguous reference to miracles. *Power* here is about moral conviction, not miraculous display.

1 Thessalonians 1:5 confirms this understanding. In Thessalonica, Paul reports, "our gospel came to you not simply with words but also with power, with the Holy Spirit." The following context makes clear that the evidence of this power was the "deep conviction" and changed lives of the Thessalonians: "you welcomed the message" (1:6). Paul tells the Corinthians the same thing. Paul insists that it is not sophisticated speech, nor even signs and wonders, but your Spirit-wrought conversion which represents the best proof of the truth of my message (cf. 1 Thess. 2:13).

### c. *Paul's Purpose Was That the Corinthians' Trust Would Be in God's Power and Not in Human Wisdom, 2:5*

**2:5** The conjunction *so that*[129] signals the purpose of Paul's preaching with "a demonstration of the Spirit's power" and not "with wise and persuasive words." He did so in order that the Corinthians might trust in God

127. Gk. δυνάμεις.

128. Gordon Fee, *God's Empowering Presence: The Holy Spirit in the Letters of Paul* (Peabody, MA: Hendrickson, 1994), 92. Elsewhere in the book, Fee turns to 2 Cor. 12:12; Rom. 15:18-19; Gal. 3:1-5 and suggests that Paul's converts normally did experience miraculous phenomena, that "the Thessalonians undoubtedly experienced such phenomena," and thus that the collocation of "Spirit" and "power" most likely implies Spirit-empowered miracles in 1 Cor. 2:4. For a balanced review of the issue in relation to Fee's book, see Peter Head, "An Extended Review of G. D. Fee, *God's Empowering Presence*," *Churchman* 111 (1997), 62-73. Head concludes that this process of argument moves away from the earlier exegetical conclusion which focused on the Spirit's powerful assistance in gospel proclamation and appropriation and prejudges the exegetical conclusions to be drawn from these other passages.

129. Gk. ἵνα.

and not in human wisdom. This verse looks back to 1:17 and hence closes off the section in bookend fashion. Hence, to *rest your faith on God's power* is the equivalent of not having "the cross of Christ emptied of its power" (to save). 1 Corinthians 1:18–2:5 is effectively an explanation of 1:17. Paul did not distance himself from the sophists in Corinth for personal reasons or because of his own tastes, but for the sake of the Corinthians. Rather than being persuaded by his cleverness and guile, Paul wants his hearers to respond to the truth clearly presented.

This response he labels faith. *Faith,* like "flesh" and "truth," is "a polymorphous concept" needing to be defined according to its context.[130] General definitions can distort or mask its meaning in any particular instance. In most of Paul's usage it refers to the human response to the proclamation of the gospel, the main components of which are belief, trust, and obedience.[131] Here the first and second of these aspects are prominent: it refers to "an intellectual conviction of truth [belief] and a stance of heart and will which exhibits trust in God's salvific act in Christ as the basis of life [trust]."[132] To have *your faith rest on God's power* in the context of 1:18–2:5 is to believe the cross to be the way of salvation, being convinced by the work of the Spirit in your own and other believers' lives, and to shun any trust in self and human wisdom as a way to God. Just as in Romans, Paul teaches that to attain righteousness a person must dismiss their own righteousness, so in 1 Corinthians to receive God's wisdom and experience his power it is necessary to relinquish your own wisdom and power.

With 2:5 the series of contrasts that Paul introduced in 1:17 is thus complete: Paul's gospel comes: (1) not with (human) wisdom, but with (God's) foolishness, (2) not with (the world's) power, but with (Paul's and God's) weakness, (3) not to the things that are, but to the things that are not, and (4) not with a demonstration of rhetorical skill, but with a demonstration of the Spirit's power. Zechariah 4:6, which Paul echoes in 2:1-5, serves as a fitting summary of this final paragraph of the section: "Not by might, nor by power, but by my Spirit, says the LORD of hosts."

## C. Affirmation of True Wisdom: The Wisdom of the Cross and the Spirit, 2:6–3:4

With the words, "We do, however," v. 6 marks a new section in Paul's argument against Corinthian factionalism. As Talbert observes, "2:6–3:4 corresponds loosely to 1:17–2:5, functioning as a contrast to the former section."[1]

130. Thiselton, 223.

131. Rom. 1:5 and 16:19 show how it can function as a synonym of "obedience." In Gal. 1:23 it refers to "the faith," meaning the message of Christianity.

132. Thiselton, 223.

1. Talbert, 5. Other commentaries disagree as to whether 3:1-4 goes with what precedes or with what follows. Our view is defended below. Bachmann agrees that 2:6–3:4

Having demolished the false wisdom that had in part led to the divisions in Corinth, Paul seeks to put genuine wisdom in its place. Up to this point Paul has emphasized the foolishness of the gospel. Now he turns to the gospel as wisdom from God.[2]

Of the 28 times Paul uses the noun "wisdom" in his letters, 15 appear in 1 Corinthians 1:17–2:13 (with another appearance in 3:19 which recaps the argument of 1:18–2:5).[3] Additionally, the adjective "wise" occurs ten times in chapters 1–3. With these data in mind, a number of commentators surmise that the Corinthians were infatuated with wisdom and that Paul is tackling the problem head-on at the outset of the letter. Thiselton makes the case that not only "wisdom" but also "maturity" and "spirituality" were Corinthian catchwords "which had become embedded in the life of the church at Corinth, and his [i.e., Paul's] most urgent task at this point is . . . to reclaim the terms for the gospel by redefining them in the light of the nature of God and of the gospel."[4]

However, it is not simply that Paul needs to correct a false view of wisdom in order to deal with divisions in Corinth. As argued in the Introduction (19-28), to Paul's mind a lack of true wisdom leads to other faults as well, especially sexual immorality and idolatry, the very vices Paul addresses negatively and positively in chapters 5–6 and 7, and 8–10 and 11–14 respectively. In Romans 1 Paul outlines his conviction that the rejection of wisdom from God (1:21-22) leads to sexual immorality (1:24, 26-27) and idolatry (1:23, 25). Thus, 1 Corinthians 2:6–3:4 has a relevance beyond chapters 1–4 in the letter. "God's wisdom" (2:7) is as much about how to live as what to believe.

Much has been written about the conceptual background of a number of key terms in the passage, such as "mystery," "the mature," and "the spiritual": is Paul adopting vocabulary from the Greco-Oriental mystery cults, Gnosticism, or Jewish wisdom and/or apocalyptic sources? While a good case can be made for the decisive nature of a Jewish apocalyptic and wisdom background for Paul's use of these words,[5] it must be admitted that they were in general usage within a variety of religious outlooks.[6]

A more significant issue for the interpretation of the passage, which sometimes receives less attention, is the precise referent of these and other

---

forms a distinct unit, giving it the heading, "Nevertheless, God's Wisdom, but Unfortunately Not among You" (our own translation). Robertson and Plummer, 16, label the section "The False Wisdom and the True."

2. Bachmann, 117.

3. The only other cluster occurs in Ephesians (3x) and Colossians (6x), which may also have particular circumstances that have prompted Paul to concentrate on wisdom.

4. Thiselton, 224.

5. See Robin Scroggs, "Paul: σοφὸς καὶ πνευματικός," *NTS* 14 (1967-68), 33-55.

6. See Birger A. Pearson, *The Pneumatikos-Psychikos Terminology in 1 Corinthians: A Study in the Theology of the Corinthian Opponents of Paul and Its Relation to Gnosticism* (SBLDS 12; Missoula, MT: Scholars Press, 1973), 27-43.

terms in the passage. The question of "who's who" is not easy to answer. Who are "we" and "us" in 2:6, 7, 10, 12, and 13? Who are "the rulers of this age" (2:6, 7)? Who are "the mature" (2:6)? Who are "the spiritual" (2:15; 3:1)? Who are "the worldly" (3:1, 3)? Who are the "infants in Christ" (3:1)?

In terms of tracing the argument of the section, the theme statement may be taken from the opening words, "we speak wisdom among the mature" (2:6a).[7] 1 Corinthians 2:6b–3:4 unpacks the three main elements of this solemn assertion. In each of the three sections Paul expounds the topic in question first negatively and then positively. A fourth section climaxes the unit with a confrontational accusation.[8]

### 1. Theme Statement: "We Speak Wisdom among the Mature," 2:6a

[6a]*We do, however, speak a message of wisdom among the mature. . . .*

**2:6a** The Corinthians could have been forgiven for thinking that Paul was totally opposed to wisdom, given that he has just declared so relentlessly that God has judged wisdom (1:18-21), outsmarted wisdom (1:22-25), and called only a few of the wise to be members of Christ's body in Corinth (1:26-31), and given that Paul's manner of preaching in Corinth was emphatically not according to wisdom (2:1-5). So in one sense, the words, *We do, however, speak a message of wisdom among the mature,* come as somewhat of a surprise.[9] In one sense it ought not to have been, since Paul and others describe Paul's work in terms of wisdom elsewhere: Colossians 1:28 — "It is he whom we proclaim, warning everyone and teaching everyone in all *wisdom,* so that we may present everyone *mature* in Christ"; 2 Peter 3:15 — "our dear brother Paul also wrote to you with the *wisdom* that God gave him."

*We* in 1 Corinthians 2:7a is a reference to Paul and the other apostles and prophets/preachers in Corinth who instruct the congregation, and not to all believers.[10] It follows hard on 2:1-5, where Paul focuses on his bring-

7. This insight builds on John Grassmick's Greek exegesis class notes from Dallas Theological Seminary.

8. 3:1-4 concludes 2:6-16 rather than belonging with 3:5-17 (Garland) or being transitional (David W. Kuck, *Judgment and Community Conflict: Paul's Use of Apocalyptic Judgment Language in 1 Corinthians 3:5–4:5* [SNTSMS 66; Leiden: Brill, 1992], 159). The whole of 2:16–3:4 concerns the lack of readiness of the Corinthians to have Paul speak God's wisdom to them because they are spiritually immature. Cf. the use of "to speak," λαλέω, in 2:6-7, 13 and 3:1.

9. TNIV is thus right to translate the δέ with the strongly contrastive, *however.* Translating σοφία as *message of wisdom* removes the possible misunderstanding that Paul is saying, "we speak wisely," in the sense of marshaling convincing arguments; as the following context indicates, the sense is, "the content we pass on may be described as wisdom."

10. This is not the case with every instance of "we" or "us" in the passage; see, e.g., vv. 10 and 12, where the reference is to all believers.

ing the message to Corinth. And 3:9 distinguishes between "we . . . God's fellow workers" and "you . . . God's field." The two groups are clearly distinguished. Paul says in v. 7 that what *we speak* is a mystery. In this connection, Ephesians 3:5-6 is significant, for there the recipients of "the mystery that has now been revealed by the Spirit" are "God's holy apostles and prophets." Although the verb "to speak"[11] here is not a technical term for Christian teaching or proclamation, nonetheless it can be used in this way, as in 2 Corinthians 4:13, Romans 15:18, Philippians 1:14, and 1 Thessalonians 2:2, 4, 16. In v. 7 it is legitimately translated as "we declare."[12] Furthermore, the exposition of *we speak* in v. 13 makes it clear that Paul has formal Christian instruction in mind.[13] The Christian leaders whom the Corinthians wanted either to lionize or deprecate, according to their score on the scale of (human) wisdom, do in fact teach *wisdom* after all.

But what is this *message* that they *speak,* and who are *the mature?*[14] Is the *message of wisdom* simply "the gospel," or is it something more far-reaching (cf. "the deep things of God" in v. 10)? Are *the mature* all believers or only a subgroup of more discerning Christians? The answers to these two questions cannot be separated. In favor of taking *the mature* as a reference to all believers is the term's cultural background, where it often denotes the initiated in a pagan religion and the basic contrast between "those who are perishing" and "those who are being saved" (1:18) throughout chapter 1.[15] However, *the mature* can also mean a person of perfect wisdom in both pagan and Jewish sources, and Paul's usage of it elsewhere seems to refer to knowledgeable, discerning, experienced Christians (Eph. 4:13; Phil. 3:15; Col. 1:28; 4:12). 1 Corinthians 14:20 is clear: "Brothers and sisters, stop thinking like children. In regard to evil be infants, but in your thinking be *mature.*" A more restricted meaning of *the mature* is also suggested by the use of similar terminology in 1 Corinthians 3:1-3, where Paul contrasts "infants in Christ" with "the spiritual," a reference to the same group as *the mature,* a point emphasized by Lightfoot.

The *message of wisdom* Paul and other Christian teachers *speak among the mature,* then, is not to be equated with the gospel, which is for all people without exception.[16] As a broad generalization, as Scroggs suggests, the

11. Gk. λαλέω.

12. The repetition of λαλοῦμεν ("we speak/declare") in 2:6 and 2:7 reflects the use of imperfective aspect in order to express a customary action, characterizing the nature of apostolic preaching: we speak wisdom.

13. See the comments on 2:12 for a discussion of the referents of the first-person plural pronouns in 2:12-16.

14. Gk. τελείοις.

15. Cf. Mare and apparently Fee (though 101 n. 13 makes it unclear how he understands the term).

16. Contra esp. Fee. To draw this conclusion is not to say that Paul presents "a two-tiered gospel" (Garland, 107) and fosters a Christian elitism. 1 Corinthians itself is evidence enough that the Corinthians need to "grow up," and that they will do so only if they heed Paul's application of the salvation that is Christ crucified.

*kerygma* is for everyone, while the "wisdom, which is a mystery" (v. 7), is for discerning, experienced Christians. This is confirmed by Paul's exposition of "the mature" in 2:14–3:4, where Paul states that he could not address them with this wisdom because of their immaturity. The *message of wisdom* is the full scope of God's teaching on salvation and the Christian life, which only "the mature" digest and appropriate. It is Christ Jesus, "our righteousness, holiness and redemption" (1:30). Lightfoot makes the intriguing suggestion that Colossians, Ephesians, and to a lesser extent Romans reflect the content of this wisdom.[17]

It is better, however, to equate "God's wisdom" (v. 7) with "the mind of Christ" (v. 16), and to take them both to refer in context to the wisdom of the cross applied to everyday life. This is precisely what Paul offers the Corinthians in the letter as a whole. In chapters 1–4 the wisdom of God is the recognition that the cross spells the end of the world's power and wisdom and provides a solid basis for Christian unity. In chapter 5 the sacrifice of Christ our Passover lamb (5:7) is the reason for purifying the assembly by removing the incestuous man. In 6:1-11 righteous suffering instead of self-assertion is recommended with the implicit example of the crucified Christ. In 6:12-20 the redemption achieved by Christ is a major reason to honor God with your body (6:20). Likewise in chapter 7 being "bought with a price" is the reason not to "become slaves of human beings" (7:22). In 8:1–11:1 it is because Christ died for our weaker brother (8:11) that we imitate Christ (11:1) and avoid causing our brother to stumble. In 11:17-34 the recollection of Christ's sacrifice for us reveals the utter unacceptability of behavior that demeans those who are members of his body. In these and other ways wisdom may be defined by Christ and his cross. The structure of this letter and hints in Paul's writings elsewhere also imply that wisdom is reflected in the rejection of immorality and idolatry and in behavior that brings glory rather than shame on God and his people.

It is not that Paul is introducing a new elitism into the church, dividing it into the spiritually mature and some lower tier of believers. That would be to "shoot himself in the foot" in his fight against Corinthian factionalism. From 1:18 onward he has insisted that there is only one division that counts, between those who are being saved and those who are perishing, those "with the Spirit" (2:15) and those without the Spirit, those in Christ (1:30) and those not. Rather, the distinction between the mature and the immature is not about status but concerns behavior in keeping with that secure and sanctified Christian identity. Paul's readiness to *speak a message of wisdom among the mature* does not betray a reluctance to address all the believers in Corinth. On the contrary, as argued above in connection with the identification of "God's wisdom," 1 Corinthians is itself evidence that he wants them all to accept the wisdom of the cross and Spirit. But a distinction among the Corinthians is clear, in the sense that some accept

17. All three letters use the term "wisdom" at significant junctures.

Paul's instructions and some do not.[18] As 3:1-4 shows, all Christians have the same status, but they show their maturity by their readiness to respond to teaching concerning the implications of "the word of the cross" for life together.

Hebrews 5:11–6:2 contains teaching comparable to that in 1 Corinthians 2:6–3:4. There "the elementary truths of God's word," "milk" (cf. 1 Cor. 3:2), are still being fed to "infants." The "solid food for the mature" is the *message of wisdom* to which Paul refers. Not unlike Paul, the author of Hebrews exhorts his readers: "Therefore let us move beyond the elementary teachings about Christ and be taken forward to *maturity.*" But significantly, the mark of maturity in Hebrews is not mere knowledge; instead, the mature are those "who by constant use have trained themselves to distinguish good from evil." It's not just what they know that distinguishes the mature from infants, but that the mature "use" what they know. Paul likewise expects all believers to become "mature" and to learn and make use of his *message of wisdom* (Col. 1:28). The mature in Corinth are those whose grasp of "Christ as the wisdom of God" (1:30) has enabled them to resist the lure of "the wisdom of the world" (1:20) and who refuse to participate in petty factionalism.

### 2. *Exposition of "Wisdom": Source and Revelation, 2:6b-12*

*(6We do, however, speak a message of wisdom among the mature,) but not the wisdom of this age or of the rulers of this age, who are coming to nothing. 7No, we declare God's wisdom, a mystery that has been hidden and that God destined for our glory before time began. 8None of the rulers of this age understood it, for if they had, they would not have crucified the Lord of glory. 9However, as it is written:*

*"What no eye has seen,*
*what no ear has heard,*
*and what no human mind has conceived —*
*these things God has prepared for those who love him" —*

*10for God has revealed them to us by his Spirit.*

*The Spirit searches all things, even the deep things of God. 11For who knows a person's thoughts except that person's own spirit within? In the same way no one knows the thoughts of God except the Spirit of God. 12We have not received the spirit of the world but the Spirit who is from God, that we may understand what God has freely given us.*

18. Cf. 1 Cor. 14:37: "If any think they are prophets or otherwise gifted by the Spirit, let them acknowledge that what I am writing to you is the Lord's command."

*a. The Source of This Wisdom Is God, 2:6b-7*

**2:6b** The second half of v. 6 underscores the contrast between God's wisdom and the wisdom of the world, which Paul had already stressed in 1:18-25. Here he calls the latter *the wisdom of this age or of the rulers of this age.* Just as earlier human wisdom is under God's judgment, here the rulers who advocate it likewise will *come to nothing.* 1 Corinthians 1:28 uses the same verb, that is, "to nullify" or "bring to nothing."[19] *The rulers of this age,* like "the things that are," are "doomed to come to nothing" (Thiselton). They have no part in the age to come. The Corinthian Christians are part of and destined for the new age. To embrace human wisdom, then, is bad eschatology, for it is an alignment with a party that God opposes and whose fate is set.

Since in v. 8 "the rulers of this age" are responsible for crucifying Christ, many commentators assume that this phrase refers to evil human rulers.[20] However, the biblical and Jewish apocalyptic background sees evil supernatural figures behind such acts against God, and comparable themes are reflected elsewhere in Paul's letters (e.g., Col. 1:26; 2:2, 15; Eph. 3:10; 6:10-12). Further, *rulers*[21] can mean "evil spirits" in the church fathers and New Testament Apocrypha.[22] While it is true that *rulers* in the plural is not used elsewhere in the New Testament for demons, John 12:31, 14:30, and 16:11 do use the term this way in the singular. 2 Corinthians 4:4 confirms that Paul did think of the progress of the gospel as being opposed on a cosmic level. Thus, with Scroggs and Bruce, it is best to take *the rulers of this age* as a reference both to the world's organized opposition to God's wisdom and to the pernicious spiritual forces behind them.

**2:7** Paul explains further that the message of *wisdom* he communicates to, and is received by, discerning believers belongs to *God* and that its nature is a *hidden mystery* now revealed.[23] Paul's other uses of the term "mystery" in 1 Corinthians 15:51, Romans 16:25-26, Colossians 1:26, and Ephesians 3:5-6 (cf. 1 Pet. 1:12) mark it as new revelation unattainable by human reason that consists of a more detailed unfolding of God's plan and purpose in the gospel. "In Jewish apocalyptic literature mystery *(raz)* has an eschatological meaning. It designates the salvific events to be revealed in the age to come."[24] The revelation of the *mystery* was no accident or afterthought, but

19. Gk. καταργέω.

20. Cf., e.g., Mare, Findlay, Godet, Ellicott, Robertson and Plummer, and Fee.

21. Gk. ἀρχόντων.

22. For example, Ignatius, *To the Trallians* 5:2; *To the Smyrnaeans* 6:1; *Acts of John* 114; *Acts of Thomas* 10, 143. Conzelmann and Barrett interpret "the rulers" in 1 Cor. 2:6 as evil spirits.

23. Gk. ἐν μυστηρίῳ, as in TNIV, is tied to "wisdom," describing the form in which the wisdom was given (Robertson and Plummer, Godet, Barrett) rather than to "we speak," in which case it would give the manner of the apostles' speaking (Findlay). Godet is right to argue that for Paul "to speak mysteriously" is not in view, for the mystery is God's and not of human origin.

24. Collins, 115.

foreordained: it was *destined before time began.* Unlike our day, in the ancient world novelty did not impress when it came to the world of ideas. On the contrary, the argument from antiquity, or here, more accurately, eternity, carried enormous weight. Not only for Jews, but also for Greeks and Romans, the more venerable a teaching was, the more credibility it attracted. Paul's point is that *God's wisdom* goes back to the very beginning.

The goal of God's plan was the ultimate good of believers: it was *for our glory.* Instead of sharing the fate of "the rulers of this age," that is, "come to nothing" (2:6b), believers anticipate an altogether better destiny (2 Cor. 3:18; Rom. 8:30; Phil. 3:21). The use of "the Lord of glory" as a title for Christ in v. 9 gives a hint as to the way in which such exaltation is possible; believers expect glory because of their union with the risen and exalted Christ. 1 Corinthians 2:7-8 thus act as a precursor to Paul's argument in chapter 15 where Christ is "the firstfruits of those who have fallen asleep" (15:20) and the link between the destiny of Christ and believers is a constant presupposition.

Daniel gives comparable teaching regarding "wisdom in a mystery." When God reveals the interpretation of Nebuchadnezzar's dream to Daniel, he responds in a prayer that shares language and ideas similar to those of 1 Corinthians 2:6-8, 10-11. In both passages wisdom (Dan. 2:20, 21, 23; 1 Cor. 2:6) from God is associated with a mystery (Dan. 2:19; 1 Cor. 2:7), and both claim that this mystery reaches to the depths: Daniel 2:22: "he reveals deep[25] and hidden things"; 1 Corinthians 2:10: "the Spirit searches all things, even the depths[26] of God."[27] The hiddenness of the mystery continues for all except believers — *for our glory* gives the result for believers only.

### b. *The Revelation of This Wisdom Came to the Apostles and Prophets through the Holy Spirit, 2:8-12*

**2:8** The evil forces of darkness, both cosmic and terrestrial, that is, *the rulers of this age,* did not "understand" God's wisdom.[28] The verb translated *understood* in the TNIV is literally "to know." But as in 1:21, the sense is not that the world did not cognitively grasp the message, but that they did not accept and welcome it personally. Instead they actively opposed the message by crucifying *the Lord of glory.*

This title refers to the grandeur of Christ. It is a qualitative genitive, meaning that he is the Lord who is characterized by glory. The paradoxical notion that the magnificent Lord would be executed in shame sums up the

25. Gk. βαθύς.

26. Gk. βάθος.

27. The similarities, though noteworthy, are not sufficient to regard it as more than a possible echo.

28. The antecedent of the relative pronoun opening v. 8 is "God's wisdom" in v. 7. The sentence contains a second class condition, meaning "if they had known, but they did not!"

foolishness of God's wisdom in the world's eyes, reminding us of 1:22-23. What is left unsaid is the heart of early Christian preaching, in the words of the apostle Peter, that "he was not abandoned to the grave but God raised him to life and exalted him to the right hand of God" (Acts 1:31-32).

**2:9** That Paul is quoting Scripture in 2:9 is suggested by the words, *as it is written.*[29] Nowhere else does he cite anything but the Old Testament using this formula. However, what follows does not match closely any particular text in Greek or Hebrew Bibles. Origen in the third century attributed the quotation to the no-longer-extant *Apocalypse of Elijah,* and a similar quotation turns up in *Gospel of Thomas* 17 as the words of Jesus. In fact, alternative hypotheses include not only that Paul is citing an apocryphal source or Jesus, but also a wisdom tradition and his opponents in Corinth. A range of Old Testament texts have also been proposed as his source. After considering the best candidate for the precursor text to 1 Corinthians 2:9, we will also note an echo of Daniel 2:19-23 in 1 Corinthians 2:6-8, 10-11.

Although we cannot be certain, the suggestion that we are dealing with a loose quotation of Isaiah 64:4 ("from of old no one has heard or perceived by the ear, no eye has seen a God besides you") has much to commend it.[30] Both texts assert that no human being is able to understand the divine revelation without God's enabling. The fact that the references to the ear and eye in Isaiah 64:4 are in reverse order compared to 1 Corinthians 2:9 does not rule out a link between the texts; such alterations were an accepted aspect of citation technique in antiquity.

The Hebrew idiom, "go up onto the heart," which appears in 1 Corinthians 2:9, is not found in Isaiah 64:4 but does occur in the Greek of Isaiah 65:17. This has led some to argue that Paul combines Isaiah 64:4 and Isaiah 65:17 in his citation. However, two differences between Isaiah 65:17 and 1 Corinthians 2:9 weigh against it: whereas the tense of the verb in Isaiah is future, in 1 Corinthians it is aorist; the Isaiah text has "their heart" rather than "the heart of man." Thiselton's conclusion is fair: "The widespread suggestion that Paul combines Isa 64:4 and 65:17, although possible, seems too imprecise for certainty, even if Paul does combine various quotations in a catena or free collection elsewhere (e.g., in Rom. 3:10-18)."[31]

In 2:8-12 Paul discusses the revelation of the wisdom that came to the apostles and prophets through the Holy Spirit. Negatively, it was not known (perceived or grasped) by the rulers of this age (2:8-9). Positively, it was revealed by God through the Spirit to the apostles and prophets who received the Spirit of God (2:10-12).

In its Old Testament context Isaiah 64:4 concerns the uniqueness of God's plan of salvation, which remains hidden. Judgment against God's enemies also appears, as in the plea for divine intervention in 64:1 and the ap-

29. See our comments on the perfect tense "it is written" (γέγραπται) in 1:19.

30. The loose form of citation precludes any discussion of textual differences.

31. Thiselton, 251.

pearance of fire in 64:2 (cf. "to make your name known to your adversaries"). In terms of its early interpretation, a range of Jewish texts associated with Isaiah 64:4 stresses the inability of humanity to understand God's ways and connect it with the stone tradition and the theme of the new creation.[32]

In its new context the text is straightforward with one grammatical exception: semantically, what does the relative pronoun, *"what,"* look back to?[33] While Conzelmann is right that the construction is difficult to unravel, Findlay and Ellicott's suggestion makes sense of the connection; *what* looks back to "we speak" in vv. 6-7, giving the sense: "we speak God's wisdom . . . what no eye has seen. . . ."[34] Thus, in citing this Scripture Paul shows that the wisdom he and other apostles and prophets preach is nothing less than the fullness of God's plan of salvation. With this citation Paul develops further the apocalyptic dimension of divine wisdom. Those who love God understand his salvation as true wisdom. Having affirmed that Paul does teach wisdom among the mature, Isaiah 64:4 reminds us that we relate to God through love and not primarily through wisdom or knowledge: *"these things God has prepared for those who love him."* Those "in the know" are not there by virtue of their own ingenuity; they receive *"what no human mind has conceived."* God prepares things beyond human comprehension for those who are his. As Paul will say in v. 16, "the mature" are not those who boast of their superior mind, but rather those who "have the mind of Christ."

**2:10** The reason Paul and other Christian teachers can declare God's wisdom, "the things he has prepared" for all believers to receive, even though these things are inaccessible to humans, is that they have been *revealed*[35] to them. The word *for* connects this verse with vv. 6, 7, and 9 and introduces the necessary explanation.[36] The Corinthians may have thought

32. Cf. Isa. 65:17; H. H. D. Williams, *The Wisdom of the Wise,* 175-84.

33. The Gk. ἅ is repeated twice in the verse. In TNIV "what" appears three times, since the first occurrence, with *what no eye has seen,* is assumed for *what no ear has heard.*

34. Godet rejects this connection, preferring to supply the verb "to be." The sense would then be: "It [i.e., God's wisdom] is things that no eye has seen." Either way the verse is saying something about the wisdom Paul preaches.

35. The aorist indicative ἀπεκάλυψεν might be construed by some to refer to a specific, once-off action in which God revealed these things to Paul. This, however, places too much weight on the verb, and demonstrates a misunderstanding of the meaning of the aorist. Being perfective in aspect, aorist indicatives simply view an action as a whole. This verb says nothing of the nature by which God revealed things to Paul by his Spirit; it simply tells us that it happened.

36. UBS$^4$ reads δέ (cf. REB, "and"; NIV, AV/KJV, "but"; NRSV, no English equivalent) rather than γάρ (cf. TNIV, NEB, "for") at the beginning of v. 10. The external evidence is not decisive. Metzger, *A Textual Commentary,* 481, prefers δέ, judging γάρ as having "the appearance of being an improvement introduced by copyists." However, Fee, 97, points out that "a copyist would scarcely have deliberately created a text with three *gars* in a row" and "a substitution of a *de* for a *gar* would have been natural and could have been deliberate or accidental." While three γάρ's in succession may have raised a copyist's eyebrow, which perhaps occasioned a correction, it is not unprecedented in Paul's letters (cf. 1 Cor. 3:2-3; 9:16;

that some of their leaders were more insightful than others, and that this explained their superior wisdom. Paul says no, knowledge of God's plan of salvation comes only *by his Spirit*.[37] The "revelation" to which Paul here refers is not the illumination given to all believers, but the disclosure of God's full purposes in the cross and Christ Jesus to the apostolic preachers, which they in turn pass on to those who love him, with the goal that they might become "mature."[38]

This is only the second reference to the "Spirit" in the book (see 2:4) and it introduces a sustained reflection on the Holy Spirit as the essential source of revelation from God. The word appears six times in five verses (2:10-14). As Thiselton and Collins note, this section establishes a framework for later material on the Holy Spirit in the letter in chapters 12–14 and 15:42-57 (cf. 15:12-28, 38-41). Paul's point in all these passages is that "the work of the Spirit remains inseparable from the work of God as revealed in Christ."[39] Thus, as we will see in later verses, to be "spiritual" is not to have some extra light from within or even somehow to be extraordinarily sensitive to the divine, as in much popular use of the term, but to appropriate and live in accordance with God's saving work through Christ by God's Spirit.[40]

A second "for," not translated by TNIV, introduces Paul's explanation as to why this "revelation" by God's Spirit is necessary: "For" *the Spirit searches all things, even the deep things of God*. The Spirit of God "searches out" (Barrett) "the depths of God's purposes" (TEV) rather than "the depths of God's nature" (NEB) or "the depths of God's own self" (Thiselton).[41] The phrase refers to the hidden but now disclosed plan of salvation to which Paul has referred in vv. 7-9. It is not that we do not learn about God through hearing of his plan, but the focus of "God's wisdom" throughout the passage is not his character and attributes in the direct sense, but rather the salvation which he bestows.

The Greek is literally "the depths of God" (NJB, NIV, NRSV), a phrase found in Jewish apocalyptic literature (e.g., *1 Enoch* 63:3; *2 Baruch* 14:8-9; *Testament of Job* 37:6; 1QS xi 18-19).[42] Using the plural, "depths," intensifies the reference. The Spirit has free and full access to this knowledge, and

---

Rom. 1:10-17; 2:11-12). Hence, the reading adopted by TNIV better explains the origin of the other reading.

37. Even though the word αὐτοῦ, "his," is not in the majority of better witnesses (e.g., 𝔓[46], א), as in other languages, such as German, the personal pronoun can be implied in the definite article, in this case in the τοῦ of τοῦ πνεύματος.

38. See on v. 6 for a defense of this view of the referent of the first-person plural pronoun to this point in the passage.

39. Thiselton, 256. Barrett compares John 16:8-15 with 1 Cor. 2:10-16 — both passages present the Spirit as the major agent in bringing the message of salvation.

40. Cf. E. Schweizer, "πνεῦμα," *TDNT* 6:436-37.

41. Gk. τὰ βάθη τοῦ θεοῦ. Paul is not saying that "God himself can be defined as βάθος" (Conzelmann, 66).

42. Wolff, 58-59.

thereby is able to reveal it to the apostolic preachers, who then declare God's wisdom to the mature. This wisdom is not attainable by human beings without the aid of God's Spirit, a point Paul emphasizes throughout the paragraph and explains further in v. 11. Several terms make this point: it is "hidden" and cannot be found, and it is a "mystery" which cannot be solved (2:6-7), reaching to the very "depths of God" (2:10). Once again, the implication of what Paul is saying deals a blow to human pride and underscores "awe and wonder at God's free choice to bestow such favor."[43]

**2:11** Paul supplies a cogent explanation, with a third use of the word *for,* as to how the Spirit of God is qualified to be the agent of revelation to the apostolic group. The type of argument he employs is the logic of minor to major. Just as a person's own spirit has exclusive access to their private thoughts,[44] so it is with *the Spirit of God* and *the thoughts of God.* Only God's Spirit is privy to the profound plan of salvation which has been revealed to the apostles. The *thoughts of God* is literally "the things of God" (AV/KJV). It is a parallel expression to "the depths of God" (v. 10). Again, it is better not to take it primarily as a reference to "what God is" (REB) or "the qualities of God" (NJB), but to "what is truly God's" (NRSV) or, as in TNIV, to "God's thoughts" which are revealed by his Spirit concerning the plan of salvation.[45]

Romans 11:33 is a helpful parallel which also uses the word "depth" and emphasizes that God's "wisdom" is beyond human ken: "Oh, the depth of the riches of the wisdom and knowledge of God! How unsearchable his judgments, and his paths beyond tracing out!" In context, the "riches" to which Paul refers are the question of "the kindness and sternness of God" (Rom. 11:22) in the "mystery" (Rom. 11:25) of his dealings with Israel and the Gentiles in the gospel. Paul goes on to ask rhetorically in Romans 11:34a, "Who has known the mind of the Lord?" a question he also asks in 1 Corinthians 2:15. In connection with our own passage, Paul humbly confesses in 1 Corinthians 2:9 that "no human mind has conceived [of God's wisdom]," before going on to trumpet the grace of God with the stunning affirmation: in the face of our inability to find God, "we have the mind of Christ."

In a world where the search for God is a given, the last clause of this verse is deeply pessimistic and unnerving: *No one knows the thoughts of God.*[46] As Gooch states, "Paul draws a thick and heavy line between things

43. Thiselton, 255.

44. Gk. τίς . . . οἶδεν ἀνθρώπων τὰ τοῦ ἀνθρώπου, literally: "who among human beings knows the things of a human being."

45. The analogy of human and divine spirits should not be pressed too far. Significantly, only the human spirit is said to be "within" a person. There is no suggestion that the Holy Spirit is "in" God. Translating Gk. τὰ τοῦ θεοῦ as "the thoughts of God" makes sense in the light of the words "we have the mind of Christ" in v. 16.

46. Different words are used for the verb "to know" in the two halves of the divine/human analogy that Paul is drawing: No one *knows* a person's thoughts except the person;

human and divine and places the things of God squarely outside the limits of human knowing."[47] When Peter confessed Jesus as the Messiah, Jesus didn't compliment him on his ingenuity, but explained: "this was not revealed to you by flesh and blood, but by my Father in heaven" (Matt. 16:16-17). Notions that we can find God through reason or intuition are cruel and misleading. No sentence in the Bible underscores more emphatically the necessity of divine revelation. In the words of Karl Barth, "God is known through God alone."[48]

**2:12** Having struck such a negative note on the score of knowing "the thoughts of God," Paul contrasts the lot of all believers, those who have the Spirit of God, with those who do not: but *we have not received the spirit of this world but the Spirit who is from God.*[49] The appearance of *we* raises again the question of to whom Paul is referring with this pronoun. To recap, we took "we" in vv. 6 and 7 and "us" in v. 10 to refer to the apostolic preachers (cf. Eph. 3:5-6) and "those who love him" in v. 9 as all believers. The first-person plural pronoun appears again in vv. 12, 13, and 16, and the commentaries are divided (or silent) over precisely whom Paul has in mind on each occasion. The best solution seems to be to understand "we" in v. 13 as another reference to the apostles and prophets/preachers; the same verb "to speak" is used as in vv. 6 and 7. However, "we" in v. 12 is almost certainly a reference to all believers, since Paul regularly defines Christian identity in terms of those who have "received" the "Spirit" (Rom. 8:15; Gal. 3:2; 2 Cor. 11:4).[50] Likewise, *us* in v. 12 refers inclusively to all Christians, with *what God has freely given us* pointing back to "God's wisdom" (vv. 6-7), "the things God has prepared for those who love him" (v. 9). The climactic "we have the mind of Christ" in v. 16 is another reference to all believers, to "those who have the Spirit" (v. 15). In other words, there is an interplay of message/messenger and response throughout the passage.

*The spirit of the world,* whom believers *have not received,* could be a reference to Satan, the spirit who leads people to oppose God (2 Cor. 4:4; Eph. 6:11; John 12:31). In that case, it would reinforce the reference to "the rulers of this age" in vv. 6 and 7 as evil supernatural figures. However, since we rejected such a narrow interpretation in vv. 6 and 7, which is better understood as a reference both to the world's human opposition to God's wis-

---

no one *knows* God's thoughts except God (Gk. οἶδα and γινώσκω respectively). The variation is probably simply stylistic. Whereas Lightfoot suggests that the first refers to direct or immediate knowledge and the second to knowledge that is attained, implying that the knowledge of God is more out of reach than knowledge about humans, in the Hellenistic period the classical distinction between the two words seems to have dissipated.

47. Paul W. Gooch, *Partial Knowledge: Philosophical Studies in Paul* (Notre Dame: University of Notre Dame Press, 1987), 36.

48. K. Barth, *CD,* 2/1, sect. 27, 179 (cited in Thiselton, 258).

49. Gk. ἡμεῖς, "we," is emphatic at the beginning of the verse. And δέ, left untranslated by TNIV, which is a legitimate option (if no other sense is compelling), probably carries a contrastive sense here, "but" (as opposed to "now" [ESV] or "and").

50. Gk. λαμβάνω and πνεῦμα.

dom and to the pernicious spiritual forces behind them, it is more likely here that *the spirit of the world* in v. 12 refers to the spirit of human wisdom that opposes God. Other references to "the world" in 1:20, 21, 27, and 28 support this identification. Paul draws the lines starkly: either you have a spirit which is oriented toward human pride and wisdom, that is, eloquence and reason independent of God, or you have God's Spirit.

The purpose[51] of receiving *the Spirit who is from God,*[52] a phrase emphasizing his very different origin from that of the spirit of the world, is that *we* as believers might "know"[53] the things that *God has freely given us.* The same verb "to know" is used as in v. 11a; believers now "know" the gift of salvation in Christ in the same direct and immediate sense as someone "knows" their private thoughts; such is their confidence and assurance. No wonder that in v. 7 Paul labeled the reception of "God's wisdom" glorious. If we were to ask for a list of the benefits of God's beneficence to which Paul is pointing in v. 12b, Godet believes that 1:30 is a good summary: "Christ Jesus," our "wisdom from God," namely, "righteousness, sanctification and redemption." *What God has freely given us* is salvation, a new state and status before God.

### 3. *Exposition of "We Speak": Words of the Spirit, 2:13*

> [13]*This is what we speak, not in words taught us by human wisdom but in words taught by the Spirit, explaining spiritual realities with Spirit-taught words.*

**2:13** In the introduction to this section we argued that the theme of 2:6-16 is "we speak a message of wisdom among the mature" (2:6a). If 2:6b-12 expounds the source and revelation of God's "wisdom," v. 13 focuses on the apostolic activity of "speaking" this message. Paul explains first, negatively, that the communication of this wisdom is not with words from human wisdom (2:13a), and second, positively, that rather it is with words from the Spirit (2:13b).

The apostles and prophets/preachers *speak*[54] "what God has freely given" all believers (2:12b), namely, the full wisdom of God expressed in Christ crucified, *in words not taught by human wisdom.* That such preachers

51. Gk. ἵνα.

52. Gk. τὸ πνεῦμα τὸ ἐκ τοῦ θεοῦ. Cf. Thiselton, 261: "the Spirit who issues from God."

53. TNIV's "understand" is accurate but a little weak, and it obscures the connection between v. 12 and v. 11.

54. Verses 13-16 once again employ present indicatives, which express their imperfective aspect through gnomic (or in some cases customary) descriptions: "we speak these things"; "natural man does not welcome what comes from God's Spirit"; "it is foolishness to him"; "he is not able to know it"; "the spiritual man evaluates everything"; "he is not evaluated by anyone"; "we have the mind of Christ."

communicate God's wisdom not in words judged by human standards to be wise, "in learned discourse" (Héring), recalls Paul argument in 1:18–2:5. As Paul says in 2:4, "my message and my preaching were not with wise and persuasive words" (cf. 1:17-18). Since in 2:6–3:5 Paul is giving a positive take on the wisdom of the cross and the Spirit, in 2:13 a negative reference to "wisdom" has to be qualified as "human wisdom" to avoid the possible misunderstanding that he is talking about God's wisdom. Another difference is that the expression in 2:13, *words taught by human wisdom,* refers not so much to the style of delivery, the emphasis of 1:17-18 and 2:4, but to the source of the content of the message. The apostolic band *speaks words taught by the Spirit,*[55] which is not surprising given Paul's insistence that the "thoughts of God" can be accessed only by his Spirit (v. 11).

The concluding clause in v. 13 is difficult to translate. The main issues to be resolved are whether the participle *explaining*[56] means "interpreting," "comparing," or "combining," and whether the word "spiritual"[57] (TNIV, *Spirit-taught words*) is neuter (spiritual things) or masculine (spiritual people). Robertson and Plummer lay out the main options.[58] The first two take the substantival adjective as neuter, the last two as masculine. Either the apostolic preachers: (1) combine spiritual things (words) with spiritual things (subject matter); (2) interpret or explain spiritual truth in spiritual language; (3) match (or combine) spiritual matters to spiritual hearers; or (4) interpret spiritual truths to spiritual hearers. In terms of the teaching of the unit overall, the differences are only a matter of nuance. Leaving aside 2:13b, 1 Corinthians 2:6-16 affirms elsewhere that the source of the message Paul speaks is wisdom from God in words of the Spirit to those who are spiritual. Adjudicating between the four alternative interpretations is quite difficult. Paul uses "spiritual" as both a neuter (cf. 1 Cor. 9:11; 10:4; 12:1; 14:1; 15:44) and as a masculine (cf. 1 Cor. 2:15; 3:1; 14:37; cf. Gal. 6:1; Eph. 6:12) substantival adjective. And the verb "to explain" means "to compare" in 2 Corinthians 10:12, "to combine" in general classical usage, and "to interpret" in various LXX texts. Since the lexical data are not decisive, the most plausible rendering depends on the flow of Paul's argument.

While TNIV's *explaining spiritual realities with Spirit-taught words* (a variation of view 2 above) is possible, the fourth view seems to fit best. The references to "the spiritual" which immediately follow 2:13 are masculine, translated as "the person with the Spirit" in 2:15 and "spiritual" (persons) in 3:1. The verb in question is used in the LXX to mean "interpret" (Gen. 40:8, 22; 41:12; Judg. 7:15; Dan. 5:8, 12; cf. *Joseph and Aseneth* 4:10) in the sense of unlocking spiritual truth revealed by God to another person.[59] The

55. Gk. σοφίας and πνεύματος are genitives dependent on διδακτοῖς (Findlay and Godet).

56. Gk. συγκρίνειν.

57. Gk. πνευματικοῖς.

58. Robertson and Plummer, 47; cf. Thiselton, 265; Merklein, 240.

59. Garland, 100.

objection that the Old Testament references almost all refer to interpreting dreams[60] misses the point; the common element both in the Old Testament and in 1 Corinthians is the presence of inaccessible revelation from God that requires explanation, in the Old Testament a dream, in 1 Corinthians "hidden wisdom." Thus, in 2:13b Paul is probably saying that the apostolic preachers speak the message in *words taught by the Spirit* by "interpreting[61] spiritual things to those who are spiritual" (NRSV).

But who are "those who are spiritual"? An identification cannot be made without also defining "the person without the Spirit" (2:14), "the worldly" (3:1, 3), and "infants in Christ" (3:1).

### 4. *Exposition of "the Mature": The Spiritual Person, 2:14-16*

*[14]The person without the Spirit does not accept the things that come from the Spirit of God but considers them foolishness, and cannot understand them because they are discerned only through the Spirit. [15]The person with the Spirit makes judgments about all things, but such a person is not subject to merely human judgments, [16]for,*

*"Who has known the mind of the Lord*
*so as to instruct him?"*

*But we have the mind of Christ.*

#### a. *The Reception of This Wisdom Is Not Possible for the Person without the Spirit, 2:14*

**2:14** With 2:14–3:4 Paul completes his reflections on his statement in 2:6a: "but (in contrast to human wisdom) we (Paul and the apostles, prophets/preachers in Corinth) speak (or declare) wisdom (the fullness of the gospel of Christ crucified) among the mature (discerning, experienced Christians)." Having pondered God's "wisdom" in 2:6b-12 and the nature of its communication by the apostolic band in 2:13, Paul turns to explain what he means by "we speak wisdom among *the mature.*" The thrust of Paul's remarks is that he wants all of the Corinthians to be "taken forward to maturity" (Heb. 6:1).

The main challenge of interpretation in these verses is working out "who's who." In talking to the Corinthians about "maturity" Paul refers to a further five groups: (1) "those who are spiritual" in 2:13, 15 and 3:1; (2) "the person without the Spirit" (TNIV) or "the unspiritual man" (RSV; NRSV: "those who are unspiritual"), literally "the natural man"[62] (NASB)

60. Lightfoot, 181; Robertson and Plummer, 47.
61. συγκρίνοντες is a participle of manner or means.
62. Gk. ψυχικὸς ἄνθρωπος.

in 2:14; (3) the "worldly" (TNIV), "men of the flesh" (RSV), or the "carnal" (NASB) in 3:1; (4) "infants in Christ" in 3:1; and (5) "the worldly" in 3:3 (using a slightly different Greek word from the one in 3:1). A satisfactory exposition depends on defining these terms clearly. A preview of the section's main characters is a helpful orientation to the passage. "Those who are spiritual" is a reference to all believers; if not all Christians are "mature," all have the conditions for such growth, thanks to the Spirit.[63] "The person without the Spirit" refers to non-Christians. "The worldly" in 3:1 refers to those made of "flesh," who are part and parcel of fallen humanity from Adam and so vulnerable to sin. "Infants in Christ" are new Christians, those who have the Spirit and thus a capacity for welcoming spiritual truth and experiencing growth but as yet limited experience of it. And "the worldly" in 3:3 are those who belong to the "flesh," that is, people who are not only part and parcel of fallen humanity but also continue to live according to its ways.

In v. 14, Paul puts the spiritual person side by side with the natural person:[64] But, in contrast to those who are spiritual, the natural person (i.e., *the person without the Spirit*) does not welcome[65] (an understatement explained by the remainder of v. 14) *the things that come from the Spirit of God* (i.e., God's full wisdom in planning and providing redemption through Christ crucified and its implications for living). The reason for this rejection is that such a person judges this message to be *foolishness.*[66] *The person without the Spirit* is volitionally prejudiced against it, and rejects it in unbelief. In fact, in as negative a statement as you can find in Paul's letters about the human condition outside of Christ, he says that the person left to their own "natural" devices "is not able[67] to know them," that is, to respond positively to the things of the Spirit.[68] In this regard, the "natural person," someone belonging to this age and not the age to come, resembles "the rulers of this age," who in 2:8 also failed to "know" or "understand" the cross.[69] The reason for this inability is that *the things that*

63. As noted in comments on 2:12, Paul regularly defines Christian identity in terms of those who have received the Spirit. Sometimes it is argued that Paul uses πνευματικός with reference to mature and discerning Christians (as perhaps in Gal. 6:1). Here, however, as BDAG observes, clearly the term is used in contrast to the natural man (ψυχικὸς ἄνθρωπος) in 2:14.

64. Cf. Gk. δέ at the beginning of the verse.

65. "Does not welcome" represents a present indicative verb (οὐ δέχεται τὰ τοῦ πνεύματος τοῦ θεοῦ· μωρία γὰρ αὐτῷ ἐστιν καὶ οὐ δύναται), the imperfective aspect of which (in light of the context, which suggests that the nature of spiritual or unspiritual people consistently dictates whether they respond one way or the other) is expressing a gnomic idea here, how things always happen, given their very nature (see Campbell, *Basics of Verbal Aspect in Biblical Greek*, 65).

66. Gk. μωρία. Cf. the comments at 1:18, 21, and 23.

67. Another present tense verb (δύναται) with its imperfective aspect expressing a gnomic idea (a statement of a general, universal fact).

68. Cf. the almost incidental sentiment of Jesus: "you, being evil" (Matt. 7:11).

69. The same verb is used in both verses and translated "to understand."

come from the Spirit *of God* are *discerned* or "inquired into"[70] only by the aid of the Holy Spirit, whom "the natural person" does not have. The word Paul uses means only "examine" when used of people (as the direct object), but means "inquire into" or "ask questions about" when used with impersonal objects. In this context (2:9-16) Paul speaks of people's ability (or lack of ability) to understand, comprehend, or know God's thoughts. In 2:10 he says that the Spirit "makes a careful or thorough effort to learn" all things, even the depths of God. It is the Spirit who knows God's thoughts (v. 11) and who was given to believers so that they might know the things God has freely given them (v. 12), things that can be known only by those who have the mind of Christ (v. 16). In light of the context and the use of the Greek verb in question, it seems Paul's idea is that the Spirit serves as a special resource to believers, who may take their questions and concerns to God. The "spiritual person" is in a position to inquire into all things and find prophetic insight from God in connection with the wisdom of the cross.

On the other hand, *the person without the Spirit of God* is like a child incapable of communicating with a parent, unable to understand the parent's mind or intentions. "The natural" person, then, is the person who belongs exclusively to the realm of their natural life and heritage from Adam, a "mere human being" (3:4). They "do not think it worthwhile to retain the knowledge of God" (Rom. 1:28a). Jude 19 describes the possible effect of such people in the church: "These are people who divide you, who follow mere natural instincts[71] and do not have the Spirit." Nonetheless, Paul's purpose is not to accuse the Corinthians of not having the Spirit, but, as will emerge in 3:1-4, as living as if they do not have the Spirit.

### *b. The Reception of This Wisdom Is Possible for the Person with the Spirit, 2:15-16*

**2:15** Before accusing the Corinthians of worldly conduct in 3:1-4, Paul must explain further what he means by "spirituality." In contrast to the undiscerning "person without the Spirit" (v. 14),[72] "the spiritual person" *makes judgments about* (or, rather, "inquires into," the same verb as in v. 14) *all things.* In context, the *all things* that those who are spiritual inquire into are God's ways that were formerly hidden.[73] Unlike the natural person, the person with the Spirit is able to bring his or her questions and challenges to God by the Spirit and discover how the wisdom of the cross applies to his/her situation. Verse 15a is thus v. 14b in reverse.

70. Gk. ἀνακρίνεται. For the lexical basis of the following interpretation, see Roy E. Ciampa, "Examining the Scriptures"? The Meaning of ἀνακρίνοντες τὰς γραφάς in Acts 17:11," *JBL* 130 (2011) (forthcoming).

71. Gk. ψυχικοί.

72. Cf. Gk. δέ at the beginning of the verse.

73. Fee, 118.

Those who are spiritual, Paul says, are *not subject to merely human judgments.* The verb in question is repeated for the third time in two verses, but this third time Paul plays on the difference between the meanings of the verb with personal and impersonal object ("to examine or interrogate" versus "to inquire into"). The spiritual person is not ultimately subject to merely human judgments since, as the end of v. 14 indicates, spiritual things (and spiritual people) are understood only via the Spirit, which the things/people of the world lack. Verse 15b is not Paul's exempting those who are spiritual from being examined by others but a way of reinforcing the argument of 1:18–2:5. Paul is placing "the spiritual" beyond the reach of the assessments of "the wisdom of the world" (1:20). The Corinthians had been examining Paul using such measures, and many of them found him wanting. Those who are spiritual are not examined by the world's false wisdom.

**2:16** Having declared that the apostles' band and those who are spiritual have received God's wisdom by the Spirit of God (2:10-11), Paul then explains the relationship the Spirit has to him and to others in 2:12–3:4. In 2:16 he quotes a question from Isaiah 40:13, "Who has known the mind of the Lord?"[74] Paul's unexpected answer in the same verse is that "we have the mind of Christ."

Paul's discussion of wisdom in 2:6-16 is not philosophical but apocalyptic in character. Derived from Old Testament and Jewish traditions, and in keeping with his use of other Old Testament texts elsewhere in chapters 1–4, Paul speaks of "this age," a "hidden mystery" "decreed before the ages," and a "glory" that is "revealed." As Hays notes, "Paul was trying to remake the minds of his readers by teaching them to interpret their lives in light of an eschatologically interpreted Scripture."[75] His quotation of Isaiah 40:13 is another link in the chain of this strategy.

One of several rhetorical questions in 40:12-14, Isaiah 40:13 expects the answer, "No one." Isaiah 40:15-17 stresses further the gulf between humans and God: even "the nations are like a drop in the bucket." In context, the "spirit of the Lord" which no one can know is God's plan of salvation (Isa. 11:2; 40:7; 59:19; 63:14). Likewise, no one is qualified to be God's "counselor" (Isa. 11:2; 19:3; 30:1). Isaiah 40 itself concerns God's intention to deliver his people, as 40:1-11 indicate. As Williams observes, 40:13a could be paraphrased, "Who is able to comprehend the salvific plan of God?"[76] Another dimension to the "spirit of the LORD" in Isaiah is its asso-

74. MT: "Who has measured the spirit of the LORD? Or what man shows him his counsel?" LXX: "Who has known the mind of the Lord? And who has become his advisor so as to instruct him?" The MT and LXX differ significantly only in regard to the verbs "to measure"/"to know" and the "spirit" (רוּחַ/*rûaḥ*)/"mind" (νοῦς). 1 Cor. 2:16 begins exactly as the LXX, with the addition of "for," but omits the middle clause. The change from "spirit" to "mind" is explicable in Paul's case since the two are virtual synonyms in 1 Cor. 2:10-15.

75. Hays, *The Conversion of the Imagination,* 407.

76. H. H. D. Williams, *The Wisdom of the Wise,* 214.

ciation with the figure of the servant who acts as God's agent in salvation (42:1; 48:16; 61:1; 63:10).

The use of the text in early Jewish literature anticipates Paul's use in a number of ways.[77] The Spirit of the Lord is connected with the mind of the Lord not only in the LXX but also in Wisdom of Solomon 9:13, 17. Furthermore, the link to God's plan of salvation is clear in various texts from Qumran which emphasize human inability to grasp God's spirit, mind, and ways. Other texts indicate that there is a group, effectively a remnant, who due to divine intervention do indeed grasp his plan of deliverance (e.g., Qumran, *2 Baruch, 1 Enoch, 4 Ezra*). All of this makes Paul's choice of the text from Isaiah 40 apt indeed.

Introduced with the conjunction "for,"[78] the question and answer conclude 2:12-16 on a positive note. That the citation leads into 3:1-4 is indicated by the words "and I"[79] at the beginning of 3:1. Paul's use of the Isaiah text clarifies a number of puzzling features of the passage. Paul's audacious claim that we have the mind of Christ represents a biting, ironic twist against the Corinthian elitists. His identification of Christ with the "spirit"/"mind" of Isaiah 40:13 is explicable in the light of its connection in Isaiah with the servant. Paul is not asserting his possession of a spiritual insight above his fellow Christians. The wisdom of which he speaks is not exclusive or esoteric but nothing more or less than the fullness of the message of the cross and the salvation it wrought, which, though available to all Christians, needs to be appropriated in order to deal with "fleshly" behavior like the divisiveness, immorality, and idolatry which are plaguing the church in Corinth.

The disjunction between the time of Isaiah and Paul is underscored in the stunning final assertion of v. 16b. *"Who has known the mind of the Lord?"* The anticipated answer is,"No one." Yet Paul follows the question with the answer, *But we have the mind of Christ. Mind* here is "not an instrument of thought" but "a mode of thought" or "mind-set."[80] The *mind of Christ,* then, is God's profound wisdom regarding salvation through a crucified Messiah which was hidden but is now revealed by the Holy Spirit. In keeping with earlier uses of the first-person plural pronoun in such statements, *we* here does refer to the apostles specifically, but also to others who are spiritual, for they receive the message of God's wisdom (2:6).

The change from "Lord" to "Christ" is a subtle indication that Paul sees himself and the Corinthians living in the messianic age of fulfillment. As Jewett puts it, "the change of expression from 'Lord' in 16a to 'Christ' in 16b binds the true divine wisdom to the crucified Christ."[81] The Spirit does

77. H. H. D. Williams, *The Wisdom of the Wise*, 216-25.

78. Gk. γάρ.

79. Gk. κἀγώ.

80. Thiselton, 275; Weiss, 68.

81. Robert Jewett, *Paul's Anthropological Terms: A Study of Their Use in Conflict Settings* (Leiden: Brill, 1971), 377.

not impart wisdom out of thin air, for the Spirit and the cross go together. The mind of Christ is not exercised by thinking about nothing. Rather, those who are spiritual habitually turn to the cross (2:8), as Paul did in the face of divisions in Corinth in 1:18–2:5. For the cross is where we find Christ's mind-set on such behavior.

### 5. *Rebuke for Immaturity: The Worldliness of the Corinthians, 3:1-4*

*[1]Brothers and sisters, I could not address you as spiritual but as worldly — mere infants in Christ. [2]I gave you milk, not solid food, for you were not yet ready for it. Indeed, you are still not ready. [3]You are still worldly. For since there is jealousy and quarreling among you, are you not worldly? Are you not acting like mere human beings? [4]For when one says, "I follow Paul," and another, "I follow Apollos," are you not mere human beings?*

**3:1-2** 1 Corinthians 3:1-4 closes Paul's positive treatment of the wisdom of the cross and the Spirit (2:6–3:4) with a confrontational accusation. The Corinthians had measured Paul against the bar of human wisdom and found him wanting. Paul's response is not only to debunk human wisdom (1:18–2:5) but to insist that he and the other Christian teachers in Corinth do in fact "declare wisdom." The problem is that only those who are spiritual are open to receiving it.

The apostle has described two classes of people, "natural" and "spiritual." But when he comes to apply what he has said about the reception of spiritual things, God's truth and wisdom, to the Corinthians, he does not address them as "natural," "those without the Spirit" (2:14), because, as "saints" (1:2) and *brothers and sisters* (3:1), they do have the Spirit. But they are not spiritual (3:1), for, he charges, they are "worldly" (3:1, 3). So at 3:1 he switches from (gnomic) present tense verbs to aorist and imperfect verbs and describes another category among those who have the indwelling Holy Spirit, which has two parts to it: (1) the *worldly* (3:1), literally those made of flesh,[82] that is, weak or baby Christians — those unaccustomed to walking in the Spirit; and (2) the "worldly" (3:3), literally those belonging to the flesh,[83] willfully rebellious Christians — those not in step with the

82. Gk. σαρκινοί.

83. Gk. σαρκικοί. Garland, 109, points out that many (including Conzelmann, 72; Schrage, 1:281-82; Wolff, 64 n. 228; Collins, 143-44) "contend that the adjectives σαρκικός and σάρκινος are essentially synonymous," while others (including Fee, 124, Witherington, 131-32; cf. Moulton-Howard-Turner 2:378) "argue that σάρκινος in 3:1 emphasizes the finitude and physical side of their existence versus the spiritual, while σαρκικός has negative ethical overtones." He points out that generally, "The -ινος suffix connotes 'made of' (cf. 2 Cor. 3:3), while the -ικος suffix connotes 'characterized by' (cf. 9:11)." BDAG points out that according to Justin and Tatian "σαρκικός means 'belonging to the σάρξ [flesh]' [opp. πνευματικός], 'fleshly'; on the other hand, σάρκινος is 'consisting/composed of flesh', 'fleshy,'" but that

Spirit, who thus prolong spiritual babyhood and invite God's fatherly discipline. As Garland points out, Paul's description of the Corinthians here is "highly ironic in a congregation that touted and prized its spiritual giftedness.[84]

An expanded paraphrase may help clarify how Paul regards the Corinthians. Paul chides them:

> "*Brothers and sisters,* in looking at your situation I must make an additional distinction to that between the natural and the spiritual (2:14-15). At the time of my initial work among you several years ago, the time of your conversion and baby Christian status, *I could not address you as* spiritually mature people,[85] but I was able to speak only as I would speak to those made of flesh, to *worldly* people, that is, as I would speak to *mere infants in Christ,*[86] as those who have the Spirit and thus a capacity for welcoming spiritual truth and experiencing spiritual growth but as yet having limited experience of it. At that time and for that stage *I gave you milk to drink,* food for babies, that is, elementary spiritual truth for baby Christians. When I was with you those eighteen months (Acts 18:11), I did not give you solid food, food for adults, that is, the wisdom of God (cf. 1 Cor. 2:6-7), that is, deeper spiritual truth for mature Christians. This was because *you were not yet ready* for solid food. But now some four or five years later *you are still not ready*!"

**3:3-4** Paul's basic accusation against the Corinthians is that in acting divisively they behave as if they belong to "this age" and as if they do not have the Spirit. In other words, they live as if they were no different from anyone else in Corinth, or, to borrow a phrase from 1 Corinthians 15:22, as if they were in Adam instead of in Christ. Paul wrote the letter to remind

---

such a distinction is not consistently reflected in the literature or the textual traditions: "The forms are generally interchanged in the tradition." While BDAG assigns the same two meanings to each word: "pert[aining] to being material or belonging to the physical realm, *material, physical, human, fleshly*" and "pert[aining] to being human at a disappointing level of behavior or characteristics, *(merely) human,*" it applies the first meaning to v. 1 and the second to v. 2. Garland, 109, follows Thiselton, 289, 292, in suggesting that "[i]n contrast to the adjectives *psychikos,* which describes the unrenewed person, and *sarkinos* (fleshy), which describes the person motivated by natural drives (fallen human nature), the adjective *sarkikos* (fleshly) is a theological evaluation that describes the person who is centered on the self."

84. Garland, 109.

85. The verb "to speak" (λαλέω; translated *address* in TNIV) links this verse back to 2:6, the beginning of the section, and confirms that "the spiritual" and "the mature" are the same group: in 2:6 Paul *speaks* wisdom among the mature; in 2:13 he *speaks* what God has freely given us, that is, wisdom, interpreting spiritual truth to spiritual people; and in 3:1 he was not able to *speak* to the Corinthians as spiritual people.

86. *Infants in Christ* are those who are spiritually immature, i.e., unaccustomed to walking in the Spirit (cf. Heb. 5:14), but growth to maturity is anticipated; thus Paul does not find fault with this nor reproach them for it.

them of their sanctified status before God and their unique identity as those belonging to the new age. He urges them to live a life worthy of this calling, to be part of God's eschatological plan to be glorified among the Gentiles (cf. the allusion to Mal. 1:11 in 1 Cor. 1:2).

In Paul's view the Corinthians are not ready for him to tell them "God's wisdom" (2:6-7) because they *are still worldly,* "belonging to the flesh."[87] In other words, they are people who are not only part and parcel of fallen humanity but also continue to live according to its pattern of life. They are still spiritual infants, when they ought by now to be spiritually mature. No one blames a baby for being immature. But Paul thinks the Corinthians have had long enough to stop behaving in an infantile manner.

Proof of their worldliness,[88] Paul says, can be seen in the fact that *there is jealousy and quarreling among you,* characterizing their corporate life. Galatians 5:13-26 is a kindred text to 1 Corinthians 2:10–3:4. Both pit the work of the Spirit against that of "the flesh" (translated "the sinful nature" in TNIV). The "works of the flesh" in Galatians 5:19-21 give a good indication as to what Paul meant by "worldly" behavior. The list includes not only "jealousy" and "quarreling,"[89] but also "selfish ambition, dissensions, factions and envy." In fact, of the fifteen items in the Galatians 5 vice list, at least six have to do with divisions.

Paul faults the Corinthian Christians for being no different from anyone else in Corinth: *you* [plural] *act like mere human beings.*[90] Paul makes this accusation three times in vv. 3-4. It opens v. 3, and the end of v. 4 repeats it in the form of a question expecting a positive response:[91] *Are you not mere human beings?* Since Paul's gospel is not "according to a man" (Gal. 1:11; TNIV: "of human origin"),[92] the lifestyle that it produces should not be either.

Verse 3b is, literally, "Don't you walk (just) like a human being?" "Walking" was a common and apt Jewish figure for daily conduct. In Galatians 5:16, 25 the solution to "indulging the flesh" is to "walk by the Spirit." Paul's complementary emphasis in 1 Corinthians 2:6–3:4 is "spiritual maturity" based on the wisdom of the cross and the new age it inaugurates.

The accusation of "worldliness" or "being governed by the flesh" in 3:3 applies to more than just the divisions in Corinth. It has prominence as the first direct word of correction from Paul and hangs ominously over the

87. Cf. Robertson and Plummer, 54, who translate σαρκικοί as "conformable to and governed by the flesh."

88. Cf. explanatory γάρ and the final question — are you not worldly? — which expects a positive answer (cf. οὐχί).

89. Gk. ζῆλος and ἔρις. In Gal. 5:21 they are translated "jealousy" and "discord" respectively. A possible distinction between the two might be that jealousy is an inward attitude and strife or discord an outward expression.

90. Cf. 15:32, where Paul accuses the Corinthians of acting as if there is no resurrection, another similarity to pagan beliefs and behavior.

91. Cf. Gk. οὐκ.

92. Both 1 Cor. 3:3 and Gal. 1:11 have κατὰ ἄνθρωπον.

rest of the letter. Corinthian problems with sexual immorality (see 1 Cor. 4:18–7:40), idolatry (see 1 Cor. 8:1–14:40), and greed (see 6:1-11) also mark them out as acting no differently from those in Corinth who do not know God. Interestingly, the "works of the flesh" in Galatians 5:19-21 include "sexual immorality, impurity, debauchery, orgies" and "idolatry." Similarly, "the world," according to 1 John 2:16, consists of "the lusts of the flesh, the lust of the eyes, and the boastful pride of life." As with Paul, John's solution to such faults is to bolster his readers' eschatology: "the world and its desires pass away. . . . this is the last hour" (1 John 2:17-18).

Nonetheless, the problem at hand is Corinthian factionalism. Paul drives home his point with another reference to two of the three Corinthian slogans he quoted in 1:12: *one says, "I follow Paul," and another, "I follow Apollos."* As we argued in the comments on 1:12, the fact that this verse concentrates on Paul and Apollos, and does not mention Peter, suggests that the followers of Apollos were more of a problem than those who protested loyalty to Peter. 1 Corinthians 4:6 supports this supposition: "I have applied these things to myself and Apollos for your benefit." Whatever the exact shape of Corinthian divisions, Paul judges them unbecoming of those who have the Spirit and belong to the age to come.

## D. Reflections on the Nature of Christian Leadership, 3:5–4:17

If in 1:18–3:4 Paul blames Corinthian factionalism on their failure to reflect on the entailments of the gospel of a crucified Messiah, in 3:5–4:17 he adds that they had not truly grasped the nature of Christian leadership.

### *1. Metaphors for the Church and Its Leaders: God's Garden Temple, 3:5-23*

The next step in Paul's response to Corinthian factionalism is to confront directly their allegiances to particular leaders. The unit ends with a startling coup de grâce, in which Paul reverses the Corinthians' claim that they belong to particular leaders; if anything, it is the other way around: the leaders belong to the Corinthians; "Paul or Apollos or Cephas . . . all are yours" (3:22 RSV)! However, Paul's final word, and main point throughout the unit, made in various ways, is that the only legitimate allegiance for members of the church is to God and Christ: "you belong to Christ, and Christ belongs to God" (3:23 TEV).

This unit is the longest discussion in the New Testament of how the leaders of the church and its members relate to each other. In it Paul attempts to renew the Corinthians' minds in order to transform their behavior away from its unthinking conformity to the prevailing pattern of relations between leaders and followers in secular Corinth. In this sense,

1 Corinthians 3:4 sets the tone for the unit with the accusation that in glamorizing (or demeaning) their ministers, the Corinthians are acting like "mere human beings" and "conforming to the pattern of this world" (Rom. 12:2). Two main points are made throughout the section. First, as mere servants of Christ, Christian leaders must not be accorded an allegiance appropriate to God alone. And, secondly, in caring for his church God holds its leaders accountable for how they build it.[1]

### *a. The Corinthians Are God's Cultivated Field, 3:5-9*

*5What, after all, is Apollos? And what is Paul? Only servants, through whom you came to believe — as the Lord has assigned to each his task. 6I planted the seed, Apollos watered it, but God has been making it grow. 7So neither the one who plants nor the one who waters is anything, but only God, who makes things grow. 8The one who plants and the one who waters have one purpose, and they will each be rewarded according to their own labor. 9For we are God's co-workers; you are God's field, God's building.*

In 3:5-9 Paul deals with the preoccupation of the Corinthians with specific leaders using an agricultural image. In terms of the Old Testament roots of Paul's use of this imagery, Hays and Williams have detected an echo here of Isaiah 5:1-7, a prominent text in early Jewish interpretation of Scripture. The features wherein the two passages overlap include the planting as the people of God, God's role as the chief worker and owner of the vineyard/field, the relative unimportance of human workers and their role as mediators, and the notion of inappropriate fruit. In particular, like 1 Corinthians 3:5-9, Isaiah 5:2 mixes building and planting metaphors (cf. Jer. 18:9; 24:6; Ezek. 36:9-10).

The main challenge for the interpretation of this passage is the question of how to understand the metaphorical language. The same is true for 1 Corinthians 3:10-17 and 12:12-27, where the church is compared to a temple and a body respectively. In the case at hand, Paul compares the Corinthians and their leaders to a cultivated field and its servant workers. Richard B. Hays's definition of a metaphor points the way for understanding such a comparison: "Metaphors are incongruous conjunctions of two images — or two semantic fields — that turn out, upon reflection, to be like one another in ways not ordinarily recognized. They shock us into thought by positing unexpected analogies."[2] If the trick is to discern the similarities

1. D. A. Carson, *The Cross and Christian Ministry* (Grand Rapids: Baker, 1993), 75.

2. Richard B. Hays, *The Moral Vision of the New Testament* (San Francisco: HarperSanFrancisco, 1996), 300. Cf. Eva Feder Kittay, *Metaphor: Its Cognitive Force and Linguistic Structure* (Clarendon Library of Logic and Philosophy; Oxford: Oxford University Press, 1987), 324, who describes the new understanding gained by the unexpected association inherent in a metaphor as a rearranging of the furniture of the mind. "A metaphor is that figure of speech whereby we speak about one thing in terms which are seen to be suggestive of an-

the comparison is drawing upon, the danger is overinterpretation. As Steven J. Kraftchick observes, "metaphor is not an isomorphic mapping of all relationships within one field to another, but a highlighting of some and suppression of others."[3] In all likelihood, the author is only drawing on a small range of possible resemblances.

Garland, following a majority of commentators, suggests that the image in 3:5-9 makes several points, including (1) the interdependence and (2) indispensability of the laborers, (3) the absurdity of rivalry between them, and (4) the absolute necessity of God as the life force of the church.[4] While all of these connections are plausible in general terms, only the first, third, and fourth are supported by Paul's use of the image in the passage. If anything, v. 7a pronounces the servants to be entirely dispensable: "neither the one who plants nor the one who waters is anything."

Along with conveying something that can be communicated in nonmetaphorical language, metaphors carry an affective impact and create a mood and tone for the passage. They cue the reader as to how to feel as much as what to think. The base character of the image, with unskilled farm laborers and a common field, impresses upon the readers the unimpressive and menial nature of the work of Christian ministers and adds weight to Paul's case "not to boast about human leaders" (3:21).

The thrust of the paragraph is evident in four parallel statements in which Paul attempts to shift the Corinthians' focus from their leaders, to whom they claim to belong, to God, to whom they really belong. Using the analogy of the church as a garden with servants, Paul points out that it makes no sense to venerate your favorite minister because (1) they are just serving God, who assigned them their tasks, v. 5; (2) it is God who causes the church to grow, v. 6; (3) in comparison with God, who gives the growth, church leaders are nothing, v. 7; and (4) God, not the Corinthians, is the one who assesses the workers and gives them the appropriate reward for their toil, v. 8.[5] Verse 9 caps off the argument: with respect to how to regard ministers and the church, the critical thing to remember is that both belong to God. God is the one who is to be "all in all" (15:28), not some human leader (who is nothing by comparison). The doctrine of church and ministers that the paragraph espouses could hardly be more theocentric.

---

other" (Janet Martin Soskice, *Metaphor and Religious Language* [Oxford: Clarendon, 1985], 15). Put another way, it is "a form of language use with a unity of subject-matter and which yet draws upon two (or more) sets of associations" (Soskice, 49). Cf. George Lakoff and Mark Johnson, *Metaphors We Live By* (2d ed.; Chicago: University of Chicago Press, 2003), 5: the function of metaphor concerns "understanding and experiencing one kind of thing in terms of another kind of thing."

3. Steven J. Kraftchick, "A Necessary Detour: Paul's Metaphorical Understanding of the Philippian Hymn," *HBT* 15.1 (1993), 23.

4. Garland, 111-12.

5. Cf. David W. Kuck, *Judgment and Community Conflict: Paul's Use of Apocalyptic Judgment Language in 1 Corinthians 3:5–4:5* (NovTSup 66; Leiden: Brill, 1992), 164.

**3:5** Having repeated the factional slogans in 3:4, which Paul claimed in 1:12 had been reported to him, Paul exposes the senselessness of Corinthian allegiance to particular Christian leaders by asking what such individuals are in themselves. In 1:18–3:4 Paul examined the main grounds on which the Corinthians preferred one leader over another, namely, their (human) wisdom and eloquence. Here he takes an even more direct tack: *What, after all,*[6] *is Apollos? And what is Paul?*[7] In one sense, 3:5-9 could follow on directly after 1:16 or even 1:12. Instead, it seems as if Paul thought it prudent to consider the style and substance of the message such figures bring before thinking about the identity and status of the messengers themselves.

Paul's answer is, Apollos and Paul, as examples of Christian leaders in general, are *only servants.* The Greek word Paul uses is often translated "deacons" (which is more of a transliteration than a translation). It refers those who assist, usually performing tasks of an unskilled nature.[8] Although to be a servant of God can be thought of as a privileged position of some dignity (cf. Abraham and David in the Old Testament), this is not Paul's point here. Especially to Gentile ears, "servant" spoke above all of a low social status. "Servant" here does not carry any claim of derived authority, as, for example, might the title of "apostle"[9] (cf. 1 Cor. 1:1). TNIV's use of the adverb *only* is not in the original, but it is true to the intention of Paul's remarks.

The Corinthians would presumably have answered the two questions in a more flattering way: "I follow Apollos, the powerful orator," or "I follow Paul, the man of God." Instead of reflected honor and glory, Paul offers the Corinthian "hangers-on" disrepute by association. Apollos and Paul are mere *servants*! In fact, it gets worse, for in v. 6 Paul and Apollos are compared to humble farm workers, the sort of the manual laborers the elite in Corinth despised. Once again, Paul is ridiculing misplaced Corinthian loyalties (cf. 1:12d-13); who in their right mind would "boast" (3:21) about

6. Gk. οὖν.

7. Metzger, *A Textual Commentary,* 483, addresses the main textual issue in this verse: "Instead of τί ("What?") the Textus Receptus, following 𝔓[46] C D F G and most minuscules, reads τίς ("Who?") in both instances. The masculine, however, appears to be a secondary accommodation to suit the personal names; moreover, the implication of the neuter τι in ver. 7 is decisive for τί in ver. 5 (since the answer is 'Nothing' the question can scarcely have been 'Who?')." Also, while D[1] Ψ 𝔐 and sy reverse the order of the names (with Paul mentioned first, then Apollos), most early witnesses reflect the order given here. The alternative order presumably arose to conform this verse to the preceding and following verses, where Paul is mentioned before Apollos.

8. Cf. A. Weiser, "διακονέω," *EDNT* 1:302: "The original frame of reference for the use of the entire word group of the διακ- stem in secular Greek was that of table service. The basic meaning of the vb., correspondingly, was *wait on tables.* From this meaning the wider sense has been derived: *care for one's livelihood,* and finally *serve* in general." The word was used of an "attendant or official in a temple or religious guild" (LSJ; cf. BDAG), but LSJ also points out that as an adjective the word means "servile, menial."

9. Andrew D. Clarke, *Serve the Community of the Church: Christians as Leaders and Ministers* (Grand Rapids: Eerdmans, 2000), 216-17.

their adoring attachment to a *servant?* In so doing Paul deliberately undermines the cultural values that lie at the root of stunted Corinthian spiritual growth.

However, Paul's real purpose is not just to put human leaders in their place, but instead to replace them with God in the affection and devotion of the members of the church in Corinth. Hence, the *servants through whom* the Corinthians *came to believe* are servants of *the Lord,* those to whom he *has assigned*[10] *each a task.*

**3:6** Logically, the work the Lord (presumably the Lord Jesus Christ) has allotted each one is essential to the success of the overall project; the "planter," the one who establishes the church, and the "waterer," the one who pastorally leads it, are both equally indispensable to its growth. But this is not Paul's point. In the end, he avers, the "increase" is not their responsibility, nor is it within their power: *God has been making it grow.*[11] Our impersonal view of the laws of nature prevents us from feeling the force of Paul's analogy. We tend to think of the growth of plants as automatic: if the soil, seed, and nutrients are right, and there is enough rain and sun, the crops grow; it is as simple as that.

However, Paul's notion that God causes the flora on earth to grow is firmly based on a Jewish theology of creation.[12] Israelite farmers routinely confessed the same, not least in prayers like Psalm 65:9-11 when they came to offer the firstfruits in fulfillment of their "vows" (65:1): "*You* care for the land and water it; *you* enrich it abundantly; the streams *of God* are filled with water; *you* provide the grain, for so *you* have ordained it. *You* drench its furrows and level its ridges, *you* soften it with showers, and *bless its growth. You* crown the year with *your* bounty, and *your* carts overflow with abundance." It is not that the farmers had not toiled over the preparation and harvest of the crop, but they did so profoundly aware of the fact that their labors would be in vain if the Lord did not "bless its growth." The ancient (and still traditional) Jewish mealtime blessing reflects the same theology of creation: "Blessed are you, O Lord, our God, King of the Universe, who brings forth bread from the earth" (cf. Ps. 104:14).

Beale points out that the "cultivating" language of 1 Corinthians 3:6-8 has affinities with Ezekiel 17 (LXX): "And God took the seed of the land and sowed it in a cultivated field planted by much water" (17:5), and this

10. Gk. ἔδωκεν.

11. The first two verbs, "planted" and "watered," are in the aorist tense, while the third is in the imperfect (Gk. ηὔξανεν; to grow or cause to grow). Garland, 112, follows Robertson and Plummer in suggesting that the imperfect is intended "to imply that God is giving growth throughout the planting and watering." This may be correct, although the imperfect only suggests an ongoing process, not how long ago it began. Since the first two verbs point to a chronological sequence (the watering followed the planting), it may be that the third verb is also to be understood to sequentially follow the first two, as the TNIV has it, "God has been making it grow."

12. Cf. the quotation of Ps. 24:1 in 1 Cor. 10:26 in the context of a discussion of food: "The earth is the LORD's, and everything in it."

"field" needed to be "watered" for "the growth of her plantation" (17:7). In particular, the words "planted," "field," and "watered" are the same in both 1 Corinthians 3 and Ezekiel 17:7.[13]

The point of Paul's analogy is that the progress of the gospel is the work of God. When it comes to church growth, whereas ministers, denominations, and institutions are contingent, only God has absolute significance. To accord Christian leaders too high a stature is to ignore their impotence without the power of the life-giving Spirit.

**3:7** "What then are (the likes of) Apollos and Paul?" Paul's answer in v. 5 was, *Only servants, through whom you came to believe.* Verse 7 supplies a second, even more demeaning answer that flows from the analogy of the church as a cultivated field: *So neither the one who plants nor the one who waters is anything.* In other words, Apollos and Paul are nothing. This low, even insulting estimation of the value of church leaders must be read in context. Using hyperbole at its best, Paul is pressing the metaphor to give perspective to the matter of assessing human leaders. Side by side, and from a human perspective, Apollos and Paul are not nothing, but when standing next to God, the owner of the field and life force of the harvest, they may as well be. Paul is not saying that believers owe no loyalty or affection to those who led or lead them or nurtured their faith in Christ. Elsewhere he can say that the Galatians would have torn out their eyes and given them to him (Gal. 4:15), and to the Thessalonians, "you became imitators of us" (1 Thess. 1:6). Ministers do have value. But when respect or fondness leads to an exclusive loyalty, and when this causes division or detracts from a proper theocentric or christocentric orientation, Paul wishes to point out that *only God, who makes things grow,* is worthy of our undivided gratitude and adoration.

**3:8** While vv. 6-7 use the image of "planter" and "waterer" to relativize the importance of individual ministers of the gospel, v. 8 develops the metaphor to make a complementary point: *the one who plants and the one who waters* (literally) "are one" (AV/KJV, RV). Does this mean they are one in status, being "equal" (RSV) with "no difference between them" (TEV), or one in task and goal, having *one purpose* (TNIV), those who "work as a team" (REB)? Since the word "one" can denote such a range of significances,[14] context is decisive. While a broad or general meaning is possible, in the previous three verses Paul's point has been that although he and Apollos performed different tasks with respect to the Corinthians (planting and watering respectively), they shared the same status as "servants" of the Lord: in v. 5 they are both servants; in v. 6 neither is ultimately responsible for the growth; and in v. 7 neither is anything (to speak of, in

13. G. K. Beale, *The Temple and the Church's Mission: A Biblical Theology of the Dwelling Place of God* (Downers Grove: InterVarsity Press, 2004), 248.

14. BAGD, 230-32, lists instances of one in type, character, class, or quality, along with one in contrast to plurality or separate parts.

comparison with God). In v. 9 both are fellow workers. The clear emphasis is that Paul and Apollos have the same rank; one is not to be preferred to the other. Their common purpose can perhaps be inferred from the fact that their planting and watering was with the hope that God would give the increase, but the text is not explicit in this regard. In v. 8 Paul drives home the same point he is making throughout the paragraph: There can hardly be any space for "rivalry, competition or ranking"[15] between and among ministers, for they share the same (low) status.

If the Corinthians wished to assess the work of various leaders over against each other (cf. 1:12; 3:4), Paul says that task is reserved for another: *each will be rewarded according to their own labor* by God. As Fee notes, "they labor under another who also determines their pay."[16] This seems to be the reason for the introduction of the puzzling notion of rewards that is developed further in 3:13-14, where the word "reward" is repeated,[17] and in 4:3-5. Paul will say in 4:4 that ministers do not even judge themselves, for "it is the Lord who judges me." Ministers like Paul and Apollos are responsible only to God for judgments about their success or failure. Obviously this does not preclude the sober evaluation of experience and gifts in gospel work, but it does make such views provisional at best (see 4:5), and rules them out of court if they lead to invidious personal comparisons.

On the nature of the "reward," see on 3:14-15 and 4:5. It is not a matter of salvation versus condemnation, but of a reward received by faithful servants, with the focus being on praise from God and knowledge of his pleasure. Paul points out in 3:10 and 15:10 that all of his work, including that for which God might reward him, is accomplished by the grace of God. Garland observes that "[t]he idea of rendering to each according to each one's work runs throughout the New Testament (Matt. 16:27; Rom. 2:6; 2 Cor. 11:15; 2 Tim. 4:14; 1 Pet. 1:17; Rev. 2:23; 20:12-13; 22:12; cf. *1 Enoch* 100:7; *2 Enoch* 44:5; Pseudo-Philo, *Biblical Antiquities* 3:10)."[18] Readers who live in more materialistic societies must resist the temptation of assuming that Paul has a materialistic reward in mind. In Paul's own context, people aspire to great honor more than they do to the acquisition of things, and most of the hints as to what Paul has in mind suggest that the reward might be that of being given special honor by God. Paul gives more indications of what he has in mind in 3:12-17, and there the reward is tied to the ability of one's work to endure into the coming age (cf. 13:13). A significant part of the reward might be the privilege of seeing the eternal results of one's work or the honor of having the enduring nature of that work recognized by the

15. Thiselton, 304.

16. Fee, 133.

17. Gk. μισθόν.

18. Garland, 112. While both R. M. Fuller ("Rewards," in *DPL* 819-20) and H. W. Hoehner ("Reward," in *NDBT*) argue that there will be eternal distinctions in rewards, Craig Blomberg ("Degrees of Reward in the Kingdom of Heaven?" *JETS* 35 [1992], 159-72), argues against this view.

Lord himself. Kuck reminds us that while Paul's argument suggests rewards will vary, "wherein the difference might lie is never made explicit."[19] That may well be intentional.

Thiselton and Garland remind us that "the image of *pay* or reward serves primarily to intensify the point that Paul and Apollos are responsible *to God,* their employer, for judgments about their success or failure, not the community."[20] Furthermore, "assessments of one's own work are pointless and misleading before all the data are open to view and God has pronounced his definitive verdict at the last day."[21]

**3:9** To cap off his argument, Paul explains that the reason exclusive allegiances to Christian leaders are illegitimate concerns the fundamental question of the identity of both ministers and the church.[22] Personal identity in the ancient world was defined chiefly by the question, whose are you? In a world where slavery was rife and sexual ethics were conceived in terms of property,[23] virtually everyone belonged to someone. Accordingly, the identity of the Corinthian Christians and their leaders to which Paul draws attention does not concern who they are so much as whose they are: both belong to God! A threefold repetition of the genitive of possession, "of God," makes this abundantly clear: *we*[24] (the apostles and prophets/ preachers, exemplified in Apollos and Paul) are fellow workers belonging to God;[25] *you* (Corinthian believers) *are God's field, God's building.*

As Carson notes, implicit in this teaching is the point that just as members ought not to pledge exclusive allegiance to particular leaders, so leaders "should refrain from presenting themselves as if they had the corner on the truth, or all the gifts, or exclusive authority or insight."[26] Church leaders must watch their own vanity and actively discourage unhealthy attachments. The church belongs to Christ and God. In the case of Corinth, however, there is no indication that Paul laid the blame for Corinthian factionalism on the leaders (see the comments on 1:12).

The words, *you are God's building,* in 3:9b introduce another metaphor;

19. Kuck, *Judgment and Community Conflict,* 168.

20. Thiselton, 304; cf. Garland, 112.

21. Thiselton, 304.

22. The verse begins with an explanatory γάρ ("for").

23. For example, a wife belonged to her husband (see 7:2-4, where Paul makes this reciprocal) and a daughter belonged to her father.

24. On the referent of "we" in this section see the comments on 2:6.

25. TNIV, "we are God's co-workers," is ambiguous as to whether Paul has in view the relationship between the servants (e.g., "God's servants working together"; NRSV) or between the servants and God ("fellow workers with God"). Garland, 113, defends the former convincingly: "In the context, it is much more likely that Paul means that they are fellow workers belonging to God. Servants (3:5) are not co-workers with the master. He is not intent on arguing that they are independent partners with God but on showing the unity of their work together, though their functions may differ. . . . The other two occurrences of the emphatic genitive 'God's' in this verse convey the idea of possession."

26. Carson, *The Cross and Christian Ministry,* 77.

they moved from agriculture to architecture. Or do they? In relation to the comparison of the Corinthians to a temple in 3:10-17, Beale notes that "the close association of 'garden' and 'temple' in the Old Testament and Judaism would plausibly have influenced a similar link in Paul's mind."[27] Thus the combination of the two images in 3:9 is not as strange as first appears. The relevant background is discussed below on 3:10-17. At this point, the comparison of the Corinthians to a *field* and a *building* serves the same end of stressing that the Corinthians are God's possession and that he is responsible for their growth.

### *b. The Corinthians Are God's Building (3:10-15)*

*[10]By the grace God has given me, I laid a foundation as a wise builder, and someone else is building on it. But each one should build with care. [11]For no one can lay any foundation other than the one already laid, which is Jesus Christ. [12]If anyone builds on this foundation using gold, silver, costly stones, wood, hay or straw, [13]their work will be shown for what it is, because the Day will bring it to light. It will be revealed with fire, and the fire will test the quality of each person's work. [14]If what has been built survives, the builder will receive a reward. [15]If it is burned up, the builder will suffer loss but yet will be saved — even though only as one escaping through the flames.*

The major Old Testament background to Paul's comparison of the Corinthians to a temple in 3:10-17 is Solomon's garden-like Temple and the end-time temple of Malachi 3–4. In terms of specific connections, Paul echoes Isaiah 3:3 in 3:10, 1 Chronicles 29:2 in 3:10, and Malachi 3:2-3 in 3:12-15. As "God's temple" (3:16), the Corinthians are the antitype of the imposing temple of Solomon and the fulfillment of Malachi's vision of an end-time temple.

Paul here envisions a scrutinizing of Christian leaders, not a judgment of all Christians, and the fire is not an instrument of punishment (as in Revelation 20), but of purification. It is not a judgment of people but of their work. Elsewhere Paul indicates that he believes that all Christians will face a similar judgment: "we must all appear before the judgment seat of Christ" (2 Cor. 5:10; cf. Rom. 14:10). The judgment in 1 Corinthians 3:10-15 is not of all humankind, of the justified over against (other) sinners, but of wise and unwise builders of the church.

**3:10** Paul picks up the image of the church as a "building" (3:9c) and develops a point he introduced only in passing in 3:8b, namely, that God holds Christian leaders accountable for how they build. This section deals with any misgivings the Corinthians may have had about their leaders being left unaccountable; 1 Corinthians 4:3a implies that the Corinthians were judging Paul ("I care very little if I am judged by you"). Paul anticipates and answers the objection that Corinthian factionalism was merely the re-

27. Beale, *The Temple and the Church's Mission,* 246.

sult of assessing the quality of their leaders' work and preferring one over against another; such assessment is God's prerogative, and he will do it with characteristic thoroughness; rest assured, *their work will be shown* [by and to God] *for what it is* (v. 13a).

Turning to the subject of "rewards," a word appearing in vv. 8 and 14, the first clause of v. 10 wipes away any misconception that the judgment to which he is about to refer somehow suggests the idea that salvation is by works: Paul's building activities were energized *by the grace God has given me.* He takes no personal credit for his achievements as a church builder or planter. As he says in 15:10a, "by the grace of God I am what I am. . . . [and with this in mind] I worked." Refusing to give any encouragement to Corinthian pride, which was so easily inflated, Paul models an appropriate humility. If Paul's work is successful, he retorts, "yet not I, but the grace of God that was with me" (15:10b). The "grace of God" in both 1 Corinthians 3:10 and 15:10 is the generous provision by God of both the calling and of "the powers and capabilities requisite for this office" (BDAG).

As noted above, the comparisons of the church to "God's field" and "God's building" may in fact be related. Beale lays out the evidence.[28] The "building" in question turns out to be a temple in v. 16, for which the most obvious model is that of Solomon.[29] As Beale states: "The only other place in Scripture where a 'foundation' of a building is laid and 'gold,' 'silver,' and 'precious stones' are 'built' upon the foundation is Solomon's temple" (1 Kgs. 5:17; 6:20-21, 28, 30, 35; cf. 1 Chr. 29:1-7; chs. 3–4). Indeed, "100,000 talents of gold and 100,000 talents of silver" were prepared for the construction of Solomon's temple (1 Chr. 22:14). Furthermore, the description of Solomon's temple combined precious metals with botanical features like wood-carved "gourds and open flowers" (1 Kgs. 6:18), "palm trees" (1 Kgs. 6:29, 32), "pomegranates" (1 Kgs. 7:18-20), "a lily design" (1 Kgs. 7:22), rows of "gourds" (1 Kgs. 7:24-26, 42), and lampstands resembling a grove of trees with blossoms (1 Kgs. 7:49-50). Significantly, later Judaism spoke of Solomon's temple as a "field" (*Targum Pseudo-Jonathan* 27:27; *Pesiqta Rabbati* Piska 39). And the early Christian *Odes of Solomon* 38:17-21 describes a "saint" being "established" on "foundations [that] were laid" and also as a "cultivation" that was "watered" by God. These traditions build upon the fact that in the Old Testament "the Garden of Eden, Israel's garden-like promised land, and Israel's future restoration in a garden-like land were either equated or associated with a temple."[30] All this suggests that in 1 Corinthians 3:5-18 Paul is comparing the Corinthians not just to any cultivated field and temple, but to nothing less than Solomon's garden temple. We will comment on the significance of this comparison when we take up v. 16.

The two parts of the "parable" of the garden temple can nonetheless

28. See Beale, *The Temple and the Church's Mission*, 245-52.

29. See v. 12 below on the building materials.

30. Beale, *The Temple and the Church's Mission*, 246.

be differentiated in terms of their portrayal of God. In 3:5-9 God is depicted as the owner of the field and as the life-force who makes things grow, and Jesus Christ is the one who assigns tasks to the workers. In 3:10-15 God is less prominent, but stands behind the judgment implicit in references to "the Day" and "the fire," and Jesus Christ is the "foundation" of the building. In one, God owns the field and makes it productive; in the other, he owns the building and inspects the quality of the work of each builder.

The analogy of Christian leaders working on a major building project is especially appropriate to Paul's argument.[31] Unlike the field, where one worker could conceivably do all the work from planting to harvest, great buildings in the ancient world, and up until the Industrial Revolution, for that matter, took many years to build, even decades. Herod's Temple in Jerusalem at the time of Paul was the work of tens of thousands of workers and took over seventy years to build. The same goes for the great cathedrals of Europe built in the Middle Ages. Workers could move on, retire, or die before the building was completed. As Carson observes, with such edifices, "it is the project as a whole that is important, and, implicitly, it is foolish to focus all praise on just one of the builders who has contributed."[32]

Paul himself plays a comparable role in both the agricultural and architectural images. Just as 'the planter' commences the work in the field, so, as the first builder on the site, Paul lays *a foundation*. Paul describes himself in this activity as *a wise builder.* This title echoes Isaiah 3:3.[33] Both passages speak of wisdom and of judgment in relation to the leaders of God's people and use the two words in combination. That Paul claims to be *wise* carries further his argument in 2:6–3:4 that he does "speak a message of wisdom among the mature" (2:6).

That *someone else is building on* the work that Paul began is in no way surprising. Nor does Paul demean such work. On the contrary, in chapters 8–14 Paul explains that the primary purpose for which the spiritual gifts are given to members of the body is so that the church might be "built up."[34] Each member is to play their own role in building up the church. Paul's point is that whether you came first or later, when it comes to gospel work in a particular setting, to translate v. 10c more literally, "each one should watch out how they build."[35]

31. It is also a common image for the church in line with the New Testament's wide usage of Psalm 118.

32. Carson, *The Cross and Christian Ministry,* 78.

33. Robertson and Plummer, 60. Only in LXX Isa. 3:3 and here do we find the combination of the two Greek words behind this title: σοφός and ἀρχιτέκτων.

34. The Greek word used here (ἐποικοδομέω), while slightly different, is based on the root verb found in chs. 8–11 (οἰκοδομέω).

35. Paul uses a third-person present imperative (βλεπέτω). Present imperatives normally indicate some kind of general action. This is a regular expression of imperfective aspect within commands — action is to be taken with reference to situations in general. Here the sense of the imperative is that all who seek to build the church upon the foundation already laid must generally take care as they do so.

**3:11** Paul explains why it is imperative that "each one build with care."[36] As Fee states, "the reason for care in building the superstructure is related to the character of the foundation."[37] *The foundation* which has *already* been *laid is Jesus Christ.* This warning is similar to the one in 1:18-25, where a style of public speaking that did not suit "the message of the cross," threatened to "empty it of its power." The church is not founded upon a style of leadership, nor even on doctrine per se, but rather upon the gospel of the crucified Messiah (2:2), which Paul preached when he first came to Corinth.

**3:12** As noted above on v. 10, the materials for the construction of the building in question point to Solomon's temple. In particular, 1 Corinthians 3:12 alludes to 1 Chronicles 29:2 (esp. LXX): "I have provided for the house of my God the gold . . . silver . . . wood . . . precious stones."[38] More generally, Paul echoes Malachi 3:2-3 in 3:12-15.[39] The two texts use similar terminology (gold, silver, day, and fire). Both envisage a judgment in which fire consumes certain materials. Both "the temple" (1 Cor. 3:16) and its leaders are seen in relation to a judgment that will distinguish valid from ineffectual service. As Beale states: "In language very close to Paul's, Malachi predicts that the Lord will 'come to his temple' in the latter days and will 'refine' the priests in the temple with 'fire . . . like silver and gold', 'burning' up every evildoer like 'stubble' and the wood of branches."[40]

Paul depicts the Corinthians as part of the end-time temple, one in which "God's name will be great among the nations, and in every place incense will be offered" (Mal. 1:11; cf. 1 Cor. 1:2), as withstanding the fiery winds of the Day of Judgment.[41] But it is not the Corinthians themselves who are under scrutiny. Rather, the work of those who have led them, or more accurately, "built" them, is being tested by fire. While the six building materials are probably listed on a "scale of descending value,"[42] Paul's point is simply that some endure in fire *(gold, silver, costly stones)*, while oth-

36. Note explanatory γάρ.

37. Fee, 139.

38. Beale, *The Temple and the Church's Mission,* 247. Missing this Old Testament background, Conzelmann, 76, imagines that Paul has some "fabulous building" in mind.

39. J. Proctor, "Fire in God's House: Influence of Malachi 3 in the NT," *JETS* 36 (1993), 9-14; Schrage. A number of Old Testament and Jewish texts swirling around a general motif of judgment may have influenced Paul in 3:12-15. However, Mal. 3:2-3 is a specific parallel.

40. Beale, *The Temple and the Church's Mission,* 251. Matt. 3:1 and Mark 1:2 also apply Mal. 3:1 to Jesus. The fact that Malachi portrays the refining of priests in the temple is no barrier to Paul's appropriation of the text. The focus of judgment in 1 Corinthians 3 is on the leaders of the church, the builders, and elsewhere he views himself as performing priestly functions (Rom. 15:16; Phil. 2:17; 2 Tim. 4:6).

41. Beale, *The Temple and the Church's Mission,* 251. The eschatological temple, composed of Christ and his people in Rev. 21:1–22:5, is constructed of similar materials: "the wall is made of jasper, and the city of pure gold, . . . the foundations . . . were decorated with every kind of precious stone" (Rev. 21:18-19).

42. BDF §460(3) (p. 241).

ers are consumed *(wood, hay, straw).*[43] If the former are worthy of the foundation, the latter are not. Whether a worker's task be primarily evangelistic or pastoral, both must be in keeping with the character of the foundation stone, who is Christ. As Paul demonstrates throughout chapters 1–4, the cross is the key both to the initial establishment and ongoing moral renewal of the church. Any doctrine of the cross that treats it only as the entry point into the Christian life is seriously deficient. The mention of three unsuitable materials recalls the ominous warning of v. 10b. "Careless" building resorts to such inferior supplies. And Paul is not talking here just about himself and Apollos. A more general application is signaled with the words, *if anyone builds.* As the next verse shows, care should be taken when building, because a most searching inspection process will certainly be undertaken at some point.

**3:13** A number of terms indicate the eschatological nature of this Day of Judgment. The verbs "to become (apparent)," "to bring it to light," "to reveal," and "to test (with fire)" are all regularly used of the final, climactic event of human history.[44] The timing of that judgment is mentioned in 4:5: it will happen "when the Lord comes." This heaping up of synonyms for the same event of examination leaves the inescapable impression that there will be no doubt about the assessment. No trace of indistinctness will be left, and no one will think a retrial necessary. The *work* of Christian leaders *will be shown for what it is.* As Thiselton puts it: "Together these terms carry the sonority and weight of what in English we might think of as an apocalyptic epiphany: a universal disclosure in which all hitherto protective veils of ambiguity and hoping-for-the-best (or, equally, fearing-for-the-worst) are removed in a definitive, cosmic act in the public domain."[45] The fact that Paul can speak of *the Day* with no further explanation indicates the central position it must have occupied in his preaching and teaching, an event he labeled more fully in 1:8 as "the day of our Lord Jesus Christ."

Seeing that we are not privy to human motivations and unable to gauge long-term effects, our judgments about Christian work will always be open to correction. "But God pronounces a definitive verdict at the last judgment which cannot be revised, for all factors have been taken into ac-

43. *Costly stones* may be precious decorative gems adorning the temple, as in 2 Chr. 3:6 ("He adorned the house with settings of precious stones"), or costly construction stones, such as in 1 Chr. 29:2 ("all kinds of fine stone and marble").

44. Gk. γενήσεται, δηλώσει, ἀποκαλύπτεται, and δοκιμάσει respectively. The phrase "to become apparent" can be used of present disclosures as in 1 Cor. 11:19 and 14:25, but in this context the future tense of the verb and the reference to "the Day" make an end-time reference clear. The verb translated *will be revealed* (ἀποκαλύπτεται) is a present indicative set in a future-referring context. Indeed, the indicative verbs surrounding this present are all in the future tense. This present is always translated as though future-referring, and is best taken this way. Present tense verbs are sometimes used with future reference in describing events that are pre-planned or pre-determined (as in those determined by God's eschatological plan, as here).

45. Thiselton, 312-13.

count in a total context."[46] Paul's words provoke fear in those who will be so judged, and humility in the Corinthians who had presumed to make judgments themselves ahead of time. This is not to say that we can never know the character of a leader's work. But we must always remember that such judgments ultimately belong to God. As Paul can say at another point to the Corinthians: "What we are is plain to God, and I hope it is also plain to your conscience" (2 Cor. 5:11).[47]

The image of a fire ravaging a group of buildings and fully consuming everything save only the most durable materials would have resonated with the Corinthians. Corinth had been destroyed by the Romans in 146 B.C. and its re-founding in 44 B.C. by Julius Caesar probably meant that some buildings in Paul's day were a patchwork of new and old materials. A mixture of building materials was regularly used in the construction of Mediterranean cities, whose dry climate made fire an ever-present danger. "Great fires" have raged in cities across the centuries to devastating effect, from Rome in A.D. 64 to London in 1666, Chicago in 1871, and San Francisco in 1906. The image is readily comprehended and evokes appropriate alarm. *The fire will test the quality of each person's work*, or "what kind of work[48] each has done." Only those Christian ministers who worked with "gold, silver and costly stones" will have anything to show for their labors.

**3:14-15** Unfortunately, exactly which criteria determine whether a person's work survives the flames are not spelled out in the passage. How do you tell the difference between "gold, silver and precious stones" and "wood, hay and straw" when it comes to building "God's temple"? To answer this question, commentators tend to read in what they think is important about Christian ministry.[49] However, as ever, context is our best guide. Three directions suggest themselves, one from the previous sections of the letter and two from chapter 4.

Although rarely noticed, strictly speaking, the judgment Paul envisages here is not of himself and other gospel workers, but only of the latter. In vv. 10-11 Paul speaks confidently of having successfully laid the foundation, which is Jesus Christ, as "a wise builder" in Corinth. It is only those who "build on this foundation" (3:12)[50] whose "quality of work" (3:13) is in question: "*their work* will be shown for what it is" (3:13). Paul believes that his "foundational" work is up to standard. But this is not mere presumption on his part. In 1:18–3:4 he has already engaged in a searching evaluation of his work and whether or not he has "emptied the cross of its power" (1:17b) and given people "human wisdom" or "God's power" on which to

46. Thiselton, 313.

47. "Plain" here translates φανερόω, the verb cognate to φανερός ("apparent, clear, evident") in 1 Cor. 3:13.

48. Gk. τὸ ἔργον ὁποῖον.

49. For example, "prayerless," "shallow" (Thiselton, 304).

50. The verb "to build upon," ἐποικοδομέω, appears three times in the passage: vv. 10, 12, and 14.

rest their faith (2:5). He did not "preach the gospel with wisdom and eloquence" (1:17), and he does not declare "the wisdom of this age," but rather "God's wisdom" (2:6-7). The foundation he laid was "Jesus Christ and him crucified" (2:2), and in a manner appropriate to the message (2:1-4). If we wonder which criteria Paul has in mind when describing the judgment of Christian prophets and teachers, we need look no further than the values Paul espouses and exemplifies in chapters 1–2. To spell it out, building materials that will be *burned up* are those in keeping with human wisdom instead of the wisdom of God, which is the fullness of the message of the cross.

The second and third criteria of judgment are mentioned in chapter 4. 1 Corinthians 4:4-5 makes many of the same points as 3:13-15 about God's exclusive prerogative to judge his workers, the thoroughness of that judgment, and the promise of rewards. The new element is the news that on the Day of Judgment the Lord Jesus "will expose the motives of people's hearts" (4:5). Disturbingly, then, God will consider not only what Christian workers said and did in their attempts to build up God's people, but why they behaved in this way. On reflection, this is not unrelated to the first criterion. As we noticed earlier, the "human wisdom" Paul so thoroughly avoids, and God so utterly condemned at the cross (1:18-20), involves not only displays of human brilliance and a message of human adequacy but also the values of self-reliance and self-promotion. In a nutshell, Paul teaches that God will judge Christian workers on the single measure of their avoidance of human wisdom and adherence to the wisdom of the cross as they go about their work. Thus, to conform to "the wisdom of the world" (1:20) in Christian ministry is not only to empty the cross of Christ of its power (1:17) and to encourage a misplaced faith (2:5), but it also leads to the minister's forfeiting *a reward* from God (3:8, 14). It is to prove not to be "faithful" to the Master (4:4). Much is at stake for building and worker alike.

But this *reward* of which Paul speaks, in what does it consist? Verse 15 confirms that Paul is not speaking of salvation as the reward in question, for *the builder* who *suffers loss will* nonetheless "himself"[51] *be saved*. The verb "to suffer loss" does not mean "to punish" but to be "deprived of something."[52] The issue then is not reward or punishment, heaven or hell, but re-

51. The pronoun αὐτός is emphatic.

52. Gk. ζημιόω. BDAG recognizes that the word often means "to experience the loss of someth[ing], with implication of undergoing hardship or suffering" but applies another meaning of the word in this case, namely, *"be punished."* A. Stumpff, "ζημία, ζημιόω," in *EDNT* 2:890 points out that v. 15 forms "a precise antithesis" to v. 14. While "[t]he natural opposite of 'to receive a reward' would seem to be 'to suffer punishment' . . . it is doubtful from the context whether the word should be taken in its juridical sense. . . . Hence we probably give the sense more correctly if we render ζημιωθῆναι by "to suffer loss," filling it out from the preceding τὸν μισθόν construed as an accus[ative] of relation." That is, "[l]oss, or the missing of the reward, is the result, or even more directly the experience, of the κατακαυσθῆναι of his work" (Stumpff, "ζημία, ζημιόω," *EDNT* 2:890).

ward or no reward. It is the builder's "work" (3:13) that will be burned up, not *the builder* himself. As Fee states, 1 Corinthians 3:14-15 is not "a soteriological statement."[53] The picture is of someone escaping from a burning building just in time, "saved by the skin of their teeth." It is hardly flattering or reassuring, and Paul does not present it as in any way normative or acceptable, but it does not undermine Paul's notion elsewhere that believers are saved by grace and not by works (e.g., Eph. 2:8-10). Paul has every confidence that all Christians, those who have been given "grace in Christ Jesus," will be "blameless" on the day of our Lord Jesus Christ" (1:8; cf. Rom. 5:1; 8:1). 1 Corinthians 3:12-15 functions as a warning to those who lead God's people to "build with care" (3:10), not only for the sake of the church but for their own sake.

The word *reward* could be translated "wages, pay, salary," the main concept being "closely bound up with that of an employer's assessment of the value of the work."[54] As Thiselton notes, the notion of a reward for workers "intensifies the point that Paul and Apollos are responsible to God, their employer, for judgments about their success or failure, not the community."[55] Some who read this passage, anxious to avoid any compromise of the doctrine of justification by grace through faith, urge that the reward of which Paul speaks is the satisfaction of work done with God's help, "by the grace of God" (3:10), as Paul puts it. An authentic ministry is its own reward. The "wise builder" who "builds with care" derives pleasure from serving God well and from watching the church being built up.

While this may be true, it can hardly be Paul's point since, as v. 13 indicates, the final outcome of a builder's work is hidden until "the day" brings it "to light." The *reward* can only be an eschatological "prize" (1 Cor. 9:24-27; cf. Phil. 3:14). Whatever its precise nature, its essence is "praise from God" (4:5). We may compare Jesus' promise in the parables of the Bags of Gold in Matthew and the Ten Minas in Luke: "well done, good and faithful servant! . . . Come and share your master's happiness" (Matt. 25:21, 23; cf. Luke 19:17). In both cases the reward for faithful service is the master's pleasure and his confidence, which leads to a further entrusting of responsibility.

### c. The Corinthians Are God's Garden-Temple (3:16-17)

*16Don't you know that you yourselves are God's temple and that God's Spirit dwells in your midst? 17If anyone destroys God's temple, God will destroy that person; for God's temple is sacred, and you together are that temple.*

53. Fee, 144.
54. Thiselton, 304.
55. Thiselton, 304.

The temple and holiness motif in 1 Corinthians 3:16-17 is a thoroughly biblical one.[56] The temple as God's dwelling and warnings to those who would profane or destroy God's temple are common in Scripture. Indeed, the conception of the community as a temple is a scriptural theme, where God's indwelling is not just of a sanctuary, but of a people (Exod. 25:8; 29:45; Lev. 26:11-12; Ezek. 11:16; 37:26-28; Ps. 114:2).[57] The Peshitta of Jeremiah 7:9 states the thought explicitly: "the temple of the Lord, the temple of the Lord, you [plural] are the temple of the Lord." This seed-thought of the community as the building or temple of God was nourished in early Jewish teaching (*The Rule of the Community* 8:4-7; Philo, *On Sobriety* 66; *On the Life of Abraham* 56).[58]

The details of 3:16-17 also bear the stamp of Paul's Bible and his Jewish heritage. The idea of "the Spirit of God" rather than simply "God" dwelling in the temple is found in Josephus' account of Solomon's temple (*Antiquities* 8.114). The connection of temple with judgment is reminiscent of Numbers 1:51; 3:10, 38; 4:20; 19:20 and 2 Chronicles 26:16-21. His concern for a purified temple also brings to mind Israel's sin offering, which was designed to cleanse the tabernacle from defilement.[59] The warning of 3:17 is stated in terms of talionic justice ("if anyone *destroys* . . . he will be *destroyed*"). This is reminiscent of LXX Joshua 7:25: "Joshua said to Achan, 'Why have you *destroyed* us? The Lord will *destroy* you.'" That Paul connects the temple metaphor with the Old Testament is clear from 2 Corinthians 6:16-18, where he quotes Leviticus 26:12 and Ezekiel 37:27.

**3:16** In his discussion of the true nature of Christian leadership, whereas 3:5-15 focuses on the status and role of Christian leaders in the congregation, 3:16-17 switches from third person to direct address in order to describe the Corinthians themselves. Ethicists of every stripe agree that identity, how a group or individual defines itself, is fundamental to their moral formation. A frequent summary of the logic of Paul's ethics is the maxim "become what you are."[60] For several reasons, 1 Corinthians 3:16-17 is a prominent text in the letter, from which and to which later discussions will proceed and refer. As such, it is anything but an isolated remark. The temple motif in the letter is more pervasive than usually recognized. The way has been paved for Paul's "startling declaration"[61] that the Corinthian Christians are *God's temple* and that *God's Spirit dwells in your midst* in the unfolding metaphor of the garden-temple in 3:5-15. In this sense v. 16 is no

56. Gk. ναός ("temple") occurs over sixty times in the LXX; ἅγιος ("holy") appears over 500 times.

57. Cf. W. Horbury, "New Wine in Old Wine Skins: ix. The Temple," *ExpTim* 86 (1974): 36-42.

58. Cf. Rosner, *Paul, Scripture, and Ethics*, 75-76.

59. See Lev. 4:1–5:13; 15:31; 16:19.

60. See the essays by Bultmann and Parsons in Rosner (ed.), *Understanding Paul's Ethics* (Grand Rapids: Eerdmans, 1995).

61. Garland, 120.

surprise, but merely spells out what has been implicit throughout the passage. Along with its ready-made contribution to the purity motif, unpacked in v. 16, the initial affective impact of the identification of the church of God in Corinth as a temple is to dignify them. It recalls in a concrete way the descriptions that opened the letter, where the fact that the Corinthians belong to God was stressed by calling them "those sanctified in Christ Jesus and called to be his holy people" (1:2).

The identification of the Corinthian believers as *God's temple* also sets the scene for the expulsion in chapter 5, where the incestuous man is "destroyed" because he has destroyed God's temple. Presumably it is because the Corinthians are God's temple that their consumption of the bread and wine in the Lord's Supper is understood in terms of participation in a sacrifice offered at an altar (10:16-22) and that Paul thought it essential for the church to be "built up" through the Spirit in chapters 12–14 (picking up on the theme from 3:10-12).

We should not miss the audacity, if not patent ludicrousness, of Paul's claim in v. 16. Whereas we might not balk at the thought of Christians' being compared to a grand place of worship, given the numerous impressive cathedrals in Europe, the early Christians were a tiny Jewish sect, paling even by comparison with the comparatively secure and established Jewish population in the Roman Empire. And Solomon's Temple was not simply an awesome building. The annual pilgrimages to Jerusalem and its temple were undertaken with the express intention of meeting with God (Pss. 42:2; 63:2; 65:1-2, etc.). According to the theology that grew up around it, the temple's foundation belonged to the creation itself and the temple would last forever (Pss. 78:69; 125:1). The destinies of the nations would be decided at the temple (Amos 1:1-15; Ps. 99:1-5), and the well-being of the whole earth depended on the one who sat on the throne in the temple mount of Zion (Pss. 29:10; 46:1-5; 93:1-4).[62] Consequently, the destruction of Solomon's Temple in 587 B.C. that accompanied the Jewish exile to Babylon was the nadir of the nation's history. To Paul's mind, its denouement was not the return from exile, nor the building of Herod's temple, but the existence of a small squabbling band in Corinth of mainly Gentile believers in Israel's murdered Messiah: *you yourselves are God's temple.*

The rhetorical question, *don't you know?*, which Paul uses to introduce the verse, occurs another nine times in the letter, the most noteworthy of which at this point is 6:19 ("your bodies are temples of the Holy Spirit").[63] The question is effectively a mild rebuke. Although on the surface the question seems to suggest ignorance or forgetfulness on the part of the Corinthians, its actual force is probably that of implying that the conduct of the Corinthians shows that they have not sufficiently thought through the implications of the following truth, even if they would claim to be familiar

62. R. J. McKelvey, "Temple," in *NDBT* 809.

63. The other eight are 1 Cor. 5:6; 6:2, 3, 9, 15, 16; 9:13, 24.

with it. Several commentators believe that what Paul wants the Corinthians to *know* probably formed part of his original oral teaching to them.[64] The tone varies from context to context, with five appearances in chapter 6 underlining Paul's growing impatience with the Corinthians' failing to act on what he had taught them only earlier, or at least to see the implications for their present conduct from his prior instruction. By 6:16, along with other stylistic features, it signals Paul's irritation and has moved from a polite admonishment to a full reprimand. At this first appearance in 3:16 the tone of the question is less sharp.

In 2:12 Paul claimed that the leaders of the church have "the Spirit who is from God." Here he tells the Corinthians that *God's Spirit dwells in your midst,* or "among (all of) you."[65] It is a stunning affirmation of their identity and status before God, recalling Paul's reference to them as "those sanctified in Christ Jesus and called to be his holy people" in 1:2. Given their behavior it sits somewhat uncomfortably, but Paul is determined to deal with the Corinthian faults that threaten to defile God's temple and compromise its holiness. That is what he sets out to do from 4:18 onward.

**3:17** With the repetition of the words *if anyone,*[66] v. 17 intensifies v. 12. According to vv. 12-16, "if anyone builds the church in a certain way, they will receive a reward if their work endures." In v. 17, the stakes are raised, and not only is their reward in jeopardy, but their very person: *If anyone destroys God's temple, God will destroy that person.* To this point in the letter Paul has given no indication that any of the leaders of the church in Corinth were remotely guilty of such a serious charge. To build with shoddy materials is one thing; to "destroy" the building quite another. While it is true that Paul can speak of other preachers of the gospel in such a drastic way, as in Galatians 1:8 ("Even if we or an angel from heaven should preach a gospel other than the one we preached to you, let that person be under God's curse"), in the case of 1 Corinthians 3:17 it may be that he is talking more generally of those who may not be in leadership doing damage to the church. The "destruction of the flesh" of the immoral man in chapter 5, or the members taking one another to secular court in 6:1-11, or the men making use of prostitutes in 6:12-20 may be in his sights. In chapter 8 Paul warns the Corinthians not to destroy a brother or sister in Christ by acting on their so-called knowledge, as by eating in an idol's temple (8:11).[67]

Some commentators ponder whether the verb "to destroy"[68] refers to

64. E.g., Barrett, 90; I. Howard Marshall, "Church and Temple in the New Testament," *TynBul* 40 (1989), 213; Hodge, 94.

65. Gk. ἐν ὑμῖν.

66. Gk. εἴ τις.

67. There Paul uses a different verb, ἀπόλλυμι, also used in 1:18-19; 10:9-10; 15:18.

68. Gk. φθείρω. A number of textual witnesses (esp. Western) have a present tense verb (φθείρει; "God destroys") rather than the future (φθερεῖ; "God will destroy") found in most witnesses. As Metzger suggests (*Textual Commentary,* 484), the present tense variant is probably a result of influence from the use of the exact word in the first clause of the verse.

the absolute demolition of the building or merely damaging it. However, this debate misunderstands the nature of metaphorical language, which should not be pressed too far. Every figure of comparison has both points of similarity and points of difference. The word has a broad semantic field. Paul uses the word twice in 2 Corinthians in similar contexts of harm to the Corinthian assembly. These give some idea of what is meant in 1 Corinthians 3:17: "We have wronged no one, we have *corrupted* [or ruined] no one, we have exploited no one" (2 Cor. 7:2); "your minds may be *led astray* [or seduced] from your sincere and pure devotion to Christ" (2 Cor. 11:3). To *destroy God's temple* is to impact a person's spiritual well-being negatively. It is to rob them of the "grace and peace . . . from God our Father and the Lord Jesus Christ" (1 Cor. 1:2) that is every believers' inheritance.

What is clear in v. 17 is that the punishment fits the crime: *if anyone destroys the temple, . . . God will destroy that person.* The measured appropriateness of God's judgment is a constant and comforting theme in the Bible to anyone concerned about the justice of God.[69] The reason God will destroy anyone who destroys the church concerns the holy status of the church:[70] *for God's temple is sacred,*[71] *and you together are that temple.* To call the church "holy" (cf. 1:2) is a way of underscoring its value to God; it is special because it belongs to him and is put to such valuable use as bringing him glory.

### *d. Reprise and Summary: All Things Belong to God (3:18-23)*

*18Do not deceive yourselves. If any of you think you are wise by the standards of this age, you should become "fools" so that you may become wise. 19For the wisdom of this world is foolishness in God's sight. As it is written: "He catches the wise in their craftiness"; 20and again, "The Lord knows that the thoughts of the wise are futile." 21So then, no more boasting about human leaders! All things are yours, 22whether Paul or Apollos or Cephas or the world or life or death or the present or the future — all are yours, 23and you are of Christ, and Christ is of God.*

In Paul's dismantling of Corinthian factionalism, the overall focus of 3:5–4:17 is on the true nature of Christian leadership. 1 Corinthians 3:18-23 connects this part of Paul's argument to what he had to say about the wisdom of the cross and the Spirit in 1:18–3:4. The paragraph applies the material expounded in those chapters to the problem of divisions in the church, drawing out its practical significance. The unit is the most direct assault on Corinthian factionalism since Paul's request for unity in 1:10. The apostle's final appeal on the subject follows in chapter 4.

69. Cf., e.g., the frightening threat of being "punished with everlasting destruction" in 2 Thess. 1:6-9, which is introduced with the explanation that God will "pay back *trouble* to those who *trouble* you" (Gk. θλίβω).

70. Note the explanatory γάρ.

71. Gk. ἅγιος.

**3:18** With his most confrontational words to this point in the letter, Paul warns the Corinthians of the danger of self-delusion: *Do not deceive yourselves.*[72] Paul's argument throughout this section suggests that some in Corinth are in fact deluded in thinking that they are wise.[73] 1 Corinthians 8:2, 10:12, and 14:37 use the same verb "to think"[74] and supply more evidence that some in Corinth thought more highly of themselves than they ought (cf. Rom. 12:3). Comparable warnings also appear in 1 Corinthians 6:9 and 15:33 (cf. Gal. 6:7).[75] Although the focus of chapters 3–4 is on Christian leaders, Paul's words here have a broader application and refer not just to teachers or aspiring teachers: *if any of you think you are wise.*[76] Sadly, inflated self-esteem is characteristic of the Corinthian church as a whole (see 4:6-7). Human wisdom measures itself over against others. At the heart of the Corinthian factionalism was each party's belief that their apostle and those who belonged to him were superior to other Christian leaders and their followers.

Paul's point is that to be wise *by the standards of this age* is nothing to boast about. This phrase recalls the extended argument in 1:18–3:4, that the cross pronounces a verdict of judgment on "the wisdom of this age" and "the rulers of this age" (2:6). *This age* refers both to a stage in history, in contradistinction to the age to come, and a world order that stands in opposition to God.

Following *do not deceive yourselves,* a second imperative, *become fools,*[77]

72. The phrase Μηδεὶς ἑαυτὸν ἐξαπατάτω *(Do not deceive yourselves)* indicates a general action, to be adhered to in situations in general. This is a normal implicature of the imperfective aspect of present imperatives.

73. The following sentence is written in the form of a "first class condition," which "indicates *the assumption of truth for the sake of argument.* The normal idea, then, is *if — and let us assume that this is true for the sake of argument — then. . .*" (Daniel B. Wallace, *Greek Grammar beyond the Basics: An Exegetical Syntax of the Greek New Testament* [Grand Rapids: Zondervan, 1999], 690). BDF §372 points out that this usage is "often closely bordering on causal 'since,'" and the local context encourages such a reading here.

74. Gk. δοκέω.

75. Robertson and Plummer, 69.

76. The function of ἐν ὑμῖν in the verse is disputable. Ellicott thinks that it goes with σοφός and suggests the meaning, "If anyone thinks he is wiser than the rest of you" (cf. Luke 1:42 for a similar usage of the preposition ἐν). But other examples of σοφὸς ἐν ("wise among") in the LXX (e.g., Exod. 36:8; Sir. 37:26) do not suggest any derogatory kind of comparison. The phrase is more likely to go with τις ("if anyone *among you* [i.e., in your midst] thinks he is wise"). The second prepositional phrase with ἐν ("in this age") is likely to modify "wise." Thus, "if anyone *in your midst* thinks he is wise in this age [i.e., in according to the wisdom of this age]. . . ." Robertson and Plummer, 70, provide a helpful suggestion regarding the significance of the second clause: "From ἐν ὑμῖν, 'in a Christian Church,' it might have been supposed that he meant the true wisdom, and he adds [ἐν τῷ αἰῶνι τούτῳ] to avoid misunderstanding." The wisdom admired *in this age* is not to be highly valued *in the church* ("among you").

77. It *may* be that the aorist imperative (γενέσθω) is used because Paul considers someone thinking themselves wise by the standards of this age a specific situation to which they would need to respond. Or it could be a case of the perfective aspect of the aorist being

sums up the positive way forward for those guilty of self-deception. Foolishness here involves focusing on Jesus and his cross and the selfless lifestyle that it entails (cf. 1:18, 23; 3:23). If the Corinthians had this preoccupation, it would lead them to eschew the values of success and human brilliance that led to their disunity. Instead of being wise *by the standards of this age,* Christians are to be foolish "by the standards of this age,"[78] and embrace the message of the cross in all its wisdom. Accordingly, the purpose[79] of becoming foolish is *so that you may become wise.* If the first use of the term "wisdom" in this verse recalls its use in 1:18–2:5, the second brings to mind its sense in 2:6–3:4, 10. The cross recommends behavior that is against what common sense would advise. To be foolish in Corinthian society was tantamount to social suicide. Similar counterintuitive paradoxes mark the teaching of Jesus: "whoever finds his life will lose it, and whoever loses his life for my sake will find it" (Matt. 10:39); "but many who are first will be last, and the last first" (Mark 10:31).

**3:19** Further to demonstrate the futility of human wisdom, Paul appeals to two more Old Testament texts in 3:19-20, which are introduced with the formula, "it is written."[80] Together they offer a pithy summary of Paul's argument in 1:18–3:21. The first, Job 5:13, declares God's ability to frustrate the goals of those claiming to be wise.[81]

The unit in which the verse appears, part of the first speech of Eliphaz, reinforces the idea of God's superiority to human wisdom and strength. In a passage depicting the God who does "great, unsearchable and marvelous things" (5:8-9), Job 5:8-16 sets up an opposition between "the wise" and "the poor." The passage in question develops the theme of God's deliverance of the latter (5:15-16: "he saves the needy from the sword of their mouth . . . so the poor have hope") and his frustration of the former (5:14: "the schemes of the wily are brought to a quick end").

A number of Jewish texts develop themes arising out of or overlapping with the sentiments of Job 5:13.[82] For example, Baruch 3:20-28 protests the futility of human striving to attain wisdom, which can only be granted

---

"used to communicate instruction in summary form, which is thereby suited to general instruction" (Campbell, *Verbal Aspect and Non-Indicative Verbs,* 87). See our comments on the tenses of the imperatives in the introduction.

78. Barrett, 93, supplies this elliptical omission in his translation.

79. Gk. ἵνα.

80. See our comments on 1:19 regarding the perfect tense of "it is written" (γέγραπται).

81. The MT, LXX, and 1 Cor. 3:19 carry an equivalent sense but differ in some details. Compared to the LXX, Paul has δρασσόμενος rather than καταλαμβάνων (both meaning "lay hold of") and ἐν τῇ πανουργίᾳ αὐτῶν ("in their craftiness") instead of ἐν τῇ φρονήσει ("in prudence/understanding"). Concerning the latter, the Hebrew is closer to Paul's rendition, using a word that implies a sly and crafty form of wisdom. The differences may be explained either as Paul's offering his own Hebraizing revision of the present LXX, his own translation of the Hebrew, or his quoting a wholly independent translation of the Hebrew text of Job (see Stanley, *Paul and the Language of Scripture,* 188-94).

82. H. H. D. Williams, *The Wisdom of the Wise,* 307-15.

by God's revelation (cf. 3:36–4:4). That God makes certain wise people ineffectual and thwarts their plans is seen in *Psalms of Solomon* 8:20 (the wise Jewish leaders when the Romans captured Jerusalem); Wisdom 17:7-11 (the wise Egyptians at the time of the exodus); 3 Maccabees 1–2 (King Ptolemy planning to enter the holy of holies); and Judith 2:2-3 (Holofernes and Nebuchadnezzar planning to lay waste Judea).

Although in the book of Job as a whole Job's friends' advice is shown to be unhelpful, misapplied wisdom, as Hays puts it, "Paul cites Job 5:13 here as an authoritative disclosure of the truth about God's debunking of human wisdom."[83] The immediate context of the quotation resonates with the themes of reversal and the mystery of divine mercy that Paul has introduced earlier in the letter (in 1:18–2:16).

**3:20** Secondly, Paul quotes Psalm 94:11.[84] If in 1:18-25 Paul says that what God does in wisdom seems foolish to the world, here we have the converse: what the world thinks is wise, God declares to be folly.[85] Psalm 94 is a prayer for God to overthrow the wicked oppressors and vindicate the righteous. Thiselton's summary is accurate: "Psalm 94 stresses that in spite of manipulative and corrupt leadership by those in authority (Ps 94:5-7, 16), the 'schemes' of these human persons fail because their best 'thinkers' are fallible (Ps 94:11)."[86] The psalm also promises that blessing awaits those who depend on God; he will not abandon them, but teach them and aid them in their time of need (vv. 12-23).

The contrast between human thinking and God's thoughts is widespread in Jewish literature.[87] The *Targum of Job* contains numerous references to the futility of the human intellect without God's revelation. Likewise, Baruch 3:29-37 asserts the inaccessibility of God's wisdom. In 1 Maccabees 2:61-64 the "plans"[88] of sinners will perish. Other texts emphasize the benefits of cooperating with God's plans and call on people to turn to God asking for wisdom.

The futility of human wisdom is a central theme in 1 Corinthians 1:19-27a, 2:4-6, and 3:18-19. However, it is not that Paul has altered the text in cavalier fashion simply to suit his argument. Paul's quotation of Psalm 94:14 in Romans 11:2 indicates that he knew the psalm well. What makes the form of his quotation in 1 Corinthians 3:20 explicable is the link Psalm 94 itself forges between "fools" and the "wise." Psalm 94:8 reads: "Under-

83. Hays, 59.

84. MT, LXX, and 1 Cor. 3:20 are equivalent except that Paul renders the verse, "the thoughts of *the wise,*" instead of "men" (ἀνθρώπων). No Old Testament MS has any other reading. A few lesser Pauline MSS agree with the MT and LXX and read ἀνθρώπων instead of σοφῶν in 1 Cor. 3:20, but this is probably a deliberate conforming of Paul's wording to the psalm. "There is little reason to doubt that the present modification goes back to Paul himself" (Stanley, *Paul and the Language of Scripture*, 195).

85. Fee, 152.

86. Thiselton, 323.

87. H. H. D. Williams, *The Wisdom of the Wise*, 315-25.

88. Gk. διαλογισμοί.

stand, O dullest of the people! *Fools,* when will you be *wise?*" The "humans" spoken of in Psalm 94:11, whose thoughts the Lord knows to be futile, are the same group described as "fools" earlier in the psalm. That Paul feels free to label them, ironically, as "the wise" fits his rhetoric and does no violence to the larger context of Psalm 94.

Psalm 94 and early Jewish literature emphasize not only that God thwarts the plans of the wise, but also that there is great blessing for those who are part of and cooperate with God's plans. Thus, not only does the citation of v. 11 signal the futility of acting or thinking independently of God, but as 1 Corinthians 3:21-23 goes on to celebrate, there are great benefits to those who boast not in human leaders but in God.

Together the texts cited in 1 Corinthians 3:19-20, which testify to the futility of human thoughts apart from God's revelation and the consequent emptiness of human wisdom, support Paul's conclusion in 3:21a: "So then, no more boasting about human leaders!" This command is as much a summary of 1:10–4:17 as the opening verse of the unit, 1:10, which calls the Corinthians to unity. God is to be glorified (6:20; 10:31), not human beings.

**3:21** The opening words of the verse, the conjunction *so then*[89] followed by an imperative, are a common construction in the letter. Paul uses it to introduce a summary command or exhortation that emerges from his previous discussion.[90] Thus, in 3:21 Paul repeats his request in 1:10 that the Corinthians be united by calling on them not to form factions around their favorite leaders. In fact, this verse sums up succinctly both the heart and one of the main grounds of Paul's appeal: "Stop boasting in your leaders, as if you belong to them, for if anything, they belong to you!"

Paul's command in Greek consists of an imperative followed by a preposition and a dative noun, literally, "do not boast in humans."[91] TNIV's *no more boasting about human leaders* accurately specifies the referent of "humans." The dative construction, *about human leaders,* could be that of sphere, "among humans," or reference/respect, "with regard to humans." The context favors the latter, especially v. 22, which mentions the specific humans Paul has in mind, along with the references in 1:12 and 3:1-4 to the leaders in question. The negative reference to improper "boasting" calls to mind the scripturally endorsed legitimate boasting in the Lord in 1:31, a thought hinted at by the prominence given Christ and God in 3:23.

The reason[92] Paul supplies for not "boasting about human leaders" is that *all things are yours.* The thought fits in with the building analogy of 3:5-15. All the workers belong to the same project. It impoverishes the church

89. Gk. ὥστε.

90. Robertson and Plummer, 71; cf. 4:5; 10:12; 11:33; 14:39; 15:58.

91. As pointed out elsewhere, present imperatives (which is what we find here in καυχάσθω) normally indicate some kind of general action. Paul is giving a general principle (that Christians should not be involved in boasting about men), not an exhortation to be applied in just one particular case.

92. Gk. explanatory γάρ.

to limit itself to one particular expression of the faith, be it in styles of leadership, worship, preaching, evangelism, or music. What belongs to God as the owner and project supervisor belongs to us. A major problem with division in the church is the fact that it is such a futile waste of resources and unnecessarily limits us in countless ways.

**3:22** This verse gives some particularity to the "all things" that belong to the Corinthians. The words, *all are yours,* by repeating 3:21b, envelop the verse and indicate its task of describing what "all things" encompasses. The ascending order of the list gives it a solemn tone and adds to the sense of wonder it engenders; possessing leaders is clearly surpassed by having life and death and the future "in the bag." However, the exuberance of its expression is matched only by the profundity of its theology.

The examples of "all things" that Paul lists fall into three categories: a triplet of leaders *(Paul, Apollos, Cephas);* a triplet of powers relating to this life *(the world, life, death);* and a doublet with respect to time *(the present and the future).*[93] The Corinthians had claimed that they belonged to particular leaders (1:11; cf. 3:5-7). In a powerful instance of "Pauline redefinition," the apostle takes the same vocabulary and phrases used by the Corinthians, but generates an entirely different meaning:[94] *whether Paul or Apollos or Cephas . . . all are yours.*[95] Paul, Apollos, and Cephas actually belong to the Corinthians because, as servants of Christ (3:5), they are engaged in the service of building the temple (i.e., the Corinthians; 3:16-17).[96] "The Church is not the property of the Apostles; Apostles are ministers of the church."[97]

Robertson and Plummer rightly note a connection to the Lordship of Christ here: "The thought is profound and far-reaching. The believer in God through Christ is a member of Christ and shares in His universal lordship, all things being subservient to the Kingdom of God, and therefore to his [i.e., the believer's] eternal welfare (vii. 31; Rom. viii. 28; John xvi. 33; 1 John v. 4, 5), as means to an end."[98] 1 Corinthians 4:1-5 returns to the question of the status of servant Christian leaders vis-à-vis their lord.

Yet the leaders the Corinthians possess are only a part of the staggering range of gifts God has given them. As 1 Corinthians 1:5 puts it, they "have been enriched in every way." The rest of the chain of gifts in 3:21 raises the stakes considerably. "The world, life, death, the present and the

93. Conzelmann, 80.

94. Thiselton, 325. Cf. John D. Moores, *Wrestling with Rationality in Paul: Romans 1–8 in a New Perspective* (SNTSMS 82; Cambridge: Cambridge University Press, 1995), 6-10, 25-28, and 132-38.

95. Findlay, 2:795, suggests plausibly that a Corinthian slogan may have been: "this leader belongs to us."

96. Mark 10:42-45 offers a similarly countercultural view of leadership.

97. Similarly, Garland, 124: "They possess all things, however, only because they belong to Christ. Their relationship to apostles and teachers comes under the scope of the lordship of Christ, just as their possession of the world does."

98. Robertson and Plummer, 72.

future" are what Fee accurately labels "the tyrannies of existence."[99] According to Romans 8:38, they are negative forces that threaten to defeat us. In short, they can be against us (Rom. 8:31b).[100] The usage of the first four terms in 1 Corinthians confirms this.

Although "the world"[101] can be used in the neutral sense of the earth as "the habitation of humanity," as in 1:27-28; 4:9, 13; 8:4; and 14:10, the appearance of "world" in 1:20-21; 2:12; and 7:33-34 marks it out as an organized force implacably opposed to God. Part of Paul's gospel is that "this world in its present form is passing away" (7:31) and will "be finally condemned" (11:32). To possess *the world* is to be free from this potent threat. Believers are not subject to the wiles of "the world," for not only does the world belong to them (3:21), but one day "God's people will judge the world" (6:2).

"Life" is a less pejorative term, but, especially in combination with "death," it can be used to point to our transience and mortality, as in the phrase, "if only for this life" (15:19). The inescapable reality of "death,"[102] which "came through [the disobedience of] a human being" (15:21), is "the last enemy to be destroyed" (15:26; cf. 54-56), overcome "through the Lord's [own] death" (11:26). Finally, *the* [things] *present*[103] is a term often used with negative associations, as in the present "crisis" (7:26), "the present evil age" (Gal. 1:4), or "the distressing times" of "the last days" (2 Tim. 3:1).

Thus, in Paul's exultant list of Corinthian belongings, of the five terms following the mention of the three leaders, only *the future*[104] is used in a consistently positive sense in Paul's letters. That "the world, life, death and things present" belong to the Corinthians is Paul's way of saying that they possess "eternal life." Nothing can separate them from the love of God that is in Christ Jesus our Lord (Rom 8:39). These insatiable powers can do the Corinthians no serious harm. Since they are like wild animals in secure captivity, there is no need to be afraid of them because *all are yours.* Indeed, in this light it is no surprise that "the future" is theirs too, as 1 Corinthians 15 will explain.

How have the Corinthians gained this unassailable position? All things are theirs because in union with Christ they are heirs, the essence of which is possession of an inheritance.[105] Put another way, Christ, in whom they now exist, the wisdom and power of God, has outsmarted and overpowered the world (1:18-25). Thiselton's description of the theology of v. 22 demonstrates the way in which Paul's brief staccato remarks sum up his response to the petty divisions in Corinth: "The Christian shares in the Lordship of Christ whereby creation and the church are restored into coopera-

99. Fee, 154.

100. The two passages share "death, life, things present and things to come."

101. Gk. κόσμος.

102. Gk. θάνατος.

103. Perfect participle of ἐνίστημι.

104. Gk. μέλλοντα.

105. Bruce, 46; cf. Rom. 8:17.

tive agencies for the well-being of humankind and for the glory of God-in-Christ, set within the providential dimension of the new order in Christ."[106]

**3:23** *You are of Christ* is Paul's counter to the Corinthian slogans of 1:12 and 3:4, "I follow Paul," "I follow Apollos," or "I follow Cephas." In both cases, the Greek is the simple genitive of possession. Paul says, "You don't belong to your favorite leaders, but to Christ!" If our interpretation of 1:12 is right, Paul had said the same there with the words, "I belong to Christ" (see the comments there). The affirmation thus acts as an inclusio around this main part of Paul's argument against disunity.

To belong to Christ could imply that the Corinthians are Christ's bride (2 Cor. 11:2), which in the sexual ethics of the ancient world involved ownership (cf. 1 Cor. 7:2-3). However, it probably places the Corinthians on the same level as their leaders as Christ's servants (3:5). 1 Corinthians 6:19-20 and 7:23 repeat the thought in reference to being slaves of God: "You are not your own; you were bought at a price."

Paul's pithy closing words, *and Christ is of God,* likewise bring to mind a theme treated in more detail later in the letter; that God is the head of Christ is touched on in 11:3 and 15:28 (cf. 8:6). Drawing attention to the ultimacy of God closes the section appropriately, for, as Richardson notes, God plays a critical role in Paul's argument in which he "offers a thoroughly theocentric understanding of both the gospel and the Christian life."[107] God chose the Corinthians (1:26-28), Paul proclaimed "the testimony of God" (2:1), their faith rested on "the power of God" (2:5), and they received "the Spirit of God" (2:12). It was God who caused the growth of the church (3:6-7), which is "God's field" and "God's building" (3:9). Not only do the church and its leaders belong to God, so even does Christ.

The finality of the words, *and Christ is of God,* reminds the Corinthians that it is God who "holds together freedom, unity and differentiated purpose."[108] Like the Corinthian leaders and the Corinthians themselves, even Christ is an agent or instrument of God. The Son, though no less than the Father in being,[109] serves the Father in obedience. His death, resurrection, and reign are all dedicated to destroying all of God's enemies and establishing a world in which all things, including Christ himself, are in perfect subjection to God (1 Cor. 15:21-28).

Paul's corrective to divisions throughout the section is not negative or small minded, but rather positive, uplifting, and expansive: believers boast in God (1:31), have the mind of Christ (2:16), and even possess *all things.* But the ultimate goal goes far beyond them. It is that God be all in all (1 Cor. 15:28).

106. Thiselton, 327.

107. Neil Richardson, *Paul's Language about God* (JSNTSup 99; Sheffield: Sheffield Academic Press, 1994), 114-15. See 1:26-28; 2:1, 5, 11, 12, 14; 3:6, 7, 9, 23.

108. Thiselton, 329.

109. See on Christ's incorporation into the very identity of God in the implied interpretation of the *Shema* in 1 Cor. 8:6.

### *2. Application: The Apostles as Models of the Wisdom of the Cross, 4:1-17*

As he continues his reflections on the nature of Christian leadership, Paul moves from providing a series of metaphors for the church and its leaders (as God's cultivated field, building, and garden-temple, 3:5-23) to showing the Corinthians how the wisdom of the cross, expounded earlier, should be applied to their appraisal of the apostles and other Christian leaders.

#### *a. Regard Ministers as God's Servants and Estate Managers, 4:1-5*

*This, then, is how you ought to regard us: as servants of Christ and as those entrusted with the mysteries God has revealed. [2]Now it is required that those who have been given a trust must prove faithful. [3]I care very little if I am judged by you or by any human court; indeed, I do not even judge myself. [4]My conscience is clear, but that does not make me innocent. It is the Lord who judges me. [5]Therefore judge nothing before the appointed time; wait till the Lord comes. He will bring to light what is hidden in darkness and will expose the motives of people's hearts. At that time each will receive their praise from God.*

The Corinthians wanted to be judged as wise in society's eyes, and to judge their leaders, only some of whom they deemed worthy of praise, by the same worldly standard. Paul's response is to assert the singular prerogative of God to judge and to bestow praise. This passage begins to wrap up the second half of Paul's response to Corinthian factionalism, with v. 1 recalling the description of leaders as "servants" (3:5-9) and vv. 2-4 reiterating the warning of 3:8, 13-15 that an evaluative judgment of such leaders is coming.

**4:1** Paul begins to summarize his response to Corinthian factionalism by telling the church what standing to ascribe to their Christian leaders: *This, then, is how you ought to regard*[1] *us. Us* here refers to leaders like Paul, Apollos, and Cephas, mentioned in 3:22 (cf. 1:12; 3:5), the same group of apostles and prophet/teachers whom Paul said "declare God's wisdom, (which is) a mystery" in 2:7. Paul is not asking the Corinthians to pretend their leaders are something they are not. Both the Corinthians and Paul get their true identities from God, not from how someone else might correctly or incorrectly identify them. Paul's identity is not established by the Corinthians but by God, and the Corinthians must simply concur with this assessment.

1. *You ought to regard us* reflects a present tense imperative (λογιζέσθω). As pointed out previously, present imperatives are normally used for general instruction, instruction that is relevant not just for a particular case or situation (even if it requires urgent application in their present context). Here Paul instructs the Corinthians (and us) on how Christian leaders are to be regarded.

Verse 1 recalls 3:5-9, in which Paul explained that leaders are "servants" and "co-workers." Here they are described as (1) *servants of Christ* and (2) *those entrusted with* a message. The TNIV's *servants* translates a different word for "servant" in 3:5. The word in question here can describe a wide range of activities and roles, from menial household worker to a junior officer who assists a superior. In second-century papyri it often means "assistant," and it might be translated here as "subordinates" (REB).[2] Church leaders are hardly worthy of ultimate loyalty or attachment, for they themselves are subsidiary to another.

The second term is often translated "stewards"[3] (NRSV, REB, AV/KJV, NJB). However, NIV/TNIV's *those entrusted with* is preferable, as "steward" is today usually associated with attendants on airplanes and ships and thus carries a sense not intended by Paul. Thiselton explains that in the ancient world the "office normally included responsibility for overseeing a household budget, purchasing, accounts, resource allocation, collection of debts, and general running of the establishment, but only as instructed within guidelines agreed by the employer or head of the house."[4] We might compare it today to an "estate manager." The Corinthians were probably familiar with such positions, especially seeing that one of their number, Erastus, was a "city administrator" (Rom. 16:23), a title which uses the same word.[5]

In all, Paul declared the status of Christian leaders using four terms. "Servant" in 3:5 and "subordinate" or "assistant" in 4:1 refer to their secondary position before Christ and the church. "Fellow workers (belonging to God)" in 3:9 defines their relationship to each other. And "manager" in 4:1, as 4:2 brings out, underscores the minister's ultimate responsibility to God himself. The "mysteries of God" which they are to dispense refer, as in 2:7, to the gospel in all its fullness. The plural noun probably points in a similar direction to the reference to the (similarly plural) "deep things of God" in 2:10. The context (vv. 2-5) suggests that the "mysteries" have to do with the message Paul has shared with the Corinthians, certain points of which had resulted in his being judged by some of them. In building the church, ministers manage a major project, the resources for which are nothing less than the fullness of the gospel of God.

**4:2** Paul makes an additional point, a further inference, about ministers as managers that sets up the rest of his comments in 4:2-5: "in this connection, then,"[6] *it is required that those who have been given a trust must prove faithful.* Those in a position of trust must be trustworthy. Garland cites an

2. Collins, 167; ὑπερέτης, a Pauline hapax, is a synonym of διάκονος in 3:5.

3. Gk. οἰκονόμος.

4. Thiselton, 336. Such a role could be filled by a slave or a free person (cf. Robertson and Plummer, 74-75).

5. Theissen, *Social Setting,* 79; cf. TNIV, "the city's director of public works." Gk. οἰκομόνος τῆς πόλεως.

6. BDAG, λοιπός, 3b. Gk. ὧδε λοιπόν (cf. BDAG, ὧδε, 2: "in this case, moreover").

ancient document recording the commissioning of a manager by his master which exemplifies the relationship Paul has in mind: "I have empowered you by this document to administer my estate in Arsinoe, and to collect the rents and, if need be, to arrange new leases or to cultivate some land yourself, and to give receipts in my name, and to transact any business connected with stewardship, just as I can transact it when I am present, and to distribute the plots in Karamis, restoring to me what remains over, as to which matter I rely on your good faith, and I confirm whatever you decide about them."[7] This commission illustrates several points about manager-master relations: the manager is charged with a range of tasks, to take the initiative and be pro-active, to represent the master in a way that befits him, and to be reliable and of "good faith." Here, as in 3:5-9, we must be aware of the risk of overinterpreting the metaphor (see the introduction to 3:5-9). While all these points may fit the analogy of ministers as God's managers, only the last point, that the ministers be found faithful, is made in the passage. This is reinforced later in the chapter when Paul commends Timothy to the Corinthians: Paul describes him as "faithful in the Lord" (4:17).

The Corinthians were assessing their leaders on the criteria of wisdom, eloquence, and impressive personal presence. In stark contrast, God's basis for judgment is very different: *those given a trust must prove faithful.* Someone or something is "faithful"[8] if you can have confidence in it to accomplish something. In the Pastoral Epistles the "faithful" sayings are those "we can trust" (e.g., 1 Tim. 1:15 — "Here is a trustworthy [*faithful*] saying that deserves full acceptance").[9] Similarly in Acts 13:34, which uses the same word, citing Isaiah 55:3, God promises "*sure* blessings." In this regard God expects no less than he himself delivers, for, as Paul reminded the Corinthians in 1:9, "God is faithful," a thought repeated in 10:13. A basic attribute of God is his dependability. Whereas we may be tempted to judge ministers on their success or initiative or giftedness in terms of interpersonal relations or speaking, the sole requirement Paul counsels them to keep in mind is their faithfulness to God.

In which connection does God insist on the dependability of his managers? For what is he relying on them? "Faithfulness" can be attached to a broad range of activities; v. 5 implies that its measurement includes testing "the motives of people's hearts." In the context of Paul's argument in chapters 1–4 it must also include the point made consistently that the presentation of the message and the messenger's own demeanor must match the message of a crucified Messiah. The faithful servant of God can be trusted to present the gospel appropriately, not "with wise and persuasive words but with a demonstration of the Spirit's power" (2:4), and as 4:8-13 goes on to demonstrate, not as a shining success, but as "the scum of the earth," a

7. Garland, 126; *BGU* 1:300.

8. Gk. πιστός.

9. Louw and Nida, 31:87.

status in keeping with their crucified Lord. The contrast with much religious practice today is marked.

**4:3** Paul's next words at first sight may appear arrogant and autocratic: but *I care very little*[10] *if I am judged by you or by any human court.* However, they are consistent with the analogy of the servant's being responsible to the owner and are not meant as an insult to the Corinthians. After all, Paul asserts not only that he is not subject to them but also that he will not be examined, literally, "by any human day."[11] The estate manager may be criticized from many quarters, but in the end only the owner's opinion counts and only the owner's assessment should concern him or her. Human "days" of judgment pale by comparison with "the Day which will bring it to light" (3:13; cf. 1:8). As Barrett notes, "here we have to do with man's feeble attempt to imitate God's judgement, and to behave as if he himself were judge."[12] Paul expresses the same sentiment to the Roman Christians: "Who are you to judge someone else's servants? To their own master they must stand or fall" (Rom. 14:4).

Further deflating any impression that he is being arrogant, Paul confesses: *indeed, I do not even judge myself.* Even Paul's verdict on himself is incidental. In contrast, Plato's *Republic* records the words of Cephalus, who writes more self-assuredly: "To him who has no sin on his conscience sweet hope is present."[13] The verb "to judge" is used three times in vv. 3 and 4.[14] It was used in 2:14-15 in the sense of "inquiring into" spiritual things. There too "the person with the Spirit . . . is not subject to merely human judgments." Likewise, here in 4:3 Paul, a spiritual man, will not be evaluated by any human being, but rather only by God (v. 4). The evaluation of Paul's "faithfulness" is God's prerogative alone. Paul's use of the same verb in 1 Corinthians 9:3 indicates that some in Corinth were indeed wishing "to sit in judgment" on Paul (cf. 2 Cor. 2:17–3:4 and 1 Thess. 2:1-2, where Paul felt it necessary to defend himself).[15]

**4:4** In context, Paul's claim, *My conscience is clear,* has a limited refer-

10. Gk. ἐλάχιστον; BDAG, 3: "pert[aining] to being considered of very little importance."

11. Barrett, 101, notes that "Rabbinic Judaism knows the contrast between 'judgements of men (or, of flesh and blood)' and 'judgements of heaven' (S.B. iii. 336)."

12. Barrett, 101.

13. *Republic* 331A (cited by Barrett, 102).

14. Gk. ἀνακρίνω, used in legal settings of judicial inquiries. See Ciampa, "Examined the Scriptures?" A judicial setting is clearly indicated by references to a human "day/court" here and to judging in v. 5.

15. This appears to conflict with 1 Cor. 5:12a, where Paul affirms that the church is "to judge (κρίνω) those inside." However, the contradiction is only apparent. The church is always to judge immoral behavior and unorthodox teaching when they manifest themselves in it (note that even Paul's teaching was expected to be evaluated in the light of Scripture; cf. Acts 17:11). We are to recognize, however, our inability to judge motives (which only God can do, v. 5) and the inappropriateness of making invidious comparisons between leaders/people or judgments regarding their importance or that of their God-given calling.

ence to his apostolic duties, the area in which some of the Corinthians were evaluating him.[16] He is not claiming sinless perfection. Rather, with respect to his faithfulness as a servant of Christ, the charges brought against him are, to his knowledge, baseless, and he is *innocent.* Paul makes pretty much the same claim in 1 Corinthians 2:1-4, where he defends his preaching to and conduct before the Corinthians. *But,*[17] Paul insists, consistent with his words in v. 3b, *that does not make me innocent* before God. Not being conscious of[18] anything against himself does not justify him.[19] The sobering truth is that *it is the Lord who judges me.* The only assessment of Christian workers that counts is not congregational (or denominational), nor even personal, but only that by "the Lord who assigned them each his task" (3:5).

**4:5** Paul draws the inescapable deduction that emerges from his discussion in vv. 1-4: *Therefore,*[20] *judge nothing before the appointed time.* The rebuke in 4:6-13 suggests that the Corinthians are currently engaged in such evaluations, whether negative or positive, of Paul and their ministers, and they are to cease this activity.[21] To so desist does not mean that the quality of the ministers' work will not be tested and revealed (see 3:13). Instead of making such judgments now, the Corinthians must *wait till the Lord* (Jesus)[22] *comes.* For, as the rest of the verse indicates, the judgment that will accompany that "revelation" (1:7) will be far more searching than any human could ever hope to achieve.

At the Second Coming, "the day of our Lord Jesus Christ" (1:8), *he will bring to light what is hidden in darkness.* Darkness is not the impenetrable veil

16. There is no need to argue, along with Lightfoot and Robertson and Plummer, that he is talking hypothetically here: "even supposing that I know nothing against myself."

17. Gk. ἀλλά.

18. The Greek has the verb σύνοιδα rather than the noun συνείδησις.

19. The verb is "to justify," δικαιόω. However, the technical sense of "declare righteous at the final judgment" (as regularly in Romans and Galatians) is not meant here (contra apparently Barrett, 102 and Fee, 162). The context in 1 Cor. 4:1-5 is Paul's evaluation by God as his faithful servant. As in 1 Cor. 3:10-15, the judgment in view is not of them but of their work. The verb is in the perfect passive form (δεδικαίωμαι) here, which is appropriately translated as being present in temporal reference: "I am not justified by this" or "that does not mean I am innocent."

20. Gk. ὥστε; see the comments on the word in 3:21.

21. The negated present tense of the imperative is used both in contexts calling for the cessation of an activity in progress and in contexts where there is no suggestion that the prohibited action is already in progress (Wallace, *Greek Grammar,* 724). Any such distinction must be based on the context. Cf. Mare, 39, and Fee, 163. Whether or not such an activity was already going on, the present imperative suggests that Paul's instruction is relevant not just for this particular case, but an exhortation that is generally valid and should be kept in mind.

22. Does "the Lord" here and in v. 4 refer to God or Jesus? That both are mentioned in v. 1 makes the question worth asking. Whereas the reference to *God's* dispensing *praise* at the end of v. 5 might suggest that he is in view, the combination of "the Lord" with the verb "to come," as in 1 Thess. 5:2, coupled with the reference to the Lord (Christ) in 3:5, means that the phrase here is a technical term for the return of Christ.

to God that it is to every human being. Psalm 139:12 prays in wonderment: "darkness is as light to you." On that day the truth of the conduct and character of Christ's servants will be revealed. A second parallel statement explains and intensifies what this means: *he will expose the motives of people's hearts.* This is the most explicit indication of the things the Corinthians are judging but should not. The one who searches the hearts is almost an Old Testament title for God (Pss. 17:3; 26:2; 44:21; 139:23). The image with reference to judgment speaks of painstaking and meticulous scrutiny.

*At that time each will receive their praise from God* contains a number of noteworthy features. This is the most explicit indication of what Paul had in mind in his earlier reference to the rewards to be received by God's servants (cf. 3:14). The judgment in question will be "then,"[23] not now; this is another damper on Corinthian eagerness to assess their leaders. Paul has in view judgment as it concerns believers in Christ. In other places Paul speaks of those in his churches as his joy, crown, and glory on the Day of Judgment (2 Cor. 1:14; Phil. 2:16; 1 Thess. 2:19-20). Testimony to his confidence in the grace of God, his predominant mood in anticipation is positive, as here. John 5:44 contains a similar view of *praise from God* and pits it over against "praise from human beings": "How can you believe if you accept praise [literally, "glory"] from one another, yet make no effort to obtain the praise that comes from the only God."

### *b. The Corinthians Are Exalted While the Apostles Are Abased, 4:6-13*

*6Now, brothers and sisters, I have applied these things to myself and Apollos for your benefit, so that you may learn from us the meaning of the saying, "Do not go beyond what is written." Then you will not be puffed up in being a follower of one of us over against the other. 7For who makes you different from anyone else? What do you have that you did not receive? And if you did receive it, why do you boast as though you did not?*

*8Already you have all you want! Already you have become rich! You have begun to reign — and that without us! How I wish that you really had begun to reign so that we also might reign with you! 9For it seems to me that God has put us apostles on display at the end of the procession, like those condemned to die in the arena. We have been made a spectacle to the whole universe, to angels as well as to human beings. 10We are fools for Christ, but you are so wise in Christ! We are weak, but you are strong! You are honored, we are dishonored! 11To this very hour we go hungry and thirsty, we are in rags, we are brutally treated, we are homeless. 12We work hard with our own hands. When we are cursed, we bless; when we are persecuted, we endure it; 13when we are slandered, we answer kindly. We have become the scum of the earth, the garbage of the world — right up to this moment.*

23. Gk. τότε.

In this passage Paul continues to reflect on ways in which apostles and other Christian leaders serve as models of the wisdom of the cross. Although vv. 6-7 and vv. 8-13 seem to be different paragraphs, the vocative in v. 6 ("brothers and sisters") suggests the beginning of a new unit of text. Even though the rest of the verse seems to summarize the point of the previous passage, in v. 7 one can already see that the transition has been made from an emphasis on their differing evaluations of various apostles and leaders (mainly at Paul's expense) to the difference between the triumphalism of the Corinthian troublemakers and the weak and foolish spectacle of Christ's apostles (with the references to their boasting about their strengths, as though they were not gifts from God). Thiselton points out that Karl Kleinknecht rightfully sees 4:8-13 as "the climax or 'high point' of 1:1–4:21 in that it provides the final step in a cross-centred critique of 'boasting in human persons' (1:29-31; 3:18-20; 4:6-7)."[24] This lay behind the schisms (1:1-11; 3:3) that plagued the Corinthians. Fee notes that this section "is dominated by two themes: their pride (vv. 6-8, 10) and his weaknesses (vv. 9, 11-13)" and that Paul uses devastating irony: "How they perceive themselves, masterfully overstated in vv. 8 and 10, is undoubtedly the way they think he ought to be. But the way he actually is, set forth in the rhetoric of vv. 11-13, is the way they all ought to be."[25]

**4:6** With the words, *Now, brothers and sisters,* Paul moves from speaking figuratively and indirectly about the church and its leaders, to speaking literally and directly to the situation in Corinth. In terms of tone and style, he shifts from polite metaphors to blunt commands, accusing rhetorical questions, and even insulting sarcasm and strong language. As Fee observes, with 4:6-13, "[t]he argument has reached its moment of truth."[26]

The *things* that Paul has *applied*[27] to himself and Apollos extend back at least as far as 3:5, where both are mentioned, but may take in all of 1:10–4:5; Paul and Apollos are first mentioned in 1:12, and Paul's own behavior in ministry is the focus of 2:1–3:4. Hence he tells the Corinthians that much of the letter to this point has been *for your benefit,* by which he means, for your sake I have tended to address the problem indirectly up to this point, but get ready for the frank things I am about to say. The fact Paul did not rush to give practical injunctions concerning the Corinthians' boasting in

24. Thiselton, 345; Karl T. Kleinknecht, *Der leidende Gerechtfertigte* (WUNT 2.13; Tübingen: Mohr, 1984), 208-304.

25. Fee, 165.

26. Fee, 166.

27. BDAG points out that the verb μετασχηματίζω usually means "to change the form of something." Here it refers to Paul, speaking metaphorically. That Apollos and Paul are "only servants" (3:5) and the church "God's field, God's building" (3:9) is to make a point only indirectly. According to BDAG, the word here means "to show a connection or bearing of one thing on another, *to apply*" and the clause means, "*I have applied this to Apollos and myself* = I have given this teaching of mine the form of an exposition concerning Apollos and myself."

their leaders (in 3:21a and then 4:6b) testifies to his pastoral sensitivity and to his conviction that mind and will must act in concert in obedience to Scripture. Simply to issue a command without giving them "the mind of Christ" (2:16) would be both unhelpful and probably unsuccessful. As Paul states in 4:14, he does not write "to shame them but to warn them," and, we might add, to change them.

Described by Conzelmann as "unintelligible,"[28] the words "not [to go] beyond the things which are written" have been subject to various interpretations.[29] Among the options are that it refers to a rabbinic adage or a slogan of Paul and/or the Corinthians.[30] In Paul's writings, "what is written"[31] always refers to Old Testament Scripture. Significantly, prior to this verse, the verb "to write" appears four times in 1 Corinthians, introducing five of the six Old Testament quotations.[32] With this in mind, v. 6a is best understood as instructing the Corinthians not to transgress the exhortations found in and constructed from the Scriptures to boast exclusively in the Lord (not in human leaders) and to recognize the unity of the people of God.

Hays defends this interpretation convincingly: "Paul has prominently spotlighted six Scripture quotations in the first three chapters of the letter (1:19, 31; 2:9, 16; 3:19, 20). In the case of the first two and the last two, the application of the texts is explicitly spelled out: No boasting in human beings. First Corinthians 3:21a links the two quotations in chapter 3 back to the quotations in chapter 1. . . . Furthermore, the two quotations in chapter 2, though they are not explicit admonitions against boasting, reinforce the same theme by juxtaposing God's gracious ways to all human understanding. The cumulative force of these citations is unmistakable: the witness of Scripture places a strict limit on human pride and calls for trust in God alone."[33] Paul's point is that to *go beyond* this witness of Scripture would be to boast in human wisdom, unwittingly supposing that the Corinthians are smarter and stronger than God.[34]

Two purpose clauses in v. 6 explain what Paul has been aiming at up to this point in the letter.[35] He wants the Corinthians, first, "to learn to live according to Scripture" (RSV) and, secondly, to refrain from arrogant rivalries. As it turns out, the two are virtually synonymous. The second purpose

28. Conzelmann, 86.

29. Garland, 133-35, lists five.

30. The τό is anaphoric and signals a quotation, as in TNIV.

31. Gk. ἃ γέγραπται.

32. Gk. γέγραπται. The only Old Testament quotation not introduced in this manner is in 2:16.

33. Hays, 69. Alternatively, J. R. Wagner ("'Not beyond the Things Which Are Written': A Call to Boast Only in the Lord [1 Cor. 4:6]," *NTS* 44 [1998], 279-87) argues that 4:6a refers back in particular to the citation in 1:31, noting echoes of 1 Kgdms. 2:10 in 1 Cor. 4:6-13.

34. Cf. Morna Hooker, "'Beyond the Things Which Are Written': An Examination of 1 Cor IV.6," *NTS* 10 (1963-64), 129-32.

35. Barrett, 107; note the repetition of ἵνα.

clause confirms our interpretation of the first (see above). What does the command mean, *Do not go beyond what is written?* It means *not [to] be puffed up in being a follower of one of us over against the other.* Arrogant claims to wisdom or rhetorical skill are at the heart of Corinthian factionalism, and they contravene Scripture's judgment on human wisdom fulfilled in the cross. "To be puffed up," a prominent term in 1 and 2 Corinthians (4:6, 18, 19; 5:2; 8:1; 13:4; 2 Cor. 12:20), is one of Paul's central accusations against the Corinthians. As Marshall notes, such pride "results from a failure of self-knowledge."[36] This is seen in Paul's rebuke in 8:1-3, where the crucial thing is not to know God but to be known by him, and in the three rhetorical questions in 4:7.

**4:7** Garland contends that Paul "punctures their inflated view of themselves with a series of [three] questions: "Who? What? Why?"[37] The first, *Who makes you different from anyone else?*, may be understood either positively ("Who made you what you are?") or negatively ("Who do you think you are, anyway?"[38]). Chrysostom's comments make both points: "Where is the evidence that you are worthy of being praised? Why, has any judgment taken place? Any inquiry proceeded? Any essay? Any severe testing? No, you cannot say it, and if men cast their votes, their judgment is not upright. But let us suppose that you really are worthy of praise and have indeed the gracious gift, and that the judgment of men is not corrupt; yet not even in this case would it be right to be high-minded; for you have nothing of yourself that you did not receive from God."[39] While the Greek may offer some support for the negative sense,[40] the context favors seeing Paul making a positive evaluation of the Corinthians Christians here and reminding them of the basis of such esteem. The fact that the Corinthians are "of Christ" in 3:23 is the basis for Paul's high regard for them. The following two questions make more sense if we take the first one as paying the Corinthians a compliment and implicitly reminding them that it was God who gave them their enviable status. The questions develop logically in sequence.

The Corinthians might have been tempted to define themselves according to their (supposed) personal accomplishments and intellectual astuteness, or their status in society, by what they assumed distinguished them.[41] "To learn from Paul" (4:6) here is eschew such human social con-

36. P. Marshall, *Enmity in Corinth*, 205.

37. Garland, 136.

38. Fee, 171.

39. Chrysostom, *Homiliae in Epistulam i ad Corinthios* 12.3.

40. BDAG argues that διακρίνω here means "to conclude that there is a difference, *make a distinction, differentiate*" and suggests that the phrase "τίς σε διακρίνει" means "*who concedes you any superiority?*" with evidence from "Appian, Bell. Civ. 5, 54 §228 δ. τινά = concede superiority to someone." This usage does not show that the language in 4:7 must be understood negatively, but only that it can be.

41. Literally, "who differentiates (or in the sense of distinguishing, [διακρίνει]) you (from anyone else)?" The singular personal pronoun (σε) addresses them as individuals.

structions and rather to locate one's personal identity in relation to God. The Corinthians are those whose very life is caught up "in Christ Jesus" (cf. Col. 3:3), a state and status they enjoy entirely "because of him" (1:30).

Hence Paul's second question: *What do you have that you did not receive?* Nothing worth having, that is, that which is not destined to "come to nothing" (2:6b; cf. 1:19), can be claimed as an achievement. The Corinthians' true wisdom, that is, their righteousness, holiness, and redemption, is a gift of God "in Christ Jesus" (1:30). That which we might legitimately take pleasure in, as Paul explains in Romans 12:3, is the result of "the grace given me . . . [and] the faith God has distributed to each of you." Paul states the same thing concerning himself in 15:10: "By the grace of God I am what I am."[42]

Just in case the Corinthians have missed the point, the third question confirms the second: *And if you did receive it, why do you boast as though you did not?*[43] Calvin's summary of the simple logic of Paul's forceful assault on Corinthian pride in this verse is accurate: "No room is left for taking pride in ourselves, when it is by God's grace we are what we are."[44]

**4:8** To complement the three rhetorical questions of v. 7, in v. 8 Paul ups the ante by launching three sarcastic and derisive statements further to humble and correct the Corinthians.[45] The exclaiming and "dashing" punctuation of the TNIV accurately captures the heightened tone.[46] Even allowing for some hyperbole (cf. 4:15a), evidently Paul thought the Corinthians viewed themselves as being fully supplied, rich, and even reigning,[47] in

42. Paul does not surmise from this, however, that God's work excuses us from needing to work. On the contrary, in the same verse (1 Cor. 15:12) Paul claims that he himself worked hard, and in Phil. 2:12-13 he commends working for the very reason that God is at work "in you."

43. This is a first-class conditional sentence in which the question in the second clause makes it clear that we are dealing with what BDF §372 calls "εἰ with the indicative of reality." Thus the first clause could be translated, "since what you have you received (as a gift from God)."

44. Calvin, 91.

45. Robertson and Plummer, 83.

46. TNIV translates it with four sentences, as do most English translations. Modern Greek editions treat it as two sentences with three clauses in the first and two in the second (literally, "Already you are filled, already you are rich; you have begun to reign without us! And would that you had indeed begun to reign, so that we might also reign along with you").

47. The verbs in this verse provide an interesting contrast. Beginning with a perfect periphrasis, the sentence continues with two aorists, with the first two verbs modified by the temporal marker ἤδη (ἤδη κεκορεσμένοι ἐστέ, ἤδη ἐπλουτήσατε, χωρὶς ἡμῶν ἐβασιλεύσατε). The perfect periphrasis naturally conveys contemporaneous temporal reference. All of these verbs are used to indicate a present state of affairs ("you are already full"; "you have become [i.e., *are now*] rich"; etc.). Since the two aorist verbs employ stative lexemes, however, these verbs view the entrance into the state in which the Corinthians now stand (i.e., they are "ingressive aorists"). They have *become* rich; they have *begun* to reign. This is a normal implication for perfective aspect when it is combined with stative lexemes (see Campbell, *The Basics of Verbal Aspect*, 87).

contrast to Paul,[48] especially in terms of their wisdom and gifts. Paul counters that the wisdom of the cross and the Spirit indicates that this inflated view of themselves is sadly mistaken. To *have all you want* sounds like an unqualifiedly good thing, as for example in feeling "full" after eating.[49] However, in the ancient world satiation was often associated with pride and licentiousness.[50] Likewise, though to *become rich* and *to reign* sound inherently positive, and can be meant this way by Paul in a spiritual sense,[51] here the descriptions are clearly meant to stamp the Corinthians' self-esteem as wildly inflated.

Many commentators take this verse as critical evidence that the Corinthian Christians suffered from an overrealized eschatology. The Corinthians were "behaving as if the age to come were already consummated, as if the saints had already taken over the kingdom (Dan. vii. 18)."[52] They had already arrived and were reigning now eschatologically. In response, throughout the letter Paul emphasizes the expectation of a future reign of Christ (e.g., 15:22-25).

The problem for this reconstruction is that, as Kuck notes, in vv. 9-13 "Paul counters their view with ethics, not with eschatology."[53] The already/not yet tension is not between existence in this life and the life to come, but between spiritual immaturity and maturity. In this sense 4:8 recalls 3:1-4: the Corinthians may think they have "already" arrived at maturity (4:8), but in Paul's view they are "not yet" there (3:2). The twice-repeated "already" of v. 8 refers to the Corinthians' thinking of themselves as morally and spiritually perfected, in Paul's view without "participation in Christ's sufferings, becoming like him in his death" (Phil. 3:10). We could paraphrase v. 8a as: "So soon and so easily you are filled . . . !"[54] It is not that they think they have experienced the eschaton that Paul still awaits, but rather that they have advanced to maturity ahead of Paul. Paul goes on in the following verses to contrast the cross-shaped lifestyle of the apostles with this Corinthian egotism. As Garland puts it: "The apostles live according to the wisdom of the cross; the Corinthians imbibe the wisdom of this age and pass themselves off as kings."[55]

A better explanation of the Corinthians' spiritual pretensions than assuming they betray a belief that the decisive eschatological events have already taken place is set forth in ancient sources. Imagining oneself to be

48. The clause *and that without us* (Gk. χωρὶς ἡμῶν) here means not that they reign without Paul's help but without his having a share in it (Fee, 173).

49. Cf. the use of κορέννυμι in the physical sense in Acts 27:38.

50. Cf. P. Marshall, *Enmity in Corinth*, 208, and Collins, 186, respectively.

51. For πλουτέω, 1 Cor. 1:5; βασιλεύω, 2 Tim. 2:12.

52. Barrett, 109. See esp. Anthony Thiselton, "Realized Eschatology at Corinth," *NTS* (1977-78), 510-26, and his 1 Corinthians commentary, 357; Fee, 172.

53. Kuck, *Judgment and Community Conflict*, 217. In Kuck's view, 218, "[i]n this section [1:10–4:21] Paul never opposes a future eschatology to the Corinthian spiritual pretensions."

54. Kuck, *Judgment and Community Conflict*, 216-17.

55. Garland, 137.

filled, rich, and reigning was in fact a claim made by Cynic and Stoic philosophers.[56] For example, according to Epictetus, the true Cynic can say, "Who, when he lays eyes upon me, does not feel that he is seeing his *king?*"[57] Plutarch's description of the Stoics is even closer to Paul's rendition of Corinthian claims: "But some think the Stoics are jesting when they hear that in their sect *the wise man* is termed not only prudent and just and brave, but also an orator, a poet, a general, *a rich man, and a king.*"[58] The Corinthians had apparently adopted the inflated self-understanding of pagan philosophy. Hays suggests plausibly that they may have argued that Christianity was the true wisdom that enabled them to attain the aims of the philosophers, not unlike the assertion of Philo of Alexandria that the law of Moses was the epitome of philosophical truth.[59] Hence, Corinthian problems are not to be attributed to their faulty theology or premature eschatology so much as to their conformity to the norms and values of pagan culture. Paul's strategy is to encourage the Corinthians "to understand themselves in terms of an apocalyptic narrative that locates present existence in between the cross and the *parousia.*"[60] It is true that the eschatological framework found throughout chapters 1–4 is at the heart of Paul's attack on Corinthian boasting. But eschatology is not so much the problem as it is the solution.

**4:9** The reason Paul wishes it was true that Christians had begun to reign is his own experience of suffering: *For it seems to me. . . .* Even if Paul can see value in suffering (Rom. 5:2, 2 Corinthians 1, etc.), he is no masochist and would prefer to be filled and free of affliction. But as 4:9-13 show, the only way to maintain the Corinthian triumphalist, prosperity theology of ease is to ignore the paradigmatic experience of the apostles. Luther's distinction between a theology of glory and a theology of the cross goes back to Pauline teaching of this order.[61] As Alister McGrath puts it, "The 'theologian of glory' expects God to be revealed in strength, glory and majesty, and is simply unable to accept the scene of dereliction on the cross as the self-revelation of God."[62]

Catalogues of hardship are not only common in Paul's letters (2 Cor. 4:7-12; 6:4-10; 11:23-29; 12:10; Rom. 8:35; Phil. 4:12) but also appear in other ancient writings as diverse as Stoic philosophy, Jewish apocalyptic, Josephus, and the Mishnah.[63] This is the first extant example from Paul. As

56. Kuck, *Judgment and Community Conflict,* 217-18; Hays, 70-71.

57. Epictetus, *Diatribai* 3.22.49.

58. Plutarch, *De Tranquillitate Animi* 472A. Philo knows and passes the maxim on in more than one place (*On the Posterity of Cain* 138; *On Dreams* 2:243-44; *On the Life of Abraham* 261; *On the Migration of Abraham* 197). It seems to have been one that was very commonly known in the Greco-Roman world.

59. Hays, 71.

60. Hays, 71.

61. Noted by Thiselton, 368.

62. Alister E. McGrath, *Luther's Theology of the Cross* (Oxford and Cambridge, MA: Blackwell, 1990), 167.

63. See John T. Fitzgerald, *Cracks in an Earthen Vessel: An Examination of the Catalogues*

Horsley notes, "[b]ecause life was difficult for the vast majority of people in antiquity it is not surprising that the variety of adversities encountered was a common literary and philosophical preoccupation."[64] The purpose of such forms varies in the literature. For example, if the Stoic use tends to stress the courage of the man under trial, the Cynic emphasizes independence from material prosperity for contentment. By contrast, for Paul, as Schrage notes, "the theme is the reflection of the cross, not heroic autonomy."[65]

Indeed, the best way to understand Paul's chronicles of woe is to note links to the death of Jesus. As Hays observes, "Paul regards these experiences not merely as misfortunes or trials to be surmounted but as identifying marks of the authenticity of his apostleship, because they manifest his conformity to Christ's sufferings."[66] In this sense, the argument from Paul's own experience in 4:9-13 is an extension of his conviction that the message of the cross is the ultimate solution to factionalism and boasting.

By way of introduction, he states explicitly that his afflictions are not outside of God's will; on the contrary, in his view[67] *God has put us apostles on display.* Various details of the list in 4:9-13 recall the sufferings of Christ. Most clearly, blessing in response to being reviled and ill treated in v. 12b is modeled on Jesus' example (Rom. 15:3). As Thiselton notes, "Christ's rejection as one 'dishonored' or 'disgraced' by the shame of the cross colors Paul's language [here]."[68] 2 Corinthians makes a specific connection between Paul's "being poor, yet making many rich" (6:10; cf. 1 Cor. 9:19-22) and the example of Jesus, who "though he was rich, yet for your sake he became poor, so that you through his poverty might become rich" (8:9). Hafemann is correct to link 4:10-13 with 2 Corinthians 1:9 and 2:14–3:3 as focusing on "dying with Christ."[69]

To depict his hardships Paul uses the disturbing metaphor of a gladiatorial show. In a public event with a cosmic audience, before the eyes of *the whole universe, angels as well as human beings,* God has put the apostles *on display* as a *spectacle.*[70] Implicitly, the Corinthians have the privileged position of spectators in the stands. On the other hand, unfortunately Paul and the

---

*of Hardships in the Corinthian Correspondence* (SBLDS 99; Atlanta: Scholars Press, 1988); Markus Schiefer Ferrari, *Die Sprache des Leids in den paulinischen Peristasenkatalogen* (SBB 23; Stuttgart: Katholisches Bibelwerk, 1991).

64. G. H. R. Horsley, "Review of John T. Fitzgerald, *Cracks in an Earthen Vessel,*" *Australian Biblical Review* 37 (1989), 83-84.

65. Schrage, 1:342 (Thiselton's translation).

66. Hays, 72.

67. Gk. δοκέω: "to consider as probable, *think, believe, suppose, consider*" or "to appear to one's understanding" (BDAG).

68. Thiselton, 367; cf. Kleinknecht, *Der Leidende Gerechtfertigte,* 221-41.

69. Scott J. Hafemann, *Suffering and the Spirit: An Exegetical Study of II Corinthians 2:14–3:3 within the Context of the Corinthian Correspondence* (WUNT 2.19; Tübingen: J. C. B. Mohr, 1986), 58.

70. Ἀποδείκνυμι, "to put on display," is used of theatrical entertainments, and θέατρον, "public spectacle," also points to a scene in an arena.

other apostles are in the ring *at the end of the procession.* The last and climactic event on the program, the criminals facing capital punishment must appear and fight to the death, "because they cannot win every combat, and their bloodied bodies will weaken until humiliation and death overtake them."[71] The apostles are *condemned to die in the arena;* reinforcing the image, Paul uses a word used for those thrown to the lions.[72] If the Corinthians think they are reigning, the apostles' lives are marked by struggle, disgrace, and failure, not unlike their Lord, who was literally executed as a criminal.

**4:10** Collins describes the rest of Paul's catalogue of woes as consisting of a sandwich structure of twelve items: (A) three contrasts between Paul and the Corinthians, v. 10; (B) six tribulations, vv. 11-12a; and (A) three contrasting actions, vv. 12b-13.[73]

Verse 10 presents the first antithetical triad in which the teaching (foolish versus wise), condition (weak versus strong), and position (dishonored versus glorified) of the apostles and the Corinthians are set in opposition.[74] Dripping with irony, and recalling the themes of 1:18–2:5 (see esp. 1:26-28), Paul effectively rebukes the Corinthians for their inflated self-esteem that takes no account of the lowly message of the cross. Appearances and reality are shown to be on collision course in view of the experience of the apostles.

The assertion that *we are fools* in the eyes of the world is clarified by the explanatory phrase, *for Christ.* It is "on account of"[75] Christ, for his sake, that the apostles have suffered humiliation. This accords with Luke's description of the apostles' response to persecution in Acts. For example, in Acts 5:41: "The Apostles left the Sanhedrin (having been flogged), rejoicing because they had been counted worthy of suffering disgrace for the Name."

Paul's assertion that the Corinthians, on the other hand, are *so wise in Christ,* is meant sarcastically. Paul stated his true opinion of them in 3:28: "you think you are wise by the standards of this age." The contrast of wisdom versus foolishness has already appeared in 1:18, 20, 21, 23, 25, and 27. In these verses "foolishness for Christ" is the prerequisite to ethical and spiritual transformation and aligns a person with God's future eschatological reversal wrought by the cross.

Likewise, in the gospel weakness and strength are turned on their heads, such that Paul can say: "I will boast more gladly of my weaknesses, so that Christ's power may rest with me" (2 Cor. 12:9). 2 Corinthians 13:4 illustrates again the relevance of the cross to Paul's remarks in these verses: "He was crucified in weakness, yet he lives by God's power. Likewise, we are weak in him, yet by God's power we will live with him in our dealing with you."

71. Thiselton, 360.
72. Gk. ἐπιθανάτιος, "under sentence of death"; *Bel and the Dragon* 31.
73. Collins, 184.
74. Robertson and Plummer, 86.
75. Note the preposition διά with the accusative.

The issue of the Corinthians' aspirations in terms of social status and prestige is summed up with the accusation: *You are honored,* but *we are dishonored.* Paul's discussion of glory and honor in 1:26-28 makes it clear that this is not intended to be an accolade. There, God chose the dishonorable in order to shame the honored! In this light the Corinthians' claim to be prudent, powerful, and of good repute disqualifies them from God's call. It is not that Paul doubts their standing before God, but rather he employs "shock tactics" to encourage them to match their conduct with their confession. In 6:20 and 10:31, using cognate terms, Paul will exhort the Corinthians to be more concerned about glorifying God than honoring themselves.[76]

**4:11-13** If the Corinthians are "already" replete, rich, and reigning (4:8), Paul counters in vv. 11-13 that his present experience is entirely otherwise; to underscore the contrast Paul repeats the word "now"[77] in the temporal phrases that mark off the subunit: *To this very hour* (4:11a) and "right up to this moment" (4:13b). Paul's point is that "[t]he present is a time of suffering, not glory."[78] In relation to the previous verse, vv. 11-13 describe the dishonor the apostles have achieved.[79] To risk understatement, the character of the apostles' ministry has been consistently nonregal. If v. 9 portrays the apostles as condemned criminals, vv. 10-13 depict them no more sympathetically, namely as maltreated strangers.

In contrast to Corinthian satiety, the apostles *go hungry and thirsty.* Instead of being rich and respectively attired, they *are in rags.*[80] To be poorly clothed was to be exposed to ridicule and shame. Although the verb is used only here in the New Testament, Revelation uses the related adjective in a text emphasizing its character as the opposite of being rich: "You say, 'I am rich . . . and do not need a thing.' But you do not realize that you are wretched, pitiful, poor, blind and *naked*" (3:17). The translation "naked" (cf. Mark 14:52) both here and in Revelation is defensible, but in both cases the word in question probably connotes an exaggerated reference to being miserably clad.

To be *brutally treated* exacerbates the ignominy and misery of the apostles. Suffering physical violence was a real possibility for many early Christians (cf. 1 Pet. 2:19-21). The verb in 1 Corinthians 4:11[81] can mean "to strike with the fist," and, by extension, can refer to being "knocked out" by a sickness (as possibly in 2 Cor. 12:7). As in other items in this hardship catalogue, it is symptomatic of being in disgrace (4:10b). In this sense it ties in with the next item, that is, being *homeless.* Respectable people can tell you where they live. The two descriptions also readily bring to mind the abuse suffered by

76. "Honored" in TNIV 4:10 translates ἔνδοξοι; cf. δοξάσατε in 6:20 and δόξαν in 10:31.

77. Gk. ἄρτι.

78. Garland, 141.

79. The verbs are plural, indicating that Paul is describing characteristic conditions that apply to the lives and work of all the apostles in general.

80. Gk. γυμνιτεύω is used only here in the New Testament and LXX.

81. Gk. κολαφίζω.

Jesus at his trial and the fact that he had "nowhere to lay his head" (Matt. 8:20; Luke 9:58). The implication of such connections is the apostles' identification with Christ and the cross, which is the subplot of the catalogue.[82]

The fact that Paul and the apostles *work hard with our own hands* may sound neutral or even positive to modern ears. However, as Hock and others point out, in the ancient world, or more specifically to the cultural elite with enough leisure time to savor the wisdom of the world, manual labor was a marker of a demeaning and low social status. In Paul's case, the tentmaker toiled in a small workplace "bent over a workbench like a slave and . . . working side by side with slaves . . . thereby being perceived by others and by himself as slavish and humiliated; of suffering the artisan's lack of status and so being reviled and abused."[83] In many cultures, the upper echelons of society still assess a man or woman's rank in the world by looking at their hands and fingernails.

With *when we are cursed, we bless,* Paul moves to speak of how the apostles respond to the ill treatment which they regularly receive. Paul could have in mind praying for those who abuse him. But the verb "to bless" outside religious contexts, which this seems to be, means "to reply with good words,"[84] those not designed to repay in kind (cf. Rom. 12:14, 17-21). Needless to say, cursing others, or "slandering" others, as the noun is translated in the vice lists of 1 Corinthians 5:11 and 6:10, has no place in the church and the kingdom of God. Nonretaliation was a central theme of Jesus' example and teaching (cf. Matt. 5:44; Luke 6:27).

The words *when we are persecuted, we endure it,* are anything but glib, given the very real possibility for the apostles of losing their life for Christ. To "put up with" serious abuse meant not to lose heart and, more specifically, not to give up the faith (cf. Mark 13:13; Matt. 10:22; 24:13; Luke 21:19; Rom. 5:3). In many cases persecution could have been deflected by simply denying Christ, whether explicitly or by falling into line behaviorally. Perseverance is an unspectacular but essential Christian virtue. Paul gets knocked down, but not knocked out.

*When we are slandered, we answer kindly* has a double edge. In one sense it reinforces the sentiment of v. 12 concerning being cursed and responding gently. On the other hand, "to answer kindly" translates a verb used on only two other occasions in these opening chapters of 1 Corinthians.[85] In both 1:10 and 4:16 it describes what Paul is trying to do in response to Corinthian boasting and factionalism: "I appeal to you . . . that there be no divisions among you" and "I urge you to imitate me" respectively. TNIV's

82. Cf. Merklein, 316.

83. Ronald F. Hock, *The Social Context of Paul's Ministry: Tentmaking and Apostleship* (Philadelphia: Fortress, 1980), 67 (cited by Thiselton, 362). Cf. Victor C. Pfitzner, *Paul and the Agon Motif: Traditional Athletic Imagery in the Pauline Literature* (SNTSMS 16; Leiden: Brill, 1967).

84. Thiselton, 363.

85. Gk. παρακαλέω.

three translations for the word ("appeal," "urge," and "answer kindly") reflect its various nuances. However, whereas most commentaries notice the function of its repetition in 1:10 and 4:16 (as an inclusio delimiting the unit), we must also not miss the significance of Paul's saying here that, when maligned, he responds with courteous exhortation. 1 Corinthians 1:10–4:17 is in fact a prime example of this insistence. At least some of the Corinthians had maligned Paul for various reasons. As 1:10 and 4:16 demonstrate, his response was not to retaliate, but rather "to exhort" them.

The contrast with the Corinthians' reigning is completed with Paul's final degrading self-description: *We have become the scum of the earth, the garbage of the world.* Whatever precise nuance may be meant by these disgusting epithets, it is clear that they are meant to recall the words, "we have been made a spectacle to the whole universe" (4:9).[86] The world's opinion of the apostles is summed up by these terms of abuse. The first phrase contains a word that has sometimes been translated as "scapegoat" or "sacrificial victim."[87] This meaning, it is thought, coincides with the ancient practice of sacrificing criminals in order to purify a city. In that case Paul would be saying that he and the apostles give their lives as offerings for the world. However, as Conzelmann notes, the fact the apostles do not die but are only "condemned to death" in v. 9 makes this interpretation unlikely.[88] Probably it is better to take the first phrase in the light of the second, as a general insult, both of which border on foul language.[89] The second term is translated by Luther as (the equivalent of English) "trash," and by Schrage as "dirt," "mud," or "excrement."[90] The apostles are "the world's scum, the scrapings from everyone's shoes" (Thiselton): "The apostle is searching for the lowest, strongest, most earthy language he can find."[91] Such a depiction of the apostles makes Paul's description of the Corinthians as "weak" and "lowly" in 1:26-27 seem like a compliment.

### c. Paul Admonishes Them as Their Father and Model, 4:14-17

*14I am writing this not to shame you but to warn you as my dear children.*
*15Even if you had ten thousand guardians in Christ, you do not have many fathers, for in Christ Jesus I became your father through the gospel.*
*16Therefore I urge you to imitate me. 17For this reason I have sent to you Timothy, my son whom I love, who is faithful in the Lord. He will remind you of*

86. Note the repetition of κόσμος in 4:9 and 4:13.

87. For example, BAGD; Barrett, 112; Gk. περικαθάρματα.

88. Conzelmann, 90; cf. BDAG, which points out that the expression "is similar to τὰ γὰρ λύματα καὶ καθάρματα τῇ χώρα ὅλῃ Jos., *Bell.* 4, 241, a description of unsavory characters" and that the initial ὡς "suggests the perception, wholly negative, that Paul's activity generates in the 'world.'"

89. See Fee, 180.

90. German *Kehricht* and *Drecke* respectively.

91. Thiselton, 365. The Greek word is περίψημα, which derives from ψάω, meaning "to wipe, rub or scrape."

*my way of life in Christ Jesus, which agrees with what I teach everywhere in every church.*

**4:14-15** In drawing such a stark contrast between himself and the Corinthians in 4:6-13, Paul effectively condemned the Corinthians for their insensitive pride; in the face of the lowly existence of the apostles, they are self-exalting and arrogant! Not surprisingly, then, in the following verse he seeks to reassure them, *I am writing this not to shame you. This* could refer to his entire treatment of their factionalism, extending back to 1:10, but the potentially offensive character of the previous paragraph, with its heavy irony and biting sarcasm, makes it the more likely antecedent for the demonstrative pronoun. Paul's directness is not intended to demolish their self-respect, "to crush them with self-recrimination,"[92] but rather to bring about change for their good.

His purpose has not been to embarrass or disgrace them *but to warn* them.[93] A favorite term of Paul's, the verb in question[94] occurs eight times in the New Testament, seven in his letters (and once in Paul's speech to the Ephesian elders in Acts 20:31). It is often translated "to admonish" or "to instruct." BDAG suggests the meaning "to counsel about avoidance or cessation of an improper course of conduct, *admonish, warn, instruct.*" According to Paul, a major responsibility of church leaders is to "warn" those for whom they care in the Lord (1 Thess. 5:12). Believers are likewise to "warn" each other (1 Thess. 5:14; Rom. 15:14; Col. 3:16). Such "warning" often takes the shape of seeking to correct those "brothers and sisters" who do not obey apostolic instruction (2 Thess. 3:15). Colossians 1:28, which resonates at many levels with the opening chapters of 1 Corinthians, is a good summary of his strategy and intention in confronting Corinthian boasting and factionalism: "We proclaim him [cf. 1 Cor. 2:2], *admonishing* and teaching everyone with all wisdom [cf. 1 Cor. 2:6], so that we may present everyone fully mature in Christ."

The basis on which Paul attempts to correct the Corinthians is his filial relationship with them: I *warn you as my dear children.* Paul regularly thinks of himself in this way in relating to the churches he founded (e.g., 2 Cor. 6:12; 1 Thess. 2:11). Indeed, "father/son" was a common image in Old Testament and Jewish wisdom literature for the teacher-student relationship (e.g., Prov. 1:8, 10; 2:1; 3:1; Sir. 2:1; 3:1)[95] and was also present in the pagan mystery religions.[96] Paul goes on to explain to the Corinthians why

92. Thiselton, 369.

93. The appropriateness of the language is seen in Josephus, *Jewish War* 1.148, where Herod threatens his sons as king and "warns" (νουθετεῖν) them as father (cited by Conzelmann, 91).

94. Gk. νουθετέω.

95. Fee, 184.

96. Lucius calls the priest who initiates him into the mysteries of Isis his "spiritual father" (Apuleius, *Metamorphoses* 11.25).

they are his children: *for in Christ Jesus I became your father through the gospel.* Through Paul they came to faith (2:4-5), for he "planted" (3:6) and laid the foundation (3:10) of the garden-temple, which is the church of God in Corinth. It is for this reason that Paul must undertake the arduous task of correcting the Corinthians. His actions are motivated by parental love; "for what children are not disciplined by their parents?" (Heb. 10:7).

To underscore the obligation Paul bears to warn the Corinthians, he stresses the uniqueness of their relationship using hyperbole: *Even if you had ten thousand guardians in Christ, you do not have many fathers.* "Ten thousand" is an idiom for an extremely high number (surpassed in the New Testament only by "ten thousand times ten thousand" in Rev. 9:16 ["two hundred million" in TNIV]). *Not many* is understatement for "one." Paul's relationship with the Corinthians is unique and cannot be replicated.

In the Greco-Roman world a "guardian" was "a slave or paid attendant who accompanied the child for the purpose of protection, guidance, and general supervision of behavior, e.g., to and from school, or on occasions when a parent was absent."[97] With no direct modern equivalent, it has been translated variously, as "tutor" (REB), "instructor" (AV/KJV), "attendant," and "custodian" (BAGD).[98] Garland points out that in the ancient world the "guardian" was sometimes caricatured as a stern, ignorant, and uncaring taskmaster and argues that Paul is referring disparagingly, if not to the other apostles or Apollos, then at least to "the local leaders of the competitive factions."[99] But on both counts this is to overinterpret Paul's metaphor. Paul's point here is not to say something about any other leader in Corinth, but to clarify the motivation for his warning; he does not do so as one whose motivation may be questioned but out of parental love, as their father.

**4:16** With *Therefore, I urge you,* Paul recalls the opening words of his response to Corinthian factionalism in 1:10 and signals the rounding off of his advice on the subject. The opening four chapters of the letter can be summarized in the command: *imitate me.*[100] Though perhaps unusual for us, this directive made perfect sense in Paul's day. Many teachers acted as models for their pupils.[101] Furthermore, the injunction in question follows on from the father imagery of 4:14-15; it is only natural for children to emulate their parents.

Paul has in fact spoken often about his own behavior and attitudes in this opening section of the letter. So it is no surprise that he should point to himself as a model. Though to us it may sound conceited, if Paul were not

97. Thiselton, 370.

98. Gk. παιδαγωγός. BDAG gives the meaning "one who has responsibility for someone who needs guidance, *guardian, leader, guide.*"

99. Garland, 146.

100. Paul uses a present imperative (γίνεσθε), which clearly implicates a command for situations in general. As we have already mentioned, this is in keeping with the imperfective aspect of present imperatives.

101. Lindemann, 114-15.

able to do this he would be guilty of hypocrisy, telling the Corinthians to act in ways he himself does not follow. But it is not that the apostle expected strict uniformity among the Corinthian Christians. In chapters 7 and 8–10 he leaves room for the role of individual conscience on various secondary matters. The command to imitate him must be understood in context.

What Paul expects the Corinthians to imitate are those things that will end the boasting and factionalism in Corinth. Garland explains: "They are to welcome being regarded as fools for Christ, and as weak and dishonored. . . . They are to recognize that all that they are and have comes to them as a grace-gift from God (3:10) and that they are not inherently extraordinary (4:7). They are to think of themselves as no better than menial field hands (3:5) and servants (4:1) awaiting God's judgment to determine if they were trustworthy (4:5). They are to rid themselves of all resentments and rivalries with co-workers so that they can toil together in God's field (3:5-9). They are to resist passing themselves off as wise or elite by using lofty words of wisdom or aligning themselves with those who do and to rely instead on the power of God that works through weakness, fear, and trembling (2:1-4)."[102] These actions and attitudes constitute the pattern of Paul's life both in the present and as he had lived it out before the Corinthians. In short, Paul is a model of the wisdom of the cross. Paul's life in its entirety had been stamped by the message of the cross, which excludes boasting and promotes humility. Indeed, later in the letter, he will say, "Follow my example, as I follow the example of Christ" (11:1). The Corinthians (and we) should make it their aim to be able to follow Paul in calling others to imitate the pattern he has modeled (2 Tim. 2:2), which is, after all, the pattern established by Christ himself.

**4:17** In order to facilitate Corinthian imitation of Paul, Paul did something concrete, along with writing to the Corinthians: *For this reason I have sent to you Timothy.* This "sending" could be an indication that Timothy is the bearer of Paul's letter.[103] However, 1 Corinthians 16:10 suggests otherwise: "When Timothy comes" implies that the Corinthians will still be expecting Timothy after receiving the letter. It is more likely that Timothy was sent by Paul on business that will include visits to both Macedonia (cf. Acts 19:22) and Corinth before the letter was written and that Paul now expects him to arrive in Corinth after its delivery.[104] Timothy, like the Corinthians, is Paul's *son,* whom he *loves.* Like Paul, he is "faithful in the Lord," the very requirement of church leaders Paul highlights in 4:2 and which is an attribute of God in 1:9. For this reason, Paul writes, Timothy *will remind you of my way of life in Christ Jesus.* Timothy lives the same way Paul does.

The reference to *my way of life in Christ Jesus* gives Paul's priority in all

102. Garland, 147.

103. In this case ἔπεμψα would be an epistolary aorist and would best be translated, "I am sending."

104. Barrett, 116.

his work. Paul is not to be compared to a university lecturer who may be interested in education only in the narrow, cognitive sense. He does teach, but his goal is to convey "how one ought to walk and please God" (1 Thess. 4:1). Doctrine and ethics are intimately related in all of his letters, perhaps preeminently in 1 Corinthians, where scarcely a paragraph concerns either belief or practice exclusively.[105] "Ways"[106] (the term is in the plural literally) reminds us of the Jewish metaphor of "walking," common also in Paul's letters, to encompass the whole of life lived out in obedience to God, *halakah.*

Paul's practical teaching to the Corinthians is not narrow or idiosyncratic but general and universal; in his words, it is *what I teach everywhere in every church.* This reassuring note is struck three more times in the letter encompassing the first three main blocks of instruction (see 7:17; 11:16; 14:33). What makes the expression of it in 4:17 distinctive is the rather redundant phrase *everywhere in every church.* It would be a mistake to write off this emphasis in the letter as a sociological ploy aimed at achieving conformity and compliance across the Pauline churches. Rather, it testifies to Paul's open agenda of contributing to the end-time universal worship of the one true God by Gentiles (see Introduction, 13-18, 25-35). It recalls the allusion to Malachi 1:11 in 1 Corinthians 1:2, where Paul writes to "all those who call upon the name of the Lord *in every place.*" This connection may also be further evidence that he is closing off this opening section of the letter on factionalism. Not only do 1 Corinthians 1:2 and 4:17 include references to "every place,"[107] but they are also the first two places in the letter where Paul uses the word "church." Furthermore, Paul's explicit reference to Christ in 4:14-17 (four times in four verses) is reminiscent of the similar accumulation in the letter opening (ten times in ten verses). While 1:1-10 introduces the letter as a whole and not just chapters 1–4, a recollection of the theme of Christ's universal Lordship in the church to end off the first major unit is fitting and suggests that 4:14-17 is the end of the section.

## III. "FLEE SEXUAL IMMORALITY" AND "GLORIFY GOD WITH YOUR BODIES," 4:18–7:40

"Practically all commentaries and translations"[1] assume that Paul finishes his treatment of divisions at the end of chapter 4, and turns to the subject of the incestuous man at the beginning of chapter 5. Doubts about this posi-

105. See Brian S. Rosner, "Paul's Ethics," in *The Cambridge Companion to St. Paul* (ed. James D. G. Dunn; Cambridge: Cambridge University Press, 2003), 212-23.

106. The word (ὁδός) appears again in 12:31 in the reference to "the most excellent way."

107. Gk. ἐν παντὶ τόπῳ and πανταχοῦ respectively.

1. Ellingworth and Hatton, 101. Ellingworth and Hatton themselves are of two minds.

tion, however, surface with Calvin, who begins the latter discourse with 4:21; Hurd, who treats 4:18-21 as a transitional passage; and Fee, who notes several links between 4:18-20 and 5:2-6. The transmission of the Greek text also shows that some of the earliest copyists disagreed on the question of where one section ends and the next begins. Various manuscripts begin new paragraphs at 4:14, 16, 17, 18, and 21 (NA[26]), while others mark 4:21 as beginning *kephalaion* 2 (an ancient system of marking divisions). Codex Vaticanus marks the new section at 4:16. The current chapter division is often defended by noting an inclusio, which in fact suggests that the unit ends earlier than 4:18-21: "The entire section (1:10–4:21) is set off by the phrase 'I exhort you' (1:10; 4:16)."[2]

The best solution is to start the new section at 4:18. 4:18-21 should not be divided since these verses deal with one subject, namely, Paul's proposed visit to Corinth. Three observations suggest that they belong with chapters 5 and 6.[3] First, the threatening tone of 4:21 ("a rod of discipline") is more in keeping with what follows than what precedes; note the contrast with 4:14, where Paul lightly admonishes the Corinthians as children. Secondly, 4:18-21 introduces ideas that are picked up in chapter 5: "being puffed up" (4:18-19; 5:2); "power" (4:19-20; 5:4); and Paul's being present (4:19; 5:3-4). Thirdly, 4:16-17 contains ideas that are found in other verses that close sections (imitating Paul [4:16; 11:1] and "the practice of all the churches" [4:17; 11:16]), and has elements that form an inclusio with 1:10 (the verb "to appeal/urge"[4] [1:10; 4:16]; the call to unity in 1:10 is reiterated with the call to imitate Paul's example in 4:16).

The main argument for taking 4:18-21 with what follows rather than with what precedes is the tone of the passage. Garland's observation is accurate even if he fails to draw the obvious conclusion: "In these opening chapters [1–4] Paul insinuates that the church is riven by unnecessary strife fed by unjustified spiritual pride. Threatening to come after them with a rod (4:21), however, seems a bit extreme to settle such problems. The three cases cited in 5:1–6:20 make that threat more understandable."[5] Paul's mood takes a turn for the worse when he discusses the pressing issues of chapters 5 and 6. Numerous rhetorical questions, exclamations, and other stylistic features point to a more emotive appeal than in the section on divisions. The stern warning of 4:18-21 sets up what Thiselton rightly calls Paul's response to "Moral Issues Which Demand a Clear-Cut Verdict (5:1–6:20)." If the Corinthians are not free of the problems of incest, lawsuits, and prostitution, Paul will indeed have to come with "a rod of discipline." 2 Corinthians 12:20-21 is an instructive parallel, where Paul expresses his

2. Garland, 39.

3. Cf. Ralph Bruce Terry, "Patterns of Discourse Structure in 1 Corinthians," *JOTT* 7/4 (1996), 8.

4. Gk. παρακαλέω.

5. Garland, 151. Garland persists in taking 4:18-21 as part of chs. 1–4.

anxiety that when he visits Corinth he not find "impurity and sexual sin" (among other sins).

Having decided that the unit under discussion begins with 4:18-21, the next question is how far it extends. Most commentators take 5:1–6:20 together, but there is disagreement as to whether to treat 7:1-40 as a separate section (e.g., Schrage, Garland), along with 5:1–6:20 (e.g., Collins), or with 8:1–11:1 (e.g., Thiselton). Starting a new section with 7:1 has in its favor the reference to the Corinthian letter: "Now for the matters you wrote about." This introduces a section in which Paul gives his "Response to Inquiries"[6] put to him by the Corinthians. However, whether or not all of chapters 7–16 should be taken as Paul's response to a letter from Corinth is uncertain.[7] Mitchell disputes whether "now concerning"[8] in 7:1, 25; 8:1; 12:1; 16:1, 12 should always be taken as a signal that Paul is taking up a topic from the letter.[9] Either way, Terry observes rightly that Paul actually alternates between responding to oral reports (1:10–6:20; 11:2-34; 15:1-58) and the Corinthian letter (7:1–11:1; 12:1–14:40; 16:1-12).[10] All this suggests that the order in which Paul addresses the church's problems in 1 Corinthians, the shape of the letter, has more to do with his own priorities and agenda than with the source of his information. Along with discourse markers, we should take content as a major indication of the demarcation of units in the letter.

1 Corinthians 4:18–6:20, covering incest, lawsuits, and prostitution, should be taken together with 7:1-40, on sexual relations, divorce, and marriage, as a single unit.[11] The first part offers a negative treatment of sexual immorality, the second a positive counterbalance.[12] This same panel structure was seen in 1:10–4:17, where Paul's discussion of wisdom begins with a negative treatment (1:18–2:5) but then moves to a more positive one (2:6–3:4). Likewise, the next main section, 8:1–14:40, deals with the issue of idolatry, beginning again with a negative treatment of its manifestations in

6. Thiselton, 483.

7. For example, Barrett, 153-54; cf. Thiselton, 483, who extends the response only through 11:1.

8. Gk. περὶ δέ.

9. Margaret M. Mitchell, "Concerning περὶ δέ in 1 Corinthians," *NovT* 31 (1989), 229-56.

10. Terry, *A Discourse Analysis of First Corinthians*, 43.

11. Cf. Alistair Scott May, *'The Body for the Lord': Sex and Identity in 1st Corinthians 5–7* (JSNTSup 278; London: T&T Clark, 2004), 3: "Paul's decision to connect his response to the oral report and the issues raised by the letter, even if only sequentially, may well indicate that the form of 5.1-7.40, although responsive, is *his* construct for *his* reasons" (italics original). 1 Cor. 4:18–7:40, as May, 3-4, argues, are also united by a number of linguistic and conceptual links. These include the boundaries of the physical body (6:12-20; 7:4); the discussion of "authority" (ἐξουσία); the argument that the Corinthians "were bought at a price" (6:20; 7:23); and more generally the compatibility of sexual and spiritual unions in 6:12-20 and ch. 7. We may add the inclusio of reference to Paul's authority in 4:21 ("a rod of discipline") and 7:40 ("I have the Spirit of God").

12. On 6:1-11, which does not concern matters sexual, see below.

Corinth (chs. 8–10) and then moving to a more positive treatment of the proper worship of the one true God (chs. 11–14).[13]

The injunction to "flee sexual immorality" (6:18a), while having obvious relevance to its immediate context (going to prostitutes), may also act as a summary command for 4:18–6:20, occurring as it does at end of this subunit. The more positive closing injunction in 6:20b, "Therefore glorify God with your bodies," a sort of hinge command, sets up Paul's treatment of sex in marriage in 7:1-40.[14] As it turns out, the following unit on idolatry and worship, 8:1–14:40, has parallel commands that function similarly: "flee idolatry" (10:14b) and "do all for the glory of God" (10:31b).

Recalling the echo of Malachi 1:11 LXX in 1 Corinthians 1:2, we believe that Paul's overriding aim for the Corinthians is that they may be part of the fulfillment of God's eschatological plan to be "*glorified* among all the Gentiles . . . *in every place.*" For this to happen, it is imperative that the Corinthian church be rid of the characteristic Gentile problems of sexual immorality and idolatry, that they flee these sins and instead glorify God with their bodies and worship.

## A. Condemnation of Illicit Sexual Relations: "Flee Sexual Immorality" (and Greed), 4:18–6:20

At first blush the three topics dealt with in this section, incest (5:1-13), lawsuits (6:1-11), and prostitution (6:12-20), seem unrelated. Attempts to identify an overarching theme which links the discussions yield different results. Each passage deals either with competitive greed (Countryman), irrational passion (Fiore), confusion about purity markers (Meeks), failures to apply the faith to moral decisions (Parry), or the community's competence to judge (Probst).[15] Garland's understanding is that "key to all three passages is Paul's concern that they do untold damage to their witness to Christ's reign by being guilty of incest, hauling fellow Christians before unbelievers to judge petty conflicts, and continuing in their former whoredom."[16]

While each of these suggestions has some validity in a general thematic sense, a more specific way of following Paul's train of thought is first to notice the common theme of sexual immorality in 5:1-13 and 6:12-20; this is more evident in the Greek, where *porn-* cognates appear nine times in eight different verses (translated variously as "sexual immorality," "sexu-

13. Schrage takes 11:2–14:40 to be one section covering "Gottesdienstfragen" (questions concerning worship). Note how 12:2 relates the following material back to the issue of idolatry.

14. The reference to "sexual immorality" in 7:2 also forges a link between 7:1-40 and 4:18–6:20.

15. Garland, 151.

16. Garland, 152.

ally immoral people," "the immoral," and "the prostitute"; 5:1, 9, 10, 11; 6:13, 15, 16, 18 [twice]).[17] Once this overall theme is identified, 6:1-11 can be seen as another pressing moral concern which shares with 5:1-13 a concern for judging; in the Greek the verb "to judge"[18] appears twice in 5:12 and three times in 6:2-3. Paul's mind, it seems, moved from judgment in the church and God judging the world (5:1-13) to the Corinthians' being judged before "the ungodly" (6:1-11).

This understanding of how 5:1-13 and 6:1-11 relate is supported by the citation of the expulsion formula from Deuteronomy in 5:13b. Sean McDonough points to the significance of the verses which follow the same words in Deuteronomy 17:7.[19] Beginning in 17:8, the discussion turns to the question of judging difficult cases within Israel. This climaxes with a repetition of the key phrase from 17:7 in v. 12: when the people enact just judgments, they will "drive out the evil from Israel." Words related to "judging"[20] occur in Deuteronomy 17:8, 9, 11, and 12, are picked up in 1 Corinthians 5:3 and 12-13, and then proliferate with the beginning of chapter 6. Paul uses the words of Deuteronomy 17:7 in 1 Corinthians 5:13, and then immediately moves on to the question of difficult cases of judgment, just as the writer of Deuteronomy had done. The fact that Deuteronomy wraps up its discussion by repeating "you will drive out the evil" makes Paul's use of this material all the more likely.

In this sense both 1 Corinthians 5:1-13 and 6:1-11 treat legal matters. This is most evident when the Old Testament distinctions between civil and criminal processes of law are recognized.[21] Incest, the problem in 5:1-13, falls into the category of criminal law, and the dispute in 6:1-11 is covered by civil law, which deals with relations within a group. Criminal cases in the Old Testament "were decided by the head of a community on his own authority or by the people as a corporate whole,"[22] both of which occur in 5:3-5, where Paul pronounces judgment and calls for the consent of the body corporate. Criminal legislation in the Old Testament "speaks of the offender in the third person and addresses the breaching community in the second" (Exod. 21:14, 23, etc.).[23] This is precisely Paul's style in 5:1-13. Old Testament civil cases, on the other hand, were to be presented to the judges described in Exodus 18, Deuteronomy 1, and related pas-

17. Peter Richardson's attempt to see a sexual matter in 6:1-11, "Judgment in Sexual Matters in 1 Corinthians 6:1-11," *NovT* 255 (1983), 37-58, finds no support in the text.

18. Gk. κρίνω.

19. Sean M. McDonough, "Competent to Judge: The Old Testament Connection between 1 Corinthians 5 and 6," *JTS* 56.1 (2005), 99-102.

20. Gk. κρίσις, κριτής.

21. Martin J. Buss, "The Distinction between Civil and Criminal Law in Ancient Israel," in *Proceedings of the Sixth World Congress of Jewish Studies* (ed. Avigdor Shinan; Jerusalem: World Union of Jewish Studies, 1977), 1:51-62.

22. Buss, "The Distinction between Civil and Criminal Law in Ancient Israel," 53.

23. Buss, "The Distinction between Civil and Criminal Law in Ancient Israel," 59: "he who does x, must be 'expelled' or 'put to death.'"

sages. It is the model of these judges that informs Paul's discussion in 6:1-11 (see below).

If Paul's main concern in 5:1-13 and 6:12-20 is to address sexual immorality, the basic fault with which he deals in 6:1-11 is greed. That greed is the reason some of the Corinthians are taking each other to court is suggested by the civil nature of the case (see below). It is also hinted at with the appearance of "the greedy" in the vice lists in 5:10, 11 and "thieves" and "the greedy" in 6:10. Jews and Christians considered pagans to be characteristically guilty of three sins, namely sexual immorality, idolatry, and greed. In the Pauline corpus, only these three vices are considered so grave that they need to be fled:[24] sexual immorality in 1 Corinthians 6:18; idolatry in 1 Corinthians 10:14; and greed in 1 Timothy 6:11.[25]

### 1. A Stern Warning: Paul's Impending Visit, 4:18-21

*[18]Some of you have become arrogant, as if I were not coming to you. [19]But I will come to you very soon, if the Lord is willing, and then I will find out not only how these arrogant people are talking, but what power they have. [20]For the kingdom of God is not a matter of talk but of power. [21]What do you prefer? Shall I come to you with a rod of discipline, or shall I come in love and with a gentle spirit?*

In this passage Paul confronts a church in which certain members are arrogant, based on their pretensions to possess wisdom and their preference for one leader over another. Some, it seems, openly repudiate Paul's authority, perhaps on the grounds that other leaders seemed more polished and sophisticated. In the most uncompromising passage in the letter to this point, Paul threatens to administer harsh discipline should the Corinthians fail to deal in particular with the disgraceful behavior he will address in the following two chapters. In these ominous verses he gives them fair warning and time to get their affairs in order, or else!

**4:18** Perhaps on hearing that Timothy and not Paul is likely to visit Corinth, some in Corinth have become inflated with arrogant self-importance.[26] As Ambrosiaster suggests, some of the Corinthians were apparently angry with Paul for not visiting them, not because they particularly wanted him to, but because they were proud and felt offended that Paul apparently thought them unworthy of a visit.[27] On the basis of 1 Corinthians 16:10-12 we may surmise that the Corinthians may have found Timothy rather timid ("When Timothy comes, see to it that he has nothing

24. Gk. φεύγω.
25. In context φιλαργυρία, "the love of money" (1 Tim. 6:10).
26. The verb "to be puffed up/conceited" (φυσιόω) always has a negative sense in Paul's writings.
27. Bray, 43.

to fear while he is with you"), especially when compared with Apollos, whom some may have preferred to visit Corinth ("Now about our brother Apollos: I strongly urged him to go to you with the brothers").

**4:19** *But I will come to you very soon* does not turn out to be the flattering news they might have hoped for. Given the current state of the church of God in Corinth, Paul does not anticipate a laudatory visit but one in which his purpose will not be to admire the Corinthians' speech but to inspect their effectiveness in life,[28] *to find out*[29] *not only how these arrogant people are talking, but what power they have.* A key word in Paul's critique of the Corinthians, "power" refers to solid, enduring effects as opposed to that which lacks substance and is shallow and passing. Paul has already spoken of the "power" of God (1:18; 2:5), of Christ (1:24), and of the gospel (2:5). Here, as in 2:4-5, the contrast is between mere words or rhetorical artistry, and the power of God to change lives and destinies.

Since in 16:8 Paul says that he will remain in Ephesus until Pentecost, *very soon* should be understood in relative terms, as "before long."[30] "If the Lord is willing" points to Paul's humility rather than any prevarication; Paul consistently qualifies his travel plans as being dependent on the will of God (1 Cor. 16:7; Rom. 1:10; 15:32; 1 Thess. 3:11; Phlm. 22). Exactly what Paul intends should he visit Corinth is difficult to say. Hays suggests that "Paul expects that if necessary God will unleash some manifestation of the power of the Spirit that will humble the arrogant ones . . . [such as] in the story of Elijah's triumph over the prophets of Baal (1 Kings 18:20-40), a story that Paul elsewhere connects to his own apostolic vocation (Rom 11:2-4)."[31]

**4:20** To make clear why he can contrast sophisticated words with substance, Paul explains that *the kingdom of God is not a matter of talk but of power.* In part a polemical rejoinder to the Corinthians who fancy themselves already to be reigning as kings (4:8), Paul asserts that God's kingdom functions differently from what the Corinthian boasters may have imagined. Their situation actually forms a contrast to the kingdom of God. Where Christ reigns, how impressive you sound is not an issue. Rather, what counts is whether your deeds are carried through effectively. As Collins observes, once again "Paul uses an apocalyptic motif to confound the inflated self-esteem of the Corinthians"[32] (cf. 2:6-16; 3:17; 4:5, 8). Though relatively infrequent in Paul, "the kingdom of God" occurs more often in

28. Thiselton, 376.

29. Whether the future form of γινώσκω here (translated *to find out*) is taken as a stative or a dynamic verb, it should probably be understood as implying the learning of information ("to arrive at a knowledge of someone or someth[ing]" or "acquire information"; BDAG), consistent which the TNIV translation.

30. Cf. the use of ταχέως in Phil. 2:19, 24 and 2 Tim. 4:9, where BDAG gives the meaning as "pert[aining] to a future point of time that is subsequent to another point of time, with focus on brevity of interval rather than on speed of activity" (cf. Garland, 148).

31. Hays, 75.

32. Collins, 202.

1 Corinthians than in any of his other letters (6:9, 10; 15:24, 50; five times and only seven elsewhere). It refers to the final coming of God as king, a reign which has been inaugurated with the cross and resurrection of Christ but has not yet been brought to consummation.

**4:21** A pair of rhetorical questions puts what is at stake in sharp perspective. The choice is in the hands of the Corinthians: *What do you prefer?* The options before them are either to act on Paul's instructions in the letter, specifically those in chapters 5 and 6 (to expel the incestuous man, to stop taking each other to court, and to cease going to prostitutes), which will mean that Paul will come to Corinth *in love and with a gentle spirit,* or alternatively to face *the rod of discipline.* This posture of Paul is reminiscent of 2 Corinthians 12:12, where he is "humble" when present but "bold" when absent. Obviously, the former is Paul's preferred mode of operation.

A "rod"[33] could be used for a number of different purposes, such as an aid to walking, herding animals, or beating people.[34] The rod that Paul threatens to brandish reluctantly is what Old Testament wisdom believed a father should use to drive out folly from the heart of his children (Prov. 22:15; 23:13-14; see 1 Cor. 4:15: "in Christ Jesus I became your father").

Whether he comes to Corinth boldly or gently, Paul expects his future face-to-face contact with the Corinthians to involve some form of correction. The choice is not between discipline or no discipline, but between harsh and gentle discipline. The "gentleness"[35] Paul hopes to employ is one commonly utilized in the context of correction, as Galatians 6:1 ("If someone is caught in a sin, you who live by the Spirit should restore that person *gently*") and 2 Timothy 2:25 ("opponents must be *gently* instructed") demonstrate. It is understood that Paul's relationship to the Corinthian church will require him to fulfill his responsibilities by exercising fatherly discipline while among them.

## 2. *A Virulent Ruling: The Case of Incest, 5:1-13*

Paul was appalled to learn that the Corinthians were condoning or at least tolerating the ongoing sexual relationship[36] of a member of their congregation with his unbelieving stepmother.[37] This is an extraordinary situation,

33. Gk. ῥάβδος.

34. Louw and Nida, 1:78 (§ 6.218).

35. Gk. πραΰτης.

36. The verb "to have" does not necessarily denote marriage as in 1 Cor. 7:2, 29 (contra Mare), since it can be used to refer to a nonmarital relationship (cf. John 4:18; Robertson and Plummer, 96). Barrett and Conzelmann's conclusion is preferable: in 1 Cor. 5:1 marriage and cohabitation are both possibilities.

37. Most commentators agree that she is the man's stepmother: there is no explicit mention of "incest," and marriage (if it is in view) was illegal between mother and son (cf. the *Institutes* of Gaius 1.63; Héring, 34). Both the Old Testament (Lev. 18:7-8) and Judaism

to risk an understatement, and it raises several questions: Since such relationships were forbidden in the Old Testament and Judaism, how could the situation have arisen in the Corinthian church? What motivated the man to enter the illicit relationship? Was it for theological, personal, or perhaps financial reasons? Why did the church fail to discipline him? We must admit that there is little evidence in 1 Corinthians to use in the task of reconstruction. Some knowledge of the social and legal background to first-century society in Corinth may help.

Andrew Clarke suggests, in the light of Roman marriage laws, that the main motivation for the relationship may have been financial.[38] Perhaps he entered the relationship either to stop his stepmother remarrying, thus keeping his father's inheritance, or to keep his mother-in-law's dowry from returning to her father, which would occur if she remained unattached. J. K. Chow believes similarly that the man was concerned that his wealthy stepmother would remarry into another family, taking her assets with her.[39] The fact that "the greedy" are listed next to the "immoral" in the vice lists of vv. 10-11 takes on new significance with this view. The simpler explanation of personal attraction cannot, of course, be ruled out. Deming supplies evidence that stepmothers "were often closer in age to the man's children than to the man himself."[40] Indeed, the stepmother may have been younger than her stepson.[41]

Paul's response to the report of incest is to insist that the man be excluded from the congregation. That Paul's instructions have links with his scriptural inheritance is clear from the use of Passover/unleavened bread imagery in vv. 7-8 and from the quotation of the Deuteronomic expulsion formula in v. 13b. As it turns out, these are just the "tip of the iceberg" of scriptural dependence. A study of biblical and Jewish teaching on exclusion reveals many points of contact with Paul's thinking in this chapter. The details are worked out in the commentary.

In short, the rationale Paul provides for the expulsion recalls teaching from the Pentateuch, where exclusion is undertaken for three reasons: for breaking the covenant; because of guilt by association; and for the maintenance of holiness. The three motifs form a package of three perspectives on the identity of Israel; people are excluded because Israel is the sanctified (holiness motif), covenant (covenant motif) community (corporate responsibility motif) of the Lord, the holy God. These motifs undergird Paul's

---

(*m. Sanhedrin* 7:4) appear to have acknowledged the distinction between a mother and a stepmother in the context of sexual relations.

38. Andrew D. Clarke, *Secular and Christian Leadership in Corinth: A Socio-Historical and Exegetical Study of 1 Corinthians* (Leiden: E. J. Brill, 1993), 80-85.

39. John K. Chow, *Patronage and Power: A Study of Social Networks in Corinth* (JSNTSup 75; Sheffield: JSOT Press, 1992), 130-41.

40. Will Deming, "The Unity of 1 Corinthians 5–6," *JBL* 115.2 (1996), 294.

41. Cf. Susan M. Treggiari, *Roman Marriage: Iusti Coniuges from the Time of Cicero to the Time of Ulpian* (Oxford: Oxford University Press), 401.

teaching throughout the passage.[42] Not only the main lines but also many of the details of Paul's instructions bear the imprint of the Scriptures. Throughout chapter 5 Paul moves within the biblical world of thought, employing vocabulary that has associations with the teaching of the Old Testament on exclusion from the community.

Paul's judgment on the case of the incestuous man in the Corinthian church is simple and to the point: the man must be removed. The command to expel the sinner occurs no fewer than six times: it is presented metaphorically in vv. 5a, 7a, and 8, in a general context in v. 11, and literally, its strongest form, at the beginning and very end of the passage, vv. 2c and 13b. In fact, each of the units in our outline closes with an equivalent command to evict the sinner.

The strength of Paul's feelings on the matter is also unmistakable. Apparently Paul considered the expulsion of the sinner imperative to protect the church's felicitous existence before God. The urgency with which Paul addresses the problem can be seen in several ways. Paul's incredulity and disquiet at the Corinthians' complacency are signaled: by the rather abrupt beginning using the word "actually" (BDAG) or "undoubtedly" (JB; cf. 1 Cor. 6:7; 15:29; Matt. 5:34);[43] by asyndeton, the lack of any connecting word like "and," "but," or "therefore," which often indicates a heightening of emotions, at the beginning of vv. 7 and 10, and in the middle of v. 13; and by exclamations and rhetorical questions. All of this reveals the urgency with which Paul expects the Corinthians to act.

Previewing the unit, in vv. 1-2 Paul rebukes the Corinthians for their inaction and tells them in no uncertain terms to remove the offender. Verses 3-5 supply authoritative support for this action, namely, Paul's presence in spirit and the name of the Lord Jesus, and tell them how to carry out the expulsion. Verses 6-8 attempt to offer further motivation, appealing to the spiritual self-interest of the Corinthians church; whereas to remove him will benefit them, not to remove him will harm them. With this Paul supplies a theological basis for the expulsion. Verses 9-11 further facilitate his removal by correcting a misunderstanding; discipline applies only to so-called brothers. Verses 12-13 assert the Corinthians' responsibility to act and close the section with a weighty command from Scripture.[44]

### *a. The Corinthians Should Remove the Immoral Man, 5:1-2*

*1It is actually reported that there is sexual immorality among you, and of a kind that even pagans do not tolerate: A man has his father's wife. 2And*

42. Paul and Ezra share the same rationale and motivations for excluding those members of the community involved in illicit sexual relationships. See Rosner, *Paul, Scripture and Ethics*, 61-93.

43. Gk. ὅλως.

44. Cf. K. Callow, "Patterns of Thematic Development in 1 Corinthians," in *Linguistics and New Testament Interpretation* (ed. D. A. Black; Nashville: Broadman, 1992), 205-6.

*you are proud! Shouldn't you rather have gone into mourning and have put out of your fellowship the man who has been doing this?*

**5:1** Paul has heard a report that is currently circulating publicly that is so scandalous that he deals with it as soon as he is finished with the problem of disunity in Corinth (1:10–4:17). Although the Corinthians have numerous problems, their most serious and pressing fault is the way they are tolerating in their midst (literally, "among you") the presence of a man committing incest. Paul is incredulous and could not be more vehement in his opposition. His dismay reveals a profound sensitivity to the holiness of God and a related concern for the holiness of God's people.[45] It is striking that Paul is so disturbed not by the Corinthians' actions, but by their inaction, which he finds utterly reprehensible.

The offense concerned *sexual immorality,*[46] a flexible term meaning "prohibited sexual relations," which in this context is specifically incest: *A man has his father's wife* tells us something of the case, the details of which were only too well known to the Corinthians. The use of the verb "to have" in this context makes it clear that it was an ongoing sexual relationship, but not necessarily a marriage.[47] And the phrase *father's wife,* reflecting the language of Leviticus 18:8, indicates that the relationship was with his stepmother, since Leviticus 18:7 forbids sexual relations with one's "mother" using a different term. That the woman is not a believer is clear since she receives no rebuke from Paul (cf. v. 12: "What business is it of mine to judge those outside the church?").

The unfavorable comparison of the Corinthians to the Gentiles, *not even among pagans,* rather than determining Paul's opposition to incest, which was set by his adherence to the relevant Pentateuchal laws, is designed to amplify Corinthian guilt. As John Calvin observes: "in making mention of the Gentiles . . . Paul intends to heighten the aggravation of the crime."[48] It was a ploy sometimes used by the Old Testament prophets. In Amos 1 and 2, the prophet heightens Israel's guilt by portraying her as worse than the surrounding nations.[49] Israel's indictment is the eighth and final, longest and most detailed judgment oracle. God's people are to be a light to the nations, not the other way around, for the sake of God's reputation and to facilitate evangelism.

45. Cf. Barclay, 45: "Our security against sin lies in our being shocked at it."

46. Gk. πορνεία.

47. This is not due to the tense or verbal aspect (which do not speak to the issue here), but to the fact that the verb "to have" (ἔχω), when used of relationships between people, is used for people who "stand in a close relationship to someone," typically with reference to relatives (including wives), but at times including illicit sexual relationships (see the evidence in BDAG, ἔχω, 2).

48. Calvin, 180.

49. Cf. 2 Kgs. 21:9, 11. In Deut. 12:29-31 and 1 Kgs. 14:24 the nations are used as a negative model for Israelite behavior.

Incest of any sort, whether with one's mother or with the wife of one's father, is prohibited in the Old Testament and early Judaism and was sufficient cause for discipline. Many commentators on 1 Corinthians 5 mention Leviticus 18:8 and 20:11 as the critical background to Paul's decision to expel the sinner, noting the shared terminology "woman" and "father" (v. 2). Sexual intercourse with the "wife" of one's father is also condemned in Genesis 49:4 (see 35:22) and Ezekiel 22:10-11. However, two verses in Deuteronomy are just as likely to have influenced Paul. First, Deuteronomy 27:20, "cursed is the man who sleeps with his father's wife," is perhaps the reason Paul "curses" the sinner in 1 Corinthians 5. Secondly, Deuteronomy 23:1 (22:30), "a man is not to marry his father's wife," may have been the impetus for Paul to quote the Deuteronomic expulsion formula in v. 13. A variation of that formula appears in Deuteronomy 22:22 ("If a man is found sleeping with another man's wife, . . . you must purge the evil from Israel"; cf. 22:24) and is presumably the penalty for the incest prohibited in Deuteronomy 23:1 (22:30). In quoting the Deuteronomic formula in 5:13, Paul, it appears, is simply following Torah.

Judaism maintained this Deuteronomic resolve that incest be punished: Mishnah *Sanhedrin* 7:4 (incest is punishable by stoning); 9:1 and *Kerithot* 1:1 (incest is one of the first offenses listed for "cutting off"); *Jubilees* 33:10-13; Tosefta *Sanhedrin* 10:1; *The Damascus Document* v; and *The Temple Scroll* lxvi. Josephus describes incest as "the grossest of sins" and "an outrageous crime" (*Antiquities* 3.274) and of incest Philo asks, "What form of unholiness could be more impious than this?" (*On the Special Laws* 3:13-14; cf. 3:20-21).[50]

The negative ways in which Paul refers to the man indicate that Paul is in no mood for wavering or compromise: v. 1c — "someone has his father's wife"; vv. 5a and 11c — "such a person"; v. 2c — "him who has done this"; v. 4 — "the one who has done such a thing"; vv. 7a and 8 — "the old leaven"; v. 8 — "the leaven of malice and evil"; v. 13b — "the wicked person." The only neutral description of the man occurs with reference to "his spirit" in v. 5b. As Kathleen Callow states bluntly, "Paul presents the person he is talking about as bad, simply by his lexical choices."[51] The very description of the man makes it clear what action needs to be taken.

**5:2** It is not clear whether v. 2a is an exclamation (as in the TNIV: *And you are proud!*) or a rhetorical question. In either case the words indicate further that Paul is shocked at their complacency (cf. v. 6a). Pride and arrogance had not only led to divisions among them (3:21; 4:6-7, 18-19), but to a callous insensitivity to sin. Pride had made them blind to the condition of the sinner and to their own sin of complicity.

50. Peter J. Tomson, *Paul and the Jewish Law: Halakha in the Letters of the Apostle to the Gentiles* (CRINT 3.1; Assen/Maastricht: Van Gorcum, 1990), 100-101, has likewise shown that Strack-Billerbeck's *Kommentar* (3:358) is mistaken in its judgment that the majority of Jewish sages did not object to a Gentile or proselyte marrying his stepmother.

51. Callow, "Patterns of Thematic Development in 1 Corinthians," 196.

Paul's rebuke of Corinthian arrogance and his call for the body to show passionate grief that will lead to action indicate that he considered the Corinthians in some sense implicated in the offense of the sinner: *Shouldn't you rather have gone into mourning?* The sin in question should bring sadness to the congregation. The alternative to pride and complacency *(shouldn't you rather)* is to mourn over the sin in their midst. The verb "to mourn"[52] is used in the New Testament for mourning over the death of a loved one (Matt. 9:15; Mark 16:10; cf. Gen. 50:10) and for grief over a great loss (Rev. 18:11, 15, 19). Hence many commentators understand Paul to be enjoining a mourning over the impending loss of the sinning brother, whose sin will lead to his destruction. It could also be taken as grief at the shame brought on the church by the incest. However, these views seem out of keeping with the fact that the word is used elsewhere by Paul only in 2 Corinthians 12:21[53] (cf. Jas. 4:9; 1 *Clement* 2:6), where its sense closely parallels the concept of godly sorrow or repentance.[54]

The use of "to mourn" in the LXX suggests that in v. 2a Paul thought the Corinthians ought to "mourn" in the sense of confessing the sin of the erring brother as if it was their own. The word occurs only six times in the LXX with reference to sin. In Ezra 10:6; Nehemiah 1:4; 1 Esdras 8:72; 9:2; and Daniel 10:2 it refers to sorrow over the sins of others, and in Nehemiah 8:9 (cf. *Testament of Reuben* 1:10) it refers to sorrow over personal sin (but still in a corporate context). For example, in Ezra 10:6, Ezra "mourned over the unfaithfulness of the exiles." In the former references the grief is given expression in prayers by Ezra, Nehemiah, and Daniel, in which the sins of others are confessed as if they are their own. Ezra 10, in particular, represents a distinct parallel to 1 Corinthians 5. It is an Ezra-like Paul who deals with the expulsion of the sinner. Just as Ezra "mourned" over the sins of the community, so Paul enjoined the Corinthians to "mourn" over the sin of the incestuous man. Just as Ezra demanded that the sinners separate from their foreign partners or else suffer expulsion themselves (10:8), so Paul demanded the expulsion of the sinner, unless he separate from his illicit partner.

Failure to deal with a seriously sinning member invites the possibility of judgment from God on the whole group. The corollary of corporate responsibility, the fear of God's judgment on the community, which we observed in Joshua 7, is also present in the incidents involving Ezra, Nehemiah, and Daniel. All three assumed that the nation stood under the covenant and that breach of responsibility could jeopardize the whole

52. Gk. πενθέω.

53. The circumstances prompting the mourning in 2 Cor. 12:21 also involve "sexual immorality" (πορνεία).

54. If Paul did not have godly sorrow/repentance in mind in 5:2a, he could have used a word other than πενθέω, such as ταλαιπωρέω (Jas. 4:9), which denotes sorrow in wretched circumstances, δακρύω (John 11:35) or κλαίω (1 Cor. 7:30), which signify weeping and crying, or even λυπέω (1 Thess. 4:13), ἀλαλάζω (Mark 5:38), or θρηνέω (John 16:20; Luke 23:27), which mean weep, especially in mourning for the dead.

group before God. A sense of urgency gripped these leaders' dealings with God and the nation.[55] As Jean Héring states, "in the OT, belief in the efficacy of mourning and fasting for warding off public misfortune is well attested by 1 Kings 21.9; Amos 5.16; 8.10."[56] Though not explicitly stated in 1 Corinthians 5, the same notion of the need to deal immediately with the sinner in order to safeguard the standing of the community before God may underlie the urgency with which Paul addresses the problem. Apparently Paul considered the expulsion of the sinner imperative to restore the church's felicitous existence before God. Paul's response to the case of incest implies that churches which do not protect the holiness of God's people as a group run the risk of forfeiting God's blessing.[57] Whether the final words of v. 2 are part of a question (as in the NIV) or a command (RSV),[58] Paul clearly wants the incestuous man to be removed, *out of your fellowship*, literally, "out of your midst."

Paul is right in v. 2 to say that such immorality is not condoned among non-Christians. In Roman society, though some forms of extra-marital sex were not universally frowned upon, such as fornication, adultery, and prostitution, a relationship between a man and his stepmother was considered incestuous, treated with a sense of outrage and disgust, and punishable by deportation to an island.[59] Dio Cassius refers to such a case as "criminal relations"[60] and Martial writes to a perpetrator, "though great Tully were recalled from the nether shades, and Regulus himself were to defend you, you cannot be acquitted."[61]

It seems fairly certain that the Corinthians (v. 2) were not boasting because of the immorality among them, but in spite of it. Those commentators (cf. RSV; TNIV) who take the former view think that the perverse Corinthian pride in the relationship was based on admiration for a display of so-called Christian liberty. However, three observations support the view that they were proud in spite of the incest among them. First, Paul does not touch on the abuse of Christian liberty until he deals with the problem in 6:12-20 (cf. "all things are lawful"). Secondly, a more specific connection between vv. 1 and 2 could have been given by using a different Greek conjunction.[62] Thirdly, that the Corinthians were already puffed up[63] is made

55. In each case πενθέω translates אבל (*'aval*), which in the Hebrew Bible often describes the reaction of those aware of the threat of deserved judgment (cf. Exod. 33:4; Num. 14:39).

56. Héring, 35. Cf. also 2 Kgs. 22:11-20.

57. Cf. John 17:11b; the church has spiritual, innate, inherent solidarity.

58. The conjunction ἵνα can introduce an imperative but very rarely with a passive verb, as we have here with ἀρθῇ.

59. See A. D. Clarke, *Secular and Christian Leadership in Corinth*, 78-80.

60. *Roman History* 58.22.

61. *Epigrammata* 4.16.

62. The particle δέ rather than the conjunction καί; cf. Callow, "Patterns of Thematic Development in 1 Corinthians," 206.

63. See 5:1-2 in Phillips, JB, and esp. NEB: "And you are *still* proud of yourselves!"

clear in 1:31 and 3:21, where Paul warns them about boasting, and 4:6, 18, 19, where they are said to be puffed up in favor of certain leaders and against Paul for not visiting them yet. Verse 6, where Paul says, "your boasting is not good," is surely a more general reference in this light rather than a specific and direct reaction to the case of incest.

We can be more specific about their boasting. It was not just pride in their church in general. The reference to being puffed up in 4:6 is perhaps an important clue, in that, being the first reference in the letter to being puffed up, it establishes a link between arrogance and their attitude toward leading figures in the church. This suggests that though the immorality is not being exalted in vv. 1-2, the offender himself may be. It is not unlikely that the incestuous man is of high social standing, a suggestion made by a number of commentaries, notably Chrysostom and H. Grotius.[64] A high status would certainly explain the Corinthians' reluctance to confront him over the matter in question. Clarke comments: "Paul is concerned here that those within the community are more concerned with the status of a person (the grounds of their boasting), than they are about his immorality."[65] He may have been a benefactor or patron of the church or a group within it. To lose such a person's favor would have been costly in a Greco-Roman society, where the generosity of such people was of great importance. Paul's firm stance on the matter indicates that in the church those who are wise, powerful, and of noble birth (cf. 1:31) receive no privileges (cf. Jas. 2:2-4) and are not exempt from discipline if they are immoral.

The Old Testament affords widespread evidence for a motif of corporate responsibility in relation to community exclusion.[66] On numerous occasions the entire nation suffers, or is threatened with, some degree of divine displeasure on account of the presence of a gravely sinning member. The most infamous is Achan's sin in Joshua 7. In Joshua 7:1 the report of Achan's sin is introduced with the words: "But *the Israelites* acted unfaithfully in regard to the devoted things." The Lord accused all Israel (7:1: "*Israel* have sinned, *they* have . . ."), yet his "fierce anger" (7:26) was turned away after the removal of only one individual, Achan (and his house).[67] At various points in her history, Israel, like the pagan sailors who felt compelled to eject Jonah in order to restore a safe passage for their ship, removed certain offenders as an exercise in corporate responsibility. While such persons remained, the nation was implicated in their sin and, it seems, impending punishment. The corporate dimension of 1 Corinthians 5 is

64. See A. D. Clarke, *Secular and Christian Leadership in Corinth,* 85 n. 57.

65. A. D. Clarke, *Secular and Christian Leadership in Corinth,* 87.

66. Cf. Calvin J. Roetzel, *Judgment in the Community: A Study in the Relationship between Eschatology and Ecclesiology in Paul* (Leiden: Brill, 1972), 116: "The Old Testament often speaks of the judgment of an individual offender for the purpose of purifying the community, and how the entire community can be implicated by the sin of one of its members."

67. For other examples see Rosner, *Paul, Scripture and Ethics,* 66-67.

marked and is particularly clear in the instruction to "mourn" over the sin of the erring brother in v. 2.

*b. Paul's Authority Stands behind the Expulsion, 5:3-5*

*3For my part, even though I am not physically present, I am with you in spirit. As one who is present with you in this way, I have already passed judgment in the name of our Lord Jesus on the one who has been doing this. 4So when you are assembled and I am with you in spirit, and the power of our Lord Jesus is present, 5hand this man over to Satan for the destruction of the sinful nature so that his spirit may be saved on the day of the Lord.*

**5:3** Verses 3-5 are one loosely structured sentence in Greek, which is something of a syntactical maze with some rather enigmatic phrases. Its overall point, however, is clear. As the word "for" indicates (omitted by NIV) at the beginning of v. 3, the verses explain how the discipline is to occur: with Paul's authority, in the context of the gathered assembly, and with the power of Christ.

In contrast to the Corinthians, Paul here (cf. TNIV, NEB: *for my part*) acts swiftly and decisively. Paul conceived of his apostolate and commission in prophetic terms,[68] and in these verses he acts like an Old Testament prophet. As the Lord's messenger, with the full authority of the divine judge, he brings God's verdict.[69]

Although not physically present, Paul is able to act as present; *I am with you in spirit.* Three interpretations of this difficult phrase are possible. First, according to some,[70] Paul is using the word "spirit" here in a psychological rather than a theological sense. He "will make his contribution, as the Corinthians reflect on what they remember of his convictions, character and ways, and on what they know of his mind in the present matter."[71] In other words, Paul is as good as present. To say that you are with someone "in spirit" in modern idiom can be merely an "earnest expression of empathetic concern and fellow feeling,"[72] something akin to "you are in my thoughts," except in reverse. Secondly, Paul's words may be a reference to life in the Spirit of God (see 2:12-13; 6:17, 19; 14:14-15). Since the Spirit is present among them, Paul is present also. Fee explains: Paul "thinks of the reading of the letter in the gathered assembly as the tangible way in which

68. See Karl O. Sandnes, *Paul — One of the Prophets? A Contribution to the Apostle's Self-Understanding* (WUNT 2.43; Tubingen: Mohr, 1991).

69. See Calvin J. Roetzel, "The Judgment Form in Paul's Letters," *JBL* 88 (1969), 305-12. Cf. 1 Cor. 10:1-14; 11:17-34; 1 Thess. 4:3-8; Gal. 6:7-10; 2 Thess. 1:5-12, and Gal. 1:6-9 for other places where Paul's words roughly approximate the judgment pronouncement of the preexilic prophets (as described by C. Westermann).

70. For example, Barrett, 123, who cites Weiss as being in agreement.

71. Barrett, 124.

72. J. D. G. Dunn, "Spirit, Holy Spirit," *NIDNTT* 3:694.

the Spirit communicates his prophetic-apostolic ministry in their midst (cf. 2 Cor. 10:10-11)."[73] In this view "my spirit" in v. 4 should thus be capitalized or written "S/spirit." Thirdly, "spirit" may be understood as the human spirit, that dimension of the human personality which is sensitive to the spiritual realm (cf. 2 Cor. 2:13; 7:13), and Paul may be thought of as saying literally that he is able to leave his body and travel via the spiritual realm into the presence of the Corinthians (cf. 2 Cor. 12:2-4, where Paul goes into heaven).

It is difficult to know with any certainty which view is correct. "My spirit" (v. 4) in such close proximity to "his spirit" (v. 5), a reference to the human spirit of the incestuous man, would favor seeing a reference to the human spirit of Paul in v. 3. However, given the dynamic character of the whole scene and the fact that prophets like Paul customarily act and speak by the Spirit of God, an ambiguous reference to the divine Spirit cannot be ruled out. For the third view it can be said that while out-of-body experiences may seem strange to us, similar phenomena are reported of Old Testament prophets such as Ezekiel (3:12; 8:3; 11:1, 24). Against the third view, however, is Colossians 2:5, where Paul's presence "in the spirit" is a more general reference to empathetic concern ("I am present with you in spirit and delight to see how orderly you are and how firm your faith in Christ is"). TNIV is ambiguous: *As one who is present with you in this way.* Views one or two are to be preferred. Either way, Paul calls the congregation together not for protracted deliberations but merely to ratify his decision. The verdict is cast: *I have already passed judgment.*[74]

What is to be done "in the name of our Lord Jesus"?[75] Is it (1) their gathering together (TNIV; JB; NEB; Lightfoot, Godet); (2) the giving over to

73. Fee, 205; cf. also J. Kremer, "πνεῦμα," *EDNT* 3:119.

74. *I have . . . passed judgment* is a translation of a perfect indicative verb (κέκρικα). Perfect verbs usually focus on the present state of affairs and not on past actions which brought that state into being. That would suggest that it might be better rendered "I am now decided," than "I have already judged" (the point not being that Paul previously made a decision, but that his mind is now made up). However, this may be pushing too hard. It appears that the present state to which the verb refers is that of one who has already rendered his judgment (the state a judge enters after giving his verdict, for which a language may or may not have a distinct term). Some present states of affairs may be expressed (in English, at least) only by reference to prior events which define them.

75. Variants include "the Lord Jesus," "the Lord Jesus Christ," "our Lord Jesus," and "our Lord Jesus Christ." The variant "Christ" has a wide geographical spread, but as Fee, 198, suggests, it may well have been added by a scribe to "heighten the solemn words of judgment" ("I have pronounced judgment in the name of our Lord Jesus Christ"; cf. also Metzger, *Textual Commentary*, 484-85). Whether "our" is original is difficult to know. It could have been added to conform with the next phrase. If original, it renders less likely the translation that implies that the deed was done "in the name of our Lord Jesus" (see the commentary); we would expect a less personal reference to Jesus in such circumstances. The variety of additions may be early testimony to the confusion over the syntax of the verse, that is, the question of to what "in the name of the Lord Jesus" attaches (see commentary). A similar set of variants occurs for the reference to Jesus at the end of the verse.

Satan (Robertson and Plummer, Findlay, Ellicott); or (3) Paul's decision/judgment (Mare, Bruce, Fee, TNIV [see the end of v. 3], RSV; GNB; Moffatt)? Or (4) does the phrase go with "the one who did this," which immediately precedes "in the name of our Lord Jesus" in the Greek?[76] In the last case, the man in Corinth was justifying his sin by appealing to his freedom in Christ. He cohabits with his stepmother, as outrageous as it may sound, "in the name of Jesus."

Literally, vv. 3-4, with the critical phrase in italics, read: "For I, though absent in the body but present in the spirit, have already passed judgment, as present, on the one who has done this thing, *in the name of the (our) Lord Jesus,* when you have gathered together, and my spirit with the power of the Lord Jesus. . . ." As can be seen, the syntax of these verses is very difficult. The word order is against views one and two. The phrase in question elsewhere in Paul follows its verb (cf. 1 Cor. 6:11; 2 Thess. 3:6; Col. 3:17).[77] View four is also unlikely since vv. 3-4 concern the setting in which the handing of the man "over to Satan" (v. 5) is to take place, not the basis on which he has acted. Furthermore, we would expect "in Christ," rather than in "the name of the Lord Jesus," if a perverse distortion of Christian freedom were being reported. View three is to be preferred, as in TNIV: *I have already passed judgment in the name of our Lord Jesus on the one who has been doing this.* Paul has handed down sentence in the name of our Lord Jesus, that is, by his authority. As C. Roetzel states: "Paul, as an apostle, possesses the authority to issue commands, but this authority is anchored in his special relation to the Lord Jesus" (cf. 2 Thess. 3:6).[78] The presence of the powerful Lord Jesus in a congregation is not always a happy thing; it can be for judgment as well as blessing, ominous as well as comforting (as in Matt. 18:20).

**5:4** The "excommunication" is to take place when the Corinthians *are assembled* and in the *power of the Lord Jesus.* Whatever else this scene implies, it is comparable to the judgment scene of Deuteronomy 19:16-20, which includes the command quoted in 1 Corinthians 5:13b. In Deuteronomy 19 the discipline also takes place in the presence of the congregation (19:20a) and the Lord (19:17: "in the presence of the LORD").[79] Numbers 15:35 ("the entire assembly must stone him" [i.e., the Sabbath breaker]), 35:24 ("the assembly must judge" a case of homicide), and Leviticus 24:14, 16 ("the entire assembly is to stone him" [i.e., a blasphemer]) are comparable. The forum for the judgment of offenders is also the gathered community in 1QS vi-vii. In biblical criminal law the whole community is involved in judgment. It is also possible that the teaching of Jesus in Matthew 18:15-20 has influenced Paul here. In particular, it is striking that the decision is taken when the church is "gathered together" (v. 3; Matt.

76. This view is taken by E. P. Sanders, *Paul* (Oxford: Oxford University Press, 1991).
77. Fee, 207.
78. Roetzel, *Judgment in the Community,* 14.
79. Jean Héring, 35, notes that, in contrast to the corporate court scene in 1 Cor. 5:3-5, in the excommunication "practised by the synagogue . . . the elders alone formed the tribunal."

18:20) and the judgment is given "in the name of the Lord Jesus" (v. 4; cf. Matt. 18:20: "in my name").[80]

A striking feature of the instructions of 1 Corinthians 5 is that they are not directed to the sinner himself but exclusively to the believers in Corinth as a group.[81] Paul addresses the church as a body throughout (the second-person plural pronoun occurs nine times). He wants the discipline to be carried out when they are assembled (literally, "brought together"; 5:4),[82] and rebukes them in 5:2, 6 as a group. The metaphor of cleansing by the removal of leaven is applied in a corporate fashion; the Corinthian Christians are to be "*a* new lump" (5:7), not new lump*s* of dough. As Meeks states, Paul "does not construe the action primarily as an action against the offender, but as a way of purging the community."[83] That the Corinthians are implicated in the offense of the immoral man is suggested by the instruction to "mourn" in v. 2. Paul's instructions are far from any brand of Christian individualism. The church, it seems, stands or falls together.

**5:5** This verse supplies the actual judgment: *hand this man over to Satan for the destruction of the sinful nature.* The man is to be consigned to Satan, literally for "the destruction of the flesh." It is commonly held that Paul here enjoins the pronouncement of a curse on the immoral man that will lead to physical suffering and ultimately death (cf. NEB: "this man is to be consigned to Satan for the destruction of the body"). The word "destruction,"[84] it is argued, is so strong a term that it can only mean death. In the LXX it frequently denotes utter ruin and sudden death (as in Exod. 12:23; Josh. 3:10; 7:25; Jer. 2:30, etc.), and Paul uses a related term in 1 Corinthians 10:10 to indicate the loss of life at the hands of "the destroying angel." Furthermore, Paul can use "flesh"[85] for the physical body (as in 1 Cor. 6:16; 15:39, 50). Supposedly parallel ancient curses can be found in secular Greek (the magical papyri) and Jewish sources, and similar tragic episodes of serious sin leading to loss of life can be pointed to in Acts 5:1-11 and 1 Corinthians 11:30. Finally, Paul's "thorn in the flesh," "a messenger of Satan" (2 Cor. 12:7), establishes a clear link between physical suffering and the work of Satan. Conzelmann states the conclusion which seems to follow: "the destruction of the flesh can hardly mean anything else but death."[86]

80. Cf. David Wenham, *Paul: Follower of Jesus or Founder of Christianity?* (Grand Rapids: Eerdmans, 1995), 210-12; McDonough, "Competent to Judge."

81. The presupposition of corporate responsibility, Christian solidarity, is introduced in 1 Corinthians in 3:23a, "you are of Christ," developed by 3:16-17 and 10:17, and receives its classic statement in 12:12-31.

82. Gk. συναχθέντων. Eduard Schweizer, *Church Order in the New Testament* (London: SCM, 1961), 192, notes that in vv. 3-5 Paul is "obviously striving to establish the church as the real bearer of responsibility."

83. Wayne A. Meeks, *The First Urban Christians: The Social World of the Apostle Paul* (2d ed.; New Haven: Yale University Press, 2003), 130.

84. Gk. ὄλεθρος.

85. Gk. σάρξ.

86. Conzelmann, 97.

However, the curse/death view of v. 5 is not the best interpretation. To hand the man over to Satan is to turn him back out into Satan's sphere, outside the edifying and caring environment of the church where God is at work.[87] In other words, v. 5 states metaphorically what Paul says literally in vv. 2 and 13: the man is to be excluded from the community of faith. A similar metaphorical elaboration is given in v. 7 with the words, "Get rid of the old yeast." "The destruction of the flesh" refers not to his death but to turning from evil desires, from his "self-sufficiency" (Thiselton), "the destruction of the sinful nature" (TNIV). That a strong term like "destruction" can be employed metaphorically, especially in reference to "flesh," is clear from Romans 8:13 (do not "live according to the flesh" but instead "put to death the misdeeds of the body"), Galatians 5:24 ("crucify the flesh"), and Colossians 3:5 ("put to death whatever belongs to the flesh"). When Paul contrasts flesh and spirit (or Spirit), as here in v. 5, flesh refers almost without exception to the corrupt, fallen, and rebellious condition of the human being, as in Romans 8:5-17 and Galatians 5:16-24. "Flesh" refers to the person oriented away from God and "spirit" to the person oriented toward God.[88] The man viewed as at enmity with God is to be "destroyed." The resemblance of v. 5 to ancient curse formulas is only superficial. The closest parallels are Old Testament formulas using the terms "to drive out" and "to cut off." Second Temple Judaism regularly replaced execution with excommunication when applying these texts to their communities.[89] Job 1:12 and 2:6 may also be parallel, where Job is "handed over" to Satan, in which case suffering led to a positive result and the loss of life was specifically excluded.[90] Acts 5:1-11 and 1 Corinthians 11:30 do report cases of what might be called capital punishment, but neither is a result of a solemn curse delivered by an assembled church. Finally, Satan's role in serving God's purposes is not out of keeping with Paul's understanding. "Satan's messenger" in 2 Corinthians 12:7 led to Paul's learning about the sufficiency of God's grace. As Findlay states, "that Satan's malignity should be (as one may say) overreached by God's wisdom and mercy . . . is nothing very wonderful: hate is proverbially blind."[91] It is not that Satan will not inflict

87. The discussion here builds upon James T. South, "A Critique of the 'Curse/Death' Interpretation of 1 Corinthians 5.1-8," *NTS* 39 (1993), 539-61; Fee, 208-13; and A. C. Thiselton, "The Meaning of *SARX* in 1 Corinthians 5.5: A Fresh Approach in the Light of Logical and Semantic Factors," *SJT* 26 (1973), 204-28.

88. Fee, 212.

89. See William Horbury, "Extirpation and Excommunication," *VT* 35 (1985), 13-38, esp. 27-30; and Rosner, *Paul, Scripture and Ethics*, 82. The exclusion of the man from the church is like the exclusion of Israel from the land.

90. Cf. G. W. H. Lampe, "Church Discipline and the Interpretation of the Epistles to the Corinthians," in *Christian History and Interpretation: Studies Presented to John Knox* (ed. W. R. Farmer, C. F. D. Moule, and R. R. Niebuhr; Cambridge: Cambridge University Press, 1967), 353: "the work of Satan is evil, but it serves God's ultimate object almost as in the book of Job."

91. Findlay, 809. Contra Morris, 88: "But it is difficult to see how handing a man over

the man with suffering, but if he does, unwittingly and ironically the suffering will be, Paul hopes, remedial.[92] That the man in 1 Corinthians 5 is not expected to die, at least immediately, is clear from v. 11, where the Corinthians are told not to "associate with" him, and from 1 Timothy 1:19-20, where Hymenaeus and Alexander are "handed over to Satan to be taught not to blaspheme" (i.e., to change their behavior). In our view the incestuous man was handed over to Satan to be taught not to commit sexual immorality.

The second half of v. 5, *so that his spirit may be saved on the day of the Lord,*[93] also makes more sense if v. 5a enjoins excluding and not cursing the man. The grammar indicates that the destruction of the man's sinful nature is the anticipated result of the action, not the express purpose, which is his salvation.[94] Whereas some strands of Judaism may have conceived of a person's death as atoning for his or her sin, in Paul only Christ's death can do this.[95] Paul's ultimate aim in excluding the man is his own good. There is the assumption, spelled out in 6:9-11, that those who persist in flagrant sin have no future with God; in this sense 6:9-11 clarifies 5:6b. Yet Paul is confident that God's faithfulness will confirm believers "until the end, blameless at the day of our Lord Jesus" (1:8). However, future salvation is not a forgone conclusion for any who claim to be fellow believers but are sexually immoral (v. 11). It is not that ethical failure results in the loss of salvation, but that assurance of salvation depends in part on ethical progress; cf. 6:11: "that is what some of you *were.*" Paul does not answer the question of whether the man is presently saved. His point is that so-called brothers who engage in blatant sexual misconduct will finally be saved "on the day of the Lord" only if "the sinful nature is destroyed."

Why must the man's flesh be *destroyed?* Why must such drastic action be taken against the man? What has he done to deserve such a punishment? Three groups of observations support the case for reading 1 Corinthians 5 (esp. v. 5) with 3:16-17 ("Don't you know that you yourselves are God's tem-

---

to Satan would have such a purifying effect. Rather, we would expect the reverse, the stimulation of those lusts."

92. The destruction of the man's sinful nature and the salvation of his spirit on the day of the Lord reflect Paul's hopes and desires for him, not Satan's. Satan has no more interest in destroying the man's sinful nature than he does in teaching Hymenaeus and Alexander not to blaspheme (1 Tim. 1:19-20), but he may accomplish those tasks in spite of himself.

93. Certain MSS add "Jesus Christ" or "our [Lord] Jesus Christ." Fee seems to think that Pauline style favors the shorter text (see 1 Thess. 5:2; 2 Thess. 2:2). However, for Paul the coming judgment is also associated with "our Lord Jesus Christ" (1:8), "the day of the Lord Jesus" (2 Cor. 1:14), "the day of Christ Jesus" (Phil. 1:6), and "the day of Christ" (Phil. 1:10). Günther Zuntz, *The Text of the Epistles: A Disquisition upon the Corpus Paulinum* (London: Oxford University Press, 1953), 184, bases his defense of "the day of the Lord" on surer grounds: "The name 'Jesus' is twice in the preceding verse: reason enough for Paul not to write it, and for scribes to add it, here." The variants in vv. 4-5 point to the fact that there are three references to Jesus in the context of the judgment on the incestuous man — Paul stresses that he is not alone in this matter.

94. Fee, 209.

95. Cf. Barrett, 126-27.

ple and that God's Spirit lives in you? If anyone destroys God's temple, God will destroy him; for God's temple is holy, and that is what you are") with an Old Testament temple/holiness motif in mind. The man must suffer "destruction" because he has destroyed God's holy temple, the church. First, certain features of 3:16-17 suggest its affinity with chapter 5. 1 Corinthians 3:16-17, in contrast to 6:19, describes the body corporate as God's temple ("you [plural] are God's temple [singular]"), which, we are claiming, is Paul's presupposition in 1 Corinthians 5. The characteristic of the temple to which Paul draws attention in 3:16-17 is its holiness, which carries a demand for the maintenance of purity, a thought which Paul develops in 5:6-8. Secondly, 1 Corinthians 3:16-17 may well anticipate 5:1-13 since it is not uncommon for Paul in 1 Corinthians and elsewhere to set up a later discussion in such a manner. 1 Corinthians 3:16-17 would have been in the forefront of the minds of the letter's recipients when chapter 5 was read. Thirdly, temple imagery is highly prevalent in both Corinthian epistles. The church is identified as the "temple of God" in 2 Corinthians 6:16. In 1 Corinthians 6:19 (significantly for 1 Corinthians 5) the need for sexual purity is linked to individual Christians' being the temple of the Holy Spirit. Furthermore, Paul associates sexual chastity with temple in 1 Corinthians 6:12-20.

There are good reasons, then, for thinking that 3:16-17 provides the theological framework for understanding perhaps the most fundamental reason for the expulsion of the sinner in 5:1-13: his flesh must be "destroyed" because he has defiled the holiness of God's temple, the church.[96] A harsh penalty attaches to a serious crime. God's justice is always measured and appropriate. The man may have thought of his behavior merely in terms of personal fulfillment or gain. Paul conceives of it as thoroughly destructive, not just of his own person and standing before God, but of the church of God with which he was associated. The destoyer must be destroyed. It seems that Paul believed, along with Deuteronomy 22:21b, that *porneia* "defiles the house" (of one's father). A corollary of this holiness theme, contamination, is also present in 1 Corinthians 5. The sinner must be removed because holiness and unholiness cannot coexist, or "a little leaven leavens the whole lump" (v. 6).[97]

William Horbury, in his study of the practice of excommunication in pre-rabbinic Judaism, argues that, throughout the post-exilic period, not only the laws of covenant but also the laws of temple admission legislated in Deuteronomy 23:2-9 (1-8) carried the implication of exclusion from the community.[98] For example, Deuteronomy 23:2-9 (1-8) was used by Ezra and

96. Adela Y. Collins, "The Function of 'Excommunication' in Paul," *HTR* 73 (1980), 263, without drawing attention to temple imagery, comes to a similar conclusion: "the more or less explicit reason for expelling the incestuous man in 1 Corinthians 5 was to guard the holiness of the community and to avoid offense to the presence of the Holy Spirit."

97. G. W. H. Lampe, "Church Discipline," 355, aptly explains the proverb as "moral contamination of the brotherhood."

98. Horbury, "Extirpation and Excommunication," 25.

Nehemiah for the exclusion of foreign wives from the community (Ezra 9:1-2 and Neh. 13:1-3, 23-27 allude to the passage),[99] and the lamentation over the destruction of Jerusalem in Lamentations 1:10 also recalls it.[100] A holiness motif is most clearly perceived in 1 Corinthians 5 in the light of this development in the use of Deuteronomy 23:2-9 (1-8).

Horbury demonstrates that during the Second Temple period the scope of the laws of admission to the assembly found in Deuteronomy 23:2-9 (1-8) were expanded beyond stipulations of physique and descent to include moral requirements.[101] Biblical evidence for this evolution includes the "entrance-*torot*" (Pss. 15; 24:3-5; Isa. 33:14-17),[102] the exclusion of "rebels" from the future congregation in Ezekiel 20:38-40, and the indictment of Israel for admitting into the sanctuary aliens who are "uncircumcised in heart" in Ezekiel 44:6-9. Josephus and Philo build upon this biblical background and "take Deut. 23 to exclude not only aliens and defective Jews, but also gravely-offending Jewish sinners."[103]

The likelihood that Deuteronomy 23:2-9 (1-8) played a role in the formation of Paul's thinking in 1 Corinthians 5 is increased by the fact that the previous verse in Deuteronomy addresses the very question with which Paul is engaged: "A man is not to marry his father's wife; he must not dishonor his father's bed." That Paul linked the two passages has every possibility since, as Horbury observes: "The admission-regulations of Deut. 23:2-9 (1-8) were linked in rabbinic exegesis with 23:1 (22:30), and correspondingly understood, as by *Targum Pseudo-Jonathan*, as marriage laws."[104] This exegesis may even have a basis in Deuteronomy. Michael Fishbane has suggested that Deuteronomy 23:1 and 23:2-9 (1-8) are linked through the mention of the Ammonites and Moabites, who, according to Genesis 19:31-38, are the offspring of incest (Lot and his daughters).[105]

It would hardly be surprising, therefore, to find in 1 Corinthians 5 the expulsion of the sinner connected with the theme of temple and holiness. Why must the offender be delivered to Satan for "destruction" (5:5)? Surely the best explanation is given only twenty-three verses before chapter 5 in the solemn affirmation: "Don't you know that you yourselves are God's temple? . . . If anyone destroys God's temple, God will destroy that

99. Michael A. Fishbane, *Biblical Interpretation in Ancient Israel* (Oxford: Clarendon, 1985), 116-17, 125-26.

100. Fishbane, *Biblical Interpretation*, 128.

101. Horbury, "Extirpation and Excommunication," 26-27.

102. Though applied in the LXX to the qualifications of a prophet, *Targum Isaiah* 33:14-17 maintains the original context of admission.

103. Horbury, "Extirpation and Excommunication," 26. For example, both apply 23:2(1) to the voluntary effeminate (not just to the born eunuch). See Philo, *On the Special Laws* 1:324-45 and Josephus, *Ant.* 4.290-91.

104. Horbury, "Extirpation and Excommunication," 25.

105. Fishbane, *Biblical Interpretation*, 120. Calum M. Carmichael, *The Laws of Deuteronomy* (Ithaca, NY: Cornell University Press, 1974), 174-76, also argues that Deut. 23:1, 3, 4-6 should be seen in the light of Genesis 19.

person; for God's temple is sacred, and you together are that temple" (3:16-17).

### *c. The Metaphor of Yeast Validates the Expulsion, 5:6-8*

*[6]Your boasting is not good. Don't you know that a little yeast leavens the whole batch of dough? [7]Get rid of the old yeast, so that you may be a new unleavened batch — as you really are. For Christ, our Passover lamb, has been sacrificed. [8]Therefore let us keep the Festival, not with the old bread leavened with malice and wickedness, but with the unleavened bread of sincerity and truth.*

**5:6** If we are correct in assuming that chapter 5 ought to be read with 3:16-17 in mind, then another element in the chapter, in addition to v. 5, should be mentioned as congruent with a temple theme, namely, vv. 7-8. Having "cleansed the temple," Paul calls upon the congregation to celebrate spiritually the festival of Passover/Unleavened Bread. That this sequence of events occurred to Paul's mind may itself testify to the influence of the Old Testament temple motif, since, in the Old Testament, there is an observable link between cleansing or restoring the temple and celebrating the Passover. Following the "removal of all defilement from the sanctuary" (2 Chr. 29:5), in order to "reestablish the service of the temple of the LORD" (2 Chr. 29:35), King Hezekiah in 2 Chronicles 30 calls upon the people to celebrate the Passover. Similarly, King Josiah, after removing the articles of idolatry from the temple and restoring the sacred ark to its rightful place, ordered the Israelites to celebrate the Passover and observe the Feast of Unleavened Bread (2 Chr. 35:1-19; 2 Kgs. 23:1-23). Ezra followed the same pattern; Ezra 6 records first the completion and dedication of the temple (6:13-18) and then a joyous Passover and Feast of Unleavened Bread (6:19-22). It is intriguing that, even in the Gospels (Matt. 21:12-13; Mark 11:15-18; Luke 19:45-47; John 2:13-22), as in 1 Corinthians 5, cleansing the temple and celebrating the Passover are connected.[106]

If in vv. 3-5 the incestuous man must be expelled for his own good, in vv. 6-8 Paul turns the Corinthians' attention to the need to remove him before he corrupts the whole congregation. In a rich and suggestive passage Paul piles one metaphor upon another to present his gospel in miniature and drive home its implications for Christian conduct. Because of the death of Christ, the church in Corinth is the new and holy people of God. They must live up to this calling and purify God's house (v. 6), become a new batch of dough (v. 7), and celebrate the Festival (v. 8) by removing the man from their midst.

Their self-confident *boasting is not good.* It is entirely inappropriate in

106. This makes the suggestion that Paul alludes to Passover because he was writing in the Passover season less likely.

the present circumstances (cf. v. 2). Instead of enjoying vibrant good health, the church was seriously ill and on the point of collapse. Only drastic surgery could save her. Paul does not, however, use medical imagery but a proverbial saying about "leaven" (cf. Gal. 5:9) put in the form of a stinging rhetorical question *(Don't you know . . . ?)*. They are in danger of being spoiled by foul fermentation. The force of this saying is similar to the modern proverb, "One bad apple spoils the whole barrel."

"Leaven" is to be preferred to the TNIV's *yeast* since, as BDAG points out, the latter term "popularly suggests a product foreign to ancient baking practice." "Leaven" is a "little" portion of a previous week's "batch of dough" which had been allowed to ferment. When added to the next batch, the leaven made the bread rise. It carried with it the slight risk of infection, especially if the process was left to go on indefinitely without starting afresh with a completely new batch.[107] Each year the Israelites, in part perhaps as a health provision, had to cleanse their homes and the temple from all leaven (Exod. 12:14-20; Deut. 20:3-8). The unleavened bread from the Feast of Unleavened Bread would supply some "fresh" leaven and start the process anew for the next twelve months of baking bread. The Israelites left Egypt in such a hurry that they did not have time to leaven their bread. The Feast of Unleavened Bread, a seven-day festival in which the Jews were forbidden to eat anything leavened, commemorates this event. Paul emphasizes (by emphatic word order in Greek) that through only a "little" part of the church, one person in fact, the evil would inevitably, slowly but surely, spread through the whole community, if left unchecked. The example of willful sin in the church can have serious effects. Like leaven in bread, unchecked sin in the church spreads through the whole and irretrievably changes it. As 1 Timothy 5:20 states, "Those who sin are to be rebuked publicly, so that the others may take warning." The unity of the church, which Paul establishes in 1:10–4:21, entails the solidarity and corporate identity of the church. Since the church is "one loaf" (10:17), even one moldy part can render the whole worthless.

**5:7** The leaven imagery leads Paul to expand further, going from a rebuke in the form of a question in v. 6 to a command: *Get rid of the old yeast.* Paul wants them to be free from leaven, "a new batch," without the evil influence of the sinning brother.[108] The sense of "get rid of"[109] is paralleled by

107. See Charles L. Mitton, "New Wine in Old Wine Skins: IV. Leaven," *ExpTim* 84 (1973), 339-43.

108. Paul uses an aorist imperative here (ἐκκαθάρατε, "clean out"; *get rid of*), since he has a specific case and situation in mind (the man who has his father's wife).

109. Gk. ἐκκαθάρατε. At the beginning of vv. 7 and 10 and in the middle of v. 13 the Majority text (and a few early witnesses) alleviates the asyndeton by supplying conjunctions in each case, which is followed by the KJV and NKJV. At a couple of points the Greek grammar also brings out that Paul wrote with strong feelings: these include the unusual placing of τινα between γυναῖκά and πατρός (isolating and making both words emphatic; BDF §473[1]), and the emphatic οὐχί (instead of οὐ) in 5:2. The changes probably amount to scribal attempts to

the use of a similar verb in Judges 20:13, where the Benjamites are called upon by the other tribes of Israel to execute certain Gibeonite sexual offenders (see 19:22-26) and thereby to "get rid of the evil from Israel."[110]

With the mention of unleavened bread, Paul's mind turns to Passover, that great founding event for God's people Israel, and the cross, its even greater equivalent. It is not that the church will become God's people when they get their house in order. That would be to put the cart before the horse and imply that a favored status before God could be a human achievement. Rather, the church is God's people because of Christ's sacrificial death ("Christ" is highlighted in the Greek by leaving it until last in the sentence), and as such they must live up to that status.

Paul customarily sets his imperatives in the context of God's prior action on behalf of believers in Christ. Verse 7 is a case in point: *Get rid of the old yeast, so that you may be a new unleavened batch — as you really are.* In this verse, as Barrett observes, "the imperative rests upon an indicative."[111] The identity of the Corinthians is to inform their behavior. In other words, "What they must become is what they already are by the grace of God."[112] We encounter it again in 6:9-11 and 6:12-20. This prominent notion in Pauline ethics, though central and much discussed,[113] is not normally linked to the Old Testament. However, it is abundantly clear that Old Testament ethical injunctions and prohibitions are, like those in the Pauline corpus, rooted in the redemptive acts of God.[114] In biblical thought human behavior is always considered in the context of the underlying and overarching relationship with God.

Deuteronomy 4:20 is a specific parallel not only to the structure of 1 Corinthians 5:7 but also to its contents. In 5:7 Paul attaches two motivations to the exhortation to cleanse out the old leaven: first, because the church has now been cleansed by Christ, and, secondly, because Christ is our Passover.[115] Deuteronomy 4:20, concluding an exhortation not to become corrupt (4:16) in idolatry, attaches two remarkably similar motivations in reverse order; first, because of the Passover, and, secondly, because you [i.e., Israel] are now the Lord's inheritance.[116]

**5:8** With *therefore,* Paul draws out a lesson from the fact that only un-

smooth out the passage. Its lack of connection and general abruptness are testimony to its emotionally charged atmosphere; Paul is writing with passionate feeling.

110. M. Newton, *The Concept of Purity at Qumran and in the Letter of Paul* (Cambridge: Cambridge University Press, 1985), 91.

111. Barrett, 128. Or as Michael Parsons says in "Being Precedes Act: Indicative and Imperative in Paul's Writing," *EvQ* (1988), 99-127: "being precedes act."

112. Fee, 217.

113. See Parsons, "Being Precedes Act," for a useful survey.

114. See Rosner, *Paul, Scripture and Ethics*, 86-87.

115. BDF §452 (3) understands καὶ γάρ in v. 7c as "for also." In other words, it introduces a second reason for the explanation of 5:7a, "be cleansed."

116. An emphasis on the present blessed status of God's people is also evident in Deut. 10:22 (cf. 10:5, 8).

leavened bread was eaten during Passover. He broadens the discussion of the unfortunate case at hand, without losing sight of it, to treat the Christian life as a whole, which he pictures most attractively as a celebration: *Therefore let us keep the Festival.* Some scholars argue that Paul here alludes to the Lord's Supper, which would perhaps tie in with v. 11.[117] While not impossible, the reference seems rather to be to holy living and moral purity in general; a reference to bread need not indicate the Lord's Table, just as a reference to water does not always indicate baptism.

With their arrogance in the face of immorality the Corinthians have been subject to the leaven of *malice and wickedness.* These vices characterized their former lives before they were called to believe. In Romans 1:29 they both appear in a list of the behavior of those without the knowledge of God. The second term turns up again in v. 13b when they are told to expel "the wicked man." The two terms have essentially the same meaning[118] and together include any and every form of iniquity.

Their old way of life (cf. 6:11b; Eph. 2:1-3; 4:17-19: "you must no longer live as the Gentiles do . . .") is to be replaced by *the unleavened bread of sincerity and truth,* which comprehensively characterizes the new way of life. Both terms indicate an authentic transparency, a perfect correspondence between their profession of faith and their new life.[119] The two positive terms are effectively antonyms to the two negative terms; *sincerity and truth* are to replace *malice and wickedness* in the church of God in Corinth. Their present situation, with the "wicked man" in their midst, makes their claim to be God's holy temple a travesty and a sham. Christ died not just to cleanse them but to transform them.

### d. The Corinthians Should Separate from Immoral Believers, 5:9-11

> [9]*I wrote to you in my letter not to associate with sexually immoral people — [10]not at all meaning the people of this world who are immoral, or the greedy and swindlers, or idolaters. In that case you would have to leave this world. [11]But now I am writing to you that you must not associate with any who claim to be fellow believers but are sexually immoral or greedy, idolaters or slanderers, drunkards or swindlers. With such persons do not even eat.*

117. Héring, 37, and Orr and Walther, 187.

118. Contra Lightfoot, 206, who believes that they cover the inward attitude (malice) and the outward expression (wickedness) of sin. According to BDAG: κακία means "the quality or state of wickedness, *baseness, depravity, wickedness, vice.* κ. is the opposite of ἀρετή and all virtue and therefore lacking in social value. W. πονηρία in the same general mng. (cp. Ael. Aristid. 33 p. 625 D.; Sir 25:17, 19) 1 Cor 5:8." And πονηρία is used "in our lit. only in the ethical sense: state or condition of a lack of moral or social values, *wickedness, baseness, maliciousness, sinfulness.*"

119. According to BDAG εἰλικρίνεια is "the quality or state of being free of dissimulation, *sincerity, purity of motive,*" and ἀλήθεια is "the quality of being in accord with what is true, *truthfulness, dependability, uprightness* in thought and deed."

**5:9** In vv. 9-11 we get some insight into the situation Paul is addressing in chapter 5: *I wrote to you in my letter.* Paul had sent a letter to the Corinthians prior to 1 Corinthians. It seems that the Corinthians had misunderstood and/or disagreed with Paul's teaching in this letter on several counts, some of which probably crop up in chapters 7–16. In response, they had written a letter back to him (see 7:1) and he had received some reports orally. In this particular instance Paul's first letter should have been enough to prevent the current fiasco of the church's ignoring the presence of a seriously sinning member ever occurring; Paul had already told them in his previous letter *not to associate* [or mix] *with sexually immoral people."*

When Paul received a report on the situation orally, perhaps from Chloe (1:11) or Stephanas (16:15), along with disturbing news of divisions in the church, he also learned that his teaching on not associating with the immoral in the church had not been followed. The Corinthians had taken Paul to mean disassociation from all immoral people, both inside and outside the church, and, it seems, concluded that such teaching was too harsh and impractical; they had no intention of cutting off all ties with those outside the church. It is possible that this was a deliberate misinterpretation designed to ridicule Paul, although a genuine misunderstanding cannot be ruled out. The church was divided internally, and many of them opposed Paul. Perhaps part of their boasting (vv. 2, 6) consisted in the fact that some of them claimed their independence from and superiority to the apostle. To remove any obstacle from before the church's way in excluding the incestuous man, Paul makes his meaning perfectly clear, both in terms of what he meant and what he did not mean.

The verb "to associate with" (cf. v. 11) means to enjoy close social intercourse.[120] Its use in 2 Thessalonians 3:14 concerns the discipline of idle busybodies who have paid no attention to a second warning (cf. 1 Thess. 4:11-12; 5:14).[121] Interestingly, in that context the one being disciplined is not to be treated "as an enemy." Rather the action is designed to "warn him as a brother" (2 Thess. 3:15), evidently in the hope that he will repent and be restored to full fellowship. Paul's instructions may thus be compared with that in Matthew 18:17, "treat them as you would a pagan or a tax collector."

**5:10** Verses 10-11 bring the needed clarification: *not at all meaning the people of this world.* These words state clearly that his instruction in the letter was not concerned with having associations with outsiders. There are of course some forms of social intercourse with unbelievers that Paul would not allow, such as dining with them in an idolatrous temple (see 10:14-22), but that is not his point here.

Paul lists four examples of people with whom social contact in the

120. Gk. συναναμ(ε)ίγνυμι. Gerhard Schneider points out (*EDNT* 3:297) that in the New Testament the verb "refers in every instance to association of believers with those who have fallen away from faith in Christ, which is warned against."

121. Fee, 222.

world is not to be avoided: *the people of this world who are immoral, or the greedy and swindlers, or idolaters.* Then in v. 11 he gives a representative list of six kinds of sinners whom the church is to judge by withdrawing from social integration with them. He then states what he takes to be obvious: it would be wrong for the Corinthian Christians *to leave the world,* that is, to be cut off from contact with non-Christians. Paul takes it for granted that believers take full part in the community and society in which they live. As Blomberg states: "Christian fellowship should be a periodic retreat from and revitalization of our regular involvement with the immoral and unbelieving in our world, and not vice versa."[122]

**5:11** Paul then states his position explicitly *(But now I am writing*[123] *to you),* so as to avoid any further misunderstanding. Close association is to be withheld from six types of professing Christians. The representative list of sinners whom the church is to judge (5:12b) is in one sense a list of covenantal norms which, when broken, automatically exclude the offender. Paul lists "sexual immorality" first, since that is the issue at hand. However, what governs his choice of the next five vices in the catalogue? Paul gives a clue in v. 13b; the sins to which the Deuteronomic formula quoted by Paul ("Expel the wicked person from among you") is connected form a remarkable parallel to the particular sins mentioned in v. 11:[124]

| **1 Corinthians 5:11** | **Deuteronomy** |
|---|---|
| Sexually immoral | promiscuity, adultery (22:21-22, 30) |
| Greedy | (no parallel, but paired with "swindlers" in 1 Cor. 5:9) |
| Idolaters | idolatry (13:1-5; 17:2-7) |
| Slanderers | malicious false testimony (19:16-19) |
| Drunkards | rebellious, drunken son (21:18-21) |
| Swindlers | kidnapping, slave-trading (24:7; LXX uses the noun "thief") |

Thus, the only item in Paul's list without such a conceptual precedent is the "greedy," which is linked with "swindlers" as one class in 5:10.[125] The

122. Blomberg, 114.

123. Paul uses what is called an epistolary aorist (ἔγραψα), by which the perfective aspect of the aorist views the activity of writing the letter (which was not even halfway complete at this point) as a (completed) whole, adopting the perspective of the readers after they received it (cf. BDF §334; Wallace, *Greek Grammar beyond the Basics,* 562-63).

124. Rosner, *Paul, Scripture, and Ethics,* 68-70; Hays, 88.

125. Morris, 88. Morris notes that "there is but one article, they are joined by *kai, and,* and separated from the rest by *or.*" Though not cited by Morris, Maximilian Zerwick (*Biblical Greek,* 59: "the use of but one article before a number of nouns indicates that they are conceived as forming a certain unity") and Nigel Turner (*A Grammar of New Testament Greek,* 3:181: the phenomenon portrays "a unified whole") support his point. Jean Héring's definition of "greedy" suggests how the two words might be related: "one who uses brute force to enrich himself at the expense of his neighbour" (Héring, 38).

five correspondences are difficult to pass off as coincidental. As Peter Zaas observes, there is usually very little overlap between any two of Paul's vice lists. Nor is there overlap between any one of Paul's lists and any list extant in ancient literature.[126]

The fact that sexual immorality, idolatry, and greed are present and prominent in all three vice lists of 1 Corinthians 5–6 gives further support to the idea that the first two vices, if not all three, are Paul's major concerns in the letter. The three vices make up three of the four vices in 5:9, are the first three items in 5:11, and the first, second, and seventh in 6:9-10. Thus each occurs three times in the vice lists of 1 Corinthians, a dubious honor otherwise only accorded to "swindlers," which is related to "greed."

*With such persons do not even eat* explains further the prohibition of close "association." Such people are to be excluded from the Lord's Table and other meals when the church gathers for fellowship. It is less certain that the church as individuals is to refuse to eat with them. The parallel teaching in 2 Thessalonians 3:15 implies that exclusion does not extend that far. However, the case of the incestuous man may be more serious than that of idle busybodies, and the words "not even" point to private meals also.[127] If Paul had meant only the Lord's Supper, there would not have been any need for these words. Titus 3:10 says to have "nothing to do" with "a divisive person," another very serious offense, after a second warning.

As Holmberg points out, that "eating together conveys a message to participants and onlookers" is "the common (and cross-cultural) perspective of cultural anthropology."[128] Who eats with whom is a powerful way of defining a social group and differentiating it from other groups. In first-century Judaism eating together was of paramount significance (e.g., Gal. 2:12). It is not surprising that Paul bans the sinner from community meals since in vv. 7-8 he has just referred to the Passover, the most nonaccessible Jewish meal, which defined the people of God for Jews (cf. Exod. 12:48). To eat or not to eat with certain people is the question again in 10:1-22.

What effect would such withdrawal of fellowship have on the immoral man? He could not simply attend another church in town. "The church of God in Corinth" was his only option. The purpose of the discipline was, as 2 Thessalonians 3:14 indicates, "in order that he may feel ashamed." Honor and praise were important values in the Roman world. Whereas honor was generally bestowed on males in the form of the giving of gifts, the arranging of marriages, the buying and selling of property, and *the invitation to meals*, shame was confined to the so-called inferior members of society.[129] Social equals in Corinthian society competed for honor, and

126. Peter S. Zaas, "Catalogues and Context: 1 Corinthians 5 and 6," *NTS* 34 (1988), 623.

127. Findlay, 812.

128. Cf. B. Holmberg, "Paul and Commensality," in Tord Fornberg and David Hellholm (eds.), *Texts and Contexts: Biblical Texts in Their Textual and Situational Contexts. Essays in Honor of Lars Hartman* (Oslo: Scandinavian University Press, 1995), 768.

129. See Witherington, 154-55.

public acclaim was regularly bestowed via inscriptions, proclamations, and celebrations. To be shunned by one's club or society was a severe disgrace, and legal proceedings were one way of shaming people in the culture (see 6:1-11). The Corinthians' reluctance to discipline the man may have been in part due to his high social standing. It was most uncommon for social inferiors to shame their superior. Paul redefines social status in the church: "let him who boasts boast in the Lord" (1:31). "For Paul it is God, not society, that can bestow real honor and disperse lasting shame."[130] Whereas for the sake of unity or of keeping a "respected" member some churches would counsel a compromise, Paul rates the purity of the church above any such consideration.

The verb "to eat"[131] appears in LXX Psalm 100 in a similar context. In Psalm 101:5, as Michael Newton observes, "banishment is equivalent to [exclusion from] table fellowship"[132] in comparable fashion to v. 11: "He who slanders his neighbors secretly, he is banished; he who is of haughty looks and of a greedy heart, with him food is not shared."[133] In both 1 Corinthians 5 and Psalm 101 (in the LXX) the faithful are not to eat with those guilty of slander, arrogance, and greed. In Psalm 101:7 the presence of God in the temple and evil are said to be incompatible, supplying a further link with the temple theme in 1 Corinthians 5: "He who practices deceit shall not dwell in my house; he who speaks falsehood shall not maintain his position before me." Psalm 101 again demonstrates the Old Testament roots of Paul's instructions about exclusion from the people of God.

### *e. The Corinthians Should "Expel the Wicked Person," 5:12-13*

*12What business is it of mine to judge those outside the church? Are you not to judge those inside? 13God will judge those outside. "Expel the wicked person from among you."*

**5:12** Paul explains why judgment must fall on those within the church with two rhetorical questions. The reason is (cf. "for" at the beginning of the verse; omitted by TNIV) that it is not the church's responsibility to judge outsiders, in the sense of censuring their behavior and undertaking discipline to change them. By "outsiders" he simply means non-Christians (Col. 4:5; 1 Thess. 4:12). The second question, which expects a positive response and puts the emphasis on "you" (plural) in the Greek, stresses their true responsibility: "those inside." The church is responsible to love, encourage, nurture, *and to discipline* those within its care.[134]

130. Witherington, 155.

131. Gk. συνεσθίω.

132. Newton, *Purity,* 95.

133. Gk. συνέσθιον.

134. The responsibility is, of course, not an unqualified one, as passages like 1 Cor. 4:3-5, Rom. 14:4-10, and Matt. 7:1-5 indicate.

**5:13** If the church judges insiders, whose responsibility is it to judge outsiders? *God will judge those outside* is the answer, according to the TNIV. A present tense verb is, however, more likely (as in KJV, RSV): "God judges those outside."[135] The sin of unbelievers will not go unchecked. God will sovereignly discipline unbelievers in the present (cf. Rom. 1:18-27), just as the church is to be a channel through which believers are called to account for high-handed sin.

Verse 13b is the quotation of a recurring expression in the LXX of Deuteronomy, where it is used on six occasions to signal the execution of a variety of offenders (13:5; 17:7; 19:19; 21:21; 22:21; 24:7; cf. Judg. 20:13). The texts are identical, apart from the verb, changing from a singular future indicative to a plural aorist imperative, presumably to suit the epistolary context.[136] Furthermore, "expel" occurs only here in the New Testament, suggesting Paul's intentional and explicit use of the formula from Deuteronomy. Paul's failure to introduce the quotation in v. 13, with "as it is written" or the like, may be explicable on rhetorical grounds; the lack of connection suits the chapter's emotionally charged atmosphere. The command, as frightening and drastic as it is, is frequent in the Bible. It closes Paul's instructions on the case of the incestuous man in an unambiguous and uncompromising way.

Why must the sinner be expelled in 1 Corinthians 5? Paul Minear concedes that "it may be easy to grasp the commands Paul gave, but it is far from easy to grasp the reasoning that lay behind these commands."[137] This commentary has held the mirror of the Old Testament up to this question and discovered three answers, each reflecting a motif of Pentateuchal community exclusion: first, the man must be removed because he is guilty of covenant disloyalty; secondly, because while he remains, the church is implicated in his sin; and thirdly, because the community is the temple of the Holy Spirit. In short, he must be driven out for the sake of the church. A fourth reason for his expulsion is that he must be ejected for his own sake.

135. In the original text, which carried no accents, the difference between "will judge" (future) and "judges" (present) could only be determined from context. External evidence, which is largely irrelevant in such cases, except as history of interpretation, favors the future tense, but only marginally; the present tense reading is spread over Western and Byzantine text-types. On internal grounds the case can be made for a future judgment in view of 6:2-4 (cf. Rom. 2:5; Acts 17:31). However, the present tense is more congruent with the immediate context. Paul is writing about the church judging its own in the present, and the contrast breaks down if v. 13a refers to eschatological judgment. In the future God will judge those inside too (3:11-15). Even a future tense would be ambiguous, not necessarily signaling an exclusively future reference, as in the last sentence of the paragraph above: "God will sovereignly discipline. . . ."

136. Deut. 13:5 is the one exception, where the verb is ἀφανιεῖς (from ἀφανίζω, "to destroy"). In all other cases the verb is ἐξαρεῖς, from ἐξαίρω: "to exclude or remove someone from a group, *remove, drive away*" (BDAG).

137. Paul S. Minear, "Christ and the Congregation: 1 Corinthians 5–6," *RevExp* 80 (1983), 341; cf. A. Y. Collins, "Excommunication," 263, who identifies the holiness of the community but adds, "there may well have been other, unspoken reasons."

This may well be the distinctively Christian and "new" element in Paul's understanding of exclusion. However, to state the purpose of church discipline only in terms of motivating the repentance and restoration of the sinner is to miss much of Paul's (and his Bible's) teaching and seriously to truncate his ecclesiology.

In all of Paul's letters no instruction speaks more forcefully about the seriousness of sin, the holiness of God's people, and their corporate standing before him than this passage, which is the longest text in the New Testament on the subject of church discipline. The church must expel the wicked man in the hope of regaining him and, above all, to protect its standing before God and the world.

The practice of church discipline today varies widely, from a complete absence and ignorance of the concept to a terrible abuse of it in cruel and harmful ways. The church must avoid being censorious and unrealistic, for people's growth in holiness is not uniform and at most the Bible calls for exclusion as a last resort in only the most serious cases (where a lifestyle of open rebellion threatens to destroy the church) and with the explicit goal of restoration. At the very least, 1 Corinthians 5 challenges us to build churches which foster not only networks of support but also a measure of accountability.

### 3. *An Exasperated Rebuke: Civil Litigation in the Family of God, 6:1-11*

In 1 Corinthians 6:1-11 Paul deals with the report that some of the Corinthian Christians were engaging one another in civil litigation in secular courts.[1] A number of details in the passage point to the case being a civil rather than a criminal matter. It is described as consisting of "the things of this life" (v. 3), a "dispute with another" (v. 1; cf. v. 5), involving one party accusing the other of "cheating" or fraud (vv. 7-8). In Roman Corinth such cases involved matters like legal possession, breach of contract, damages, fraud, or injury. That greed may be the driving motivation which led to the conflict is suggested by the appearance of the vice in all three vice lists in chapters 5 and 6. To follow Paul's advice in vv. 7-8 is to follow one of two alternative courses of action which would keep this scandal from being played out in the public courts. It would be preferable for the church to learn to arbitrate disputes among its members in a wise and God-honoring way. If they actually find they are not prepared to do so, it would be better to diffuse the situation by accepting some monetary setback. Most civil cases deal with disputes over money or possessions, even if pride some-

1. Contra A. Stein, "Wo trugen die korinthischen Christen ihre Rechtshändel aus?" *ZNW* 59 (1968), 86-90, who makes the improbable suggestion that the Corinthians were submitting their cases to Jewish judges.

times takes over as the basic motivation for pursuing the case. While one function of vv. 9-11 is to warn believers about the greatest consequences of a life marked by immorality (including greed and the related acts of swindling or robbing), another function of those verses is to hold out the inheritance of the kingdom of God as an encouragement to those who might suffer financial loss due to following Paul's guidance on this issue. At stake from the litigants' point of view is both material advantage and honor. It was presumably greed which caused the offense in the first place, and greed could also motivate the more powerful or influential of the conflicting believers to take the case to the secular court. To flee greed is to nip such cases in the bud.

Paul considers all pagan/secular courts to be inappropriate places for Christians to take their internal disputes, in part because those running those courts and adjudicating the issues brought to them are the "ungodly" (see the comments on v. 1), that is, people who have not experienced the transforming power of Jesus Christ, who do not make judgments in light of the true wisdom revealed in his cross, and who operate in a system that is governed or severely contaminated by very different values and a different worldview. While Paul's concerns may apply as much to courts in our own time and cultures, it would be a mistake to imagine that the courts to which the Corinthians were turning were just like the ones with which many of us are familiar. Perhaps we imagine a court and jury conducting matters in a restrained and civil manner under the assumption of equal rights to both parties. The situation in Corinth could not be more different. Some understanding of judicial process in a Roman colony is necessary to appreciate the finer nuances of Paul's instructions. What was civil litigation like in Corinth?

Ancient Roman courts could not be relied upon to administer justice impartially since they were open to bribes and were partial to the status and power of the prosecutor or defendant or both.[2] The Roman judicial system was damaged by "improper influences" that "made equality before the law unattainable."[3] In fact, "the principal criterion of legal privilege in the eyes of the Romans was *dignitas* or honor derived from power, style of life, and wealth."[4] Furthermore, going to court was very expensive and beyond the reach of most people. The system favored people of higher status.

2. Winter, "Civil Litigation in Secular Corinth and the Church: The Forensic Background to 1 Corinthians 6.1-8"; Witherington, 162-65; P. Garnsey, *Social Status and Legal Privilege in the Roman Empire* (Oxford: Clarendon, 1970), 183-85; and A. D. Clarke, *Secular and Christian Leadership in Corinth,* ch. 5. A judge and not a jury was probably involved in the case (cf. A. D. Clarke, *Secular and Christian Leadership in Corinth,* 62; contra Winter, "Civil Litigation in Secular Corinth and the Church." The plural "unrighteous" (6:1) and "unbelievers" (6:6) are a reference to the court system in general.

3. Garnsey, *Social Status,* 207.

4. Garnsey, *Social Status,* 279. Cf. *Digest* 48.19.28.16: "Our ancestors used to punish slaves more severely than freemen, the notorious than persons of uncorrupted repute in every punishment."

Cicero complained that excessive favor, great resources, and money with which to offer bribes hindered justice in the provinces east of Rome.[5] "Although Roman jurists strove to formulate a definition of justice that would be valid for all times and all peoples, in practice the Roman legal system, which was controlled, of course, by the upper class, reinforced the distinctions between the classes in Roman society."[6] The modern notion of equal standing in law did not pertain.

In all likelihood one, if not both, of the Christians in dispute in Corinth was powerful and wealthy, and the one with greater power or wealth could expect to have some advantage over their less influential "brother," and greater hope of escaping any serious financial loss. However, more than money was at stake in civil proceedings. Someone of high status would scrupulously avoid being taken to court because loss of reputation was a genuine concern. Bribery of judges, advocates, and witnesses occurred regularly in courts which were frequently swayed by fear and personal connections. With reputation on the line, the courts were awash with personal enmity. As Winter states, "the proceedings were not conducted dispassionately by the parties but with great acrimony."[7] Advocates were not expected to show any restraint: "the advocate . . . was permitted to use the most unbridled language about his client's adversary, or even his friends or relations or witnesses."[8] Young orators learned their trade with colorful character assassination, often playing to crowds of onlookers. Civil litigation was inevitably vexatious. It is little wonder that the church in Corinth suffered strife, jealousy, and discord with members entangled in such circumstances.

Paul is concerned that such strife is occurring in the family of God. The word "brother"[9] occurs four times in vv. 5-8 to refer to those involved in the dispute, translated in the TNIV as "believers," "brother," and "brothers and sisters" respectively. "Brother" in Greek can be generic, referring to both or either male and female believers. In spite of the assumption of virtually every commentator, the passage does not actually indicate that the "brothers" involved are men. That "brothers" can include women is clear from 11:2-16 and Philippians 4:1-3. Women were not excluded from civil litigation, even if they were often represented by men in court. And women are just as prone to the faults that lead to such action (cf. Phil. 4:2). We simply do not know whether the culprits in Corinth were male or female or male and female.

There can be little doubt that Paul's concern that judicial matters be

5. Cicero, *Pro Caecina,* 73, cited in Witherington, 164.

6. Jo-Ann Shelton, *As the Romans Did: A Sourcebook in Roman Social History* (2d ed.; New York: Oxford University Press, 1998), 9-10.

7. Winter, *Paul and Philo among the Sophists,* 94.

8. J. W. Jones, *The Law and Legal Theory of the Greeks* (Oxford: Oxford University Press, 1956), 151.

9. Gk. ἀδελφός.

settled internally was the common Jewish attitude of his day. That Jews sometimes handled their own disputes can even be seen from Paul's own experience in Corinth when Gallio passed Paul's case onto a Jewish tribunal (cf. Acts 18:12-16). It is also possible that the administration of justice in ancient Israel as presented in the Scriptures may have influenced Paul's thinking in the appointment of judges in 6:1-6. Roland de Vaux explains that Israel had three different jurisdictions involving priests,[10] elders, and professional judges instituted by the authority of the king.[11] All three groups are mentioned in the Pentateuch and take part in judicial affairs in other parts of the Scriptures. It is the tradition of the regal appointment of judges which provides the best background for 1 Corinthians 6:1-6. Such judges find their prototypes in the competent laymen appointed to dispense justice by Moses upon the advice of Jethro, his father-in-law, in Exodus 18:13-26 and Deuteronomy 1:9-17.[12] Deuteronomy 16:18-20 and 17:8-13 give further directions for these judges.

Paul vigorously opposes the behavior of the Christians in Corinth who take one another to court, judging it sheer audacity. Numerous rhetorical questions (disguised rebukes) and the use of "dare he"[13] (6:1; cf. Rom. 5:7) betray Paul's disdain. As v. 5a indicates, Paul writes to shame the Corinthians over such behavior. He insists on the inappropriateness and regrettable nature of the Corinthians' behavior in 6:1-6 by depicting the situation as a family altercation between brothers. The word "brother" is used three times in vv. 5 and 6 and once in v. 8 for this very purpose.[14] The term "brother" was in standard use (see, e.g., 1 and 2 Maccabees and many rabbinic texts) in Jewish communities and may well have enjoyed a relatively technical sense in early Christian communication (cf. "brother" in semilegal contexts in Matt. 18:15 and Gal. 6:1). Exodus 18 and Deuteronomy 1 likewise share Paul's concern that disputes between *brothers* be settled peacefully. In Genesis 13:8, a passage which records the legal controversy between Abram and Lot over the Promised Land, Abram says that there should not be strife between[15] Lot and himself "because we are brothers." Psalm 133:1 captures Paul's sentiment well: "Behold, how good and how pleasant it is for *brothers* to dwell together in unity." Paul was concerned that *brothers* in the family of God not squabble.

Paul's opposition to the use of secular courts to adjudicate between members of the body of Christ must not be taken as a condemnation of

10. Priests functioned as judges in cases concerning the cult or religious practice.

11. Roland de Vaux, *Ancient Israel: Its Life and Institutions* (Grand Rapids: Eerdmans, 1997), 152-55.

12. See Rosner, *Paul, Scripture and Ethics*, 95-99, on its influence in other parts of the Old Testament and on Jewish custom contemporary with Paul.

13. Gk. τολμάω.

14. RSV's "brother" (replaced in NRSV by "another") in v. 1 is not in the Greek.

15. The preposition ἀνὰ μέσον is used five times in Gen. 13:6-11.

government or even secular courts in general.[16] In Romans 13 he discusses in more sober fashion the attitude of Christians to government officials in general and their administration of criminal law and concludes that government is God's servant, reflecting the teaching of the wisdom tradition of the Old Testament.[17] 1 Corinthians 6:1-11 deals with the use of secular courts for civil cases between Christians. It does not concern criminal law, which in Corinth would have covered crimes such as high treason, embezzlement, bribery at elections, extortion in the provinces, forgery of wills or coins, violent offenses, and adultery. On this score he might have taken a different view. This passage could not be used, for example, to justify the covering up of child abuse or murder, even if such crimes were committed within the church fellowship. It also does not cover the case of a believer and a nonbeliever entangled in legal matters.

The injustice of secular courts was not Paul's only reason for opposing their use to settle disputes between Christians. He is also concerned about the reputation of the church before outsiders and about unity and concord within the body. Paul argues that an eschatological worldview, which the Corinthians lacked or at least failed to appreciate, properly understood would have led them to seek to settle the dispute internally (6:2-3) or, if that were not possible, to prefer to suffer the financial loss over which the dispute arose than to take their brother to the courts of the ungodly (6:7-11). Property and material possessions are of little consequence to those destined to inherit the kingdom. Once again, who Christians are, or rather will be in the future, should determine how we behave in the present.

The apostle's case against lawsuits comprises two closely related points:[18] in 6:1-6 he insists that Christians ought to be able to settle their own disputes,[19] and in 6:7-11, going a step further, he intensifies this point by pointing out that no matter who wins the case in a pagan court everyone actually loses. Paul challenges the Corinthians to allow themselves to be wronged and cheated rather than to do wrong to each other and the church by taking the matter to a secular court.

### *a. The Corinthians Should Settle Their Own Disputes, 6:1-6*

> [1]*If any of you has a dispute with another, do you dare to take it before the ungodly for judgment instead of before the Lord's people?* [2]*Or do you not know that the Lord's people will judge the world? And if you are to judge the world, are you not competent to judge trivial cases?* [3]*Do you not know that we will judge angels? How much more the things of this life!* [4]*Therefore, if*

16. In view of his experience as listed in the catalogues of woe (1 Cor. 4:9-13; 2 Cor. 11:23-28), it is not surprising that Paul did not trust Roman justice. Cf. K. Wengst, *Pax Romana and the Peace of Jesus Christ* (Philadelphia: Fortress, 1987), 76.

17. Cf. Dan. 4:25; Eccl. 8:2-5; Rosner, *Paul, Scripture and Ethics*, 112-15.

18. Cf. Barrett, 135; Talbert, 28.

19. 6:1 and 6:6 form an inclusio (note the repetition of κρίνω and ἐπί).

*you have disputes about such matters, do you ask for a ruling from those whose way of life is scorned in the church? [5]I say this to shame you. Is it possible that there is nobody among you wise enough to judge a dispute between believers? [6]But instead, one brother goes to law against another — and this in front of unbelievers!*

**6:1** Paul turns his attention to another issue that involves judging: *If any of you has a dispute with another.* The connection with 5:1-13 is clear from vv. 12-13. As Fee states: "If the church does not 'judge' those outside, neither does it go outside with inside affairs [for judgment]."[20] Paul is indignant that *the Lord's people* (literally, "the saints"), that is, members of the church in Corinth, are suing each other in secular courts. He cannot believe that a Christian would have the gall to take another Christian to court. His indignation is signaled by the word order in Greek (*dare* is the first word in the sentence) and by the use of a rhetorical question, which in this case is a thinly disguised rebuke.

Paul is dismayed by the fact that Corinthian believers have taken their grievances *before the ungodly for judgment.* The reasons for Paul's horror, although not explicit, can be surmised from the rest of the passage and from our knowledge of Paul and Corinth. First, Paul considered secular courts unsuitable for settling disputes. Paul describes the judges before whom the Corinthians were taking their disputes as "unrighteous."[21] Does "unrighteous" here simply identify the judges as non-Christians, or does it also characterize them as people who can be expected to act unrighteously? Several commentators understand the term "unrighteous" as standing in contrast to the "saints" in the same verse, as being simply synonymous with the "unbelievers" in v. 6, and as thus denoting the "unrighteous" in a religious not a moral sense, despite its appearance in a moral sense in v. 9.[22] The clear antithetical parallelism suggested by the opposition between the terms "unrighteous" and "saints" (or "holy ones")[23] suggests that Paul is thinking about the contrast between believers and unbelievers. That does not, however, mean that the moral connotation is absent. BDAG correctly defines the meaning of the former word as "pert[aining] to acting in a way that is contrary to what is right, *unjust, crooked*" and goes on to suggest the paraphrase "those who are from your Christian perspective impious unbelievers." That is, Paul's description of them as *ungodly* simultaneously identifies them as unbelievers and rebellious sinners who did not know God's true wisdom, righteousness, or transforming power and therefore were less qualified to serve as judges than anyone who had been sanctified by the Spirit of God (cf. 1:2). Paul knew that the secular courts in Corinth

20. Fee, 228.

21. Juries were used more commonly in criminal jurisdiction.

22. For example, Lang, 79.

23. Gk. κρίνεσθαι ἐπὶ τῶν <u>ἀδίκων</u>
καὶ οὐχὶ ἐπὶ τῶν <u>ἁγίων</u>;

could not be trusted to deliver a fair decision on the matter and that their use would inevitably lead to a hardening of the divisions in the church. Going to law changes relationships for the worse; acquaintances (or even family members) become adversaries, and the drive for victory replaces the hope of reconciliation. If the members involved in the dispute included leaders of the congregation, which is not unlikely given the Corinthians' reluctance to intervene, the situation would be all the worse.

That Paul considers *ungodly* or "unrighteous" judges unsuitable is explicable in terms of the qualifications of judges taught throughout the Old Testament, especially in Exodus 18/Deuteronomy 1 and related passages. LXX Deuteronomy 16:18-20a states, for example, that judges must be righteous: "Appoint judges and officials for each of your tribes in every town the LORD your God is giving you, and they shall judge the people *justly.* Do not pervert justice or show partiality. Do not accept a bribe, for a bribe blinds the eyes of the wise and twists the words of the *righteous.* Follow *justice justly.*"[24] In all these cases the judges are to act in light of their knowledge of justice which was informed by God's revelation of himself and of his law, which the ungodly are unable and/or unwilling to do. A second reason is Paul's concern for the reputation of the church. "Airing dirty laundry in public" will bring shame upon them and harm the cause of the gospel in Corinth. We shall deal with this matter further in v. 5, where Paul writes to shame the Corinthians. Thirdly, Paul thinks it unnecessary that the Christians in Corinth dispute before outsiders "instead of before the saints." As vv. 2-3 explain, the church has the resources and competence with which to settle such disputes.

**6:2** In vv. 2-3 Paul argues against the practice of taking disputes before secular judges by insisting on the superior competence of the saints to handle such cases: *Are you not competent to judge trivial cases?* The reason the Corinthians ought to settle their feuds internally is that believers will judge the world (v. 2) and even angels (v. 3), to say nothing of ordinary earthly matters.

Most commentators acknowledge the Old Testament as the major source of Paul's conviction that the saints will judge the world (6:2), contending that it derives from the Jewish hope that God's people will participate in the judgment of the last days expressed in Daniel 7:22,[25] developed by postbiblical Jewish writings (e.g., Wis. 3:7-8; *Jubilees* 24:29; Sir. 4:11, 15; *1 Enoch* 1:9, 38; 38:5; 95:3; 96:1; 98:12; 108:12; 1QpHab. v 4-5) and picked up in early Christian teaching (e.g., Matt. 19:28; Luke 22:30; Jude 14-15; Rev. 2:26-27; 20:4).[26]

24. Words in italics use δικ- words; cf. Exod. 23:6-8; Lev. 19:15; 1 Sam. 8:3; Isa. 5:23; 32:1; Mic. 3:9.

25. For example, C. H. Dodd, *According to the Scriptures: The Sub-Structure of New Testament Theology* (London: Fontana, 1952), 68: Dan. 7:22 "supplies the implicit scriptural authority for Paul's doctrine that the saints shall judge the world (1 Cor. vi. 2)."

26. Cf. esp. Lietzmann, 25.

Turning his attention from the parties involved in the litigation, Paul focuses upon the church and their duty to deal with such cases. Verses 2-3 supply the theological basis for not going "before the unrighteous." Paul employs the transparent logic of arguing from the greater to the lesser (cf. v. 4: "how much more . . ."). His argument with the Corinthians once again concerns not just their behavior, but their identity. The Corinthian Christians are eschatological people. If they will someday "judge the world," then "trivial cases" should be a matter of course.[27] From the perspective of the everlasting kingdom, the Corinthian litigation is "trifling" (NEB, JB) and totally insignificant.

Paul is not contradicting what he said in 5:12. *Present* judgments of the people who belong to the world are not their responsibility. Believers will, however, be involved in the *future* and final judgment of the world. As so often with Paul, the critical question is, What time is it? Eschatology for Paul is not a divine jigsaw puzzle to be solved, but a sure hope to be reckoned with now; the future carries weighty implications for conduct in the present.

**6:3** Paul presses his point by asserting that the scope of the judicial authority of believers in the End Time will include the judgment of angels. Presumably Paul has evil angels in mind, the judgment of whom is referred to in Jude 6 (cf. *1 Enoch* 10:12; 12:3-5; 22:11; 54:5-6). In referring to the subjection of all forces opposed to God, 1 Corinthians 15:24 probably alludes to the same notion.[28] Good angels will also aid in this future judgment (Matt. 13:41; 16:27; 25:31). The Corinthians' shame is all the worse when it is recognized that they will participate in judging matters of cosmic proportions. And, in this light, the Corinthian dispute seems mundane and small.[29] Judging everyday affairs should be no problem for those destined for such high office and responsibility.[30]

The dispute in Corinth concerned "the things of this life," mere matters of business.[31] Corinth was a city in which the rich would have employed working people of lower status to provide a wide range of services.[32] Many of these would have constituted "the things of this life." Quite possi-

27. "Cases" is κριτηρίων, which can mean a court of justice ("Are you unfit to form even the most insignificant courts?" NASB; Barrett, 136) or the legal action itself. As we have argued, the context favors the second sense, which is also clearly attested by two inscriptions cited by BDAG (cf. W. Schenk, "κριτήριον," *EDNT* 2:321).

28. Cf. Godet, 288.

29. "Trivial" in v. 2 reflects the superlative form of the word "small" (Gk. ἐλαχίστων is the superlative form of ἐλαχύς but is used as the superlative form of μικρός). As Sampley, 854, puts it, "The sublimity of Paul's eschatological vision . . . mocks the trifling insignificance of the disputes that some Corinthians have dragged before public tribunals."

30. On the origin of the notion of believers judging angels, see Rosner, *Paul, Scripture and Ethics*, 112.

31. Gk. βιωτικά.

32. Cf. Donald W. Engels, *Roman Corinth: An Alternative Model for the Classical City* (Chicago: University of Chicago Press, 1990), 43-65.

bly the situation Paul addressed involved a rich person suing a poor person over the services he or she had provided.[33] Alternatively it was two rich people involved in a dispute over some business dealing. In either case, the issue was not nearly as weighty as those which God has in mind for them in the eschaton! "If they are destined to be participants in the celestial judgment of the world and of the angels, they ought to be able to handle mundane matters of far less consequence. If they cannot settle minor rifts between themselves, they are hardly worthy to participate in the judgment of the world, let alone of the angels."[34] Since God intends to allow them to participate in the judgment of the world and of angels, however, they should at least get started in figuring out how they might arbitrate in simple cases such as the ones they are presently bringing to the courts.

**6:4** Paul says, with heavy irony, if you do have petty "matters of business" to settle between yourselves, "appoint as judges even men of little account in the church" (NIV). In other words, since all of you are qualified, destined to judge the world and angels, anyone will do. Some translations and commentators adopt a different interpretation and, along with the NIV, treat the words as a question instead of an ironic imperative and take the "men of little account" to be a reference to the judges of the secular courts rather than members of the church in Corinth: "Do you ask for a ruling from those whose way of life is scorned in the church?" The Greek is ambiguous. The word order is unusual for both a question and a command.[35] Both views make reasonable sense in context; rejecting the settling of disputes externally or recommending that they be settled internally amounts to the same thing. The problem for both views is the pejorative term, "those whose way of life is scorned," which is translated too mildly in the NIV. The verb means to think nothing of,[36] to despise, to scorn, to hold in contempt (cf. 2 Cor. 10:10; Rom. 14:3, 10; Gal. 4:4; 1 Thess. 5:20). For Paul to describe either the non-Christian judges or his fellow Christians in such terms seems harsh.

On balance, the text of the NIV makes better sense. It is not likely that Paul would describe the non-Christian judges as despised since some of the Corinthian Christians at least did not share this view; after all, they thought enough of them to seek their judgment! That Paul is using irony is clear from the previous reference to "the despised" in the letter in 1:29, which is a reference to the majority of believers in Corinth, who are de-

33. See Alan C. Mitchell, "Rich and Poor in the Courts of Corinth: Litigiousness and Status in 1 Corinthians 6.1-11," *NTS* 39 (1993), 583.

34. Garland, 203.

35. Cf. Fee, 235: "this interpretation [ironic imperative] faces the nearly insuperable difficult[y] of having an imperative appear as the final word in a sentence"; and Lightfoot, 211, who notes "the awkwardness of the interrogative coming at the end of so long a sentence."

36. Gk. ἐξουθενέω, "to show by one's attitude or manner of treatment that an entity has no merit or worth, *disdain*" (BDAG). In the passive here, "despised, of no account."

spised in the eyes of the world. And the ironic reference to "the wise" in v. 5 makes a similar use of irony in v. 4 all the more likely. Paul does not risk dividing the church by calling on "the despised" in the church to settle the dispute because it is not a serious proposal. In the light of 1:29 no one would have been offended. They are despised only in the world's eyes, as 1:29 makes clear. In effect, Paul says: "Don't use the 'somebodies' in the world. You will judge the world one day! Therefore, even the 'nobodies' in the church would be better than they."[37] As the Geneva Bible states, Paul writes that "they end their private affairs between themselves by chosen arbiters out of the church: for which matter and purpose, the least of you, he says, is sufficient."[38] The least of the Corinthians can deal with the smallest matter.

**6:5-6** Whereas Paul did not consider the Corinthians' factiousness a cause of shame (4:14), their litigation is another matter. But more particularly, what he has just said in v. 4b about appointing "the contemptuous" among them to judge was said to shame them. When the problem arose, there should have been someone wise enough in the church to help the parties settle the dispute amicably.

This is precisely what Paul says in v. 5b: *Is it possible that there is nobody among you wise enough to judge a dispute between believers* (literally, "between a brother"[39])? The question has an ironic twist since the Corinthians are so enamored with wisdom ("you are so wise in Christ!"; 4:10). These words reveal the source and basis for Paul's insistence in vv. 1-6 that disputes be handled internally, namely, Old Testament teaching about judges in Exodus 18, Deuteronomy, and related passages.[40]

37. Of course, as Paul will make clear in 12:21-25, the church is not to be seen in terms of status and influence. In reality there are no "men of little account" in the church.

38. Several church fathers seem to have understood the verse similarly. Severian of Gabala took Paul to mean "the lowest person in the church is preferable in judgment to an unbeliever" (Bray, 16). Chrysostom (*Homiliae in Epistulam i ad Corinthios* 16.6 [NPNF[1] 12:92]) paraphrases Paul this way: "Even though none be wise," says he, "I bid you entrust things to those who are of least weight." So also Augustine, *Of the Work of the Monks,* 37.

39. 6:5b contains a grammatical irregularity — singular ἀδελφοῦ ("brother") — for which no wholly satisfactory explanation has been proposed. The Greek text reads literally, "between his brother." Several ways of resolving the problem have been considered by scholars (see Rosner, *Paul, Scripture and Ethics,* 104-6, for details). Perhaps we may regard 6:5b as a loose reminiscence of the LXX of Deut. 1:16 which has led to rather abrupt, but nevertheless comprehensible, Greek. It was sufficiently clear to be taken without comment by people whose mother tongue was Greek. Two fourth-century Greek-speaking exegetes, Chrysostom and Theodoret, do not balk at the Greek of 6:5b, quoting it without drawing attention to it, and the Vulgate translates it literally. Lightfoot, 212, asserts that "the sentence is much abridged." Perhaps Paul may have been abridging Deut. 1:16. This solution recognizes the Greek Bible milieu of 1 Cor. 6:1-6 in general, and of the preposition ἀνὰ μέσον ("between") in particular, and it does not resort to speculative emendation, but nonetheless acknowledges the awkwardness of the phrase in koine Greek.

40. See Rosner, *Paul, Scripture and Ethics,* 94-121; and Rosner, "Paul and Moses Appointing Judges: An Antecedent to 1 Cor 6.1-6?" *ZNW* 82.3/4 (1991), 275-78.

The situations in which Moses in Exodus 18/Deuteronomy 1 and Paul in 6:1-6 find themselves are not without similarity. Both Moses and Paul are overwhelmed by the judicial problems of the people of God.[41] Both leaders decide to handle the more difficult cases themselves,[42] with the Lord's help[43] (Paul pronounces judgment on the incestuous man in chapter 5), and appoint judges to adjudicate the lesser cases by deciding between their brothers. The situations of Moses and Paul are of course not alike in every respect. Moses was not rejecting unsuitable judges, but appointing suitable ones. Without doubt, Paul's main task was more the former. This difference, however, is not so great that Paul could not have seen any relevance in the Moses incident to his own situation. Verses 6:1b, 4b, and 5b indicate that Paul recommended as one option that some people from within the community settle the dispute. Furthermore, patristic interpretation of 1 Corinthians 6:1-11 certainly saw the passage as relevant to the issue of the appointment of judges.[44] There are also impressive terminological links between 6:1-11 and LXX Exodus 18/Deuteronomy 1 (and related passages). A total of eight terms, some of which occur rarely in both the LXX and Paul's letters, can be traced from 6:1-8 to the tradition of Moses appointing judges in the Greek Old Testament. That these data represent more than merely the coincidence of terms one normally expects to find in any two discussions of judicial affairs is suggested by the comparison of v. 5b with LXX Deuteronomy 1:16. In these two texts Moses and Paul appoint wise judges (cf. LXX Deut. 1:15) to judge between their brothers.[45] Paul's words echo Deuteronomy 1:16.

In 6:1-6 Paul applies the lessons of Exodus 18/Deuteronomy 1 (and related passages) to the problem of lawsuits in Corinth. He follows the implications of the Moses material (because Moses was the most important biblical precedent for what he was doing), but does not find it necessary to signal his use of Scripture to the Corinthians either by quotation or allu-

41. See Deut. 1:12; Exod. 18:13, 14, 18; and Paul's disquiet in 1 Cor. 5:1; 6:1.

42. Exod. 18:22, 26; Deut. 1:17; 1 Cor. 5:3-5; cf. M. Delcor, "The Courts of the Church of Corinth and the Courts of Qumran," in *Paul and Qumran* (ed. J. Murphy-O'Connor; London: Chapman, 1968), 76: "In the Epistle to the Corinthians the office of supreme judge has fallen on the Apostle himself."

43. Cf. Exod. 18:19b and 1 Cor. 5:3-5.

44. BiPa 1.452 and 2.381 assemble over 50 patristic discussions of 1 Cor. 1:1-11 (or parts thereof), about which see *NewDocs* [= *New Documents Illustrating Early Christianity* (ed. G. H. R. Horsley and S. Llewelyn; North Ryde, NSW: The Ancient History Documentary Research Centre, Macquarie University Press, 1981-)] 3:152, and conclude correctly that "this passage provided the basis for what became the institution of the episcopal court set up under Constantine."

45. A computer search of *TLG* (*Canon of Greek Authors and Works*, ed. Luci Berkowitz and Karl A. Squitier) confirms the significance of LXX Deut 1:16 in relation to 1 Cor. 6:5. The only places in both literary and nonliterary Greek where the three words "judge between a brother" occur in that order are LXX Deut. 1:16, 1 Cor. 6:5, and commentaries on the latter verse by Origen and Theodorus Studies (and a reference to the same verse in Basil the Great's commentary on Isaiah).

sion; v. 5b is an echo of Deuteronomy 1:16. Just as Moses appointed wise and righteous laity to decide lesser civil cases (including fraud) between their brothers, so also Paul rejected unrighteous judges and told the Corinthians to appoint wise laity to decide such cases between their brothers. Paul is, despite the absence of explicit indication, in effect, depending upon and obeying Torah as he understands its application to his new situation. To make this explicit he could have quoted Deuteronomy 25:1, which declares, "If there should be a dispute between men, they are to take it to the judges," but he does not. Nevertheless, the weight of the evidence bears the conclusion that Exodus 18/Deuteronomy 1 had some influence upon the conception and expression of Paul's instructions to the Corinthians in vv. 1-6 that disputes between brothers should be handled internally.

Many commentators assume that behind Paul's insistence that Corinthian lawsuits be handled internally rather than externally stands his concern for the reputation of the church.[46] Though disputed by some,[47] this contention is supported by Paul's rebuke in v. 5a: "I say this to your shame." The only other place in the New Testament where this expression is used is in 15:34, where the cause for shame is the unhappy relation of the Corinthians toward outsiders. In v. 5a he writes to shame the Corinthians at least partly because of the disrepute they have brought upon themselves by airing their dissensions in public before "unbelievers" (6:6). That Paul is concerned about what outsiders think of the behavior of the Corinthian church is clear from 14:23-25.

In Judaism contemporary with Paul there was both a negative and a positive reason for keeping a good reputation for the community of God's people: to protect the honor of God's name and to win the heathen.[48] That the Old Testament contains both threads of the concern that God's people maintain a good reputation before the heathen is clear. Evidence can be gathered from sources as diverse as the intercession of Moses on behalf of God's people in Exodus 32 (see 32:12, 25), Numbers 14:13-19 (see vv. 15-16) and Deuteronomy 9:25-29, the prophets (cf. Isa. 52:5; Ezek. 36:20), and even Wisdom literature (Prov. 3:4; 22:1; 25:10; Eccl. 7:1a). It is clear from Romans 2:24 that Paul knew and valued this tradition. In a discussion of Jewish shortcomings, he

46. Delcor, "The Courts," 69, e.g., writes: "Everything suggests that the Apostle wishes especially to prevent the private scandals of the community from being known by judges who did not share their faith."

47. For example, Fee, 232, stresses instead Paul's point that the Corinthians are "eschatological people." The two themes, eschatology and a good reputation, may, however, both be operating in the passage. Elsewhere (229) Fee appears to admit the good reputation theme (Paul is aggravated because the Corinthian action "totally destroys the community before the world [v. 6]").

48. Cf. Willem van Unnik, "Die Rücksicht auf die Reaktion der Nicht-Christen als Motiv in der altchristlichen Paränese," in *Judentum, Urchristentum, Kirche: Festschrift für Joachim Jeremias* (ed. Walther Eltester; Berlin: A. Töpelmann, 1960), 221-34, who has traced the desire to make a good impression on one's heathen neighbors as an ethical motive in 2 *Clement*, the New Testament, and the intertestamental Jewish writings.

states that "the name of God is blasphemed among the Gentiles because of you, as it is written," quoting Isaiah 52:5 (cf. Ezek. 36:20).[49]

Two texts in 1 Corinthians evidence the concern. In 9:19-23 Paul claims that he behaves circumspectly before all outsiders so that he might save some (cf. 9:12b). This stands in contrast to the Corinthians, who air their "dirty laundry" with its consequent harm to the cause of the gospel's progress. 1 Corinthians 10:31-32, the conclusion to Paul's discussion of whether or not to eat food sacrificed to idols (8:1–11:1), ties together both the negative and positive motives of this good reputation theme: "So whether you eat or drink or whatever you do, do it all for the glory of God. Do not cause anyone to stumble, whether Jews, Greeks or the church of God." At least part of Paul's opposition to the Corinthians' taking their disputes before pagan judges was that such behavior damaged the reputation of the church, of the gospel, and of God himself, a concern which Paul, in all likelihood, received from the Scriptures.

Verses 4b and 5b call for the same response: a fellow Christian is to intervene and resolve the dispute between members of God's family. This is no idle and impractical suggestion. As Winter explains: "Provision existed in Greek, Roman and Jewish legal systems for the use of arbitrators who acted in a legal capacity with the agreement of the defendant and the plaintiff."[50] Some in the Corinthian congregation may well have had legal training. Secular education often included instruction in forensic matters.

Paul closes the section (vv. 1-6) by repeating his charge (cf. v. 1) that *brothers and sisters* in Christ, members of God's family, ought not to dispute in front of unbelievers. Paul injects the emotive term "brother" twice (literally, "But brother goes to law with brother") to further shame the Corinthians involved (cf. 8:11, "the brother for whom Christ died").[51] As Winter reminds us, "Romans considered it highly inappropriate to engage in intrafamily litigation," pointing out that "Cicero wrote about a dispute relating to property, 'Do not allow brothers to engage in litigation and to settle their differences in a proceeding involving charges of scandalous conduct.'"[52] Paul's "brother" language signals the kind of "deep resocialization"[53] that was typical of his missionary strategy. It is not that he is calling for a permanent court to be set up in the church. Instead, he calls for constructive intervention to save a situation which threatened the church's unity and reputation.

49. On Paul's desire that the community make a good impression on outsiders both for the sake of evangelism and for the honor of God's name, see Rosner, *Paul, Scripture and Ethics*, 110.

50. Winter, *Paul and Philo among the Sophists*, 96.

51. David G. Horrell, *Solidarity and Difference: A Contemporary Reading of Paul's Ethics* (London: T&T Clark, 2005), 114, highlights this as one of several texts where "the sibling language is used with an apparently deliberate and repeated emphasis to impress an ethical demand."

52. Winter, *After Paul Left Corinth*, 71.

53. Meeks, *Moral World*, 129.

### *b. The Corinthians Should Be Willing to Suffer Wrong, 6:7-8*

*[7]The very fact that you have lawsuits among you means you have been completely defeated already. Why not rather be wronged? Why not rather be cheated? [8]Instead, you yourselves cheat and do wrong, and you do this to your brothers and sisters.*

**6:7** In vv. 7-8 Paul states that the very presence of "lawsuits" is a defeat.[54] It is important to note that Paul is referring here to judicial cases, not just to a dispute among Christians; Paul has used the legal term[55] in this verse, as opposed to his use of the more general term for "dispute"[56] in v. 1. The problem is not the dispute, but the taking of the dispute before the secular courts. This understanding makes sense of Paul's previous teaching in the section about correct handling of such disputes. Paul is advocating a nonjudicial judgment ethic, not a non-dispute ethic. Thus one does not need to see v. 4 as a concession to the ideal presented in vv. 7-8.[57] The dispute itself is not a defeat, but if it is taken before an unrighteous judge it is nothing but a defeat. Jesus had established the ideal for dealing with conflicts within the community (Matt. 18:15-17). It entailed going and speaking with the offending person alone (Matt. 18:15). "Only if this private face-to-face remonstration fails may the person who feels a sense of grievance seek a further step," which entailed bringing one or two witnesses (in keeping with the standard established in the Old Testament; Matt. 18:16). One could take the issue to be judged by the church only if these previous steps had failed.[58] We do not know whether the Corinthians' plaintiffs had taken those first steps, but they certainly had not allowed the church to serve as the final arbiter.

While there is plenty of blame to go around in the situation Paul describes, Paul's "stinging rebuke pertains particularly to the one who initiated the court action but also to the entire church body."[59] Chrysostom notes that "the act itself of going to law brings each party under his censure, and in that respect one is not at all better than another. . . . Say not then, 'which did the wrong?' For on this ground I condemn you at once, even for the act of going to law."[60] Paul, however, does not clearly judge the person being taken to court as much as he does the one taking them (for using secular courts to resolve the issue) and the church as a whole (for not intervening and finding a God-honoring way to resolve the dispute within

54. There is a string of present indicatives in vv. 7-8 (ἔστιν; ἔχετε; ἀδικεῖτε; ἀποστερεῖτε) which express their imperfective aspect by creating a descriptive setting. The many presents create a scene that characteristically represents the Corinthians.

55. Gk. κρίματα (cf. BDAG).

56. Gk. πρᾶγμα.

57. Contra Rosner, *Paul, Scripture and Ethics*, 115; thanks are due to Carl Matthei for this correction.

58. Thiselton, 436.

59. Garland, 209.

60. Chrysostom, *Homiliae in Epistulam i ad Corinthios* 16.7 (NPNF[1] 12:92).

the context of the church). Paul himself may not have known whether or not the person being taken to court was guilty or innocent.

In any instance of litigation the goal is to achieve a personal victory. Paul states as emphatically as he can that the outcome of the present case is already known: no matter what the result of the lawsuit, whether the plaintiff or the defendant wins, it is a defeat for both parties, with the church as a whole becoming the real loser. They were defeated the moment the legal proceeding began, since its initiation served as testimony to the church's failure to resolve the conflict as a healthy family would be expected to do. Garland draws out the devastating social implications of such a legal proceeding for the church: "Litigation by its very nature promoted enmity from the slander that was part and parcel of a trial and could only have fueled the church's factionalism. . . . Church members who were clients of one of the parties would have to side with their patron, if they were to remain clients, over against a fellow Christian."[61]

Paul employs two rhetorical questions that both emphasize the preferable alternatives to their actions as described in the following verse. They should prefer to be wronged or cheated (v. 7) over cheating and doing wrong to their brothers and sisters (v. 8).[62] To be wronged or cheated is to be greatly preferred to wronging or cheating another, especially a brother or a sister in Christ. Both questions are directed at the plaintiff, the one who brought the case to court. Their meaning is equivalent to: "do not return evil for evil; overcome evil with good" (Rom. 12:21b). By enduring undeserved injury believers follow the example of Christ (Phil. 2:1-11; 1 Pet. 2:19-21).

Paul calls for believers not just to forgo their rights but willingly to suffer injustice and abuse rather than take their disputes before pagan courts. Willingness to suffer injustice and abuse for the cause of Christ is a major theme in Paul's ethics. He recommends, "not repaying evil for evil" (1 Thess. 5:15; Rom. 12:17), "not taking vengeance" (Rom. 12:19), and "not cursing" (Rom. 12:14). The concepts of "forbearance" (1 Cor. 13:4; 1 Thess. 5:14; Gal. 5:22; 2 Cor. 6:6) and "endurance" (1 Cor. 4:12; 2 Cor. 11:20;[63] 1 Cor. 13:7; 2 Cor. 6:4; Rom. 12:12[64]) are kindred thoughts. Christians should avoid secular courts, which are based on the principle of retaliation for wrongs done.[65] The motivation here is not so much forgiving love as in 13:5c ("love keeps no record of wrongs"), but harmony in the body and witness before the world.

61. Garland, 209.

62. Gk. μᾶλλον serves as a "marker of an alternative to someth[ing], rather," here, "why do you not rather suffer wrong (instead of doing wrong to others)?" (BDAG). Ambrosiaster's view is that a believer "ought not to engage in litigation at all, but if the matter is too serious to be disregarded he should bring the case to the church, so as not to incur an immediate penalty and personal downfall" (Bray, 52).

63. Gk. ἀνέχομαι.

64. Gk. ὑπομένω.

65. Cf. S. Meurer, *Das Recht im Dienst der Versöhnung und des Friedens: Studie zur Frage des Rechts nach dem Neuen Testaments* (ATANT 63; Zürich: Theologischer Verlag, 1972).

LXX Leviticus 19:13a states: "You shall not *wrong* your neighbor." Paul is in agreement, contending that it would be better for the Corinthian Christians to suffer *wrong*.[66] Several commentators confidently ascribe the source of Paul's teaching in these verses to the words of Jesus in Matthew 5:39-42 (cf. 5:40, "If anyone wants to sue you and take your coat, give your cloak as well").[67] However, the nonretaliatory ethic of Jesus stands solidly in a tradition of ethics of the Old Testament and early Judaism.[68] Jesus' teaching is not unique at this point.

In asking the Corinthians to be wronged and defrauded rather than compromise Christian standards of love Paul is, in effect, urging them to imitate himself. In 4:16 the exhortation to follow his example involves in its immediate context suffering for the sake of Christ (see 4:11-13). In chapter 9 Paul exemplifies the attitude of being willing to suffer loss which he expects of the Corinthians in 6:7-8;[69] though possessing "the right of support" Paul says: "We did not use this right. On the contrary, we put up with anything rather than hinder the gospel of Christ" (9:12b). Indeed, the theme of suffering righteously and related notions punctuate the Corinthian correspondence (1 Cor. 4:8-13; 15:3-8; 2 Cor. 1:3-8; 4:7-12, 16-18; 6:3-10; 7:5-7; 11:23-30; 12:7-10; 13:4). It is within the province of this material that the provenance of the sentiments expressed in 6:7-8 must be sought. The biblical theme of the suffering righteous forms the dominant background for the various Pauline discussions of suffering, including those found in 1 Corinthians. Paul applies this theme as a help to understanding not only the sufferings of Jesus but also his own sufferings and, in this case, the sufferings of his churches.

**6:8** Paul does not, however, leave the defendant free of blame. Repeating the language of the previous verse, he spares no punches: the offenders did not prefer to suffer wrong or be cheated; rather, Paul says, *you yourselves cheat and do wrong, and you do this to your brothers and sisters.*[70] Paul addresses the whole church as if personally responsible and involved in the action (note second-person plural verbs in vv. 7b and 8), even if his words have particular significance for the parties in dispute.

Oster thinks that we "have no way of knowing what particular legal and moral transgressions these Corinthian believers had committed."[71] But the terms Paul uses provide the needed hint. As Sampley points out, Paul's terms for "doing wrong" in both vv. 7 and 8 serve as an inclusio, linking

66. Both texts use ἀδικέω.

67. For example, Fee, 241, describes it as "a sure instance" of how the teaching of Jesus has influenced Paul."

68. See Gordon Zerbe, *Non-Retaliation in Early Jewish and New Testament Texts* (JSPSup 13; Sheffield: Sheffield Academic Press, 1993).

69. The lesson of self-denial exemplified by Paul in 1 Corinthians 9 was to be applied by the Corinthians to the problem of meat sacrificed to idols, but it is also applicable here in a secondary way.

70. The two verbs are repeated from v. 7.

71. Oster, 135.

"back to Paul's first description of civil judges as ones who 'wrong' others" (6:1, where the term is translated "ungodly").[72] "What characterizes the judgments rendered by unbelieving judges — namely, their wronging of others, is precisely what Paul sees has ironically become operative within the community of believers." This is "yet another irony and yet one more reason why the community needs to redefine itself as distinct from the world."[73] It is quite likely that we are not merely dealing with a parallel between unbelieving judges who (as fallen and unregenerate people operating on the basis of the world's understanding of wisdom) by nature do wrong and fail to reflect true justice in their courts and separate wrongdoing on the part of the Corinthian plaintiffs. Rather, it is in the very act of subjecting their brother or sister to the judgment of such ungodly/wrongdoing judges that the Corinthians themselves become guilty of doing wrong to them. To expose one's own brother or sister in Christ to that environment is truly to be "completely defeated already" (v. 1).

### *c. The Corinthians Should Suffer Now and Inherit Later, 6:9-11*

> *9Or do you not know that wrongdoers will not inherit the kingdom of God? Do not be deceived: Neither the sexually immoral nor idolaters nor adulterers nor male prostitutes nor practicing homosexuals 10nor thieves nor the greedy nor drunkards nor slanderers nor swindlers will inherit the kingdom of God. 11And that is what some of you were. But you were washed, you were sanctified, you were justified in the name of the Lord Jesus Christ and by the Spirit of our God.*

**6:9-10** Following the train of the argument in 6:1-20 is not an easy task. If Paul addresses the problem of lawsuits in 6:1-8 and going to prostitutes in 6:12-20, where does 6:9-11, which concerns inheriting the kingdom, fit? Most commentators understand these verses to go with what precedes rather than what follows. But there is far from unanimity,[74] and little help is given with appreciating their relevance to Paul's instructions not to fight lawsuits. What could have led Paul to speak of "inheriting the kingdom of God," a phrase he uses only twice outside of these verses in his letters (1 Cor. 15:50; Gal. 5:21)?

Part of the problem is the fact that the verses in question can be justifiably seen to look both ways. With the initial reference in the vice list to the

72. The adjective ἄδικος is used in v. 1 (reappearing in v. 9), and the verb ἀδικέω is used in both vv. 7 and 8 (the noun ἀδικία appears in 13:6). The Corinthians "do wrong" (ἀδικέω) by subjecting their brothers and sisters to the judgments of a wrongdoer (ἄδικος).

73. Sampley, 855.

74. See Winter, "Civil Litigation in Secular Corinth and the Church," 559-72; Kenneth E. Bailey, "Paul's Theological Foundation for Human Sexuality: I Cor. 6:9-20 in the Light of Rhetorical Criticism," *Near East School of Theology Theological Review* 3 (1980), 27-41; and Orr and Walther, 193-98, who divide the section 6:1-9a and 6:9b-20.

"sexually immoral," they introduce Paul's instructions in 6:12-20 (as well as look back to 5:1-13). Furthermore, if temple prostitution is in Paul's sights, the second item, "idolaters," may also be significant. However, the contextual links with 6:1-8 are even more impressive. The conjunction "or" connects the two, as does the appearance of words in Greek from the same root: "unrighteous" in v. 9 and "justified" in v. 11 recall "unrighteous" in v. 1 and "to wrong" in vv. 7-8.[75]

Before considering how vv. 9-11 function in the argument of chapter 6, it is worth inquiring as to their possible origin. Here we are not asking from where Paul derived this possibly traditional piece of paraenesis, but what led him to include it at this point in the argument. 1 Corinthians is riddled with scriptural quotations and allusions. We have argued that two such passages from the Old Testament seem to have played a formative role in 6:1-8, even though they are not explicitly cited: Daniel 7:22 in 6:2-3; and Exodus 18/Deuteronomy 1 in 6:1-6. The broader Old Testament contexts of both of these represent sources of influence for Paul's reference to inheriting the kingdom of God in vv. 9-11.

In Deuteronomy 1 and Exodus 18 Moses is depicted as appointing judges in comparable fashion to Paul in vv. 1-6. Both passages from the Pentateuch precede the giving of the law. In Deuteronomy 1–6 the point is made repeatedly that the people of God will *inherit* the land if they obey the covenant stipulations enshrined in the Ten Commandments.[76] For example, Deuteronomy 6:1 states: "Now this is the commandment, the statutes and the ordinances which the Lord your God commanded me to teach you, that you may do them in the land to which you are going over, to inherit it." Furthermore, in Deuteronomy 3:21 the land they will inherit is described as "the kingdoms" of the peoples they will dispossess. In Exodus 19 they are told that keeping this covenant will enable them to become a "*kingdom* of priests and a holy nation." In vv. 9-11 Paul connects inheritance with a list of *ten* vices. Whereas the Decalogue and Paul's vice list overlap in content, the similarity is not so marked as to suggest dependence. It is not that Paul is giving a second Decalogue. Nonetheless, that Paul and Moses both gave God's people ten words to ensure they would receive their inheritance and become part of a kingdom is intriguing. Paul acts like Moses in a number of places in his letters.[77] Furthermore, Paul has a high view of Exodus traditions, not least in 1 Corinthians.[78] That Paul could have reflected on the Moses material typologically, seeing a similarity in his situation and theirs, and been led to speak of inheriting the kingdom is quite possible. He could in fact have easily quoted Deuteronomy 16:20 as a way of moving from the notions of judging righteously to inheritance: "Justice

75. Gk. δικαι-.

76. In the LXX, "to inherit" occurs more often than in any other book.

77. See Rosner, *Paul, Scripture and Ethics*, 102-3.

78. See, e.g., J. K. Howard, "Christ Our Passover: A Study of the Passover-Exodus Theme in 1 Corinthians," *EvQ* 41 (1969), 97-108.

and only justice you shall follow, that you may live and inherit the land which the Lord your God gives you" (RSV).

In Daniel 7 "the saints" are said to have been given judgment to exercise (7:22), a function Paul echoes for "the saints" (1 Cor. 6:1) in vv. 2-3. In the case of Daniel we do not even have to move outside of the chapter to find as many as nine references to the *kingdom.* In fact, in the same verse, Daniel 7:22, it is stated that not only was "judgment given to the saints," but "the saints received the kingdom." Whereas in Deuteronomy the inheritance, though desirable and from God, is temporal and limited, namely, the land, in Daniel 7 the kingdom, as in 1 Corinthians 6:9-11, is everlasting and universal (see esp. 7:27). Thus we need look no further for the inspiration of references to "inheriting the kingdom" such as we find here.[79] The Old Testament texts which influenced him in vv. 1-6 continued, it seems, to make an impact in vv. 9-11.

That Paul's words in vv. 9-11 function as a warning to those Corinthian Christians fighting lawsuits against one another (and to those going to prostitutes) is manifestly clear: people who act in that fashion will not inherit the kingdom. However, the likely origin of 6:9-11 suggests another function for the verses in context. In Exodus, Deuteronomy, and Daniel the references to inheriting the kingdom are set in the context of suffering. Whereas in the former texts the people have come out from slavery in Egypt (Exodus) or have endured the wilderness wanderings (Deuteronomy), in Daniel the theme of hardship and destruction matches both the courses of the four kingdoms which are narrated in rapid succession and the historical setting of God's people in exile. In both cases inheriting the kingdom is held out as encouragement to fidelity and obedience in difficult circumstances in the knowledge that the wicked will one day face judgment when God's people are vindicated.

It is this notion, with both its components of warning and its hope-inspiring promise, that provides a bridge between 1 Corinthians 6:7-8 and the following three verses. Paul states in 6:9 that *wrongdoers will not inherit the kingdom of God.*[80] The word translated *wrongdoers*[81] here is the same one

79. The idea of "inheriting the kingdom" seems to predate Paul (cf. Matt. 25:34 and references to inheriting the earth [Matt. 5:5] or eternal life [Matt. 19:29; Mark 10:17; Luke 10:25; 18:18], which seem to reflect a similar transformation of Old Testament land theology; cf. Garland, 211) and had probably already been used by him in Gal. 5:21 (depending on one's dating of that letter).

80. The characterizing use of present tense verbs in vv. 7-8 gives way to speaking of future judgment with two future indicatives in vv. 9-10 (κληρονομήσουσιν; κληρονομήσουσιν). The future judgment of the unrighteous (cf. 1 Cor. 4:5; 5:13) is a biblical theme (Dan. 12:1-2; Eccl. 12:14; Pss. 96:10, 13; 98:9; Amos 5:18-20; Isa. 24:1-23) which is developed in early Jewish literature: *4 Ezra* 7:45-61; *2 Baruch* 30:2-5; 51:1-6; *1 Enoch* 10:1-6; 22:11; 54:6; 55:3–56:4; 91:6-9, 19; 94:9; *Jubilees* 15:34; *Testament of Levi* 4:1-6; *Testament of Benjamin* 10:8-10; in rabbinic literature cf. the phrase, "such and such have no share in the world to come," e.g., in *m. Sanhedrin* 10:1-4; *m. 'Abot* 3:16.

81. Gk. ἄδικοι, plural of ἄδικος.

translated "ungodly" in v. 1, which also shares the same root as the verb used to describe the Corinthians as people who "do wrong" to their brothers and sisters in the previous verse. Paul implies that the litigious Corinthians have been acting the part of unrighteous people who would face rejection in the final judgment and that they had better change their ways so as to distance themselves as far as possible from such behaviors.

If wrongdoers or unrighteous people *will not* inherit the kingdom, it is natural to ask, Who *will* inherit the kingdom? The answer is, those whose faith commitment to Christ leads them to reject the immoral, greedy, and idolatrous behavior which marks the lives of pagans, and, more precisely in this context, those who do not wrong and cheat others and who would prefer to suffer righteously than to subject their brothers and sisters to the injustices of unrighteous courts (vv. 7-8). Vv. 9-11 provide encouragement to the Corinthians to follow Paul's difficult advice in vv. 7-8 (not to dispute with one another, even if it means you suffer); those who choose to suffer wrong are the kind of people who will inherit the kingdom, a curious paradox. With respect to vv. 1-8, vv. 9-11 act as both a warning and an encouragement to follow Paul's instructions. That Paul has a positive purpose for these verses as well is clear from v. 11, which assures the Corinthians that Paul thinks better of them.

It is not uncommon in Paul's letters for the apostle to follow up the thought of present suffering with the encouragement of future glory. It is a biblical pattern of thought with which he is apparently quite familiar. Romans 8:17 demonstrates that in Paul's mind suffering is linked with inheritance: "Now if we are children, then we are *heirs* — *heirs* of God and co-*heirs* with Christ, if indeed we share in his *sufferings*." The example par excellence of suffering leading to glory is of course Christ himself. In 2 Corinthians 4:17 suffering and glory are also connected in Paul's own experience: "Our light and momentary troubles are achieving for us an eternal glory that far outweighs them all."

In context, vv. 9-11 serve as both a warning and an encouragement not to do wrong to one another as by taking each other to court. Paul argues that an eschatological worldview, which the Corinthians lacked or at least failed to appreciate, properly understood would have led them to seek to either settle the dispute internally (vv. 2-3) or gladly suffer the financial loss over which the dispute arose (vv. 9-11).[82] Property and material possessions are of little consequence to those destined to inherit the kingdom! An indifferent attitude to material possessions in the light of eschatological realities is further pressed upon the Corinthians in 7:29-31.

The vice list in vv. 9-10 contains ten items, six of which are repeated

82. Of course, since internal efforts to resolve such disputes would not always result in a solution that was equally satisfying to both parties, there would/will still be times when one would feel that they had made a significant sacrifice by not taking the issue to the public court, where they might possibly have received a more favorable outcome.

from 5:11. The other four expand the most relevant vices in chapters 5 and 6, namely, sexual immorality (adultery and different types of homosexual behavior) and greed (thieves). The order of the vices changes for no apparent reason. In the table below the new vices are in italics.

| **1 Corinthians 6:9-10** | **1 Corinthians 5:11** | **1 Corinthians 5:9** |
|---|---|---|
| 1. sexually immoral | sexually immoral | sexually immoral |
| 2. idolaters | idolaters | idolaters |
| 3. *adulterers* | | |
| 4. *male prostitutes* | | |
| 5. *practicing homosexuals* | | |
| 6. *thieves* | | |
| 7. greedy | greedy | greedy |
| 8. drunkards | drunkards | |
| 9. slanderers | slanderers | |
| 10. swindlers | swindlers | swindlers |

Whereas one new term, "thieves,"[83] belongs especially to the concerns of 6:1-11, the other three deal with sexual sin, and are thus in line with the main subject matter of the rest of 1 Corinthians 5–7. "Adulterers"[84] refers to married people having sexual relations outside marriage. The same term is employed in the Decalogue (LXX Exod. 20:13; LXX Deut. 5:18 [17]) and the Holiness code (LXX Lev. 20:10).

With the next two terms Paul refers to homosexual behavior of one form or another.[85] Rather than referring to "male prostitutes and practicing homosexuals" (TNIV), they are better understood as referring to those who willingly play the passive and active roles in homosexual acts. Paul is not discussing "homosexuals" per se, but homosexual acts (commonly engaged in by Roman men who were also active in heterosexual relationships). In the Roman world, homosexual relations were invariably exploitative relations between men of quite contrasting social statures. It was not uncommon for married men to practice heterosexual sex with their wives (and female slaves and prostitutes) and to also en-

83. Gk. κλέπτης.

84. Gk. μοιχός. In the Greco-Roman world "adultery" was thought to apply only in cases involving non-exempt married women. The Jewish and Christian view was more comprehensive.

85. Gk. μαλακός and ἀρσενοκοῖτης. On the complicated question of translation see Robin Scroggs, *The New Testament and Homosexuality: Contextual Background for Contemporary Debate* (Philadelphia: Fortress, 1983). John Boswell's thesis in *Christianity, Social Tolerance, and Homosexuality* (Chicago: University of Chicago Press, 1980) that ἀρσενοκοῖτης refers to active male prostitutes has been soundly refuted by J. Robert Wright, "Boswell on Homosexuality: A Case Undemonstrated," *Anglican Theological Review Supplement* 66 (1984), 79-94, and David F. Wright, "Homosexuals or Prostitutes? The Meaning of ἀρσενοκοῖται (1 Cor. 6:9; 1 Tim. 1:10)," *Vigiliae Christianae* 38 (1984), 125-53.

gage in homosexual relations with male prostitutes or slave boys or other young men of lower class who had little freedom to refuse.[86] Romans did not think in terms of sexual orientation or identities, but that proper masculinity was to be expressed in taking the active, dominant role in any sexual act. To desire or willingly play a passive homosexual role was considered shameful, but it was expected that men of stature would penetrate people of lesser status (whether women or men) but not be penetrated themselves. The Jewish and Christian perspective affirmed by Paul was quite different.

Paul's opposition to all homosexual behavior (clearly targeting those who engaged in it freely and willingly) seems to derive from Leviticus 18:22 and 20:13, which represent absolute bans.[87] Paul's opposition to homosexual acts was not because he had not thought about the subject[88] or had simply taken over a conventional list of vices from Hellenistic authors, whether Jewish or secular (the view of Scroggs). Paul opposed homosexual behavior on the basis of creation theology[89] and because it is marked as a vice in the Torah and was stressed as a vice by Jews.[90]

86. On homosexual behavior in the Roman world see D. M. Halperin, "Homosexuality," in *OCD* 720-23, and Craig A. Williams, *Roman Homosexuality* (Oxford: Oxford University Press, 2010).

87. Cf. Robert A. J. Gagnon, "A Comprehensive and Critical Review Essay of *Homosexuality, Science, and the 'Plain Sense' of Scripture,* Part 2," *HBT* 25 (2003), 230-32. David F. Wright, "Homosexuals or Prostitutes," 126ff. The connection of Paul's ἀρσενοκοῖτης with Lev. 18:22; 20:13 lends support to taking "male" as the object in the compound word ("intercourse with males," i.e., male homosexual). William L. Petersen's critique of Wright's article, "Can Ἀρσενοκοῖται Be Translated by 'Homosexuals'? (1 Cor 6.9; 1 Tim 1:10)," *Vigiliae Christianae* 40 (1986), 187-91, complements it in this area (187: "Wright has performed a service in calling attention . . . to the LXX echoes in the word"). For Wright's response to Petersen's criticisms see Wright, "Translating Ἀρσενοκοῖται (1 Cor 6:9; 1 Tim 1:10)," *Vigiliae Christianae* 41 (1987), 396-98. For a useful survey of the biblical data on homosexuality see Wright, "Homosexuality: The Relevance of the Bible," *EvQ* 61 (1989), 291-300. On the biblical evidence as well as the medical and behavioral questions see Thomas E. Schmidt, *Straight or Narrow: Compassion and Clarity in the Homosexuality Debate* (Downers Grove, IL: InterVarsity Press, 1995).

88. Contra E. P. Sanders, *Paul,* 116.

89. Cf. G. J. Wenham, "the Old Testament Attitude to Homosexuality," *ExpTim* 102 (1990-91), 359-63, who convincingly traces the Old Testament opposition to homosexual behavior to Israel's doctrine of creation in Genesis 1–3.

90. For surveys of the evidence of Judaism's uniformly negative attitude to homosexuality, employing other terms, see Scroggs, *Homosexuality,* 66-98; L. M. Epstein, *Sex Laws and Customs in Judaism* (New York: Ktav, 1967), 134-37; Victor Paul Furnish, *The Moral Teaching of Paul* (Nashville: Abingdon, 1979), 64-67; and James B. De Young, "A Critique of Prohomosexual Interpretations of the Old Testament Apocrypha and Pseudepigrapha," *BSac* 147 (1990), 437-54. Further support may be gleaned from 1 Tim. 1:10, the only other occurrence of ἀρσενοκοῖτης in the New Testament. Gagnon, "A Comprehensive and Critical Review Essay," points out (233-34) that the vice there appears in a list said to derive from the law of Moses (1:8-9), suggesting a link with the Levitical prohibitions; at least half the vices in the list derive from the Decalogue. See also the commentaries on Paul's condemnation of both male and female same-sex conduct in Rom. 1:26-27.

The vice lists in 5:9-11 and 6:9-10 have obvious relevance to the paragraphs in which they occur. They also function as a thinly veiled threat as Paul deals with other subjects in the letter. Those guilty of such sins will not inherit the kingdom and ought to be excluded from the congregation in Corinth. For the Corinthian Christians guilty of going to prostitutes, the lists, both of which begin with "sexual immorality," would have been ringing in their ears when they heard Paul's instructions in 6:12-20. Those whom Paul accuses of "objective" idolatry in 10:1-22 (see the comments there) would have recalled the reference to "idolaters" in 6:9 and the serious way in which the incestuous man was dealt with in chapter 5. Likewise 11:21, Paul's comment about abuses at the Lord's Supper ("For in eating each one goes ahead with his own meal; one is hungry and another is *drunk*") recalls the "drunkard" in 5:11 and 6:10. The vice lists hang over Paul's instructions at least through chapter 11. On rereading the letter, or on hearing it again, the vice lists are passages that would come to the foreground, especially for some of the original audience.

**6:11** The ten terms used in the previous two verses are nouns that stand for individuals whose lives are characterized by the sin in question. It is not that any person who ever commits one of the sins will not inherit the kingdom; Paul is thinking of persistent rebellion against God, not the temporary backsliding or lapse of the believer. With pastoral sensitivity Prior explains: "Paul is not talking about isolated acts of unrighteousness, but about a whole way of life pursued persistently by those who thus indicate that they would be aliens in the kingdom of truth and light."[91] The New Testament teaches consistently that perseverance is a sign of election (cf. 1 John 3:4-10, etc.). Professing Christians who live such lives are tragically among those who will not inherit God's kingdom.

The warning of vv. 9-10 is not properly understood without v. 11, which injects a positive note of affirmation and hope: "That is what some of you were. But [now things are different]."[92] Paul stresses the change that many of the Corinthian Christians had undergone. Some of them were enmeshed in such vices, but no longer. The words "some of you" do not indicate that Paul considers only some in the church to be *washed, . . . sanctified, . . . justified* (truly saved),[93] but that only some were saved from

91. Prior, 9.

92. After the characterizing of the present indicative verbs in vv. 7-8 and the references to future judgment with future indicatives in vv. 9-10, Paul uses a series of aorist indicatives in v. 11 to undergird moral behaviour with the past facts of cleansing, sanctifying, and justifying (ἀπελούσασθε; ἡγιάσθητε; ἐδικαιώθητε). Such aorist indicatives might be misunderstood by some as specifying the point at which these actions occurred, perhaps even stretching the point to argue that all actions occurred at the same time (i.e., at the point of conversion). While such conclusions may be justified from a theological point of view, the aorists themselves do not make it so — they simply convey the fact that such actions occurred.

93. Cf. Robertson and Plummer, 119: "Not all of them, not even many, but only some, are said to have been guilty; and it is all a thing of the past."

an overtly sinful lifestyle. If for Christians the future has invaded the present, a decisive break has also been made with the past; the once/now motif is just as important as the already/not yet. Paul uses the concept of inheritance to refer to that which all believers will receive in the kingdom because they are sons of Abraham through faith (cf. Rom. 4:13; 8:17; Gal. 3:29; 4:4-7; Titus 3:5, which forge a link between being an heir and a son to faith and promise).

Three verbs underscore the change: the Corinthians were washed, sanctified, and justified. Each is preceded in the Greek by the strong adversative, "but," to stress the transformation that has been effected by God. First they have been cleansed from the filth of the types of sin listed in vv. 10-11. The Corinthians are clean before God. Since the washing is only one part of Paul's threefold description of their conversion, the reference is primarily to spiritual transformation and only by implication to baptism which signifies it. Secondly, they have been sanctified, separated from a godless lifestyle, having received a holy status (cf. 1:1, 30). The Corinthians are holy, possessed by God.[94] Thirdly, they have been justified or declared righteous in spite of their many vices, set in a right relation to God (cf. 1:30). The Corinthians stand vindicated by God. God has done something dramatic in and for the Corinthian believers. As different people, they ought to live differently (learning to resolve their differences in healthy and edifying ways rather than fighting lawsuits against one another). The indicative implies the imperative. All three actions refer to a break with the old life (vv. 9-10) and the beginning of a new life that leads to a new lifestyle. The three metaphors describe the same reality, namely, their conversion. The words also recall the temple motif, so prominent in the letter: in biblical and Pauline thought only those who have been sanctified and cleansed can enter into God's presence and be used in the worship of God.

The unselfconscious trinitarianism of the description of how the change came about is striking: "in the name of *the Lord Jesus Christ* and in the *Spirit* of our *God*." The most explicit instance of trinitarian thought in Paul's letters occurs in the famous benediction of 2 Corinthians 12:14. It is foundational to Paul's understanding of salvation that it involves the cooperative work of all three persons of the Godhead, to use the language of Chalcedon. 1 Corinthians 1:4-7, 2:4-5, 2:12, and 6:19-20 are other places in the letter (cf. 2 Cor. 1:21-22) where salvation is predicated either explicitly or implicitly on the threefold work of the triune God.[95] The terms also reinforce the eschatological nature of the transformation the Corinthians (along with all other believers in Christ) have experienced. God's establishment of

94. Cf. the title of David Peterson's book: *Possessed by God* (Grand Rapids: Eerdmans, 1995).

95. Gordon D. Fee, "Christology and Pneumatology in Romans 8:9-11 — and Elsewhere: Some Reflections on Paul as a Trinitarian," in *Jesus of Nazareth: Lord and Christ* (ed. J. B. Green and M. Turner; Grand Rapids: Eerdmans, 1994).

the Messiah (Christ) as Lord over all and his transformation of his people by the cleansing and renewing power and presence of the Holy Spirit were both part of the Old Testament picture of the wonderful changes that would be introduced with the in-breaking of the age to come and its overcoming of this present evil age.[96]

### 4. A Firm Correction: Temple Prostitution, 6:12-17

*12"I have the right to do anything," you say — but not everything is beneficial. "I have the right to do anything" — but I will not be mastered by anything. 13You say, "Food for the stomach and the stomach for food, and God will destroy them both." The body, however, is not meant for sexual immorality but for the Lord, and the Lord for the body. 14By his power God raised the Lord from the dead, and he will raise us also.*

*15Do you not know that your bodies are members of Christ himself? Shall I then take the members of Christ and unite them with a prostitute? Never! 16Do you not know that he who unites himself with a prostitute is one with her in body? For it is said, "The two will become one flesh." 17But whoever is united with the Lord is one with him in spirit.*

1 Corinthians 6:12-20 is widely acknowledged to be one of the most difficult passages in Paul's letters. Commentators have described the unit as "disjointed," "obscure," "unfinished,"[1] "imprecise," "extravagant," and even "incoherent."[2] Gordon Fee notes, without exaggeration, that "the passage is full of unique, and in some cases difficult expressions, which in turn have given rise to equally unique interpretations."[3] Bruce N. Fisk rightly states that "[s]cholars continue to puzzle over the meaning and rhetorical function of 1 Corinthians 6:12-20."[4]

The difficulty of interpretation arises chiefly from our incomplete knowledge of the historical setting of the passage. Much of Paul's language here is clipped and elliptical. By the end of v. 15 it is clear that Paul is addressing a matter of sexual immorality, probably involving prostitution. But the precise nature of the objectionable behavior and some of the details of Paul's response are indistinct. Do the instructions concern sexual immo-

96. For example, note God's establishment of his Son over all other powers in Psalm 2 and, in Ezek. 36:23-27, his sanctification of his name by the cleansing and sanctification of his people by the Spirit so that they no longer profane his name among the nations but, rather, obey him from the heart.

1. See Héring, 47.

2. T. A. Burkill, "Two into One: The Notion of Carnal Union in Mark 10:8; 1 Cor. 6:16; Eph. 5:31," *ZNW* 62 (1971), 118, 120.

3. Fee, 251.

4. Bruce N. Fisk, "Πορνεύειν as Body Violation: The Unique Nature of Sexual Sin in 1 Corinthians 6.18," *NTS* 42 (1996), 540.

rality in general or a particular manifestation of *porneia?* If, as commonly agreed, Paul is quoting the Corinthians, where do the citations begin and end? In what sense is the Lord "for the body"? What exactly do "body" and "spirit" signify in this context? What does the quotation of Genesis 2:24 contribute to Paul's argument? What does it mean to sin against your own body? According to Paul, what is the nature of sexual intercourse? Why does Paul consider the believer's union with Christ so critical? Perhaps no section in the New Testament invites mirror reading — "reading between the lines" — more than this one.

While not minimizing the historical difficulties, it is possible to exaggerate their significance for reading 6:12-20 confidently and with profit. The passage must be read as part of 1 Corinthians, the overall thrust of which is Paul's opposition to Roman influence in the church belonging to God in Corinth, particularly the archetypal Gentile sins of sexual immorality and idolatry. Then it makes good sense, contributes to Paul's main agenda, and renders a marked contribution to Christian sexual ethics. We must not lose sight of these benefits, even if some uncertainties linger.

In terms of historical background, it is still legitimate to ask what Corinthian fault Paul is addressing in these verses. The five main hypotheses for the subject under discussion in 1 Corinthians 6:12-20 are: (1) sexual immorality in general; (2) the incest mentioned in 5:1; (3) sacred prostitution; (4) temple prostitution; and (5) secular prostitution. Weighing the pros and cons of these alternative scenarios highlights many distinctive features of the passage, its setting and place in the letter, even if settling on one is not *the* key to the passage's interpretation.[5]

Some commentators argue that Paul is concerned in 6:12-20 not with a particular manifestation of *porneia* but with *sexual immorality in general.* In 1987 Fee called this "the standard view, found in most of the older commentaries."[6] Robertson and Plummer, for example, state: "He [Paul] now takes up the subject of *porneia* generally, dealing with it in the light of first principles."[7] According to Morris, "Paul has spoken of a specific case of incest (ch. 5). Now he deals with the general principle governing sexual practices."[8] However, Paul's explicit mention of prostitution in vv. 15-16 points to an acute case giving rise to his instructions. Holtz explains: "This fact does not force us to assume that Paul's line of thought was not quite clear and did not take true aim from the beginning [of 6:12-17]. It rather means that the apostle is dealing very concretely with a situation in the church, a church which knew what was at stake. Paul is from the start

5. Contra Brian S. Rosner, "Temple Prostitution in 1 Corinthians 6:12-20," *NovT* 40.4 (1998), 336, who called it "the most fundamental question of interpretation." See this article (336-51) for a full discussion of the proposed backgrounds.

6. Fee, 250.

7. Robertson and Plummer, 121.

8. Morris, 95.

dealing with arguments which concern the matter in question in this particular church."[9]

The main proponent of the view that the subject under discussion in 6:12-20 is *the incest of 5:1* is Will Deming.[10] He argues that all of chapters 5 and 6 should be understood as Paul's response to the sexual offense mentioned in 5:1. In an elaborate reconstruction Deming proposes that the Corinthian church is divided over a member who has breached accepted sexual norms. Some want the man to be punished; others do not. The former take the man to the public courts, but lose the case. When Paul writes 5:1–6:20 in response to the matter, the divisions have already been exacerbated by the animosity of the court battle. In Deming's view the Corinthian slogan that Paul quotes in 6:12, "all things are lawful for me" (ESV), was used by Stoic and Cynic philosophers to describe people who felt immune from legal interference in their affairs and were consequently legally permitted to do certain things. Thus the slogan in 6:12 "represents the position of the immoral man in 5:1, who has been exonerated by the courts."[11] And the "prostitute" of 6:16 is "the step-mother [who] sold her services as a prostitute."[12] Although it fits some pieces of the puzzle, Deming's imaginative proposal is gravely flawed. A specific technical legal sense of the Corinthian slogan is not the best candidate for the meaning of the slogan in 1 Corinthians (see below on 6:12). The suggestion that the stepmother was selling herself to her stepson strains credulity. Most tellingly, Paul would not have made the claim in 5:1 that the sexual offense in question is "of a kind that even pagans do not tolerate" if he knew that a secular court in Corinth had already refused to condemn the deed.

If 6:16 points to prostitution as the subject under discussion, with which kind of prostitute were some of the Corinthians involved? The most specific answer to this question is *sacred prostitution.*[13] Sacred or cultic prostitution is defined by Karel van der Toorn as "religiously legitimated intercourse with strangers in the vicinity of the sanctuary . . . organized or at least condoned by the priesthood."[14] In the strictest sense the purpose was to increase fertility. Two lines of evidence are thought to support the identification of the sacred prostitution. First, Paul's opposition in 6:12-20 is couched in terms of religious allegiance using sacral language. In nine verses "God" and "Lord" each occur four times, "Christ" twice, and "Holy Spirit" once. Paul's citation of Genesis 2:24 in v. 16 may function not only to prove the seriousness of sexual union with a harlot but also to introduce the notion of the believer's nuptial union with Christ. This decidedly theo-

9. Traugott Holtz, "The Question of the Content of Paul's Instructions," in Brian S. Rosner, *Understanding Paul's Ethics,* 53.

10. Will Deming, "The Unity of 1 Corinthians 5–6," *JBL* 115.2 (1992), 289-312.

11. Deming, "The Unity of 1 Corinthians 5–6," 303.

12. Deming, "The Unity of 1 Corinthians 5–6," 295.

13. See, e.g., the commentaries of Weiss and Fee.

14. Karel van der Toorn, "Cultic Prostitution," *ABD* 5:510.

centric response to *porneia* would certainly be a fitting rebuttal of sacred prostitution, in which the participant is both immoral and unfaithful to God. However, it is not decisive since in the Old Testament unfaithfulness to God was described simply as adultery, not sacred prostitution. Sexual immorality of any kind was seen as an affront to God.

Secondly, more significantly, several details of the passage, read in the larger context of 1 Corinthians, point to a link with idolatry. The call to "flee sexual immorality" in 6:18 is matched by a comparable call to "flee idolatry" in 10:14. The temple imagery of 6:19-20 is also suggestive. Paul could be saying, "Don't go to the temple (to use prostitutes); you are the temple!" The juxtaposition of sexual immorality and idolatry in 10:7-8 likewise takes on new significance if read in the light of the presence of sacred prostitution in Corinth. That the first two items in the vice list of 6:9-11 are the immoral and idolaters may also be regarded as a pointer. Finally, the appearance of the words, "I have the right to do anything," both in 6:12, with reference to the use of prostitutes, and in 10:23, in connection with the consumption of temple food, may indicate that some Corinthians defended both practices on one occasion.

The main objection to finding a form of prostitution connected with pagan cultic practices behind the text is that there is no solid evidence that sacred prostitution existed there in Paul's day. Even if internal evidence suggests it, the external evidence is critically lacking. The ancient geographer Strabo's famous account of 1,000 prostitutes in the temple of Aphrodite refers to the Corinth destroyed in 146 B.C. by the Romans and not to new Corinth, which was founded by Julius Caesar as a Roman colony. Some have even disputed the accuracy of Strabo's remark with reference to old Corinth. Murphy-O'Connor, for example, writes that "sacred prostitution was never a Greek custom, and were Corinth an exception, the silence of all other ancient authors becomes impossible to explain."[15] Hans Herter concludes that besides the report of Strabo on Corinth, sacred prostitution was to be found only in Cyprus and eastern Asia Minor, the periphery of the Greek world; it was an "un-Greek practice."[16] More recent publications in fact raise doubts about the reality of cult prostitution anywhere in the ancient world.[17]

If sacred prostitution must be ruled out on historical grounds, another form of prostitution may lay claim to the same internal evidence and should be considered, namely, *temple prostitution.* Although sacred prostitution probably did not exist in the Corinth of Paul's day, there is evidence that many of the temple precincts hosted dinners after which

15. J. Murphy-O'Connor, *St Paul's Corinth: Texts and Archaeology*, 56.

16. H. Herter, "Die Soziologie der Antiken Prostitution im Licht des heidnischen und christlichen Schrifttums," *JAC* 3 (1960), 72-73.

17. See, e.g., S. M. Baugh, "Cult Prostitution in New Testament Ephesus: A Reappraisal," *JETS* 42.3 (1999), 443-60; and Stephanie Budin, *The Myth of Sacred Prostitution in Antiquity* (Cambridge: Cambridge University Press, 2008).

prostitutes were on offer. In such cases the prostitution was a part of the festivity rather having any ritual significance; hence the label, *temple*, rather than sacred, prostitution. There is considerable evidence in pagan, Jewish, and Christian writings that feasting and sexual immorality went together.[18] And in the Greco-Roman world prostitution at pagan cultic events was not uncommon. As Catherine Edwards notes, various ancient texts indicate that sexual pleasure was often the expected sequel to a banquet, and sometimes prostitutes were explicitly mentioned as part of the after-dinner entertainment.[19] Elsewhere in the New Testament, Revelation 2:14 may supply evidence of such activity in Asia Minor: the church at Pergamum is guilty of eating food sacrificed to idols and of sexual immorality. Acts 15 may also be a witness to this phenomenon. Some scholars argue that the purpose of the apostolic decree was to discourage Christians from any connection with the idolatrous worship of pagan cults.

In the end it is not possible to be certain which type of prostitution Paul opposes in 1 Corinthians 6:12-20. Even if the cumulative weight of evidence points toward some kind of temple prostitution, *secular prostitution*, prostitution of an entirely non-religious nature, cannot be ruled out. It was common in Jewish texts for idolatry and sexual immorality to be linked, not least because these two vices were considered to be the distinctive marks of the Gentiles.[20] In Corinth itself, whether the offending Corinthians were making use of prostitutes after a meal in a temple (at the sanctuary of Demeter, the Asklepion, or some temple in connection with the Isthmian games), or simply in a setting not associated with idolatry is impossible to know. The Corinthians could well have argued, "I have the right to do anything," in the contexts of both sexual behavior and eating food sacrificed to idols, without the two being connected. In the Scriptures, other forms of *porneia*, and not just sacred or temple prostitution, are treated as a sin against God (e.g., Gen. 39:9; Ps. 51:3; cf. *Testament of Reuben* 1:9). Although cult prostitutes and harlots are distinguished in the Hebrew Scriptures, the Greek Bible generally uses the *porn-* group of words for both. Thus in the LXX prostitution in general is viewed as apostasy. As it turns out, most of the references to prostitution in Paul's Bible are figurative, referring to Israel's unfaithfulness to the Lord and worship of other gods, which might also help explain Paul's treatment of *porneia* in terms of unfaithfulness to God.

Central to Paul's argument against sexual immorality is the citation of Genesis 2:24 in 6:16: "The two will become one flesh." He uses this text to explore the implications of the statement that "the body is for [service of

18. Rosner, "Temple Prostitution in 1 Corinthians 6:12-20," 348-50.

19. C. Edwards, *The Politics of Immorality in Ancient Rome* (Cambridge: Cambridge University Press, 1993), 188. Cf. Winter, *Seek the Welfare of the City*, 174, who cites Dio Chrysostom as saying that brothel-keepers "drag their stock" to the "great festive occasions."

20. See Rosner, *Greed as Idolatry*, 111-15.

and communion with] the Lord" (v. 13). However, as argued below (see on 6:16), its influence can be felt throughout the unit and on into chapter 7.[21]

The place of 1 Corinthians 6:12-17 in the argument of 4:18–7:40 is more straightforward than its precise interpretation. Even if in it the apostle responds to the specific sin of prostitution, the way Paul addresses it acts as a fitting conclusion to his treatment of sexual immorality in the wider unit of 4:18–6:20. This is especially clear in 6:18-20, which acts as a final warning, not only for prostitution, but for all sorts of sexual immorality (including incest, adultery, and homosexual activity). Paul's reference to sexual immorality in the plural in 7:2 (see the comments there) is further indication of the general applicability of these verses.

In terms of what follows, the relationship between 6:12-20 and 7:1-40 has caused problems for commentators. On the one hand, 6:12-20 clearly indicates that some Corinthians were either going to prostitutes or were contemplating doing so, while 7:1-40 has usually been taken as evidence that other Corinthians favored abstaining from sexual relations altogether. This traditional view holds that within the same church some Corinthians were extremely loose, while others were extremely uptight about sexual relations (with the question being which position may have led to the other as a reaction). However, as we will argue in the commentary, chapter 7 is best understood not against a background of two equally radical and opposing views of sexuality, but in terms of two very common views of sex within the Roman world. Both views believed in restrained sexual relations within marriage (usually only for the purposes of procreation), with one holding that sexual pleasure and gratification should not be pursued at all and the other holding that it was to be found in relations with slaves, prostitutes, or other people outside of the marriage. In our view, 6:12-20 suggests that some Corinthians were in agreement with the latter view (sexual gratification was to be found outside the marriage), which was the most common view, while 7:1-40 suggests that other Corinthians were in agreement with the former view (that sex was to be restricted to the marriage and not for pleasure). Paul agrees that sexual relations are to be engaged in only within the marriage relationship but recognizes the need to be sensitive to each others sexual needs (so that restricting sexual relations to the intent to procreate would be likely to leave some tempted to find their sexual needs satisfied elsewhere).

The focus on the problem of contact with prostitution in 6:12-17 is embedded within the broader section focusing on sexual immorality in general and concluding in 6:18-20, with the warning to flee sexual immorality and the call to honor God with one's body. In chapter 7 Paul will more fully address ways in which Christian men and women could glorify God with their bodies in a variety of contexts which would provide potential tempta-

21. Loader, *The Septuagint, Sexuality, and the New Testament*, 86-95, also assigns a central role to the text in Paul's argument.

tions to sexual immorality. Maintaining healthy sexual relations with one's wife is part of a married man's strategy for avoiding sexual immorality in general and the temptation of prostitution in particular.

What does 6:12-20 offer to Christian sexual ethics? Its importance lies in the fact that it is not our usual discourse. In response to sexual immorality, we talk of faithfulness to one's partner, the detrimental psychological effects of obsessive lust and casual sexual experience, and the abusive treatment of the other as a sexual object. Instead of such things, Paul is concerned with impurity and contamination, and especially the question of ownership.[22] The key concepts for Paul are power, authority, and the body. Assuming the Corinthian men involved were married, rather than emphasizing keeping faith with one's partner, Paul points instead to the intimate union of believers with Christ. In terms of its contribution to Christian thought, the unit is every bit as surprising and profound as it is frustrating and elusive.

The passage divides into two subunits: vv. 12-14 and 15-17. In 6:12-14 Paul corrects the Corinthians' misapplication of Christian freedom and asserts that believers' bodies come under the lordship of the risen Christ. In 6:15-17 he applies the doctrine of union with Christ to the question of what a person does with their body.

### a. *The Bodily Resurrection of Christ Underscores the Sanctity and Future of the Believer's Body, 6:12-14*

**6:12** In vv. 12-14 Paul tackles the Corinthian excuses for their immoral behavior head-on. Commentators and translations generally agree that this subunit contains slogans, or at least arguments, from the Corinthians which Paul counters with his own pithy formulations. Even though the Greek does not signal these elements formally, there are good reasons for using quotation marks in the English versions for the sentences that represent the viewpoint of some of those in Corinth. The TNIV takes this approach, and also adds the words "you say" in vv. 12 and 13 for further clarification. Each time Paul quotes the Corinthians here he corrects them with an assertion of his own, introduced with an adversative conjunction (italicized in the table below): "but," "but," and "however."[23] The first slogan, which is repeated twice, turns up again twice in 1 Corinthians 10:23.[24] We may tentatively reconstruct the "conversation" as follows:[25]

22. Cf. the title of William Countryman's book on New Testament sexual ethics, *Dirt, Greed and Sex* (Minneapolis: Fortress, 2007).

23. Gk. ἀλλά, ἀλλά, and δέ respectively.

24. Less direct evidence that Paul is quoting the Corinthians is the fact that the subject of prostitution is not introduced until the end of v. 15; the Corinthians presumably already know that what Paul is talking about in vv. 12-14 is connected to the subject of going to prostitutes.

25. Cf. esp. Hays, 102.

| **The Corinthians** | **Paul** |
|---|---|
| "I have the right to do anything" | *but* not everything is beneficial |
| "I have the right to do anything" | *but* I will not be mastered by anything. |
| "Food for the stomach and the stomach for food, and God will destroy them both." | The body, *however,* is not meant for sexual immorality but for the Lord, and the Lord for the body. By his power God raised the Lord from the dead, and he will raise us also. |

It is impossible to know for sure whether the words *"I have the right to do anything"* are an exact quotation or not of the Corinthians who were defending the use of prostitutes.[26] Did Paul's response influence the way he reports the Corinthian rationalization, or vice versa?[27] Paul may have composed both in the light of the Corinthian defense of their "right" to use prostitutes (and food sacrificed to idols). What is clear is that some Corinthians were asserting their freedom to do certain things that Paul objected to — here, involving prostitution; in chapter 10, eating food explicitly identified as having been offered to idols.

The origin of the Corinthian position is difficult to pinpoint. In general terms it was something of a commonplace in pagan moral philosophy for a person to assert their supreme autonomy. Dio Chrysostom, for example, could say, using language similar to that in 1 Corinthians 6:12: "[t]he wise . . . are permitted to do anything they wish."[28] The sentiment was also used of the authority of kings. Several plausible identifications have been suggested. Mark Allen Plunkett relates the claim, *I have the right to do anything,* to 1 Corinthians 4:8, where the Corinthians apparently claim to be kings ("you have begun to reign").[29] P. Marshall and Bruce Winter claim that the social elite used the catchphrase with reference to their (arrogant) use of power and privilege.[30]

In any case, Paul opposes the Corinthians' appeal to the exercise of their personal freedom in the area of sexual relations. His correction is twofold (see the chart above). First, Paul says, *but not everything is beneficial.* Unfortunately, Paul moves on before explaining, beneficial for whom or what? Generally in 1 Corinthians that which is beneficial relates to what benefits others.[31] According to Thiselton, "The issue for Paul [here] is what helps and

26. In ch. 10 the words "for me" are missing. Possibly Paul includes it here for the sake of symmetry; he uses the pronoun "I" in the second rebuttal.

27. See below on the play on words in v. 12b.

28. Dio Chrysostom, *Orations* 14.17 (reported in Garland, 228).

29. Mark Allen Plunkett, "Sexual Ethics and the Christian Life: A Study of 1 Corinthians 6:12–7:7," unpublished Ph.D. thesis, Princeton Theological Seminary, 1988.

30. Marshall, *Enmity in Corinth,* 215, 284-85, 289-90; Winter, *After Paul Left Corinth,* ch. 5.

31. Cf. Fee, 252. The Gk. συμφέρει (BDAG: "to be advantageous") appears again in 10:23 and 12:7 ("for the common good").

what hinders in constituting credible corporate Christian identity as a community in corporate solidarity with Christ."[32] The emphasis in the rest of the chapter is more on the implications of going to prostitutes for the individual. Here at the outset the corporate is in view, that is, "the common good" (12:7). Paul does not elaborate here how individual freedom might affect the body corporate. His thought may relate to the "well-known paradox that if everyone claims unqualified autonomy, no one can be free, for everyone is threatened by the freedoms of the other."[33] The kindred thought of the priority of edification and love for others over personal gain will take center stage in the next major unit of the letter, chapters 8–14. The use of prostitutes, like any form of sexual immorality, is not just an issue of personal ethics, but will have a negative impact on others. Even if we have a right to do something (and in the case of using prostitutes, we don't), we must never forget the extent to which our behavior affects the lives of those to whom we are connected. 1 Corinthians 8 is effectively an exposition of *not everything is beneficial* in the context of eating food sacrificed to idols. Every deliberation about behavior pleasing to God will have a social dimension.

Paul's objection to intercourse with prostitutes also has an individual aspect: *"I have the right to do anything"* (you say) — *but* (Paul says) *I will not be mastered by anything* (or anyone). The Greek contains a clever play on words.[34] A few translations try to preserve the rhetorical impact of Paul's retort:

> "I am free to do anything, but I will not let anything make free with me" (REB);
> "'Liberty to do anything' — but I will not let anything take liberties with me" (Thiselton);
> "All things are in my power, but I shall not be overpowered by anything" (Edwards).

How does having sex with a prostitute bring someone under such power? It is tempting to think, in psychological terms, of a destructive obsession. But this would probably be anachronistic. The way that Paul thinks the "mastery" happens will become clear in the following verses. As Loader contends, Genesis 2:24, cited in 6:16, "is in the background [here] . . . [that is,] sexual intercourse leads to people becoming one flesh."[35] According to Paul, such contamination compromises the integrity of the Christian as belonging to Christ (see v. 15). In 6:11 Paul has already raised the issue of to whom we

32. Thiselton, 462.

33. Thiselton, 461.

34. The two halves of v. 12b contain two forms of ἐκ + εἰμί — ἔξεστι, "it is permitted" and ἐξουσιασθήσομαι, "to be mastered/put under the authority of." The word ἐξουσία, "right," becomes key in chs. 8 and 9; cf. 8:9; 9:4, 5, 6, 12, 18, where some Corinthians are claiming the "right" to eat food sacrificed to idols.

35. Loader, *The Septuagint, Sexuality, and the New Testament*, 88.

belong: the Corinthians are under the power of the Lord. The issue of authority will also be raised in relation to marriage in the opening verses of chapter 7, where the husband and the wife have authority over each other's bodies.[36]

Paul counters arrogant Corinthian claims to masterful independence with the ironic assertion that their supposed freedom will actually lead to a form of bondage! Far from being a master (with the right to do anything), they are themselves mastered and under the authority of something antithetical to pure devotion to Christ. Sin as a power finds eloquent expression in Jesus' words, "the one who sins is a slave of sin" (John 8:34), and in Romans 5–8, especially chapter 6, where either sin or righteousness is said to reign over a person.

**6:13** At first blush Paul's next response to Corinthian rationalizations for involvement with prostitutes seems to be a diversion. He quotes them as saying (or at least believing): *"Food for the stomach and the stomach for food, and God will destroy them both."*[37] As it turns out, it is not off the subject since the Corinthians used the sentiments of v. 12a about being free to do anything with respect to both going to prostitutes and eating idol food. As Loader notes, the ancient world regularly linked sexual appetite and appetite for food.[38] Further, if we 'read between the lines' it is not difficult to infer the logic of the Corinthian position. The *stomach*[39] or belly, as "the organ of nourishment" (BDAG, 1), was associated, along with food, with that which is physical and therefore transient. The Corinthians probably also believed that just as food is meant for the stomach and vice versa, so also sexual activity is meant for the body and the body for sexual activity. The stomach and the body are useless unless we eat and have sex. Such natural bodily processes have no abiding significance and are thus of no moral consequence.

In a style typical of Greek dualistic thought, the Corinthians apparently reasoned that God is concerned only with those aspects of a person that survive death, that is, their soul or spirit.[40] When Paul reports that some of the Corinthians believed that *God will destroy both* the stomach and food, the verb "to destroy"[41] has eschatological connotations,[42] as else-

36. Schrage, 2:19.

37. Some take the quotation to end with ". . . the stomach for food," and understand "but (δέ) God will destroy both" as the beginning of Paul's response (e.g., RSV, NRSV, NIV, NEB). The difficulty is that the Greek conjunction δέ can be translated in an adversative ("but") or a continuative sense ("and"); the beginning of Paul's counterassertion is not clearly signaled. We prefer the TNIV's decision to include all of v. 13a as part of a quotation on the grounds that the shorter slogan "seems banal" (Thiselton, 462) and Paul's comeback in vv. 13b-14 makes better sense this way.

38. Loader, *The Septuagint, Sexuality, and the New Testament*, 88.

39. Gk. κοιλία.

40. See the comments on the resurrection body in ch. 15.

41. Gk. καταργέω.

42. While future indicative verbs are used in other ways as well (as in vv. 12, 16), they are frequently used in reference to eschatology in this part of the letter, especially future judgment or vindication (cf. 5:13; 6:2-3, 9-10, 13-14).

where in the letter (1:28; 2:6; 13:8, 10-11; 15:24, 26). However, he interrupts their reasoning and objects that the body is not like the belly and food in this regard: *The body, however, is not meant for sexual immorality* (as you surmise) *but for the Lord, and the Lord for the body.* Byrne is right that "the nub of the dispute between Paul and the Corinthians concerns the value to be placed upon present bodily existence."[43]

Paul's concise expression here needs to be unpacked. We may paraphrase: "The body is for service of and fellowship with the Lord Jesus Christ;[44] and the Lord Jesus Christ stands for the sanctity and future of the believer's body." A "whiff" of Genesis 2:24, to be quoted in v. 16, can be detected in Paul's words. As Loader points out, the mutuality of the formulation, "body for the Lord and Lord for the body," "echoes the structure of mutuality assumed to be created in Gen 2:24 between a man and a woman and may stand under its influence indirectly."[45] At 7:1 we will find a contrasting Corinthian position: It is not good for a man to treat sex as a basic appetite to be satisfied as one sees fit (see the comments there).

**6:14** The significance attached to the future of the body is clear in v. 15: *By his power God raised the Lord from the dead* [bodily], *and he will raise us also.* That Jesus was raised *bodily* is carried over from the two references to "the body" in the previous verse (and once each in vv. 16 and 17); the point is made explicit in 15:12-58. Paul does not say that God will raise believers' *bodies;* he uses the personal pronoun, *us,* since it forms a better parallel to God's raising *the Lord* in the first half of the verse.

Far from an overrealized eschatology, it is a Corinthian underestimation of eschatology that Paul seeks to correct to change their behavior. The body is not insignificant and transient; on the contrary, it will be raised.[46] And since it will be raised, it is important now how we behave with our bodies. It is the destiny of being raised from the dead bodily that gives "meaning, responsibility and significance to bodily existence in the present."[47] Käsemann is right that it is "[i]n the bodily obedience of the Christian [that] . . . the lordship of Christ finds visible expression."[48]

Making a link between the resurrection of Christ and that of believers is the major motif of the crowning unit of the letter, 1 Corinthians 15.[49] It is also implicit in the words Paul uses to describe believers' resurrection in

43. B. Byrne, "Sinning against One's Own Body: Paul's Understanding of the Sexual Relationship in 1 Corinthians 6:18," *CBQ* 456 (1983), 608-16 (here 611).

44. The use of "the Lord" being raised by God in v. 15 indicates that its referent throughout the unit is Jesus Christ.

45. Loader, *The Septuagint, Sexuality, and the New Testament*, 89.

46. A textual problem attaches to the verb translated, "he will raise." The three main variants, covering the aorist, present, and future tenses, each have considerable external evidence in their favor. As Metzger, *Textual Commentary,* 486-87, concludes, "[t]he context makes the future necessary as the correlative of 'will destroy' in ver. 13."

47. Thiselton, 465.

48. E. Käsemann, *New Testament Questions for Today* (London: SCM, 1969), 135.

49. Conzelmann, 111: "The commentary is provided by chap. 15."

several letters, which are roughly the same as when he speaks of the resurrection of Christ.[50] This is true of all of the main terms, including: "to raise up," "to raise," "resurrection," and "to live."[51] In fact, only the related compound verbs "raise up" and "resurrection,"[52] which occur once in 1 Corinthians 6:14 and Philippians 3:11 respectively, with reference to the resurrection of believers, are not used of Christ's resurrection. But in both cases the connection with Christ's resurrection is apparent in the context. Here in 1 Corinthians 6:14 it is Paul's main point. The use of the prefix "together" in four verbs that the apostle uses elsewhere actually make the link between the two explicit at the lexical level: "we live together with [him]" (Rom. 6:8; 2 Tim. 2:11); "we are glorified together with [him]" (Rom. 8:17); we "rise up together" (Col. 2:12; 3:1), and "he made alive together with [him]" (Col. 2:13; Eph. 2:5).[53] 1 Corinthians 6:15 will press the point further. Our resurrection is tied to Christ's because we are members of his body. The added point here is that Christians *as bodies* are members of the resurrected Christ.

Grammatically, the phrase *by his power* may qualify either verb in the sentence: Does God raise the Lord (NIV, TNIV) or us (RSV, NRSV) *by his power?* The words in question appear at the end of the sentence in Greek to make them emphatic. Thus their closer proximity to the resurrection of believers is not decisive. For Paul, the resurrection of Christ manifests the power of God (Rom. 1:4; 2 Cor. 13:4; Eph. 1:19; Phil. 3:10), just as it is always God who raises him.[54] However, Paul's use of the same noun, "power,"[55] in 1 Corinthians 15:43 favors the connection to the resurrection of believers. There, in the context of expounding the nature of believers' resurrection bodies, Paul explains that such bodies, although "sown in weakness," are "raised in *power.*" In the argument of 1 Corinthians 6 it serves Paul better to stress the power of God in raising believers bodily from the dead, a point some doubted,[56] than to remind them that God powerfully raised the Lord Jesus Christ.[57] In 6:14 the significance of both Christ's and our resurrections is underscored with reference to God: in the former, the divine agency is explicit ("*God* raised the Lord"); in the latter, the manner in which we will be raised, by God's power (cf. 4:20), closes the subunit.

50. For a detailed chart see M. E. Dahl, *The Resurrection of the Body* (London: SCM, 1962).

51. Gk. ἀνίστημι, ἐγείρω, ἀνάστασις, and ζάω respectively.

52. Gk. ἐξεγείρω and ἐξανάστασις respectively.

53. Gk. συζήσομεν, συνδοξασθῶμεν, συνεγείρω, and συνεζωοποίησεν respectively.

54. See 1 Cor. 15:38 and the divine passives in 15:14, 20 ("raised [by God]"; cf. Gal. 1:1; Rom. 8:11; 2 Cor. 4:14).

55. Gk. δύναμις.

56. See the introduction to ch. 15.

57. Cf. Robertson and Plummer, 124: "There was need to remind the Corinthians of God's power, in order to confirm their belief in their own future resurrection."

### b. Union with Christ Excludes Union with a Prostitute, 6:15-17

**6:15** Paul's response to the Corinthian use of prostitutes comprises two points: If in vv. 12-14 *the bodily resurrection of Christ* underscores the sanctity and future of the believer's body, in vv. 15-17 *union with Christ* is shown to be utterly incompatible with union with a prostitute. With v. 15 the tone changes from deliberation and reasoned persuasion to accusation and impassioned pleading. The verse contains two forceful rhetorical questions and an outburst of strong denial. As Conzelmann notes, the ideas of v. 15 are "grounded on what follows" in vv. 16-17.[58]

The beginning of the first question, "do you not know," represents the sixth time (of ten) in the letter (3:16; 5:6; 6:2, 3, 9) that Paul reminds the Corinthians of something they should have known. The unstated implication is that if they had known it, they would not have gone astray: *Do you not know that your bodies are members of Christ himself?* The repetition of the words "do you not know" sounds more impatient as the letter goes on. The fourth time in fifteen verses, the question at this point is not a polite enquiry but a barely disguised rebuke.

The content of the first question continues the focus on the individual believer's relation to Christ. Every believer's being part of the body of Christ is given full attention in chapter 12. If there the emphasis is on interdependence, here Paul wishes to underscore the authority of Christ over the bodies of every Christian. Our use of the word "member" for an individual's voluntary association in a sporting club or society makes the translation potentially weak and misleading. Paul uses the term[59] as part of his metaphor of the body of Christ. The connection implied by the imagery is living and organic. REB's two-word translation, "limbs and organs," is helpful, in that it evokes "the double context of public action in the world and sexual intimacy," both of which are integral to Paul's argument.[60] The term appears three times in the verse.

Given Paul's presuppositions and symbolic world, both halves of the second question underscore the unthinkable nature of sex with a prostitute:[61] *Shall I then take the members of Christ and unite them with a prostitute?* The action of "taking away"[62] something from Christ reminds us of Paul's first "shock tactic" in the letter in 1:13 (in the context of factionalism), where he asks the question, "Is Christ divided?" Quite literally, at the heart of Paul's world stands Christ the risen Lord, for whom all believers live and in whom they find their purpose and identity. The translation "to take away" is probably too soft.[63] Even though the verb can mean "remove," it

58. Conzelmann, 111.

59. Gk. μέλος.

60. Thiselton, 465.

61. Gk. πόρνη; BDAG: "one engaged in sexual relations for hire, *prostitute*."

62. Gk. αἴρω.

63. AV/KJV, "take," is weaker still.

can also carry more forceful connotations such as "seize control" (BDAG, 3) or "destroy, do away with" (Louw and Nida, 20.43).

Paul asks incredulously: "Shall I then tear from Christ his limbs and organs and make them the limbs and organs of a prostitute?"[64] He does not have in mind the prostitute as an individual, but, opposite the corporate Christ, she appears as a symbol of that which is inimical to the sanctified status of God's people. Whether of the temple or secular variety, the prostitute here is a symbol of darkness and defilement. It is an argument from the incompatibility of two realms. Paul uses the same logic in 1 Corinthians 10:14-22 and 2 Corinthians 6:14–7:1. In both of these texts that which is opposed to God is named as the demonic. Here in chapter 6 the worry is not explicitly fellowship with the demonic, but rather the notion of contamination and uncleanness, a concern that is raised again in 1 Corinthians 7:14-15.

Paul's response to the second question is emphatic: *Never!*[65] More common in Romans, where the idiom marks a transition and advances the argument, here it functions only as the ultimate repudiation.[66] In going to prostitutes, the Corinthians not only renounce the lordship of Christ over their bodies and deny their resurrection life to come, but they act in a way that sullies and even does violence to Christ's body.

**6:16** With increasing exasperation, for a fifth time in this chapter, Paul asks, *Do you not know?* A central plank in the argument, this verse spells out the reason that union with Christ excludes any thought of union with a prostitute. In Paul's view, *he who unites himself with a prostitute is one with her in body.* However it is understood, this assertion underscores the serious nature of having sex with a prostitute. Many, both today and in Paul's day, think of such sex as casual and passing. Paul's view could hardly be more different. We would expect Paul to use the language of *one body* with respect to Christ and the church (cf. ch. 12), or of the union established in marriage (cf. Eph. 5:28-33). Here, surprisingly, Paul uses it of the outcome of sex with a prostitute. In Jewish moral teaching, uniting oneself, or cleaving, to God or an evil thing was not uncommon. Ecclesiasticus 19:2 and 2:3 are especially close to Paul's sentiment: respectively, "the man who cleaves to a prostitute is reckless" and "Cleave to him [i.e., God]." In 1 Corinthians 6:16a the verb "to unite"[67] sets up the quotation of Genesis 2:24 in v. 16b.

In the second half of v. 16 Paul cites a text from the Genesis creation narrative to explain why union with a prostitute is unthinkable: *For it is*

64. TNIV removes the third instance of "members" for the sake of English style and introduces the verb "to unite," which anticipates v. 16.

65. Gk. μή γένοιτο. This negated optative verb is used by Paul "to express strong rejection" (always in response to a question; BDF §384). He uses it to convey, in the strongest terms possible, his wish that something might never happen.

66. Contra Garland, 234.

67. Gk. κολλάω.

*said, "The two will become one flesh."*[68] The introduction to the citation, literally, "he says," or "it is said,"[69] may refer to Adam, Moses, or God, or simply to Scripture, as its source. Paul may well be implying that God "says" the words since the verb in question regularly appears in the LXX translation of "thus *says* the Lord," and the Matthew 19:5 citation of Genesis 2:24 attributes it to God. In its original context Genesis 2:24b forms part of a description of the first, prototypical marriage. There it emphasizes the real and enduring bond that is created in a marriage through sexual union. The text is also used within the Old Testament to prohibit divorce, as in Malachi 2:15-16: "Has not the LORD made them one?" The text was customarily used in discussions of marriage (e.g., in Philo), and served to explain the nature of marital union, as in Matthew 19:5 and Ephesians 5:31.

In general terms Paul's reflections on the nature of the bond established in sexual relations via Genesis 2:24 are intended further to impress upon the Corinthians a high view of the body and behavior involving the body. Throughout the paragraph the apostle seeks to demolish Corinthian notions about the transience and consequent insignificance of the body. The text also supports the notion that our bodies are not our own but belong to the Lord (not unlike spouses in marriage; cf. 7:4), a point he will make explicit in v. 19 ("you are not your own"). Genesis 2:24 gives credence to Paul's assertions that "the body is for [service of and communion with] the Lord" (6:13b) and "you are not your own" (6:19b).

The quotation functions specifically in Paul's argument in at least two ways. First, Paul uses it to prove that sexual intercourse with a prostitute is not an insignificant affair. The "for"[70] introducing 6:16b indicates that Genesis 2:24 gives a reason for the assertion in 6:16a that "he who unites himself with a prostitute becomes one with her in body." A compound of the verb "to unite" occurs in the part of LXX Genesis 2:24 that is not quoted in the new 1 Corinthians context ("for this reason a man will leave his father and mother and be united to his wife"). The thought introduced by Genesis 2:24, that of the intended permanence of sexual relationships, highlights the uniqueness of the sin of *porneia*, something underscored in v. 18b.

Secondly, and more subtly, Genesis 2:24 draws attention to the spiritual marriage of the believer to Christ, a union that Paul assumes calls for faithfulness and purity. Paul presents two mutually exclusive alternatives in 6:16-17: cleaving to a prostitute and cleaving to the Lord. Thus the Genesis text is used not only to prove the seriousness of sexual union with a prostitute, but to introduce the notion of the believer's nuptial union with

68. In matters textual, Stanley, *Paul and the Language of Scripture*, 195, notes accurately that "[a]part from the intrusion of the introductory formula ["For it is said"], . . . which occurs only here in the Pauline corpus, the quotation in I Cor. 6.16 follows the unanimous wording of the LXX tradition of Gen 2.24."

69. Gk. φησίν, third singular present active of φημί.

70. Gk. γάρ.

Christ.[71] Several features of the text, and its place in 1 Corinthians, point in this direction.[72] Paul is concerned about the union of believers with the "Lord" (Jesus Christ) in v. 17, a good fit with nuptial imagery, and not simply with "God." He could also have used a word other than "to unite" in vv. 16 and 17, which did not recall the Genesis marriage text.[73] Back in v. 13, as Talbert notes, "to be for" language ("the body for the Lord; the Lord for the body") appears with reference to marriage in the Song of Songs 2:16 and Romans 7:2-3.[74] The idea of spiritual marriage is also implicit in 1 Corinthians 7:32-35, where pleasing the Lord and pleasing one's marriage partner are compared. The Corinthians' marriage to Christ is made plain in 2 Corinthians 11:2, where Paul states: "I promised you to one husband, to Christ, so that I might present you as a pure virgin to him." Ephesians 5:32, commenting on the same phrase from Genesis 2:24 ("the two shall become one flesh"), also makes the connection to the marriage of Christ and the church. Thus, with the image of spiritual marriage in view, some of the disconnected elements of 6:12-20 harmoniously converge. Verses 13b and 19b protest the Lord's right over the believer's body, a right given additional credence in the light of their nuptial union. The implication of ownership of the body of one's partner in a physical marriage is taught in 1 Corinthians 7:4. The same implication carries for spiritual marriage, as Ezekiel 16:8b attests with reference to God's marriage to Israel: "you became mine."

**6:17** In order to correct any misunderstanding of the application of marriage imagery to the believer's relationship with Christ, Paul clarifies that believers are not simply one body with Christ: *But whoever is united with the Lord is one with him in spirit.* Calvin is right to see here an argument from lesser to greater: "The union of Christ with us is closer than that of husband and wife. . . . For if a man who is joined to a wife in marriage ought not to have union with a prostitute, it is far more serious in the case of believers, who are not . . . one flesh with Christ, but one Spirit."[75]

The TNIV renders the critical phrase (literally, "is one spirit") into an English idiom that might suggest that Christ and the believer are in harmonious relations: *one with him in spirit.* Other English versions, such as NRSV, bring out the connection with the quotation of Genesis 2:24 in the previous verse more explicitly: "But anyone united to the Lord becomes one spirit with him." Fee is probably right to see a reference to the divine Spirit: "Paul is probably referring to the work of the Spirit, whereby through the 'one

71. Cf. Calvin, 218: Gen. 2:24 is used to "magnify the efficacy and dignity of the spiritual marriage which subsists between us and Christ." Also Prior, 101: "Paul uses the vocabulary, explicitly in connection with marriage, to describe the relationship between Christ (the Bridegroom) and the church (his Bride)."

72. See Rosner, *Paul, Scripture and Ethics,* 132-34.

73. See Rosner, *Paul, Scripture and Ethics,* 132.

74. Talbert, 30.

75. Calvin, 131.

Spirit' the believer's 'spirit' has been joined indissolubly with Christ. . . . The way to express that union is in terms of the Spirit."[76] Thiselton follows Fee and translates: "But the person who is intimately united with the Lord is one Spirit." In the context of 1 Corinthians, Paul has told the Corinthians in 3:16 that "God's Spirit dwells in your midst" and will soon inform them, in 6:19, that their "bodies are temples of the Holy Spirit." Both texts have considerable prominence (see the commentary) and resonate strongly with more incidental references to "S/spirit" in the rest of the letter, such as the one in 6:17b. The role of the Spirit of God in effecting union with Christ is also evident in Romans 8:9-11 and 2 Corinthians 3:17. As Paul affirms in 1 Corinthians 15:45, Christ himself may be described as a "life-giving spirit."

### 5. A Strong Admonition: The Incongruence of Sexual Immorality and Christian Identity, 6:18-20

*[18]Flee from sexual immorality. All other sins people commit are outside their bodies, but those who sin sexually sin against their own bodies. [19]Do you not know that your bodies are temples of the Holy Spirit, who is in you, whom you have received from God? You are not your own; [20]you were bought at a price. Therefore honor God with your bodies.*

These verses deserve to be treated as a discreet unit, since they form the fulcrum on each side of which the surrounding chapters pivot. They include the two injunctions that we use to summarize the whole of 4:18–7:40: "flee sexual immorality" and "glorify God with your body." The negative injunction to "flee sexual immorality" (6:18a), while concluding Paul's immediately preceding teaching against using prostitutes, also acts as a summary command for 4:18–6:20, which treats and mentions other forms of *porneia*, namely, incest, adultery, and homosexual acts. The more positive closing injunction in 6:20b, "Therefore glorify God with your bodies," sets up Paul's treatment of sex in marriage in 7:1-40.

Some have questioned the relevance of the Old Testament to Paul's ethical teaching on the grounds that Paul overlooks the opportunity to quote Scripture in such a context. He could have cited any number of texts forbidding prostitution, premarital sex, or extramarital sex.[77] The fallacy with such reasoning is that the most fundamental reason someone is opposed to something will not necessarily be made explicit in their arguments against it. Paul's arguments in 1 Corinthians 6 against the use of prostitutes in effect presuppose that prostitution is wrong. Paul is like a passenger trying to convince the driver who is speeding to slow down with

76. Fee, 260.

77. See Rosner, *Paul, Scripture and Ethics,* 121-26. Cf. on prostitution (some mercenary, some religious): Gen. 34:31; Lev. 21:7, 9; Deut. 22:21; 23:17 (esp. LXX); Amos 7:17; 2 Kgs. 23:7; Jer. 2:20; Ezek. 23:37, 40, 41; Hos. 6:9-10; 7:4; 8:9-10.

appeals to road safety, expensive fines, no need to hurry, and so on. The use of such proofs does not betray a lack of interest in the law; even if left unmentioned, the relevant law might rest at the heart of their opposition. As it turns out, a possible quotation of *Testament of Reuben* 5:5 in v. 18 reveals Paul's indebtedness to the Genesis account of Joseph fleeing Potiphar's wife in Genesis 39.

**6:18** The heart of Paul's appeal to the Corinthians against going to prostitutes is an appeal to their identity. According to Paul, the Corinthians' sanctified status (1:2) demands their sexual purity. They are obliged to maintain the holiness of God's temple (3:16-17). Thus the case of incest (ch. 5) and the use of prostitutes (6:12-17) represent a threat to their core identity as people belonging to God. In this light it is hardly surprising that Paul issues the strongest possible command with the words: *flee sexual immorality.*[78] The lack of grammatical connection to what precedes heightens their emotive force.[79] Equally, the verb "to flee" carries a sense of urgency; in the LXX people "flee" from enemies, snakes, the kinsman avenger, and other potent dangers. The sin to be fled here is sexual immorality, *porneia*, a target broader than just prostitution. An apt concluding appeal to chapters 5–6, the injunction is a blanket condemnation of all illicit sexual relations. Words cognate to *porneia* occur in 5:1, 9, 10, 11; 6:13, 15, 16, 18 (twice).[80] As Barrett puts it: "Temptations to fornication were so common in Corinth that mere disapproval was likely to be inadequate; strong evasive action would be necessary. The same was true of idolatry (x. 14)."[81]

The central command of 4:18–6:20 in v. 18, *flee sexual immorality,* finds an exact parallel in a piece of early Jewish moral teaching, *Testament of Reuben* 5:5.[82] Even though the individual words are not uncommon, the specific injunction occurs in only these two places in ancient Greek literature (along with quotations of 1 Cor. 6:18 in the church fathers). On the other hand, Gregory of Nyssa suggested a link between Paul's advice in 1 Corinthians 6 and the example of Joseph in Genesis 39. LXX Genesis 39:12 uses the same verb "to flee"[83] to describe Joseph's successful escape from Potiphar's wife: "he *fled* out of her house" (cf. Gen. 39:13, 15, 18). Another suggestive link with 1 Corinthians 6 is the fact that Genesis 39 forms a contrast to Tamar's prostitution in Genesis 38.[84]

78. This is a present imperative (Φεύγετε). As we have pointed out previously, present imperatives are used for generally relevant instruction rather than instruction intended to address one particular situation. It is always right to flee sexual immorality.

79. Findlay, 821, describes the exhortation as beginning with "vehement abruptness."

80. Outside of chs. 5–6 πορν- words occur only in 7:2 (reprising the warnings of the previous two chapters) and 10:8.

81. Barrett, 150.

82. Paul adds the conjunction οὖν, "therefore," not translated in TNIV. On the connection between the texts see Rosner, *Paul, Scripture and Ethics*, 123-46; and "A Possible Quotation of *Test. Reuben* 5:5 in 1 Corinthians 6:18a," *JTS* 43/1 (1992), 123-27.

83. Gk. φεύγω.

84. Gk. πόρνη occurs in LXX Gen. 38:15, 21, 22; πορνεία in 38:24.

It is possible that both sources influenced Paul. As it turns out, the *Testament of Reuben* 5 was itself written with Joseph in mind.[85] Along with calls to "flee" sexual immorality, both texts in fact share two other features in common with 1 Corinthians 6:18-20. The author of the *Testament of Reuben* also noted the relevance of God's indwelling to the state of chastity (10:1-3; cf. 1 Cor. 6:19) and concluded that Joseph had "glorified" God (8:5; cf. 6:20). The Genesis Joseph account likewise describes Joseph as "one in whom is the Spirit of God" (41:38) and that his chief motivation in the action was not to sin against God (39:9), akin to glorifying him. Thus *Testament of Reuben* witnesses to a traditional interpretation of Genesis 39 that may also have influenced Paul. Alternatively, Paul quotes *Testament of Reuben* 5:5 directly, not as sacred Scripture but as an appropriate ethical maxim, a text to which he was driven because of its effective use of Joseph in its warnings against *porneia.*

The second half of v. 18 bolsters Paul's warning against sexual immorality: Why flee sexual immorality? Because *[a]ll other sins people commit are outside their bodies, but those who sin sexually sin against their own bodies.*[86] The basic point is clear: sexual immorality is to be fled because it is worse in some way than other sins. Unfortunately, the sense in which *porneia* is distinctive over against other sins is debated. Paul's statement is one of the most puzzling in the letter. Some have suggested that the sentence represents another example (see 6:12-13) of Paul's quoting and then correcting the Corinthians: "You say, 'every sin a person commits is outside the body'; but I say that he who sins sexually sins against his own body."[87] While it is conceivable that the Corinthians may have argued that bodily actions are of no significance, v. 18 contains less justification than the other examples in the letter for detecting a Corinthian slogan. As Garland points out, the "but" in the second half expresses an exception, rather than functioning contrastively.[88] Either way, we are left to ponder the sense in which Paul thinks *porneia* a sin "against one's body."

By "body"[89] Paul is referring to human life viewed as physical. It is not that we have a body, but that we are embodied. As Schrage defines it, the body is "the locus where we experience life, death, sickness and sexuality."[90] It is better to think of Paul's anthropological terms as aspects rather than parts of the human person. That Paul is referring to the whole

85. See *Testament of Reuben* 4:8, which speaks of Joseph "protecting himself from a woman."

86. The word "other" is not in the Greek, but is legitimately supplied in most English versions. For another clear example of "other" being elided in Greek, but needed in English translation, see Matt. 12:31: "people will be forgiven every [other] sin . . . , but blasphemy against the Spirit will not be forgiven."

87. Cf., e.g., Murphy-O'Connor, "Corinthian Slogans"; Talbert; Hays.

88. Garland, 236.

89. Gk. σῶμα.

90. Schrage, *The Ethics of the New Testament*, 238.

person with the term "body," and not to some part, is clear from the following two verses. There he uses the second-person pronoun, "you," and "body" interchangeably.

To ask why certain other sins, such as drunkenness, gluttony, self-mutilation, or suicide, are any less against the body ignores the context of Paul's assertion. As noted earlier, the foundation of Paul's teaching against *porneia* in 6:12-20, and even on into chapter 7, is the argument in v. 16, based on Genesis 2:24, that "he who unites himself with a prostitute is one with her in body." In v. 18b Paul is not saying that only *porneia* damages the body, but rather that only *porneia* establishes a "one-flesh" union that is "against the body." Sexual sin is against the body because, as Fisk states, it is "uniquely body-joining, . . . [and] uniquely body-defiling."[91] As with so many other compressed expressions in the section, we need to supply something to complete our understanding of Paul's thought. Here we might add that *porneia* is a sin against the body's "rightful ownership"; the believer's body is under the authority of Christ the Lord (vv. 12-15), is a temple of the Holy Spirit (v. 19), and was purchased by God (v. 20). No other sin threatens to put the body under the mastery of something or someone else (v. 12b).

**6:19-20** With yet another rhetorical question Paul reinforces the notion that believers' bodies belong to God. Here the tone is less impatient than it is imploring. Unlike the questions of vv. 15b and 16a, v. 19a adds information that is positive and affirming of the Corinthian Christians: *Do you not know that your bodies are temples of the Holy Spirit, who is in you, whom you have received from God?*

Paul has already described the whole congregation as God's sacred temple in 3:16-17. See on those verses for the meaning and significance of such a designation. Here Paul applies the corporate imagery to the individual believer, with particular reference to the believer's body. Every phrase underlines the need to flee sexual immorality (v. 18a). Naming the indwelling Spirit as *Holy* carries the implication that the privilege of being God's temple carries with it the obligation not to desecrate (or destroy; 3:17) the temple. Jewish history had been marked, and would continue to be so, by appropriate and inappropriate behavior in the temple of God. The purpose of the temple was to bring glory to God and to sanctify his name. The fact that the Holy Spirit resides in the believer's body adds further weight to the responsibility not to sin against that body. The Spirit's origin as a gift *from God* (cf. Ezek. 36:22-32) further emphasizes both the fact that believers "stand in grace" (Rom. 5:2) and that God's authority stands over their lives (1 Thess. 4:8).

In case the Corinthians needed reminding, Paul states his main point in response to sexual immorality in the church of God in Corinth in the simplest terms: *You are not your own;* or as Thiselton puts it, "you do not belong to yourselves." This truth is a major theological motif in the letter with

91. Fisk, "Body Violation," 558.

profound implications for everyday life. It strikes at the heart of the modern and postmodern notions that we establish our own identities and prize autonomous freedom. The answer to Corinthian factionalism and inappropriate attachment to human leaders is to realize that "you belong to Christ" (3:23a). In 7:22-24 the implication of being "Christ's slaves" is that we are ultimately "responsible only to God." Here is Paul's basic answer to "I have a right to do anything" (6:12). It was announced in the opening address of the letter — the Corinthians are the church belonging to God (1:2a).

Moving from cultic imagery to that of slave market, Paul adds support to his assertion that the Corinthian Christians belong to God: *you were bought at a price.* On slavery in the first century, see on 7:21-23. In short, the status and conditions of a slave depended on to whom you belonged. Along with inevitable contemporary associations, Paul drew on the Old Testament theology of redemption. Here in 1 Corinthians 6:20 Paul has in view a change of ownership, not a manumission resulting in unqualified freedom. As Thiselton explains, "The imagery stresses primarily the new ownership, and secondly a costly act on the part of the new owner which makes the believer legitimately and contractually the one to whom the believer now *belongs.*"[92] The genitive of price may be translated "with a price" (NRSV, KJV/AV, ESV) / "for a price" (Moffatt) or "at a price" (TNIV, REB, NIV, NJB). The latter emphasizes the cost of their purchase, a note struck elsewhere in the New Testament with reference to the blood of Christ (Acts 20:28; 1 Pet. 1:19; Rev. 5:9).

A more specific parallel to this verse is Hosea 3:2-3. Just as Paul exhorted the Corinthians not to go to prostitutes, so in Hosea 3:3 Hosea commanded Gomer not to be a prostitute ("you must not be a prostitute"). Both admonitions to sexual fidelity are argued on similar grounds. Hosea's demand is based upon his special relationship with Gomer: he is her husband (3:1) and, having redeemed her from the slave market ("I bought her," Hos. 3:2), he is her master. George L. Klein spells out the comparison: "In Hosea 3 the prophet redeemed his wife out of a degrading life to a life bound by sexual decorum. Similarly, in 1 Corinthians 6 the audience has been redeemed out of bondage to sin (including licentiousness) to a life in which sexual sin was unconscionable."[93] An analogy from Homer-Gomer to God–his people is made plain in 3:1 ("Love her as the LORD loves the Israelites"). Klein concludes that 1 Corinthians 6:19b-20 alludes to Hosea 3:1-3. However, lack of common terminology cautions against too confident an identification of any literary connection between the passages. Still, it is a Hosea-like Paul we encounter when we read Paul warning against prostitution. Calling God's people to repentance on the grounds that he is their husband and master places Paul in the tradition of the best of Israel's prophets.

92. Thiselton, 477.

93. George L. Klein, "Hos 3:1-3 — Background to 1 Cor 6:19b-20," *Criswell Theological Review* 3/2 (1989), 373-75 (here 374).

Paul's closing words are a command that acts as a hinge between the positive (7:1-40) and negative (4:18–6:20) sections of his treatment of sexual ethics for the church of God in Corinth. It arises out of both the temple (v. 19) and slavery (v. 20a) fields of meaning he has just evoked. The glory of God is the ultimate purpose of God's temple, and the bodies of slaves literally belonged to their masters. *Therefore honor God with your bodies.*

TNIV's *honor* gives an accurate sense of the verb,[94] but it obscures the critical nature of the Corinthians' being called not only to "glorify" God with respect to fleeing sexual immorality but also by fleeing idolatry in the next major unit of the letter (10:31: "glorify God in everything you do"). The word "body" makes its seventh appearance in nine verses. Schrage is right that "[t]he decisive argument against unchastity [in 6:12-20] . . . is the question, to whom does your body belong?"[95]

## B. Affirmation of Sexual Purity: "Glorify God with Your Bodies," 7:1-40

Collins asserts that "[t]he basic theme of chs. 5 and 6 is the purity of the community. What does it mean for the community to be God's holy people?"[1] The same is true for chapter 7. As argued in the introduction to 4:18–7:40, chapters 5–7 form a single unit addressing principally the sin of sexual immorality, first negatively (4:18–6:20) and then positively (7:1-40). In Barnett's words, chapter 7 "completes Paul's 'Holiness Code' begun in chapter 5."[2] Even though in this chapter Paul begins to answer questions put to him in the Corinthian letter (see 7:1, 25), "he has so arranged his letter that his replies fall within the block of teaching on sexual holiness."[3] This is in keeping with the practice of ancient Jewish moral teachers who regularly treated sexual sin and sexual relations in marriage in tandem. In short, Paul's commands to "flee from sexual immorality" (6:18) and to "glorify God with your bodies" (6:20) can be achieved either by self-restraint (cf. 5:1-13; 6:12-20) or by "having sexual relations with one's spouse" (7:2; cf. 7:1-40). The apostle's exhortation to the Thessalonians, penned in Corinth, applies equally well here: "It is God's will that you should be sanctified: that you avoid sexual immorality; that each of you should learn to control your own

94. Gk. δοξάζω. We would normally expect a present imperative here (rather than the aorist δοξάσατε) since the context does not suggest that Paul is addressing a specific case or situation rather than giving a generally relevant exhortation. It may be that Paul has the Corinthians' particular problems with sexual immorality in mind. Or this could be a case of an aorist imperative being used "to communicate instruction in summary form" (Campbell, *Verbal Aspect and Non-Indicative Verbs*, 86-91 [87]).

95. Schrage, *New Testament Ethics*, 134.

1. Collins, 203.

2. Barnett, 106, an allusion to Leviticus 18–20.

3. Barnett, 106-7.

body in a way that is holy and honorable, not in passionate lust like the pagans, who do not know God" (1 Thess. 4:3-5).

The chapter throws up some formidable exegetical challenges. It is not always clear to whom the apostle is speaking, and at several key junctures his language is ambiguous, at least for those who, unlike the original readers, experience the disadvantage of reading at a temporal and cultural distance. Also, ascetic strands in the teaching are assessed differently in the commentaries. Does Paul discourage marriage or not? What about the Corinthians in their letter to him? Murphy-O'Connor thinks that asceticism in Corinth "struck a chord in Paul. He himself lived a life of sexual asceticism (vv. 7-8), and believed that someone like him could . . . live a more ordered (v. 35), less anxious (v. 32), less troubled (v. 28) and happier life (v. 40)."[4] This raises the question of whether the seemingly ascetic elements in the discussion reflect a radical commitment to celibacy on the part of some Corinthians, or is more directly related to Paul's own personal preferences.

Most scholars believe that some in Corinth were saying that "it is good for a man not to have (any) sexual relations with a woman" (7:1) and were consequently advocating celibacy in marriage, divorce from unbelieving partners, and remaining single if you were a "virgin" or a widow. In other words, they were promoting celibacy as a rule or norm and considered sex to be a sin (cf. "sin" in 7:28, 36). How they arrived at this stance is a matter of speculation. Suggestions range from the influence of the Essenes at Qumran, who were celibate, to an early form of Gnosticism, to a misunderstanding of the arrival of the new age in Christ wherein the order of marriage is marginalized. Special circumstances in Corinth, such as a famine or some other social crisis (see on 7:26), may also have encouraged some not to marry or to put their marriages on hold. A more general explanation might be that a low view of the body, which was rife in Greek and Roman thought, may have impacted the Corinthians not only with regard to their denial of a bodily resurrection (see the comments introducing ch. 15) and their resort to prostitutes (see 6:12-20), but also to their movement in an ascetic direction. Stoic and Cynic philosophy taught that the unmarried may have an advantage in the pursuit of wisdom. Similarly, Greek popular piety viewed virginity as a means to religious power, as, for example, with the priestesses of the Oracle at Delphi.[5] Thus, some in Corinth may have taken the irrelevance of the body to things of the spirit (cf. "body and spirit" in 7:34) to imply license and libertinism in sexual matters (see 6:12-20), while others took it as an encouragement to celibacy and denial of bodily pleasures (see 7:1-40). Hays has suggested that some even more perversely wanted to "have their cake and eat it too": "In order to understand

4. Murphy-O'Connor, 59.

5. Evidence of Paul's writing against ascetic impulses in his letters includes Col. 2:20-23 (cf., literally, "Do not touch") and 1 Tim. 4:3, which oppose those who "forbid marriage" and "abstain from certain foods."

Paul's concern, we must picture the sadly comic scenario in which a Christian married couple plays a charade of sexual abstinence with one another while indulging in clandestine extramarital affairs."[6] As we shall see, interpreting Corinthian positions in this chapter, as elsewhere in the letter, in light of dominant Roman views rather than quite exotic ones, leads to a less comic and more realistic understanding of the situation.

This commentary interprets the situation rather differently than most others, understanding the Corinthians in light of such Roman perspectives. For example, closer examination of the euphemism of "touching" used in what is taken to be a quote from the Corinthians in 7:1 reveals that it was probably not used for sexual relations in general, but for a range of sexual activities which would have been frowned upon by most Greco-Roman moralists in Paul's day (see on 7:1). Thus the Corinthians who used the expression were more likely to be stating their disapproval of certain kinds of sexual relations than a commitment to complete abstinence or celibacy.

Furthermore, much of Paul's teaching in this chapter (and certainly the contents of chapters 5–6 and 10:6-8) seems to suggest that Paul has in mind readers who are considering marriage or remarriage, or struggling with avoiding sex outside of marriage, and are quite unprepared to do without sex altogether:

- Paul's statement in 7:4 that "the husband does not have authority over his own body but his wife does" would have been a pointed reminder to husbands who thought they were free to continue sexual relationships with household slaves, prostitutes, or consorts that they were not in fact free to do so.
- 1 Corinthians 7:5 indicates that Paul does not think the couples he is addressing are prepared permanently to abstain from sex, but would be in danger of being tempted by Satan because of their "lack of self-control" if they were to abstain for any but the shortest of periods.
- In vv. 8-9 Paul expresses both his own preference that widows and other single people remain unmarried and his concern that they may not be able to "control themselves" and may "burn with passion."
- Paul's counsel that a wife should not separate from her husband, but "if she does, she must remain unmarried or else be reconciled to her husband" (vv. 10-11) would hardly seem to serve to dissuade a wife from separating from her husband if remaining unmarried (and celibate) was what she had in mind in the first place! Rather, Paul's counsel seems more directly aimed at dissuading a woman who was thinking of leaving her husband in order to marry someone else (rather than out of a preference for celibacy).

6. Hays, *The Moral Vision of the New Testament*, 50.

- Our reading of vv. 25-35 also suggests that Paul is responding to people whose preference would be to marry and who need reassurance from him that he is not adamantly opposed to the idea. He is the one who thinks it would be best for virgins to remain single, but they are free to marry and need to know that if they do they will not be sinning (vv. 25-28). He wants to spare them the troubles they will experience in life if they get married (v. 28). He wants them to be free from the concerns they will experience if they go ahead and marry (v. 32). He is concerned that his words might be interpreted as an attempt "to restrict" them (v. 35).
- In vv. 36-38 the Corinthian man Paul has in mind clearly "feels he ought to marry"; that is what "he wants." Paul is thinking of a man struggling with "control over his own will." He feels that those who are not compelled to marry do best not to do so (at least in the context of the temporary crisis in Corinth; see on v. 26), but he wants them to know that he will not blame them if they do.
- Finally, in vv. 39-40, Paul indicates that a widow "is free to marry anyone she wishes," but it is his view that she would be happier if she stays single.

These texts all have subtle indicators suggesting Paul has in mind men and women who want to marry and/or have sex, and that he is probably more inclined toward a fundamental commitment to celibacy (or total abstinence) than they are.

It seems that three different factors combined to raise questions in the minds of some Corinthians about the appropriateness of sex and/or marriage. The most important of these was probably the letter Paul sent them and to which they were replying in the letter to which Paul refers in 7:1 ("Now for the matters you wrote about"). In 5:9 Paul says that he wrote to them in an earlier letter "not to associate with sexually immoral people," and he indicates that there was some confusion about exactly what it was that he had in mind. In 6:9-11 Paul writes that some of the Corinthians had previously fallen under the categories of the sexually immoral, but he stresses in v. 11 that although that is what they used to be, they were washed, sanctified, and justified "in the name of the Lord Jesus Christ and by the Spirit of our God." Wives and husbands who did not fully understand what Paul had in mind in his warning about sexually immoral people may have thought that it implied that they should divorce or refrain from sexual relations with spouses who had been involved in sexual immorality even before their conversion (7:1-5; thus Paul's stress that they had been washed and sanctified from that experience and that those labels no longer applied to them). Others may have wondered if one implication would be that they should divorce unbelieving spouses (7:12-14), perhaps especially those who continued to exercise the immoral sexual freedoms that were commonly practiced at the time (especially by men),[7] and thus Paul emphasizes that the unbelieving husband or wife (regardless of their behavior!) "has been sanctified" through their relationship with their believing spouse (v. 14). In Paul's day there was a very influential debate raging about whether it was appropriate to enjoy sex for pleasure or inspired by passion, or if it was only appropriate when engaged in for the procreation of children. Evidence suggests many married Roman men regularly engaged in recreational (or hedonistic) sex with people other than their wives[8] and only (or primarily) engaged in procreational sex with their wives. Some Corinthians may have interpreted his warning about sexual immorality in terms of that Greco-Roman debate and concluded, along with late Stoic and Pythagorean moralists, that all recreational sex should be avoided and that even within marriage sex should take place only when procreation was intended.[9]

This brings us to the second factor that seems to have raised questions about sex and marriage in the minds of some Corinthians, namely, "the present crisis" mentioned in v. 26. In times of famine or other severe economic and social hardship family responsibilities became exponentially more difficult to fulfill. Marital sex (unlike sex with prostitutes or consorts) was likely to result in another mouth to feed and another person's welfare to attend to[10] in a situation where one's own survival could be enough of a challenge. This may have encouraged some Corinthians to think twice about marrying or remarrying during such times of social stress.[11] It could also have meant a deliberate decision to refrain from sex within marriage in cases where one spouse or another felt it was immoral to engage in sexual relations within marriage except for the explicit purposes of procreation.

The third factor would have been the Corinthians' own awareness of Paul's personal commitment to a celibate lifestyle, mentioned above. He reminds them of his preference throughout the chapter (see esp. v. 7, "I wish that all of you were as I am"; v. 8, "It is good for them to stay unmar-

7. Later, Tertullian will categorically state "that believers contracting marriages with Gentiles are 'guilty of fornication' and should be excommunicated" (Margaret Y. MacDonald, "The Role of Women in the Expansion of Early Christianity," in *Early Christian Families in Context: An Interdisciplinary Dialogue* [ed. David L. Balch and Carolyn Osiek; Grand Rapids: Eerdmans, 2003], 179, citing Tertullian, *To His Wife* 2.3 [ANF 4]).

8. Options included female and male household slaves, street prostitutes, consorts (call girls), and adulterous affairs with married women.

9. For fuller discussion of the Roman context and both the Corinthians' and Paul's response to it, see Roy E. Ciampa, "Revisiting the Euphemism in 1 Corinthians 7.1," *JSNT* 31 (2008), 325-38.

10. While Greeks and Romans sometimes used contraceptives and/or abortifacients, they are not thought to have been particularly effective.

11. Such a decision, however, may have led some to be tempted to find sexual release through prostitutes or consorts, since they would not be expected to know or be responsible for any offspring that could result from such sexual relations.

ried, as I do"; vv. 26-28, "those who marry will face many troubles in this life, and I want to spare you this"; vv. 32-35, "I would like you to be free from concern").

Rather than interpreting the questions from the Corinthians as indicators that they are committed to celibacy, whether within or outside of marriage, it seems better to understand them as a reaction to Paul's warnings about sexual immorality and to the crisis Corinth was experiencing at the time in light of contemporary debates about the proper place and purposes of sex in Roman society (see the comments on 7:1). This approach has the added advantage of attributing to the Corinthians one of the more dominant views of sex in the Roman world, rather than the rather exotic view (of a commitment to celibacy even within marriage) that is customarily attributed to them.

Confronted with extremely personal and practical questions about sex and marriage in response to his earlier letter to them and fueled by a dominant moral perspective in Roman society and by a local social crisis in Corinth at the time, Paul offers balanced advice on practical freedom, personal inclination and giftedness, and conviction in the light of circumstances, both internal and external, in order to clear a path to the goal of glorifying God with their bodies (6:20) and offering undistracted devotion to the Lord (7:35).

For all its difficulties, 1 Corinthians 7 shows Paul the pastor at his best. No passage in his letters contains a more sustained and nuanced ethical reflection on concrete issues of everyday life, aside from 1 Corinthians 8–10. And dealing with such concrete questions does not diminish the relevance of the teaching. Paul's counsel can help us as relatively detached observers to reflect more objectively on our own particularity. Even though our concerns may not coincide with theirs, the chapter's sexual ethics have much to offer to contemporary discussions.

In answer to a number of questions put to him in a letter (cf. "Now for the matters you wrote about"; 7:1) Paul's basic advice to the married, the unmarried, the "virgins," and the widows is to prioritize pure and undistracted devotion to the Lord, which, in most cases, Paul suggests, would be best served by not experiencing major changes in one's life situation, certainly not in a time of crisis. Thus, believers are discouraged from seeking a change in status (7:2, 8, 10, 11, etc.). This guiding principle of seeking the most effective way to serve the Lord in whatever life situation one finds oneself in is taken up directly and reinforced in 7:17-24 with reference to circumcision and slavery. Hence, as in chapters 8–10 and 12–14, the structure of the larger unit has an "ABA" shape in which the matter at hand is treated in two blocks (here 7:1-16 and 7:25-40) interrupted by an apparent aside in which a major tenet is illustrated and reinforced.

The chapter may also be understood in light of a two-part parallelism (A-B; A′-B′) in which Paul addresses married people (7:1-7) and then unmarried people and widows (7:8-9) and then goes back and addresses each of these groups again (married people in vv. 10-16; and then unmarried people and widows in vv. 25-38 and 39-40, respectively).

Although not explicit, much of what Paul says here finds its roots in the Old Testament.[12] Key background texts include Genesis 2:24, Exodus 19:15; 21:10-11,[13] and Deuteronomy 20:5-7; 24:1-4. Despite no explicit reference to Torah in the chapter, Paul's advice would not have taken shape without the influence of this material.[14]

### 1. *Counsel Concerning Various Marital Statuses, 7:1-16*

#### a. *For the Married: Maintain Sexual Relations, 7:1-7*

*1Now for the matters you wrote about: "It is good for a man not to have sexual relations with a woman." 2But since sexual immorality is occurring, each man should have sexual relations with his own wife, and each woman with her own husband. 3The husband should fulfill his marital duty to his wife, and likewise the wife to her husband. 4The wife does not have authority over her own body but yields it to her husband. In the same way, the husband does not have authority over his own body but yields it to his wife. 5Do not deprive each other except perhaps by mutual consent and for a time, so that you may devote yourselves to prayer. Then come together again so that Satan will not tempt you because of your lack of self-control. 6I say this as a concession, not as a command. 7I wish that all of you were as I am. But each of you has your own gift from God; one has this gift, another has that.*

**7:1** *Now for the matters you wrote about* signals the first issue from the Corinthian letter to Paul that the apostle chose to deal with. The letter evidently raised a number of concerns, to which the following chapters respond. But the sequence of Paul's response is his own. Some material in chapters 7–16 came to Paul from oral reports, and he has collected his responses to the concerns about sexuality in 4:18–7:40 and about worship in 8:1–14:40 (both in negative and positive panels).

A consensus of commentators and translations regards v. 7:1b as a pithy summary, if not a direct citation, of a main point from the Corinthians' letter: *"It is good for a man not to have sexual relations with a woman"* translates literally "it is good for a man not to touch a woman." "To touch a woman" was a sexual euphemism, and does not mean "to marry" (contra

12. Rosner, *Paul, Scripture and Ethics*, 147-75.

13. See esp. David Instone-Brewer, *Divorce and Remarriage in the Bible: The Social and Literary Context* (Grand Rapids: Eerdmans, 2002), 189-212. Rabbinic interpretation of Exod. 21:10-11 divided the obligations of marriage into two groups: emotional obligations and material obligations. Instone-Brewer finds Paul's discussion reflecting these emphases in 7:1-9 and 7:32-35 respectively.

14. The outline for chapter 7 is adapted from Hays, 112.

NIV, "it is good for a man not to marry").[15] On the basis of a study of eight examples of the euphemism[16] Fee (followed by other scholars) understood it to refer to sexual relations in general (as it is translated by the TNIV and most recent translations) and thought it reflected an antisex perspective.[17] As already noted, others have considered it antimarriage.[18] Both of these views are mistaken.

Fee's influential study was not in fact an exhaustive treatment of the relevant extrabiblical texts. A fuller study of twenty-five known instances of the euphemism provides a more precise understanding.[19] As it turns out, the euphemism is applied to the following cases: Acting on sexual passions for the sake of pleasure or sexual release (Plato, *Leges* 8.837b-d; 8.840a), including the specific cases of using the following kinds of people for one's own sexual gratification: slaves or people taken forcibly into one's household (Gen. 20:4, 6; Josephus, *Antiquities* 1.163-64; 4.257; Plutarch, *Alexander* 21.9; Marcus Aurelius, *Meditations* 1.17), a defenseless woman (Ruth 2:9), a virgin placed in one's protective care (Euripides, *Electra* 50–51), a wife during her menstrual period (Philo, *On the Special Laws* 3:32). It is also used of a pederast's relation with their love interest (Plutarch, *Quaestionum Convivialum* 634a), of "unnatural" homosexual relations (Plato, *Leges* 8.836c), of incestuous relations (Plato, *Leges* 8.838b), of rape or adultery (Euripides, *Hippolytus* 885, 1026, 1044; Josephus, *Antiquities* 2.57; Prov. 6:29), of sex with one's defiled concubine (*Testament of Reuben* 3:15), of sex with any wellborn or free person other than one's wife (Plato, *Leges* 8.841d) or with anyone at all other than one's wife (Aristotle, *Politics* 7.14.12 [1335b]).

One of the earliest of these examples is that of Plato, *Leges* 8.837b-d. In the midst of the conversation about sexual desires or cravings and how to get young people to abstain from them the issue is raised of a man who, "drawn in opposite directions by the two loves [namely, the love of the body and love of the soul], . . . finds himself at a loss, with one bidding him to pick [literally, touch] the bloom of youth[20] and the other telling him not to. For the man who loves the body, hungering for the bloom as for ripe fruit, bids himself take his fill without honoring the disposition of soul of the beloved. The other sort of lover holds the desire for the body to be sec-

15. Schrage, 2:59; Fee, 275; and idem, "1 Corinthians 7:1-7 Revisited," in *Paul and the Corinthians: Studies on a Community in Conflict: Essays in Honour of Margaret Thrall* (ed. T. J. Burke and J. K. Elliott; Leiden: Brill, 2003), 197-213.

16. Plato, *Leges* 8.840a; Aristotle, *Politics* 7.14.12 [1335b]; Gen. 20:6; Ruth 2:9; Prov. 6:29; Plutarch, *Alexander* 21.9; Josephus, *Antiquities* 1.163; Marcus Aurelius, *Meditations* 1.17.

17. See Fee, 275; and idem, "1 Corinthians 7:1 in the *NIV*," *JETS* 23.4 (1980), 307-14; idem, "1 Corinthians 7:1-7 Revisited," in *Paul and the Corinthians: Studies on a Community in Conflict: Essays in Honour of Margaret Thrall*, 197-213.

18. Instone-Brewer, *Divorce and Remarriage in the Bible*, 193.

19. These twenty-five examples include three different Greek verbs meaning "to touch." There are nineteen examples of the euphemism employing the verb ἅπτω, four that use the verb θιγγάνω, and two that use the verb ψαύω.

20. Gk. κελεύοντος τῆς ὥρας ἅπτεσθαι.

ondary; looking at it rather than loving it, with his soul he really desires the soul of the other and considers the gratification of body by body to be wantonness."[21] Here the problem is not sex itself, but acting out of a desire to gratify the body rather than a concern for the soul of the other. According to Plato, it is self-gratification that leads the man to "touch" the object of his desire. Here "to touch" seems to be equated with "taking one's fill without honoring the disposition of the soul of the beloved." Plato thinks that it is better not to do so.

Another example comes from Plato's *Republic* 5.461e, which concludes an extended discussion on relations that should be prohibited by referring to "that which we have just now said, (which is) not to touch one another.[22] But the law will allow brothers and sisters to cohabit[23] if the lot so falls out and the Delphic oracle approves."[24] Here the prohibited relations are referred to in terms of the insistence that people not touch one another, while the next line refers to approved sexual relations using a different verb.

In a world where there was significant debate about whether pleasure and passion were acceptable motivations for sexual relations, or whether sexual relations should be engaged in solely for the purposes of procreation, it is quite remarkable that this particular euphemism is consistently used for sexual relations motivated by pleasure or passion rather than procreation (or reason or marital friendship, which would also have been acceptable motivations for some Stoics).[25] Further, in virtually all cases the authors indicate that in their view it was good (or would have been good) for the man not to touch the woman (or other person), without suggesting that they were committed to celibacy or opposed to sex in general. Thus, there is no sound reason for concluding that the euphemism is antisex. Rather, along with a prominent point of view in Paul's world, it is much more likely to reflect a concern about certain kinds of (and motivations for) sexual relations than a rejection of sexual relations in general. It would probably be preferable, then, to translate the Corinthian position as "it is good for a man not to use a woman for sexual gratification," or "it is good for a man not to have sex with a woman for the sake of pleasure." This is in contrast to the other Corinthian view which was cited in 6:13 (according to which sex should simply be understood as a basic human need,

21. Thomas L. Pangle, *The Laws of Plato: Translated, with Notes and an Interpretive Essay* (New York: Basic Books, 1980), 228-29.

22. Gk. ὃ νυνδὴ ἐλέγομεν, ἀλλήλων μὴ ἅπτεσθαι.

23. Gk. συνοικεῖν.

24. The end of the first sentence reflects our translation, while the second sentence is Shorey's (LCL). For that previous sentence Shorey has "This will suffice for the prohibitions of intercourse of which we just now spoke."

25. See further Ciampa, "Revisiting the Euphemism in 1 Corinthians 7.1," 325-38. Plato and Aristotle both suggest that men and women outside the ideal ages for procreation should not engage in sexual relations (Plato, *Republic* 5.461a-b; Aristotle, *Politics* 7.14.12 [1335b]).

like food, with which the stomach should be supplied). While some are saying (with reference to sex), "food for the stomach and the stomach for food" (i.e., sex is merely the natural feeding of a basic human need/appetite), others are saying "it is good for a man not to touch a woman" (i.e., it is not good to use a woman [or any person] to meet a man's hunger for sexual gratification).

As in 6:12 (cf. 10:23) and 8:1, Paul cites a Corinthian opinion to which he gives partial assent before going on to qualify it in terms of present application. Here most of the kinds of sex that would be referred to with this euphemism would also fall under the category of *porneia* (sexual immorality). In fact, the more Hellenized Corinthians may have used it to put into their own words what they thought Paul might have had in mind when he warned them about contact with sexually immoral people in his previous letter to them (5:9). The objection to touching a woman may have been somewhat more restrictive, however, than a rejection of *porneia,* since Scripture does not suggest that there is anything wrong with engaging in sex with one's spouse motivated by pleasure or passion (something idealized by the Song of Solomon). Furthermore, a commitment to engaging in sex with one's wife solely for the purposes of procreation could easily lead to such an austere sexual life that spouses could easily be tempted to find sexual relief with other people (especially since people who did not believe in limiting themselves to sex for the purposes of procreation typically found that further release in extramarital sexual activity). Thus, in the following verses Paul will emphasize the importance of both avoiding sexual immorality and (therefore) meeting the normal, appropriate, sexual needs of one's spouse.

The statement *it is good* most likely reflects the recommendation some Corinthian believers have made to less chaste members of their congregation which they hope Paul will ratify. He does so with a minor qualification.[26] He would certainly not object to married people who were happy to refrain from sex except for the purposes of procreation. In fact, he thinks unmarried people should seriously consider a life of singleness or celibacy (cf. 7:8-9, 27, 32-35, 40). The sexual euphemism of "touching" does not point to a sexual experience engaged in by men and women in the same way. "Touching" was something that a man did to the object of his sexual interests. Women and men did not "touch" each other. The English language, especially in its more colloquial forms, has a number of similar expressions. To render the euphemism into idiomatic, if indelicate, English, the Corinthians were saying something like: "it is good for a man not to bed/bang/shag a woman." Paul agrees, and in vv. 2-5 he expresses his own views about sex and marriage in rather different terms.

**7:2** While the Corinthians' concerns about sex were evidently expressed in the euphemism of "touching," one that refers to a unilateral act

26. See Ciampa, "Revisiting the Euphemism in 1 Corinthians 7.1," 336-37.

on the part of a man, in vv. 2-5 Paul's own thinking about sex and marriage is consistently expressed in terms of mutual and symmetrical rights and responsibilities. *But since sexual immorality is occurring* translates literally, "but because of sexual immoralities." The plural noun[27] has puzzled interpreters. Whereas some take it as a general reference to licentious behavior (cf. TNIV), others restrict it to adultery, or link it to the use of prostitutes in 6:12-20. The best choice of referent is to notice the appearance of the term or its cognates not only in chapter 6 but also chapter 5; "sexual immoralities" in 7:2 refers to the sins which Paul has already spoken against in the section, namely, incest and prostitution (both using terms cognate to "sexual immorality" in 7:2), along with adultery and homosexual behavior (using three other terms in the same broad semantic field; see on 6:9), and presumably premarital sex, which Paul indicates some would be tempted to fall into (7:9, 36-37).[28] In Paul's world men were not tempted to various forms of sexual immorality by wives committed to sexual abstinence, but were generally expected (except by Stoic and Pythagorean moralists) to find their primary sexual satisfaction with people other than their wives, restricting their sexual relations with their chaste and virtuous wives to the purpose of procreation. Of course, Paul's congregations would presumably have been taught that all such extramarital relations were prohibited to the Christian. Jennifer Glancy reflects on the fact that in the Roman world "the master's right to have sexual relations with one of his slaves was not accompanied by moral judgment against the master or the slave" and points out that Christian slaveholders who heard that such relations were prohibited to them as Christians "could choose to redirect their sexual attention to their wives."[29] Paul's teaching in vv. 2-5 may be based in part on a sense that such wives might need some apostolic encouragement to be prepared for that potentially unexpected (and potentially unwanted) increased sexual attention from their husbands.

In Paul's mind, the way to avoid the perils of extramarital sex is literally "to have" your own wife or husband, not in the sense of acquiring one, but by maintaining regular sexual relations with the one you already have.[30] The verb "to have" may mean "to stand in a close relationship to someone" and thus simply point to a family relationship: to have a son or a father or a wife or a husband (BDAG [2a]). And so Paul could mean simply

27. Gk. πορνείας.

28. Paul's concern that husbands and wives not be tempted by their lack of self-control during periods of abstinence points to the broad range of sexual offenses that could be included in the term *porneia,* since it would presumably include sexual relations with anyone other than one's own spouse, including relations with one's household slaves or with courtesans, or other unmarried women. Such relations were not considered "adulterous" in the Roman world, where the term "adultery" applied only to sex with someone else's legitimate wife. Paul, however, is clearly concerned about the possibility that a spouse might seek sexual relief or gratification with anyone other than their own spouse.

29. Jennifer A. Glancy, *Slavery in Early Christianity* (Minneapolis: Fortress, 2006), 67.

30. Fee, 278.

that each man should have his own wife.[31] In some cases, however, the verb seems to mean to have sexual relations with the woman.[32] Some texts are ambiguous (Aristotle, *Categories* 15b; Exod. 2:1; Tob. 7:13 [S]; Mark 6:18). If it is taken in the simple sense of having a wife Paul's sense here would be simply "each one should be married to his own wife, and each woman should be married to her own husband." This would mean that the verb has the same meaning in vv. 2, 12, 13, and 29. It would be left to the following verse to explain that within marriage it is important to maintain ongoing sexual relations. However, Paul's later indication that his own preference is for unmarried men and women to remain single is a problem for this interpretation (although vv. 6-7 may be taken to signify that his verb in v. 2 is a "permissive imperative" rather than a reflection of his true preference). One factor that works against this interpretation (besides the fact that it would be at odds with Paul's clearly stated preference later in the chapter) is the use of the imperative: "each one should have." The verb is usually used in the indicative mood to refer to the present or prior existence of an established marriage ("he has/had a wife"), while the verb "to take" is normally used for the establishment of a new marriage.[33] Here the imperative[34] for each one to "have" his own[35] wife suggests the maintenance of sexual relations from time to time (cf. on 5:1 and the TNIV on 7:1). The verb in 7:1 links the present discussion with that of incest in chapter 5: in one sense the solution to "having" (sex with) your father's wife (or any other inappropriate woman) is to "have" (sex with) your own wife.

Paul's discussion reflects the uniform biblical stance on sex. Fundamentally, in the Bible there are only two types of sex: sex within marriage and sexual immorality, *porneia.* 1 Corinthians 7:2 makes it inescapably clear that while there may be a number of types of the latter, the only valid alternative to them is the former. As Thiselton observes, "in 1 Corinthians 5–7 Paul envisages either physical union within marriage or celibacy."[36] The alternative to *sexual immorality* is that *each man should have sexual relations with his own wife, and each woman with her own husband.*

31. This seems to be the usage in 2 Chr. 11:21; Isa. 54:1; 1 Esdr. 9:12, 18; Jdt. 10:19; Tob. 3:8; Mark 12:23; Luke 20:28, 33; 1 Cor. 7:12(-13), 29.

32. Cf. H. Hanse, "ἔχω," *TDNT* 2:817 n. 5: "In the expressions γυναῖκα ἔχειν and ἄνδρα ἔχειν, ἔχειν implies more than a legal relationship, but for the most part it is used, not for personal fellowship, but as a technical term for sexual intercourse; even outside marriage one may 'have' a woman or a man." This seems to be the usage in Deut. 28:30; Isa. 13:16; Matt. 22:28; 1 Cor. 5:1.

33. Gk. λαμβάνω: e.g., Gen. 4:19; 6:2; 11:29; 12:19; Mark 12:19, 20; Luke 20:28, 29.

34. The imperatives in this pericope (vv. 2, 3, 5; ἐχέτω; ἐχέτω; ἀποδιδότω; ἀποστερεῖτε) are all present imperatives, consistent with the generally relevant instruction Paul is providing on the subject.

35. The use of the adjective ἴδιος ("one's own"; each one should have *his own* wife), probably also points to a reference to a previously established marriage within which sexual relations are to be continued.

36. Thiselton, 495.

Married people should not get in the habit of refraining from enjoying sexual relations for extended periods "because of the danger that one of the partners might be tempted outside the marriage into fornication." Bluntly realistic, this may jar as a rather low view of the purpose of marriage. According to 7:2, Paul views marriage as a release for sexual desires, "a way of avoiding danger."[37] Certainly the notion that sexual relations within marriage ought to act as a check on immorality is reflected in Paul's Jewish inheritance: for example, "Drink water from your own cistern. . . . rejoice in the wife of your youth. . . . Why should you be infatuated, my son, with a loose woman?" (Prov. 5:15, 18, 20); "Be on your guard against the spirit of immorality. . . . take for yourself a wife" (*Testament of Levi* 9:9-10); and: "Beware, my son, of all immorality. First of all take a wife from among the descendants of your father" (Tob. 4:12).[38] This biblical and Jewish perspective is remarkably different from the Roman view that men were to take wives in order to have legal heirs, while sexual pleasure, if it was to be sought at all, would typically be found outside the marriage. Of course, as noted earlier, the specific occasion for Paul's remarks warns against taking his comments too sweepingly. As Schrage demurs, "We must avoid the misconception that 1 Corinthians 7 provides something like a complete Pauline teaching concerning marriage."[39] Marriage was many things in Paul's thinking. Ephesians 5, for instance, contains a more lofty estimation: "Husbands, love your wives, just as Christ loved the church. . . ." And he would have agreed with Hebrews 13:4: "Marriage should be honored by all." In fact, vv. 4-5 are not actually lewd, but offer a profound definition of marriage as the total giving of yourself to your spouse.

**7:3** To support his comments about the prophylactic effects of a healthy marriage against the dangers of sexual immorality Paul expounds the intimacy and mutuality of marriage. Paul's views were starkly different from his contemporaries who were not Jews or Christians. Even if some of his language in the chapter overlaps with Stoic-Cynic debates concerning the advantages and disadvantages of marriage,[40] the emphasis on sexual gratification stands out as distinctive. Carolyn Osiek and David L. Balch point out that "[i]n surprising contrast to the predominant political, philosophical, and medical focus on generating legitimate children, Paul never refers to procreation, even when discussing Christian heterosexual couples' relationships."[41] Ward explains: "Paul, in effect, redefines marriage as

37. William R. G. Loader, *Sexuality and the Jesus Tradition* (Grand Rapids: Eerdmans, 2005), 155.

38. The two postbiblical Jewish texts use the same word as in 1 Cor. 7:2, πορνεία, for "immorality."

39. Schrage, *Ethics of the New Testament*, 226.

40. See the work of Balch, Wimbush, Yarbrough, and Deming.

41. Carolyn Osiek and David L. Balch, *Families in the New Testament World: Households and House Churches* (Louisville: Westminster/John Knox, 1997), 118.

a context for the mutual satisfying of erotic desires" in contrast to the pagan philosophical idea that "the purpose of marriage was the procreation of legitimate heirs who would inherit and continue the name, property and sacred rites of the family."[42] Indeed, the positive bodily union advocated in vv. 3-5 complements his insistence on abstinence in 5:1-13 and 6:12-20. The quotation of Genesis 2:24 in 6:16 prepares the way for the present discussion; for Paul, marriage is grounded in the goodness of creation. "One flesh," while denoting more than sexual union, does not signify less. As Colin Brown puts it, "Paul sees the normal married life as the divine provision for man's natural needs."[43]

To the Corinthians who would have overly restricted their own married sexual life or that of other members of their community, Paul's response is clear: *The husband should fulfill his marital duty to his wife, and likewise the wife to her husband.* Simply put, married men and women are obligated to have sex with their partners. To press his point Paul uses the language of submission to authority and of debt or robbery in vv. 4 and 5 respectively. The "authority" of which he speaks is that of a master who owns the body of his slave, a thought never far from the passage (see 6:19-20; 7:21-23). Paul's convictions may be traced to Exodus 21:10-11, which concerns the rights of the slave wife.[44] The Law of Moses taught that the husband "shall not diminish her [i.e., his wife's] food, clothing *or her marital rights* [a euphemism for sexual relations]." Instone-Brewer explains: "This passage said that even a slave wife had the right to expect love from her husband, and so the rabbis and Paul deduced that a free wife and a husband also had the right to expect this."[45]

How frequently did Paul's contemporaries think married people should have sex in order to provide their spouse with their marital rights? In *Solon* 20.3 Plutarch (who did not feel that intercourse needed to be restricted to the purpose of procreation but did suggest that men might be expected to find sexual satisfaction with women other than their wives) suggests that even if a wife does not produce children, a husband should have intercourse with her three times per month as a reflection of the "honour and due affection which a husband ought to pay to a virtuous, chaste wife."[46] Jewish tradition took one's marital duty much more seriously. Ac-

42. R. B. Ward, "Musonius and Paul on Marriage," *NTS* 36 (1990), 286-87. Concerning the interpretation of Gen. 2:18-24 in *Jubilees*, and its positive affirmation of sex within marriage, apart from the question of procreation, see William Loader, *Enoch, Levi, and Jubilees on Sexuality: Attitudes Towards Sexuality in the Early Enoch Literature, the Aramaic Levi Document, and the Book of Jubilees* (Grand Rapids: Eerdmans, 2007), 237-44.

43. Colin Brown, "Separate: Divorce, Separation and Re-marriage," in *NIDNTT* 3:536 (cited by Thiselton, 492).

44. The verb used in Exod. 21:10 LXX prohibiting the deprivation of sexual rights (ἀποστερέω) is the same used by Paul in v. 5.

45. Instone-Brewer, *Divorce and Remarriage in the Bible*, 193.

46. Cf. S. B. Pomeroy, *Plutarch's Advice to the Bride and Groom and A Consolation to His Wife* (New York: Oxford University Press, 1999), 54.

cording to Rabbi Eliezer, one's marital duty depended upon one's status or employment: "Men of independent means — every day, workmen — twice a week, ass drivers — once a week, camel drivers — once a month, and sailors — at least once every six months" (*m. Ketubbot* 5:6). The fact that the first two categories are much broader than the last three suggests that in practice most Jewish men were expected to observe their marital duty at least twice a week, although those in specific occupations that would make such a practice impossible were given a special dispensation.

In this context it is important to note that the verse speaks of an obligation to give love, not of the right to demand love.[47] BDAG indicates that the key word[48] here means "to meet a contractual or other obligation." Indeed, as mentioned above, this passage, in contrast with the unilateral idea of "touching," is full of the striking language of reciprocity. The word *likewise,* repeated in v. 4 and a notion developed throughout the chapter, underscores the essential nature of marriage as an equal partnership, at least in the area of sexual relations.

**7:4** Paul offers a cogent explanation of why sexual relations are due in marriage: the spouse's body belongs to his or her partner.[49] A property ethic applied to sexuality was common in the ancient world,[50] including the Old Testament. In Deuteronomy 20:5-7 and 28:30 the acquisition of a house, a vineyard, and a wife are routinely equated. That adultery was considered an offense against sexual property can be seen in Job's assertion that the appropriate punishment of an adulterer would be that the offender's own wife become the servant and sexual property of another (Job 31:9-10). The close proximity of adultery and theft in the Decalogue makes sense in this light (Exod. 20:14-15, 17). Furthermore, incest "uncovers the father's nakedness" (Lev. 18:7-8), and prostitution is a wrong done to the father of the harlot's household, since, being unmarried, she is his property (Lev. 21:9; Deut. 22:13-21). When Paul uses the common expression for a married woman as, literally, "under a man"[51] (Rom. 7:2), he implies the authority and ownership of the husband and reflects the same teaching.[52]

The marked mutuality of Paul's comments (the husband has author-

47. Note that *b. Pesaḥim* 72b deals with the husband's marital duty to provide his wife with sexual pleasure.

48. Gk. ἀποδίδωμι.

49. The main biblical ways of conceiving of sexual ethics are in terms of purity and property. Both permeate Paul's teaching throughout chs. 5–7.

50. Yarbrough surveys the evidence, *Not like the Gentiles: Marriage Rules in the Letters of Paul* (Atlanta: Scholars Press, 1986), 31-63.

51. Gk. ὕπανδρος.

52. Paul's affirmation that the two belong to one another in total mutuality may derive from Gen. 2:24 quoted in the previous chapter (1 Cor. 6:16), "the two will become one flesh." A full quotation of this text is the basis of the statement in Eph. 5:28, "In the same way, husbands ought to love their wives as their own bodies. He who loves his wife loves himself."

ity over[53] his wife's body, and she has authority over his) was, however, revolutionary in the ancient world where patriarchy was the norm. For the husband to have authority over his wife's body was nothing special. In fact, it was understood that the husband had authority over the bodies of virtually all the members of his household (at least those of his wife, children, and household slaves). In fact, the idea that he had authority over all those bodies was reflected in the common understanding that both female and male slaves were subject to the sexual exploitation of the *paterfamilias* (male head of the household).[54] It may well have been due in part to husbands who were tempted to continue to follow through on that understanding that led to concerns within the community about husbands' "touching" women. Paul's following statement affirming the reverse, that "the husband does not have authority over his own body, but the wife does," clearly pointed to a radical and unprecedented restriction on the husband's sexual freedom. It communicates, negatively, his obligation to refrain from engaging in sexual relations with anyone other than his wife and, positively, his obligation to fulfill his marital duty to provide her with sexual pleasure and satisfaction. To our knowledge, the only other place a similar thought is recorded prior to Paul is in the poetic notes of mutual belonging in the Song of Solomon (2:16a; 6:3a; 7:10a): "I am my beloved's and he is mine." Other lines in the Song confirm that such language, though open to abuse, properly belongs to the realm of love and desire. Far from feeling threatened by such sentiments, the female lover swoons, "his desire is for me" (7:10b) and "his banner over me is love" (2:4b).

**7:5** Paul has strongly affirmed the importance of fulfilling sexual responsibilities with respect to one's spouse by maintaining a healthy love life (in part at least) as a prophylactic against sexual immorality. As Corinthian men, especially, adjust to the biblical restriction of sexual relations to those with their spouse, and the leanings of some who might even limit sex to the purpose of procreation, Paul reinforces his point with remarkably forceful language here: *Do not deprive each other.* If v. 3 speaks in general terms of marital dues, v. 5 is even more strident and explicit. The verb translated "deprive"[55] usually means "to cause another to suffer loss by taking away through illicit means" and is translated *"rob, steal, despoil, defraud"* (BDAG; cf. 1 Cor. 6:7-8 TNIV).[56] It is the same verb used in Exodus

53. The Greek word used, ἐξουσιάζω, means "to have the right of control" (BDAG). The TNIV rendering, suggesting that each one *yields* their authority to the other, is weaker than the Greek, which simply says that each spouse has authority over the other's body, rather than that each one has authority over their own body which they (may or may not) choose to yield to the other.

54. See, e.g., Margaret Y. MacDonald, "Slavery, Sexuality and House Churches: A Reassessment of Colossians 3.18–4.1 in Light of New Research on the Roman Family," *NTS* 53 (2007), 94-113; Glancy, *Slavery in Early Christianity,* 67.

55. Gk. ἀποστερέω.

56. BDAG has a softer meaning here: "to prevent someone from having the benefit of

21:10 LXX to prohibit the deprivation of sexual rights. Paul's point (and the point in Exodus) is that to refuse to have relations with one's spouse is to withhold what is properly theirs, just as an employer might "*keep back by fraud* . . . the wages of the laborers who mowed your fields" (Jas. 5:4 NRSV). If today "cheating" refers to extramarital affairs, in Paul's idiom it means depriving your spouse of the sexual relations that are their due. Paul's concerns regarding sexual immorality, an emphasis (or, even more likely, the emphasis) of his earlier letter to the Corinthians (5:9), should not have been understood as in any way supporting an artificial restriction of sexual pleasure within marriage, or a call to refrain from sexual relations with spouses who had had a history of sexual improprieties. Rather, rightly understood, a proper concern with sexual immorality should lead to a greater awareness of a potential danger of failing to provide a spouse with their "conjugal rights."

Having made his point about the need to provide for the sexual needs (and rights) of one's spouse, Paul does allow for limited periods of abstinence. Those who are married must maintain sexual relations "except perhaps in case you may"[57] abstain *by mutual consent and for a time.* The concession is constrained in two ways. First, the decision to refrain from having sex must not be unilateral; it must be an agreed decision between the husband and wife. Literally, it is to be "with a common voice."[58] Intriguingly, Paul's instructions assume that husbands and wives will communicate openly about sex; he was no prude. Again, this sentiment is radically countercultural. In the Greco-Roman world, as the head of the household, the husband was sovereign. To Paul's mind, however, if authority over the husband's body belongs to the wife, and vice versa (v. 4), then any decision regarding those bodies must be consensual. The egalitarian orientation of Paul's instructions here is all the more remarkable in light of the discrepancy in ages between husbands and wives in the Roman world, with wives being significantly younger and less mature (and experienced) than their husbands. For a husband's will to be dependent upon his younger wife's agreement would be quite counterintuitive.[59]

---

someth[ing], *deprive,"* although from examples given in LSJ, M-M, and *EDNT,* it seems clear that it has to do with deprivation of something that people have a right to, and thus the idea of stealing or defrauding is still present.

57. Edwards, 159. Paul's diffidence is expressed by the clause translated in the TNIV as *except perhaps.*

58. Gk. ἐκ συμφώνου. The adjective σύμφωνος means "pert[aining] to being in agreement" (BDAG).

59. Paul probably anticipates that it would be the wife whose interest in refraining from sexual relations for a while would need to be agreed upon by her husband. Collins, 253, suggesting that "sexual asceticism was 'in the air' in first-century Corinth," refers to Juvenal's *Satires* 6.535-37, Ovid's *Amores* 1.8.74, and Propertius's *Elegies* 4.5.28-34. But those texts all speak of a woman's desire to refrain from engaging in sex for a few days, and the use of excuses (such as the arrival of special holy days, a headache, etc.) to achieve that goal. In the latter two texts the suggestion is made that the occasional night's delay will heighten

Secondly, the withdrawal must not be permanent, but only *for a time.* We should take our cue from Paul's diffident tone in this verse and throughout the chapter and refrain from speculating concerning the specific span of time Paul may have had in mind. As Baumert argues, *for a time* may simply mean "according to the situation."[60] Nothing in the passage compromises the integrity of individual marriages. As Furnish puts it, Paul's concession is "an allowance made empathetically, out of concern, with constructive good will."[61]

The purpose of the temporary and harmonious abstinence is *that you may devote yourselves to prayer.* Periodic abstinence for the purpose of prayer in v. 5 brings to mind similar voluntary sexual abstinence before cultic activities in Judaism (e.g., Exod. 19:15; Lev. 15:18; 1 Sam. 21:4-6) and finds a specific parallel in the *Testament of Naphtali* 8:8: "there is a time for having intercourse with one's wife, and a time to abstain for the purpose of prayer." Some have conjectured that in v. 5 Paul reveals an underlying concern that sexual activity in and of itself raises purity issues of a religious nature. But as Garland contends, "Paul does not say that sexual contact makes one impure or that it impedes spiritual activity."[62]

Rather than concerns about purity motivating Paul's advice, it is more likely, given the emphasis on the importance of respecting one's spouse's sexual rights, that the point is that only the most serious situations, those requiring special dedication to extended prayer, may be expected to impinge on their fulfillment. Paul acknowledges that occasions may arise when it is appropriate to retreat in prayer, and, if acceptable to both spouses, pause from all potential distractions, including one's normal sexual obligations. There is a textual variant which results in the reading "that you may devote yourselves to fasting and to prayer."[63] While the text is certainly not original (Metzger believes that it is an interpolation, "introduced in the interest of asceticism"[64]), it may point to an accurate interpretation in the sense that refraining from sexual relations was understood to be a form of fasting, that is, refraining from some good, God-given blessing as a sign of one's greater concern with some issue being brought before God. In this view marital sex is not seen as a necessary evil, or hindrance, but as a blessing that may be given up under special circumstances.

---

a husband's (or lover's) desire for sex. While these texts certainly do not reflect a commitment to asceticism, celibacy, or a kind of serious abstinence like that which is routinely attributed to the Corinthians, they do point to a kind of unilateral (and deceptive) approach to temporary sexual abstinence that would not fit with Paul's instructions.

60. N. Baumert, *Ehelosigkeit und Ehe in Herrn: Eine Neuinterpretation von 1 Kor 7* (Wurzburg: Echter, 1984), 27-28. BDAG points out that πρὸς καιρόν means "for a limited time" and perhaps also "for the present moment."

61. Furnish, *The Moral Teaching of Paul,* 35.

62. Garland, 262.

63. Supported by ℵ², 𝔐, and *sy,* among others (see Metzger, *Textual Commentary,* 488).

64. Metzger, *Textual Commentary,* 488.

When it comes to purity, it is not sex that concerns Paul, but sexual immorality. Recalling the advice of v. 2, Paul shores up his directive that the concession to abstinence be short-lived with a warning about the temptation to *porneia: Then come together again so that Satan will not tempt you because of your lack of self-control.* Jews like Paul customarily believed that Satan tempted people to commit acts of sexual immorality (CD iv 15-17; *1 Enoch* 69:4; *Testament of Reuben* 6:3). Thiselton explains the dynamics Paul feared: "When voluntary consent begins to degenerate into frustration, . . . the whole experience [of undistracted prayer] becomes counter-productive."[65] Paul has the realistic concern that abstinence may make the Corinthians susceptible to sexual temptation, the solution to which, if you are married, is to "drink water from your own cistern." The word for *lack of self-control*[66] appears in the New Testament elsewhere only in Matthew 23:25, where it is translated "self-indulgence." Self-restraint, as becomes clear in 1 Corinthians 8–10, is a key ethical principle that the apostle commends in the letter.

**7:6** Paul makes it clear that his approval of a married couple's abstaining for the purpose of unhurried prayer is a yielding to special circumstances: *I say this as a concession, not as a command.* The antecedent of *this,* that which Paul allows but does not command, is best understood as v. 5b. In other words, the *concession,* what Paul somewhat reluctantly allows, refers to a temporary agreed abstinence from sex.[67] For Paul, a full marriage relationship is the norm, from which any divergence may take place only in exceptional conditions and for a limited time.

Paul is not normally shy to exercise authority (e.g., 7:12, 25; 14:37; cf. Phlm. 8), nor does he shrink from presenting himself as a model to be emulated (cf. 4:6; 9:24-27; 11:1; 1 Thess. 1:6; 2 Thess. 3:7-9). The word for *command* that Paul uses refers to a specific and authoritative directive and might even be translated "decree."[68] In the New Testament it appears only in Paul's letters: three times with reference to a divine command (Rom. 16:26; 1 Tim. 1:1; Tit. 1:3); three times in a context where Paul backs away from giving an order (1 Cor. 7:6, 25; 2 Cor. 8:8); and only once in a positive sense of human commands (Tit. 2:15). 1 Corinthians, and especially chapter 7, exposes the caricature of Paul as a severe authoritarian figure intent on establishing uniformity and enforcing compliance. The apostle recognizes

65. Thiselton, 509.

66. Gk. ἀκρασία.

67. The precise antecedent is debated by commentators. See Schrage, 2:67-72; Thiselton, 510-12. Verses 2-5 in fact contain a number of specific commands: each husband is to "have" his own wife and each wife her own husband (7:2); the partners are to fulfill their marital duty (7:3); and they must not deprive each other (7:5a). Also decisive is the fact that the singular demonstrative pronoun most naturally refers to a single concession. Winter's argument that *this* looks forward (Bruce W. Winter, "1 Corinthians 7:6-7: A Caveat and a Framework for 'The Sayings' in 7:8-24," *TynBul* 48 [1997]: 57-65) is a conceivable but unnecessary hypothesis given that 7:5b adequately explains the linguistic and exegetical data.

68. Gk. ἐπιταγή; cf. BDAG.

that nonmoral questions like the sex life of married couples cannot be regulated deontologically; he offers advice and counsel, not rules and casuistry.

**7:7** It is possible that Paul's own celibacy was held up as a model of sexual restraint by some Corinthians. It is also possible that some felt that there was a tension between Paul's personal lifestyle and his affirmation of marriage. Either way, Paul is concerned not to allow his example to be misused. He does not hide his personal preference for celibacy. Indeed, he admits that his own "ability of living without marriage"[69] has its advantages for the service of Christ (see 7:32-35; 9:5): *I wish that all of you were as I am.* The language of "wishing" or individual preference, as Thiselton explains, is "personal, not moral."[70] His assertion may be compared to those in Christian ministry "wishing" that all people were as they are. Such sentiments commend that person's circumstances and calling (such as that of ministers or the celibate) without suggesting necessarily that there is anything "wrong" with that of those in other situations (such as those not in ministry or those who are married).

As the rest of the verse indicates, in Paul's mind both the single and the married states are equally valid and blessed by God: *But each of you has your own gift from God; one has this gift, another has that.* The general thought may be compared to Matthew 19, where Jesus responds to the disciples' assertion that it is better not to marry with the caution: "Not everyone can accept this word, but only those to whom it has been given" (Matt. 19:11). "Gifts" are a key theme in 1 Corinthians; the same term[71] appears in 1:7 and then receives concentrated attention in chapters 12–14 (see 12:4, 9, 28, 30, 31). Although "gift" can have a broad meaning for Paul, ranging from the general benefits of salvation to specific endowments, two constants are evident across the usage: a gift is freely and graciously bestowed by God; and gifts are given by God for the building up of the body of Christ.[72]

In v. 7 the *gift from God* is not celibacy itself,[73] especially conceived as a perpetual state. To start with, Paul's own marital status may in fact not have been "single." Since from ancient Jewish sources we know that Jewish men devoted to the study of Torah in pharisaic or rabbinic circles were almost invariably married (cf. *m. Yebamot* 6:6; *b. Yebamot* 62b-63b, *b. Qiddušin* 29b; *b. Sanhedrin* 36b), it is quite possible that Paul the rabbi would have been married at an earlier point in his life.[74] Furthermore, the states of celi-

69. Calvin, 141.

70. Thiselton, 154.

71. Gk. χάρισμα.

72. Schrage, 2:73.

73. The issue is not whether an individual has some elusive gift of celibacy, but whether he or she can concentrate on living a life worthy of the gospel to the glory of God without being distracted by sexual desires.

74. Collins, 260, thinks it "likely that Paul would have been married at some point in his life." Cf. Joachim Jeremias, "War Paulus Witwer?" *ZNW* 25 (1926), 310-12; Hays, 119. If he were once married, it seems that he is most likely now a widower, for if he were sepa-

bacy/singleness and marriage are common gifts of providence to all creation. When Paul talks of "gifts" in his letters, he means those having reference not to creation but to the new creation of the kingdom and the gospel, gifts that carry responsibilities specifically to God and God's people. The gifts that Paul has in mind in v. 7 refer to the contentedness contributing to a life of service rather than to a lifelong calling to "eunuch-hood" (cf. Matt 19:12). Thiselton explains: "[T]he parallel [in the words *one has this gift, another has that*] is not celibacy versus marriage, but the gift of a positive attitude which makes the most of the freedoms of celibacy without frustration, and the positive attitude which caringly provides the responsibilities, intimacies, love, and 'dues' of marriage while equally living out the gospel."[75]

That Paul's "gift" concerns the capacity to concentrate on the work of the gospel without being distracted by sexual desires, whether unexpressed, as in the case of the celibate, or expressed, as for those married, is suggested by what follows in v. 9.

*b. For Unmarried and Widows: Stay Unmarried, 7:8-9*

*8Now to the unmarried and the widows I say: It is good for them to stay unmarried, as I do. 9But if they cannot control themselves, they should marry, for it is better to marry than to burn with passion.*

**7:8** Having counseled the married couples in the church to maintain sexual relations, Paul moves on to give advice to a different group: *Now to the unmarried and the widows I say.* In referring to *the unmarried* Paul may have had widowers in particular in mind.[76] The word[77] he used may be employed to refer to any person who is not presently married, including those who are single (never married), separated, divorced, or widowed (cf. 7:11, where it has a divorced person in view).[78] Two reasons in particular have been suggested in support of the idea that *widowers* is the best understanding of the word in v. 8: first, the Greek word for "widower"[79] was seldom used. Also, throughout the chapter Paul discusses situations involving men and women in "mutuality";[80] *widowers* is the expected complement of

rated or divorced it would surely have emerged in his discussion of these issues in 1 Corinthians 7. For evidence that some Jewish leaders in the prerabbinic period were committed to celibacy, see John P. Meier, *A Marginal Jew: Rethinking the Historical Jesus,* vol. 1, *The Roots of the Problem and the Person* (The Anchor Bible Reference Library; New York: Doubleday, 1991), 336-41 (cf. Martin Hengel, *The Pre-Christian Paul* [London: SCM, 1991], 67).

75. Thiselton, 513-14.

76. Cf. Fee, Hays, Collins, Schrage, and Deming, *Paul on Marriage and Celibacy.*

77. Gk. ἄγαμος.

78. The other two occurrences are to an unmarried man (7:32) and an unmarried woman (7:34).

79. Gk. χῆρος. Using "unmarried" to refer to widowers is analogous to Greek's using "man" and "woman" to refer to husband and wife respectively.

80. Fee, 228.

*and the widows,* just as Paul addresses males and females in similar circumstances throughout the chapter (7:2-3, 4, 12-13, 14-15, 27-28, 32-34).[81] Neither argument is convincing. For starters, although the word may be used to refer to people of any subcategory of single person, there is no evidence that it ever means "widower," "divorcé," "never married," and the like.[82] Thus, in v. 11 it refers to a divorced or separated woman but simply means "unmarried" (and is consistently translated "unmarried" or "single"). And while the context makes it clear that Paul is thinking of a divorced or separated woman in that verse, the context in v. 8 is ambiguous, as reflected by those translations and commentaries that suggest Paul has unmarried people in mind here.[83] It may be that Paul is thinking about potential couples where one of the potential spouses is a widow. That is, he may be thinking of widows and their suitors.[84]

It is not actually the case that Paul always deals in parallel terms with men and women in each category discussed in this chapter. In vv. 36-38 Paul addresses the struggle of the engaged man who is unsure about whether he should marry his fiancée without addressing the same problem from the side of the engaged woman, and in vv. 39-40 he discusses the situation of a widow without addressing widowers. In fact, as pointed out in the introduction to this section, we probably have a case of an A-B, A′-B′ parallel structure in which Paul addresses married people (7:1-7) and then unmarried people and widows (7:8-9) and then goes back and addresses each of these groups again (married people in vv. 10-16, and then unmarried people and widows in vv. 25-38 and 39-40, respectively). Garland follows Schrage in suggesting that Paul "may have highlighted their case simply because there were more widows than widowers and they faced more serious economic problems by remaining single."[85] The advice Paul gives

81. Only in 7:10 is the female addressed first; see below.

82. The failure to distinguish between denotation and reference is a common interpretive error. See John Lyons, *Linguistic Semantics: An Introduction* (Cambridge: Cambridge University Press, 1995), 77-82; Moises Silva, *Biblical Words and Their Meaning: An Introduction to Lexical Semantics* (Grand Rapids: Zondervan, 1983), 103-8; Peter Cotterell and Max Turner, *Linguistics and Biblical Interpretation* (Downers Grove, IL: InterVarsity Press, 1989), 82-90.

83. See most English versions and Lightfoot, Robertson and Plummer, Barrett, Héring, Witherington, and Thiselton.

84. This would be consistent with our interpretation of vv. 25-38, where the topic introduced as that of "virgins" actually deals more with actual or potential suitors (or fiancés) of virgins. Although there were divorcées and other single people in the Roman world, the three main categories of adult women mentioned in the sources (probably considered the most honorable women) are married women, widows, and virgins: "It seems that the axiom voiced in the mid-second century B.C. by a slave in Plautus's *Curculio* still held in Augustan Rome: 'Love whatever you want, as long as you stay away from married ladies, widows, virgins, young men and free boys'" (Plautus, *Curculio* 35–38; cited by John R. Clarke, *Looking at Lovemaking: Constructions of Sexuality in Roman Art, 100 B.C.-A.D. 250* (Berkeley: University of California Press, 2001), 84. See also Plutarch, *Roman Questions* 289A; Philo, *On the Special Laws* 2:30; 3:26; *Virtues* 114; Josephus, *Antiquities* 3.277.

85. Garland, 272, referencing Schrage, 2:94.

in vv. 8-9 is elaborated upon and reinforced when he returns to discuss the unmarried and widows again in vv. 25-40.

Paul's statement to the unmarried and widows that *"It is good . . . to stay unmarried"* does not primarily reflect agreement with the Corinthian slogan quoted in 7:1, but his own practice *(as I do)* and recommendation. He agrees with the Corinthian slogan that many kinds of sexual relationships (not merely adultery as understood in his context) are inappropriate. Furthermore, he indicates that for many people it may be preferable to refrain from marriage and sex altogether, as he does. As Thiselton explains, as in 7:7a, Paul's counsel here "is not a comparative evaluation in terms of any negative entailment for others."[86] He is not saying that it is wrong for the widowed to marry, as 7:39-40 confirm (cf. "free to marry"), but only that in his view it is better to remain as they are. The apostle's counsel in 7:25-38 fills out Paul's reasons: staying unmarried is preferable because of the "present crisis" (7:25-28), because of the end of the world (7:29-31), and because of the distractions of married life (7:32-35). Notwithstanding these reasons, Paul allows those unmarried the freedom to choose whether to get married or not (7:36-38). The following verse suggests Paul is responding to normal "red-blooded" Corinthian men and women who are not prepared to abstain from sexual relations and adopt a life of celibacy.

**7:9** Paul's advice in v. 8 comes with an important rider: *But if they cannot control themselves, they should marry.*[87] The lack of self-control Paul refers to is not necessarily some form of sexual immorality, but may only be the struggle with erotic desires. If sexual desire is a chronic distraction and temptation,[88] disrupting a life lived out for the gospel, Paul advocates marriage. If Paul's preference for singleness is expressed tentatively, *they should marry* is an unequivocal imperative.

The reason Paul thinks that those who feel the compulsion of sexual desire should get married is given in v. 9b: *for it is better to marry than to burn with passion.* Hays explains: "Here again the specter of *porneia* looms in the background. Paul is concerned that [unmarried believers] might find themselves lured into illicit sexual activity."[89] This is the same reasoning as in 7:5b, where Paul insisted that married couples maintain sexual relations on a regular basis so as to avoid sexual "temptation." The word for "self-control"[90] that is used in 7:9a appears again in 9:25, where Paul models the

86. Thiselton, 516.

87. *They should marry* is an aorist imperative (γαμησάτωσαν) since Paul is describing the proper response to a specific situation.

88. The problem of sexual passions was a constant concern for Greco-Roman and early Jewish writing. Two prime examples are Plato's *Laws,* which has an extended section dedicated to a discussion of ways to keep young men from getting caught up in sexual desires (8.835-842), and 4 Maccabees, which is also dedicated to the topic of the mastery of the passions, this time through devout reason (see 4 Macc. 1:1).

89. Hays, 119.

90. Gk. ἐγκρατεύομαι.

"strict training" of an athlete for the sake of the gospel. A couple whose physical attraction has become so powerful that they cannot live for God and are at risk of *porneia* ought to conclude that they do not have Paul's gift (7:7) and should get married.

To *burn with passion* is literally "to burn," prompting the suggestion by some commentators that Paul is referring to the Day of Judgment.[91] In this case v. 9 would be saying that it is better to get married than to commit sexual immorality and face the fires of hell. Paul, it is thought, is alluding to 1 Corinthians 3:15 and the fires of judgment, and 6:9 where sexual sins lead to being excluded from the kingdom. Against this interpretation, Alexander has shown that "burning" was a widespread metaphor for the forces of erotic passion in both Jewish and pagan sources.[92] The context of 7:1-8, which deals entirely with sex, and the parallel with 1 Corinthians 7:5b favor taking it in this sense. What distinguishes Paul's use of the image over against the pagan sources is that "the fire is not to be doused by fleeting, illicit sexual encounters or by grim repression of natural sexual desire,"[93] as in various pagan sources, but by getting married and having sex with your spouse.[94] In our comments on v. 1 we suggested that the Corinthian slogan referred to in 7:1 ("it is good for a man not to touch a woman") had in mind sexual relations that were incited and motivated by erotic passion rather than an intent to reproduce.[95] Paul's reference here to the problem of unmarried people burning with passion suggests that the Corinthians may well have mentioned that specific problem in their letter to him. Paul clearly does not share the late Stoic view, accepted by the church fathers who attributed it to him, that sex was to be engaged in only for the purpose of procreation.[96]

### *c. For Christian Married Couples: Do Not Divorce, 7:10-11*

*[10]To the married I give this command (not I, but the Lord): A wife must not separate from her husband. [11]But if she does, she must remain unmarried or else be reconciled to her husband. And a husband must not divorce his wife.*

**7:10-11** In response to further questions from Corinth likely posed to him in their letter (see 7:1), Paul turns his attention back to the married

91. For example, Bruce, 68; Snyder, 97.

92. L. A. Alexander, "'Better to Marry than to Burn': St. Paul and the Greek Novel," in R. F. Hock et al., *Ancient Fiction and Early Christian Narrative* (SBLSymS 6; Atlanta: Scholars Press, 1998), 235-56. In Jewish/biblical tradition see Prov. 6:27-28; Sir. 9:8; *Testament of Joseph* 2:2; Philo, *On the Decalogue* 122; *On the Special Laws* 3:209.

93. Garland, 275.

94. Cf. the advice to younger widows in 1 Tim. 5:14.

95. See the discussion there and the more detailed evidence given in Ciampa, "Revisiting the Euphemism in 1 Corinthians 7:1."

96. Cf., e.g., Augustine, *The Good of Marriage;* Clement of Alexandria, *Miscellanies* 2:23; 3:1.

couples within the church: *To the married.*[97] The most common mirror reading of this chapter suggests that some of these in Corinth were advocating celibacy in marriage and that here Paul is responding to some of the anti-sex persuasion who were going a step further, seeking to be celibate by simply divorcing their partners. Although we know of a few Cynic philosophers who divorced their wives based on their strongly held (and minority) view that marriage was an excessive burden, most people divorced their spouses in order to marry someone else, and there is no reason to think the Corinthians were acting any differently. In fact, Paul's directive in v. 11 would have little or no dissuasive power if the woman's intention was in fact to remain celibate and unmarried.[98] It could very well dissuade someone from divorcing their husband, however, if that divorce was being sought in order to marry someone else.[99]

A mirror reading that attends more to the fact that Paul is responding to the letter written to him by the Corinthians (7:1) after they received his letter warning them not to associate with sexually immoral people (5:9) may point in a more specific direction. According to the standard Jewish and Christian opinion, Gentiles were in general sexually immoral people. Philo places this view on the lips of Joseph: "Other nations are permitted after the fourteenth year to deal without interference with harlots and strumpets and all those who make a traffic of their bodies, but with us a courtesan is not even permitted to live, and death is the penalty appointed for women who ply this trade. But before lawful union we know no mating with other women, but come as virgin men to virgin maidens. The end we seek in wedlock is not pleasure but the begetting of lawful children."[100] In Corinth wives who knew that their husbands had a history of sexual immorality may have wondered whether or not Paul expected them to aban-

97. *The married* represents a perfect active participle (γεγαμηκόσιν, from γαμέω), a fine example of the perfect tense expressing a present state — here the state of marriage. David Instone-Brewer, *Divorce and Remarriage in the Bible: The Social and Literary Context* (Grand Rapids: Eerdmans, 2002), 200, argues that "to the rest" in v. 12 should be translated, "But concerning other matters" (rather than other persons), and that consequently vv. 11-12 apply to mixed marriages as well. However, the parallel plural dative constructions translated "to the unmarried" (v. 8), "to the married" (v. 10), and "to the rest" (v. 13) point to Paul addressing three distinct groups and support the conclusion that vv. 11-12 concern Christian married couples.

98. So also Garland, 283 n. 11.

99. The incestuous marriage between Herod Antipas and Herodias that was so severely criticized by John the Baptist (Mark 6:17-18; Matt. 14:3-4; Luke 3:19) and subsequently cost him his life was one that was entered into only after they had each divorced their prior spouses in order to marry each other. That Jesus describes divorce and remarriage as adultery (Mark 10:11-12; Matt. 5:32; 19:9; Luke 16:18) and that in the Sermon on the Mount he discusses this issue immediately after warning that "anyone who looks at a woman lustfully has already committed adultery with her in his heart" (Matt. 5:28) may reflect this background in which divorce and remarriage frequently served as a way of committing legalized adultery.

100. Philo, *On the Life of Joseph* 43 (LCL).

don their husbands. In 6:11 Paul admitted that some of them used to be guilty of sexual immorality including specific behaviors as adulterers and those who engaged in homosexual acts, but God had washed and sanctified them, so that they were no longer to be thought of (or acting) in those ways. In 7:14 Paul will refer to the sanctification of unbelieving spouses of believers as part of his argument in favor of honoring and maintaining those marriages. In both cases the references to sanctification are probably intended, in part, to explain why Paul's letter about avoiding sexually immoral people should not be taken as an argument in favor of divorcing one's husband The fact that Paul addresses wives first in 7:10-11 suggests that it was a woman (or women) instigating the divorce(s) in Corinth; elsewhere in the chapter Paul gives instruction in the order males and females (7:2-3, 4, 12-13, 14-15, 27-28, 32-34).

Unlike the question of whether the widowed ought to marry in 7:8-9, Paul's response in 7:10-11 is sharp and direct: *I give this command.*[101] Giving a "charge" or "order" recalls Paul's tone in addressing incest, lawsuits, and prostitution in chapters 5–6. Divorce is a moral question rather than an issue of prudence. The reason he can be so uncompromising is signaled in two short phrases: *not I, but the Lord.* Paul's prohibition of divorce for Christian married couples is based on the teaching of Jesus, which was later preserved in Mark 10:2-12/Luke 16:18. Barrett thinks that Paul cites the words of Jesus here because they disagree with teaching found in the Old Testament.[102] Hence, Paul opposes incest, lawsuits, and prostitution because these activities are opposed by Scripture, and divorce because of the teaching of Jesus. However, to label it a departure from Old Testament teaching is somewhat misleading; for while Deuteronomy 24:1-4 presupposes the legitimacy of divorce, other texts disallow it under certain circumstances (Deut. 22:19, 28-29; Mal. 2:15-16). Jesus' teaching on divorce is presented as the authoritative interpretation of Deuteronomy 24:1-4,[103] and Paul's appeal to the teaching of Jesus shows that the Old Testament and the Lord's teaching (which frequently consists of such scriptural interpretations) are both norms for Christian ethics.[104]

101. Gk. παραγγέλλω, "to make an announcement about someth[ing] that must be done, *give* orders, *command, instruct, direct*" (BDAG). The verb highlights the (real or supposed) authority of the one who is the subject of the verb, who in the New Testament includes Jesus, the Jewish authorities, God, magistrates, Paul, and Timothy. Paul generally uses the verb with respect to his own commands/orders to the church or to Timothy, although he uses it four times in 1 Timothy with respect to Timothy's own responsibility to direct the affairs of the church (1 Tim. 1:3; 4:11; 5:7; 6:17).

102. Barrett, 162; cf. Rosner, *Paul, Scripture and Ethics,* 167.

103. See Instone-Brewer, *Divorce and Remarriage in the Bible,* 133-88.

104. Clearly, various sayings of Jesus were known in the churches that Paul founded or visited. In this instance Paul probably has in mind teaching that ended up recorded in Mark 10:9, 11-12: "What therefore God has joined together, let not man put asunder. . . . Whoever divorces his wife and marries another, commits adultery against her; and if she divorces her husband and marries another, she commits adultery" (cf. Luke 16:18; Matt. 5:32). Other

That Paul does not quote the relevant sayings of Jesus here does not betray a lack of interest. On the contrary, as Dunn argues, the allusive character of Paul's reference shows that Paul and the Corinthians were well aware of the teaching of Jesus on this subject and that its authority can be taken for granted: "the allusion implies an accepted authority."[105] What is implicit throughout the letter on every subject is made explicit here; the Corinthians are to live under Christ's lordship.

Regardless of the particular circumstances in Corinth, Paul "articulates a general norm in vv. 10-11":[106] *A wife must not separate from her husband. . . . And a husband must not divorce his wife.*[107] Contrary to how they are used today, the verbs "to separate" and "to divorce" here refer to the same thing, namely, the disavowing of the marriage. Mark 10:9 uses "separate" in the sense of divorce: "Therefore what God has joined together, let no one separate." And in 1 Corinthians 7:15 and 13 respectively they describe the same action. In the Greco-Roman world men and women could divorce their partners by enacting what has been called a "divorce by separation,"[108] that is, simply by telling their partner to leave or by leaving themselves. Divorce was very common, and probably most marriages ended before the death of a partner.[109] Instone-Brewer observes that "Graeco-Roman marriage certificates were worded as though they expected the marriage to end in divorce, not death."[110] One funeral inscription from the first century B.C. commented on an exception: "Uncommon are marriages which last so long, brought to an end by death, not broken apart by divorce; for it was our happy lot that it should be prolonged to the 41st year without estrangement."[111] In this context, Paul's decree, on the authority of the Lord Jesus, that Christian married couples who were former Gentiles should stay married is highly countercultural.

Further evidence that Paul is addressing a wife (or wives) in the congregation who is seeking to end their marriage(s) is given by v. 11a: *But if she does, she must remain unmarried or else be reconciled*[112] *to her husband.* That

---

appeals to the authority of Jesus in the letter include 9:14 (cf. Luke 10:7/Matt. 10:10) and 11:24-25 (cf. Luke 22:19-20). Allusions also appear in 13:2 (cf. Mark 11:23) and 13:3 (cf. Mark 10:21).

105. James D. G. Dunn, *1 Corinthians* (New Testament Guides; Sheffield: Sheffield Academic Press, 1995), 101.

106. Hays, 119.

107. It seems that vv. 11a-b may be functioning as a parenthesis (as suggested by ESV, NRSV, NAB, NET).

108. Instone-Brewer, *Divorce and Remarriage in the Bible*, 190 and ch. 4.

109. This is even more striking given the fact that women married very young, contraception and abortion were dangerous, and one in five pregnancies was fatal (Thiselton, 523).

110. Instone-Brewer, *Divorce and Remarriage in the Bible*, 191.

111. G. H. R. Horsley, ed., *New Documents*, 3:33-36.

112. Reconciliation here implies the restoration or reassertion of the marriage relationship. This is the only "mundane" use of reconciliation language in the New Testament

Paul gives the woman only two options[113] and bars her from marrying someone else is reminiscent of the reasoning in Mark 10:11-12, where divorcing one's partner is judged to be a legalized form of adultery. As pointed out above, this makes it unlikely that the woman would have been motivated by a desire to be celibate and abstain from sex. Paul makes it clear that whatever her motivation she is not to use her divorce as a way of marrying someone else. Ever the realist, having reckoned with the possibility of her not obeying the Lord's command, Paul repeats his wishes in v. 11b to make it clear, with customary reference to the other gender, that the continuance of the marriage is the goal: *And a husband must not divorce his wife.*

The question arises whether the commands of vv. 10b and 11b are meant to be taken as an absolute prohibition of divorce for Christians. A long history of interpretation has viewed them in that way. The most thorough examination of Paul's teaching in light of the relevant scriptural, Jewish, and Greco-Roman background is that of David Instone-Brewer. He shows that Paul is clearly dealing with Greco-Roman "divorce by separation," which was a "no fault" type of divorce, and that Paul does not approve of it any more than Jesus approved of the Hillelite version which permitted a man to divorce his wife for any reason that might occur to him.[114] In the context, Paul is clearly dealing with people who are asking about whether they should divorce their spouses on grounds that Paul considers unacceptable, and thus he tells them that they should not do so. Paul stands with Jesus in holding that divorce may be justified only where one partner clearly manifests a radical refusal to respect one's marital commitments and maintain the fundamental integrity of the marriage.[115]

---

(although there is one other in the alternative reading of Acts 12:22 found in MS D). Paul uses the noun (καταλλαγή; Rom. 5:11; 11:15; 2 Cor. 5:18-19), the verb (καταλλάσσω; Rom. 5:10; 2 Cor. 5:18, 19, 20), and the related verb (ἀποκαταλλάσσω; Eph. 2:16; Col. 1:20-21) of humans being reconciled to God and of Jews and Gentiles being reconciled in the body of Christ. Paul's use of the aorist passive imperative here (καταλλαγήτω) is interesting, but *TLG* indicates that present imperatival forms of this verb do not appear until the fourth century A.D., suggesting little should be made of the aorist here. This probably reflects a standard idiomatic usage of the verb or an intuitive understanding of the relationship between lexical and verbal aspect (see Fanning, *Verbal Aspect in New Testament Greek,* 340-79, for a full discussion of exceptions to the rule). In fact, all but one of the following imperatives in this chapter are present imperatives, consistent with the understanding that he is providing generally relevant moral instruction rather than teaching that is expected to be applied to just the particular case at hand. The one exception is the aorist χρῆσαι in v. 21, but *TLG* points out that the verb does not appear in the second-person singular present middle imperative in all of Greek literature, suggesting that Paul's use of the aorist in that verse is also unremarkable.

113. Cf. Collins, 269-70. The command to remain unmarried both eliminates the most common motivation for divorce and safeguards a necessary condition for the restoration of the marriage.

114. Instone-Brewer, *Divorce and Remarriage in the Bible,* 199-200 (see 189-212).

115. See Instone-Brewer, *Divorce and Remarriage in the Bible,* 196. Instone-Brewer's argument that divorce may be justified in cases where material support, emotional support,

### *d. For Christians Married to Unbelievers: Stay Married, 7:12-16*

*[12]To the rest I say this (I, not the Lord): If any brother has a wife who is not a believer and she is willing to live with him, he must not divorce her. [13]And if a woman has a husband who is not a believer and he is willing to live with her, she must not divorce him. [14]For the unbelieving husband has been sanctified through his wife, and the unbelieving wife has been sanctified through her believing husband. Otherwise your children would be unclean, but as it is, they are holy.*

*[15]But if the unbeliever leaves, let it be so. The brother or sister is not bound in such circumstances; God has called us to live in peace. [16]How do you know, wife, whether you will save your husband? Or, how do you know, husband, whether you will save your wife?*

**7:12-13** Paul gives advice to another group in the church in Corinth, those married to unbelievers, concerning the question of divorce: *To the rest* [of those married] *I say this.* Religiously mixed marriages represented a serious problem in the ancient world where household solidarity and male headship were assumed. Plutarch's "Advice to Bride and Groom" makes the point: "A wife ought not to make friends of her own, but to enjoy her husband's friends in common with him. The gods are the first and most important friends. Wherefore it is becoming for a wife to worship and to know only the gods that her husband believes in."[116] Likewise, Jews were to marry only those belonging to their religion (Deut. 7:3; Neh. 13:25), and there was even biblical precedent for divorcing pagans (Ezra 10:3, 19). In the postbiblical *Joseph and Aseneth* (8:5-7) Joseph gives some reasons for this thinking: "It is not fitting for a man who worships God, who will bless with his mouth the living God and eat the blessed bread of life and drink a blessed cup of immortality, . . . to kiss a strange woman who will bless with her mouth dead and dumb idols and eat from their table. . . . Likewise, for a woman who worships God it is not fitting to kiss a strange man, because this is an abomination before the Lord God."[117]

In this light it is not surprising that some believers in Corinth were wondering whether to continue in their marriages to non-Christian partners. The problem had been caused by the intrusion of the gospel. Ominously, Matthew records Jesus as having said: "I did not come to bring

---

or marital rights are withheld is susceptible to a dangerously broad interpretation including any complaints regarding the inadequacy of the emotional, sexual, or material support provided by one's spouse. Wives and husbands are not well served by either overly lax or overly restrictive interpretations of biblical teachings on divorce and remarriage, and it is incumbent upon Christian leaders to provide counsel that takes seriously both God's commitment to the preservation of marriage wherever possible and his commitment to the protection of the vulnerable (those who continue to suffer due to the hardness of human hearts).

116. Plutarch, *Moralia* 140D.

117. Cited in Garland, 284-85.

peace but a sword. . . . your enemies will be the members of your own household" (Matt. 10:34-36). Some Corinthians may have raised concerns about purity, arguing that the believer is defiled by sexual contact with a pagan (or even Jewish) spouse. They would have been aware of Paul's own intense disdain for idolatrous partnerships, as reflected in his teaching in 2 Corinthians 6:14–7:1 ("Do not be yoked together with unbelievers. . . . what does a believer have in common with an unbeliever? What agreement is there between the temple of God and idols?"). They may have appealed to the logic of defilement inherent in Paul's instructions concerning the incestuous man in 1 Corinthians 5 and the prostitute in 1 Corinthians 6: "a little yeast leavens the whole batch of dough" (5:6), and union with a prostitute defiles Christ (6:15-17). Since Paul is responding to the letter the Corinthians wrote him in response to his warning to them about not associating with sexually immoral people (1 Cor. 5:9-10), some may have been concerned that sexual relations with unbelieving (and thus presumably sexually immoral[118]) spouses were illegitimate (and perhaps fell under the category of "touching"; see on 7:1), leading them to wonder if they should refrain from sexual relations with, or even divorce, those spouses.[119] Wouldn't the impurity of the unbelieving spouse infect their Christian husband or wife? And where do the children stand? If on some subjects we feel impatient with the Corinthians, on this score their concerns are perfectly understandable within a Jewish and Christian worldview.

Unfortunately for Paul this issue was not addressed by the teaching of Jesus. In some respects Paul's Gentile mission was more complicated than the ministry of Jesus, which was primarily to Jews. The apostle must draw on other resources: *I say this, I, not the Lord.* What Paul has to "say" here, however, is not his "take-it-or-leave-it" opinion. Ultimately, his apostolic judgments derive their authority from Jesus even when a saying of the Lord is not directly involved (7:40; 14:37; 2 Cor. 10:8 and 13:10: "the authority the Lord gave me for building you up"). 1 Corinthians 14:34 and 15:51 show that the verb "to say" may introduce an authoritative word.[120] In this case, Paul's teaching reflects his own unpacking and extended application ("one is tempted to say his own *halakah*") of the Lord's command.[121]

Paul's advice to both men *(he must not divorce her)* and women *(she must not divorce him)* believers in mixed marriages is the same: religious differences are no reason to end the marriage. Thiselton points out the

118. It is remarkable that in 6:9-11 Paul talks about the sanctification that believers have received, so that they no longer fall under the category of sexually immoral people, and he will use the same verb two more times in 7:14 in explaining why Christian spouses need not divorce their pagan spouses.

119. Note that if Corinthians were arguing for celibacy as a general principle it would not seem necessary for Paul to address the specific question of whether to continue in marital (and sexual) relations with unbelieving spouses.

120. Findlay.

121. Hays, 121. So also Conzelmann, 121 n. 25, and Garland, 285.

remarkably "evenhanded mutuality of Paul's exhortation, which stands in contrast to what we might have expected from a first-century writer, but which coheres with Gal 3:28."[122] In both cases Paul uses a resolute third-person imperative properly translated as an uncompromising command.[123] The obvious condition for the continuation of the marriage (cf. v. 15a) is that the unbelieving partner *is willing to live with him* or *her.* This bolsters further Paul's teaching in this chapter on marriage as a genuine partnership. He does not urge Christian men to force submission or conversion on their wives; the patriarchal setting would certainly have allowed this (as the quote from Plutarch above illustrates). Indeed, "willingness" in this context carries no sense of reluctance with it but rather implies free consent and approval.[124] Paul, as his knowledge of Genesis 2:24 (see 1 Cor. 6:16) shows, knew that marriage was a creation ordinance and was not to be willingly dissolved except under extreme circumstances. As Garland points out, "to live with" means "to live together in a marriage commitment (cf. 1 Pet. 3:7)."[125]

To be more specific about the experience of the early Christians in Corinth, it is possible that, given Paul's understanding of marriage as an exclusive partnership, this might include a commitment on the part of the unbelieving spouse to abstain from all kinds of extramarital relationships. Given, however, the general expectation in the Greco-Roman world (criticized by some Stoic/Pythagorean moralists) that husbands would engage in extramarital sexual relationships with slaves, prostitutes, or courtesans, it is possible that Christian wives would be expected to have to endure such behavior on the part of unbelieving husbands. Thiselton reminds us of the case from the second century reported by Justin at the beginning of the second chapter of his *Second Apology.* Justin relates the story of a woman who had come to Christian faith in the context of a marriage where both she and her husband had been unchaste. Upon becoming a Christian she became a chaste wife and tried to persuade her husband to adopt a similarly chaste lifestyle based on Christ's teachings. He alienated her, however, by continuing to live a sexually immoral lifestyle. "[I]n spite of her deep desire to leave him, her friends advised her to stay to try to win her husband. Her husband so declined in unnatural vice, however, that in the end she gave him a writ of divorce. Upon this, her husband reported her to the authorities for her Christian faith."[126]

**7:14** The reason Paul counsels that Christians married to unbeliev-

122. Thiselton, 527.

123. The present imperative is the normal tense for "general precepts . . . concerning attitudes and conduct" (BDF §335).

124. Gk. συνευδοκέω, "to join in approval, *agree with, approve of, consent to, sympathize with*" (BDAG); cf. Rom. 1:32; Luke 11:48; Acts 8:1; 22:20 (in every case properly translated by "approve" or "approval" in the TNIV).

125. Garland, 285.

126. Thiselton, 527.

ers ought to stay married[127] is that *the unbelieving husband has been sanctified through his wife, and the unbelieving wife has been sanctified through her believing husband.* To calm concerns about purity, Paul asserts that the status of unbelieving spouses is significantly altered by their intimate association with their believing spouse, so that mixed marriages have the same status in God's eyes as fully Christian marriages.[128] The Corinthians, on the other hand, may have assumed the opposite, namely, that the pure person would be defiled by the unclean person.[129] In 4QMMT and *Jubilees,* for example, marriage to an outsider results in ritual defilement. The Corinthians may have thought it impossible to be truly holy while married to a pagan spouse. Indeed, they could be excused for such thinking in the light of teaching in Leviticus and Haggai 2:11-14, where it is clear that holy and clean things may be profaned by that which is unclean, and texts such as Numbers 4:15, 20 make it clear that contact between that which is holy and that which is profane brings disastrous results. And as they heard the letter read, Paul may have inadvertently increased their fears by identifying both their assembly (3:16) and each believer as the holy temple of God (6:19). The notion that holiness rather than uncleanness is contagious has only marginal biblical support (cf. Exod. 29:37; 30:29; Lev. 6:18) prior to the ministry of Jesus. When Jesus touched unclean people, however, rather than becoming unclean himself his own holiness proved to be contagious, making the unclean clean (e.g., Mark 1:40-44//Matt. 8:2-3//Luke 5:12-14; Mark 5:25-34, 39-42). So also in Paul's view, perhaps due to the example of Jesus, holiness is more powerful than impurity, at least the holiness that comes through Christ's sanctifying work.

But in what sense has the unbelieving spouse actually *been sanctified,* or made holy, by their Christian husband or wife?[130] It clearly does not mean that they have been saved or now benefit from the covenantal status of the believing spouse, since 7:16 shows that that is an effect that can only be hoped for as the marriage unfolds. And there is no suggestion that it

127. Note the explanatory γάρ.

128. Cf. Fee, 298.

129. See Yonder Moynihan Gillihan, "Jewish Laws on Illicit Marriage, the Defilement of Offspring, and the Holiness of the Temple: A New Halakic Interpretation of 1 Corinthians 7:14," *JBL* 121 (2002), 711-44 (esp. 729).

130. The perfect indicative ἡγίασται occurs twice in v. 14. It had been thought that the perfect tense "combines in itself, so to speak, the present and the aorist in that it denotes the *continuance* of *completed action*" (BDF §340) so that the verb tense itself would indicate here that the unbelieving spouse has been made holy through their marriage (which would be the completed action with a continuing effect). More recent studies of verbal aspect have suggested, however, that what the perfect expresses is the current status of the marriage relationship and the fact that it is regarded as holy by the Lord. As such, it is a description of the unbeliever that is communicated by the choice of tense, not how or when this change of state took place. These perfects, therefore, are best and most naturally rendered as "is sanctified." The following discussion addresses the question of the historical and social background for understanding the sanctification that Paul has in mind and is not based on the verb tense per se.

means that such unbelievers experience serious moral transformation upon the conversion of their spouses (and experience shows that this is not the case).

Several scholars have noted the likelihood that Paul is employing Jewish terminology for betrothal and marriage: "In Jewish society the concept of marriage as a transfer of ownership had already disappeared by the first century. The Old Testament word for betrothal, *erubin,* suggested that a wife was 'acquired,' and so the word *kiddushin,* 'sanctified,' was used instead, which suggests that the bride and groom set themselves apart, or sanctified themselves, for each other."[131] Thus "a man could no longer declare that the woman was his wife, or betrothed to him, but would *sanctify* her and say that she was *sanctified* to him."[132] Among other things the language affirmed that the forthcoming marriage would be licit. "The rabbis assumed that the act of betrothal, or 'sanctification,' implied the licitness of the marital union."[133] Gillihan explains how Paul has taken up and transformed this background:

> Paul used Jewish betrothal language in a new way when he ruled that an unbeliever is "sanctified" by a believing spouse. Given the prohibition of Jesus against divorce, any marriage in which there was a believer was ruled to be licit, and Jewish language of betrothal provided a linguistic proof that the sanctification of the spouse and the licitness of the union were guaranteed. . . . While he recognizes a boundary separating the community of believers from unbelievers, analogous to the boundary between Jews and Gentiles, he does not agree with MMT and *Jubilees* that insider-outsider marriage results in the ritual defilement of offspring. Instead, like the rabbis, Paul allows that (at least preexisting) marriage between an insider and an outsider may be sanctified — that is, licit — although it is not the superior form of licit marriage.[134]

While in the Jewish context "the 'sanctification' presupposed the licitness of the marital union on the basis of the pre-betrothal status of both spouses, . . . Paul wrote his ruling to address the status of already existing marriage."[135] Gillihan suggests that Paul "meant that the act or state of being married to a believer, and not the premarital status of the spouses, literally sanctifies the unbelieving spouse as an eligible partner and effects the licitness of the union. We might say that the Pharisaic/Rabbinic betrothal idiom has come under the influence of the commandment of the Lord against divorce, so that licitness of marriage is now judged on the basis of

131. Instone-Brewer, *Divorce and Remarriage in the Bible,* 233.

132. Ze'ev Wilhelm Falk, *Introduction to Jewish Law of the Second Commonwealth, Pt. 2* (AGJU 11; Leiden: E. J. Brill, 1978), 285 (cited by Garland, 288).

133. Gillihan, "Jewish Laws on Illicit Marriage," 718.

134. Gillihan, "Jewish Laws on Illicit Marriage," 729.

135. Gillihan, "Jewish Laws on Illicit Marriage," 718.

the indissolubility of the marital bond (by the believer) rather than on the basis of the premarital status of each spouse."[136]

Several things can make a marriage licit or illicit, among them the religious or spiritual compatibility of the intended. But in a case where a person has already entered into a marriage before knowing Christ (or being known by him), their marriage is deemed licit or valid as a consequence and extended blessing of their conversion. It is evidently understood that the Christian's prior decision to commit themselves to their spouse now entails an act of having set that spouse apart to themselves, and thus to their sphere of influence.

Remarkably, the passive verb that is always used of the woman (who "is sanctified" by her husband) in the rabbinic context (cf. *m. Qiddušin* 2:1–3:11) is used by Paul of the unbeliever, male or female, who is sanctified by their believing spouse. Gillihan says that "Paul's usage puts the believer, male or female, in the more powerful 'male' role of sanctifying/causing licit betrothal, while the unbeliever implicitly becomes 'feminized.'" That is, Paul's argument attributes to the unbelieving spouse "a legal status typically associated with the female spouse."[137] Thus the believer-unbeliever distinction takes the place normally reserved for the male-female distinction, while the latter is replaced by a gender-indifferent power which applies to both men and women. "Contending that the Christian wife has the same power to sanctify her unbelieving husband as the Christian husband has to sanctify his unbelieving wife is quite novel. It accords with Paul's emphasis throughout the chapter on the mutuality of spouses . . . , but it also expresses his conviction that Christians live in a new and potent field of God's holiness that works irrespective of gender."[138]

How is it that the unbeliever is sanctified by their believing spouse? It seems there are three interrelated ideas from his biblical and Jewish background that are informing Paul's thought here: the holiness of people in God's temple (cf. 3:16-17; 6:19); the transferability of that holiness (Exod. 29:37; 30:29; Lev. 6:18; contrast Num. 4:15, 20); and the interrelatedness of families.[139] The idea of a "holy family" takes up Jewish ritual language and rests securely on the presupposition of family solidarity. That God's loving concern extends to the whole family is illustrated in various Old Testament texts (e.g., Gen. 6:18; 17:7-27; 18:19; Deut. 30:19; Ps. 78:1-7). As Garland notes, a key part of the biblical idea of the solidarity or interrelatedness of families, which is likely at the heart of the transferability of the holiness of God's people, probably "hinges on the two becoming one flesh (Gen. 2:24; cited in 1 Cor. 6:16) and on God's blessing of marriage." He explains how it is that the positive transference of holiness to such a spouse differs from the

136. Gillihan, "Jewish Laws on Illicit Marriage," 719.

137. Gillihan, "Jewish Laws on Illicit Marriage," 717-18.

138. Garland, 289.

139. See Rosner, *Paul, Scripture, and Ethics*, 169-70.

negative contamination Paul refers to in 6:15-17 when someone joins himself to a prostitute and becomes one body with her: "A Christian who has relations with a prostitute cannot convey holiness, because that union is outside the will of God. Fornication is the antithesis of holiness. Marriage, on the other hand, is a divine institution that accords with God's will for man and woman."[140] That is, one of the acts takes place within the proper context of family solidarity while the other does not. It is clear, of course, that the holy status experienced by the unbelieving spouse is not the same as that experienced by those who know Christ.

What are the implications of being sanctified, or set apart, for the spouse? Gillihan believes that, among other things, those who are thus sanctified "have full access to the temple constituted by the sanctified community."[141] This is consistent with the standard meaning of the verb Paul uses. When used of things it means to "set aside someth[ing] or make it suitable for ritual purposes, *consecrate, dedicate,*" and when used of people it means to "include a pers[on] in the inner circle of what is holy, in both cultic and moral associations of the word, *consecrate, dedicate, sanctify*" (BDAG). In this case, the sanctification of the unbelieving spouse, while reflecting a special, technical usage of the verb, still seems to suggest that the unbeliever is included in the inner circle which consists of those who "have full access to the temple constituted by the sanctified community." Thus, the key to the meaning of the two uses of *sanctified* in v. 14a is found in Paul's reference to being "unclean" or "holy" in v. 14b. Both "holiness" and "uncleanness" are scriptural terms well known in Second Temple Judaism for their importance with respect to access to God's temple. Most Old Testament references to holiness are found in cultic-ritual texts. Everything which belongs to the cult is holy. It is this priestly-cultic holiness, which is a central concern in the Qumran literature, the apocryphal writings, Philo, and Josephus, rather than prophetic-ethical holiness, which Paul has in mind here.[142]

This second, related idea brings in benefits that others have suggested constituted what it meant to "be sanctified" by the believing spouse. Here they are seen not as the meaning of the sanctification, but as natural consequences flowing from it. That is, while others believe the following blessings constitute being sanctified, we suggest that the blessings follow from being sanctified, that is, they follow from the blessing of being in a spiritually/religiously licit and valid (not merely legally licit and valid) marriage relationship with a believer (part of God's temple). Thus, Laney and Fee think that the "pagan partner is 'set apart' to receive a Christian witness and influence that he or she might not otherwise have,"[143] and indeed they pre-

140. Garland, 288-89.

141. Gillihan, "Jewish Laws on Illicit Marriage," 729.

142. See Rosner, *Paul, Scripture and Ethics,* 169-70.

143. J. C. Laney, "Paul and the Permanence of Marriage in 1 Corinthians 7," *JETS* 25 (1982), 283-94; Fee, 300-301, summarized by Garland, 287 (where he also rightly critiques Fee's use of Rom. 11:16 as a parallel).

sumably will receive a greater witness than they would have if their marriage with the believer were not allowed to continue because it was deemed spiritually unacceptable. The recognition of the marriage as spiritually acceptable also means that to a certain degree the unbelieving spouse is brought into association with the church and "into a power sphere of holiness that somehow neutralizes the non-Christian's potential to contaminate the Christian."[144] As Thiselton suggests, the lifestyle of the believing spouse, their "example, witness, prayer, and living out of the gospel," is bound to "affect the ethos and to some extent the values and lifestyle of the home, whether this be the husband or the wife."[145] They are in a position to receive Christian influence and witness. They live in a "sacred environment," "a sphere in which God's holiness and transforming power operate,"[146] in which there is increased potential for their salvation (cf. v. 16).

The early Christians, a tiny Jewish sect, had a keen sense of their vulnerable identity and the dangers outside. In 1 Corinthians 7:14 Paul allays Corinthian fears that their mixed marriages might somehow make them unclean and separate them from God unless they were to separate or divorce themselves from their unbelieving spouses. Rather, their marriage, by God's grace, receives the same status as any other Christian marriage, and should be nurtured and protected rather than abandoned.

As pointed out above, the second part of the verse, *Otherwise your children would be unclean, but as it is, they are holy* (with its references to that which is *unclean* or *holy*), clarifies that the holiness Paul had in mind in the first part related to the biblical and Jewish concerns with ritual purity. For Paul it seems uncleanness is "something which belongs by its very nature to the pagan world outside the church."[147] Paul's warning in his earlier letter about not associating with sexually immoral people (5:9) was not intended to cause people to question whether they should remain in their pre-Christian marriages with unbelievers or to worry about the status of children born within such marriages. Having assured them that unbelieving spouses have been sanctified through their marriage to one who has now become a believer, he points out that their children have also benefited from the parent's conversion, and are rendered "holy."

Gillihan shows that at this point Paul differs from rabbinic teaching since, unlike them, "he does not rule that offspring born within an exogamous marriage take on the status of the inferior spouse (see *m. Qiddušin* 3:12); instead he affirms that the children are 'holy,' that is, have full access to the temple constituted by the sanctified community."[148] In

144. Garland, 288.

145. Thiselton, 530. His suggestion, however, that it is in fact the example or lifestyle of the Christian that "make[s] the spouse (and the children) in this sense holy" (emphases removed) goes too far.

146. Hays, 122.

147. E. Best, "1 Corinthians 7:14 and Children in the Church," *IBS* 12 (1990), 161.

148. Gillihan, "Jewish Laws on Illicit Marriage," 729.

calling these children "holy" Paul does not mean that they are automatically saved (any more than the unbelieving spouses), but that rather than being held at arm's length by members of the church they are to be fully embraced in exactly the same way as children born into families where both parents are believers.[149] As a result of this, those children "will be marked by an element of shaping and 'difference' from a wholly pagan environment."[150] This result should bring great blessings that would otherwise be lost to the children of such families, but they are not what make them "holy" rather than "unclean." It is the Lord's sanctioning of their parents' marriage which accomplishes that and allows them to experience the blessing of living within a community inhabited by the Spirit of God. Both parts of v. 14 serve to support Paul's injunction to believers in mixed marriages not to divorce their partners (vv. 12b and 13b).

**7:15** It seems that vv. 15a-b may be functioning as a parenthesis, along the lines of vv. 11a-b (many suggest a more concise parenthesis in v. 12), in which "but if" introduces a potentially undesirable situation which is background information with respect to the main focus on his positive instructions. In this case the undesirable situation is that of the unbelieving partner wishing to end the marriage. Paul says that if this unfortunate situation arises, let your partner leave: *But if the unbeliever leaves, let it be so.*[151] *The* [Christian] *brother or sister is not bound in such circumstances.* Using the language of "being bound" does not mean that the Corinthians regarded their marriages to unbelievers as slavery.[152] As Instone-Brewer notes, "Jewish marriage was based on a concept of bondage — both husband and wife were bound to keep the obligations outlined in their marriage contract, and divorce required a certificate of freedom for the wife."[153] *Not bound*[154] here refers to freedom to remarry. Instone-Brewer explains: "The only freedom that makes any sense in this context is the freedom to remarry. . . . [A]ll Jewish divorce certificates and most Greco-Roman ones contained the words 'you are free to marry any man you wish,' or something very similar."[155] Although Deming argues on the basis of Stoic texts that Paul refers here to marriage to an unbeliever as a form of

149. Rabbinic Judaism's view that proselyte children constituted full members of Israel is roughly parallel.

150. Thiselton, 530.

151. Paul's imperative is one of toleration or, as Wallace, *Greek Grammar*, 488, suggests, it "could almost be called 'an imperative of resignation,'" which is often used for an act which is seen as a *fait accompli.* So also Garland, 290.

152. Contra Deming, *Paul on Marriage and Celibacy*, 148, who fails to take the Jewish background into account.

153. Instone-Brewer, *Divorce and Remarriage in the Bible*, 191.

154. The use of the perfect tense here (δεδούλωται) provides a fine illustration of its focus on a present state. The idea is not that he has not been bound, but on the person's unbound state — he "is not bound."

155. Instone-Brewer, *Divorce and Remarriage in the Bible*, 202. Rabbi Judah would later refer to the divorce certificate as, among other things, a "deed of liberation" (*m. Giṭṭin* 9:3).

slavery,[156] the texts he cites simply suggest that marriage was frequently thought of as a form or slavery or bondage, and do not support the idea that marriage to an unbeliever is being described differently than others. In fact, if there is a special condition that is being referred to as slavery here, it is more likely to be that of having to maintain the status of a married person despite being abandoned by one's spouse than the prior state of being married to an unbeliever. Paul says that *in such circumstances*[157] (namely, that of being abandoned, not merely that of being married to an unbeliever) a Christian spouse is not bound. That is, spouses are not stuck in the slavery of a no-man's-land where they have no spouse (because they have been abandoned) and yet are not able to remarry (because they remain married). They are free.[158] And although a different verb is used to refer to the "bondage" of marriage in v. 39 and Romans 7:2, in both of those texts Paul explicitly refers to the freedom gained upon the dissolution of a marriage as freedom to remarry, assuming that his readers would want to remarry (also implied in v. 27), rather than suggesting that he is dealing with people who would prefer to remain single (and celibate). This is in keeping with the fact that in the Roman world, most people remarried (and were expected to remarry) after getting divorced.

Some unbelievers feel threatened by the conversion of a spouse to Christ, as they now live with someone whose ultimate loyalties and commitment is beyond their understanding, and not all recover from the experience. Unfortunately, new converts may also need to be warned about the subconscious temptation to start life over again and find a believing spouse by "locking-out" their unbelieving spouse and completely immersing themselves in their new Christian world to the point that their spouse feels completely abandoned and estranged from them and finally gives up and divorces the believer. The unbelieving spouse of a Christian ought to find in them a model of self-sacrificing love that is even more committed to the health of the marriage and to blessing their spouse than ever before, such that only a radical prejudice could explain their unwillingness to continue in the marriage.

There are several ways in which the next phrase may operate in the passage: but *God has called us to live in peace.* Either (1) this "calling"[159] refers to staying in the marriage in contrast to the separation of v. 15a;[160] or (2) it signifies not being overly distressed if a divorce occurs, as in v. 15b;[161] or

156. Deming, *Paul on Marriage and Celibacy,* 145-49.

157. Gk. ἐν τοῖς τοιούτοις.

158. Of course, if the Christian really wanted to remain celibate, being abandoned by their spouse would probably not be considered a problem or a situation in which they would be likely to feel the least bit bound or enslaved.

159. Garland, 293, notes that one's calling "becomes the leitmotif in the next unit" (7:17-24), with the verb used eight times and the noun once.

160. Lightfoot; Barrett.

161. Ellicott; Godet.

(3) since v. 15c embodies a principle capable of varied application, it applies both to keeping the marriage bond in peace and allowing a determined unbelieving partner to depart in peace.[162] In favor of this third fuller meaning is the fact that v. 15c is sandwiched between references to both separation (v. 15b) and a continuing marriage (v. 16). However, the problem for the second interpretation is that it gives *peace* an unusual sense in the light of New Testament usage. "Peace" for Paul refers to reconciliation, both vertical with God and horizontal between human beings. "Peace" is the opposite of division in Luke 12:51 and can be said to characterize a household in Matthew 10:34-36. Paul is saying in v. 15 that if your unbelieving spouse leaves, you are free to remarry, but don't forget that at the core of your Christian identity is the recognition that you are those who restore relationships as peacemakers.

The *peace* to which Paul refers here is not the absence of hostility after a marital breakup (in most cases a dubious notion anyway) but the peace of continued relationship. Harmony, or *concordia,* was a fundamental ideal in Roman marriages, frequently referenced on epitaphs of spouses who enjoyed long and happy marriages.[163] Thus, as suggested above, vv. 15c-16 go back to pick up the line of thought where it was left off in vv. 12-14, and the calling to peace should be understood as being related to the solidarity of family, in this case, one which exists together in a state of ritual purity or holiness (v. 14). In this context, since believers are called to peace (v. 15c), it would be inappropriate for them to be so un-peace-loving as to divorce a spouse who is part of the sanctified family unit and is willing to live with them (vv. 12-13). Rather than being antagonistic, they should take a peace-loving approach. Romans 12:18 makes the point of v. 15 more generally: "If it is possible, as far as it depends on you, live at peace with everyone." Paul's statement in v. 15 reflects his Jewish heritage, "which for the sake of peace did certain deeds toward the less favored, or even toward the Gentiles, with a view toward winning the favor of Judaism with them."[164]

**7:16** Paul's final words to Christians in mixed marriages have been taken as striking an optimistic or a pessimistic note.[165] The TNIV favors the latter, while the NRSV the former: *How do you know, wife, whether you will save your husband? Or, how do you know, husband, whether you will save your wife?* (TNIV); "Wife, for all you know, you might save your husband. Husband, for all you know, you might save your wife" (NRSV). Does Paul end his instructions to those in mixed marriages optimistically, with the

162. Bruce.

163. See Suzanne Dixon, *The Roman Family* (Baltimore: Johns Hopkins University Press, 1992), 70.

164. Fee, 304-5. For example, *m. Giṭṭin* 5:8-9: "They do not try to prevent the poor among the gentiles from gathering gleanings . . . in the interests of peace. . . . Moreover, greetings [meaning *shalom,* peace] may be offered to gentiles in the interests of peace."

165. The majority of commentators take the verse optimistically. For the pessimistic interpretation see Ellicott, and Robertson and Plummer.

thought that perhaps they will be the catalyst to the salvation of their unbelieving spouse, or pessimistically, discouraging the Christian spouse from hanging on in their marriage pointlessly. In other words, grammatically does the word "for" at the beginning of the sentence (not translated by TNIV) connect the verse to vv. 12-14 or to v. 15? In other words, is v. 16 giving a further encouragement to stay in the mixed marriage or to let the unbelieving partner leave?

The context favors an optimistic thrust, since Paul's main stress is on reasons why such marriages should be preserved rather than abandoned.[166] Verse 16 provides both Christian husbands and wives one more reason for staying in their mixed marriages (recall NRSV above). Peter certainly gives women hope that wise Christian living might lead to the conversion of their unbelieving spouses (1 Pet. 3:1-4). Paul's point that the unbelieving spouse has been sanctified by their marriage to a believer (v. 14) with the result that they have been brought into an unusually powerful position from which to receive Christian influence and witness in the midst of God's temple, the "sphere in which God's holiness and transforming power operate,"[167] would certainly raise one's hopes for the potential conversion of the unbelieving spouse. Also, the idiom "how do you know" is used positively in a range of Greek sources.[168] Lightfoot summarizes pithily: "What he [Paul] is really advising is the sacrificing of much [the supposed ease of divorce from a difficult partner] for the possible attainment of what is a great gain [the conversion of your spouse], though an uncertain one."[169] Later in this same letter Paul will stress his own willingness to sacrifice himself in many ways in the hope of being able to win others over to Christ (9:19-22). Garland recognizes that Paul's "own missionary concern to win others at all costs is likely to color his advice about marriage."[170]

For a full discussion (and bibliography) tending toward the pessimistic view see Thiselton. That view suggests, as mentioned above, that Paul's idea is, "It is no use hanging on in the hope of converting him/her, because how do you know that this will happen?"[171] It seems an Achilles' heel of the pessimistic view, overlooked by its proponents, that there really was no such thing as "hanging on" in a Roman marriage once one of the spouses had decided to divorce. Once either spouse clearly indicated that the mar-

166. Paul is not being sarcastic with the use of the verb "to save"; it can be a missionary term meaning "to convert" (Barrett, 167; e.g., 1 Cor. 9:22: "that I might *save* some").

167. Hays, 122.

168. Gk. τί οἶδας; cf. 2 Sam. 12:22; Esth. 4:14; Joel 2:14; Jonah 3:9; *Joseph and Aseneth* 11; *Liber Antiquitatem Biblicarum* 9.6; Epictetus, *Diatribai* 2.20.30; cf. Garland, 294; Conzelmann, 124 n. 47.

169. Lightfoot, 227 (1895 ed.).

170. Garland, 294.

171. Thiselton, 537-38, following an old tradition. Cf. Robertson and Plummer, 144, "If the unbeliever demands divorce, grant it: you are not bound to refuse. If you refuse, you will have no peace."

riage was over, it was over. Nothing more needed to be done to effect the divorce, and nothing could be done to avoid it.[172]

Those Corinthians in mixed marriages, reassured by Paul that their mixed marriages are special to God (i.e., holy), may even take heart from the thought that their husband or wife may one day be saved and they will no longer be married to an unbeliever (vv. 12-13; cf. 1 Pet. 3:1-2).

### 2. *Exposition of the Principle of Remaining as You Were When Called (Illustrated by Circumcision and Slavery), 7:17-24*

The place of this paragraph in the argument of chapter 7 is not immediately obvious. What do circumcision and slavery have to do with singleness and marriage? While there is a link with the language of "calling" in v. 15, there is no question that Paul digresses. Nothing else in the letter suggests that circumcision or slavery is a special problem at Corinth that Paul needed to address.[173] On the other hand, it may not be much of a digression, however, especially if the main theme of the letter is understood to revolve around the relationship between marriage, singleness, and sexual purity (i.e., questions revolving around *porneia* and "touching"), since slaves could neither legally marry nor exercise any significant control over their own sexual purity (i.e., they were often the objects of the sexual "touching" of their masters),[174] and, according to Philo, circumcision symbolized the excision of the pleasures and passions[175] typically associated with sexual "touching" and changes in either status (e.g., the circumcision of an uncircumcised Christian man or the manumission of a young slave woman) may have been motivated by marital intentions (cf. comments on vv. 18, 21). Even if it is something of a digression, however, as observed by Collins and many others, 7:17-24 is a digression with a definite purpose. Similar rhetorical strategies appear with chapter 9 in the unit chapters 8–10 and chapter 13 in chapters 12–14. In all three cases Paul turns aside from the issue at hand to illustrate a basic principle that he wishes to underscore.

1 Corinthians 7:17-24 is the central element in a ring composition or

172. See Susan Treggiari, "Divorce Roman Style: How Easy and How Frequent Was It?" in *Marriage, Divorce, and Children in Ancient Rome* (ed. Beryl Rawson; Oxford: Oxford University Press, 1991), 31-46; Judith Evans Grubbs, *Women and the Law in the Roman Empire: A Sourcebook on Marriage, Divorce and Widowhood* (London: Routledge, 2002), 187-218.

173. Judith Gundry-Volf, "Male and Female in Creation and New Creation: Interpretations of Galatians 3: 28 in 1 Corinthians 7," in *To Tell the Mystery: Essays on New Testament Eschatology in Honor of Robert H. Gundry* (ed. Thomas E. Schmidt and Moisés Silva; JSNTSup 100; Sheffield: JSOT Press, 1994), 97.

174. Note, e.g., Glancy, *Slavery in Early Christianity*, 21: "Sexual access to slave bodies was a pervasive dimension of ancient systems of slavery. Both female and male slaves were available for their owners' pleasure. . . ." This was in keeping with "the widespread ancient recognition of slaves as benign sexual outlets for their owners."

175. Cf. Philo, *On the Migration of Abraham* 92; *On the Special Laws* 1:9.

ABA pattern,[176] the function of which is to reinforce Paul's advice to be content in one's life situation. Paul states repeatedly in the chapter not to seek a change in marital status (7:2, 8, 10, 11, 12-16, 26-27, 37, 40). Then in vv. 17-24 he pleads three times to remain in the situation in which you were called, with reference to the two great social dividers of his day, namely, the questions of race and social class (7:17, 20, 24). Whether a Christian is married or single, circumcised or uncircumcised, slave or free, makes no difference to God, or more accurately "before God" (as v. 24 literally says), so there is no need to change. Deming rightly points out that vv. 17-24 run directly counter to Corinthian preoccupations with social status distinctions and their enhancement.[177]

That Paul chose circumcision and slavery to make his point takes on greater significance in the light of Galatians 3:28, where Paul lists the same three pairs relevant to 1 Corinthians 7 when he proclaims that "in Christ Jesus . . . there is neither Jew nor Greek, neither slave nor free, neither male or female."[178] The great divisions of the ancient world are redundant in the light of the new creation. What matters in Galatians 3 is being "children of God through faith" (3:26). The deeper our recognition of the imminence of the final transition to the fullness of the new creation, the greater our indifference to the distinctions and distinctive concerns of life in this present age (cf. 1 Cor. 7:29-31). The tension and relationship between the "already" and the "not yet" aspects of Christian eschatology must inform the moral and ethical thinking and behavior of the believer.[179] "In one sense, the new eschatological reality of the gospel abolishes 'human' categorization; but in a deeper and more realistic sense it relativizes and redefines them."[180] Paul addresses the deeper and more existential question of when and how outward circumstances matter and when they do not.

The order of the two examples in vv. 17-24 also advances Paul's argument. If circumcision reinforces the basic principle of not changing one's status, the illustration of slavery allows Paul to introduce an analogous exception. As Garland puts it, "change of status is unnecessary as it relates to God's call, but that does not mean that change of status is prohibited."[181] In v. 21 Paul allows that if a slave has the opportunity for freedom, they should take it. Similar exceptions also appear in the A sections of chapter 7:

176. See John J. Collins, "Chiasmus, the 'ABA' Pattern and the Text of Paul," in *Studiorum Paulinorum Congressus Internationalis Catholicus* (AnBib 17-18; Rome: E Pontificio Instituto biblico, 1963), 575-83.

177. Deming, *Paul on Marriage and Celibacy*, 159.

178. S. Scott Bartchy, *Μᾶλλον Χρῆσαι: First-Century Slavery and the Interpretation of 1 Corinthians 7:21* (SBLDS 11; Missoula, MT: Society of Biblical Literature, 1973), 164.

179. Cf. Loader, *Sexuality and the Jesus Tradition*, 173: "The station in which one finds oneself has no validity in itself. . . . the underlying assumption is that at the eschaton it will cease to apply. . . . [Hence they are] to be considered interim states." Cf. Mark 12:25 — in the resurrection there will be no marrying or sexual relations.

180. Thiselton, 547.

181. Garland, 300.

in vv. 8-9 and 28 the single and widowed respectively may marry or remarry; and in v. 15 those divorced by a non-Christian spouse may remarry. Paul's advice in the chapter about marriage is not uniformly or rigidly conservative. Thus, the second example of slavery "illustrates both the ultimate indifference of one's state of life (v. 21a) and the possibility of having a preference where circumstances allow (v. 21b)."[182]

In terms of structure within the subunit, vv. 17a and 24 form an inclusio around the paragraph with several repeated terms and ideas. At its center, v. 20 repeats the same thought: remain as you were when called. The two main points of the chapter — remain as you are and change if you can or must, but only under certain circumstances — are both reinforced and illustrated in this paragraph (although most commentators see only the first).

*a. Analogy of Circumcision/Uncircumcision, 7:17-20*

> [17]*Nevertheless, each of you should live as a believer in whatever situation the Lord has assigned to you, just as God has called you. This is the rule I lay down in all the churches.* [18]*Was a man already circumcised when he was called? He should not become uncircumcised. Was a man uncircumcised when he was called? He should not be circumcised.* [19]*Circumcision is nothing and uncircumcision is nothing. Keeping God's commands is what counts.* [20]*Each of you should remain in the situation you were in when God called you.*

**7:17** Paul signals that he is drawing back from the intense task of instruction to expound a principle with the opening word, *Nevertheless,* literally, "if not." The sense is to interrupt the subject at hand with something of general relevance and might be better translated "At all events" (Thiselton), "However that may be" (NRSV, REB), or even "Anyway" (NJB).[183] His general point is that *each of you should live as a believer in whatever situation the Lord has assigned to you, just as God has called you.* Literally: "To each as God apportions, each as God has called, thus walk." Three key terms demand comment, namely, "apportion," "call," and "walk."

That God "apportions" or distributes spiritual gifts to the body of Christ is not uncommon in Paul's letters, and Paul uses the word in question in that sense in Romans 12:3 and 2 Corinthians 10:13. He also uses the verb "to give" for that divine activity in 1 Corinthians 3:5 and 12:7. However, the context in 1 Corinthians 7 is not ministry in the church but rather the circumstances of daily life. Is Paul then teaching in v. 17 that there is not only a call of God to salvation but also to a particular situation in everyday

182. G. W. Dawes, "'But If You Can Gain Your Freedom' (1 Corinthians 7:17-24)," *CBQ* 52 (1990), 681-97, 697.

183. Cf. BDF §376. The adversative "nevertheless" or "but" (KJV) is too strong in this context.

life?[184] The problem is that what the Lord "assigned" is not clear since the object of the verb is not given.[185] Is it the gift of salvation or the individual's lot in life? The next phrase is parallel and clarifies the matter.

The verb "to call" occurs eight times in 7:17-24.[186] The verb often means to "choose for receipt of a special benefit or experience" (BDAG), and Paul's most frequent use of the word is as an authoritative summons to salvation and service.[187] As his use of the word in 7:15 shows, he employed it with other referents as well. This seems to fit well in the context of 1 Corinthians 7. Paul is dealing with issues of marital, racial, and social status, and makes the far-reaching point that these circumstances are what the Lord in his purposes assigns to each Christian. Thiselton spells out the profound implications: "This Pauline concept of call and service varies greatly from that of secular modernity, which gives a privileged place to 'autonomy,' and from that of secular postmodernity, which gives privilege to self-fulfillment and to power interests. These stand nearer to Corinth than to Paul, and gives this section fresh relevance to the present."[188] In Paul's view, my station in life is under the sovereign and gracious direction of God. He *assigned* it to me and *called* me to it.

Paul tells the Corinthians, no matter what circumstances they find themselves in, whether married or not, circumcised or not, free or not, to conduct their lives, or *live,* accordingly: "thus walk."[189] "Bloom where you are planted."[190] There is no need to change to improve yourself in relation to God. God does not reckon one condition better than another in terms of serving him. In fact, God placed the Corinthians in these circumstances. The Corinthian Christians' lot is part of their "assignment" and "calling." "Walking" is Paul's most comprehensive way of talking about conduct (see

184. Martin Luther certainly took the verse in this way and translated the word for "call" in v. 20 as "occupation" *(Beruf).* It formed part of his polemic against the view that only the "religious," monks, priests, and nuns, were called by God.

185. Several translations supply "the life" the Lord has assigned (CSB, ESV, NRSV). The NIV supplies "the place in life," while the NJB supplies "the part." The NAB translates, "should live as the Lord has assigned" (similarly, NET), and the TNIV, "should live as a believer in whatever situation the Lord has assigned to you" (similarly, NLT).

186. The perfect indicative used here and in v. 17 (κέκληκεν) may be best understood as the equivalent to an aorist verb, either due to the occasional use of a perfect tense in place of an aorist (see Caragounis, *The Development of Greek,* 110-12) or because it is a historical perfect used with a lexeme related to discourse (the indirect discourse implied by "as the Lord called him"; see Campbell, *Basics of Verbal Aspect,* 107-8).

187. Cf. the verb in 1 Cor. 1:9, the noun in 1:26, and the adjective in 1:2, 24. See also Rom. 11:29; Eph. 1:18; 4:1, 4; Phil. 3;14; 2 Thess. 1:11; 2 Tim. 1:9.

188. Thiselton, 548.

189. As pointed out earlier, all but one of the following imperatives in this chapter are present imperatives, which, as a natural implication of imperfective aspect, suggests that Paul is providing generally relevant moral instruction rather than teaching that is expected to be applied to just a particular case at hand (for the exception see the comments on the last verb in v. 21).

190. Hays, 123.

on 1 Cor. 3:3) and is a thoroughly Jewish metaphor. In Judaism one was to "walk," or conduct one's life, according to teachings of the Law of Moses. The exposition of the legal requirements of the Mosaic covenant were referred to as *halakah,* based on the Hebrew word "to walk" *(halak).* Paul's use of the metaphor usually reflects the idea that the gospel or the Spirit provides a new basis or compass for guiding Christian living. His use of the metaphor here is remarkable in light of the fact that two verses later (v. 19) he will say, *Circumcision* [one of the most fundamental requirements of Jewish *halakah*] *is nothing and uncircumcision is nothing. Keeping God's commands* [what *halakah* was all about] *is what counts.* That seemingly paradoxical verse, as well as the words "responsible to God" or, more literally, "before God" in v. 24, fill out Paul's meaning here.

To encourage Corinthian assent Paul assures them that what he is teaching here is no ill-considered novelty: *This is the rule I lay down in all the churches.* The second of four such statements in the letter (4:17; 11:16; 14:33), it emerges not just from a pragmatic impulse but from eschatological convictions. As announced in 1:2 (alluding to Mal. 1:11), Paul's open agenda is to contribute to the end-time *universal* worship of the one true God by Gentiles. This involves helping them to live holy lives, to walk before God, and to please him in every respect.

**7:18** Up until the end of v. 17 the Corinthians would have been thinking only in terms of being married, single, divorced, or widowed with reference to not changing their circumstances. Verse 18, using two questions and two corresponding commands, introduces, by way of illustration, another area of application: *Was a man already circumcised*[191] *when he was called? He should not become uncircumcised. Was a man uncircumcised when he was called? He should not be circumcised.* This example is chosen because presumably it was uncontroversial to the Corinthians; there is no point to introducing a premise in an argument if the audience disagrees with it. Fundamental to Paul's vision of the church is that it transcends ethnic boundaries and unites Jews and Gentiles in one body. In the churches in which Paul worked Gentiles did not need to become Jews, and Jews did not need to become Gentiles. Paul's letter to the Galatians reveals how vociferously he responded to Gentile believers wanting to become Jews by being circumcised in order to be part of the people of God. This was not a problem in Corinth; otherwise Paul would have tackled it head-on. As 1 Corinthians 9:17-23 will show, diversity in the church has a positive purpose in that it can serve the interests of the witness of the gospel.

Winter contends that some Jewish Christians may have wanted to hide their circumcision (through epispasm) in order to give them a higher status in society.[192] Indeed, Philo states that circumcision was "ridiculed by

191. The perfect passive participle (περιτετμημένος) refers to the state of the man at the time, in keeping with the perfect tense's tendency to express a current state of affairs.

192. Winter, *Seek the Welfare of the City,* 147-52.

many."[193] The fact that Paul simply includes it as the complement to Gentiles wanting to be circumcised may suggest that this was also not a problem in the Corinthian church. Given the context here, of a discussion of marriage and singleness, however, it may be that a Gentile believer could have felt some pressure from his present or future Jewish bride (or her family) to become circumcised,[194] and a Jewish believer may have felt similar pressure from a Gentile bride or virgin (or her family) to have his circumcision undone. Such pressure would have had little to do with issues of justification or religious adherence, but with a potential fiancée's personal feelings about the presentation of her spouse's genitals. The following verse, however, seems to imply (with its reference to what "matters" or "counts") that Paul has in mind someone's sense of moral obligation to accept or undo circumcision rather than simple social pressure coming from a potential spouse (or in-laws). On the calling referred to here, see the comments in v. 17.

**7:19** This verse is properly described by E. P. Sanders as one of the most amazing sentences that Paul ever wrote.[195] Indeed, it is hard to imagine a more un-Jewish statement than Paul's opening words, *Circumcision is nothing and uncircumcision is nothing.*[196] Circumcision was a sign of membership in the covenant community, and virtually all Jews considered it a principal command. When Antiochus Epiphanes wanted to eradicate Judaism, for example, one of the basic things he did was have all those who circumcised their children killed (1 Macc. 1:60-61). Philo firmly criticizes some who argued that the Mosaic laws (including that regarding circumcision) had merely symbolic significance and thus did not need to be literally obeyed (*On the Migration of Abraham* 89–93).

In one sense, Paul's sentiments in vv. 18-19 concerning the relative irrelevance of circumcision, despite the obvious contradiction of Genesis 17:10-14 and other passages, find some sympathy in passages like Deuteronomy 10:16 and Jeremiah 4:4, where membership in the covenant community is a matter of the heart, not an outward sign. Other figurative uses of circumcision (Exod. 6:30; Jer. 6:10; 9:26, which speak of uncircumcised lips, ears, and heart respectively) also point in Paul's direction. Nonetheless, v. 19a is radical in comparison with these Old Testament sentiments. It is one thing to say that circumcision has a deeper significance, quite another to say it has no significance.

However, Paul's next words come as even more of a surprise and apparently create a confusing paradox: literally, "but (or instead) keeping

193. Philo, *On the Special Laws* 1:2.

194. For one first-century Jewish perspective on intermarriage with Gentiles see Philo, *On the Special Laws* 3:29.

195. Sanders, *Paul, the Law and the Jewish People,* 161-62. Cf. Justin [Martyr], *Dialogue with Trypho* 10.

196. Gk. οὐδέν ἐστι: "means nothing, is unimportant" (BDAG). Cf. Matt. 23:16, 18; John 8:54; Acts 21:24.

God's commands," an idiom well translated as, *Keeping God's commands is what counts.*[197] Both main terms, "keeping" and "commands," point to Paul's being meaning that what is paramount is observing the law of Moses. Apart from here in v. 19, the noun "commandments" or "commandment"[198] is used thirteen times in Paul's letters. In the majority, ten times, it refers unambiguously to the Jewish law (Rom. 13:9; Eph. 2:15; 6:2; Tit. 1:14; and six times in Romans 7; the other three [1 Cor. 14:37; Col. 4:10; 1 Tim. 6:14] refer to Paul's own instructions). The verb "to keep"[199] can mean "obey" in the New Testament and is used regularly with reference to keeping the law of Moses, namely, "God's commandments" (Rev. 12:17; 14:12), the "commandments" (of Moses; Matt. 19:17), "the law of Moses" (Acts 15:5), the Sabbath commandment (John 9:16), and "the whole [Jewish] law" (Jas. 2:10).[200] In this verse the related noun[201] is used, which refers to "persisting in obedience" (BDAG). Thielman is right to observe that "keeping the commandments/laws" in Jewish and Christian literature regularly referred to obeying the Mosaic law (Sir. 29:1; 32:23; Wis. 6:18; Matt. 19:17; Josephus, *Antiquities* 8.120, 395; 17.159).[202] Since circumcision was an essential part of the law (Gen. 17:10-14; 23-27), what could Paul have possibly meant when he said that *circumcision is nothing* but the important thing was *keeping God's commands?* How is this paradox to be resolved?

The problem of Paul and the law is notoriously complex. As v. 19 demonstrates, Paul says things that are evidently contradictory. While midstream in a commentary is no place to dive into this debate, a few caveats and observations may help us to navigate toward a solution that accounts for the evidence of 1 Corinthians and helps us arrive at an accurate appreciation of this verse. A common way to resolve the paradox of v. 19 is by drawing on the venerable distinction between different parts of the law (civil, ceremonial, and moral), dating back, in part at least, to the time of Origen.[203] According to Thielman, for example, Paul distinguishes between parts of the law that count and parts that do not count. Circumcision falls

197. Translations differ on whether the relationship between the clauses suggests simply that while (un)circumcision does not matter, keeping God's commandments does, or whether opposites are implied, such that while (un)circumcision means nothing, keeping God's commandments means everything. Other translations say that keeping God's commandments "matters" (NAB, NASB), or is "what counts" (NET, NIV), "what is important" (NJB, NLT), or "is everything" (NRSV).

198. Gk. ἐντολή.

199. Gk. τηρέω.

200. The other "commandments" that are to be "kept" are those of Jesus in John 14:15, 21; 15:10; 1 John 2:3, 4; 3:22, 24; 5:3.

201. Gk. τήρησις, also in Wis. 6:18 and Sir. 32:23.

202. F. Thielman, "The Coherence of Paul's View of the Law: The Evidence of First Corinthians," *NTS* 38 (1992), 238-39.

203. See Christopher J. H. Wright, "The Ethical Authority of the Old Testament: A Survey of Approaches: Part I," *TynBul* 43 (1992), 102; and idem, "The Ethical Authority of the Old Testament: A Survey of Approaches: Part II," *TynBul* 43 (1992), 205.

squarely into the latter category.[204] But (most of) the rest of the law is still valid as *God's commands*. However, this approach does not do full justice to the absolute nature of Paul's negative statements about the law and misses the rhetorical function of the other statements.

Roughly speaking, Paul does three things with the law, and each one must be fully heard without prejudicing the others: (1) polemical repudiation; (2) radical replacement; and (3) wholehearted reappropriation. These correspond to treating the law as *legal code, theological motif,* and *source for ethics* respectively. These three ways of treating the law seem to reflect three different aspects of how both Jesus and Paul think of the law as being "fulfilled" in Christ and in Christian teaching. When studying the law in Paul's thought, such differentiation is vital. Broadly speaking, in terms of the history of interpretation, Luther emphasized the first, Calvin the third, and the new perspective has concentrated on the second motif. In one sense, all three are right in what they affirm but wrong in what they deny.[205] The first move can be seen in the negation of circumcision in v. 19a. Another instance is in 1 Corinthians 9:20, where Paul says simply, "I am not under the law."

Verse 19b is an example of the second move. Instead of obeying the law, Paul says that the important thing is to obey *God's commands,* which, we submit, the Corinthians would have understood as Paul's own instructions in the letter. The only other place where "commands" appears in 1 Corinthians is in 14:37: "what I am writing to you is the Lord's *command.*"[206] Paul's words in 7:19 are formulated in a deliberately polemical fashion. Christians don't "keep" the commands of the Mosaic law, but instead "keep" some other commands (that are nonetheless from God). When Paul speaks of Christians positively vis-à-vis the law, he does not usually say that they "keep" it or "obey" it but rather that they "fulfill" it.[207] Both Jesus and Paul think of the law as being "fulfilled" in Jesus and in Christian teaching. Moo observes correctly: "Paul reserves this language for the eschatological 'filling up' of the basic demand of the law that has been made possible with the coming of Christ."[208] Elsewhere in 1 Corinthians replacement of the law of Moses can be clearly seen in 9:21, where Paul says, "I am under the law of Christ."

The third move, that of using the law for questions of conduct can be

204. Thielman, "The Coherence of Paul's View of the Law," 237-40.

205. Luther denies the third, Calvin underestimated the second, and the new perspective is reductionistic with regard to the first.

206. Cf. Col. 4:10 and 1 Tim. 6:14 where "command" likewise refers to apostolic instruction.

207. Gk. πληρόω (Rom. 8:4; 13:8; Gal. 5:14; ἀναπληρόω in Gal. 6:2; πλήρωμα in Rom. 13:10). See Stephen Westerholm, *Israel's Law and the Church's Faith: Paul and His Recent Interpreters* (Grand Rapids: Eerdmans, 1988), 202-4; cf. Hans Dieter Betz, *Galatians: A Commentary on Paul's Letter to the Churches in Galatia* (Hermeneia; Philadelphia: Fortress, 1979), 275.

208. D. J. Moo, *Romans* (Grand Rapids: Eerdmans, 1996), 170.

seen in 9:24, where Paul asserts that Deuteronomy 25:4 "was written for us," and in 10:11, where it is said that the events of the exodus and wilderness wanderings "were written down as warnings for us." The question to ask in these cases is not *which bits* of the law are valid, but *in what sense* is the law valid for Christians. Christians are instructed by the law not *qua* Jewish law but *qua* Christian Scripture. The subtle influence of Scripture in 7:17-24 also points indirectly to a rejuvenated role for the law in determining Christian conduct. Paul conceives of conduct as "walking" (in v. 17) "before God" (v. 24), appeals to a saving event as forming the identity of the people of God in v. 23a (reminiscent of the exodus), possibly alludes to Leviticus 25:42 in v. 23b, and gives the "call of God" a key place in everyday life throughout the paragraph. All these show that Paul continues to draw on the Jewish Bible when he formulates moral teaching and seeks moral guidance.[209]

To summarize, the following chart suggests that Paul's approach to the law in 1 Corinthians consisted of three moves.

**Paul and the Law in 1 Corinthians**

| *Text* | *Repudiation* | *Replacement* | *Reappropriation* |
|---|---|---|---|
| 1 Cor. 7:19 | "circumcision is nothing" | "Keeping God's commands is what counts" | |
| 1 Cor. 9:20-21 | "I am not under the law" | "I am under the law of Christ" | |
| 1 Cor. 9:9 | | | Deut. 25:4, "was written for us" |
| 1 Cor. 10:11 | | | The exodus and wilderness wanderings "were written down as warnings for us" |

Without entering into the complexities of Paul's other letters, the same pattern can be observed elsewhere. In Romans, repudiation and replacement are evident in 6:15, where believers are said to be "not under the law but under grace," and all three moves are arguably present in 8:1-4. In Galatians, Paul asserts that believers are "no longer under the supervision of the law" (Gal. 3:25), nor "under the law" (Gal. 5:18), but instead are "led by the Spirit" (Gal. 5:18); nonetheless, "the entire law is fulfilled in keeping" the love command (Gal. 5:14). In Ephesians, Christ "abolishes the law in his flesh" (Eph. 2:15), the church being built instead "on the apostles and

209. The full story is that Paul reappropriates the law not only *as wisdom* for living, but also *as prophecy*, as a witness to the gospel. On this hermeneutical solution to the puzzle of Paul and the law, see Brian S. Rosner, *Paul and the Law* (New Studies in Biblical Theology; Downers Grove, IL: Apollos/InterVarsity, forthcoming).

prophets, with Christ Jesus himself as the chief cornerstone" (Eph. 2:20); yet Paul can quote approvingly the commandment to "honor your father and mother" (Eph. 6:1-3).

Treating 1 Corinthians 7:19 as a piece of polemic rather than a paradox is supported when it is compared to two parallel texts in Galatians. In both cases the thing contrasted with the irrelevance of circumcision is not part of the law that remains (contra Thielman et al.) but something that replaces the law entirely: "In Christ Jesus neither circumcision nor uncircumcision has any value. The only thing that counts is *faith expressing itself through love*" (Gal. 5:6); "Neither circumcision nor uncircumcision means anything; what counts is *a new creation*" (Gal. 6:15). In all three cases the complement to the repudiation of circumcision is a substitute. Since "faith through love" and "a new creation" cannot be understood as the law of Moses in part or in any sense, it seems that *keeping God's commands* should probably not be taken that way either.

But can more be said about the precise referent of the divine *commands* Paul expects the Corinthians to *keep* in 1 Corinthians 7:19b? Can we be more specific than saying that Paul is referring to God's will?[210] Without developing the thought, Garland suggests that v. 19b might be a reference to avoiding *porneia:* "What matters is keeping the commandments of God (7:19), in particular, avoiding fornication (7:2). . . . Paul implies that the important distinction is not between those who are married and those who are celibate but between those who avoid fornication and those who fall prey to it."[211] The context supports this reading of the text.[212] As argued in the introductions to 4:18–7:40 and 7:1-40, the commands to "flee sexual immorality" in 6:18 and "glorify God with your body" in 6:20 dominate chapters 5–7 and are never far from view. As it turns out, from 6:12–7:16 Paul uses ten imperative verbs. Interestingly, six of these refer either directly or indirectly to keeping away from sexual immorality: 6:18, 20; 7:2, 3, 5, 9.[213] And it would certainly not be unlike Paul to give this command prominence, as 1 Thessalonians 4:3, penned by Paul in Corinth, demonstrates: "It is God's will that you should be sanctified: that you avoid sexual immorality." In its broader context, then, 1 Corinthians 7:19 resonates with Paul's argument in chapter 7, and its significance would not have been lost on the Corinthians. The better readers would have seen its relevance to the main

210. Barrett, 169, suggests that Paul has in mind "an obedience to the will of God as disclosed in his Son [which is] far more radical than the observance of any code, whether ceremonial or moral, could be." Cf. Furnish, *The Theology of the First Letter to the Corinthians*, 62: keeping God's commands means "leading one's life in accordance with God's call (v. 17a), as one who belongs to Christ (v. 22)."

211. Garland, 299, 306.

212. In the broader context of the whole letter, perhaps a second basic command of God that Paul would have the Corinthians think of is the avoidance of idolatry (cf. 10:14 and 10:31).

213. The other four consist of commands concerning divorce: 7:11, 12, 13, 15.

message in the chapter and "connected the dots" to conclude that "Marriage is nothing and singleness is nothing, but keeping God's commandments is what counts, especially avoiding sexual immorality."

**7:20** Having used circumcision as an illustration, Paul reiterates the basic guiding principle for all of his instructions in chapter 7, which he introduced in v. 17, before moving on to another example: *Each of you should remain in the situation you were in when God called you.*[214] Paul is not against making any change to one's circumstances, as v. 21b proves. Rather, he is responding to the opinion that such changes will enhance one's calling to live as a Christian.[215] A third rendition of the principle in v. 24 will add the phrase "before God." As Paul insists in vv. 29-31, human social categories are not ultimate. Those Corinthians who thought that by changing their marital or other social status they would enhance their spiritual life are indirectly rebuked by Paul in this verse. Just as there is no need for the Corinthian Christians to change their ethnic status by becoming Jews to live a life pleasing to God, so too there is no need for them to change their marital status to do so.

### *b. Analogy of Slavery/Freedom, 7:21-23*

> [21]*Were you a slave when you were called? Don't let it trouble you — although if you can gain your freedom, do so.* [22]*For those who were slaves when called to faith in the Lord are the Lord's freed people; similarly, those who were free when called are Christ's slaves.* [23]*You were bought at a price; do not become slaves of human beings.*

**7:21** To buttress his advice on the unimportance of marital status to one's relationship with God, Paul moves from drawing an analogy with ethnic status in vv. 17-20 to one involving social status in vv. 21-23. If for modern readers, whose societies have done away with the practice of slavery, his words appear "opaque and troubling,"[216] Hays is correct that Paul's original audience would probably have found them "clear and reassuring." Some comment on the ancient institution and experience of slavery is needed to understand this passage.

While estimates vary, Corinth's population broke down three ways: approximately one third were slaves, one third were emancipated slaves, and one third freeborn citizens. Unfortunately, Barclay is right that there are "more than enough difficulties in attempting to grasp the true character and significance of slavery in the Graeco-Roman world of the first century."[217]

214. Literally, Paul tells them, "Each one in the calling in which he or she was called, in it remain."

215. Fee, 309.

216. Hays, 126.

217. J. M. G. Barclay, "Paul, Philemon and the Dilemma of Christian Slave-Ownership," *NTS* 37 (1991), 161-86, 161.

Byron's survey of thirty-five years of research points out that there are still widely differing views.[218] Scholars who have investigated legal texts tend to depict slavery as a benign form of mass employment for the under classes. People sold themselves into slavery, slaves could be highly educated, legal action and public opinion supported better treatment of slaves, and slaves might even aspire to upward social mobility.[219] On the other hand, sociological definitions of slavery have produced less flattering depictions. Slaves were persons without honor, and they were stripped of their former identity when they became slaves. Masters exercised unlimited power over their slaves, and the institution itself was created and maintained by violence.[220] Both views may be right. Since slavery was diverse in practice and ideology, it is difficult to generalize. Treatment of slaves varied from protection and provision to abuse and exploitation.[221] Dale Martin's conclusion is judicious: it mattered less that someone was a slave than whose slave one was.[222]

If the Corinthians thought of a change in their ethnic status neutrally, they may well have valued highly improvements in their social status. Christian slaves, for instance, might have been saving up to buy their freedom, and many may have looked at their freed and born-free brothers and sisters in Christ with envy. Slavery, even benign, would have placed considerable limitations on their Christian lives and service, humanly speaking. Hence Paul's counsel concerning slavery was more pertinent and concrete than his comments on circumcision.

In fact, in the context of a discussion on singleness, marriage, and sexual purity a discussion of slavery versus freedom becomes remarkably pertinent since slaves could neither legally marry nor exercise any significant control over their own sexual purity. As Glancy notes, "Sexual access to slave bodies was a pervasive dimension of ancient systems of slavery. Both female and male slaves were available for their owners' pleasure. . . ." This was in keeping with "the widespread ancient recognition of slaves as benign sexual outlets for their owners."[223] In other words, they were often the

218. John Byron, "Paul and the Background of Slavery: The *Status Quaestionis* in New Testament Scholarship," *Currents in Biblical Research* 3.1 (2004), 116-39.

219. For example, Bartchy, *Μᾶλλον Χρῆσαι: First-Century Slavery and the Interpretation of 1 Corinthians 7:21;* F. Lyall, *Slaves, Citizens and Sons: Legal Metaphors in the Epistles* (Grand Rapids: Zondervan, 1984).

220. For example, O. Patterson, *Slavery and Social Death: A Comparative Study* (Cambridge, MA: Harvard University Press, 1982); K. R. Bradley, *Slaves and Masters in the Roman Empire: A Study in Social Control* (New York: Oxford University Press, 1987).

221. Cf. Barclay, "Paul, Philemon and the Dilemma of Christian Slave-Ownership," 167.

222. D. B. Martin, *Slavery as Salvation: The Metaphor of Slavery in Pauline Christianity* (New Haven and London: Yale University Press, 1990), 122.

223. Glancy, *Slavery in Early Christianity,* 21; Carolyn Osiek, "Female Slaves, *Porneia,* and the Limits of Obedience," in *Early Christian Families in Context: An Interdisciplinary Dialogue* (ed. David L. Balch and Carolyn Osiek; Grand Rapids: Eerdmans, 2003), 262-64. See also the fuller discussions in MacDonald, "Slavery, Sexuality and House Churches," 94-113,

objects of the sexual "touching" of their masters.[224] She thinks it plausible that Paul raises the slaves issue "in the midst of his discussion of marriage because he is aware that slaves, who are unable to contract marriages, are the sexual property of their owners."[225] Elsewhere she has suggested that "by limiting the legitimate range of sexual expression to marriage, Paul implicitly suggests that slaves who oblige their masters sexually are engaged in *porneia*."[226] Unless there was a prior understanding that slaves were not morally accountable for sexual activities over which they had no control, Paul's warning about not associating with those guilty of *porneia* would have presumably raised serious questions for some of the slaves within the Corinthian congregation. One of the many motivations behind slaves' desire to achieve freedom (besides the obvious benefits) would have been the ability to exercise some sovereignty over their own sexual behavior and the freedom to enter into a formal and legal marriage.

That also raises another way in which the discussion of slavery is pertinent to a broader discussion of marriage and the possibility of changing one's social status: one of the primary reasons for the manumission of female slaves in the Roman world, it seems, was in order that they might marry their former masters.[227] Male slaves were also sometimes manumitted by their female masters in order to marry them, although this was considered rather scandalous.[228] The issues of Jew/Gentile and slave/free, and of status hierarchies in general, may have been raised in relation to marriage due to typical Roman (and Jewish[229]) concerns about the appropriate status of wedding partners: "If both marriage partners were not to be of

---

and Jennifer A. Glancy, "Obstacles to Slaves' Participation in the Corinthian Church," *JBL* 117 (1998), 481-501 (although Glancy's view that Paul's teaching would have marginalized slaves due to their sexual obligations is unjustified).

224. See on 7:1, and Ciampa, "Revisiting the Euphemism in 1 Corinthians 7:1."

225. Glancy, *Slavery in Early Christianity*, 68.

226. Glancy, "Obstacles to Slaves' Participation in the Corinthian Church," 496.

227. C. Wayne Tucker, "Women in the Manumission Inscriptions at Delphi," *TAPA* 112 (1982), 231. See Osiek, "Female Slaves, *Porneia*, and the Limits of Obedience," 261; Osiek and Balch, *Families in the New Testament World*, 61. Martin, "Slave Families and Slaves in Families," in *Early Christian Families in Context* 216-22, admits that this may be true but points out that "we have few means to test the hypothesis" (216) and provides evidence of other motives behind the manumission of women. Our point is not that it was the usual or most common reason for the manumission of a woman, but only that it seems to be a well-known motivation at the time. One interpretation of vv. 36-38 suggests that it deals with just such a scenario of a slave owner besotted with a female slave (see the comments there).

228. See Judith Evans Grubbs, "'Marriage More Shameful than Adultery': Slave-Mistress Relationships, 'Mixed Marriages,' and Late Roman Law," *Phoenix* 47 (1993), 125-54.

229. Josephus, *Antiquities* 4.244, adds his views regarding this very concern in his paraphrase of Deut. 22:13-21: "Let your young men, on reaching the age of wedlock, marry virgins, freeborn and of honest parents. He that will not espouse a virgin must not unite himself to a woman living with another man, corrupting her or wronging her former husband. Female slaves must not be taken in marriage by free men, however strongly some may be constrained thereto by love: such passion must be mastered by regard for decorum and the proprieties of rank" (Thackeray's translation [LCL]).

equal social status, then only the woman should be inferior, not the man. . . . The prejudice against freedmen and freedwomen, in favor of the freeborn, was always present. Yet marriages of nonelite women with men of lower social status . . . were not infrequent."[230] Lining up acceptable marriages in a small community like the Corinthian church would have been complicated by the intersection between such Roman concerns and "Paul's preference . . . that believers marry 'in the Lord,' that they marry other believers."[231] Either an unusual number of people would have to remain unmarried or some other preference would have to give: the preference for marrying people of the same religious commitment or the preference for marrying men of the same or a higher social status.

While he discussed the circumcision issue in the third person (v. 18: "a man"; literally, "someone") in this verse, Paul addresses the slave reader with a series of second-person singular verbs.[232] He begins by asking the question directly: *Were you a slave when you were called?* Some may have wondered, "Isn't my ability to honor and serve God profoundly compromised by the fact that I live the life of a slave? Isn't this especially the case where it pertains to living a life of sexual purity and integrity? Wouldn't I have a better standing with God if only I were free?"

If the case of the slave were truly parallel to that of the circumcised person, Paul would undoubtedly have responded in a way parallel to v. 18: "If you were called as a slave, don't be freed!" But the radical difference, of course, was that a man could choose to be circumcised or to have the circumcision undone, while the slave really has no ability to change his status. Only his master can decide whether or not to free him. There would be no sense, then, for Paul to counsel the slave not to seek a change in status. Either one will be thrust upon him or her, or it will not. Given the different circumstance Paul's counsel is also rather different: *Don't let it trouble you.* The verb translated "to trouble [someone]"[233] is rendered elsewhere in the New Testament as "paying no attention to" (Matt. 22:16; Mark 12:14), "caring nothing" (Mark 4:38; Luke 10:40; John 10:13), and "not showing concern" (Acts 18:17; 1 Cor. 9:9). The Corinthian Christian slaves are not to worry about their low status or about presumed negative spiritual implications resulting from it. If Paul is thinking about the sexual and moral implications of the life of a slave, part of his subtle point would presumably be that slaves are responsible only for those actions over which they have some control, not for those which are forced upon them due to their social status (otherwise they could hardly not be troubled by their situation).[234] Before offering

230. Osiek and Balch, *Families in the New Testament World*, 61.

231. Meeks, *The First Urban Christians*, 101.

232. Second-person singular verbs appear in only ten verses in 1 Corinthians: 4:7; 7:16, 21, 27, 28; 9:9; 14:16, 17; 15:36, 37 (there are twenty-four such verbs in those ten verses, three in this one verse).

233. Gk. μέλω, "be a source of concern" (BDAG).

234. The general view of the time was that in these situations slaves were "not dis-

an eloquent explanation for this remarkable counsel in vv. 22-23, the rest of v. 21 considers what to do if the opportunity for freedom presents itself.

Paul addresses a hypothetical situation which would surely have been on the mind of some members of the church in Corinth. Literally, he says: "but if you are able to become free, rather [or "more," or "all the more"; cf. BDAG] make use [or make the most of]." Readers must supply that which is left understood. The question is, make use of what? The answer could be "your slavery" or "your freedom." This text has divided interpreters since the early church.[235] Modern English translations are also divided: "Even if you can gain your freedom, make use of your present condition [i.e., your slavery] now more than ever" (NRSV); *although if you can gain your freedom,*[236] *do so* (TNIV).[237] While something can be said for both interpretations, the evidence favors the TNIV understanding of the verse.[238]

Elliptical expressions are common to most languages, and it is a general "rule of thumb" to supply a word from the immediate context. An uncontroversial example is 1 Corinthians 4:15: "Even if you had ten thousand guardians in Christ, *you do* not *have* many fathers." In the second clause there is no verb ("have") in the Greek (which literally reads, "but not many fathers"), but no one disputes that it can be supplied from its presence in the previous clause. Correspondingly, in the case of 7:21, the preceding clause mentions "freedom," and it is therefore the most likely referent. The other critical terms also make sense if the verse is read this way. Recalling our literal translation above, the verb[239] means "make use of, employ"

honored or regarded as acting immorally" (Susan M. Treggiari, "Marriage and Family in Roman Society," in *Marriage and Family in the Biblical World* [ed. Ken M. Campbell; Downers Grove, IL: InterVarsity, 2003], 166).

235. While Chrysostom, *Homiliae in Epistulam i ad Corinthios* 19.5, e.g., thought it was an encouragement to remain in slavery, he admits that others thought otherwise: "Now we are not ignorant that some say, the words, "use it rather," are spoken with regard to liberty: interpreting it, 'if you can become free, become free.'"

236. In the context slavery and freedom are the two different legal statuses. Paul does not have in mind an opportunity to gain one's freedom by running away, even if Ulpian, the famed Roman jurist, said flight was "'a form of liberty' for the slave, that at once brought relief from the power of the master" (K. R. Bradley, *Slavery and Society at Rome* [Cambridge: Cambridge University Press, 1994], 128, citing *Digest* 21.1.17.10).

237. The majority of translations supply something along the lines of "your freedom" (cf. RSV, NIV, JB, NEB ["but if a chance of liberty should come, take it"]; NAB and NJB agree with the NRSV). B. R. Braxton's view, *The Tyranny of Resolution: 1 Corinthians 7.17-24* (SBLDS 181; Atlanta: Society of Biblical Literature, 2000), that the verse is deliberately ambiguous because Paul did not want to speak to the issue directly, supposing problems pertaining to slavery in the church, is unlikely. The apostle had no track record for "shy diplomacy," and, as argued above, a careful assessment of the evidence points to "your freedom" as the ellipsis Paul intended.

238. Garland, 308-12, offers a thorough defense; see also J. A. Harrill, *The Manumission of Slaves in Early Christianity* (HUT 32; Tübingen: Mohr Siebeck, 1995).

239. Gk. χράω. Here we find a second-person singular aorist middle imperative form of the verb (χρῆσαι). It has been pointed out earlier that this is the only imperative that is not a present imperative from v. 12 until the end of the chapter (see also the comment on

(BDAG) and not "make the most of" or "put up with."[240] And the conjunction[241] means "to a greater or higher degree, *more*"[242] or "for a better reason, *rather, all the more*"[243] (BDAG). Alternatively, Harrill's exhaustive survey of usage concludes that in combination with the verb this conjunction should be understood adversatively as "instead" or "preferably,"[244] which also supports supplying "your freedom" to complete the verse.[245]

In terms of structure and logic vv. 21-22 follow a similar pattern to that of vv. 18-19 and v. 27. In all three cases there are three elements: a rhetorical question, an imperative, and an explanation. The only difference is that in vv. 21-22, v. 21b breaks the pattern and introduces an interjection that would most naturally be taken as some kind of exception.[246] The imperative in v. 21a also points in this direction. As pointed out above, we might have expected Paul to say, "Were you called as a slave? Do not seek to become free." Instead, he writes: *Don't let it trouble you.* Deming concludes plausibly that "[t]his deliberate softening of the imperative . . . would seem to rule out the idea that 7:21b is somehow an attempt to heighten the imperative's impact."[247]

Dawes points out that on two other occasions in 1 Corinthians when Paul uses paired illustrations, in 3:5-7 (the field and building) and 15:35-44a (sowing and different kinds of bodies), the second image extends and complements rather than just repeats the first.[248] In the case at hand, Paul's first illustration of circumcision is absolute, whereas his second allows an exception; after all, Paul does not say "slavery is nothing." As mentioned in the introduction to 7:17-24, this makes good sense of Paul's counsel concerning marriage and singleness throughout the chapter.[249] On some issues he allows no exceptions. In particular, he insists on no extended abstinence for those married (7:5) and no divorce for those married to Christians. On the other hand, exceptions to Paul's main advice do punctuate his counsel, all of which are introduced by the word "if,"[250] as in v. 21b. The exceptions from the rule of "remaining as you are" include: (1) v. 5 — occasional tem-

---

καταλλαγήτω in v. 11). According to *TLG*, a second-person singular present middle imperative form of this verb does not appear in all of Greek literature, suggesting that Paul's use of the aorist here is unremarkable.

240. Barrett, 170; cf. 1 Cor. 7:31; 9:12, 15; 2 Cor. 1:17; 3:12; 13:10.

241. Gk. μᾶλλον.

242. Cf. Matt. 8:13; Phil. 1:9; 3:4; Phlm. 16.

243. For example, 1 Tim. 6:2; Phil. 2:12.

244. Harrill, *The Manumission of Slaves in Early Christianity*, 108-21.

245. Cf. Garland's translation: "Were you a slave when you were called? Do not let it bother you. But if you are able to become free, instead make use of freedom."

246. Harrill, *The Manumission of Slaves in Early Christianity*, 123-26.

247. W. Deming, "A Diatribe Pattern in 1 Cor 7:21-22: A New Perspective on Paul's Direction to Slaves," *NovT* 37 (1995), 137.

248. Dawes, "'But If You Can Gain Your Freedom' (1 Corinthians 7:17-24)," 688.

249. See Garland, 311-12.

250. Either Gk. εἰ or ἐάν; all but the first, in common with v. 21b, also include the word δέ.

porary abstinence from sex in marriage; (2) vv. 8-9 — marriage or remarriage of unmarried and widows; (3) vv. 10-11 — the separated remaining unmarried or being reconciled; (4) vv. 13-15 — separation from unbelieving spouses; (5) v. 28 — marriage of a single man or "virgin"; (6) v. 36 — marriage to one's "virgin"; and (7) v. 39 — marriage of widows.

Much hangs on Paul's few words in v. 21b. What is Paul's attitude to slavery? Does he unwittingly join hands with oppressive social forces by consigning slaves to perpetual slavery? In short, he does not. As Barnett concludes,[251] "Paul saw no good in slavery and gave his strongest and unqualified support for slaves to gain their freedom": *if you can gain your freedom, do so.*[252] As Glancy suggests, Paul's concerns regarding their sexual vulnerability may well have been a key part of what "prompted him to advise slaves to take advantage of opportunities for freedom as they arose."[253] That Paul does not regard slavery as "a desirable institution" is confirmed in v. 23 with the general exhortation, *do not become slaves of human beings.*[254]

The fact that Paul explicitly mentions the possibility that slaves would be freed, and encourages them to take full advantage of that new status would certainly have put the topic of manumission in the mind of both the slaves and masters in the congregation, and perhaps opened up space for further discussion of the topic, if it had not already been an open subject among the believers in Corinth.

Of course our churches have many people in them who feel trapped either in their marriages or in their singleness. And even in countries where slavery is no longer legal, it is not uncommon for there to be people who either are virtual slaves, or who at least feel, and may be, trapped in their circumstances. Such people also need to know that their ability to serve and honor God is not actually determined or diminished by their circumstances. Like the Corinthian believers they need to know that they should not nurture the belief that God would be more pleased with them or more willing to use them if only their circumstances would change. And like the Corinthians, they need to know that if opportunities arise that would allow them to transition to a more empowering and less oppressive situation without compromising their Christian integrity, they should feel free to do so. The rhetoric and preaching of much Western Christianity often falsely assumes that all people (perhaps especially all Christians) experience numerous opportunities and great social mobility, and suggests that Christians should expect to have their life dreams fulfilled. Such teaching is completely foreign to Paul's thought and to the experience of people in most cultures and times throughout history.

251. Barnett, 121-22.

252. D. G. Horrell, *The Social Ethos of the Corinthian Correspondence* (Edinburgh: T&T Clark, 1996), 162; Philemon, even given its own difficulties of interpretation, shows that Paul was not opposed to the freeing of slaves.

253. Glancy, *Slavery in Early Christianity*, 69.

254. Horrell, *The Social Ethos of the Corinthian Correspondence*, 162.

Paul realized that many slaves in the church with slim prospects of freedom had to cope with their limitations. On this point it is significant that marriage is also conceived as a form of bondage (see on v. 15), one that limits a person's capacity to serve the Lord with "undivided devotion" (7:32-35). His message is the same to both groups: "Just as slaves should not become absorbed in anxiety over their slavery, so those who are married should not become absorbed in their anxiety over being married."[255] The next two verses supply an explanation for this assessment of the state of being a slave.

**7:22** The reason not to worry about being a slave,[256] if you don't have the opportunity to be free, is that *those who were slaves when called to faith in the Lord are the Lord's freed people; similarly, those who were free when called are Christ's slaves.* Paul's point is that "[a]ll, regardless of worldly social status, are now under the authority of Christ."[257] Slaves knew better than most that, when it comes to personal identity, the key issue is not who you are but whose you are.

The verse announces a status reversal that is nothing short of revolutionary: the *slaves* are given the higher rank as *the Lord's freed people,* as opposed to the *free* in the church, who are described as *Christ's slaves.* The implicit message to status-conscious believers was that social differences have no place in the church. God prefers the "lowly things of this world" over the "wise" or "influential" by "human standards" (cf. 1:26-29). God's values are not our values. Rather than confirm them in their own prior social status as slaves or free, Christ has already seen fit to alter each person's status, showing, it would seem, that the maintenance of that prior status is not an extremely high value. From this perspective this verse does not provide strong support for the interpretation of v. 21 that sees it as committing the slave to their slave status come what may.

To understand Paul's reference to the Lord's "freedman," it is important to know that upon being manumitted, or freed, most slaves did not then become independent of their former master. Rather, the master became their patron, committed to their well-being and social advancement, and the former slave continued to be obligated to him in a variety of ways (the master could dictate the terms of the former slave's future obligations and responsibilities in the manumission document): "[T]he master, now the slave's patron, looks after the welfare of the freedman. As Christ's freedman, the former slave takes on the name of the master, is directed by him, and owes him allegiance."[258] As Martin stresses, Paul's formulation em-

255. Garland, 313.

256. The explanatory γάρ connects what follows not to the interjection of v. 21b but to the imperative of v. 21a, "Don't let it trouble you."

257. Hays, 125.

258. Garland, 314. See Garland's fuller discussion there, as well as Susan Treggiari, *Roman Freedmen during the Late Republic* (Oxford: Clarendon, 1969), 68-81; and Markus Barth and Helmut Blanke, *The Letter to Philemon: A New Translation with Notes and Commentary* (The Eerdmans Critical Commentary; Grand Rapids: Eerdmans, 2000), 41-53.

phasizes "the benefits of clientage to Christ over clientage to a human patron,"[259] in that the slave's true status is bound up in "his or her placement in a different household entirely: the household of Christ. The slave is a freedperson of the Lord and shares in the benefit, status, and obligations that relationship brings."[260] As Byron explains:

> The call of God creates paradoxical freedom. Those called while slaves are not freed to live a life of self-determination, but a life of restricted service to the Lord. Those called while free persons are made slaves of Christ. Both are in a similar situation in the context of God's call regardless of any actual social status.[261]

As Christ's slaves and freed people, all believers owe him obedience and allegiance.[262] They are his. The experience of being a slave (or having been a slave) does not have any prejudicial impact on one's ability to honor Christ. In fact, such experience may help one better understand the way life is to be lived in the service of another (namely, Christ, an infinitely better master), in a way that freeborn people may have difficulty grasping. Grasp it they must if they are going to learn to live as *Christ's slaves.*

The terms "free" and "slave" in relation to Christ are not denotative but connotative, and the purpose is rhetorical. Paul is not trying to create a new hierarchy in the church, but rather to encourage believers who are slaves not to despair at their condition. "Paul consigns honor and status to Christian slaves by designating them as the 'freedmen of Christ.' The slave no longer is simply the slave of so-and-so but a freedman belonging to the Lord."[263] Both phrases, "the freed of the Lord" and "the servant of the Lord," employ genitives of possession, that is, "[b]oth individually and corporately they belong to Christ and therefore to God."[264] As believers they "have been claimed by the Lord, and in their belonging to him they have been granted a new identity and status."[265] This fits with the letter's overriding eschatology, namely, that Christ's lordship is what matters and that its establishment relativizes all other social statuses.

259. D. B. Martin, *Slavery as Salvation,* 64.

260. D. B. Martin, *Slavery as Salvation,* 65.

261. John Byron, *Slavery Metaphors in Early Judaism and Pauline Christianity: A Traditio-Historical and Exegetical Examination* (WUNT 2.162; Tübingen: Mohr Siebeck, 2003), 238.

262. For a recent and detailed discussion of Phil. 2:6-11 and its presentation of Christ as the paradigmatic slave of God whose example calls believers to a similar obedience to God (and expectation of exaltation), see Byron, *Slavery Metaphors in Early Judaism and Pauline Christianity,* 150-80.

263. Garland, 315. Byron, *Slavery Metaphors in Early Judaism and Pauline Christianity,* 236-37, shows that Paul's earlier discussion of one's "calling" and the subject of circumcision militates against D. B. Martin's suggestion (*Slavery as Salvation,* 65-67) that Paul intends to create a new hierarchy.

264. Furnish, *The Theology of the First Letter to the Corinthians,* 49.

265. Furnish, *The Theology of the First Letter to the Corinthians,* 65.

The two designations, *the Lord's freed people* and *Christ's slaves,* combine two of the letter's key themes, namely, that of belonging to Christ and that of living under his lordship. Both have far-reaching social and ethical implications, for they inform and even define self-identity and perception. The example of Christ, who served God through situations of constraint (cf. Phil. 2:6-11), shows how fundamental to Christian identity is Paul's teaching here.[266]

**7:23** If v. 22 explains v. 21a, why slaves ought not to be perplexed by their lot, with the thought that ultimately the slaves belong to Christ and not their earthly master, v. 23 explains v. 22. Believers in Corinth belong to Christ because *you were bought at a price.* The same words appeared in 6:20a as an explanation for the assertion that "you are not your own" (6:19b). Here they support Paul's contention that "you do not belong to any other human being either: You belong to God."

As Robertson and Plummer note, "In one sense Christ's death was an act of emancipation, it set free from the thraldom of sin; in another sense it was a change of ownership."[267] Paul's point focuses on the second point here. His words do not suggest that the Corinthians were simply bought out of slavery and are now free and on their own. The notion is not so much that "of Christ's purchase of believers *out of* slavery," since *the price* "brings the believer into Christ's own possession as his or her Lord, who then takes over the responsibility and care of the purchased one. The Christian *belongs to Christ,* not to himself or to herself."[268] This is part of what may be the most fundamental theme of this letter: the lordship of Christ under which all believers are to live their lives.

Paul's thinking is consistent with Old Testament and Jewish thinking about the significance of the exodus event. As noted in the comments on 6:19-20, the Jewish background to "being bought with a price" antecedent to the Christ event in 7:23a, "you were bought with a price," is the exodus. The Israelites were slaves in Egypt, and God redeemed them from their bondage. But he did not set them free to go off and live however they might like. Indeed, they were freed to serve the Lord.

Paul's teaching on slavery in vv. 21-23 is comparable to the ceremony in Exodus 21:5-6 of piercing the ear lobe of a slave who, at the end of seven years' service, instead of becoming free chooses to remain with his master. Daube points out that the *Mekilta* commentary on this passage forms a remarkable parallel to 1 Corinthians 7:21-23 in that it not only recommends that slaves become free if the opportunity arises, but it cites the notion that God is the master of every Jew on account of the exodus event.[269]

Paul's final words on the subject of slavery are more general: *do not*

266. Thiselton, 549-50.

267. Robertson and Plummer, 149.

268. Thiselton, 561.

269. David Daube, *The Exodus Pattern in the Bible* (London: Faber and Faber, 1963), 46.

*become slaves of human beings.*[270] Paul is playing on an implied contrast between their divine Lord, who bought them at a price and now owns them as his own, and the mere human beings to whom they might be tempted to turn over the governing of their lives. He may be alluding to Leviticus 25:4, where the same contrast is at work: "Because the Israelites are my servants, whom I bought out of Egypt, they must not be sold as slaves" (cf. 25:55). Having told the Corinthians' Christian slaves to take their freedom if they can (v. 21b), it seems redundant to tell those who are free not to sell themselves into slavery. According to Winter, Paul has in mind "Christian free men willing to sell themselves into slavery for social and financial benefit."[271] Martin has argued that "because of their positions and their connections with powerful patrons," slaves who played managerial roles on behalf of their owners enjoyed unusual opportunities for social advancement. In his view, "[f]or a select few, slavery could bring access to financial resources, citizenship, education, and the patronage of higher status persons."[272] In fact, it has been suggested that the Corinthian church might have had an outstanding example of just such an approach to upward mobility: Osiek and Balch think that Erastus, Corinth's city treasurer (Rom. 16:23), "was probably at the time a public slave through self-sale, then a freedman with Roman citizenship, who went on to more responsible positions."[273] If Erastus is such an example, and that is far from clear, it may be that others were thinking of following a similar course.

It may be, however, that Paul's words are meant in a spiritual rather than a literal sense. That is, Paul was urging the Corinthians "to avoid entanglements with those who would ensnare them in immoral practices" and thus he was "encouraging a 'spiritual' freedom."[274] Robertson and Plummer explain that the bondage in view is "some condition of life which is likely to violate God's rights of ownership."[275] Given the remoteness from chapter 1, the "slavery" Paul has in mind is probably not specifically to party leaders (cf. 1:11-12). Thiselton points to patronage and possessions, citing 1:26–2:5, 5:1-5, 6:1-8, and 9:15-18 as evidence of such problems in Corinth, and the "bondage of an honor-shame culture" as Paul's target.[276]

270. Note that the address changes from second-person singular to second-person plural.

271. Winter, *Seek the Welfare of the City: Christians as Benefactors and Citizens*, 146. See Glancy, *Slavery in Early Christianity*, 80-85, for a careful examination of the limited evidence for self-sale into slavery, concluding that the evidence "supports the claim that self-sale into slavery was known and at least occasionally practiced in the Roman Empire" but that we do not "have sufficient evidence to support the stronger claim that the practice was common" (84).

272. D. B. Martin, *Slavery as Salvation*, 30, 32. For a brief critique of Martin's thesis, see Byron, *Slavery Metaphors in Early Judaism and Pauline Christianity*, 10-12.

273. Osiek and Balch, *Families in the New Testament World*, 98. See the discussion of Erastus in Florence Morgan Gillman, "Erastus (Person)," *ABD* 2:571.

274. Glancy, *Slavery in Early Christianity*, 84.

275. Robertson and Plummer, 149.

276. Thiselton, 561-62.

Garland agrees with Barrett that Paul means, "Do not make yourselves dependent on the value judgments of men."[277] That is in keeping with Bartchy's suggestion that "to become slaves of men would be to regard social or religious status as more decisive than the calling from God in Christ."[278] In the context of this particular part of Paul's letter the most obvious danger of this kind would be that of allowing the cultural prejudices of others regarding singleness or marriage govern one's own decisions about how best to serve the Lord. Robertson and Plummer capture the tenor of Paul's prohibition: "Do not let social relations or public opinion or evil advisers interfere with the absolute service which is due to him who bought you with his Son's blood."[279] As such, *do not become slaves of human beings* is a remarkably comprehensive maxim for Christian ethics.

### *c. Enunciation of the Principle, 7:24*

*[24]Brothers and sisters, all of you, as responsible to God, should remain in the situation in which God called you.*

**7:24** This verse repeats the general principle already announced in vv. 17 and 20: "Do not seek a change in your (marital, ethnic or social) status." Along with the inclusio formed with v. 17, the broad address of *Brothers and sisters,*[280] *all of you,* also signals the end of the paragraph (7:17-24). Paul makes his appeal on the basis of being part of the family of God established through redemption (v. 23a) and expresses his genuine affection for them. Since it is no small matter to be a slave, Paul has been careful not to make light of the circumstances of Christian slaves. His counsel throughout reflects his "tenderness of heart and robustness of judgment."[281]

The rest of the verse repeats the earlier renditions with one additional element. The final two words in Greek, which modify the verb "to remain," are, literally, "before" or "alongside God."[282] They are variously translated as "in the presence of God" (REB, NJB) or "with God" (KJV, NRSV). While these translations of the phrase are neutral, the TNIV's *as responsible to God* and Thiselton's "with God at their side" go in different directions. Is the purpose of the words to call the Corinthians to account (the former), or to reassure them (the latter)? Paul probably intends something of both ideas: As they remain with/before God, they should be aware that whatever their

277. Garland, 315; Barrett, 171.

278. Bartchy, *Μᾶλλον Χρῆσαι: First-Century Slavery and the Interpretation of 1 Corinthians 7:21*, 182.

279. Robertson and Plummer, 149.

280. Gk. ἀδελφός. The words "all of you," or "each one of you," make this a clear instance of inclusive language.

281. Robertson and Plummer, 148.

282. Gk. παρὰ θεῷ.

situation they 1) are not alone in it, and 2) are responsible before God (who bought them at a price) for how they live within it.[283]

### 3. *Counsel for Single Adults, 7:25-38*

Barnett comments despondently that "[t]his passage [7:25-35] and the next (7:36-40) are the most difficult in the epistle, as witnessed by the divergent opinions of commentators and translators."[284] Murphy-O'Connor agrees: "This is probably the most difficult and controverted section of the letter."[285] While 1 Corinthians 11:2-16 may come close to the second half of chapter 7 for obscurity of detail, these verses do present formidable challenges to a secure interpretation. The problem is not the number of exegetical problems involved so much as their critical nature. The biggest questions concern the referents of a key term and phrase: Who are "the virgins" (vv. 25, 28, 34, 36, 37)? And what was "the present crisis" (v. 26)? Once these questions are answered, the task then is to trace the argument in the section and discern how Paul's counsel here coheres with the rest of the chapter. These difficulties notwithstanding, the section has much to offer by way of guidance in the application of a Christian worldview to common and complex issues of life. As with the preceding verses, some of the issues addressed in these verses are faced by believers of every time and culture (e.g., whether to marry or remain single, how deeply to invest oneself in the various ups and downs of our daily life) while others reflect particular, complex social realities of first-century Corinth. Even the latter are important for us today since a foreign situation can actually enhance relevance by helping us look at our own situations through new eyes which have been informed by insights applied in other complex settings. In so many ways 1 Corinthians provides us with case studies of "Ministry in Complex Urban Settings" which can be fruitfully applied in similarly complex, even if different, settings.

The basic thrust is clear. In vv. 1-16 the apostle addressed married couples (7:2-7), the unmarried (in general terms), widows (or widows and their suitors) (7:8-9), those contemplating divorce (7:10-11), and those in mixed marriages with unbelievers (7:12-16). In vv. 25-38 Paul addresses the question of "virgins," mainly from the point of view of their potential suitors and actual fiancés, and he advises them to stay unmarried for three reasons: (1) because of the "present crisis" (7:25-28); (2) because of the end of the world (7:29-31); and (3) because of the distractions of married life (7:32-35).[286] However, this advice is tempered with the proviso of freedom to

283. Cf. 1 Cor. 3:19 — "in God's sight."

284. Barnett, 124.

285. Murphy-O'Connor, *Corinthians* (New Testament Message, vol. 1; Wilmington, DE: Glazier, 1978), 171.

286. A key question concerns whether reasons 1 and 2 are in fact the same reason; see below in the commentary.

choose whether or not to marry (7:36-38). Verse 38 sums up Paul's stance: "he who marries the virgin does right, but he who does not marry her does better."

All three grounds that Paul gives for "the virgins" not to marry are structured around inclusios. Paul introduces something at the beginning of each paragraph which he then confirms and clarifies at its closing:

1. Because of "the present crisis," that is, "troubles in this life" (7:26a, 28b);
2. Because "the time is short," that is, "this world in its present form is passing away" (7:29a, 31b); and
3. Because it is better "to be free from concern," that is, "to live in a right way in undivided devotion to the Lord" (7:32a, 35b).

Paul goes to greater lengths to explain his advice in this case than in any of the earlier cases — some fourteen verses compared with only a few to each of the previous four groups. This may be, in part at least, because it was an issue of particular concern raised in the Corinthians' letter to Paul. He began this chapter by introducing "the matters you wrote about" with the expression "now concerning. . . ." He uses that expression again as he introduces this verse. This is different from the ways he introduced the earlier subdivisions of the chapter, where he addressed himself "to" the unmarried and widows (v. 8) and then "to" those who were already married (v. 10) and "to" the rest (those married to unbelievers). Here he does not address himself "to" the virgins, but deals with issues related to them *(about virgins)*, mainly addressing those who are engaged to a virgin or who might consider pursuing one. Paul's guidance in these verses seems to support and expand on some of his earlier instructions in the chapter. This pattern can be seen elsewhere in ABA structures in this letter, as well as the impression that Paul's primary target or concern is finally addressed in the second "A" unit (e.g., the issue of tongues vs. prophecy [ch. 14] as the primary concern of his extended discussion of spiritual gifts in chs. 12–14).

Men who were struggling with the temptation to "touch a woman" (see on v. 1) might have been expected to deal with their sexual needs within the context of their own marriage or through establishing a newly formed marriage with a virgin.[287] The Corinthians may have written to Paul about particular challenges relating to the desirability or lack of availability of virgins (we don't know how many there were in the Corinthian church) or the issue of prior commitments of marriage engagement (perhaps made before knowing Christ or the implications of knowing Christ for marriage plans). Verses 36-38 may well suggest that the Corinthi-

287. There would be rarer opportunities for widows or divorced women (who were both expected, if they were young enough, to remarry soon after becoming single). Virgins and widows were considered the most honorable women to marry.

ans (or possibly Chloe's people) had mentioned to Paul a case (or cases?) where a man was torn between canceling or holding off on his planned marriage with his fiancée and either his overpowering desire or his sense of social responsibility which compelled him to consummate the marriage. The new Christian expectations (parallel to Jewish expectations; see again Philo, *On the Life of Joseph* 43) that men should guard their sexual purity by engaging in sexual relations only within the context of marriage would have required quite an adjustment on the part of those raised in Roman culture where men were generally free to engage in a wide range of sexual experiences before marrying in their mid to late twenties. Some Corinthian men may have felt pressured to marry earlier than usual in order to avoid an extended period of celibacy before marriage. The new sexual expectations for male converts would have created a number of complex dynamics within the Corinthian church.

Paul's assumption in all three arguments noted above is that it takes more effort and resources to be married as opposed to being single and that, especially in the context of the ongoing crisis the Corinthians were experiencing, in most cases it would be best for everyone to maintain the status quo in the midst of such turbulent times.

### a. Stay Unmarried Because of the "Present Crisis," 7:25-28

25*Now about virgins: I have no command from the Lord, but I give a judgment as one who by the Lord's mercy is trustworthy.* 26*Because of the present crisis, I think that it is good for a man to remain as he is.* 27*Are you pledged to a woman? Do not seek to be released. Are you free from such a commitment? Do not look for a wife.* 28*But if you do marry, you have not sinned; and if a virgin marries, she has not sinned. But those who marry will face many troubles in this life, and I want to spare you this.*

**7:25** *Now about virgins* addresses a fifth group in the church who needed Paul's counsel. *Now about* repeats the opening words of 7:1, where Paul indicated that he was taking up questions and issues from the Corinthians' letter. Even though, technically speaking, they could introduce a subject of Paul's own choosing,[288] their immediate placement following the purposeful aside of vv. 17-24 almost certainly indicates that Paul is again addressing directly concerns the Corinthians had raised in their letter.[289] Who the *virgins* were and what the Corinthians wanted to know about them are debated. The term appears in vv. 25, 28, 34, and 36-38.

Fee summarizes the three main views.[290] First, for centuries the text

288. Cf. Mitchell, "Concerning περὶ δέ in 1 Corinthians."

289. See Hurd, *The Origin of 1 Corinthians*, 61-71, and the comments introducing the passage.

290. Fee, 326-28.

was read as addressing the issue of fathers giving their "virgin" daughters in marriage. Lightfoot explains this interpretation: "St Paul generalized, first stating the guiding principle (v. 27), then applying it to both sexes (vv. 28-35), and finally dealing with the special point which the Corinthians had put to him (vv. 36-38)."[291] In this understanding, in vv. 36-38 Paul instructs fathers concerning "their virgins" about the question of whether "to give them in marriage" or not.[292] While fitting some of the details, this view has trouble accounting for others. In particular, if Paul were addressing such a situation, we would have expected more explicit address to fathers, guardians, daughters, and the like, terms which are conspicuous by their absence from the passage.

A second view takes issue with restricting *virgins* to females, referring it to both men and women who are living in a "spiritual marriage," that is, without sexual relations.[293] Many scholars believe that Paul addressed something like this already in 7:2-6 (see above for our contrasting view), and "spiritual marriages" were known in Christian circles from the second to the fifth centuries. The second-century *Acts of Paul and Thecla* 5, for example, blesses "they who have wives as if they had them not, for they shall inherit God." However, there is no clear evidence of such relationships within the first century, and since vv. 2-6 have already made it clear that Paul would be opposed to such forms of marriage it is not clear why he would address it again here in a more conciliatory way. Perhaps an even stronger objection to this view is that although the genitive plural "virgins" in the phrase, *now about virgins*, gives no indication of gender and the word can be used in reference to men, the only cases where it does so is in reference to certain Israelite or Jewish men (such as Joseph, Abel, Melchizedek, and the apostles John and Paul), and, in a spiritual sense, to the church (Rev. 14:4).[294] It should also be remembered that it is very unlikely that any of the (Roman) Corinthian men thinking about getting married would have been virgins, since, unlike Roman women, Roman men were expected to begin engaging in sexual relations (with prostitutes or slaves, etc.) after reaching adolescence.[295] Since the Corinthian church had

291. Lightfoot, 231.

292. Importance is attached to Paul's use of γαμίζω in v. 38, which is translated in the Gospels as "to give in marriage" (Matt. 22:30; 24:38; Mark 12:25; Luke 17:27; 20:35), instead of γαμέω. But see below on v. 38 on the legitimacy of the translation "to marry."

293. The first advocate in modern times was H. Achelis, *Virgines subintroductae: Ein Beitrag zum VII. Kapitel des 1. Korintherbriefs* (Leipzig, 1902); cf. NEB, Hurd, *The Origin of 1 Corinthians*, 170-80, Thrall, Ruef, and Murphy-O'Connor.

294. Nonnus of Panopolis and *CIG* 4:8784b use it of the apostle John, *Joseph and Aseneth* (4:9 and 8:1) uses it of Joseph; the *Legend of St. Pelagia* 27.1 uses it of Abel; and the *Suda* uses it of Abel and Melchizedek (BDAG). For the exception that proves the rule, cf. Achilles Tatius 5.21.1: It is claimed that Clitophon is a virgin (παρθενία), "if at any rate there is male virginity" (cited in *TLNT* 3:47 n. 22).

295. Spicq cites the examples from *Joseph and Aseneth* mentioned in the previous note in support of the view that Paul "means men as well as women" here (*TLNT* 3:50), suggest-

been in existence for only around four years, and most Roman men did not marry until their mid to late twenties, those who were thinking of marriage were very unlikely to be virgins at the time. This point is reinforced by the fact that all subsequent uses of the word in vv. 28, 34, 36, 37, and 38 are feminine. Thus, while it is theoretically possible that Paul intended the generic sense in v. 25 before going on to address specific female cases,[296] the linguistic evidence and the historical and social context militate against such a view.

The third view is that *virgins* refers to betrothed young women. It infers that some engaged couples in the church were wondering whether to go through with their marriages. It is suggested that they may have felt under pressure from ascetic thinking in the church that it is not good to have sexual relations with a woman (cf. 7:1b). Or some other circumstance may have put them off (see below on *the present crisis* in v. 26). Paul addresses their male fiancés in vv. 27-28 and 36-38, insisting that it is not a sin to marry and to consummate the marriage. This is perhaps the most widely held view among commentators today. A problem for this view is that there were a variety of ways in which a Greek could and did refer to betrothed virgins or betrothed young women,[297] and the word "virgin," by itself, is not used in that way elsewhere. It becomes clear in vv. 36-38 that Paul has betrothed virgins in mind at least in those verses (where they are repeatedly referred to as "his virgin"). It may be that the Corinthians had referred to "betrothed virgins" in their letter to Paul and that he responds by referring to "the virgins," meaning "the [betrothed] virgins you mentioned," but that is speculation. It seems just as possible that vv. 25-35 address a broader question regarding virgins (or young unmarried women) in general, as those most commonly to occupy the attention of unmarried men who are struggling with issues of sexual purity and possible advantages to marrying. In suggesting that *it is good for a man to remain as he is* (v. 26), Paul almost certainly does not mean for him to continue to remain engaged forever, and v. 27 clearly addresses both men who are and men who are not presently bound or pledged to a woman. The first part of v. 28, *But if you do marry, you have not sinned,* does not seem to be addressed to one pledged (or possibly married) to a woman, but to the one mentioned at the end of v. 27 who is not bound or pledged to a woman. It is not clear from v. 28 that the

---

ing that "Paul is careful to explain the superiority of virginity to recent converts from paganism in secular terms: 'beauty/nobility,' a Greek word connoting honorableness, excellence, and moral good (τοῦτο καλόν, 1 Cor 7:26; καλῶς ποιεῖ, 7:37-38)" (51 n. 36). But it is more likely that Paul is encouraging the men in question to remain single (and celibate) than that they should remain virgins (which, as pointed out above, they were unlikely to be).

296. Lightfoot, 231.

297. For example, Philo, *On Agriculture* 152 has ταῖς ὁμολογηθείσαις παρθένοις (betrothed virgins), while *On Agriculture* 157 refers to ἐγγυηθείσης γυναικός (betrothed wife); Josephus, *Against Apion* 2.201, refers to παρθένον ἑτέρῳ προωμολογημένην (a virgin who has been promised).

virgin in mind was one already betrothed to a man rather than a general reference to any virgin who decides to marry (certainly what Paul says in the verse applies to all who marry). Verses 32-35 refer to married and unmarried men and women without any indication that currently engaged men and women are particularly in view (v. 34 gives no hint that the virgin mentioned there is engaged). Verses 36-38, however, as we have already mentioned, clearly seem to be dealing with engaged couples, and leave the impression that the Corinthians may have mentioned something about issues with previously established betrothals.

While it may be that Paul was responding to a question that dealt only with betrothed virgins (we might say, "engaged young ladies"), young (virgin) ladies were considered the most desirable potential wives,[298] and given that the Corinthians were evidently responding to Paul's comments in his earlier letter about avoiding people contaminated by sexual immorality, it would seem natural for them to raise the question of the desirability of marrying virgins (as well as the wisest course of action for virgins themselves in a world full of *porneia*). We tentatively prefer the conclusion, in fact, that the Corinthians raised the issue about the wisdom of marrying virgins/maidens in general as well as the problem of whether to follow through with betrothal commitments at this time (see on vv. 36-38).

As best we can tell, in response to Paul's warnings in his previous letter about sexual immorality (and avoiding those involved in it), some Corinthian men were wondering if they should find a virgin to marry (or, in some cases, go ahead and marry the virgin to which they are already betrothed) in order to better avoid such temptations, although the crisis Corinth was experiencing at the time did not make it a propitious time to start a family. Paul first admits that for this issue *I have no command from the Lord.*[299] Unlike the question of whether to divorce in vv. 10-11, on which Paul does have a command from the Lord, on this subject he is left to his own devices. But it is not that Paul himself cannot give a command. On the contrary, in vv. 2-16, when the apostle addresses other questions of marriage and divorce, he does give some commands. The difference here is that Paul is not addressing an issue with one right answer. The matter calls for the decision and consent of those advised, and the distinction is not between right and wrong but between "right" and "better" (v. 38).

However, it is also not that Paul is like a counselor in the modern sense of giving neutral help designed to assist autonomous individuals come to their own decision; Paul responds to the issue *as one who by the Lord's mercy is*

298. For the Jewish view, see Michael L. Satlow, *Jewish Marriage in Antiquity* (Princeton: Princeton University Press, 2001), 118-19; on the Roman side, see Susan Treggiari, *Roman Marriage: Iusti Coniuges from the Time of Cicero to the Time of Ulpian* (Oxford: Clarendon, 1991), 315-16.

299. As Barnett notes, 125, Paul's "care in distinguishing the words of Jesus from his own words fill us with encouragement about the integrity of the words of Jesus we find in this Letter and in the Gospels."

*trustworthy.* The *mercy*[300] to which he refers is not his salvation but his apostleship and his call to proclaim Christ among the nations; 2 Corinthians 4:1: "through God's mercy we have this ministry" (cf. Gal. 1:15-16). And "trustworthiness" or "faithfulness"[301] is that quality required of all qualified Christian ministers according to 1 Corinthians 4:2. As a predominantly Gentile church, the Corinthians can hardly ignore what Paul has to say.

What Paul *gives* in response to Corinthian quandaries he calls his own *judgment.* Other translations render the term in question his "opinion."[302] Deming, reading 1 Corinthians 7 alongside Stoic-Cynic discussions of marriage, suggests that the word points to an appeal to what is fitting in the present situation.[303] However, Collins is right to underscore Paul's rhetoric of reminding the Corinthians that his "opinion" is from someone who is reliable.[304] Personal "opinion," with its connotations of polite civility, hardly fits Paul's persona as "an apostle of Christ Jesus by the will of God" (1:1); even if not as categorical as a command, in a situation where people are making major life-changing decisions the apostle gives his *judgment* or "rule of conduct."[305] However, as vv. 36-38 show, Paul does this without compromising the Corinthians' personal responsibility to live "before God" (v. 24). In Thiselton's words, "Paul the pastor thinks aloud" but also "leaves them free to make responsible decisions about advantages and disadvantages for the Kingdom of God, for others, and for themselves."[306]

**7:26** Paul introduces his guidance with the words (literally): "Therefore, I think this is good."[307] He uses the same language the Corinthians used in their maxim, *It is good for a man not to touch a woman,* which he quoted at the beginning of the chapter (7:1b). Consciously responding to the concerns they raised with him, his counsel in v. 26b is that (literally) "it is good for a man to be thus."[308] Although on first sight it seems Paul may mean it is good "to remain a virgin," looking back to v. 25, it is more likely that his words are looking ahead to v. 27 and mean, it is good not to make any change in your marital status.[309] Thus, this verse is another application of the principle Paul illustrated in vv. 17-24: "remain as you are."

300. Paul describes his present state (using the perfect passive participle ἠλεημένος from ἐλεέω) as that of one who is a recipient or object of God's grace.

301. Gk. πιστός.

302. NRSV, REB, NJB; Gk. γνώμην. BDAG suggests that γνώμη means "a viewpoint or way of thinking about a matter, *opinion, judgment, way of thinking,*" and to "give" one (γνώμην διδόναι) is to "express an opinion, appraise a matter, offer counsel or direction."

303. Deming, *Paul on Marriage and Celibacy,* 175-77.

304. Collins, 289.

305. Collins, 289.

306. Thiselton, 577.

307. This verse is awkward in Greek and contains some redundancy ("good" is repeated in the first and last clause). It is smoothed out by TNIV without any loss of sense.

308. We can translate ἄνθρωπος as "man," as does TNIV, in view of the use of γυνή, "woman/wife," in v. 27.

309. There is little difference in meaning.

The reason given that it is good not to seek a change in your marital status is *because of the present crisis.* Fee captures Paul's underlying logic: "In light of the troubles you are already experiencing, who needs the additional burden of marriage as well?"[310] Or as Morris puts it, "when high seas are raging, it is no time for changing ships."[311] In the absence of effective contraception in the ancient world, marriage inevitably led to having children and, all too often, to the death of the mother. The added responsibilities of the married state would be felt more acutely in times of economic or other social crises. As Francis Bacon observed, "children sweeten labours, but they make misfortunes more bitter."[312]

But which troubles does Paul have in mind? Bruce Winter has suggested that *the present crisis* being experienced in Corinth was "dislocation in the city's life caused through a series of acute grain shortages and the attendant social unrest."[313] He cites evidence for grain shortages in the East during the forties and fifties in Eusebius, Pliny, Suetonius, and several strands of nonliterary evidence. Tiberius Claudius Dinippus was curator of the grain supply in Corinth during this period, an office filled only in times of famine.[314] Such famines invariably caused serious social upheaval. Garnsey claims that "the fear of famine rather than famine itself was enough to send people on the rampage."[315] Indeed, Paul would not have been the first to describe such a situation as a "crisis": Thucydides uses the same term to sum up the plight of cities facing conditions of dire necessity, including severe famine.[316] Unfortunately, the precise dating of those fam-

310. Fee, 329. Whatever the *present crisis* was, Paul clearly saw that it would create "troubles in this life" (v. 28) for married people rather than singles. The words "crisis" (ἀνάγκη) and "troubles," or tribulation (θλῖψις or the verb θλίβω), are often used as a word pair in the LXX and New Testament (Pss. 24:17; 106:6, 13, 19, 28; 119:143; Job 15:24; 20:22; Zeph. 1:15; 2 Cor. 6:4; 1 Thess. 3:7), suggesting that they should be interpreted in tandem here, tying together vv. 26-28.

311. Morris, 116.

312. Cited by Robertson and Plummer, 154.

313. B. W. Winter, "Secular and Christian Responses to Corinthian Famines," *TynBul* 40 (1989), 86-106 (93); Winter, *After Paul Left Corinth*, 216-25.

314. He seems to have assumed the role in A.D. 51 and held it for many years. See the thorough discussion of the subject in Barry N. Danylak, "Tiberius Claudius Dinippus and the Food Shortages in Corinth," *TynBul* 59 (2008), 231-70. Danylak points to "the possiblility that the food crisis in Corinth may have persisted for as long as five years" (270). He also corrects the commonly cited idea that Dinippus served in the role three different times (242-44).

315. P. Garnsey, *Famine and Food Supply in the Graeco-Roman World: Responses to Risk and Crisis*, 31.

316. Thucydides, 3.82.2; 85.2. Garland, 324, notes a significant parallel that supports taking the present crisis as a specific local set of circumstances that has implications for the question of whether to go ahead with plans for marriage. A textual variant of 3 Macc. 1:16 uses the same words to describe the desecration of the temple by Antiochus IV Epiphanes: "Then the priests prostrated themselves and entreated the supreme God to aid in the present crisis [text: the present situation]." 3 Macc. 1:19-20 continues: "Those women who had recently been arrayed for marriage abandoned the bridal chambers prepared for wedding union. . . . Mothers and nurses abandoned even newborn children here and there."

ines escapes us.[317] It is quite possible that Paul had a grain shortage or famine in Corinth in mind when he counseled Corinthian engaged couples to remain as you are *because of the present crisis,* or it may be that a few years after such severe famine other types of social upheaval and economic stress may have resulted as part of its aftereffects.

The majority of commentators, on the other hand, understand Paul to be referring to the tribulation or messianic woes which are the lot of all Christians and will herald the Second Coming of Christ. On this reading, vv. 29-31 reinforce the same point. Many see Paul here exercising his conviction that the parousia was imminent. Indeed, the two words translated *present crisis* can be construed in an eschatological sense. "Crisis"[318] is used in Luke 21:23 in connection with the destruction of Jerusalem, a portent of the End. And the word for "present"[319] can mean "to be about to occur" (BDAG). Mark's eschatological discourse presents similar sentiments to 1 Corinthians 7:25-31 with its warnings to "pregnant women and nursing mothers" and reference to "a shortening of days" (Mark 13:17, 20; cf. 1 Cor. 7:29).

Moore points out that the key word, *crisis,* does not have an established usage in eschatological contexts.[320] While Luke employs it, Matthew 24:21, 29 and Mark 13:19 prefer another word,[321] and Paul uses it elsewhere with no thought of the End Time. Elsewhere in Paul's letters it means "duress" (2 Cor. 9:7; Phlm. 14), "calamities" or "disaster" (2 Cor. 6:4; 12:10), or "distress" (1 Thess. 3:7). It actually turns up in 1 Corinthians 7:37, where it is translated "compulsion." BDAG defines the word as covering a range of meanings involving some outer or inner pressure.[322] Furthermore, Paul's use of the other key word does not support the sense of "impending." He uses it to refer to that which is already present in contrast to the future: "the *present* or the future" (1 Cor. 3:22); "the *present* nor the future" (Rom. 8:38); "*present* evil age" (Gal. 1:4). The main difficulty for this view is the relationship of v. 26 to vv. 29-31. Moore's suggestion that the opening words of v. 29 mark a clear break[323] and supply a new point is not entirely satisfactory since the two paragraphs are clearly related in some way.

Paul may be referring to the eschatological crisis of the entire interadvental period (much as "tribulation" sometimes refers to the entire period), making the point that nothing that belongs to this present world,

317. Much of Winter's discussion (as well as that of Bradley B. Blue, "The House Church at Corinth and the Lord's Supper: Famine, Food Supply and the Present Distress," *CTR* 5 [1991], 221-39) revolves around the year 51 (*After Paul Left Corinth,* 218-23), while Paul was still in the city. This letter, however, was written a few years later.

318. Gk. ἀνάγκη.

319. Gk. ἐνίστημι.

320. Arthur L. Moore, *The Parousia in the New Testament* (NovTSup 13; Leiden: E. J. Brill, 1966), 115-17.

321. Gk. θλῖψις.

322. BDAG, 61.

323. Cf. Héring, 57.

which is passing away, is ultimately significant. If this is correct, the "crisis" is not "temporary" (i.e., a few years or a decade or two) except in the sense that everything connected with this passing world order between the first and second comings of Jesus is temporary. This fits perfectly with the point of vv. 29-31. But the word *crisis* is usually employed for temporary periods of crisis or distress (the first usage above), and it seems unlikely that Paul is arguing that people should opt to maintain their current marital status until the return of Christ.

We are not left with the options of simply equating the two sections (so that they both are purely eschatological in focus) or of building a wall between them (so that they are dealing with two unrelated issues). Paul himself probably would not have known whether or not *the present crisis* in Corinth was a part of the final woes that would come on the earth. Jesus had predicted that the earth would experience severe famines and plagues before the End (Matt. 24:7; Mark 13:8; Luke 21:11; cf. Rev. 6:8; 18:8), and in Romans 8:35 Paul's list of trouble, hardship, persecution, famine, nakedness, danger, and sword may well reflect his understanding that he and some of his readers were already living in the time of eschatological tribulations. Acts 11:28 tells us that Agabus "predicted that a severe famine would spread over the entire Roman world" and that it was referring to the one that took place during the reign of Claudius. That particular famine happened between A.D. 45 and 48. Paul would probably have recognized that *the present crisis* in Corinth was like that of the End and might even have been a part of it; the present woes are typical, at least, of the parousia woes, if they are not in fact the first and outlying clouds spinning around the ultimate hurricane on the eschatological horizon (see further below on v. 29).[324] Paul was not expecting the world to come to an immediate end, it seems, or he would not have been warning people about the implications of singleness and marriage for a life with more or less stress. It seems likely that even if he understood the *present crisis* to be part of larger eschatological developments, it would pass at some point.

In any case, in v. 26 Paul is saying that the unusually difficult circumstances in Corinth mean that staying single is advisable, at least for the time being. Paul's advice regarding marriage in this passage may be due as much to the extenuating circumstances in the church as to abstract theological convictions. The wisdom (or not) of marrying or making other critical life decisions that will effect the lives of others may depend on the presence or absence of a more-or-less stable social environment. Important decisions in life (as well as mundane ones), if made wisely, will take into consideration the social context. Times of great social and economic upheaval and instability that reflect the extreme frailty and passing nature of this world (of which our eschatology reminds us) in tangible and threatening ways call for great caution and reflection upon our ultimate goals and mission in life and how

324. Cf. Horrell, *Solidarity and Difference*, 147 n. 41.

such decisions cohere with them. We need wisdom to discern the times and understand our circumstances so as to know the best way to glorify God and avoid putting ourselves or others under unnecessary duress.

The significance of this conclusion is that Paul's negative stance on getting married here and throughout the chapter is to some extent a "refraction" of his ethics, to borrow Helmut Thielicke's helpful term. His instructions assume "the character of a necessary emergency measure"[325] rather than being his sober direction for all the churches. The fact that other passages in Paul's letters are more positive about marriage demonstrates that what he says here is not the whole of his teaching on marriage.[326] Paul's teaching about marriage in 1 Corinthians 7 is "a practical reflection on concrete circumstances."[327]

**7:27** Paul clarifies what he meant in v. 26 by "it is good for a man to be thus" with two direct questions each with a corresponding imperative (cf. the same structure in v. 18). A debate over their meaning is reflected in the NIV and TNIV translations. The Greek reads literally: "Are you bound to a woman? Do not seek to be loosed. Are you loosed from a woman? Do not seek a woman." Three terms generate the ambiguity: "bound," "loosed,"[328] and "woman." In short, the first can refer to marriage or betrothal,[329] the second to divorce or breaking off the engagement,[330] and the third to a wife or a fiancé.[331] Hence the NIV translates with marriage and divorce in view: "Are you married? Do not seek a divorce. Are you unmarried? Do not look for a wife."[332] And the TNIV with betrothal and 'breaking up': *Are you pledged to a woman? Do not seek to be released. Are you free from such a commitment? Do not look for a wife.*[333]

If we must choose between these two views, the second is to be preferred. Paul is not addressing a general audience of married people. As

325. Helmut Thielicke, *Theological Ethics* (Philadelphia: Fortress, 1966), 380.

326. Cf. 1 Cor. 11:11-12; 2 Cor. 11:2; Eph. 5:21-33; Tit. 2:2-6. Even if one regards Ephesians and the Pastorals as inauthentic, there is no reason to think that their teaching on marriage is un-Pauline. It is unlikely that followers of Paul would correct their mentor on this subject since, as Fee, 276, observes, "the entire history of the early church moves in the other direction" (i.e., toward asceticism).

327. Thiselton, 577.

328. The perfect passive indicatives "bound" and "loosed/free" (δέδεσαι; λέλυσαι) refer, as is usual with perfect verbs, to the current state of their subjects. So also in v. 39.

329. Greek perfect passive of δέω, "to bind." The word is used in Rom. 7:2 of the bond between a husband and a wife. It is also used more broadly of legal obligations in the papyri (which could fit with a betrothal).

330. Greek noun λύσις, from the verb λύω, "to loose," used in the next clause. The word could be used in context to refer to divorce (although the New Testament generally uses other terms for divorce). In the papyri it can mean "discharge of bonds" or "discharge of debts or obligations" (MM).

331. Gk. γυνή can mean "adult female" or "wife," depending on the context.

332. Cf. REB, NRSV.

333. Thiselton, 577, argues for this position on the grounds of "continuity of topic and argument" in the passage.

Schrage points out, such an address would be an unnecessary repetition of vv. 10-16, where he did in fact have a command from the Lord concerning divorce.[334] While the verb translated "pledged" (TNIV) or "bound" (NRSV, ESV, NET, NAB, NASB, etc.) is clearly used elsewhere by Paul to refer to a binding marriage commitment, including just twelve verses later (v. 39; cf. Rom. 7:2), elsewhere Paul uses two other words for divorce in 1 Corinthians 7, suggesting that the language of "loosing" in v. 27 may have a different meaning.[335] The reason the language is ambiguous and may apply to either situation is that in the ancient world "an engagement created the same ties as marriage," so that the "vocabulary of relationship by marriage was used from the time of betrothal."[336] Paul uses language that is broad enough to apply clearly to both married and betrothed men. His focus here is on unmarried men, but married men are still listening in and would not suffer from the reinforcement of the point. There is overlap with the counsel he already gave to married couples, since the counsel is similar for those who are married and those who are betrothed. Finally, only the betrothal view of the verse explains Paul's failure to give a corresponding word to women. Whereas throughout the chapter Paul almost always balances instructions to both men and women, in v. 27 and vv. 36-38 he addresses only men.[337] As Garland notes, "This change in pattern is attributable to cultural mores, which assume that males take the initiative in betrothal arrangements."[338]

It is not clear how Paul would have looked upon the breaking of a betrothal. While according to both Roman and Jewish views betrothal placed the couple in the legal framework of marriage already, for Romans it was a very simple thing to dissolve a betrothal or a marriage, while for many Jews (like Jesus and Paul), marriage (and presumably betrothals since betrothed couples were considered legally married) could be broken only under rather extreme circumstances. Did Paul think that because Roman betrothals were not taken as seriously as Jewish ones they could legitimately be dissolved on lesser grounds than a marriage, or perhaps on any grounds (thus treating them much like engagements in many modern Western countries)? In this verse Paul says that a man betrothed to a woman should not seek to break such a commitment, but according to the most common interpretation of vv. 36-38, Paul there suggests that the person who decides not to marry his fiancée makes the best choice (so the TNIV). The latter passage is one of the most difficult in the New Testament, and we will address its problems in our comments there. The fact is that in two other places (v. 39 and Rom. 7:2) Paul uses the verb[339] translated here as *pledged* or "bound" to refer to the lifelong

334. Schrage, 2:158.

335. ἀφίημι in vv. 11, 12, and 13, and χωρίζω in vv. 10, 11, and 15.

336. Treggiari, *Roman Marriage,* 159.

337. He finishes the chapter by addressing just women in vv. 39-40.

338. Garland, 326.

339. Gk. δέω.

bond of marriage. That he tells such people not to seek a dissolution of the bond suggests that he does not think betrothals should be taken lightly, or broken except on serious grounds. It seems that what Paul lacks is a command from the Lord regarding whether or not a single man should consider marrying a virgin. Whether or not a betrothed man should dissolve the betrothal may well have been understood to fall under the Lord's command regarding divorce.[340] The first part of the verse makes better sense if Paul's counsel to the unmarried men in the following verses is "a necessary emergency measure" and not his general position. The fact that Paul does not recommend a dissolution of the betrothal commitment suggests that at some point in the future (when *the present crisis* is over) the couple might, or perhaps should, go ahead with the marriage.

The men Paul has in mind in this verse would have been either betrothed to one of the "virgins" mentioned in v. 25, or thinking about finding a virgin to marry. Paul is saying, "if you are betrothed to 'a virgin' (or married), stay as you are (the Lord's command applies here); if you are single, do not seek betrothal and marriage." The second part of the verse is clearly not addressed to engaged men,[341] but to single men who are not engaged. This supports the view that the passage as a whole is (mainly) addressing single men who may (vv. 27a, 36-38) or may not (vv. 27b-28, 32-35) be engaged already.

The logic of v. 28, and the following verses, suggests that vv. 28-35 are addressing unbetrothed men who are considering marrying virgins, and unbetrothed young (virgin) women who are thinking about getting married, while vv. 36-38 turn to focus on men who are already betrothed to a virgin.

**7:28** Even if in Paul's "judgment" (v. 25) single men should not get married (v. 27b), at least at this time of crisis (v. 26a), it was not a position to which they were required to submit. What matters is "keeping the commandments of God" (v. 19), such as avoiding sexual immorality. Whether to marry or not is not of the same order: *But if you do marry, you have not sinned; and if a virgin*[342] *marries, she has not sinned.* These words would apply to both engaged (v. 27a) and unengaged (v. 27b) men and women, although even more clearly to the latter, since Paul had already said that engaged people should not dissolve the engagement (suggesting they should go

340. On the Roman side, see Treggiari's comment above. Matt. 1:18-20 reflects the similar view on the Jewish side.

341. Even if the last clause, translated *Are you free from such a commitment?* (literally, "Are you free of a woman/wife?"), means simply "Are you unmarried?" (NIV), an engaged man would not have to *look for a wife.* Only an unbetrothed single man might be expected to do that.

342. It is literally, *the* virgin, meaning one of those referred to in v. 25. Although the article is omitted in B, F, G, and 429, it is found in $\mathfrak{P}^{15, 46}$, א, A, D, K, L, P, and most minuscules. Copyists probably deleted it because it seemed out of place here (Metzger, *Textual Commentary*, 490).

through with the marriage at some point). If they should not break their engagement, it can hardly be "sin" to follow through on what it represents.

Many scholars think that Paul feels the need to reassure Corinthian couples that "it is not a sin" (NJB) to marry because some in Corinth argued that it was. In their view it is only a short step from saying, "it is good for a man not to have sexual relations with a woman" (7:1b), to saying that it is sin for single people to marry. However, Paul is probably simply clarifying the force of his own recommendation in favor of not changing one's status, right now, including the status of "engaged/betrothed." The fact that in his judgment it is best not to make such life-changes in the present context (v. 26) does not mean that someone who decides to go ahead and marry is sinning. "Those who do not accept his advice do not in fact commit sin."[343] In cases such as these there is, as Thiselton observes, "freedom where Christians must take responsibility for their own actions after weighing carefully the factors which others (including Christian teachers or pastors) have brought to their attention in a non-directive manner."[344] Whether to marry or not is not a matter of "sin," but of discerning what is best (cf. v. 38).

To end this phase of his counsel to unmarried men (and young women) Paul returns to his "judgment" that it is better for them to stay as they are: *But those who marry will face many troubles in this life, and I want to spare you this.* "Many troubles in this life" translates the phrase "afflictions of the flesh."[345] Other English versions show the range of possible meanings: "distress in this life" (NRSV); "worldly troubles" (RSV, ESV); "affliction in [one's] earthly life" (NAB); "difficult circumstances" (NET). Scholars usually choose between thinking that Paul is referring to the distractions of marital life which he expounds in vv. 32-35 or that he is reprising v. 26, his only stated grounds to this point for the counsel for betrothed couples to stay as they are, namely, "because of the present crisis" (v. 26; possibly a food shortage in Corinth or enduring economic problems coming in its wake). Here "flesh" refers to our weakness and frailty characteristic of existence in this life, while "afflictions" ("distress" or "pressure" [Thiselton]) calls to mind more readily "the present crisis" than the less distressing "concerns of married life," and seems too strong a word for what Paul expounds in vv. 32-35. We may do best to see that these are not unrelated, since the concerns of married life, like life itself, become much more distressing in times of social crisis.

As Garland points out, upon a superficial reading "Paul would seem to resonate with those who had a dismal view of marriage." He has in mind those who suggested that marriage was "a great struggle" or "full of care" (Antiphon, *On Harmony* 357.15-16; 360.1), or "burdensome and grievous" (Hierocles, *On Marriage* 505.24-25, mentions and rejects this view), or an ex-

343. Fee, 333.
344. Thiselton, 577.
345. Gk. θλῖψιν τῇ σαρκί.

perience similar to being "quite loaded down with burdens" (*Ecclesiastes Rabbah* 1.2).[346] As Garland points out, Calvin also "identifies the affliction as 'the responsibilities and difficulties' that marriage brings, springing 'from the affairs of the world.'"[347] Some of those authors may in fact have a dismal view of marriage. Even those with a much more positive view of marriage may agree, however, that in times of great social and economic crisis one's marriage may add greatly to the burdens a person must endure. Paul is explicitly talking about troubles or afflictions suffered especially by *those who marry,* troubles and afflictions that will not be experienced as fully by single people. In times of "crisis" the blessing of a spouse and children can become a grievous burden. As a good father himself (4:14-15), Paul hopes to keep his children from unnecessary distress, *to spare* them, by persuading single men and women who are at or approaching the normal time to marry to remain single. Paul ends the paragraph where he started, judging that for practical reasons (perhaps the impact of a famine in Corinth, or some other crisis) it would be better not to marry.

*b. Stay Unmarried Because of the End of the World, 7:29-31*

> [29]*What I mean, brothers and sisters, is that the time is short. From now on those who are married should live as if they were not;* [30]*those who mourn, as if they did not; those who are happy, as if they were not; those who buy something, as if it were not theirs to keep;* [31]*those who use the things of the world, as if not engrossed in them. For this world in its present form is passing away.*

**7:29** With a solemn introduction, startling assertions, poetic rhythm, and paradoxical content, vv. 29-31 are among the most profound in the letter. Scholars debate their background in Stoic and Jewish apocalyptic traditions[348] and speculate about their non-Pauline origin.[349] Such is their allure that many treat them in isolation and forget to read them in the context of Paul's counsel that single men and women stay unmarried and compare them with comparable teaching in other parts of 1 Corinthians (esp. chs. 1–2).

Verses 29-31 inject another factor into Paul's discussion of whether to get married or not. TNIV's *What I mean, brothers and sisters* gives the impression that what follows explains what was said in vv. 25-28, especially the

346. Garland, 327.

347. Calvin, 158, cited by Garland, 327.

348. See Garland, 345-46, for a summary of views. The similarities with Jewish apocalyptic texts are marked (cf. esp. 2 Esdr. 16:40-48; Zech.12:12-14; also Jer. 16:2-8). The links to Stoic thought are limited to the idea of detachment from the world; Schrage's judgment, "Die Stellung zur Welt bei Paulus, Epiktet und in der Apokalyptik," *Zeitschrift für Theologie und Kirche* 61 (1964), 125-54, 138, that such resemblances are coincidental and "illusory" is sound.

349. For example, V. L. Wimbush, *Paul the Worldly Ascetic: Response to the World and Self-Understanding in 1 Corinthians 7* (Macon, GA: Mercer University Press, 1987).

"afflictions of the flesh" of v. 28 and "the present crisis" of v. 26. Verse 29's note of eschatological urgency thus identifies these troubles with the time of tribulation that apocalyptic thought frequently associated with the end of the world. But Robertson and Plummer are right that the opening words of v. 29 mark a transition to a new point: "But this I do declare."[350] The verb translated "to declare" carries more weight than the more common verb "to say" or "mean,"[351] and the demonstrative pronoun points forward rather than back. Vocatives, such as *brothers and sisters* here, often introduce new points as well.

It is not that the two paragraphs are unrelated. But the first must not be collapsed into the second. Paul's point is that "the present crisis" (the famine) is *like* that of the End, which is approaching; in other words, the present woes of vv. 25-28 are in some senses typical of the parousia woes alluded to in vv. 29-31. Both types of troubles give those Corinthians considering marriage cause for "concern," to use the language of v. 32. But they are not the same thing. The new idea is that since believers know where the world is headed, they are not to allow it to dictate their existence. The primary purpose of vv. 29-31 is to set the question of whether to marry or not in proper proportion and perspective. The prospect of a new heaven and new earth takes the edge off prevailing troubles on this earth and may even enable a believer to endure a marital or social status they consider unsatisfying or undesirable and glorify God within it. According to Paul, being married or not is not central to the Corinthians' (or our) identity, but rather being "in Christ Jesus" (1 Cor 1:30).

Why does Paul counsel unmarried men in the church that "it is good for a man to remain as he is" (v. 26b) and not get married? The reason in v. 26 is "because of the present crisis." Paul's disarmingly simple assertion in v. 29 is that they should not get married because *the time is short.* Both terms in this statement raise questions.

What "time" is he referring to? The time until what? The word Paul uses for "time" here has been regularly overinterpreted (and overly theologized) since the publication of Cullmann's *Christ and Time.*[352] Even the discussion of the word's meaning in BDAG is a bit more complicated than it needs to be.[353] Often discussions on the word's meaning fail to re-

350. Robertson and Plummer, 154.

351. Gk. φημί rather than λέγω (cf. 1 Cor. 1:12; 6:5; 15:6): "Paul uses φημί in 1 Cor 7:29; 10:15, 19; 15:50 to formulate authoritatively apostolic doctrine and instruction" (V. Hasler, "φημί," *EDNT* 3:421). Cf. 15:50 (TNIV: "I declare to you"), where it also introduces an apocalyptic announcement.

352. Oscar Cullmann, *Christ and Time* (London: SCM, 1951).

353. BDAG provides the following meanings: (1) "a point of time or period of time"; (2) "a defined period for an event"; (3) "a period characterized by some aspect of special crisis." It seems to us that their first definition mixes two different meanings together while their second and third import elements that are not actually part of the word's meaning or denotation but include ideas based on the particular point or period of time referred to in particular contexts. For the second definition given in BDAG the local context defines the

spect an appropriate distinction between meaning (or denotation, or lexical meaning) and reference. The evidence suggests that the word denotes either 1) a point in time (often with the added idea of being the appropriate or right time), or a period/span of time; or 2) a season. In this context it is clear that the definition that applies is that of a "period of time." Other meanings attributed to the word are better seen as meanings not of the word itself but of phrases or clauses of which it is a part, or have more to do with the particular point or period of time which is being referred to. In a number of New Testament contexts the word refers "to the distinctive period between the eschatological event set in motion by Christ's death and resurrection and his final revealing."[354] In this context the particular period to which Paul seems to be referring is that of "the time remaining until the parousia and the judgment."[355]

Is Paul taking about the quantity of time remaining until then, or is he saying something about the character or quality of time of the present period?[356] We should probably see both at work. That is, Paul says that the remaining time is limited and that the fact that the End is coming affects the character and quality of the time we have left. The key phrase literally reads, "the time has been compressed" or "gathered in."[357] There is an interesting parallel to Paul's language in Josephus's *Jewish War* where he says that the Zealot leaders were not sure what to do upon hearing that the Romans were coming after them because of "the shortness of the time that they had."[358] Here "the shortness of the time" is, literally, "the forcibly compressed time."[359] The parallel suggests that "compressed time" was a way of referring to very limited time.[360] It seems, then, that Robertson and Plummer

---

period or span of time to which the word refers, and in those texts included in the third definition the relationship with some special crisis is not suggested by the word itself but by other words or elements in the context. With their third definition BDAG includes references where the word clearly has the distinct meaning of "seasons."

354. Garland, 328. That is, "the eschatological time that began with the sending of Christ" (W.-G. Kümmel, cited by J. Baumgarten, "καιρός," *EDNT* 2:233).

355. Baumgarten, "καιρός," *EDNT* 2:233. So also Robertson and Plummer, 154.

356. See Thiselton, 580-83, for a discussion of the distinction between a "theology of eschatological imminence" and "a chronology of eschatological imminence," including the opposition between "Schweitzer's view that Paul believed in the imminence of the parousia in the near future and Bultmann's view that this language is merely a device to promote a sense of existential urgency" (580) and the mediating positions of Caird and Wimbush.

357. Greek perfect passive participle of συνστέλλω.

358. Whiston's translation. Thackeray's translation captures the idiom: "being so hard pressed for time" (LCL).

359. Gk. οὕτως καιρὸν συνεωσμένους; συνωθέω: "force together, compress forcibly" (LSJ).

360. The verb could be a divine passive signaling "the theocentric perspective of apocalyptic," that is, that it is God's action that has changed the nature or extent of time (Wimbush, *Paul the Worldly Ascetic*, 40). The fact that the cited example from Josephus also uses a perfect passive verb (like the one Paul used) leaves open the possibility that such constructions simply comment on the time available and not on the one who might have caused a limitation.

summarize the idiom accurately as time which "has been drawn together so as to be small in amount."[361] This shortness of time radically affects the way believers are to live their lives in the here and now.

The reminder about the limited time at our disposal underlines that there is a special quality to the time between the cross and glory. The Corinthians are in the final stretch of history (as we all have been since the coming of Christ) such that the events of the end are happening around us. Just as the future coming of the Romans conditioned the thinking and actions of the Zealots as they prepared for their arrival, as Christians our knowledge that we are in the end times and that this world will be brought to a conclusion ought to condition how we think about all of our activities and priorities in the meantime.[362] The future has broken into the present, resulting in a relativizing of human social commitments, such as marriage. This teaching is reinforced in the parallel assertion that closes the paragraph in v. 31: *this world in its present form is passing away.*[363]

The statement that time is "short" does not quantitatively limit the time that is left. The context implies that Paul expects the Corinthians to live long enough, for example, that it would make a significant difference whether or not they marry in the near future. Additionally, as Oster notes: "Even though the time was short, Paul continued to talk to the Corinthians about his own future plans to visit them (4:19; 11:34; 16:5-8) and the need for them to make and execute plans for a donation to aid in relief work among churches in Judea (1 Cor 16:1-4; cf. 2 Cor 8–9), plans whose consummation was two or three years in the future."[364]

As a contemporary parallel, concerns about future changes that could be brought about by global warming may end up impacting many generations that will live out their lives in light of those concerns, not necessarily knowing if or when major global changes will significantly change their lives or that of their children and/or grandchildren. Each generation may "hand over the baton" to the next, with the understanding that even if they and their children live out their whole lives without seeing radical changes brought about by global warming they are not exempt from the need to live their lives differently in light of those concerns. Thus the future of a world transformed by global warming is already breaking into our present, conditioning the attitudes and behaviors of people today.

To say the time is short is not to say that any given generation will not live a full lifetime, but that there is no generation of believers that is exempt from the responsibility to "give [them]selves fully to the work of the Lord," knowing that their "labor in the Lord is not in vain" (15:58). The conclusion

361. Robertson and Plummer, 154.

362. As contemporary parallels, consider the effect a big examination or a critical business deadline has on the character of the present time.

363. Hays, 128, connects the two assertions. See our introduction to 7:25-38 (p. 329) on the presence of three such inclusios in the unit.

364. Oster, 173.

to chapter 15 reinforces many other eschatological elements in this letter (4:5; 6:2-3; 10:11; 11:26; 13:9-12; 15:23-26; 16:22), including the one here.

To tease out the implications of the time being short and the world passing away, Paul issues five parallel commands in vv. 29-31 in the form of "those who . . . live as if. . . ." Paul's first application of his eschatological framework, in 7:29b, is ambiguous: *From now on those who are married should live as if they were not.* Literally, he tells "those who have a wife, be as not having a wife." The verb "to have" can mean "to have sexually," as in 1 Corinthians 5:1 and 7:2. Thus it could be imagined that Paul is opposing sexual relations in marriage, a view commonly attributed to the Corinthians (see the introduction to this chapter and the comments on 7:1-2). However, such a view founders on the clear statements of vv. 2-5, where Paul commands them: "Do not deprive each other" (v. 5a). And here it is much more likely that the verb simply refers to the existence of a familial relationship: to have a wife = be married (cf. BDAG and the comments on 7:2). The point here is that Paul wants the Corinthians to "learn how to sit loose to all earthly ties."[365] He is not advocating "withdrawal from, or renunciation of, the world"[366] and marital obligations, but a relativizing of the importance of the things of this world.[367] Paul counsels a clear-sighted measure of detachment based on the conviction that the cross has judged the present age and the goal of history looms; such eschatological realities change forever the value to be put on current circumstances and happiness. Clearly, marriage is of this world, since death breaks the commitment (v. 39; cf. Rom. 7:2), and is one of the things that should be assessed differently in the light of eternity.

**7:30** Strictly speaking, Paul's second example of how a Christian view of time impacts the present moves away from the issue of marriage: *those who mourn* [ought to live] *as if they did not*. However, the "weeping," "crying" (BDAG), or "mourning" that may have come first to mind to the Corinthians was the hurt caused by their unconsummated relationships, or the present crisis (v. 26) that would have made such marriages even more difficult than usual; Paul's counsel not to marry may well have brought grief to those couples looking forward to getting married. The apostle is not recommending a kind of Stoic imperviousness to life's knocks. Elsewhere he recommends "mourning with those who mourn" (Rom. 12:15), using the same word as here, and reports that at times he himself felt intense emotional pain (Rom. 9:2; 2 Cor. 2:4; Phil. 3:18; this last reference uses the same verb). In spite of this, as Garland notes, "Paul's clear-sighted eschatological vision leads him to neutralize the sadness associated in the OT with virginity and never producing children (cf. Judg. 11:37; Gen. 19:8)."[368] Such setbacks are real, but for those in Christ Jesus they are not the last word.

365. Robertson and Plummer, 156.

366. B. Witherington, *Jesus, Paul, and the End of the World* (Carlisle: Paternoster, 1992), 29.

367. Cf. Thiselton, 601; cf. Wimbush, *Paul the Worldly Ascetic*, 16.

368. Garland, 330.

Thirdly, just as sadness is not decisive for Christians, so neither is its positive counterpart: *those who are happy* [ought to live] *as if they were not.* Joy is a major theme in Paul's letters and experience (1 Cor. 16:17; 2 Cor. 7:4-10; Phil. 1:12-19; 4:10). In fact, he can give a command that seems to contradict his dour sentiment here: "rejoice always" (Phil. 4:4). However, as the following two examples demonstrate, Paul is not disparaging a full-blooded engagement with the world (cf. 5:10b), but wants it to be tempered by a sober assessment of life's ups and downs in the light of something of greater significance.

In the first three paradoxical commands Paul uses the same word to describe both the state of those addressed and its corresponding negation: (1) those *having* a wife, live as if not *having* one; (2) those *mourning,* live as if not *mourning;* (3) those *rejoicing,* live as if not *rejoicing.* The fourth and fifth depart from this pattern. In literary terms, the variation of the final elements in a list helps bring it to climax.

In vv. 30b-31a Paul generalizes still further, applying his end-time reasoning to ever broader categories: *those who buy something* [ought to live] *as if it were not theirs to keep.* Heavenly-mindedness does not mean that the Corinthians will no longer need to "do business."[369] But such activities are not to divert a believer in Christ from the real business of life. Two of the parables of Jesus are especially pertinent here: In the parable of the Great Banquet (Luke 14:15-24) some of those invited miss out because they are distracted by marriage or commerce; likewise, in the parable of the Coming of the Son of Man (Luke 17:26-37) some miss out because they are taken up with marriages, buying and selling, among other things. Jesus strikes a similar note to Paul's five paradoxes: "Those who try to keep their life will lose it, and those who lose their life will preserve it" (Luke 17:33). Material things can cost spiritually. Paul's advice is not "to hold firmly"[370] to them, to possess them but not to let them possess you. TNIV's paraphrase, *as if it were not theirs to keep,* captures the sense. As regards possessions, Paul recommends living "as not entering upon full ownership."[371]

**7:31** Paul's fifth and final example in v. 31a is his most general and appropriately climaxes the set: to summarize, *those who use the things of the world* [ought to live] *as if not engrossed in them.* It contains a memorable play on words and introduces the term "world," which v. 32b picks up and reinforces. To *use* something is the same verb as in v. 21, where slaves were encouraged to "make use of the opportunity" to gain their freedom if it presented itself. Paul counsels here, seemingly churlishly, that those able to take advantage of worldly conditions, whether in business, by getting married, or through manumission, should not "make full use" of these advan-

369. Gk. ἀγοράζω: "to acquire things or services in exchange for money" or "to secure the rights to someone by paying a price" (BDAG).

370. Gk. κατέχω: "to keep in one's possession" (BDAG, def. 3).

371. Robertson and Plummer, 156.

tages. The second verb (TNIV: "to be engrossed") is the same as the first ("use"), except it has an intensifying prefix.[372] Paul uses it in 1 Corinthians 9:18, where he refuses "to take full advantage" of his rights as an apostle to receive financial support. Though difficult to preserve the connection in translation, Calvin does well with, "And those who *use* this world, as not *using it to the full.*" His explanation is also helpful: "Paul therefore suggests using things in a moderate and disciplined way, such as will not hinder or delay us on our journey, but enable us to keep pressing on to the goal."[373] Luther's comments spell out the practical benefits for both good and ill fortune, for "happiness" or "mourning": Christians should use what is available but "not sink too deeply into it either with love and desire or suffering and boredom, but should rather behave like guests on earth, using everything for a short time because of need."[374] Paul's stance toward *the world* is the opposite of that inspired by a denial of eschatology in 15:32b, where "full use" of the things of the world is encouraged: "If the dead are not raised, 'Let us eat and drink, for tomorrow we die.'"

Having completed his five examples of how to live when the future has "squashed" the present, Paul sums up the main idea of the paragraph in v. 31b. His words supply the rationale for the ethic of vv. 29b-31a[375] and reprise and clarify v. 29a: *For this world in its present form is passing away.* This sentiment comes as no surprise, since almost half the references to the "world" in 1 Corinthians refer to its rejection and judgment (1:20, 21, 27, 28; 2:12; 3:19; 6:2; 11:32). The Corinthian Christians are described as being different from "the people of this world" (5:10) and destined to "judge the world" (6:2). There is no point to getting wrapped up in the world because it is under God's judgment and we do not belong to it.

Here in v. 31b it is not the world itself that is said to be *passing away,*[376] but rather *the world in its present form.*[377] Although it may mean a number of things, *form* here takes its meaning from the admonitions in the previous verses. Paul has warned against placing too much importance on marriage, the highs and lows of human life, and the acquisition of goods. He summarizes these as "the uses of the world" in v. 31a. Hence "the form of this world" describes "the world's social and economic infrastructure . . . that makes these activities possible."[378] Paul has reflected on the most basic experiences of human life — experiencing joy and sadness, buying goods, and

372. Gk. χράομαι and καταχράομαι. The choice of words is intentional and significant since, as noted above, in the first three he chose simply to repeat the verb in question from the first half of the saying.

373. Calvin, 160. KJV's "use/abuse" reduces the saying's shocking nature. The prefix on καταχράομαι is better taken as one of intensity than as giving a bad sense to the term.

374. Luther, *Works,* 28:52; cited in Thiselton, 584.

375. Note explanatory γάρ.

376. Gk. παράγω, "to go out of existence" (BDAG, def. 4).

377. Gk. σχῆμα: "the generally recognized state or form in which someth[ing] appears" or, more likely here, "the functional aspect of someth[ing], *way of life*" (BDAG).

378. Deming, *Paul on Marriage and Celibacy,* 181.

engaging the world around us — because these are in the same category as living as a married or a single person, and like those experiences they are not to be treated as the ultimate meaning or significance in life. What matters is glorifying God (6:20; 10:31) and doing the work to which he has called us (and thus awaiting his reward in glory; 1:7-8; 2:7; 3:13; 4:5; 9:18-27; 15:43, 58). Augustine elaborates: "We cannot love what is eternal unless we cease to love what is temporal. . . . Learn to dismiss it before you are dismissed by it."[379] As in 1 Corinthians 1–2, ultimately worldliness is a form of pointless folly, "for the external structures of this world are slipping away."[380]

### c. Stay Unmarried Because of the Distractions of Married Life, 7:32-35

*32I would like you to be free from concern. An unmarried man is concerned about the Lord's affairs — how he can please the Lord. 33But a married man is concerned about the affairs of this world — how he can please his wife — 34and his interests are divided. An unmarried woman or virgin is concerned about the Lord's affairs: Her aim is to be devoted to the Lord in both body and spirit. But a married woman is concerned about the affairs of this world — how she can please her husband. 35I am saying this for your own good, not to restrict you, but that you may live in a right way in undivided devotion to the Lord.*

**7:32** The opening words of this verse indicate that Paul is taking his recommendation that single men and women remain unmarried a step further.[381] He writes: Now (or but) *I would like you to be free from concern.* The argument moves from the mundane and practical in vv. 25-28 ("the present crisis" and "troubles in this life") and the eschatological in vv. 29-31 ("the time is short"; "this world in its present form is passing away") to the christological in vv. 32-35. This third point makes explicit what underlies the first two, namely, that Paul wants the Corinthians to live lives of undistracted devotion to the Lord.

The key word in this section is *concern* or "anxiety." It appears five times in vv. 32-34 as both a noun and a verb. In Paul's view, whereas the married person is anxious to please their spouse, the unmarried person is anxious to please the Lord. The word can be used in both a negative and a positive sense. For instance, Paul wrote to the Philippians, "Do not be anxious about anything." But in the same letter he can also commend Timothy as one who is "genuinely anxious for [the Philippians'] welfare" (RSV). Context determines whether the anxiety in view is good or bad. In the case of vv. 32-34 it is not that either of the "anxieties" (for the spouse and for the

379. Augustine, *Sermon* 161.11, PL 38:884, cited by Kovacs, *The Church's Bible*, 122-23.

380. Thiselton, 585.

381. Wimbush, *Paul the Worldly Ascetic*, 49, notes the adversative or transitional force of δέ following the verb "to wish" and the second-person plural pronoun "you" (ὑμᾶς), which does not appear in vv. 29-31. Taken together these mark "a significant turn."

Lord) is necessarily negative.[382] While it may be possible to be overly anxious to please the Lord, that is not what Paul has in mind, and married people are right to concern themselves with the happiness of their spouses. Paul's concern is for them to have as few distractions from their service and devotion to the Lord as possible.

Paul does not want to eradicate *concern,* which would be a dubious goal at best, but to refocus it and to set priorities. The story of Mary and Martha in Luke 10:40-41 illustrates the same concern. When Jesus came for a meal, Martha was "distracted by all the preparations that had to be made." Jesus rebukes her for being "*anxious* and upset about many things," using the same word for *concern* prominent in 1 Corinthians 7:32-35. Mary, on the other hand, "has chosen what is better . . . [for, as Jesus explains,] few things are needed — or indeed only one." Both in Luke and here in 1 Corinthians the point is not to disparage household duties or marriage respectively, but to put the accent on something of greater concern.

The unit exhibits the careful address to males and females characteristic of the chapter. Paul addresses single men in vv. 32b-34a and single women, with some variation, in v. 34b. Verse 35 reprises v. 32a, forming an inclusio, thereby reinforcing Paul's overriding aim to secure "undistracted devotion to the Lord."

Throughout vv. 32-35 Paul explains that he prefers singleness because marriage makes life more complicated and can be a distraction from devotion to the Lord. Even if Stoics and Cynics also warned about the distractions of married life, the priority of pleasing God in these verses has more in common with biblical and Jewish thought. Specifically, it may have been derived from Deuteronomy 6, which Paul alludes to in the next chapter (8:6): "Love the Lord your God with all your heart." Martin McNamara notes the Palestinian Targum to the Pentateuch's treatment of Deuteronomy 6 and its relevance to New Testament teaching on the undivided heart: "Israel was commanded to love God 'with all her heart' [Deut. 6:5]. In the targum full devotion to God is described as 'a perfect heart,' i.e., one completely set on God, not divided between him and created things."[383] Furthermore, in several rabbinic texts, worldly preoccupations, such as a wife, are seen as a potential distraction from the study of Torah.[384] Paul's sentiments in this section are thus a subtle polemic reminiscent of his words in v. 19. It would not be the first time that Christ replaces the law in Paul's appropriation of traditional teaching.[385]

382. Contra Barrett, 179.

383. Martin McNamara, *Targum and Testament: Aramaic Paraphrases of the Hebrew Bible: A Light on the New Testament* (Grand Rapids: Eerdmans, 1972), 122-23.

384. For example, *'Abot de Rabbi Nathan* a. 20, which includes in its warnings against distractions from the study of and devotion to Torah, "the wife of a man." The phrase could refer to one's own wife or the wife of another, in which case the distraction would not be marriage but adultery.

385. Cf., e.g., the use of Deut. 30:12-13 in Rom. 10:6-8.

Paul observes that *an unmarried man is concerned about the Lord's affairs — how he can please the Lord.* Unencumbered by the legitimate concerns to look after a wife and children, *the unmarried man* is free to concentrate his undivided attention on other things. The other things that Paul has in mind are "the things of the Lord," defined as being occupied with the question of *how he can please the Lord*[386] instead of how he may please his wife. This conclusion is doubtless based on Paul's own missionary experience, which included various hardships not conducive to having a wife (e.g., 1 Cor. 9:5, 12; 2 Cor. 11:23-27). It recalls his comments in v. 7a: "I wish that all of you were as I am."

"Pleasing the Lord" is one of Paul's crisply comprehensive ways of distilling what is important in life (cf. v. 19b). The equivalent of "keeping the commandments of God" (v. 19b), he uses it in contexts of divine judgment: "we make it our goal to please him, whether we are at home in the body or away from it" (2 Cor. 5:9). The referent of "Lord," which occurs five times in vv. 32-35, is probably not God, but Christ. Although Paul can speak of "pleasing God" (1 Thess 4:1; cf. 2:15), in 2 Corinthians 5:8-10 "pleasing *the Lord*" is associated with "the judgment seat of *Christ.*" Further, the comparison of pleasing one's spouse with pleasing Christ is implicitly nuptial imagery, and throughout the New Testament the believer's spiritual marriage is to Christ (cf. 2 Cor. 11:2; see also comments on 6:16-20). As Paul will write only thirteen verses later, "for us . . . there is but one Lord, Jesus Christ" (8:6).

**7:33** Paul completes his advice to single men with the words: *But a married man is concerned about the affairs of this world — how he can please his wife.* This verse is the exact complement of v. 32b except that *a married man* replaces "an unmarried man," *the affairs of this world* replaces "the affairs of the Lord," and *please his wife* replaces "please the Lord."

Paul is not saying that those who are married cannot please the Lord. Just as vv. 29-31 contain sharp paradoxes, here we find arresting hyperbole — Paul is not saying that married men are concerned only about their wives and about nothing else. Nonetheless, this verse and the next both validate the proper concern married Christians should have for the happiness of their spouses. Otherwise Paul would have said that married people should simply decide to concern themselves with pleasing the Lord rather than pleasing their spouses, and single people could go ahead and marry with the same understanding. A married person who neglects or alienates their spouse by dedicating themselves solely to the service of God has misunderstood what devotion to the Lord requires of them and fails to honor God. It is Paul's recognition of the very real and legitimate concerns that married people have for the other members of their family that plays such a significant part in his preference for singleness. It is better, he says, not to be in a position where one must give significant time and attention to family members rather than to the Lord.

386. The two phrases are in apposition.

Paul's reference to *the affairs of this world* should be understood in light of his earlier comments to the effect that "this world in its present form is passing away" (see on v. 31). In his view it is better to invest one's life in the service of the one who is eternal than in being occupied with concerns about transient things. As in 7:7a, Paul reveals his preference for singleness, but it should not be read absolutely.[387] Just as 7:7b allowed for a different assessment of personal circumstances, so in vv. 36-38 Paul will allow engaged couples the freedom to choose. Paul is not giving direction in a casuistic fashion, but offers a godly perspective, informed by eschatology and Christology, from which to make responsible choices "before God" (v. 24b).

**7:34** Here Paul explains that he is concerned that the Corinthians serve Christ wholeheartedly. In his experience, "a married man" is worse off in this respect than the unmarried because *his interests are divided.* Paul uses the same verb as he did in 1:13: "Is Christ *divided?*"[388] Thiselton explains well Paul's thinking here: "The married man finds himself apportioned to both his wife and to the Lord; and it is this parceling out of time, attention, energies, and tasks that means he is 'pulled in two directions' [REB]."[389]

Having counseled the single men in vv. 32b-34a, Paul addresses the women in the rest of v. 34. The same advice is given with two differences. First, the women are addressed with a more complex description, as (literally) "the woman, the unmarried (woman) and the virgin," which either means "the unmarried woman and the virgin" or "the unmarried and virgin woman." The grammar is ambiguous, and multiple construals are possible.[390] There could be (1) one noun modified by two adjectives ("unmar-

387. The contrast between v. 32b and v. 33 is not between good and bad anxieties, but between the objects of the anxieties, single-focused concern for the Lord and concern for one's wife (as well).

388. Gk. μεμέρισται, perfect indicative passive of μερίζω, which refers, once again, to the present state of the subject. The concerns of a married man *are divided.* There is no hint of a past action leading to this state, as traditional analyses tended to assume. Rather, the perfect tense is being used to describe the current situation of the subject.

389. Thiselton, 590.

390. The difficulty in construing Paul's text has also led to a variety of textual variants in the MSS. The text supported by NA[27] is witnessed to by some ancient and important MSS, as well as some important versions ($\mathfrak{P}^{15}$, B, P, 6, 104, 365, 1175, 1505, *pc*, t, vg, co, Eusebius). It reads ἡ γυνὴ ἡ ἄγαμος καὶ ἡ παρθένος ("the unmarried woman and the virgin"). Other ancient and important witnesses (e.g., $\mathfrak{P}^{46}$, א, A) have ἡ γυνὴ ἡ ἄγαμος καὶ ἡ παρθένος ἡ ἄγαμος ("the unmarried woman and the unmarried virgin"). Finally, Western MSS, some ancient versions and Fathers, and the vast majority of minuscules (D, F, G, Ψ, 𝔐, ar, b, sy[p], Cyprian, Ambrosiaster, Speculum [Ps.-Augustine]) have ἡ γυνὴ καὶ ἡ παρθένος ἡ ἄγαμος ("the woman and the unmarried virgin"). At first sight the final version seems more difficult, but only when, with most modern translations, we understand the first part of this verse to complete the thought of v. 33. Scribes who thought v. 34 began a new thought read the beginning of the verse as "And there is a difference also between . . ." (cf. ERV, KJV). The fact that it is hard to see how any distinction between an unmarried woman and a virgin would

ried and virgin woman"), or (2) two nouns acting as a compound subject ("the unmarried woman and the virgin"), or (3) an epexegetical phrase referring to one woman ("the unmarried woman, that is, the virgin"). The first option is unlikely; because "the virgin" is normally understood to function substantivally since it does so everywhere else in 1 Corinthians and the New Testament, it should be understood that way here as well. What Paul says about the opportunity to be devoted to the Lord clearly applies equally to all categories of unmarried women; therefore, the third option would seem unlikely since it would seem to unduly limit the application to virgins. The second option could be interpreted in two different ways. If two exclusive categories are intended, the first presumably refers to "the woman who is currently free of wedlock" (i.e., divorcees and widows) and the second to "the woman who has never married" (Thiselton).[391] On the other hand, Paul may be referring to two overlapping categories, all unmarried women (including divorcees, widows, and young single women who have never been married ["virgins"]) and virgins in particular (the unmarried woman and [our special interest] the virgin [in particular]"). Since Paul's point applies equally to virgins and other unmarried women (as v. 32 applies to all unmarried men), he probably references the broad category of which his statement will be true and then highlights the particular subset of women he is most directly addressing in this section. That is, it applies to unmarried women (in general) and virgins (in particular). A second difference from Paul's advice to the men is that instead of "how to please the Lord" he adds: *Her aim is to be devoted to the Lord in both body and spirit.* Some have suggested that this phrase, "holy both in body and in spirit," is a quotation from "the Corinthian ascetical party"[392] which they used to describe "a specific group of well-intentioned and zealous unmarried women in Corinth."[393] However, such speculation is unwarranted, given Paul's consistent, apparently independent concern with holiness and purity issues throughout the letter (see Introduction, 21-22). Holiness here is not a reference to avoiding sexual intercourse, but carries the general Old Testament sense of "belonging exclusively to God,"[394] as in 1:2. The combination of *body and spirit* describes

---

make sense of the rest of the verse (since neither has to worry about a husband) "may have led copyists to shift the adjective ["unmarried"] from γυνή to παρθένος" (Metzger, *Textual Commentary*, 490), leaving the distinct categories of a wife (who has to worry about a husband) and an unmarried virgin (who does not). The second variant (with "unmarried" after both "woman" and "virgin") probably reflects a conflation of the other two readings (so also Metzger). The first variant presented above best explains the origin of the other two and is therefore most likely to be original.

391. The singular verb *is concerned* does not decide the case since it could be used of "a sense construction for the singular collective category" (Thiselton, 590).

392. Barrett, 181.

393. Collins, 292; cf. A. C. Wire, *The Corinthian Women Prophets* (Minneapolis: Fortress, 1990), 90-97.

394. Thiselton.

the whole person and simply serves to heighten and extend Paul's description of the goal of total devotion to the Lord.[395]

**7:35** *I am saying this* refers to Paul's counsel to single believers to stay unmarried because of the distractions of married life. This he says to them *for your own good,* profit, or advantage, for practical and pastoral rather than ascetic reasons.[396] This is a positive way of saying that he writes "to spare you . . . troubles in this life" (v. 28b). That he writes *not to restrict you* (literally, "not to throw a noose over you"[397]) reinforces the point made in v. 28 that those who choose to marry in spite of Paul's advice are not sinning. Coercive restraint is not Paul's intention. Rather, his purpose is to promote orderly, undistracted conduct: *but that you may live in a right way in undivided devotion to the Lord.*

Three terms define the existence Paul has in mind: *to live in a right way* translates the adjective "seemly," "proper," or "fitting,"[398] and *undivided devotion* reflects both an adjective[399] meaning "being in constant attendance, *constantly in service*" (BDAG) and an adverb meaning "without distraction."[400] The adjective and adverb work together to reinforce the idea of constant, single-minded service. The line may be taken to refer to two separate concerns: 1) dedicating themselves to what is proper/appropriate, and 2) serving the Lord with undistracted devotion (so ESV, NRSV, NAB, NASB, CSB, NJB). Or it may be taken to promote one priority through a combination of adjectives and an adverb that are to be taken together: "so that without distraction you may give notable and constant service to the Lord" (NET), "that you may live in a right way in undivided devotion to the Lord" (NIV, TNIV), "I want you to do whatever will help you serve the Lord best, with as few distractions as possible" (NLT). "Propriety" as an abstract value has not been a concern in this context, but in 1 Corinthians 14:40 Paul clearly affirms that the worship of God "should be done in a fitting and orderly way"; therefore, it seems likely that Paul has the propriety of worship itself in mind here as well. In other words, Paul's intention is that they might dedicate themselves to serving the Lord in the most fitting or proper way and with undivided attention.

### *d. Stay Unmarried, with the Proviso of Freedom to Choose, 7:36-38*

*[36]If anyone is worried that he might not be acting honorably toward the virgin he is engaged to, and if she is getting beyond the usual age for marrying and he feels he ought to marry, he should do as he wants. He is not sin-*

395. Schrage, 2:180.

396. Gk. σύμφορος.

397. Gk. βρόχον ὑμῖν ἐπιβάλω; cf. Thiselton, 592.

398. Gk. εὐσχήμων, "pert[aining] to being appropriate for display, *proper, presentable*" (BDAG); cf. 12:23-24, where parts of the human anatomy are presentable or unpresentable.

399. Gk. εὐπάρεδρος.

400. Gk. περισπάστως.

*ning. They should get married. [37]But the man who has settled the matter in his own mind, who is under no compulsion but has control over his own will, and who has made up his mind not to marry the virgin — this man also does the right thing. [38]So then, he who marries the virgin does right, but he who does not marry her does better.*

**7:36** Reading other people's mail can be confusing. There is probably no better example of this problem in Paul's letters than this verse, which sets the scene for the subunit of vv. 36-38. The difficulty lies in trying to work out to whom Paul is speaking and what he is talking about. Paul may not know the person by name, or the whole situation, but he knows enough to give some needed guidance to the troubled man.[401]

The passage is dogged by uncertainty concerning its subjects and by ambiguous terms. Who is the *anyone* Paul is addressing? What does it mean not to be *acting honorably toward* (literally) "his virgin"? Who exactly is this "virgin"? Does the main term of the second independent clause refer to the woman and mean "past maturity" (as in TNIV, *getting beyond the usual age for marrying*) or to the man and mean "uncontrollably passionate"? What does the phrase (literally) "it ought to happen thus" mean (TNIV, *he should do as he wants*)?

In spite of these uncertainties, vv. 36-38 show us the apostle dealing with delicate issues of personal choice and responsibility. What emerges is "Paul's constant concern to be pastorally positive and constructive, while also emphasizing the importance of determining what is helpful in special cases and circumstances."[402] The matter does not concern right and wrong, but in Paul's terms in v. 38, some conduct which is "good" and other which is "better."

The three interpretations of this passage which have historically competed for primacy can be illustrated in major English translations.[403] Either the situation in view involves: (1) a father deciding whether or not to give his virgin daughter in marriage — see NASB below (cf. ASV); or (2) couples living in a "spiritual" marriage, without sexual relations, struggling to maintain their abstinence — see NEB below; or (3) as argued in the introduction to 7:25-38, Christian engaged couples contemplating whether or not to get married — see NRSV below and TNIV above (cf. NIV, REB, ESV, NJB, NLT).

1. "But if any man thinks that he is acting unbecomingly toward his virgin *daughter,* if she should be of full age, and if it must be so, let him do what he wishes, he does not sin; let her marry." (NASB)

401. The sentence begins with a first-class condition, what BDF calls "Εἰ with the indicative of reality," which often has the sense "as you say, as is believed, as you see, etc." (§372).

402. Thiselton, 601.

403. For a full treatment of the issues, see Thiselton, 593-602.

2. "But if a man has a partner in celibacy and feels that he is not behaving properly towards her, if, that is, his instincts are too strong for him, and something must be done, he may do as he pleases; there is nothing wrong in it; let them marry." (NEB)
3. "If anyone thinks that he is not behaving properly toward his fiancée, if his passions are strong, and so it has to be, let him marry as he wishes; it is no sin. Let them marry." (NRSV)

The first view was held by many church fathers and is expressed by Calvin: "Paul now turns to address the parents, who had children under their control."[404] In this view *anyone* is the father, and "his virgin" is his daughter. According to this view, fathers would have been holding back from giving their daughters in marriage either because of the social instability of the "present crisis" or (since most if not all potential Roman husbands would have been sexually active as young single men) due to questions raised by Paul's warning about associating with sexually immoral people in his previous letter to the Corinthians (5:9; see the comments introducing the chapter) and over concerns about the problem of sexual "touching" (see on 7:1). They feel that what they are doing might be shameful, and Paul counsels that the father may "do what he wishes, he does not sin; let her marry . . . if she should be of full age" (NASB).[405] This interpretation was standard among the church fathers. The main piece of evidence in favor of this view is the different verb "to marry" that Paul uses in v. 38. Elsewhere in the chapter (vv. 9, 10, 28, 33, 24, 36, 39) the more common verb meaning "to marry" is used and the switch in v. 38 to a verb which usually means "to give in marriage" is thought to be compelling.[406] Thus NASB translates v. 38: "So then both *he who gives his own virgin daughter in marriage* does well, and he who does not *give her in marriage* will do better."[407]

Despite its age this view is difficult to sustain. Father-daughter relationships appear nowhere explicitly in the chapter.[408] It would also be unusual to refer to a father's daughter as "his virgin." As counterevidence, Acts 21:9 calls Philip's "four unmarried daughters" (literally) his "virgin *daughters*," not his "virgins." Along with these arguments from silence, this view cannot account for the plural subject of v. 36's closing imperative: "Let them marry." NASB's "let her marry" is based on a textual variant[409] that is only weakly attested and may itself be testimony to a deliberate scribal change to accommodate the father-daughter interpretation of the passage.

404. Calvin, 164. Among modern commentators see Grosheide, Morris, and Barnett.

405. In an ancient context this would mean that she has reached puberty.

406. The two verbs are γαμέω and γαμίζω respectively. They are attested in the Gospels (Matt. 22:30/Mark 12:25/Luke 17:27) with this distinction: "they neither marry (γαμέω) nor are given in marriage (γαμίζω)."

407. Gk. γαμίζων in both parts of the sentence.

408. Fee, 326.

409. Gk. γαμείτω instead of γαμείτωσαν.

Finally, the verb in v. 38 does not need to be translated "to give in marriage." Paul probably chose it here because he was using it transitively while he had used the other verb intransitively.[410]

The assumption that Paul is addressing celibate couples living together as "brother" and "sister" is also unlikely.[411] This view suggests that Paul is addressing a husband who is in a "spiritual marriage" (marriage without sexual relations because they consider sex sinful or because they consider abstinence a superior lifestyle) who is having trouble coping with his sexual desires and wishes to engage in sexual relations with his wife. Paul counsels them not to feel guilty about having sex; "he may do as he pleases; there is nothing wrong in it [literally, "he does not sin"]" (NEB). The imperative "let them marry" is then understood as "let such a couple engage in marital relations." However, against this view is the fact that Paul opposed any extended periods of marital abstinence in vv. 1-5, and that the verb used does not have that sense.[412]

The third view, that Paul is addressing betrothed Christian couples, is followed by most recent English translations and the majority of modern commentaries.[413] It makes sense of the details of the passage and is congruent with Paul's advice elsewhere in the chapter. In v. 36 the two parties concerned are addressed with the words *anyone* (the betrothed male) and *his virgin* (his fiancée). TNIV is clear: *If anyone is worried that he might not be acting honorably toward the virgin he is engaged to. . . .* The word "virgin" refers to a single "young woman of marriageable age" (BDAG), that is, an eligible young woman. When such a young woman is called "his virgin," it suggests that she is spoken for.[414]

The man *might not be acting honorably toward the virgin he is engaged to* either because he is giving in to sexual temptation,[415] or because he has been holding off on the marriage longer than was considered appropriate. Much of Paul's language in these verses is open to being interpreted in terms of either sexual temptation or social/moral pressure.[416] In the context

410. Cf. Fee, 355, and Garland, 338.

411. Advocates include Weiss; Héring; Hurd, *The Origin of 1 Corinthians*, 169-78; Murphy-O'Connor; cf. Moffatt's translation: "spiritual bride."

412. Deming, *Paul on Marriage*, 40-47 and 206-9, lodges the strongest objections to the "spiritual marriages" view. It is noteworthy that REB has departed from NEB and adopts the "betrothed Christians" view.

413. Cf. Barrett; Fee; Schrage; Wolff; Bruce Winter, "Puberty or Passion? The Meaning of ὑπέρακμος in 1 Corinthians 7:36," *TynBul* 49 (1998), 71-89; Collins; Thiselton.

414. In *Aethiopica*, Heliodorus's third-century-A.D. romance novel, Charicles, the love-sick maiden, refers to herself as "your virgin" (τὴν σὴν παρθένον) when speaking to her beloved Theagenes, whom she hopes to marry someday (*Aethiopica* 6.8.6.9).

415. Gk. ἀσχημονέω.

416. The church fathers (explicitly Theodore of Mopsuestia, Chrysostom, Theodoret, Augustine, and Ambrosiaster) all took it in nonsexual ways (Conzelmann, 135 n. 38; Thiselton, 595). Paul uses the same verb in 13:5 (the only other place it appears in the New Testament) without any suggestion of a sexual connotation in the context.

of this chapter's focus on *porneia* and concerns about "touching" women, it seems natural to take it as a reference to sexual impropriety. However it should also be noted that the last explicit reference to sexual temptations was back in v. 9, and that much or most of vv. 10-35 deal with social expectations and obligations. The man thinks or worries[417] that he may not be treating his virgin properly. We hold that the nature of the man's inappropriate behavior is suggested later on in the verse, when Paul indicates what the man thinks *he ought to* do. That is, he ought to marry the girl who has now come of age.

As Findlay notes, Roman society looked down on keeping an adult "daughter at home, without any apparent reason"; he contends that such behavior was considered "dishonorable."[418] In fact, Susan Treggiari points out that "[t]he Augustan marriage laws forbade a *paterfamilias* to prevent the marriage of his daughter," but the practice persisted and later emperors "ordered provincial governors to enforce this rule" and interpreted the law to "cover fathers who did not look for a match for their children."[419] Some men engaged themselves to underage girls in order to benefit from the privileges given to married men by law. Although they would not actually become married until the girl was older, they could claim the benefits of a married man right away.[420]

The next clause, as noted above, has been translated in two ways: *and if she is getting beyond the usual age for marrying* (TNIV) and "if his passions are strong" (NRSV). Part of the problem is that the subject of the dependent clause is unexpressed. It could be either the subject of the previous clause, the man *(anyone)*, or the most recently mentioned person, the virgin.[421] The relevant word[422] has been taken to refer "either to puberty on the part of a woman or 'full of passion' with reference to men."[423] A reexamination of the evidence suggests that the word means to have passed through puberty, that is, to have arrived at full adulthood.[424] As such, it most likely ap-

417. Gk. νομίζω. As BDAG suggests, the word means "to form an idea about someth[ing] but with some suggestion of tentativeness or refraining from a definitive statement, *think, believe, hold, consider.*"

418. Findlay, 836.

419. Treggiari, *Roman Marriage*, 147, citing *Digest* 23.2.19. That Jewish fathers worried about marrying off their daughters is suggested by Sir. 42:9-14.

420. Treggiari, *Roman Marriage*, 154.

421. Fee, 351, points out that it is more usual for such a construction to pick up the subject of the preceding clause, namely the man, but he admits that this is not decisive and that it could refer to either the man or the woman.

422. Gk. ὑπέρακμος.

423. Winter, *After Paul Left Corinth*, 246; idem, "Puberty or Passion," 77. On the one side translations have "if she is past marriageable age" (CSB); "if she is past her youth" (NASB); "if she is past the bloom of youth" (NET); "if she is getting along in years" (NIV). On the other side: "if his passions are strong" (NRSV, ESV, NJB); "and will inevitably give in to his passion" (NLT). The NAB leaves it quite ambiguous with "if a critical moment has come."

424. Despite Winter, "Puberty or Passion," all ancient usages of the word are consistent with the conclusion that when applied to people the word ὑπέρακμος refers to arrival at

plies to the woman (since men usually married at a later age). Since most women would be expected to marry as adolescents, TNIV's *getting beyond the usual age for marrying* probably reflects Paul's meaning.

The sequence of ideas — "if she has come of age, and so it ought to happen, . . . let them marry" — suggests that the man feels an "obligation to meet certain social or moral expectations,"[425] namely, that of following through on his promise to marry the girl (a promise which may well have brought him legal benefits in the interim) now that she has come of age. To not do so would be to have exploited her and her family, an unseemly thing to do. The "it" to which Paul is referring is made explicit at the end of the verse: *They should get married*[426] (which employs a permissive imperative), given the man's sense of moral obligation in light of the girl's arrival at a critical age.

The fact that Paul says, *He is not sinning,* has been taken by many to indicate that he is dealing with Corinthians who are promoting celibacy and who have suggested to the man that it would be wrong, a sin, to go ahead and marry his fiancée. But it is Paul himself who has been advocating celibacy and who has indicated that he does not want anyone to seek to change their status but, rather, wants each one to remain in the situation in which they already found themselves (vv. 17, 20, 24, 26). In light of the various ways he has driven home this point, it is not surprising that when giving his permission to marry Paul feels the need to clarify that this would not be a sinful course of action. Paul might have preferred that the man be and feel free not to follow through with the marriage, but he respected his right to decide whether or not this was the best course of action. This man is concerned, as he should be, not to do anything unseemly or disgraceful. He is concerned about his own moral integrity and the reputation of the gospel. He too wants to "glorify God with [his] body" (6:20). It is not a preference for marriage or singleness that counts, but "Keeping God's commandments" (7:19).

7:37 Just as Paul gave no "command" to single adults not to marry "because of the present crisis" in vv. 25-26, his counsel to a male fiancé in v. 36 to get married if he feels he ought to is also not compulsory. In v. 37 he affirms that not all those who are betrothed must get married. Remaining single is still an acceptable option. Both the man who marries and the one

a particular stage of human development. There is no clear evidence that the word ever meant, or was thought to mean, "full of sexual passion."

425. BDAG, ὀφείλω, 2. Winter's suggestion (*After Paul Left Corinth,* 250; idem, "Puberty or Passion," 84) that this clause be translated "and thus it is bound to happen" (where "it" refers to an assumed temptation to engage in sexual relations) is based on a misunderstanding of the entry on ὀφείλω in LSJ.

426. The textual variant in D*, F, G, 1505, *pc,* d, $vg^{st}$, $sy^{p}$, which reads "let him/her marry" (γαμείτω), clearly reflects an attempt to smooth over a difficulty for the common view in the early church that the passage dealt with a father considering whether or not to give his daughter away in marriage.

who does not may do *the right thing.* The action is not the sole determinant of "pleasing the Lord" (7:32). Verse 37 spells out the conditions that validate deciding not to get married. They are not general moral principles but continue to relate directly to the man's state of mind, as in v. 36, where the man's particular social situation and his relationship with his betrothed play such a significant role. Nonetheless, and perhaps for the very reason that they relate to concrete circumstances, they have far-reaching ethical implications in analogous settings.

The verse lists four criteria for not getting married that turn out to be two interrelated criteria; repetition of words and ideas reveals an ABBA structure.[427] The first and fourth read literally: the man must be "firmly established *in his heart*"; he must have "decided this [not to change his relationship with his virgin] *in his own heart.*" As well as touching the emotions, the "heart" can be the place of volition. Hence TNIV translates it as *mind* in both parts of the verse. Romans 14:5 is a parallel instruction, where in a context of scruples over certain days Paul advises that "everyone should be fully convinced in their own mind." In Paul's moral world there are grey areas and matters on which Christians differ, but there is to be no equivocation. "Everything that does not come from faith [confident trust and assurance before God] is sin" (Rom. 14:23b). Along with two references to the man's heart (and one to his will — see below), the verse contains three self-reflective pronouns. Together these elements point to the man's arriving at "an independent personal conviction."[428] Whereas on some issues there are commands to keep, on others each person must form their own judgment "as (personally and directly) responsible to God" (v. 24). The two brief remarks at the beginning and end of v. 37 anticipate Paul's fuller discussion of related matters in the following three chapters of the letter.

The second and third criteria that Paul lists for deciding not to get married are also synonymous. The man is literally to "*have* no necessity" but to "*have* authority[429] concerning his own will." Both phrases have been thought to refer to his sexual self-control. "Necessity" or *compulsion*[430] can refer to sexual need, but the word is used for all manner of necessities or compulsions and does not have a particular association with sexual desires. Treggiari mentions that "[a] daughter who compelled her *paterfamilias* to consent to her marriage need not have been acting alone: her mother may well have taken the initiative in making a match for her."[431] If the

427. A — He stands firm in his heart;
B — He has no necessity/compulsion;
B′ — He has freedom to exercise his own will;
A′ — He has decided in his own heart. Cf. Garland, 341-42.

428. Thiselton, 601.

429. Gk. ἐξουσία. A key term in the next unit, this noun occurs again in 8:9; 9:4, 5, 6, 12, 18; 11:10; and 15:24.

430. Gk. ἀνάγκη.

431. Treggiari, *Roman Marriage,* 147. She reminds us that although "either party was

daughter could compel her *paterfamilias* to consent, and has her mother's support as well, the engaged man may well have felt the compelling power of at least that threesome if he were to consider breaking off or indefinitely extending the engagement a year or two after entering into it.

Many think the "will"[432] Paul has in mind here also concerns "sexual desire."[433] That usage is rather rare, however,[434] and the nonsexual usage is clearly more common in the LXX and New Testament, even omitting references to the will of God.[435] Paul does not use the word with a sexual connotation in any of its other twenty-three occurrences in his letters. In many cases the noun "will/desire" is found in the same context as the verb "to will/desire,"[436] and in such cases the two typically have the same basic meaning and reference. That is the case here, where the verb appeared in v. 36 ("as he wants") with reference to the man's desire to marry. Here by *his own will* Paul probably has in mind the man's own wish to marry or not to marry, independent of external pressures like those that have led the man mentioned in v. 36 to feel that he ought to marry his fiancée.

The two clauses translated *who is under no compulsion but has control over his own will* share the same verb ("to have"), could be more literally (and woodenly) rendered "not having necessity/compulsion but has authority/freedom with regard to his own will," and should be taken as mutually interpretive.[437] That is, one who is compelled or needs to take a certain course of action may not exercise their will freely, while one who is not compelled by some external force is free to act according to their own will. The TNIV translation of the next clause, *and who has made up his mind,* misses a nuance of the Greek text that ties this clause more closely to the previous two. It reads "and has decided this in his own heart. . . ."[438] The

---

legally free to break [an engagement] at any time and there was little social disadvantage attached," still "it was correct for an engagement to be broken only for strong reasons" (158).

432. Gk. θέλημα.

433. Winter, "Puberty or Passion," 85; cf. W. G. Kümmel, "Verlobung und Heirat bei Paulus (1 Cor 7, 36-38)," in *Neutestamentliche Studien für Rudolf Bultmann zu seinem siebzigsten Geburtstag* (ed. W. Eltester; BZNW 21; Berlin: Töpelmann, 1954), 283-84. John 1:13 has such a usage.

434. BDAG affirms only that "acc[ording] to many [the word in our verse] has the connotation of sexual desire." The only parallels mentioned there, besides John 1:13, are three occurrences in two magical papyri (PG 4.1430, 1521, 1533).

435. When the word is used in the LXX and the New Testament to refer to the will of humans, it is usually in a nonsexual sense (2 Sam. 23:5; 1 Kgs. 5:22, 23, 24; 9:11; 2 Chr. 9:12; Esth 1:8; Pss. 1:2; 27:7; 106:30; 144:19; Eccl. 12:1, 10; Job 21:21; Sir. 8:15; 32:17; Isa. 58:3, 13; Jer. 23:26; Dan. 11:16, 36; Dan (Theodotion). 4:35; 8:4; 11:3, 16, 36; Luke 12:47; 23:25; John 5:30; 6:38; 1 Cor. 16:12; 2 Pet. 1:21).

436. Gk. θέλω/ἐθέλω.

437. This is suggested by the chiastic structure (verb-object/object-verb) of the key terms (μὴ ἔχων ἀνάγκην, ἐξουσίαν δὲ ἔχει) which places necessity (ἀνάγκην) in opposition to freedom/authority (ἐξουσίαν).

438. Gk. καὶ τοῦτο κέκρικεν ἐν τῇ ἰδίᾳ καρδίᾳ.

previous clause referred to "his own[439] will," and this one does to "his own heart." BDAG recognizes this as a usage that points "to a striking connection or an exclusive relationship" so that "own will" and "own heart/mind" contrasts with "not being under compulsion" and "is not simply equivalent" to the possessive genitive in "in his heart/mind" at the beginning of the verse. The man who does not feel obligated or compelled has the freedom to follow his own will and to make up his own mind independently, rather than having to negotiate a course whose boundaries have been set by serious social obligations or expectations.

The middle two criteria, then, bring us back again to the importance of arriving at "an independent personal conviction."[440] The man's ability to decide and stand firm in his own heart (A, A′) depends to a significant degree on whether or not some necessity or compulsion diminishes this ability to freely exercise his own will (B, B′). In first-century Corinth part of the compulsion may have had to do with the expectations of the fiancée, her parents and family, as well as other members of the church or neighbors in the city. In modern Western societies the factors that might impinge upon a decision to marry, to extend an engagement, or to end it may be either similar to or different from those in Corinth.

One of the most difficult phrases in this passage is the one translated *not to marry the virgin* (so also NIV). Translated literally, it reads "to keep his own virgin" (CSB, NAB, NET). The NASB has "to keep his own virgin *daughter,*" while the ESV and NRSV render the same clause "to keep her as his betrothed [NRSV: fiancée]," and the NJB has "and decides to let her remain as his fiancée." BDAG translates the key clause "*keep his virgin inviolate* as such,"[441] but one would normally expect a second accusative for such a meaning (as in "keep her pure" or "keep her unblemished"). If the man chooses to end the betrothal, the woman would no longer be "his virgin" and could be expected to be married to a different man. The man cannot really determine whether or not the woman will be kept inviolate; he can only decide whether or not he will marry her himself, either now or after a more prolonged engagement.

Although it is a very difficult exegetical decision, it seems to make the most sense, in light of vv. 26-27, to see Paul distinguishing between two kinds of betrothed men: one who feels he should not wait any longer before marrying his fiancée, and one who feels free to follow Paul's advice not to change his (and her) status during "the present crisis" (v. 26) and who prolongs the engagement for the time being, keeping his girl as his fiancée rather than marrying her. He is bound to her, but he seeks neither to be released from her nor to conclude the engagement with a marriage for the time being (v. 27). In other words, it is acceptable not to get married now if

439. Gk. ἴδιος, in this phrase and the next.

440. Thiselton, 601.

441. See BDAG on τηρέω.

he can wait. If other contextual (moral and social) factors compel him to marry now rather than wait until later, however, "he ought to marry" (v. 36). In either case, if he follows Paul's guidance in making the decision, he *does the right thing*. In the context of vv. 25-38, to "do well" is to make a choice "before God" that is realistic, decent, and fitting, and in due vigilance against sexual immorality and that promotes undistracted service of the Lord Jesus and aims to please God.

The previous occurrences of the adverb "good" in chapter 7 are revealing. Paul says that it is "good" for the widowed to remain unmarried (v. 8) and for single adults not to marry ("because of the present crisis"; v. 26). The first appears in Paul's quotation of the Corinthian slogan in v. 1: "it is good for a man not to 'touch' a woman." In vv. 2-5 Paul responds to the maxim with his own guidance for avoiding *porneia*. Here Paul affirms the man who will not rush into a marriage but is prepared to wait for a more appropriate or propitious time before marrying and having sex with his virgin. He has done a good thing.

**7:38** With the words *So then*, Paul brings his counsel concerning the marriage of betrothed couples in vv. 36-38 to a close. Having instructed the betrothed concerning several factors and principles that should be considered in making the decision of whether to marry one's fiancée, Paul offers encouragement to those inclined both ways, and to the married and single who were "listening in" to the conversation: *he who marries the virgin does right, but he who does not marry her does better.*[442]

Paul is not "damning . . . [those who decide to marry] with faint praise,"[443] nor is he saying that celibacy is a morally superior state.[444] As Garland explains, "Regarding one choice as better does not make the other choice bad."[445] This verse is to be read in the light of everything he has said in the chapter regarding circumstances and inclinations, motives and obligations, personal freedom and convictions. Paul's preference arises from his own experience of a practical freedom in that state which he employs in the single-minded service of Christ. He still leaves the betrothed with the genuine freedom to choose.

442. Literally, "he who marries his (own) virgin does right, but he who does not marry does better." There is no explicit direct object in the second clause. Although it is possible that the first clause addresses engaged men and the second one men who are not yet engaged, it is more likely that the direct object is elided in the second clause, being understood due to its presence in the first. In this case, it may be understood (in light of vv. 26-27, 37b) that the one not marrying the virgin at this time of crisis will most likely go ahead and marry her at a later point in time, if she is still amenable to the idea.

443. Thiselton, 602.

444. Contra D. B. Martin, *The Corinthian Body*, 211, who speaks of a hierarchy of virtue here.

445. Garland, 342-43.

### 4. *Counsel for Christian Widows, 7:39-40*

> [39]*A woman is bound to her husband as long as he lives. But if her husband dies, she is free to marry anyone she wishes, but he must belong to the Lord.* [40]*In my judgment, she is happier if she stays as she is — and I think that I too have the Spirit of God.*

**7:39** Paul had already addressed widows in vv. 8-9. The reason they are again spoken to here is to "continue the pattern of alternating instructions to males and females."[446] Also, the order unmarried and widows mentioned in v. 8 is reprised in the fuller sections of vv. 25-38 and 39-40. In vv. 25-38 Paul advised those thinking of marrying virgins as to whether or not to get married. In vv. 39-40 he does the same for widows in the congregation. The latter section is brief presumably because the question of widows marrying was less pressing than that of those considering their first marriage. The letter of the Corinthians to Paul (see 7:1a) almost certainly asked about "the virgins" (v. 25); Paul may have addressed widows for the sake of completeness.

Paul makes three points regarding the termination of marriage and remarriage for the benefit of Christian widows in Corinth. Peter Tomson argues that all three use "formulations directly related to Rabbinic halakha."[447] Biblical roots are also evident. What Paul says and the way he says it shows that he stands in the biblical and Jewish tradition on the subject.

In 7:39a Paul indicates that the death of a husband terminates the marriage bond (cf. Rom. 7:2), so that the widow has the right to remarry: *A woman is bound to her husband as long as he lives.* Deuteronomy 24:3 stipulates the same provision with the words, "if the latter husband dies." To read this as a prohibition against all divorce and remarriage is to ignore its context. Paul states the general and ideal in connection with a particular class of individuals. He is assuming, for the sake of his point, that there are no legitimate grounds for divorce (especially since his view reflects a conservative Jewish view that put strict limits on grounds for divorce in comparison with Roman and more liberal Jewish views). Contrary to what was done in the Roman culture in which she lived, a Christian woman was not (morally) free to divorce her husband at her own discretion (although v. 15 shows that Paul condoned divorce in certain circumstances).

In 7:39b Paul states that widows may remarry: *But if her husband dies, she is free to marry anyone she wishes.* According to Jewish custom, a widow whose husband died without an heir was supposed to marry her brother-

446. Garland, 343.

447. Peter J. Tomson, *Paul and the Jewish Law: Halakha in the Letters of the Apostle to the Gentiles* (CRINT 1; Assen [Netherlands]: Van Gorcum, 1990), 120-22. Cf. Rosner, *Paul, Scripture and Ethics,* 171-73.

in-law and produce an heir for her deceased husband through him (see Deut. 25:5-10). This was called levirate marriage. It has been suggested that "the obvious message of these verses" is that a Christian widow was not subject to levirate marriage.[448] It is questionable, however, whether it would ever have occurred to any Corinthian that levirate marriage might apply to them. On the other hand, Paul's statement here is similar to *m. Giṭṭin* 9:3, a tractate expounding the halakic implications of Deuteronomy 24:1-4 for divorce which includes this line which was part of the standard Jewish divorce certificate: "you are free to marry any man." For Paul, widows were to have the same freedom that was granted to divorcées according to Jewish law,[449] a freedom that Roman divorcées also experienced.

Paul adds a restriction, however, in 7:39c: *but he must belong to the Lord*[450] or, literally, "only in the Lord." Does Paul mean that the new husband must be a Christian believer or that "[s]he must remember that she is a member of Christ's body and not forget her Christian duties"?[451] In other words, must he be "in the Lord" or must she undertake the marriage "in the Lord"? Probably the former is intended. Whereas "in Christ" language is amenable to a range of meanings, Paul does use the phrase "in the Lord" in Romans 16:11 unambiguously to mean "Christians." Similar clauses were in Jewish circulation in Paul's day. For example, a Bar Kokhba divorce deed has an analogous specification: "you may go and be married to *any Jewish man* you want."[452] The exclusion of marriage to a non-Jew has its basis in Scripture (Deut. 7:3; Josh. 23:12; Ezra 9:1-4; Neh. 13:23-27).[453]

However, it would be wrong to take Paul's words as a universal command. For a Christian to marry someone else who is in Christ is rather, as Fee puts it, "good sense."[454] One thing that 1 Corinthians 7 definitely shows is that in many areas of sexual ethics Paul's teaching cannot be reduced to "following orders." Elliptical expressions like "only in the Lord" need something to be supplied to be accurately understood; in this case, "my advice would be . . ." fits the tenor of Paul's instructions. We do not actually know whether or not the betrothed virgins discussed in vv. 36-38 were believers. It may well have been a complicating factor if men were betrothed to virgins and then converted to Christ before the betrothal was transformed into marriage. The question about virgins may also have arisen in part due to the challenges of finding a spouse from within the Christian community when it was undoubtedly a rather small group. What was a man to do if he did not feel that he could live the life of a celibate single

448. Instone-Brewer, *Divorce and Remarriage in the Bible,* 208.

449. See Instone-Brewer, *Divorce and Remarriage in the Bible,* 208-9.

450. Cf. REB, "within the Lord's fellowship."

451. Lightfoot, *Notes,* 225.

452. *DJD* 2, no. 19.

453. Meeks, *First Urban Christians,* 101, points out that Paul's "phrase 'a sister as wife' in 1 Cor. 9:5 presupposes the norm" of believers marrying other believers.

454. Fee, 356.

man but there were no good options within the church? The question is not one of sin and not sin, but of good and better.

Incidentally, Paul uses the pleasant image of sleep here for the death of a Christian; he says literally, "But if the man sleeps."[455] While this may have been a polite euphemism among Greeks for centuries,[456] for Christians it came to serve as an allusion to the hope of the resurrection (cf. Eph. 5:14, where a different Greek verb[457] is used for the same euphemism and where it is explicitly tied to the resurrection hope).[458] As 15:54-55 shows, it is based on the conviction that Christians face death as the last enemy which has "lost its sting" because of Jesus Christ. Pannenberg observes that the notion of sleep implies the expectation of waking: "The familiar experience of being awakened and rising from sleep serves as a parable for the completely unknown destiny expected for the dead."[459]

**7:40** Paul's final words to Christian widows reflect his personal experience and preference: *In my judgment, she is happier if she stays as she is.* The word "judgment"[460] might give the impression that Paul is finally "laying down the law" and excluding any real scope for free decisions of personal conviction. However, the same word was used in v. 25 in contrast to giving a "command" and may here be better translated as "opinion" (as in NRSV, REB, NJB) or even "view." From Paul's perspective the unmarried state is preferable (cf. v. 7a). There is no need to read his advice as more binding than this. As Robertson and Plummer observe, throughout the chapter "the preference given to celibacy is tentative and exceptional."[461]

The word for "happier"[462] can have religious connotations (cf. Rom. 4:7-8; 14:22). Thus Findlay, for example, thinks that Paul means that the widow will be more "blessed" by staying single and devoting herself to the work of the Lord.[463] Certainly widows sometimes had a special status in some parts of the early church. Probably Paul's intention here is broader. He believes that the widow's life will be less complicated if she stays single,

455. Cf. 11:30; 15:6, 18, 20, 51; 1 Thess. 4:13-15.

456. It was used as early as Homer's *Iliad* (11.241) and by other Greek authors after him. It was also commonly used in Greek epitaphs (see LSJ, BDAG).

457. Gk. καθεύδω.

458. See M. Völkel, "κοιμάομαι," *EDNT* 2:302: "The demarcation of the circle of those for whom κοιμάομαι is used is illuminating: It is in all instances, including 1 Cor 7:39, used consistently of Church members, David (Acts 13:36), or the ἅγιοι (Matt 27:52)." For Paul the term "is used primarily in connection with questions about the fate of Church members who die before the parousia (1 Thess 4:13ff.) or before the resurrection (1 Cor 15:12ff.)." While "the Pauline occurrences are not sufficient to justify the long-held view that expectation of the resurrection was inherent in κοιμάομαι," still, one may affirm that it "is a term directly relevant to death and the associated Christian hope."

459. W. Pannenberg, *Jesus — God and Man* (Eng. trans.; Philadelphia: Westminster and London: SCM, 1968), 74; cited in Thiselton, 604.

460. Gk. γνώμη.

461. Robertson and Plummer, 162.

462. Gk. μακαριωτέρα, a comparative form of μακάριος.

463. Findlay, 838.

especially in view of "the present crisis" (v. 26) and the distractions of married life (vv. 32-35). In effect, he counsels widows to be content and not to seek a change in their status, his default position throughout the chapter (see vv. 17, 20, 24).

Paul's final appeal reminds the Corinthians that his counsel in general must be taken seriously: *and I think that I too have the Spirit of God.* There were strong personalities in the church in Corinth who held views different from Paul's. Given Corinthian infatuation with spiritual gifts and manifestations, Paul implies with his *I too* that he, no less than others in the church, speaks "in words taught by the Spirit" (2:13).

## IV. "FLEE IDOLATRY" AND "GLORIFY GOD" IN YOUR WORSHIP, 8:1–14:40

Paul turns from his extended section dedicated primarily to questions of sexual immorality (chs. 5–6) and the need to glorify God with our bodies (chapter 7) to a section dedicated to the issues of idolatry (specifically food offered to idols; 8:1–11:1) and the proper worship of God (11:2–14:40). As with the previous extended sections, this one also begins with a negative treatment, here of the idolatry that needs to be vigorously rejected, and follows up with a positive one, in this case dealing with the proper worship of God.

### A. Condemnation of Idolatrous Practices: "Flee Idolatry" (Food Offered to Idols), 8:1–11:1

This section, like other parts of the letter (cf. esp. chs. 12–14), reflects an A-B-A structure. Paul raises the question of food offered to idols in 8:1-13. He then seemingly moves to a different topic in 9:1-23, where he discusses his own example of waiving rights for the sake of the gospel. Then he returns to the question of food offered to idols in 9:24–11:1. As it turns out, 9:1-23 is not really a digression, but a section in which Paul provides crucial ethical guidance that informs his teaching on the issue of food offered to idols (as ch. 13 provides the crucial ethical foundation for the issues raised concerning spiritual gifts in chs. 12 and 14).

While the issue of eating food offered to idols strikes many Western readers as irrelevant, it continues to be a live issue in many Asian contexts. Paul's discussion also provides indirect guidance for a number of issues on which believers with different convictions about debatable issues need to learn to distinguish between issues on which Christians might agree to disagree, respecting the convictions and conscience of others and acting out of sensitivity to their spiritual well-being, and other issues that call for a clear and unambiguous rejection of behavior that undermines the central tenets and values of the Christian faith.

Can it be wrong for one believer to watch R-rated movies but alright for another to do so? Or for one to observe the Sabbath but not for another? Or for one to use Eastern medical treatments? Or for one to drink alcoholic beverages? And so on. Paul's arguments in these chapters are crucial for sorting through such important and perennial issues.

Although a mirror reading of Paul's argument will be subjective, to read the section accurately and profitably we must attempt to understand the views to which Paul is responding. Our approach is strongly influenced both by the contents of these chapters and the fact that Paul is responding to a letter (and other news) sent in response to his earlier letter to them which some Corinthians evidently understood as an exhortation not to associate with their ungodly and immoral pagan neighbors (cf. 5:9-10; 7:1).[1] It seems that the Corinthians had written Paul something like the following:

> "Your call not to associate with immoral people has exacerbated a point of conflict among us. Some members of the church are upset because others have accepted invitations to dinners held in idol temples and freely eat food that has been sacrificed to idols. But we all possess knowledge and so we know that an idol has no real existence since there is no God but one. So there is no such thing as "idol food"; just food. The others, however, are frightened and upset about what we eat and question our right to eat any food we want. We are trying to build them up so that they too can enjoy their freedom in Christ and the right to eat any food, as long as they are thankful to God for it. We have explained to them that eating this food commends us to our neighbors. We'll be worse off if we do not eat it and better off if we do since we will offend our friends and neighbors (and hurt our chances of social advancement by building relationships with potential patrons) if we snub them by rejecting their invitations or their food. Only by accepting their invitations and eating their food will we have opportunities for outreach and advancement. Those other believers, being weak, think that we are actually condoning idolatry and encouraging them to participate in it as well."

There are three contexts in which people ate food that had been offered to idols. *Celebrations held in dining halls* attached to pagan temples would have served food that had been offered to the god of the temple as

1. Cf. J. Fotopoulos, *Food Offered to Idols in Roman Corinth* (Tübingen: J. C. B. Mohr, 2003), 187, for the relationship between this section of Paul's letter and the issues raised in the earlier correspondence with the Corinthians, and 179-87 for his cogent arguments against J. C. Hurd's view (*The Origins of 1 Corinthians* [London: SPCK, 1965], 240-70) that Paul is attempting to impose the decree of the Jerusalem Council (cf. Acts 15:20, 29; 21:25) after having supported a more liberal attitude when the church was founded.

patron of the event, whether they were primarily religious or social events (see the comments on 8:10-11). It was also common for food eaten at *a dinner in the private home* of a pagan neighbor to be offered to a god whose presence and patronage were acknowledged by the host. Much of the *food sold in the meat market* would have also been food that had originally been sacrificed to an idol before finding its way to the market. As it turns out, a large percentage of the meat available for consumption would have been previously offered to an idol. Other kinds of food were also susceptible to being offered to idols.

A traditional interpretation of chapters 8–10 holds that Paul's concern about food offered to idols is based on the damage that may be caused to the conscience of Christians who associate that food with idolatry. Others hold that the problem Paul has is with the idol food itself, which has become spiritually contaminated by being offered to idols. Our understanding is that the problem is not with the food per se, nor merely with the conscience of "weaker brothers," but with any association with idolatry (sharing in the offering regardless of how one construes it) and the risk of leading others, by example, into idolatry.

In chapters 8–10 Paul seems to wrestle with two kinds of idolatry: *subjective* and *objective.* By "subjective idolatry" we mean an occasion when a person consciously participates in an activity that they consider idolatrous. Whether or not others judge it to be so may be beside the point. By "objective idolatry" we have in mind people who do not consider themselves idolaters (they do not believe in idols or other gods) who participate in an activity that they consider innocent but which in fact is idolatrous. Karl Barth proposed a similar distinction: "To be in contact with this atmosphere and not to be severed from paganism, that which the Corinthians cherish and prize as their freedom, may, regarded objectively, be communion with devils every time, and the subjective element, their human knowledge, will not prevent its actually being so."[2]

The "knowledgeable" Corinthians do not realize that they are in danger of leading other believers to commit subjective idolatry and that they themselves are in danger of committing objective idolatry despite their touted knowledge of monotheism. The two groups involved are probably distinguished socially, with those receiving and accepting invitations to temple dinners and denying that the eating of idol food has any spiritual significance being from the upper echelons of Corinthian society. These are the social climbers who are impressed by their own philosophical sophistication and the lack of sophistication of those complaining about them. Those considered "weak" by that first group probably come from the lower social levels and reflect less sophistication and/or respectability (see the discussion on "weakness" in 8:7-12).

Seyoon Kim has suggested that "[i]n 1 Cor 10:14–11:1 Paul summa-

2. Karl Barth, *Resurrection of the Dead* (London: Hodder and Stoughton, 1933), 56.

rizes and concludes his long, careful discussion of the problem of eating the meat offered to idols (1 Cor 8–10) in terms of the principles of Christian liberty and the double command of love, the wholehearted devotion to God which excludes idolatry, and the love to neighbors which demands giving up one's right for the sake of the weak brethren."[3] More generally Youngman has summarized the theme of 1 Corinthians 8:1–11:1 as "do everything out of love for God and people; restrict the exercise of your rights for the sake of the gospel."[4] Such summaries recognize that the double command of love (Deut. 6:5; Lev. 19:18), though not cited here, clearly underlies Paul's thinking. The more explicit stress on love in 13:1–14:1 and on edification in chapter 14 (and the connection Paul established between them in 8:1) suggest that the double command of love undergirds all of 1 Corinthians 8–14.[5]

The issue of food sacrificed to idols would naturally be expected to be dealt with in the light of Old Testament teaching on idolatry. In early Judaism concerns regarding idolatry tended to revolve around food. The association between eating and idolatry was established in key Old Testament texts. In chapter 10 Paul will cite the first of those texts, Exodus 32:6, relating to the golden calf. There the description of Israel's worship of the calf includes a reference to sitting down to eat and then rising up to engage in "play" — generally understood as a reference to pagan revelry. Exodus 34:14-15 discusses the need to destroy pagan altars due to the danger that an Israelite might be invited to eat of the sacrifices offered there. That worst-case scenario came to be realized in the event narrated in Numbers 25:1-3, where the daughters of Moab invited the Israelites to their sacrifices and the Israelites went and ate and worshiped their gods, inciting God's anger against them. Paul's discussion of food offered to idols reflects a similar concern with invitations to social and religious events in pagan contexts.

Concern to avoid idolatry coexisted with a fundamental conviction that there was only one God in reality, the creator of heaven and earth. Those things which others worshiped as gods were often described as nonentities.[6] In other places they are described as demonic spirits masquerading as gods (Lev. 17:7; Deut. 32:17; Ps. 106:37; reflected also in *Jubilees* 1:11; *1 Enoch* 99:7; *Testament of Judah* 23:1).[7] In 1 Corinthians 8–10 the creational

3. Seyoon Kim, *Paul and the New Perspective* (Grand Rapids: Eerdmans, 2001), 26 n. 94.

4. Scott Youngman, "Stratificational Analysis of a Hortatory Text: I Corinthians 8:1–11:1" (M.A. thesis, University of Texas at Arlington, 1987), 128.

5. Michael Gorman (*Cruciformity* [Grand Rapids: Eerdmans, 2001], 100) points out Walter Brueggemann's suggestion that Israel's covenant obligations could be summarized in terms of love for people as the expression of love for God (Brueggemann, *Theology of the Old Testament* [Minneapolis: Fortress, 2005], 424; cf. 417-34).

6. See Isa. 40:19-20; 42:17-19; 44:9-20; 45:16-20; 46:1-7; 48:5; Jer. 10:1-12; Pss. 115:3-8; 135:15-18; Hab. 2:18-19; the Epistle of Jeremiah; Bel and the Dragon; Josephus, *Antiquities* 2.237-54.

7. Some Jewish literature reflects both ideas in different parts of their polemic. See Peter J. Tomson, *Paul and the Jewish Law* (CRINT 1; Assen: Van Gorcum, 1990), 154-63, for a careful discussion.

monotheism of the Old Testament plays a significant role in Paul's approach to dealing with issues related to food offered to idols (8:4-6; 10:26-30).

Disputed issues in this chapter include the amount of material included in Paul's citations of Corinthian positions in 8:1, 4(-5), the meaning of "food offered to idols," the nature of the "right" Paul affirms in 8:9, the identification of "the weak" (whether they are a real or merely hypothetical group of people), whether the Corinthians were divided or united in their views on food offered to idols, and the meaning of "conscience" in 8:7, 10, 12; 10:25, 27-29. We will address these below.

Since Romans 14 also deals with eating or abstaining from certain kinds of food and proper attitudes toward "weaker" believers, many read 1 Corinthians through a prism informed by that chapter. But it seems that they actually deal with two rather different issues. While Romans 14 concerns Jewish food laws (*kashrut;* cf. Lev. 11:1-23), which Paul considers an issue of indifference (one may eat or not eat according to one's convictions but must avoid judging others who take a different approach), 1 Corinthians 8–10 deals with idol food, a subject of much greater concern to Paul.[8] In Acts the question of clean and unclean foods is dealt with in Acts 10:9-15, while idol food is handled in a very different way at the Jerusalem council (Acts 15:20-29). This section (1 Cor. 8:1–11:1) ties together questions of conscience and debatable matters as well as Paul's fundamental commitments to the spiritual health of others (both believers and unbelievers) and the avoidance of any association with idolatry.

On food sacrificed to idols (8:1–11:1), simply put, Paul has three basic things to say: (1) in relation to their fellow Christians (8:1-13), the Corinthians are warned not to do anything that might cause someone to stumble by falling into subjective idolatry; (2) in relation to God (9:24–10:22), the Corinthians are warned not to provoke the Lord to jealousy by a lack of self-restraint in the form of participation in objective idolatry (despite their intellectual rejection of any such thing); (3) in relation to their neighbors (10:23–11:1), the Corinthians are told to be careful not to give offense to anyone and to value the glory of God more than the exercise of their own freedom (10:31–11:1).

### *1. Instructions concerning Subjective Idolatry and the Downfall of "the Weak" in Corinth, 8:1-13*

*1Now about food sacrificed to idols: We know that "We all possess knowledge." But knowledge puffs up while love builds up. 2Those who think they*

8. See Alex T. Cheung, *Idol Food in Corinth* (JSNTSup 176; Sheffield: Sheffield Academic Press, 1999), 135-36; Thomas R. Schreiner, *Romans* (BECNT 6; Grand Rapids: Baker, 1998), 705-6; Douglas J. Moo, *The Epistle to the Romans* (NICNT; Grand Rapids: Eerdmans, 1996), 829-31. Romans 14 seems to address abstention from eating meat based on various Jewish concerns, but idol food, the primary issue in Corinth, is never mentioned.

*know something do not yet know as they ought to know. [3]But whoever loves God is known by God.*

*[4]So then, about eating food sacrificed to idols: We know that "An idol is nothing at all in the world" and that "There is no God but one." [5]For even if there are so-called gods, whether in heaven or on earth (as indeed there are many "gods" and many "lords"), [6]yet for us there is but one God, the Father, from whom all things came and for whom we live; and there is but one Lord, Jesus Christ, through whom all things came and through whom we live.*

*[7]But not everyone possesses this knowledge. Some people are still so accustomed to idols that when they eat sacrificial food they think of it as having been sacrificed to a god, and since their conscience is weak, it is defiled. [8]But food does not bring us near to God; we are no worse if we do not eat, and no better if we do.*

*[9]Be careful, however, that the exercise of your rights does not become a stumbling block to the weak. [10]For if anyone with a weak conscience sees you, with all your knowledge, eating in an idol's temple, won't they be emboldened to eat what is sacrificed to idols? [11]So this weak brother or sister, for whom Christ died, is destroyed by your knowledge. [12]When you sin against them in this way and wound their weak conscience, you sin against Christ. [13]Therefore, if what I eat causes my brother or sister to fall into sin, I will never eat meat again, so that I will not cause them to fall.*

### *a. Love Must Take Priority over Knowledge, 8:1-3*

Paul introduces the issue of food sacrificed to idols and its relationship to our knowledge of God and our love of our brothers and sisters in Christ in vv. 1-3 and then discusses the specific theological knowledge the Corinthians have in mind in vv. 4-6. There are several steps in the argument of vv. 1-3: Paul introduces the topic (v. 1a); cites the basis for the stand taken on the issue by some or all of the Corinthians, namely, their shared knowledge (v. 1b); and then hints at two problems with their emphasis on knowledge (its detrimental effect on those "in the know" and its incomplete or faulty nature; vv. 1c-2) before pointing to a more theocentric orientation (loving God and being known by him) that should guide the Corinthians' behavior (v. 3). Paul begins his discussion of the Corinthians' argument in favor of eating food offered to idols in vv. 4-6.

**8:1** This verse begins with the third use of Paul's favorite topic marker in this letter, *Now about* (7:1, 25; 12:1; 16:1, 12).[9] While Mitchell is correct to point out that the expression itself does not necessarily introduce a subject raised in the Corinthians' letter to Paul, the expression is used for the first time in 7:1, where that letter is first mentioned and Paul indicates that he is responding to its contents. Except for those places where Paul

9. Gk. περὶ δέ. See M. M. Mitchell, "Concerning περὶ δέ in 1 Corinthians," and also her *Paul and the Rhetoric of Reconciliation*, 190-92.

says that he is responding to information found elsewhere (e.g., 11:18), it is probably best to understand most topics introduced in such a fashion after 7:1 as responses to that letter. It does not follow, however, that Paul is taking up each issue in the order in which it was raised by the Corinthians. Paul's own logic seems to be reflected in the way in which he has organized his response (see the Introduction, 21-25).

Scholars debate whether the topic is "meat offered to idols" (NAB) or, more generally, *food offered to idols* (TNIV, with most translations).[10] While meat may have been the most desirable food resulting from a pagan sacrifice and/or the food most likely to be "contaminated" in that way,[11] the expression itself is likely to refer to any of a variety of foods used in pagan offerings.[12] The word used by Paul reflects a Jewish perspective which was shared by early Christians. Pagans used the word Paul refers to in 10:28: "food offered to a god."[13] The word used by Paul is also found in 4 Maccabees 5:2 in reference to Antiochus's approach to forcing Jews to apostatize by eating food that was known to have been offered to idols. It is also used in Acts 15:29 and 21:25 in reference to abhorrent practices that Gentile converts were to avoid in order to make fellowship between Jewish and Gentile Christians possible (cf. also Rev. 2:14, 20). Paul's use of this term places his whole discussion in the context of Jewish and biblical concerns regarding idolatry and the historical role of avoiding such food out of loyalty to the God of Israel.

At issue were portions of animal or other sacrifices that had been offered to a god but then removed for consumption in the god's temple or in the home of someone who participated in the offering, or for sale in the market.[14] Most of the meat sold in the market would have been previously offered in such sacrifices, but evidently one would not know for certain unless one inquired.

Most scholars agree that Paul cites a Corinthian position in this verse, but there is debate regarding which words are the Corinthians' and which

10. Gk. εἰδωλόθυτα (plural). In favor of "meat offered to an idol" is the fact that the second part of the word is a verb (θύω) that usually means to sacrifice by killing an animal. But LSJ give as the first definition of the word, "*offer by burning* meat or drink to the gods," and reference an offering of cheese. According to John P. Dickson, *Mission-Commitment in Ancient Judaism and in the Pauline Communities* (WUNT 2.159; Tübingen: Mohr Siebeck, 2003), 232 n. 18, "[t]hat εἰδωλόθυτα refers to more than just 'meat' is clear from several expressions in Paul's discussion," including the reference to drinking the cup of demons in 10:21, the reference to "anything sold in the meat market" (where more than meat was sold) in 10:25, and the reference to eating "whatever is put before you" during a meal in 10:27.

11. Paul's reference to meat in 8:13 suggests that the eating of meat was particularly likely to cause problems based on association with idols.

12. See Peter David Gooch, *Dangerous Food* (Waterloo, ON: Wilfrid Laurier University Press, 1993), 53-55; Fotopoulos, *Food Offered to Idols in Roman Corinth,* 63, 208.

13. Gk. ἱερόθυτος. See BDAG on εἰδωλόθυτος and ἱερόθυτος.

14. For information regarding temples and offerings in Corinth in Paul's time see chs. 2–5 of Fotopoulos, *Food Offered to Idols in Roman Corinth.* For more general information on Greek and Roman sacrifices see *OCD* 1344-46.

are Paul's. Did the Corinthians write to Paul saying, "We know that we all possess knowledge," or does Paul write in the first-person plural ("we know/recognize"), affirming (in part) their simpler statement that "we all possess knowledge"? The answer would be obvious to the Corinthians but is perhaps unattainable today, and the difference does not greatly affect our exegesis, once we understand the ways in which Paul both agrees and disagrees with those to whom he is responding.

Verse 4 gives the clearest indication of the particular knowledge the Corinthians have in mind. It seems that their view of monotheism, based on the *Shema* (Deut. 6:4: ". . . the LORD our God is the only God"), served as the basis (or rationalization) for their approach to food offered to idols.[15] The recognition that there is only one true God, the God of Israel, the God who raised Jesus from the dead, was certainly a *sine qua non* of early Christian faith. "Recognition of this fact," Garland points out, "is fundamental to conversion to both Judaism and Christianity, and would have been a critical component of Paul's missionary preaching."[16] The Old Testament (especially Ezekiel) is full of references to a time when not only Israel, but also other nations (i.e., the Gentiles) would come to recognize the God of Israel as the true Lord (Isa. 19:21; 49:26; Ezek. 21:5; 25:11; 28:22-24; 29:6; 30:19, 25-26; 32:15; 35:4, 9, 12, 14-15; 36:23, 36; 37:28; 38:23; 39:6-7).[17] Tobit 14:6 looked forward to the day when all the nations of the world would reject their idols and offer true and sincere worship to God.

Paul is probably affirming that all Christians have some knowledge that they share in common, especially the knowledge that the God who raised Jesus Christ from the dead is the one true God. In the following argument, however, Paul refers to a kind of knowledge that was not shared

15. The approach the Corinthians used to rationalize their stance on the issue should not necessarily be identified with the reasons why they adopted their approach in the first place. The psychological and sociological pressure to maintain old social relationships and develop new ones would have been great. Much of the food eaten in the context of important social celebrations such as weddings, birthdays, and festivals would have been offered to idols either before or during the celebration itself. To avoid such social events would have resulted in seriously weakening one's social status and connections in a world where such connections were considered essential to one's well-being and that of one's family.

16. Garland, 367 (cf. Cheung, *Idol Food in Corinth,* 122). Garland also argues, on the basis of the lack of an article before "knowledge" in the Greek, that Paul does not have some specific knowledge in mind, but knowledge in general. Chrysostom, whose knowledge of Greek is unquestionable, understands the text to refer to a claim "to know God with total precision" (τὸν θεὸν εἰδέναι μετὰ ἀκριβείας ἁπάσης). See his *Homiliae in Epistulam i ad Corinthios* 20.3 (NPNF[1] 12:112; PG 61.162.21).

17. Other kinds of knowledge (γνῶσις) are also referred to in this letter, most of them in favorable ways (cf. 1:5; 12:8; 13:2, 8; 14:6). The use of the language of knowledge (γνῶσις) does not itself suggest Gnostic tendencies in Corinth (that would be an anachronistic association). The Corinthians were evidently convinced that God had given them superior understanding (knowledge) in a number of important areas, but there is no clear evidence of concepts that distinguished later Gnostic thought.

by all Christians, a knowledge that separated Christians who possessed it from Christians who did not (cf. vv. 7, 10-11). That knowledge seems to have been what they incorrectly considered a logical implication of biblical monotheism, namely, that idols and idolatry carried no meaning or significance whatsoever.

Paul's statement, *knowledge puffs up while love builds up*, raises questions about his attitude regarding knowledge. Does Paul have in mind knowledge in general or the particular knowledge valued by some Corinthians? Does he mean to indicate that any knowledge always puffs one up, that the views held by the Corinthians always puff people up, or that that this particular knowledge is puffing people up in this case? The ESV suggests that the problem is with the particular knowledge the Corinthians value ("this 'knowledge' puffs up"). The NLT maintains a fine ambiguity that allows for knowledge to be a potential but not a necessary problem ("knowledge may make us feel important"). Paul's positive statements about knowledge make it unlikely that he means that knowledge usually or consistently causes this problem. Chrysostom comments that "when [knowledge] is without love, it lifts men up to absolute arrogance."[18] To "puff up" is a figurative use of a word meaning to huff, puff, blow up or inflate. Figuratively it means "to cause to have an exaggerated self-conception" (BDAG), that is, to make one haughty or arrogant. Paul is contrasting the negative effects knowledge is having on the Corinthians (in this particular case) with the positive effects that would be expected if love were being exercised.

Paul gives a fuller explanation of the Christ-like love he has in mind in chapter 13. Love is the most basic and fundamental ethical expectation Paul has of Christians. While the word generally meant "the quality of warm regard for and interest in another" (BDAG), it came to be used as Christian shorthand for the kind of other-oriented behavior that was modeled and taught by Christ.[19] To "build (up)" is figurative speech, employing a word referring to the construction of buildings. Used figuratively it suggests the development of people who are stronger and more complete. Paul's use of the motif of "building/edifying"[20] is based on its background in Old Testament prophetic promises regarding God's future plans for the redemption and restoration of Israel. In Jeremiah it is normally God who does the planting and building, but in Jeremiah 1:10 these activities (as well as those of tearing down and uprooting) are ascribed to Jeremiah's own prophetic activity. Jeremiah tears down and builds as he proclaims God's

18. Chrysostom, *Homiliae in epistulam i ad Corinthios* 20:2 (NPNF$^1$ 12:112).

19. Despite the popular view that ἀγάπη (love) is a special word that signifies divine Christ-like love per se, it was used in the LXX to refer to both innocent and corrupt forms of romantic or erotic attraction (2 Sam. 13:15; Song 2:5, 7; 3:5; 5:8; 7:7; 8:4, 7).

20. See οἰκοδομέω or ἀνοικοδομέω in the LXX: Isa. 44:26, 28; 49:17; 54:14; 58:12; 60:10; 61:4; Jer. 1:10; 12:16; 24:6; 30(37):18; 31(38):4, 28, 38; 33(40):7; 42(49):10; Ezek. 36:36; Amos 9:11, 14; Zech. 1:16; 6:12, 15; 8:9.

prophetic word, or, alternatively, God acts through the prophet to tear down and build up his chosen nation/people.

This background informs Paul's language of "building up" or "edifying" the church. As O. Michel points out, in the New Testament building "is primarily an apocalyptic and Messianic concept. . . . The Messiah will build the future temple and the new community."[21] The edification of the church is now an activity for which the Spirit empowers the whole eschatological community, as Paul will make clear in chapters 12–14. It is probably not coincidental that those chapters will give special attention to the edifying value of prophetic ministry in the church. Paul will place great stress on the centrality of love as a key to the edification of the church, a key which leads the church to value ministries and activities like prophecy that promote the edification of the whole community over those with more limited edifying value.

While the puffing up affects the one who has knowledge, Paul's discussion of love in chapter 14 indicates that it leads to the edification of others. In chapters 8–14 Paul draws a series of contrasts between the effects knowledge is having in the Corinthians and the effects love would have if it were more clearly present. Paul associates both knowledge and love with processes that cause something to increase in size. Whereas knowledge is leading those "in the know" to expand through inflation with hot air, love leads others to increase in something more substantial, akin to the growth of a solidly constructed building.

**8:2** Paul's use of the conditional clause (literally, "If someone thinks they know something"[22]) adds subtlety to his statement. He does not attack anyone outright but discusses the issue as if it were a possibility. Some Corinthians *do* believe that they have significant knowledge, and he addresses them indirectly. In saying that they *do not yet know as they ought to know* Paul may be making a generally applicable statement that anyone who thinks that they know something is self-deceived, or he may be commenting strictly on those in Corinth who feel that they have great theological insight when in fact they are blinded to the serious problems of their position. Paul clearly thinks he knows certain things and, in fact, thinks there are many things Corinthians should know but do not (3:16; 5:6; 6:2, 3, 9, 15, 16, 19; 9:13, 24). The last clause of this verse refers to things that one ought to know. Some hold that Paul refers to people who believe they have some sort of comprehensive or complete knowledge[23] (the NLT refers to those who claim "to know all the an-

21. O. Michel, "οἰκοδομέω," *TDNT* 5:139 (cf. 140).

22. Ambrosiaster and 𝔓[46] omit "something," leaving the verb without an explicit object.

23. According to Fee, "The perfect tense of the infinitive implies that they consider themselves to have arrived as far as knowledge is concerned," but that seems to be based on an unchecked grammatical presupposition. Fee also thinks that the object, "something" (τι), "is not original, and once it was added ἐγνωκέναι was eventually changed to the more com-

swers," while the NJB indicates those who have "full knowledge of something"). In 13:9-12 Paul contrasts the imperfect/incomplete nature of all of our present knowledge with the perfect/complete knowledge that will be ours when we see the Lord face to face. Paul's words that the person does *not yet*[24] know as they must could suggest that he has that eschatological contrast in mind, but that is unlikely. It is not everyone who does not yet know as they ought to know, but those Corinthians who think they have come to some significant insight.[25] The contrast between this verse and the following one suggests that the way one ought to know is related to love. Probably, in light of 13:12, the point is that they are infatuated with abstract theological or philosophical knowledge but remain woefully deficient in their knowledge (and love) of God. True theological understanding, and certainly true knowledge of God, does not lead one to act in a way which is insensitive to others and offensive to God. As Ambrosiaster put it, "Only when a person has love can he be said to know as he ought to know."[26] If the Corinthians had understood the issues with true Christian insight, they would not need to be reminded of their responsibilities to their brothers and sisters in Christ, nor would they have required warnings to flee idolatry.

**8:3** This verse contains a surprising twist. Conzelmann explains: "We expect: 'The man who loves God knows him rightly.' But the thought is deliberately given a different turn":[27] *But whoever loves God is known by God.* Whereas we anticipate the active voice, Paul uses the fact that God knows us as a way of deflating the pride of the Corinthian "know-it-alls." Paul reasons that while "[w]e all possess knowledge" (8:1a), the knowledge that really counts is not one we possess. This is not merely a rhetorical turn, but a fundamental theological and spiritual insight which ought to promote a proper humility about whatever knowledge we do have.[28] As Richard Hays puts it, "what counts is not so much our knowledge of God as God's knowledge of us. That is the syntax of salvation."[29] This is part of a biblical tradition of confessing the simple but profound truth that God

---

mon εἰδέναι, which had lost its perfect force." In commenting on this text Chrysostom does refer to "complete/perfect knowledge" (τελείαν γνῶσιν), but he does not see it as utopian, but something that Paul would encourage his readers to achieve, as long as it is accompanied by love (cf. NPNF[1] 12:112). But why would a scribe have added τι in the first place if it did not make sense with the original verb? The evidence suggests that most scribes did not understand the perfect to imply arriving at some sort of complete knowledge, but probably only implies that one had come to possess some significant insight.

24. Gk. οὔπω.

25. Paul does not say, "If someone thinks they know something, they should realize that none of us yet knows as we ought to."

26. Cited in Bray, 75.

27. Conzelmann, 141.

28. Cf. Brian S. Rosner, "'Known by God': The Meaning and Value of a Neglected Biblical Concept," *TynBul* 59 (2008), 223.

29. Hays, 138.

knows us better than we know him.[30] It is in his knowledge of us that our true identity is found. The Enlightenment dictum of "I think, therefore I am" might be revised to, "I am known, therefore I am."[31]

Why does being known by God lead to his unconditional acceptance? How can God know us and yet, given our sinfulness, not reject us? The reason is that he sees us in Christ. Calvin explains: "When God beholds his image in us He does that not by looking at that which He has put into us by nature, but at that which He has put into us by grace."[32] Being known by God may be defined theologically as his gracious knowing or regarding of us as we are in Christ. All humans are created in the image of God, yet in one sense only believers in Christ are being renewed in that image and are part of the one new man that is Christ. So too, all humans are defined by being known in the general sense, as relational definitions of anthropology also affirm. However, it is believers in Christ who receive the fullest affirmation of their humanity in being known by God.[33]

The reference to the love of God[34] in the context of a controversy over idolatry and monotheism probably echoes Deuteronomy 6:4-5, where the confession that the Lord is the only God is immediately followed by a command to love him with the totality of one's being. The love of God, reflected in sincere, wholehearted, and exclusive worship of him, is the fundamental mark of his people. To be "known by God" is to be the object of his gracious elective purpose, to be one of his special people, called to serve him in the world and to be held accountable for one's faithfulness to the mission assigned by God.[35] To know God and to be known by him is to be in covenant with him.[36] In Galatians 4:9 Paul refers to Christian conversion in terms of coming to be known by God.

As affirmations of one's covenant relationship with God, to love God, to know him, and to be known by him all entail a recognition that he

30. Rosner, "Known by God," 222.

31. Others have similarly revised Descartes's dictum, "I think, therefore I am," switching the active to the passive voice. For example, Joseph Cardinal Ratzinger prefers, "I am thought, therefore I am" (*Introduction to Christianity* [trans. J. R. Foster; New York: Herder and Herder, 1970], 185), while N. T. Wright, claiming the support of the apostle Paul, favors, "I am loved, therefore I am" (*Paul: Fresh Perspectives* [London: SPCK, 2006], 173).

32. Calvin, *Sermon on Job* 10:7-8.

33. For further discussion, see Rosner, "Known by God," 226-28.

34. Both $\mathfrak{P}^{46}$ and Clement have more simply, "but if someone loves, that one knows" (εἰ δέ τις ἀγαπᾷ, οὗτος ἔγνωσται), with the second verb understood as a middle rather than passive form. Minuscule 33 and the original hand of ℵ also omit "by him." The words were probably omitted in order to assimilate the wording of v. 3 to the more generic kind of statements made in v. 2 (see the fuller discussion in Metzger, *Textual Commentary,* 490-91). For a fuller discussion of the textual issues see Thiselton, 625-26 (who prefers the shorter text), and Garland, 376-77 (who prefers the longer text).

35. For individuals chosen for special roles, see Gen. 18:19 (Heb.); Exod. 33:12, 17; Jer. 1:5. For God's people in general, see Amos 3:2; John 10:14-15; 2 Tim. 2:19.

36. In Exod. 33:12-13, being known by God (v. 12) serves as the basis for Moses' request to know him (v. 13).

alone must be worshiped, and are relevant to any discussion of idolatry. As Garland points out, being known by God "draws sharp boundaries that set [the Corinthians] apart from worshipers of false gods and delimits what they may and may not do."[37] The same can be said for loving God (cf. Deut. 6:5, 14; 11:1, 13, 16, 28; 13:2, 3; 30:6, 16, 17; Josh. 23:7, 11; Ps. 97:7-10) and knowing God (e.g., Isa. 19:21; 49:26; Ezek. 21:5; 25:11; 28:22-24; 29:6; 30:19, 25-26; 32:15; 35:4, 9, 12, 14-15; 36:23, 36; 37:28; 38:23; 39:6-7). Paul returns to the relationship between human knowledge and being known by God in 13:12, making it clear that the knowledge that must be our ultimate goal is the knowledge of the One who already knows and loves us perfectly.

### *b. Christians (unlike Pagans) Acknowledge Only One God and One Lord, 8:4-6*

In vv. 4-6 Paul reintroduces the issue (v. 4a) of food sacrificed to idols, citing the more precise theological basis referred to by the Corinthians (Jewish monotheism; v. 4b) and then comments briefly on the relationship between pagan and Christian understandings of the existence of gods and lords (v. 5) and the Christian commitment to christological monotheism (v. 6).

**8:4** Paul resumes his argument, having broached the subject and undermined any "knowledge" that was not consistent with the love for God or others that is foundational to any Christian ethic. He cites the Corinthians' viewpoint and agrees with them in principle,[38] but will go on in the following verses to clarify the proper implications for Christian behavior, which are rather different from what the Corinthians had in mind. Here he turns to address those who were puffed up with their knowledge: *So then,*[39] *about eating food sacrificed to idols: We know that "An idol is nothing at all in the world" and that "There is no God but one."* Paul refers explicitly to the "eating" of food offered to idols, thus anticipating the argument that suggests that the issue is not with the food itself but with the actions of believers. The rest of the verse seems to include two citations from the Corinthians' letter to Paul.[40] The first statement, literally, "there

37. Cf. Garland, 371.

38. As Thiselton puts it, Paul agrees with the Corinthians "even if there is more to be said" (629). That is, he "generally but not precisely endorses" the Corinthian formulations (630).

39. *So then* (οὖν) here serves as a "marker of continuation" (BDAG). Thiselton's translation, "To return to the topic of eating meat associated with idols, then . . ." (613), is less subtle than the Greek, but communicates the idea.

40. Possibly one citation, if the claim to know these facts is not Paul's but the Corinthians'. In that case the verse should read, "So then, about eating food sacrificed to idols: 'We know that an idol is nothing at all in the world and that there is no God but one.'" Even if the Corinthians said, "we know that . . . ," it is likely that they would acknowledge learning these truths from Paul (even if other teachers may have drawn different implications from them).

is no idol in the world,"[41] seems to represent a possible inference from the second statement, that "there is no God but one." Garland uses the following logic: "Idols purport to be images of various gods; but if the gods do not exist, then idols do not exist."[42] That an idol does not exist "in the world" does not suggest that they exist elsewhere. By "the world" Paul means the created universe.[43] The theme of this world as God's creation is reflected in the references to heaven and earth (cf. Gen. 1:1) in this verse and to all things coming from God and through Christ in the following verse.[44] Both of the cited statements are formulated negatively since the stress of the Corinthian argument would have been on the negative conclusions drawn from monotheism for the existence of idols or other gods. The second statement alludes to the *Shema,* cited twice daily by faithful Jews. It begins, "Hear, O Israel: The LORD our God, the LORD is one" (Deut. 6:4). Both Corinthian statements may be seen as inferences drawn from the *Shema.* They are not merely theoretical inferences, of course, but affirmations (or, rather, denials) that serve to guide the behavior of those who make them.

**8:5-6** While there is disagreement over whether all of this verse is from Paul or whether most of it is from the Corinthians,[45] it seems best to take it as Paul's own confession in which he expands on the points made by the Corinthians. Verse 6 also has a creedal sound to it (and is set off in poetic form in NA[27]), leading many to believe that Paul is citing (or slightly modifying) creedal material from the early church. Wright is not exaggerating when he asserts that the writing of this text ranks "as one of the greatest pioneering moments in the entire history of Christology."[46] We do not

41. As in the NAB. Alternatively it could be literally translated, "no idol exists in the world." There is a clear parallel structure in the Greek ("no idol . . . no God"), but the Greek has an elided verb and it is not clear whether the key words are to be taken as predicate nominatives ("there is no idol . . . there is no God") or as the subject ("No idol exists . . . no God exists"). Schrage and others argue that the first clause should be translated, "An idol is nothing [i.e., has no real existence] in the world." Chrysostom's comments ("What then? are there no idols? no statues? Indeed there are; but they have no power: neither are they gods, but stones and demons") may suggest that he thought the surface meaning of Paul's words would be taken to say, "there is no idol in the world."

42. Garland, 371.

43. BDAG has (following the *Twentieth Century New Testament*), "no idol has any real existence in the universe," in the context of a series of texts where the nature of the universe as God's creation is stressed.

44. In the LXX the word κόσμος (here, "world") was used to refer to the host of heaven (employing the meaning "ornamentation," often in contexts warning the readers not to worship them [cf. Deut. 4:19; 17:3; Isa. 24:21; 40:26]). Paul might be asserting that idols do not actually represent gods who are reflected in the host of stars in heaven.

45. Willis and Fotopoulos hold that vv. 4-6, with the exception of v. 5b, consist of Corinthian affirmations (Wendell L. Willis, *Idol Meat in Corinth* [Chico, CA: Scholars Press, 1985], 83-88; Fotopoulos, *Food Offered to Idols in Roman Corinth,* 210-14).

46. N. T. Wright, "Monotheism, Christology, and Ethics: 1 Cor. 8," in his *The Climax of the Covenant* (Minneapolis: Fortress, 1992), 136.

know whether Paul wrote this beautifully crisp and profound text or if it existed in some form before the writing of this letter. The text is so theologically profound and so perfectly fits Paul's argument here[47] and his theology and expression as found elsewhere in his writings[48] that we are inclined to think that he wrote it himself.[49] Paul does not actually qualify the Corinthians' statements but rather is "engaging in the twofold task of building rapport and anticipating objections."[50]

The sentence is grammatically incomplete (i.e., an anacolouthon),[51] but Paul's meaning is clear enough. He contrasts the polytheistic understanding of pagan society with the Christian christological form of strict Jewish monotheism. Paul begins with an explanatory *for*[52] since he will elaborate on the concise affirmations of the Corinthians. His concessive *even if*[53] signals that the statement he is about to make will be strongly qualified shortly. He will qualify all of v. 5 with his creedal affirmation in v. 6. The reference to *so-called gods . . . in heaven* or *on earth* may point to the presence of physical idols (on earth) which are supposed to represent actual gods existing in the atmosphere (in heaven). Alternatively, it may "signify a distinction between the gods presumed to operate in the upperworld and those in the underworld."[54] It may be, however, that Paul simply prefers an all-inclusive expression to discuss the existence of so-called gods anywhere in all creation (so that *heaven* and *earth* together here equal *the world* in v. 4).

Since Paul has already referred to the things worshiped by others as *so-called gods* in v. 5a, it seems appropriate to place *gods* and *lords* in quotation marks in v. 5b, as do the NIV, TNIV, ESV, and other interpreters.[55] Paul affirms that there are many entities in the world referred to as *gods* or *lords*, without suggesting that they are what people suppose them to be (as is made clear by v. 6). The language of Deuteronomy 6:4 ("the LORD our God, the LORD is one") has governed Paul's wording and argument in these verses:

47. This could possibly be explained by the suggestion that he wrote this paragraph with this particular creedal text in mind.

48. The fatherhood of God and the lordship of Christ are constant and associated themes in Paul's writings. For some of the language used here see also Rom. 11:36 and Col. 1:16.

49. See also Fee, 374.

50. Cheung, *Idol Food in Corinth*, 123-24.

51. $\mathfrak{P}^{46}$, B, 33, b, sa, and Ir$^{lat}$ eliminate the anacoluthon by omitting the ἀλλ' ("but") from v. 6.

52. Gk. γάρ.

53. Actually he uses a combination of conjunctions which is unique in the LXX and New Testament: "for even if" (καὶ γὰρ εἴπερ).

54. Garland, 374. He also raises the possibility that by *gods on earth* Paul has in mind those worshiped through the emperor cult.

55. Including Thiselton, Fee, and Barrett. Quotation marks were not used in ancient Greek, but the readers would have understood Paul's attitude from his qualification in v. 5.

*For even if there are so-called gods, whether in heaven or on earth (as indeed there are many "gods" and many "lords"), yet for us there is but*

*one God, the Father,*
*from whom all things came and for whom we live;*
*and there is but*

*one Lord, Jesus Christ,*
*through whom all things came and through whom we live.*

He expands his opening statement that "there are many 'so-called' gods" so as to allow the plurality of "lords" in the pagan world as well. While references to "gods" are common in the Old Testament, they are not frequently referred to as "lords." While some have suggested that Paul has a distinction in mind between *gods* and *lords*,[56] it seems more likely that Paul is simply setting up the interpretation he wants to provide of Deuteronomy 6:4, so that the *one Lord* and *one God* are contrasted with the *many gods and many lords* of the pagan world. That "there are many 'so-called' gods" and indeed "many gods and many lords" affirms the Old Testament's recognition that pagan gods, while not really gods in any sense comparable to the God of Israel (and thus only "so-called" gods), do represent some reality. This may echo Deuteronomy 10:17, where, just a few chapters after the *Shema*, the Israelites are told, "the LORD your God, he is God of gods and LORD of lords." That is the only text of the Hebrew Bible where "gods" and "lords" appear in the same sentence as in 1 Corinthians 8:5, and in that sentence Israel's God is referred to as both Lord and God (as in the *Shema*), and his superiority over any other hypothetical claimant to that title is strongly affirmed, as in 1 Corinthians 8:5 (cf. Ps. 136:2-3).

It is notable that Paul's christological modification of the *Shema* comes in a passage where he hopes this statement might fulfill the very same roles that the *Shema* did in Judaism. The *Shema* was important both for its theological affirmation and its sociological function. Early Judaism rallied around the one God who had redeemed them, and their allegiance to that one God was reflected in their worship of him and rejection of all other claims to deity. If the Corinthians would rally together in loyalty to God the Father and the Lord Jesus Christ, giving Christ the priority that they had been giving their own agendas, it would go a long way toward promoting unity within the Corinthian congregation and toward maintaining a distinct identity in contrast to the pagan environment. The deity of Christ may not be his main point, but his incorporation of Christ the Lord into the very definition of the God of Israel is consistent with the central role that Christ held in the worship and theology of the early church.

56. See Garland, 374; Fee, 373; Hays, 139.

While the rest of the world may be enamored with a multitude of gods and lords, *for us,* that is, for all those who have that knowledge common to all Christians (vv. 1, 4), things are different. We know that there is in fact only one true God and one true Lord. The key words of v. 6, "Lord," "God," and "one," are taken from Deuteronomy 6:4 ("the LORD our God, the LORD is one"), in which *Lord* and *God* both refer to the same *(one)* God. Here Paul "has glossed 'God' with 'the Father', and 'Lord' with 'Jesus Christ,' adding in each case an explanatory phrase: 'God' is the Father, 'from whom are all things and we to him', and the 'Lord' is Jesus the Messiah, 'through whom are all things and we through him.'"[57] Paul thus simultaneously reaffirms strict Jewish monotheism and the highest possible Christology imaginable. Christ finds his identity within the very definition of that one God/Lord of Israel.[58]

The reference to God as the Father has several potential connotations. In Philo God's role and title as Father is usually associated with his role as creator (*On the Ceation of the World* 7, 74, 77; *Allegorical Interpretation* 1:18; *On the Cherubim* 23, 49; *On the Posterity of Cain* 175; *That God Is Unchangeable* 30; *On Drunkenness* 30; *On the Confusion of Tongues* 144, 170; *Who Is the Heir?* 98, 200, 205, 236; *On Flight and Finding* 84, 177; *On the Change of Names* 29; *On Dreams* 1:35, 190; *On the Life of Abraham* 9, 58; *On the Life of Moses* 1:158; 2:48, 238, 256; *On the Decalogue* 51, 105; *On the Special Laws* 1:34; 2:6, 256; 3:178; 4:180; *On the Virtues* 34, 64, 77, 179; *On Rewards and Punishments* 24, 32; *On the Contemplative Life* 90; *On the Embassy to Gaius* 115, 293; *Questions and Answers on Genesis* 1:58; 2:13; 3:62).[59] Elsewhere in biblical and Jewish writings the fatherhood of God is often associated with the exodus or the hope of restoration/second exodus.[60] Here both creation and eschatological restoration seem to be in mind. Paul first refers to him as *the Father, from whom all things came* (i.e., the creator). The next clause is more enigmatic.[61] It is commonly translated (as in the TNIV) *and for whom we live,* but it could also be translated "and he is the goal of our existence,"[62] suggesting God as the destiny of all things, complementing God's role as the originator of all things. Creation comes from God and is being brought to him. It is all about God, *from beginning to end.*

The statement of the unique lordship of Jesus Christ is central to Paul's theology in general and to this letter in particular.[63] The "christological monotheism" affirmed here distinguishes the Christian community from both non-Christian Judaism and Gentile paganism. Jewish monothe-

57. N. T. Wright, "Monotheism, Christology and Ethics: 1 Cor. 8," in *The Climax of the Covenant* (Minneapolis: Fortress, 1992), 129.

58. See Hays and N. T. Wright, "Monotheism."

59. See also Deut. 32:6; Mal. 2:20.

60. See Ciampa, *The Presence and Function of Scripture in Galatians 1 and 2,* 40-44.

61. Gk. καὶ ἡμεῖς εἰς αὐτόν.

62. See Thiselton, 636-38; Garland, 375.

63. See esp. 1:2; 12:3, and the discussion of this theme in the introduction to the letter.

ism is affirmed against all forms of pagan polytheism (or atheism), while, against non-Christian Judaism, Christ is understood to participate in God's identity.[64]

The roles attributed to the Father and to Christ in creation (*from whom* and *through whom*) reflect traditional biblical and Jewish affirmations of the roles of God and of Wisdom (for the latter see Prov. 8:22-31; Wis. 9:4, 9; Philo, *On Flight and Finding*, 109).[65] According to the prophets, Yahweh's absolute power as creator of heaven and earth is what sets him apart from idols (which are human creations; see, e.g., Jer. 10:3-16; Isa. 44:9-24). The description of Christ in terms normally attributed to Wisdom (Wis. 8:1-6; 9:1-2, 9; Sir. 24) suggests that just as Jesus takes the place of "the Lord" in the *Shema* he also takes the place of "Wisdom" within Hellenistic Judaism.[66] As Wright asserts, "Paul has indicated that everything one might hope to gain through possessing [Wisdom] can be gained rather by possessing Christ."[67]

The relationship between the last clause of v. 6 and the first half of the verse (about God the Father) challenges interpreters. Literally it reads, "and we through him." The earlier part of the verse affirmed that all things came into existence through Christ. It would be redundant to say we also came into existence through Christ since we were already included in "everything." Paul is probably highlighting Christ's role in both creation and our participation in new creation (i.e., "all creation has come into being through him and our experience of new creation was through him as well"). In this way both statements about Christ may be understood as coming logically between the two affirmations made about the Father. Thiselton, quoting Langkammer, puts it this way: "'Paul is the first to outline a sketch of a formal link between Protology [cosmology] and soteriology' which proclaims before the community 'God the Father, the originating Ground of all and the end-goal,' alongside 'the one Lord, the Mediator of the first creation and the Mediator of the reality of salvation.'"[68] This suggests a pervasive "sense of movement 'from . . . through . . . to.'"[69] Christ is understood to be the means of accomplishing all of the Father's intentions for his creation.

Paul's statement puts emphasis on the first-person plural personal

64. N. T. Wright, "Monotheism," 135-36.

65. Any possible association with Stoic or syncretistic thought (see the discussion in Thiselton, 635) is overshadowed by the clear Jewish understanding of God as creator and redeemer of the universe. Paul explicitly contrasts ("but for us") the Christian understanding with that of others.

66. N. T. Wright, "Monotheism," 130.

67. N. T. Wright, "Monotheism," 130. Contra James D. G. Dunn, *Christology in the Making* (Grand Rapids: Eerdmans, 1996), 182-83, the preexistence of Christ is presupposed in both his identification with the "Lord" in the *Shema* and his identification with the role of Wisdom which was present at the time of creation.

68. Thiselton, 637, citing P. H. Langkammer, "Literarische und theologische Einzelstücke in 1 Kor VIII:6," *NTS* 17 (1970-71), 197.

69. Thiselton, 637.

pronoun throughout this verse *(but for us . . . and we . . . and we)*.[70] He thus stresses the unique covenantal relationship between all Christians and the God who created the universe (in contrast with the delusions of the pagan world). *We* know the truth of one God and one Lord. We know that all creation comes from the Father and that he is the reason and goal of *our* existence.[71] We know the Lord Jesus, the agent of all creation and the one to whom *our* new existence is due as well. The structure of the text implies both a relationship and a contrast between us and the rest of creation. All of creation originated with the Father through the Son. We are a part of that creation, and our existence comes from the Father through the Son as well. But both this text and its context highlight a contrast between Christians and the non-Christian world. For them there are *many "gods" and many "lords,"* but for us there is only *one God* and *one Lord*. They are part of God's creation, but we represent the restoration, renewal, and destiny of God's creation, his new creation (cf. 2 Cor. 5:17), which is accomplished through Christ.

The verse can be outlined as follows to show both the parallels and implied contrasts:

But for us
1. One God, the Father
 A *From whom*
  B *all things* [came into existence]
  B′ and *we* [are being brought]
 A′ *to him*
2. And one Lord, Jesus Christ,
 A *through whom*
  B *all things* [came into existence]
  B′ and *we* [have come into existence (in new life)]
 A′ *through him.*

### c. Subjective Idolatry Is Still a Danger for Some Christians, 8:7-8

**8:7** Up to this point Paul seems to have been discussing knowledge that was universally shared within the Christian community, but here he explicitly says, *not everyone possesses this knowledge*. If the "all" or "everyone" Paul refers to in v. 7 included those who were not yet Christians, it would alleviate the problem, but the context indicates that he has Christian believers in mind. Paul seems to have shifted from those facets of knowledge that Christians have in common to a particular conclusion that some Corinthians have drawn which is related to them. Their conclusion is implied in this verse where Paul declares, *Some people are still so accus-*

70. Cf. Fee, 375.
71. Cf. Fee, 375.

*tomed to idols that when they eat sacrificial food they think of it as having been sacrificed to a god.* The Corinthians have evidently concluded that since idols have no real existence, "food offered to idols" is a category that lacks any meaning. What they eat they eat as mere food (cf. v. 8),[72] something which they have received as a gift of God,[73] not as something that has been offered to idols (regardless of where it has been and what others have done with it). Others, however, continue to associate food offered to idols with their former experience as idolaters, *and since their conscience is weak, it is defiled.*[74]

What was the danger facing the "weaker brothers and sisters," and what is the relationship, if any, between this passage and the discussion of "weaker brothers" in Romans 14?[75] Most scholars (especially those who think that Paul's argument here closely parallels that found in Romans) are of the opinion that they are simply in danger of doing something that would violate their conscience. Others think that the danger is that the particular act of rebellion against the conscience would be one of idolatry.

It appears that the "knowledgeable" Corinthians do not realize that they are in danger of leading brothers and sisters in Christ to commit subjective idolatry. That is, their example may lead weaker brothers and sisters in Christ to consciously participate in an activity that they consider idolatrous (even though the "stronger" Corinthians do not consider it to be so).[76]

Paul suggests that there may be Christians whose lengthy[77] experience with idolatry and idol food makes it difficult for them to distinguish between the two. If they eat food that they know has been offered to an idol, it is with a conviction (rejected by other Corinthian Christians) that they are committing an idolatrous act. That they would actually do such a thing is a testimony to the social pressures within Corinthian society, which, rather than being lessened within the church of Corinth, were intensified since even brothers in Christ were participating in and justifying such activities. One would need to have a very strong conscience or "psy-

72. So Cheung, *Idol Food in Corinth,* 128.

73. Severian of Gabala (c. 400) suggested that the Corinthians justified their eating of food offered to idols by saying, "to us it is not something offered to an idol — since I sanctify these things by pronouncing the name of Christ over them before eating them" (οἱ Κορίνθιοι τὰ εἰδωλόθυτα ἤσθιον, λέγοντες ὅτι ἡμῖν οὐκ ἔστιν εἰδωλόθυτον — ἁγιάζω γὰρ αὐτὰ τῇ ἐπονομασίᾳ τοῦ Χριστοῦ καὶ ἐσθίω; see Karl Staab, *Pauluskommentare aus der griechischen Kirche,* 253-54).

74. *Is defiled* represents not a perfect verb (which would call to mind a defiled state), but a present passive (μολύνεται) suggesting that the conscience is defiled in the act of eating.

75. See Mark Reasoner, *The Strong and the Weak: Romans 14:1-15.13 in Context* (SNTSMS 103; Cambridge: Cambridge University Press, 1999), 45-58, on "strong" and "weak" as terms of social status in first-century Rome and the summary in K. K. Yeo, *Rhetorical Interaction in I Corinthians 8 and 10* (Leiden: Brill, 1995), 90; Thiselton, 706.

76. See our comments introducing 8:1–11:1.

77. A long association is suggested by *still so accustomed to idols* (literally, "through intimate idol-experience until now").

chological faculty which can distinguish between right and wrong"[78] not to cave in under such pressure.

One usage of "weak" or "weakness" in the Roman world had to do with one's incapacity for sound independent judgment as a basis for legal protection.[79] It was especially associated with womanly weakness, but also applied to young people in general. While Paul probably does not have women and young people in particular in mind, the description he gives of those with "weak consciences" being led astray by a misunderstanding of the example of others invokes a similar concept. These "weaker" brothers and sisters cannot eat the food without understanding the act as idolatrous, but their non-Christian friends will not understand if they refuse while other Christians from the same church are not abstaining.

The Old Testament and Jewish background suggests that social pressure was the most common instigator of idolatry in Israel. During the intense persecution under Antiochus (see 4 Macc. 5:2-3) it would have been very convenient for Jews simply to eat idol food with the rationalization that they did not recognize any god but their own and that therefore the act of eating the idol food signified nothing. But the act itself was understood to be idolatrous, and it was the monotheism of the Jews that led them to (fight and/or) die rather than perform it; it did not serve as an excuse or justification for eating it. Many Gentiles who had been properly engrafted into the Jewish and apostolic understanding of the dangers of idolatry would have understood the eating of idol food in a similar manner. If the strength of their own convictions is not sufficient to resist the social pressure (if *their conscience is weak*), they may cave in and defile themselves. That Paul does not have some "mere" contradiction of one's conscience in mind is suggested by the rest of the passage. Verses 11-12 say that the weak person whose conscience is wounded is "destroyed" by the knowledge of the strong. In v. 13 Paul says that he would rather give up meat altogether than allow such a consequence.

The language of "weakness" appeared earlier in the letter (1:25, 27; 2:3; 4:10), but it will be concentrated in this chapter (vv. 7, 9, 10, 11, 12). In

78. Louw and Nida, *Greek-English Lexicon*, entry 26.13 (for συνείδησις ["conscience"]). There is a great debate over whether the word means "conscience" or "consciousness" or something else altogether (see, e.g., Thiselton, 640-44; Cheung, *Idol Food in Corinth*, 130-33; Willis, *Idol Meat*, 89-92; Robert Jewett, *Paul's Anthropological Terms* [AGJU 10; Leiden: Brill, 1971], 401-46). The Greek word seems to suggest an internal moral arbiter (healthy or corrupt) that may be qualified by the strength or weakness of one's ability to act according to its leading. That is, conscience as seen not primarily as something that judges past actions, but which governs future behavior.

79. According to the Rules of Ulpian (early third century) II.1, "Guardians *(tutores)* are appointed for both males and females, but for males only as long as they are below puberty, on account of the *weakness* of their age; however, for females both below puberty and above, both on account of the *weakness* of their sex *(sexus infirmitas)* and on account of their ignorance of legal affairs" (cited in Judith Evans Grubbs, *Women and the Law in the Roman Empire* [London/New York: Routledge, 2002], 29).

some places Paul refers to people with weak consciences, while in others he simply refers to the same as those who are weak. The use of the language of weakness probably originated with the Corinthians. Those who had serious misgivings about eating food offered to idols were probably considered theologically and morally immature by the others, and "thought that these weak Christians needed to be 'built up.'"[80] Paul's argument recognizes the moral instability of some of the Corinthians, but, as Cheung points out, he "exhibits no concern to change the weak as he shows every concern to change the knowers."[81] Still, the following verse, along with 10:25-27, suggests that there is nothing wrong with the food per se, so that the strong Corinthians should not be judged so much for eating food that was offered to idols (as though that bestowed some negative spiritual significance to the food itself), but for being recklessly insensitive to the impact their actions are having on those who observe them eat food that has been explicitly identified as idol food. The "weaker" brothers and sisters would do well to recognize that their "stronger" brothers and sisters (and they themselves) are free to eat whatever food they wish, as long as they do not do things which seem to condone idolatry and which may lead others to fall into what they perceive to be idolatrous behavior.[82]

**8:8** Whether various parts of this verse consist of citations from the Corinthians or responses to them is unclear. The first clause may be understood in either a positive or a negative manner. The TNIV supports the positive reading, *food does not bring us near to God* (or commend us to him; cf. ESV, NIV, NRSV, NET, NLT, NASB, NJB). Thiselton follows the negative reading suggested by Murphy-O'Connor and Jeremias: "Food will not bring us into God's judgment."[83] This reading presumes that the text is a citation of the position of some Corinthians, who are defending their practice against any suggestion that it puts them in spiritual danger. The point being made by Paul or the Corinthians has to do with the role of food versus people. People present food to gods; the food does not present them to the gods. Food is the object of human action, not a subject whose action need concern us. The problem is not with what the food does to us but with what we might do with some food. In the next clause the subject of the verbs changes from the food to us and what we do, or do not do, with it.

The words *we are no worse if we do not eat, and no better if we do* are often

80. Cheung, *Idol Food in Corinth,* 125.

81. Cheung, *Idol Food in Corinth,* 125.

82. As Fotopoulos suggests, Paul's position reflects "an opposition to idol-food consumption in idolatrous contexts for the sake of the Weak" which also "allow[ed] idol-food consumption from the *macellum* [i.e., the meal market] or at meals hosted by pagans only if it was clear that such food was indeed not idol-food. The general prohibition of idol-food and the conditional allowance of idol-food consumption from the *macellum* and at meals hosted by pagans would also serve Paul rhetorically as a way to appeal to both the Weak and the Strong who were divided over the issue" (*Food Offered to Idols in Roman Corinth,* 187).

83. Thiselton, 647.

taken to mean that eating or abstaining is a matter of indifference, something that is morally neutral.[84] It is probably Paul's point, however, being made in response to a suggestion by some Corinthians that in fact they are worse off if they do not eat food offered to idols and better off if they do (for the sake of maintaining or building relationships outside the church). If they were not going to snub their neighbors and if they were going to advance up the social ladder of Corinthian society, it would have been advantageous to participate in the many important social contexts where idol food would be served.

As we noted in the introduction to this section of the letter, the Corinthians had probably written something to the effect that "Eating this food will bring us into contact with (*or* commend us to) our neighbors. We'll be worse off if we do not eat and better off if we do since we will offend our friends and neighbors (and hurt our chances of social advancement through relationships with important patrons) if we snub them by rejecting their invitations or their food. Only by accepting their invitations and eating their food will we have opportunities for outreach and advancement." In the Roman world the establishment and nurturing of relationships with wealthier and more well-connected members of society were important for social and economic survival. Everyone needed to have connections with more influential individuals who might help them navigate through the difficult political, legal, or financial challenges they would face.

Paul's response is that the Corinthians need to be more concerned about what will please God (not their pagan neighbors) and benefit their fellow Christians (rather than themselves). By eating idol food (out of concern to please their pagan friends and neighbors) they are putting themselves in danger of divine judgment since their behavior reflects a lack of concern for their brothers and sisters in Christ (cf. v. 7 and the development of the theme in vv. 9-13).[85] By focusing on their social standing with their Corinthian neighbors (rather than the well-being of their Christian brothers and sisters) they have missed the weightier question of what will lead to being better off with God and may do eternal damage to themselves and others. "Rather than implying that neither eating nor abstaining from idol food makes any difference, this verse lays the foundation for his statement in 8:13, 'I will absolutely never eat meat.' Abstinence, in this case, benefits

84. See Barrett, Witherington, and Fee.

85. Translations are divided as to whether or not the conjunction δέ should be translated "but," left untranslated, or treated in some other way. Stephen Levinsohn's treatment of δέ in nonnarrative texts suggests that its primary function is to signal that the text it introduces is "to be processed as developing from the previous material." The nature of the development is indicated by the content of the material, not by the conjunction itself (Levinsohn, *Discourse Features of New Testament Greek* [Dallas: SIL International, 2000], 112-13). The use of this conjunction at the beginning of vv. 8 and 9 suggests that the discussion of "our" welfare in v. 8 is to be understood in relation to the discussion of the welfare of our brothers and sisters in Christ in vv. 8 and 9-13.

others and oneself."[86] Christians must avoid any behavior that would put the spiritual well-being of others in such grave danger.

### *d. The Corinthians Should Forego Their Rights to Avoid Destroying Other Believers, 8:9-13*

**8:9** We believe that v. 9 builds upon and develops Paul's previous statements and should probably not be understood in contrast with the previous verse (i.e., we prefer "Be careful that . . ." to *Be careful, however, that* . . .). The warning "be careful"[87] is used for grave warnings (Matt. 24:4; Mark 13:5; Luke 21:8; Acts 13:40; Gal. 5:15; Col. 2:8; Heb. 12:25; 2 John 1:8), already suggesting the seriousness of the consequences of a failure to give heed.[88]

What the Corinthians need to be careful about is *that the exercise of your rights does not become a stumbling block to the weak.* The language of *rights* probably comes from the Corinthians themselves. Paul will focus on the question of *the exercise* of one's rights in the following chapter (where the word appears six times: vv. 4, 5, 6, 12 [2x], 18). Paul's language seems to suggest that he accepts that there is a legitimate right in question, but that its exercise must be conditioned by factors the Corinthians have overlooked. Many understand the "right" to be that of eating idol food and/or eating social meals in pagan temples. Each of those proposals creates difficulties with Paul's argument in the rest of chapters 8–10. We think that Paul would agree that Christians do not have to fear idol food and may, in theory, accept any food as a gift from God to be received with thanksgiving. The problem is not with eating food that has been offered to an idol per se, but with eating food that has been explicitly identified by others as idol food. If a weak brother or sister in Christ could fall into subjective idolatry by following the practice of the knowledgeable Christian (or if a pagan could naturally interpret the Christian's behavior as participation in, or affirmation of, idolatry), that practice is to be rejected. The right to eat any food God provides is qualified by the gospel priority of guarding against any possible association with, or complicity in, idolatry.

The particular danger that concerns Paul is that by exercising a right to eat food without worrying about its history certain Corinthian believers might become a *stumbling block*[89] to others. While the idea of a *stumbling*

86. Garland, 386.

87. Gk. βλέπετε μή. In contrast to the series of imperatives in ch. 7, this is the only imperative in this chapter (there is just one more at 9:24 before another extended series of imperatives in ch. 10). This imperative, like most of the others in the letter, is a present imperative, suggesting generally relevant moral instruction. It is not in just one case, but in general, that Christians must beware of letting their liberties become a stumbling block to others.

88. The use of μή πως (literally, "lest somehow") suggests a feared outcome that is to be avoided.

89. Gk. πρόσκομμα (Heb. *mik̲šôl*).

*block* may sound like a minor obstacle to us (we stumble and then catch ourselves or get back up), the metaphor of the stumbling block was used in the New Testament (mainly by Paul) to describe an obstacle that keeps someone from finding their way to ultimate salvation (Rom. 9:32, 33; 14:13, 20; 1 Cor. 8:9; 1 Pet. 2:8).[90] The context here implies that the stumbling would be that of falling into idolatry. Interestingly, there is an association between stumbling blocks and idolatry in the Old Testament and Jewish literature.[91] By describing the behavior of the "knowing" as a potential *stumbling block,* Paul may be associating their behavior with a metaphor associated with idolatry in the Old Testament.

**8:10-11** Paul asks his "knowledgeable" readers to think about what might happen if a Christian with a "weak conscience" should see them eating[92] in an idol's temple: *For if anyone with a weak conscience sees you, with all your knowledge, eating in an idol's temple, won't they be emboldened to eat what is sacrificed to idols?*

Archeological and documentary evidence has been interpreted by some in a way that suggests that many social events would have been held in dining halls associated with idol temples without any considerable religious significance. Some scholars believe that the Corinthian Christians could have frequented such dining halls for wedding, birthday or other social celebrations without being associated with the worship of the idol whose facilities were being used.[93] Others have suggested that such a compartmentalizing of religious and social events reflects a modern dichotomy between sacred and secular rather than the realities or perceptions of the ancient world.[94] One wonders why someone would be led to eat idol food upon seeing another Christian *eating in an idol's temple* unless it could be assumed that food eaten on the premises would be idol food. It is unlikely that Paul is insinuating that the person with a weak conscience would go a

90. On the eschatological connotation of falling (pointing to ultimate rejection by God) see the comments on 10:12.

91. Cf. LXX Exod. 23:33; 34:12; Ezek. 14:3, 4, 7; 1QH$^{a}$ xii 15 and 4QH$^{d}$ i I 3; *b. 'Abodah Zarah* 6a, 14a; *b. Menaḥot* 109a.

92. Literally, "reclining" (Gk. κατάκειμαι), referring to the standard posture for eating meals.

93. Willis, *Idol Meat in Corinth,* 42, points to two papyrus invitations that mention explicit events being celebrated (a coming-of-age celebration and a birthday party): "If one restricts oneself solely to the explicit reasons, these dinners seem to have been familial celebrations. It is certainly begging the question to assume they refer to a sacramental cult meal." His fixation on the concept of a sacramental meal has blinded him to the idolatrous associations explicit in virtually all such invitations. The invitation to the coming-of-age celebration reads as follows: "Apollonius requests you to dine at the table of the lord Sarapis on the occasion of the coming of age of his brothers in the temple of Thoeris" (quoted from Willis, 41). Quite apart from the context of being a pagan temple, the invitation is to celebrate the event by dining at the table of the god Sarapis!

94. For the most thorough discussion of the archeological evidence (concluding that eating in the precincts of an idol's temple would have had religious connotations and entailed eating idol food) see Fotopoulos, *Food Offered to Idols in Roman Corinth* (esp. 65-70).

step further than the person they were observing. Rather, assuming that the person was eating idol food (based on familiarity with the context), they would be tempted to eat similar food, thus falling into subjective idolatry. They would eat it not as mere food, however (like the person they are observing), but as an act of participation in the worship of the idol (the significance they attached to the consumption of idol food).[95] The logic of this verse (someone sees you, the one with knowledge, eating in the idol temple) suggests that the special knowledge of this Christian has led them to feel free to eat in the idol's temple despite its association with idolatry.[96] The knowledge involved is not that the social situation is innocent of idolatrous associations, but that since there is only one true God, what others think of as idol food is merely food (cf. vv. 1, 4, 7); the idolatrous associations made by others are considered meaningless and insignificant by the one who has this special knowledge.

Paul says that a person with a weak conscience (unstable due to a lack of confidence in the correctness of his or her own convictions[97] or a lack of strength to stand by them) will be *emboldened* [literally, "built up"] *to eat what is sacrificed to idols.* Probably that is exactly what the "knowledgeable" Christians think should happen. In their view the weak Christian needs to gain the moral and theological strength necessary to overcome their qualms about eating such food. But Paul has already explained that the so-called edification leads not to greater Christian maturity, as the "knowing" supposed, but to an idolatrous spiritual breakdown. Paul introduced the language of "edification" or "building up"[98] in the first verse of this chapter, and he will develop the theme later (10:23; 14:4, 17). It is clear that this is not the kind of "edification" that he had in mind!

Paul's adopts a highly emotive tone and describes the result bluntly: *So this weak brother or sister,*[99] *for whom Christ died, is destroyed by your knowl-*

95. That Paul has concerns even about the practice of the "knowing" Christian will be made clear in ch. 10 (where Paul addresses the reality of objective idolatry on the part of those who subjectively reject the existence of idols). Here he focuses on the danger of leading others to participate in objective or subjective idolatry.

96. The actions of both people are explained by participial phrases that modify the main verb. The first person, "having knowledge" (because of his knowledge), eats in the idol temple. The conscience of the second person, "being weak" (because it is weak), leads him to follow the example of the other.

97. In this sense there would be a parallel with Rom. 14:23: "everything that does not come from faith is sin."

98. Gk. οἰκοδομέω.

99. Paul employs terms that are grammatically masculine but which are semantically generic. Masculine substantival adjectives and participles are commonly used to refer to "people" in general (neuter forms are used for "things" in general). The masculine word for "brother" is also often used generically (as it continues to be used in some Latin languages). The use of the masculine and feminine forms together ("brother and/or sister" or "brothers and/or sisters") is typically restricted to places where one seeks to itemize the relevant family relationships or emphasize the application to both genders (cf. Num. 6:7; Josh. 2:13; Ezek. 44:25; Hos. 2:1; Matt. 12:50; 19:29; Mark 3:35; 10:29-30; Luke 14:26; 1 Cor. 7:15; Jas. 2:15).

*edge* (v. 11). Each word seems carefully chosen to present the consequences in the most powerful way: The person is described as 1) a weak person; 2) a brother; and 3) one for whom Christ himself gave his life. How would one be expected to treat a weaker brother, especially one for whom the Lord laid down his life? Paul highlights the incredible value Christ places on the lives of these brothers and sisters. These are ones *for whom Christ died.* 1 Peter 1:18-19 strikes a similar note: "it was not with perishable things such as silver or gold that you were redeemed. . . . but with the precious blood of Christ"! These Corinthians are acting in a way that could lead to the destruction of such cherished people! The word "destroy" points to the ultimate ruin of the people involved,[100] reinforcing the seriousness of the "stumbling" referred to in v. 9 (see the comments there).

The sentence structure of v. 11 (in Greek) is arranged to stress the first and last words. The first word in the Greek is the verb "is destroyed";[101] the last word is the verb "died." In this way the potential effect of the Corinthian approach is contrasted with that of Christ. Christ died to save these brothers, but they are promoting their destruction, all for the sake of their so-called "knowledge!" Paul has been working to get the Corinthians to rethink the relative value they are placing on their special knowledge since the first verse of this chapter (knowledge is puffing you up, but love builds up), and vv. 9-13 continue to force the issue.

**8:12-13** In v. 12 Paul reinforces the identification between Christ and his people: *When you sin against them in this way and wound their weak conscience, you sin against Christ.*[102] The logic of the verse builds on that of the preceding one. Since Christ identified with us and died for us, including the weak (and we were all weak; Rom. 5:6), when we destroy those whom Christ died to save we sin against him. Paul uses the metaphor of "striking a blow"[103] to the weak conscience (moral arbiter) of their brother or sister in Christ to describe the effect of the Corinthians' behavior.

Recall from the context just what it is that is described as being a "stumbling block" (v. 9), destroying fellow Christians (v. 11), sinning against them and Christ by striking a blow to their weak conscience (v. 12), and causing them to fall (v. 13). All these statements are related to the scenario described in v. 10, where a fellow Christian happens to see one of them having a meal in an idol's temple and winds up eating idol food as a

100. Gk. ἀπόλλυμι. See H.-C. Hahn's discussion, "Destroy, Perish, Ruin," in *NIDNTT* 1:464.

101. "Is destroyed" (ἀπόλλυται) is a present passive indicative (rather than a perfect tense) expressing the idea that they experience or suffer destruction thanks to the insensitive believer (a perfect tense would suggest that they are in a state of destruction).

102. Verse 12 has something of a chiastic structure, with the verb "sinning" coming at the beginning and end of the verse and those sinned against being named after the first occurrence of the verb and before the last one: ἁμαρτάνοντες εἰς τοὺς ἀδελφοὺς καὶ . . . εἰς Χριστὸν ἁμαρτάνετε (*sinning* against the brothers . . . against Christ you *sin*).

103. Gk. τύπτω.

result. The "weak" Corinthians should certainly refrain from imitating any behavior they consider idolatrous, and would do well to learn, as Paul suggests in Romans 14:3, not to judge the strong (at least not on the basis of the history of the food they consume). The "strong" Corinthians should refrain from any behavior that might lead others into subjective idolatry or confirm them in it. They must learn, as Paul asserts in Romans 14:3, not to despise the weak.

Paul says, *if what I eat causes my brother or sister to fall into sin, I will never eat meat again, so that I will not cause them to fall* (v. 13). The food in question, of course, is food that *my brother or sister* knows to have been offered to idols. In chapter 10 Paul will deal with problems with the attitude and behavior of those who would associate themselves with objective idolatry (including eating food that has been identified by others as idol food). For now he deals with the issue of leading others to fall into sin (in this case idolatry) through thoughtless (or misconceived) behavior. The word translated *fall into sin* in the first clause and *fall* in the third clause[104] is often translated "cause to stumble." BDAG gives as its meaning "to cause to be brought to a downfall," which better communicates the dire implications.[105] Paul stresses his concern over the potential downfall of brothers and sisters in Christ by repeating the key word and by stressing the radical choice he would take to avoid ever contributing to such a consequence with a redundant idiomatic expression[106] that communicates the strongest absolute negation possible (which is translated somewhat weakly in the TNIV as *will never . . . again*). It combines that standard expression for emphatic negation (essentially "I will *never* [or *certainly not*"])[107] with the somewhat redundant *for eternity*.[108]

Paul presumably refers to eating meat in this verse (the only place in the letter where meat is specifically mentioned) not because meat was the only food of concern, but because it would have been the most difficult kind of food to come by without some questionable history, since most of the meat available in the market (or served at dinners) would have been previously part of an offering to an idol. He does not actually promise that he will never eat meat, but he states as strongly as possible that he would absolutely give it up forever rather than allow someone to suffer spiritual ruin by eating it. He expects the Corinthians, the ones "in the know," to do likewise.

104. Gk. σκανδαλίζω.

105. Cf. H. Giesen, "σκανδαλίζω," *EDNT* 3:248.

106. Found only here in Paul's writings. It appears six times in John's Gospel (John 4:14; 8:51, 52; 10:28; 11:26; 13:8).

107. Gk. οὐ μή with the aorist subjunctive, "the strongest way to negate something in Greek" (Wallace, *Greek Grammar*, 468). This usage of the aorist subjunctive is related to its association with remoteness (here, remoteness from reality). The usage adds prominence to Paul's declaration.

108. Gk. εἰς τὸν αἰῶνα.

### 2. Exposition of Paul's Example: Waiving Rights for the Sake of the Gospel, 9:1-23[1]

*1Am I not free? Am I not an apostle? Have I not seen Jesus our Lord? Are you not the result of my work in the Lord? 2Even though I may not be an apostle to others, surely I am to you! For you are the seal of my apostleship in the Lord.*

*3This is my defense to those who sit in judgment on me. 4Don't we have the right to food and drink? 5Don't we have the right to take a believing wife along with us, as do the other apostles and the Lord's brothers and Cephas? 6Or is it only I and Barnabas who don't have the right not to work for a living?*

*7Who serves as a soldier at his own expense? Who plants a vineyard and does not eat of its grapes? Who tends a flock and does not drink of the milk? 8Do I say this merely on human authority? Doesn't the Law say the same thing? 9For it is written in the Law of Moses: "Do not muzzle an ox while it is treading out the grain." Is it about oxen that God is concerned? 10Surely he says this for us, doesn't he? Yes, this was written for us, because when farmers plow and thresh, they should be able to do so in the hope of sharing in the harvest. 11If we have sown spiritual seed among you, is it too much if we reap a material harvest from you? 12If others have this right of support from you, shouldn't we have it all the more?*

*But we did not use this right. On the contrary, we put up with anything rather than hinder the gospel of Christ.*

*13Don't you know that those who serve in the temple get their food from the temple, and that those who serve at the altar share in what is offered on the altar? 14In the same way, the Lord has commanded that those who preach the gospel should receive their living from the gospel.*

*15But I have not used any of these rights. And I am not writing this in the hope that you will do such things for me, for I would rather die than allow anyone to deprive me of this boast. 16For when I preach the gospel, I cannot boast, since I am compelled to preach. Woe to me if I do not preach the gospel! 17If I preach voluntarily, I have a reward; if not voluntarily, I am simply discharging the trust committed to me. 18What then is my reward? Just this: that in preaching the gospel I may offer it free of charge, and so not misuse my rights as a preacher of the gospel.*

*19Though I am free and belong to no one, I have made myself a slave to everyone, to win as many as possible. 20To the Jews I became like a Jew, to win the Jews. To those under the law I became like one under the law (though I myself am not under the law), so as to win those under the law. 21To those not having the law I became like one not having the law (though I am not free*

1. Our outline for this section is indebted to that of Fotopoulos, *Food Offered to Idols*, 201-3.

*from God's law but am under Christ's law), so as to win those not having the law.* [22]*To the weak I became weak, to win the weak. I have become all things to all people so that by all possible means I might save some.* [23]*I do all this for the sake of the gospel, that I may share in its blessings.*

Many scholars think that the rhetoric of this chapter suggests that some Corinthians have questioned Paul's apostolic authority and that this is his response to that challenge. They take this chapter to be something of a digression from the subject of food offered to idols. Others see a sandwich structure (A-B-A) in chapters 8–10 similar to that found in chapters 12–14, a view we affirm. In both instances an issue is raised in a section which is followed by another one that appears to address a different subject but which turns out to be a key to the issue raised in the first section.[2] We think it unlikely that Paul was aware of any serious doubting of his apostolic authority in Corinth, if it existed.[3] In fact, although he seems to be aware that others have questioned his apostolic authority and/or practices, his argument presupposes the Corinthians' acceptance of his apostolic status. The series of rhetorical questions at the beginning of the chapter (*Am I not free? Am I not an apostle? Have I not seen Jesus our Lord? Are you not the result of my work in the Lord?*) depend upon the Corinthians' agreement for their rhetorical power in support of the argument that follows. Paul affirms his right to support based on his status as an apostle and expects the Corinthians to accede to both points. He explains how his seemingly strange behavior of self-support actually reflects a refusal to exploit his rights due to his commitment to the priority of the gospel.

It is the priority of the gospel and its implications for Christian attitudes towards one's rights (and the well-being of oneself and others) that turns out to be a key to how one should handle the issue of food offered to idols. This is consistent with the theme of edification with which Paul introduced this main section (8:1; cf. Rom. 14:19). The relationship between one's freedom (v. 1) and the qualms of other brothers and sisters in Christ may have been an issue raised by the Corinthians. One can easily imagine them complaining that to prohibit them from knowingly eating food offered to idols would constitute an infringement on the freedom purchased for them by Christ (including a right to eat such food), something they should resist for the sake of the gospel (cf. Gal. 2:4; 5:1). Paul's response highlights his own freedom and rights as an apostle and his commitment to subject that freedom and those rights to gospel priorities, for his own sake and that of others. In this way he models a commitment to making life-choices in line with the priority of the gospel (as would be expected of anyone who has truly come under its power). Paul provides us with a "study

2. There are several vocabulary links between ch. 9 and chs. 8 and 10, including "free," "right" "weak," "share," and obstacles ("stumbling block" and "hindrance"); cf. Garland, 396, n. 1.

3. Contra Fee, 394-400. 2 Cor. 10–13 suggests that it existed, and Paul was aware of it, later.

of claimable rights that go unclaimed for a purpose,"[4] all in the interests of the effective ministry of the gospel.

Most of the chapter is dedicated to an exposition of Paul's own practice as an example of a gospel-centered approach to one's rights. That exposition begins and ends with material relating to the exploitation or qualification of freedom in the broadest terms possible (vv. 1-2, 19-23). Embedded within that broader material is a discussion focused on the specific issue of Paul's right to support as an apostle of Christ (vv. 3-18). Both parts (the broader material and the discussion of support) are divided into two parts each, one establishing the apostle's freedom or rights (vv. 1-2, 3-14), and the other explaining why Paul has not exploited his rights or freedom (vv. 15-18, 19-23). The pattern could be outlined as follows:

Paul's freedom and rights (vv. 1-14)
  a. Paul's freedom and status (vv. 1-2)
  b. Paul's right to support (vv. 3-14)
Paul's refusal to exploit his rights and freedom (vv. 15-23)
  b. Paul's refusal to exploit his rights (vv. 15-18)
  a. Paul's refusal to exploit his freedom (vv. 19-23)

### *a. Paul Enjoys Elite Apostolic Status and Freedom, 9:1-2*

**9:1-2** *Am I not free? Am I not an apostle? Have I not seen Jesus our Lord? Are you not the result of my work in the Lord?*[5] The first three rhetorical questions in v. 1 seem to reflect a sequential order going from each affirmation to its logically preceding basis: Paul must be at least as free (in Christ) as any other Christian would be (1a); since he is an apostle, after all (1b); and his apostleship (1b) is based upon his vision of Christ and commissioning by him (1c). The fourth rhetorical question, along with the contents of v. 2, provides further confirmation of Paul's apostleship, seen in the Lord's work through his ministry in establishing the Corinthian church (cf. Gal. 2:7-9).

The issues raised by the rhetorical questions are unlikely to have been disputed in Corinth, since Paul would not gain anything by asking rhetorical questions that might have been answered negatively by the Corinthians.[6] The wording of the questions indicates that he expects the Corinthians to respond to each question in the affirmative,[7] and that he expects the

4. Sampley, 903.

5. The first, second, and fourth verbs are present indicative forms of the stative verb "to be" (εἰμί). The third verb ("I have seen") is a perfect indicative (ἑόρακα), which also stresses Paul's present state and status as an eyewitness of the Lord. The verbs all work together to provide description and characterization of Paul as background for the following discussion.

6. Cf. Garland, 398.

7. By using the negative οὐ rather than μή for "not" in the rhetorical question (cf. BDF §427).

questions to be sufficient in themselves to establish his Christian freedom on the basis of his apostolic status.

The freedom to which Paul refers *(Am I not free?)* is not the legal status he discusses in 7:21, 22b and 12:13 but, in context, refers to freedom in Christ (cf. 9:19; 10:29; 7:22a; Gal. 2:4; 4:26–5:1), a divinely given freedom from the imposition of the norms of this world to live by the norms of the Spirit.[8] In the previous verse (8:13) Paul declared that he would rather give up eating meat than let his eating practices cause a brother to fall. "Some of his auditors may well have thought, 'Some freedom!'"[9] Such a response would also be consistent with the extreme individualism so often found in modern Western thinking. But the freedom to which Christ has liberated us is not a freedom to do as we please, but a freedom to serve God and others in the newness and power of the Spirit (cf. chs. 12–14 and Gal. 5:13-26), a freedom to do as we ought. It is a freedom to live out the life of Christ in a community that glorifies God as it follows the sacrificial example of the Lord Jesus Christ.

As an apostle commissioned by Christ (v. 1b-c) Paul is accountable to him and must live according to Christ's agenda rather than any other. He already mentioned his role as an apostle in 1:1, 17; 4:9. The stress of 1:17 is on being sent by Christ to preach the gospel. Elsewhere it is clear that Paul's understanding of his apostolic ministry is formed on the basis of certain prophetic callings in the Old Testament.[10] He understands his vision of Christ, referred to in v. 1c, in terms of prophetic commissioning visions. His vision of Christ is not in the same category as that of the 500 who saw Christ (1 Cor. 15:6), since his vision entailed being commissioned by Christ to preach the gospel to the Gentiles (Gal. 1:11-12, 15-16; Acts 26:15-18). The conjunction of ideas suggests that the reference to Jesus as "our Lord" may not simply reflect Paul's common use of the title as elsewhere, but reflects the fact that his vision was precisely that of Jesus reigning in glory as Lord.[11]

8. See the discussion in Ciampa, "Freedom," *NDBT* 503-6 (esp. 505).

9. Sampley, 903.

10. See K. O. Sandnes, *Paul — One of the Prophets? A Contribution to the Apostle's Self-Understanding* (WUNT 2.43; Tübingen: J. C. B. Mohr, 1991), 64-65; Ciampa, *Scripture in Galatians 1 and 2,* 111-16. Note 2 Cor. 3:16-18, where Paul relates Christian freedom to our ability to see Christ.

11. See Kim, *The Origin of Paul's Gospel,* 55-66, 104-111. Presumably the Corinthians would have known this from Paul's earlier testimonies to that effect. As others have pointed out, the reference to seeing the risen Jesus leaves no room for any separation between the earthly, historical Jesus and the risen Christ. Thiselton has an extended discussion of "apostle" and apostleship (667-73) in which he argues (among other things) that apostles "above all performed self-involving acts of witness which were transparent in their cruciform and Christocentric lifestyle" (668, emphasis removed). "The instantiation of the cruciform, Christlike stance toward others in practical lifestyle constitutes both part of what it is to be an apostle and an instantiation of the Christ-centered principle urged in 8:1-13" (668, emphasis removed). While Thiselton clearly identifies a key element of Paul's own thinking

As in Galatians 2:7-9, in the last question of v. 1 and the follow-up material in v. 2 Paul indicates that the effectiveness of his ministry to the Gentiles confirms the authenticity of his apostolic calling. His statement that the Corinthians are *the result of* his *work* in the Lord anticipates the argument in vv. 7-14. Paul's right not to work for a living is based on the fact that his ministry is his work and that the very existence of the Corinthian church is one of its results.

Others might question his apostolic authority, but surely the Corinthians know better! *Even though I may not be an apostle to others, surely I am to you! For you are the seal of my apostleship in the Lord.* His statement that he might not be an apostle *to others* may mean that he was not sent to everyone, but to the Corinthians. It is more likely that by *to others* he means "in the eyes of others," suggesting awareness that some have questioned his apostleship. Paul's stress is on the certainty of the Corinthians' acceptance of his apostolic role and status, not on the attitudes of others. The point is not that others deny that he is an apostle, but that even if others might not recognize him (or know what to make of him) since they have not personally experienced God's presence through his ministry, the Corinthians have had that experience and therefore know that Paul was commissioned by God.

The reference to *the seal of* Paul's *apostleship* entails a figurative use of the word for a signet or the impression left by a signet[12] which "confirms or authenticates" (BDAG) the thing so marked. The very existence of the Corinthian church testifies to the authenticity of Paul's apostleship.

As elsewhere, *in the Lord* at the end of both v. 1 and v. 2 probably refers to life lived under the reign of the resurrected Lord. It often qualifies activities performed in the light of Christ's reign, or status established through his reign.[13]

---

about apostleship as reflected in this and his other letters, this is not what the word "apostle" connotes in 9:1. In 9:1 apostleship is associated with Paul's spiritual freedom and serves as the foundation for his presumed rights. The logic of the chapter is that although he is an apostle (and therefore has certain rights that should apply), he has not exploited his freedom or rights but has reflected a Christ- and gospel-centered lifestyle that surrenders rights for the sake of others (and, ultimately, oneself). The concessive logic would not work if Thiselton's meaning is read into the word in 9:1 (i.e., it does not make sense to say, "Although I am an instantiation of the cruciform and Christ-centered lifestyle, I did not exploit my freedom and rights"). Paul's logic assumes that apostleship is already associated with elements of status and authority. His larger argument will clarify that such status and authority (like Christian freedom in general) are to be employed only in a cruciform, Christ- and gospel-centered manner. Thiselton's conclusion (673) that apostleship "fundamentally points away from the self . . . to Christ as crucified and raised" can be accepted as a key point in Paul's thinking about his apostolic role, but not as a commonly recognized semantic element of the word "apostle" (ἀπόστολος) in New Testament texts.

12. Gk. σφραγίς.

13. BDAG states that the preposition ἐν is especially found in Pauline and Johannine usage "to designate a close personal relation in which the referent of the ἐν-term is viewed as the controlling influence," with possible glosses including "under the control of, under

### *b. Paul Has a Right to Support, 9:3-14*

**9:3** *This is my defense to those who sit in judgment on me.* The demonstrative pronoun, *This,* may point back to vv. 1-2 (if Paul is defending his apostolic status), or ahead to vv. 4-18 (if he is defending his refusal to charge for his teaching). The early Greek fathers are divided on the issue.[14] Verses 1-2 would serve as a poor defense for those who question Paul's authority. The second question would surely be considered a case of begging the question. The verses' greatest apologetic value would be for those who (like the Corinthians) owed their Christian life to his ministry. The following verses, however, do explain why Paul refuses to carry out ministry for payment, preferring to preach the gospel for free. Verses 4-14 suggest that at this point the Corinthians probably had no doubts about Paul's apostleship, but may have been baffled by his decision to use a self-supporting approach to his ministry.

Paul's use of legal language — *defense, sit in judgment* (or "conduct a judicial hearing")[15] — ties it to the language of "rights" found in the following verses (cf. vv. 4-6, 12, 18) as well as tying it back to 8:9. It is also a remarkable rhetorical device which invites the Corinthians to consider his arguments carefully. This is not the kind of defense we would expect someone to give in our legal system. Rather, "the rhetorical questions are employed in such a fashion as to put the readers on the stand, so to speak . . . being led by the inquisitor, Paul, through a series of questions" whose required answers are clearly indicated in the Greek.[16] Paul offers a *defense* that attacks the defenses of anyone opposing him.

**9:4-6** Each of the three rhetorical questions in these verses deals with some aspect of support (food/drink, marital/sexual companionship, and working for a living respectively). The first two questions begin with identical wording and thereby stress the key issue of the use of "rights": *Don't we have the right. . . ?*[17] The first question *(Don't we have the right to food and drink?)* relates directly to the subject discussed in the previous and fol-

---

the influence of, in close association with." In many cases (as here) it is difficult to know whether an element of means could be involved (*you are the result of my work* thanks to/through *the Lord*). Note BDF §219 (4): "The phrase ἐν Χριστῷ (κυρίῳ), which is copiously appended by Paul to the most varied concepts, utterly defies definite interpretation!" On the variety of possible meanings see Murray Harris, "Prepositions and Theology in the Greek New Testament," *NIDNTT* 3:1192-93. While such phrases usually seem to reflect the usage suggested in the previous note, it is sometimes difficult to know whether an instrumental idea is entailed (e.g., Rom. 3:24; 6:11, 23; 12:5; 14:14; 1 Cor. 1:2, 4, 7:22; 9:1-2; 11:11; 2 Cor. 2:12, 17; 3:14; 5:19; Gal. 2:4, 17; 3:14, 28).

14. For Theodoret see Bray, 80 and PG 82:293, lines 24-27; on Chrysostom see *Homiliae in Epistulam i ad Corinthios* (NPNF[1] 12:119) and PG 61:171, lines 53-60.

15. Gk. ἀπολογία (cf. apologetics — the defense of the faith) and ἀνακρίνω, respectively. For the definition of the second term see BDAG.

16. Sampley, 904.

17. Gk. μὴ οὐκ ἔχομεν ἐξουσίαν.

lowing chapters: rights relating to food and drink. The verbs "to eat" and "to drink"[18] are paired together nine times in chapters 9–11 (9:4; 10:7, 31; 11:22, 26, 27, 28, 29 [x2]) but only twice outside of those chapters in Paul's writings (1 Cor. 15:32; Rom. 14:21). The reference to (literally) "the right to eat and to drink" suggests that this example was chosen because it parallels the Corinthians' concern with their perceived right to eat whatever food they wanted (cf. 8:9). While the Corinthians defended their right to eat as they wished (including idol food), Paul discusses his right to material support, a right he chooses not to exploit. The right to material support in the form of food and drink will be established in vv. 7-11 and 13-14. As v. 6 will make clear, *we* refers to Paul and Barnabas.

The second rhetorical question, *Don't we have the right to take a believing wife* [literally, "a sister [as a] wife"] *along with us, as do the other apostles and the Lord's brothers and Cephas?* (v. 5), touches on another key issue already addressed in 1 Corinthians, namely, that of sexual needs (cf. chs. 5–7, esp. 7). It probably also relates more directly to the central issue of support in that it would presumably have lessened Paul's workload if he had a wife working alongside him or possibly working to support him as he carried out his ministry.[19] Paul's next question, *Or is it only I and Barnabas who don't have the right not to work for a living?* may suggest that he and Barnabas could have married women wealthy enough to support their ministry and free them from having to work. That any wife Paul or Barnabas might bring along would be a *believing* (literally, "sister") *wife* reflects the biblical expectation that believers should marry within the family of God.[20] This verse suggests that Paul and Barnabas were single men who could have married and benefited from the support of wives but did not exercise the right to do so.

Paul indicates that the norm among early Christian leaders was to marry and bring along a wife when traveling. It has been suggested that Paul's list of Christian leaders follows an order of ascending importance, going from *the other apostles*, to the even more important "brothers of the Lord," to *Cephas* (Peter), who was thought of as the most authoritative of them all. We should not read a strict and clear hierarchy (much less that of a papacy) into Paul's text. His discussion of his own role and his relationship to the Christian leadership in Jerusalem in Galatians 2:6-9 imply that he and Peter are the two "point men" in God's global mission strategy (with

18. Gk. ἐσθίω and πίνω.

19. Note Acts 18:3, which indicates that, while in Corinth, Paul stayed with Aquila and Priscilla, who worked together in the same trade. See Richard Saller, "Women, Slaves, and the Economy of the Roman Household," in *Early Christian Families in Context* (ed. David L. Balch and Carolyn Osiek; Grand Rapids: Eerdmans, 2003), 185-204, for background on women's contributions in the family and the workplace.

20. Suggestions that Paul is actually referring not to a wife but to a female attendant who would help him in his ministry are misdirected (*pace* Allo, 212-14); the word γυνή (literally, "woman/wife") would be quite redundant since ἀδελφή ("sister") would have sufficed if Paul had in mind a "Christian woman" who was not a wife (so also Thiselton, 681; Héring, 77).

Peter leading the ministry among Jews and Paul leading the ministry to Gentiles), with James (the Lord's brother) and John (the apostle) also exercising considerable influence in the church in Jerusalem. Notably, Paul indicates that whatever rights apply to these other key Christian leaders ought to apply to himself and Barnabas as well.

Verse 6 suggests that those named in v. 5 do not work for a living due to the fact that they have the support of a wife.[21] Barnabas was, of course, Paul's partner during the early part of his ministry (cf. Acts 9:26-27; 11:22-30; 12:25–15:39; Gal 2:1-9). There are no other indications that Paul and Barnabas were working together at the time Paul wrote this letter. Barnabas may have been mentioned simply as the only other key leader Paul could think of whose ministry was carried out under the same conditions as his own. Paul's indication that he (and Barnabas) should not have to work for a living picks up the language of v. 1, where he says that the Corinthians are *the result of my work in the Lord.*[22]

**9:7** Paul introduces three more rhetorical questions: *Who serves as a soldier at his own expense? Who plants a vineyard and does not eat of its grapes? Who tends a flock and does not drink of the milk?* Each reinforces the point that "[i]n everyday life one expects to be sustained by one's labors."[23] One cannot justify the adoption of an opulent lifestyle by Christian leaders on the basis of this text. As Garland notes, Paul's analogies "refer only to maintenance for basic subsistence, and questions about wages for the work are far from Paul's mind."[24] As Fee puts it, Paul is not arguing that he has the right "to be 'paid' for services rendered" but [that he has the right to have his basic needs] 'provided for' by those who owe their lives to him."[25]

Each question begins with the interrogative "who?" and expects the answer "no one." Each stresses the active work/labor for which the worker expects to be supported.[26] The expectation of support is not predicated on status, but on work carried out for the benefit of others. The first question makes the point that a soldier "does not have to provide for his own subsistence."[27] The word used by Paul may refer specifically to the soldier's ra-

21. Thiselton and Héring contend that Paul means that the apostles had the right "not only to be married and to be accompanied by their wives on their journeys . . . but also to have them supported by the Church" (Héring, 77, cited by Thiselton, 681). If so, it would suggest that those not needing to work included the other leaders mentioned and their wives, who traveled with them.

22. Cf. Paul's statement to the Corinthians in v. 1, "you are my work" (τὸ ἔργον μου ὑμεῖς ἐστε), with his "right not to work" (ἐξουσίαν μὴ ἐργάζεσθαι) in v. 6.

23. Fee, 405.

24. Garland, 409.

25. Fee, 405 n. 44.

26. The people involved are not referred to as "soldiers," "farmers," or "shepherds," but as those who "serve," "plant," or "shepherd" (cf. Ellingworth and Hatton, 197).

27. Spicq, "ὀψώνιον," *TLNT* 2:603. For details, see J. B. Campbell, "Stipendium," *OCD* 1444, or the much fuller discussion in G. R. Watson, *The Roman Soldier* (Ithaca, NY: Cornell University Press, 1969), 89-114. Roman soldiers were provided with food, clothing, and

tions or provisions, or more generally to their pay or salary. Even in the latter case the idea would be payment provided to the soldier for the purchase of food and other necessities.[28] Heidland suggests that "there may also be allusion to the thought that the support of the congregation never can or will be adequate compensation for the apostle's work" but that it serves merely as a food ration,[29] the modern equivalent of reimbursement for meals eaten while traveling on business. The implied analogy assumes that Paul's work is also carried out under the authority of another who would be expected to arrange for his support.

One who planted a vineyard would be expected to enjoy some of its fruit (see the application of this principle in Deut. 20:6), and one who tends a flock would also be expected to receive "compensation that derives intrinsically from the work," such as drinking the milk produced by the flock.[30] As Ellingworth and Hatton point out, in the second and third examples "Paul is probably thinking of a farm worker and a shepherd, that is, people employed by someone else; he does not seem to be thinking of a landowner. Such an interpretation would make a better parallel to 7a: *Who serves as a soldier at his own expense?*[31]

Godet thinks that the examples of a soldier, vinedresser, and shepherd came naturally to Paul "because the people of God are often described in the prophets as an army, a vine, a flock."[32] In 3:5-9 Paul presented his ministry as one of planting[33] "God's field." In vv. 9-11 Paul returns to the agricultural analogy, describing apostolic missionaries as spiritual counterparts to agricultural laborers, working in God's fields.

**9:8** Paul employs another rhetorical question to emphasize that his point is also supported by divine authority established through Scripture:[34]

---

equipment, but the costs for those things were deducted from their pay, and there were complaints that not much was left after those deductions (cf. Tacitus, *Annales* 1.17; Polybius, *History* 6.39.15; for an apparently temporary exemption to the deduction for clothing see Plutarch, *Tiberius et Caius Gracchus* 5.1). Given the agricultural contexts of the next two analogies, Paul might have in mind not the official support the soldier receives from his commanders, but his right to requisition food (or eat from the fields through which he passes) during the course of his duties. See Brian M. Rapske, "Acts, Travel and Shipwrecks," in *The Book of Acts in Its Graeco-Roman Setting* (ed. David W. J. Gill; The Book of Acts in Its First-Century Setting 2; Grand Rapids: Eerdmans, 1994), 14.

28. Cf. C. C. Caragounis, "Ὀψώνιον: A Reconsideration of Its Meaning," *NovT* 16 (1974), 51-52; C. Spicq, "ὀψώνιον," *TLNT* 2:600-603; Garland, 408; Thiselton, 683-84.

29. H. W. Heidland, "ὀψώνιον," *TDNT* 5:592.

30. Garland, 409.

31. Ellingworth and Hatton, 197.

32. Godet, 2:10, followed by Garland, 409.

33. Using the same verb as 9:7 in 3:6, 7, 8 (the only places in Paul's writings where the verb appears).

34. According to BDAG, κατὰ ἄνθρωπον ("in a human way, from a human standpoint") generally "emphasizes the inferiority of human beings in comparison w[ith] God." Paul may be using what appears to be a *merely human* set of arguments, but in fact he is not speaking merely on human authority since his teaching is supported by divine revelation.

*Do I say this merely on human authority? Doesn't the Law say the same thing?* The question is worded to indicate that the answer to the first part (does Paul speak *merely on human authority?*) is expected to be negative, while the answer to the second part *(doesn't the Law say the same thing?)* is expected to be positive.[35] The Greek could be literally translated, "Do I say these things on merely human authority, or is it not true that the Law says these things as well?" Paul's words express a parallel between "I say these things" and "the Law says these things"[36]: the law of Moses (God's revelation) agrees with Paul. It says the same thing that he does. In fact, v. 10, which provides a principle derived from the citation of Deuteronomy 25:4 in v. 9, is almost an exact parallel to v. 7: the one who carries out his work in the fields expects to partake of the fruits of their labor.

**9:9-10** Paul introduces his quotation from Deuteronomy 25:4 with a citation formula[37] indicating that it provides a foundation for the previous verse: *For it is written in the Law of Moses: "Do not muzzle an ox while it is treading out the grain."* On first sight the verse seems to deal with something rather removed from the issue of Paul's right to be supported in his ministry. Paul's use of the verse has often been considered allegorical.[38] It is probably more accurate to understand it as an argument from the lesser to the greater, as some early Jewish usage suggests.[39]

Philo cites Deuteronomy 25:4 in the midst of a section (*On the Virtues* 125–47) that he tells us will address the extension of the same principles of humanity and compassion which were applied to all types of people "even to the race of irrational animals" (*On the Virtues* 125). As he concludes that section, he suggests that if we learn how to treat lower forms of life humanely we will not fail to do the same with humans (160).

Josephus discusses Deuteronomy 25:4 in *Antiquities* 4.233, where it is both immediately preceded and followed by his discussion of the laws of gleaning (Lev. 19:9; 23:2) and those which allow people who pass through a field to pluck ears with their hands (Deut. 23:25), respectively. By placing Deuteronomy 25:4 in the midst of various laws that provide people with access to food Josephus may be treating the law concerning work animals as an extension of those that apply to people. That may also be indicated by the word he uses to refer to the animals in this context. He says that one is

35. With μή embedded within the first clause and οὐ within the second.

36. Gk. ταῦτα λαλῶ . . . ὁ νόμος ταῦτα οὐ λέγει.

37. See our comments on the perfect tense "it is written" (γέγραπται) on 1:19.

38. See most commentaries, esp. Schrage, 2:298-300, and the views cited in Walter Kaiser, "The Current Crisis in Exegesis and the Apostolic Use of Deuteronomy 25:4 in 1 Corinthians 9:8-10," *JETS* 21 (1973), 11-14.

39. Called *qal waḥomer* in rabbinic literature and referred to in Latin as an argument *a minore ad majus* or *a fortiori.* See below and the discussion in Instone-Brewer, "1 Corinthians 9:9-11: A Literal Interpretation of 'Do Not Muzzle the Ox,'" *NTS* 38 (1992), 554; and in R. E. Ciampa and B. S. Rosner, "1 Corinthians," in the *Commentary on the New Testament Use of the Old Testament* (ed. G. K. Beale and D. A. Carson; Grand Rapids: Baker Academic, 2007), 718-22.

not "to bind the mouth of the oxen treading out the corn on the threshing floor, since it is not right to restrain our *co-workers* of the fruit. . . ."[40]

The Talmud's treatment of the verse reflects some significant (and later) developments in the rabbinic interpretation of the text. In *b. Baba Meṣiʿa* 88b the Mishnah's teaching that men may eat from the loose produce of the field in which they work (cf. *m. B. Meṣiʿa* 7:2) is defended on the basis of an argument from the lesser to the greater from Deuteronomy 25:4, perhaps influenced by Deuteronomy 23:24 as well.[41]

The broader context of Deuteronomy 25:4 shows a more general concern for the humane treatment of people.[42] Deuteronomy 24:10–25:3 addresses the need for humane treatment of poor and marginalized people, and Deuteronomy 24:19-22 discusses the need to allow sojourners, orphans, and widows to benefit from what is left in the field at the end of the harvesting process. The command of Deuteronomy 25:4 comes soon after these passages which are concerned to make sure that *not only* those who work get to benefit from the product of their labor (*eating* it), but that other needy and marginalized people should also be able to eat it. Given that context, it is natural to understand the command as an extension of an already implied principle that those who work are allowed to partake of the fruit of their labors since, when it comes to humans, that benefit even extends beyond those whose labors contributed to the harvest or production of food.

C. K Barrett argues against understanding this text in terms of an argument from the lesser to the greater. In his view Paul is not saying, "If God cares for oxen how much more for people," but rather, "God does not care for oxen but for people."[43] Barrett's argument rests on a common reading of the last clause of v. 9 and the first clause of v. 10. However, 1 Corinthians 9:10a should probably not be translated "Does he not speak *entirely* for our sake?" (cf. ESV, NRSV, NASB, NJB), but rather "Doesn't he surely say it for our sake?" (cf. TNIV, NIV, NET, NLT).[44] That is, Paul's statement need not (and should not) be taken as an absolute denial that the law was given for the sake of animals, but as a strong assertion that God is even more concerned about humans (and that he was particularly concerned to give guidance for the eschatological community of the church).

This is in keeping with the common Jewish understanding. Following the same line, in his lecture on Deuteronomy 25:4 Martin Luther cleverly quipped that the verse was obviously not written for oxen since "oxen can't

40. Gk. τοὺς συνειργασμένους τοῦ καρποῦ; *Antiquities* 4.233.

41. See Tomson, *Paul and the Jewish Law,* 125-31.

42. See Hays, 151.

43. Barrett, 206.

44. BDAG notes that the adverb Paul uses (πάντως), when "pert[aining] to strong assumption," means "by all means, certainly, probably, doubtless," and suggests that this verse be translated, "Is he (not) certainly speaking in our interest?" See the discussion in Thiselton, 686-87.

read"![45] As a general principle, ancient Jewish interpreters agreed that the law was written for human consumption. Philo said, "The Law was not given for the sake of unthinking creatures, but for the sake of those who can think and reason" (*On the Special Laws* 1:260).

Paul's question, *Is it about oxen that God is concerned?*, is formulated to indicate that the obvious answer is "no."[46] At first glance it appears that the cited text does indeed reflect concern for oxen (rather than people), but as pointed out above,[47] the near literary context of Deuteronomy 25:4 points to a concern for human well-being.

Paul has set up the argument from the first verse of this chapter where he argues that the Corinthians are his "workmanship,"[48] suggesting that just as the vineyard worker gets to eat some of the fruit and a shepherd gets to have some of the flock's milk (9:7) and even an ox can eat some of the grain it treads out, so also the one whose labor has resulted in the Corinthian community has the right to enjoy some compensation from that which has been produced. They are the field he has sown, and he has the right to reap some fruit from its harvest (9:11). The logic of Deuteronomy 25:4 fits the logic of the other examples given in 1 Corinthians 9:7.

Paul says, *Surely he says this for us, doesn't he? Yes, this was written for us, because when farmers plow and thresh, they should be able to do so in the hope of sharing in the harvest.* For whom exactly does Paul suggest Deuteronomy 25:4 was written? By *for us* Paul may have in mind the sake of human beings rather than simply the sake of animals (like oxen). That would make perfect sense of the contrast between a concern *about oxen* (v. 9b) and one *for us* (v. 10a). In other places, however, Paul indicates that scriptural texts were written (especially) for the community of the last days (cf., e.g., 10:6, 11). This might suggest that *for us* means "for the guidance of the church in the last days." Richard Hays convincingly argues, however, that Paul has his apostolic team specifically in mind.[49] It seems likely that Paul's use of the argument from the lesser to the greater presupposes a previously established apostolic interpretation according to which apostolic missionaries are understood to be spiritual laborers, sowers, and reapers (Matt. 9:37-38; 10:10; Luke 10:2, 7; John 4:36-38; Rom. 1:13; 1 Cor. 3:6-9; 9:11; 1 Thess. 5:12; 1 Tim. 5:17-18). In light of this background we suggest that Paul has not only his own missionary team in mind, but also a biblical principle that applies to all who labor (remember, in v. 8 Paul says that the text he will quote in v. 9 teaches the things he just affirmed in the rhetorical questions of v. 7), and which is applied to him and his team as well as to all apostolic missionaries, since they also fall under the category of field laborers.

45. Cf. Martin Luther, *Lectures on Deuteronomy* (Luther's Works, vol. 9; ed. Jaroslav Pelikan; St. Louis: Concordia, 1960), 248.

46. By introducing the question with μή.

47. See p. 405.

48. Or the result of his work (Gk. τὸ ἔργον).

49. Hays, *Echoes of Scripture*, 165-68.

This background may help solve a key question regarding the second half of v. 10. It is not clear wether it is to be understood as a quotation (". . . for it is for our sake it is written that 'whoever plows should plow in hope and whoever threshes should thresh in hope of sharing in the crop'") or as a justification of Paul's interpretation of Deuteronomy 25:4 (*this* [Deut. 25:4] *was written for us, because when farmers plow and thresh, they should be able to do so in the hope of sharing in the harvest*). The first option is difficult since we do not know of any text that Paul could be citing. The strongest argument against the second option is the balanced parallel (poetic) nature of the two clauses and the apparently un-Pauline vocabulary.[50] Instone-Brewer suggests that Paul's words are "almost a paraphrase of *m. Baba Meṣiʿa* 7:2: 'These may eat [of the crop in which they labour] by virtue of what is enjoined in the Law: he who labours on what is still growing after the work is finished [i.e., from ploughing to reaping], and he who labours on what is already gathered before the work is finished [i.e., threshing].'" In fact he thinks it "likely that Paul had this specific mishnah in mind," which presumably existed in oral form in his day.[51] If Paul is summarizing an orally transmitted halakic interpretation of Deuteronomy 25:4 and related texts, it would explain the formalized language and its relationship to the prior citation.[52]

Paul argument may seem somewhat strange to our way of thinking, but in his context he is demonstrating tremendous skill as a biblical exegete. He knows how to address a very practical issue that is not explicitly discussed in Scripture (namely, the question of support for gospel workers) through a hermeneutically informed application of what might otherwise seem an obscure text. It is rhetorically powerful as an act of biblical interpretation and speaks both to the issue of his support and to that of his apostolic credentials as a divinely authorized interpreter of Scripture and the gospel. It also commends Scripture as a source of Christian moral instruction.

Paul's argument asserts that we should deduce from a proper interpretation of Deuteronomy 25:4 that Christian workers have a right to be supported in their ministries. Thus, it is not merely a matter of acceding to an affirmation of Paul's apostolic authority on this subject, but rather of learning to understand how Scripture should inform our ethical understanding of such issues.

**9:11** Paul expands upon the agricultural metaphor, describing gos-

50. See Stanley, *Paul and the Language of Scripture,* 197 n. 52.

51. D. Instone-Brewer, "1 Corinthians 9:9-11, A Literal Interpretation of 'Do Not Muzzle the Ox,'" *NTS* 38 (1992), 558. He provides clear evidence that by Paul's time "an 'ox' in Scripture implied any labourer, of any species of animal, including human" (564; cf. 559-64). Paul's words could reflect a loose citation or interpretation of Sir. 6:19, but it seems more likely that Sir. 6:19 simply reflects a similar traditional interpretation of Deuteronomy's teaching about oxen.

52. Cf. Instone-Brewer, "1 Corinthians 9:9-11," 558-59; K. Koch, *The Prophets,* vol. 2, *The Babylonian and Persian Period* (London: SCM, 1983), 42 n. 33.

pel workers as farmers: *If we have sown spiritual seed among you, is it too much if we reap a material harvest from you?* The suggestion that a *qal waḥomer* argument (or "argument from the lesser to the greater") is present in vv. 9-10 is strengthened by the observation that v. 11 operates by means of a reversed *qal waḥomer* argument: "If a labourer may eat of a valuable crop he is working on, much more should he be allowed to eat from a less valuable crop instead."[53]

The words translated *spiritual* and *material*[54] are part of a dichotomy that is frequently found in Paul between the "Spirit" and the "flesh" (or "sinful nature"). They are often taken to refer to a contrast between non-physical or immaterial reality and physical or material reality. Paul's wider usage of these terms, however, reflects an eschatological dualism contrasting the things and power of this age with those of the age to come. Fee thinks that we may see that contrast reflected here as well since the word translated material here "has to do with the material needs of this earthly life" while Paul's reference to having *sown spiritual seed* "refers to the gospel, in which the Spirit plays such a key role." Thus even here Paul is referring to the "things of the Spirit."[55] The Corinthians like to think of themselves as people of the Spirit, but they "must not forget who sowed among them the things of the Spirit that made it possible for them to be so."[56]

Paul highlights the irony of the contrast between what is sown and what is reaped with the word translated *too much* (literally, "a great thing" or a "big deal").[57] The great thing or big deal is not for Paul to *reap a material harvest* but for them to have received the spiritual seed which brought them to life in Christ! Chrysostom contends that it was "to prevent them from getting big[58] heads" that "Paul points out that while in other cases the seed is material and the fruit is as well, it is not that way here since the seed is spiritual but the return is material."

**9:12** Paul ties together the language of rights from vv. 4-6 with that of sharing in a harvest[59] from v. 10 in the rhetorical question at the beginning of this verse: *If others have* (or *share in*) *this right of support from you, shouldn't we have it all the more?* The contrast between *others* and *we* is signaled and stressed in the Greek text by placing them at the beginning and end of the question, respectively.[60]

We do not know who the *others* are who have received support from

53. Instone-Brewer, "1 Corinthians 9:9-11," 559; see his fuller discussion.

54. Gk. πνευματικός and σαρκικός. The same pair of words shows up in Rom. 15:27.

55. Gordon D. Fee, *God's Empowering Presence: The Holy Spirit in the Letters of Paul* (Peabody, MA: Hendrickson, 1994), 31-32.

56. Fee, *God's Empowering Presence*, 141.

57. Gk. μέγας. BDAG has, "Is it an extraordinary thing (i.e., are we expecting too much = our colloquial 'is it a big deal')."

58. Using μέγας for "big."

59. Gk. ἐξουσία and μετέχω, respectively.

60. "If others . . . not more we?" (Εἰ ἄλλοι . . . οὐ μᾶλλον ἡμεῖς;).

the Corinthians or had the right to such support.[61] The logic of Paul's statement implies that their right (whether or not they or the Corinthians have conceived of it as a right) is the same one to which Paul is entitled, suggesting that they are people who have carried out gospel ministry among the Corinthians. Still, since they were not the founders of the church, they are not as entitled to the right as Paul is.

In the second half of this verse Paul anticipates the point he has had in mind since the first verse of this chapter and that he will return to in v. 15: that despite having an unquestionable right to support from the Corinthians (the point of vv. 1-12a), he has not made use of that right due to his greater concern for the effectiveness of the gospel ministry. *But we did not use this right. On the contrary, we put up with anything rather than hinder the gospel of Christ.* He has not actually finished his set of arguments regarding his right to support (see vv. 13-14), but having mentioned others who had chosen to exercise their right to support in v. 12a, Paul anticipates in 12b the conclusion he will make in v. 15 by pointing out that he chose not to exercise that right. That Paul has taken a break from arguing that he has a right to support is signaled by the interruption in the series of rhetorical questions in v. 12b. That series will be completed in v. 13.

Paul and his colleagues *put up with all things rather than cause any hindrance to the gospel of Christ.* There is a contrast between *all things*[62] and *any hindrance*[63] that highlights the apostle's manner of assessing and applying the priority of the gospel. By *anything* Paul has especially in mind the extra difficulties they endured due to their willingness to forgo the exercise of certain rights for the sake of the gospel (especially the need to work for a living and go without the companionship of a wife).[64] Chrysostom picks up on the contrast. First he points out that Paul's hardships included the terrible things he refers to in 4:12, and he suggests that "by saying, 'we bear all

61. They may not be mentioned in the letter. Since Paul does mention a number of people who have evidently ministered among them, those mentioned are natural candidates (esp. Apollos, who is frequently mentioned and whose ministry among the Corinthians is compared to Paul's as a waterer following a planter [1:12; 3:4-6, 22; 4:6; 16:12], and Cephas/Peter [1:12; 3:22; 9:5; 15:5], who is mentioned in this very passage as one who has not needed to *put up with* all the deprivations Paul has experienced). Many think that Paul has in mind the pseudo-apostles mentioned in 2 Corinthians, and that may be correct. But although Paul does not exercise this right, he clearly considers it legitimate and would not necessarily look down on others who would take advantage of it. Paul does not actually say that they have exercised such a right; only that they might also have such a right (like Paul). It seems likely, however, that he is aware that some have received support from the Corinthians. In the context of the logic of Paul's question, the conditional clause certainly must refer to a real situation of which Paul is aware.

62. Gk. πάντα.

63. Gk. τινα ἐγκοπήν.

64. As BDAG points out, *all things* often refers to "a 'whole' that is implied fr[om] the context," citing Matt. 18:26; Mark 4:34; Luke 1:3; Rom. 8:28; 2 Cor. 6:10; Gal. 4:1; Phil. 2:14; 1 Thess. 5:21; 2 Tim. 2:10; Tit. 1:15; 1 John 2:27. Here the implied "whole" is all that they suffer due to their commitment to the priority of the gospel.

things,' he intimates both hunger and great straits and all the other things."[65] So the lengths to which Paul was willing to go were very great. Then, commenting on what Paul seeks to avoid, Chrysostom points out that Paul "did not say 'subversion' [a stronger word] but 'hindrance'; nor simply 'hindrance,' but 'any' hindrance." That was, he says, so as not to "cause so much as the slightest suspense and delay to the course of the Word."[66] So Paul is willing to go to the greatest lengths in order to avoid the very least of hindrances to the progress of *the gospel.* The *gospel* is mentioned for the first time here since 4:15, and it serves as the key to Paul's explanation of his decision to forgo the use of certain rights. The concept of the gospel is explicitly referred to in vv. 14 (x2), 16 (x2), 18 (x3), and 23, and it is the dominant concept in the remainder of the chapter. The primacy of the gospel trumps all other considerations when it comes to Paul's use of his rights. A gospel (evangelical) Christian is not someone who merely believes the gospel, but one whose life reflects gospel priorities.

The question remains, why did Paul feel the gospel might be hindered by receiving support from the Corinthians? He does not tell us. In the following verses he does discuss his need or desire to preach the gospel in a way that demonstrates that he is doing it willingly rather than as a result of being pressured, and that while he, in fact, has no choice but to preach the gospel, he does have a choice regarding the attitude with which he does it, and he chooses to demonstrate his pleasure to do so by not accepting support from those to whom he is ministering. But all of this does not really answer the question of why accepting support from the Corinthians could hinder the gospel.

Recent studies of friendship and its relationship to the patronage system in ancient Roman society have helped us understand a number of dynamics in early Christian worship and ministry that are rather foreign to our ways of doing things today. In Paul's context, the giving and receiving of gifts was part of a much larger system in which friendships and obligations were established, managed, and maintained.[67] Such friendships and obligations entailed commitments of loyalty, future favors, and privileged status with respect to those who were not part of the relationship. Peter Marshall explains: "The offer of a gift constituted an offer of friendship. While in theory it was voluntary and disinterested, it was intended to place the recipient under an obligation to repay. Acceptance was conditional; the

65. *Homiliae in Epistulam i ad Corinthios* 21.7 (NPNF[1] 12:122).

66. *Homiliae in Epistulam i ad Corinthios* 21.7 (NPNF[1] 12:122).

67. See Peter Marshall, *Enmity in Corinth: Social Conventions in Paul's Relations with the Corinthians* (WUNT 2.23; Tübingen: J. C. B. Mohr [Paul Siebeck], 1987), 1-34; John K. Chow, *Patronage and Power: A Study of Social Networks in Corinth* (JSNTSup 75; Sheffield: JSOT Press, 1992); Ronald F. Hock, *The Social Context of Paul's Ministry: Tentmaking and Apostleship* (Philadelphia: Fortress, 1980), 50-65. For a popular introduction to the subject of patronage in the Roman world see David A. deSilva, *Honor, Patronage, Kinship and Purity: Unlocking New Testament Culture* (Downers Grove, IL: InterVarsity Press, 2000), 95-119.

recipient must respond with a counter-gift or service, immediately or at some later time, and numerous and popular conventions governed the behaviour of both benefactor and recipient."[68] Through this system, "people of high status . . . used their wealth not only to cater for their social and economic needs, but to form alliances, to secure power, as a form of security and protection against personal and political enemies."[69]

Marshall points out that "[w]hether the leaders of one of the factions made the offer to Paul is not indicated. That similar offers were made to others (1 Cor. 9:11-12a) who accepted is known; that these recipients were made figureheads of the factions and the means of comparison and opposition to Paul is probable."[70] He has also suggested that some Corinthians offered a gift to Paul which was an offer of friendship but which also "represented the vested interests of a group for people from the higher ranks in Corinth who wished to put Paul under obligation to them."[71] Marshall's description of the patronage system, like most modern descriptions, may be overly prejudicial or cynical,[72] but even if the motivations of those offering the support were not so objectionable, such an offer would entail social consequences that could negatively impact Paul's ministry and the advance of the gospel. For Paul to accept such a gift would probably have suggested to the Corinthians and others, not only that they were friends, but also that they were Paul's patron and he their client. Such a perception would have had potentially disastrous results for the ministry of the gospel. Paul would no longer be free (cf. vv. 1, 19a) to be all things to all people (vv. 19b-22), but would be expected to be what his Corinthian patrons wished. He may also have not felt free to correct them as he saw fit. Others to whom he ministered (both within and outside the Corinthian church) could well think that he represented the interests of the Corinthians who supported him rather than God's interests or their own.

In fact, the language of vv. 13-18 (as well as much else in Paul's theology) strongly implies Paul's understanding that God is his patron, and he is under obligation to serve his agenda rather than anyone else's (see our comments in the introduction to ch. 12 and on 12:4-6). Paul's comment that the support he is entitled to would be merely material wealth while the Corinthians have received superior spiritual benefit from him (v. 11), along with the suggestion that he works for the Ultimate Patron, might have suggested to the Corinthians that any idea that they should be his patrons would be to get things backward.

**9:13** Paul returns to the use of rhetorical questions establishing his right to support, and to his favorite in this letter: *Don't you know?* (cf. 3:16;

68. P. Marshall, *Enmity in Corinth,* 242.

69. P. Marshall, *Enmity in Corinth,* 243.

70. P. Marshall, *Enmity in Corinth,* 232.

71. P. Marshall, *Enmity in Corinth,* 233.

72. deSilva's description of the patronage system (*Honor, Patronage, Kinship and Purity,* 95-119) is more sympathetic.

5:6; 6:2, 3, 9, 15, 16, 19; 9:13, 24). Once again there is a certain sting to the questions since some Corinthians evidently prided themselves on their knowledge. What they should know is *that those who serve in the temple get their food from the temple, and that those who serve at the altar share in what is offered on the altar.* They should know these things based on either their knowledge of the functioning of the temple in Jerusalem, or their knowledge of pagan temples which functioned in a similar manner with regard to the point at issue.

While vv. 7-11 established the right of support for gospel workers on the basis of a preestablished analogy with agricultural field-workers, vv. 13-14 establish the same right based on the parallel between the manner of support of those dedicated to sacred service elsewhere and those dedicated to the service of the gospel of Christ. Christians do not have a physical temple or priests dedicated to the service of one, but we do have apostles and gospel workers who have been called to dedicate their lives to the ministry of the gospel. Paul reminds the Corinthians how such people are supported, and in the following verse he states that the Lord established that gospel workers/preachers should be supported in a manner similar to temple workers. His statement that "those employed in the temple service" partake of the sacrificial offerings is a principle that was reflected in the administration of both the Jerusalem temple (Lev. 6:16-18, 26 [9-11, 19 HB]; 7:6-8; Num. 5:9-10; 18:8-20; Deut. 10:9; 18:1-5; 1 Sam. 2:28; 2 Chr. 31:4, etc.) and pagan temples. It is much more likely, however, that Paul has the Jerusalem temple and its priests in mind since the connection to the following verse ("so also")[73] probably implies that the Lord's teaching about the support of those who preach the gospel is based on the Old Testament pattern rather than merely (or accidentally) parallel to other religious practices.[74]

It is not clear whether Paul intends to distinguish two groups of people in the two different parts of this verse, or whether he is simply using two different expressions that stress the ongoing nature of the sacred. Garland follows Chrysostom, Héring, and Collins in suggesting that Paul may have in mind the distinction "between those who work in the temple precincts, such as the Levites in the Jewish temple, and priests who serve at the altar."[75]

Paul's point seems to be that those dedicated to divine service are

73. Gk. οὕτως καί.

74. The word used for "altar" here (θυσιαστήριον) generally refers to altars erected to the God of Israel in the LXX and New Testament. BDAG states that in this case it refers to "the altar of burnt offering in the inner forecourt of the temple at Jerusalem." Garland mistakenly identifies the word translated "serve" (παρεδρεύω) in the second half of the verse as one not found in the LXX, perhaps based on the incomplete information found in BAGD. BDAG properly identifies examples in Prov. 1:21; 8:3. The word is not a technical term related to worship, and although it is used by pagan authors in relation to the work of priests at pagan altars, Chrysostom clearly understood Paul to be discussing the Jewish temple.

75. Garland, 414. Cf. Chrysostom (NPNF[1] 12:126).

supported through that very service.[76] This support is not to be expected by anyone who serves God in some way or other, but only by those whose "working lives" are dedicated to the service of God. As Garland points out, the "cultic motif" with its references to temples and altars and the issue of worshipers sharing in the offerings "tie back into the central issue, food offered to idols. It also connects with the idea that those who eat the sacrifices are sharers in the altar — an idea he will develop in 10:18."[77]

**9:14** The parallel suggested between v. 14 and v. 13 by *in the same way* is reinforced by a syntactical parallelism between the verses as well.[78] The parallel highlights the relationship between preaching the gospel and serving in the temple or at the altar. The command of the Lord Paul refers to, *that those who preach the gospel should receive their living from the gospel,* is evidently based on the tradition recorded in Luke 10:7 and Matthew 10:10: "the laborer deserves to be paid." That saying, in the exact form recorded in Luke 10:7, is cited in 1 Timothy 5:18 following a citation of Deuteronomy 25:4. It was on the basis of this teaching that Jesus sent out his disciples without support. Luke 10:7 explicitly mentions "eating and drinking" what others provide them (cf. 1 Cor. 9:4). As Fee points out, "the casual way in which Paul introduces" Jesus' teaching suggests that the Corinthians may have already been familiar with it.[79] The word for "laborer"[80] in Luke 10:7 and Matthew 10:10 was especially used to refer to agricultural laborers (BDAG). As such, the agricultural analogy Paul used in the previous verses is consistent with Jesus' approach.

There has been some discussion of whether or not Paul should have complied with the Lord's "command." D. L. Dungan has argued that Paul disobeyed or set aside Christ's command.[81] As Fee points out, however, the command Paul is referring to "does not have to do with his [Paul's] action but theirs" since it "is not given *to* the missionaries, but *for* their benefit."[82] The whole thrust of Paul's argument from v. 4 onward suggests that "Paul did not understand himself to be disobeying a decree from the Lord, but interpreted it as a right that he was free to accept or refuse."[83]

76. Harry Nasuti has argued that in this passage Paul moves from mere physical reward for normal human labor to the idea of spiritual reward for spiritual service ("The Woes of the Prophets and the Rights of the Apostle: The Internal Dynamics of 1 Corinthians 9," *CBQ* 50 [2001], 251-54). Paul's point, however, is that he has refrained from exercising his right to material support from the Corinthians. He clearly hopes to receive some reward for that service.

77. Garland, 414.

78. The content of the Lord's command in v. 14 closely parallels the syntactical structures found in the previous verse.

79. Fee, 413.

80. Gk. ἐργάτης.

81. See D. L. Dungan, *The Sayings of Jesus in the Churches of Paul* (Philadelphia: Fortress, 1971), 3-40.

82. Fee, 413 n. 96 (emphasis his).

83. Garland, 415.

Paul's reference here to Jesus' teaching about support, taken with other evidence within this letter and elsewhere, indicates that he knows more about Jesus than simply of his death and resurrection. That Paul would cite Jesus' teaching to clinch the argument implies that the weight both Paul and his readers placed on the teaching of the Lord and, consequently, that Paul would have been familiar with more of his teaching than one might otherwise suppose based on the number of references to it in his letters.

As Schrage points out, the word *gospel* has two somewhat different meanings in this verse.[84] As the object of the verb "to preach" or "proclaim," it refers to "the content of the gospel, the message of salvation through Jesus Christ." In the final phrase of the verse, *live from the gospel,* however, the word *gospel* serves as a verbal noun referring to the act of proclamation of that message (thus in the second half of the sentence the word *gospel* serves as shorthand for the fuller expression *preach the gospel* in the prior clause). Nasuti (followed by others) has suggested that Paul may also have had two different meanings in mind by the final expression, *to live from the gospel.* He argues that with vv. 13-14 Paul switches from an emphasis on material support to the idea of spiritual rewards that are accrued by those in God's service.[85] Garland follows him in suggesting that Paul may mean that "the preacher also receives spiritual sustenance from the gospel."[86] However, BDAG provides evidence that "*to live from* (something)" is to "obtain one's living fr[om] someth[ing]."[87] Furthermore, Paul goes on in v. 15 to say that he has not made use of or employed the rights he has referred to in this and the previous verses. It seems unlikely that he would say that he has not exercised the right to live from the gospel in the sense of drawing spiritual life from it or that he has not benefited spiritually from his ministry.

Fee properly reminds us that Paul is compelled to establish his right to material support as a prelude to his defense of his decision not to exercise that right. "Contemporary ministers," on the other hand, "seldom feel compelled so to argue!" Although Paul tends to be the primary reference point for many evangelical thinkers, he has not often served as a model in terms of his refusal of support, despite Hafemann's point that Paul "intended his apostolic life-style to be an authoritative standard for his churches."[88] As Fee correctly reminds us, "the key . . . must be for us what it was for Paul — 'no hindrance to the gospel.'" Of course, Paul's situation, as

84. Cf. Schrage, 2:309.

85. Nasuti, "The Woes of the Prophets," 250-53.

86. Garland, 416.

87. Gk. ζῆν ἔκ τινος. BDAG cites Aristophanes, *Ecclesiazusae* 591; Demosthenes, *Contra Eubulidem* 36 (57.36); Papyrus Oxyrhyncus 1117, 19; 1557, 12; *Testament of Job* 47:1, 2, as well as this verse.

88. Scott J. Hafemann, *Suffering and the Spirit* (WUNT 2.19; Tübingen: J. C. B. Mohr [Paul Siebeck], 1986), 129.

a traveling apostle ministering in a variety of situations and to very different groups of people (cf. vv. 20-22), while navigating through the potential complications of the Roman system of patronage, was rather distinct from that of most ministers of the gospel in both the first and twenty-first centuries. Most ministers today live on quite modest salaries. When others become known for opulent lifestyles or justify luxurious salaries on the basis of Paul's argument here, "the objective of this text is lost" due to an attitude that reflects "bald professionalism rather than a concern for the gospel itself."[89] Chrysostom highlights the relationship between v. 13a ("eat from the temple") and 14b ("live from the gospel"). "Just as there [it is written] 'to eat,' here [it is written] 'to live'; not to engage in business or build up treasures." Clearly "to live" or "make a living" suggested a way of subsisting, not of gaining wealth.

### *c. Paul Refuses to Exploit His Right to Support, 9:15-18*

**9:15** With this verse begins the section where Paul focuses on the main point he anticipated in v. 12b. *But I have not used*[90] *any of these rights. And I am not writing*[91] *this*[92] *in the hope that you will do such things for me, for I would rather die than allow anyone to deprive me of this boast.* Paul "wants to eliminate the possibility that the Corinthians might take his extended defense of the legitimacy of being paid as an apostle in 9:6-14 to be a hidden plea that he too now be paid by the Corinthians."[93] His third sentence contains an anacoluthon (grammatical break): "I would rather die than — no one will deprive me of my grounds for boasting!" (cf. NET).[94] The emotional weight suggested by both what Paul says and the grammatical break indicating his inability or unwillingness to complete the thought support the conclusion that "there is nothing more important to Paul, even his very life, than the fact that he offers his gospel free of charge."[95] The decision to preach the gospel free of charge entailed significant sacrifice on Paul's part since it meant that he would have to support himself through labor in addition to his gospel ministry.

89. Fee, 414.

90. If there is any distinction between Paul's use of the perfect tense here (κέχρημαι) and his use of the aorist in v. 12, it may be simply that that perfect form has slightly more prominence (or stress) than the aorist (see Campbell, *Basics of Verbal Aspect*, 111).

91. On the epistolary aorist (ἔγραψα), see our comments on 5:11.

92. Paul uses demonstrative pronouns and an adverb to tie this verse back to the previous argumentation: *these rights* (τούτων) are the ones defended in vv. 4-14; *this/these things* (ταῦτα) which he wrote refers to the same verses, as does the reference to *such things* (οὕτως), which he is not hoping they will do.

93. Hafemann, *Suffering and the Spirit*, 138.

94. Technically this is called aposiopesis — "a sudden breaking off of a thought in the middle of a sentence, as though the speaker were unwilling or unable to continue." There are some variants in the MSS, but the external support for this reading (including $\mathfrak{P}^{46}$, א*, B, D*c, 33, 1739, 1881; b; Tertullian, Ambrosiaster, and Pelagius) is strong, and internal evidence indicates that the other readings arose as attempts to smooth out Paul's grammar.

95. Hafemann, *Suffering and the Spirit*, 138.

The language Paul uses in vv. 15-18 reflects both similarities to and differences from the experiences of the prophets of Israel. Nasuti has pointed out that Paul's language echoes the language prophets sometimes used in response to the sufferings they or others would experience as a result of their prophetic ministry.[96] The prophets suffered terribly for their ministries, and some, like Jeremiah, bemoaned the suffering inherent in the prophetic ministry. Paul does not bemoan his suffering, however, but boasts of it! Jeremiah is so disturbed by the message he has to communicate that he wishes he had never been born (Jer. 15:10; 20:14-18). Paul would rather die than give up his ministry of preaching the gospel freely.[97] Paul did not think of his extra work as suffering or sacrifice. It was his *boast* or *glory*! The Corinthians did not want to be deprived of their freedom to eat whatever food they might. Paul does not mind depriving himself of the right to material support; in fact he insists on it. What he will not let anyone do is deprive him of the privilege he has of preaching the gospel without charge, since the gospel is the ultimate priority of his life. He insisted on a course of action by which the priority he himself gave to the advance of the gospel would be clearly manifest to all.

**9:16** Paul continues his explanation of his decision to preach the gospel without asking for support, and why his particular approach is so important to him. *For when I preach the gospel, I cannot boast, since I am compelled to preach. Woe to me if I do not preach the gospel!* The verse consists of two conditional statements that discuss the implication for Paul of either preaching or not preaching the gospel.[98] On the one hand, if he does preach the gospel (and the reader knows that he does), he has nothing to boast about, since he does not have a choice in the matter; he is compelled to do so. On the other hand, if he does not preach the gospel, he will face the ultimate calamity.[99] Both parts reinforce the same idea: Paul does not really have any choice in the matter of *whether* he will preach the gospel or not.

His description of his compulsion to preach the gospel reflects the prophetic call on his life. As Hafemann and others have pointed out, "in speaking of the 'constraint' laid upon him, Paul is portraying his own apostolic experience of preaching the gospel in terms of the experience of those OT prophets who felt compelled to deliver the divine message entrusted to them, regardless of their own desire, or lack of desire to do so."[100] As Abra-

96. Nasuti, "The Woes of the Prophets," 256-58.

97. Cf. Nasuti, "The Woes of the Prophets," 258.

98. The contrast is highlighted syntactically by placing the opposing elements at the beginning and end of the verse: *"if I preach the gospel . . . if I do not preach the gospel"* (ἐὰν γὰρ εὐαγγελίζωμαι, . . . ἐὰν μὴ εὐαγγελίσωμαι).

99. In some contexts a "woe" (οὐαί) may refer to the most dreadful human hardship. In most cases, however, esp. in the prophets and the New Testament, it refers to the calamity of divine judgment. Cf. vv. 23-27.

100. Hafemann, *Suffering and the Spirit*, 138-39. Hafemann (139 n. 130) points to Jer.

ham Joshua Heschel puts it, "The prophet does not volunteer for his mission; it is forced upon him. He is seduced, he is overwhelmed. There is no choice."[101] Paul's role as preacher of the gospel is not something he has chosen for himself, but a task which has been assigned to him by God. Since Paul has no choice in the matter, but is compelled or constrained[102] to preach the gospel, he cannot boast or take any special pride in the fact that he does so.

Nasuti has suggested that Paul's exclamation, *Woe to me if I do not preach the gospel!* entails an inversion of the self-directed woe sometimes declared by biblical prophets (related to Jeremiah's wish that he had never been born; Paul's preference to die).[103] Jeremiah declared a woe on himself (Jer. 10:19; 15:10; 45:3) for being constrained to proclaim the message of judgment entrusted to him by the Lord. Paul declares a woe on himself if he does *not preach the gospel.* His master has entrusted him with a mission, and he cannot refuse to fulfill it. "The servant sent by the Lord does what he has to do even if he is not willing, because if he does not do it he will suffer for it. Moses preached to Pharaoh even though he did not want to, and Jonah was forced to preach to the Ninevites."[104] Of course, Paul is happy to carry out his commission, and insists on adopting a way of going about it that communicates his eagerness to fulfill his calling. A key difference between Paul and Jeremiah is found in the fact that Paul does not find himself, like Jeremiah, at the stage of salvation history where judgment and exile are the key messages. He has the privilege of preaching the message of salvation to all nations. Paul's message is one that brings salvation (rather than judgment) to all the groups he mentions in vv. 19-22, and he is happy to do whatever he must for the sake of the gospel in order that he "may share with them in its blessings" (9:23).

**9:17** Like the previous verse, this one also consists of two contrasting conditional sentences.[105] *If I preach voluntarily, I have a reward; if not vol-*

20:9 as well as Jer. 4:19; Isa. 21:3; Amos 3:8; Mic. 3:8, and the "hand of God" motif found in Isa. 8:11; 10:10; 28:2; Jer. 15:17; Ezek. 3:14, 24; 37:1. On Paul's prophetic self-understanding see also Sandnes, *Paul — One of the Prophets?;* and R. E. Ciampa, *The Presence and Function of Scripture in Galatians 1 and 2,* 111-15.

101. Abraham Joshua Heschel, *The Prophets* (New York: Harper & Row, 1962), 2:224.

102. BDAG defines ἀνάγκη as "necessity or constraint inherent in the nature of things," which sounds rather like impersonal fate. Louw and Nida render it "an obligation of a compelling nature." Hafemann is correct to emphasize that what Paul has in mind is not "the inescapable 'necessity' of an impersonal fate, but is rather the 'necessity' or 'constraint' which results from the call of God itself" (*Suffering and the Spirit,* 139).

103. Nasuti, "The Woes of the Prophets." In the context of his vision of the throne of God (Isa. 6:5), Isaiah declares a woe on himself due to his sinfulness and that of the people of Israel which would inevitably lead to judgment (though Isaiah himself is spared through the intervention of the angel in vv. 6-7). Other such woes include Isa. 24:16; Jer. 10:19; 15:10; and 45:4.

104. Ambrosiaster, cited in Bray, 84.

105. The verse is tied to the previous one by the γάρ, which indicates that Paul will expand on his obligation to preach, and by the demonstrative pronoun, literally *if I do this willingly* (*this* [τοῦτο] = what I was just discussing in the prior verse, namely, preach the gospel).

*untarily, I am simply discharging the trust committed to me.*[106] While the previous verse contrasted the implications of preaching versus not preaching the gospel (making it clear that Paul has no choice but to preach the gospel), this one refers to two different conditions under which one might carry out such a task, as a free person who chooses to accept a given task, or as a slave who is given a task by the master and does not have the luxury of choosing his own projects. The former carries out his work *voluntarily,* while the task is imposed on the latter. The former is entitled to a reward for what he does, while the latter is not.[107] Paul falls under the latter category, not the former. As God's trusted slave, steward of his household, Paul is not entitled to a reward (or entitled to boast) for carrying out his assigned task.[108] Paul is not referring to his personal attitude toward the task, but reinforcing the understanding that he does not carry out his work on his own initiative.[109] Even if Paul were not disposed to preach the gospel on his own initiative, he would still have to do so, since his master has entrusted him with this commission/task. The language Paul uses of being entrusted with a task would normally be used in reference to a slave or a freedman still under the authority of his master, one who executes tasks without expecting to be thanked or rewarded.[110]

**9:18** Paul expands on his reference to a reward from the previous verse. *What then is my reward? Just this: that in preaching the gospel I may offer it free of charge, and so not misuse my rights as a preacher of the gospel.* It is not clear what *reward* Paul has in mind in these verses. Most take it to be an example of a Pauline paradox, "my reward is to receive no reward."[111]

Hafemann and Gardner, among others, strongly argue that it refers to the eschatological reward Paul expects from the Lord.[112] As Gardner points

106. *Committed to me* reflects the perfect indicative πεπίστευμαι, and points to Paul's present status as one entrusted with a commission or task.

107. Fee, 419.

108. Cf. Hafemann, *Suffering and the Spirit,* 140-42. Paul has already identified himself as a servant of Christ and steward/administrator of the mysteries of God, who must be faithful to his task (cf. 4:1-2).

109. The two Greek words (ἑκών and ἄκων) could be translated "willingly" and "unwillingly" (cf. Louw and Nida), but that would mislead most readers, since the issue is not whether the person is willing but whether they are free to pick and choose their tasks according to their own will. Thiselton's suggested translation gets it right, contrasting that which is "entirely by personal choice" with that which "does not arise from my own initiative" (Thiselton, 676, 696).

110. Gk. οἰκονομία. Cf. *TLNT* 2:569 n. 5; Garland, 426; Dale B. Martin, *Slavery as Salvation: The Metaphor of Slavery in Pauline Christianity* (New Haven: Yale University Press, 1990), 74; BDAG, "I have been entrusted with a commission/task"; *EDNT* 2:499, "managerial activity in connection with certain [entrusted] affairs."

111. Conzelmann, 158, citing Wettstein; cf. Ernst Käsemann, *New Testament Questions of Today* (Philadelphia: Fortress, 1969), 223; Schrage, 2:326; Garland, 426.

112. Hafemann, *Suffering and the Spirit,* 142-43; Paul D. Gardner, *The Gifts of God and the Authentication of a Christian: An Exegetical Study of 1 Corinthians 8-11:1* (Lanham, MD: University Press of America, 1994), 94.

out, Paul's "woe" in v. 16 has an eschatological connotation and in 3:8, 14 the word "wage/reward" also has eschatological overtones. Clearly the last part of this passage (vv. 23-27) is marked by a focus on eschatological rewards. Hafemann helpfully distinguishes Paul's two categories of (1) preaching per se and (2) preaching free of charge and suggests that while there is no reward for the former, a reward is expected for the latter.[113] He outlines the two as follows:

| **Preaching per se** | **Preaching free of charge** |
|---|---|
| Done by compulsion | No compulsion to do so |
| Not voluntary (at one's discretion) | Voluntary (at one's discretion) |
| Woe if not done (no reward expected if done) | Reward expected if done |
| An imposed task | A ground for boasting |

In his view, although Paul expects no reward for preaching the gospel (since that task has been entrusted to him by his master), he does expect a reward for preaching the gospel free of charge, since that was not required of him. Hafemann helpfully points out that "Paul's summary statement in I Cor. 9:18 is therefore best interpreted as a restatement of verse 15, with Paul's question in verse 18a taken to refer to that for which he expects to be paid in the last judgment."[114] It certainly would make sense for Paul to understand his strategy as outlined in v. 18b to be that for which he will be rewarded. What he says, however, is not that he will be rewarded for taking his approach to ministry, but that his reward is to carry out his ministry in the way he does. It may be that Paul is employing metonymy, with the word "reward"[115] signifying the basis for a reward, but the word has not been used that way elsewhere. The connection to v. 15, however, is important, since, as Fee and Schrage point out, Paul's description of his "reward" in this verse is parallel to his reference to his "boast" in that one.[116] It does not follow, however, that Paul's eschatological reward is in sight. Rather, Paul says that his reward is *Just this: that in preaching the gospel I may offer it free of charge, and so not use my rights as a preacher of the gospel.* He considers the privilege of preaching the gospel free of charge (the privilege of not exercising his right) reward in and of itself and the source or basis of his pride.[117]

113. Hafemann, *Suffering and the Spirit,* 143 (cf. his argument in 142-43).

114. Hafemann, *Suffering and the Spirit,* 143.

115. Gk. μισθός.

116. Cf. Fee, 421, "the way the argument is structured implies that his 'pay' and his 'boast' refer to the same reality, preaching the gospel without accepting support so as to put no hindrance before the gospel." Similarly, Schrage, 2:325-26.

117. While μισθός ("reward") is not used elsewhere for the basis for a reward, καύχημα ("boast") is regularly used for the basis for one's boast (cf. Rom. 4:2; 2 Cor. 1:14; 5:12; Gal. 6:4; Phil. 1:26; 2:16), and the ESV, NRSV, NET, and NLT all translate it that way in this verse.

The word translated *misuse*[118] in the TNIV and "use" in other translations is related to the word[119] translated "use" or "employ" in vv. 12 and 15, and its meaning "differs little, if at all" (BDAG) from that of the simpler form used in those verses. The word itself means to use, employ, or take advantage of someone or something. The context, not this word, is the key to deciding whether such usage is or would be appropriate or not.[120] Since Paul has already said, twice (in vv. 12 and 15), that he has not used the right to which he was properly entitled, it seems best to understand him to be reinforcing that point here again.[121]

Paul's reward is the privilege of "offering the 'free' gospel 'free of charge,'" and in doing so "his own ministry becomes a living paradigm of the gospel itself."[122] If the Corinthians learn from Paul, they will reconsider their ardent defense of the eating practices that have endangered the spiritual health and survival of their brothers and sisters in Christ. The reward they ought to be pursuing is not that of being able to eat food sacrificed to idols, but the privilege of freely abstaining so that the gospel might not be hindered. That would hardly approximate the kind of commitment Paul showed them (and others) by working to support and feed himself rather than be supported by them, but it would reflect the preeminence of the gospel in their moral reasoning. As Thiselton, puts it:

> if Paul cannot "freely" give his apostolic work (since to this he is pressed by God without choice), what is left to give "freely" is his toil and labor as a leather worker and salesman in the commercial agora. This he gives to relieve others of bearing his costs and more especially avoiding the obligations of patronage which might compromise his voice on behalf of less influential groups within the church.[123]

*d. Paul Refuses to Exploit His Apostolic Status and Freedom, 9:19-23*

**9:19** At this point in his argument Paul goes back to his initial statement in v. 1 where he affirmed his freedom as an apostle of Christ. *Though I am free and belong to no one, I have made myself a slave to everyone, to win as many as possible.* He has established his freedom to accept support and explained why he does not do so, namely, for the sake of the gos-

118. Gk. καταχράομαι.

119. Gk. χράομαι.

120. That the same word would have the lexical meaning of "use" or "misuse" is linguistically unlikely (despite the lexicons). The texts cited in support of the usage "misuse" indicate that it was inappropriate not by the use of this word, but by referring, in the immediate context, to something that should not be or should not have been used or employed.

121. The NIV translates "make use," while the ESV, NRSV, NET, and NASB translate "make full use" and the NLT suggests "never demanding." The question is whether the compound form of the verb makes a subtle change to the meaning.

122. Fee, 421.

123. Thiselton, 697.

pel.[124] The discussion of his right to material support (to eat and drink) is embedded within the larger discussion of his personal and apostolic freedom in general and his decision to freely enslave himself to others for their benefit.

Paul's relationship to *everyone* (literally, "all") is stressed by the way the two main parts of the opening clause of this verse end and begin, respectively, with different forms of the word "all."[125] There is an implied concessive relationship[126] between his status as a free person (*though* I am free) and his decision to enslave himself (the two key Greek words "free" and "I enslave myself" begin and end the clause, providing a chiastic structure[127]). The TNIV has helpfully clarified Paul's statement that he is "free from all people"[128] by pointing out that to be free from someone is not to belong to them. Thus *I am free and belong to no one.* The slave-free dualism was as basic to Roman society as the Jew-Gentile dualism was to Jewish thought. According to the *Institutes* of the Roman jurist Gaius (second century A.D.), the "principal distinction made by the law of persons is this: that all human beings are either free or slaves."[129] "In the ancient Greek and Roman world, the polarity between 'slave' and 'free' seemed as natural a way of dividing up the human race as those between men and women or young and old."[130] For a person to become a slave was to give up their identity and experience what has been referred to as "social death."[131] Essentially "the slave serves as surrogate body for the slaveholder."[132]

In the context of the foregoing argument we might add that there is more than one sense in which Paul does not belong to anyone (besides the Lord). He is no one's slave, but he is also free from the entanglements that

124. See the discussion of the structure of this chapter at the beginning of the commentary on it.

125. "Being free of all (πάντων) to all (πᾶσιν) I have enslaved myself."

126. The concession is communicated through the adverbial participle (ὤν) in combination with the logical relationship between the clauses themselves.

127. "Being free (Ἐλεύθερος γὰρ ὤν)
of all people (ἐκ πάντων)
to all people (πᾶσιν)
I have enslaved myself (ἐμαυτὸν ἐδούλωσα)."

128. The form used for *all* (πάντων) could mean all people or all things, but several elements of the context make it clear that Paul has all people in mind (e.g., the proximity to πᾶσιν ["to all"], which refers to people in this case, and the reference to enslaving himself to people).

129. *Institutes* 1.8; cited in Thomas Wiedemann, *Greek and Roman Slavery* (London: Routledge, 1981), 24.

130. Wiedemann, *Greek and Roman Slavery,* 15.

131. Cf. O. Patterson, *Slavery and Social Death: A Comparative Study* (Cambridge, MA: Harvard University Press, 1982); John Byron, "Paul and the Background of Slavery: The *Status Quaestionis* in New Testament Scholarship," *Currents in Biblical Research* 3 (2004), 119-20, 123.

132. Glancy, *Slavery in Early Christianity,* 10.

would come with obligations to wealthy patrons who might have accepted him as a client. He does not belong to the knowledgeable in Corinth, or to any other patron or special interest group that might wish to own him. Shockingly, even though he is not obligated to any particular person or group, he has decided to act as the slave of all of them! "Since as Christ's slave (household manager) he cannot receive 'pay' (vv. 17-18), he is thereby also 'free' from all people (i.e., free from the restrictions that patronage might impose), so that he may 'freely' become the 'slave' of all."[133] The decision to become a slave for the sake of the salvation of others reflects the pattern established by Christ.[134]

Paul's self-identification as a slave also helps us understand why he had no qualms about working as a manual laborer among the Corinthians. Since such laborers were deemed to be "low-lifes" by the culturally elite, Paul's practice of self-support by that means had already raised the issue of the propriety of his lifestyle. His ultimate concern for the gospel and utter lack of concern for the social prejudices of others could hardly be stated more bluntly than to say that for the sake of the gospel he, though free, willingly became the slave of all.

What Paul means by his outlandish metaphorical reference to making himself *a slave to everyone* is explained in the following verses. One does not usually think of slavery as a position of influence. Paul's language throughout this section continues the idea of the inversion of values that he introduced earlier in the letter when discussing the wisdom of the cross versus the wisdom of this world. Paul adopts the position of the powerless slave to bring salvation to those he serves. "Paul does not lead from a secure position above others but from a position below them, incarnating the folly of the cross."[135] One can only imagine how a member of the Corinthian elite might respond to the idea that another free person would willingly become their slave in order to save them. It has been suggested that a free person might sell themselves into slavery "to pay off debt, to secure a more stable life or to climb socially."[136] Paul makes him a slave of all not to gain some advantage for himself but for those he would serve.[137] As Chrysostom points

133. Fee, 423.

134. So, among others, Fee, 426.

135. Garland, 429.

136. James S. Jeffers, *The Greco-Roman World of the New Testament: Exploring the Background of Early Christianity* (Downers Grove, IL: InterVarsity Press, 1999). Jeffers thinks it "likely that Erastus, the Christian and city treasurer of Corinth (Rom 16:23), had to sell himself temporarily into slavery to the city in order to hold this important position." For a careful discussion of the (rather weak) evidence regarding self-sale, see Glancy, *Slavery in Early Christianity*, 80-85.

137. Cf. Cyril of Alexandria's comment (his Letter 76), cited in Bray, 84, that Paul acted "not in order that he might gain some sort of advantage but that, with the loss of a part, he might gain all." Clement speaks of Christians who surrendered themselves to slavery so that others might be freed with the money which was paid for them (*1 Clement* 55:2). Did they get the idea from Paul's language here?

out, Paul's attitude reflects his "zeal and love for Christ" and his "insatiable desire for the salvation of mankind."[138]

Although Paul is free of all and has enslaved himself to all, he knows that he will not be able to save all people, so the final clause of the verse indicates that his strategy is intended *to win as many as possible.*[139] The same verb[140] appears four more times in the next three verses, and only one other time in Paul's writings (Phil. 3:8). It usually means to "*gain, derive profit* or *advantage*" (LSJ) through business of some sort. As Siede points out, in this and the following verses it "corresponds with 'saving' in 1 Cor. 9:22" and refers to "the goal of missionary work" (as it is also used in Matt. 18:15 and 1 Pet. 3:1).[141] Paul's intentional approach to ministry never loses its focus on the priority of reaching others with the gospel message. Just prior to this chapter he had to admonish the Corinthians for behavior that could cause someone to stumble and fall short of salvation (8:9-13).

**9:20** In this and the next two verses Paul clarifies what it means to make himself a slave of all people. His explanation has to do with the way he ministers in different contexts to different kinds of people. He takes as examples Jews (v. 20a), those under the law (v. 20b), those outside the law (v. 21), and the weak (v. 22a). Verse 22b indicates that these are just a few examples of Paul's adaptive mission strategy. The first three examples Paul uses are drawn from the most basic differences among those to whom he ministers (Jews, by birth or choice, and Gentiles). The fourth example, the weak, is chosen due to its direct relevance to Paul's discussion of food offered to idols in ch. 8 and the contrast it draws between his own approach to such people and that of some of the Corinthians. While the first two categories are Jewish categories, it may be that the latter two are generally Gentile categories (since the weak of ch. 8 are accustomed to idols).

It has been suggested that the passage reflects a chiastic arrangement. Garland sets out the following:

A I made myself a slave to all in order that I might gain more (v. 19).
  B I became to the Jews as a Jew, in order that I might gain Jews (v. 20a).
    C To those under the law as [one] under the law . . . to gain those under the law (v. 20b).
    C′ To those outside the law as [one] outside the law . . . to gain those outside the law (v. 21).

138. *Homiliae in Epistulam i ad Corinthios* (NPNF[1] 12:128).

139. Gk. τοὺς πλείονας could also be translated "more people," as in the ESV and NRSV. Either way, Paul's intention is clear: more people would be won to Christ by his strategy than if he were to set a higher priority to his rights than to the ministry of the gospel.

140. Gk. κερδαίνω.

141. B. Siede, "κέρδος," *NIDNTT* 3:137. D. Daube, "κερδαίνω as a Missionary Term," *HTR* 40 (1947), 109-20, argues for a background in early Jewish missionary terminology.

B′ I became to the weak weak in order that I might gain the weak (v. 22a).

A′ I have become all things to all persons in order that I might in all circumstances save some of them (v. 22b).[142]

The parallels are clear enough between A and A′ as well as between C and C′, while that between B and B′ is not (the evidence of the rest of the letter does not support the idea that the "weak" serve as either a synonym or antonym of "Jews"). It may work better to collapse B and C together as Jewish categories and C′ and B′ as fundamentally Gentile categories (as suggested above), as follows:

A I made myself a slave to all in order that I might gain more (v. 19).

B I became to the Jews as a Jew, in order that I might gain Jews; to those under the law as [one] under the law . . . to gain those under the law (v. 20).

C To those outside the law as [one] outside the law . . . to gain those outside the law; I became weak to the weak in order that I might gain the weak (vv. 21-22a).

A′ I have become all things to all persons in order that I might in all circumstances save some of them (v. 22b).

The weak, mentioned in v. 22, do not represent a generally recognized group of people like the others, but evidently do represent a subgroup within the church (according to our interpretation of the previous chapter). The parallel between 9:19-22 and 10:32-33[143] leads to the possibility that Paul's categories here reflect those given in 10:32, where he appeals to the Corinthians to avoid giving offense to Jews, Greeks [Gentiles], or the church of God, with the weak referred to in ch. 8 being the part of the church of God most likely to be offended by the rest of the Corinthians.

The logical relationship between being a slave to all people (v. 19) and becoming like them (vv. 20-23) would have been clear to the Corinthians. As Wiedemann puts it, a slave "was an outsider who brought no rights with him from the society he came from, and had no claims on the society which maintained him. The extent of this deracination is symbolised by the fact that he had to accept the religion of his new owner's household."[144] While Paul would not adopt the religions of those among whom he worked, he would adapt himself to his environment as much as his faith would allow, much as a slave would be expected to adjust to the cultural reality of the family they served.

142. Garland, 427.

143. These two texts are the two places in this section that use the verb "to save" (σῴζω).

144. Wiedemann, *Greek and Roman Slavery*, 33.

Paul has divided up humanity (in vv. 20b-21) with a version of the standard Jewish dualism; one is either under the law of Moses or outside that law. Yet he does not place himself within either or any of the categories he uses. His statement, *To the Jews I became like a Jew, to win the Jews* seems especially strange coming from the pen of a Jew.[145]

This way of putting it "shows how radically he conceives the claim that in Christ he is 'free with respect to all,' that is, in a position transcending all cultural allegiances." His expressions *like a Jew* and *like one under the law* are "especially revealing of Paul's theology of the new creation."[146] Paul's way of qualifying his adaptation to those under the law and those outside the law reveals an understanding of his identity in Christ that transcends all others and that refuses to be lost or dictated by his roles as a slave of others.

As pointed out above, Paul's self-description also matches that of a slave whose cultural adaptation is part of his job requirements. A slave captured through war and sold to a Roman household will be expected to adapt to the Roman culture of the household. If sold to a Jewish household or a household of another cultural background, he or she will need to adapt to the culture of that new household, to become like them. The slave's cultural adaptability is a reflection of the requirements of his life's situation, but the fact that Paul sees himself having to adjust to whatever cultural context he might minister within (whether Jewish or Gentile) reflects the transcendent identity flowing from his participation in a greater reality (new creation). Paul has willingly and strategically placed himself in the role of such a slave because he sees that such an approach, though extremely difficult for him to carry out, is of strategic advantage for the gospel.

Paul's determination to adapt himself to the different cultures and contexts in which he would work established a basic mission strategy reflective of an important understanding of the relationship between the gospel and culture that has been essential to effective mission work throughout history. The Christian church could have simply decided that the gospel was a Jewish message sent throughout the world and that a proper response to the gospel should result in adopting the same cultural incarnation in all places. In that way Christians would all look and act the same, all have the same culture, wherever (or whenever) they lived. Paul understands that the gospel does not belong to any particular culture. As the gospel takes root among different peoples and cultures, its essence will remain the same but its "look and feel" may be somewhat different.

Paul's ability to adapt his life and culture according to the context in which he worked would have been strategic not only for the initial communication of the gospel but also for the ability of his converts to understand what it would look like for them to become members of Christ's body. Gen-

145. Cf. Gal. 1:13-14; 2:15; Rom. 11:1; Phil. 3:5; 2 Cor. 11:22; Acts 21:39; 22:3; 23:6.
146. Thiselton, 702.

tile converts would not have to adopt Jewish culture to be members of Christ's community, and Jewish converts to Christ would not need to become Gentiles or reject their Jewish heritage and lifestyle as part of their recognition of Christ's lordship.

The word *Jew(s)* often has a "focus on adherence to Mosaic tradition," suggesting "conformity to Israel's ancestral belief and practice" (BDAG). By *Jews* here Paul means the same thing, or nearly the same thing, as he does by *those under the law.* The latter phrase might more clearly include Jewish proselytes than the former (so Theodore of Mopsuestia). Although Paul is a Jew in terms of his ethnicity and heritage, he no longer understands himself to be part of Judaism, and would not consider himself a Jew if that word is defined by those who understand their relationship with God to be based on their adherence to the Mosaic covenant.[147] To become like a Jew in order to win Jews would entail adapting his language and lifestyle to better communicate the gospel message in way that would not seem foreign to one who (like Paul) was raised in a Jewish household.

Today many Jews would certainly feel, upon attending a Christian church, that they would need to jettison key aspects of their cultural and ethnic heritage in order to be assimilated into a Gentile-dominated Christian culture. To many people, nonethnic churches of the West may seem more like the Borg of the *Star Trek* films, which assimilated all people and cultures into one utilitarian culture in which all diversity was eliminated, than the amazingly diverse body of Christ of which Paul speaks in his letters. Of course there is no reason why the gospel (or its incarnation in the church) should seem foreign to a Jew, since it is an essentially Jewish message that first took root among Jews. Acts 16:1-3 and 21:20-26 are suggestive of Luke's understanding of how Paul would become like a Jew for the sake of the Jews, even if the latter text deals with an event after Paul wrote this letter.

Would the socially influential members of the Corinthian church have expected Jewish converts to Christ to assimilate to an essentially Roman cultural expression of Christianity, or would they rejoice in the cultural diversity that might flourish in their midst as the gospel reached people of different backgrounds and brought them together?

*To those under the law I became like one under the law (though I myself am not under the law), so as to win those under the law.* As suggested above, *those under the law* would be essentially equivalent to *the Jews,* but would more clearly include proselytes as well as Jews "by nature" (Gal. 2:15). To become like those under the law, if it can be distinguished at all from becoming like the Jews, would presumably entail living according to the law of Moses with or without adapting to other aspects of traditional Jewish culture.

147. On Paul's use of the term "Judaism" in Gal. 1:13, see Ciampa, *The Presence and Function of Scripture in Galatians 1 and 2,* 106-8. Paul calls himself a Jew twice in Acts (21:39; 22:3), but it may be significant that he prefers to call himself an "Israelite" in his letters (Rom. 9:3-4; 11:1; 2 Cor. 11:22; Phil. 3:5).

Paul did not qualify his statement that to the Jews he became like a Jew (since he was a Jew, in the most basic sense). He does qualify his statement that he became like someone under the law when working among those under the law by pointing out that he himself was *not under the law.* This latter phrase refers to his understanding of the fact that the Mosaic covenant has been superseded by Christ (Rom. 6:14-15; 7:6; Gal. 3:23-24; 5:18). There is nothing inappropriate about keeping the law as a matter of tradition or preference, as long as such law-keeping is not imposed on Gentiles and does not undermine the fellowship of brothers and sisters in Christ (cf. Gal. 2:11-14).[148] Although Paul understood himself to live under the conditions of the new covenant in Christ rather than under the law of Moses, he was happy enough to observe the law when living among those who might have stumbled if he had not. Paul probably has in mind issues like the observance of food and Sabbath laws as well as the halakic standards of the communities where he ministered.[149] As Fee puts it, "The difference" between Paul's behavior "and that of his social companions is not in the behavior itself, which will be identical to the observer, but in the reasons for it. The latter abstain because they are 'under the law'; it is a matter of religious obligation. Paul abstains because he loves those under the law and wants to win them to Christ. Despite appearances, the differences are as night and day."[150]

**9:21** Paul moves from those who were under the law to those who were not. *To those not having the law I became like one not having the law (though I am not free from God's law but am under Christ's law), so as to win those not having the law.* The same word for "without law"[151] is used four times in this text, with two different referents in mind (as recognized by BDAG). The implied contrast with the previous reference to those "under the law" indicates *those not having the law* refers to Gentiles as people who are not under the Mosaic law. Paul's statement that he became *like one* of them implies that he adapted to the ways and customs of the Gentiles among whom he worked. Of course, under those circumstances halakic concerns would not have been a concern.

Since the same word, *not having the law,* usually meant "evil" or "wicked" in the LXX (LEH), however, and since Paul would not want the Corinthians to think that he would ever act like a person who is not committed to obeying God he adds, *though I am not free from God's law but am un-*

148. As Conzelmann (160) points out, Paul "does not have to deliver the Jews from their practice of the Law, but from their 'confidence' in the Law as a way of salvation."

149. Cf. the standards established in the Mishnah, many of which would have coexisted in Paul's day with somewhat different standards in some Jewish communities as there were a number of issues over which disputes were common.

150. Fee, 429.

151. Gk. ἄνομος. As BDAG affirms, in the first part of this verse it refers "to the Mosaic law, used of gentiles as persons who do not know it" and "those without (Mosaic) law (= 'gentiles')."

*der Christ's law. Free from God's law* contains the third use of the same word for "without law" in this verse, but this time the near context suggests the meaning "free fr[om] obedience to God" (BDAG). In one sense Paul is "without law," but in another he is not. Paul uses an antonym to "without law," here translated *under law*,[152] to clarify his meaning.

The translation suggested by BDAG helpfully clarifies the significance of all the legal language in this verse: "I identified as one outside Mosaic jurisdiction with those outside it; not, of course, being outside God's jurisdiction, but inside Christ's." He is not bound by the law of Moses but is bound to obey God as one living under the authority of the Lord Jesus Christ. As Fee explains, "This does not mean that in Christ a new set of laws has taken the place of the old, although in terms of specifics it would certainly refer to those kinds of ethical demands given, for example, in Rom. 12 and Gal. 5–6."[153] 1 Corinthians asserts that "lawlessness" (especially in the forms of idolatry, sexual immorality, and greed) was prevalent in Corinth, and that may also have led Paul to emphasize that the fact that he is not under the law does not mean that he participates in such "lawless" behavior. Like Paul, the Corinthians must live under Christ's lordship.

Paul says that he accommodates himself to the Gentile context *(to those not having the law)* in order to win Gentiles. It may be that there were ways in which Paul did not adapt to Corinthian customs which they would have liked, but he obviously accommodated enough to establish a church that, even if poorly and inconsistently, expressed the gospel in the midst of Corinthian culture. In fact, Paul's accommodation was so great that the evidence of this letter suggests that the Corinthians had more difficulty in understanding where Corinthian culture was to be resisted than where it might be embraced.

**9:22** Paul now moves beyond the basic Jew-Gentile dualism to address part of the question raised in the previous chapter: How should the Corinthians relate to those they consider "weak"? *To the weak I became weak, to win the weak. I have become all things to all people so that by all possible means I might save some.* The knowledgeable, or strong, Corinthians should have already recognized the adjustments Paul made in order to more effectively minister to them and win them for Christ. They must consider the implications for the way they should relate to those who understand idol food differently than they do.[154]

In the previous chapter Paul's references to the weak had to do with Christian brothers and sisters whose weakness of conscience (i.e., moral instability) was such that they could be led to fall into idolatry by caving in to

152. Gk. ἔννομος.

153. Fee, 430.

154. Chrysostom sees the logic of Paul's structure, suggesting that he is "in this part coming to their case, with a view to which also all these things have been spoken. However, those were much greater things, but this more to the purpose; whence also he hath placed it after them" (*Homiliae in Epistulam i ad Corinthios* 22.5; NPNF[1] 12:128).

the pressure or example of other Christians. Since Paul says that he became weak (or like the weak)[155] in order *to win* them, it would seem unlikely that he is talking about believers here, unless he is talking about their ultimate salvation (concern over which motivates his argument in 8:9-11) rather than their conversion. Weakness is a motif that appears throughout this letter (cf. 1:25, 27; 2:3; 4:10; 8:7, 9-12; 9:22; 11:30; 12:22; 15:43), however, and Paul both "experienced considerable weakness in Corinth (see on 2:1-5; 4:9-13; cf. 2 Cor. 4:7-18; 11:16–12:10)" and indicated that "he considered this to be a paradigm of the Christian life."[156] In fact, Paul suggested in 1:26-31 that most of the Corinthian congregation would be categorized as the weak rather than the powerful. As Fee points out, it is "probably a more purely sociological category than a socio-religious one" here.[157] Even if Paul sought *to win* the powerless, the motif of seeking the salvation of *the weak* would still relate back to spiritual concern for the welfare of those Christians for whom association with idolatry remained a temptation. Fotopoulos thinks that "the rhetorical thrust in naming these groups is directed at the reference to the Weak to whom Paul has accommodated himself," revealing that "Paul's behavior is once again antithetical to that of the Strong. The Strong do not accommodate themselves to the Weak, thus bringing about their downfall (8:9) and destruction (8:11) by consuming sacrificial food as a freedom and a right."[158] It is noteworthy that Paul never says that he "became strong to the strong."[159]

The second part of the verse (v. 22b; *I have become all things to all people so that by all possible means I might save some*) uses totalizing language[160] to draw out the main point of vv. 20-22a and provide the climax to the sequence. It should be interpreted in the light of that preceding text. By becoming *all things to all people* Paul means that he adopted the most appropriate and effective approach for each group of people with which he worked. He did not become more than one thing for more than one person or group, but since he worked with all sorts of people he ultimately adopted all possible approaches along the way.

Verse 22b also plays on the structure of vv. 20-22a. In the previous se-

155. This is the only one of the statements that lacks the comparative "as/like" (ὡς), although it is added by a number of witnesses ($\aleph^2$, C, D, F, G, Y, 33, 1881, 𝔐, vg$^{ms}$, sy, co), in order to maintain the pattern found in the previous statements. It may be that Paul simply elided it, expecting the reader to infer that it was based on the established pattern and the unlikelihood that he would actually become weak rather than become like those who are.

156. Fee, 431.

157. Fee, 431 (and n. 49). Cf. the NLT: "When I am with those who are oppressed, I share their oppression." See Mark Reasoner, *The Strong and the Weak: Romans 14:1–15:13 in Context* (SNTSMS 103; Cambridge: Cambridge University Press, 1999), 45-58, on "strong" and "weak" as terms of social status in first-century Rome and the summary in Yeo, *Rhetorical Interaction*, 90; Thiselton, 706.

158. Fotopoulos, *Food Offered to Idols*, 226.

159. Cheung, *Idol Food in Corinth*, 143; Fotopoulos, *Food Offered to Idols*, 226.

160. Gk. πᾶσιν, πάντα, πάντως (all things, all people, all means).

ries of lines a key word has been repeated three times in each line: To the [x/y/z] I became (as) [x/y/z] in order to win the [x/y/z]. *I have become all things to all people so that by all possible means I might save some* modifies that pattern in a subtle but significant way. He still uses the variants of a key word (in this case "all") three times in the sentence. However, he is not so bold (or unrealistic) as to say that he had become all things to all people in order to win all people.[161] He may not be able to save all people, but he is willing to use all possible means[162] to save as many as possible. The stress found in the previous lines on the goal of winning others for Christ is heightened here. Paul switches from the aorist tense used in vv. 20, 22a (translated *I became*) to the perfect tense here (translated *I have become*) to sum up his practice throughout his ministry.[163] Paul does not mean that he became more than one thing to any group of people, of course, but that he identified with and adapted to each group, in turn, in the most appropriate manner.

Paul is willing to surrender his right to live according to his own culture, context, and preferences and adapt to the realities and ways of those with whom he works and whom he hopes to reach for Christ. He is not concerned about staying within his own "comfort zone," but about overcoming artificial barriers inhibiting those who have not yet responded to the gospel from coming into the life of Christ. Paul offers an example of promoting the gospel at great personal cost. To *become all things to all people* required considerable versatility and sensitivity and often led to suffering and even persecution.

The way this adaptation is related to the question of hindering or not hindering the gospel is suggested by some of Paul's earlier usage of the language of salvation in this letter, where it tends to appear in association with the preaching of the gospel. Other texts (1:18, 21; 15:1-2) stress that it is the preaching of the gospel that leads to the conversion/salvation of the hearers. Here Paul's goal of saving members of these different groups presumably relates to his ministry of preaching the gospel among them. But these verses help clarify that it is not merely the preaching of the gospel per se that is important, but the preaching of the gospel through a messenger who

161. Although that ([τοὺς] πάντας instead of πάντως τινάς) is the reading found in D, F, G, 33, latt, Cl, Did$^{pt}$, it seems clearly intended to impose the same structure found in the preceding lines.

162. Gk. πάντως.

163. Stanley Porter has suggested that the perfect is a "frontground" tense-form which is "used to mark prominent features" (*Idioms of the Greek New Testament* [Biblical Languages: Greek 2; Sheffield: JSOT, 1992], 302). Such features are "selected for grammatical as well as conceptual emphasis" (ibid.). Similarly, Constantine Campbell believes that the perfect tense usually has the pragmatic implicature of intensification or prominence: "The concept of prominence is here taken to refer to the degree to which an element stands out from others in its environment. Thus, prominence is here roughly synonymous with stress." *Verbal Aspect, the Indicative Mood, and Narrative: Soundings in the Greek of the New Testament* (Studies in Biblical Greek 13; New York: Peter Lang, 2007), 206 (cf. 199-210).

incarnates its message such that the hearers can both understand it clearly from one who obviously empathizes with them and can see what it would look like if it took root in them. The term *save* also interprets the meaning of the term "win" in the previous verses. Fee points out that "[w]hereas he is intransigent on matters that affect the gospel itself, whether theological or behavioral (e.g., 1:18-25; 5:1-5, etc.) . . . that same concern for the saving power of the gospel is what causes him to become all things to all people in matters that don't count."[164]

Paul's statement that he adapts his approach according to the community in which he is ministering does not contradict his statements elsewhere that he is committed to pleasing God rather than humans (Gal. 1:10; 1 Thess. 2:4). In those texts Paul is talking about behaviors that please people but displease God. Here Paul is discussing his limited accommodation in ways that would not be offensive to God but that were strategically important for bringing people into life-transforming contact with the gospel.

As Carson puts it, Paul's accommodating approach to his ministry "is not a license for unlimited flexibility."[165] Garland is equally clear:

> He does not think that fundamental and distinctive demands are negotiable, depending on the circumstances. . . . He did not tone down his assault on idolatry to avoid offending idolaters or to curry favor with them. His accommodation has nothing to do with watering down the gospel message, soft-pedaling its ethical demands, or compromising its absolute monotheism. Paul never modified the message of Christ crucified to make it less of a scandal to Jews or less foolish to Greeks.[166]

A commitment to making a good impression on pagan neighbors in order to win them over (and thereby protect or enhance God's reputation) is an ethical motive found also in other early Jewish and Christian writings.[167] An important background to this ethical motif is found in the Old Testament (e.g., Exod. 32:12, 25; Num. 14:13-19; Deut. 9:25-29; Isa. 52:5 LXX; Ezek. 20:9-22; 36:20-23).[168] Of course, the commitment to becoming like those one seeks to save has never been as perfectly incarnated as in the case of Christ himself, who "became what we are . . . in order that we might become what he is."[169] As Ambrose put it, "He who did not think it robbery to

164. Fee, 431.

165. D. A. Carson, "Pauline Inconsistency: Reflections on I Corinthians 9.19-23 and Galatians 2.11-14," *The Churchman* 100 (1986), 33.

166. Garland, 435.

167. Cf. van Unnik, "Die Rücksicht auf die Reaktion der Nicht-Christen als Motiv in der altchristlichen Paränese."

168. Cf. Paul's quotation of Isa. 52:5 LXX in Rom. 2:24; Rosner, *Paul, Scripture and Ethics*, 110-11.

169. Morna Hooker, "A Partner in the Gospel: Paul's Understanding of Ministry," in *Theology and Ethics in Paul and His Interpreters: Essays in Honor of Victor Paul Furnish* (ed. Eugene H. Lovering Jr. and Jerry L. Sumney; Nashville: Abingdon, 1996), 91.

be equal with God took the nature of a slave. He became all things to all men to bring salvation to all. Paul, an imitator of him [1 Cor. 11:1], . . . spent his life for the advantage of those he wished to win."[170] Paul follows Christ's model of taking on the form of a servant for our sakes (Phil. 2:7; 1 Cor. 9:19).

**9:23** The priority of the gospel is stressed again as *all this*[171] is done *for the sake of the gospel, that I may share in its blessings* (more literally, "that I might be a partner in it"). The context suggests (cf. the series of purpose clauses in vv. 12, 19-23) that *for the sake of the gospel* means "that it might not be hindered, but, rather, have the greatest impact possible."

The meaning of the very last clause and its relationship to the one preceding are debated. Many translations render it, "that I may share in its blessings" (cf. ESV, NRSV, NIV, TNIV, NLT). A few remain more literal and ambiguous (e.g., "so that I can be a participant in it"; NET, NAB, NASB, KJV). The NJB has, "that I may share its benefits with others." The key word means "participant" or "partner."[172] As BDAG points out, the genitive case is used with "the thing in which one shares" and it recommends the translation "that I might jointly share in it." It takes "it" to mean "the benefits promised by the gospel" (thus agreeing with the first set of translations above). Many commentators take that as a reference to eschatological salvation and think that it fits with Paul's statements in vv. 25-27 to the effect that he runs to win a prize and does not want to be disqualified at the end.

It may be that Paul is already transitioning to the theme of the following verses, but his reference to partnership or participation in the gospel may be best understood in the light of other references to partnership in the gospel in Philippians 1:5, 7. There the Philippians are praised for being partners with Paul in his ministry of preaching the gospel. Through the material support they provided Paul they participated in the spread of the gospel through him. Paul has willingly, even if unnecessarily, supported himself in the ministry (his labor playing the same role as the support of the Philippians) and thereby participated in an even more effective spread of the gospel. While he claims to be compelled to preach the gospel, he was not compelled to provide his own financial support or to take the approach of missionary accommodation that he did. By doing so he more explicitly identified himself as one who was personally committed to the ministry of the gospel.

This suggests that the last two clauses may provide parallel explanations for Paul's actions, two different ways of saying that he is committed to doing whatever it takes for the gospel to have the greatest impact possi-

170. "Letters to Priests," 54, cited in Bray, 87.

171. Gk. πάντα. As pointed out earlier, the scope of this word (πᾶς) is frequently indicated by the near context.

172. Gk. συγκοινωνός; cf. BDAG.

ble. He could be a mere servant of the gospel, but his actions reveal a greater personal investment. As Collins puts it, "by becoming all things to all people he himself shares in the preaching of the gospel."[173] "He portrays himself as a partner with the gospel in the common enterprise of winning others."[174] As in one of the usages in v. 14, the word *gospel* here serves as a verbal noun having to do with the proclamation and ministry of the message of Christ.

Paul's argument regarding the limitations of his own rights for the benefit of others is one that may be applied to an endless number of rights which one might wish to protect at others' expense and that of the gospel. As Thiselton reminds us, "we should not allow anything to obscure the force of this chapter for current debates today about 'autonomy' and 'the right to choose.'"[175] The concept of absolute autonomy is diametrically opposed to the Christian view of our identification with Christ, our solidarity as members of his body, our recognition of his lordship, and our calling to use the freedom we have in the interests of the well-being and salvation of others. The gospel leads us to live in ways that will win others to Christ and promote their best interests, not to promote our own personal interests and freedom at others' expense.

### 3. *Warning regarding Objective Idolatry and the Downfall of "the Knowledgeable" in Corinth, 9:24–11:1*

**9:24–11:1** The place of vv. 24-27 within Paul's argument is construed in various ways.[1] It seems to be a transition passage moving from Paul's example of foregoing rights to the issue of keeping or forfeiting one's eternal reward. These verses may relate to vv. 1-23 as an appeal to the Corinthians to follow Paul's example and receive a reward.[2] Clearly Paul continues to serve as an example in vv. 24-27. Those verses do not clearly refer to the issue of one's rights, however, but do raise the issue of self-restraint as the distinguishing mark of a subset of people who stay in God's favor, while those who fail to exercise self-restraint find themselves rejected. One may also recognize a pattern whereby illustrations from human experience (9:7, 24-27) are followed by scriptural support for the same point (9:8-10; 10:1-10).

We follow Senft's suggestion that we "regard these verses as an introduction to 10:1ff.: the Israel of the exodus, having started off well on its course but not reaching its goal, is comparable with the athlete who does not persevere in the hard discipline which leads to success. May the Corin-

173. Collins, 356. See the helpful discussion in Robert L. Plummer, "Imitation of Paul and the Church's Missionary Role in 1 Corinthians," *JETS* 44 (2001), 226-30.

174. Garland, 437.

175. Thiselton, 676.

1. Cf. M. M. Mitchell, *Paul and the Rhetoric of Reconciliation*, 239 n. 297.

2. Conzelmann, 162, points to a link between v. 27 and v. 23.

thians, like Paul himself, do everything to arrive at the goal!"[3] Chrysostom seems to have seen the same thing back in the fourth century. He suggests a parallel structure to 9:4-11 (or 23) with that of 9:24–10:13 (or 22). In introducing chapter 10 he looks back and comments that "as above he alleged the examples of the Apostles and those of common custom and those of the priests, and his own, so also here, having set forth those of the Olympic games and those of his own course, he again proceeds to the histories of the Old Testament."[4]

Our understanding of the thrust of this passage will be directly related to the role we think it has in the ongoing argument. If we think that the passage relates most closely to what precedes, we may understand the goal to be the salvation of others. Chrysostom, despite his observation above, imagines Paul's point here to be that "whatever I do, I do for the sake of the salvation of my neighbor."[5] That interpretation reflects the thrust of vv. 19-23, but does not closely reflect Paul's language or imagery in vv. 24-27 where the stress is on the reward the runner himself receives and Paul's own concern to keep from disqualifying himself for the prize. In our view, if vv. 19-23 indicate that Paul's adaptive approach to his ministry is for the sake of the effectiveness of the gospel, vv. 24-27 suggest that his disciplined self-restraint keeps him from failing to receive the ultimate prize.

The subject headings for the following three parts of this section reflect their relationships with this opening pericope:

- 10:1-13 demonstrates that the history of Israel shows that those who lack self-restraint are condemned. The Corinthians need to learn the dire lesson from Israel's history and find God's way out of their temptation to follow the same destructive path.
- 10:14-22 argues that those who worship God must refrain from any association with idolatry. Paul's exhortation to "flee idolatry," which serves as a summarizing plea for this whole section, is unpacked in such a way as to warn the Corinthians against allowing others to associate them with idolatry in any way. In this section the emphasis falls on the particularly egregious issue of participating in meals offered in idol temples and Paul's adamant opposition to that practice.
- 10:23–11:1 urges that freedom be used for (and not to the detriment of) the glory of God. Here our interpretation differs from that of Fee

3. Senft, 126.

4. Chrysostom, *Homiliae in Epistulam i ad Corinthios* 23.3 (NPNF[1] 12:133). Although Fee makes a key division at 10:1, he relates the texts as follows: "in the immediately preceding argument Paul has urged the Corinthians to run (the Christian life is implied) as those intent on obtaining the eschatological prize; the application of the imagery to himself in vv. 26-27 serves as a warning that those who fail to exercise 'self-control' may also fail of the prize itself. In the present section (10:1-13) that warning is now vigorously pursued."

5. Chrysostom, *Homiliae in Epistulam i ad Corinthios* 23.2 (NPNF[1] 12:132).

and others who think that Paul objects only to Christian participation in meals which take place in the precincts of an idol temple[6] as well as others who think Paul took an even more tolerant view.[7] While idol food in the meat market and in meals hosted in private homes raises more complex questions and requires a more nuanced answer, Paul's basic response is to urge the Corinthians to avoid any practice that would allow others to associate them with idolatry in any way.[8] This is for the sake of the spiritual well-being of those who are making up their minds about the possibility of serving God and/or idols. It is not their personal freedom which is to be their ultimate concern, but the glory of God.

### *a. Athletes Who Lack Self-Restraint Do Not Receive the Prize, 9:24-27*

*[24]Do you not know that in a race all the runners run, but only one gets the prize? Run in such a way as to get the prize. [25]Everyone who competes in the games goes into strict training. They do it to get a crown that will not last; but we do it to get a crown that will last forever. [26]Therefore I do not run like someone running aimlessly; I do not fight like a boxer beating the air. [27]No, I strike a blow to my body and make it my slave so that after I have preached to others, I myself will not be disqualified for the prize.*

**9:24** Once again Paul introduces ideas that should be familiar to the Corinthians with *Do you not know?* They certainly would have known about games and stadiums based on the proximity of Corinth to the Isthmian games, which were held under the patronage of the city of Corinth and which attracted thousands of visitors to the city every other year (in-

6. Cf. the discussion in Gordon D. Fee, "Εἰδωλόθυτα Once Again: An Interpretation of 1 Corinthians 8–10," *Bib* 61 (1980), 172-97, and B. N. Fisk, "Eating Meat Offered to Idols: Corinthian Behavior and Pauline Response in 1 Corinthians 8-10 (A Response to Gordon Fee)," *TrinJ* 10 (1989), 49-70.

7. John Dickson, e.g., believes that Paul supports a right to eat in the precincts of pagan temples: "In chap[ter] 8 he even acknowledged the right of the 'knowledgeable' to dine with pagans in a sacred precinct, a situation he again endorses in 10:27 and 10:31" (John Dickson, *Mission-Commitment in Ancient Judaism and in the Pauline Communities: The Shape, Extent and Background of Early Christian Mission* [WUNT 2.159; Tübingen: Mohr Siebeck, 2003], 255).

8. The concern that others might be tempted back into idolatry or have their idolatrous practices tacitly affirmed is central to our interpretation of Paul's argument. Paul seems to agree with ancient Jewish concerns about the variety of ways in which Jews might be associated with idolatry through the eating of food handled or prepared by (unconverted) Gentiles, a concern that extended even to converted Gentiles in the earliest days of the church. See the comments on 10:27, where the background in the interpretation of Exodus 34:15 reflected in texts like Dan. 1:8; *Jubilees* 22:16; Acts 11:3; Gal. 2:12; *t. ʿAbodah Zarah* 4:6; *b. ʿAbodah Zarah* 8a; *Seder Elijah Rabbah* 9 (8) 46-48 is discussed. Such concerns extended beyond the context of pagan temples to the use of any food which might have been offered to idols. Paul is concerned only about food which is explicitly identified as having been offered to idols.

cluding A.D. 49 and 51).[9] The Isthmian games were one of the four major Greek athletics competitions, the others being the Olympic, Pythian, and Nemean games.[10] Paul may or may not have attended the games.[11] While all but the most Hellenized Palestinian Jews considered them out-of-bounds, Murphy-O'Connor suggests that the same attitude may not have prevailed elsewhere, pointing out that "many Hellenized Jews had no compunction about attending the games" and that "Jews had specially reserved seats in the theatre at Miletus in western Asia Minor."[12]

Perhaps this was one of the areas in which Paul (like Hellenized Jews) became as one not under the law when among Gentiles. Ethical objection to the games themselves could stimulate as easily as squelch a fascination with what went on there and certainly would not require a rejection of the positive ideals that may have been associated with the discipline of those who competed. In fact, much philosophical usage of athletic motifs emphasized the idea that there were much more important goals (honors, prizes, rewards) toward which one should strive than those for which the athletes aimed. Pfitzner speaks of the "favourite antithesis between the 'holy' and 'profane' contests" in literature influenced by Greek philosophy.[13] Certainly anyone who lived in Corinth would have known all about the games. Paul almost certainly would have done business with those visiting the games, and probably with those competing in them as well. He may have made some of the tents in which many of the visitors stayed.[14]

Paul employs a series of athletic metaphors in vv. 24-27, referring specifically to two of the events that made up the games, namely, running (racing; vv. 24, 26a) and boxing (vv. 26b-27).[15] He also makes reference to competitors in general (v. 25). As noted above, illustrations drawn from the world of the famous athletic games were, in fact, quite popular in pagan moral philosophy.[16] The paragraph begins in v. 24 with a focus on the Corinthians marked by forms in the second-person plural (you know, you run), then moves to a contrast between them and us in v. 25, and concludes by personalizing the material in vv. 26-27 (which is marked by forms in the first-person singular).

9. For ancient accounts of the games see cf. Murphy-O'Connor, *St. Paul's Corinth,* 12-15.

10. For a brief description of Greek athletics see *OCD* 206-7.

11. O. Broneer, "The Apostle Paul and the Isthmian Games," *BA* 25 (1962), 1-31, thinks that he did.

12. Jerome Murphy-O'Connor, *St. Paul's Corinth,* 15; cf. Emil Schürer, *The History of the Jewish People in the Age of Jesus Christ* (3 vols.; ed. G. Vermes, F. Millar, and M. Black; Edinburgh: T&T Clark, 1973-87), 2:54-55; Victor C. Pfitzner, *Paul and the Agon Motif: Traditional Athletic Imagery in the Pauline Literature* (Leiden: E. J. Brill, 1967), 38-75.

13. Pfitzner, *Paul and the Agon Motif,* 62.

14. See Broneer, "The Apostle Paul and the Isthmian Games," 5, 20.

15. Paul uses a series of present indicative verbs in vv. 24-27 (τρέχουσιν; ἐγκρατεύεται; τρέχω; πυκτεύω; ὑπωπιάζω; δουλαγωγῶ; "they run"; "he exercises restraint"; "I run"; "I box"; "I treat [my body] roughly"; "I enslave [it]") which express their imperfective aspect by creating a series of descriptive scenes through the metaphors.

16. See Pfitzner, *Paul and the Agon Motif,* 23-37.

The Corinthians obviously know *that all the runners in the stadium*[17] *run the race but only one gets the prize.* They should learn from the analogy and themselves *run*[18] *in such a way as to get the prize.* It would be dangerous, of course, to overinterpret the athletic metaphor, as though every facet of the athlete's situation (or even most or many of them) found an exact parallel in the life of the Christian. (See the discussion of the interpretation of metaphorical language in our comments introducing 3:5-9.) The sentence here stresses the contrast between *all* and *one* with slightly more stress placed on the *one.* Pfitzner suggests that "Paul, by pointing directly to the example of the runners in the arena who exert all their strength and energy to become the 'one', sets the stage for the theme of [self-control][19] which follows. All the endeavours of the athlete are in vain if he has not trained his body and abstained from all that may in any way harm his physical condition."[20] In his view the key point of comparison in vv. 24-27 lies solely in v. 25 with the central theme of self-control:

> It is only by isolating the two verses that commentators have concluded that the major stress lies on the necessity of the Christian's total strength, of maximum endeavor in the struggle to attain to the heavenly prize. This conclusion is only possible by falsely subordinating the central theme of [self-control], and by raising the preparatory picture of the striving runner and the complementary image of the victor's crown to a position of independent importance. Not the thought of maximum exertion but rather the theme of self-restriction (as developed in vv. 19-23) dominates in Paul's mind.[21]

Pfitzner is correct to question an emphasis on striving or struggle per se, and a tendency to focus solely on the issue of eternal reward rather than self-restraint. However, he may be guilty of underinterpreting the passage. Both are present in the passage. Fee properly recognizes that "the primary point of the metaphors is the imperative of v. 24b, which controls the entire paragraph. Paul is urging the Corinthians to "run" the Christian life in such a way, in this case *by exercising proper self-control* (the emphasis in vv. 25-27), as to obtain the eschatological reward."[22] Paul does not elaborate on

17. The stadium is mentioned to clarify that Paul is not talking about all people who run, but about those who run in the competitive games (taking place in the stadium).

18. As with the majority of the imperatives used in this letter, the imperfective aspect of the present imperative here (τρέχετε) suggests that Paul is giving instruction that is of general and continual relevance. Pfitzner, *Paul and the Agon Motif,* 88-90, argues that the word should be taken as an indicative ("You are running") rather than an imperative ("Run") and denies that this passage is parenetic/hortatory in nature. His argument is linguistically possible but unlikely on contextual grounds and has not persuaded many.

19. Gk. ἐγκράτεια.

20. Pfitzner, *Paul and the Agon Motif,* 87.

21. Pfitzner, *Paul and the Agon Motif,* 87.

22. Fee, 434 (his emphasis).

the prize he has in mind for the Christian. Fee suggests that Paul has in mind "the eschatological victory itself." Here again our proper understanding of where we are in God's eschatological program provides the most basic orientation for our lives; we live as those existing during the in-between time of the "already" and the "not-yet"; inhabiting the world over which Christ already reigns as people who will be rewarded by the king at the consummation of the age. The figure of the eternal reward "is intended to impress upon them that the goal, being eternal in nature, is of such value that it should affect the way they live in the present."[23]

The point, of course, is not to suggest that Christians are to think of each other as competitors, seeking to win a prize that might otherwise go to a brother or sister in Christ! Although team sports did not exist as we know them, Paul obviously expects many Christians to run in such a way as to receive a heavenly reward. Christians must do whatever it takes to finish well since "the laurels go only to the victor, in this case, a multitude of victors."[24] The Corinthians are not to seek to be like all the runners, but like the one who receives the prize. As Pfitzner emphasizes, the following verses will clarify that the way to run in order to win is through the discipline of self-control.[25] As Garland puts it, the Corinthians "are to run as if their life depended on it. It does."[26]

**9:25** What makes for a winning athlete? Uncontroversially, Paul reckoned that it was self-control or self-restraint: *Everyone who competes in the games goes into strict training.* The Greek word translated by TNIV as "strict training" is helpfully defined by BDAG as "to keep one's emotions, impulses, or desires under control, *control oneself, abstain.*"[27] The TNIV here fails to catch the precise emphasis on self-control suggested by Paul's more literal statement, "Everyone who contends for a prize exercises self-control in all respects."[28] Athletes were held to be excellent models of self-control.

While their self-discipline, as Paul suggests, needed to apply to all areas, Mitchell points out that the example of the athlete's bodily discipline is "particularly apt" since "the athlete's self-renunciation is precisely in those areas of Corinthian dispute: sexual behavior and diet.[29] The same need for self-control is no less relevant in the modern world where immediate hedo-

23. Fee, 437.

24. Garland, 440.

25. Chrysostom understands and clarifies this, linking the two verses by citing the last part of v. 24 ("run so that you may obtain the prize") followed by "And having said this, he teaches how it is done (v. 25), 'Everyone who competes . . .'" (Καὶ εἰπὼν οὕτω, καὶ τὸν τρόπον διδάσκει· *Πᾶς δὲ ὁ ἀγωνιζόμενος πάντα ἐγκρατεύεται).*

26. Garland, 440.

27. Gk. ἐγκρατεύομαι. See on 7:9.

28. Spicq suggests that the last part be translated "submits to every kind of abstinence" (*TLNT* 61).

29. The motif of "the athlete's rigorous diet" is common. Cf. Garland, 441; Epictetus, *Diatribai* 3.15.10; Philo, *On Dreams* 2.2 §9; Horace, *Ars poetica* 412–14; Xenophon, *Symposium* 8.37.

nistic gratification is a given and fulfilling one's desires is taken to be a healthy response irrespective of the context or social implications. The athlete forgoes present pleasures for the sake of a later ultimate good, which is the advice which Paul urges on the Corinthians."[30] She points out that in his comments on this verse Chrysostom refers to the athlete's need to exercise self-control by refraining, in particular, from getting drunk with wine and from sexual immorality.[31] It is particularly important when reading figurative language in an ancient text, as with Paul's metaphor in these verses, to locate accurately the nature of the imagery, and not to read into the text modern associations. An athlete's self-restraint is exalted as an example to be passed on in Plato's *Laws* 8.839e-840c.[32]

Paul uses the athletic metaphor to provide an inspirational image of a person who is looked up to for their remarkable self-discipline in the pursuit of excellence and glory.[33] Today great athletes are still looked up to as people who have mastered their skills by mastering their bodies. People usually want to emulate such heroes, and Paul hopes that the Corinthians will be inspired by the metaphor to emulate their famed self-control.

Athletes exercise such self-control in order *to get a crown that will not last* (literally, "a perishable crown"); *but we do it get a crown that will last forever* (literally, "an imperishable one").[34] This reflects the standard philosophical use of the athletic motif, whereby the award sought by those pursuing athletic victory is contrasted with the greater one pursued by the one dedicating their life to virtue and philosophy.[35] Seneca provides a good example of the motif: "What blows do athletes receive on their faces and all over their bodies! Nevertheless, through their desire for fame they endure every torture, and they undergo these things not only because they are fighting but in order to be able to fight. Their very training means torture. So let us also win the way to victory in all our struggles, — for the reward is not a garland or a palm or a trumpeter who calls for silence at the proclamation of our names, but rather virtue, steadfastness of soul, and a peace that is won for all time."[36]

In the local Isthmian games, the victor's crown was woven out of

30. M. M. Mitchell, *Paul and the Rhetoric of Reconciliation*, 249.

31. M. M. Mitchell, *Paul and the Rhetoric of Reconciliation*, 249 n. 346, citing PG 61.189.

32. Spicq cites Philostratus, *De Gymnastica* 52: "If athletes have just yielded to the pleasures of Venus, it is better not to exercise them. Are they perhaps men who will take shameful pleasure rather than wreaths and the proclamations of heralds?" (C. Spicq, *TLNT* 61 n. 9).

33. See our comments on the affective impact of metaphors in the comments introducing 3:5-9.

34. Paul stresses the contrast by placing *perishable* and *imperishable* at the beginning and end, respectively, of the two clauses.

35. Cf. Pfitzner, *Paul and the Agon Motif*, 82 (and 23-72 passim).

36. *Epistulae Morales* 78.16. Richard M. Gummere's translation (Lucius Annaeus Seneca, *Moral Epistles;* trans. Richard M. Gummere; LCL; Cambridge, MA: Harvard University Press, 1917-25).

withered celery,[37] while Christians anticipate an eternal reward from the God who called them. Hays paraphrases Paul's thought this way: "If these athletes push themselves to the limit in training to win that pathetic crown of withered vegetables, how much more should we maintain self-discipline for the sake of an imperishable crown?"[38]

Hays rightly reminds us that Paul's argument does not suggest that the body is the enemy of the spiritual life; "rather it is the *instrument* of that life" and "the 'punishment' of the body refers to grueling training for the contest, seeking to bring the body to peak efficiency. To 'enslave' the body means, in this context, to devote it unreservedly to God's service through service to others (cf. 9:19), not to practice self-denial for its own sake."[39] These verses bring to mind Paul's imperative to "honor God with your bodies" in 6:20 and the central role it plays in chapters 5–7. Paul's high view of the body, in the light of the resurrection of Christ, is a pervasive theme in the letter.

**9:26** Paul personalizes the argument by moving to the first-person singular in describing his approach in terms of two metaphors from the context of the athletic games. The first continues the metaphor of running which began in v. 24, while the second is grammatically and rhetorically parallel but introduces the metaphor of boxing. In stating that he does *not run like someone running aimlessly*[40] (literally, "uncertainly"), Paul evidently means "not as one who has no fixed goal" (BDAG).[41] He is very deliberate in how he lives his life and carries out his ministry. Obviously he does not feel that the Corinthians are being very intentional or disciplined in their approach. Paul is not like an occasional jogger who appreciates the value of a run now and then. His approach is more like the dedicated athlete who is strictly disciplined, knowing that his success depends on it.

Paul's reference to *a boxer beating the air* could refer to one who is shadowboxing (not engaged in a real contest) or to "unskillful boxers, who miss their mark" (BDAG). As Schmidt points out, the parallel language in the two parts of the verse, *"I do not run/fight like . . ."* suggests that they should be understood together and probably make the same point, such that not beating the air is similar to not running aimlessly. "I run as one who is not without a sure goal (i.e., who has a precise goal), I fight as one who does not swing aimlessly in the air (but I train systematically)."[42] Johannes Weiss argues similarly that a boxer who fails to hit his opponent

37. Cf. Broneer, "The Apostle Paul and the Isthmian Games," 186; Murphy-O'Connor, *St. Paul's Corinth,* 15, 104-106.

38. Hays, 156.

39. Hays, 156.

40. Literally, "So that is how I run, not as one running uncertainly."

41. So Chrysostom (*Homiliae in Epistulam i ad Corinthios* 23.2; NPNF[1] 12:132; PG 61.189): "what is, 'not uncertainly?' Looking to some mark/goal" (Τί δέ ἐστιν, Οὐκ ἀδήλως; Πρὸς σκοπόν τινα βλέπων); cf. NLT, "I run straight to the goal"; NASB, "as not without aim"; NJB, "not without a clear goal."

42. K. L. Schmidt, "πυγμή," *TDNT* 9:916 n. 15: "Twice we have ὡς οὐ . . . rather than οὐχ ὡς, . . . and the exact sense is to be gleaned from the par. οὐκ ἀδήλως."

and only manages to flay the air "is unskillful, careless, undisciplined."[43] Robertson and Plummer compare the body to "the horses in a chariot race, which must be kept well in hand by whip and rein if the prize is to be secured."[44] What Paul has in mind with the image of a boxer who does not beat the air is clarified not only by its relationship with the previous clause, but also by the contrast in the following verse.

**9:27** While a boxer is trained to beat his opponent, Paul's metaphor surprises us with its suggestion that his opponent is his own body! *I strike a blow to my body,* he says, *and make it my slave.* It is his body that must be dominated and mastered. He must "make it strictly serve my purposes, bring it under strict control."[45] That, he says, is *so that after I have preached to others, I myself will not be disqualified for the prize.* Whether or not Paul continues the athletic metaphor here is a contested issue. Some hold that the "preaching to others" refers to the role of "the herald who has called the athletes to the line (although in his illustration he remains an athlete himself)."[46] But the word is used frequently enough by Paul to refer to Christian preaching (Rom. 10:8, 14-15; 1 Cor. 1:23; 15:11-12; 2 Cor. 1:19; 4:5; 11:4; Gal. 2:2; 5:11; Phil. 1:15; Col. 1:23; 1 Thess. 2:9; 1 Tim. 3:16; 2 Tim. 4:2) that it is unlikely that readers would not have understood it in that sense here,[47] especially since any metaphorical interpretation would have required a significant role change for Paul in any case (from athlete to herald). It is also unlikely that the herald's role in the games would have been simply referred to as "preaching to others."

There is a greater likelihood that the last part of the verse might reflect a return to the athletic metaphor. Sampley argues that the word *disqualified*[48] is "a technical term of athletics in which a competitor fails the test or is thrown out of the competition."[49] Such a technical usage, however, is not attested in any of the lexicons or dictionaries.[50] Whether understood

43. Weiss, *ad loc.;* cited by Schmidt, *TDNT* 9:916 n. 16.

44. Robertson and Plummer, 197.

45. Thiselton, 716 (emphasis removed). David J. Williams suggests that Paul's "image is of the victor leading the vanquished into slavery" (*Paul's Metaphors: Their Context and Character* [Peabody, MA: Hendrickson, 1999], 117). While suggestive, it does not fit the athletic context of Paul's metaphor.

46. D. J. Williams, *Paul's Metaphors,* 269. Cf. the translation of the NJB and Robertson and Plummer, 197. Williams admits that in practice "it was probably the umpires who instructed the athletes in the rules, not the herald, but for Paul's purposes a reference to the herald was near enough" (289 n. 112).

47. Gk. κηρύσσω. Schrage argues that it is "mission terminology" and not related to the previous athletic metaphor but relates back to Paul's mention of the gospel (εὐαγγέλιον) in v. 23 (2:371-72).

48. Gk. ἀδόκιμος.

49. Sampley, 910.

50. Cf. the entries in LSJ, BDAG, *EDNT, NIDNTT, TDNT,* and *DGE.* Spicq, without providing evidence, thinks that Paul "is alluding to the preliminary test at athletic competitions, where the judge, after an examination, 'eliminated' certain contestants who were 'not acceptable,' or in the case of defeat, refused to award the prize" (*TLNT* 1:361).

within the context of the previous athletic metaphor or not, the word clearly refers to God's potential eschatological judgment on Paul (and also on the Corinthians).[51] It suggests being rejected as unworthy by the ultimate judge. Philo describes the history of Israel after receiving the law with its "gentle instructions and exhortations" as well as "threats and warnings" through the use of the image of the athletic contests, and allegorically describes the defeated as "whole lives that fall, which once overthrown can hardly be raised up again."[52] The image of "falling" (as in the previous sentence) is used both in Philo and Paul to refer to ultimate divine rejection. This is an important part of the rhetorical motivation (or parenesis/moral exhortation) essential to keeping the Corinthians from underestimating the dangerous position in which their attitudes and practices have placed them. As Garland puts it, "Paul is engaged in moral exhortation and not discoursing on the security of the believer."[53] He wants the Corinthians to ask, as does Chrysostom, "Now if Paul feared this, who had taught so many, and feared it after his preaching . . . ; what can we say?"[54] One of the ways in which God secures the perseverance of believers is by such stern warnings.

The athletic metaphors may ironically relate to the Corinthians' issues with "weaker brothers and sisters" in their midst, suggesting that they need to pay more attention to their own potential "weaknesses" to make sure they do not keep them from falling short of the finish line.

It would be a grave error to think that Paul is somehow relating salvation to the adoption of an ascetic lifestyle, as though harsh treatment of the body were the key to salvation. Rather, Paul's language about self-restraint rather than self-indulgence probably has more to do with the motifs of fleeing sexual immorality and idolatry, in this case, idolatry associated with food. As noted above, athletes were famous for their discipline especially in the areas of sex and food, the areas that most preoccupy Paul's arguments in this letter. In the context of Paul's references to the discipline of his body, we should recall that the body is sometimes especially associated with its appetites for food or sex (Rom. 1:24; 6:12; 1 Cor. 6:13, 18).[55]

In the following passage (10:1-13) Paul will remind the Corinthians of the dismal failure of the Israelites who gave in to their "evil cravings" and were destroyed due to their apostasy, which manifested itself principally through idolatry, sexual immorality, and greed. When we recall the prominence of these vices in the lists of 5:11 and 6:9-10 (which points out that

51. Paul's language reflects a concern not to be the kind of person referred to in Sir. 37:19: "One kind of person is clever at teaching others, yet is no good whatever to himself" (NJB).

52. Philo, *On Rewards and Punishments*, 4–6.

53. Garland, 445.

54. Chrysostom, *Homiliae in Epistulam i ad Corinthios* 23.2 (NPNF[1] 12:132).

55. BDAG lists Rom. 4:19 and 1 Cor. 7:4 as places where the body is referred to "as the seat of sexual function."

those who practice such vices will not inherit the kingdom of God), we can see a pattern in Paul's thought. The Corinthians do not need to adopt every aspect of Paul's lifestyle, but they do need to take much more seriously the potential for apostasy by following uncritically their appetites for food (including idol food) and sex (including illegitimate sex). They are to show the kind of discipline modeled by Joseph while in Potiphar's house (see on 6:18) or perhaps Daniel with regard to the table of Nebuchadnezzar (cf. Dan. 1:8). Whether they eat or drink, or in whatever they do (perhaps especially in their diet and sexual relations), they are to glorify God and flee from sexual immorality and idolatry. To do otherwise is to run headlong into apostasy.

### *b. The History of Israel Shows That Those Who Lack Self-Restraint Are Condemned, 10:1-13*

Paul continues to warn the Corinthians about their need to exercise greater discipline in view of the danger of spiritual failure. Fee explains: "In the immediately preceding argument Paul has urged the Corinthians to run (the Christian life is implied) as those intent on obtaining the eschatological prize; the application of the imagery to himself in vv. 26-27 serves as a warning that those who fail to exercise 'self-control' may also fail of the prize itself. In the present section (10:1-13) that warning is now vigorously pursued."[56]

The key issue of idolatry will be mentioned again in v. 7, and the more specific topic of food sacrificed to idols is resumed in v. 14. Paul moves now from warnings based on the illustrations drawn from the athletic games to more direct warnings based on the example of Israel through the exodus and wilderness periods.[57] He provides a typological (ecclesiological) interpretation of the exodus, wilderness wandering, and apostasy of Israel which is informed by both Jewish interpretive traditions and the worship experience of the early Christian communities. The logical link between the two is easily discerned: all the runners run but not all win; so also, all the Israelites experienced the blessings of the exodus and divine provision, but not all made it to the Promised Land. Just as in the previous passage the Corinthians were to interpret their situation in the light of the analogy of the athletic games, in this passage Paul uses the Israelites' experience of re-

56. Fee, 442.

57. Paul switches from the descriptive use of present indicative verbs in 9:24-27 to a series of mainly aorist and imperfect verbs used to narrate Israel's experience in the exodus and wilderness in 10:1-6. In vv. 7-10 he alternates between present imperatives (and hortatory subjunctives) and aorist (and imperfect) indicatives within each verse, drawing generally valid and relevant principles from the negative example found in Israel's history. All but one of the imperatives in ch. 10 are present imperatives (see v. 15 for the exception), and their imperfective aspect suggests that Paul employs them to give generally relevant (as opposed to situationally particular) instruction.

demption, idolatry, and destruction as a prism through which the Corinthians are to understand their own situation.

Mitchell has pointed out that Philo (*On the Special Laws* 4:129; *On the Life of Moses* 1:161-64, 305; 2:174, 283; *On the Posterity of Cain* 182–85; *On Drunkenness* 95) and Josephus (*Antiquities* 3.295; 4.12, 140) refer to the same incidents Paul mentions in 1 Corinthians 10:1-13 as notorious instances of factionalism (cf. 1 Cor. 1:10-13; 11:18-19; 12:25).[58] Corinth was not the first place God's people had experienced divisions relating to idolatry and sexual immorality! In a way similar to that of Psalms 78 and 106, Nehemiah 9:5-37, and Deuteronomy 32:1-43, 1 Corinthians 10:1-13 rehearses the consequences of earlier rejections of God's mercy as a warning to the author's own generation of readers.[59]

The expressions "all" (5x in vv. 1-4), "most of them" (once, in v. 5), and "some of them"[60] (4x, once per verse in vv. 7-10) provide keys to this passage. Verse 6 serves as a kind of transition and focal point which provides a basic explanation, elaborated upon in vv. 7-10, of how most of those Israelites who all shared the same experiences ended up being judged by God, namely, by giving in to their evil cravings. There were a variety of ways in which various Israelites fell short (some gave in to one craving and some to another).

The basic structure of the argument is as follows:

- Verses 1-4 discuss the redemptive blessings experienced by the whole community of Israel as parallels to those blessings experienced by Christian believers.
- Verses 5-10 discuss Israel's experience as a warning for "us" in light of the fact that God's judgment fell on *most* of Israel due to the various things that *some* of them did.
- Verses 11-13 conclude the passage with a final warning. The first-person plural pronoun[61] marks key transitions at vv. 1, 6 (2x), and 11.

As Sampley points out, Paul retells of Israel's experience "in ways designed to encourage his auditors to identify with its characters." They were "our fathers" (v. 1), who, like us, were baptized (v. 2) and partook of spiritual food and drink (vv. 3-4) and, like us, "were related in a special way to Christ."[62] In vv. 6-13, however, "the persons with whom the readers were encouraged to identify in 10:1-4 turn out to be those who desired evil (v. 6), were idolaters (v. 7), committed sexual immorality (v. 8), tested the Lord (v. 9), and grumbled against him (v. 10).[63] This is another case where Paul is

58. M. M. Mitchell, *Paul and the Rhetoric of Reconciliation*, 138-40.

59. Fee, 442.

60. Gk. πάντες, τοῖς πλείοσιν αὐτῶν, and τινες αὐτῶν, respectively.

61. Gk. ἡμῶν/ἡμᾶς.

62. Sampley, 913.

63. Sampley, 913.

interpreting the experience and situation of his readers in the light of a scriptural typology.

> [1]*For I do not want you to be ignorant of the fact, brothers and sisters, that our ancestors were all under the cloud and that they all passed through the sea.* [2]*They were all baptized into Moses in the cloud and in the sea.* [3]*They all ate the same spiritual food* [4]*and drank the same spiritual drink; for they drank from the spiritual rock that accompanied them, and that rock was Christ.* [5]*Nevertheless, God was not pleased with most of them; their bodies were scattered in the wilderness.*
>
> [6]*Now these things occurred as examples to keep us from setting our hearts on evil things as they did.* [7]*Do not be idolaters, as some of them were; as it is written: "The people sat down to eat and drink and got up to indulge in revelry."* [8]*We should not commit sexual immorality, as some of them did — and in one day twenty-three thousand of them died.* [9]*We should not test Christ, as some of them did — and were killed by snakes.* [10]*And do not grumble, as some of them did — and were killed by the destroying angel.*
>
> [11]*These things happened to them as examples and were written down as warnings for us, on whom the culmination of the ages has come.* [12]*So, if you think you are standing firm, be careful that you don't fall!* [13]*No temptation has overtaken you except what is common to us all. And God is faithful; he will not let you be tempted beyond what you can bear. But when you are tempted, he will also provide a way out so that you can endure it.*

**10:1-2** *For I do not want you to be ignorant of the fact. . . .* Garland points out that by beginning this passage with *For* Paul "thereby indicates that he now gives the grounds for his warning in 9:24-27 about the possibility of disqualification."[64] In other places Paul asks, "Don't you know?" In using the epistolary "disclosure formula"[65] *I do not want you to be ignorant*, he does not imply that they should know the following information, but that it is important for them to know it.[66] If, as we have argued, however, the knowledge they have prided themselves on is (partly at least) theological knowledge based on their knowledge of Scripture (cf. on 8:1, 4), the suggestion that they could be ignorant of the lesson to be drawn from Israel's experience may still be aimed at their pride.

*. . . brothers and sisters, that our ancestors. Our ancestors* is literally "our

64. Garland, 447. So also Schrage, 387-88; Robertson and Plummer, 199, who paraphrase Paul's idea as follows: "Failure through lack of self-discipline is not an imaginary peril: if you lack it, your great spiritual gifts will not save you from disaster."

65. The disclosure formula consisted of the verb "I want" (θέλω), the identification of the addressee(s), a verb of knowledge in the infinitive followed by a ὅτι ("that") clause with contents of the information the author wishes to make known. Cf. Terence Y. Mullins, "Disclosure: A Literary Form in the New Testament," in *NovT* 7 (1964), 44-50.

66. As Collins points out, by using a double negative (not . . . not-know; οὐ . . . ἀγνοεῖν) Paul gives added emphasis to the formula (368).

fathers,"[67] and Paul's reference to the readers as his *brothers and sisters*[68] reflects his understanding that the Corinthians are to understand themselves in the light of a new identity formed through their adoption into the covenant people of God. Even the Gentile readers of this letter are now to think of the Israelites of the exodus as their adopted "fathers" through their inclusion in the covenant community.[69]

*. . . were all under the cloud and that they all passed through the sea. [2]They were all baptized*[70] *into Moses in the cloud and in the sea.* The reference to *all* the Israelites having a similar experience with the cloud and the sea is just the first of a series of analogies Paul will suggest between experiences common to all Israelites and those common to all Christians (including the Corinthians).

The phraseology Paul employs of being *under the cloud* and of having *passed through the sea* may have been intended to approximate the experience of ancient Christian baptism as being dipped under the water and/or passing through it. The fact that the Israelites were "under the cloud" and "passed through the sea" (v. 1) is understood to correspond to the baptism experienced by the Corinthian Christians (v. 2). The second verse makes the parallel explicit, thereby guaranteeing that it will not be missed. Those experiences were part of what it was for Israel to pass from Egyptian bondage to freedom in their own land. Baptism was understood to be the act that initiates the person into the new covenantal relationship, and references to the sea and the cloud are interspersed within Exodus 14:2-27. That the Israelites were able to pass through the sea was considered not only the greatest miracle of the exodus, but also the climactic act of redemption as the people faced extermination at the hands of the army of Egypt.

The importance of the exodus traditions in Israelite consciousness, thought, and imagination can hardly be overestimated.

67. It is unlikely that Paul is using the first-person plural pronoun in an exclusive manner here. It is because the ancient Israelites are also the fathers of the Corinthians (through the adoption of the latter into the covenant people) that the Corinthians can be expected to learn from them.

68. Gk. ἀδελφοί.

69. So also Hays, 160.

70. Some MSS ($\mathfrak{P}^{46}$, B, 1739, 1881, 𝔐, Or) have a middle form (ἐβαπτίσαντο), while others (א, A, C, D, F, G, Ψ, 33, 81, 104, 365, 630, 1505, 2464, *al*, latt) have the passive form (ἐβαπτίσθησαν). Bruce Metzger and A. Wikgren believe that it "is more probable that copyists replaced the middle ἐβαπτίσαντο (which corresponds to Jewish practice, according to which the convert baptized himself) with the passive (which is the usual expression in the case of Christian baptism, e.g., 1.13, 15; 12.13, etc.), than vice versa" (Metzger, *A Textual Commentary*, 493). The majority of the UBS[4] committee, however, felt the external evidence superior enough and Pauline usage consistent enough to suggest that ἐβαπτίσθησαν was original. Collins points out that the original reading of $\mathfrak{P}^{46}$ (ἐβαπτίζοντο) was later "corrected" to ἐβαπτίσαντο, and he takes it as evidence of a tendency of "a corrective dynamic operating in the textual tradition" which sought "to distinguish 'baptism into Moses' from 'baptism into Christ'" thus implying a secondary origin for all the middle forms (cf. Collins, 368).

> Within Israelite historical consciousness the exodus held a central place. The exodus was recalled as the major formative event in Israelite history. It was seen as the event in which Israel was created; their history as a people was perceived to have begun at the exodus. As a result, the exodus was recalled as that which formed the identity of the Israelite people; they were people who had once been slaves but had been saved from slavery by the Lord their God.[71]

The exodus is now to play a central role in forming the identity not only of Jews but of Gentile believers as well. And the parallel between the exodus and the experience of salvation the Corinthians have had at the turn of the ages was something to be expected by all those who knew the biblical story. It was

> because Israel knew that God had acted for them in the past [that] they could be sure that God would act similarly for them in the future. Hence the prophetic books envision God's restoration of Israel in terms of a new exodus event. Israel will once again be gathered from the nations and be led through the wilderness to her inheritance. In the words of Michael Fishbane, the exodus informed Israel's "projective imagination" (Fishbane 1979: 121), their expectation of how God would interact with them in the future.[72]

The pillar of cloud served as a theophanic guide for the people during the day as they traveled through the wilderness. The two events both speak of God's redemptive power and presence in the midst of his people. The idea that the fathers were "under the cloud" is suggested in Exodus 14:24, which says that the Lord "looked down" on the Egyptians trailing the Israelites from the pillar of fire and of cloud (see also Exod. 13:21, 22; Num. 9:15-23; 14:14; Deut. 1:33; Ps. 78:14). That the Israelites passed through the midst of the sea is indicated in Exodus 14:22, 29. Paul's language facilitates the identification between the experience of the Israelites and that of the Corinthians.

There is no antedated concept of "baptism into Moses,"[73] and the ex-

71. Sylvia C. Keesmaat, "Exodus and the Intertextual Transformation of Tradition in Romans 8.14-30," *JSNT* 54 (1994), 35.

72. Keesmaat, "Exodus and the Intertextual Transformation of Tradition in Romans 8.14-30," 35-37. The reference is to Michael Fishbane, "The 'Exodus' Motif/The Paradigm of Historical Renewal," in his *Text and Texture: Close Readings of Selected Biblical Texts* (New York: Schocken, 1979), 121-40. On the prominence of the exodus as a central and formative pattern in Jewish thought see Yair Zakovitch, *"And You Shall Tell Your Son . . .": The Concept of the Exodus in the Bible* (Jerusalem: Magnes, 1991); David Daube, *The Exodus Pattern in the Bible* (London: Faber and Faber, 1963); and Michael Fishbane, *Biblical Interpretation in Ancient Israel* (Oxford: Clarendon, 1985), 358-68, 375, 412-13.

73. Judaism was, however, developing the concept and practice of proselyte baptism at the time Paul was writing (cf. Scot McKnight, "Proselytism and Godfearers," in *DNTB* 845).

pression is evidently formulated by Paul in order to make the metaphorical parallel to baptism into Christ as clear as possible.[74] Just as Christ is identified as the founder of the new covenant established through his death and resurrection, Moses was understood to be the (human) founder of the covenant established at the time of the great exodus redemption. Just as the people were expected to obey the covenantal expectations established by Moses, we are expected to obey all that Christ commands us. As Thiselton points out, baptism "into" Christ or Moses signifies "not locality, sphere or movement but *adherence to* the one in whose name the candidate is baptized."[75]

**10:3-4** Paul says that they *all ate the same spiritual food and drank the same spiritual drink.* The two clauses are clearly set out in parallel manner. In Greek the first five words are identical in each clause (literally, "and all [ate/drank] the same spiritual"),[76] with the last two words playing the same syntactical role in the same order but with "drank drink" substituting for "ate food." The theme of food and drink, of course, clearly points us back to the issue of food (and drink) offered to idols in chapter 8 (and the dietary discipline of the athlete in ch. 9). By calling the food and drink *spiritual* "Paul does not mean *immaterial,* but *that which* is provided by the Spirit of God (cf. 9:11; 12:1; 15:44, 46), with all the 'hallmarks' of what is regarded as a miraculous provision."[77] Fee goes a step further by suggesting that Paul chose the word "to accomplish two ends simultaneously: (1) to refer to that food and drink which for Israel were supernaturally given and thus divinely sustained them in the desert; and (2) at the same time to suggest the analogy or type of the Lord's Supper, the special food and drink of Christians."[78]

Many interpreters have thought that the reference to *spiritual food* and *spiritual drink* relates to a Corinthian sacramentalism that led them to think they gained some sort of spiritual security through their participation in the Lord's Supper. According to this view, Paul seeks to undermine their hypersacramentalism by pointing out that although the Israelites participated in similar sacraments, many of them still perished in the desert; the sacraments offer no guaranteed protection. Others have pointed out, however, that the context does not suggest that Paul has a concern with a false sacramentalism on the part of the Corinthians, but with idolatry.[79] There is no evidence that the Corinthians attributed some sort of magical qualities to the Lord's Supper which they were counting on for spiritual protection in the midst of idolatry. They did not think that idolatry was a reality that

74. Chrysostom suggests that "because he wishes to bring the type near the truth, . . . he uses the terms of the truth even concerning the type."

75. Thiselton, 725.

76. Gk.: καὶ πάντες τὸ αὐτὸ πνευματικὸν βρῶμα ἔφαγον
καὶ πάντες τὸ αὐτὸ πνευματικὸν ἔπιον πόμα·.

77. Thiselton, 726 (his emphases).

78. Fee, 447.

79. See Fee, 447 n. 31; Garland, 453-55.

required any sort of protection, since there is only one God anyway. Paul's point is that even after having been fully initiated into the redeemed community many Israelites still fell under God's judgment through their participation in idolatry and sexual immorality. Like the Corinthians, they had experienced redemption and had committed themselves to adhere to the one true God but behaved in a way that brought the judgment of the one they were committed to honoring.

In v. 7 Paul points out that it was due to eating and drinking food that should have been rejected that the Israelites suffered destruction in the wilderness. Collins notes that the reference to *spiritual food* "suggests a contrast between the food craved by the Israelites and the food given by God."[80] That God had provided them with (presumably superior) *spiritual food* and *spiritual drink* and that they had still chosen to partake of the (inferior) food and drink of other gods stood as a serious warning to the Corinthians. They also knew what it was to partake of spiritual food and drink and were similarly tempted to settle for that which would bring condemnation rather than be content with the food God had provided. Later in the chapter Paul will point out the unacceptability of partaking of the cup and table of pagan deities when one participates in the cup and table of the Lord, evoking the motif of divine jealousy (cf. vv. 16-22).

In terms of specific Old Testament background, God's provision of quail and manna is related in Exodus 16 and Numbers 11 and celebrated in Deuteronomy 8:3, 16; Nehemiah 9:20; Ps. 78:24; 105:40. The water from the Rock is mentioned in Exodus 17:6 and Numbers 20:8-11 and then celebrated in a series of texts, including Deuteronomy 8:15; Nehemiah 9:15; Psalms 78:20; 105:41; 114:8; and Isaiah 48:21.

The early church's (and Paul's) understanding of the last supper and the Lord's Supper in terms of the Jewish Passover and the promised second exodus would have made the parallel between the Lord's Supper (see below on 1 Cor. 11:23-26) and the Israelites' experience in the exodus a natural one for Paul and his readers. Paul understands the water and manna to have been provided by the Spirit, and he also understands the elements of the Lord's Supper to be food and drink of the Spirit, who communicates the presence of Christ to his community.

While Paul is building on an analogy (and typological relationship) between Israel's experience and that of believers in Christ (as the earlier reference to baptism and the following identification of the rock as Christ make clear), the references to *the same* here would logically relate to the *all* mentioned earlier in the sentence, especially in the light of the later references to *some of them*. In other words, all the Israelites of the exodus had the same experience of redemption, but they did not all respond to it in the same way. They all started out the same, but they did not end up the same way.

80. Collins, 369.

Paul draws on a rich Jewish exegetical tradition when he speaks of the rock that followed Israel (v. 4):[81] *they drank from the spiritual rock that accompanied them. . . .* In inquiring how the interpretive tradition of a moveable well developed, Enns notes that "the miraculous provision of water in the desert is mentioned only at the beginning of the wilderness wandering period (Exod. 17, Rephidim; also the waters of Elim in Exod. 15:22-27; see *Bib. Ant.* 11:15 . . .) and at the end (Num. 20, Kadesh; Num. 21, Beer)."[82] He suggests that the exegetical tradition provided an answer to the natural question of what the Israelites had done for water between those times. The answer was that "the rock of Exodus 17 and the rock of Numbers 20 are one and the same. Hence, this rock must have accompanied the Israelites through their journey." That interpretation was facilitated by a potential ambiguity in Numbers 21:16-20. When God promised to give the Israelites water from the well, was it a one-time offer? When the text says, "This is the well *of which the LORD said to Moses,* 'Gather the people and I will give them water'" (v. 16) does it mean that God will give them water *from the well* or that he will give them *the well itself,* and, thereby, water? Jewish tradition came to understand the latter. In the following verse the Israelites sing to the well, calling on it to spring up (or go up), using a verbal form which in every other context (Num. 21:17; 1 Sam. 25:35; Isa. 21:2; 40:9; Jer. 22:20; 46:11) entails movement from one place to another, a thought that could have been encouraged by the fact that the succeeding verse (Num. 21:18) begins to recount the itinerary of Israel's travels. The understanding that the well/rock traveled with Israel was based on an interpretation that Paul and other Jewish interpreters evidently inherited from their fathers.

Paul's use of the basic conclusion regarding the traveling nature of the rock should be distinguished from suggestions that he is indebted to the fuller (and fanciful) legends found in later rabbinic material.[83] As Garland puts it: "Paul may have incorporated a traditional Jewish interpretation of the following rock, but he gives it a uniquely Christian twist: 'The rock was Christ.' He is not thinking of a material rock following them, or a movable well, but of the divine source of the water that journeyed with them. He understands the replenishing rock in a spiritual sense, not a physical sense."[84] The Israelites were replenished by actual water throughout

81. For example, *Liber Antiquitatem Biblicarum* 10:7; 11:15; *t. Sukkah* 3.11, *b. Šabbat* 35a; *b. Pesaḥim* 54a; *Genesis Rabbah* 62:4; *Numbers Rabbah* 1:2; 9:14; 19:25-26; *Targum Onqelos* Num. 21:16-20; cf. E. Earle Ellis, "Note on 1 Corinthians 10:4," in his *Prophecy and Hermeneutic in Early Christianity: New Testament Essays* (Grand Rapids: Eerdmans, 1978), 209-13; and Peter E. Enns, "The 'Moveable Well' in 1 Corinthians 10:4: An Extra-Biblical Tradition in an Apostolic Text," *BBR* 6 (1996), 23-38.

82. Enns, "The 'Moveable Well' in 1 Corinthians 10:4," 30.

83. See Garland, 455-57, and the fuller discussion in Enns, "The 'Moveable Well,'" and Thiselton, 727-30.

84. Garland, 456-57. So also Chrysostom, who argues that "it was not the nature of the rock which sent forth the water, (such is his meaning,) else would it as well have gushed out before this time: but another sort of Rock, a spiritual One, performed the whole, even

their wilderness experience, and such constant provision of food and water reflected the same reality as the constant presence of the pillar of cloud or fire: God's presence in the midst of the community, accompanying the community and guiding, protecting, and sustaining it (and bringing judgment when necessary).[85]

Paul identifies Christ as the one who provided Israel with water:[86] *and that rock was Christ*. The identification of the rock with Christ involves a distinctively Christian hermeneutical step beyond that of a moveable well or rock common in Jewish interpretation. It may be questioned whether Paul means to establish an analogy between the role of the rock in Israel's experience and the role of Christ in the church's experience, whether he is employing allegorical interpretation,[87] or whether he means to make a stronger statement regarding the actual identity of the rock in Israel's experience.[88] Philo identified the rock with the wisdom of God (*Allegorical Interpretation* 2:86). Since such hypostatization of that particular divine attribute has been shown to underlie other important christological statements of Paul (1 Cor. 1:24, 30; 8:6; Col. 1:15-17), it may be that Philo's understanding of the rock is genealogically related to Paul's. In 1 Corinthians 10:20-22 Paul will clearly draw on Deuteronomy 32. As Meeks says, Paul found "in Deuteronomy 32 phrases that were suggestive for his admonition to the Corinthian Christians."[89] That opens the possibility that his reference to the rock being Christ may have been influenced by the rock motif found in that chapter (32:4, 13, 15, 18, 30, 31). As Meeks points out, "Rock" is "the preferred name for God" in the Hebrew text of that chapter. Interestingly, the only other place the word is used in Deuteronomy outside chapter 32 is in 8:15, which affirms that God "brought you water out of the flinty rock." As Garland and others have pointed out, Paul "may have made the shift from God as the Rock in the Scriptures to Christ as Rock in the same way that he applied the references to God as 'Lord' in the Scriptures to Christ."[90]

---

Christ who was everywhere with them and wrought all the wonders. For on this account he said, 'that followed them'" (*Homiliae in Epistulam i ad Corinthios* 23.3 [NPNF[1] 12:133]).

85. The cloud pointed more to theophanic guidance and protection. The image of the Rock usually signified protection or judgment, but the image of water from the rock suggested the motif of sustenance. As implied here, the reference to the Rock accompanying the community should be interpreted in the light of Paul's previous mention of the cloud which also accompanied the community. We shall see that the references to the judgment on Israel in the following verses also relate to the "rock" motif as a metaphor for God's strength in defending or meting out judgment on his community.

86. See Thiselton, 729; Witherington, 218; Schrage, 2:395-96.

87. Cf. Dietrich A. Koch, *Die Schrift als Zeuge des Evangeliums: Untersuchungen zur Verwendung und zum Verständnis der Schrift bei Paulus* (BHT 69; Tübingen: Mohr Siebeck, 1986), 211-16.

88. Cf. Anthony T. Hanson, *Jesus Christ in the Old Testament* (London: SPCK, 1965), 17-22.

89. Wayne A. Meeks, "'And Rose Up to Play': Midrash and Paraenesis in 1 Corinthians 10:22," *JSNT* 16 (1982), 72.

90. Garland, 457; cf. Godet, 2:57-58; Fee, 449.

**10:5** *Nevertheless, God was not pleased with most of them; their bodies were scattered in the wilderness.* While vv. 1-4 were marked by the experience of "all" of Israel, this verse presents a contrast in that while they all experienced the blessings associated with redemption, *most of them* did not please God. *Most of them,* in fact, is understatement. If the Corinthians remember the story, they will recall the fact that of the original exodus generation only Joshua and Caleb were spared (Num. 14:29-30, 38; 26:65; 32:11-12)! That the whole community had experienced such wonderful blessings did not keep almost all of them from incurring God's wrath due to rebellion. The contrast is marked by *Nevertheless* or "But."[91] Paul indicates that one can deduce that *God was not pleased with most of them* on the basis of what happened to them.[92] They would not have been destroyed were it not for the fact that they stirred up God's anger against them. Paul's statement that *their bodies were scattered in the wilderness*[93] serves as his summary of the experience of so many Israelites. He is paraphrasing Numbers 14:16, where Moses asks God to show mercy on his people lest the nations end up saying that God "scattered their bodies in the wilderness."[94] As it turned out, Paul would have us understand, God did not ultimately wipe his people from the face of the earth, but those who rebelled against him were destroyed in the wilderness.

**10:6** Linguistically Paul structures vv. 6-11 in a chiastic manner, tying the verses together as a unit. The first and last verses both begin with references to "these things" which are understood to be examples or "types."[95] Paul employs second-person plural imperatives ("do not") in vv. 7 and 10 and first-person plural hortatory subjunctives ("let us not") in vv. 8 and 9. The structure ties vv. 7-10 together as a unit which "unpacks" the point of v. 6 and prepares for the similar summarizing point in v. 11.

Within 10:6-11 Paul lists the sins which brought God's wrath upon Israel (mentioned in v. 5) in vv. 6-10. Four of them echo texts from Numbers. 1 Corinthians 10:6 mentions that they "craved evil things," echoing Numbers 11, where vv. 4 and 34 serve as an inclusio around the narrative of Israel's rebellious "craving" to eat meat.[96] Collier also points out that two key verbs from Exodus 32:6, "to sit down" and "to rise up,"[97] are found at the beginning (v. 4) and end (v. 32) of Numbers 11 LXX.[98]

91. Gk ἀλλά.

92. In Greek the two clauses are linked by γάρ ("for"). The TNIV correctly assumes that the logical relation is clear from the context.

93. The TNIV does a fine job with the verb (καταστρώννυμι), whose primary meaning is "spread out" but in this context has to do with "laying low" or "killing off" the people in the wilderness (cf. BDAG).

94. Compare Num. 14:16, κατέστρωσεν αὐτοὺς ἐν τῇ ἐρήμῳ, with 1 Cor. 10:5, κατεστρώθησαν γὰρ ἐν τῇ ἐρήμῳ.

95. Verse 6 begins with ταῦτα δὲ τύποι, while v. 11 begins with ταῦτα δὲ τυπικῶς.

96. Gary D. Collier, "'That We Might Not Crave Evil': The Structure and Argument of 1 Corinthians 10:1-13," *JSNT* 55 (1994), 63.

97. Gk. καθίζω and ἀνίστημι, respectively.

98. Collier, "'That We Might Not Crave Evil,'" 65.

As Collier suggests, the linguistic ties provided Paul with "a midrashic link to Exod. 32.6 as a kind of summary of Numbers 11. Exod. 32.6 is understood midrashically as Numbers 11 writ small."[99] Paul ties together Exodus 32:6 and the theme of "desire" or "craving"[100] found in Numbers 11 and related Old Testament texts that mention food and the craving of evil things.[101] So "when Israel sat down to eat, they sinned, for they craved the food of their own choosing rather than what God had provided: (1) in *idolatry* (v. 7), it was eating and drinking in an idol feast in an attempt to fulfill their own desires (Exod. 32.6); (2) in *harlotry* (v. 8), it was a desecration against God himself as 'the people blatantly practiced harlotry' . . . , primarily a forsaking of God in idolatry, since the people 'ate the [Moabite] sacrifices and worshipped their idols' (. . . Num. 25.1-2); and (3) in *testing* (v. 9), it was the speaking against God . . . that was at issue, for the people said, 'there is no food or water' (. . . Num. 21.4-7)."[102]

In terms of delimiting the subunit, Collins points out that Paul's "negative injunctions are characterized not only by their parallelism but also by the fact that they been incorporated into a literary unit delimited by the encompassing notion of 'example'" in vv. 6 and 11 and that that "*inclusio* defines vv. 6-11 as a discrete sub-unit within Paul's scriptural exposition."[103]

In v. 6 Paul says that the examples listed in vv. 1-5 *(these things)* happened to serve as lessons from which we should learn: *Now these things occurred as examples to keep us from setting our hearts on evil things as they did.* The word Paul uses for *examples* (or warnings, or patterns;[104] possibly "types") provides the background for the concept of typology, the understanding that patterns found in persons, actions, events, and institutions can be expected to find correspondences (with some eschatological "heightening") in God's future redemptive works.[105] Typological interpretation goes back to the Old Testament and the way the prophets described God's postexilic redemption in terms of a second exodus. The use of "type" (v. 6) and "typical"[106] (v. 11) as technical terms for typological interpretation is established by the time of the early fathers. Goppelt argues that Paul was the first to use these words for "the prefiguring of the future in prior history."[107] Two of the key texts for this argument are found in this passage (1 Cor. 10:6, 11; cf. also Rom. 5:14).

Goppelt is surely correct to understand Paul's point to be that "[b]y

99. Collier, "'That We Might Not Crave Evil,'" 65.

100. Gk. root ἐπιθυμ-.

101. Collier, "'That We Might Not Crave Evil,'" 65-66.

102. Collier, "'That We Might Not Crave Evil,'" 66.

103. Collins, 366.

104. Gk. τύποι.

105. See Leonhard Goppelt, *Typos: The Typological Interpretation of the Old Testament in the New* (trans. Donald H. Madvig; foreword by E. Earle Ellis; Grand Rapids: Eerdmans, 1982), 17-20.

106. Gk. τύπος and τυπικῶς, respectively.

107. Goppelt, *Typos*, 4.

his dealings with the first people of God, the forefathers (1 Cor 10:1), God reveals to the people of God who are living at 'the fulfillment of the ages' what they may expect from him."[108] Still that seems to fall somewhat short of what typology is usually understood to entail (a correspondence between the past and the future which has been designed by God). Paul clearly establishes a typological relationship between Israel and Christian experience in vv. 1-4. It could be argued, however, that in vv. 5-11 he does not point to divinely established patterns but rather to patterns which the Corinthians must avoid fulfilling.[109]

Some interpreters understand typology to consist merely of retrospective interpretation by New Testament authors, whereby they find correspondences between their own experience and that described in the Old Testament. Many texts seem to reflect such an approach. Garland suggests that the key word "reveals a pattern or correspondence, observed after the fact, that contains a teaching."[110] If the Old Testament text was written as a warning or pattern to guide the church in the last days (cf. vv. 6, 11), however, it could be so only if it were understood that the experience of God's eschatological community would follow patterns established in the Old Testament such that one could deduce a lesson from Israel's exodus experience and apply it to a context that was significantly different in its historical particularities. That the second exodus would follow the general pattern of the first exodus was an expectation found already in Old Testament texts. While Davidson, for example, pushes the predictive element of typological exegesis too far, the basic understanding that the church's experience would correspond to patterns found already in Israel's experience seems to be required by Paul's argument.[111] The pattern would not require that believers experience destruction similar to that of the Israelites, but that behavior similar to that of the Israelites would result in a judgment that was also similar to theirs.[112]

As mentioned above, Paul's reference to Israel's "craving" echoes Numbers 11, especially vv. 4 and 34, which serve as an inclusio around the narrative of Israel's rebellious "craving" to eat meat.[113] "Craving evil" serves

108. Goppelt, *Typos*, 146.

109. Cf. Garland, 459.

110. Garland, 459.

111. Cf. Richard M. Davidson, *Typology in Scripture: A Study of Hermeneutical* τύπος *Structures* (Andrews University Seminary Doctoral Dissertation Series; Berrien Springs, MI: Andrews University Press, 1981), 193-297.

112. Collins argues forcefully that Paul's language (τύπος and τυπικῶς) refers to examples and that Paul "is not to be seen as a proponent of patristic hermeneutics. He [Paul] uses *typos* to present a model, the *paradeigma* of Hellenistic rhetoric, from which the Corinthians are to learn" (370). His warning is salutary. Paul may not have used the language the way the Fathers did, but their understanding reflects a development of Paul's understanding (and that found in the Old Testament and other early Jewish and Christian writers) that the eschatological redemption would follow certain patterns seen in the exodus redemption.

113. Collier, "'That We Might Not Crave Evil,'" 63.

as a general description of the problem that led to the series of specific sins listed in the following verses.[114] That information should guide us in our understanding of what the idolatry, sexual immorality, testing, and grumbling in vv. 7-10 have in common. The "evil things" which the Israelites craved and which led them to test the Lord and grumble when their cravings were not satisfied tended to be based on a willingness to gratify appetites (either sex or food) in ways prohibited by the Lord or an insubordinate attitude toward the Lord arising from his failure to gratify those appetites as they wanted. What those who died in the wilderness judgments had in common was that they craved evil things. In the following verses we will see the variety of ways such a craving manifested (and tends to manifest) itself.

**10:7** With this verse Paul begins a series of references to things "some of them" (i.e., one subset of those who perished in the wilderness) did but that the Corinthians must reject. Each item in the list is introduced with the same negative particle.[115] First on the list is idolatry, one of the two key themes of this letter and the key issue of chapters 8–10. That this is the primary concern here will be indicated again in v. 14.

*Do not be idolaters, as some of them were; as it is written: "The people sat down to eat and drink and got up to indulge in revelry."* That some of them were idolaters is supported by a quotation from Exodus 32:6. Exodus 32 describes the episode of the golden calf, one of the most notorious moments of sin in the Old Testament. The incident is reiterated in the Exodus narrative (Exod 32:4, 8, 24, 35), and that narrative is itself reiterated in Deuteronomy (9:8, 12, 16). The golden calf is also alluded to or echoed in Judges 2:17 and 1 Kings 12:28 and retold in Deuteronomy 9:8-21, Nehemiah 9:16-18, and Psalm 106:19-23.

Deuteronomy 32:6 depicts a perversion of the covenant ceremony/meal that had been described in Exodus 24:5-11 (note the references in both texts to burnt and peace offerings followed by eating and drinking). Exodus 32:6 is distinctive in that it says that the community "rose up to play," suggesting, as indicated by the TNIV, that they *"got up to indulge in* [pagan] *revelry."* The previous verse indicated that the behavior described in v. 6 was understood to consist of a "feast to the LORD," using language that had previously been used in Exodus to refer to the Passover (Exod. 12:14; 13:6). In Exodus 32:4 Aaron had suggested that the golden calf represented the gods who had delivered the Israelites from the land of Egypt. In these ways the true worship of the God who had actually redeemed them from Egypt had been twisted into pagan worship of idols which were now receiving credit for the exodus.

114. So also Chrysostom: "For having said, 'that we should not lust after evil things,' which was general, he subjoins that which is particular, implying that each of their sins arose from evil lusting" (*Homiliae in Epistulam i ad Corinthios* 23.4 [NPNF[1] 12:134]).

115. μηδὲ εἰδωλολάτραι γίνεσθε ("do not be idolaters"; v. 7), μηδὲ πορνεύωμεν ("and let us not commit sexual immorality"; v. 8), μηδὲ ἐκπειράζωμεν τὸν Χριστόν ("and let us not test Christ"; v. 9), and μηδὲ γογγύζετε ("and do not murmur"; v. 10).

That the golden calf fiasco held a strong place in Jewish thinking is clear.[116] The story is recounted in Acts 7:39-43 as an example of Israel's hard-heartedness and idolatry. Philo refers to the event in *On the Life of Moses* 2:161-62, 270 and in *On Drunkenness* 95 and alludes to it in *On the Special Laws* 1:79. It is retold once again in *Liber Antiquitatem Biblicarum* 12. It is notable for being one of very few incidents omitted from Josephus's retelling of the Old Testament[117] an omission that Thackeray calls "the most glaring exception" to Josephus's promise to omit nothing.[118] The verse is cited in *t. Soṭah* 3:10, where the context suggests that the focus on eating and drinking points to an arrogant, self-absorbed attitude on the part of the people of Israel, and in *t. Soṭah* 6:6, where the clearly idolatrous reference to "playing" in Exodus 32:6 is used to interpret Genesis 21:9 in terms of idolatrous acts on the part of Ishmael. The event left an indelible mark on the history of Jewish thought about idolatry and functioned as the archetypal act of apostasy.[119]

Paul's text reproduces the LXX of Exodus 32:6, which is a literal rendering of the text found in the MT.[120] The quotation serves as proof that the Israelites committed idolatry. The text's statement that the people "rose up to play" (TNIV: *"got up to indulge in revelry"*) has been associated with idolatry and sexual debauchery since antiquity.[121] Unlike the following verses, this one does not mention a punishment for the Israelites' sin. Koet has suggested that this is because the punishment mentioned in the following verse actually fuses together elements of the punishments of both Exodus 32 and Numbers 25 (see the discussion on the following verse).

The references to eating and drinking in association with idolatry make Exodus 32:6 an obvious reference point for issues related to food sacrificed to idols. Although Collier has suggested that Numbers 11 was Paul's main text with Exodus 32:6 being a supplementary text, it is more likely that we should understand things the other way around, with Exodus 32:6 marked as Paul's main text by its explicit citation (and important use of the key words for eating, drinking, and rising up), while allusions to Numbers 11 and 14 (see the comments on 10:5-10) fill out the picture by pointing to subsequent situations where the same association between eating, drinking, and idolatry (and Israel's postredemption apostasy) can be seen along with other temptations the Corinthians are facing.

116. Cf. Brevard S. Childs, *The Book of Exodus* (OTL; Philadelphia: Westminster, 1974), 573-81.

117. Cf. *Antiquities* 3.99.

118. Thackeray, 4:363.

119. Scott J. Hafemann, *Paul, Moses, and the History of Israel: The Letter/Spirit Contrast and the Argument from Scripture in 2 Corinthians 3* (Tübingen: Mohr Siebeck, 1995).

120. In a very few citations of the LXX text or MSS of the New Testament singular forms, ἀνέστησεν or ἀνέστη ("[it] rose up") is substituted for the plural found everywhere else (ἀνέστησαν — "they rose up"). This is a result of a desire to have the final verb agree with the singular subject, ὁ λαός ("the people"), of the previous verb, "sat down" (cf. Stanley, *Paul and the Language of Scripture*, 197 n. 54).

121. See Meeks, "'And Rose Up to Play,'" 69-70.

The structure of Paul's argument suggests that he is using the wording of Exodus 32:6 "to recall the Israelite's eating the food (the manna) and drinking the water (from the rock) that God had provided for them. Their idolatry was all the more egregious after their experience of God's graciousness to them."[122] Having been provided with spiritual food and drink, they had the "slap-in-the-face audacity" to eat and drink in honor of and worship in the presence of idols.[123]

Fee points out that if Paul were merely interested in general parenesis against idolatry he could have chosen a more direct citation, such as Exodus 32:8, in which God complains that the Israelites "have made for themselves a golden calf and have worshiped it and sacrificed to it and said, 'These are your gods, O Israel, who brought you up out of the land of Egypt!'" or v. 31c, where Moses complains to the Lord that they "have made for themselves gods of gold."[124] Clearly he chose 32:6b because it mentions eating and drinking — the behavior that raised the issue of idolatry in Corinth. Fee goes further and argues that by citing this particular text Paul is "specifically identifying the idolatry as a matter of cultic meals in the idol's presence."[125] That may be pushing the details too far. Fee and others have also argued that the reference to "rising up to play" "almost certainly carries overtones of sexual play" and that such an understanding is supported by the Old Testament context and was the interpretation of the rabbis and of the early church.[126] Exodus 32:19 describes the "playing" in terms of "a circular dance"[127] including that "performed round the altar of Dionysus,"[128] or "the *dance* as a public religious ceremony" (LSJ). Regarding the rabbis, Fee points out in a footnote that while such a view is attributed to R. Eliezer b. R. Yosé the Galilean, in the same passage Akiba argues that "only idolatry is in view." He does not mention that in the same passage, R. Ishmael says that it is referring to bloodshed and Simeon b. Yoḥai says that it has to do with inheritance (all in *t. Soṭah* 6.6; cf. *Genesis Rabbah* 53:11). It is clearly erroneous to refer to any one interpretation as the understanding of the rabbis, although the most consistent interpretation is that it referred to idolatry (*Genesis Rabbah* 53:11; *Exodus Rabbah* 1:1; 41:7). With respect to the Fathers, a

122. Collins, 371.

123. Collins, 371, quotes Hays's point that "The slap-in-the-face audacity of the people's idolatry is underscored by Paul's device of reading the eating and drinking as a reminiscence of the earlier narrative of God's gracious provision" (*Echoes of Scripture*, 92).

124. Fee, 454.

125. Fee, 454.

126. Fee, 454-55.

127. The Hebrew word (מחלה) means "dance in a ring" (*HALOT*).

128. Cf. "χορός," in Henry George Liddell, *A Lexicon Abridged from Liddell and Scott's Greek-English Lexicon* (abr. ed.; Oxford: Clarendon, 1994). For a description of the Dionysian dance and its association with "play" see Karl Kerényi, *Dionysos: Archetypal Image of Indestructible Life* (trans. from the German by Ralph Manheim; Mythos; Bollingen series 65; Archetypal Images in Greek Religion 2; Princeton, NJ: Princeton University Press, 1996), 264-65 and the citation from Plato, *Euthydemus* 277d.

variety of interpretations may also be found.[129] While they may understand "rising up to play" variously, they consistently understand it to refer to some inappropriate behavior that followed from the prior act of eating and drinking. If Paul understands the text in a similar manner in this context, it would seem that he takes the eating and drinking to have led to idolatry, since that is the particular sin to which he relates the text.

Paul's argument follows a "neither-nor" structure such that the Corinthians should *neither* be like the Israelites who "rose up to play" *nor* should they commit sexual immorality. That structure would not seem to suggest that Paul had already broached the issue of sexual immorality in the immediately preceding words. On the other hand, however, the same structure continues in vv. 9-10 despite the fact that Israel's grumbling against the Lord is understood as testing him in Exodus 17 (cf. vv. 2, 3, 7) and Numbers 14 (cf. vv. 2, 22, 27). Not too much stress, it seems, should be put on the significance of that structure.

Paul uses Exodus 32:6 to inform the Corinthians' understanding of the ethical and spiritual danger they are facing. As Hays suggests, "by coaxing the reader to recall the golden calf story, he links the present Corinthian dilemma . . . to the larger and older story of Israel in the wilderness. This metaphorical act creates the imaginative framework within which Paul judges — and invites his readers to judge — the proper ethical response to the problem at hand."[130] The text serves as a warning for the Corinthians to avoid fulfilling a potential typological role by repeating the experience of Israel.

It would probably come as a surprise to certain Corinthians that they would need to worry about being guilty of idolatry. They had expressed their complete rejection of the very notion of other gods (cf. 8:1, 4)! Paul's argument in the following verses will clarify that even those who explicitly and consciously reject the existence of other gods may yet be condemned as idolaters. While subjectively they reject the notion, objectively their actual behavior implicates them as participants in idolatrous activities.

It may be important that Paul does not explain how the Israelites conceived of the behavior he cites from Exodus 32:6. He simply states that they *"sat down to eat and drink and got up to indulge in revelry."* Whether they thought of themselves as worshiping the Lord or worshiping other gods may not be as relevant as we or the Corinthians might tend to assume. They were participating in idolatrous behavior whether they conceived of it that way themselves. This may be an important warning for modern readers

129. In NPNF[1] 12:134 (*Homiliae in Epistulam i ad Corinthios* 23.4) Chrysostom interprets it as a reference to idolatry. His comments in *Homiliae in Acta Apostolorum* 27 (NPNF[1] 11:177) could be taken to refer to play as self-indulgence, or perhaps as sexually immoral behavior. In *Homiliae in Matthaeum* 6.9 (NPNF[1] 10:42) it seems to be taken as a case of frivolous mirth. In *The Book of Pastoral Rule* 3:19 (NPNF[2] 12:43) Gregory the Great seems to take it as a case of "levity of conduct."

130. Hays, *Echoes*, 92.

who cannot imagine how ancient peoples ever practiced idolatry. Modern people do not tend to give idols any more credence than some of the Corinthians did. That does not exempt them or us from the dangers of behaving in idolatrous ways. We are not innocent simply because we ourselves would not conceive our relationship to those other things in our society that fascinate us and compete for our loyalties and our priorities as idolatry. As Martin Luther affirmed, reflecting on the first commandment in his Larger Catechism, "whatever your heart clings to and relies upon, that is your God; trust and faith of the heart alone make both God and idol." We may broaden Luther's definition to include the biblical themes of love and service: a god is that which one loves, trusts, and serves above all else.[131]

**10:8** Second on Paul's list of the sins that led to the demise of so many Israelites is sexual immorality, the other great theme of this letter, which received concentrated attention in chapters 5–7. He warns that *We should not commit sexual immorality, as some of them did* (literally, "as some of them committed sexual immorality") — *and in one day twenty-three thousand of them died.* As he will do in the next two verses as well (but differently from the previous verse), Paul repeats the main verb (here "to practice sexual immorality"), using it both in his direct appeal to the Corinthians in the first clause and in his reference to the Israelites' failure in the same area. Paul is not concerned with the precise manner or circumstances in which Israel failed, but with the fact that their failure was in the area of sexual immorality.[132] Paul is referring to the incident in Numbers 25:1-9 where the first verse recounts Israel's participation in gross sexual immorality[133] with Moabite women and the last refers to the death of 24,000 as a consequence.

In this verse Paul highlights the Israelites' involvement in sexual immorality, but it is noteworthy (given the fact Paul is dealing with the issue of food sacrificed to idols) that that sin took place in the context of an idolatrous meal. Numbers 25:2 indicates that the incident began when, having been invited by Moabites to the sacrifices to their gods, Israelites ate and then bowed down to those gods (according to the LXX they "ate of their sacrifices and bowed down to their idols"). Thus idolatry and sexual immorality are tied together in both Numbers 25:1-2 and 1 Corinthians 10:7-8 (not to mention the broader structure of this letter). Cole thinks that the Numbers text suggests "a process that led from general sexual immorality with the Moabite women to full-scale idolatry that probably included ritual prostitution in the Baal Peor cult."[134]

131. On idolatry see Rosner, *Greed as Idolatry: The Origin and Meaning of a Pauline Metaphor.*

132. The word Paul uses (πορνεύω) is the same one which served as the primary concern in chs. 5–7. It is used for general preoccupation with any form of "unsanctioned sexual intercourse" (BDAG).

133. Gk. ἐκπορνεύω.

134. R. Dennis Cole, *Numbers* (The New American Commentary 3B; Nashville: Broadman & Holman, 2001), 435.

Ashley agrees: "The first acts may have been physical, but they quickly led to cultic and spiritual acts."[135] Not only was there a process from sexual immorality to idolatry, but that process, in Numbers 25, included eating pagan meals. After some Israelites had sexual relations with the Moabite women, those women invited them to their sacrifices. The Israelites "went to the sacrificial rites and *then* partook of meat that had been offered to the Moabite gods and *then bowed themselves down* to these gods (i.e., worshiped them)."[136] It may be that Paul is simply combining warnings about idolatry and sexual immorality in this context, or it may be that in this and the prior verse he is suggesting that idolatry tends to follow from (among other things) a lack of self-restraint with respect to the appetites of the stomach and the libido. Garland points out that "[i]n the minds of most Jews, sexual immorality and idolatry were two sides of the same coin (Wis. 14:12; T. Reub. 4:6; Philo, *Mos.* 1.55 §302)."[137]

While the Numbers text is clearly in mind, Paul refers to 23,000 casualties, while Numbers 25:9 indicates that the death toll was 24,000. The discrepancy of "the missing thousand" has been dealt with in a number of ways. Some suggest that Paul's memory slipped slightly (perhaps recalling the number 23,000 from Numbers 26:62 — the total of the Levites in the census).[138] Grotius's solution was to posit that 23,000 died in the same day while the others died subsequently.[139] It has also been suggested that the actual number was between twenty-three and twenty-four thousand and that Numbers and Paul rounded the number in opposite directions. These last two suggestions both leave one wondering how Paul would be privy to such information since there is no biblical or pre-Pauline tradition supporting it.[140]

Bart Koet has put forward the possibility that Paul is intentionally fusing together elements of the punishments mentioned in Numbers 25:9 and Exodus 32:28.[141] Although Exodus 32:28 mentions the death of just 3,000 men rather than twenty-three or twenty-four thousand, several aspects of Paul's reference have more in common with Exodus 32:8 than with Numbers 25:9: Numbers 25:9 says nothing about the deaths occurring in a single day, while Exodus 32:28 states that the men died "that day." Whereas Numbers 25:9 says simply that the twenty-four thousand "died," Paul uses

135. Timothy R. Ashley, *The Book of Numbers* (NICOT; Grand Rapids: Eerdmans, 1993), 516.

136. Ashley, *The Book of Numbers*, 516-17.

137. Garland, 461-62.

138. See Witherington, 222 n. 16; Collins, 371.

139. Cited in Thiselton, 739.

140. All other sources consistently maintain the number 24,000. While Paul may have received the number by direct inspiration, that would seem an argument of desperation. Paul writes as one who expects his readers to recognize the biblical source of his statements, not as one who is communicating newly revealed information about the events.

141. Bart J. Koet, "The Old Testament Background to 1 Cor. 10:7-8," in *The Corinthian Correspondence* (ed. R. Bieringer; Leuven: Leuven University Press, 1996), 607-15.

the exact word found in Exodus 32:28 — "fell."[142] Koet's suggestion is that Paul may have fused the two texts together so that the reference to Numbers 25:9 would still be recognizable but that the echo of Exodus might also be heard. He thinks that this explains why there is no mention of a punishment in v. 7 (unlike in vv. 8-10); in other words, the punishment for the sin of Exodus 32:6 is incorporated into the reference to the punishment for the sin of Numbers 25 in the subsequent verse. Koet's suggestion deserves serious consideration as it would not only clarify the numerical discrepancy but would also explain other features of Paul's text. Still, unless or until other examples of such an approach to intertextuality can be found in early Jewish or Christian literature, it cannot be deemed ultimately convincing.

As Fee points out, there "is not an entirely satisfactory solution" to the question of "the missing thousand."[143] Thiselton points out that patristic writers show no awareness of or concern regarding the issue.[144] While the exact number may be of interest to us, the point Paul was making was not dependent upon it. Paul's point is that Numbers 25 serves as a warning to us since a huge number of people were wiped out due to their lack of self-restraint in the area of sexual immorality (and idolatry).

Paul points to a variety of ways (all related to food and drink) in which different groups of Israelites offended God and brought his severe judgment on themselves. In each case the judgment came about in a different way. Paul mentions three of the judgments: the thousands who died from the plague in Numbers 25 (v. 8); those who were killed by serpents in Numbers 21 (v. 9); and those who were killed by "the Destroyer" in Numbers 14 (v. 10). God used a variety of methods, but in each case those who rebelled against him suffered utter destruction. Although Koet's explanation of why Paul does not mention the judgment meted out in Exodus 32 in v. 7 should be given consideration, it may well be that Paul does not mention it simply because, unlike in the other cases, judgment did not come from direct divine intervention but as Israelites faithful to the Lord killed their brothers, companions, and neighbors (Exod. 32:26-28) and he did not want for a moment to suggest that such an approach would be applicable to the church.

**10:9** The relationship between this and the following verse and the Corinthian context (and Paul's broader concerns in this letter) is not quite as transparent as in the case of the prior verses. When we allow the near context to inform our reading, however, the relationship becomes clearer. Paul warns that *We should not test Christ,*[145] *as some of them did — and were killed by*

142. Gk. ἔπεσαν.

143. Fee, 456.

144. Thiselton, 740.

145. While our earliest MS, 𝔓[46], a series of other MSS, and a variety of versional and patristic witnesses reflecting wide geographical distribution (versional support includes the Old Latin, the Vulgate, Syriac, Sahidic, and Bohairic, while patristic witnesses include Irenaeus [Gaul], Ephraem [Edessa], Clement of Alexandria, and Origen [Palestine]) have

*snakes.* This is how some of the Israelites experienced divine judgment during the wilderness experience. Paul is alluding to Numbers 21:5-6, where the Israelites spoke against God, criticizing him and his provision, complaining, in particular, about a lack of *food and water* (ironically mentioning that they detested the food they had). Elsewhere in the Old Testament such complaining is described as "testing the LORD" (Exod. 17:2-3, 7 [concerning water *to drink*]); or "testing God" (Ps. 78:18 [demanding *food they craved*], 41, 56 [provoking him through idolatry]; Ps. 106:14/105:14 [due to their *craving*]). In contrast with other cases where Israel complains to the Lord, this one, as Ashley notes, "has no verbal reaction from either Yahweh or Moses. One reads only of the punishment, *the fiery serpents.*"[146] In this case Israel's impudence results in an immediate and deadly response.

Hays suggests that the parallel between the two halves of this verse does not necessarily imply that that Israelites had put *Christ* to the test.[147] Paul could be understood to say, "We should not put Christ to the test like some of them tested God." On the other hand, Paul has already identified Christ with the rock which provided water (and followed Israel) in 10:4, and in Exodus 17:2, 7, the people of Israel are twice described as testing "the LORD," perhaps leading to Paul identify Christ the Lord as the one tested there. Furthermore, in Numbers 21:6 it is "the LORD" who sends the serpents in response to the complaining. Paul has already identified Christ as "the Lord" named in the *Shema* (see on 1 Cor. 8:6), making the identification between Christ and the Lord in those other Old Testament texts a natural one. Numbers 21:5-6 is probably being read in the light of Psalm 78:18, where the incident is related to *craving* food, a theme found throughout this passage.[148] The Corinthians are warned against following the example of those in Israel who tested the Lord's patience by insisting on eating the food they craved or desired even if it entailed provoking him. Such insolence can expect to be met with judgment.

The theme of testing the Lord will be raised again in vv. 21-22 when Paul warns against provoking the Lord and the motif of God's strength (see the comments there). While Paul would certainly vehemently oppose any behavior or attitudes that could be interpreted as putting the Lord to the test, the context indicates that his present concern is with the possibility of

---

"put *Christ* to the test," some other strong witnesses (including א, B, C, P, 33, and others) have "put *the Lord* to the test," and a few others (including A and 81) have "put *God* to the test." As Metzger (*Textual Commentary,* 494) points out, *Christ* is the reading that best explains the origin of the others, since the "difficulty of explaining how the ancient Israelites in the wilderness could have tempted Christ" would have "prompted some copyists to substitute either the ambiguous ['Lord'] or the unobjectionable ['God']." The latter two variants also bring Paul's wording into conformity with the Old Testament texts listed above, which also militates against the likelihood of either of them being the original text.

146. Ashley, *The Book of Numbers,* 404.

147. Hays, 165.

148. See Hays, 164, and Collier.

testing the Lord's patience through participation in idolatrous activities. In Corinth that was most likely to happen through persistent consumption of food associated with idols.

**10:10** Paul's concern with possible attitudinal problems seems to be reflected here again in this warning about grumbling: *And do not grumble, as some of them did* [literally, "as some of them grumbled"] — *and were killed by the destroying angel.* The key word[149] can mean simply "to express oneself in low tones that are not readily distinguishable," but it typically means "to express oneself in low tones of disapprobation," thus the usual translation, "grumble" or "murmur" (BDAG).

There is no agreement on what passage or passages Paul has in mind in this verse. Hays's suggestion is Numbers 14, where the whole nation is condemned due to their insistent complaining against the Lord (see Num. 14:1-2, 27-38).[150] He thinks that Paul might have concluded his exhortation with this passage "because it represents the most comprehensive judgment" since "here it is not merely a few thousand who are punished, but the whole nation." Others see that as a point against Numbers 14, since Paul indicates that "some of them" grumbled and were destroyed.[151] Collier believes that Paul has Numbers 11 in mind again since 11:1 begins "and the people were grumbling," while vv. 33-34 describe the very great plague of the Lord, and, as he points out, "all of this takes place in the context of rampant [craving] . . . described as an insatiable (and deadly) craving for meat."[152] Garland suggests Psalm 105 LXX (106 MT and Eng.) as the "best backdrop" based on the numerous vocabulary parallels between the two passages (including "craving"[153] in Ps. 105:14 and 1 Cor. 10:6; "testing"[154] God in Ps. 105:14 and 1 Cor. 10:9; "grumbling"[155] in Ps. 105:25 and 1 Cor. 10:10; spiritual or physical "adultery"[156] in Ps. 105:39 and 1 Cor. 10:8; "destruction"[157] in Ps. 105:23 and 1 Corinthians 10:9-10, etc.).[158] We agree with Thiselton who, along with Orr and Walther, holds that the reference to "grumbling" serves as a general allusion to the various Pentateuchal texts that cite Israel's guilt in this area.[159]

Paul's reference to "the destroyer"[160] seems to evoke Exodus 12:23,

149. Gk. γογγύζω.

150. Hays, 165.

151. So Meyer and Heinrici, but Schrage (2:402 n. 110) thinks that this is pushing Paul's exegesis too far. In the other situations the guilt of "the people" (as a whole) is usually highlighted, even if only some of them end up being destroyed in each case.

152. Collier, "'That We Might Not Crave Evil,'" 66.

153. Gk. ἐπιθυμέω.

154. Gk. ἐπείρασαν.

155. Gk. ἐγόγγυσαν.

156. Gk. ἐπόρνευσαν.

157. Gk. ἐξολεθρεύω/ὀλοθρευτής.

158. Garland, 464.

159. Thiselton, 742-743.

160. Gk. ὁ ὀλοθρευτής.

but Schneider is probably correct: "In good Old Testament fashion" Paul has in mind the destroying angel who carries out any divine judgment.[161] Ultimately, of course, all the adult Israelites except Joshua and Caleb were destroyed as God waited for the whole generation to perish before leading his people to the Promised Land.

It is not clear whether Paul thought that the Corinthians were already guilty of grumbling against the Lord or against him (which might be considered the equivalent since Israel's grumbling against Moses was considered grumbling against the Lord; Exod. 16:2-8). Their letter to him seems to have had some questions and raised a number of issues in which they shared their own "insights." The "knowledge" they shared with Paul regarding idols not being real and there only being one God (cf. 8:1, 4) may have been in response to their knowledge that Paul (like other early Jewish and Christian leaders) opposed eating food that was known to have a cultic history.[162] It is possible that Paul is making a preemptive move to try and keep the Corinthians from responding inappropriately to Paul's argument in this letter by complaining about the restrictions he imposes on the use of their "freedoms" and "rights" in the area of diet. On the other hand, since it is clear that each of the other warnings (about idolatry, sexual immorality and testing the Lord) are based on attitudes and/or behaviors that Paul believed to have already been manifested in the midst of the church in Corinth, it may well be that the inclusion of grumbling in this list of warnings reflects his sense that they have already begun to manifest that parallel to Israel's behavior as well.

**10:11** Paul wraps up vv. 6-11 by returning to the point of v. 6: that we must learn from Israel's experience in the desert so as not to end up repeating it. Paul says Israel's experiences (literally, "these things,"[163] referring back to the experiences recounted in the previous verses) *happened to them as examples*[164] *and were written down as warnings for us.*[165] The understanding that Scripture is always relevant to God's people is common to ancient Jewish and Christian literature.[166] Remarkably, the word Paul uses for instruction or warning occurs only once in the LXX, in Wisdom 16:6, which, speaking of Numbers 11, says that "they were provoked as a warning[167] for a short time."

161. J. Schneider, "ὀλοθρευτής," *TDNT* 5:169-70; see Exod. 12:23; Wis. 18:25; 2 Sam. 24:16; 1 Chr. 21:12, 15; 2 Chr. 32:21; Sir. 48:21, and Garland, 463.

162. On this general rejection see chs. 2 and 4 of Cheung, *Idol Food in Corinth.*

163. Some witnesses have "all these things" (either πάντα δὲ ταῦτα or ταῦτα δὲ πάντα) rather than merely "these things" (ταῦτα δέ). Metzger (*Textual Commentary,* 494) admits that "it is possible that πάντα may have been omitted by copyists who recalled ver. 6," but he and his colleagues decided that it is "more probable that the original ταῦτα (A B 33 630 1739 1881) was expanded by the addition of πάντα, whose varying position in the manuscripts suggests that the word is a gloss, inserted to heighten the narrative."

164. Gk. τυπικῶς.

165. Gk. πρὸς νουθεσίαν ἡμῶν.

166. See Rosner, "'Written for Us,'" 98-102.

167. Gk. νουθεσία.

Paul understands, however, that the Scripture has particular relevance *for us, on whom the culmination of the ages has come.*[168] This understanding of Scripture is similar to the view of the Qumran community that the Scriptures were written down with particular relevance to the eschatological community of the last days. Old Testament texts which suggested that God's revelation was written with a future time (or the last days) in mind, such as Daniel 8:26; 9:24; 12:4, 9 (and possibly Isa. 8:16), may have promoted such an understanding. The superscription found in fifty-six of the psalms in the LXX, "for the end,"[169] may also have suggested an eschatologically focused reading of Scripture. As Fee points out, here "one captures a sense of Paul's view that both the historical events and the inscripturated narrative are not simply history or isolated texts in Scripture; rather, behind all these things lies the eternal purposes of the living God, who knows the end from the beginning, and who therefore has himself woven the prefigurement into these earlier texts for the sake of his final eschatological people."[170]

Like some other Jewish groups in the New Testament period (most notably the Qumran community), Paul understands that he and his communities are living in the days of the eschatological fulfillment of the Old Testament promises and prophecies, related to the theme of the "latter days" (Deut. 4:30; Jer. 23:20; 30:24; 48:47; 49:39; Ezek. 38:16; Dan. 2:28; 10:14; Hos. 3:5).

Paul's statement that *the culmination of the ages has come* upon us clearly reflects the eschatological understanding found elsewhere in the New Testament as well, namely, that "the last days" have been upon us since the first coming of Christ. He does not explain precisely what he means because it is such a standard part of his teaching.[171] This eschatological understanding is especially relevant to this point of Paul's argument for at least two reasons. First, it is because the age of eschatological salvation has dawned that Paul can confidently point to Israel's exodus experience as a model from which we should learn. It was understood from the time of the Old Testament prophets that God's eschatological redemption of his people would follow patterns established at the first exodus. Isaiah, in particular, describes the coming salvation as a second exodus. The fact that we live in a time of eschatological crisis, the time of *the culmination of the ages,* also implies that God's ultimate acts of salvation and judgment are particularly imminent. Since God has begun the process of wrapping up history, it is of utmost urgency to learn from Israel's example in order to assure that

168. Besides this verse, see Rom. 4:23-24; 15:4, and the discussion in Hays, *Echoes,* 166-68.

169. Gk. εἰς τὸ τέλος; also found in Theodotion's text of Dan. 11:13.

170. Fee, 458-59.

171. As Fee points out (459), "the precise nuance of the wording itself is not certain," but "there is little question about Paul's point. Through his death and resurrection Jesus Christ marks the turning of the ages; the old is on its way out, the new has begun."

the devastating judgment that fell on the nation does not end up being repeated in our own experience. The eschatological point of departure found in this verse casts its shadow over the next two verses as well.

**10:12** Paul draws a conclusion from vv. 1-11: *So,*[172] *if you think you are standing firm, be careful that you don't fall!* As suggested by this verse's relationship with the preceding one, the language of standing and falling here carries eschatological connotations. In a military or judicial context to stand or fall refers to the possibilities of surviving or not the crisis of a military attack or the judgment of one's master (cf. Pss. 17:39; 35:13; Rom. 14:4).

Paul uses the same word, "fall,"[173] here to describe the danger of the one who thinks that they stand that he used in v. 8 to describe what happened to the Israelites who engaged in sexual immorality. Here the word carries the same eschatological connotation as that found in Psalm 19:9 LXX; 35:13 LXX; *Psalms of Solomon* 1:5; Romans 11:11; 14:4-5; and 1 Corinthians 13:8.[174]

Some of the Corinthians, at least, clearly thought of themselves as possessing an unassailable spiritual security based on their knowledge and spiritual experiences. They thought that they had nothing to fear from the practice of their freedoms in the areas of diet or sexual gratification. They considered themselves spiritually strong and knowledgeable enough to enter into theological debate with Paul. Paul's warnings throughout this passage are intended to help them see that their behavior suggests that they are not nearly as secure as they suppose and that reconsideration of their present attitudes and practices is a matter of great urgency.

**10:13** In case they had not picked up on the implications of vv. 1-12, Paul reminds the Corinthians that their situation is not new or unique. *No temptation has overtaken you,* he says, *except what is common to us all.* In other words, "the temptation you struggle with is common to all humanity."[175] Being tempted by the appetitive sins of forbidden food and illicit sex does not make them unusual.

172. Gk. Ὥστε.

173. Gk. πίπτω.

174. See Philo's discussion in *On Rewards and Punishments* 4–6, where he refers to athletes who fall "but can easily stand once more erect" whereas in the race of life "it is whole lives that fall, which once overthrown can hardly be raised up again."

175. Chrysostom suggests that the word here translated *common to us all* (ἀνθρώπινος) refers to trials or temptations that are "small, brief, moderate" (μικρός, βραχύς, σύμμετρος), basing his understanding here on his interpretation of Rom. 6:19 and Heb. 12:4. The fact that he senses the need to base his interpretation (and explanation for his readers) on his understanding of other texts shows that the Greek was not transparent (to him or them). Fee also feels that it "refers to the nature of the trial. It does not require superhuman effort for them to abstain since it is a merely human trial" (460 n. 51). Collins (373) and Witherington (224) also take it to mean "merely human." These interpretations take Paul's word to suggest a contrast between human and divine (or superhuman) temptations. It is not clear, though, that Paul or any other ancient Christian ever contemplated a divine-sized or superhuman-sized temptation. We are suggesting that the clauses say two different things, namely, (1) "The temptations you are facing are ones all humans face," and (2) "God will not let these (or other) temptations attain irresistible proportions."

Paul's point is not just the abstract one that there is no such thing as a unique temptation, but that the one or ones the Corinthians are dealing with (whether they realize it or not) are not new. They are ones Israel struggled with (vv. 6-10) and are common to Gentiles as well. Garland is correct to point out that the temptation should be understood "in the context of the warning examples he has just enumerated and the exhortation to flee idolatry that immediately follows."[176] That the Old Testament and ancient Judaism considered idolatry the most common and fundamental temptation of humanity (with sexual immorality as a related sign of human corruption and greed a particular manifestation of idolatry), along with the context of Paul's statement (in 1 Corinthians 8–10 in general and immediately before the exhortation to flee idolatry in particular) suggests that he has the common human pull toward idolatry in mind. According to the Old Testament and early Jewish understanding, virtually all Gentiles and many Jews were guilty of idolatry.

The immediately following reference to God's faithfulness should probably be understood in contrast to Paul's reference to our human tendency to be unfaithful to him (i.e., idolatrous).[177] Fee believes that Paul's point is "that in ordinary human trials one can expect divine aid. There is no danger of 'falling' here. But it is otherwise with idolatry. The 'way out' in that case is simply put: 'Therefore, flee idolatry.' That is the concern of the next paragraph."[178] This seems to miss the mark, as though Paul had digressed from his discussion of idolatry to talk instead about "ordinary human trials" or temptations, as though idolatry was not such an ordinary temptation. The Corinthians may not have realized it, but they are tempted to participate in idolatrous activities. That temptation is not irresistible or insurmountable, and they must resist it, take the way out, or suffer destruction as did the Israelites mentioned in the previous verses.[179]

Thiselton, however, suggests that the temptation Paul has in mind is the "craving" that was mentioned in v. 6.[180] While the primary issue Paul deals with in chapters 8–10 is idolatry (esp. in relation to idol food), his discussion in 9:24–10:13 seems to have recalled the concerns with sexual immorality that he had more directly addressed in chapters 5–7 (esp. in 9:25; 10:6, 8). As was pointed out above, the sins of idolatry and sexual immorality often were considered together as the fundamental weaknesses of Gentiles, and Thiselton is right to point to the centrality of v. 6 within Paul's argument.

The word translated *temptation*[181] can also mean "test" or "trial" in the right contexts. Here, however, there is no indication that the Corinthians

176. Garland, 467.
177. For the Old Testament background on God's faithfulness, see on 1:9.
178. Fee, 461-62.
179. Cf. Witherington, 224.
180. Thiselton, 748.
181. Gk. πειρασμός.

are suffering an unusual trial, while the context suggests that they are tempted to fall into some of Israel's sinful patterns.

*And God is faithful; he will not let you be tempted beyond what you can bear. But when you are tempted, he will also provide a way out so that you can endure it.* The last two clauses are structured by a "not . . . but" logic which controls how the clauses are to interpret each other. As Collins points out, the parallel structure is reinforced by the use of "tempt/temptation" and "can" in each of the clauses.[182]

Paul's statement that God's faithfulness (see comments on 1:9a) leads him to provide a way to endure the temptation should probably be understood in the light of the references in vv. 7-10 to the various things that "some" of the Israelites did. The implication is that the temptations were not irresistible. Not all the Israelites fell. In each case many were able to endure the temptations and remain faithful to God. "God always provides his people with a choice" and with an "exit path."[183] That God does not allow us to be exposed to irresistible temptations is a reflection of his faithfulness to his commitments to us as his covenant people. In some cases God may remove us from the situation of seemingly unbearable temptation, while in other cases he may provide strength or other resources within the situation to strengthen his people so that they may endure the temptation and remain faithful to him.

A concern with unbearable trials or temptations may be related to traditional Jewish expectations regarding the crisis that would accompany the onset of the new age and the transition of the ages and the expectation that many would be overwhelmed and fall away under the pressure (Sir. 15:11-12; *Jubilees* 23:23-27; *1 Enoch* 94:5; *2 Enoch* 66:5-7; *4 Ezra* 5:1-13; 6:14-25; *Sibylline Oracles* 3:796-809; *2 Baruch* 27; 48:31-37; 70:2-10; Mark 13:20; Matt. 24:10-13; 22). Israel faced such tremendous trials and temptations during their wilderness wandering, as they were on the threshold of entering into the Promised Land. Many, in fact most, fell away, but not of necessity. There was *a way out* in each situation, and while many did not choose it, others did. The Corinthians must be like those who followed the way out that God always provides. "The imagery of exit and escape continues the motif of the Exodus experience, written for the benefit of the Corinthians."[184]

This passage has focused primarily upon the great danger in which some Corinthians find themselves, but it ends with a more general focus on the wonderful faithfulness of our God, who can be trusted not to leave us without hope or escape, but to provide for us the way out so that we might not cave in to the temptations around us. We call on our faithful God to "lead us not into temptation, but deliver us from the evil one" (Matt. 6:13),

182. Collins, 374.
183. Thiselton, 748 (emphasis removed).
184. Collins, 374.

and when we find ourselves in trials and temptations, we can know that he will not put us in a situation we cannot endure, but will make it possible for us to glorify him either in the situation or in thanksgiving for our escape from it.

### c. Those Who Worship God Must Refrain from Any Association with Idolatry, 10:14-22

As Paul moves toward his conclusion, he starts with the most basic exhortation on the subject ("flee idolatry"). This exhortation, as we have argued in the Introduction to the commentary (21-25), sums up the main point of chapters 8–10. The rest of the chapter develops two basic arguments: first, that participation in pagan meals may have disastrous consequences for Christian participants (vv. 15-22); and secondly, in all situations one must act in ways that promote rather than threaten the salvation and spiritual well-being of others (vv. 23-33).

The first section unpacking the fundamental exhortation to flee idolatry in v. 14 (namely, vv. 15-22) is rich in the theology of the Lord's Supper. The passage has been remarkably underused in most churches' theology and liturgy of the Lord's Supper, for which all the weight ends up resting on 11:23-29. It complements and fills out the material in chapter 11 by explaining that the Supper entails participation in the blood and body of Christ, that the single loaf speaks to the heart of the unity that must mark the life of the church, and that the meal serves to renew the exclusive covenant with God established through Christ, and that its abuse constitutes a foolish and dangerous challenge to the God who is present in its celebration.

> *14Therefore, my dear friends, flee from idolatry. 15I speak to sensible people; judge for yourselves what I say. 16Is not the cup of thanksgiving for which we give thanks a participation in the blood of Christ? And is not the bread that we break a participation in the body of Christ? 17Because there is one loaf, we, who are many, are one body, for we all partake of the one loaf.*
>
> *18Consider the people of Israel: Do not those who eat the sacrifices participate in the altar? 19Do I mean then that food sacrificed to an idol is anything, or that an idol is anything? 20No, but the sacrifices of pagans are offered to demons, not to God, and I do not want you to be participants with demons. 21You cannot drink the cup of the Lord and the cup of demons too; you cannot have a part in both the Lord's table and the table of demons. 22Are we trying to arouse the Lord's jealousy? Are we stronger than he?*

**10:14** As Paul approaches the end of his treatment of food sacrificed to idols, he provides a summarizing exhortation similar to that given near the end of his treatment of sexual immorality in 6:18. *Therefore, my dear friends, flee from idolatry.* In doing so he indicates that he is drawing the conclusion[185] from his previous argumentation, which also indicates to the reader how Paul expects the illustrations and warnings in vv. 1-13 to be understood. This is indeed "the directive that all of chs. 8–10 has been arguing for,"[186] and indicates that idolatry is "the root issue in the whole discussion."[187] It is hardly a question of merely causing someone to act against their conscience. Here Paul introduces a section (10:14-33) in which he draws his conclusions on the subject.[188] This is only the second time in the letter (cf. 4:14) that he refers to them as his "dear friends,"[189] and the first time he has used the word in a vocative form (cf. 15:58). By referring to the Corinthians in this intimate way, he leaves no doubt about his personal affection and concern for them. The urgency of the main exhortation (here, as also in 6:18) is indicated by the use of the word "flee"[190] with its connotation of extreme imminent danger. In the context of the previous verse's promise that God would always "provide a way out" so that we can endure whatever temptation comes our way the exhortation to "flee" suggests that this is the way out from the temptation to idolatry, and that there is a narrow window of opportunity that they had best not let pass by. Thiselton notes that the combination of the reference to the "way out" in v. 13 and the call to *flee* in v. 14 "conjures up the image of an army caught [in a narrow gorge] and urged to flee at all speed through a mountain pass."[191] Or, perhaps, of a seemingly defenseless people trapped between an attacking army and the shore of a sea who are urged to flee at all speed through a divinely provided opening in the sea (cf. Exodus 14)?

**10:15** *I speak to sensible*[192] *people; judge*[193] *for yourselves what I say.* Witherington points out that the first clause of this verse "should likely be seen as rhetorical irony. Paul calls the audience 'wise,' though their behavior indicates otherwise." He goes on to point out that "Paul knows, like any good rhetorician, that he must rely on the power of persuasion."[194] His

185. Paul marks the role of this sentence with Διόπερ ("Therefore"), a strong inferential conjunction.

186. Witherington, 224.

187. Collins, 378.

188. As argued by Schrage (2:435), Thiselton (754), and others, the combination of the vocative (ἀγαπητοί μου) and the inferential conjunction (Διόπερ) suggests the beginning of a new section, one that wraps up the previous discussion.

189. Gk. ἀγαπητοί. Traditionally translated "beloved," that word has come to take on formal or stilted connotations in English. Thiselton, 755, renders the word "my very dear friends."

190. Gk. φεύγετε, a present active imperative from φεύγω. See on 6:18.

191. Thiselton, 755.

192. Gk. φρόνιμος; "pert[aining] to understanding associated w[ith] insight and wisdom, *sensible, thoughtful, prudent, wise*" (BDAG).

193. This is the one aorist imperative (κρίνατε, from κρίνω) in the chapter (the first since 7:21). The perfective aspect of the aorist imperative calls to mind that Paul is not exhorting the Corinthians to judge his ideas as a general rule, but is calling on them to use good judgment in considering the argument he now expounds.

194. Witherington, 224.

power of persuasion would be significantly reduced, however, if the Corinthians perceived that he was being ironic in calling them wise.[195] Rather, as Collins suggests, it seems that "[t]he *captatio benevolentiae*[196] of v. 14 is continued as Paul describes the Corinthians as prudent folk."[197] Paul surely writes to them in this way since some of the Corinthians "had prided themselves in their understanding of things, and surely had intimated as much in their letter to him" and he wants "to show them how sensible [his position] is, based on their own experience of the Lord's Table."[198] He will appeal to their own self-perception as wise people, trusts that their critical faculties are sufficient to allow them to perceive the soundness of the following argument, and therefore calls on them to judge for themselves the logic of his following argument.

While Paul is certainly sincere in his appeal to their abilities to discern a sound argument, there is also an implication that if they are indeed wise and sensible people, they will recognize the soundness of his thinking. If they fail to see the weight of Paul's argument, it would serve as an indictment of the wisdom they claimed for themselves and that Paul was willing to grant them. They are expected "to judge for themselves that Paul is right!"[199] The rhetorical element of Paul's appeal to them to exercise their abilities to discern a sound argument is reflected as well in the series of rhetorical questions that Paul employs in the argument found in vv. 16-22.

Paul's statement that he addresses himself to wise or *sensible* people also reinforces the traditional opposition between wisdom and idolatry (e.g., Pss. 96:5; 97:7; 115:3-8; 135:15-18; Isa. 40:18-20; 41:7; 44:9-20; Jer. 10:1-14; 51:15-17; Wis. 14-15; Rom. 1:19-25) that underlies the relationship between chapters 1–4 and 8–10 (see our discussion of the letter's structure in the Introduction, 21-25). As Paul argued in Romans 1:21-23, those who lack wisdom lapse into the worship of idols.

**10:16** Here Paul begins the series of rhetorical arguments[200] that

195. Some translations (e.g., ESV, NRSV) translate the ὡς ("*as* sensible people"), while others (e.g., NIV, TNIV, NET, NLT) do not. The word functions as a "marker introducing the perspective from which a pers[on], thing, or activity is viewed or understood as to character, function, or role" (BDAG). If it were to be translated here, it would have to be along the lines of "I speak to you as people I consider wise people" and not as though it suggested, "I speak to you as though you were wise people." Fee (464-65) regrets that the NIV did not translate it, but he also argues that, as in 5:3, it "refers to an actual reality, not a merely hypothetical one."

196. A rhetorical move intended to gain favor with the audience. Chrysostom agrees, calling Paul's reference to them as sensible people an *encomium* and implying that he builds them up further "when he discourses not as commanding nor as laying down the law, but as advising with them and as actually pleading before them" (*Homiliae in Epistulam i ad Corinthios* 24.2 [NPNF$^1$ 12:139]).

197. Collins, 379.

198. Fee, 464.

199. Fee, 465.

200. In vv. 16-22 Paul uses a series of present tense indicative verbs and infinitives (with one present tense imperative in v. 18a) whose imperfective aspect fits his choice to ad-

mark this part of his argument. *Is not the cup of thanksgiving for which we give thanks a participation in the blood of Christ?* Literally Paul's question begins, "Is not the cup of blessing which we bless . . . ," but the TNIV translation faithfully represents the idea of the blessing.[201] Early Jews and Christians understood that they did not need to bless food or drink. They did not bless the cup itself, but blessed God (gave thanks to God) for providing them with the good gifts of food and drink. The ancient and still traditional Jewish blessing begins, "Blessed are you, O Lord, our God, King of the Universe, who brings forth food from the earth. . . ."[202] Chrysostom, in the fourth century, has a similar understanding[203] and finds in Paul's words the motif of God's grace and mercy and a rebuke of the Corinthians, suggesting that Paul means to ask, "How then are you not acting inconsistently, . . . blessing God for delivering you from idols, yet running again to their tables?"[204] Chrysostom sees in the reference to the *cup of thanksgiving* an acknowledgment that the Christian faith is all of grace and mercy because of which thanksgiving to God plays a central role in what is the heart of Christian worship — namely, the Lord's Supper.[205] That Paul is discussing the church's practice of the Lord's Supper is made perfectly clear by the time we finish Paul's next question: *And is not the bread that we break a participation in the body of Christ?*

---

vance his argument at this point through a series of definitions, rhetorical questions, and assertions about the nature of things.

201. The Gospels alternate between references to blessing bread and giving thanks for it, indicating that the references to blessing bread are to be understood as references to blessing or thanking God for it: Matt. 14:19 (blessed); 15:36 (gave thanks); 26:26 (blessed); Mark 6:41 (blessed); 8:6 (gave thanks); 14:22 (blessed); Luke 9:16 (blessed); 22:19 (gave thanks); 24:30 (blessed); John 6:11 (gave thanks), 23 (gave thanks); Acts 27:35 (gave thanks). All three references in the Gospels to the cup use "gave thanks" (Matt. 26:27; Mark 14:23; Luke 22:17). The *Thanksgiving Hymns* of Qumran similarly alternate between the set expressions "Blessed be you, Lord" (1QH$^{a}$ v 4; vii 8; viii 17; xiii 20; xviii 14; xix 27) and "I give you thanks, Lord" (1QH$^{a}$ x 20, 31; xi 19, 37; xii 5; xiii 5; xv 6, 26, 34; xvi 4; xvii 38). Some witnesses (F, G, 365, *pc;* Ir$^{lat\ pt}$) have "cup of εὐχαριστίας" (thanksgiving). The evidence is too weak to be considered original but does offer further evidence of the way "blessing" was understood by certain scribes. Thiselton (792 n. 70) points out that "[t]he Greek translation of the Hebrew may take a double accusative, in which God is sometimes implicit rather than explicit."

202. Cf. Marvin R. Wilson, *Our Father Abraham: Jewish Roots of the Christian Faith* (Grand Rapids: Eerdmans, 1989), 177. The standard blessing over wine was "Blessed are you, O Lord, our God, King of the Universe, Creator of the fruit of the vine" (cf. *m. Berakot* 6:1-3).

203. Commenting on this verse, he has Paul saying that he calls the cup the cup of blessing because "I unfold all the treasure of God's goodness, and call to mind those mighty gifts," and says that we too recount "over the cup the unspeakable mercies of God and all that we have been made partakers of, so draw near to Him, and communicate; giving Him thanks" (*Homiliae in Epistulam i ad Corinthios* 24.3 [NPNF[1] 12:139]).

204. *Homiliae in Epistulam i ad Corinthios* 24.3 (NPNF[1] 12:139; PG 61:200).

205. He paraphrases Paul's thought as follows (*Homiliae in Epistulam i ad Corinthios* 24.3 [NPNF[1] 12:139]): "For when I call it 'blessing,' I mean thanksgiving, and when I call it thanksgiving I unfold all the treasure of God's goodness, and call to mind those mighty gifts."

The word translated *participation* has generated serious debate. BDAG suggests that here, as in some other cases, it may mean "the common possession or enjoyment of someth[ing]." The issue is whether in the context of worship the word suggests common possession or enjoyment of a relationship "with the deity (in the Christian's case, with Christ himself), or with fellow participants in the meal as they worship the deity by sacrifice and by eating in his/her honor."[206] According to Friedrich Hauck, they "enter into a spiritual communion with the risen Lord."[207] He argues on the basis of this text that "[p]articipation in Christ, which is known basically and perfectly in faith, is achieved and experienced in enhanced form, with no dogmatic implication, in the sacrament."[208] Furthermore, "In terms of the common belief of antiquity it is self-evident for him that those who partake of the cultic meal become companions of the god."[209]

J. Hainz, on the other hand, argues strongly that the context indicates that Paul is referring primarily to "partnership with the other partakers in the meal" since his "concern is the various relationships between those who partake at the table of the Lord and those who partake at the altar, i.e., at the table of demons," and he "does not allude directly to the relationship of the one who eats at the altar to God . . . but to the partnership that they enter by eating." In the end, however, he concludes that one "enters into partnership with the powers to which the sacrifices are dedicated *and* with those who share in the offerings."[210]

Fee[211] suggests that the reference to Christ's "blood" may have more of a vertical orientation (pointing to our relationship with God) while the one to his "body" may have a more horizontal orientation (pointing to our relationships with other members of Christ's "body," the church). While Paul does develop the theme of our relationship with the rest of the church under the motif of the "body" in the next chapter, there is no indication here that he has two different ideas in mind rather than simply referring to the body and blood of Christ that are associated with the Lord's Supper. In fact, in this context Paul's stress seems to be on the divine aspect of the fellowship throughout. In contexts where food and drink are being shared the word used here, often translated "fellowship," is typically used to describe the sense of fellowship, camaraderie, and friendship that is experienced by those enjoying food and drink in the presence of

206. Fee, 466.

207. Friedrich Hauck, "κοινωνός," *TDNT* 3:804.

208. Hauck, "κοινωνός," *TDNT* 3:805.

209. Hauck, "κοινωνός," *TDNT* 3:805, referring back to 803 n. 45, where he points out that "Philo speaks of a close fellowship between the righteous and God in the cultus, esp[ecially] in the sacrificial meal," citing *On the Special Laws* 1:221 (God "makes the whole company of those who offer the sacrifice, partakers at the altar and table companions, only admonishing them not to look upon it as their own feast, for they are but stewards of the feast").

210. J. Hainz, "κοινωνία," *EDNT* 2:304. Emphasis added.

211. Fee, 468-69.

friends.[212] It is probably just such "fellowship," with the social and political advantages that would come from sharing in it, that probably drew some Corinthians to join their neighbors at meals where pagan gods/idols were honored. Paul's argument, with its emphasis on participation in the blood and body of Christ, seeks to stress that where God is (or gods are) invoked as the host or patron (or hosts/patrons) of the meal, the fellowship is not merely with the men and women gathered around the table, but with the deity as well. Through our fellowship with Christ we participate in the benefits of his sacrifice, which serves to establish or renew our covenantal relationship with God.

The wonder of the Christian faith is that our participation in Christ (i.e., in his blood and body) is not based on a sacrifice that we make to please the god (as in the Greco-Roman and other pagan religions), but on Christ's own sacrifice of his *body* and *blood,* that we might indeed participate in the life that only he can provide for us through that sacrifice. Pagan sacrifices offer only a reflection of the human longing for communion with the divine and a human attempt to establish that communion. Christ's sacrifice of his body and blood for us establishes what we could never achieve otherwise: true communion with God and participation in the life he has won for us through the cross.

The Lord's Supper, like the last supper, was based upon the Passover *Seder,* and Paul's comments here should be understood in the light of that context.[213] The final cup of the Passover meal (and the last supper) was called the "cup of blessing." Just as participation in the Passover celebration entailed participation in the benefits of the Passover sacrifice (on which see Exod. 12:27; 34:25; Deut. 16:2, 5, 6; 2 Chr. 35:1, 6, 11), so participation in the Lord's Supper entails participation in the benefits of his sacrificial death on the cross. In 11:25 the cup will be interpreted as a reference to "the new covenant in [Christ's] blood." Paul evidently has in mind the Christian's participation in the benefits of Christ's covenant-establishing sacrifice.[214] The Lord's Supper is best understood as a covenant-ratifying meal in which the whole community was to participate.[215]

As Thiselton points out, the blessing which was uttered at the Passover *Seder* was one in which God was blessed or thanked for the (exodus) redemption commemorated in the *Seder.* For the Christian to share in the cup of

212. See the uses of κοινωνία in Plutarch's *Quaestionum Convivialium* ("table-talk"): 614.E.9; 615.A.3; 618.A.7; 643.A.3; 643.B.4; 643.D.4; 643.F.4; 644.A.8; 644.D.2; 679.A.6; 679.A.9; 697.C.6; 707.C.8; 708.D.4; 709.B.3; 709.D.2; 726.E.4; 728.A.3; 741.D.1.

213. See the extended discussion in Thiselton, 756-60.

214. William Lane has shown the importance of the covenantal background to Paul's concerns with the Corinthians in this letter (Lane, "Covenant: The Key to Paul's Conflict with Corinth," *TynBul* 33 (1982), 3-29; cf. esp. 23-24).

215. Gordon Hugenberger describes the Lord's Supper "as a covenant-ratifying oath-sign" (*Marriage as a Covenant: Biblical Law and Ethics as Developed from Malachi* [Biblical Studies Library; Grand Rapids: Baker, 1998], 209 n. 171).

blessing in the Lord's Supper "represents a participation . . . in the redemption achieved in this context not by liberation from the oppression of Egypt, but the costly purchase of freedom from sin (1 Cor 6:19; 7:23) won through the 'body and blood' of Christ."[216] He correctly emphasizes the covenantal context of Paul's thought and its Old Testament and Jewish background.[217]

To "break bread" was a common way of referring to the sharing of a meal. Bread was baked in larger or smaller loaves and would be broken by hand, usually by the father as a signal that the meal had begun.[218] The expression was naturally applied to meals shared by early Christians.[219]

While Fee and others insist that Paul's only problem with food offered to idols was with its consumption in the context of an official pagan cult meal, Paul's argument in this verse should caution us against too narrow a view of what Paul opposes. Christian worship, in which a meal was shared by a group sharing fellowship in someone's house (with bread, wine, singing and theological discussion), would, in many ways, have looked and seemed more like a large social event than a formal pagan cultic meal where animals were sacrificed and then eaten in the presence of the god. This is especially so given the way the Corinthians seem to have been carrying out their worship (with some getting drunk and sated while others go hungry).

Paul's language stresses the religious context that is established for Christians by "merely" saying a blessing over the cup and eating the bread as a spiritual life-giving gift from Christ. While Willis seeks to describe many pagan meals (both within and outside the precincts of pagan temples) as merely social events, others have pointed out that such a dichotomy between sacred and secular was foreign to the Roman world and is not supported by the evidence. Even in gatherings for meals intended to celebrate birthdays or other important social events, the attendees were invited to dine at the table of the god (even if the event were not in the god's temple), whose name would be invoked and in whose name a blessing would have been said over the wine and food. The great religious significance that Paul attributes to those same actions in Christian contexts suggests that he would not have considered them innocent of religious significance at pagan meals.

Hanson has argued that the references to bread and wine (with the latter described as "blood") in Deuteronomy 32:14 (which recounts God's provision for Israel, including "the best of the wheat" and "wine, the blood of the grape") would have been "quite enough to point Paul to the Eucharist, which he is of course discussing in 1 Cor. 10:14-21."[220] He goes so far as

216. Thiselton, 758.

217. Cf. esp. Thiselton, 759.

218. Cf. BDAG on κλάω ("to break").

219. Cf. Jer. 16:7; Matt. 14:19; 15:36; 26:26; Mark 8:6, 19; 14:22; Luke 22:19; 24:30; Acts 2:46; 20:7, 11; 27:35.

220. Anthony T. Hanson, *Studies in Paul's Technique and Theology* (Grand Rapids: Eerdmans, 1974), 115.

to affirm that "1 Cor. 10:14-21 is a Christian midrash on Deut. 32:17-21."[221] It may be that sometime before writing 1 Corinthians Paul was led from his reading of Deuteronomy 32 to certain reflections on the Lord's Supper. In this context however, the requirements of his argument are more likely to have led him to bring the Lord's Supper (with its echoes of Deuteronomy 32) into his argument than that the echoes of Deuteronomy 32 play a significant role in his argument here.

**10:17** *Because there is one loaf, we, who are many, are one body, for we all partake of the one loaf.* This verse can be and has been interpreted in a way that emphasizes a purely social implication of partaking of the Lord's Supper. Certainly the theme of the unity of the body is crucial, and relates to the persistent issue of the divisions within the Corinthian church. That there is only one loaf is mentioned both at the beginning and at the end of the verse.[222] But while one can imagine a father making a similar statement to his family as they share a loaf of bread at dinner, Paul probably understands the special nature of the bread (as the body of Christ) to be the explanation for its ability to unite such a diverse group. Paul's statement, that our common eating of the one loaf makes us one people, clearly implies the common ethical relationship between the "indicative" and the "imperative." That is, the Corinthians were to live out (better than they had been doing) the unity that was expected of a group of people who had been united by Christ's death on their behalf. As Exodus 12:43-48 indicates, the Passover was to be celebrated by the whole community of Israel as a common and unifying experience for the nation. The Lord's Supper should have had (but apparently had failed to have) a similar role for the church in Corinth.

Given the argument of the near context, with its concern regarding the need to flee from idolatry and any association with pagan offerings, the point that all who partake of the bread and wine of the Christian meal become united by doing so is probably intended to prepare the way for vv. 21-22, where the ethical impossibility of eating at both the Lord's table and "the table of demons" is stressed. If all those who eat the bread together in the church are thereby made into one body, presumably all those who share food or drink which is associated with a pagan idol become one together through their joint sharing of that food.

**10:18** Paul's explanation of the religious/spiritual involvement implied in Christians' participation in the Lord's Supper is supported by a consideration of the experience of the Israelites. *Consider the people of Israel: Do not those who eat the sacrifices participate in the altar?* Paul continues his use of rhetorical questions. This one serves to assert that in Israel *those who eat the sacrifices participate in the altar.*

221. Hanson, *Studies in Paul's Technique,* 115.

222. They are the second and third words from the beginning and the end of the verse (ὅτι εἷς ἄρτος . . . ἑνὸς ἄρτου μετέχομεν).

The verse begins, however, with an exhortation to learn from, literally, "Israel according to the flesh" (TNIV, *the people of Israel*). Significant debate continues over the question of whether Paul is referring to Jewish practice in his own day or to more ancient Israel. Gardner, Hays, and Thiselton argue that Paul has in mind sinful Israel, especially Israel as the nation that worshiped the golden calf. This proposal is supported by the evidence of other references to and echoes of that event and of Exodus 32 and of Deuteronomy 32 in this chapter.[223] The use of the present tense participle to refer to the people Paul has in mind ("those who eat"),[224] as well as the present indicative verb ("are participants"),[225] seems to suggest that Paul had the present experience of his own day in mind, or a general ("gnomic"[226]) principle in mind rather than some specific previous event.[227]

Witherington argues that the expression "surely means OT Israel and implies a distinction from an Israel according to the Spirit," namely, the church.[228] Since v. 1 already indicated that the Corinthians were the heirs of the Israelites (who were their "fathers"), this verse may clarify the relationship by implying that the Corinthians are "Israelites according to the Spirit" (since the Spirit is the expected contrast with the flesh in Pauline thought).[229]

The reference to "Israel according to the flesh" suggests a distinction between the Judaism which found its identity in the Jerusalem cult and believers who considered themselves the true heirs of Israel (and whom Paul elsewhere refers to as the true circumcision [Rom. 2:28-29], or the children of the Jerusalem above rather than the present Jerusalem [Gal. 4:25-26]). This distinction is simply a variation of the distinction made in the Old Testament and ancient Judaism between the faithful remnant and those citizens of Israel who were considered unqualified to be counted as true

223. See the discussion in Thiselton, 771-72. It may be noteworthy that the key vocabulary of the crucial clause, "eat," "sacrifices," and "altar" (ἐσθίοντες . . . θυσίας . . . τοῦ θυσιαστηρίου), is all found in Exod. 32:5-6. But they are common terms used even more frequently in relation to the proper offering of sacrifices at the tabernacle or temple (cf. Lev. 6:8-9; 10:12-13; Deut. 12:27; 27:6-7; Hos. 8:12-13).

224. The present substantival participle (used here) is rarely used to refer to people who carried out their actions in the past.

225. Gk. οἱ ἐσθίοντες and κοινωνοὶ . . . εἰσίν, respectively.

226. Cf. Wallace, *Greek Grammar beyond the Basics*, 523.

227. See the discussion of our approach to the Greek tenses and verbal aspect in the Introduction to the commentary (42-46). Although present time is not the essence of present tense verbs (and the normal temporal significance of indicative verbs is cancelable), there is nothing in the context here to indicate to the reader that the normal temporal understanding is cancelled. Paul's readers might have expected some such linguistic clue if he expected them to understand his reference to be to something that was no longer the case.

228. Witherington, 218.

229. So also Chrysostom and Collins, among many others. The latter (380) points out that, "[g]iven the experience of some of the Israelites during the wandering through the desert (10:6-11), some negativity may be implied in Paul's use of this term to describe historical Israel." Cf. Rom. 8:4-6, 9, 13; 1 Cor. 5:5; Gal. 3:3; 4:29; 5:16-17; 6:8; Phil. 3:3.

members of God's covenant people (cf. the need to have a circumcised heart in Deut. 10:16; Jer. 4:4; 9:24). Thus, Paul points to the cultic practices of the Judaism of his day, based on Old Testament teaching. While some sacrifices were consumed only by the priests and others by the whole community, to eat the food that had been offered in sacrifice was to participate in the cultic act of the sacrifice, that is, to participate in the worship of the God of Israel.[230]

By "participating in the altar" Paul evidently means that those eating the meal from the food taken from the altar are counted as those who offered the worship through the sacrifice that was offered there (and expect to benefit from the efficacy of that offering). The implication for eating food offered to idols is clear. Paul implies that to knowingly eat food that has been clearly identified as such makes one a willing participant of the offering from which it was taken. Such is understood to be the case in Christian participation in the Lord's Supper and in the offerings made at the temple in Jerusalem as well, and it would be only reasonable to assume that it applies to food offered to idols also. That very implication brings Paul back to the issue of the significance of idols and idol food, an issue that he touched on in 8:4, 7 and that he addresses again in the following verses.

**10:19** Verse 19 continues the use of rhetorical questions to lead the Corinthians to the proper conclusions. *Do I mean then that food sacrificed to an idol is anything, or that an idol is anything?* The introductory question, literally, "What am I saying then?" (TNIV, *Do I mean then*), indicates that Paul is about to draw conclusions from (or summarize the point of) the previous verses. The follow-up, *that food sacrificed to an idol is anything, or that an idol is anything?* raises a potential misunderstanding that could have arisen from Paul's previous arguments. The Corinthians may think that Paul's argument (that those who knowingly/intentionally eat food offered to idols are thereby spiritually united to that to which the food is offered and to the others who also eat the food with them) works only if the idols to which the food is offered are real gods after all (and that his argument assumes that they are).

Since 10:16 Paul has been discussing the spiritual significance of participation in Christian and Jewish cultic meals as part of his argument against participating in pagan religious meals. Earlier (see on 8:4) he affirmed (in agreement with some of the Corinthians) that idols are not real and that there is only one real God. In 10:19 he concedes that food itself does not become spiritually contaminated by being sacrificed to idols. The rhetorical question clarifies that Paul has not gone back on his affirmation that idols (and gods) are not real and that food does not become spiritually contaminated by being offered to an idol.

**10:20** Paul takes a break from the series of rhetorical questions to

230. See Daniel G. Reid, "Sacrifice and Temple Service," in *DNTB* 1038-44 for discussion of the various sacrifices and who could eat which.

make some very strong assertions in response to them in this verse and the next. *No, but the sacrifices of pagans are offered to demons, not to God, and I do not want you to be participants with demons.* Here Paul clarifies that his objection to participation in pagan religious meals reflects his understanding that although the idols themselves do not have any valid spiritual reality and do not represent actual gods, there is a spiritual reality behind them in that they have been created at the instigation of demons posing as gods and those worshiping them worship those demons. The rhetorical question of the previous verse does not need or receive an answer (*No* is supplied by the context in the TNIV and other translations), although the contrastive *but* makes Paul's meaning clear. He says, literally, "but that which they offer they offer to demons and not to God."

A key question is whether "they" refers to the Israelites mentioned in the previous verses or to pagans. In most ancient manuscripts and witnesses the subject is explicitly identified as "the pagans," but in some there is no explicit subject.[231] The editors of UBS[4] considered the inclusion of the subject "an ancient gloss" intended to prevent the understanding that Paul was referring to the offerings made by "Israel according to the flesh" (cf. v. 18).[232] Some interpreters argue that it is a gloss that misrepresents Paul's meaning,[233] but the majority is probably correct that even if it is a later gloss it represents an accurate interpretation of Paul's meaning. This is not a critique of Jewish offerings in Jerusalem (which, according to Acts, Paul himself participated in from time to time even after his conversion to Christ), but is consistent with ancient Jewish understandings of pagan offerings.

The words *[offered] to demons, not to God*[234] are a quotation from (or allusion to) Deuteronomy 32:17, and the recognition that he is doing so will have to play some part in our evaluation of Paul's meaning. The verse comes from the Song of Moses, which recounts Israel's unfaithfulness to the Lord despite his goodness to them. They provoked him to jealousy by strange and abhorrent gods (32:16) and "sacrificed to demons, not God, to gods they had not known; to new ones who had recently appeared, ones your ancestors had not known" (v. 17). While Israel had a long history with the God who had raised them up and redeemed them, they showed a lack of faithfulness to him. The Hebrew word translated "demons"[235] in Deuteronomy 32:17 does not refer to deities but less-powerful spirits which in

231. The textual history of the relevant portion of 1 Cor. 10:20 is rather complex. "The gentiles/pagans" (τὰ ἔθνη) is found in 𝔓[46 vid], א, A, C, P, Ψ, 33[vid], 81, 104, 365, 630, 1175, 1505, 1739, 2464, as well as the Latin, Syriac, and Coptic versions. The majority of the Byzantine tradition and the lectionaries also have it, along with a modification of the verb (from plural to singular to agree with the plural neuter subject). Witnesses lacking the subject include B, D, F, G, Ambrosiaster, and Speculum (Pseudo-Augustine).

232. Metzger, *Textual Commentary*, 494.

233. See Thiselton, 773; Kistemaker, 346-47.

234. Gk. δαιμονίοις καὶ οὐ θεῷ.

235. Heb. שֵׁדִים / *šēdîm*.

Mesopotamian texts are treated as spiritual protectors of persons or places.[236] They were not originally considered malevolent demons (as understood by Jews [and Christians] since Hellenistic times) but were thought of as second-tier spiritual beings, obviously utterly unworthy of being treated with the respect and worship due to Israel's God. This understanding of "demons" developed since the time of Deuteronomy 32:17 in the light of later experience and revelation, and this passage played a significant role in its development.

In this text God is upset with his "sons and daughters" (32:19) for sacrificing to demons. In Psalm 106:37 Israel is condemned for sacrificing *their own sons* and daughters to demons.[237] The latter text is the only other place in the Old Testament where the Hebrew word for "demons" appears. It refers to later, even more shocking, events which are probably understood in the light of Deuteronomy 32:17. In Baruch 4:7 the exile is attributed to the fact that Israel provoked their Maker, "sacrificing to demons and not to God."[238] The reference to God's nursing of Israel in Baruch 4:8 probably reflects the influence of Deuteronomy 32:10-15 (esp. vv. 13-14). In *1 Enoch* 19:1 Enoch is told that the spirits of the angels who cohabited with women in Genesis 6 (see 1 *Enoch* 6) will lead the people to offer sacrifices to demons as though they were gods. In the *Testament of Solomon* 5:5 Solomon, who has been given magical power over demons, is told by one who identifies himself as one born of a human mother and an angelic father (again, cf. Jewish tradition regarding Gen. 6:1-4) that, after being held by Solomon for a little while, the demons will again be loosed and will deceive the human race into worshiping them as gods. Revelation 9:20 describes humanity stubbornly continuing to worship demons despite the evidence of God's wrath falling on the earth. *Leviticus Rabbah* 22:8 associates Deuteronomy 32:17 with the sacrifices to goat idols/demons mentioned in Leviticus 17:7, and explains that the laws insisting that sacrifices could be offered only at the door of the tabernacle (Lev. 17:3-4) were intended to prevent such forbidden sacrifices.

Two different emphases may be found within ancient Jewish thinking about false gods. An apocalyptic Jewish tradition tended to affirm the reality of demons as spiritual enemies of God's people, while a Hellenistic Jewish tradition (reflecting an emphasis in the prophets) tended to reject them as nongods (or perhaps nonentities).[239] Some have seen a tension in Paul's thought that reflects his acceptance of elements of both Jewish traditions.[240] He does use the language and rhetoric of both traditions, but it is important

236. See *HALOT* and *TWOT*, 906.

237. Heb. שֵׁדִים/*šēdîm;* Gk. δαιμόνια.

238. Gk. θύσαντες δαιμονίοις καὶ οὐ θεῷ. The last four words agree perfectly with Deuteronomy 32:17 LXX, and the fifth from the last is merely a different form of the verb.

239. See Richard A. Horsley, "Gnosis in Corinth: 1 Corinthians 8:1-6," *NTS* 27 (1980), 37-39; and the discussion in Thiselton, 634-35.

240. Paul refers to "demons" only here (vv. 20-21) and in 1 Tim. 4:1.

to recognize that they are not ultimately in conflict. The prophetic and Hellenistic traditions ridicule the preposterous idea that there could be more than one God and point to the weak and powerless nature of the idols, which are human artifacts. The apocalyptic tradition recognizes that there is some spiritual reality behind the human tendency to worship those things which are not gods.

Thiselton affirms Bruce's assertion that for Paul these demons "were probably not personal beings but impersonal forces which exerted a powerful influence over unregenerate man."[241] But BDAG properly understands Paul's use of the word to refer to "a hostile transcendent being w[ith] status between humans and deities," with the understanding that they were the "objects of polytheistic worship" and that here Paul is making "satirical reference to the secondary status of these members of the spirit-world relative to deity."[242]

Paul quotes the first five words of Deuteronomy 32:17 LXX exactly except that the tense of the verb has been altered.[243] But while Deuteronomy 32:17 referred to the abhorrent unfaithfulness of Israel, most readers understand Paul to be speaking of the practices of the Corinthian Christians' pagan neighbors (as did many ancient scribes). Paul's other references to the scene of the golden calf in the context (and elsewhere) suggest that "Paul sees the Corinthian controversy about idol meat (v. 19) in double exposure with Israel's wilderness idolatry."[244] On the basis of Paul's use of Deuteronomy 32 a number of scholars believe that he is not thinking of pagan sacrifices but of the failure of the Israelites.[245] While Paul is clearly thinking of Israel's failure in the past, it seems fair to say that the sacrifices referred to in both Deuteronomy 32:17 and 1 Corinthians 10:20 are pagan sacrifices and that "Paul's real concern, like that of the Song of Moses, is that *God's own people* are becoming implicated in this 'abhorrent' practice."[246] Paul does not suggest that the Corinthians (like the Israelites) were themselves tempted to (consciously or intentionally) offer sacrifices to pagan gods (what we have called "subjective idolatry"), but he does indicate that by knowingly partaking in meals where sacrificial food was consumed they were still to be considered participants in the sacrifices themselves (which we have called "objective idolatry"), establishing the relevance of his argument in vv. 16-18 to his use of Deuteronomy 32:17.[247]

241. Bruce, 96, cited in Thiselton, 775.

242. BDAG, δαιμόνιον.

243. While the LXX uses an aorist verb (they "sacrificed"; ἔθυσαν), Paul uses a present tense verb (they "sacrifice"; θύουσιν).

244. Hays, *Echoes*, 93.

245. Cf. esp. Hays, *Echoes*, 93; Thiselton, 774-75.

246. Hays, 169. Hays thinks that the gloss reflects a failure on the part of scribes to recognize the allusion to Deut. 32:17.

247. If Paul has Christian practice in mind in vv. 16-17, Jewish practice in mind in v. 18, and pagan practice in mind in this verse, it could reflect his three-part focus explicitly laid out in v. 32: "Jews . . . Greeks . . . the church of God."

Paul's argument suggests that the problem is not with the food (or drink) itself, but with the social and spiritual significance of eating (or drinking) it in contexts that may naturally be understood as condoning and/or participating in the pagan offering itself. On the issue of eating food offered to idols the Corinthians reason purely on the basis of the nature of the food. Paul argues on the basis of the potential significance of the act of eating it.

Paul's statement, *I do not want you to be participants with demons,* reflects the connection between vv. 15-19 and the first part of this verse. If pagan offerings are actually offerings made to demons (and neither to gods, as the pagans suppose, nor to "thin air," as some Corinthians suppose), to knowingly and intentionally eat food from that offering in a context where it is acknowledged as such is to establish oneself as one in communion[248] with those demons (whether knowingly or not). Corinthians who do participate in such meals have fallen into the same error as the Israelites who practiced pagan idolatry in the instance of the golden calf.

**10:21** Paul moves from the language of "wanting" to the stronger language of moral impossibility in declaring, *You cannot drink the cup of the Lord and the cup of demons too; you cannot have a part in both the Lord's table and the table of demons.* That is, if they are to continue to be considered worshipers and servants of the Lord, they must absolutely reject any association with the cup and/or table of demons. The expression "Lord's table"[249] is used in Malachi 1:7, 12 LXX to refer to the altar. Ezekiel 41:22 also describes the altar in the vision as "the table that is before the Lord"[250] and in Ezekiel 44:16 the Lord refers to it as "my table." In Isaiah 65:11 LXX the Lord complains against unfaithful Israelites who "prepare a table for the devil and fill up the mixture [of wine as an offering] for Fortune."[251] Paul is clearly referring to participation in the Lord's Supper as a participation in the Lord's Table, implying that the celebration of Christ's sacrifice which takes place there now serves as a centerpiece for Christian worship as did the temple in the Old Testament. He also makes clear that the church is also committed to "the radically *exclusive* character of Israel's monotheistic faith."[252] One cannot worship the one true God and participate in any other worship.

Ancient invitations to family celebrations were frequently worded explicitly as invitations "to dine at the table of the lord Sarapis [or the like]." Some of those celebrations were held in the temple of that "god," while others were held in other temples or in private homes. Many of Willis's examples of social events where idol food would have been consumed are based on such invitations where it is clear that the invitation to eat at the ta-

248. Gk. κοινωνός, one who is a "companion, partner, sharer" (BDAG) with them. In the context of a meal the word implies one who enjoys fellowship with the others at the table (here the demons are understood to be the honored guests at such meals).

249. Gk. τράπεζα κυρίου.

250. Gk. ἡ τράπεζα ἡ πρὸ προσώπου κυρίου.

251. Gk. ἑτοιμάζοντες τῷ δαίμονι τράπεζαν καὶ πληροῦντες τῇ τύχῃ κέρασμα.

252. Hays, 170.

ble of the god is occasioned by some significant social event in the life of the person issuing the invitation. Obviously Paul would rule out explicitly religious meetings. Although there is significant debate on the issue, it seems that he would likely have had very serious qualms about any context where the name of a pagan god would be invoked over food or drink before being consumed by those gathered for any occasion.

**10:22** Paul returns to the series of rhetorical questions which he had left off at v. 19. *Are we trying to arouse the Lord's jealousy? Are we stronger than he?* Paul's words (literally), "Shall we provoke the Lord?" echo the Lord's complaint against Israel in Deuteronomy 32:21 LXX: "They have provoked me with what is no god; they have angered me by their idols."[253] He essentially asks if he or the Corinthians would be foolish enough to follow in Israel's footsteps by participating in pagan worship as they did, provoking him by engaging in idolatrous associations or actions. Paul's follow-up question, *Are we stronger than he?* signals that the expected answer is clearly "No!"[254] This question probably also reflects Deuteronomy 32 and its emphasis on the strength of the Lord which is highlighted in that chapter in more than one way. According to Deuteronomy 32, one of the purposes of the coming judgment will be to impress on the nation their lack of strength and the Lord's great power. Verse 30 depicts Israel's impotence without the Lord's help: one man will chase a thousand Israelites; two will put ten thousand to flight. Verses 36-38 indicate that judgment will bring an end to Israel's strength, including any they may have derived from "the gods": The Lord will desist from punishment "when he sees that their strength is gone" (32:36).

As Peter C. Craigie explains: "Since Israel's defection was largely a result of the arrogance of believing in their own strength, that arrogance and belief in human strength had to be totally demolished before the people were in a position to realize their need of God's strength. The rhetorical question posed in vv. 37-38 is designed to create awareness that other possible sources of strength were also useless."[255] The motif of God's strength is also reflected in Deuteronomy 32 through the repeated use of the epithet "the Rock."[256] In fact, in translating the chapter the Targumim employ several titles which interpret "rock" as a figure for God's strength (most frequently, "the Strong One").[257] In Deuteronomy 32, especially in the Targu-

253. Compare παρεζήλωσάν με ("they provoked me") of Deut. 32:21 LXX with παραζηλοῦμεν τὸν κύριον ("Shall we provoke the Lord?") of 1 Cor. 10:22. Chrysostom recognized the allusion. He cites Deut. 32:21 LXX and says that Paul was "reminding them of an ancient history and of their fathers' transgression" (*Homiliae in Epistulam i ad Corinthios* 24.6 [NPNF[1] 12:141]).

254. Through the incorporation of the negative μή ("not") into the question.

255. Peter C. Craigie, *The Book of Deuteronomy* (NICOT; Grand Rapids: Eerdmans, 1976), 387.

256. Heb. צוּר/*ṣûr;* Deut. 32:4, 15, 18, 30, 31.

257. See Rosner, *Paul,* 200.

mim, the question of Israel's participation in idolatry and the Lord's jealousy and discipline is set in terms of strength and power. Israel follows other gods when they feel strong (cf. 1 Cor. 10:11, "Let him who thinks he stands . . ."), and, in response, the Lord purposes to show himself strong(er) by punishing the Israelites. Paul's question is designed not only to underscore the impotence of believers, but also to stress the omnipotence of God: surely we are not stronger than the Strong One! Understood in the light of this background, 1 Corinthians 10:22b can be seen as a frightening threat of judgment upon those Corinthian Christians who provoke God to jealousy.[258] Here, as in Deuteronomy 32, the strength and jealousy motifs are responses to the inexplicable and inexcusable involvement of God's people in objective idolatry.[259]

### d. Freedom Should Be Used for the Glory of God, 10:23–11:1

*23"I have the right to do anything," you say — but not everything is beneficial. "I have the right to do anything" — but not everything is constructive. 24No one should seek their own good, but the good of others.*

*25Eat anything sold in the meat market without raising questions of conscience, 26for, "The earth is the Lord's, and everything in it."*

*27If an unbeliever invites you to a meal and you want to go, eat whatever is put before you without raising questions of conscience. 28But if someone says to you, "This has been offered in sacrifice," then do not eat it, both for the sake of the one who told you and for the sake of conscience. 29I am referring to the other person's conscience, not yours. For why is my freedom being judged by another's conscience? 30If I take part in the meal with thankfulness, why am I denounced because of something I thank God for?*

*31So whether you eat or drink or whatever you do, do it all for the glory of God. 32Do not cause anyone to stumble, whether Jews, Greeks or the church of God — 33even as I try to please everyone in every way. For I am not seeking my own good but the good of many, so that they may be saved. 11:1Follow my example, as I follow the example of Christ.*

Paul quotes from a Corinthian slogan, twice, and responds to it, twice (10:23), before providing a general moral principle to guide Christians in their relationships with others (10:24). That is followed up by a series of instructions intended to address both specific scenarios (10:25-30) and general guidelines (10:31–11:1).[260]

258. Chrysostom understood Paul's intention similarly, asking, "Are we tempting Him, whether He is able to punish us, and irritating Him by going over to the adversaries and taking our stand with His enemies?" (*Homiliae in Epistulam i ad Corinthios* 24.6 [NPNF¹ 12:141]).

259. See Brian S. Rosner, "'Stronger than He?' The Strength of 1 Corinthians 10:22b," *TynBul* 43.1 (1992), 171-79.

260. In 10:24–11:1 Paul moves from a more expository style (with 10:16-23 filled pri-

**10:23** In 9:24–10:22 Paul focused especially on the threat to one's own spiritual (and general) health and well-being posed by a lack of self-restraint with respect to idol food. In 10:23–11:1 he returns to focus again on the question of the danger posed to the well-being of others (cf. 8:1–9:23). As Paul moves toward the conclusion of this negative section on idolatry, he cites the same slogan from the Corinthians' letter that he cited back at 6:12 (see the comments there): *"I have the right to do anything."*[261] Here, as there, he cites the slogan once and then qualifies it and then cites it a second time and provides a second qualification. In both verses he qualifies the slogan the same way the first time *(but not everything is beneficial)*, but the second qualification is different in each case. While in 6:12 the second qualifier is "I will not be mastered by anything," here the second qualification is that *not everything is constructive.* The word translated *constructive*[262] is usually translated "edifies" (as in TNIV 14:4 [2x], 17) or "builds up" (as in TNIV 8:1). The TNIV translation reflects a creative usage of the building/construction imagery but may keep people from seeing the relationship with the motif. It should also be pointed out that in English for something to be "constructive" usually means that it is helpful or advances a discussion or a cause. In this letter the building metaphor is more directly related to the well-being of a person or a community (which is how "edify" or "build up" have come to be used in the spiritual vocabulary of English-speaking Christians).

While both texts (6:12 and 10:23) discuss what is beneficial, the first one follows up with a stronger emphasis on one's own well-being (not to be mastered by anything), while the latter text follows up with a greater emphasis on the well-being of others (that they should be edified). That is reflected in the emphasis given to those issues in the two sections. They affect both the individual and the group, but Paul puts somewhat more emphasis on the welfare of the self in his discussion of sexual immorality (esp. in 6:12-20) and somewhat more emphasis on the welfare of others in his discussion of idol food (esp. in 8:1–9:23; 10:23–11:1). This verse marks the shift back to a focus on the well-being of others, which continues through the end of this major section.[263] Paul indicates that our behavior should not

---

marily with present indicative verbs by which he developed his argument) to a hortatory style, with seven imperatives (all present imperatives) found in the space of these eleven verses.

261. Literally, "all things are permitted." At 6:12 Paul writes, "all things are permitted to me." The Majority text includes the words "to me" (μοι) here as well, but as Metzger says, "That the word crept into the text from 6.12 seems to be almost certain, especially in view of the overwhelming testimony supporting the shorter text," which includes ($\mathfrak{p}^{46}$, ℵ*, B, C (C* in the first instance), D (F, G, and P in the first instance [these MSS omit the second πάντα οἰκοδομεῖ by homoeoteleuton), $it^{d}$, vg, and $cop^{sa, bo}$" (*Textual Commentary*, 495).

262. Gk. οἰκοδομέω.

263. Chrysostom (*Homiliae in Epistulam i ad Corinthios* 24.6 [NPNF[1] 12:141]) suggests, regarding the two qualifications in this verse, that Paul writes "the former with reference to one's self, the latter, to one's brother: since the clause, 'are not expedient,' is a covert intima-

be dictated by what we may consider to be our rights or what freedoms we may have, but by that which will benefit (ourselves and especially) others and will make for individual Christians who are stronger in their faith and commitment to Christ and a Christian community which is stronger in its unified reflection of the lordship of Jesus Christ. As Fee puts it, Paul's focus is on using one's "rights" "to 'benefit' and 'build up' others in the body."[264] At the end of chapter 8, evidently the practices of some Corinthians in eating idol food has served not to build up the community or the spiritual health of their brothers and sisters in Christ but to bring (or threaten to bring) destruction (see on 8:9-13).

**10:24** Paul clarifies whose benefit and edification should preoccupy us (cf. v. 23) by way of an aphorism or crisply stated moral principle which was likely a consistent part of his moral teaching: *No one should seek their own good, but the good of others.* Paul teaches the same principle as an attribute of love in 13:5, and it also appears in Romans 14:7; 15:2; Galatians 6:2; Philippians 2:1-7. It is understood to be based on the model of Christ, for whom all things, including the sacrifice of his own life, were done for the benefit of others. Chrysostom and Thiselton both point out that Paul's teaching in this verse had already been more fully unpacked earlier. Chrysostom thinks that Paul can express his thought so concisely here because he had made the point at length in 9:19-23, showing that he had used his own rights and liberty for the benefit and in the service of others. Given that prior exposition, he was content to make the point briefly here and to use these few words to prod them to recall what had been said in that earlier passage.[265] Thiselton points out that "Paul's demonstration of how this axiom should operate at Corinth has been set forth in 8:7-13, where concern for the brother or sister for whom Christ died takes priority over one's own concerns."[266]

The "others" Paul has in mind are understood by the contrast with oneself. It is not any other person in particular, but precisely anyone who would be overlooked and suffer the consequences of our selfish preoccupation with our own rights and benefits. Verse 32 suggests that in the Corinthians' situation those others might be fellow believers (members of the church of God) or unbelieving Jews or Gentiles — which are the broadest possible categories Paul could have expressed.

---

tion of the ruin of the person to whom he speaks; but the clause, 'edify not,' of the stumbling block to the brother." He may be right, but it would appear that the verb may just as easily have the benefit of others in mind here. Usually the one whose benefit is in mind is indicated through the use of a noun or pronoun in the dative case (cf. Deut. 23:6 [23:7 LXX]; Esth. 3:8; 3 Macc. 6:24; Prov. 19:10; Sir. 30:19; 37:28; Jer. 33:14; Bar. 4:3; Matt. 5:29, 30; 18:6; John 11:50; 16:7; 2 Cor. 8:10). In cases where such clear syntactical indications are lacking, either the reference may be to the common good or the context may suggest a more specific reference, often the addressee (cf. 2 Macc. 11:15; 4 Macc. 5:11; John 18:14; 1 Cor. 12:7; 2 Cor. 12:1; Heb. 12:10). There is a close parallel in Sir. 37:28.

264. Fee, 479.

265. *Homiliae in Epistulam i ad Corinthios* 24.6 (NPNF[1] 12:141).

266. Thiselton, 782.

**10:25-26** How Paul's principle, stated in v. 24, impinges on the ways the Corinthians should handle a couple different situations where they may be confronted with the possibility of consuming idol food is sketched out in vv. 25-30. The two particular contexts he discusses are the two easiest and most innocent ways to come into contact with idol food: at the marketplace or at a dinner hosted by a friend, neighbor, or patron.[267] It is not clear whether vv. 28-30 should be understood as explicitly qualifying the Christian's freedom in both scenarios (vv. 25-26 and v. 27) or only the second of them (while implicitly qualifying the Christian's freedom in the first scenario as well). The structural parallel between v. 25 and v. 27b[268] suggests that Paul's remarks in vv. 28-30 explain why one should not raise questions of conscience in either situation and thus apply to any situation where a Christian is informed that the food they are about to eat (or purchase to eat) was previously offered to an idol. In short, Paul's comments qualify a Christian's freedom in any circumstance where their behavior may be reasonably interpreted by others as participation in or support of idolatry.

*Eat anything sold in the meat market without raising questions of conscience* (v. 25). That is, they need not (and should not) ask any questions about the potential religious history of the food for sale. The market to which Paul refers would have been a meat market "that sold other food provisions as well."[269] Paul's statement makes sense on the assumption that much of the food sold there (esp. the meat) would have been previously offered to one god or another but that the possible religious history of any particular piece of meat or other food would not be immediately apparent to the shopper. One could perhaps discover any possible religious history by asking the seller, but Paul discourages the Corinthians from doing so. Why they should feel free to eat any food sold in the market is clarified in v. 26. Why they should not ask questions that about the religious history of the food is further clarified in vv. 28-30. In order to discuss the significance of not asking questions of conscience we will have to anticipate our discussion of the significance of vv. 28-30.

By not asking questions about the food sold in the market the Christian allows for the possibility that they may in fact end up eating food that had previously been offered to an idol (which suggests Paul's issue must not be with the food per se). On the other hand, they eliminate the possibility that anyone will be able to interpret their purchase as one intended to condone or promote idolatry. To ask questions and refuse to eat food which is explicitly identified as idol food would seriously reduce the food options

267. Paul had already discussed the issue of eating meals in the precincts of an idol temple in 8:10-12, indicating that such a context was so utterly fraught with extreme danger for the spiritual well-being of anyone who might observe the Christian there that it should not be considered a viable option.

268. Both use the formula: "Eat whatever is . . . without raising questions of conscience."

269. Fotopoulos, *Food Offered to Idols*, 141.

available. To ask questions and then go ahead and eat food that had been explicitly identified as idol food could be interpreted (by the one selling the food or by someone observing the transaction) as a willingness to be considered a supporter of or participant in the sacrifice that was made.[270] To avoid asking questions was to avoid giving anyone the ability to associate the purchase with any religious intention on the part of the buyer.

The application of vv. 28-30 to this situation suggests that if the seller or another person were gratuitously to identify a certain piece of food as one that had been previously offered to an idol, the Christian would be expected to choose another piece of food instead in order to avoid making a purchase that could be misconstrued.

One of the questions that Paul needs to address is the question of whether food sacrificed to idols is inherently inconsumable due to what has been done to it, or whether the problem is primarily a matter of avoiding any clear personal association with, or participation in, the pagan offering itself. In v. 26 Paul cites Psalm 24:1 *(for, "The earth is the Lord's, and everything in it")*[271] to explain why Christians should feel free to eat any food without having to know about its religious history. Psalm 24 boldly declares that the Lord, the God of Israel (and no other deity), is sovereign Lord over all the earth. The earth does not belong to Baal or to any other god, but to the Lord of Israel! *He* is the glorious King who reigns over all the earth and over all of its inhabitants![272] The rest of the psalm discusses the Lord's victory procession and the qualifications of those who may join it.[273]

According to Kraus, the two offenses in the psalm that are listed as precluding one from participating in the worship procession are the worship of idols and perjury.[274] Commentators are divided as to the nature of the first qualification. As Broyles indicates, the "phrases are ambiguous, perhaps intentionally so, whether they forbid vain pursuits and lying/perjury in general or forbid appealing to idols (so NIV) and false gods in par-

270. Gerd Theissen has pointed out that the "have-nots" would only rarely have had opportunity to eat meat (*The Social Setting of Pauline Christianity Essays on Corinth* [Philadelphia: Fortress, 1982], 125-29). So also Meeks, *The First Urban Christians,* 69. Justin Meggitt demonstrates, however, that while meat was not a regular part of the diet of the poor, it was available to them and consumed by them in lower-class eating establishments (*popinae* or *ganeae*) (Justin J. Meggitt, *Paul, Poverty and Survival* [Studies of the New Testament and Its World; Edinburgh: T&T Clark, 1998], 108-12). Even this meat would have been of poor quality and served in modest quantities (Meggitt, *Paul, Poverty and Survival,* 111), so that the opportunity to purchase or eat a good cut of meat would have been unusual for the non-elite members of society.

271. The LXX translates the Hebrew quite literally, and Paul's citation follows it exactly, with only the introduction of postpositive γάρ ("for") to connect the citation to the context.

272. Peter C. Craigie, *Psalms 1–50* (WBC 19; Waco, TX: Word, 1983), 209.

273. See Craig C. Broyles, *Psalms* (NIBCOT 11; Peabody, MA: Hendrickson, 1999), 127-28.

274. Hans-Joachim Kraus, *Psalms: A Continental Commentary* (2 vols.; trans. H. C. Oswald; Minneapolis: Fortress, 1993), 314.

ticular."[275] The word used[276] suggests "vain thing" and is sometimes used to refer to idols in a vague but derogatory manner (since they did not merit anything better). The first verse of the following psalm begins with the psalmist declaring "To you, Lord, I have lifted up my soul" (Ps. 25:1), suggesting a reference to worship, which is what it means to lift up one's soul elsewhere in the Psalms (86:4; 143:8).

Psalm 24 closes with an emphasis on the identification of the Lord as the "King of glory," mentioned four times in the last five verses. Within those verses the motif of the Lord's strength (see on v. 22) is stressed: The king of glory is the Lord "strong and mighty," the Lord "mighty in battle."

Psalm 24:1 is most commonly cited in rabbinic literature to teach the obligation to thank God for one's food. On the basis of Psalm 24:1 it was taught that one should not taste any food until after having recited a benediction over it (*t. Berakot* 4:1; *b. Berakot* 35a; *b. Šabbat* 119a).[277] Paul's citation of Psalm 24:1 is consistent with the prevalent Jewish understanding of its relevance for the way God's people approach the food that he graciously provides. Paul is thoroughly Jewish and biblical in his understanding that creation is good and that the food we receive has been provided for us by God and should be received with thanksgiving (cf. 1 Cor. 10:30) and with the understanding that food, like everything else in creation, exists to fulfill the purpose God has in mind for it, namely, his glory (see 1 Cor. 10:31). The doctrine of creation Paul finds in Psalm 24:1 indicates that there is nothing wrong with the food itself, regardless of the way others have misused it in their religious ignorance. Psalm 24:1 says, it all belongs *to the Lord,* and not to any god or demon to whom it may have been offered (regardless of what the pagans who offered it may have thought). As far as the Christian is concerned, whatever food is found in the market is part of God's gracious provision and should be thankfully received as such.

If Paul and the Corinthians would have read Psalm 24:4 as a reference to idolatry, a citation from the psalm could have simultaneously reminded them not only of the goodness of God's creation, but also of his sovereignty over all creation (with its references to his strength and might) and of the requirement that all those who recognize his sovereignty avoid involvement with idolatry or risk a confrontation with the strong and mighty king of glory! Paul draws an ethical application from the text's statement of

275. Broyles, *Psalms,* 129.

276. שָׁוְא.

277. According to *t. Berakot* 4:1 (similarly, *b. Berakot* 35a; *Šabbat* 119a), "One must not taste anything until he has [first] recited a benediction [over it], as Scripture states, *The earth is the Lord's and all that it contains* (Ps. 24:1). One who derives benefit from this world [by eating its produce] without first having recited a benediction has committed sacrilege [viz., it is as if he ate sanctified temple produce, thereby misappropriating God's property]. . . . One should make use of his face, his hands, and his feet only for the honor of his creator, as Scripture states, *The Lord has made everything for its purpose* (Prov. 16:4 read as 'Everything that God has made [should be used] for his sake, for his glory')" (Neusner's translation).

God's ownership of and sovereignty over all creation. Since all food belongs to the Lord and comes from him, it can be received with thankfulness, regardless of how it has been used by others.

**10:27** The particular concern regarding food sacrificed to idols and the contamination of idolatry from eating food in 10:27-30 is based on Exodus 34:15, which, in the midst of a passage preoccupied with the avoidance of contamination from idolatry, warns that the danger of allowing the inhabitants of the land to remain would be that "when they prostitute themselves to their gods and sacrifice to their gods, someone among them will invite you, and you will eat of the sacrifice." That verse was a key text in the development of an important strand of Jewish thinking on the whole issue of eating with Gentiles, as reflected in *Jubilees* 22:16, "Separate yourself from the gentiles, and do not eat with them, and do not perform deeds like theirs. And do not become associates of theirs. Because their deeds are defiled, and all of their ways are contaminated and despicable, and abominable."[278] Along similar lines is Rabbi Shimeon ben Eleazar's teaching that "Israelites outside the land worship idols in purity. How? If a non-Jew prepared a wedding feast for his son and sent out to invite all Jews in his town — even if they have food and drink of their own and have their own servant waiting at them, they worship idols. Thus it is said: '[. . . Lest you make a covenant . . . when they sacrifice to their gods and] when one invites you, you eat of his sacrifice' (Exod. 34:15)."[279] The position of *Seder Elijah Rabbah* is similar: "One should observe in his heart not to eat with a gentile at table. . . . Thus they taught: anyone who eats with a gentile at table, worships idols and eats sacrifices to the dead."[280]

Paul's permission to accept an invitation to a meal and to eat whatever is served (v. 27) would seem to contradict Exodus 34:15,[281] but Paul's more detailed instructions (vv. 28-30) suggest that he has a simple dinner invitation in mind, and that the believer was to be careful to avoid eating any food that was explicitly identified as having been offered to an idol. This clearly does not follow the Jewish tradition cited above, but may still be understood as a more "liberal" approach to avoiding association with pagan sacrifices (and thus in the spirit of Exod. 34:15) while still allowing believers to maintain and develop social relationships with their nonbelieving neighbors.

*If an unbeliever invites you to a meal and you want to go, eat whatever is put before you without raising questions of conscience.* The second most common and innocent way of coming into contact with idol food (after visiting the

278. Wintermute's translation, *OTP* 2:98.

279. *T. ʿAbodah Zarah* 4:6; *b. ʿAbodah Zarah* 8a; cited by Peter J. Tomson, *Paul and the Jewish Law: Halakha in the Letters of the Apostle to the Gentiles* (Minneapolis: Fortress, 1990), 234.

280. *Seder Elijah Rabbah* 9 [8] 46-48, cited by Tomson, *Paul and the Jewish Law*, 234.

281. So Hans Hübner, *Vetus Testamentum in Novo* (vol. 2; Corpus Paulinum; Göttingen: Vandenhoeck & Ruprecht, 1997), 277.

local meat market) would be that of accepting an invitation to a dinner hosted by a non-Christian friend, neighbor, or patron. Such dinners were extremely common and served as a key to establishing the social and political network that was essential to advancement and even social survival (for free people) in that society.[282] Any respectable person would hope to be receiving invitations to dinners in the homes of others or hosted in other facilities, including the dining facilities which were incorporated into the precincts of some idol temples. To fail to receive such invitations would be a sign of social marginalization. To refuse to accept such invitations would tend to lead to social isolation. Paul recognizes that some of the Corinthians are receiving such invitations and will naturally want to accept them and maintain or improve their standing within the city's social world. The problem (and the reason Paul needs to address the issue) is that even when such meals were primarily social events, there were almost always religious components that could not be ignored. The wine would almost certainly be offered in the name of Dionysus, and gods were likely to be sung to or honored in other ways. Usually some of the food, at least, would have been previously offered to a god to whom thanks were being given for the joyful occasion of the dinner.

How could a Christian possibly navigate such a context without being seen as a willing participant in the idolatrous practices taking place? Some things go unstated but are probably assumed by Paul, including the presumption that Christians would not actually sing the praises of idols and that if they pronounced any name over their own cup of wine, it would be that of the Lord Jesus Christ. When he tells the Corinthian Christians to *eat whatever is put before you without raising questions of conscience,* he is suggesting that they treat their food options at the meal the same way they would treat them in the market. His suggestion that they not ask questions of conscience certainly implies that the religious history of the food in question was not expected to be known with certainty by the guests. If it has not been made explicit, the Christian may feel free to eat without fear that their actions can be interpreted as idolatrous.

**10:28** Food with an unknown (and potentially ambiguous) history is not a problem for the Christian (v. 27). *If,* however, *someone says to you, "This has been offered in sacrifice,"* the Christian should not eat that particular food selection *(then do not eat it).* If that is the only food (or the main dish), it may place the Christian in a very awkward position, since a rejection of the host's food would be a serious *faux pas.*[283] Paul is probably assuming, how-

282. For a fine overview of the place of the banquet in the early Christian world, see Dennis E. Smith, *From Symposium to Eucharist: The Banquet in the Early Christian World* (Minneapolis: Fortress, 2003). See also Peter D. Gooch, *Dangerous Food: I Corinthians 8–10 in Its Context* (Studies in Christianity and Judaism = Études sur le christianisme et le judaïsme 5; Waterloo, ON: Published for the Canadian Corporation for Studies in Religion by Wilfrid Laurier University Press, 1993), 27-46; Cheung, *Idol Food in Corinth,* 27-38.

283. In question 10 of Plutarch's *Table Talk* (II.10, 642F-644D) he discusses different ap-

ever that the meal (as would be typical) might be one in which many different food choices were being passed around.[284] That would provide two different "ways of escape." First, in such a context one might not be expected to know which items had or had not previously been offered to an idol (or to the guests in the name of the idol) and which had not been used in a religious offering. Secondly, the Christian would not have to go without food altogether but could choose from those items that had not been explicitly associated with an idol. If the Christian could not simply choose strategically from the food offered at the dinner, they might feel the need from time to time to excuse him- or herself from the dinner. Dickson thinks that this could serve a positive function in the spread of the gospel. He argues plausibly that "the occasional withdrawal from pagan banquets hinted at in 10:28 would present a clear critique of paganism and would very likely lead to an opportunity for believers to explain or defend the Christian position, a scenario made all the more conceivable in light of the important place of 'table-talk' at Greco-Roman banquets."[285]

Several questions remain about the scenario Paul describes. Is the person informing the Christian of the religious history of the food thought to be another Christian or a pagan, and why are they offering that information? Paul seems to depict the informant as a pagan since they do not use the pejorative term for "idol food" used elsewhere by Paul and other early Jews and Christians, but the neutral or positive term for "food offered to a god/divinity."[286] They presumably mention the idolatrous association of the food because they are aware that Jews and Christians (the latter being considered a Jewish offshoot) had severe qualms about eating such food. They could be merely interested in the Christian's response, or, more likely, they might think that they are helping the Christian by informing them so that they might make an informed decision regarding whether or not they would abstain from eating that item.[287] Paul is not interested in the particular motivation or specifics of the hypothetical situation. What seems to be important is that the Christian has been informed that the food had been offered to an idol and someone knows it to be so and knows that they are aware of it.

---

proaches to serving food at dinner parties, including one approach where the host measures out equal portions of food to each guest and another where all the guests share the food from a common table. In the former context the pressure to eat what is put before one would presumably be greater. If there were a common table to which the guests had access, one would have greater freedom to pick and choose according to taste or religious sensitivities.

284. J. Robert Sallares ("Meals," *OCD* 942) suggests that the main part of the meal could comprise "up to seven courses (fercula), with one chief item," which "might be a whole roasted pig, accompanied by smaller, but substantial courses (e.g., lampreys, turbot, roast veal)."

285. Dickson, *Mission-Commitment*, 259.

286. Gk. ἱερόθυτον.

287. The word Paul uses for "informing" (μηνύω) in the following clause ("the one who informed you") *may* suggest information that is shared as a service or favor to the one to whom it is provided.

Paul says that in such a situation the Christian should abstain *both for the sake of the one who told you and for the sake of conscience.* How does the Christian's behavior affect the one who informed him or her about the food? The friendly pagan was aware of Jewish/Christian scruples with respect to idol food and probably expected the Christian to abstain after discovering the food had a religious history. If the Christian does not abstain, their pagan friend may decide the Christian is not consistent with their own convictions, or is a hypocrite. Or they may decide that not even all Jews or Christians think that there is any serious problem with pagan religion. If their awareness of Jewish and Christian qualms had caused them to wonder about their own pagan practices, they would perhaps wonder or worry no further. Paul's initial reference to the particular concern for the other person was ambiguous. His concern *for the sake of the one who told you and for the sake of conscience* could be taken as either "concern for the other person and their conscience" or "concern for the other person and for your conscience." In vv. 29-30 he clarifies that he had the former in mind and why the other person's conscience is important for the Christian's ethical decision.

**10:29-30** Paul clarifies that he has the other person's conscience in mind *(I am referring to the other person's conscience, not yours)* and thus continues the motif of concern for "the other" which pervades this letter. He follows up with two more rhetorical questions that are intended to clarify (thus the *For*) why the Christian should be concerned about the conscience of the person who informs them of the idolatrous background of the food they are being offered. The meaning of the rhetorical questions has not been transparent to many readers, however, and they have wished that Paul had gone on to answer them![288] He asks, *For why is my freedom being judged by another's conscience? If I take part in the meal with thankfulness, why am I denounced because of something I thank God for?* The questions seem to discredit the other person's right to judge or denounce the behavior of the Christian who would eat the food identified as idol food. That is, they sound like the arguments of one justifying the practice of eating the food rather than those of one explaining why it should be rejected. Fee, in fact, thinks that Paul abandons the issue of the benefit of the other person and has suddenly turned to defending his own practice against those who criticize him. But, as Collins points out, Paul's use of the first-person singular in these two questions reflects "a classic construction in which the 'I' is used to illustrate something universal (BDF §281). Use of the first person in this way is especially characteristic of the diatribe."[289] We need not, therefore, conclude that Paul has left the issue of the one who might eat such food in order to defend his own practice. Paul may be using himself as an example,

288. Fee (486) points out that Paul's response "is so sudden and apparently non sequitur that it has created a notorious crux for interpreters."

289. Collins, 388.

but he is not defending his own practice of eating idol food here but explaining that he does not give anyone the opportunity to judge him as a consumer of idol food.[290]

It is a Corinthian's own view of their freedom and their conviction that their own personal attitude toward the food (one of thanksgiving[291]) is all that should matter, that may lead them to eat food which has been identified to them by someone else as idol food. The theme of freedom and rights has governed all of chapters 8–10[292] due to the role those concepts evidently played in the Corinthians' justification of their own approach to the issue of idol food. The theme of thanksgiving reflects the theme of blessing mentioned by Paul in v. 16 (we bless God, thanking him for the food he provides) and the reference to Psalm 24:1 in v. 26, which was understood to provide the reason for giving thanks for whatever good things we enjoy from God's creation. The citation of the verse probably served as an endorsement for one aspect of the understanding of the "knowledgeable." The point is that freedom and thankfulness are not (as some Corinthians might think) the keys to ethical discernment. Rather, not even one's freedom and thankfulness to God justify putting oneself in a situation where others' consciences may lead them to think idolatry is being practiced or condoned.[293]

Paul suggests that the act of (purchasing and/or) eating such food may result in someone else judging them or denouncing them. Two key words in these verses are those used for the response to the Christian's decision to eat the food in question. First, "to be judged" here means more specifically "to be unfavorably judged" (BDAG). To "be denounced" is to be spoken of "in a disrespectful way that demeans, denigrates, maligns" (BDAG), or, as Thiselton helpfully puts it, "to suffer defamation of character."[294] As Thiselton further points out, Paul is raising the potential for the Christian to be maligned for being "inconsistent in belief and practice." Since the person pointed out to them that the food they were on the verge of purchasing or eating was idol food, they evidently expected the Christian's rejection of idolatry to require them to avoid such food.

The rhetorical question in v. 29 begins *Why,* or more specifically, "For

290. As others have pointed out (cf. Schrage, 2:471; Thiselton, 789), Paul's use of "for" (γάρ) rather than "however" or "but" (δέ or ἀλλά) suggests that he is explaining or defending what he has just said rather than defending his own use of his freedom.

291. The theme of thanksgiving appears twice in v. 30: the reference to partaking "in thankfulness" (χάριτι, indicating a "response to generosity or beneficence"; BDAG) is followed up by a more explicit reference to that which "I thank God for."

292. "Freedom" (ἐλευθερία; cf. 9:1, 19) here is parallel in meaning to "right" (ἐξουσία; cf. 8:9; 9:4-6, 12, 18).

293. This is similar to Thiselton, 790, who notes that Paul's point is, "What would be the advantage of my exercising my freedom if I thereby suffer defamation of character? If it genuinely does not matter whether I eat or not, why choose the path that raises unnecessary difficulties? What is the point of 'freedom' if I cannot choose not to cause problems?"

294. Thiselton, 790.

what reason," "To what end,"[295] or, as Findlay has suggested, "What good end will be served by . . . ?"[296] Given Paul's general concern for the reception of the gospel and the benefit of others, these rhetorical questions were probably designed to stress the undesirability of any behavior that would lead others to malign Christian teaching or practice.[297] Those who are unnecessarily drawn to denigrate Christian teaching or practice are not experiencing the same reaction which was promoted by Paul's gospel-centered approach of adapting to the needs of those he sought to reach. If the other person's sense of moral judgment convinces them that the Christian is acting in a hypocritical or unethical manner and leads them to judge the Christian and think less of the gospel and its effects, the Christian is not promoting the gospel but hindering its success. Verses 24, 32-33 clarify (along with 8:9-13; 9:19-23) that it is the primacy of the gospel as a guide to dealing with difficult moral issues that governs Paul's thinking on this issue.

**10:31** Paul concludes his discussion of idol food strongly in 10:31–11:1, using the inferential conjunction "so" or "therefore"[298] at the start of v. 31 and employing three imperatives in these four verses. In these verses he returns to the biblical motif of maintaining a good reputation before outsiders for the dual (negative and positive) motives of protecting the honor of God's name and winning over the heathen (vv. 31-33):[299] *So whether you eat or drink or whatever you do, do it all for the glory of God. Do not cause anyone to stumble, whether Jews, Greeks or the church of God — even as I try to please everyone in every way. For I am not seeking my own good but the good of many,*[300] *so that they may be saved."* Such an unselfish approach to life is to be expected of anyone who follows the example of Christ. The Suffering Servant is described in Isaiah 53:11-12 LXX as one who gave himself for the good of "many."[301]

Paul begins his conclusion[302] by postulating three alternatives, or rather two alternatives followed by a universalizing catchall phrase. Each of the three alternatives is linguistically marked by the term "whether": (literally) "whether you eat, whether you drink, whether you do something [else], do everything for the glory of God."[303] It has sometimes been suggested that Paul's point is that even in the most mundane aspects of life (such as eating and drinking) we should concern ourselves above all

295. Gk. ἱνατί; cf. BDAG, which points out that the same expression was "oft[en] written separately; for ἱνα τί γένηται; 'to what end?'"

296. The basis for Fee's (486 n. 52, 487 n. 55) rejection of Findlay's suggestion is unclear, but Thiselton, 790, points out (along with BDAG; see n. 291 above) that the construction most likely is similar to what Findlay offers.

297. Cf. how this theme is treated in Rom. 14:16; 1 Tim. 6:1; Tit. 2:5; 2 Pet. 2:2.

298. Gk. οὖν.

299. See Rosner, *Paul, Scripture, and Ethics,* 109-11.

300. Gk. τὸ τῶν πολλῶν.

301. See the use of πολλοῖς and πολλῶν ("many") in those verses.

302. Marked as such here by οὖν ("so" or "therefore").

303. Gk. Εἴτε . . . εἴτε . . . εἴτε.

with the glory of God. Of course that is true, but Paul does not mention eating and drinking primarily because they are mundane activities but because those activities have been the focus of his discussion since the beginning of chapter 8 and because they were particularly dangerous contexts, in Paul's world, for potential entanglement with idolatrous activities. The point is that when the Corinthians think about issues related to food and drink (or any other issue), their overriding concern should not be with the exercise of their own rights and freedom or desires but with the potential implications for God's honor and glory. If their practice leads others to judge them unfavorably or to denigrate them and the Christian faith (vv. 29-30), God's glory has not been well served. God's glory is served by the progress of the gospel.

Karl Barth correctly recognized that this verse "is the goal of this section."[304] Paul's exhortation to do everything (including eating and drinking) to God's glory as he concludes his section on idol food parallels the exhortation to glorify God with our bodies in the conclusion to his section on sexual immorality (cf. 6:20). God is to be glorified in the world through his people. Sexual immorality (chs. 5–6) and idolatry (chs. 8–10) are the antithesis to the glorification of God. They are to be countered by the manifestation of Christian sexual purity (ch. 7) and God-honoring worship (chs. 11–14) which reflect true wisdom (cf. chs. 1–4) as we await the return of the resurrected Son of God (ch. 15). Any behavior that detracts from God's glory is to be rejected in favor of ones that promote it.

**10:32** Part of what glorifying God entails in this context is the avoidance of offense to others. The first clause of this verse is often translated "Give no offense" (e.g., ESV, NRSV, NASB, NET, NLT), and that is in keeping with the recommendation of BDAG.[305] As Fee points out, the adjective Paul uses here is "the negative form of the noun that appears in 8:9"[306] as "stumbling block." In our comments on that word we pointed out that Paul uses the metaphor of the stumbling block (as well as stumbling or falling) to describe an obstacle that keeps someone from finding their way to ultimate salvation, to the proper destination of life's journey. The reference to falling in 10:12 reflects the same idea. The TNIV translation, *Do not cause anyone to stumble,* reflects well the relationship to 8:9 and the motif Paul has used elsewhere in the letter. As John Dickson puts it, "Paul's exhortation in v. 32 calls on the Corinthians so to modify their social intercourse that the salvation of insiders and outsiders would in no way be put at jeopardy."[307]

The three-part description of those who are not to be offended, *whether Jews, Greeks or the church of God,* casts the net as widely as possible.

304. Barth, *The Resurrection of the Dead,* 41.

305. See BDAG on ἀπρόσκοπος ("pert[aining] to not causing offense, *giving no offense*").

306. Fee, 488 n. 63.

307. Dickson, *Mission-Commitment,* 252. See his full discussion of the motif of falling or stumbling on pp. 250-52.

*Greeks* here "represents all non-Jewish pagans within the so-called civilized world"[308] and is virtually synonymous with "Gentiles." In Jewish and Christian writings the dualism reflected in "Jews and Greeks/Gentiles" is usually sufficient to refer to all peoples. Paul's addition of *the church of God* reflects the transformation effected by Christ in the lives of Jews and Greeks/Gentiles that makes them something different from what they were previously. Even if Gentiles become true or spiritual Jews or part of true/spiritual Israel, in Christ neither they nor converted Jews can simply still fall under the category of *Jews.* Jews and Greeks may still serve to refer to all nonbelievers. But those who believe in Christ are *the church of God,* his eschatological people (cf. the comments on 1:2). Paul's language points "to a discontinuity, as if to imply that 'the people of God' are partly redefined, although not in exclusivist terms since their roots and basis of divine promise and covenant remain in continuity with Israel's history."[309] That Paul intends to include all people under the categories of *Jews, Greeks* and *church of God* is verified in the following verse where Paul speaks of his attempt to please "everyone." Paul stressed this same theme in 9:19-22, where he discussed his approach to ministering to Jews, those under the law, those not under the law and the weak. There he finished up, "I have become all things to all people so that by all possible means I might save some," which is clearly parallel to the following verse (10:33).

The context suggests how Paul might imagine the Corinthians could cause members of these different groups to stumble. Dickson helpfully comments: "The reference to Jews probably reflects an awareness on the part of Paul of a large Jewish community in Corinth which could easily have taken offence at the 'liberal' social habits of the 'knowledgeable' in the Corinthian church. Of course, Paul does not think that attendance at pagan banquets will lead Jews into idolatry. His point is probably that such behaviour might give Jews of the city another reason (cf. 1:23) to denounce the church and so to avoid Christians and Christian tradition."[310] That would result in stumbling and missing out on the saving power of the gospel. The stumbling of the *Greeks* could easily come about if some Corinthians were to eat food in such a way that could be interpreted as "a tacit affirmation of idolatrous beliefs thereby strengthening the 'Greeks' in a form of 'piety' destined for destruction."[311] As he points out, this scenario is "analogous to that described in 8:7-13 in relation to believers" and therefore may also explain how those who are identified as *the church of God* could be led to stumble if the Corinthians are not more careful. A "weaker brother who 'up until now' had been accustomed to idols" could

308. Fee, 489 n. 67.

309. Collins, 795.

310. Dickson, *Mission-Commitment,* 255.

311. Dickson, *Mission-Commitment,* 255. Dickson seems to think that the "tacit affirmation of idolatrous beliefs" would come about only through participation in "a banquet explicitly 'hallowed/tainted' by a pagan deity."

be led back into idolatry, which would be a stumbling block and result in their destruction "since idolatry stands under the eschatological judgement of God."[312]

**10:33** Verse 33 picks up the theme of 9:22, where Paul said, "I have become all things to all people so that by all possible means I might save some." Here he says that the Corinthians must be careful not to cause anyone to stumble (v. 32), even *as I try to please everyone in every way. For I am not seeking my own good but the good of many,*[313] *so that they may be saved* (v. 33). So the Corinthians are to follow Paul's example, which is briefly summarized here since Paul had more fully described it for them in 9:19-23. In the comments on those verses it was pointed out that while Paul emphasizes elsewhere that he is committed to pleasing God rather than humans (Gal. 1:10; 1 Thess. 2:4), there and in this passage he highlights his commitment to working in such a way as to positively impress those among whom he lives and works. His love for and commitment to God keep him from doing anything inappropriate merely to please humans. It is that same love for God and commitment to him and the gospel that led him to adapt his life and ministry to the needs and context of those among whom he lives and ministers in order to bring them into life-transforming contact with the gospel message God has entrusted to him.

**11:1** This verse clearly belongs to the preceding discussion, despite its unfortunate separation by the later division of the letter into chapters. As the last verse of this passage, it clarifies that Paul himself is following and passing on to the Corinthians the example set by Christ himself: *Follow my example, as I follow the example of Christ.* That Paul had Christ's example in mind may have been telegraphed by his reference in v. 33 to "the good of many" since Isaiah 53:11-12 LXX describes the Suffering Servant as the righteous one "who serves many well"[314] and "who bore the sins of many."[315] Paul referred to the example of Christ that he has in mind in 8:11, where he pointed out that Christ died for the weak, and the reference to Christ's blood and body in 10:16 points in the same direction. It is evoked again in Paul's references to Christ's body, blood, and death in his discussion of the Lord's Supper in 11:24-26, and in 15:3 the fact that "Christ died for our sins" is affirmed to be at the heart of the gospel message, the gospel message for the advance of which Paul said he was willing to sacrifice anything in 9:23. Christ's example of putting the needs of others before his own freedom or rights, and especially of doing whatever is necessary to secure their salvation (see again the preceding verse), was clearly the motivating force behind Paul's own approach to ministry as he has described it to the Corinthians and promoted it as a model for them to follow.

312. Dickson, *Mission-Commitment*, 255.
313. Gk. τὸ τῶν πολλῶν.
314. Gk. δίκαιον εὖ δουλεύοντα πολλοῖς.
315. Gk. πολλῶν.

Paul's call to the imitation of his example as he follows that of Christ is not about the reinforcement of his own power and imposing an ideology of "sameness," as some have suggested,[316] but, as Andrew Clarke has shown, "[t]he substance of this imitation is presented in the preceding verse, namely that they are not to seek their own good, but the good of many."[317] His review of Paul's use of the motif of imitation shows a consistent pattern in which "the object of imitation is not exclusively Paul, but is always ultimately Christ."[318]

As suggested in the introduction to 8:1–11:1, the relationship between the two great commandments to love God and neighbor (Deut. 6:5; Lev. 19:18), though not cited in this book, may be seen to underwrite Paul's argument throughout this section and particularly this final section. In Paul's view, our love for God must be reflected in our love for others. That perspective is reflected in the relationship between v. 31 and vv. 32-33, where doing "all for the glory of God" (v. 31) entails doing what it takes to keep others from stumbling unnecessarily (v. 32) and seeking their good and salvation (v. 33). That is the model Paul set for the Corinthians and which Christ set for Paul through the giving of his very life (11:1).[319]

## B. Affirmation of Edifying Worship: "Glorify God" in Your Worship, 11:2–14:40

**11:2–14:40** Having dealt with the issue of idolatry in 8:1–11:1, Paul now turns to discuss issues relating to proper Christian worship in 11:2–14:40.[1] As N. T. Wright has argued, "Being grasped by the gospel as Paul has expounded it . . . means worshipping the true God, and so reflecting this God by becoming a more complete human being. Genuine humanness resulting from true worship: that is Paul's vision."[2] Paul will try to lead the Corinthians to better reflect what Wright calls "God's renewed hu-

316. See Elizabeth A. Castelli, *Imitating Paul: A Discourse of Power* (Literary Currents in Biblical Interpretation; Louisville: Westminster/John Knox, 1991).

317. Andrew D. Clarke, *Serve the Community of the Church: Christians as Leaders and Ministers* (First-Century Christians in the Graeco-Roman World; Grand Rapids: Eerdmans, 2000), 226. See his very helpful discussion of the issues in *Serve the Community of the Church,* 224-28 and his article, "'Be Imitators of Me': Paul's Model of Leadership," *TynBul* 49 (1998), 329-60. See also David Horrell's discussion of "Other-Regard and Christ as Moral Paradigm," in his *Solidarity and Difference,* 204-45.

318. Clarke, *Serve the Community of the Church,* 228.

319. For a helpful discussion of the significance of this verse for the evangelistic orientation of the church see Robert L. Plummer, "Imitation of Paul and the Church's Missionary Role in 1 Corinthians," *JETS* 44 (2001), 222-26.

1. Conzelmann, 181, provides the title "Questions of Divine Worship" for 11:2–14:40; so also Schrage, 2:487.

2. N. T. Wright, *What Saint Paul Really Said: Was Paul of Tarsus the Real Founder of Christianity?* (Grand Rapids: Eerdmans, 1997), 140.

manity" in these chapters. Of course chapter 15 will bridge the gap from the incomplete renewal of humanity experienced before bodily resurrection with that ultimate and complete renewal and restoration that will be experienced only when we experience resurrection like that of the Lord for whom we wait.

The conclusion to the previous section included (like the conclusion of ch. 6) a call to do everything to "the glory of God" (10:31). The "everything" of 10:31 focused especially on eating and drinking, not because those activities represent the most mundane of human activities, but because they were especially related to the context of worship and the specific problem Paul was addressing in Corinth.[3] The focus on worship that brings glory (and not dishonor) to God is reflected throughout this section, even if that particular term does not frequently appear.

In 11:2-16 the issue of male and female (or husband and wife) behavior that reflects glory or shame is treated. Whatever glory or shame might be produced is implicitly understood to be reflected up a hierarchical chain that ultimately brings glory or shame to God.[4] The church's way of celebrating the Lord's Supper will either reflect well or poorly on Christ and promote or diminish the health of the congregation. Chapters 12–14 stress the theme of edification which embraces all of chapters 8–14 (see 8:1). The edification motif should be understood as part of the motif of the church as God's Spirit-indwelt temple, which is being rebuilt in this time of Christ's inaugurated kingdom. Those chapters begin with a reference to the Spirit-inspired declaration of Christ's lordship (12:3) and toward the end include a reference to the expectation that all nations will come to worship God as he makes his presence known in the midst of his people's worship (14:24-25, echoing Isa. 45:14 and perhaps Zech. 8:23 as well). Chapters 11–14 are framed by discussions relating to men and women in worship (11:2-16; 14:34-35). There may be several reasons for this. For one, given that the issue of sexual immorality was a central concern for Paul in this letter, the possibility that the behavior of men and women gathered together for worship could be marred by some impropriety may be a natural concern for him.[5]

3. That is, eating food offered to idols (chs. 8–10), eating in pagan temples (8:10), eating the Jewish temple sacrifices (10:18), and eating and drinking at the table of our Lord or of demons (10:16, 21).

4. Cf. William R. G. Loader, *The Septuagint, Sexuality, and the New Testament: Case Studies on the Impact of the LXX in Philo and the New Testament* (Grand Rapids: Eerdmans, 2004), 101.

5. A Greek marriage certificate from 92 B.C. (Papyrus Tebtunis 1:104) stipulates that "it shall not be lawful" for the wife "to spend the night or day away from the house of [the husband] without [her husband's] consent or to have intercourse with another man or to dishonor the common household or to bring shame upon [her husband] in anything that causes a husband shame" (see David Instone-Brewer, "1 Corinthians 7 in the Light of the Graeco-Roman Marriage and Divorce Papyri," *TynBul* 52 [2001], 108). Here the context suggests that shame would be most likely due to inappropriate contact with other men. Paul's

The precise arguments Paul uses and themes he emphasizes are driven by those things he knows about the Corinthian church through their correspondence or through his other sources. In chapter 11 he seems to be responding to certain ways in which the Corinthians are honoring or dishonoring some of the traditions he passed on to them. He begins by praising them in v. 2 when he introduces the question of man and female attire while praying or prophesying, but he introduces his discussion of the Lord's Supper by saying that he cannot praise them (v. 17), a statement he repeats within the passage (v. 22). Interestingly, vv. 2-16 relate especially to traditions concerned with the relationships between the sexes (cf. chs. 5–6) in the context of the church, while the rest of the chapter relates to traditions having to do with eating and drinking (cf. chs. 8–10) the Lord's Supper. While chapter 7 may be seen as Paul's positive Christian response to the issue of sexual immorality as raised in chapters 5–6, and chapters 11–14 may be considered Paul's positive Christian response to the issue of idolatry raised in chapters 8–10, the two parts of chapter 11 seem to address relationships between the genders and eating and drinking in the specific context of Christian worship with respect to the Corinthians' faithfulness (or lack thereof) to traditions they received from Paul.

In vv. 2-16 Paul indicates that the Corinthians have eagerly sought to honor the traditions he passed on to them about appropriate relations and attire in worship, even if they do raise some issues or questions with him about those traditions and their proper implementation. In the remainder of the chapter he discusses the shameful manner in which they have been celebrating the Lord's Supper and invokes the shared tradition about that practice in order to correct their behavior.

Despite the difficulties of discerning what the Corinthians might have said to Paul, one must exert the necessary energy to make the most sense of his argument. They may have said something like this:

> "Paul, we want you to know that we have faithfully kept the traditions you passed on to us, but some of us are wondering whether those traditions have been faithfully implemented even in the way we have worshipped since you founded this church. For instance, as things are now, our men come to worship with their heads uncovered, but women have been covering their heads. Some of us wonder why we continue to distinguish between men and women in this way since among the traditions you passed on to us is the fact that we are all parts of God's new creation and that in this new creation there is no longer Jew nor Greek, slave or free, or even "male and female."[6] More and more women are

statement in 14:35 that the women should ask their questions of "their own husbands" at home rather than in the church may point in a similar direction.

6. There is no reason to think that the Corinthians were familiar with Gal. 3:28, but some understanding of that part of Paul's thinking on their part (esp. some misunderstanding) would explain significant elements in this passage.

out in public these days with their heads uncovered, just like men. Some find this very offensive, but others feel that the offended are merely old-fashioned and that the gospel would have us celebrate our sameness in Christ."[7]

Most of the rest of chapters 11–14 seems to respond not to things that were mentioned in the Corinthians' letter, but to things Paul has heard about behavior that was humiliating poorer members of the church during the Lord's Supper and about the superiority that was being attributed to certain members who seemed to be the recipients of special spiritual powers which were understood to more clearly reflect God's presence in them. Someone may have communicated something like the following to Paul:

> "When the church was gathered at so-and-so's house for the Lord's Supper, they had their best friends (other richer families of the church) with them in the triclinium (dining room) where all the food was served (and where some were even getting drunk as in a common drinking party). The rest hung around out in the atrium and hardly got to eat or drink anything. It was apparent from where and what each one was served (if anything) how they ranked in terms of their social status.
>
> "Also, those who speak in other tongues during our worship service are being held out as the most important contributors to our worship. Everything seems to revolve around them. They think their behavior is clear evidence that God is in them and that through them he is present in our worship. Most of us do not have that gift and wonder whether or not we have anything significant to offer to our church's worship. Some of those more important people (the pillars of our church) also take a significant amount of time prophesying to the rest of us. Sometimes they say the strangest things in the style of a manic prophet! And why is it that only part of the church seems to have these special gifts?"

Some parts of the above reconstructions are more speculative than others. Clearly Paul knows of church members who were being treated shamefully in the celebration of the Lord's Supper and walking away hungry (11:21-22) and that there was an unhealthy preoccupation with one spiritual gift in particular, namely, speaking in tongues (see chs. 12–14). The possibility that social distinctions underlie several of the issues is suggested by both elements in the text itself and familiarity with social realities within the Roman, and particularly Corinthian, context.

Breaking down the larger unit of chapters 11–14, we see that in chap-

7. If Paul had written 2 Corinthians 3 before rather than after this letter, one would expect the Corinthians to ask the question this way: *As we come together as a body to worship our true head, Jesus Christ, shouldn't we be uncovered like Moses was when he entered the presence of God, so that we can all reflect the Lord's glory and be fully transformed into his image?*

ter 11 Paul deals with commendable and condemnable ways in which the Corinthians are relating to traditions Paul passed on to them. In chapters 12–14, he will focus on issues related to spiritual gifts and their use in the Christian worship gathering. In 11:2-16 creation traditions (original creation and new creation traditions) will be in the foreground as Paul explains the ways in which men and women are to worship together in this new community. In 11:17-34 traditions relating to the first exodus and the new exodus will take center stage as Paul explains the implications of the celebration of the new covenant meal for the way rich and poor are to worship together in the new community. In chapters 12–14 themes relating to the rebuilding of the new restored community and the role of the eschatological Spirit in that edification process will be most prominent.

### *1. Directions regarding the Proper Application of Traditions Relating to Worship, 11:2-34*

#### *a. Men and Women Should Honor God and Others by Maintaining Proper Gender Distinctions in Worship, 11:2-16*

This passage, dealing with honorable attire for prayer and prophecy, is one of the most difficult passages in the letter, due in part to Paul's use of expressions and ideas that he apparently expects to be transparent to the Corinthians but which have been opaque to most readers ever since. Some of the problems to be addressed in this passage include the meaning(s) of the word "head" throughout the passage; the unclear implications of Paul's argument (can men and women minister in similar ways or not?); what kind of head covering Paul has in mind; whether Paul implies that woman is not made in the image of God in v. 7; what "authority" he has in mind in v. 10; what Paul means by "because of the angels" in v. 10. Some of our difficulty undoubtedly comes from our inability to know exactly what Paul had previously taught the Corinthians on this subject and what they had written to him about it. Most likely some Corinthians wanted to develop Paul's teaching that in Christ "there is neither Jew nor Greek, there is neither slave nor free, there is no 'male and female'" (Gal. 3:28; perhaps as one of the traditions he delivered to them; cf. 11:2) in such a way that distinctions between men and women would be avoided in worship. The wearing of veils seems to have been a contentious issue. It is not clear whether women or men (or both) were promoting the view Paul is confronting.

Despite its obscurities, Paul's teaching in this passage clearly affirms three things: a balance between (1) respect for a creation mandate to maintain and even celebrate the gender distinctions with which we have been created; (2) a respect for culturally specific approaches to guarding moral and sexual purity; and (3) a commitment to fully integrating women and their gifts into the experience of the worshiping community.

Paul's arguments seem to reflect a certain tension between lessons learned from creation (or nature) and new creation (or life in the Lord), related to the well-known tension between the "already" and the "not yet" but presented in terms of intersecting interpretations of the early chapters of Genesis (see on vv. 7-12). Although the text is not cited and there is no clear linguistic tie to it, it may be that the promise in Joel 2:28-29 that in the last days God would pour out his Spirit on all people (v. 28), even on "the male and female servants" (v. 29), and that then "your sons and your daughters shall prophesy" (v. 28) may have played a role in his thinking about both men and women praying and prophesying in the church.

Paul's ultimate concern seems to be related to the manifestation of glory and shame in worship, particularly that all be done to the glory of God (cf. 10:31), and not to glorify or shame anyone else. Humanly directed glory is to be avoided, as well as humanly or divinely directed shame. Paul's language about the man being the head of the woman has often been used as part of an argument which limits the ministries in which women are allowed to engage. It is remarkable, however, that this passage makes no distinction between the ministries in which men and women may engage. Paul distinguishes not between their roles (both men and women are free to pray and prophesy), but between the proper attire expected for either of them to engage in those activities.

> [2]*I praise you for remembering me in everything and for holding to the traditions just as I passed them on to you.* [3]*But I want you to realize that the head of every man is Christ, and the head of the woman is man, and the head of Christ is God.* [4]*Every man who prays or prophesies with his head covered dishonors his head.* [5]*But every woman who prays or prophesies with her head uncovered dishonors her head — it is the same as having her head shaved.* [6]*For if a woman does not cover her head, she might as well have her hair cut off; but if it is a disgrace for a woman to have her hair cut off or her head shaved, then she should cover her head.*
>
> [7]*A man ought not to cover his head, since he is the image and glory of God; but woman is the glory of man.* [8]*For man did not come from woman, but woman from man;* [9]*neither was man created for woman, but woman for man.* [10]*It is for this reason that a woman ought to have authority over her own head, because of the angels.* [11]*Nevertheless, in the Lord woman is not independent of man, nor is man independent of woman.* [12]*For as woman came from man, so also man is born of woman. But everything comes from God.*
>
> [13]*Judge for yourselves: Is it proper for a woman to pray to God with her head uncovered?* [14]*Does not the very nature of things teach you that if a man has long hair, it is a disgrace to him,* [15]*but that if a woman has long hair, it is her glory? For long hair is given to her as a covering.* [16]*If anyone wants to be contentious about this, we have no other practice — nor do the churches of God.*

*i. Introductory statement of commendation, 11:2*

**11:2** Paul begins this verse with a verb *(praise)* that appears three times in this passage and nowhere else in his writings except for an Old Testament citation in Romans 15:11.[8] *I praise you,* he says, *for remembering me in everything and for holding to the traditions just as I passed them on to you.* This expression of praise is remarkable since Paul does not use similar language elsewhere and throughout the letter he deals with serious problems of every kind (spiritual, theological, moral, social, etc.). As pointed out above, this passage introduces a section concerned with the glorification of God in our worship (cf. 10:31). The hierarchical chain that is outlined in the following verses and their references to shame and glory suggest concern that the Corinthians' "worship" will result in dishonor rather than honor accruing to God. The language of praise is often associated with glory or honor (cf. 1 Chr. 16:27; Eph. 1:6, 12, 14; Phil. 1:11; 1 Pet. 1:7). That which the Corinthians do which is praiseworthy brings them honor (or glory), and that honor and glory presumably also reflect to Christ and God the Father. Paul introduces this text with an affirmation of his praise for the Corinthians; in the following verses he will clarify how their behavior can and should remain praiseworthy through their obedience to his instructions. Worship that is not praiseworthy does not glorify God.

Presumably Paul is responding to the Corinthians' own claim to have faithfully remembered him and the traditions he passed on to them. That the Corinthians were keeping the traditions *just as [Paul] passed them on* is stressed. Whether the point was originally made by the Corinthians in their letter to Paul, or by Paul in his response, his words here serve as a strong affirmation, even if they are qualified by the teaching in the following verses. This verse suggests that a positive relationship still holds between Paul and the Corinthians, and he hopes that his present argument will be well received in the light of that relationship.

The concept of *remembering* will be evoked again in Paul's discussion of the Lord's Supper. There, however, it is not Paul or his traditions that are remembered, but Christ's covenant-establishing death for us. To *remember,* as usual in Scripture, does not recall something that was forgotten, but something that is kept in mind. Thus Thiselton has, "keeping me in mind" here, and BDAG renders the relevant part of this verse, "you think of me in every way."

In the New Testament "traditions" are frequently criticized or spoken of in critical ways (as "the traditions of the elders" or "the traditions of men"; cf. Matt. 15:2, 3, 6; Mark 7:3, 4, 5, 8, 9, 13; Gal. 1:14; Col. 2:8). Thanks in part to the influence of those passages, traditions are frequently looked down upon in many evangelical circles. Three out of the five times that

8. Gk. ἐπαινέω. The exact form of the verb (ἐπαινῶ) appears again in vv. 17 and 22, but is negated in both of those verses ("I do not praise you").

Paul refers to traditions, however, he does so with very positive connotations (here and in 2 Thess. 2:15; 3:6). Traditions, when they do not undermine the teaching of God's word but preserve valid interpretations and/or applications of it, are of great value to the church. In 2 Thessalonians 2:15 and 3:6 Paul refers to the standards for Christian teaching and living as the "traditions"[9] he passed on. In this chapter he seems to have the standards for Christian worship particularly in mind. Although it has been suggested that in the following verses Paul will provide arguments that are intended to get the Corinthians to change worship patterns they have followed since Paul was with them, it seems more likely that he is merely providing them with arguments to support the worship practices he passed on to them, practices that some of them had begun to question (perhaps in light of some of Paul's other teachings).[10] By pointing out that he is clarifying traditions that he passed on to the Corinthians, Paul reminds them that these are not simply his personal preferences. He wants to help the Corinthians understand the implications of Christian teachings which predated Paul's ministry among them and which are accepted by the churches in general (cf. 11:16). In this verse Paul brings both the Corinthians' respect for him and their respect for the traditions of the church to bear, and he hopes that he can leverage both in his attempt to move the Corinthians toward more healthy kinds of behavior — behaviors which glorify God.

*ii. Statement of the basis for Christian practice, 11:3*

**11:3** In saying *I want you to realize* Paul suggests that there is some aspect of the traditions mentioned in the previous verse that the Corinthians have not applied or understood as well as he would like. What he wants them to realize is that *the head of every man is Christ, and the head of the woman is man, and the head of Christ is God.* To Paul's mind, everyone (except God) has a head, and it is important to understand who your head is. The order of the pairs mentioned seems unexpected to many readers: man-Christ, woman-man; Christ-God. It has been suggested that if Paul were trying to establish an order of hierarchy he would have said something like "God is the head of Christ, and Christ is the head of every man, and man is the head of the woman."[11] But Paul is interested especially in the way men

9. Gk. παράδοσις.

10. Chrysostom has a similar understanding, suggesting that earlier Paul had passed the traditions on to the Corinthians but that now he provides them with the rationale behind those traditions (*Homiliae in Epistulam i ad Corinthios* 26.1 [NPNF$^1$ 12:149]).

11. For example, Francis Watson: "Although the Pauline statement *lends itself to* hierarchical rearrangement along these lines, it is not its *intention* to assert any such account of being as hierarchy. As the threefold statement stands, there is no descending or ascending hierarchy: only a series of assertions in which a 'head' is assigned to man, to woman and to Christ. The reference is probably to pre-eminence and authority rather than to relations of origin" (*Agape, Eros, Gender: Towards a Pauline Sexual Ethic* [Cambridge: Cambridge University Press, 2000], 43).

and women fit into a broader hierarchical framework. That explains both why he begins not with God or Christ but with the identification of the head of *every man* and goes next to the head of *the woman* and why he does not name the head first (i.e., "Christ is the head of every man" or "the man is the head of the woman") but introduces the man and then his head, the woman and then her head. The observation that God is the head of Christ, at the end of the verse, highlights the fact that the hierarchy in which the man and woman find themselves continues all the way up to God the Father. The following verses will clarify that Paul is concerned with behavior in the context of worship (where men and women would be praying and prophesying), and for that reason as well it is natural to bring *God* into the discussion even in this verse.[12] Those following verses will also discuss the need to avoid shaming one's head. By bringing up God's relationship to Christ as his head Paul completes the line so that his following discussion about shaming one's head will be understood to have implications for bringing shame or honor to God, who stands at the top of the series of heads and is to be glorified and honored in the Corinthians' worship, not dishonored by it.[13]

The significance of the view that Paul points to a hierarchy going from God to Christ to man to woman has been a matter of significant discussion in the history of interpretation and must be addressed here. It should first be pointed out that Paul's presentation would have been seen as a rather subversive view of things for good Roman citizens, where it was understood that ultimate authority passed from the gods to the Roman emperor and from him down through the ranks to the lowest in society. The lowest in society were expected to respect those over them out of their respect for the emperor (and gods), who stood at the top of the hierarchy. The Corinthian Christians, on the other hand, are to look to God as the one who gives ultimate meaning to the way they fulfill their appointed role in life, not to the emperor or his (or other) gods. Jorunn Økland has pointed out that in the struggle to understand the proper relationships between men and women in worship in the Roman world cosmological hierarchies often played a significant role.[14] It is not surprising that Paul also appeals to a hierarchy as part of his explanation for why men and women were not to participate in worship in exactly the same way. Below it will be noted that it is remarkable how little Paul actually does with this, in comparison with his

12. Remarkably, prophets, prophecies, and prophesying are mentioned thirty-seven times in Paul's letters and fully twenty-two of those references appear in chs. 11–14 of this letter.

13. Thus Watson's statement that "The sequel will show that it is only the first two assertions that play any role in the argument" (*Agape, Eros, Gender,* 43-44) is only partly true. The relationship of the behavior of those first two to honoring or dishonoring God is fundamental to Paul's concern in this section of the letter.

14. Jorunn Økland, *Women in Their Place: Paul and the Corinthian Discourse of Gender and Sanctuary Space* (JSNTSup 269; London and New York: T&T Clark, 2004), 125-27.

contemporaries, in terms of differentiating the places of men and women in worship.

It is not clear whether Paul has men and women in general in mind in these verses, or husbands and wives in particular.[15] When the words for men/husbands and women/wives are found together and discuss the relationships between one and the other,[16] usually husband-and-wife relationships are being discussed, and that is probably Paul's primary concern here,[17] even though the dynamics of the marriage relationship in his context reflected (and influenced) the broader issue of how men and women were expected to relate within society.

The language of the husband as the "head" of the wife does not seem to predate this letter. Great care must be taken to avoid the assumption that the Greek word for "head" has the same meaning(s) as our English word, and the sense that many have that the meaning of the word is transparent may be due, in part, to reading the text in light of the common use of "head" in English to refer to those who are in charge of a department or area of responsibility. The word "head," when used metaphorically in the New Testament, usually occurs in passages that deal with an explicit metaphorical relationship between a head and a body (Eph. 1:22-23; 4:15-16; 5:23; Col. 1:18; 2:19). That raises the question whether its meaning is the same or different in a context like 1 Corinthians 11, where the term "body" does not appear in the argument.

The meanings of the Hebrew and Greek words for "head" in the Old Testament and LXX[18] and their relationship to Paul's meaning here have been the subject of much debate. It has been argued that one of the word's meanings, and the one most appropriate for this context, is that of "source."[19] A number of scholars have argued against this, suggesting that the word in this context means "authority over."[20] Both of the previous views have received serious criticism, and there has been a recent tendency to reject both "source" and "authority over" as possible meanings for the word or the best meaning here. Those rejecting those two possibilities have

15. The Greek word ἀνήρ could mean "man" or "husband," while γυνή could mean either "woman" or "wife."

16. That is to say, between an ἀνήρ and a γυνή.

17. Thus the TNIV alternative reading, "the head of the wife is her husband."

18. ראש and κεφαλή, respectively.

19. See Collins, 405; Fee, 501-5; S. Bedale, "The Meaning of *Kephalē* in the Pauline Epistles," *JTS* 5 (1954), 211-15; Catherine C. Kroeger, "The Classical Concept of Head as 'Source,'" Appendix 3, in G. G. Hull, *Equal to Serve* (Old Tappan, NJ: Revell, 1987); idem, "Head," *DPL* 375-77; A. Mickelsen and B. Mickelsen, "What Does *Kephalē* Mean in the New Testament?" in *Women, Authority and the Bible*, ed. A. Mickelsen (Downers Grove, IL: InterVarsity Press, 1986).

20. J. A. Fitzmyer, "Another Look at ΚΕΦΑΛΗ in I Corinthians 11.3," *NTS* 35 (1989), 503-11; W. A. Grudem, "Does *Kephalē* Mean 'Source' or 'Authority over' in Greek Literature? A Survey of 2,336 Examples," *TrinJ* 6 (1985), 38-59; idem, "The Meaning of *Kephalē* ('Head'): A Response to Recent Studies," *TrinJ* n.s. 11 (1990), 3-72.

tended to a more nuanced understanding of "head" as meaning "prominent," "preeminent," or "foremost."[21] Even if by "head" Paul means "more prominent/preeminent partner" or (less likely) "one through whom the other exists," his language and the flow of the argument seem to reflect an assumed hierarchy through which glory and shame flow upward from those with lower status to those above them. In this context the word almost certainly refers to one with authority over the other.[22] In BDAG the word means "a being of high status" and "in the case of living beings [is used] to denote superior rank."[23] Louw and Nida suggest "one who is of supreme or pre-eminent status, in view of authority to order or command — 'one who is the head of, one who is superior to, one who is supreme over'" and hold that this verse should be rendered "Christ is supreme over every man, the husband is supreme over his wife, and God is supreme over Christ." Of course, our understanding of Paul is complicated by the fact that he engages in wordplay, going back and forth between a literal meaning and a metaphorical meaning for the word.[24] That also suggests that we should not be surprised if the metaphorical meaning of "head" in Greek may not be the

21. Thiselton, 812-22; R. S. Cervin, "Does *Kephalē* Mean 'Source' or 'Authority' in Greek Literature? A Rebuttal," *TrinJ* 10 n.s. (1989), 85-112; A. C. Perriman, "'His Body, Which Is the Church . . .': Coming to Terms with Metaphor," *EvQ* 62 (1990), 123-42; idem, "The Head of a Woman: The Meaning of κεφαλή in 1 Cor 11:3," *JTS* 45 (1994), 602-22; G. W. Dawes, *The Body in Question: Metaphor and Meaning in the Interpretation of Ephesians 5:21-33* (Leiden: Brill, 1998), 122-49.

22. See the discussion in Thiselton, 812-22 and in Loader, *The Septuagint, Sexuality, and the New Testament*, 100-101.

23. *A Greek-English Lexicon of the Septuagint* (rev. ed.; ed. Johan Lust, Erik Eynikel, and Katrin Hauspie; Stuttgart: Deutsche Bibelgesellschaft, 2003) gives the meaning "leader" for Judg 10:18 (MS A). MS B has ἄρχων, "ruler," at the same point. This textual issue is interesting and suggestive since ἄρχων ("ruler" or "leader") is used to translate רֹאשׁ ("head") over 100 times in the LXX, raising the possibility that κεφαλή may have gained similar associations or meanings since it could be considered a more "literal" translation of the Hebrew word. According to Heinrich Schlier ("κεφαλή, ἀνακεφαλαιόομαι," *TDNT* 3:675), "The implied element of what is superior or determinative is expressed in the LXX along with the sense of 'man' or 'person.' κεφαλή is used for the head or ruler of a society." Cf. the antithesis between head and tail (κεφαλή and οὐρά) in LXX Deut. 28:13 (cf. 28:43-44) and in Isa. 9:13. In Isa. 9:14 κεφαλή is used for "head" (רֹאשׁ) in the Hebrew. It is also "used for 'head,' 'ruler,' 'leader' of others or of a society" in Judg. 10:18 (3:675). In *On the Creation of the World* 119 Philo says that the head "is the most princely [or authoritative — τὸ ἡγεμονικώτατον] part in an animal," and in *On the Special Laws* 3:184 he says that "nature conferred the sovereignty of the body on the head (κεφαλή) when she granted it also possession of the citadel as the most suitable position for its kingly rank" and "conducted it thither to take command and established it on high with the whole framework from neck to foot set below it, like the pedestal under the statue" (Colson's translation).

24. David Horrell (*The Social Ethos of the Corinthian Correspondence: Interest and Ideology from 1 Corinthians to 1 Clement* [Edinburgh: T&T Clark, 1996], 171) holds that Paul uses this word "not to talk about authority and subordination but *precisely because* he wants to talk about the way in which men and women must attire their *kephale* in worship. Nevertheless, the theological legitimation which the *kephale* analogy provides clearly gives man priority over woman."

perfect word for the metaphor Paul has in mind, since the wordplay may have pushed him to adopt an unusual meaning. David Horrell points to another potential conclusion regarding the relative importance of the two meanings (literal and metaphorical) of "head" in this passage:

> Paul's specific and contextual concerns clearly motivate the whole passage: he uses the word ["head"] precisely because his concern is with the way in which the [head] must be attired in worship. He follows the assertion of woman's secondary place in the order of creation (vs. 8f.) not with a command for her to be subordinate, but with an insistence that her correct attire is a sign of her [authority] to pray and prophesy. Paul's purpose seems to be the establishment of "proper" distinction between men and women rather than with male superiority or authority. The practical issue of attire is uppermost in his mind.[25]

The Old Testament reflects a patriarchal context and understanding of the relationship between husbands and wives (even if a "softer" patriarchalism than in some other cultures). Whether or not a patriarchal relationship is understood to exist between Adam and Eve before the fall is debated,[26] although most ancient readers of Genesis 1–2 may have assumed that they had that type of relationship (the only kind of marriage they knew). Genesis 3:15, given as part of the curse following the sin in the garden, suggests that the stratification that had been established in creation (humans having dominion over creation but as vice-regents under God's dominion) will now be explicitly extended such that the woman will also come under the dominion of the man as a result of her role in the fall. If some Corinthians were arguing that Christ, as head of the church, was head over men and women in the same way (since in the new creation there is no longer any "male and female") Paul seems to be affirming that the creation pattern is still significant and cannot be shrugged off. While there is a tension between creation and new creation (esp. *fallen* creation and new creation), creation is the context in which Christians live out their lives, and it cannot be passed off as irrelevant.[27]

25. David G. Horrell, "The Development of Theological Ideology in Pauline Christianity," in *Modelling Early Christianity: Social-Scientific Studies of the New Testament in Its Context* (ed. Philip F. Esler; New York: Routledge, 1995), 230 (translations have been provided in brackets at those places where Horrell used Greek).

26. For contrasting views cf. Bruce K. Waltke, *An Old Testament Theology: An Exegetical, Canonical and Thematic Approach* (Grand Rapids: Zondervan, 2006), 232-47, and Rolf Rendtorff, *The Canonical Hebrew Bible: A Theology of the Old Testament* (Tools for Biblical Study 7; Leiden: Deo, 2005), 427-28.

27. Jorunn Økland suggests that "Paul draws on different patriarchal discourses of gender to which there were no real alternatives in his day, they only came in different packages. Naturally, there could be subversive practices to the dominant discourses and we could even view Paul's own attempt to incorporate women in the *ekklesia* as one such subversive practice" (*Women in Their Place*, 176). Scholars differ as to whether Paul's adaptation

This passage played an important role in patristic discussions of the doctrine of the Trinity. Specifically, v. 3 was used by heretics to argue that Christ was inferior to the Father. Chrysostom pointed out that the term "head" must be understood not in terms of a consistent level of distinction, since God and Christ are infinitely superior to us and the relationship between men and women (or husbands and wives) cannot be marked by such an infinite distinction.[28] He points out that it would be absurd to think that the relationship between Christ and God and/or that which applies between the man and the woman is the measure of the other relationships. Rather, although the language used for each relationship is the same, the precise nature of the relationship is determined "according to the occasion."[29] Chrysostom himself may have assumed the male-female or husband-wife relationship would hold to a standard static pattern of submission, but his argument at least suggests that the use of headship language does not predetermine the nature of the relationship that might be described by that language.[30]

### *iii. Description of shameful behaviors, 11:4-6*

**11:4-5** The next two verses address in sequence the issue of men and women praying and prophesying in the church and the conditions under which they should do so in order to avoid shaming their "heads": [4]*Every man who prays or prophesies with his head covered dishonors his head.* [5]*But every woman who prays or prophesies with her head uncovered dishonors her head — it is the same as having her head shaved.* Although there were already female prophets in the Old Testament (Exod. 15:20; Judg. 4:4; 2 Kgs. 22:14; Neh. 6:14; Isa. 8:3), Joel 2:28 [3:1 LXX and HB] indicated that one of the marks of the last days would be the generous outpouring of the Spirit on all God's people with the result that Israel's "sons and daughters shall prophesy." Paul indicates that doing so in an inappropriate manner would bring shame on one's head, evidently meaning one's husband (in the case of a

---

of the culturally normative hierarchical relationship and his use of it to justify different head styles in worship provides an eternal endorsement of that hierarchy and its application in the church or whether it reflects a contextualized theology which might need to be recontextualized in other cultures. Either way, Paul's commitment to fully integrating women and their gifts in the life of the church is clear.

28. NPNF[1] 12:150 (*Homiliae in Epistulam i ad Corinthios* 26.3).

29. NPNF[1] 12:150 (*Homiliae in Epistulam i ad Corinthios* 26.3): Gk. κατὰ τὸ αἴτιον.

30. Chrysostom makes it clear that in his view the subordination of the woman is a result of the fall. He says that the woman "was not subjected as soon as she was made; nor, when [God] brought her to the man, did either she hear any such thing from God, nor did the man say any such word to her: he said, rather, that she was 'bone of his bone, and flesh of his flesh' but he made no mention to her at all of rule or subjection. But when she made an ill use of her privilege and she who had been made a helper was found to be an ensnarer and ruined all, then she is justly told for the future, 'your turning will be to your husband'" (NPNF[1] 12:150-51 [*Homiliae in Epistulam i ad Corinthios* 26.3]).

woman) or Christ (in the case of a man). Paul's ultimate concern, in the broader context is with the glory of God/Christ. The immediate concern seems to be that the behavior of some wives would bring shame to their husbands. It is interesting to note that the two verses before Joel 2:28 both stress that in the eschatological time of restoration and salvation God would see to it that "my people will never again be put to shame" (Joel 2:26, 27). For either men or women to act in a way that would bring inappropriate shame on themselves or others in worship would be to undermine God's intentions for his people and for their worship, and would dishonor God himself.

In vv. 4-16 Paul will address the question of the propriety of covering or not covering one's head (or possibly of varying hair styles) while praying or prophesying. It was his concern regarding what people did with their heads in worship that led him to introduce the discussion with the reference to the different "heads" of the man, woman, and Christ. Much discussion has focused on whether Paul is referring to head coverings or hair styles.[31] If hair styles are in view (men wearing long hair and/or women letting their hair down rather than putting it up), it may suggest that homosexual influences were penetrating the church, since long hair was associated with homosexuality in the Roman world.[32] If the issue has to do with head coverings the question remains whether Paul's concern is more directly related to general expectations of women in public settings[33] or to the roles of head coverings in Roman worship.[34] The decisions are difficult ones, and no real consensus has been reached. It may be that Paul's approach reflects more than one of the concerns highlighted by various interpreters. Since the early Christian house church turned what would normally be the more or less private context of a household into a public place for the worship of the God of Israel, the private versus public issue would have been raised as well as standard questions regarding the proper dress of men and women in worship and the proper distinctions between men and women in places of worship.

Paul starts by addressing how this question relates to the first of the key players mentioned in the previous verse: the man. In vv. 4-16 he will focus especially on how it relates to women. Although Paul begins with the men and mentions them again in vv. 7a, 14, it seems that the issue of the man's covering (or lack of one) is raised as a foil to clarify how the issue re-

31. See the discussion in Witherington, 232-35; Thiselton, 823-26; David E. Blattenberger, III, *Rethinking 1 Corinthians 11:2-16 through Archaeological and Moral-Rhetorical Analysis* (Studies in the Bible and Early Christianity 36; Lewiston, ME: Mellen, 1997); Økland, *Women in Their Place,* 190-91; and esp. Watson, *Agape, Eros, Gender,* 45-48.

32. So Jerome Murphy-O'Connor, "1 Cor 11:2-16 Once Again," *CBQ* 50 (1988), 265-74.

33. So Bruce W. Winter, *Roman Wives, Roman Widows: The Appearance of New Women and the Pauline Communities* (Grand Rapids: Eerdmans, 2003), 77-96.

34. So R. E. Oster Jr., "When Men Wore Veils to Worship: The Historical Context of 1 Corinthians 11:4," *NTS* 34 (1988), 481-505; and Witherington, 232-36.

lates to women. The way it relates is by contrast: Whatever is appropriate for the man would be inappropriate for the woman — and vice versa. This strict antithetical relationship seems to suggest that "[c]lear gender boundaries is the point."[35]

*Every man who prays or prophesies with his head covered dishonors his head.* It is not clear why it would bring shame on Christ for a man to pray or prophesy with his head covered. Paul's words in 2 Corinthians 3:13-16, however, may suggest a potential biblical background for both Paul's understanding that men's heads should be uncovered and for some Corinthians' support for both men and women to be uncovered in God's presence. Paul says, "we are not like Moses, who put a veil over his face" (2 Cor. 3:13), for having turned to the Lord, "the veil is removed" (3:16); as a result "we all *with unveiled faces*" reflect the glory of the Lord and are transformed into the image by the work of the Spirit (3:18). The conceptual and lexical ties between 1 Corinthians 11:4-7 and 2 Corinthians 3:13-18 are remarkable, including the use or rejection of veils in God's presence, glory, and image. Paul is referring to Moses' experience as explained in Exodus 34:33-34, when he decided to wear a veil when in the presence of the people but removed it when he went into the presence of the Lord. If the Corinthians were already familiar with Exodus 34:33-34 and had heard Paul express something similar to 2 Corinthians 3:13-18, one could easily see how some might deduce that the women also should act like Moses and remove the veil when entering into God's presence, since Paul indicated "we all"[36] should approach God with "unveiled faces." Paul now needs to explain why women should in fact continue to wear veils even when in the presence of the Lord. Of course, there is a difference in that in this letter Paul is talking about covering one's "head" (the special concern is likely to be the hair) rather than one's "face" (as in 2 Corinthians).

Davina Lopez has suggested that since "statues of head-covered emperors showing 'correct' masculine ritual behavior" were common in Paul's world, his teaching that it would be shameful for a man to cover his head while worshiping would have been not merely odd "but also politically scandalous. . . . Piety, expressed by men covering their heads in ritual, is also a visual identification with 'faithful images of the emperor.'"[37] It clearly was not obvious to most Romans that it would be shameful for them to cover their heads while in worship. The fact that it was the normal approach to Roman worship may have something to do with Paul's attitude toward it. It may well be, as Garland suggests, that for Paul (and presumably some other early Christians) to cover one's head in worship would evoke a "clear association . . . with pagan devotion." If that were the

35. Økland, *Women in Their Place,* 191.

36. Gk. ἡμεῖς . . . πάντες.

37. Davina Lopez, "Review of Jorunn Økland, *Women in Their Place: Paul and the Corinthian Discourse of Gender and Sanctuary Space,*" *Review of Biblical Literature* [http://www.bookreviews.org] (2005), 4.

key issue for the men, however, one would wonder why Paul would not have similar problems with women covering their heads, since that was also the norm for Roman worship.

Perhaps more central to Paul's thinking is the need to maintain a strict distinction between the sexes, one that was traditionally associated with some type of antithetical manifestation (e.g., men were associated with public life, women with the privacy of the household, men were to be in the open air and women covered, etc.).[38] Plutarch wonders why "sons cover their heads when they escort their parents to the grave, while daughters go with uncovered heads and hair unbound." One solution he offers is that it may be because "the unusual is proper in mourning, and it is more usual for women to go forth in public with their heads covered and men with their heads uncovered." He points out that "in Greece, whenever any misfortune comes, the women cut off their hair and the men let it grow, for it is usual for men to have their hair cut and for women to let it grow" (*Quaestiones Romanae* 267 A-B).[39] Plutarch's comments relate, of course, to the other observations about long and loose hair being a mark of some Roman homosexuals — such men attempted to identify themselves as females not by ignoring, but by employing, the antithetical distinction between the sexes in the area of head styles. In Paul's context, men and women were expected to have contrasting head styles, especially in public. Women were more commonly expected to have their heads covered while in public. In most Roman worship settings the proper places for men and women were clearly distinguished. Where the places were not distinguished, their roles would be distinguished (usually in a way that reflected a hierarchical distinction between men and women).[40]

It may be a combination of the above factors that led Paul to decide that since men and women would share the same space in the worship setting, it would be necessary to maintain a clear gender distinction through the use/avoidance of head coverings. If the need was felt to have men's and women's heads distinguished in the public worship of the church, Paul's main issue may have been simply that of deciding whose head would be covered, and whose would not. In vv. 14-15 Paul will indicate one of the places where he found his clue as to which person should have their head covered and which should not.

The question is still raised as to why Paul speaks of heads covered or uncovered only during prayer and prophecy, rather than when in public or in worship. It may be that Paul thinks of prayer and prophecy as central aspects of Christian worship and therefore means to distinguish the appearance of men and women in that act. It may also be that for Paul participa-

38. Cf. Jerome H. Neyrey, "What's Wrong with This Picture? John 4, Cultural Stereotypes of Women, and Public and Private Space," *BTB* 24 (1994), 78-80.

39. Translation of Frank Cole Babbitt (Loeb).

40. Økland, *Women in Their Place*, 92, 125-28.

tion in worship may be summarized as "praying or prophesying" (that is, to engage in speaking to either God [in prayer] or those gathered [in prophecy])[41] and that by "to pray or to prophesy" he means the same as we would by speaking of those who "worship God in church on Sunday." On the other hand, in Roman worship it was only the person offering a sacrifice that would cover their head. In this case it seems that Paul thinks that it is most important to guard some gender distinction in the public act of leading in worship (see the further discussion in the comments on v. 5).

For the man to worship in a manner that did not reflect his proper distinct identity as a male by leaving his head uncovered would bring shame on his own head (and thereby bring shame on Christ/God).

Paul's teaching (and presumably the tradition he passed on to them) regarding the women is the exact opposite of that regarding the men: *every woman who prays or prophesies with her head uncovered dishonors her head.* As in the previous verse, it is not clear whether prayer and prophecy are understood as two very distinct practices for which women should cover their heads or whether Paul is using a synecdoche, in which prayer and prophecy, as prominent kinds of worship activities, serve together as a general reference to active participation in worship. Prayer and prophecy are highlighted both here and in chapter 14. In pagan Roman piety the person (male or female) offering the sacrifice would cover their head as the sacrifice was offered (a ritual act referred to as *capite velato*), and there could be a parallel here, if Paul's thought is that in the act of praying or prophesying the woman would cover her head. Although praying is mentioned again in v. 13, Paul's discussion in the following verses seems to many to reflect a concern (and follow a line of argumentation) for covering the female head (and leaving the male head uncovered) not merely in the act of prayer or prophecy. In fact there is evidence that the covering of the female head in public settings was a cultural expectation in flux, with sensitivities raised when it was not being practiced.

While most scholars believe that Paul is arguing in favor of having women wear a veil (or pull their mantle over their head),[42] some believe that he is talking about having them bind their hair up on their heads in a special (culturally modest) hair style. At the heart of the debate are images

41. Cf. Fee, 506: "The two verbs are neither exhaustive nor exclusive but representative: they point to the two foci of Christian worship — God and the gathered believers."

42. For a helpful discussion of the standard head-covering practices of the Roman world, see Gerd Theissen, *Psychological Aspects of Pauline Theology* (trans. John P. Galvin; Edinburgh: T&T Clark, 1987), 158-63. Theissen argues that more liberal views regarding the covering of women's heads would have been common: "One cannot therefore claim that there was social pressure in Greece which made head covering a requirement for women. When the veiling of women is required in some literary documents, a conservative ideal of women, not everyday reality, stands behind this" (162). Theissen's own references to veiling "required in some literary documents" and to "a conservative ideal of women" suggest social disagreement over the practice of women appearing in public with an uncovered head, however common it may have been.

and statues of women from Paul's time. Some of them depict women with their heads covered (or veiled), and others with their heads uncovered. It has been suggested that the expectation that upper-class women would cover their heads in public had given way in western parts of the early Roman Empire and that images of women with uncovered heads and literary references to women's hairstyles being noted in public confirm that they were no longer expected to cover their heads in public.[43] It seems clear that some prominent women were not, in fact, covering their heads in public, but it is not so clear that this was uncontroversial. On any given day today one may turn on a TV or open a popular magazine and find men and women dressed in ways that draw crowds of paparazzi and raves (and sometimes, even if rarely, shock) from commentators. Special events such as the red carpet entrance to the Academy Award ceremonies are especially well known for new and sometimes radical fashion statements.[44] Yet most (or at least many) Christians, even today, would be shocked, or at least think it inappropriate, if women attended or participated in church services dressed in similar ways.

The evidence that some, or even many, women were not covering their heads in worship may have been a point of significant concern for those with a traditional sense of sexual and moral propriety.[45] As Judith Lynn Sebesta points out, the traditional costume of the Roman matron "signified her modesty and chastity. . . . It consisted of her distinctive dress, the woolen *stola,* which was worn over a tunic; the protective woolen bands which dressed her hair; and the woolen *palla* or mantle, which was used to veil her head when she went out in public."[46] Sebesta points out that although "to modern women of Western countries, the Middle Eastern custom of veiling women seems to signify social inequality and even inferiority, to modern

43. See, e.g., R. MacMullen, "Women in Public in the Roman Empire," *Historia* 29 (1980), 208-18.

44. This parallel is closer than it might appear at first if, as Laetitia La Lollette points out, "Roman practice may go back to the age-old notion, still prevalent in the Middle East, that a woman's sexual powers are concentrated in her hair" ("The Costume of the Roman Bride," in *The World of Roman Costume* [ed. Judith Lynn Sebesta and Larissa Bonfante; Wisconsin Studies in Classics; Madison, WI: University of Wisconsin Press, 2001], 55). Today the focus has shifted to the extent to which women expose other parts of their bodies.

45. It was pointed out above that Plutarch affirmed, "it is *more usual* for women to go forth in public with their heads covered and men with their heads uncovered" (*Quaestiones Romanae* 267A, emphasis added).

46. Judith Lynn Sebesta, "Symbolism in the Costume of the Roman Woman," in *The World of Roman Costume,* 48. Cf. Carolyn Osiek and Margaret Y. MacDonald, with Janet H. Tulloch, *A Woman's Place: House Churches in Earliest Christianity* (Minneapolis: Augsburg Fortress, 2006), 8: "Considerable evidence indicates that covering a woman's head with a veil was once customary throughout both Greek and Roman spheres of influence, but that it was much less prevalent in western Roman areas by the middle of the first century. Many official portraits of women continued to feature the suggestion of a veil, but it was more symbolic than concealing." See the fuller discussion in Winter, *Roman Wives, Roman Widows,* 78-85.

women of the East it is a symbol of their honor and of the sanctity and privacy of their family life." For a married woman to neglect the covering of her head while in public would traditionally be understood as "a sign of her 'withdrawing' herself from matronage," and the decision of a Roman husband to divorce his wife for doing so would amount to "a ratification of the exclusion her bare head had expressed."[47] We have argued that in this letter Paul is concerned, above all, with the infiltration of Roman and Corinthian values and lifestyles into the church. Of special interest is the influence of sexual immorality and idolatry for which pagan Gentiles were infamous in Jewish thinking. A move toward the abandonment of the female head covering would have struck many at the time as a move toward a more licentious, a more sexually provocative, way of appearing in public, precisely the kind of social influence Paul is anxious to avoid.[48]

As pointed out above, the question of a woman bringing shame on her husband was such a fundamental concern that it is addressed in a Greek marriage contract of the time (Papyrus Tebtunis 1.104) which stipulates that the wife is not permitted "to dishonor the common household or to bring shame upon [her husband] in anything that causes a husband shame." In the world of Paul and the Corinthians contact between men and women who were not married to each other was highly regulated and any deviation from the cultural expectations was bound to bring shame on the woman and her husband. References to shame in husband-wife or male-female relationships most often have to do with the transgression of some sexual expectation. As Watson notes, the shame Paul has in mind "appears to be the shame of physical nakedness."[49] He thinks, however, that that means the head covering he has in mind must cover the face, and not merely the hair since Paul indicates that a woman's hair counts as a "covering" or "garment" and "the absence of a hair-covering cannot be associated with nakedness."[50] But even if one does not accept Troy Martin's (unlikely) proposal that the word normally translated "covering"[51] in v. 15 should be understood as a reference to the male testicle,[52] there is sufficient evidence to suggest that women's hair was understood to be an object of intense sexual attraction and even possibly as part of her genitalia.[53] It has been sug-

47. Sebesta, "Symbolism in the Costume of the Roman Woman," 48-49.

48. See the discussion of the "new Roman woman" in Winter, *Roman Wives, Roman Widows*, 21-31.

49. Watson, *Agape, Eros, Gender*, 48.

50. Watson, *Agape, Eros, Gender*, 48.

51. Gk. περιβόλαιον.

52. See Troy Martin, "Paul's Argument from Nature for the Veil in 1 Corinthians 11:13-15: A Testicle instead of a Head Covering," *JBL* 123 (2004), 75-84.

53. Again, the former is supported by Laetitia La Lollette's suggestion that "Roman practice may go back to the age-old notion, still prevalent in the Middle East, that a woman's sexual powers are concentrated in her hair." She points to the "importance the Romans attached in early times to the covering of the head of the sexually mature woman" and the understanding that "a chaste woman was one who kept her hair covered" ("The

gested that for a mature Roman woman to expose herself (or her hair) to the penetrating sexual gaze of a man other than her husband was the virtual equivalent of announcing that she was available for other types of sexual penetration. In fact, as Watson points out, the apocryphal story of Susanna suggests that the ability to gaze openly on the face of a beautiful woman could be interpreted as a substitute for the thwarted attempt to enjoy sexual relations with her.[54] A similar association is reflected in the Ethiopic version of the *Apocalypse of Peter* 7:22, where we are told that for their divine judgment various groups of wicked people are hung by their offending parts. Those who blasphemed are hung up by their tongues, adulterous women are hung up *by their hair,* and the men who committed adultery with them are hung up by their penises.

Although more and more women may well have begun to appear in public without having their head covered by the *stola, palla,* or other covering, and it was becoming more and more acceptable, it seems that any public behavior, and especially attire (or lack thereof),[55] by married women that served to invite the attention of men was perceived to be scandalous.[56] Paul does not seem to require women to have their head covered if they are simply attending the meeting, but he does require them to have their head covered if they are going to draw attention to themselves by leading in some way (praying or prophesying) in the public meeting. In these cases a woman might be expected simply to pull her *stola* or *palla* over her head before speaking up. Some women may well keep their heads covered whenever they are in public, but others could at least be expected to take this simple step in the interests of propriety.

Paul says that for the woman to have her head uncovered would be *the same as having her head shaved.*[57] The women themselves would evidently not think of it as being the same as having their heads shaved since more

---

Costume of the Roman Bride," 55). On the latter, see T. Martin, "Paul's Argument from Nature for the Veil in 1 Corinthians 11:13-15," 77-82.

54. See F. Watson's interpretation of Susanna (*Agape, Eros, Gender,* 49): "The moment of unveiling is the satisfaction of the elders' desire for Susanna. Having failed to persuade her to lie with them, the 'desire' they announce to her *(en epithymia sou esmen,* v. 21) remains unfulfilled. But the sight of her naked, unveiled face at her trial provides a substitute for what Susanna refused them: in a climactic moment, they look and are satisfied."

55. Different authors point to different kinds of scandalous self-presentation, including bright, colorful, and flashy clothing or makeup, fancy or merely exposed hairstyles, and the (male) toga. For a full and helpful discussion see Kelly Olson, "*Matrona* and Whore: The Clothing of Women in Roman Antiquity," *Fashion Theory* 6 (2002), 387-420, or the abbreviated version, "*Matrona* and Whore: Clothing and Definition in Roman Antiquity," in *Prostitutes and Courtesans in the Ancient World* (ed. Christopher A. Faraone and Laura McClure; Wisconsin Studies in Classics; Madison, WI: University of Wisconsin Press, 2006), 186-204.

56. Olson, "*Matrona* and Whore," 399-401.

57. *Shaved* here is the perfect passive participle ἐξυρημένῃ. The perfect tense here is functioning similarly to the normal adjective "uncovered" earlier in the verse, as a simple description of the state in which her head should be found (shaved, rather than uncovered, if it comes to that).

and more "liberated women" of the time were beginning to appear in public without covering their heads but were not generally tempted to be seen in public with a shaved head. We will discuss the disgrace associated with the shaved head in the commentary on the next verse. In the meantime it simply needs to be pointed out that if Paul can get the Corinthians to view an exposed woman's head in public worship as being as shameful as they would consider it to be for a woman to have her head shaved, he will have succeeded in providing a strong reinforcement for the tradition he passed on to the church and which was evidently generally accepted in the early church.

Part of the regulation of contacts between men and women in the Roman world was reflected in the understanding that when it came to worship men and women were to occupy distinct places and/or distinct roles. "Women were either excluded from public and private religious life or confined to its 'alien' and fringe aspects. Women participated in the ceremonies of imported cults, those governed (in Roman eyes at any rate) by the Greek Rite. When they exercised religious responsibilities, they did so at night or behind closed doors or in suburban or frontier temples."[58] Jorunn Økland points out that "[t]o a certain extent this applies also to Corinth. All of the sanctuaries that gave women more prominent space were located outside of the city center, especially the Acrocorinth."[59]

Furthermore, even in "mixed sanctuary places" (where both men and women would be involved in worship at the same time), "a distinction between the place of men and that of women is still seen as crucial" and "a fundamental notion . . . seems to be that some physical places are for men and some for women, or some ritual roles are for men and some for women. Often the spaces or roles for men are placed closer to the ritual center, or in other ways hierarchically placed over those for women."[60] Where sanctuary spaces were shared by both genders, gender differentiation tended to be by way of role differentiation.[61]

Given the consistent concerns regarding the proper places of men and women in sanctuaries in the ancient world, in a letter concerned about issues of boundaries within and around the church, it is not too surprising that Paul would feel the need to clarify how, or the extent to which, men and women could participate together in the worship of the God of Israel. In Økland's words, "Paul is drawing on flexible discourses of sanctuary space and he combines these also with other ideas to accommodate women into a ritual space in which their presence is problematic. But Paul is cre-

58. John Scheid, "The Religious Roles of Roman Women," in *From Ancient Goddesses to Christian Saints* (ed. P. S. Pantel; Cambridge, MA: Belknap, 1992), 397, cited in Økland, *Women in Their Place*, 128.

59. Økland, *Women in Their Place*, 128.

60. Økland, *Women in Their Place*, 92.

61. Cf. Økland, *Women in Their Place*, 125-26. "Boundaries between women's and men's ritual spaces were set by walls, times, and by gender-specific rules" (126).

ative enough to at least try."[62] His strategy was generally consistent with cultural expectations: "since women are integrated in the communal space, the boundaries must be maintained by differentiation."[63] Økland suggests that Paul's thinking about proper behavior in and use of worship spaces is especially informed by his understanding of the Jerusalem temple and a desire he shared with other Jews of his time to replicate the temple experience in some way.[64] Steven Fine has argued that ancient thinking about the synagogue developed along similar lines.[65] It may be that Paul is following a pattern familiar to the ancient synagogue. While we do not know how men and women were distinguished in the ancient synagogue, it seems that, as in the early church, men and women were not segregated in that context. Some have thought that women were separated by worshiping from a balcony, but Eric Meyers's research suggests otherwise: "In all of the ancient synagogues discovered, there is no evidence for the separation of women into a designated area or balcony. Surely a medieval development, the segregation of women is not borne out by the archaeological data."[66] Of course, the Jerusalem temple had a separate court for women, who were not allowed to advance into the court of Israelites, which was restricted to men. If a spatial separation was not replicated in the synagogue, it may be that some other distinction such as what Paul proposes for the church was practiced there as well.

Thus by passing on a tradition that entailed maintaining the traditional antithetical gender distinction in the public display or covering of the head, Paul would both provide the minimal gender distinction that would be expected in any worship context and also avoid any suggestion that Christian women were promoting the sexual looseness of the "new Roman women" who were known for their disregard of the traditional marks of female modesty and purity.[67]

**11:6** Here Paul develops the parallel between an uncovered and a

62. Økland, *Women in Their Place*, 169.

63. Joseph Marchal, "Review of Jorunn Økland, *Women in Their Place: Paul and the Corinthian Discourse of Gender and Sanctuary Space*," *Review of Biblical Literature* (http://www.bookreviews.org) (2005), 3.

64. Økland, *Women in Their Place*, 161-65.

65. See Økland, *Women in Their Place*, 162-64.

66. Eric M. Meyers, "Ancient Synagogues: An Archaeological Introduction," in *Sacred Realm: The Emergence of the Synagogue in the Ancient World* (ed. Steven Fine; New York: Oxford University Press, 1996), 18.

67. In applying this passage to contemporary readers modern Western Christians usually assume that the veil is not an issue and that there are no cultural situations in which a veil could actually be a valid resource. However, even in Western culture today we usually consider it important to know whether the person we are speaking with is male or female, and find it awkward if we are not sure. In many other cultures strong distinctions between men and women remain important for understanding how and where people of different genders are to relate to each other. The question of how the gospel intersects with culture in addressing healthy relationships between the genders will always require great wisdom and sensitivity.

shaved female head that was introduced at the end of v. 5. *For if a woman does not cover her head, she might as well have her hair cut off*[68]; *but if it is a disgrace for a woman to have her hair cut off or her head shaved, then she should cover her head.* For a woman to appear in public with a shaved head was to suffer extreme public humiliation. Although it is from the fifth century B.C., a passage from Aristophanes' *Thesmophoriazusae* (838) is helpful: "There are many reproaches we have the right to bring against men. The most serious is this, that the woman who has given birth to a useful citizen, whether *taxiarch* or *strategus,* should receive some distinction; a place of honor should be reserved for her at the Stenia, the Scirophoria, and the other festivals that we keep. On the other hand, she of whom a coward was born or a worthless man, a bad trierarch or an unskillful pilot, should sit with shaven head, behind her sister who had borne a brave man."[69] Not only do we find that this was an extreme form of humiliation, but we also learn that this was the most serious reproach that could be brought against *a man,* which confirms that the humiliation of the woman serves as a humiliation and reproach against her husband. As in our passage, Aristophanes' text makes it clear that shame and honor may be transmitted from the wife to the husband (and in our text, through the husband to Christ and God).[70]

In the *Testament of Job* (first century B.C. or A.D.) 23:7–25:8 Job's wife is reduced to having her hair cut off in exchange for food. It is done "disgracefully in the market, while the crowd stood by and marveled" (24:10).[71] The following chapter of the *Testament* consists of a lament for her which focuses on her great losses and humiliation by comparing her former wealth and generosity with her present situation, summarized by the refrain, "Now she sells/exchanges/gives her hair for loaves!" which is repeated five times. In the *Sibylline Oracles* 3:356-62, Rome is described as a virgin that has lived in splendor but which is about to be humiliated: "Often the mistress will cut your delicate hair and, dispensing justice, will cast you from heaven to earth" (359-60).[72] While the shame was probably based on association with nakedness, the humiliation of having a woman's hair shaved off may also have to do with the suggestion that she has forfeited her very identity as a woman (which is marked by the possession of her

68. This verb (κειράσθω) is an aorist imperative, whereas *she should cover her head* (later in the verse) is a present imperative. Either an aorist or a present would make sense (the aorist due to the summarizing nature of its perfective aspect or because Paul has a particular situation in mind, or the present because he is providing a general rule for how such a scenario should be handled). *TLG* indicates that there are no cases of the present imperative in the middle and passive voices of κείρω (which is the expected alternative) in all of Greek literature (probably due to the relationship between lexical and verbal aspect). So Paul's use of the aorist is probably not of exegetical significance. Paul is providing a general rule for how such a scenario should be handled.

69. Translated by Eugene O'Neill Jr. (Perseus Project).

70. See also, Tacitus's *Germania,* 19.

71. Translation of R. P. Spittler in *OTP* 1:849.

72. Translation of J. J. Collins in *OTP* 1:370.

hair) similar to the way in which a married woman's failure to cover her head in public could be understood as suggesting that she had forsaken her identity as a married woman. In the case of the lesbian the move indicated a desire to abandon a female identity for that of a man.[73]

Paul does not want anyone to suffer *disgrace* in the congregation's worship, so the option of having the woman shave her head is not a real one, but it would have a similar effect to her uncovering her head, since in the latter case she would dishonor her head (cf. v. 5). *Head* in this last case probably refers both to her own head/self and also to her husband, who also serves as her head. She would bring shame on herself and her husband. The only real option, if honor is to be maintained for all those participating in the worship experience (and thus, presumably, for God to be honored as well), is for the woman to cover her head, at least when she prays or prophesies in church.

### *iv. Development of the basis for Christian practice, 11:7-12*

In these verses Paul will develop the theme of men and women in creation and in the Lord.[74] The Greek text of v. 7 suggests that these verses serve to support the conclusion[75] reached in v. 6 (or vv. 5-6), namely, that women should cover their heads in worship (or at least when they pray or prophesy). Paul's thinking on men and women is developed especially in the light of creation (as expressed primarily in Gen. 1:26-27 and Gen. 2:18-23). Man, woman, and God are all explicitly mentioned in vv. 7 and 12, and the intervening verses focus on the relationship between men and women in light of their respective relationships with God, especially as reflected in the origins of the first man and woman and those of men and women ever since. The traditional (and majority) reading of vv. 7-9 takes them to reflect Paul's understanding that Genesis 2 establishes a functional hierarchy reflected in the order in which the man and woman were created and in their respective purposes.[76] Others think that the point is that gender distinctions are reflected in the distinct origins of men and women (Adam and Eve) and should be maintained in the church.[77]

73. Similarly, for a man to grow long hair suggested that he had become effeminate (see Pseudo-Phocylides 212; Philo, *On the Special Laws* 3:37; *On the Life of Moses* 1:54; *On the Contemplative Life* 50–51).

74. Paul builds his argument in vv. 7-12 out of indicative verbs (with infinitives) and verbless clauses (ὀφείλει κατακαλύπτεσθαι, ἐστιν [v. 7]; ἐστιν [v. 8, with an elided verb in the second part of the verse]; ἐκτίσθη [v. 9, with an elided verb in the second part of the verse]; ὀφείλει ἔχειν [v. 10]; vv. 11-12 are verbless). This reflects an argument from the structure of reality (how things are or came to be and how things therefore ought to be).

75. The verse begins with the Greek conjunction γάρ ("for").

76. For an intriguing study of the translation of the creation narrative in the LXX and its potential importance for understanding the New Testament texts, cf. Loader, *The Septuagint, Sexuality, and the New Testament*, 27-59, 99-104.

77. See esp. L. Ann Jervis, "'But I Want You to Know . . .': Paul's Midrashic Inter-

Jewish interpreters struggled to understand the relationship between Genesis 1:26, 27 and the narratives in Genesis 2. Many distinguished between the accounts and applied them in very different ways. Philo distinguishes between "the heavenly man" of Genesis 1:26-27 and "the earthly man" of Genesis 2:7 (*Allegorical Interpretation* 1:31; 2:4-5; *On the Creation of the World* 134). The former is "born" in the image of God and does not partake of the corruption of earthly existence. The latter is made out of clay and partakes of the vagaries of earthly existence and "has a helpmeet for him." Paul's own understanding of the significance of the relationship between those texts of Genesis is reflected in these verses.

**11:7** In the previous verses Paul indicated that a woman should cover her head in worship and a man should not, and he indicated that not to do so would be disgraceful, but he did not explain why it was so, except to say that "the head of every man is Christ, and the head of the woman is man." Here Paul explains further why this distinction holds. While this verse and the following could be taken to support the point that the man is the head of the woman (v. 3), the context suggests that it is intended to support the point that the woman should cover her head, since that is not only the final point made in v. 6 but also the implied point of v. 10 and the stress of v. 13 as well. Paul begins this verse with the case of the man, who *ought not to cover his head.* This is not his main concern, but it provides a foil for the point he wants to make about the woman. The reason[78] the man should not cover his head is that *he is the image and glory of God.* The *woman,* on the other hand, *is the glory of man* (and therefore she should cover her head). That mankind was created in the image of God is clear from Genesis 1:26-27. The image of God is interpreted in Psalm 8 as having to do with humanity being "crowned . . . with glory and honor" (8:5). Paul probably uses the term "glory" both because it is associated with "image"[79] and because it is sometimes substituted for "likeness" or "image" in references to Genesis 1:27.[80] As Garland points out, Paul moves smoothly from "image" to "glory," which "then becomes the key term in 1 Corinthians 11:7-9 and counterbalances the notion of 'shame' in 11:4-6."[81]

The references to the *glory of God* and *the glory of man* should be under-

---

textual Response to the Corinthian Worshipers (1 Cor 11:2-16)," *JBL* 112 (1993), 231-46; Judith M. Gundry-Volf, "Gender and Creation in 1 Corinthians 11:2-16: A Study in Paul's Theological Method," in *Evangelium, Schriftauslegung, Kirche: Festschrift für Peter Stuhlmacher zum 65 Geburtstag* (ed. J. Ådna et al.; Göttingen: Vandenhoeck & Ruprecht, 1997), 151-71; Craig S. Keener, *Paul, Women and Wives: Marriage and Women's Ministry in the Letters of Paul* (Peabody, MA: Hendrickson, 1992).

78. The participle ὑπάρχων ("being" [the image and glory of God]) is understood to be causal, pointing to the reason why the prior statement holds; thus the TNIV translation *since.*

79. Morna D. Hooker, "Authority on Her Head: An Examination of 1 Cor. 11:10," *NTS* 10 (1964), 415. Cf. Ps. 106:20; Rom. 1:23; 2 Cor. 3:18; 4:4.

80. Cf. Ps. 8:5; 4QDibHam[a] 8 i 4.

81. Garland 523.

stood as keys to what this passage is about, as understood from the stress on "the glory of God" in 10:31. Paul's statement in v. 7 that man *is the image and glory of God; but woman is the glory of man* causes some to think that Paul understood Adam to be created in the image of God, but not Eve. In 15:49 however, he says that "just as we have borne the image of the earthly man, we shall also bear the image of the heavenly one," suggesting that he understands all humanity to share (even if imperfectly) in the image of God as it has been passed down to us through Adam, and that part of our redemption in Christ entails the restoration of God's perfect image in Christ (cf. Rom. 8:29; 1 Cor. 15:49; 2 Cor. 3:18; Col. 3:10; 2 Cor. 4:4; Col. 1:15). Understanding 11:7 in the light of 15:49 suggests that for Paul Adam was created directly in the image of God and that the rest of us (from Eve on) are made in God's image as we inherit it from Adam and our parents (cf. Gen. 5:3; 9:6).

That is similar to a rabbinic way of interpreting Genesis 1:26-27 and understanding the relationships between those verses and the narratives in Genesis 2. As D'Angelo has shown (following Boucher), some rabbinic debates over the interpretation of Genesis 1:26 implied that the plural forms ("let us"; "our") referred to God's intention to create the first man and woman in unique manners after which every other man and woman would be created by God in conjunction with (through) a human father and mother (thus "our" image would be the image of God and the parents). Thus, "[i]n the past Adam was created from dust and Eve was created from Adam; but henceforth it shall be "in our image, after our likeness" [Gen. 1:26]; "neither man without woman nor woman without man, and neither of them without the Shekinah" (*Genesis Rabbah* 8:9; cf. *Genesis Rabbah* 22:2; *y. Berakot* 9:1). Thus Adam and Eve were created in different manners, and neither of them was created in the manner of the rest of humanity (through a mother and father). The rest of humanity, however, was to come about through God working through both a mother and a father.[82]

The close relationship between Paul's clear allusion to Genesis 1:26 in v. 7b and his statement that the woman is the glory of the man in v. 7c calls to mind that he understands Adam to have been uniquely made in God's image (without any human contribution), while God's image was passed to Eve through Adam. Verse 7 is therefore probably best understood as an interpretation of Genesis 1:26-27 "through the creation account in Gen. 2."[83]

Gundry Volf[84] argues that Paul's point is that "man and woman are both *the glory of another* and therefore both have an obligation not to cause shame to their heads." This is true, but the question of whose glory each one reflects (and not just that it is of another) seems important to Paul's ar-

82. On the variety of Jewish sources that relate to this theme, see Mary R. D'Angelo, "The Garden: Once and Not Again: Traditional Interpretations of Genesis 1:26-27 in 1 Corinthians 11:7-12," in *Genesis 1–3 in the History of Exegesis: Intrigue in the Garden* (ed. G. A. Robbins; Studies in Women and Religion 27; Lewiston, NY: Edwin Mellen, 1988), 7-21.

83. Garland, 522.

84. Gundry-Volf, "Gender and Creation in 1 Corinthians 11:2-16," 157.

gument. It is important because it is appropriate for the glory of God to be reflected in worship, but not that of man. For man's glory (the woman) to be uncovered in worship does not bring glory to him and/or God but shame.

One of the reasons that Paul does not mention that the woman was also created in God's image is probably "because he wants to stress the point that she is the glory of man."[85] Thus Paul's point is not that women are not made in God's image but that the way the creation narrative distinguishes between the origin and purpose of the man and the woman suggests that the man (not originating from the woman or being created to complete her) does not reflect the woman's glory (but only God's), while the woman does reflect the glory of the man. Verses 8-9 use details from Genesis 2 to explain why the man cannot be understood as the glory of the woman, while the woman can be understood as the glory of the man.[86]

On the basis of the use of the word "glory" in texts like 1 Thessalonians 2:20 and Philippians 3:19 Watson has suggested that in the second part of this verse (where it refers to the woman) the word means "the object of a person's joy, love and devotion" such that "man as the manifestation of God should not be veiled, but woman as the object of man's erotic joy, love and devotion should be veiled" since the veil covers a "focal point for the male erotic drive."[87] While this suggestion fits well with Paul's broader concerns about the understanding of the church's need to protect itself against the presence or threat of sexual immorality and with the understanding that an uncovered woman drawing attention to herself would likely have been considered sexually provocative by many in Paul's context, it does not ultimately convince. Watson contends that Paul is using the word "glory" in two different ways in this verse. He understands man to be *the glory of God* in the sense of God's "manifestation or revelation," but he does not think that meaning makes sense for the woman. She is not the manifestation or revelation of man "for, unlike God, man is not hidden and does not need a manifestation external to himself. Even if he did, why would it need to be concealed behind a veil?"[88] We may be able to answer

85. Garland, 523; cf. Gundry-Volf, "Gender and Creation in 1 Corinthians 11:2-16," 156.

86. Proverbs 11:16 says that "a kindhearted woman gains honor [or glory]." In the LXX the same verse is rendered "a grateful wife brings glory to her husband." BDAG points out that the term used for "grateful" (εὐχάριστος) in that text is found "oft[en] in ins[criptions] of cities and their people who are grateful to their benefactors." The text may suggest that a wife who is grateful to her husband (as her spousal benefactor) brings him glory. In our passage the woman's appropriate response to her "head" (husband as patron/benefactor?) should lead her to keep from bringing him shame in the worship service (as well as elsewhere, certainly). 1 Esdras 4:17, in the midst of a speech extolling the strength of women, declares that women "make men's [impressive] robes; they bring men glory; men cannot exist without women" (NRSV).

87. F. Watson, *Agape, Eros, Gender,* 56.

88. F. Watson, *Agape, Eros, Gender,* 56.

Watson's question best without proposing two different meanings for "glory" in a context where the point of contrast seems to be based on the different people who might be revealed, manifested, or honored in the context of the worship of God.

BDAG states that the word "glory" means "reflected radiance" in this verse (evidently in both parts). That is consistent with the understanding of the image of God (or images of gods) in the ancient biblical and pagan contexts. Beale points out that "the notion that Adam was set in a sanctuary as a royal 'image' of his God is an ancient concept found even outside Israel." He points out that Ashurbanipal II "created an icon of the goddess Istar . . . from the finest stones, fine gold . . . making her great divinity resplendent."[89] Beale also shows that "[t]he resplendent glory of the image was to reflect the luminescent glory of the goddess herself. Accordingly, the light of the deity was to shine out from the temple into the faces of humanity. Consequently, the idols in Assyria were made of precious metals in order to reflect the heavenly glory of the god they represented."[90] This idea of the god's image reflecting and/or representing his glory is not restricted to ancient Near Eastern texts[91] but is found elsewhere in the Bible, especially in Paul's thinking. In 2 Corinthians 3:18 Paul refers to believers as people who "with unveiled faces reflect the Lord's glory, [and] are being transformed into his image [literally, "the same image"] with ever-increasing glory."[92] In the following chapter Paul refers to "the light of the gospel that displays the glory of Christ, who is the image of God" (2 Cor. 4:4). Here Paul describes Christ as God's image, manifest in glory which transforms those who look upon it into the same glorious image. The thought suggests that the glory reflects/reveals/manifests the one whose glory it is and leads others to be caught up in admiration of that one. Paul's discussion in 2 Corinthians 3–4 also recalls the role of a veil in keeping people from seeing the glory shining recalls an image, which also suggests that Paul has a similar glory in mind for the woman and that it is appropriate for her to wear a veil to keep people from gawking at man's glory in the church.

The cultic associations of any reference to an "image of God" (or an image of any god, which is expected to be found in cultic contexts and to serve as a conduit for worship of the god represented by the image) are significant in our context since Paul is dealing with proper behavior and adornment in the context of Christian worship. Paul's ultimate point seems to be that nothing should happen in worship that would detract from God's

89. G. K. Beale, *The Temple and the Church's Mission: A Biblical Theology of the Dwelling Place of God* (New Studies in Biblical Theology; Downers Grove, IL: InterVarsity Press, 2004), 88, citing A. K. Grayson, *Assyrian Rules of the Early First Millennium* B.C. (Toronto: University of Toronto Press, 1996), 296.

90. Beale, *The Temple and the Church's Mission*, 88.

91. For which, see more examples in Beale, *The Temple and the Church's Mission*, 88-89.

92. Adopting the marginal reading of the TNIV, which translates κατοπτρίζω "reflect." BDAG has the definition "look at someth[ing] as in a mirror." Cf. NET, NLB, NJB.

glory, including behavior that would draw attention to the glory of man. Hooker points out that the woman's head should be covered "not because she is in the presence of man, but because she is in the presence of God and his angels — and in their presence the glory of man must be hidden."[93]

**11:8** By beginning verses 8-10 with *For*[94] Paul indicates that he will explain further the point he made in v. 7. As it turns out, he does not focus on the issue of man being the image and glory of God (except implicitly), but on the issue of the woman being the glory of the man. God is not explicitly mentioned in these verses, but *man* and *woman* are. Paul supports the principle he drew in v. 7 from the creation of Adam and Eve as described in Genesis 2. That *man did not come from woman* is patent in Genesis 2:7: he was "formed . . . from the dust of the ground." That the *woman* came *from man* is taught in Genesis 2:23. In fact, it is given as the explanation of her name: "she shall be called 'woman,' for she was taken out of man." How does this relate to one being the glory of the other? The artist's work brings honor and glory to the artist. While both men and women were created by God, according to Genesis 2 the man played a role in the making of the woman, but the woman played no role in the making of the man. She was not around when the man was made, and he can in no way be considered a reflection of her nature or character. She, on the other hand, was not simply made after the man, but the man was the raw material from which she was made. One could say that she is the glory of the man in that she is a reflection of the quality of the materials used! What is said of the woman is consistent with what could also be said about any child with respect to his or her parents: they came from them and exist because of them. In fact, when Philo explains why the woman was made from the man instead of from the earth (like the man) he answers as follows: "First, because woman is not equal in honour with man. Second, because she is not equal in age, but younger. . . . Third, he wishes that man should take care of woman as of a very necessary part of him; but woman, in return, should serve him as a whole. Fourth, he counsels man figuratively to take care of woman as of a daughter, and woman to honour man as a father." Furthermore, he says that the woman "should give to him who has taken her the honour which she showed those who begot her."[95] The parallel with a father and daughter is also tied to the proper respect of the honor (or glory) of the parent.

Paul uses a chiastic structure (inverted parallelism) both in this verse and the next, as his comments alternate between the sexes (man . . . woman; woman . . . man). This is not for the sake of any theological point, but flows naturally in the course of making alternating statements about men and women in relation to each other.

93. Hooker, "Authority on Her Head: An Examination of 1 Cor. 11:10," *NTS* 10 (1964): 415.

94. Gk. γάρ.

95. Philo, *Questions and Answers on Genesis* 1:27 (Loeb).

**11:9** Paul goes on and points out that *neither was man created for woman, but woman for man.* That the man was not *created for woman* goes without saying in Genesis 2. She was not even on the scene yet. That *woman* was created *for man*[96] is based on Genesis 2:18, where God said, "It is not good for the man to be alone. I will make a helper suitable for him." The context suggests that he would have been the only one of God's creatures without a corresponding mate, and that was not good. As Watson points out,

> The Pauline language and the Genesis narrative are "androcentric" in the sense that woman's being is determined by the being of the man; her existence rectifies the deficiencies of his, and nothing is said of the meaning of her existence in itself and apart from his. Yet his own existence in itself and apart from her has been described as "not good." If man-in-himself is an abstraction contrary to the will of the creator and the nature of the creature, then he hardly constitutes a "centre" in relation to which woman's existence is peripheral and dependent.[97]

The woman is not created for her own sake, but so that the human being might be complete, might be all that God intended.[98] The original man and the original woman had different origins and different original purposes. The origin and purpose of each suggest that in some way the woman's existence as narrated in Genesis 2 points to the man as the source and reason for her existence. Thiselton points out that "for the most part [Paul] stresses gender equality in the gospel (cf. Gal 3:28; 1 Cor 7:2-4) but 'objects to *symbolic* disregard for sexual differences in the dress of male and female prophets.'"[99] The dress code that Paul had in mind was not seen merely as a symbolic expression of gender distinction to be maintained for the sake of respect for "that which God wills, decrees, and expresses in creation or in the creation order,"[100] however, but was, at least in Paul's con-

96. Gk. διὰ τὸν ἄνδρα.

97. F. Watson, *Agape, Eros, Gender,* 58.

98. That the woman originated from the man and was made because of him implies the anteriority of the man: the one coming into existence from and for the other comes into existence after the other. This point is made explicit in 1 Tim. 2:13 (cf. Philo, *Allegorical Interpretation* 2:5: the helper "is younger than the one being helped"). In Paul's context wives would almost always have been significantly younger and less mature than their husbands, providing a more consistent relationship between the pattern of Adam and Eve as described by Paul in his letters and their own marriages than would be seen in many Western marriages today. On the nature of the husband-wife relationship in the Roman world see Susan Treggiari, *Roman Marriage: Iusti Coniuges from the Time of Cicero to the Time of Ulpian* (Oxford: Clarendon, 1993); Beryl Rawson, "Adult-Child Relationships in Roman Society," in *Marriage, Divorce, and Children in Ancient Rome* (ed. Beryl Rawson; Canberra: Humanities Research Centre, 1991), 27, and (more concisely) Witherington, 170.

99. Thiselton, 836, citing Wayne Meeks, *The First Urban Christians,* 161 (Thiselton's footnote, referencing Barth, is mistaken).

100. Thiselton, 836.

text, understood to be essential to avoiding the infiltration of anything that might distract worshipers' attention away from the glory of God. Clearly gender distinctions are important to Paul, and they are most certainly to be maintained by the church. Paul's concern, however, is ultimately with the need for an exclusive focus on God's glory (which would certainly be diminished by any apparent disrespect for gender distinctions in worship) which jealously avoids the promotion of human glory, and even more zealously avoids any behavior which would inappropriately introduce shame into the context of Christian worship.

**11:10** This verse is fraught with exegetical difficulties. Paul says, *It is for this reason that a woman ought to have authority over her own head, because of the angels.* Questions are raised about the *reason,* the *authority,* and the *angels.*

By *for this reason* Paul could mean either the reason(s) just offered in the previous verses or the reason given at the end of the verse *(because of the angels).* The fact that Paul has clearly been providing reasons why a woman should have her head covered in the previous verses suggests that that is what he has in mind. The sentence structure itself reveals that the *reason* is *because of the angels.* It is probably best to understand Paul to have both in mind.[101] In fact, given the fact that the significance of the angels is unclear, an interpretation that relates the reference to the angels to the preceding arguments should probably be preferred.

Angels are associated in such diverse ways with creation, worship (including prayer and prophecy), and women in the Old Testament and in Jewish literature that it is difficult to discern which one(s) Paul might have had in mind here. It is also unclear whether he is referring to good angels or evil ones. Some think that Paul may be concerned about the women's vulnerability to angelic attention based on the common Jewish understanding that Genesis 6:2 referred to angels who mated with women (Philo, *On Giants* 16–18; Josephus, *Antiquities* 1.73; *1 Enoch* 6–19; 21; 86–88; 106:13-15, 17; *Jubilees* 4:15, 22; 5:1; CD ii 17-19; 1QapGen$^{ar}$ ii 1; 4QAgesCreat [4Q180 1 i 7-8; 4Q181 2 i 1-2]; *Targum Pseudo-Jonathan on Genesis* 6:1-4; *Testament of Reuben* 5:6-7; *Testament of Naphtali* 3:5; *2 Baruch* 56:10-14).[102]

According to two different Jewish traditions, the angels worshiped Adam when he was created (e.g., *Life of Adam and Eve* 13–16; *Genesis Rabbah* 8:10).[103] If Paul has any reason to think that his readers are familiar with this

101. So also Chrysostom (NPNF$^1$ 12:153 [Chrysostom, *Homiliae in Epistulam i ad Corinthios* 26.5]): "For all these [reasons] which have been mentioned," he says, or rather, "not only for these, but also 'because of the angels.'"

102. Richard J. Bauckham points out that "[t]his was how the account of the 'sons of God' in Gen 6:1-4 was universally understood (so far as our evidence goes) until the mid-second century A.D." (*Jude, 2 Peter* [WBC 50; Dallas: Word, 1983], 51).

103. In the account given in *Life of Adam and Eve* 13–16 it was due to their refusal to worship Adam, at the urging of Michael, that the devil and his underlings were cast out of heaven. In the account given in *Genesis Rabbah* 8:10 God caused Adam to fall asleep so that the angels would know that he was not divine (and would not worship him).

tradition, it could be that he would expect them to understand that by covering the face of the glory of the man (i.e., by covering the woman's face) he hopes to avoid distracting angelic attention from the worship of God to the worship of man, just as he does not allow anyone but God to receive glory in the church's worship.[104] In Isaiah 6:2 the seraphs cover their faces in the presence of God, and it could be that Paul thinks that women should behave in a similar fashion. It is not clear why men would be granted an exception; however, it is clear that for Paul the fact that man is God's image and glory does in fact mean that some special distinction applies.

According to Acts 12:23, an angel killed Herod Agrippa I for accepting praise as though he were a god rather than giving glory to God. This presupposes an understanding of a great angelic zeal for the protection of God's glory. If Paul's concern is not that of distracting angelic attention from God's glory, it may well be that he is concerned that angelic guardians of God's honor and glory would be offended (and perhaps required to intervene) if women's attire were to either draw attention to the glory of man or in any way be considered inappropriate for those worshiping God. According to a significant Jewish tradition, angels were the guardians of creation order, and some therefore suggest that Paul was concerned to make sure that nothing in the worship service would offend them.

One of the concerns of the worship of Israel was the exposure of nakedness in the act of worship (Exod. 20:26; 28:42; cf. *4QReworked Pentateuch[a]* 7-8 8). Of course, shame and nakedness are almost used as synonyms in Scripture (Lev. 20:17; 1 Sam. 20:30; Isa. 47:3; Mic. 1:11; Nah. 3:5; Rev. 3:18). This same concern with avoiding the exposure of nakedness and shame in the presence of God is reflected in the Dead Sea Scrolls. 1QM x 1 tells how the readers were told "to keep ourselves from any shameful nakedness, and he [Moses] told us that You are in our midst, a great and awesome God." What makes this even more interesting for our purposes is that a little earlier in the same work we find a similar concern, but this time rather than the presence of God among the people it is the presence of "holy angels" that requires the avoidance of the shame related to sexual uncleanness or nakedness: "Any man who is not ritually clean in respect to his genitals on the day of battle shall not go down with them into battle, for holy angels are present with their army. There shall be a distance between all their camps and the latrine of about two thousand cubits, and no shameful nakedness shall be seen in the environs of all their camps."[105] Paul may well be referring to the angels as divinely appointed auditors of the community's worship who, like God, would be offended by any shameful displays during the worship.[106]

104. Cf. Hooker, "Authority on Her Head," 415 n. 2.

105. 1QM vii 5-7 (trans. of Wise, Abegg, and Cook, *The Dead Sea Scrolls: A New Translation*).

106. Cf. Loader, *The Septuagint, Sexuality, and the New Testament*, 102: Paul's statement probably "reflects the concern about nakedness and shame: nakedness is inappropriate in

In the presence of the angelic protectors of the purity of divine worship the use of the veil allowed the women simultaneously to respect the men/husbands in the congregation and freely exercise a newly found authority to pray and prophesy alongside them in the sacred space of the church gathered for worship. Watson suggests that the veil "is a prophetic sign to the angels that the new creation has dawned and that their jurisdiction has passed away," and that the authority of the woman prophet, "represented by the veil, is greater than theirs."[107] It is not clear why the angels would have interpreted the use of the veil in that way without having read Paul's argument. That women would simultaneously respect the men/husbands in the congregation and freely exercise a newly found authority to pray and prophesy alongside them may have served as such a sign for angels observing the scene.

Ideally, Christian women were worshiping side-by-side with the men of the community, even praying and prophesying along with the men, but in a way that did not bring shame or disgrace on those men or anyone else. They were worshiping in a way that respected the proper decorum expected in the presence of God and his angelic attendants, such that the community's full attention was on the glory of God without being distracted by either human glory or shame. It is just possible that Paul is thinking of behavior which is not only acceptable to the angels but also of behavior by which "the manifold wisdom of God might now be made known to the rulers and authorities in the heavenly places" by the church as men and women (as well as Jews and Gentiles) worship God together as one (Eph 3:10).

What is the *authority* the woman was to have *over her own head?* Some (Chrysostom, Theodoret, etc.) have suggested that it would be the veil as a sign of man's (or her husband's) authority over her.[108] Most church fathers understood the reference to authority "as metonymy for *a sign of power over.*"[109] Others (Hooker, Barrett, Bruce) hold that it is the veil as a sign of the woman's own authority to pray and prophesy in the church. Watson helpfully suggests that "the covering of the head gives woman the 'authority' to proclaim the word of God to the congregation irrespective of her relation to any other 'head.' The fact that 'the head of woman is man' is a potential deterrent to woman's proclamation which the covering of her head will effectively nullify."[110]

---

the presence of the holy angels. That understanding may also have gone so far as seeing potential danger to women (and to angels) if women's naked beauty (at least in relation to the head and face) is exposed in the presence of angels, given the story of the fall of angels in Gen 6:2 and the traditions it spawned."

107. F. Watson, *Agape, Eros, Gender,* 71.

108. In commenting on this verse Chrysostom asserts that "being covered is a mark of subjection and authority" (NPNF[1] 12:153 [Chrysostom, *Homiliae in Epistulam i ad Corinthios* 26.5]).

109. Thiselton, 838. See his excursus on the meaning of "authority" (ἐξουσία) here.

110. F. Watson, *Agape, Eros, Gender,* 44.

Garland points out that this view "requires the head covering to do double (and dissonant) duty as a symbol. On the one hand, it serves to efface man's glory in the presence of God; on the other hand, it serves as a symbol of the woman's authorization to pray and prophesy. . . . It is more likely that the covering serves only one primary function: the cloaking of man's glory."[111] In his view "the head covering represents the 'woman's control over her own head, by which she demonstrates her faithfulness to her husband or her acknowledgement of her status.'"[112] He quotes Lucius's confession in Apuleius's *Metamorphoses (The Golden Ass)* that the central concern of his life has been "to observe in public the heads and tresses of beautiful women, and then to conjure up the image at home for leisurely enjoyment" and suggests that "Paul wishes to curb the erotic potential of the uncovered female head in the context of worship."[113] This helpful suggestion also seems to extend the function of the veil beyond the simple "cloaking of man's glory" to the cloaking of the woman's beauty.

BDAG point out that "[m]any now understand it as a means of exercising power," with the abstract word "authority" serving in place of the more concrete "veil." It gives a parallel from Diodorus Siculus 1.47.5 which refers to a stone figure with "three kingdoms [i.e., three symbols of royal power] on its head."[114] We are reminded that those with authority were often recognized by the symbols of authority that were placed on their heads (crowns, diadems, etc.). As Dionysius of Halicarnassus put it, "even today the Romans give kings scepters and diadems to establish their authority" (*Roman Antiquities* 3.61).[115] The Roman world was full of statues and other images of men and women who had "authority on their heads" in the form of signs of royal power. In such a context (and given the parallel just cited), it is likely that this verse should be translated as in the NRSV, NIV, NET, and ESV: the woman should have "a symbol of authority on her head" as opposed to "have authority over her own head."[116]

This last observation, along with the conjunction of references to glory, (dis)honor, and angels, leads us back to Psalm 8, which understands

111. Garland, 525.

112. Garland, 525, citing J. D. BeDuhn, "'Because of the Angels': Unveiling Paul's Anthropology in 1 Corinthians 11," *JBL* 118 (1999), 303-4.

113. Garland, 525-26, citing Lindsay's translation of *Metamorphoses* 2.8.

114. Gk. ἔχουσα τρεῖς βασιλείας ἐπὶ τῆς κεφαλῆς. See the full bibliography in BDAG.

115. Cf. Josephus, *Against Apion* 1.98; Manetho, *History,* Fragmenta 50a; Polybius, *History* 29.23. Cf. *3 Baruch* 7:4; *Testament of Abraham* B 7:5; 10:8; *Joseph and Aseneth* 3:11; 5:6; 16:13; 18:5; 21:4. For an example of someone wearing authority on his head that was not his own see Diodorus Siculus 17.116.2-3.

116. The collocations would seem to point in two different directions since ἐξουσία ἐπί normally suggests "authority over" something while ἐπὶ τῆς κεφαλῆς would normally designate something "on one's head" (esp. in a context where that is what has been under discussion). When we look at the fuller expression, however, "authority over a head" is a less likely collocation while "[symbol of] authority on a head" would be something found on many coins, statues, and other images throughout that culture.

the creation of mankind in Genesis 1 to entail human dominion (authority), having been "made a little lower than God [or the heavenly beings; LXX = angels] and crowned with glory and honor." John Paul Heil says that "the woman should take account not only of her creational status as the glory of man, but also of the creational status of both men and women as having a glory and honor that approached that of the angels." He cites Psalm 8 and suggests that a woman "should exercise authority over her head by having it covered . . . not only to maintain her status as the glory . . . of man (11:7b), but also to do her part in order that both men and women can maintain their lofty creational status of a glory and honor that is just short of that of the angels (11:10b)."[117] While in the future the Corinthians will judge angels (1 Cor. 6:3), in the meantime they find themselves just below the angels,[118] who zealously guard the honor and glory of God. By wearing her veil during public worship the woman signals her own status as created by God even while covering up any trace of human glory in the presence of God and his angelic court.

The woman's head is not one over which others have authority. God has granted her authority to pray and prophesy. She exercises that authority in a dignified way by respecting both herself and the rest of the congregation through the avoidance of provocative attire or any dress or behavior which would bring shame on herself, others, or God, in a context where all eyes and every heart should be focused on God's glory in the midst of his holy people.

**11:11** In vv. 11-12 Paul discusses the origins of men and women since Adam and Eve. In doing so he follows a chiastic structure "in which 'woman' frames 'man'" (woman-man-man-woman) and which "asserts the dependence not only of the woman upon the man but especially of the man upon the woman 'in the Lord,' as confirmed by the fact that man is now given birth into the world through woman in accord with God's scriptural plan of creation":[119] *Nevertheless, in the Lord woman is not independent of man, nor is man independent of woman.* The meaning of this verse is not immediately apparent; it literally reads: "Nevertheless, neither woman apart from man nor man apart from woman, in [or *by*] the Lord." But, as we shall see, the verse becomes clearer in the light of similar statements about men and women that Jewish rabbis made based on Genesis 1–2. After establishing a principle for the behavior of men and women in worship from the narrative of the unique creation of the first man and woman in vv. 8-9, Paul now qualifies the potential implications of those narratives in light of the origin of every man and woman since that first pair. 1 Esdras 4:14-17, a dis-

117. John Paul Heil, *The Rhetorical Role of Scripture in 1 Corinthians* (Studies in Biblical Literature 15; Atlanta: Society of Biblical Literature, 2005), 183-84.

118. See the interpretation of Psalm 8 in Heb. 2:7-9, where it is understood that Christ (and Christians) were made to experience life below the status of angels for a limited time, until their glory would be fully realized.

119. Heil, *The Rhetorical Role of Scripture in 1 Corinthians*, 185.

cussion of the power of women, contains several ideas related to our passage: "Gentlemen, is not the king great, and are not men many, and is not wine strong? Who is it, then, that rules them, or has the mastery over them? Is it not women? Women gave birth to the king and to every people that rules over sea and land. From women they came. . . . Women make men's clothes; they bring men glory; men cannot exist without women" (1 Esdr. 4:14-17 NRSV). Three verses later the speaker clearly alludes to Genesis 2:24 ("A man leaves his own father, who brought him up, and his own country, and clings to his wife"). Here woman's power ("reign") is related to the fact that all men come from women and are raised by them and that without women men cannot even come into existence.

As pointed out in the comments on v. 7, rabbinic tradition also distinguished between the origin of Adam and Eve and that of the rest of humanity. The language they used is very close to Paul's language here: "In the past Adam was created from dust and Eve was created from Adam; but henceforth it shall be "in our image, after our likeness" [Gen. 1:26]; *neither man without woman nor woman without man,* and neither of them without the Shekinah" (*Genesis Rabbah* 8:9; emphasis added). D'Angelo sees three features in common between 1 Corinthians 11:7-12 and the rabbinic statements: "First, Paul advances the formula 'neither woman without man nor man without woman' as an interpretation of Gen. 1:26. Second, Paul also contrasts that phrase with the creations of Adam and Eve (1 Cor. 11:7-9). Third, Paul also makes a temporal distinction between creation and its aftermath, and on that basis rejects the creation of Eve as the basis for prescriptions about women."[120] It is not clear that Paul's statement in v. 11 reflects his interpretation of Genesis 1:26 (although his allusion to the text and the use of his phrase elsewhere as an interpretation of that text raises that possibility). It may be based on a broader understanding of the relationship between Genesis 1 and Genesis 2, one which later rabbis based on Genesis 1:26 itself. Also, it is not the case that Paul rejects the creation of Eve as the basis of prescriptions about women. Paul introduces the verse with *Nevertheless,*[121] which introduces a qualification, not a rejection, of the prior statement. Paul is in agreement with other ancient interpreters of Genesis 1–2 in deducing some principles from the creation of Adam and Eve, while qualifying them in light of the recognition that their creation was unique and that other principles may be applied in the light of the way all men and women have come into being ever since.

Chrysostom's interpretation is similar. It is "in order not to either lift up the men more than was appropriate nor to abase the women. . . . he brings in the correction, saying, 'Nevertheless neither man without the

120. D'Angelo, "The Garden: Once and Not Again," 21.

121. Gk. πλήν, which, according to BDAG, serves as a "marker of someth[ing] that is contrastingly added for consideration."

woman nor woman without man, in the Lord.' 'Do not only consider the first things and that creation,' he says. 'For if you investigate what comes after those things you will find that each of the two is the cause of the other, or, rather, not even that each is the cause of the other, but that God is the cause of everything.' Therefore he says, 'neither man apart from woman nor woman apart from man, in the Lord.'"[122]

Paul's statement that "neither woman without man nor man without woman" applies *in the Lord*[123] seems strange at first sight, since clearly the same reality applies to all of humanity, not merely to Christians. D'Angelo suggests that Paul has taken the temporal distinction other interpreters applied between the creation of the first pair and the formation of the rest of humanity and has applied it to the distinction between all creation and new creation in Christ.[124] The point, presumably, would be similar to that made in the rabbinic texts: that the community's application of the principle drawn from the narration of the creation of the first human couple is tempered by the way God has determined to bring every other human being into his creation.

If one were to take the final prepositional phrase (translated here and elsewhere as *in the Lord*) instrumentally ("by/through the Lord"),[125] Paul's meaning would correspond perfectly to the Jewish exegetical tradition cited above about the Lord's role in the formation of every human being (based in part on Gen. 4:1): "neither of them without the Shekinah" (*y. Berakot* 9:1; *Genesis Rabbah* 8:9; 22:2). It would also strengthen the parallel between v. 11 and v. 12:

1) "neither woman without man" in v. 11 is equivalent to "woman is from man" in v. 12.
2) "nor man without woman" in v. 11 is equivalent to "the man through the woman" in v. 12.
3) "by/through the Lord" in v. 11 is equivalent to "all things are from God" in v. 12.

In this case the only difference between Paul's statement and the rabbinic view would be that *the Lord* in v. 11 refers specifically to Christ.

Many scholars find in Paul's *in the Lord* a reference to the new creation context established by the gospel. Thiselton sees Paul turning here to "his third 'lens' or 'point of reference' as that of eschatology or the order of the gospel" (the first two lenses being the order of creation and societal convention): "Whereas the creation order entails a differentiation that may also embody a hint of priority, at least in terms of the Genesis narrative, Paul

122. Cf. NPNF[1] 12:153 (*Homiliae in Epistulam i ad Corinthios* 26.5).

123. Gk. ἐν κυρίῳ.

124. D'Angelo, "The Garden: Once and Not Again," 24-25.

125. This seems to be the interpretation suggested by the quotation from Chrysostom given above.

adds that in the gospel differentiation is determined more explicitly by a principle of mutuality and reciprocity. *There could be no reciprocity or mutuality unless each was differentiated from the other.* Even so, the very experience of human birth in the natural or created order demonstrates that the principle of mutual interdependence does not originate, Marcion-like, with the new order of the gospel *in the Lord*."[126]

In Paul's case, it is the community established *in the Lord* which is to live in the light of these truths. Paul's *in the Lord* seems to suggest that the new creation in Christ relativizes the distinctions between men and women in a way similar to the observation based on the distinction between Adam and Eve and the rest of us.

**11:12** Verse 12 summarizes the interpretation of Genesis 1–2: *For as woman came from man, so also man is born of woman. But everything comes from God.* The first clause, *as woman came*[127] *from man*, refers to Eve (or to her and to women in general) and reminds the reader again of Genesis 2:21-23: "So the LORD God caused the man to fall into a deep sleep; and while he was sleeping, he took one of the man's ribs and then closed up the place with flesh. Then the LORD God made a woman from the rib he had taken out of the man, and he brought her to the man. The man said, 'This is now bone of my bones and flesh of my flesh; she shall be called "woman," for she was taken out of man.'"[128] The second clause, *so also man is born of woman*, points not to the creation of the first man but to that of every man (and woman) since Adam (perhaps evoking Gen. 4:1). In the naming of Eve in Genesis 3:20 her role is established as "the mother of all the living." Gundry-Volf points out that "[t]his comparison cancels out the exclusive privilege of man: just as in the beginning Eve was made from Adam's rib, in all subsequent history man is born through woman. Thus both man and woman are 'from/through' each other, though in different ways." Furthermore, "Paul's frame of reference for the idea of the woman's priority is thus the created order, while for the man's priority it is creation in primal history."[129]

Like Thiselton, Watson sees Paul pointing to an aspect of the new creation in Christ which was foreshadowed in the narratives of Genesis 2. He suggests that the earlier discussion pointed to

> an imbalance in the first creation that the veil is to screen out in the new creation. Having moved forward from the old creation to the situation "in the Lord" (vv. 7-10), Paul is now in a position to look back at the old creation from the new perspective and to see the togetherness of man

126. Thiselton, 842.

127. There is no verb in the Greek, and the statement could be understood to refer to the way things continue ("woman comes from man"), but the context suggests that the original creation of the first woman is especially in mind.

128. Gk. κληθήσεται γυνή ὅτι ἐκ τοῦ ἀνδρὸς αὐτῆς ἐλήμφθη αὕτη.

129. Gundry-Volf, "Gender and Creation in 1 Corinthians 11:2-26," 162-63.

> and woman in the Lord already foreshadowed there. The new creation redresses an imbalance in the old; but, seen retrospectively, the old creation is also prophetic of the new. Anticipations of the togetherness of man and woman in the Lord may be found in the simplest and most obvious phenomena of the first creation. Woman is from man: as we have already seen, this intimate original unity is represented by the Genesis narrator as the basis of the erotic movement of man towards woman which is the original foundation of their relationship. But, even in the first creation, the relation of man and woman is not wholly determined by *eros*. Woman is from man, but man is also through woman. Man is the origin of woman, but it is no less true that woman is the origin of man. . . . Eve claims: "Through God, I have created a man" (Gen. 4.1).[130]

As Thiselton points out, "Paul insists that true human relationality entails otherness and indeed respect for the otherness of the other as a necessary basis for true reciprocity, mutuality, and relationality that constitutes what it is to be human."[131]

The final clause, *everything comes from God*, reminds the reader that God is the ultimate origin of every man and woman — of every human being and all creation (see LXX Gen. 1:1, 31; Eccl. 3:11; Isa. 45:7; Amos 5:8; Jonah 1:9), apparently relativizing the significance of other factors in the creation of men and women and clearly emphasizing that it is *his* glory and honor that must govern all that is done. That everything comes from God has been asserted already in 8:6, with the reminder that we (and presumably all things) exist for his pleasure and purposes, or, more to the point for Paul's reference here, for his glory (cf. 10:31). Of course in 3:21-23 Paul had already made the point that everything belongs to God, and in 15:28 he will emphasize that all things are destined to be perfectly submitted to him so that in the end he will be "all in all," as he should be.

### *v. Appeals to common sense, nature and consensus, 11:13-16*

**11:13** Verses 13-15 follow the structure woman-man-woman, suggesting, again, that the woman's behavior is of central concern. Having provided theological arguments in favor of having the women continue to cover their heads in the worship setting Paul now appeals to the readers to take a hint from nature regarding the most appropriate attire to use.

Paul begins v. 13 with an appeal to the readers to use their own critical faculties: *Judge for yourselves*.[132] Of course the following text indicates

130. F. Watson, *Agape, Eros, Gender*, 79.

131. Thiselton, 843.

132. Paul uses an aorist imperative (as in 10:15), suggesting that he is inviting the Corinthians to think carefully about this present argument (rather than making a general appeal to judge things for themselves). There are eleven imperatives in this chapter, and all but the ones found here and in v. 6 (see the note there) are present imperatives.

that they are not to continue judging on whatever basis they had been previously applying. Paul's whole argument suggests that some of the readers have not been thinking clearly about this subject; otherwise he would not need to address it. His previous discussion and that found here and in the following two verses are intended to help guide the Corinthians in their ability to judge for themselves.

*Is it proper for a woman to pray to God with her head uncovered?* The question of what is *proper* raises the issue of the context in which one finds oneself. Here it is the worship of the God to whom all things owe their origin (11:12c) that provides the crucial context. As Heil explains, "In other words, is it proper or appropriate not just in the eyes of society but most especially in the eyes of the God . . . who, as the ultimate origin of both man and woman (11:12c), created woman to be the glory of man (11:7b), the God . . . for whose glory we are to do all things (10:31), to pray to this God . . . with her rather than the man's head uncovered. . . ?"[133] Although it is not unusual in other literature for the verb "to pray"[134] to be followed by an object (like "to God" or "to the Lord"),[135] it is unusual for Paul to use such a construction. Paul uses the verb nineteen times in his letters and eight times in this letter alone, but this is the only place where he provides the object: "to God." Lockwood points out that this addition "reminds the Corinthians of the solemn nature of worship. Here they approach the almighty and holy God. . . . In his presence the women [as well as the men!] should show decorum."[136] In the Roman world both men and women covered their head when offering a sacrifice to a god (although not when merely attending or participating in someone else's act of sacrifice). As pointed out above, Paul's earlier argument would serve to explain why it was appropriate for a man to participate in worship without covering his head, but traditional interpretations of decorum for men and women in worship — and for women whenever in public — would have suggested that the woman

133. Heil, *The Rhetorical Role of Scripture in 1 Corinthians,* 186. The last ellipsis represents Heil's "uncovered by long hair," a part of his argument that we find unconvincing. The other ellipses represent places where Heil provides Greek (τοῦ θεοῦ; θεοῦ; τῷ θεῷ).

134. Gk. προσεύχομαι.

135. *Pace* Lockwood, 376. Cf., e.g. (with a form of θεός or θεά ["G/god/goddess"] as the object), Philo, On the *Contemplative Life* 66; Josephus, *Antiquities* 10.252, 256; Aristophanes, *Peace* 560; Aristophanes, *The Rich Man* 958; Aristophanes, *Frogs* 892; Plato, *Republic* 1.327; Plato, *Critias* 106a; Euripides, *Andromache* 1118; Euripides, *Electra* 415; Euripides, *Heracles* 1307; Aeschylus, *Agamemnon* 281; Xenophon, *Cyropaedia* 1.6.1; 2.1.1; 3.3.57; 6.4.19; Xenophon, *Anabasis* 6.3.21; Plutarch, *Cimon* 5.3; Plutarch, *Themistocles* 30.2; Diodorus Siculus, *Library* 13.16.7.

136. Lockwood, 376. Chrysostom (cf. NPNF[1] 12:153 [*Homiliae in Epistulam i ad Corinthios* 26.5]) has a similar understanding, suggesting that Paul "hints at something more awful here [than in his similar statement in 10:15]. For he says that the affront here passes on to God: although he does not actually state it that way, but uses something of a milder and more enigmatical form of speech: 'is it proper for a woman to pray to God unveiled?'"

should have her head covered in a context such as that of offering worship to God in a public setting.

**11:14-15** Paul turns from an intuitive sense of decorum to an argument from nature or convention: *Does not the very nature of things teach you that if a man has long hair, it is a disgrace to him, but that if a woman has long hair, it is her glory? For long hair is given to her as a covering.*[137] Some think that by *the very nature of things*[138] Paul is referring to the way God created the universe. It would be consistent with the biblical and Jewish wisdom tradition to take a lesson from the way God created the world. The closest parallel to Paul's language is found in Plato's *Poetics* 1460a, which says, "Nature itself teaches[139] that [the heroic hexameter] is the right meter." Plato is referring back to his earlier statement that "experience has shown that the heroic hexameter is the right meter."[140] "Experience" in Plato's text (and thus "nature") has to do with trial and error and the observation of what works well and what does not. Chrysostom shares a similar understanding of Paul's statement. He says that Paul is here adopting his "constant practice of stating commonly received reasons . . . , betaking himself to the common custom, and greatly abashing those who waited to be taught these things from him, which even from men's ordinary practice they might have learned."[141] This "common custom" is understood by Chrysostom to constitute a law enacted by nature: "'And if it is given to her for a covering,' you say, 'why does she need to add another covering?' So that not only nature, but also her own will may share in her acknowledgement of her subjection. For Nature herself, in anticipation, enacted a law indicating that you should be covered. Do your own part, then, so that you will not seem to be subverting the very laws of nature."[142]

Some interpreters believe this passage suggests that the women did not need any other head covering because it is affirmed that God has given them long hair as a head covering. According to this view, the long hair itself, or a manner of pinning and fixing the long hair up (so that it served as a covering), could serve as the required covering so that no other covering would be necessary. This seems unlikely. The woman's hair is precisely what was perceived to be in need of covering in that culture and context, not its display. However, it is more likely that Paul is suggesting that the pattern established by nature or human custom provided a clue that women's heads should be covered. As Watson argues, "the point is that women's long hair

137. Paul builds his argument in vv. 14-22a mainly out of present indicative verbs (with a perfect indicative in v. 15 and an aorist subjunctive in v. 19) which make statements or form rhetorical questions about how things are or how different people (Paul, the Corinthians) are responding to their environment.

138. Gk. ἡ φύσις αὐτή; literally, "nature itself."

139. Gk. ἡ φύσις διδάσκει.

140. Found at the end of 1459b.

141. NPNF[1] 12:153-154 (*Homiliae in Epistulam i ad Corinthios* 26.5).

142. NPNF[1] 12:154 (*Homiliae in Epistulam i ad Corinthios* 26.5).

(as opposed to men's short hair) is *analogous* to the additional covering represented by the veil. In seeking to impose this extra covering on women but not on men, Paul is following the example of nature itself, which has similarly seen fit to provide women with an extra covering."[143]

These verses continue to reflect the concerns regarding shame and honor that have marked the whole passage. For a man to have long hair is a *disgrace,* but a woman's long hair is her *glory.* The covering of her head may be understood to cover her glory so that only God's glory is recognized in the worship setting,[144] or it could be understood to be a glorious sign of the authority that she has to worship side-by-side with the men of the community (cf. Psalm 8, where mankind is "crowned with glory and honor"). Paul would have the women think of their head coverings as a sign of their honor, and would have them know that to omit it would be to bring them disgrace (just as long hair would bring disgrace to a man). Since glory is something typically reflected in kings and other royalty or bestowed by royalty,[145] that God has bestowed *glory* on the woman, in the form of her hair, supports the idea that the authority mentioned in v. 10 is her own. Since she has been bestowed with glory, she should cover her head with a veil as a sign of the authority she has received.

**11:16** Paul concludes this part of his argument with a warning against dissension: *If anyone wants to be contentious about this, we have no other practice — nor do the churches of God.* Paul's *practice* (or "custom" — it is the same word used by Chrysostom in commenting on the meaning of "the nature of things" in v. 14) is not only his, but it is the only practice known among *the churches of God.* This is Paul's final argument at the end of an extended discussion of the subject. That extended discussion employed several different kinds of arguments to the effect that men and women should continue to attire themselves differently in keeping with the established practice of the churches and the warrants found in the narratives regarding the creation of the first man and woman.

Some have suggested that Paul means to say that he does not want to be contentious so that if the readers decide they disagree with him that will ultimately be acceptable to Paul. This is a serious misreading of Paul's argument and its conclusion. Paul's point is that our behaviors are not merely a matter of personal preference (as is often thought in the modern [or postmodern] Western world) but are lived out in a community context, and so the well-being of the community (and of the other) must play an integral

143. F. Watson, *Agape, Eros, Gender,* 87. This was also Chrysostom's view (cf. NPNF[1] 12:152-53 [*Homiliae in Epistulam i ad Corinthios* 26.4]).

144. Theodoret, 205, feels that the woman should realize "that she dishonors the one who gave the hair if she does not come with the due respect and honor."

145. Cf., e.g., 1 Kgs. 3:13; 1 Chr. 29:25; 2 Chr. 1:12; 17:5; Esth. 1:4; 5:11; 6:3; 10:2; Pss. 8:5; 24:7-10; 145:11-12; Prov. 14:28; 25:2; Isa. 6:1; Jer. 13:18; Dan. 2:37; 4:30; 7:14; 11:20; Bar. 5:6; Sir. 47:11; *Psalms of Solomon* 5:19; 17:6; Matt. 4:8; Luke 19:38; 1 Thess. 2:12; 1 Tim. 1:17; 2 Tim. 4:18; Rev. 21:24.

role in our decisions regarding the attitudes and postures we assume with respect to those around us.

Paul began this passage by commending the Corinthians for continuing to hold to the traditions he had passed on to them. As he comes to its conclusion, he reminds them that what he has been defending are the traditions practiced by all *the churches of God*. If his commendation of them is to stand, those who are uncomfortable about the universal practice of the church will need to learn how to deal with the conflict between their own perspectives and those who support the traditional practice of the churches without becoming contentious.

### *b. Wealthy Believers Should Honor the Lord and Their Poorer Brothers and Sisters in the Way They Practice the Lord's Supper, 11:17-34*

As Garland notes, these verses seem to reflect another A-B-A′ structure, with the discussion of the Corinthian abuses of the Lord's Supper framing the recitation of the Words of Institution and a brief interpretation of them.[146] While in the previous passage Paul praised the Corinthians for holding to the traditions he passed on to them, here he turns to address the question of the Corinthians' manner of celebrating the Lord's Supper, and especially the way in which the behavior of some Corinthians contradicts the meaning of that traditional celebration. A key issue in this passage, as in much of this letter, is that of the unity of the church. Perhaps even more fundamental is the importance of honoring Christ by honoring his body, the church (as a whole), rather than dishonoring him and bringing judgment on oneself and the body by humiliating members of the body. While in the previous passage the concern was with the possibility of dishonoring God by shaming oneself and bringing shame or dishonor on one's spouse (or people of the opposite gender), in this passage the concern is with the reality that people were dishonoring Christ by humiliating members of the body of Christ who were of a lower social and economic level. Class issues may have been involved in both cases since the forsaking of head coverings was probably a greater temptation for more well-to-do women who were tempted to follow the model of the "new Roman woman." Here the class issue comes out even more clearly.

For what Paul may have heard about the problems in Corinth related to this passage see the comments introducing 11:2–14:40. Paul's response is based on well-known Jesus traditions (the Last Supper) and the early Christian tradition of the Lord's Supper as well as Christian appropriation of the Old Testament traditions upon which those were based, namely biblical and Jewish traditions regarding Passover. Paul's teaching on the Lord's Supper in these verses must be understood in light of his prior statements in 10:16-17 (described by Günther Bornkamm as "the only authentic

146. Garland, 535.

commentary in the New Testament itself on the words of institution"[147]). Those words will be taken into consideration in the following comments.

The heart of Christian worship consisted of remembering the significance of, and giving thanks to God for, the bread and wine that would be consumed at the meal (and for other blessings that were recognized to have come from his hand). This did not require a special sanctuary or an elaborate liturgy and may have had more in common with formal dinner parties in which a god was blessed or invoked than with more elaborate religious liturgies of the time. The difficulties many believers would have had when they or their brothers or sisters attended dinner parties in pagan homes where another god would naturally have been invoked at the beginning or during a meal may be more easily understood in light of the parallel with the fairly informal nature of early Christian worship.

> [17]*In the following directives I have no praise for you, for your meetings do more harm than good.* [18]*In the first place, I hear that when you come together as a church, there are divisions among you, and to some extent I believe it.* [19]*No doubt there have to be differences among you to show which of you have God's approval.* [20]*So then, when you come together, it is not the Lord's Supper you eat,* [21]*for when you are eating, some of you go ahead with your own private suppers. As a result, one person remains hungry and another gets drunk.* [22]*Don't you have homes to eat and drink in? Or do you despise the church of God by humiliating those who have nothing? What shall I say to you? Shall I praise you? Certainly not in this matter!*
>
> [23]*For I received from the Lord what I also passed on to you: The Lord Jesus, on the night he was betrayed, took bread,* [24]*and when he had given thanks, he broke it and said, "This is my body, which is for you; do this in remembrance of me."* [25]*In the same way, after supper he took the cup, saying, "This cup is the new covenant in my blood; do this, whenever you drink it, in remembrance of me."* [26]*For whenever you eat this bread and drink this cup, you proclaim the Lord's death until he comes.*
>
> [27]*So then, whoever eats the bread or drinks the cup of the Lord in an unworthy manner will be guilty of sinning against the body and blood of the Lord.* [28]*Everyone ought to examine themselves before they eat of the bread and drink of the cup.* [29]*For those who eat and drink without discerning the body of Christ eat and drink judgment on themselves.* [30]*That is why many among you are weak and sick, and a number of you have fallen asleep.* [31]*But if we were more discerning with regard to ourselves, we would not come under such judgment.* [32]*Nevertheless, when we are judged in this way by the Lord, we are being disciplined so that we will not be finally condemned with the world.*
>
> [33]*So then, my brothers and sisters, when you gather to eat, you should all*

147. Günther Bornkamm, *Early Christian Experience* (London: SCM, 1969), 139 (cited in Horrell, *Solidarity and Difference*, 107).

*eat together.* [34]*Those who are hungry should eat something at home, so that when you meet together it may not result in judgment.*

*And when I come I will give further directions.*

*i. Rebuke for abuses at the Lord's Supper, 11:17-22*

This passage consists of an opening rebuke (v. 17), a statement of the report of Corinthian misconduct (v. 18), Paul's assessment of that report (vv. 19-21), and a further rebuke (v. 22).

**11:17** While in the previous passage (esp. v. 2) Paul praised the Corinthians for continuing to hold to the traditions he passed on to them, *In the following directives* he says that he has *no praise* for them. Both passages have to do with things that are remembered properly or improperly. He praised them for remembering him and the traditions he gave them. He has no praise for the way they are practicing the Lord's Supper because it reflects a failure to properly consider the implications of remembering Christ as he is proclaimed in that Supper. Paul's oblique manner of explaining why he is unhappy with them is that their *meetings*[148] *do more harm than good.*[149] The harm rather than good that Paul has in mind is clarified in the following verses. The following verse highlights the divisions that have been created in the church, but Paul goes on to accuse the Corinthians of "sinning against the body and blood of the Lord" (v. 27) and eating and drinking judgment on themselves (v. 29), which is why some members of the community were sick and some have died (v. 30). The good the meetings should have done would be, according to the broader context, that of building up the church through love (8:1; chs. 12–14), bringing glory to God (10:31), and receiving his approval (11:19).

**11:18-19** Paul's first concern is that he has heard a report of *divisions* among the Corinthians when they *come together as a church.* To *come together as a church* was supposed to represent the coming together of one body (10:17) of people who together participate in the body and blood of Christ (10:16). BDAG indicates that the term "church" or "assembly" was used by early Christians "for chiefly two reasons: to affirm continuity with Israel through use of a term found in Gk. translations of the Hebrew Scriptures, and to allay any suspicion, esp[ecially] in political circles, that Christians were a disorderly group." The sad irony was that the Corinthians were not actually "coming together" when they came together, but gave clear indications of being a divided and disorderly group, which reflected poorly on Christ and on themselves.

Paul's comment, *to some extent I believe it,* seems a bit strange, since all

148. Gk. συνέρχομαι: "to come together w[ith] others as a group, *assemble, gather*" (BDAG).

149. BDAG has, "you hold your meetings in such a way that they turn out not to your advantage, but to your disadvantage."

the evidence from the rest of this passage and this book clearly indicates that he thought it clear that the Corinthian church was a divided church. It is probably intended to introduce his own ironic comment in the following verse[150] with the sense, "I suppose, *to some extent,* it stands to reason that there would be divisions among you since *No doubt there have to be differences among you to show which of you have God's approval*!"[151] Paul is most likely referring ironically to a view that was reported to him as being held by some Corinthians. They thought the differences among them were a reflection of those who had God's special approval. The following verses make it clear, however, that the divisions were provoked by the insensitive behavior of some of the social elites within the Corinthian church and that that behavior most certainly did not meet with *God's approval.* If anyone could be said to *have God's approval* in the Corinthian church, it would not be any of those wealthier and more socially advanced Christians who were snubbing their brothers and sisters! The behavior that, according to worldly wisdom, would have distinguished some of the members as socially superior members of the church who were "considered worthy of high regard, respected, esteemed"[152] was actually shown to be unworthy of high regard, respect, or esteem since that very behavior was a disgrace to the community and an insult to God. That which distinguished the social elites in the Corinthian church was not worthy of praise (cf. v. 22) but had already brought God's judgment on them (vv. 29-32) and now Paul's sarcastic blame. They needed to recognize that behaviors that they thought merely marked them as social elites in fact ironically marked them as standing under divine judgment.

As will be pointed out in the comments on vv. 23-26, the Lord's Supper entailed a reappropriation and reapplication of the Passover tradition in which Christ's death on the cross was understood to provide the basis for the new and final redemption of God's people, the second exodus. Peter Craigie points out that "the Passover became the act, symbolically speaking, of the one large family of God."[153] In 2 Chronicles 30 the celebration of the Passover is depicted as a unifying and sanctifying event that "fit well into Hezekiah's designs to reunify the nation."[154] The Lord's Supper, like

150. This is supported by the fact that the following verse is introduced with a γάρ ("for"), suggesting that v. 19 plays an explanatory role.

151. The reference to "God's approval" is reflected in the translation of the NIV, TNIV, and NLT (the NET refers to "those who are approved"). ESV and NRSV have, "those who are genuine among you." The text literally means those who are δόκιμος, which BDAG defines in this case as "pert[aining] to being genuine on the basis of testing, approved (by test), *tried and true, genuine.*"

152. This is another meaning given by BDAG for δόκιμος in other contexts which, if applied here, may help communicate the irony suggested by Paul's words.

153. Peter C. Craigie, *The Book of Deuteronomy* (NICOT; Grand Rapids: Eerdmans, 1976), 242; see also Robin L. Routledge, "Passover and the Last Supper," *TynBul* 53 (2002), 203-21, 207, 212, 216.

154. Victor Harold Matthews, Mark W. Chavalas, and John H. Walton, *The IVP Bible Background Commentary: Old Testament* (Downers Grove, IL: InterVarsity Press, 2000), 453.

the Passover meal on which it was based, should have served as an experience that strengthened the unity of God's people, not one that would divide them.

**11:20-21** *So then, when you come together, it is not the Lord's Supper you eat,* [21]*for when you are eating, some of you go ahead with your own private suppers. As a result, one person remains hungry and another gets drunk.* Certainly the Corinthians imagined that they were eating the Lord's Supper when they gathered together. Paul, however, wants them (and us) to understand that the identity of the meal cannot be distinguished from the manner in which it is carried out. The distinctions Paul had mentioned in the previous verses are made clearer here. Certain members were not waiting for each other (cf. v. 33), but rather some, presumably the wealthier members, were going ahead before the others arrived and satiating themselves with food and drink while others ended up getting little or nothing. This was a common complaint in other dinner parties in the Roman world. In many cases the seating of the guests and the distribution of the food were orchestrated in such a way as to reflect the social pecking order as perceived or imposed by the host.[155] Ancient writers complained of being insulted by the lower quality or lesser quantity of food served to them in comparison with more highly esteemed dinner guests. It seems that the social elite of the church, who would not have been constricted by work obligations, gathered and began their meal before the arrival of the poorer members of the church, who would not have had such flexibility of work and schedules. Also, even a large Roman home in Corinth would have room for only a limited number of people in the dining room (the Roman *triclinium*),[156] usually about nine people who would be served by the household servants, so that even if all the members of the church arrived at approximately the same time only those who were invited into the *triclinium* would have been likely to be served a full meal. Even there distinctions might have been made by the proximity of each guest to the host and the quality and quantity of food served to each. Other members may have gathered in an outside atrium where sparser offerings, if any, would have been found. As already mentioned, the household slaves would have normally been expected to serve the dinner guests. One can only imagine what kind of dynamic might have been created when, as in Corinth, slaves were also part of the church and technically, at least, participants in the Lord's Supper as well.

What the Corinthians were participating in could not be considered *the Lord's Supper* since that supper was marked by the unity of those who had become one body in Christ and by a recognition that the Lord who presided over that supper was the one who had given up his own prerogatives

155. This is the second question addressed in Plutarch's Table-Talk (*Quaestionum Convivialum* 615c–19a).

156. The *triclinium* was a room in which three of the four walls were taken up with couches which would accommodate three people each who would eat while reclining on them.

and sacrificed his own life for those who were unworthy. Indeed, the Lord to whom they belonged is the one who took the nature of a servant (Phil. 2:7) and died a shameful death (2:2; see 11:23-24 below). Consequently the *Lord's Supper* must be marked by clear manifestations of unity and concern for others, and since their supper reflected none of those values it could not rightfully be so described.

That some members of the church were satiating themselves and getting drunk at these meals may have suggested that they were carrying on as would be expected at a meal eaten in the name of Dionysus, the god identified with merry (and usually excessive) feasting in the Roman world.[157] In fact, it was suggested that any activities that distracted from informal friendly conversations and merry entertainment were an abuse of Dionysus (also known as Bacchus).[158] If Dionysus/Bacchus was abused when merry entertainment and libertine partying were inhibited, Christ is abused when his self-sacrifice and other-orientation[159] is not reflected in the fellowship that sees in the wine not merry entertainment but sacrifice for others. Christians who understand the true nature of the Lord's Supper should be expected to manifest a commitment to laying their lives down especially for the sake of the poorer and more fragile (the "weaker") members of their church.

**11:22** Paul's indignation is poured out in a blistering interrogation followed up by a solemn indictment: *Don't you have homes to eat and drink in? Or do you despise the church of God by humiliating those who have nothing? What shall I say to you? Shall I praise you? Certainly not in this matter!* The suggestion that they *have homes to eat and drink in* raises the question of Paul's understanding of the context of the church meeting. Although it is possible that the church met in a shop or some other context, it is most likely that it met in the home of a wealthier member of the church who served as a patron/benefactor of the community. If so, one could imagine the adults of that home replying that they were indeed eating and drinking in their home. Paul's language, however, suggests that the physical structure of someone's home needed to be reconceptualized as church-meeting space, "sacred space," when it was serving as the meeting place of the local Christian community.[160] Christians who participate in the Lord's Supper might *eat and drink,* but they are not merely eating and drinking as they do so and they must not act as they might in other mundane contexts of eating and drinking. They are, as they are about to be reminded again, gathered in remembrance of their Lord and to proclaim his death until he returns. If they want to have a drink or a meal on their own terms, they must wait until they are in the privacy of their own homes or in the home of a friend. They

157. Cf. Plato, *Leges* 2:666; *Cratylus* 406c; Plutarch, *Quaestionum Convivialum* 613c–15c.

158. Cf. Plutarch, *Quaestionum Convivialum* 614e–15b.

159. Horrell unpacks the motif of "love" in Paul's ethics under the interpretative labels of "corporate solidarity" and "other-regard" in chs. 6–7 of *Solidarity and Difference.*

160. For much more on this see Økland, *Women in Their Place,* 131-67.

are not free to do so when gathered as *the church of God*, even if that happens to take place in what serves at other times as their own home. Of course they are to represent and incarnate the presence and attitude of Christ at home as well as in other contexts, so that the behavior Paul is criticizing would not be acceptable even at other times, but it is all the more reprehensible when done in the context of the gathered church.

By humiliating those who have nothing they were despising *the church of God*, the society belonging to God and not to their city.[161] The humiliation was carried out by distinguishing between the "haves" and the "have nots" in the provision of food before, during, or after the Lord's Supper. That they were gathered as *the church of God* should have been enough to remind them that they constituted a covenant community in which each member found a place through God's gracious redemption and not through their own social status, achievements, or qualities. Paul's reminder that it was in fact *God's* church that was being despised hinted at the great danger that was involved. That this danger had already come to realize some of its grave potential and might continue to do so is stressed in vv. 27-34. One may not despise God's church without inviting the wrath and judgment of God! God's concern for the poor, caring for the poor as a mark of piety, and the oppression of the poor as a mark of the wicked are key themes of the Old Testament.[162] God's special concern for his covenant people would make such humiliation of the poor among his people by other members of the same community even more egregious.

Paul is dumbfounded by the insensitivity of this behavior and wonders out loud how the Corinthians expected him to respond upon finding out how their celebrations of the Lord's Supper were being conducted. He reiterates the point made upon introducing this subject: he certainly has no praise for them in this area![163] The tie between this verse and v. 17 may also clarify the thought in that previous verse where he told them that their meetings "did more harm than good." In this verse it is the humiliation of the poorer members of the church that is highlighted. Rather than serving to build up the church in love (8:1), which would be for the better, their meetings served to tear down and humiliate some members in the presence of others.

This verse also reveals another tie between this passage and the previous one. Not only do both have to do with traditions being faithfully or scandalously implemented and followed, but they both have to do with

161. Cf. on "church of God" at 1:2.

162. See Ciampa, *The Presence and Function of Scripture in Galatians 1 and 2*, 153 n. 94.

163. The Greek verb ἐπαινέω ("I praise" or "I commend") is used four times in this letter — all in this chapter. Paul praises the Corinthians in v. 2 for being faithful in remembering some other traditions he passed on to the Corinthians. Then he introduced this passage by saying that he had no praise for them with respect to the way they implemented the tradition of the Lord's Supper (v. 17). He uses the verb twice in this verse for rhetorical emphasis, literally saying, "Shall I praise you? I do not praise you in this area."

practices that would either potentially dishonor or humiliate members of the congregation or are actually doing so. The same word[164] translated *humiliate* in this verse is translated "dishonor" in vv. 4 and 5. In this passage Paul has no praise for the Corinthians, for they are not honoring the tradition of the Lord's Supper by dishonoring poorer members of their congregation. In the previous passage Paul praised the Corinthians for keeping traditions he passed on to them and warned them about a misapplication (or rejection) of those traditions that would result in dishonoring themselves and their "heads" (especially the women's husbands). In both cases it is clear that the shaming, humiliation, or dishonoring of other members of the community entailed a failure to honor the God who established and ruled over that community and whose honor was tied to that shown to and among the members of his covenant community.

### *ii. Recitation and interpretation of the words of institution of the Last Supper, 11:23-26*

**11:23-24** The way Paul introduces this restatement of the words of the institution of the Lord's Supper *(For)* indicates that it will clarify why praise for the Corinthians' practice of it was unthinkable: *For I received from the Lord what I also passed on to you: The Lord Jesus, on the night he was betrayed, took bread, and when he had given thanks, he broke it and said, "This is my body, which is for you; do this in remembrance of me."*[165] Here again Paul makes it clear that his teaching is not idiosyncratic but reflects the standard and traditional teaching that had been passed down from the very beginning, from the Lord himself. The language of "receiving" and "passing on" was the standard language for the transmission of authoritative traditions. Paul's statement that he received it *from the Lord* did not suggest that Christ had revealed it to him in a vision, but that those who had passed this on to Paul had received it either directly from the Lord himself or from others who had. It was Paul himself who had brought the Corinthians into this stream of tradition that had come from the Lord, and now it was his responsibility to straighten out the abuses that had been introduced. The reminder that he was the one who had passed this on to the Corinthians also served rhetorically to reinforce his moral and spiritual authority in the community since it has to do with one of the most fundamental touch-

164. Gk. καταισχύνω.

165. In vv. 23-26 the aorist tense provides the backbone for the narrative (a common role for the perfective aspect of the aorist in narrative texts): "he took bread, . . . broke it, . . . and said." The imperfect "night he was betrayed" (v. 23) provides some off-line, supplementary (contextual) material informing the following mainline events of the mini-narrative, and the aorist participle, "when he had given thanks" (εὐχαριστήσας), provides other off-line background material introducing the breaking of the bread (see Campbell, *Basics of Verbal Aspect*, 62). The direct discourse in vv. 24-25 is marked by present indicatives, subjunctives, and imperatives.

points for their community experience and self-understanding. It reinforces the Corinthians' awareness that Paul plays the role of the spiritual father of this community, the one who established the original connection between the Corinthians and the Lord who redeemed them. The language of the passing on of traditions also ties this passage to the beginning of the chapter, where Paul referred to the keeping of the traditions he had passed on to them.

Major studies have been written to determine the relationship between the wording preserved in this passage and that found in the gospel traditions, and those studies should be consulted by those interested in such problems.[166]

The Lord Jesus is described as the patron overseeing the meal who gives the blessing and distributes the food. He is Lord of all creation and Lord, in particular, of all those who eat at his table. The reference to the betrayal of the Lord *(on the night he was betrayed)* reminds us that from its very institution the meal has always been in danger of being eaten by those who fail to live out its meaning. It also serves as an indirect way of referring to his death since in the passion narratives the multiple references to Christ's betrayal serve as pointers anticipating his crucifixion.[167] Since the verb translated *betrayed*[168] can also be rendered "handed over" or "given over," Paul may be echoing the LXX rendering of Isaiah 53:6 ("the Lord gave him up for our sins") and 53:12 ("his life was given up to death, and . . . he was given up on account of their sins"), where the same word was used.[169] It is clear from evidence elsewhere in Paul's letters that he understands Jesus' death as the fulfillment of God's plan as foreshadowed in Isaiah 53.

The description of Jesus' actions reflects those of the head of a household at the beginning of a meal. Paul says that Jesus gave thanks before breaking the bread *(when he had given thanks)*.[170] This refers to the traditional act of blessing God that was discussed in the comments on 10:16. Jesus would have blessed God, that is, given thanks to him, for his wonderful provision. In a normal meal the thanksgiving would have been for the provision of the food that was about to be gratefully received. In the context of the Passover the thanksgiving or blessing would have also recognized God's goodness in the redemption of his people which was being com-

166. See I. Howard Marshall, *Last Supper and Lord's Supper* (Grand Rapids: Eerdmans, 1981), and Joachim Jeremias, *The Eucharistic Words of Jesus* (London: SCM, 1987). For a brief treatment see I. Howard Marshall, "Lord's Supper," *DPL* 569-75.

167. Many other occurrences of the same verb (παραδίδωμι) are found where it is tied to betrayal unto death (Matt 10:21; 17:22-23; 20:18-19; 24:9; 26:2; 27:26; Mark 9:31; 10:33; 13:12; 15:15; Luke 18:32-33; 21:16; 24:7, 20; John 19:16).

168. Gk. παραδίδωμι.

169. Hays, 198.

170. Normal patterns of usage suggest that the contextual background information provided by the pre-posed (appearing before the main verb) aorist adverbial participle (εὐχαριστήσας) is likely to be temporal location in this case ("upon/immediately after giving thanks") as other common usages do not fit well here.

memorated. Paul is describing Jesus' actions in breaking the unleavened bread served at the Passover meal he shared with his disciples just before his death,[171] and it is notable that in the shadow of that death Christ still recognized God's faithful and generous provision for him and his disciples as he shared his last meal with them.

Paul has already alluded to the unleavened bread and referred to Christ as "our Passover lamb" who has been sacrificed (see on 5:7), suggesting that he understood Jesus' words at the Last Supper to mean that he was fulfilling the role of the sacrificial lamb in the establishment of the new covenant. Deuteronomy 16:3 calls the unleavened bread "the bread of affliction," referring to the sufferings of Israel. Jesus, in saying that the bread represents his body *which is for you,* makes it refer to the redemption he is about to accomplish by his own suffering. In these verses the theme of unity is seen in the (one) bread which is broken and distributed (cf. 10:16-17). In the following verse it will be seen in the concept of the unifying covenant.

The words *this is my body* have been an epicenter of controversy for centuries. BDAG indicates that when used in explanations the verb involved[172] is used "to show how someth[ing] is to be understood, *is a representation of, is the equivalent of,*" and in the formula used here ("this is . . .") means either "this or that means" or "that is to say."[173] The bread should be understood to represent Christ's body just as the different elements of the Passover Seder represented and reminded them of different aspects of Israel's experience of redemption at the time of the exodus. In the Seder they ate unleavened bread to remind them of their forefathers who baked cakes from unleavened dough "that they had brought out of Egypt, for it was not leavened, because they were thrust out of Egypt and could not wait" (Exod. 12:39), and they ate bitter herbs (Exod. 12:8; Num. 9:11) "because the Egyptians embittered the lives of our fathers in Egypt" (*m. Pesaḥim* 10:5). The bread of the Lord's Supper represented and was to remind the disciples of the Lord's body which was given or broken for them.[174]

When Christ told his disciples that the broken bread representing his body was *for you,* he clearly meant for all those who were members of his community. As the Corinthians (and we as well) reflect on these words in

171. Exod. 12:8; cf. Routledge, "Passover and the Last Supper," 215-17.

172. Gk. εἰμί.

173. Cf. Matt. 27:46; Mark 7:2; Acts 1:19; 19:4; Rom. 7:18; 9:8; 10:6-8; Phlm. 12; Heb. 2:14; 7:5; 9:11; 10:20; 11:16; 13:15; 1 Pet. 3:20.

174. The best texts simply say, "which is for you" ($\mathfrak{P}^{46}$, ℵ*, A, B, C*, 6, 33, 1739*, *pc,* vg$^{st}$, Cyprian), although some texts have the word "broken" (κλώμενον) and scribes later added that word to most of the earlier MSS (the word is found in ℵ$^2$, C$^3$, D$^2$, F, G, Ψ, 1739$^{mg}$, 1881, 𝔐, sy). As is often the case, the scribes may well have unpacked the meaning of the clause accurately even if the word itself is not part of the original text. Other later attempts to supply a predicate are reflected in D*, which has the synonym "broken into pieces" (θρυπτόμενον), and in the Coptic tradition, which has "given" (which brings it into agreement with Luke 22:19).

light of Paul's criticism of their practice of the Supper, it should lead to an awareness that Christ did not discriminate but rather included all the members of the community at his table.

Christ told the church to *do*[175] *this in remembrance of me.*[176] What they were to do *(this)*, presumably, was to reenact the dinner as Christ shared it with them, with the breaking and distribution of the bread and wine, the word of blessing or thanksgiving to God, and the explanation of the significance of the bread and wine. That Paul can recount the event so precisely for the Corinthians reflects the fact that the early church did indeed continue to recall that evening and relive it together on a regular basis ever since.

Of course to participate in the meal *in remembrance* of Christ does not simply mean that those eating should recall, give thanks for, and celebrate who Christ is and what Christ did for them, but also that they should partake in a way that befitted the occasion that it was intended to evoke. Jesus' statement that we are to partake of the Lord's Supper in his *remembrance* reflects the nature of the Passover as a "memorial" (Exod. 12:14) during which the Israelites were to remember the day of their exodus redemption (Deut. 16:3). Each Jewish father (including those who lived generations and centuries after the fact) was to explain to his son that he celebrated the Passover Seder the way he did "because of that which the Lord did for me when I came forth out of Egypt" (*m. Pesaḥim* 10:5). This background suggests that the act of remembrance entailed profound meditation upon and proclamation of that which was remembered, a suggestion which finds confirmation in v. 26, where Paul affirms that participation in the Lord's Supper entails the proclamation of his death. It is also crucial for our understanding of the Lord's Supper that the *remembrance* is not an act of remembering a long-lost friend, present only in the memories of the community. It is understood by all that the Lord who is being remembered and whose death is being proclaimed did not remain dead but is living and present with the community as they celebrate what he accomplished when he first came, not "to be served, but to serve, and to give his life as a ransom for many" (Mark 10:45; Matt. 20:28) and as they look forward to his return to consummate his redemptive work (cf. v. 26 — "until he comes"). See the further comments on vv. 26-29.

At the celebration of the Lord's Supper each one should have the opportunity to rejoice in "that which the Lord did for me" when he provided for the forgiveness of our sins and our inclusion in God's covenant people through the sacrifice of his body on the cross. Any behavior that would marginalize members of the community or treat them as lesser members of the body must be strictly avoided.

175. Here and in the following verse, the present imperative "do" (ποιεῖτε) indicates that Jesus did not mean that the disciples should follow his lead simply for that evening, but that he was providing general instruction to be followed on other occasions as well.

176. The words here (Gk. τοῦτο ποιεῖτε εἰς τὴν ἐμὴν ἀνάμνησιν) are identical to those found in Luke 22:19.

In 10:16-17 Paul affirmed that "the bread that we break" is "a participation [or fellowship/sharing] in the body of Christ" and that "because there is one loaf, we, who are many, are one body, for we all partake of the one loaf." These words from the previous chapter are expected to inform our understanding of the present text. It would have been one loaf of bread that was broken and shared among the believers, and as we partake of the bread of the Lord's Supper in Christ's remembrance we participate in or share in his body as a group of people who have been formed into one community by the Lord of the Supper. It is not merely a question of a group of individuals sharing in the redemption found through the breaking of Christ's body, but of a group whose identity is formed in light of that in which they all share together — namely, the redemption won through Christ's death on our behalf. Some of the Corinthians had found a way of participating in the Lord's Supper that completely undermined that part of its message.

**11:25** *In the same way, after supper he took the cup, saying, "This cup is the new covenant in my blood; do this, whenever you drink it, in remembrance of me."* The cup was handled *In the same way* inasmuch as it too was provided with an interpretation which tied it to Christ's redemptive death and was to be taken in Christ's remembrance.

The words *after supper* are not given any special emphasis here. It is probably a noncontroversial part of the tradition. As in the case of the last supper the Corinthians were evidently celebrating their version of the Lord's Supper in the context of a full meal (full, at least, for some of the members but not for all of them). The meal was evidently sandwiched between the opening blessing associated with the bread and the final words regarding the cup. In this way the entire meal was provided with religious significance. This verse as well as vv. 27-32 makes it clear that the meal itself was to be understood in terms of the reaffirmation and ratification of the new covenant between God and his people.

As explained above (with regard to the bread which represents Christ's body), the words *This cup is the new covenant in my blood* should be understood to provide the theological significance of the cup. It represents and serves to reaffirm the new covenant established by Christ's sacrificial death on the cross for us. The *cup* was often used figuratively "of undergoing a violent death" (BDAG). Jesus' statement that the cup "is the new covenant in my blood" fuses together the language of Jeremiah 31:31 ("a new covenant") and Exodus 24:8 ("This is the blood of the covenant that the LORD has made with you"). The latter text refers to the establishment of the covenant at Sinai, while the former consists of God's promise to establish a new covenant in the time of postexilic restoration. By fusing the two texts together Jesus interprets his impending death as the sacrifice that establishes the new covenant associated with the second exodus.

The theme of unity is found in the reference to the new *covenant*, since a covenant is something that binds people together within a relationship or community. The Corinthian believers were bound together as God's new covenant people through their participation in the benefits of Christ's death on their behalf. The theme of sacrifice for others is clearly present in the identification of the wine not with merriment (as in the typical Roman dinner party) but with Christ's sacrificial blood and the understanding that the meal is to serve as a proclamation of "the Lord's death."

On the expression *do this . . . in remembrance of me,* see the comments on the similar statement with respect to the bread. The words here are identical to those found in the previous verse (with the words *whenever you drink it* embedded within those words in this case), which are identical to those found in Luke 22:19. The parallel is part of the reason that Paul says that Jesus addressed the issue of the cup *In the same way.* The theme of remembrance suggests that those who participate in this meal are to do so in full recognition of its relationship to the redemption that was won for them only through Christ's sacrifice, a redemption which has washed away those worldly distinctions and created a community of people who are all — rich and poor, slave and free — saved by grace and not by works or social standing. For the Corinthians to truly celebrate the *Lord's* Supper, they would need to take more seriously its nature as a celebration of new covenant redemption brought about through Christ's *self-sacrificing* death for them on the cross. To recognize it as such would necessarily require a change in the ways the Corinthian Christians were treating each other.

In our comments on 10:16 we pointed out that Paul's statement that "the cup of thanksgiving for which we give thanks" is "a participation [or fellowship/sharing] in the blood of Christ" stressed that participation in this supper does not merely bring one into fellowship with the other men and women gathered around the table, but with Christ himself and that through our fellowship with Christ we participate in the benefits of his sacrifice, which serves to establish or renew our covenantal relationship with God. That is the new covenant of which Paul speaks in this verse.

**11:26** Paul now begins to comment on the significance of the words of institution for the Corinthians, albeit in an indirect way. *For whenever you eat this bread and drink this cup, you proclaim the Lord's death until he comes.* Here it becomes clear that Paul's recitation of the words of institution was particularly interested in the references to Christ's body and blood and the Supper as an act of remembrance. To partake of the bread/body and cup/blood in remembrance of Christ is to proclaim his death. Paul's recitation was clearly intended to "remind the community of the narrative which gives the meal its meaning, with its focus on the death of Christ, and so, at least implicitly, raises the question as to whether their conduct towards one another reflects the pattern of Christ's self-giving death for others."[177] Clearly their behavior was not consistent with the proclamation which served as the heart and meaning of the meal.

177. Horrell, *Solidarity and Difference,* 109.

Not merely Christ's death is in view, of course, since Paul says that we proclaim his death *until he comes.* The one whose death is proclaimed clearly did not remain dead but lives now and will return one day! This verse places the church, as it partakes of the Lord's Supper, in the precise eschatological situation of living between the first coming of Christ, when he died (and rose) to accomplish our redemption, and the second coming of Christ when he will return to consummate our redemption. The reference to Christ's return raises the question of the kind of community he will ultimately establish and reminds the reader that as the church awaits the consummation it must endeavor to be a community whose *koinonia* or fellowship is marked by Christ's self-sacrificing commitment to the well-being of others.

The reference to the coming of Christ also reminds the reader of that final public vindication of Christ and his people when he comes to judge his enemies and consummate the redemption of his people and world. In the following verses Paul will stress that Christ's role as judge is not an exclusively future role or limited to the judgment of the (external) enemies of his people, but is being carried out in the present even against his own community due to their sin against him and those with whom he has identified himself even through death.

### *iii. Warnings and instructions to correct the abuses at the Lord's Supper, 11:27-34*[178]

This passage consists of a warning regarding the consequences of the improper practice of the Lord's Supper (vv. 27-30), a statement of the lessons to be learned from the Corinthians' recent experience (vv. 31-34a), and a promise of further instruction (v. 34b).

**11:27** Since the practice of the Lord's Supper entails the proclamation of the Lord's death, there are clear consequences for practicing it in a way that undermines the significance of that "self-giving death for others." *So then, whoever eats the bread or drinks the cup of the Lord in an unworthy manner will be guilty of sinning against the body and blood of the Lord.* Paul's introductory *So then* indicates an inference to be drawn from his prior explanation of what the Lord's Supper is all about. The reference to participating in the Lord's supper *in an unworthy manner* must be understood in light of the context, where the Corinthians were practicing the supper in a way that humiliated other members of Christ's body. To eat and drink in *an unworthy manner* is to eat and drink in a way that demeans, humiliates, or disrespects other members of Christ's community. What does Paul have in mind by *sinning against the body and blood of the Lord?* He could mean sinning against those who by their participation in Christ have come to constitute the body and blood of the Lord or he could mean that they sin against the (new) cov-

178. Similarly, Garland, 535.

enant which the Supper itself represents (v. 25) and reaffirms and thereby sin against the one who established that covenant and Supper and who presides as Lord of that table. Given the identification that is established between Christ and his people through their participation in his death and the other-centered focus of the new covenant Christ has established, it is probably best to understand that both ideas are in mind. To worship Christ in a way that shows disrespect toward those who are have been "united with the Lord," have become "one with him in spirit" (6:17), and who share or participate in his body and blood (10:16) is to sin not just against them but also against the covenant reaffirmed in the meal, against the Lord of the meal and of those brothers and sisters in Christ.

**11:28-29** Verses 28-34 are tied together by their constant reference to the motif of the judgment which comes on the church for the members' failure to treat each other as is appropriate for those who constitute the body of the Lord Jesus Christ. To sin against the body and blood of the Lord (v. 27) is to sin against the new covenant established by Christ's body and blood, calls down judgment on oneself and on the community, and thus is to be avoided at all costs (vv. 28-34). Since Paul clearly believes that the Corinthians have in fact been sinning against Christ's body and blood and have brought judgment on themselves, he explains what needs to be done to correct the situation and to avoid inciting further judgment.

Paul warns that *Everyone ought to examine themselves before they eat of the bread and drink of the cup. For those who eat and drink without discerning the body of Christ*[179] *eat and drink judgment on themselves.* To *examine oneself* and to *discern the body of Christ* do not merely mean, in this context, to solemnly recognize that the bread and cup represent Christ's body and blood rather than being mundane food and drink. To *examine oneself* means to examine one's compliance with the covenant as reflected in their ways of relating to other members of the community and to *discern the body of Christ* must include recognizing that those other members of the community represent Christ himself (since they have also been united with him) and must be treated as people for whom Christ chose to give up his life and to shed his blood.

Gordon Hugenburger points out that "Paul's threat that whoever eats and drinks unworthily will 'eat and drink judgment upon himself'" reflects the nature of the Lord's Supper "as a covenant-ratifying oath-sign" implying "a self-maledictory symbolism" such that "our infidelity deserves the same dreadful curse which overtook Christ, whose death is symbolized in the elements."[180] This is consistent with Paul's depiction of the

179. The words *of Christ* are not in the original text but have been added for the sake of clarity. The oldest and best texts say simply "without discerning the body" ($\mathfrak{P}^{46}$, ℵ*, A, B, C*, 6, 33, 1739, 1881*, *pc*, vg, co, Pel). The words "of the Lord" (τοῦ κυρίου) were later added to ℵ, C, and 1881 and are found in the majority of MSS. The words were evidently added to clarify the meaning.

180. Gordon P. Hugenberger, *Marriage as a Covenant: Biblical Law and Ethics as Developed from Malachi* (Biblical Studies Library; Grand Rapids: Baker, 1998), 209 n. 171.

judgment that fell on Israel as a result of their infidelity to God's covenant in 10:8-10. Paul's allusion to the divine judgment that has fallen on the Corinthian community makes it clear just how seriously the Supper and its practice is to be taken.

**11:30** Paul now explains what has come about due to their eating and drinking without discerning Christ, respecting his covenant and the fact that those other members are also part of Christ's body: *That is why many among you are weak and sick, and a number of you have fallen asleep.* This verse may be (and has been) easily twisted to suggest that were it not for sin in the community no one would get sick or die. It is not that all the sicknesses and deaths in the community are to be attributed to their sinning against Christ's body and blood, but that that is responsible for *many* of the health problems that have wracked that community. To *fall asleep* was a well-known figure for death in the Greco-Roman world.[181] It should not be assumed that the sick or dying were particularly guilty of the sin, but, like most plagues of divine judgment in the Old Testament, the plague could fall indiscriminately on the community as a whole (e.g., Exod. 32:35; Num. 8:19; 11:33; Deut. 32:24; Josh. 22:17).[182] Paul's teaching here is consistent with teaching about divine discipline elsewhere in that, as the following verses make clear, he clearly hopes that the church will learn from its experience and respond in a way that will not only be less prejudicial to the physical health of church members but also more likely to result in the kinds of edifying behaviors that will lead to the development of a community that truly glorifies God in all it does.

**11:31** Paul explains how to avoid the judgment which the church has been experiencing due to its insensitivity to its covenant commitments, including the needs and dignity of its own members: *But if we were more discerning with regard to ourselves, we would not come under such judgment.*[183] The word translated *discerning* is based on the root word *judgment* at the end of the verse and has to do with judging or evaluating,[184] although it is not as strong as the latter word. The point is that something as simple as more self-evaluation, more self-examination, could help us avoid divine judgment by leading us to catch and correct ourselves before God decided to

181. See BDAG, κοιμάω 2, for a list of ancient sources going back to the *Iliad.*

182. In some cases a plague would be visited on the guilty people in particular (e.g., Num. 14:37).

183. Paul uses what is known as a "second class conditional" structure, a contrary-to-fact conditional structure marked by the presence of εἰ with an imperfect or aorist indicative in the protasis and ἄν with an imperfect or aorist in the apodosis (see Wallace, *Greek Grammar beyond the Basics,* 694-96; Porter, *Idioms of the Greek New Testament,* 259-61). Here Paul has imperfects in both the protasis and the apodosis (εἰ δὲ ἑαυτοὺς διεκρίνομεν, οὐκ ἂν ἐκρινόμεθα). Unfortunately, the Corinthians (the "we" Paul has in mind) were clearly not discerning with regard to themselves and had therefore come under the judgment to which Paul refers.

184. For the first word (Gk. διακρίνω) BDAG gives the meaning "to evaluate by paying careful attention to," with *"evaluate, judge"* as possible translations. The Greek word translated "judgment" at the end of the verse is κρίνω.

take matters into his own hands and bring about a very undesirable external motivation that might lead us to finally correct what we had consistently ignored. To worship God is also to expose oneself to the extreme danger that comes from treating what is holy as though it were profane. In our case our brothers and sisters in Christ have been sanctified (cf. on 1:2), that is, made holy in God's sight, and for us to treat them as mere objects or in ways that are not worthy of the God who has sanctified them is to invite divine wrath for our disrespect of the God we claim to worship.

In much of the Western world today (perhaps especially in some evangelical contexts) the idea that God would judge his people in the way Paul suggests here is completely foreign, and people may be tempted to think that Paul's language reflects an antiquated and unenlightened view of God. Such an attitude reflects the extent to which the modern world has lost the biblical understanding of God's transcendence and fearsome holiness. In *The Chronicles of Narnia* C. S. Lewis emphasized the idea that Aslan was not "a tame lion," but in much evangelical culture at the beginning of the twenty-first century the Christian God is a tame God, into whose presence people feel free to enter in a trifling or frivolous manner. Paul would have us know that the way we behave in worship and the way we treat other members of God's holy people are not to be taken lightly, but require the most serious circumspection.

**11:32** Even God's judgment has the good of his people in mind: *Nevertheless, when we are judged in this way by the Lord, we are being disciplined so that we will not be finally condemned with the world.* Like the previous verse, this one has two words based on the same root. The word translated *judged* is the same as "judgment" in the previous verse. The word translated *condemned*[185] is based on that same root word but is stronger. The line of thought from the previous verse to this one is that self-examination may help us avoid (the stronger) judgment, and that judgment is intended to help us avoid (the even stronger) condemnation. The relationship between the Greek words for "judged" and "condemned" is stressed in the Greek by placing them as the first and last words of the sentence, respectively. God's judgment has a holy purpose — that of better preparing us to exist in his holy presence through a process of redemptive discipline.[186] The difference between God's designs for his people and his plans for the rest of *the world* is stressed by the two alternatives of *being disciplined* or *condemned.* The world in rebellion against God is destined to be condemned by him. God's discipline is intended to spare us from that and to ensure our perseverance in our relationship with God, whose discipline reflects his fatherly commitment to his people (since *discipline* is most commonly meted out by a father to his children with the intention of developing their character and safe-

185. Gk. κατακρίνω.

186. Gk. παιδεύω; "to assist in the development of a person's ability to make appropriate choices, *practice discipline*" (BDAG).

guarding their future). Paul's statement that God's discipline is intended to spare us from ultimate condemnation also serves as a solemn warning to the Corinthians of the danger they face if they fail to respond appropriately to that divine discipline. Implicit in the statement is the idea that condemnation is an open threat for those who continue to act in the way that has brought God's judgment on them in the first place.

**11:33-34** We arrive at Paul's conclusion to his discussion of the Corinthians' problems with the Lord's Supper: *So then, my brothers and sisters, when you gather to eat, you should all eat together.* In this case Paul's *So then* does not lead to a theological conclusion, but to a very practical one. Paul's appeal to the readers as *my brothers and sisters*[187] highlights the importance of this passage which brings the topic to its conclusion.[188] The reference to gathering *to eat* could suggest that the church did not share the Lord's Supper whenever they gathered, but had special meetings to participate in the Lord's Supper. On the other hand, the reference to gathering *to eat* may simply be intended to indicate the explicit resumption of the theme of eating which was kept on the surface throughout vv. 21-29 but was not mentioned in vv. 30-32.

Some scholarly debate has focused on whether the verb and reflexive pronoun translated above as *eat together*[189] mean "to receive each other" or "to wait for each other." The first interpretation would suggest that the emphasis is on the need for the Corinthians to accept each other and treat each other not only with due respect and courtesy, but also with true care and affection. This certainly fits with Paul's teaching and emphasis throughout this section. Unfortunately, the verb used does not seem to be used with the sense of receiving another person with hospitality but when it has to do with "receiving" is a matter of receiving something from someone. When used with a person as an object, it usually means "to remain in a place or state and await an event or the arrival of someone" and calls for a translation such as "expect" or "wait" (BDAG; Thiselton, 899). This fits with our interpretation of v. 21, which rebukes the Corinthians for not waiting for each other but going ahead and eating their meal before less privileged members of the community have arrived. In fact, Schrage (finding a temporal element to the key verbs in each verse) has suggested that this verse forms an inclusio with v. 21.[190] It seems that v. 21 refers to the precise practical offense while v. 33 provides the precise practical correction to that offense. The translation adopted by the TNIV, *you should all eat together,* fits perfectly with the interpretation defended here (especially thanks to the

187. BDAG notes that, even when used literally rather than metaphorically, ἀδελφοί can mean not merely "brothers" but "brothers and sisters" (as translated by the TNIV). See on 1:10.

188. The vocative ἀδελφοί is often used to introduce a new passage, but here its function is to signal that one is coming to its conclusion.

189. Gk. ἀλλήλους ἐκδέχεσθε.

190. Cf. Schrage, 3:56.

*all*): Paul's exhortation to "wait for each other" is intended to guarantee that any eating that is done is enjoyed by the whole community together rather than by certain parts of the community who are insensitive to the rest.

Every Christian community needs to think very carefully about its worship practices and whether or not they are being carried out in ways that disadvantage or show insensitivity to any of its members. Subgroups (potential cliques) within the church also need to be alert to whether or not the fellowship they enjoy with each other sends a message of exclusiveness which is inconsistent with the reality of the oneness of Christ's body. The previous and following verses stress how serious the danger may be when such sensitivity is lacking.

**11:34** Since the members of the community should wait for each other so that they can eat together, *Those who are hungry should eat something at home.* By having something to eat before the meeting they will not be tempted to go ahead and start the meeting early (before all have arrived) in order to assuage their hunger. The idea is not that they would not eat anything at the church meeting, but that their participation in the meal which included the Lord's Supper would be focused on the significance of the meal itself and the fellowship with other members of the community and not on satisfying one's own natural hunger. It is just possible to take Paul's words to say "If someone is hungry let them eat in the house," with the point being that as part of one's Christian love for others the host of the church gathering (the person in whose house the church would be meeting) must make sure that no one goes away hungry and that if the food is being served in the house (more specifically in the triclinium?) anyone who is hungry would have access to it, and not merely those who share the social status of the host or special favor with them. This is unlikely, however, since the expression used[191] means "at home" (cf. BDAG), and it is clearly used that way in 14:35. Of course generous hospitality is a Christian virtue, and the person hosting the church gathering would presumably be providing some food for all those gathered, but they would be better able to serve the whole community if those who gathered were not famished when they came and were not looking forward to the food more than they were to fellowship with the community as a whole.

The precaution of eating at home (before the church gathering) if one is hungry is to be taken *so that when you meet together it may not result in judgment.* Divine judgment would be incurred if, out of concern for their own felt needs, people continued to display a lack of consideration for others and attended to their own desires and pleasures rather than the well-being of others, especially those who may have greater needs than their own.

*And when I come I will give further directions.* We obviously do not know what further directions Paul had in mind or why he did not share them in

191. Gk. ἐν οἴκῳ.

the letter. Perhaps he had some specific instructions about a more effective way of sharing the Lord's Supper that would have been too complicated to write out in a letter, or he had some words of direction or correction to share with some particular members of the church which would have been tactless to include here. It is also possible that Paul recognizes that he does not have a full picture of exactly what was going on (and had not heard both sides or every side of this issue) and decided that some conclusions could be drawn (and guidance given) only after arriving and seeing what was going on for himself. Since the further directions could evidently wait until he arrived in Corinth, they were presumably of lesser urgency than the guidance he provided in the letter. The fact that he was anticipating another visit to Corinth and yet sent this letter ahead of time suggests that what Paul did include in this letter addressed issues he considered rather urgent. In this particular passage it is clear that he is dealing with a matter of life and death and which needed to be dealt with immediately for the sake of the spiritual, social, and physical health of the congregation.

## 2. *Guidance in the Use of Gifts of the Spirit in Worship, 12:1–14:40*

### *a. The Proper Worship of the One True God Is Governed by the Unity and Diversity Reflected in the Gifts of the Holy Spirit, 12:1-31*[1]

In this section of the letter Paul continues the theme of worship which he had already begun to develop in chapter 11 (chs. 8–10 dealt with the avoidance of association with *pagan* worship). That this material relates back to chapters 8–10 is suggested by Paul's reference to idols in 12:2. In fact, 12:1-3 indicates that it is the Spirit who causes one to recognize the lordship of Jesus Christ and reject idolatry and other apostatizing influences. That it is the same/one Spirit/Lord/God who acts in various ways in the community is stressed in 12:4-11. This same/one Spirit or God evokes the motif of the *Shema* that was highlighted in 8:4-6 and which is the most basic Jewish and Christian antidote to idolatrous thought or behavior. Chapters 12–14 reflect the ABA structure found in chapters 8–10, and chapter 7, where the middle unit, which at first sight appears to be a digression, turns out to provide a key to the apostle's approach to the issue introduced in the previous section and developed in the following. Chapter 12 introduces the issue of spiritual gifts and their function within the body of Christ. Chapter 13 stresses the importance, nature, and permanence of love, which is the only proper basis for the use of the gifts. Chapter 14 returns to the gifts of tongues and prophecy in particular and stresses the superiority of prophecy due to its superior ability to edify the body (the goal established by

1. This entire chapter is marked by expository discourse. It contains no imperatives until v. 31, and that one is debated (some take it to be an indicative).

love). Chapter 13, at the heart of the chiastic structure, is also at the heart of Paul's ethical thrust throughout this letter.

The only biblical quotation in this section is found in 14:21, where Paul quotes Isaiah 28:11-12. The only other allusion to Scripture that has been identified is to Isaiah 45:14 (cf. Zech. 8:23) in 14:25.

The opening verse introduces the topic of spiritual things (often translated "spiritual gifts"). The second verse provides the reason why Paul is concerned about the Corinthians' potential ignorance on the subject. The third verse distinguishes between things that must and must not be attributed to the Holy Spirit (statements which clearly identify a speaker as being either with Christ or against him), and vv. 4-11 stress the oneness of the Spirit who provides the church with a diversity of gifts. Verses 12-31 emphasize the oneness of the body which is constituted by the Spirit. The main emphasis of the chapter, then, turns out to be the oneness of the Christian community based on the oneness of the God/Lord/Spirit who establishes and serves as the patron of the community (in implied contradistinction to divisions, or at least lack of unity, that might be expected to exist among pagans pursuing diverse blessings from different patron gods/idols, each presumed to offer different benefits/gifts to its followers).

> [1]*Now about the gifts of the Spirit, brothers and sisters, I do not want you to be uninformed.* [2]*You know that when you were pagans, somehow or other you were influenced and led astray to mute idols.* [3]*Therefore I want you to know that no one who is speaking by the Spirit of God says, "Jesus be cursed," and no one can say, "Jesus is Lord," except by the Holy Spirit.*
>
> [4]*There are different kinds of gifts, but the same Spirit distributes them.* [5]*There are different kinds of service, but the same Lord.* [6]*There are different kinds of working, but in all of them and in everyone it is the same God at work.*
>
> [7]*Now to each one the manifestation of the Spirit is given for the common good.* [8]*To one there is given through the Spirit a message of wisdom, to another a message of knowledge by means of the same Spirit,* [9]*to another faith by the same Spirit, to another gifts of healing by that one Spirit,* [10]*to another miraculous powers, to another prophecy, to another distinguishing between spirits, to another speaking in different kinds of tongues, and to still another the interpretation of tongues.* [11]*All these are the work of one and the same Spirit, and he distributes them to each one, just as he determines.*

### *i. Presentation of the christological criterion for discerning Spirit-led worship, 12:1-3*

**12:1** The TNIV translation *gifts of the Spirit* may be getting just a bit ahead of Paul's thought at this point. Literally he says, "Now I do not want you to be ignorant concerning spiritual things [*or* concerning matters of spirits]" or possibly "concerning spiritual people."[2] BDAG and most translations (for rare exceptions, see CSB, NJB) support translating the key word as "spiritual gifts" or "those who possess spiritual gifts," but the word is much broader in its meaning. By the time we get to the next appearance of this word in 14:1 it may well be that Paul could expect his readers to know that the spiritual things he has in mind are spiritual gifts, but that is not yet clear in 12:1. In fact, in 12:1-3 Paul probably has in mind the difference between acting under the power of God's Spirit and acting under the influence of other spiritual powers (cf. Eph. 6:12). To be ignorant of spiritual things or spiritual matters would include being ignorant of the fact that someone who says "Jesus be cursed" is operating under the influence of another spirit whereas one who testifies that "Jesus is Lord" has come under the influence of the Spirit of God. Spiritual gifts will be the focus of most of chapters 12–14, but these introductory verses seem to deal with broader issues.

Here the vocative reference to the readers, *brothers and sisters*, precedes the introduction of a new topic (or sub-topic), as well as reinforcing Paul's relationship to the readers and respect for them. Paul's concern that they not be *uninformed* or "ignorant" recalls his similar statement in 10:1 and, as there, may have a touch of irony given the Corinthians' apparent overconfidence in their superior knowledge (see on 8:1-4).

The reason why the Corinthians might be uninformed (or misinformed) about spiritual things is indicated in the following verses: their former experience as pagans may have poorly prepared them to understand these realities. In our own time also, many are ignorant of spiritual things or misinformed about them. In the post-Enlightenment context naturalistic and rationalistic presuppositions and habits of thought tend to guide our thinking, so that the existence and influence of spiritual powers or beings tends to be either doubted or kept to the periphery of our consciousness. There has been a reaction to this post-Enlightenment rationalism recently, and a greater openness to learning from other cultures that previously were simply looked down upon for their supposed superstition based on their beliefs in spirits and their influence in the world. We are very much in need of very careful thinking about spiritual things today, and we must be equally careful about either assuming an unbiblical naturalistic worldview or falling prey to superstitious thinking as an overreaction to rationalism. Interestingly, Paul did not think that the Corinthians' previous experiences with spiritual realities was helpful to them, but rather that they had to have their thinking about spiritual things transformed in light of divine revelation. Their knowledge of spiritual realities had been

2. The Greek adjective is πνευματικός (also in 2:13, 15; 3:1; 9:11; 10:3-4; 12:1; 14:1, 37; 15:44, 46). The genitive plural form used here (πνευματικῶν) could be construed as masculine or neuter in this context. The neuter noun used for (spiritual) "gifts" is χάρισμα (plural: χαρίσματα; also in 1:7; 7:7; 12:4, 9, 28, 30-31).

seriously distorted and needed to be reshaped in light of a true understanding of God and the difference between true and false religion.

**12:2** Having just said that he did not want the Corinthians to be uninformed or ignorant about spiritual things, he now reminds them of that which they already know. In this case, what they know is not particularly flattering: they had formerly fallen under the influence of idols: *You know that when you were pagans, somehow or other you were influenced and led astray to mute idols.* The word for *pagans*[3] is usually translated "Gentiles," but here Paul seems to be stressing their religious background and not simply the fact that they were not ethnic Jews (which would still be the case). Still, the language suggests that the word "Gentiles/pagans" no longer applies to the readers as it did before. This is consistent with 10:1, where Paul refers to the ancient Israelites as "our fathers" (with "our" meant to include the readers). The Corinthians are no longer what or who they used to be and must no longer think or act in the ways to which they were accustomed before knowing Christ. Nor are we.

The text translated *somehow or other you were influenced and led astray* is actually rather difficult. The TNIV translation seems to suggest that the contingency[4] is not one of unknown time(s) but of unknown manner *(somehow or other).* If that is the meaning, it may well imply that since there are innumerable idols in the world there would have been innumerable ways in which any given pagan might have been led astray. Each idol temple would have offered something slightly or significantly different to its potential worshipers, and worshipers of each idol may have been (mis)led differently. The following passage will stress that for Christians there is only one God and Spirit. That same God is experienced by all of his people and blesses them all in the most diverse ways. In paganism there may have been many gods, but each one tended (tends) to be associated with a particular and distinct type of experience.[5] In Christ there is one God, who makes himself known to his people in a great diversity of ways (all consistent with his perfect character). We do not need different gods for different needs or blessings, for there is only one God, and he provides for our every need. While the points made in the previous sentences are true and suggested by vv. 4-11, most of the linguistic evidence suggests that the construction used by Paul in this clause points not to a variety of ways in which people might have been led astray, but to "repeated action in past time,"[6] suggesting a translation such as "whenever you were led, you were led astray to dumb idols." If this is correct, the point would be that the Corinthians' pre-

3. Gk. ἔθνος; plural: ἔθνη.

4. Suggested by the Gk. ὡς ἄν.

5. So also Theodoret, 209: "not convinced each was capable of everything, they supposed one was source of wisdom, another of military arts, and another of nautical skills."

6. BDAG ἄν a. α. (cf. BDF §367, and BDAG on ἄγω, which suggests that the relevant text be translated, *"how you were attracted, carried away again and again to mute idols,* where ἄν denotes repetition . . .").

Christian spiritual experiences were thoroughly marked by deception. It is not as though some of their experiences were valid and others were not. Their previous spiritual experience is completely untrustworthy as a guide to the ways of the one true God they have now come to know in and through Christ.

Terence Paige has made a strong case for understanding Paul's reference here to the constant processions that were a part of normal life in the Roman world (including Corinth).[7] Such processions took place as part of religious festivals "in which the participants normally proceeded along a sacred route" which brought them to an image in a sanctuary.[8] Paige points out that in Corinth there would have been processions related to the worship of Demeter and Kore, Apollo, Dionysus, Isis, as well as other gods.[9] It should be recalled that the word translated *led astray*[10] in the TNIV and in most other translations usually means simply "to lead off" or "to lead away [from someplace]" and does not necessarily entail being misled.[11] Paige points out that animals would also have been included in the *pompe,* animals that would have been sacrificed after arriving in the sanctuary of the god. He suggests that Paul may have been playing "on this 'leading' of both people and animals by implying that in their former practices the Corinthians were like the animals themselves, led away captive to slaughter. . . . The pompe then symbolizes the ignorance and slavery of the Corinthians' pre-conversion life, in which they simply followed where they were led."[12] In sum, "[t]he Corinthians are reminded that in their former life they were enslaved, in ignorance of the true God and his workings, to evil powers associated with the pagan cultus."[13] Whether Paul has cultic processions, demons, or self-deception in mind, the Corinthians' experience of idolatry was not one that prepared them to discern the true nature of spiritual experiences. Since they had participated in the worship of *mute idols,* they were not equipped to know what one might properly expect to be announced in the name of the one true God of Israel. Clearly they were previously led about in a state of spiritual ignorance, and Paul recognizes the urgency of having that ignorance replaced by a proper understanding of how the Holy Spirit works in the lives of God's people.

The Old Testament and ancient Jews and Christians know of only two types of people: idolaters and those who only worship the one true God, the God of Israel. The central section of the *Shema,* Deuteronomy 11:13-21,

7. Terence Paige, "1 Corinthians 12:2: A Pagan *Pompe*?" *JSNT* 44 (1991), 57-65.

8. Paige, "1 Corinthians 12:2: A Pagan *Pompê*?" 59; cf. Garland, 566.

9. Paige, "1 Corinthians 12:2: A Pagan *Pompê*?" 60.

10. Gk. ἄγω.

11. BDAG does state that in this and a few other cases the word means "to cause to depart from correct behavior" or, in the passive voice, to "be misled, carried away." Other examples include Lucian, *Cataplus* 26; *Diognetus* 9.1; and *Acts of Paul* 1:10.

12. Paige, "1 Corinthians 12:2: A Pagan *Pompê*?" 63.

13. Paige, "1 Corinthians 12:2: A Pagan *Pompê*?" 64.

establishes only two alternatives: one will either "faithfully obey the commands I am giving you today — to love the LORD your God and to serve him with all your heart and with all your soul" (11:13), or "turn away and worship other gods and bow down to them" (11:16).[14] Before coming to Christ, the Corinthians were on the wrong side of that divide.

That idols are *mute* or "dumb" is an Old Testament theme taken up many times in Jewish sources (cf. Hab. 2:18-19 [and 1QpHab xii 12]; Isa. 46:7; Jer. 10:5; Pss. 115:5; 135:16; *Genesis Rabbah* 84:10; *m. Sanhedrin* 7b). The Lord is known throughout the Law and the Prophets as the true and living God who speaks to his people through his prophetic messengers. The contrast with idols is made explicit in Isaiah 41:22–42:9. Since the idols are mute, their worshipers were never able to receive any actual revelation from them, leaving them in the dark, even when they thought they had found enlightenment. If any of the Corinthians are especially proud of or confident in their level of understanding or perception of intellectual or spiritual things, they are reminded by Paul that their superior education and social status did not keep them from being completely duped before coming to know Christ. Now they must continue to have their thinking "reprogrammed" in light of the true knowledge of God that comes through the work of the Spirit within the community.

**12:3** Since the Corinthians have such an impoverished background when it comes to understanding the things of the Spirit, Paul feels the need to clarify the most basic matter of spiritual discernment: *Therefore I want you to know that no one who is speaking by the Spirit of God says, "Jesus be cursed," and no one can say, "Jesus is Lord," except by the Holy Spirit*. Spiritual discernment begins by recognizing that which should and should not be attributed to the Spirit of God. Acclamations of lordship and pronouncements of a curse (or *anathema*) are two very different kinds of declarations that might be made in the name or presence of a god or idol in the world of the Corinthians. Whom one curses or acclaims as lord serves as clear testimony of a person's affiliation and allegiance. Paul's examples are extreme opposites.

To declare *"Jesus be cursed"* would be to express a complete rejection of him and to place oneself on the opposite side of a fundamental divide.[15] There is some question as to whether or not anyone actually ever would

14. Cf. W. A. Meeks, "Social Functions of Apocalyptic Language in Pauline Christianity," in *Apocalypticum in the Mediterranean World* (ed. D. Hellholm; Tübingen: J. C. B. Mohr, 1983), 690. The *Shema* consisted of Deut. 6:4-9; 11:13-21 and Num. 15:37-41 (cf. *m. Berakot* 2:2).

15. Each of the Greek statements has an elided verb (literally, "Jesus [is/be] cursed" and "Jesus [is] Lord"). Several scholars suggest that the two statements must have the same implied verb and that since the indicative "is" is the only verb that would make sense of the second statement, "is" should be supplied in the first statement (i.e., "Jesus is accursed"). One might naturally expect the same verb in each case, but if the statements are understood to express diametrically opposed attitudes toward Jesus, a statement cursing him and one declaring him to be Lord would best fit. In this case it is not grammatical parallelism that we should expect, but antithetically parallel speech acts.

have made such a statement. Some[16] interpreters suggest that Paul simply formulated this hypothetical statement as a radical and antithetical alternative to the following statement *(Jesus is Lord),* which is the central confession of the truly spiritual person.[17] However, this statement was most likely made by Jews reacting to the Christian sect.[18] If the statement was declared by Jewish detractors, it is just possible that the Corinthians would not understand it since the key word involved (here translated *cursed*[19]) was often used in Greek literature for a votive offering, a gift offered in worship to a god in fulfillment of a vow. Thus if a Greek or Roman were to hear of someone saying "Jesus is a votive offering" in a worship (or any other) context, they may have thought it simply incoherent.[20]

The declaration *"Jesus is Lord"* is the most fundamental of all Christian statements of faith. In it the historical figure, Jesus of Nazareth, is identified with or as Yahweh.[21] We have already seen that Paul's christological monotheism finds the true identity of Jesus Christ in the reference to the LORD in the *Shema* (Deut. 6:4; see our comments on 1 Cor. 8:4-6). Of course, this was also a politically loaded affirmation in the context of the Roman Empire, where that title was expected to be attributed to Caesar. *Jesus is Lord* is not merely a statement of theological conviction but of personal allegiance. His role as Lord, according to Paul's theology, has to do with his exaltation to the final eschatological role of the ideal Davidic (Adamic) vice-regent.[22] Paul's thought may go back to Joel 2:32 (3:5 LXX), which, following up on God's promise to pour out his Spirit on all people (2:28-29 = 3:1-2 LXX) testifies that at that time "all who call on the name of the Lord will be saved." It is one of the OT texts about Yahweh that Paul applies to Christ elsewhere (Rom. 10:13; cf. Acts 2:21). For Christians, "the name of the Lord" is now known to be Jesus.

Both potential declarations have to do with Christ, highlighting the Christocentric nature of the discernment process. For Paul, everything depends upon what one says about and how one positions oneself with respect to Jesus.

That true prophetic speech originated by God's Spirit is made clear by many Old Testament passages (see esp. Num. 11:25-29; 24:2-3; 1 Sam.

16. For example, Schrage, 3:116-17.

17. See Conzelmann, 206, and Sampley, 941.

18. See Garland, 570.

19. Gk. ἀνάθεμα. The first definition given in BDAG is "that which is dedicated as a votive offering."

20. It is possible that some scribes thought the sense should be, "[This is offered as] a votive offering to Jesus" since a few textual witnesses (F, 629, *pc*, lat; Spec) have Ἰησοῦ (genitive or dative) rather than Ἰησοῦς (nominative).

21. See David B. Capes, *Old Testament Yahweh Texts in Paul's Christology* (WUNT 2.47; Tübingen: J. C. B. Mohr, 1992).

22. See Roy E. Ciampa, "The History of Redemption," in *Central Themes in Biblical Theology: Mapping Unity in Diversity* (ed. Scott J. Hafemann and Paul R. House; Grand Rapids: Baker Academic, 2007), 254-308.

10:6, 10; 19:20, 23; 2 Sam. 23:2; Neh. 9:30; Isa. 61:1; Joel 2:28; Mic. 3:8; Zech. 7:12) and was a commonplace of early Christian teaching (see, e.g., Luke 1:67; Acts 2:17-18; 19:6; 28:25; Eph. 3:5 1 Pet. 1:21; 1 John 4:1; Rev. 19:10). That is abundantly confirmed throughout 1 Corinthians 12–14.

### *ii. Exposition of the trinitarian basis for unity in light of the diversity of spiritual gifts, 12:4-7*

**12:4-6** In these verses Paul stresses that there is but one God, who provides various manifestations of his Spirit.[23] The verses function much like synthetic parallelism, with each new line not exactly repeating but reinforcing and slightly developing the thought of the previous ones. Each refers to that which is *different* and that which is the *same* (with the latter relating to the three persons of the Trinity, referred to, respectively, as *Spirit, Lord,* and *God*) and raises the issue of "the one and the many" with the understanding that although God is one, he is reflected in a tremendous diversity of ways. Or, rather, since there is only one God, it is that same God who provides all the gifts that are needed. Chrysostom rightly points out that Paul "implies that there is no difference in the gifts of the Father, and the Son, and the Holy Spirit," that he does not confuse the persons of the Trinity but declares "the equal honor of the Essence" since "that which the Spirit bestows . . . God also works [and] the Son likewise ordains and grants."[24]

It has been suggested that the references to Spirit, Lord, and then God anticipates the structure of the following passages, with vv. 7-11 focusing on the Spirit (see references to the Spirit in vv. 7, 8, 9, 11), vv. 12-14 focusing on the body of Christ (the Lord), and vv. 15-31 focusing on God and the way he put the body together (cf., e.g., vv. 18, 24, 28).

*There are different kinds of gifts, but the same Spirit distributes them.* Part of the significance of the fact that all believers receive their various gifts from the same Spirit (Lord and God) may be that they are all direct clients of the same benefactor/patron. It is not that the wealthy among them are the patrons of the poorer members of the congregation, but that each member of the church has received a gift directly from God[25] which he or she then shares with the rest of the community, with even the poorer members of the community having gifts to share with the wealthy and well-

23. Paul builds his exposition in vv. 4-6 (a series of affirmations) on the back of three uses of εἰσίν (the present indicative third-person plural form of εἰμί). There is also a substantival participle in v. 6, but that is off the main line.

24. Chrysostom, *Homiliae in Epistulam i ad Corinthios* 29.4 (NPNF[1] 12:171).

25. Cf. Chrysostom, *Homiliae in Epistulam i ad Corinthios* 29.4 (NPNF[1] 12:171): "in that it has been granted to you to receive from the same source as the other . . . you have equal honor. For certainly you cannot say that the Spirit bestowed the gift on him, but an angel on you: since the Spirit bestowed it both on you and him. Wherefore he added, 'but the same Spirit.' So that even if there is a difference in the gift there remains no difference in the Giver."

connected so that each member is dependent upon the free sharing of the gifts of all the other members of the community. Each one has something they have received directly from God and have been empowered to share with the rest. Collins suggests that Paul's choice of the word "gifts" to refer to these spiritual realities "functions as a theological corrective" to the understanding expressed in the Corinthians' preferred terminology of "spiritual phenomena," which highlighted "the ecstatic and the extraordinary." Paul, Collins points out, wants to redefine the concept to underscore "the idea that authentic spiritual phenomena are gifts."[26] The stress is thereby transferred from the individuals expressing the various phenomena to the God who has freely given them to each of the members of the body. This emphasis is partially masked by the translation *different kinds* in this and the following two verses. The word used has to do with "division or distribution of someth[ing] to pers[ons]" and here suggests "allotments of spiritual gifts" (BDAG). As Sampley notes, "By Paul's choice of the term ["allocations"] for his description of the diversities among the Corinthians (vv. 4-6), he anticipates the point with which the passage will emphatically conclude: The Spirit is the source of all charismata and allocates them to each person as the Spirit chooses."[27]

The understanding of these special abilities as *gifts* ("given" by God, v. 7) may be particularly significant in light of the patronage system in the Roman world, where a patron was expected to receive praise and glory from his or her clients for their lavish generosity. 1 Corinthians 1:5-7 ties the Corinthians' enrichment with the charismata they have received from God.[28] This would relate to the social discrepancies between church members, suggesting that those who were poorer in normal Corinthian (and human) eyes should understand themselves (and be understood by their materially richer brothers and sisters) as actually being among a privileged group which has found true enrichment from Christ.

Such an understanding also helps to explain two aspects of chapters

26. Collins, 450. Similarly, Thiselton points out that "Paul redefines what *counts as spiritual* by talking about what God 'freely gives,' on his own initiative and in his own sovereign choice (12:11), as empowerments (ἐνεργημάτων, v. 6) through the agency of the Holy Spirit for practical service of God and of other persons (διακονιῶν, v. 5)" (930, his emphasis, bold font changed to single quotes).

27. Sampley, 943.

28. On God as benefactor and patron and the proper response of his people, see David A. deSilva, *Honor, Patronage, Kinship and Purity: Unlocking New Testament Culture* (Downers Grove, IL; InterVarsity, 200), 126-56. The motif of God as "benefactor" (εὐεργέτης) is common in Philo (*On the Creation of the World* 169; *Allegorical Interpretation* 1:96; 2:56; 3:78, 137; *That God Is Unchangeable* 110; *On Planting* 87, 90; *On Sobriety* 55, 58; *On the Change of Names* 28; *On Dreams* 1:163; *On the Life of Moses* 2:256; *On the Decalogue* 41; *On the Special Laws* 1:152, 209, 272, 300; *On the Embassy to Gaius* 118; *Questions and Answers on Genesis* 1:55, 91; 2:50). In *Embassy* 118 Philo speaks of God as "the Benefactor of the whole world, who through His power bestows blessings poured in unstinted abundance on every part of the All" (trans. F. H. Colson [LCL]).

12–14. First, it suggests how the spiritual gifts in chapters 12–14 tie in to the motif of the proper worship of the one true God (who should be recognized [and glorified] as the infinitely generous patron of the community[29]). As deSilva stresses, "The first component of a fulsome response of gratitude is simply giving thanks to the Giver."[30] It entails "proclamation of God's favors and publicly acknowledging our debt" as we "simply and honestly give God public praise for the gifts and help we have received from God."[31] It also relates to the idea that the proper worship of God would naturally call for a similar lavish use of spiritual gifts for the well-being of the other members of the community. That a "prominent kind of exhortation in the New Testament promotes imitation of the virtues and generosity displayed by God and Jesus"[32] is natural since one is expected "to respond in accordance with what benefactions one has received," which would mean sharing our gifts with others as generously as God has shared them with us.[33] deSilva applies this directly to spiritual gifts:

> Divine endowments of this kind (whether teaching, prophetic utterance, wisdom, tongues or even monetary contributions) become opportunities and obligations for service. The proper response to receiving such gifts is not boasting (1 Cor 4:7), which in effect suppresses the acknowledgment that these qualities stem from God's endowment, but sharing God's gifts with the whole church and the world. We are to exercise stewardship of the varied gifts that God has granted with the result that the honor and praise offered to God increases (1 Pet 4:10-11; see also Rom 12:3-8; 1 Cor 12:4-11; Eph 4:7-16).[34]

29. Discussing the proper response to a gift from a patron, Seneca says that one should "accept cheerfully, professing [one's] pleasure and letting the giver have proof of it. . . . Let us show how grateful we are for the blessing that has come to us by pouring forth our feelings, and let us bear witness to them, not merely in the hearing of the giver, but everywhere" (*On Favors* 2.22.1, trans. John W. Basore [LCL]). Philo stresses that God's role as benefactor should lead his people to worship him in a number of places. In *On Sobriety* 58 he speaks of the need of one who has been richly blessed by God to "requite his Benefactor with the words of his lips with song and with hymn" (trans. Colson and Whitaker [LCL]). In *On the Life of Moses* 2:256 he asks, "What should Moses do but honour the Benefactor with hymns of thanksgiving?" (trans. Colson [LCL]). In *On the Special Laws* 1:272 he speaks of those who "offer the best of sacrifices, the full and truly perfect oblation of noble living, as they honour with hymns and thanksgivings their Benefactor and Saviour, God" (trans. Colson [LCL). In *Questions and Answers on Genesis* 2:50 he says that it is proper that one "who had received good by the grace of God should give thanks with a willing disposition. But one who waits for a command is ungrateful, being compelled by necessity to honour his benefactor" (trans. Marcus [LCL). Josephus reserves the word εὐεργέτης for human benefactors, but he refers to God as "patron" (προστάτης) in *Antiquities* 2.122; 4.185; 7.340, 380. This term is also used for Jesus in *1 Clement* 36:1; 61:3; 64:1.

30. deSilva, *Honor, Patronage, Kinship and Purity,* 142.

31. deSilva, *Honor, Patronage, Kinship and Purity,* 143.

32. deSilva, *Honor, Patronage, Kinship and Purity,* 146.

33. deSilva, *Honor, Patronage, Kinship and Purity,* 147.

34. deSilva, *Honor, Patronage, Kinship and Purity,* 148.

The status implied by the reception of any of the gifts is suggested by v. 5: *There are different kinds of service, but the same Lord.* The gifts are distributed by the Lord so that those receiving them might use them in his service. While service is clearly to be rendered to the rest of the community, in contexts where the terms *service* and *Lord* are used in close relationship with each other, it is normally understood to be a reference to a service or ministry to which one has been appointed by the Lord (e.g., Acts 20:24; Col. 4:17; 1 Tim. 1:12). One implication, then, is that every member of the community is to be respected as one who has been deemed worthy of a particular assignment in the service of the Lord. Another is that in exercising one's gift one is performing a royal and holy service. That there are *different kinds of service* to which the Lord has called the various members of the body means that there is no one type or group of ministries that is to be seen as more closely associated with the Lord's service than others. That they are all appointed by *the same Lord* suggests again that no member of the community has a gift that should be looked down upon as though it had been bestowed upon him or her by some lesser power or authority. As Collins points out, "Mention of the single Lord prepares for the discussion of the body of Christ in vv. 12-26."[35]

Verse 6 points to the effects, results, or outworking of the gifts that have been bestowed by the Spirit. *There are different kinds of working, but in all of them and in everyone it is the same God at work.* The word translated *working*[36] has to do with the effects or outworking of something.[37] In this context it is presumably the presence of the divine gift in each one which manifests itself in the effect which God produces in the life of the one on whom it has been bestowed. It is *the same God* who causes such diverse effects, which are manifestations of the gift he has bestowed for use in his service. Wright points out that "the basis of the church's unity — the fact that it is the same Spirit, the same lord, the same god 'who works all in all' (12.6) — looks on once more to chapter 15, where the end of the whole story is that this god, the creator and lord of history and the world, will eventually be 'all in all' (15.28)."[38] He is the one behind each of the various manifestations at work in every member of the community. If one were to trivialize or marginalize the contribution made by any member of the community, one would be trivializing something which God himself was doing in and through that person.

Later on Paul would point out that when the gifts were operating in the church as God desired, it would lead others to come to recognize the presence of God within the community and to fall down to worship him (14:24-25). The gathering of the church for worship is not merely a matter of a group of human beings coming together to practice certain traditions or

35. Collins, 449.
36. Gk. ἐνέργημα.
37. "[T]o bring someth[ing] about through use of capability" (BDAG).
38. N. T. Wright, *The Resurrection of the Son of God*, 295-96.

liturgy, but entails the presence and activity of God himself in and through his people as they worship and build each other up in his presence.

Prophetic texts that looked forward to the outpouring of the Spirit anticipated a variety of manifestations. Joel 2:28-32 (3:1-5 LXX and HB), one of the more influential texts, refers to prophesying, dreaming (revelatory) dreams, seeing visions, and God-given wonders. Other texts also look forward to the manifestation of a variety of behaviors or qualities through the work of God's Spirit (e.g., Isa. 11:1-5; 32:15-17; 44:3-5; 61:1-4). That all such manifestations must be understood to originate from the *same* God (rather than a *variety* of spiritual beings [cf. 12:2]) is based on the presupposition of biblical monotheism (see on 8:4-6).

**12:7** *Now to each one the manifestation of the Spirit is given for the common good.* The motif of "gifts" is reflected here not in the usual term for "(spiritual) gift" but in the more common verb here translated *given.*[39] It is clarified that each gift is a *manifestation of the Spirit,* that is, an ability or ministry which the Spirit actualizes within the believer and which reveals the presence of the Spirit — of God — among his people.[40] In 14:25 a visiting outsider, exposed to the manifestation of the Spirit through prophetic ministry, will "fall down and worship God, exclaiming, 'God is really among you!'" The promise of the revelation of God's saving presence, promised in Isaiah 40 and many other prophetic texts, is coming to fulfillment (partially, at least) in the church through the Spirit's work in her midst. The gifts of the Spirit may be *manifestations of the Spirit* which celebrate God's attributes (wisdom, knowledge, power to heal, power over nature, wisdom, discernment, etc.) by actualizing or manifesting those attributes in ways which promote *the common good* and in doing so bring God glory.[41]

The word translated *common good*[42] here is the same one that was used in 6:12 and 10:23 for that which "is beneficial" in the repeated phrase "not everything is beneficial." Once we understand this verse in relation to those previous statements about what is beneficial, the place of the gifts of the Spirit in Paul's thought becomes clearer. They are not given for our own indulgence, but to benefit the community of which we are a part. The expression in 6:12 and 10:23 suggests that our entire lives should be oriented around that which will benefit those around us (and ourselves as well, ulti-

39. Gk. δίδωμι.

40. This suggests that "of the Spirit" (τοῦ πνεύματος) reflects a "subjective genitive"; that is, the Spirit is understood to be the subject of the action or activity implied in the previous noun (manifestation). In other words, the Spirit manifests different things in different people. As Hays, 210, points out, "Here 'Spirit' stands in for all three persons of the Trinity, and the word 'manifestation' is employed as the generic category that includes 'spiritual gifts' in the narrower sense as well as other activities inspired by God in the church."

41. 4QShirShabb$^{f}$ 23 ii 12 speaks of "tongues of knowledge" in the heavenly worship of the angels which "bless the God of knowledge in all the works of his glory" (Florentino García Martínez's translation).

42. Gk. συμφέρω.

mately). It is entirely natural, then, that the gifts God gives us are intended for the same purpose.

That the Spirit would be manifest in *each one* was already suggested by Joel 2:28-29 as well as Ezekiel 36:26-27; 37:14, and may be understood as the fulfillment of the desire expressed by Moses in Numbers 11:29 (cf. Isa. 32:15; 44:3). We argued above that the passage from Joel (with its explicit reference to pouring out the Spirit on men and women) probably played a key role in informing Paul's argument in 11:2-16.

*iii. Sample listing of some gifts of the Spirit, 12:8-11*

Here we find the first extended list of gifts in this letter, provided, as Fee points out, "to illustrate the thesis of v. 7."[43] Although there has been great interest in discerning the nature of the various gifts Paul mentions, "that lies outside Paul's own interest, which is simply to illustrate the *diversity* of the Spirit's activities/manifestations in the church."[44] The role of the Spirit in bestowing the gifts is stressed especially at the beginning and end of the list (vv. 8-9, 11). Some of the particular gifts mentioned by Paul were already associated with the Spirit (or were referred to in terms of "a spirit of . . .") in the Old Testament, including wisdom and knowledge or understanding (Exod. 32:3; 35:31; Isa. 11:2; Dan. 1:4; 5:11-12; 1QS iv 3-4, 20-22 [interpreting Ezek. 36:25-27]; 4QpIsa$^a$ 8-10 iii 11-12 [interpreting Isa. 11:2]; some texts highlight the particular knowledge that Israel's God is the Lord [e.g., Ezek. 37:6, 14]), healing (Isa. 61:1; 2 Kgs. 2:15-16; 4:32-36; 5:3-14 [healings through Elisha]; 1QS iv 6), and prophecy (e.g., Num. 11:29; Joel 2:28; 1 Sam. 10:6, 10; 19:20, 23; 2 Sam. 23:2). Miracles were especially associated with God's special intervention in the exodus and in the ministries of Elijah and Elisha. It is unclear whether the order of the gifts is according to a strict hierarchy or other structural principle. Paul consistently places tongues and the interpretation of tongues at the end of his lists, and in doing so he seems to be intentionally demoting the gift on which the Corinthians evidently placed inordinate value.

This list of gifts has been variously categorized.[45] In v. 8 we have two gifts relating to speech (message of wisdom and message of knowledge). In

43. Fee, 590.

44. Fee, 590, his emphasis.

45. Cf. Witherington, 257: "In the first list Paul groups together gifts of instruction (wisdom and knowledge), then gifts of supernatural power (miracles, healings) and of inspired utterance (prophecy, tongues)" (see also Hays, 211-12). Fee, 590-91, points out that these are popular groupings but argues (591) that "[i]f grouping is legitimate at all, it is most likely to be found in some clues Paul himself has given, by starting the third and eighth items (faith and tongues) with a different word for 'another.' If so, then the first two are chosen for very specific *ad hoc* purposes; 'wisdom' and 'knowledge' held high court in Corinth. He then adds a random list of five items that have as their common denominator a supernatural endowment of some kind, and concludes with the 'problem child' and its companion, tongues and interpretation."

vv. 9-10a there are three gifts relating to miracles (faith [to move mountains; 13:2], healing, miraculous powers), in v. 10b we have two gifts related to prophecy (prophecy and distinguishing between [prophetic] spirits), and in the remainder of v. 10 we have the two gifts related to tongues (speaking in tongues and interpreting them). It may be that Paul is using an A B A′ B′ structure[46] so that he twice begins with gifts of prophecy and speech before going to the more "spectacular" gifts, whether of miracles or tongues:

| | | | |
|---|---|---|---|
| Speech: | Message of wisdom | Speech: | Prophecy |
| | Message of knowledge | | Distinguishing of spirits |
| Wonder: | Faith (prerequisite to . . .) | Wonder: | Tongues (and their |
| | Healing | | interpretation) |
| | Miraculous powers | | |

Of the gifts that Paul lists, the ones that we have good reason to believe were being practiced in Corinth are those of prophecy and tongues, which are the two that Paul extensively compares in chapter 14.[47] The gifts of faith, healing, and miraculous powers may have been practiced within the church in Corinth (cf. Galatians 3:1-5), but it is also possible that they are mentioned in order to serve comparative purposes to keep the Corinthians from being overly impressed with tongues, the variety of wonder-instilling gifts that seemed to have them enthralled. Since Paul exercised many (if not all) of the gifts mentioned here (Acts 16:16-18; 19:11-12; 28:8; 1 Cor. 14:18), it may also serve to remind them that the apostle writing this letter is much more experienced in these things than any of the Corinthians are likely to have been.

Nowhere does Paul provide a complete list of spiritual gifts. He provides us, instead, with a variety of partial lists (1:5; 12:8-10, 28, 29-30; 13:1-3, 8-9; Rom. 12:6-8; Eph. 4:11 [cf. 1 Pet. 4:11]), no two of which agree completely, and there is no reason to believe that we would come up with an exhaustive list simply by compiling those gifts that Paul happens to mention in these different *ad hoc* lists of representative examples; "Other and different gifts are conceivable."[48] We have no grounds for believing that Paul himself thought he knew (or could possibly know) the complete range of potential gifts.

46. Collins, 451, sees a different, 2+5+2, A-B-A′ chiastic structure: "Paul begins with two gifts of the word (v. 8). 'To someone else' *(heterō)* introduces a series of five charisms (vv. 9-10c). Another 'to someone else' introduces the final pair. The first two charisms have to do with wisdom and knowledge, Pauline understanding of which was developed in chs. 1–4. The last two charisms have to do with talking in tongues, another matter of Pauline concern (see ch. 14)." His chiasm, then, is based on the numbers of gifts and the fact that the first and last pairs have to do with speech (although some in the middle do as well).

47. Chapter 14 revolves around those two gifts and the relative value of each one. In 14:26 Paul suggests that things which people might contribute to the Corinthian worship service include "a hymn, or a word of instruction, a revelation, a tongue or an interpretation." In 1:5 Paul says, with respect to spiritual gifts, that the Corinthians have been enriched "with all kinds of speech and with all knowledge."

48. Barnett, 230.

Anticipating the results found in the comments on these verses, we may briefly summarize our view of the gifts Paul mentions in vv. 8-10 as follows. A "message of wisdom" is most likely the ability to give guidance for dealing with challenging circumstances in a way that is consistent with Christ's stress on self-sacrifice for the well-being of the other. A "message of knowledge" would seem to be a message marked by theological understanding, including understanding based on (Spirit-inspired) study of Scripture. The gift of "faith" seems to be an extraordinary God-given confidence in his saving power and presence informed by the knowledge that he is now acting to sanctify his name in the eyes of all the nations. The gift of "healing" would be the privilege of being the recipient or the channel of miraculous healing. The gift of "miracles" would be the privilege of serving as a channel for the (miraculous) eschatological manifestation of God's power to save and to judge. The gift of "prophecy" entails the communication of a message given by God as a response to and tailored to the special needs and issues of those gathered to hear it. The gift of "distinguishing between spirits" is a special ability to evaluate the origin, authority, and application of a prophetic message. The gift of "speaking in different kinds of tongues" is the ability to speak to God in unlearned human (and possibly also angelic) languages. The gift of "the interpretation of tongues" would be the ability to translate or interpret what was said to God through the gift of tongues.

The argument of chapters 12–14 as a whole suggests that Paul is most concerned about the overvaluing and abuse of the gift of tongues. Even though there does not seem to be a strict hierarchy to the order of the gifts listed, it is probably not accidental that tongues and their interpretation are placed last. It is also probably not accidental that messages of knowledge and wisdom come first. As Garland points out, they are "closely related to the message delivered by apostles (2:6-7, 11-16; 2 Cor. 11:6), prophets (1 Cor. 13:2), and teachers (14:6, 26). It is this ministry of the word that most benefits the church and strengthens its mission to the world."[49]

**12:8** *To one there is given through the Spirit a message of wisdom, to another*[50] *a message of knowledge by means of the same Spirit.* As Witherington points out, "The three lists of gifts and functions in vv. 8-10, 28, and 29f. (cf. 14:26) are representative, not exhaustive. Paul's point is simply to show that there are varieties of gifts. He does not explain or comment at any length on the gifts, except those that were causing problems in Corinth. We are not at all sure what some of these gifts were."[51] As mentioned above, wisdom and knowledge (or understanding) were already associated with God's Spirit in the Old Testament and early Jewish texts (e.g., Exod. 32:3; 35:31; Isa. 11:2; Dan. 1:4; 5:11-12; 1QS iv 3-4, 20-22 [interpreting Ezek. 36:25-

49. Garland, 581.

50. Verses 8b-10 are marked by a lack of verbs, with "is given" (δίδοται) understood from its presence in vv. 7-8a.

51. Witherington, 257.

27]; 4QpIsa[a] 8-10 iii 11-12 [interpreting Isa. 11:2]), and some of those texts highlight in particular the knowledge that Israel's God is the Lord (e.g., Ezek. 37:6, 14). The relationship or distinction between a message of wisdom and a message of knowledge is unclear. Our tendency is to think of wisdom as a more practical thing that has to do with the way one deals with challenging circumstances. BDAG renders wisdom as "the capacity to understand and function accordingly." Knowledge is taken to be more abstract and less practically oriented. BDAG defines it as "comprehension or intellectual grasp of someth[ing]." In the LXX and early Jewish and Christian literature wisdom and knowledge often go together as a word pair or in parallelism (cf. Prov. 2:6; 9:10; 30:3; Eccl. 1:16, 18; 2:21, 26; 9:10; *Barnabas* 2:3; 21:5; 4 Macc. 1:16; Sir. 21:18; Dan. (Theodotion) 1:4; Rom. 11:33; Col. 2:3). In some cases texts seem to suggest that wisdom leads (or is expected to lead) to knowledge (cf. Philo, *That God Is Unchangeable* 143; *On Flight and Finding* 82 [?]; 2 Sam. 14:20; Prov. 8:12; Wis. 9:17; 10:8; 1 Cor. 1:21 [?]). In fact, Wisdom teaches knowledge (Wis. 7:21). Although knowledge is not usually said to lead to wisdom, wisdom is something that can be known (Eccl. 7:25; 8:16; Wis. 6:22). As a word pair or in the same verse, wisdom almost always comes before knowledge (17 cases of wisdom followed within eight words by knowledge and only two cases of the opposite).

According to Psalm 111:10 and Proverbs 9:10, "the fear of the LORD is the beginning of wisdom." As we have argued in the discussion of the structure of this letter, Paul understands that true wisdom keeps one from idolatry and sexual immorality and leads to the proper worship of God (what Ps. 111:10 and Prov. 9:10 refer to as "the fear of the LORD"). The *message of wisdom* Paul has in mind must be understood in light of his extensive treatment of the subject of true and false wisdom in chapters 1–4 of this letter. Any message that Paul would recognize as a message of wisdom would have to be a message that reflects the upside-down (or right-side up in a very surprising way) wisdom which recognizes in Christ crucified not foolishness but God's power and wisdom (1:24). Someone "wise enough to judge a dispute between believers" (6:5) might have a *message of wisdom* to speak to them and to the congregation. A message of wisdom would presumably be one that reflects Christ's stress on self-sacrifice for the well-being of the other.

In many texts knowledge has to do with personal acquaintance and experience, sometimes on a very intimate level (such as in the well-known usage of the word as a euphemism for sexual relations but also in other texts referring to the knowledge of people or of God). Within this letter Paul speaks of knowledge in a variety of ways. Sometimes he has personal knowledge in mind, and at other times he seems to be thinking of information or theology or other things.[52]

52. Personal knowledge (to know a person or their thoughts or mind): Rom. 1:21; 1 Cor. 1:21; 2:16 (?); 3:20; 8:3; 13:12 (?). Knowledge of things: Rom. 2:18; 1 Cor. 2:8, 11, 14; 4:19; 8:7, 10, 11; 13:2 (?); 14:7, 9. Unclear: 1 Cor. 8:1, 2; 13:8, 9; 14:6.

In popular Pentecostal and charismatic teaching a "word of knowledge" is thought to refer to the supernatural communication of personal information about someone who is listening to the speaker, such as a revelation that someone in the congregation is suffering from a particular kind of cancer or that someone in the congregation has been carrying on an adulterous affair. Of course the Holy Spirit may communicate such information,[53] but it is unlikely that that is what Paul has in mind. If we are to discern what Paul has in mind from his own context, we will need to pay careful attention to hints in his writings about what a message or word of wisdom or knowledge would suggest to him and his readers.

Perhaps one of the clearest hints may be found in 8:1-4, 7, where Paul refers to the Corinthians' vaunted possession of "knowledge," which turns out to be more specifically the knowledge that "an idol is nothing at all in the world" and that "there is no God but one" (8:4). This is knowledge that was not shared by all the Corinthians (8:7). In a related matter, although Paul does not express it in these exact words, it seems that these Corinthians had come to some important knowledge but lacked the wisdom to know how to apply it properly, wrongly thinking that it meant that idolatry was not a real danger. Paul first mentions knowledge in 1:5 when he says that they have "been enriched . . . with all knowledge," which presumably is related to his comment that they "do not lack any spiritual gift" in 1:7. Chrysostom believes that "the word of knowledge" is something "which most of the faithful had, possessing indeed knowledge, but not thereupon able to teach nor easily to convey to another what they knew."[54] While we may not be certain, it is quite possible that for Paul a word or message of knowledge would simply be a message marked by theological understanding, including understanding based on (Spirit-inspired) study of Scripture, such as that reflected in 8:4. The assumption that the knowledge must be something that could not be humanly discerned (i.e., that it could not be discerned using Spirit-guided human reason) is based on a grace-nature dichotomy that assumes that what is truly spiritual must be completely distinct from our human abilities. That is, that grace is always at odds or in tension with nature and not in harmony with it. Such a view usually results from an inadequate understanding of nature (and the human being) as God's creation and of the role of human reason and meditation in the pro-

53. It may be that that is how Peter knew the truth about Ananias and Sapphira in Acts 5:1-4, but the text does not inform us. The way the "word of knowledge" is usually practiced in contemporary church life raises the question why God reveals some truth about someone but not who that person is. That is, it usually consists of a strange combination of knowledge and ignorance at the same time. The way it is practiced in some churches today also reflects the anonymity that tends to mark so many of our churches (esp. larger churches), where the personal information supposedly revealed would not already be known to the congregation. In small first-century house churches it is likely that everyone already knew everyone else's business.

54. *Homiliae in Epistulam i ad Corinthios* 29.5 (NPNF[1] 12:172).

cess of prophetic inspiration (which usually reflects evidence of profound scriptural study/contemplation as a framework within which inspiration occurs and is to be understood).

The knowledge reflected in the apostles and prophets was a God-given knowledge that flowed from a Spirit-guided saturating of the heart and mind in the Scriptures.

**12:9-10** *to another faith by the same Spirit.* Since all Christians have faith in Christ, and Paul indicates that the faith he has in mind here is one that (like the other gifts) is not shared by all, most scholars understand Paul to be referring to faith that works miracles.[55] Many refer to 13:2 in making that suggestion, and that intuition is confirmed by the fact that the reference to faith in 13:2 seems to be part of another (mini-)list of gifts which includes tongues, prophecy, faith, and self-giving (martyrdom/self-sacrifice). Thus it is a particularly important clue to what Paul has in mind here. We should bear in mind that in 13:2 Paul indicates that he would have the ability to move mountains if he were to have the extraordinary gift of "all faith" (see the comments there). The reference to faith here (even without the special modifier of "all" faith) should probably still be understood to refer to miracle-working faith, even if it would not be expected that one could actually move literal mountains.[56] The reference to "mountain-moving" faith in 13:2 echoes Jesus' promise about the power of even mustard-seed sized faith to move mountains (Matt. 17:20; 21:21; Mark 11:23). The moving (or razing) of mountains is an eschatological motif associated with God's judgment and/or the removal of obstacles to the restoration of his presence to his people (Isa. 40:4; 41:15; 42:15; 49:11; 54:10; Luke 3:5; Rev. 6:14; 8:8; 16:20). This understanding of *faith* as miracle-working suggests a close relationship between the gift of faith and the following references to gifts of healings and miracles.[57] According to Thiselton, "rather

55. Cf. Witherington, 257. So also Chrysostom, *Homiliae in Epistulam i ad Corinthios* 29.5 (NPNF[1] 12:172), who says that Paul means not "the faith of doctrines, but the faith of miracles." Bruce speaks more broadly of "a special endowment of faith for a special service" (119). Carson helpfully clarifies that this special faith "enables a believer to trust God to bring about certain things for which he or she cannot claim some divine promise recorded in Scripture, or some state of affairs grounded in the very structure of the gospel" (D. A. Carson, *Showing the Spirit: A Theological Exposition of 1 Corinthians 12–14* [Grand Rapids: Baker, 1987], 39). Calvin, 262, supports the unlikely view that Paul has in mind a type of faith "which does not lay hold of Christ in His wholeness for redemption, justification and sanctification, but only in so far as miracles are performed in His name. Judas had faith like that, and even he carried out miracles by it."

56. Maureen Yeung properly points out that it is a serious mistake for scholars to segregate miracle faith from salvation/kerygma faith (*Faith in Jesus and Paul: A Comparison with Special Reference to 'Faith That Can Remove Mountains' and 'Your Faith Has Healed/Saved You'* [WUNT 2.147; Tübingen: Mohr Siebeck, 2002], 47-50). They are not two distinct kinds of faith since the miracle-working faith is simply an extension of the same kind of faith that is bound to salvation. She believes that Paul's understanding of faith might best be described as "miracle-salvation faith" (50).

57. Garland (582) suggests that faith may be at the head of the next group of gifts "be-

than focus on the category of miracle, it is more helpful to consider the conceptual entailments of faith in the God who is Almighty and sovereign in relation to his own world."[58] In other words, faith in an almighty and sovereign God entails an understanding that he is capable of intervening in the most dramatic or supernatural (or even more subtle and mundane) ways. It is important to note, however, that Paul is working from an eschatological understanding of the significance of the outpouring of the Spirit and of other signs of God's long-awaited grace, favor, and presence among his people. This is not merely a question of a timeless doctrine of the nature of God, but one of understanding the possibilities now that God has acted and chosen to manifest his presence among the people "on whom the culmination of the ages has come" (10:11).

Thiselton thinks that his view ties the faith of this verse to the "message of knowledge" in v. 8 (which has to do with the knowledge of God; cf. 8:4-6). He is right to see a connection, but it is not based simply on God's eternal existence as the only true God, but with the fulfillment of the eschatological expectation that the Gentiles would come to recognize the God of Israel when he would sanctify his name before them through powerful acts of redemption (cf., e.g., Ezek. 36:22-27). The Corinthians are among those Gentiles who have come to call on the name of the God of Israel. Faith in this context is most likely to be an extraordinary God-given confidence in his saving power and presence informed by the knowledge that he is now acting to sanctify his name in the eyes of all the nations.

*to another gifts of healing by that one[59] Spirit, to another miraculous powers.* Just as it is not clear what distinction Paul might have had in mind between the "message of wisdom" and the "message of knowledge" (see above on v. 8), it is also not clear whether Paul makes any distinction between the gifts of healings and miracles or even whether Paul would think either of them would operate apart from the gift of faith, or would be special manifestations of that gift. That *gifts of healing* and *miraculous powers* are mentioned in the plural (as opposed to a "gift of healing" or the "working of miracles") suggests that each healing and miracle may be understood to be a separate gift from God.[60] Paul "does not refer to the power to heal all diseases but to instances of actual healing."[61]

---

cause they depend especially on the power of faith." Cf. also Carson, *Showing the Spirit*, 40: the gifts of faith, healings, and miracles are "not quantum packages, each discrete from the others. Rather, there is considerable overlap."

58. Thiselton, 946.

59. Some ancient witnesses have "the same Spirit" (א, $C^3$, $D^{gr}$, G, K, P, 614, *Byz Lect*, $it^g$, $syr^{p,h}$, $cop^{sa,bo}$, arm, *al*), but that seems to reflect an attempt to conform the language of this clause to that of the previous ones. Textual support for *that one Spirit* is strong and diverse (A, B, 33, 81, 104, 1739, $it^{ar,\ d}$, vg, Ambrose, Speculum, Hilary, Basil, *al*).

60. So Fee, 594.

61. Garland, 582. As Carson notes (*Showing the Spirit*, 39-40), a believer who has "been granted the χάρισμα *(charisma)* to heal one particular individual of one particular disease at one time . . . should not presume to think that the gift of healing has been bestowed

Thiselton argues that the plural "implies various kinds of healings" and that the "kinds may appear to include sudden or gradual, physical, psychosomatic, or mental, the use of medication or more 'direct' divine agency, and variations which are not to be subsumed in advance under some stereotypical pattern of expectation."[62] He also argues that healers "are given varied gifts at varied times for varied tasks, and we should not impose a post-eighteenth-century dualism of 'natural' and 'supernatural' upon the ways in which God chooses to use, or not to use, regular physical means."[63] His whole discussion of healing reflects great theological and pastoral insight, and we find ourselves in basic agreement with his concerns. However, in this context, with *gifts of healing* given by the Spirit tucked between references to special Spirit-given gifts of faith and of miraculous powers, it seems unlikely that Paul has normal bodily or humanly advanced healing processes in mind, even granting that God heals people in those ways. It is one thing to address the reality that God heals in a myriad of ways and the need to avoid a grace versus nature dichotomy that fails to appreciate God's work in and through his wonderful (even if fallen) creation. It is another thing to answer the question of what kinds of healings Paul most likely has in mind in this particular context. Here Fee is right to remind us that Paul is discussing "manifestations of the Spirit's presence in their midst" which are "most likely chosen because they are, like tongues itself, extraordinary phenomena. It would scarcely do for Paul at this point to attempt to broaden their perspective by listing less visible gifts. That will come in time (especially through the analogy of the body and in the lists in vv. 28-30); but for now the emphasis is on the supernatural."[64] Carson is right: "There can be little doubt that Paul understands these healings to be as miraculous as those of the Lord Jesus himself."[65]

Acts tells us that on various occasions Paul himself exercised healing power (Acts 14:8-10; 19:11-12; 28:7-9), but there is no indication that this was the norm in his life. While Epaphroditus survived his illness, he was clearly in danger of dying despite being with Paul (Phil. 2:27), and there is no evidence that he was healed through Paul. He did not bring healing to Trophimus or to his own thorn in the flesh (2 Tim. 4:20; 2 Cor. 12:7-9). As Paul clarifies in 13:8-12, the Spirit allows believers to experience partial foretastes of the blessings that will be ours when we see Christ face to face. Healings are wonderful but temporary blessings, but they remind us of the complete renewal and transformation of our bodies (and the rest of creation) that awaits us with Christ's return.

As mentioned above, it is not clear whether or not Paul has a distinc-

---

on him or her, prompting the founding of a 'healing ministry.'" We need to avoid an inappropriate "institutionalizing of gifts" (39).

62. Thiselton, 948.

63. Thiselton, 948.

64. Fee, 591.

65. Carson, *Showing the Spirit,* 39.

tion in mind between healings and miracles.[66] Chrysostom argues that the two gifts are to be distinguished since "he that had a gift of healing only performed cures while the one with powers for working miracles used to punish as well. For miracles were not only for healing but also for punishing such that Paul inflicted blindness and Peter killed people."[67] All of these examples have to do with the eschatological manifestation of God's power to save and to judge. In the Old Testament and early Judaism healing was expected to accompany forgiveness and the restoration of God's people (Deut. 32:39; 2 Chr. 7:14; Job 5:18; Pss. 41:4; 103:3; 107:20; 147:3; Isa. 6:10; 19:22; 29:18; 30:26; 35:5-6; 42:4-6; 53:5; 57:18-19; 58:8; 61:1; Jer. 30:17; 33:6; Ezek. 47:12; Hos. 6:1; 7:1; 14:4; Mal. 4:2; 2 *Baruch* 73:1-2; 1 *Enoch* 96:1, 3). The Gospels (see esp. Matt. 11:4-5) make it clear that Jesus' ministry of healing was understood as a fulfillment of such prophetic promises (perhaps esp. Isa. 42:6-7).

Miracles, such as those that were experienced at the exodus and through Elijah and Elisha, were also expected at the time of the new exodus when God's presence would be fully restored to his people and would manifest itself in great power. That the Corinthians are participating in a new exodus was already suggested by Paul's stress on the parallels between their experiences and those of the Israelites during the first exodus and wilderness journey in 10:1-11.

*to another prophecy*. There is a tremendous amount of literature on the nature and understanding of prophecy in the ancient world and in the New Testament in particular.[68] Fee asserts, primarily on the basis of chapter 14, that for Paul prophecy consisted of "spontaneous, Spirit-inspired, intelligible messages, orally delivered in the gathered assembly, intended for the edification or encouragement of the people."[69] In an extended discussion of the relationship and distinction between prophecy and preaching, Forbes contends that preaching has to do with "the proclamation of *past* revelation. Prophecy, on the other hand, is proclamation of revelation only just re-

66. Witherington, 257, thinks that the latter may refer to exorcisms.

67. *Homiliae in Epistulam i ad Corinthios* 29.5 (NPNF[1] 12:172). In this he is followed by Calvin, 262-63.

68. See David E. Aune, *Prophecy in Early Christianity and the Ancient Mediterranean World* (Grand Rapids: Eerdmans, 1983); M. E. Boring, "Prophecy (Early Christian)," in *ABD* 5:495-502; T. Callan, "Prophecy and Ecstasy in Greco-Roman Religion and in 1 Cor," *NovT* 27 (1985), 125-40; E. Earle Ellis, *Prophecy and Hermeneutic in Early Christianity* (Grand Rapids: Eerdmans, 1978); Gordon D. Fee, *God's Empowering Presence: The Holy Spirit in the Letters of Paul* (Carlisle: Paternoster and Peabody, MA: Hendrickson, 1994); Christopher Forbes, *Prophecy and Inspired Speech in Early Christianity and Its Hellenistic Environment* (WUNT 2.75; Tübingen: Mohr, 1995); Thomas W. Gillespie, *The First Theologians: A Study in Early Christian Prophecy* (Grand Rapids: Eerdmans, 1994); W. A. Grudem, *The Gift of Prophecy in 1 Corinthians* (Lanham, MD: University Press of America, 1982); D. Hill, *New Testament Prophecy* (London: Marshall, 1979); K. O. Sandnes, *Paul — One of the Prophets?* (WUNT 2.43; Tübingen: Mohr, 1991). For a fuller bibliography see Thiselton, 903-7.

69. Fee, 595.

ceived."[70] That is, "today's prophecy is tomorrow's preaching or teaching."[71] The temporal distinction may be true, but it may be missing the key issue. Prophecy seems to be more highly occasion- or situation-focused. That is, it tends to be a responsive phenomenon. It is not about the passing on of traditional teaching and ethics, but the communication of a divine message that is understood to be especially given as a response to and tailored to the special needs and issues of those gathered to hear it.

Paul's best clues as to his own understanding of prophecy are given in 13:2; 14:3, 24-25, 30-32, 37, although it is not always clear where the prophetic gift is being distinguished from others and where various terms should be understood to refer to essentially the same phenomenon.[72] At the very end of chapter 14 Paul seems to indicate that the argument he has just completed is to be understood as a prophetic message, carrying the authority of Christ himself, and that such an understanding will be confirmed by any true prophets that the Corinthians have in their midst (14:37). This supports Boring's suggestion that the prophetic message "may well include material taken from tradition and the prophet's own reflection, consciously or unconsciously, with or without re-interpretation, but it is not presented as material which a past authority once said, but as what the deity now says."[73] The best definition is that of Thiselton: prophecy "combines pastoral insight into the needs of persons, communities, and situations with the ability to address these with a God-given utterance or longer discourse (whether unprompted or prepared with judgment, decision, and rational reflection) leading to challenge or comfort, judgment, or consolation, but ultimately building up the addressees."[74] As will become clearer in chapter 14, Paul understood prophetic ministry to be essential to the building up of the church. The presence of the prophetic word in the ministry of the church was one of the sure signs that the Spirit had been poured out and that the end of the ages had arrived (Joel 2:28-29).

*to another distinguishing between spirits.* The last four gifts in the list con-

70. Forbes, *Prophecy and Inspired Speech,* 228 (his emphasis).

71. Forbes, *Prophecy and Inspired Speech,* 228 (his emphasis).

72. For instance, is prophecy to be fully distinguished from a message of knowledge or wisdom, or might a message of knowledge or wisdom come in the form of a prophecy (12:8-10)? Is prophecy understood to entail the fathoming of mysteries and knowledge, or are those two different but related abilities (13:2)? Are revelation, knowledge, prophecy, and a word of instruction all to be clearly distinguished, or are they overlapping terms (14:6)? Has a reference to prophecy been omitted from 14:26, or is it understood to be included under one or more of the terms used there? Collins (451-52) helpfully suggests that Paul's list of gifts in vv. 8-10 "is characterized by the rhetorical device of *repetitio,* used for emphasis' sake. The accumulation of several gifts serves to illustrate and highlight the rich giftedness of the community. Awareness of this fact is more important than is the determination of the precise nature of any single gift."

73. M. E. Boring, "What Are We Looking For? Toward a Definition of the Term 'Christian Prophet,'" *SBL Seminar Papers* (Missoula, MT: Society of Biblical Literature, 1973), 149, cited in Forbes, *Prophecy and Inspired Speech,* 226-27.

74. Thiselton, 964.

sist of two pairs, each main gift (prophecy and tongues) having a complementary gift having to do with its confirmation or clarification. The gift of *distinguishing between spirits* is most likely that of weighing or evaluating the origin, authority, and application of a prophetic message.[75] Grudem argues against the idea that it has to do with the weighing of prophecies. Quoting Robertson and Plummer, he suggests a more general understanding, such as "the ability to recognize the influence of the Holy Spirit or of demonic spirits in a person."[76] Carson points out that "[s]pectacular displays often attest the power of the spirit world; they do not in themselves attest the power of the Holy Spirit. . . . There is ever a need to distinguish demonic forces from the Holy Spirit. This gift is apparently designed to meet that need."[77] While that may be a primary function of this gift,[78] its placement in this list (following prophecy rather than directly after miracles), and Paul's standard way of pairing prophecy with its evaluation, suggest that this particular application of the gift is foremost in his mind here. Paul will discuss this further in 14:29-30, and the fact that in 14:27-29 Paul discusses tongues and their interpretation as well as prophecy and its weighing strongly supports the suggestion that those are the gifts that he has in mind here as well.[79] He also refers to it in 1 Thessalonians 5:20-21, where he says that prophecies are to be tested. As Thiselton explains, "claims to prophecy must be weighed and tested" since "[w]hile the speaker believes that such utterances or discourses come from the Holy Spirit, mistakes can be made, and . . . believers, including ministers or prophets, remain humanly fallible." Evaluation need not be limited to the two options of divine or demonic origin. Thiselton also points out that it "would go beyond the limits of exegesis to assume that the gift of prophecy belongs any more *permanently* to some specific individual as an 'office' than the gifts of faith or kinds of healings."[80]

The expression *distinguishing between spirits* seems a bit strange to most readers, but Fee points out that Paul uses the term *spirits* "in a much more flexible way than most of us are comfortable with. The Spirit who speaks through the prophets is understood to be speaking through 'the spirit' of the prophet; when Paul is praying in the Spirit, he speaks of 'my spirit' praying (cf. on 5:3-4). The Corinthian zeal for 'spirits' in 14:12, therefore, is zeal for manifestations of the Spirit (esp. tongues) as he quickens their spirits to pray."[81]

75. See the fuller discussion in Thiselton, 965-70.

76. Grudem, *The Gift of Prophecy,* 59.

77. Carson, *Showing the Spirit,* 40. This is in basic agreement with Chrysostom, *Homiliae in Epistulam i ad Corinthios* 29.5 (NPNF[1] 12:172; similarly, Theodoret, 211-12), who believes that it has to do with "knowing who is spiritual, and who is not: who is a prophet, and who a deceiver."

78. Cf. Grudem, *The Gift of Prophecy,* 59-60.

79. So also Fee, 596.

80. Thiselton, 965 (some emphasis removed).

81. Fee, 596-97. Cf. 1 John 4:1.

*to another speaking in different kinds of tongues.* Much has been written about the gift of tongues, especially since the start of the modern charismatic movement. As Fee points out, this is "the 'controversial gift,' both then and now," and based on Paul's argument in chapter 14 it seems that "the Corinthians' singular preference for this manifestation is what lies behind this entire argument."[82] The nature of this gift continues to be greatly debated.[83] Some have argued that it entailed ecstatic babbling or "a kind of sub- or pre-linguistic form of speech, or possibly . . . a kind of coded utterance, analogous but not identical to speech," something "articulate, though in modern terms non-linguistic."[84] As Forbes stresses, while this view may make sense of scientific analyses of the modern practice of glossolalia which have concluded that it does not have the marks of actual language,[85] it "demands rather more linguistic sophistication of Paul than is reasonable." It is doubtful "that Paul, without the benefit of training in modern linguistics, can be expected to conceive of something analoguous to language, possessing cognitive content, but of no recognizable linguistic structure. Such concepts were simply not available to him. If this is what glossolalia actually was, Paul would almost certainly simply have assumed that it was just a (real) language that he did not know."[86]

Thiselton endorses Luke Timothy Johnson's assertion that Paul "could hardly make clearer his conviction that tongues are an intrinsically noncommunicative form of utterance (1 Cor. 13:1; 14:2, 4, 7-9, 16-17, 23)."[87] But it is hard to see how any "intrinsically noncommunicative form of utterance" can be interpreted, even in Thiselton's sense of making articulate something that was inarticulate. Paul does not say that it is "an intrinsically noncommunicative form of utterance" but that it is not understood by mere humans unless it is interpreted (or translated). Those who speak in tongues "do not speak to other people but *to God*" since "no one [else] understands them" (14:2).

Fee and others suggest that Paul has in mind angelic tongues or languages, based on 13:1. That verse seems to contain another embedded par-

82. Fee, 597.

83. For a full discussion see Forbes, *Prophecy and Inspired Speech,* 53-72. Several scholars refer to studies suggesting that the word "tongue" was sometimes used as a technical term for archaic words or phrases. See Heinrici, 382-83; Thiselton, 978; Witherington, 258. This may be true, but it is irrelevant here. The word γλῶσσα ("tongue") was most commonly used for normal and contemporary human languages — not least the Greek language of Paul's day. The only way one could attribute one of the other unusual meanings proposed for the word would be in the light of strong contextual indications — precisely the evidence that is lacking here. How would any ancient reader of this text be expected to know that Paul had such a particular usage in mind without the provision of such linguistic clues?

84. Forbes, *Prophecy and Inspired Speech,* 57.

85. W. J. Samarin, "The Linguisticality of Glossolalia," *Hartford Quarterly* 8 (1968), 49-75.

86. Forbes, *Prophecy and Inspired Speech,* 57 n. 30.

87. Luke Timothy Johnson, "Tongues, Gift of," in *ABD* 6:597, cited by Thiselton, 978.

tial list of gifts (tongues, prophecy, faith, martyrdom), and thus it may serve as an important clue regarding Paul's meaning here. Arguably, the closest parallel to speaking in tongues from ancient texts may be found in the *Testament of Job*, from around the time of the New Testament.[88] There Job's daughters are not given a normal inheritance but a special one of cords or sashes which God had given to Job. When the first daughter, Hemera, wrapped hers around her, she "took on another heart — no longer minded toward earthly things — but she spoke ecstatically [or "spoke out"][89] in the angelic dialect, sending up a hymn to God in accord with the hymnic style of the angels. . . . Then Kasia bound hers on and had her heart changed so that she no longer regarded worldly things. And her mouth took on the dialect of the archons and she praised God for the creation of the heights" (48:1–49:2). The third sister, called Amaltheia's Horn, put hers on, and "her mouth spoke ecstatically [or "spoke out"] in the dialect of those on high, since her heart also was changed, keeping aloof from worldly things. For she spoke in the dialect of the cherubim, glorifying the Master of virtues by exhibiting their splendor" (50:1-2).

This passage has many parallels to New Testament thinking regarding the role of the Spirit in the Christian life, including the Spirit's (and cords') role as a stand-in for or alternative to the expected inheritance (*Testament of Job* 46–47), its effect of changing one's heart (48:2; 49:1; 50:2), and the fact that Job tells his daughter that the cord will "lead you into the better world, to live in the heavens" (47:3). Job also explains how the cords brought healing and prophetic insight to him (47:6-9). Forbes tries to minimize the importance of this parallel by pointing out that it is not clear whether it should be dated before Paul or after him, or even whether the text has suffered Christian interpolations. If the passage is a Christian interpolation or has experienced Christian influence, it would then reflect an early Christian understanding of the sort of phenomenon that was occurring in Corinth and elsewhere. If the text is from before Paul or from around his time, but not based on a Christian interpolation, it would suggest that other Hellenistic Jews were familiar with the idea that followers of the God of Israel might sing praises to God in the tongues of angels. Either way the text would seem to be relevant (as background to the Corinthian experience or the earliest interpretation of experience similar to the Corinthians').

In Luke Timothy Johnson's view, "The obvious problem with this hypothesis is that it is unhelpful for determining the linguistic or psychological dimensions of the speech as it was practiced by early Christians,"[90] but that is hardly a problem for its historical or exegetical likelihood. The

88. In the introduction to his translation of the book in *OTP* 1:829, 833, Russell Spittler argues for a date somewhere in either the first century B.C. or the first century A.D.

89. Gk. ἀποφθέγγομαι, which, according to BDAG, means "to express oneself orally, w. focus on sound rather than content, *speak out, declare.*" See the discussion of this in Forbes, *Prophecy and Inspired Speech,* 183 n. 3 and 163 n. 35.

90. Johnson, "Tongues, Gift of," in *ABD* 6:597.

greater problem with this view is that 1 Corinthians 13:1 is the only place in the Bible that makes any mention of the idea of "angelic languages."[91] But the verse also mentions human languages, and the rhetorical patterns of 13:1-3 suggest that each verse moves from a reference to a normal spiritual gift to a reference to an idealized or extreme version of the same (see the comments there). The only verse that mentions angelic tongues, then, actually provides even stronger evidence that the normal gift was understood to consist of human languages. We cannot rule out the possibility that the Corinthians themselves (if not Paul) thought of the gift of tongues in just such an idealized way. If they were familiar with the ideas found in *Testament of Job* 48–50, they may have understood the phenomenon in their midst to be the same. It seems clear that the Corinthians had a special fascination with this gift. Dale Martin has argued that the ability to speak through spiritual power and not through the use of the mind (such as in ecstatic speech)[92] would have been considered a high-status activity, lending itself to be abused as a sign of spiritual superiority.[93] Clearly the phenomenon in the *Testament of Job* was understood to represent an extraordinary spiritual privilege. Paul's own reference to the insignificance of speaking "in human or angelic tongues" without love in 13:1 suggests that such behavior would generally be associated with a very high level of spirituality (keeping company with a prophetic gift that enables one to "fathom all mysteries and all knowledge" with "a faith that can move mountains," with giving away all one's earthly goods to the poor or even one's very body; 13:2-3). Paul himself may leave open the possibility that tongues could consist of unknown human or *even* angelic languages.

Forbes has provided the strongest exegetical arguments for the view that Paul understands glossolalia to consist of "the miraculous ability to speak unlearned human and (possibly) divine or angelic languages."[94] The most common usage of the word translated *tongues* here is in reference to ordinary human languages.[95] This was Josephus's[96] normal usage and is also

91. It is not clear that any relationship exists between the gift of tongues and Paul's reference to the inward or "wordless groans" of Rom. 8:23, 26.

92. Forbes, *Prophecy and Inspired Speech,* rightly argues against the suggestion that speaking in tongues fit the profile of typical ecstatic speech (in part because the speakers were understood to control themselves enough to follow Paul's guidance regarding appropriate and inappropriate times to speak [as in 14:28-29]). On the other hand, the fact that one's speech was not controlled by one's own mind, and was not even understood by one's own mind (14:14-15), suggests that it could fall into some intermediate category between normal speech and what is normally thought of as ecstatic speech, and would probably be perceived as a special type of high-status inspired speech.

93. See Dale B. Martin, *The Corinthian Body* (New Haven and London: Yale University Press, 1995), 87-103, and his article, "Tongues of Angels and Other Status Indicators," *JAAR* 59 (1991), 547-89.

94. Forbes, *Prophecy and Inspired Speech,* 64.

95. See also Forbes, *Prophecy and Inspired Speech,* 60-61.

96. *Antiquities* 1.34, 284, 305, 333; 2.108; 3.134, 144, 159, 163, 166, 291; 4.73; 5.201, 226,

common in Philo,[97] the LXX, and the New Testament.[98] As pointed out above, 13:1 mentions both human and angelic languages and does so in a way that suggests that the normal phenomenon of glossolalia would have consisted of the speaking of unlearned/unknown human languages (see also the comments on 13:1). Fee and others have argued that Paul's "use of earthly languages as an *analogy* in 14:10-12 implies that it is not a known earthly language, since a thing is not usually identical with that to which it is analogous."[99] Forbes points to the weakness of this argument when he reminds us that "Paul is comparing naturally known languages with what he sees as special gifts of languages."[100] That is, he may be comparing languages that people both speak and understand by normal rational processes with a special and unusual ability to articulate languages without engaging the mind or understanding what they are saying (unless they are also given a separate but related gift). These are not similar phenomena but dissimilar.

All the evidence of chapter 14 seems to be consistent with the understanding of tongues as discourse directed toward God. Paul explicitly says that those who speak in tongues "do not speak to other people but to God" (14:2). He refers to praying in a tongue (14:14), which is the same as praying "with my spirit" (14:14-15). He refers to singing "with my spirit" (14:15) and remarks that "when you are praising God in the Spirit, how can the others . . . say "Amen" to your thanksgiving? . . . You are giving thanks well enough, but the others are not edified" (14:16-17). The ambiguous evidence regarding the exact nature of tongues raises the question of whether even Paul himself or the other earliest Christians knew the exact nature of the phenomenon. Clearly Paul knew that it was a blessing from God that was intended to edify the body of Christ but that was having a negative effect due to the way it was being abused. Evidently experience led him to assume that no one in the congregation was likely to understand the tongues unless God provided someone with a special ability to do so.[101] If 13:1 reflects Paul's view of tongues, it may just as well reflect a lack of precise knowledge, leaving open the issue of whether those speaking might be speaking human or angelic languages.[102]

---

323; 6.22, 302; 7.10, 67; 8.95, 142, 156; 9.283, 290; 10.8, 158, 218, 243f; 11.329; 12.1, 14; 18.228; 19.208; 20.71; *War* 1.3; 3.92; 4.145; 5.151, 272, 361; 6.438; *Against Apion* 1.82, 173; 2.21).

97. *Allegorical Interpretation* 1:69; *On the Posterity of Cain* 93; *On Sobriety* 28, 45; *On the Confusion of Tongues* 68; *On the Life of Abraham* 27, 57; *On the Life of Moses* 2:31; *On the Decalogue* 159; *On the Special Laws* 2:41, 145; *On Rewards and Punishments* 14).

98. Gen. 10:5, 20, 31; 11:7; Zech. 8:23; Isa. 19:18; 28:11; 66:18; Jer. 5:15; Ezek. 3:6; Dan. 3:4, 7; 4:21; 6:26; Jdt. 3:8; Acts 2:11; Rev. 5:9; 7:9; 10:11; 11:9; 13:7; 14:6; 17:15.

99. Fee, 598.

100. Forbes, *Prophecy and Inspired Speech*, 63.

101. Garland (584) thinks that this is a significant assumption on Paul's part since Corinth was quite a metropolitan city where one could expect to find people from all kinds of language backgrounds. The Corinthian church would have been small enough, however, that the actual number of languages known to the members would have been limited.

102. Acts 2:26 may possibly suggest that tongues-speaking was understood as a par-

Much of our fascination with this gift probably misses the point. Whether modern tongues-speaking is the same as that practiced in Corinth or not (and regardless of the nature of ancient or modern tongue-speaking) the key questions have to do with whether a Christian congregation recognizes it as a gift from God that can be used in public to strengthen (build up) the body of Christ or in private for personal edification. Given Paul's emphasis on the diversity of gifts that God was showering on the church (and can be expected to shower on the church) for its well-being, we cannot be content simply to try to understand the experience of the ancient Corinthian church but must be prepared to recognize the gifts God may be giving to members of our own congregations (be they the same or different from those given in Corinth) and to sort out how they might best be employed for the building up of the whole body of Christ.

*and to still another the interpretation of tongues.* Just as prophecy was (and is) to be weighed and evaluated, tongues need to be interpreted. Sustained debate continues over the meaning of the word translated "interpretation."[103] Thiselton has argued that in over 75 percent of the cases, it (and related terms) "refers to the articulation of thoughts or feelings in intelligible speech"[104] and that in Philo and Josephus the word was sometimes used "to mean the capacity to express in *words* or articulate speech wonders which had otherwise left a person speechless, or able to react only emotively with awe or joy."[105] Thiselton does not argue that it must mean that here, but that it may (and that the context suggests it does). He contends that it "means to *translate* only when the context clearly relates to translation."[106] The whole argument seems to assume that Paul knew the phenomenon that he and his churches experienced was a nonlinguistic reality, a sort of verbal but inarticulate communicate of emotional and psychological feelings and longings. That may be a matter of letting Romans 8 play a greater role in the exegesis of 1 Corinthians 12–14 than it should, especially since 1 Corinthians 13:1 seems to suggest that Paul has some

---

ticipation in the rejoicing of Christ's tongue in his postresurrection life. Acts 2:4, 16-19 and 19:6 understand speaking in tongues (along with prophecy) as a fulfillment of Joel 2:28-32 (3:1-5), although it is not mentioned explicitly in the latter text. Speaking in tongues and prophesying will be the two gifts on which Paul focuses in ch. 14. Acts 2:4-11 has the story of a clear but unique case of "speaking in other tongues," which was clearly understood to be a case of *xenoglossia,* speaking unknown human languages. Luke Timothy Johnson argues that "a careful reading indicates that the miracle consisted precisely in the *hearing,* not the mode of speaking" (Johnson, "Tongues, Gift of," in *ABD* 6:597). But this ignores the fact that v. 4 states that they were speaking in different languages (λαλεῖν ἑτέραις γλώσσαις) and also ignores the simple explanation (provided by the text itself) that the reason people *heard* the Galileans speaking in all those different languages (vv. 8, 11) was that the Spirit had enabled those Galileans to *speak* in them (v. 4).

103. Gk. ἑρμηνεία.

104. Anthony C. Thiselton, "The 'Interpretation' of Tongues? A New Suggestion in the Light of Greek Usage in Philo and Josephus," *JTS* 30 (1979), 18, cited in Thiselton, 976.

105. Thiselton, 976.

106. Thiselton, 976.

kind(s) of language(s) in mind (human and/or angelic). In a case where what is being interpreted (or translated) are "tongues" or "languages"[107] rather than sighs, groanings, or some other thing, preference should probably be given to the suggestion that the term refers to the translation or interpretations of whatever language is being spoken.[108]

**12:11** In concluding this part of his argument Paul goes back to themes he emphasized in vv. 4-9: *All these are the work of one and the same Spirit, and he distributes them to each one, just as he determines. All these* recalls "all of them" in v. 6[109] and stresses (esp. by being placed first in the sentence) the diversity of gifts listed in the previous verses. It should not be taken to imply that the list given was a complete one since Paul will mention other gifts later in this same section of the letter. The *work* recalls the use of the same word for "work" in v. 6.[110] There God was the subject of the verb. The alternation here suggests that we should not think that Paul sees a hard-and-fast distinction between the roles of the persons of the Trinity. *One and the same Spirit* recalls "the same Spirit" in v. 4[111] and reaffirms the same motif found in vv. 5-6 ("the same Lord," "the same God") and in the five references to the work of the Spirit in vv. 7-9.[112] *He distributes them* (or "allots them") recalls "different kinds" (or "allotments"), repeated three times in vv. 4-6, which introduced this theme.[113] *To each one* recalls the same expression in v. 7[114] and also refers back to the references in vv. 8-10: "To one . . . to another . . . to another . . . to another . . . to another . . . to another . . . to another . . . to still another. . . ."[115] As a whole the verse puts great stress on three main points. First, *All these,* that is, the diversity of gifts, is stressed by being placed in front. Secondly, the singular origin of all the gifts in the initiative and governing role of the Spirit is stressed by the use of the dual modifiers, *one and the same* Spirit (when either one would have normally been sufficient) and by the three different verbs which are all governed by the Spirit (literally, "[the Spirit] works . . . distrib-

107. In Greek we are dealing with the ἑρμηνεία γλωσσῶν. The collocation of these two words in this way is likely to suggest the translation or interpretation of some sort of language, despite Thiselton's objection that "appeals to the 'normal' use of γλῶσσα to mean *language*" are inappropriate "when we are hardly discussing 'normal' uses of the term!" Whether or not we are dealing with a normal use of the term is subject to debate, and the collocation of these two terms in this way is an important datum to be considered in that debate.

108. BDAG indicates that although the word can mean "interpretation," its most likely meaning here is "translation," a meaning found also in *Berliner Griechische Urkunden* 326 I, 1; II, 15; Papyrus Oxyrhyncus 1466, 3; Sir. prologue 20; *Letter of Aristeas* 3, 11, etc.; Justin.

109. Gk. τὰ πάντα in v. 6 and πάντα ταῦτα here.

110. Gk. ἐνεργέω in both cases.

111. Gk. τὸ δὲ αὐτὸ πνεῦμα in v. 4 and τὸ ἓν καὶ τὸ αὐτὸ πνεῦμα here.

112. "of the Spirit . . . through the Spirit . . . by means of the same Spirit . . . by the same Spirit . . . by that one Spirit."

113. The verb used here (διαιρέω) is related to the noun used at the start of vv. 4, 5, and 6 (διαίρεσις). "Distributes them" in the TNIV of v. 4 is a clarification of the meaning where Paul elided (omitted) a verb.

114. Gk. ἑκάστῳ in each case. See also ἐν πᾶσιν in v. 6.

115. Alternating in Greek between ἄλλῳ and ἑτέρῳ.

utes . . . determines").[116] Thirdly, that the gifts are distributed on a strictly individual basis is stressed by the two words translated *each one*[117] (where either would have been sufficient).

Thiselton points to the connection between this passage and the next: "If no single individual is likely to receive the full range of the gifts of the Spirit, each needs others also; hence 12:12-31 expound this principle."[118]

### *iv. Exposition and application of the church's identity as Christ's body, 12:12-31*

The remainder of this chapter deals with the understanding of the church as Christ's body. Verses 12-14 introduce the theme with an emphasis on the idea that one body has many parts. Verses 15-26 focus on the interdependence of all the parts of the body, with vv. 15-20 approaching the subject from the perspective of those who perceive themselves to be inferior members of the community and with vv. 21-26 approaching the subject from the perspective of those who perceive themselves to be superior members of the community. Verses 27-31 complete this section by reinforcing the point that each believer is a member of the body (v. 27), highlighting a number of functions members might have within the body (v. 28) and the fact that no function is carried out by all members of the body (vv. 29-30), and by introducing the idea of proper priorities in thinking about the pursuit and use of the gifts (v. 31).

#### 1) Introduction of the Analogy: Like a Human Body, Christ's Body Has Many Parts, 12:12-14

Paul uses the body as a metaphor for the relationship between the various members of the church. He introduces the metaphor in v. 12 and provides the theological foundation for it in v. 13. Finally, he reiterates the original point in v. 14.

> [12]*Just as a body, though one, has many parts, but all its many parts form one body, so it is with Christ.* [13]*For we were all baptized by*[119] *one Spirit so as to form one body — whether Jews or Gentiles, slave or free — and we were all given the one Spirit to drink.* [14]*Even so the body is not made up of one part but of many.*

**12:12** Paul's opening word, *just as,*[120] makes it clear that he is using the body as an analogy or metaphor for understanding the relationship between the diverse members of the Christian community. As Garland sug-

116. Gk. ἐνεργεῖ . . . διαιροῦν . . . βούλεται.
117. Gk. ἰδίᾳ ἑκάστῳ, "individually, to each one" (cf. Thiselton, 989).
118. Thiselton, 989 (bold emphasis omitted).
119. Or *with;* or *in.*
120. Gk. καθάπερ.

gests, *so it is with Christ* "is awkward only because 'Christ' is shorthand for the church as the body of Christ (12:28). He leaves it to the reader to complete the thought: Just as the body has many limbs and organs and despite their number and differences make up one body, so Christ's body has many limbs and organs and despite their number and differences make up one body."[121] Thiselton reminds us that "Christ remains the main *subject* whom the rhetoric serves" and that he also "retains an emphatic position as a nominative at the end of the long sentence."[122]

The word translated *parts*[123] is often translated "members" (e.g., NRSV, NET, NASB, ESV). The latter is a perfectly appropriate translation as long as it is kept in mind that "member" in this case would mean a part or organ of the human body and not "member" in the sense of a member of a social organization or church-member. Given that the social meaning is more common in popular English usage, the choice of the TNIV and some others (including the NAB, NIV, NJB, NLT) is a wise one. Paul is not the first to use the body as a metaphor to explain the nature of a social group. In fact, it was a very common rhetorical device.[124] However, Paul's use of it is significantly different from the way it was typically employed. Dale Martin points out that "[w]hereas traditionally the body analogy is invoked to solidify an unquestioned status hierarchy, Paul's rhetoric questions that hierarchy" in 12:22-25.[125]

Stress is placed on the paradox of the one and the many, with both terms repeated. In fact, the middle of the verse consists of a bit of synonymous parallelism in the form of a chiasm:

A *a body, though one,*
  B *has many parts;*
  B′ *all its many parts*
A′ *form one body.*

It is important to stress that the body metaphor or analogy is not used to impose uniformity upon the church. "There is unity in plurality, but not uniformity. Individual integrity remains."[126] Indeed, Paul's "insistence that a functioning body needs diverse body parts . . . reminds us of the need to distinguish and not equate solidarity and sameness."[127]

The following verse also points to a theological justification (rather than a merely pragmatic one) for the use of the body analogy, and suggests that the comparison is a proper one due to real ontological parallels be-

121. Garland, 590. So also Fee, 693, and others.
122. Thiselton, 996 (his emphasis).
123. Gk. μέλη, the plural of μέλος.
124. See M. M. Mitchell, *Paul and the Rhetoric of Reconciliation*, 157-64.
125. D. B. Martin, *The Corinthian Body*, 94.
126. Garland, 590.
127. Horrell, *Solidarity and Difference*, 122.

tween the nature of the human body and the nature of the church. The image of the church as the body of Christ was raised already in 10:17 and 11:29, and part of its basis may already have been hinted at in 6:16-17. We will comment a bit further on the possible theological background for the idea in the following verse. The thought of the many varied body parts, and a potentially disjointed mix of them, may have been common in Corinth, where archeological excavations of the temple of Ascelpius (the Greek god of healing) have unearthed a "huge number of terra cotta ex-votos [i.e., votive offerings] representing heads, hands and feet, arms and legs, breasts and genitals, eyes and ears" which represented ailing body parts for which the god was credited with healing.[128]

**12:13-14** *For we were all baptized by*[129] *one Spirit so as to form one body — whether Jews or Gentiles, slave or free — and we were all given the one Spirit to drink. Even so the body is not made up of one part but of many.* Verse 13 has several exegetical problems. One has to do with whether we are baptized *by one* Spirit (NASB, NIV, TNIV, NLT), or in(to) one Spirit (ESV, NAB, NET, NJB, NRSV; cf. TNIV marginal note).[130] Another is whether we are baptized in/by the Spirit *so as to form* one body (TNIV) or whether we are baptized in/by the Spirit into one body (virtually all other English translations).[131] Finally, the verb translated *given . . . to drink*[132] is interpreted in a variety of ways. Carson suggests that here the word means to flood or pour out, as in irrigation. In support of this he points out that a "connection between this verb and Spirit is found in only one other biblical passage (Isa. 29:10 [LXX]) where it bears this meaning." He concludes that our text should be translated, "we were all drenched [or flooded]."[133] Hays considers it "a vivid expression for Paul's conviction that the one Spirit has been given in overflowing abundance to everyone in the community."[134] Gerhard Schneider thinks that Paul's use of this verb "presupposes that the Spirit can be 'poured out' (cf. Acts 2:17; Joel 3:1 LXX)." While some see a connection with the Lord's Supper, he thinks that "Paul is probably thinking more of baptism . . . than of the eucharist."[135] Paul's statement that the Corinthians were all baptized into one body and were all given the one Spirit to drink

128. Jerome Murphy-O'Connor, *St. Paul's Corinth*, 190.

129. Or *with;* or *in.*

130. Gk. ἐν ἑνὶ πνεύματι. The preposition could point to the sphere into which one is baptized or introduce the agent through which the action is carried out. Wallace, *Greek Grammar beyond the Basics*, 375, argues for the latter.

131. Gk. εἰς ἓν σῶμα. The preposition εἰς may suggest the sphere into which one is baptized or the goal toward which the action is intended to lead. The translation *so as to form one body* may also suggest that the baptism establishes the body rather than introduces such people into a body that already existed beforehand. The latter idea is unlikely (see Carson, *Showing the Spirit*, 44).

132. Gk. ποτίζω.

133. Carson, *Showing the Spirit*, 46.

134. Hays, 214.

135. Gerhard Schneider, "ποτίζω," *EDNT* 3:142.

(v. 13) seems to echo his interpretive description of Israel's exodus and wilderness experience in 10:2-4. The Israelites were all "baptized into Moses" and drank the same spiritual drink" (cf. Ps. 78:15 [77:15]).[136]

Carson points out that if the Spirit is the agent of the baptism here, this would be the only place in the New Testament where that was so. "In the other six instances, related to the prophecy of John the Baptist, Christ as the agent does the baptizing, and the Holy Spirit is the medium or sphere in which we are baptized. Moreover, whenever the verb *baptize* is used in the New Testament, it is the *medium* of the baptism — water, fire, cloud, and so forth — that is expressed using this preposition . . . , not the *agent*.[137] It is remarkable, though, that a Greek father like Chrysostom seems to assume without hesitation that Paul is referring to the Spirit as the one who baptizes us.[138]

Fee is probably right to suggest that Paul's lines,

*For we were all baptized by [or "in"] one Spirit . . .*
*and we were all given the one Spirit to drink,*

reflect "a piece of semitic parallelism, where both clauses make essentially the same point."[139] If these two statements are to be read in light of each other, the drinking or drenching with the Spirit is the experience of the Spirit that is also referred to as the baptism by or of the Spirit here and elsewhere. All of this is our experience as believers now that the Spirit has been poured out as the prophets promised (Isa. 32:15; 44:3; Ezek. 39:29; Joel 2:28-29).

While those two statements stand out in our English translation (thanks to our consistent placement of prepositional phrases), the syntactical parallel is not as clear in Greek,[140] although the conceptual parallel

136. Gk. πάντες τὸ αὐτὸ πνευματικὸν ἔπιον πόμα.

137. Carson, *Showing the Spirit*, 47. The Greek preposition referred to is ἐν. So also Hays, 214: "The Spirit is not the agent who does the baptizing, but the figurative element into which the new converts were immersed, being plunged into a new world of Spirit-experience" (cf. James D. G. Dunn, *Baptism in the Holy Spirit: A Re-examination of the New Testament Teaching on the Gift of the Spirit in Relation to Pentecostalism Today* (Philadelphia: Westminster, 1970), 128.

138. This despite the fact that the translator renders the preposition ἐν as "in." Chrysostom (*Homiliae in Epistulam i ad Corinthios* 30.2 [NPNF[1] 12:176]) says that Paul's "meaning is this: that which established us to become one body and regenerated us, is one Spirit: for not in/by [ἐν] one Spirit was one baptized, and another [in] another. And not only is that which has baptized us one, but also that unto which He baptized us, i.e., for which He baptized us, is one. . . . So that both He who formed it is one, and that into which He formed it is one." The point seems to be that both the agent of the baptism (namely, the Spirit) and the sphere into which we were baptized (namely, the body) are one. Theodoret, 202, commenting on this verse, says, "we were all renewed by one Spirit" (ὑφ' ἑνὸς ἅπαντες ἐνεουργήθημεν Πνεύματος).

139. Fee, 604 (see 603-4).

140. Gk. καὶ γὰρ ἐν ἑνὶ πνεύματι ἡμεῖς πάντες εἰς ἓν σῶμα ἐβαπτίσθημεν,
καὶ πάντες ἓν πνεῦμα ἐποτίσθημεν.

should probably be recognized. In Greek the parallel between the lines referring to the body and the Spirit is at least as strong. Literally:

"We all into one body were baptized
and all one Spirit were given-to-drink."[141]

This may reflect part of Paul's logic. The new humanity into which we have been incorporated reflects standard biblical anthropology: it consists of one body indwelt by one spirit (which in this case happens to be the Holy Spirit). We have all been baptized into the same Spirit and therefore into the same body. Earlier in this very letter (10:2), Paul used the same preposition used here with respect to the baptism into[142] (TNIV, *so as to form*) the body. There he spoke of baptism "into Moses," where (the covenant and people of) Moses is understood to represent the body or sphere into which the Israelites were baptized. In Romans 6:3 and Galatians 3:27 Paul uses the same preposition again to speak of being baptized "into Christ," who represents the new sphere of covenantal life into which we are introduced by the Spirit. In all the other New Testament cases where the verb "to baptize" is used with the preposition "into," used here in relation to the body, some form of water baptism seems to be in mind,[143] even though in most cases the preposition does not refer to the element into which the people are baptized, but the sphere or reality into which they enter through their water baptism. This is not to say that their water baptism accomplishes these things, but there was such a close and intimate association between baptism and conversion that references to the former could serve to point to all that was entailed in the latter by way of synecdoche.

Both *one* and *all* are stressed in this verse, with *one* occurring three times and *all* twice. There is a spiritual solidarity that exists between believers due to the fact that they *all* have experienced the same *(one)* Spirit and entered the same *(one)* body. As Fape puts it, Paul seeks "to validate the conversion experience of all believers in the sense of experiencing in full an inward spiritual transformation" which is "a common experience that comes from the Spirit of God." That is, "conversion is a universal experience for all believers and it is rooted in the activities of the one Spirit of God."[144]

There has been much speculation about the source of Paul's identification of the church as the body of Christ. Seyoon Kim has argued that two of the elements that may have contributed to Paul's conception are Jewish

141. Gk. ἡμεῖς πάντες εἰς ἓν σῶμα ἐβαπτίσθημεν,
καὶ πάντες ἓν πνεῦμα ἐποτίσθημεν.

142. Gk. εἰς. See p. 591 n. 131.

143. Gk. βαπτίζω + εἰς. Cf. Mark 1:9; Acts 19:3, 5; Rom. 6:3; 1 Cor. 1:13, 15; 10:2; 12:13; Gal. 3:27 and M. Olusina Fape, *Paul's Concept of Baptism and Its Present Implications for Believers: Walking in the Newness of Life* (Toronto Studies in Theology 28; Lewiston, NY: Mellen, 1999), 127.

144. Fape, *Paul's Concept of Baptism,* 133.

mystical *(merkabah)* speculation about the measurement of the body of the "likeness of a man" in Ezekiel 1:26 and about other visionary figures (including the one "like a son of man" in Daniel 7) and their roles as representatives of Israel.[145]

Fee suspects that "this is not simply an *ad hoc* theological construct, but rather is inserted precisely because it reflects the heart of Pauline theology. What makes the Corinthians one is their common experience of the Spirit, the very Spirit responsible for and manifested in the great diversity just argued for in vv. 4-11."[146] Paul seems to give potentially clearer hints regarding the background in a few related texts. In 1 Corinthians 6:15-17 he asks, "Do you not know that your bodies are members of Christ himself?" That our bodies are members of Christ is known since "whoever is united with the Lord is one with him in spirit." The language of this last clause is built out of the previous sentence about one "who unites himself with a prostitute" and becomes "one with her in body" on the basis of Genesis 2:24: "The two will become one flesh." The same word for "unite"[147] is used in both cases. The concept of a union in or through (the) "S/spirit"[148] and the association with Genesis 2:24 are suggestive, and the explicit reference to the members of Christ's body is important, as well as Paul's easy alternation between "flesh" and "body." Genesis 2:24 is also cited in Ephesians 5:31, where it also justifies Paul's statement "for we are members of his body" (5:30). Paul goes on to indicate that his quotation of Genesis 2:24, while clearly applied to the husband-wife relationship in Ephesians 5:28-33, also applies to "Christ and the church" (5:32).[149] In 1 Corinthians 10:17 Paul said, "[b]ecause there is one loaf, we, who are many, are one body, for we all partake of the one loaf." In the verse just prior to that he indicated that "the bread that we break" is "a participation in the body of Christ" (10:16). The parallels between this verse and Galatians 3:27-28 have already been mentioned. In that text Paul says, "all of you who were baptized into Christ have clothed yourselves with Christ." Thus, "There is neither Jew nor Gentile, neither slave nor free, neither male nor female, for you are all one in Christ Jesus."

These various texts, taken together, suggest that one is united with Christ by the Spirit in baptism[150] in a way which is analogous to the union

145. Seyoon Kim, *The Origin of Paul's Gospel* (WUNT 2.4; Tübingen: J. C. B. Mohr, 1984), 252-56.

146. Fee, 603.

147. Gk. κολλάω.

148. In the Greek, of course, there is no orthographic distinction between "spirit" and "Spirit."

149. Gen. 2:24 may also be echoed in Eph. 2:14-15 in the language of two people becoming one (Christ "has made the two one"; his purpose was "to create in himself one new humanity [or "man"] out of the two").

150. Whether Spirit baptism and/or water baptism need not detain us since both were associated with the conversion experience, with the latter serving as "the outward and visible sign" of the former (Bruce, 121, cited in Carson, *Showing the Spirit*, 43).

of man and woman into one flesh or body (Gen. 2:24). All share one S/spirit and therefore have been incorporated into one new man who partakes of the resurrection life in which the former distinctions no longer carry the same significance. All those who have been united to Christ have become part of the same body — Christ's body. Wright points out that "[w]hen [Paul] develops his picture of the church as the body of the Messiah, he seems to be aware that this is not a metaphor chosen at random." Rather,

> what the creator god has accomplished in and through Jesus is the renewal of the human race, that for which humankind was made in the first place. What better image, then, to use for its corporate life than that of a human body, with limbs and organs working as they were meant to do? The present unity of the church is important not least because it will thereby anticipate the perfect harmony of the resurrection world, when members of the *soma Christou*, the Messiah's body, who have each exercised their *pneumatika*, spiritual gifts, are finally raised to life, to be given the *soma pneumatikon* (15.44-46), the entire body energized and animated by the divine Spirit.[151]

There may be some relationship between Paul's understanding of the church as the Spirit-indwelt temple of God and Jesus' identification of his body with God's temple (Matt. 26:61; 27:40; Mark 14:58; 15:29; John 2:19-21). Elsewhere we learn that the body is something intended to be offered to God in worship (Rom. 6:13, 19; 12:1; 1 Cor. 6:13-20). This idea is probably related to the understanding that the Spirit inhabits the body, as he does the temple, and leads it to worship God (1 Cor. 3:16-17; 6:19). Paul's descriptions of the church as temple and body are interrelated.

This verse may reflect very early baptismal tradition similar to that found in Galatians 3:27-28. Other early Christian texts also "reflect a similar tradition in referring to the ways in which various kinds of opposites become united as one." Furthermore, "the conviction that Paul is drawing on such a tradition in these two texts is strengthened by the observation that the pairs he cites [i.e., Jews/Gentiles, slave/free] in each case are not all of particular relevance to their epistolary contexts."[152] Those pairs "express the two basic distinctions that separated people in that culture — race/religion and social status."[153] In 7:18-22 Paul cites these distinctions as ones that one should not commit oneself to eliminating, but it is clear that part of the reason why they need not be eliminated is that they have lost any ultimate significance (and therefore it would be a mistake to focus one's energy on them one way or another). To these pairs Paul adds that of "male and female" in Galatians 3:27-28 (from Gen. 1:27). Garland notes that it is

151. N. T. Wright, *The Resurrection of the Son of God*, 295.

152. Horrell, *Solidarity and Difference*, 104.

153. Fee, 606.

likely that this pair (male and female) was omitted here because the church's primary division was sociological.[154]

Thiselton rightly stresses that all believers participate in the new identity established by the experience referred to in this verse, "whatever the variety and difference of their pre-Christian status (or 'natural' status) as Jews or Gentiles, or as slaves or freepeople. Any theology that might imply that this one baptism in 13a in which believers were baptized by [or in] one Spirit might mark off some postconversion experience or status enjoyed only by some Christians attacks and undermines Paul's entire argument and emphasis. Paul's constant use of . . . one, and . . . all,[155] constitutes a direct onslaught against categorization or elitism within the church."[156] Garland speaks eloquently to this point: "What may polarize the world does not or should not divide the church. The segmentation of the Corinthian congregation into cliques is the by-product of human depravity and spurs individuals to treat their differing spiritual experiences as a pretext for reinstating class divisions — now employing spiritual classifications — so as to elevate themselves over others."[157] The baptism in or by the Spirit which Paul speaks of here is an experience common to all believers, to all those who are part of the body of Christ. The variety of gifts mentioned in this and other passages suggests that believers may have very different experiences of God and his Spirit, but the thrust of Paul's whole argument here is that any hint that some believers are second-class Christians because they have not shared some experience that another group has must be utterly rejected. Christians may not only have different gifts, but also different experiences of God. A recognition that God gives different gifts to different believers and that he might manifest himself in one person's life differently from the way he does in another's should lead to a greater respect for the authenticity of another believer's relationship with God, even if it happens to manifest itself somewhat differently than one's own. In v. 14 Paul simply reiterates the point he made in v. 12 and justified in v. 13: *Even so the body is not made up of one part but of many.* As the Geneva Bible paraphrases it, "The unity of the body is not prevented by this diversity of members, and furthermore it could not be a body if it did not consist of many members, and those being different."

### 2) Exposition of Implications for Powerful Members of the Body: You Need Me, 12:15-20

This section and the next are marked by the personification of body parts which are given lines expressing either the view that they themselves do

154. Garland, 592. Others have argued that Paul omitted the reference to the two genders due to concerns that his teaching on the subject had contributed to the problems discussed in 11:2-16 (so Hays, 214).

155. Gk. ἕν and πάντες.

156. Thiselton, 997 (emphases removed).

157. Garland, 592.

not belong to the body (vv. 15-20) or that they do not need the other parts of the body (vv. 21-27). Paul's statements in vv. 18 and 24 and the intervening text affirm God as the creator of the human body, whose design reflects his wisdom (Gen. 2:7; Ps. 139:14-15). The wisdom of the church's body-like function reflects God's wisdom in creating the human body.

Paul is not the first person to personify the body parts and give them speech. In the fifth century B.C., Menenius Agrippa gave a famous speech to persuade the plebeians to end their revolt against the patricians. In that speech he described the functioning of a city-state by analogy with a human body. The speech is passed on to us by the first-century-B.C. Greek historian and rhetorician Dionysius of Halicarnassus among others. Menenius Agrippa is recorded as arguing as follows (*Antiquitates Romanae* 6.86.1-4):

> A commonwealth resembles in some measure a human body. For each of them is composite and consists of many parts; and no one of their parts either has the same function or performs the same service as the others. If, now, these parts of the human body should be endowed, each for itself, with perception and a voice of its own and a sedition should then arise among them, all of them uniting against the belly alone, and the feet should say that the whole body rests on them; the hands, that they ply the crafts, secure provisions, fight with enemies, and contribute many other advantages toward the common good; the shoulders, that they bear all the burdens; the mouth, that it speaks; the head, that it sees and hears and, comprehending the other senses, possesses all those by which the thing is preserved; and then all these should say to the belly, 'And you, good creature, which of these things do you do? What return do you make and of what use are you to us? Indeed, you are so far from doing anything for us or assisting us in accomplishing anything useful for the common good that you are actually a hindrance and a trouble to us and — a thing intolerable — compel us to serve you and to bring things to you from everywhere for the gratification of your desires. Come now, why do we not assert our liberty and free ourselves from the many troubles we undergo for the sake of this creature?' If, I say, they should decide upon this course and none of the parts should any longer perform its office, could the body possibly exist for any considerable time, and not rather be destroyed within a few days by the worst of all deaths, starvation? No one can deny it. Now consider the same condition existing in a commonwealth. For this also is composed of many classes of people not at all resembling one another, every one of which contributes some particular service to the common good, just as its members do to the body.[158]

158. *The Roman Antiquities of Dionysius of Halicarnassus*, vol. 4, trans. Earnest Cary (LCL 364; Cambridge, MA: Harvard University Press; London: W. Heinemann, 1943), 109, 111. See also M. M. Mitchell, *Paul and the Rhetoric of Reconciliation*, 157-60. Livy, *History of Rome* 2.32.7-33.1, records a more concise version. The illustration of the interdependence of

From there he identifies the city council or senate with the stomach, which is nourished by all the other body parts and "duly distributes that which is beneficial to each and all."[159] Similarly, the senate "administers the affairs of the public and provides what is expedient for everyone." The role of the city council here is remarkably similar to that of God (12:18, 24, 28) or the Holy Spirit (12:8, 9, 11) in Paul's thought, with a key distinction being that in Dionysius's use of the analogy the city council represents the stomach which is a part of the body, and which needs to be defended from the perception that its role is self-serving (thus preserving the status quo). In Paul's discussion God/the Holy Spirit is obviously not a part of the body, but distributes the members/gifts within the body for the well-being of the body itself.[160] Of course, as Witherington points out, "Paul, unlike the Stoics or Seneca, uses the body imagery to speak not of a natural unity of all humans or of the republic, but of a community that is a supernaturally created unity with diversity, the product of God's creative Spirit."[161] Paul "is concerned about the pride of the so-called superior members."[162] He does not use the body metaphor to convince the "weak" members to give rather than withhold their support for the "strong," but rather he "urges the strong (probably the well-to-do) to give more honor and respect to the weak, and so cease their fractious behavior."[163]

> [15]*Now if the foot should say, "Because I am not a hand, I do not belong to the body," it would not for that reason cease to be part of the body.* [16]*And if the ear should say, "Because I am not an eye, I do not belong to the body," it would not for that reason cease to be part of the body.* [17]*If the whole body were an eye, where would the sense of hearing be? If the whole body were an ear, where would the sense of smell be?* [18]*But in fact God has placed the parts in the body, every one of them, just as he wanted them to be.* [19]*If they were all one part, where would the body be?* [20]*As it is, there are many parts, but one body.*

**12:15-17** There is some question regarding the proper punctuation of vv. 15 and 16. The standard Greek texts punctuate the last part of each verse as a rhetorical question: "would it for that reason cease to be part of

---

the parts of the body is also mentioned by Cicero, *De Officiis* 3.5.22; and Plutarch, *Marcius Coriolanus* 6. Garland, 593 n. 5, thinks that this fable "is probably more familiar to commentators than it was to the original recipients of the letter," but given the number and diversity of references in ancient Greco-Roman literature, it would be surprising if it were not rather well known. Plutarch refers to it as a "celebrated fable" (*Coriolanus* 6.4).

159. Gk. τὸ πρόσφορον ἁπάντων.

160. According to Dionysius, the city council or senate (βουλή) distributes the city's resources as it sees fit, while in Paul's understanding the Holy Spirit distributes the gifts to the members of the church as he wills (καθὼς βούλεται).

161. Witherington, 261.

162. Garland, 594.

163. Witherington, 253-54.

the body?" There are three other rhetorical questions in this paragraph: two in v. 17 and one more in v. 19. The three rhetorical questions in vv. 17 and 19 are all clearly marked by the interrogative pronoun, "where?"[164] while there is no similar marking in vv. 15-16. In fact, one would expect a different marker if a question were intended.[165] The vast majority of English translations translate these texts as assertions. Fortunately, the meaning is the same either way, even if the rhetorical feel is slightly different.

Paul uses two extremities (the foot and hand) and two sensory organs of the head (the ear and eye) as examples of body parts that could potentially be considered of inferior value but which must recognize themselves to be every bit a part of a whole body as any other and of tremendous importance for the proper functioning and full health of the body.[166] Fee points out that "[i]n both cases these parts carry on comparable functions in the body; there is no hint that one is superior to the other."[167] He goes further to argue against Grosheide and others who hold that some parts consider themselves or other parts inferior. "Neither in the analogy itself nor in Paul's own application (vv. 17-20) is there a hint that one of these is superior to the other. That comes in the second application (and then he allows that it is only apparent), but it is totally lacking here, where the parts are of the same kind in each case (limbs, sensory organs)."[168] In fact, it is "precisely this kind of application, based on the metaphor alone, that seems to do injustice to Paul's own concern."[169] But he has no explanation for why one body part would say something like what is attributed to the foot or the ear. He simply observes that those statements (of the foot and ear) are "obviously absurd."[170] This seems to unnecessarily divorce this text from its context and to dismiss a logical inference. The ear feels that it would be part of the body if it were an eye and the foot feels the same about the hand. Fee is right to say that Paul's words hardly suggest that the foot is inferior to

164. Gk. ποῦ.

165. Normally we would expect μή rather than οὐ to mark a rhetorical question that expects a negative or hesitant answer. Cf. Thiselton, 1003. BDAG defines μή as a "marker of expectation of a negative answer to a question," although it also points out that in some cases (such as Rom. 10:18-19; 1 Cor. 9:4-5) "μή is an interrog[ative] word and οὐ negates the verb. The double negative causes one to expect an affirmative answer." Thus, we must weigh the possibility that the avoidance of μή could be intended to preserve the expectation of a negative answer.

166. Paul employs what are known as third-class conditional structures in vv. 15-16. These are marked by the use of ἐάν with a subjunctive verb in the protasis (with virtually any verb form in the apodosis). The third class is a "more tentative" conditional structure which "simply projects some action or event for hypothetical consideration" (Porter, *Idioms of the Greek New Testament*, 262). Paul encourages the Corinthians to consider and learn from the hypothetical scenarios he presents with the body metaphor.

167. Fee, 610.

168. Fee, 610 n. 10.

169. Fee, 610.

170. Fee, 610.

the hand or that the ear is inferior to the eye, but their hypothetical statements indicate that those members, absurdly perhaps, do feel inferior.[171] And v. 21 certainly does suggest that some parts consider others to be unnecessary. Fee admits that "many others" see it this way,[172] but does not think that the Corinthians would have. Given the social issues that most commentators see behind the Corinthians' problems, it seems unlikely that they would not have read Paul's comments the way so many other interpreters have. This does not mean that Fee's suggestion that the analogy points to "the disquieting desire on the part of many to be something in the body other than what they are" is not apropos, or his suggestion that this "is a plague on our house."[173] We are reminded, however, that "the ear does not say that it wants to be an eye, and the foot does not say that it wants to become a hand."[174] They merely state that since they are not eyes or hands, they do not belong to the body. The implication is that they do not really matter. This may reflect a fundamental perception that one's place in the larger scheme of things is predetermined and unalterable. In our own Western society we may be more likely to aspire to becoming the equivalent of eyes or hands. In many cultures and contexts the simple sense of being an outsider with no hope or contemplation of becoming an insider may be more common.

As pointed out above, the personification of human organs was not new to Paul, but had been done before, at least by Menenius Agrippa in the passage cited above, which shares some interesting parallels to Paul's thought. One of the parallels is in the speaking foot, with Dionysius's "if . . . the feet should say . . ." (*Antiquitates Romanae* 6.86.2) paralleling Paul's *if the foot should say* . . . (12:15). In Dionysius's case the feet participate in sedition against the stomach and seem to have an exalted sense of their own self-importance. In our text the foot seems to suffer from a sense of inferiority or a crisis of identity. It thinks that it is not a part of the body because it is not a hand (v. 15a). The ear feels the same way because it is not an eye (v. 16a). "[E]ars that constantly hear someone say how beautiful the eyes are can

171. "In both cases the inferior member seems to suppose that the superior member certainly must belong to the body" (Grosheide, 294).

172. Fee, 610 n. 10. Chrysostom is among them (cf. *Homiliae in Epistulam i ad Corinthios* 30.3 [NPNF[1] 12:177]). For other ancient interpreters who understood Paul similarly, see also the comments of Theodoret of Cyrus, Severian of Gabala, and Ambrosiaster in Bray, 125.

173. Fee, 610. So also G. Deluz, *A Companion to 1 Corinthians* (Eng. trans., London: Darton, Longman & Todd, 1963), 179-80 (cited by Thiselton, 1004): "Christians must give up anxiously comparing themselves with each other. . . . It leads to jealousy [cf. 1:10-12; 3:1-4] and discouragement. . . . They complain that they are not like so-and-so. . . . They develop an inferiority complex and lose all the joy of salvation. The foot grumbles because it walks in the dust and carries the whole weight of the body. . . . Others would like to be the eye which oversees or [esp.!] the mouth which speaks. . . . God knows why he has made each one of us as we are; he knows [of] what use each one of us can be."

174. Garland, 594.

easily get the idea that they are inconsequential, and the eyes can easily get the idea that they are all-important."[175]

Paul insists that each is indeed a part of the body, regardless of what they might say (vv. 15b, 16b). Each body part or organ plays an important role, and it is essential for each one to play the particular role for which it was created. If any part were not to fulfill its proper role, the whole body would suffer from its absence.

In v. 17 Paul uses rhetorical questions to stress that the body needs all its parts, including its eyes, ears, and nose: *If the whole body were an eye, where would the sense of hearing be? If the whole body were an ear, where would the sense of smell be?* There would be no hearing (or speaking, or smelling, or tasting, or anything other than seeing) if the whole body were an eye. A similar problem would exist if the whole body were an ear. The fact that all the parts are needed is stressed by the ridiculous image[176] that is evoked by these rhetorical questions. "A well-functioning body requires a multiplicity of members with a multiplicity of functions," and a church full of just one kind of gift (or even just a few different ones) "would quickly shrivel up and die from the loss of its other senses and its lack of nourishment."[177]

**12:18-20** *But in fact* reflects a transition "introducing the real situation after an unreal conditional clause or sentence."[178] "The hypothesis and the analogy is over and done with: now for realities as God has arranged them."[179]

God, Christ, and the Spirit have not been mentioned since v. 13. Here the stress falls on God's action, which both introduces and concludes the verse. The body is fit together not accidentally or haphazardly, but *God has placed the parts in the body, every one of them, just as he wanted them to be* (v. 18). Here Paul is building on the point he made in vv. 4-11: God is sovereign over the placement of the body's parts (both in the typical human body and in the church). To disparage or deny one's own place in the body (or anyone else's) is to insult God's wisdom and sovereign choice.[180] *If they were all one part, where would the body be?* It could not function because there would be no body. Paul concludes this unit with the same point stressed in vv. 12 and 14: *there are many parts, but one body* (v. 20). That is how God put together the human body, and that is how he put together the body of Christ.

175. Garland, 594.

176. Garland calls it a "freakish object" (595).

177. Garland, 595.

178. BDAG on νυνὶ δέ here.

179. Thiselton, 1003.

180. Similarly, Thiselton, 1004: "To try to rank some gifts as 'more essential' than others, let alone as necessary marks of advanced status to which all should aspire, is to offer a blasphemous challenge to God's freedom to choose whatever is his good will for his people both collectively and individually."

### 3) Exposition of Implications for Marginalized Members of the Body: I Need You, 12:21-27

While in the previous passage the focus was on a possible sense on the part of some that they themselves did not belong to the body, this passage shifts the focus to those who may not question their own place in the body but that of other parts for which they feel they have no need. Body parts that may mistakenly be considered dispensable are referred to in a variety of ways within this passage: those *that seem to be weaker* (v. 22), *less honorable* (v. 23), *unpresentable* (v. 23) or parts that lack(ed) honor (v. 24).

The TNIV and others end this paragraph with v. 26, but v. 27, like the previous verses, is marked by the semantic domain of the body and its parts, while that language is absent from vv. 28-31. Also, the two previous paragraphs each concluded with summarizing references to the body and its parts (12:14, 20). It makes sense to see Paul concluding this paragraph in the same way in v. 27.

> [21]*The eye cannot say to the hand, "I don't need you!" And the head cannot say to the feet, "I don't need you!"* [22]*On the contrary, those parts of the body that seem to be weaker are indispensable,* [23]*and the parts that we think are less honorable we treat with special honor. And the parts that are unpresentable are treated with special modesty,* [24]*while our presentable parts need no special treatment. But God has put the body together, giving greater honor to the parts that lacked it,* [25]*so that there should be no division in the body, but that its parts should have equal concern for each other.* [26]*If one part suffers, every part suffers with it; if one part is honored, every part rejoices with it.* [27]*Now you are the body of Christ, and each one of you is a part of it.*

**12:21** Here Paul changes the hypothetical dialogue partners. No longer are they divided between the parallel or related parts (hand/feet or eye/ear) but between the different categories. We now hear of a hypothetical claim addressed by the eye to the hand, and to the head (rather than the ear) to the feet. These pairings may be more likely to reflect some hierarchical assumptions, with the head itself and its organs assumed to be of greater value or importance than others. As pointed out in the introduction to this passage, the previous paragraph (12:15-20) addressed those who may have felt inferior, and therefore not really belonging to the body, while here Paul addresses those who may have considered themselves self-sufficient, or at least without need of certain other parts of the body.[181]

*The eye cannot say to the hand, "I don't need you!" And the head cannot say to the feet, "I don't need you!"* Jerome allegorizes the parts, and reflects knowledge of the fable of Menenius Agrippa, cited above (in a reference to

181. So also Chrysostom (*Homiliae in Epistulam i ad Corinthios* 31.1 [NPNF[1] 12:181]), and Fee, 612.

the scorning of the belly). According to Jerome, "The church has real eyes: its teachers and leaders who see in sacred Scripture the mysteries of God. . . . It also has hands, effective persons who are not eyes but hands. Do they plumb the mysteries of sacred Scripture? No, but they are powerful in works. The church has feet: those who make official journeys of all kinds. The foot runs that the hand may find the work it is to do. The eye does not scorn the hand, nor do these three scorn the belly as if it were idle and unemployed."[182] Paul is not promoting such direct identifications, but the basic point of the allegory (that different people in the church have different roles, all of which are needed) is sound. "It is hardly mere speculation to imagine that those who perceived themselves as possessing the 'high-status' gifts of knowledge and wisdom, or of the power to heal or to speak in tongues, could be tempted to think of themselves as *the* inner circle on whom the identity and function of the church really depended."[183] The evidence of the rest of the epistle suggests that it would have been members of the social elite who considered themselves "*the* inner circle on whom the identity and function of the church really depended," raising the likelihood that they are also the ones who were more likely to have been exercising the most highly prized gifts. Although it is impossible to know who was speaking in tongues[184] or practicing certain other gifts, the social elite would have been the ones most likely to be recognized for their knowledge, wisdom, and oratorical skills, that is, the ones most likely to have been considered enriched "with all kinds of speech and with all knowledge" and therefore not lacking "any spiritual gift" (1:5, 7).[185]

It is not just that all these parts are needed by the body as a whole, but no individual part may claim that they do not need some other part that God has placed in the body, since their own well-being depends on the health of the whole body, and for that the functioning of each part is necessary.

182. Homily 85 on Matt. 18:7-9, cited in Bray, 126. Garland, 595, thinks that Paul has these same groups in mind: "'Eye' and 'head' are transparent metaphors for those in leadership roles, who are likely to be more affluent and better educated. The 'hands' and 'feet' represent the laboring class or slaves. 'Eyes' and 'heads' in the church always get special treatment and then begin to think that they are special."

183. Thiselton, 1005.

184. It may be that believers from humble backgrounds were the ones who tended to speak in tongues, and that they emphasized the gift, sensing that it had the potential to bring them parity with their more elite brothers and sisters who seemed to have a corner on wisdom and knowledge. It may even be that Paul had something of the sort in mind in v. 24, when he said that "God has put the body together, giving greater honor to the parts that lacked it." Theissen (*Psychological Aspects*, 301) believes that "glossolalia could have exerted great attraction precisely for the less educated and the weak. For this is, after all, an ability that is not tied to educational presuppositions. . . . Danger of embarrassment does not exist, since the clear criteria necessary for that are lacking." Garland, 596, suggests that the problem with tongues was "not only its unintelligibility but also its contribution to the conflict between those of higher and of lower status in the church."

185. So also Hays, 212 (cf. 220).

**12:22** Verse 22 begins with a clear adversative, here translated *on the contrary.*[186] The parts that one might be tempted to consider dispensable are those *that seem to be* [i.e., are thought by others to be[187]] *weaker.* That is, they are thought to be "experiencing some incapacity or limitation" or to reflect some "relative ineffectiveness, whether external or inward" (BDAG). They seem to be weaker, or less impressive, in comparison with some other parts. Paul's reference to those who seem to be weak "recall to mind God's choice of what is weak in the world (1:27; cf. 4:10; 9:22)."[188]

Thiselton and (evidently) Garland endorse Moltmann's suggestion that "the gift of the weaker, unpresentable members to the church is that they give others a concrete opportunity to practice love and patience."[189] While there is certainly edifying truth in this suggestion, when accepted as an interpretation of Paul's meaning here it ultimately seems to confirm their status as weak rather than recognize that as a misperception and would seem to tend to patronize such members as having no special contribution to make to the community beyond the opportunity to serve people who have little or nothing of their own to contribute.

Paul says that those that seem to be weaker are, in fact, *indispensable* (or necessary).[190] Chrysostom points out that "when he calls them 'weak' and 'less honorable,' he uses the expression, 'which seem'; but when he calls them 'necessary,' he no longer adds 'which seem,' but himself gives his judgment, saying, 'they are necessary.'" This, he thinks, is because those parts of the human body "are useful to procreation of children and the succession of our race."[191]

One could imagine a comparison between a car's oil drain plug and its electronic ignition system. One is as low-tech (and unimpressive) as could be, while the other is highly sophisticated. But a car won't last long without its oil drain plug no matter how impressive its ignition system! The various hoses used to deliver fuel or other fluids from one part of the car to the places where they are needed are not impressive or technological wonders, but it would be ridiculous to think that the car could get along without them. As Garland reminds us, "The failure of one little valve can shut down the whole bodily system. The implication is that there is no unimportant gift or person in the body of Christ."[192] It would be just as ridicu-

186. Gk. ἀλλά.

187. Gk. δοκέω, "to appear to one's understanding" (BDAG), here and in v. 23. Chrysostom (*Homiliae in Epistulam i ad Corinthios* 31.2 [NPNF[1] 12:181]) notes the same: "And he well said, 'which seem,' and, 'which we think'; pointing out that the judgment arises not from the nature of the things, but from the opinion of the many."

188. Garland, 596.

189. Garland, 597. Cf. Thiselton, 1009; Moltmann, *The Spirit of Life* and his "The Knowing of the Other and the Community of the Different," in *God for a Secular Society* (Eng. trans., London: SCM, 1999), 135-52.

190. Gk. ἀναγκαῖος.

191. *Homiliae in Epistulam i ad Corinthios* 31.2 (NPNF[1] 12:182).

192. Garland, 594.

lous for someone with the gift of encouragement or giving to feel threatened by someone with the gift of tongues or some other more "impressive" gift, or for someone with a more impressive gift to think that they could dispense with those will less remarkable ones.[193]

**12:23-24a** This text *(and the parts that we think are less honorable we treat with special honor. And the parts that are unpresentable are treated with special modesty, while our presentable parts need no special treatment)* is marked by lexical oppositions. While *less honorable* contrasts with *special honor* in English as well as in Greek,[194] the contrast between *unpresentable* parts and those treated with *special modesty* stands out in Greek more than in English.[195] BDAG offers a literal translation along the lines of "our unpresentable [parts] receive greater presentability."

There is debate regarding the possible social references in Paul's varied use of language having to do with honor and shame.[196] Everyone agrees that the *unpresentable* parts which *are treated with special modesty* refer in the first place to the sexual organs (v. 23). The question is whether or not Paul is thinking of them (and of the weaker and less honorable parts) as a metaphor for low-status members of the community. Carson argues that "Paul is not here interested in the varied social strata that made up the Corinthian church, but in the perceived stratification of the [gifts]."[197] It seems not only possible, but even likely, however, that there was a perceived correlation between social stratification and the stratification of the gifts. That may even partly explain how Paul moves so freely from a discussion of the divine distribution of the gifts in vv. 4-11 to a discussion of the divine distribution of the members of the body itself in vv. 12-27, and to a discussion that identifies people somewhat with the gifts they have received (vv. 28-31). Witherington suggests that Paul's language here needs to be understood in light of "the *cursus honorum,* the pecking order of power and dignity in a Roman colony," since "the Romans divided society into two groups with regard to honor: the *honestiores,* or privileged and 'honorable' strata of society, and the *humiliores,* who did not qualify for reasons of birth, lack of wealth, or possibly education to be among the elite."[198] Thus, "[w]hen Paul speaks of the 'more presentable ones' who do not need extra honor (v. 24), he is likely referring to the socially more elite Christians, who would include the likes of Erastus and perhaps Gaius (Rom. 16:23). They may have been freedmen or veterans or the sons of such who had prospered in a situation where consid-

193. Carson, *Showing the Spirit,* 48.

194. Gk. ἀτιμότερα contrasts with τιμὴν περισσοτέραν.

195. Gk. ἀσχήμονα contrasts with εὐσχημοσύνην περισσοτέραν.

196. D. B. Martin, *The Corinthian Body,* 94, points out that "[i]n these verses Paul uses a variety of terms whose status significance is often lost in translation: *ta dokounta* ('the esteemed'), *asthenestera* ('weaker'), *anankaia* ('necessary'), *atimotera* ('less honorable'), *timē perissotera* ('abundantly honored'), *hysteroumenos* ('lacking')."

197. Carson, *Showing the Spirit,* 49.

198. Witherington, 259-60.

erable upward mobility was possible. At least some of these people were by their behavior not only belittling but humiliating some of the *humiliores*. Paul seeks to correct this in various ways."[199]

Chrysostom sees God's wisdom in our much greater compulsion to cover our sexual organs than other parts of our body: "For to some parts by their nature He has given not to need it [namely, special honor]; but to others, not having granted it by their nature, He has compelled us to yield it."[200]

The thought of treating *the parts that we think . . . less honorable . . . with special honor* and those *that are unpresentable . . . with special modesty* reinforces the point of 10:24: "No one should seek their own good, but the good of others." That was part of doing whatever one did (whether eating or drinking or whatever) "all for the glory of God" (10:31). The following verse points out that when God himself put the body together, he gave "greater honor to the parts that lacked it."

**12:24b-25** Here Paul draws the conclusion from the analogy of the body in vv. 22-23. We recognize the importance of all the parts of our body and we give special honor to those body parts that might seem to lack honor by "dressing them up." God has put the body of Christ together in a similar way. *But God has put the body together, giving greater honor to the parts that lacked it, so that there should be no division in the body, but that its parts should have equal concern for each other.* The verb translated *put the body together*[201] suggests "compounding various elements together."[202] If it was not good for the man to be alone (Gen. 2:18), it is also not good for the parts of the body to be separated or divided from each other.

God put the various parts of the body together in an intentional way. He gives gifts that the body needs to people who might otherwise be thought of as unimportant or dispensable. Sometimes he gives such people especially desirable spiritual gifts. That is, he gives *greater honor to the parts that lacked it*. It would seem to follow that since God has acted in this way he would be honored when his people also make sure that they give special honor to those who seem to lack it so that honor might be, on the whole,

199. Witherington, 260.

200. *Homiliae in Epistulam i ad Corinthios* 31.2 (NPNF[1] 12:181). Cf. D. B. Martin, *The Corinthian Body*, 94-95: "The remarkable thing about Paul's imagery is . . . his claim that the normally conceived body hierarchy is actually only an apparent, surface hierarchy. The genitals, he says, may *seem* to be the most shameful part of the body; but our very attention to them — our constant care to cover them and shield them from trivializing and vulgarizing public exposure — demonstrates that they are actually the most necessary of the body's members, those with the *highest* status."

201. Gk. συγκεράννυμι.

202. Adapted from Thiselton, 1010. BDAG has, "to effect a harmonious unit, *compose*," as a figurative extension of the meaning "to bring about a blend by mixing various items" (cf. Thiselton, 1010, "composing a harmonious work or substance"). That suggestion seems to move a bit too far in the direction of the intention or result of the action to which the verb refers rather than to the action itself. Chrysostom (61.259.20) thinks that the word refers to "that which is mingled" (τὸ κιρνώμενον) and which thereby "becomes one" (ἓν γίνεται).

equally shared in the body of Christ. To fail to give honor to those in need of it would not honor God but bring shame to his name.[203] "All are of equal value; but if there is to be any overcompensation, it is to be for the less favored. The church is not to be like its surrounding society, which always honors those who are already honored. It is to be counter-cultural and bestow the greatest honor on those who seem to be negligible."[204]

Paul is hardly trying to create a new division in which those who had honor in human society are now to be diminished or lacking in honor and perhaps envious of those who have now been compensated in some way through God's distribution of spiritual gifts and abilities. He wants all members of the body to enjoy equal honor *so that there should be no division in the body.* The need for the church to be marked by unity rather than divisions is a constant theme of this letter. So constant is it that it has frequently been considered its primary objective. While we have argued in the introduction to this commentary and elsewhere that unity is not the letter's ultimate goal,[205] it is most certainly one of its primary themes. The theme needed to be addressed in the light of the divisions which had entered into the Corinthian church (see esp. on 1:10-17; 11:18-19). Paul's reference to the "parts that lacked honor" fits with other clues in the letter (e.g., 11:21-22) that suggest that those divisions tended to reflect tensions between believers from opposite ends of the spectrum in terms of social status. The very way God had put the body together indicated that unity rather than divisions should mark its life.

The *equal concern*[206] Paul mentions is not merely emotional anxiety, of course, but giving care and attention to each other's needs (which will entail mainly the care and attention of the well-to-do to the needs of the have-nots). This, like much of Paul's practical teaching in this letter, reflects the motif of "love" which "builds up" (8:1) and anticipates the extended treatment on the theme of love in the following chapter.[207]

Large churches must be careful about the human tendency to facilitate the formation of subgroups by means of which those of elevated social status and the appearance of self-sufficiency are able to isolate themselves from those with whom they would not naturally tend to associate. As we have seen, this seems to have happened in Corinth (see, e.g., 11:21-22). God

203. Chrysostom, *Homiliae in Epistulam i ad Corinthios* 31.4 (NPNF[1] 12:183).

204. Garland, 596.

205. Ciampa and Rosner, "The Structure and Argument of 1 Corinthians: A Biblical/Jewish Approach."

206. Gk. μεριμνάω. BDAG defines it as "to attend to, *care for, be concerned about.*" Louw and Nida suggest "to have an anxious concern, based on apprehension about possible danger or misfortune."

207. Note Hays, 216: "The high-status Corinthians may look down their noses at their uncouth lower-class brothers and sisters in the faith, regarding them as something of an embarrassment, but Paul insists that they must be 'clothed' with dignity and honor. This echoes his earlier insistence that the strong must accommodate their behavior to the needs of the weak (8:7-13; 10:28-29a), as Paul himself has done (9:19-23; 10:31–11:1)."

put the body together in such a way that those who experience honor in this life and those who do not are to astound the world by their unity and their concern for one another.

**12:26** Paul does not have some minimal or superficial unity in mind, but one that entails a profound solidarity between the members of the body: *If one part suffers, every part suffers with it; if one part is honored, every part rejoices with it.* Calvin's comment on v. 23, that Paul argues that we look after our more modest parts because "their shame would bring disgrace upon the whole body,"[208] is clearly informed by this verse. As Lionel Thornton points out, it follows from Paul's argument "that in the Body of Christ there are, strictly speaking, no private sufferings. All are shared because there is one life of the whole. Accordingly, wrong done to one member is wrong done to the whole Church, and therefore to Christ himself."[209] Paul's words here are reminiscent of his argument in 11:3-12, where it was implied that honor and shame were understood to travel upward from the church to Christ and God. As Hays notes, "In view of the way Paul has spoken of giving honor to 'the inferior member' in verses 23-24, the last sentence of this unit should also be read as an implicit exhortation: The more obviously honorable members of the church should rejoice in showing honor to the less honorable."[210] The very next verse will point out again that this body of which each one is a part is the body of Christ, bringing out the connection not only between the suffering or honored members of the body but between those members and Christ himself.

**12:27** While most of the preceding argument has spoken generally in terms of the metaphor of the body and implicitly of the church as a similar organism, at this point Paul wants the precise identity of the implied references to be clear: *Now you are the body of Christ, and each one of you is a part of it.* As Garland observes, "In case the Corinthians have not realized it, [Paul] clarifies that he is talking about them."[211] They themselves are the body he has in mind, and it is not just any body, but the body of Christ. Such memorable descriptions of the church are prominent in the letter and are used by Paul to clinch an ethical argument. In 3:16-17 and 6:19-20 the identifications of the church as the temple of the Holy Spirit are high points in the apostle's opposition to divisive factions and sexual immorality respectively. In this case, Paul tells each member of the church *(each one of you)*, no matter how humble their social position in the world, that they are not just a part of a peculiar social group (that may seem in the eyes of the

208. Calvin, 268.

209. Thornton, *The Common Life in the Body of Christ* (London: Dacre, 1950), 36, cited in Thiselton, 1012, where he also points out that "if the ear and fingers of a musician are praised, or if the hands and feet of an athlete are praised, a person receives congratulations for his or her coordination *as a whole.* The whole person is described as a good musician or as a good athlete, and indeed some intrusive bodily distraction could wreck the performance."

210. Hays, 216.

211. Garland, 598.

world to lack any significance) but instead are a part of Christ the Lord's own body. That is an incredible honor. It is an honor in which they all participate individually, and it is an honor which they all share as a group, reinforcing again the solidarity of the members. To dishonor any part of Christ's body would be to dishonor Christ himself.

### 4) Preliminary Conclusion: Our Worship Should Reflect God's Priorities in the Use of the Gifts, 12:28-31

In these verses Paul establishes proper priorities in two different ways. First he sets up something of an order of importance to the gifts and exhorts the Corinthians to desire or pursue the gifts in light of those priorities (vv. 28-31a). Then he transitions to the following chapter by suggesting an even greater priority than that of acquiring or manifesting spiritual gifts (v. 31b). The list of gifts is probably not given in an absolute order of value, but the first three gifts or offices are clearly ordered and set above the others and it is not accidental that speaking in and interpreting tongues are last in the list.[212] In between we find "a diverse sampling of ministries, supernatural grace-gifts, and services" the point of which is "to illustrate briefly the broad spectrum of spiritual manifestations in the church."[213] Verses 29-30 reinforce the point that no gift is common to all believers.

> [28]*And God has placed in the church first of all apostles, second prophets, third teachers, then miracles, then gifts of healing, of helping, of guidance, and of different kinds of tongues.* [29]*Are all apostles? Are all prophets? Are all teachers? Do all work miracles?* [30]*Do all have gifts of healing? Do all speak in tongues?*[214] *Do all interpret?* [31]*Now eagerly desire*[215] *the greater gifts. And yet I will show you the most excellent way.*

**12:28** Paul's statement that *God has placed in the church* recalls 12:18 ("God has placed . . . in the body"). Hays suggests that "[t]he numbering of the first three items (apostles, prophets, and teachers) may indicate a certain hierarchy of authority (cf. Eph. 4:11), but it may also indicate something about the temporal order in which these gifts come into play in the construction of the Christian community: the itinerant apostle comes first and founds the church, while prophets and teachers follow to continue the work of constructing and instructing the community. Just this sort of sequence has been described already in 3:5-14."[216] There is probably a correlation among the three first crucial gifts that are needed for the establishment of a church and the three most valuable gifts that might function within the

212. So also Sampley, 949.
213. Garland, 599.
214. Or *other languages.*
215. Or *But you are eagerly desiring.*
216. Hays, 217.

body of Christ.[217] Paul does not seem to have a "hierarchy of authority" in mind here, but the reference to the "greater gifts" in v. 31 probably relates back to the order given here, which reflects not a hierarchy of authority but a hierarchy of value or profitability, with value or profitability measured in terms of the ability to (establish and) edify a church.

The order Paul presents here clearly "does not reflect the evaluation of the surrounding culture. The ranking of apostles as first and tongues as last is a reversal of the world's appraisal of apostles as society's scum (4:9-13)."[218]

*first of all apostles.* The word "apostle"[219] is used in more than one way in the New Testament. BDAG points out that in earliest Christianity the word "denoted one who proclaimed the gospel, and was not strictly limited." Besides referring to himself as an apostle (Rom. 1:1; 11:13; 1 Cor. 1:1; 9:1-10; 15:9; 2 Cor. 1:1; Gal. 1:1; Eph. 1:1; Col. 1:1; 1 Tim. 1:1; 2:7; 2 Tim. 1:1; Tit. 1:1), Paul uses the same title for Barnabas (Acts 14:14; 15:2), Andronicus and Junia (Rom. 16:7), and James, the Lord's brother (Gal. 1:19). With that in mind, some believe that by *apostles,* Paul has in mind missionaries or church planters.[220] Fee argues that "there is no other evidence that Paul thought of a local church as having some among it called 'apostles,' who were responsible for its affairs,"[221] and most would agree with Dunn that Paul has in mind the more "limited circle of individuals (though much wider than 'the twelve'), a select circle which was soon closed, though not before Paul had been added to it."[222] Dunn outlines three "key characteristics" of these apostles: 1) "they had been commissioned personally by the risen Jesus in a resurrection appearance"; 2) "they were missionaries and church founders"; and 3) they had "a distinctively and decisively eschatological role."[223] Fee thinks that "with this word [Paul] is reflecting on his own ministry in this church" and that "the plural is in deference to others who have had the same ministry in other churches." As Sampley points out, "Paul's claim of priority for the apostles . . . reaffirms his standing, his authority, as did his references to the Corinthians earlier as babies (3:1) and as did his claim to being their father in the faith (4:14)."[224]

*second prophets.* Paul dedicates considerable space to the importance of the prophetic ministry for the edification of the church in chapter 14. For a fuller discussion of the gift of prophecy, see our comments on v. 10. We

217. Garland rightly points out that the first three gifts or offices, "with their threefold ministry of the word, are essential for both the founding and the continued edification of the church" (598).

218. Garland, 599.

219. Gk. ἀπόστολος.

220. Cf. Theodoret, 214; Witherington, 261.

221. Fee, 620.

222. James D. G. Dunn, *Jesus and the Spirit: A Study of the Religious and Charismatic Experience of Jesus and the First Christians as Reflected in the New Testament* (Grand Rapids: Eerdmans, 1997 [1975]), 273. See the discussion in Witherington, 262.

223. Dunn, *Jesus and the Spirit,* 273, cited also by Thiselton, 1015.

224. Sampley, 949.

find Thiselton's argument convincing that the gift consists primarily of "the proclamation of revealed truth in relation to a pastoral situation."[225] While Paul indicates that any believer could prophesy, evidently those who did so on a regular basis came to be known as prophets. Calvin thinks that Paul has in mind "those who were blessed with the unique gift of dealing with Scripture, not only by interpreting it, but also by the wisdom they showed in making it meet the needs of the hour."[226] He sees them, furthermore, as both "outstanding interpreters of Scripture" and "men endowed with extraordinary wisdom and aptitude for grasping what the immediate need of the Church is and speaking the right word to meet it."[227] The second emphasis, on having a special ability to understand "the immediate need of the Church" and to speak "the right word to meet it," thus communicating the divine will, is very similar to our own understanding of the prophetic gift (for which the predicting of future events was a secondary and not essential feature). This verse raises some issues for Grudem's view that New Testament prophecy was of a less authoritative nature since it always needed to be weighed and evaluated, something that is not explicitly stated about teaching in general. But the importance of evaluating teachings was probably assumed,[228] whereas, were it not for the repeated emphasis on weighing and evaluating prophecies, it may have been considered presumptuous to treat them in that way.

Thiselton points out that "Paul's language about prophets' 'inspiration' here need not imply a *Deus ex machina* event, but the *pastoral insight inspired* by instruction set forth by teachers."[229] Garland is right that "it is difficult to see how prophets and teachers rank differently."[230] In any case, prophets seem to have been more attuned to the particular message a church needed to hear at any given moment while teachers were expected to pass on the same Christian teaching that needed to be learned by all believers in all places.

*third teachers.* See above (in the comments on "prophets") on the possible distinction between teachers and prophets. Dunn suggests that the teachers were those with "the responsibility of passing on the tradition, received presumably, in the first instance at least, from the founding apostle," as well as "the interpretation of tradition and thus its development."[231] Thiselton argues that teachers worked "to expound and explain what is the case about God's dealings with the world through Christ by the Spirit, on

225. Thiselton, 1016.

226. Calvin, 271.

227. Calvin, 271.

228. Cf. Acts 17:10-12, where Luke, Paul, and the Bereans seem to have all felt it to be appropriate.

229. Thiselton, 1018.

230. Garland, 598. It is just possible that prophets were more associated with a "message of wisdom" and teachers with a "message of knowledge."

231. Dunn, *Jesus and the Spirit*, 282 (emphasis removed).

the basis of which the pastoral and situational speech-acts of prophets can have their effect."[232] Thus, "teachers perform speech-acts of transmission, communicative explanation, interpretation of texts, establishment of creeds, exposition of meaning and implication, and, more cognitive, less temporally applied communicative acts."[233] It would be a mistake to think that teachers were focused on teaching abstract theological truths while prophets entered into practical application and appeals. That might fit with some teaching in the formal educational contexts today, where children and adults are taught subject contents but little or nothing about how they should live, and where moral norms are often considered trespassers on school property. Such a mistaken understanding of teaching in the Bible could be encouraged by the common use of the word "doctrine" to translate the key New Testament word for "teaching." "Teaching" in the New Testament (and the surrounding philosophies and religions) typically was moral teaching. The teacher of Romans 2:21 teaches others not to steal or commit adultery. In 1 Cor. 4:17 Paul refers to his "ways," which he teaches everywhere. In Ephesians 4:21-24 Paul says that the readers "were taught, with regard to your former way of life, to put off your old self, which is being corrupted by its deceitful desires; to be made new in the attitude of your minds; and to put on the new self, created to be like God in true righteousness and holiness." He then goes on to the end of the chapter and beyond, covering a number of other moral teachings.

Barrett's suggestion that teachers were "mature Christians who instructed others in the meaning and moral implications of the Christian faith"[234] is properly balanced. The difference with prophets, then, would not be that the latter are the only ones applying the Christian faith, but that the teachers would pass on the traditional Christian theological and moral teachings that were valued and needed to be known by all believers everywhere, while the prophets were especially gifted at addressing the particular, context-specific needs of a gathered congregation with inspired pastoral insight.

*then miracles, then gifts of healing.* On these two gifts, see the comments on vv. 9-10. Here they appear in reverse order from that found there. It seems unlikely that Paul thinks of either of them as being "greater" than the other, so the order is most likely arbitrary. God himself is known for his miracle-working power, including his power to heal from disease.[235] Since

232. Thiselton, 1017.

233. Thiselton, 1017.

234. Barrett, 295. Similarly, Theodoret, 214, and Collins, who suggests, "The teacher is one who instructs with regards to God's will, whether in catechesis (cf. 14:9) or as an interpreter of the Scriptures" (469).

235. On God as the one who works wonders/miracles, see 1 Chr. 16:12; Neh. 9:17; Job 5:9; 9:10; Pss. 77:11, 14; 78:12; 105:5; 106:7, 21-22. For God as healer, see Gen. 20:17; Exod. 15:26; Num. 12:13; Deut. 32:39; 1 Sam. 6:3; 2 Kgs. 20:5; 2 Chr. 30:20; Pss. 6:2; 30:2; 103:3; 107:20; Isa. 19:22; 30:26; 57:18; 57:19; Jer. 17:14; 30:17.

God is also known as the one who helps his people when they are in need and who guides or governs the universe (see the following gifts *of helping* and *of guidance* or governance), it may be that we are supposed to recognize in some of these spiritual gifts the ability not only to do what only God could empower people to do, but to do what God himself is famous for doing for his people and his creation.

*of helping.* That scholars do not know precisely what Paul had in mind should not surprise us since even Chrysostom felt the need to explain to his congregation (who spoke Greek) what Paul had in mind. In his view, it meant "To support the weak" and had to do with "aptness for a patron's office,"[236] referring to the ancient role of the patron or benefactor. Calvin suggests that this gift was either "both an office, and a gift, in the Church of long ago, but of which we have no knowledge now; or it has to do with the work of the diaconate, that is to say, the care of the poor."[237] He prefers the second explanation. Garland points out that when the related verb[238] appears in Paul's speech in Acts 20:35, it is used with respect to helping the weak. He thinks that it may have to do with "assisting the socially disadvantaged."[239] In the LXX this word most often refers to help God granted his people (1 Esdr. 8:27; 2 Macc. 8:19; 15:7; 3 Macc. 2:33; 5:50; Pss. 21:1, 20; 83:6; 88:19; *Psalms of Solomon* 7:10; 16:1).

*of guidance.* The noun Paul uses is a substantivized form of the verb meaning "to steer a ship" and usually refers to the act of piloting a ship. It is just as closely related to the noun used for a "pilot" — one who carries out this role on a regular basis.[240] The latter word is used in the LXX of 4 Maccabees 7:1; Proverbs 23:34; Ezekiel 27:8, 27, 28 and in Acts 27:11 and Revelation 18:17. Witherington says that the "important word" used here "is often unfortunately translated 'administration.' It really refers to those who give guidance or wise counsel."[241] It depends on what one means by administration or giving guidance. In some contexts "administration" calls to mind clerical work while in others it refers to senior management. The word used here favors the latter. In some cases "giving guidance" suggests a personal counselor or advisor while in others it suggests that the guidance of an organization is provided by its senior management. Again, it is the latter idea that is suggested by the word choice, that of effective governance or leadership. The role of the pilot or helmsman was well known, both in its literal sense and as a metaphor for governance.[242]

236. *Homiliae in Epistulam i ad Corinthios* 32.3 (NPNF[1] 12:187).

237. Calvin, 272.

238. The Greek verb in Acts is ἀντιλαμβάνω; the word here is ἀντίλημψις.

239. Garland, 599.

240. The Greek word used here is κυβέρνησις. The verb "to pilot" is κυβερνάω, while the word for the pilot himself is κυβερνήτης.

241. Witherington, 261.

242. See Josephus, *Antiquities* 10:278; Philo, *On the Creation of the World* 46, 88; *Allegorical Interpretation* 3:80 (cf. 3:118, 224); *On the Cherubim* 36; *On Dreams* 1:186; *On the Confusion*

"The clarity of the image of the work of the helmsman made it obviously suitable for fig[urative] use for the statesman," and the "conception of the deity as [pilot] became a favourite one."[243] Margaret Mitchell has shown that the role of the ship captain was a commonplace in discussions of factionalism and concord, recalling the kind of leadership that guides a community through difficult waters [times/challenges] as a strong and harmonious unit.[244]

In Beyer's view, Paul's reference "can only be to the specific gifts which qualify a Christian to be a helmsman to his congregation, i.e., a true director of its order and therewith of its life."[245]

*and of different kinds of tongues.* This gift comes last again, due to the fact that it has caused such problems in Corinth (as it has often done in other contexts where it comes to be considered a mark of the spiritual elite).

**12:29-30** Paul has been stressing the diversity of the gifts given to the church and the fact that no one has all of the gifts. Now he makes it clear that no spiritual gift is given to everyone. Most of the other believers will not have whatever gift any particular person in that same church might have and will therefore be in need of it. *Are all apostles? Are all prophets? Are all teachers? Do all work miracles? Do all have gifts of healing? Do all speak in tongues? Do all interpret?* Each of these rhetorical questions is framed in Greek[246] in such a way as to indicate that the only appropriate response would be "no." The readers should understand why none of these gifts are shared by all, since "Paul has said four different ways in this chapter, *the gifts are apportioned as God or the Spirit sees fit* (12:11, 18, 25, 28)."[247] Thiselton criticizes Fee for suggesting that Paul is emphasizing the need for diversity. "Paul is not saying, 'Look at how varied your gifts are.' No, he is asserting, 'since none on his or her own receives this extensive range of necessary gifts, *you need others, and others need you.*'"[248] It is not clear that Fee's point is different from Thiselton's. He certainly does not mean that Paul is saying, "Look how varied your gifts are." Fee's view is that Paul is saying, "The church needs people with a variety of different gifts to function properly."

---

*of Tongues* 98 (cf. *On the Migration of Abraham* 6; *Who Is the Heir?* 228; *On the Life of Abraham* 70, 115–16; *On the Eternity of the World* 83; *Questions and Answers on Genesis* 2:34); *On the Life of Abraham* 272; *On the Special Laws* 4:186; *On the Virtues* 61 (cf. *On the Virtues* 186; *On Rewards and Punishments* 51); *On the Embassy to Gaius* 149.

243. H. W. Beyer, "κυβέρνησις," *TDNT* 3:1035.

244. M. M. Mitchell, *Paul and the Rhetoric of Reconciliation,* 163-64. Cf. Thiselton, 1021-22.

245. H. W. Beyer, "κυβέρνησις," *TDNT* 3:1036. In his view the "combination of ἀντιλήμψεις and κυβερνήσεις makes it certain that the ἐπίσκοποι . . . and διάκονοι . . ., who are first mentioned in Phil. 1:1, are to be regarded as the bearers of this gift" (ibid.).

246. By introducing each question with the Greek negative μή.

247. Sampley, 949 (his emphasis).

248. Thiselton, 1023. Calvin (272) also sees Paul's main point as being that "nobody is so fully equipped with everything, as to be replete in himself, and not feel the need of other people's help."

The evidence of the New Testament suggests that there were few apostles, miracle workers, or people with gifts of healing in the early church (mainly the twelve apostles, Paul and Barnabas, Stephen, and Philip),[249] while quite a few evidently spoke in tongues (cf. Acts 2:4; 10:46; 19:6; 1 Cor. 14:5, 13, 18, 23, 27, 39; Mark 16:17). Paul's argument in chapter 14 will attempt to tip the balance away from an emphasis on tongues, toward a larger number of people exploring and exercising the gifts of prophecy and teaching (note esp. 14:6, 26).

**12:31** Paul prepares for his focus on love in the following verses: *Now eagerly desire the greater gifts. And yet I will show you the most excellent way.* The Greek verb translated *eagerly desire*[250] could be understood as either a statement (indicative mood), "you are zealous for the greater gifts," or as an imperative, "seek/desire the greater gifts." It is clear from Paul's way of addressing the issue that some Corinthians were seeking or eagerly desiring what they considered to be the greater gifts (esp. tongues) and that that had created problems in the community. In that light it may seem strange for Paul to encourage such behavior and exhort them to continue such pursuits,[251] while a simple statement that they are behaving in such a way seems quite natural.[252] The precise verb form used here will appear two more times in chapter 14 (vv. 1 and 39), however, and in both of those cases it is clearly used as an imperative. The parallels between the uses here and in chapter 14 are too great to allow us to interpret the verb any differently in each case.[253] Thus, virtually all interpreters and English translations understand it to be an imperative.[254]

Of course, not all imperatives carry the same sense. Smit thinks that

249. Cf. Acts 2:43; 5:12; 6:8; 8:13; 14:3; 15:12; 19:11; Rom. 15:19; 2 Cor. 12:12. On the other hand, Gal. 3:5 and Heb. 2:4, along with 1 Cor. 12:10, 28-29, suggest that such things were more frequent than we might otherwise gather, and texts such as Matt. 24:24, Mark 13:22, and 2 Thess. 2:9 warn that signs and wonders could not automatically be thought to originate from God or one of his authorized messengers.

250. Gk. ζηλοῦτε.

251. Smit feels that "in its presentation of charismata and love and in the behavior it demands of the Corinthians I Cor 12:31 is diametrically opposed to I Cor 13:1-13" (J. F. M. Smit, "Two Puzzles: I Corinthians 12:31 and 13:3: A Rhetorical Solution," *NTS* 39 [1993], 250). Prior, 223, follows Arnold Bittlinger, *Gifts and Graces: A Commentary on I Corinthians 12–14* (trans. Herbert Klassen; London: Hodder & Stoughton, 1967), 73-75, and G. Iber, "Zum Verständnis von 1 Cor. 12:31," *ZNW* 54 (1963), 43-53, in thinking that the verb is indicative rather than imperative. Ralph Martin takes the verb to be indicative and possibly interrogative (*The Spirit and the Congregation: Studies in 1 Corinthians 12–15* [Grand Rapids: Eerdmans, 1984], 34-35). David L. Baker, "The Interpretation of 1 Corinthians 12–14," *EvQ* 46 (1974), 226-27, thinks that here and in 14:1, 19 Paul is citing and responding to a Corinthian slogan about the importance of seeking spiritual gifts.

252. See also Hays, 217-18.

253. 12:31, "eagerly desire the greater gifts" (Gk. ζηλοῦτε δὲ τὰ χαρίσματα τὰ μείζονα); 14:1, "eagerly desire spiritual gifts" (Gk. ζηλοῦτε δὲ τὰ πνευματικά); 14:39, "eagerly desire to prophesy" (Gk. ζηλοῦτε τὸ προφητεύειν).

254. As a present imperative it suggests that this is not merely occasional instruction, but guidance that is generally relevant and valid.

Paul is using an ironic *permissio* with which he "ridicules in an ironic manner the Corinthians' pursuit of these gifts as their highest goal."[255] In this case the imperative would have the sense, "Continue to strive for the greater gifts! It will be to your ruin!" but Garland rightly objects that Paul is unlikely to have introduced his sublime discussion of love with mockery.[256] The imperative could also have a nonironic but still permissive sense, as in "Go ahead [if you must] and seek the greater gifts. And yet I will show you the most excellent way."

Thiselton provides the best explanation of this part of the verse and how it relates to the Corinthians' issues. They had demonstrated "a zealous concern, even a striving, for the gifts of the Spirit that were deemed to be greatest in the sense of their supposedly constituting a mark of a high social and/or spiritual status." But Paul redefines the terms since he completely rejects the Corinthians' approach to deciding what counts as high spiritual status and the way gifts relate to such a status. Ironically, he urges them, "Do not stop being zealously concerned about the 'greatest' gifts, provided that you follow me in transposing and subverting your understanding of what counts as 'the greatest.'"[257] Of course, Paul will lead them to understand that the greatest gifts "are not those that minister to status or to self, but those which serve the good of others and build the community. I now show you that what is an even greater way still is the way of love."[258] "Paul urges the Corinthians . . . to seek earnestly or be eager for the greater gifts, the intelligible ones that build up the body. They are greater only because they more easily function to strengthen the body."[259] Paul's statement in 14:21, "Since you are eager[260] for gifts of the Spirit, try to excel in those that build up the church," suggests a similar idea. He does not discourage them from being eager for certain gifts, but seeks to change their view of the gifts in which they should seek to excel.

Further insight into another difficulty with this verse may be provided by 14:21-22. Paul has stressed that the gifts are distributed according to God's will (12:11, 18, 24, 28) and that each one should appreciate both their own gifts and contribution to the body and those of the other parts of the body. That raises a couple of questions: How "can one strive for or eagerly desire something that can only be given? Does Paul expect them to try to attain gifts that they do not have?"[261] Garland rejects the suggestion that Paul is encouraging the Corinthians to pray to receive certain gifts, since "[h]e does not tell them to pray for these greater gifts."[262] But Paul

255. Smit, "Two Puzzles," 253.
256. Garland, 601.
257. Thiselton, 1024 (emphases removed).
258. Thiselton, 1024 (emphases removed).
259. Witherington, 261.
260. Gk. ζηλωταί, related to the imperative translated "eagerly desire" (ζηλοῦτε).
261. Garland, 602.
262. Garland, 602. That Paul expects his readers to pray for other gifts is supported by Godet, 232; Robertson and Plummer, 282; and Barrett, 296.

does in fact explicitly tell those who speak in tongues to "pray that they may interpret what they say" (14:22). And, remarkably, that comes immediately after saying that since the Corinthians eagerly desire the gifts of the Spirit, they should "try to excel in those that build up the church." The interpretation of tongues is more likely to build up the church than uninterpreted tongues, so one who has the gift of speaking in tongues should pray for the gift of interpreting them as well. Since that is the case, it would seem logical for believers to pray that they might be able to provide prophetic insight for the church, especially since Paul indicates that he would be very happy for them all to prophesy (14:1, 5, 24, 31, 39).[263] Prior believes that when love "controls and prevails in a church, then every member will be freed to bring his particular gift and to ask God for more gifts, not for his own sake, but for the benefit of all."[264]

Van Unnik points out that "the gifts of God's grace do not work automatically; they are not in the state of permanent activity."[265] Furthermore, they "need not be continually active," may "be neglected or quenched (1 Thess. 5:19)," and may "fall into disuse and need reviving."[266] In Chrysostom's view, Paul "gently hinted that they were the cause of their own receiving the lesser gifts, and had it in their power, if they would, to receive the greater. For in saying, 'desire earnestly,' he demands from them all diligence and desire for spiritual things."[267] Is *the most excellent way* the best way to pursue spiritual gifts or things of the Spirit or the most excellent way to live (and glorify God), or both? Chrysostom feels that Paul intends to "point out . . . a fountain of gifts"; "one way which leads to all [the gifts]."[268] It seems best not to think that Paul was talking about pursuing love as a way to gain greater gifts rather than the way to live and prioritize life, but as one uses one's gifts in constant loving service to others, God may see fit to provide further enablements to allow one's service to be even more creative and effective.

Another question is whether Paul is urging the Corinthians (and us) to *desire* the greater gifts or to "seek" them. Many translate *zēloute* as "eagerly [or earnestly] desire" (TNIV, NIV, ESV, NASB, NLT); others with "strive [eagerly]" (NAB, NRSV). NET suggests, "you should be eager for," and NJB, "set your mind on." Thiselton translates it "continue to be zealously concerned about."[269] There is ultimately little difference between these translations. The conclusion of BDAG, that the verb means to "be

263. That does not mean, of course, that Paul would want them all to lose or abandon whatever other gifts they might already have.

264. Prior, 223.

265. Willem C. van Unnik, "The Meaning of 1 Corinthians 12:31," *NovT* 35 (1993), 156-57, cited in Garland, 602.

266. Garland, 602.

267. *Homiliae in Epistulam i ad Corinthios* 32.5 (NPNF[1] 12:188).

268. *Homiliae in Epistulam i ad Corinthios* 32.5 (NPNF[1] 12:188).

269. Thiselton, 1024 (emphases removed).

positively and intensely interested in someth[ing]," clarifies how the various translation possibilities, including "strive, desire, exert oneself earnestly, be dedicated,"[270] are related.

Chrysostom points out that this most excellent way is different from the gifts in that it "is open in common to all," while "the gifts are entrusted, to some these, to others those, but not all to all people." In that sense, love "is a universal gift."[271]

Paul's promise to show the Corinthians a superior path to follow reflects an Old Testament motif that is usually associated with the exodus or second exodus. That God showed Israel the way or path by the pillar of cloud and fire is pointed out in Exodus 13:21 and Deuteronomy 1:33. Micah 4:2 tells us that in the time of salvation the nations will go to the house of God and be shown the way established by the Lord, while in Isaiah 48:16-17 the speaker affirms that the Lord will direct his people in the way they should go. Samuel was also committed to showing Israel the good and right way (1 Sam. 12:23). According to Jesus, the two love commands summarize the way we should follow God (Matt. 22:37-39; Mark 12:30-31; Luke 10:27; citing Deut. 6:5 and Lev. 19:18), and Paul will expound on the way of love in extended fashion in the following chapter (see also Rom. 13:9; Gal. 5:14). That Paul needs to show them a more excellent way suggests that the way they are on right now is not the superior way that is to mark God's people.[272]

Wright's remarks on Paul's understanding of the divinely intended way of being human, although not commenting directly on this passage, are apropos. He argues that while paganism consistently leads to "the fracturing of genuine humanity," as when "one category of human beings define themselves against another,"[273]

> Paul articulated . . . *a way of being human* which he saw as the true way. In his ethical teaching, in his community development, and above all in his theology and practice of new life through dying and rising with Christ, he zealously articulated, modelled, inculcated, and urged upon his converts a way of life which he saw as being the genuinely human way of life. And he saw this as the way of life to which Judaism had been called, but to which, without the Messiah, Judaism had not attained and could not attain.[274]

That is the way he expounds in the following chapter.

270. See BDAG on ζηλόω. The second definition given by BGAG is "to have intense negative feelings over another's achievements or success, *be filled w[ith] jealousy, envy.*"

271. *Homiliae in Epistulam i ad Corinthios* 32.5 (NPNF[1] 12:188).

272. Garland, 603.

273. N. T. Wright, *What Saint Paul Really Said,* 145-46.

274. N. T. Wright, *What Saint Paul Really Said,* 136 (his emphasis).

### *b. Love Is the Most Perfect and Only Eternal Way to Worship God, 13:1-13*

This famous "love chapter" is certainly one of the most well-known chapters in the entire Bible, and probably the best-known passage in Paul's letters. This, of course, is due in large part to the fact that many Christian weddings include a reading from this passage. Given that particular exposure, many Christians assume the chapter is primarily about love between a man and a woman — that it was written to provide guidance and insight for married couples. It is perfectly appropriate, of course, for married people to learn how to love each other better through the reading and study of this passage, even if its original and primary purpose was somewhat different.

The chapter is primarily about living in Christian community in a way that glorifies God, and that is by learning to treat other members of Christ's body the way God has treated us — with self-sacrificing, other-oriented love. This is what has come to be referred to as *agapē* love, based on the Greek word used for it here. That word is used ten times between 13:1 and 14:1. Many Christians seem to assume that the word *agapē* was invented by Christ or his followers and always meant divine, Christ-like love. Although the word did come to be the preferred word among Christians for the love shown and expected by Christ, its basic meaning, as indicated by BDAG, is "warm regard for and interest in another."[1]

The word did not come with a tremendous amount of preestablished content, which is why the New Testament texts (and especially this chapter) dedicate so much space to explaining exactly what love means for and requires of believers. The key sources for such understanding are the love commands of the Old Testament and Christ's example of self-sacrificing love for others (Lev. 19:18; Deut. 6:5; Rom. 13:9; Gal. 5:14; Rom. 5:8; 14:15; 2 Cor. 5:14; Gal. 2:20; Eph. 2:4; 5:2, 25). There is a long tradition of unpacking the meaning of the command to love one's neighbor (Lev 19:18).[2] Love is a central theme of Paul's Christian ethical teaching (Rom. 12:9-10; 13:8, 9, 10; 14:15; Gal. 5:13-14; Eph. 1:15; 4:2, 16; 5:2), and in Romans 13:10 Paul makes clear that he understands his teaching on love to be a reflection of Leviticus 19:18, which he considers a summary of the law.

This commentary has argued that purity and holiness are major themes in this letter, especially in chapters 5–14 with their concerns about

1. BDAG also points out that the word ἀγάπη ("love") is used "without limitation to very intimate relationships, and very seldom in general Greek of sexual attraction." It is frequently used in the LXX of the Song of Solomon for sexual attraction (Song 2:4-5, 7; 3:5, 10; 5:8; 7:7; 8:4, 6-7), and it is even used of the rapacious attraction to Tamar in 2 Sam. 13:15.

2. Cf. Tob. 4:13; 2 Macc. 15:14; Matt. 5:43 (Jesus citing a contemporaneous interpretation); 5:44-46; 19:19; 22:39-40; Mark 10:21; 12:31-33; Luke 6:27-38; 10:27-37; John 15:12-17; Jas. 2.8; 1 Pet. 1:22; 2:17; 4:8; 1 John 2:10; 3:10-18, 23; 4:7, 11-12, 21; 5:1; 2 John 1:5-6; *m. Nedarim* 9:4; *Genesis Rabbah* 24:7; *Leviticus Rabbah* 24:5; *b. Pesaḥim* 75a; *b. Yebamot* 62b; *b. Ketubbot* 37b; *b. Nedarim* 65b; *b. Soṭah* 8b; *b. Qiddušin* 41a; *b. B. Qamma* 51a; *b. Sanhedrin* 45a, 52a-b, 76b, 84b; *b. Niddah* 17a.

sexual immorality *(porneia)* and idolatry, and the Christian commitment to sexual purity and the proper worship of the one true God. The concentrated focus on love in this chapter, along with these other themes, reminds us that the holiness code in Leviticus 18–20 also puts great emphasis on love, most crisply expressed in the love command itself, Leviticus 19:18.

This chapter occupies the middle of an A-B-A structure, similar that found in chapters 8–10, where the first and last of the three chapters clearly deal with the same subject matter (food sacrificed to idols in chs. 8 and 10 and spiritual gifts in chs. 12 and 14) and the middle chapter focuses on a key for dealing with the issue in the proper manner. In this case, the middle chapter not only provides a key to guide all believers in the use of spiritual gifts, but it also provides the most important key for dealing with all of the conflicts that have divided the Corinthians (and those that have divided Christian congregations ever since).[3]

The structure of the chapter itself also reflects an A-B-A pattern, with the central section on the nature of love (vv. 4-7) sandwiched between two sections dealing with the relationship between gifts and love (vv. 1-3 [on the uselessness of gifts apart from love] and 8-12 [on the enduring nature of love and the transitory nature of the gifts]).

Wright points out that the zealous energy that previously led Paul to persecute Christians had been transformed by Christ and that "energy was now characterized by the thing that Paul saw at the very heart of the God he learnt to worship afresh: the quality which he called *agapē* — love."[4] In his view, Paul stresses that love is about "those who worship God in Christ Jesus" functioning "as a family in which every member is accepted as an equal member, no matter what their social, cultural or moral background," and "the existence and flourishing of such a community is the thing that is going to reveal to the pagan world that the gospel of Jesus Christ is what it claims to be":[5]

> That is why, when writing 1 Corinthians, Paul builds up his argument step by step, showing at point after point the way in which this community is radically different from its pagan neighbours, until at last he reaches chapter 13, when, like the chorale theme in Sibelius's "Finlandia," the clear poetry in praise of love, *agapē*, rings out, and we realize that this was all along the subtext of the entire letter.
>
> Everything Paul has said so far on every topic has been, after all, an appeal for *agapē*. This is the lifestyle that reveals what genuine renewed

3. Collins, 471, is incorrect to say, "Embedded between two chapters with an ecclesiological perspective, ch. 13 is anthropological and theological." This chapter is both theological and ecclesiological. As Hays (*The Moral Vision of the New Testament*, 35) recognizes, "Paul interprets love in terms of the ecclesial context elaborated in the surrounding chapters. . . . Love binds the body of Christ together." Indeed, for Paul, "love has its primary locus in the common life of the church."

4. N. T. Wright, *What Saint Paul Really Said*, 135.

5. N. T. Wright, *What Saint Paul Really Said*, 146.

humanity is all about. Paganism is always trying to ape it, but all it can do is collapse into personality cults, factional fighting (it's very easy, after all, to "love" everyone else in your faction; that's the point of having a faction in the first place), and blatant eroticism, which parodies the life of *agapē* at the same time as it progressively distorts, defaces, and destroys the human beings who live in that way.[6]

Thiselton notes that this chapter on love "takes its place among the themes which concern worship, from idol foods (chs. 8–10), dress in worship (11:2-16), and the Eucharist (11:17-34) to the use of charisms during worship (12:1–14:40)."[7] The theme was already evoked in 8:1 (see the comments there), and it underlies all of chapters 8–14 (cf. also 16:14), a major division of the letter that both begins and ends with a call to love and edification (8:1; chs. 13–14).

Some have questioned whether Paul wrote this chapter as he was composing this letter or if he is using something he himself or someone else had written at an earlier time for a different situation. The material fits this context extremely well. Spiritual gifts are mentioned in vv. 1-3, 8 (especially tongues and prophecy, the main topics of ch. 14) and are still referred to in v. 12, and most interpreters recognize that at least several (if not all) of the qualities that Paul attributes to love suggest that this is an ad hoc list pointing to some of the key attitudes and behaviors that a number of the Corinthians have been lacking and that Paul has had to address in this letter.[8]

This passage is commonly and appropriately classified as an encomium,[9] that is, discourse dedicated to the praise of a person or thing.[10] Here

6. N. T. Wright, *What Saint Paul Really Said*, 146, 147.

7. Thiselton, 1027.

8. Cf. also M. M. Mitchell, *Paul and the Rhetoric of Reconciliation*, 274 n. 500. As Witherington notes (265), "love is said to be not the very things that Paul has already said that the Corinthians are: jealous (cf. 3:3), self-promoting, puffed up (cf. 4:6), shameful (cf. 5:2; 11:4), each one a seeker of his or her own advantage (cf. chs. 8–10), easily provoked, and reckoners of wrongdoing (cf. ch. 6)."

9. James G. Sigountos, "The Genre of 1 Corinthians," *NTS* 40 (1994), 246-60; Burton L. Mack, *Rhetoric and the New Testament* (Minneapolis: Fortress, 1990), 64-66; Hans Dieter Betz and Margaret Mitchell, "Corinthians, First Epistle to the," in *ABD* 1:1145; M. M. Mitchell, *Paul and the Rhetoric of Reconciliation*, 165 (on 274 n. 499 she limits the application to 13:3-7, as does Hays, 221); Kennedy, *New Testament Interpretation*, 156; Collins, 442-43; Sampley, 950-51; Garland, 606-7; cf. Witherington, 264; R. P. Martin, *The Spirit and the Congregation*, 41-42. Chrysostom thinks that vv. 1-3 precede the encomium rather than serve as part of it (*Homiliae in Epistulam i ad Corinthios* 32.5 [NPNF[1] 12:188]: "Then intending to proceed to the discourse concerning it [viz., love] and the encomium of this virtue, he first lowers these [viz., the gifts] by comparison with it, intimating that they are nothing without it"). Later (*Homiliae in Epistulam i ad Corinthios* 34.5 [NPNF[1] 12:203) he seems to indicate that each of the praiseworthy statements about love is an encomium, referring to v. 13 as "another encomium of love" given because Paul was not "content with those before mentioned, but he strives to discover yet another." Origen also refers to "the encomia [plural] of love."

10. It is not surprising, given the nature of the chapter, that it does not contain any imperatives.

it is love that receives this extended praise. James Sigountos has provided the fullest and most valuable discussion of the classification of the chapter's formal classification. Sigountos's structure fits our passage well, even if it is not so clear that all encomia had such strict structures. The term could also be used more generally for any spoken or written piece of praise for a person or thing,[11] and certainly there can be no objection to the application of the term to this passage at least in this less formal sense. The passage has been referred to as a hymn or prose hymn, not because it was to be sung, but in recognition of its lofty, exalted prose. It is clearly marked by rhetorical amplification, by which Paul takes what could have been stated in one or two concise prose clauses and slows down his argumentative and topical progression to a near stop in order to develop this expanded and elaborate tribute to love.[12]

It should have been clear by the end of the previous chapter that no person would be deserving of an encomium for manifesting any spiritual gift, since the gifts were all bestowed by God and are manifestations of his power, not those of the believer. Still, encomia usually focused on a person's deeds and one could easily imagine Corinthians anticipating praise from God on the last day (perhaps a "'Well done, good and faithful servant!'" as in Matt. 25:21, 23) on the same basis as those Jesus quoted who said, "'Lord, Lord, did we not prophesy in your name and in your name drive out demons and in your name perform many miracles?'" (Matt. 7:22). Jesus says that he will tell them, "I never knew you. Away from me, you evildoers!" (7:23). They may have imagined that they would be commended for their use of eloquent speech or their ability to speak in tongues or for their employment of other spiritual gifts. Paul makes it clear that not even he would receive any such praise for the use of his extraordinary gifts, and that that would be the case even if he exercised gifts that were exponentially greater than he actually experienced. Rather, none of it would count for anything. He would count for nothing in God's eyes if his deeds were not empowered by love.

Most epideictic speeches reinforce or give voice to values already held by the audience or community being addressed. Typically such a speech is given about a person, and what is highlighted is the way they fulfilled or upheld the values of the community. Paul's speech does this in part but also subverts some of the values of certain members of the Corinthian church.

11. For more informal usages cf. Esth. 2:23 LXX; Josephus, *Antiquities* 2.195, 346; 14.68; 19.274; Philo, *Allegorical Interpretation* 2:67; *Who Is the Heir?* 162; *On the Life of Abraham* 247; *On the Life of Moses* 2:240.

12. This is consistent with Aristotle's guidance on epideictic rhetoric (the rhetoric of praise and/or blame), recommending that one "employ many of the means of amplification" in order "to attribute beauty and importance" to the object of praise (*Rhetoric* 1368a, tran. J. H. Freese [LCL]). Witherington, 264, points out that "the differences between ch. 13 and the surrounding chapters is not between what is rhetorical and what is non-rhetorical, but between showpiece epideictic rhetoric and plainstyle deliberative rhetoric."

Certainly the Corinthians already value love, and are aware that it serves as the core of Christian ethics. It is impossible to imagine a church founded by Paul (or any other apostle) which would not be aware of the centrality of love for Christian life and ethics. They also value tongues, prophecy, and other spiritual gifts. Paul's argument in this letter recognizes and affirms all of these values, but rather than merely to confirm their previous status, Paul works to restructure the prioritization of these values. He does so in such a way that the practical meaning of love is clarified and that it is established as an exponentially greater value than any of the gifts. In the process he also clarifies the way in which the practice of the gifts by some Corinthians has been inconsistent with love. By reinforcing the mutually shared value of love and clarifying its implication for the practice of the gifts, Paul hopes to put the church on a path towards spiritual health.

Söding highlights "the eschatological and theocentric dimension" of love in this chapter.[13] The eschatological nature of love is seen in Paul's affirmations that it "endures" (v. 13) even when most things will be abolished or set aside (vv. 8, 10, 11), that it "never falls/fails" (v. 8), and that its presence or absence has eschatological and soteriological implications (see on vv. 2-3). The theocentric nature of love in this chapter is reflected in that much of what Paul says about it in this chapter was previously affirmed of God in the Old Testament and/or early Judaism, and is said about God by Paul himself elsewhere (see below on vv. 4-7). It is also reflected in the fact that, while God is constantly being mentioned in the surrounding chapters, Paul does not explicitly refer to him in this one, contenting himself with an exposition on love (though see v. 12 on seeing [God] face to face). Söding states that Paul refers to "love" here as "God's eschatological power."[14] Similarly, Stauffer says that "[f]aith and hope bear the marks of this defective aeon" while with love, which never fails, "the power of the future age already breaks into the present form of the world." Thus it "is the only vital force which has a future," for it "is seen to be no longer of this world but to stretch into the future aeon."[15] As Thiselton puts it, love "is that quality which distinctively stamps the life of heaven, where regard and respect for the other dominates the character of life with God as the communion of saints and heavenly hosts."[16]

### i. *Encomium in praise of love's significance in comparison with other gifts of the Spirit, 13:1-3*

*[1]If I speak in human or angelic tongues, but do not have love, I am only a resounding gong or a clanging cymbal. [2]If I have the gift of prophecy and can*

13. Thomas Söding, *Das Liebesgebot bei Paulus: Die Mahnung zur Agape im Rahmen der paulinischen Ethik* (NTAbh 26; Munster: Aschendorff, 1995), 130.

14. Söding, *Das Liebesgebot bei Paulus*, 131.

15. E. Stauffer, "ἀγαπάω, ἀγάπη, ἀγαπητός," *TDNT* 1:51-52.

16. Thiselton, 1035.

*fathom all mysteries and all knowledge, and if I have a faith that can move mountains, but do not have love, I am nothing.* [3]*If I give all I possess to the poor and give over my body to hardship that I may boast, but do not have love, I gain nothing.*

As Mitchell suggests, "The deliberative argument by appeal to advantage is . . . fully operative in 13:1-3, in each case stressing that tongues, prophecy, knowledge, faith and heroic acts are not the most advantageous thing the Christian should seek."[17] She also points out that, as in other parts of this letter, "Paul here appeals to himself as the example to be imitated" but with the important twist that "here he is a hypothetical negative example to be rejected."[18] That is, if (and only if) he were to exercise such remarkable gifts without an underlying basis of love, it would all be for naught. This encomium of love indicates that even those who have the most extraordinary spiritual accomplishments will still fail to receive an encomium from God if they lack love. Paul refers to himself in these verses but does so in a manner that shows he is not speaking of his actual actions, gifts, or attributes but of what his condition would be under such hypothetical conditions. Sampley holds that this approach allows Paul to "lay out some stern warnings to his auditors without risk of unduly offending them" since they "can hear much more forceful and blunt criticism of themselves precisely because it is Paul's critique of his imaginary, contrary-to-fact self."[19]

In each of the verses there seems to be a three-step heightening that moves from reference to a remarkable gift to a truly marvelous gift to the most excellent way of love without which it surprisingly turns out that those seemingly impressive gifts turn out to be of no value whatsoever.[20]

17. M. M. Mitchell, *Paul and the Rhetoric of Reconciliation,* 278.

18. M. M. Mitchell, *Paul and the Rhetoric of Reconciliation,* 273. So also Sampley, 951-52. Witherington, 268, summarizes the ties between these verses and Paul's role as an example: "First, Paul later claims explicitly that he speaks in tongues (14:18). Second, Paul's prophetic status is apparent at various points (1 Cor. 2:2-16; 7:40; 14:37). Third, he claims both to know and to teach mysteries (cf. 2:1, 10; 4:1, 15:51; 2 Cor. 12:1-7) and to have special revelatory knowledge (1 Cor. 2:16). Fourth, Paul claims and Acts confirms that he was a miracle-worker (2 Cor. 12:12; Rom. 15:19; Acts 14:3; 16:16-24; 19:11; 28:3-6). In regard to a self-chosen poorer state, one must bear in mind what Paul says in ch. 9 about refusing patronage and working with his hands as an enslaved leader, as well as the tribulation catalog in 4:11f. (cf. also 2 Cor. 6:3-10). In regard to Paul boasting, besides what he says in chs. 4 and 9, one will think of the mocking self-commendation in 2 Corinthians 10–13."

19. Sampley, 951-52.

20. Similarly, Daniel B. Wallace, *Greek Grammar beyond the Basics,* 698: "The fourfold condition is used in a very broad way. Paul builds his argument from the actual (he does have prophetic powers) to the hypothetical (he does not understand all mysteries nor have all knowledge [otherwise, he would be omniscient!]). This is his pattern in the first three verses of 1 Cor 13 — an argument from the actual to the hypothetical. It is therefore probable that Paul could speak in the tongues of human beings, but *not* in the tongues of *angels* (v. 1). 1 Cor 13:1, then, offers no comfort for those who view tongues as a heavenly lan-

Such heightening was also known as amplification in rhetorical terms. Chrysostom sees that going on here not only in terms of the steps within each verse, but also in the progression from tongues to prophecy and then from prophecy to total self-abnegation: Paul "preferred to conduct his argument by amplification, he begins from the less and ascends to the greater. For whereas, when he indicated their order, he placed the gift of tongues last, this he now numbers first; by degrees, as I said, ascending to the greater gifts."[21] The eschatological nature of love is reflected in the affirmation that whether or not one "is" anything before God (v. 2) or "gains" anything from one's actions (v. 3), both of which have soteriological connotations, depends on the presence or absence of love.

**13:1** This verse has played a remarkable role in some modern discussions of the viewpoints of the Corinthians and their theological problems. Those who conclude that the Corinthians were suffering from an overrealized eschatology have found in this verse a hint that they may have thought that by speaking in tongues they were already participating in angelic experience as all believers would upon the resurrection from the dead. This thought, that some Corinthians aspired to or imagined themselves to be participating in angelic life and experience, is also considered to be related to their abstinence from sexual relationships (7:1), among other things.[22] We find the texts employed in support of such interpretations to have more convincing interpretations that do not depend on overrealized eschatology as the key background issue.

Some interpreters have suggested that by speaking *in human or angelic tongues* Paul refers to "sublime oratory," picking up on the theme of wise and lofty speech from the first two chapters.[23] The other references to spiritual gifts and to speaking in tongues in the near context make it clear that Paul has the gift of speaking in tongues in mind. The first two gifts Paul mentions in these verses (13:1-2a), tongues and prophecy, are those that will receive extended discussion in chapter 14; the first is the one that seems to be valued most highly by the Corinthians, while the second is the one Paul himself seems to value most highly as an alternative.

Two factors govern our interpretation of the reference to human and angelic tongues. The first factor is that each of the other abilities mentioned

---

guage." Each of the first three verses of this chapter employs third-class conditional structures (marked by the use of ἐάν with a subjunctive verb in the protasis). This structure "simply projects some action or event for hypothetical consideration" (Porter, *Idioms of the Greek New Testament*, 262). Paul is not asserting that he or anyone else actually has or could have such idealized forms of the gifts mentioned.

21. *Homiliae in Epistulam i ad Corinthios* 32.7 (NPNF[1] 12:189).

22. Cf. Fee, 12, 269, 276, 330, 498, 502, 516, 573.

23. See Calvin, 274 ("eloquence"); Carl R. Holladay, "1 Corinthians 13: Paul as Apostolic Paradigm," in *Greeks, Romans and Christians — In Honor of A. J. Malherbe* (ed. D. L. Balch, E. Ferguson, and W. A. Meeks; Minneapolis: Fortress, 1990), 92; Mack, *Rhetoric and the New Testament*, 65.

in vv. 1-3 seem to be spiritual gifts. That leads us to reject interpretations of either speaking in human tongues or angelic tongues to be a great but merely human achievement. The second factor is that there seems to be a repeated three-step pattern of heightening in each verse, from a remarkable gift to a truly marvelous gift to the most excellent way of love. In light of that contextual evidence, it appears that Paul recognizes the ability to speak (presumably unknown) human languages as a spiritual gift and that the ability to speak angelic languages would be "a deluxe version" of that same gift. In practice, of course, one would presumably never know (and Paul himself probably was not sure himself) when or whether the unknown language being spoken was a human or angelic language. The praise angels give to God is mentioned in Psalm 103:20 and 148:2. The Qumran community manifested an extraordinary fascination with praise that is offered from the tongues of angels (cf. 4QShirShabb[a] 2 i 1-8; 4QShirShabb[d] i 1-8; ii 26-37; 4QShir[b] 35 i 3-5). Forbes has provided strong evidence that speaking in tongues would have been understood as unknown human languages, while Martin provides evidence that angels and divinities were understood to have their own languages.[24] There does not seem to be any reason to think that we are restricted to just one or the other, although the rhetorical pattern would suggest that speaking in tongues would most frequently entail speaking of (unknown) human languages, with the ability to speak angelic languages seen as an even more wonderful version or extension of the same gift.[25] Since it would presumably be impossible to tell the difference (as long as no one understood the language anyway), it may be that some Corinthians were making the extraordinary claim to speak in angelic languages.[26]

That Paul mentions tongues here at all indicates that it was generally thought to confer high spiritual status in Corinth, since the point of these opening verses is the surprising assertion that even these extraordinary spiritual powers count for nothing if they are not empowered by love. By including tongues in this set of examples Paul tacitly confirms the value of speaking in tongues even as he denies that it retains any value if such speaking is not governed by love for others.

24. Forbes, *Prophecy and Inspired Speech*, 53-72; D. B. Martin, *The Corinthian Body*, 88-90 and "Tongues of Angels," 558-61 (cf. *Testament of Job* 48–50; Dio Chrysostom, *Discourses* 10.23; 11.22).

25. Thiselton recognizes in Paul's rhetoric "a climactic escalation from gifts-as-they-are to scenarios or imagined projections of the utmost that they could be" (1044, emphasis removed). Theodoret, 215, and Calvin, 274, both see hyperbole here. Garland points out that in the following two verses "a second condition is appended with ἐάν that escalates the glory quotient of the gift" (610) and that "[s]ince the second ἐάν does not appear in 13:1, speaking in the tongues of angels may not be an exaggeration of speaking in the tongues of humans" (610 n. 7). It is difficult to know how much to make of that syntactical difference, and thus it is best not to be dogmatic regarding whether Paul thinks of speaking in angelic tongues as a normal glossolalic experience or as hyperbole.

26. Cf. Blomberg, 259: "'Tongues of angels' probably refers to the Corinthians' estimation of this gift."

If Paul exercises such gifts and does *not have love,* he is *only a resounding gong or a clanging cymbal.* This is the first mention of love since 8:1. The word occurs nine more times between 13:1 and 14:1. To have or *not have love* is not about emotions or feelings but about living and relating to other people in a way that either does or does not reflect their great worth in God's eyes and therefore in ours. Paul will expand on just what kinds of behaviors he has in mind in vv. 4-7. The same phrase, *but do not have love,*[27] is repeated in each of the first three verses of this chapter. Garland points out that "[o]ne can put on a show of love without having love, but one who truly has love cannot help but show it. Consequently, Paul emphasizes having love."[28]

While referring to himself, Paul clearly has in mind that some Corinthians have in fact been exercising this and other gifts while failing to exercise love. They are to recognize themselves in this less direct approach taken by the apostle and realize that while they may have anticipated receiving great praise from God for their spiritual accomplishments, they actually amount to nothing more than noisy gongs or cymbals. Carson reminds us that "[t]his value judgement is meant to be shocking. . . . It is not the gift of tongues that is only a resounding gong . . . but I, myself,"[29] that is, the Corinthians themselves (and we ourselves).

What does Paul have in mind by *a resounding gong or a clanging cymbal?* According to BDAG, the word translated *gong*[30] refers to "a metal of various types, such as copper, brass, or bronze" or to "anything made of such metal,"[31] and the participle modifying it means "to sound" or "ring out." There are a few references to sounding bronze in ancient Greco-Roman literature. Herodotus tells of a blacksmith who discovered secret tunnels by hitting a bronze shield on the ground: "all the other places which he struck returned a dull sound; but where there were tunnels, the bronze of the shield rang clear."[32] According to Plato (*Protagoras* 328e-329b), the problem with most public speakers is that they don't know how to answer questions or interact with interlocutors: "suppose you put a question to one of them — they are just like books, incapable of either answering you or putting a question of their own; if you question even a small point in what has been said, just as brazen vessels ring a long time[33] after they have been struck and prolong the note unless you put your hand

27. Gk. ἀγάπην δὲ μὴ ἔχω.

28. Garland, 610.

29. Carson, *Showing the Spirit,* 59, cited in Thiselton, 1035.

30. Gk. χαλκός.

31. Corinth was famous in antiquity for its bronze, although it is not clear whether this has anything to do with our text. See Jerome Murphy-O'Connor, "Corinthian Bronze," *RB* 90 (1983), 80-93, as well as his *St. Paul's Corinth,* 202-18.

32. Herodotus, *Histories* 4.200 (A. D. Godley's LCL trans.). Gk. ἠχέεσκε ὁ χαλκὸς τῆς ἀσπίδος.

33. Gk. τὰ χαλκία πληγέντα μακρὸν ἠχεῖ.

on them, these orators too, on being asked a little question, extend their speech over a full-length course."[34] Ovid refers to Bacchus's attendants causing their bronze cymbals to resound.[35]

Both implements mentioned by Paul have been translated in a variety of ways. Virtually all English translations translate the first noun as *gong* and the participle as "noisy" (NRSV, ESV, RSV, NASB, NET, NLT) or "resounding" (TNIV, NIV, NIV, NAB), although the NJB goes with "booming." The second noun has been consistently translated as "cymbal," while the participle has usually been rendered as either "clanging" (TNIV, NIV, NRSV, ESV, RSV, NASB, NET, NLT) or "clashing" (NAB, NJB), although the KJV has translated it as "tinkling."

BDAG suggests that the meaning of the first term here may be "a noisy (brass) gong" or possibly an "'acoustical vase' used in theaters." W. V. Harris and William W. Klein have provided the strongest evidence that Paul has in mind a bronze acoustic jar; they base their view on comments by Vitruvius Pollio in his *On Architecture* 5.5.1, 7-8 and archeological evidence found in a few ancient theaters.[36] Anathea Portier-Young offers several telling arguments against this view: (1) "no one has discovered a "sounding-vase" at Corinth or elsewhere"; (2) "[o]nly Vitruvius makes mention of this device," and he does not identify it with the term used by Paul; (3) "the Corinthian theater that allegedly made use of these vases did not stand in Paul's time, and had not stood for nearly a hundred years"; (4) "[t]here is no guarantee that either Paul or his audience knew of the existence or function of such objects."[37] She points out that "one must keep in mind that there are no extant biblical, classical, or Hellenistic references to a musical instrument or device" known by the term Paul uses here.[38]

That Paul has in mind a *gong* is supported by the fact that this term seems to be in a parallel relationship with another that clearly means *cymbal*, suggesting that this, too, may be a reference to a musical instrument. This view may find further support in 14:7-8 where Paul refers to "lifeless things that make sounds" like the pipe or harp, whose tunes will not be recognized "unless there is a distinction in the notes," and to the trumpet, which will be useless if it "does not sound a clear call."

An even more likely interpretation of the parallelism between the

34. Plato, *Plato in Twelve Volumes*, vol. 3, trans. W. R. M. Lamb (Cambridge, MA: Harvard University Press; London: William Heinemann Ltd., 1967).

35. Ovid, *Fasti* 3.740-42; "aeriferae comitum concrepuere manus . . . sonitus aera."

36. W. Harris, "'Sounding Brass' and Hellenistic Technology," *BAR* 8 (1982), 38-41, and "Echoing Bronze," *The Journal of the Acoustical Society of America* 70 (1981), 1184-85, and William W. Klein, "Noisy Gong or Acoustic Vase? A Note on 1 Corinthians 13:1," *NTS* 32 (1986), 286-89.

37. Anathea Portier-Young, "Tongues and Cymbals: Contextualizing 1 Corinthians 13:1," *BTB* 35 (2005), 100. See also Jerome Murphy-O'Connor's comments in *St. Paul's Corinth*, 76.

38. Portier-Young, "Tongues and Cymbals," 100-101. That is, none referred to as a χαλκός.

first two clauses is offered by Portier-Young: "Paul has begun his analogy with a very generic reference to a metal well known for its capacity to produce a ringing sound. At this point, any number of interpretations might be suggested by the material mentioned. . . . Anticipating the need for clarification, however, Paul has added a more concrete image, 'a loud-sounding cymbal.'"[39]

> In the phrase "ringing bronze-thing or loud-sounding cymbal," the latter descriptive element serves to fill out and therefore "disambiguate" the meaning of the first. . . . In the case at hand, while the words are not synonyms, they in fact describe the same thing. Compare Paul's description of two musical instruments, the pipe and lyre: "just as soulless things giving sound, either a pipe or a lyre . . ." (14:7). Taken by itself, the expression "soulless things giving sound" could refer to anything from falling rocks to a babbling brook, or shoes slapping on stone pavement. The two instruments named clarify and limit Paul's meaning, thereby providing the substance of the metaphor.[40]

In the case of the two expressions in 13:1, we should probably understand not only that the second expression, *clanging cymbal,* clarifies the reference to the "resounding brass" but that Paul's intention in mentioning a resounding or clanging brass cymbal[41] is further disambiguated in the following chapter with the references to "lifeless things that make sounds" but that lack "a distinction in the notes" (14:7).[42]

According to K. L. Schmidt, the word translated *cymbal*[43] "denotes a shallow metallic basin which, when struck against another, gives out a resounding note." Such instruments "were particularly used in the cultus." He suggests that Paul's contrast between clanging cymbal and love evokes the image "of a prophet of the old covenant speaking of the noisy, empty and futile nature of an external cultus."[44] In the LXX the bronze (or brass) utensils are frequently referred to as part of the temple worship (Exod. 27:3; 38:23; Lev. 6:21; 1 Kgs. 7:31; 2 Kgs. 25:14, 16; 1 Chr. 18:8; 2 Chr. 4:16, 18; 1 Esdr. 8:56; Ezra 8:27; Jer. 52:18). Schmidt conjectures (based on Tiberius

39. Portier-Young, "Tongues and Cymbals," 101.

40. Portier-Young, "Tongues and Cymbals," 101.

41. It is possible that there is a heightening here just as there is between human languages and angelic languages. In that case the version of the gift that results in speaking human languages could possibly be compared to "sounding brass," while speaking angelic languages would be like a clanging cymbal. Neither would be something to which one would aspire.

42. Chrysostom seems to tie these texts together in commenting on the expression "sounding brass," asserting that it suggests "a thing senseless and inanimate" because it emits sound "but at random and in vain, and for no good end" (*Homiliae in Epistulam i ad Corinthios* 32.6 [NPNF[1] 12:189]).

43. Gk. κύμβαλον.

44. K. L. Schmidt, "κύμβαλον," *TDNT* 3:1038.

Caesar's reference to Apion as the "world's cymbal" [*cymbalum mundi*]) that "a sounding cymbal might well be a term for an empty-headed and boastful prattler."[45]

Thiselton points out that "[m]odern musicologists distinguish the *crotal*, which goes back thousands of years and is a thick metal plate, from the modern *orchestral cymbal*, which is of Turkish origin. The *crotal* had 'a definite pitch' and could be hit head-on (unlike the modern orchestral cymbal) or struck by a club or hammer." He thinks that this may explain the use of the singular, cymbal, here.[46] But virtually all of our references to cymbals (or *crotals*) up to and including the first century are in the plural (or dual),[47] suggesting that they were not used as individual instruments but in pairs or in sets, with each one tuned to a definite pitch like the various bars that make up a xylophone. Portier-Young also points out that "[a]ccording to the biblical record, the cymbals were never played alone, but always together with other instruments."[48] That is most likely true outside the Bible as well. In any case, one could not play a song with just one cymbal or pair of cymbals. There would be no variety of notes, no way to play a tune, that could be recognized.[49] As Garland puts it, those who speak in tongues but lack love "are no more than a bunch of loud clangers,"[50] or, possibly, no more useful than a xylophone or piano with only one functioning note.

We should remember that Paul's statement "I am only sounding brass or [more specifically] a clanging cymbal" "is parallel with 'I am good for nothing' (v. 2) and 'it is not to my advantage' (v. 3)"; thus, we should probably not stretch it to mean much more than those two statements.[51] Robertson and Plummer's suggestion that the point of this apodosis is that "I produce nothing of value" complements the points of the next two ("I am of no value" and "I gain nothing of value")[52] is on target.

45. K. L. Schmidt, "κύμβαλον," *TDNT* 3:1038.

46. Thiselton, 1037.

47. Based on a search of *TLG* which found approximately fifty occurrences. Exceptions include our verse, *Sibylline Oracles* 8:114, Xenophon, *Hippos* 1.3, Megasthenes, *Fragmenta* 38a.78-79, Flavius Arrianus, *Historia Indica* 14.6.1-2, *Periplus Ponti Euxini* 9.1.3, Pseudo-Clementine, *Recognitiones* 8.29.3.8. Josephus describes them in *Antiquities* 7.306 as being "broad and large instruments . . . made of brass" (κύμβαλά τε ἦν πλατέα καὶ μεγάλα χάλκεα).

48. Portier-Young, "Tongues and Cymbals," 104.

49. See Thiselton's discussion and proper rejection of Todd Sanders' argument in favor of taking the word translated *or* here (Gk. ἤ) as "rather than" and the two clauses to mean "I have become only a resonating acoustic jar rather than a flourish of cymbals" (Thiselton, 1038-39; cf. Todd K. Sanders, "A New Approach to 1 Corinthians 13:1," *NTS* 36 (1990), 614-18. Sanders' approach is followed by Horsley, 176). When authors or speakers intended the word to be understood as the comparative particle ("than" or "rather than") rather than the disjunctive particle ("or"), they introduced linguistic markers (e.g., μᾶλλον ἤ) so as not to leave their auditors in the dark. It is a mistake to argue in favor of a meaning that requires some sort of linguistic clue even when such a clue is missing.

50. Garland, 613.

51. M. M. Mitchell, *Paul and the Rhetoric of Reconciliation*, 473.

52. Robertson and Plummer, 291.

**13:2** Paul moves from tongues (which the Corinthians value so highly) to the gift of prophecy (which ch. 14 contends is the one to which they should give more attention), and then on to other highly valued gifts (see above on the elements of heightening and amplification in these verses). While the previous verse referred to just one gift (with two versions) in the conditional "if" clause (or protasis) leading up to its conclusion or apodosis, this verse mentions two different gifts (prophecy and faith) leading to the same conclusion or apodosis. We will look at each gift before commenting on the concluding statement.

*If I have the gift of prophecy and can fathom all mysteries and all knowledge.* Paul does have the gift of prophecy, and describes his apostolic calling in language echoing famous prophetic calls of the Old Testament.[53] Indeed, his prophetic standing as an apostle is understood to out-trump any other prophetic gift in Corinth or in the churches he has planted (cf. 14:37-38). Garland states: "The mysteries of God have been revealed to Paul (2:1, 9-10; 15:51), and he regards himself as a 'steward of God's mysteries' (4:1)."[54] The reference to "knowing all mysteries" evokes the portrayal of Daniel in Daniel 2 and 4, especially in 4:9 in Theodotion's version, where because "the Holy Spirit of God" is in him "no mystery is too hard for him."[55] And yet not even Paul would claim the ability to *fathom all mysteries and all knowledge.* In vv. 9-12 he stresses that in this age "we know in part and we prophesy in part," for "now we see only a reflection as in a mirror." It is only at Christ's return that "completeness comes" and "we shall see face to face" and "know fully" (see the comments there). Paul is describing what it would be like, in hyperbolic terms, to have the most perfect prophetic gift imaginable, what it would be like if he knew fully even now. His thought reflects "a climactic escalation from gifts-as-they-are to scenarios or imagined projections of the utmost that they could be."[56]

The mention of mysteries is interesting since in 14:2 Paul says that those who speak in tongues "utter mysteries by the Spirit." The contrast between prophecy and tongues is that those with the former gift have a God-given ability to understand the things of God while those who have the latter gift utter divine mysteries but have no understanding of what they are saying.

That there is an important relationship between *prophecy* and *knowledge* is clear, even if its exact nature is not.[57] Prophets are people who know

53. See Karl O. Sandnes, *Paul — One of the Prophets? A Contribution to the Apostle's Self-Understanding* (WUNT 2.43; Tübingen: J. C. B. Mohr [Paul Siebeck], 1991), and Roy E. Ciampa, *The Presence and Function of Scripture in Galatians 1 and 2* (WUNT 2.102; Tübingen: Mohr Siebeck, 1998), 111-14, 332-33.

54. Garland, 610.

55. Gk. καὶ πᾶν μυστήριον οὐκ ἀδυνατεῖ σε.

56. Thiselton, 1044 (emphasis removed).

57. Fee, 633 n. 35, points out that the terms "mysteries" and "knowledge" are frequently found together in Jewish apocalyptic literature, pointing to Dan. 2:19-23, 28, "where

God and/or the things of God (cf. Num. 12:6; Ps. 74:9; Luke 7:39; Acts 2:30; Rom. 16:25-26 [where we find knowledge and understanding of a mystery through prophetic ministry]; Eph. 3:5). Knowledge and prophecy are mentioned together again in 1 Corinthians 13:8-9, where it seems they are separate gifts (as also appears to be the case in 12:8) but may still be very closely related. In this verse Paul describes a prophetic gift that subsumes understanding of *all mysteries and all knowledge* within it, presumably as the necessary foundation for the most perfectly infallible explanation imaginable of God's will for his people in a particular place and time.

*and if I have a faith* [literally, "all faith"] *that can move mountains.* Mountain-moving faith was "a proverbial expression for accomplishing something impossible in a miraculous way (see Matt. 17:19-20; 21:21; Mark 11:22-24; Luke 17:6; *b. Ber.* 64a; *b. Sanh.* 24a)."[58] Of course Paul "has faith and has performed miracles (2 Cor. 12:12; Rom. 15:19)."[59] That Paul has in mind the most perfect possible manifestation of the gift of faith is indicated by a third use of the word "all" in this verse (after "all mysteries" and "all knowledge") which modifies faith in Greek; literally, "and if I have all faith."[60] In the comments on 12:9 it was pointed out that the moving (or razing) of mountains is an eschatological motif associated with God's judgment and/or the removal of obstacles to the restoration of his presence to his people (Isa. 40:4; 41:15; 42:15; 49:11; 54:10; Luke 3:5; Rev. 6:14; 8:8; 16:20). But Paul may be speaking hyperbolically here of a literal (and quite amazing) power to move mountains. Remarkably, while Paul's reference to "mountain-moving" faith here echoes Jesus' promise about the power of even mustard-seed-sized faith to move mountains (Matt. 17:20; 21:21; Mark 11:23), what Jesus says (probably speaking metaphorically or even more hyperbolically than Paul) can be done with mustard-seed-sized faith Paul can only imagine doing in some more perfect state in which he might have "all faith."

*but do not have love, I am nothing.* Even if Paul had such extraordinary faith as could actually move mountains, if it were not accompanied by love, he would be nothing. Mitchell points out that here "the rhetorical force of the argument is strengthened by the contrast between the thrice-repeated 'all' and Paul's single 'nothing.'"[61] Even with all that knowledge and all that understanding and faith, he would still be nothing. As pointed out

---

in the LXX the repeated language includes σοφία, γνῶσις, μυστήρια, and ἀποκαλύπτω," and to "the recurring 'he showed me all the mysteries of . . .' in 1 Enoch (41:1; 52:2; 61:5; 63:3; 68:5; 71:4)." There is also some association between angels and mysteries in Jewish apocalyptic literature (1QH$^{a}$ ix 11; 4Q403 fr. 1 ii 23; *3 Baruch* 1:6-8; 2:5; *1 Enoch* 106:19; *Testament of Levi* 2:9-10).

58. Garland, 614. For a full and careful discussion of mountain-moving faith, see Maureen Yeung, *Faith in Jesus and Paul* (WUNT 2.147; Tübingen: Mohr Siebeck, 2002), 21-50.

59. Garland, 610.

60. Gk. καὶ ἐὰν ἔχω πᾶσαν τὴν πίστιν.

61. M. M. Mitchell, *Paul and the Rhetoric of Reconciliation*, 474.

above, the eschatological nature of love is reflected in the affirmation that whether or not one "is" anything before God[62] (which has soteriological connotations) depends on the presence or absence of love. We need to recall Carson's comments regarding v. 1 since here also "[t]his value judgement is meant to be shocking" and it is not the gifts themselves that would amount to *nothing,* "but I, myself."[63] Paul, of course, although he is incredibly gifted, still does not have gifts reflecting the ideal level of perfection he is describing. And yet it should be clear to any reader that Paul could not possibly be thought of as amounting to *nothing.* If that is so, one would have to conclude that it is only so because it is love, in fact, that motivates and empowers all that he does on behalf of Christ and his kingdom. It was his love for others that he was speaking of in chapter 9 when he said he had made himself "a slave to everyone, to win as many as possible" (9:19) and had "become all things to all people so that by all possible means [he] might save some" (9:22). The only way to rise above not "square one" but "square zero" is to operate out of love, which, of course, is a gift of God and fruit of the Spirit's work in our lives (Gal. 5:22).

These first three verses of the chapter raise the readers' anticipation for vv. 4-7 since the elaborate amplification on the necessity of love raises the question of what such love looks like in real life. The anticipation will not be resolved immediately, however, as Paul goes on in the next verse to develop this theme one step further.

**13:3** *If*[64] *I give all I possess to the poor and give over my body to hardship that I may boast, but do not have love, I gain nothing.* This verse contains one of the more difficult textual problems in the New Testament.[65] Witnesses are divided between *give over my body . . . that I may boast*[66] and "give over my body that I may be burned,"[67] with a number of other subsidiary variants of

62. Fee also argues that "nothing in the sight of God" is "surely what Paul means by "nothing" in this sentence and "profit nothing" in the next (632, n. 33).

63. Carson, *Showing the Spirit,* 59.

64. Gk. κἄν is formed by crasis (contraction) from καὶ ἐάν ("and if" or "even if") and has the same meaning. Thiselton thinks that it means "even if" here and "signals the escalating rhetoric" of the passage (1044).

65. For more on the textual issues see Chrys C. Caragounis, "'To boast' or 'to be burned': The Crux of 1 Cor 13:3," *SEÅ* 60 (1995), 115-27; J. F. M. Smit, "Two Puzzles: 1 Corinthians 12.31 and 13.3. A Rhetorical Solution," *NTS* 39 (1993) 246-64; J. H. Petzer, "Contextual Evidence in Favour of ΚΑΥΧΗΣΩΜΑΙ in 1 Corinthians 13:3," *NTS* 35 (1989), 229-53; James K. Elliott, "In Favour of καυθήσομαι at 1 Corinthians 13:3," *ZNW* 62 (1971), 297-98; as well as Metzger, *A Textual Commentary,* 497-98, and Thiselton, 1042-44.

66. Read by 𝔓[46], א, A, B, 048, 33, 1739*, *pc,* co, goth[mg], Hier[mss], Clement, Origen, Jerome, and Greek MSS mentioned by Jerome.

67. Read by C, D, F, G, L, 81, 1175, 1881*, *al,* latt, sy[hmg], Tertullian, Ambrosiaster, Aphraates, Cyprian, Origen, Basil, Chrysostom, Cyril, Theodoret, Euthalius, Maximus the Confessor, John of Damascus, and some of Jerome's MSS. The difference in Greek between these two readings is very slight. The first is καυχήσωμαι, while the second is καυθήσομαι. The two different letters are easily switched due to the fact that their pronunciations were not that different.

the second choice.[68] The second reading would echo Daniel 3:95 LXX, where Daniel's friends "gave their bodies to be burned,"[69] but both external and internal considerations indicate that the first reading ("that I may boast") is to be preferred.[70] We take *that I may boast* to be the original text, which was altered once martyrdom by fire became a more common experience.

*If I give all I possess to the poor.* English translations are divided between those that simply mention giving away all that is owned (ESV, NRSV, NAB, NET) and those that indicate that everything is given away *to the poor* (TNIV, NIV, NASB, NJB, NLT, CSB, KJV). BDAG suggests that the word[71] here means "to give away, prob[ably] in installments" and that the relevant part of this text means to "give away all one's property bit by bit, dole it out" or "divide in small pieces = fritter away in the process of such charitable activity," explicitly asserting that "the text makes no mention of feeding 'the poor' as KJV." On the other hand, even BDAG gives "to cause someone to *eat, to feed*" as the first definition of the word, and LSJ indicates that the meaning here is to "give food by hand." The two meanings in the LEH lexicon of the LXX are "to feed [somebody] with [something]" and "to feed [somebody] with morsels." Gerhard Schneider notes that the word generally means "give to eat, feed; distribute (as alms)" and that the meaning in this verse is "*use* all my possessions to feed the needy," that is, "*distribute as alms*."[72] This seems correct, and while both kinds of translations are acceptable, even those that do not mention the poor explicitly should probably be understood to have the welfare of the poor implicitly in view. As we will see below, that this is what Paul has in mind may help explain the reference to boasting in the middle of the verse.

The context makes it clear that the actions mentioned here are understood to reflect the practice of spiritual gifts (since the examples in vv. 1-2 were clearly spiritual gifts and the relationship between gifts and love dominates this chapter). It is not as clear whether or not they are embodiments of one or two of the gifts mentioned in 12:8-10 or 12:28-30. In Romans 12:8 Paul refers to the gift of (alms)giving — of sharing one's resources with those in

68. The other variants are attempts to improve the awkward grammar of the second option, one of them adopting a verb form (καυθήσωμαι, found in Ψ, 1739[c], 1881[c], 𝔐) that was used in the Byzantine period but not in New Testament times (the future subjunctive) and that cannot be original. The other changes to a third-person verb (καυθῇ) to smooth the expression to "give over my body that it might be burned" (as in 1505, *pc*, sy[h]).

69. Gk. καὶ παρέδωκαν τὰ σώματα αὐτῶν εἰς ἐμπυρισμόν.

70. Scribes would have been tempted to change the "boasting" reading into the "burning" reading after martyrdom by burning became an all-too-common experience in the early church. It is much harder to find sufficient motives for the opposite change to take place. Metzger also points out that "[t]he argument that the presence of the statement, 'that I may glory,' destroys the sense of the passage loses some of its force when one observes that for Paul 'glorying' is not invariably reprehensible; sometimes he regards it as justified (2 Cor 8.24; Php 2.16; 1 Th 2.19; 2 Th 1.4)" (Metzger, *Textual Commentary*, 498).

71. Gk. ψωμίζω.

72. Gerhard Schneider, "ψωμίζω," *EDNT* 3:503.

need. He may well have the same or a similar gift in mind when he mentions the gift of "helping" in 1 Corinthians 12:28, and that may be what he has in mind here as well. The impression that he is moving from less highly valued to more highly valued gifts may militate against this idea, since the gift of helps does not seem to rate more highly than the gift of prophecy in Paul's thinking. Paul probably has saved the gift or gifts mentioned in this verse for last, however, because of the theme he has been developing in this passage: that the practice of spiritual gifts motivated and empowered by anything other than love is of no value whatsoever.[73] One could imagine someone speaking in tongues, prophesying, or exercising faith out of other motivations, but the thought that someone might give away all their belongings to help the poor out of some other motivation is rather counterintuitive. One would presume that such actions were done out of concern for the poor. Paul will say, however, that even these things may be done out of other motivations, and that when that is so, such helping of the poor is of no spiritual benefit to the helper whatsoever.

These gifts may also be listed at the climax of this passage because almsgiving appears to have been (along with prayer and fasting) perhaps the most highly regarded form of piety within some strands of Second Temple Judaism, including the teaching of Jesus and the apostles.[74] While the apostles did not necessarily give everything to the poor, they did leave everything behind in order to follow Jesus for the benefit of others. In 4:9-11 Paul indicates some of the things he has given up to serve Christ and bring the gospel to others: "To this very hour we go hungry and thirsty, we are in rags, we are brutally treated, we are homeless" (v. 11).[75]

*and give over my body to hardship that I may boast.*[76] The TNIV supplies

73. Cf. Garland, 614: "If the rich man had followed Jesus' directive to a tee and sold all his goods to give to the poor (Mark 12:17-22), but did so selfishly, solely to possess an inheritance in the kingdom of God, then it would have been for naught."

74. This is especially reflected in Tobit, Sirach, Matthew, and Luke/Acts. See Tob. 1:3, 16; 2:14; 4:5-11, 16; 12:8-9; 14:2, 8-11; Sir. 3:30–4:10; 7:10; 12:3; 17:15-24; 29:8-13; 31:8-11; 35:1-4; 40:17, 24; Matt. 6:2-4; Luke 11:41; 12:33; Acts 3:2-3, 10; 9:36; 10:1-31; 24:16. For a fuller listing of related texts in the Bible and Second Temple Jewish literature, see Ciampa, *The Presence and Function of Scripture in Galatians 1 and 2*, 152-53 and nn. 94 and 97 on those pages. Sirach 3:30 asserts that "almsgiving atones for sin." Jesus told the rich young man, "Go, sell everything you have and give to the poor, and you will have treasure in heaven" (Mark 10:21//Matt. 19:21). In the same context Peter exclaimed, "We have left everything to follow you!" (Mark 10:28//Matt. 19:27). Zacchaeus responded to the Lord's grace by saying, "Look, Lord! Here and now I give half of my possessions to the poor" (Luke 19:8).

75. By way of the rhetorical questions in 1 Cor. 9:4-6 Paul suggests that he may have given up even more than Peter: "Don't we have the right to food and drink? Don't we have the right to take a believing wife along with us, as do the other apostles and the Lord's brothers and Cephas? Or is it only I and Barnabas who don't have the right not to work for a living?"

76. The textual problem was discussed in the introduction to this verse, where it was concluded that the giving over of the body was not for the sake of being burned (through martyrdom).

the words "to hardship" with a footnote explaining that they were included in the translation "[t]o achieve clarity" where words "not in the original texts" are "required by the context" but are enclosed in corner brackets because of the translators' uncertainty. What the translators had in mind remains uncertain, although they are probably trying to be as ambiguous as the text itself, without leaving a sentence that is overly awkward. As in the previous verses, we are undoubtedly dealing with a case of "a climactic escalation from gifts-as-they-are to scenarios or imagined projections of the utmost that they could be."[77] Thus we should interpret this clause in a way which reflects the closest possible relationship with the preceding one. The relationship of escalation is to be found in the difference between giving up one's belongings and giving up one's *body*, or whole self.[78]

*1 Clement*, written from Rome to the church in Corinth around the end of the first century, gives examples of sacrifices made by people full of love: "Many kings and princes, in times of pestilence, when they had been instructed by an oracle, have given themselves up to death, in order that by their own blood they might deliver their fellow-citizens [from destruction]. . . . We know many among ourselves who have given themselves up to bonds, in order that they might ransom others. Many, too, have surrendered themselves to slavery, that with the price[?] which they received for themselves, they might provide food for others."[79] As Thiselton points out, "Handing over one's body could in theory refer to selling oneself into slavery in order to provide the funds for the needy," but he thinks that this is reading in an overly specific scenario.[80] Speaking more generally, Paul has in mind "putting one's whole being, including the physical body, at the disposal of others."[81] Presumably, in keeping with the first part of the verse, this would be done in some way that would bring benefit to others, perhaps especially the poor. There are a variety of scenarios that could be imagined: selling oneself into slavery to provide funds for the poor, metaphorically making oneself a slave for the benefit of others (cf. 9:19), perhaps by taking on extra work to earn funds to help the poor, doing projects requiring physical labor for their benefit, and more. Paul may have in mind a willingness to sacrifice everything, including the totality of one's life, for the benefit of others, without focusing specifically on helping the poor. Of course, the gospel is about Christ's giving over his body for our salvation and the glory he gained for himself and for us in the process (cf. Phil. 2:5-11). "Christ died for our sins" and was "raised from the dead, the firstfruits of those who have fallen asleep" (15:3, 20). Christ's giving over of his body

77. Thiselton, 1044 (emphasis removed).

78. As Petzer ("Contextual Evidence," 241) paraphrases, Paul has in mind an approach to proving one's piety by "giving up not only your own belongings, but even your own body, with the result that you may be able to legitimately boast about it."

79. ANF 1:19.

80. Thiselton, 1044 (emphasis removed).

81. Thiselton, 1044.

for us is what is celebrated in the Lord's Supper in the words given us by Paul himself in 11:24: "This is my body, which is [given/broken?] for you."[82] Horrell speaks of "the normative pattern of Christ's self-giving for others" as the key to Paul's "christologically shaped morality."[83] In fact, he reminds us that it was precisely in his self-giving that "Christ's love . . . is given substance" (Gal. 2:20).[84] That Paul may very well have Christ in view here is made more plausible by the recognition that the references to "mountain-moving faith" and to giving away all one's possessions to the poor in the previous clauses seem to reflect on Christ's own teaching.

Paul speaks of his own commitment to such a pattern of life in a variety of ways (see the last paragraph of our commentary on the first clause of this verse). In discussing the resurrection of the dead Paul speaks of his willingness to "endanger [himself] every hour" and "face death every day" (15:30-31), and "to [metaphorically or not] fight wild beasts" (15:32). Horrell summarizes the basic pattern of Paul's life, which he calls others to imitate, as "self-giving and self-lowering *for the sake of the other.*"[85] As Garland summarizes, Paul "understands that he is being given up to death for Jesus' sake and for others (2 Cor. 4:11; Col. 1:24). But love rules his apostolic work (cf. 1 Cor. 16:24; 2 Cor. 2:4; 11:11; 12:15). If he did not do all in love, it would all be for naught."[86]

Calvin thinks that there is "no doubt that Paul is speaking about martyrdom here, which is the finest and supreme action of all. For what is more admirable than that unconquerable firmness of character, where a man has no hesitation about pouring out his life for his witness to the gospel?"[87] Of course his language reflects Paul's own in Philippians 2:17 ("But even if I am being poured out like a drink offering on the sacrifice and service coming from your faith, I am glad and rejoice with all of you")[88] and 2 Timothy 4:6 ("For I am already being poured out like a drink offering, and the time for my departure is near"). Calvin's thoughts are based on the textual variant we have rejected, but this may well be one of many cases where a textual variant that should be rejected as unoriginal points in the direction of the proper interpretation of the text nonetheless. That is, that Paul does not have in mind giving over his body to be burned in martyrdom does not mean that he does not have in mind the possibility of giving over his body to death by some other form of martyrdom. Although martyrdom was not all that common at the time of Paul's writing, it would still have been rec-

82. Cf. Petzer, "Contextual Evidence," 247.

83. Horrell, *Solidarity and Difference*, 242.

84. Horrell, *Solidarity and Difference*, 242. Cf. Hays, *The Moral Vision of the New Testament*, 202.

85. Horrell, *Solidarity and Difference*, 243.

86. Garland, 610.

87. Calvin, 275.

88. Interestingly, these words follow immediately after a reference to Paul's hope to "be able to boast on the day of Christ that I did not run or labor in vain" (v. 16).

ognizable as a possibility for one utterly committed to obeying God. In Romans 16:3-4 Paul greets Priscilla and Aquila as co-workers who "risked their lives for me." In Philippians 2:25-30 Paul commends Epaphroditus as one who "was ill, and almost died" and as one whom the Philippians should honor "because he almost died for the work of Christ. He risked his life to make up for the help you yourselves could not give me."

A willingness to sacrifice one's body or life for the benefit of others is a fundamental Christian value, one that is ultimately sustained by the message of the resurrection of the dead, which is extensively defended in chapter 15. It is the promise of the resurrection which warrants whatever sacrifices we might make as we live out our love for God and others. Thanks to the promise of the resurrection, we know that all our labors of love are not in vain (15:58), but will result in great *gain* (13:3b).

*but do not have love, I gain nothing.* It would be strange and unusual for someone to give away all of their belongings and/or sacrifice their very body in the service of Christ and others without being led and motivated by the power of love within them, but Paul has suggested in the previous clause that it might be done out of a sense of duty and commitment to God and the hope to be able to rejoice in God's presence on the last day for having been able to follow through with such sacrificial service. If one were to carry out even such self-sacrificing service and yet not have love, it would ultimately bring no gain or advantage on that last day. As pointed out above, the eschatological nature of love is reflected in the affirmation that whether or not one "gains" anything from one's actions (which has clear soteriological connotations) depends on the presence or absence of love. The advantage, in the case of *giving over* [*one's*] *body,* is presumably eschatological gain experienced as divine vindication at or before the resurrection of the dead. Here, despite what would appear in human eyes to be the most remarkable demonstration of spiritual commitment imaginable, the person should expect no praise or reward from God. They will *gain nothing* from him. "The 'totality of the gift' contrasts dramatically with 'the nothingness of the result.'"[89]

Collins points out that "Paul's argument is couched in the language of the rhetorical argument from advantage (cf. 14:6). . . . Paul has previously urged the Corinthians to consider what is to their own advantage (6:12; 7:35; 10:23, 33; 12:7). Now he offers himself as an example of one who has considered what is to his own advantage and has come to the conclusion that there is no advantage whatsoever that would accrue to himself if he does not have love."[90] Ironically, love is all about seeking *gain* (benefit or advantage) for others (see on vv. 4-7), so that, paradoxically, the only way to gain a benefit or advantage from God is to love others, that is, to dedicate one's life to seeking to gain benefit or advantage for those around us.

89. Garland, 616, citing Spicq, *Agape in the New Testament* (vol. 2; trans. M. A. McNamara and M. H. Richter; St. Louis and London: Herder, 1965), 149.

90. Collins, 477.

*ii. Pointed description of some of love's key attributes, 13:4-7*

> [4]*Love is patient, love is kind. It does not envy, it does not boast, it is not proud.* [5]*It does not dishonor others, it is not self-seeking, it is not easily angered, it keeps no record of wrongs.* [6]*Love does not delight in evil but rejoices with the truth.* [7]*It always protects, always trusts, always hopes, always perseveres.*

In contrast with vv. 1-3 and 8-12, which compare love with qualities of spiritual gifts, these four verses are marked by an "exclusive concentration" on love's qualities.[91] They are also distinct in their rhetorical style since "[t]he encompassing sections contain sentences with a complex grammatical structure, but those in Paul's central section are short and simple."[92] Both of those observations support the point made earlier, that this chapter reflects a chiastic structure with these verses serving as the centerpiece of the chiasm. These four verses also reflect a chiastic structure, with positive affirmations about love found in vv. 4a-b and v. 7 and negative affirmations in vv. 4b-6.[93]

Today, more than ever, "love is a vague and over-used term, which requires definition and substance to be made meaningful."[94] Witherington argues that "love is a matter of behavior, not feeling. In particular it is other-directed behavior, not self-directed action."[95] Although this view is widespread in New Testament interpretation,[96] it is based on a misunderstanding of emotion. While love is not just a feeling, it is not less than or other than a feeling. The noncognitive approach to the emotions, now largely discredited by modern psychology, holds that emotions are something to be contrasted with rational thought and consequently cannot be commanded; the emotions are regarded as an independent noncognitive system. The cognitive approach regards emotion as an indicator of what we believe and value and as such is an integral part of our reason and ethics. As Matthew Elliott observes: "Love is an emotion. As with any emotion, a Christian worldview will have unique reasons for love and distinct ideas about what action and behaviour it should motivate."[97] 1 Corinthians 13 elaborates on these behaviors.

91. Collins, 478.

92. Collins, 478.

93. Collins, 478.

94. Horrell, *Solidarity and Difference,* 242, paraphrasing Hays, *The Moral Vision of the New Testament,* 202.

95. Witherington, 269.

96. Cf. Schrage, *The Ethics of the New Testament,* 212: "Human love, like God's love, is not an attitude or an emotion, but an act."

97. Matthew Elliott, *Faithful Feelings: Emotion in the New Testament* (Leicester: Inter-Varsity Press, 2005), 161. Elliott's book is a full defense of the cognitive view of emotion in relation to New Testament interpretation. See also his stirring popular application to Christian living: *Feel: The Power of Listening to Your Heart* (Carol Stream, IL: Tyndale House, 2008).

Horrell notes that the expression "other-regard" serves as "a concise way of defining what love implies, according to Paul."[98] Another way of putting it might be to say that love entails "being for someone," just as God, who loves and knows us fully (v. 12), is "for us" in Romans 8:31, which in context, Paul implies, is equivalent to "the love of God that is in Christ Jesus" (Rom. 8:39), the two expressions forming an inclusio for the unit Romans 8:31-39. It is God's love for us which serves as the model and foundation for the love we have for him and each other, and that love is seen and felt in the fact that he is for us. Love is what Paul has been talking about through much of this letter.[99] He signaled the theme back in 8:1, and although he did not use the term in chapter 9, the description he gives there of the way he relates to others will, on the basis of his description of love here, now be seen as one of further examples of loving behavior.

In these verses Paul personifies love, describing it not by way of adjectives, but through verbs — in terms of its behavior.[100] As Spicq argues, while other kinds of love, like those extolled in society today, "can remain hidden in the heart, it is essential" to Christian love "to manifest itself, to demonstrate itself, to provide proofs, to put itself on display."[101]

Interestingly, Paul spends more time on what love does not do than on what it does. As most commentators have noted, this is in large part due to the fact that Paul's comments about love here are not based on some abstract, context-free meditation on the subject, but on providing a stinging contrast to the behavior of some Corinthian Christians. Most, if not all, of the descriptions of love given here reflect concerns Paul has with the church in Corinth. As others have pointed out, "omitting the negatives in each clause leaves us with a good description of the Corinthians' behavior. They are impatient and unkind, filled with jealousy, vainglorious, and puffed up. They insist on their own way, are cantankerous and resentful, and rejoice in wrong rather than right."[102] Paul's praise of love is highly ironic, since it is primarily characterized by listing behaviors that implicitly reflect blame on the Corinthians.[103] It should be clear through their reading

98. Horrell, *Solidarity and Difference*, 242.

99. So also N. T. Wright (*What Saint Paul Really Said*, 147): "Everything Paul has said so far on every topic has been, after all, an appeal for *agape*."

100. Paul uses fifteen verbs in these four verses. English translations commonly translate several of the more active Greek verbs with the English verb "is," followed by an adjective.

101. Spicq, *TLNT* 1:12. Spicq is right that "it would almost always be necessary to translate *agapē* as 'demonstration of love,'" but this is one case where that does not apply, since Paul is in fact distinguishing love from its manifestations, proofs, and displays.

102. Garland, 616, crediting J. C. Hurd, *The Origin of 1 Corinthians* (London: SPCK, 1965), 112.

103. Sigountos, "The Genre of 1 Corinthians," 256-57; Garland, 616; Horsley, 177. According to the Geneva Bible, Paul provides this discussion of love so that "the Corinthians may understand both how profitable it is in the church, and how necessary: and also how far they are from it, and therefore how vainly and without cause they are proud."

of this passage that "although the gifts of the Spirit are conspicuous in their assembly, their lack of love is even more conspicuous."[104]

If love "is the lifestyle that reveals what genuine renewed humanity is all about,"[105] the Corinthians still seem to be revealing something else. Wright suggests that all paganism can do "is collapse into personality cults, factional fighting . . . , and blatant eroticism, which parodies the life of agape at the same time as it progressively distorts, defaces, and destroys the human beings who live in that way."[106] In Paul's view paganism's parody of community is supposed to be confronted by the true community found in the creation of God's renewed family.[107]

The theocentric nature of love in these verses was mentioned above. In light of that, it is not surprising that the attributes of love that Paul describes in these verses are also "qualities generally attributed to God."[108] It has also been suggested that "[t]he positive qualities typify Paul's personal behavior. Paul is to be imitated (11:1)."[109] That this is so is supported by Paul's references to himself in vv. 1-3 and 11-12. Given the close association of some of these motifs with God's own nature, it seems more likely that, as is common in Pauline ethics (e.g., Eph. 5:1-2, 25) and New Testament ethics generally (e.g., John 13:34-35; 15:9, 12; 1 John 1:5-7; 3:16; 4:7-11, 16, 19), Paul's thinking is focused more on the imitation of God/Christ (11:1b). The reason that even with the most extraordinary gifts imaginable Paul would still be nothing without love is not that love is part of his own nature but that love reflects God's nature. Imitation is said to be the purest form of flattery. It is also at the core of what is expected of those who truly worship God. Love is at the heart of this section dealing with the proper worship of the one true God because that God has manifested himself to us in the love of Christ and expects his loving nature and work in our lives to be reflected in our relationships with one another.

**13:4a** Paul begins his description of love with two of its positive attributes. *Love is patient, love is kind.* These two clauses reflect a chiastic structure.[110] Patience is one of God's attributes in the Old Testament (in the LXX, cf. Exod. 34:6; Num. 14:18; Neh. 9:17; Pss. 7:12; 85:15; 102:8; 144:8; Wis. 15:1; Sir. 5:4; 18:11; Joel 2:13; Jonah 4:2; Nah. 1:3) and in Paul (Rom. 2:4; 9:22).[111] The same can be said for kindness (in the LXX cf. Pss. 24:7-8; 30:20; 33:9; 67:11; 85:5; 99:5; 105:1; 106:1; 119:68; 135:1; 144:9; Wis. 15:1; *Psalms of Solo-*

104. Garland, 616-17.

105. N. T. Wright, *What Saint Paul Really Said,* 147.

106. N. T. Wright, *What Saint Paul Really Said,* 147.

107. N. T. Wright, *What Saint Paul Really Said,* 148.

108. Collins, 480; cf. Garland, 617.

109. Collins, 479.

110. Subject-verb; verb-subject (literally, "love waits patiently; acts kindly — love; Gk. ἡ ἀγάπη μακροθυμεῖ, χρηστεύεται ἡ ἀγάπη).

111. Collins, 480, points out that patience "frequently appears in the NT's catalogue of virtues, where it is often joined with kindness (2 Cor 6:6; Gal 5:22; Col 3:12) and other social qualities (Eph 4:2; Col 1:11; 2 Tim 3:10)."

*mon* 10:7; Jer. 40:11; Dan. 3:89; 1 Esdr. 5:58; cf. Rom. 2:4; 11:22; Titus 3:4). Fee suggests that these two attributes "represent respectively love's necessary passive and active responses toward others. . . . In Pauline theology they represent the two sides of the divine attitude toward humankind (cf. Rom. 2:4) . . . Thus, Paul's description of love begins with this twofold description of God, who through Christ has shown himself forbearing and kind toward those who deserve divine judgment. The obvious implication, of course, is that this is how his people are to be toward others."[112]

The word translated *patient*[113] can simply mean "to remain tranquil while waiting," but here the meaning is "to bear up under provocation without complaint, *be patient, forbearing*" (BDAG). That is, it is to be "patient in suffering."[114] As a divine attribute, patience "is especially characteristic of God, suggesting God's forbearance of sinners."[115] Thiselton translates the first verb "waits patiently" in order to preserve the active verb idea of the Greek. He believes that love waits patiently "not only because it deals patiently with the loved one but also because it recognizes that *the right timing* plays a huge part in securing the welfare of the other."[116] Sirach 29:7-8 uses the same verb in a context that echoes 1 Corinthians 6:7-8 (using the same verb for "defraud" that is used in those two verses): "Many refuse to lend, not because of meanness, but from fear of *being defrauded* needlessly. Nevertheless, *be patient* with someone in humble circumstances, and do not keep him waiting for your alms." A more *patient* attitude, then, may have led the one who felt defrauded in 6:7-8 to take a less aggressive approach to the brother they took to court. In other circumstances as well the patience love manifests would keep us from responding rashly or irritably toward those who cause us trouble or inconvenience, remembering the infinite patience with which the Lord has treated each one of us.

The rarely used verb translated *is kind*[117] means to "be *kind, loving, merciful*" (BDAG). While the verb is rare,[118] cognate nouns are not, such that, as Thiselton concludes, "(a) there is no doubt about the meaning of the verb; and (b) the choice of the dynamic verbal form is deliberate, even if only to play its part in a chain of active temporal processes."[119] As suggested by Fee's comment cited above, kindness is the more active counterpart to patience. It has to do with reaching out through deeds that demonstrate compassion and mercy. Chrysostom says that such kindness works

112. Fee, 636-37.

113. Gk. μακροθυμέω.

114. Garland, 617.

115. Collins, 480.

116. Thiselton, 1047.

117. Gk. χρηστεύομαι.

118. Found also in *Psalms of Solomon* 9:6 and *1 Clement* 13:2; 14:3, where it is associated with mercy and forgiveness.

119. Thiselton, 1047, commenting on the cognate noun χρηστότης (kindness, generosity, uprightness).

"to appease and extinguish" the community fires set by the anger of others "not only by enduring nobly, but also by soothing and comforting." Thus "they cure the sore and heal the wound of passion."[120] Garland helpfully suggests that love "responds to others with the same tender heart and forgiveness that God has shown to us in Christ (Eph. 4:32). Kindness recognizes that everyone carries a heavy load."[121]

**13:4b-5** Having provided two positive attributes of love, Paul now moves to a list of eight negative behaviors that love does not manifest. These "eight negations follow rapidly one after another so as to give a staccato effect."[122]

*It*[123] *does not envy.* The word translated "envy" here can have a positive or negative meaning. BDAG defines it as either "be positively and intensely interested in someth[ing]," with possible translations including "strive, desire, exert oneself earnestly, be dedicated," or "to have intense negative feelings over another's achievements or success," or "be filled w[ith] jealousy, envy." Here Paul clearly has the negative meaning in mind.

The Corinthian congregation was being eaten away by the destructive power of envy or jealousy. Paul alludes here to his comments in 3:3, where he mentioned the "jealousy and quarreling" among them that showed that they were still "worldly," still "acting like mere human beings." While we need not doubt that the Corinthians were marked by jealousy or envy with respect to each other's spiritual gifts, there is no reason to think the problem was confined to that issue. The contrasts that would have existed between the social elites in the congregation and those brothers and sisters who were less well off would have provided many opportunities for envy, especially as those who had nothing were humiliated (11:22) as one person remained hungry while another became drunk (11:21), or as the wealthier members were able to use the legal system to their advantage while those of lesser means could not (6:1-8). As Thiselton points out, "The envy which is carried over from a status-seeking, non-Christian Corinthian culture into the Christian church is . . . deemed to be incompatible with love, which does not begrudge the status and honor of another, but delights in it for the sake of the

120. *Homiliae in Epistulam i ad Corinthios* 33.1 (NPNF[1] 12:195). According to Theodoret, 216, that "love is kind" means "it employs gentleness and courtesy."

121. Garland, 617.

122. Collins, 478.

123. Most textual witnesses (א, A, C, D, F, G, Ψ, 048, 0243, 1739, 1881, 𝔐, sy) include a third occurrence of "love" either following the verb translated *does not envy* (where it could serve either as subject of that verb — "Love does not envy" or, more likely, of the following one — "Love does not boast"). One ($\mathfrak{P}^{46}$) places it after the following verb. Some other excellent witnesses (B, 33, 104, 629, 1175, 2464, *pc*, lat, sa, bo$^{ms}$, Cl, Ambst) have only the two references to love included in the TNIV translation given here. While this is a particularly difficult textual decision to make (cf. Metzger, *A Textual Commentary on the Greek New Testament*, 498, and English translations differ widely on the number and placement of explicit uses of the word "love" in these verses), fortunately it makes no difference to the meaning of the text.

other."[124] In Christ, of course, they had all been "enriched in every way — with all kinds of speech and with all knowledge" (1:4). It is possible that some who were better off financially and socially found themselves envious of the spiritual gifts of some of the poorer members of the congregation. That would have been very new territory for both parties! Love teaches us not to envy but to ask, "How best do I serve these for whom Christ died, whatever my own desires?"[125]

*it does not boast.* The verb here[126] means "to heap praise on oneself" or "behave as a braggart" (BDAG). According to Braun, the emphasis of the word is "on the rhetorical or literary form of boasting, on the element of exaggeration, obtrusiveness, offensiveness, unsettlement, or flattery, on the mere show as opposed to genuine culture."[127] Although Paul uses a different term here than earlier,[128] this attribute of love reminds the reader of his several previous criticisms of the Corinthians in this letter for acting precisely this way (1:29-31; 3:21; 4:7; 5:6). Again Paul "underlines the issue of status seeking and triumphalism at Corinth. Even believers seemed to come to act the part of braggarts, which was at odds with cruciform, Christlike love."[129] Paul may particularly have in mind those who "think of themselves as having 'wisdom' (3:18) and 'knowledge' (8:2), and especially as being 'spiritual' (14:37)."[130] As Fee points out, "It is not possible to 'boast' and love at the same time. The one action wants others to think highly of oneself, whether deserving or not; the other cares for none of that, but only for the good of the community as a whole."[131]

*it is not proud.* The word used here[132] was already contrasted with love in 8:1, where it was translated "puffs up." Paul is the only New Testament author to use the word, and six of his seven uses are in this letter, where it serves as a key term for one of Paul's concerns about the Corinthians.[133] It means "to cause to have an exaggerated self-conception, *puff up, make proud*" (BDAG). Love leads one to an exaggerated self-conception. Once again, "Paul hammers home the incompatibility of love as respect and concern for the welfare of the other and obsessions about the status and attention accorded to the self."[134] Thiselton asks an important question for

124. Thiselton, 1048 (emphasis removed).

125. Fee, 637.

126. Gk. περπερεύομαι.

127. H. Braun, "περπερεύομαι," *TDNT* 6:93-94.

128. Hays, 226, suggests that Paul may use a different verb here "because he has just used the verb 'boast' in a positive sense in 13:3."

129. Thiselton, 1049 (emphasis removed).

130. Fee, 638.

131. Fee, 638.

132. Gk. φυσιόω.

133. Cf. 1 Cor. 4:6, 18, 19; 5:2; 8:1; 13:4; Col. 2:18. Fee asserts that it is the Corinthians' "greater sin, to be arrogant in the face of so much that is unholy and unloving, and therefore unchristian" (638).

134. Thiselton, 1049 (emphasis removed).

Christian leaders today: "How much behavior among believers and even ministers is actually 'attention seeking' designed to impress others with one's own supposed importance?"

*It does not dishonor others.* The only other place this verb[135] appears in the New Testament is in 7:36. It means to act contrary to a standard of decency, that is, to "behave disgracefully, dishonorably, indecently" (BDAG). The cognate noun meaning "behavior that elicits disgrace"[136] appears in a vice list in Romans 1:27, and 12:23 uses the cognate adjective[137] referring to something "that is not openly done, displayed, or discussed in reserved society because it is considered 'shameful, unpresentable, indecent,' or 'unmentionable'" (BDAG). Thiselton translates, "it does not behave with ill-mannered impropriety," and understands its antithesis to be "thoughtless pursuit of the immediate wishes of the self regardless of the conventions and courtesies of interpersonal life."[138] He thinks that this relates to Paul's concern "that worship services should be conducted with "propriety," that is, with order, good taste, courtesy, and the absence of an egocentric concern to draw attention to one's own gifts and rhetoric at the expense of the decorum of the whole."[139]

While Thiselton's concerns are valid and undoubtedly appropriate applications of the text, Paul's own target, as indicated by his vocabulary and the previous context is more likely to be that identified by Hays, who understands that Paul has used "a stronger term referring to shameful behavior":

> For example, Paul uses the cognate noun in Romans 1:27 to characterize the "shameful act" of male homosexual intercourse. In the context of 1 Corinthians, the only previous explicit use of this word has been in the hypothetical reference to an unmarried man who is "behaving shamefully" in relation to his betrothed virgin (7:36), but Paul's use of the term here probably also reflects the sexual misconduct that he has condemned in 5:1-2 (note the link with "puffed up" in 5:2) and 6:12-20, as well as the "shameful" behavior of women prophesying with heads uncovered (11:2-16) and the humiliation of the poor at the Lord's Supper (11:20-22). All of these Corinthian offenses would constitute the sort of "acting shamefully" that Paul sees as contrary to love.[140]

*it is not self-seeking.* This verse has been translated in a variety of ways: "does not insist on its own way" (NRSV, ESV, RSV), "is not self-seeking" (TNIV, NIV), "is not self-serving" (NET), "does not seek its own interests"

135. Gk. ἀσχημονέω.
136. Gk. ἀσχημοσύνη.
137. Gk. ἀσχήμων.
138. Thiselton, 1049 (emphasis removed).
139. Thiselton, 1049-50 (emphasis removed).
140. Hays, 226-27. So also Fee, 638.

(NAB), "never seeks its own advantage" (NJB), "does not demand its own way" (NLT), "is not selfish" (CSB). Paul's language is elliptical; literally it says that love "does not seek its own [blank]." Gorman points out that the "precise missing element in the idiomatic phrase 'one's own X' must be supplied from the context, though the Greek idiom normally refers to one's own (proper or improper) interests or welfare." The language here echoes Paul's exhortation in 10:23-24 and his statement of his own *modus operandi* in 10:33, and his meaning here is clarified by his use of the similar language in those texts, especially 10:33, which is less elliptical. There Paul says that he does not seek his own advantage, interest or benefit[141] but that of others. In 10:33 the expression is parallel to others in v. 23 which speak again of what is "profitable" or "beneficial" and of what "builds up."[142] "Love, then, according to 1 Corinthians 13:5 (in light of 1 Corinthians 10) does not seek its own interest or edification but seeks, instead (implicitly), the interest and edification of others."[143]

This is what Horrell has in mind by "other-regard" as one of Paul's fundamental moral norms (see above). Gorman's study of Paul's ethic concludes that love "seeks the good, the advantage, the edification of others. It is characterized by regard for them. Love, according to the apostle, is the dynamic, creative endeavor of finding ways to pursue the welfare of others rather than one's own interests. It is not self-centered but others-oriented."[144] Of course there is no greater example of this than Christ himself, who, in keeping with the model of Isaiah 53, gave himself up for all of us (Mark 10:45; Matt. 20:28; Gal. 1:4; 2:20; Eph. 5:2, 25; 1 Tim. 2:6; Tit. 2:14). This may in fact be "the fullest expression of what Christian love is all about."[145] Love "does not believe that 'finding oneself' is the highest good; it is not enamored with self-gain, self-justification, self-worth. To the contrary, it seeks the good of one's neighbor — or enemy (cf. Phil. 2:4)."[146]

*it is not easily angered.* BDAG suggests that this verb[147] means "to cause a state of inward arousal" and in the passive may be translated "become irritated, angry." Horst Balz has, "let oneself be carried away (in anger)."[148] As Fee points out, that "the one who loves is not easily provoked to anger by those around him or her" is "a further expression of the forbearance with which the list began."[149]

*it keeps no record of wrongs.* This expression[150] could also be translated

141. All of these are possible translations of the Gk. τὸ . . . σύμφορον.
142. The two Greek terms are συμφέρω and οἰκοδομέω.
143. Gorman, *Cruciformity,* 159.
144. Gorman, *Cruciformity,* 160.
145. Fee, 638.
146. Fee, 638.
147. Gk. παροξύνω.
148. Horst Balz, "παροξύνω," *EDNT* 3:43.
149. Fee, 639.
150. Gk. οὐ λογίζεται τὸ κακόν.

more ambiguously, "does not contemplate evil" (either in the sense of thinking about doing evil acts or in the sense of suspecting others of evil). Chrysostom makes a point that Paul "did not say 'does not carry out evil' but 'does not even think about it,' that is, so far from contriving any evil, it does not even suspect it of the one it loves."[151] But most modern scholars interpret and translate it in light of the fact that the term translated *keeps . . . record*[152] was originally "a mathematical and accounting term" which was also used for "cognitive processes" (BDAG). Paul employed the term in both ways, but especially in the former way when discussing God's justification of the sinner, counting him or her as righteous and not crediting them with sins (Rom. 4:3-11, 22-24; Gal. 3:6, based on its use in the LXX in texts such as Gen. 15:6 and Ps. 31:2). Fee's summary underlines the theological basis of this aspect of love: "Just as God in Christ does not 'reckon our sins against us' (2 Cor. 5:19), so the one who loves does not take notice of the evil done against him/her in the sense that no records are kept, waiting for God or man to settle the score."[153]

**13:6** The two parts of this verse reflect Paul's transition from his list of negative behaviors that love does not manifest (ending with *delight in evil*) to the final series of positive characteristics of love (beginning with *rejoices with the truth*). *Love does not delight in evil but rejoices with the truth.* Collins points out that "The antithetical structure of v. 6 together with the parallelism of the following verse suggests that v. 6b is to be read with v. 6a." and that "[t]he antithesis focuses on lawlessness and truth."[154] The antithetical structure is highlighted by the use of the same root verb for rejoicing in both parts (with only the first negated).[155]

As BDAG stresses, *truth*[156] here has to do with "the content of what is true," especially "the content of Christianity as the ultimate truth." It is contrasted with unrighteousness (evil) since it "expresses itself in virtues like righteousness and holiness." Here the idea is that it rejoices when the truth (righteousness and holiness) wins out.

Söding reminds us that God is the one who supremely "hates injustice (cf. Rom. 1:28; 2:8) and bears all truth in himself (v. 6)."[157] The reference to truth here suggests that for Paul "love implies the biblical notion of 'jus-

151. *Homiliae in Epistulam i ad Corinthios* 33.4 (NPNF[1] 12:198).

152. Gk. λογίζομαι.

153. Fee, 639. Not keeping count of evil (v. 5) "is God's prerogative and salvific will (cf. 2 Cor. 5:19; Rom. 4:7-8)" (Söding, *Das Liebesgebot bei Paulus*, 131).

154. Collins, 481.

155. The second part of the verse has a compound verb formed from the verb found in the first part along with a prepositional prefix (Gk. χαίρει . . . συγχαίρει). In fact the two parts of the verse have other elements of assonance as well, with the vowels of τῇ ἀδικίᾳ resonating in those of τῇ ἀληθείᾳ. Although it is to a much lesser degree, there is also much assonance in the rest of this passage, thanks to the repetitions of οὐ and οὐκ and the numerous similar verb endings (i.e., verbs ending in -ει or -ται).

156. Gk. ἀλήθεια.

157. Söding, *Das Liebesgebot bei Paulus*, 131.

tice,' right relationships with God and other people. Love implies a commitment to justice."[158]

Thiselton is right to suggest that, "along with virtually every other declaration in these verses, Paul probably alludes to a situation of contrast at Corinth." He outlines the various possibilities:

> (i) the sense of inflated self-importance and complacency . . . with which people at Corinth viewed the wrongdoing of the incestuous men in 5:1-5, especially if patronage, property, or social status was involved (see above on 5:1-5); or (ii) the tacit or overt approval of the injustice entailed in seeking to use the manipulative machinery of a local Gentile magistrate's court for the acquisition of property rights; or (iii) more broadly, to the competitive, status-seeking culture at Corinth which would encourage taking pleasure at the loss of esteem suffered by another if their complicity or involvement in some wrongdoing came to be exposed.[159]

As he points out, there may be something to F. F. Bruce's suggestion that Paul is referring to "malicious joy or gloating . . . over people's failures" *(Schadenfreude)* or to "overly ready pleasure in prophetic rebuke and pronouncing judgment on failures within the congregation."[160]

**13:7** This verse seems to be less ironically tied to the failures of the Corinthians than the previous ones. Here Paul "seems to be glorifying the qualities that he himself most values,"[161] although he is clearly also setting up the final part of his argument about the enduring nature of love versus the temporary nature of the spiritual gifts. The TNIV reflects the remarkable staccato structure of the verse, consisting of four sets of paired words, each consisting of the word which the TNIV translates as *always*[162] followed by a present indicative verb with the same ending,[163] lending even greater assonance to the verse. That word translated *always* or "all things" is technically the (accusative) direct object of the verb, but, as BDAG notes, the "acc[usative] of specification stands almost in the sense of an adv[erb] . . . *in all respects, in every way, altogether*" and perhaps as *always.*

Like the chapter as a whole, and some other parts within it (e.g., vv. 4-7), this verse has a chiastic structure: "The four verbs form a chiasmus, the middle two ('believes' and 'hopes') focused on the future in an intense trust and hope that enables endurance and perseverance ('bears' and 'endures') in the present."[164] Failure to recognize this leads many to insist on a mean-

158. Collins, 481.

159. Thiselton, 1054 (emphasis removed).

160. Thiselton, 1054 (emphasis removed), citing Bruce, 127.

161. Horsley, 177.

162. Gk. πάντα, from πᾶς.

163. Each verb ends in -ει (πάντα στέγει, πάντα πιστεύει, πάντα ἐλπίζει, πάντα ὑπομένει).

164. Horsley, 177. So also Fee, 639: "Most likely they form a chiasm, the first and fourth dealing with present circumstances, the second and third looking to the future."

ing for the first verb which has no overlap with the meaning of the fourth, assuming Paul would not be redundant.[165] It seems, rather, that Paul has intentionally used verbs with related meanings to establish another chiastic structure. Thus the love that endures/perseveres is also that which establishes persevering faith and hope.[166]

*It always protects.* The translation of the TNIV and NIV, *always protects,* reflects one of the two common meanings of the verb, "to keep confidential, *cover, pass over in silence*" (BDAG). This is the meaning found in Ecclesiastes 8:17 LXX and the one supported by Gerhard Schneider, "'love *covers* all things,' i.e., all unpleasantness from other people ('with the cloak of love')," although he admits that the meaning he applies in 1 Corinthians 9:12, "*enduring* anything," could also apply here.[167] The understanding of the NJB, which says love "is always ready to make allowances," is similar.

Paul is the only New Testament author to use this verb, and the three other times he uses it (1 Cor. 9:12; 1 Thess. 3:1, 5) all bear the same meaning, "to bear up against difficulties" (BDAG). Paul's usage in 9:12 is particularly important, given the use of the same direct object.[168] Our discussion above concerning the chiastic structure of this verse also supports this meaning here. If there is any difference between this first verb in the verse and the fourth verb, it may be that this one has more of the idea of "not giving in" while the fourth has the idea of "not giving up." That is to say, this verb is used in a way that has to do with giving resistance to things or forces. It is when Paul could no longer resist his felt need to send help to the Thessalonians (1 Thess. 3:1) and to find out how they were doing (1 Thess. 3:5) that he sent Timothy to them. He resists all pressure to take advantage of his rights and thereby "hinder the gospel of Christ" (1 Cor. 9:12).[169] In fact, this clause, with its echo of 9:12, suggests again that Paul may be pointing to himself as a model of the kind of love that should mark the Corinthian church.

This is the meaning reflected in most English translations — "bears all things" (NRSV, ESV, NASB, CSB, NET, NAB, KJV). Thiselton thinks

165. W. Kasch ("στέγω," *TDNT* 7:587) asserts that "it may be taken for certain that στέγω does not mean the same as ὑπομένω, for Paul would not spoil his fine three-membered formula for the sake of a term of the same meaning, especially as πιστεύω, ἐλπίζω, and ὑπομένω here agree with the πίστις, ἐλπίς and ἀγάπη of v. 13." With Kasch's approach Paul seems to have a four-member formula rather than a three-member formula.

166. Chrysostom and others take the four verbs all to have one's attitude toward other believers in mind, such that the one who loves always supports, believes the best of others, hopes the best for them, and endures or bears it all if his faith and hope in others turns out to be ill-founded (*Homiliae in Epistulam i ad Corinthios* 33.4 [NPNF[1] 12:198]). While this approach is consistent with the previous context, it does not fit Paul's other discussions of faith and hope and it unwisely attributes to Paul the kind of Pollyannaish view of love and Christianity that have been soundly criticized (see the discussion below).

167. Gerhard Schneider, "στέγω," *EDNT* 3:272.

168. Gk. πάντα (1 Cor. 9:12: πάντα στέγομεν; 13:7: πάντα στέγει).

169. For similar usages, see Philo, *Against Flaccus* 64; Josephus, *War* 4.24.

that this is "a lexicographically safe but theologically dangerous" translation.[170] It is dangerous only, we would argue, if it is taken the way Thiselton fears, as support for "Marx's notion of Christianity as the opium of the people, or Nietzsche's concept of Christianity as 'servile mediocrity.'"[171] That is, it is not safe if it is taken as a call to be a people who are happy to accommodate all manner of unjust and oppressive conditions rather than to work to overthrow or transform them. Thiselton is right to insist that the love of which Paul speaks "is precisely *not* 'docile' or conformist; it does not seek a quiet life by 'servile mediocrity' but 'is creative, innovative, transforming.'"[172]

If we were merely interested in reproducing Paul's thought, with no concern for rhetorical or literary power, we might recommend, love "always bears up" (or "always bears the strain" or "never caves in to the pressures of the world"),[173] "never loses faith, never exhausts hope, never gives up." Or love "never gives in (to the pressures of the world), never gives up its faith (in the Lord), never loses its hope (in the future he has for us), never fails to endure." If a desire to reflect Paul's rhetorical and literary power is to play a role in the translation, we might alter the TNIV only slightly to love "always perseveres, always trusts, always hopes, always endures." Of course, any concise translation of such taut lines will be susceptible to misunderstanding and will require explanation.

*always trusts.* This has nothing to do with a naïve credulity. As Fee puts it, "Paul does not mean that love always believes the best about everything and everyone, but that love never ceases to have faith," which "is why it can endure."[174] This is not about always trusting those around us, who are often not worthy of such trust, but about trusting the one who calls us to love others and living out that love for others as a reflection of our trust in him. In Paul's other passages drawing together two or more elements of the three key virtues of faith, hope, and love, the faith and hope are faith and hope in God (while the love is "love for all the saints").[175] As Collins points out, "In the context of 1 Corinthians faith is a matter of finding one's self-definition in the saving power of God, which is revealed in the cross of Christ (see 1:18-25)."[176]

*always hopes.* Here again, this has nothing to do with a naïve optimism. This is not about hoping for the best in those around us. It is about maintaining the hope set before us by the one to whom we have entrusted our lives and our futures, and being empowered by that eschatological

170. Thiselton, 1058.
171. Thiselton, 1056.
172. Thiselton, 1057.
173. The NEB has the right idea with "there is nothing love cannot face."
174. Fee, 640.
175. Cf. 1 Cor. 13:2; Gal. 5:6; Eph. 1:15; Col. 1:4, 23; 1 Thess. 1:3; 3:6; 2 Thess. 1:3, 5; Phlm. 5; cf. 1 Pet. 1:21.
176. Collins, 482.

hope for our future to take the risk of loving those around us in the present (see comments on the previous clause).

*always perseveres.* Love never gives up. It never quits. It never dies or comes to extinction. It *perseveres* or endures through all the challenges of this life and finds itself alive and well in all the ages to come.[177] As Deluz puts it, "Like Christ on the cross, love endures scorn, failure, ingratitude. . . . At the end shines out the light of Easter. For *love never ends.*"[178] It is never a mistake to replicate the love of Jesus Christ in our relationships with those around us since it is that love and those loving actions which have eternal significance (cf. vv. 1-3) and whose influence and benefits will reach into eternity after all else has melted away and failed to endure the final transition to the ultimate manifestation of the kingdom of God. The following verses will develop this idea of love's permanence in the light of the temporary nature of the gifts.

*iii. Encomium in praise of love's endurance in comparison with other gifts of the Spirit, 13:8-13*

> [8]*Love never fails. But where there are prophecies, they will cease; where there are tongues, they will be stilled; where there is knowledge, it will pass away.* [9]*For we know in part and we prophesy in part,* [10]*but when completeness comes, what is in part disappears.* [11]*When I was a child, I talked like a child, I thought like a child, I reasoned like a child. When I became a man, I put the ways of childhood behind me.* [12]*For now we see only a reflection as in a mirror; then we shall see face to face. Now I know in part; then I shall know fully, even as I am fully known.* [13]*And now these three remain: faith, hope and love. But the greatest of these is love.*

The eschatological nature of Paul's thinking about love is evident throughout these verses. He uses a variety of images to distinguish between that which is permanent and that which, being temporary, will pass away. Hays points out that "[l]ove is mentioned only in the beginning and end of the unit (vv. 8a, 13); all the intervening material (vv. 8b-12) highlights the temporary status of spiritual gifts, especially tongues, prophecy, and knowledge (vv. 8b-9)," thus confirming that the chapter as a whole and this unit in particular were "composed to deal with the specific problem of the evaluation of spiritual gifts" and not as a general "hymn to love."[179]

For Paul, love, as Wright explains, "is not so much a virtue to be worked at, though it is surely that as well, as the ultimate bridge, in terms

177. As Hays, 228, puts it, "love persists in a hostile world, awaiting the coming of the Lord."

178. Deluz, *Companion to 1 Corinthians*, 193, cited by Thiselton, 1060.

179. Hays, 228. Similarly, Fee, 642.

of human character, from present Christian living into the future kingdom."[180] Thus,

> this exquisite chapter looks forward . . . to the final discussion, which will concern the resurrection, the new world that God will make, *and the continuity between the resurrection life and life here and now.* The point of 13.8-13 is that the church must be working *in the present* on the things that will last *into God's future.* Faith, hope and love will do this; prophecy, tongues and knowledge, so highly prized in Corinth, will not. They are merely signposts to the future; when you arrive, you no longer need signposts. Love, however, is not just a signpost. It is a foretaste of the ultimate reality. Love is not merely the Christian duty; it is the Christian destiny.[181]

Chrysostom has insightfully suggested that among Paul's objectives was a desire "to persuade those who seemed to be accounted inferior that it is in their power to have the chief of all signs, and that they will be no worse off than the possessors of the gifts, if they have this, but rather much better" as well as to humble those with the most esteemed gifts and "show that they have nothing unless they have this," so that "they would both love one another."[182]

This passage begins with a thesis statement (love never ends but the gifts will; v. 8). This is followed by the grounds or warrant for the thesis (the arrival of the complete version will mean the dispensing of the partial; vv. 9-10). Paul then provides a personal illustration (as an adult Paul dispenses with their childish ways; v. 11), and some further explanation (present perception is like perceiving something in a mirror [partial], but in the eschaton there will be face-to-face or complete perception; v. 12). Finally this passage and the chapter as a whole reach their conclusion (v. 13). The passage continues the theme of the relationship between love and spiritual gifts, with another partial gift list (as they all are) serving as the point of comparison (in this case, prophecy, tongues, and knowledge, with extra, subtle attention given to prophecy and knowledge in v. 12). The praise of love reaches its zenith in Paul's declaration that it is greater than any spiritual gift and all other virtues, even the other two cardinal virtues of faith and hope.

**13:8** Love is again contrasted with gifts. This time the contrast is made on the basis of the permanence of the former and the temporary nature of the latter. Paul's statement that *love never fails* (literally, "never falls"[183]) reflects the eschatological connotations associated with the same verb in some other texts (see on 10:12), having to do with failing to pass the

180. N. T. Wright, *The Resurrection of the Son of God*, 296.

181. N. T. Wright, *The Resurrection of the Son of God*, 296.

182. *Homiliae in Epistulam i ad Corinthios* 34.1 (NPNF[1] 12:201).

183. Gk. πίπτει. The word *never* (οὐδέποτε) is strong; this is the only place where it appears in Paul's letters.

ultimate judgment[184] and enter into its reward, being judged and failing to "make the cut." Here it seems to introduce vv. 8-13 by summarizing the point made in v. 7 and contrasting with the remaining verbs in this verse, and with the verb "remains" in v. 13 as well.[185] Love does not fail or fall in the end precisely because it never gives in, never surrenders its faith or hope, and never gives up (v. 7).

In contrasting love with the spiritual gifts Paul starts with the gift whose value he will stress in the next chapter (prophecy), and then moves to the two gifts that seem to be most highly valued by the Corinthians themselves (tongues and knowledge). By starting out with his own preferred gift, he makes it clear that he is not simply picking on a couple gifts that have some special flaw. The expression *where there are/is* is not meant to make a special point about the particular gifts mentioned, but to say, "whether one has the gift of prophecy, or of tongues, or of knowledge (or whatever gift one might have). . . ."[186] In each of these cases, "and therefore in all cases, these are manifestations of the Spirit for the church's present eschatological existence, in which God's new people live 'between the times' — between the inauguration of the End through the death and resurrection of Jesus with the subsequent outpouring of the Spirit and the final consummation when God will be 'all in all' (see 15:20-28)."[187]

This part of the verse has a chiastic structure, with the same verb used to describe what will happen to prophecies and to knowledge and a different verb used to describe what will happen to tongues.

*But where there are prophecies, they will cease.* Paul's references to things that *cease* or *pass away* in vv. 8 (twice) and 10 (also "put behind" in v. 11) employ a word that regularly has an eschatological connotation in this letter, referring to those things that do not survive the transition from this age into the fullness of the age to come (1:28; 2:6; 6:13; 13:8, 10; 15:24, 26), reflecting the influence of the Old Testament and Jewish apocalyptic, especially that of the "day of the Lord" (cf. Isa. 13:6-13; 65:17; 66:22; Joel 1:15-

184. Those who are vindicated "stand" when it is complete. Those who are not "fall." See Ps. 19:9 LXX; 35:13 LXX; *Psalms of Solomon* 1:5; and Rom. 11:11; 14:4-5.

185. Cf. Fee, 643. W. Michaelis, "πίπτω, κτλ.," *TDNT* 6:165-66, points out that πίπτει "is usually related to what follows," but he notes that "[f]ormally and materially the statement also resembles the short sayings in 13:4-7 in which ἀγάπη is again the subj[ect]. One may thus ask whether this is not the conclusion of the section 13:4-7. If so, the fourfold πάντα of 13:7 (= in all circumstances) is contrasted with the οὐδέποτε of 13:8 (= in no circumstances)."

186. According to Robertson and Plummer, 296, "The repeated εἴτε is depreciatory; it suggests indifference to the gifts of which the use was at best temporary." More likely it suggests indifference with respect to which particular gift a person might have. Paul's use of εἴτε . . . εἴτε is not normally depreciatory (cf. Rom. 12:6-8; 1 Cor. 3:22; 8:5; 10:31; 12:13, 26; 13:8; 14:7, 27; 15:11; 2 Cor. 1:6; 5:9-10, 13; 8:23; 12:2-3; Eph. 6:8; Phil. 1:18, 20, 27; Col. 1:16, 20; 1 Thess. 5:10; 2 Thess. 2:15). Despite Thiselton, 1061, we do not see anything "almost pejorative" in the reference to this verse in BDF, which merely says that "The sense of εἴτε . . . εἴτε comes very close to that of καὶ . . . καί in such passages [as in Rom. 12:6-8 and 1 Cor. 13:8] and the two constructions are in accord" (237).

187. Fee, 643.

2:11; 3:14-16; Zeph. 1:14-18; Mal. 3:2; 4:1-2). Unlike love, the gift of prophecy will not survive the transition through the resurrection to the fullness of the new creation. The following verses explain why that is so. Thiselton thinks that the passive voice of the verb "does not suggest simply that prophecies melt away of their own accord as they are fulfilled, but that the cosmic, eschatological, public deed of divine judgment brings them to an end. How can preachers and prophets have anything to say when the last judgment not only reveals, but evaluates and pronounces judgment upon, everything."[188] Furthermore, the gift of prophecy provides us with a limited (although still inspired and remarkable) understanding of and ability to communicate God's will for a given community, while we will all have a complete understanding of that will and perfect communication and communion when we are in his presence.

Some of the texts that *may* inform Paul's thinking about the temporary nature of our partial knowledge and prophecy include Jeremiah 31:34 (in the restoration all will know the Lord and will not need to be taught to know him), Isaiah 54:13[189] (in the eternal covenant of peace the children of God's people will "all be taught by the LORD"), and Zech. 13:3-6 (prophesying a time when there would be no more prophets [they had been false]).

*where there are tongues, they will be stilled.* The verb here is technically in the middle voice,[190] suggesting that tongues "will stop" or will "come to an end" rather than *be stilled* (cf. BDAG), although the meaning is not significantly different. Some have argued that the different verb and the middle rather than passive voice imply the tongues will come to an end on their own, before the time when prophecies and knowledge will cease.[191]

188. Thiselton, 1061.

189. See Stephen E. Witmer, "θεοδίδακτοι in 1 Thessalonians 4.9: A Pauline Neologism," *NTS* 52 (2006), 239-50, on Isa. 54:13 as background to Paul's reference to being "taught by God" in 1 Thess. 4:9.

190. See Wallace, *Greek Grammar*, 422-23.

191. See S. D. Toussaint, "First Corinthians Thirteen and the Tongues Question," *BSac* 120 (1963), 311-16. Wallace, *Greek Grammar*, 422, provides a grammatical argument for distinguishing between the situation applying to prophecy and knowledge and that which applies to tongues: "If the voice of the verb here is significant, then Paul is saying either that tongues will cut themselves off (direct middle) or, more likely, cease of their own accord, i.e., 'die out' without an intervening agent (indirect middle). It may be significant that with reference to prophecy and knowledge, Paul used a different verb (καταργέω) and put it in the *passive* voice. In vv. 9-10, the argument continues: 'for we *know* in part and we *prophesy* in part; but when the perfect comes, the partial shall be done away [καραργηθήσονται].' Here again, Paul uses the same passive verb he had used with prophecy and knowledge and he speaks of the verbal counterpart to the nominal 'prophecy' and 'knowledge.' Yet he does *not* speak about *tongues* being done away 'when the perfect comes.' The implication *may* be that tongues were to have 'died out' of their own *before* the perfect comes." He goes on to provide a strong argument against considering παύσονται a deponent verb. He concludes, "this is not to say that the middle voice in 1 Cor 13:8 *proves* that tongues already ceased! This verse does not specifically address *when* tongues would cease, although it is giving a *terminus ad quem:* when the perfect comes" (423).

This reflects a failure to synthesize the information provided by both grammar and context. The "for" which introduces vv. 9-10 indicates that those verses explain why the things affirmed in this verse are so. That is, they explain why (and in the process, when) prophecies, tongues, and knowledge will come to an end. It should be understood that these three gifts are chosen merely as examples so that what is said about them is understood to apply to the other spiritual gifts as well. There is nothing about the middle voice to suggest that tongues would stop or come to an end at any point in time other than that which is clarified in the following verses — at the final consummation.

The different verb and voice were probably chosen for stylistic purposes[192] — to add color and create one more chiasm in a passage that is full of them. Imagine how boring the text would sound if Paul simply repeated the same verb in each case! The TNIV and NIV translators evidently thought that the English translation would be stylistically weak if they even repeated the same translation for the same verb which Paul applied to prophecies and knowledge.

One of the arguments against the view that Paul thinks that speaking in tongues has to do with speaking in angelic languages is that it would hardly make sense for such a gift to cease at the very point when we would be entering into regular interaction with angels![193] While there is little to commend the idea that Paul believes that tongues typically entail speaking angelic languages, this argument against that view misses the point that a spiritual gift entails a partial ability which will be discarded in the light of the arrival of perfect reality to which it points.[194]

*where there is knowledge, it will pass away.* The context makes it clear that what *will pass away* is the gift of knowledge, and not knowledge itself. The following verses indicate that all our present knowledge, including that of those with the special gift of knowledge, is partial and will be replaced by complete and perfect knowledge when we see God face to face.

192. So also, e.g., Fee, 643 n. 17; Garland, 622 n. 13.

193. So, e.g., Thiselton, 1061 (emphasis removed): "This must surely call into question the notion that tongues are either, in Paul's view, a language of heaven, or a paradigmatic way of expressing exalted intimacy with God. If this were so, why should they cease at the *eschaton?*" Thiselton is right to argue that this counts against the view that tongues reflects the "paradigmatic way of expressing exalted intimacy with God," but he goes too far when he says that it could not represent angelic languages. We would hardly be well served in the resurrection by the ability to articulate prayers and praise without either knowing what we are saying or what any angel might say in response. It is not as though anyone has argued that the gift of tongues entails complete understanding of and fluency in angelic dialects.

194. This is made most clear in the case of knowledge, since in 13:12 Paul says, "Now I know in part; then I shall know fully, even as I am fully known" — thus making it clear that we will not be lacking knowledge in God's presence, but only the limited version of it that was available through the spiritual gift offered in our present time between the first and second comings of Christ.

**13:9** The *for* at the beginning of this verse signals that vv. 9-10 provide a basis for Paul's statement about the temporary nature of gifts in v. 8. *For we know in part and we prophesy in part.* This may have been news to the Corinthians, some of whom probably "thought their knowledge was full (6:12; 8:1, 4; 10:1-4), not partial (13:10); and . . . thought they were 'mature' or 'perfect,' as opposed to being mere children (2:6–3:4) — the opposite of what Paul insinuates in verse 11."[195] Paul's comment makes it clear that all human knowing is partial — including even his own and that of the most gifted and knowledgeable believers in Corinth. Paul will repeat and clarify his idea in the second half of v. 12 when, being more explicitly self-referential, he says: "Now I know in part; then I shall know fully, even as I am fully known." Prophecy always entails the communication of a limited amount of knowledge, which cannot compare to the full disclosure of God's heart and mind, of constant "real time" knowledge of his will, and of his ultimate judgment on all creation.

**13:10** *but when completeness comes, what is in part disappears.* This verse has been at the center of a controversy. What does *when completeness comes* mean, and when will or did it arrive? It is agreed that the key term[196] of the first clause has to do with perfection[197] or completeness[198] here (in other contexts it has to do with maturity, as in 2:6). The meaning of the corresponding term[199] in the second clause is clearer, almost always being translated "the partial" (NRSV, ESV, NET, NAB, NLT, NASB, CSB) or *what is in part* (TNIV, KJV).[200] Some scholars have argued that the "perfect/complete" thing to which Paul was referring was the completion of the canon or the maturing of the church, one or the other of which they attribute to the disappearance of the more spectacular gifts from most if not all churches in the postapostolic period. The context (esp. v. 12) makes it abundantly clear, however, that the point at which Paul expects the gifts to pass away or disappear is when we see the Lord "face to face" and "know [him] fully, even as [we are] fully known." It is unlikely that Paul has in mind some particular perfect or complete thing or person, but the dawning of the age which brings with it the perfect or complete realities to which each of the spiritual gifts pointed as very partial manifestations of the same. If my friend tells me, "I have a partially functioning television and a partially functioning radio, but when that which is fully functioning arrives I'll put away what is only partially functioning," I would understand that he is

195. Horsley, 178.

196. Gk. τὸ τέλειον.

197. For example, "the perfect" (ESV, NAB, NASB, CSB), "perfection" (NIV, NJB), "what is perfect" (NET). Cf. BDAG, *EDNT.*

198. For example, *completeness* (TNIV), "the complete" (NRSV), "full understanding" (NLT).

199. Gk. τὸ ἐκ μέρους.

200. It was translated "the imperfect" by the NIV (cf. NJB), but that translation was dropped in the TNIV.

waiting for a new (or at least a fully-functioning) TV and radio to be delivered. In Paul's context, it appears that he is waiting for complete or perfect versions of that which is manifested in the gifts of prophecy, tongues, and knowledge (i.e., perfect communication, communion, and interpersonal knowledge between God and his people), which will arrive when we experience the fullness of the new creation in the presence of the Lord himself. Thus, when all the complete versions of the partial realities we experience through spiritual gifts in this life arrive, those partial realities will be laid aside and will disappear.

**13:11** The thought of this verse may have been triggered in part by the use of the word translated "completeness" in the previous verse, since it often has to do with maturity: *When I was a child, I talked like a child, I thought like a child, I reasoned like a child. When I became a man, I put the ways of childhood behind me.* Human arrival at maturity was a common metaphor in Paul's world. He uses it as a figure of speech for eschatological transition in Galatians 4:1-7 (in Christ [in the fullness of time — the time appointed by the father] those who were children come to experience full adulthood and enter into the status of legal heirs). Paul speaks autobiographically again (as he did in vv. 1-3) as an example of typical human development.[201] The point is not to insult the Corinthians and suggest that they are immature (although he does that elsewhere) or that the gifts themselves or their use in Corinth or elsewhere is immature. They are perfectly appropriate for this time in the church's life. But when we go through the final transition at the end of this age, from this old creation to the fullness of the new heavens and the new earth, we will leave behind many of the things that were natural, good, and healthy in this world as being unsuitable for the world into which we are introduced at that point. As Garland writes: "There is an age appropriate to certain activities, but there comes a time when those activities are no longer appropriate."[202]

Thiselton points out that Heinrici and Wolff think that the words translated *talked, thought,* and *reasoned*[203] relate to tongues, prophecy, and knowledge, respectively.[204] While the possible association with the three gifts Paul has chosen as his examples is remarkable, Paul is not simply trying to make a point about those three particular gifts. That the three verbs Paul chose all have to do with human communication and thinking probably reflects the

201. The four imperfect indicative verbs in this verse (ἤμην, ἐλάλουν, ἐφρόνουν, ἐλογιζόμην) should be understood as progressive or descriptive imperfects, where their imperfective aspect helps Paul "describe an action or state that is in progress in past time from the viewpoint (or, more accurately, portrayal) of the speaker" (Wallace, *Greek Grammar beyond the Basics*, 543). That is, Paul uses them to paint a picture of children's behavior. The imperfects are followed by two perfect indicatives (γέγονα, κατήργηκα) at the end of the verse that describe Paul as one who reached a state of adulthood, one in which childish things were a thing of the past.

202. Garland, 623.

203. Gk. ἐλάλουν . . . ἐφρόνουν . . . ἐλογιζόμην.

204. Thiselton, 1067 citing Heinrici, 423 and Wolff, 323.

fact that his attention is especially focused on gifts that have to do with communication between God's mind and our own. As Chrysostom suggests, in this verse and the next Paul is pointing out just how great the distance is between our present knowledge of God and that which we will enjoy once we fully enjoy his presence in the resurrection life. Furthermore, he points out that if Paul himself, "who knew so much," could refer to even his own experience and knowledge as analogous to that of a child compared to an adult, the transformation that awaits us must be incredible![205]

**13:12** Paul continues with the temporal distinction brought out in the previous verse, suggesting that the distinction made there between a child's thinking and that of a man is analogous to the difference between our present experience *(now)* and that which awaits us in the future *(then). For now we see only a reflection as in a mirror; then we shall see face to face. Now I know in part; then I shall know fully, even as I am fully known.* That this verse has not left behind the subject of spiritual gifts is clarified by the recognition that in the first sentence Paul alludes to Numbers 12:6-8, which contrasts Moses' own prophetic experience with that of all other prophets. There the Lord says:

"When there are prophets of the LORD among you,
 I reveal myself to them in visions,
 I speak to them in dreams.
But this is not true of my servant Moses;
 he is faithful in all my house.
With him I speak face to face,
 clearly and not in riddles;
 he sees the form of the LORD."

The first clause of our verse could be more literally translated, "For now we see in a mirror, indirectly [*or* by a riddle]." The last word of the clause[206] may mean either "indirectly" or "by a riddle" (cf. BDAG), making the allusion clearer in Greek than in English translation. While other prophets receive revelation through visions and dreams (12:6; cf. Joel 2:28 [3:1]), Moses experiences the presence of the Lord face to face,[207] not indirectly,[208] and he sees his form (LXX: glory). Paul says, "now we see in a mirror[209] indirectly,[210] but then face to face.[211] Now I know in part; then I shall know fully, even as I am fully known."

According to *Leviticus Rabbah* 1:14 there was a debate regarding the difference between Moses and the other prophets based on Numbers 12:8.

205. Chrysostom, *Homiliae in Epistulam i ad Corinthios* 34.2 (NPNF[1] 12:202).
206. Gk. αἴνιγμα.
207. LXX: στόμα κατὰ στόμα.
208. LXX: οὐ δι' αἰνιγμάτων.
209. Gk. δι' ἐσόπτρου.
210. Gk. ἐν αἰνίγματι.
211. Gk. πρόσωπον πρὸς πρόσωπον.

Both sides held that Moses, like the other prophets, saw the Lord through a mirror, reading the word for "appearance"[212] in Numbers 12:8 as though it meant "mirror," another meaning of the word used for "vision"[213] in Numbers 12:6 (the two words were written the same way in unpointed Hebrew, but pronounced slightly differently). Some thought the difference was that the other prophets saw the Lord through a series of mirrors, while others thought Moses saw the Lord through a polished mirror while the other prophets saw him through a blurred one. Fishbane argues that this midrashic reading "may have preceded Paul or have been common coin among ancient homileticists."[214] Paul's reference to a mirror in the context of an allusion to the same text would be a strange coincidence if he does not share some interpretive tradition with its authors. As it turns out, Paul's argument has more in common with the one found in *Leviticus Rabbah* than Fishbane seems to have realized.

Fishbane correctly points out that Paul's interpretation is different in that the rabbis "backed off from the possibility of such a public and unmediated vision of God" as that suggested by Numbers 12:8, presumably on the basis of texts such as Exodus 33:20 and Deuteronomy 4:12. In their view even Moses "could only aspire to envisage God through one clear mirror, not directly."[215]

Fishbane contrasts Paul and the rabbis in terms of their view of the uniqueness of Moses' experience. He correctly attributes to Paul the anticipation of "a time when all would know divine truths directly, 'face to face' like Moses." He attributes to the rabbis the view that "the highest state of prophetic knowledge was limited to the greatest of the prophets — Moses." The conclusion of *Leviticus Rabbah* 1:14, however, seems to suggest the same hope that Paul had, namely, that in the eschaton all would have an experience similar to that of Moses: "R. Phinehas said in the name of R. Hoshayah: This may be compared to a king who allowed himself to be seen by his close friend [only] by means of his image. In this world the Shekinah manifests itself only to chosen individuals; in the Time to Come, however, 'The glory of the Lord shall be revealed, and all flesh shall see it together; for the mouth of the Lord hath spoken it'" (citing Isa. 40:5). The contrast between this age and the age to come matches Paul's thinking precisely. The reference to the vision of "the glory of the Lord" (in the citation from Isa. 40:5) helps us connect to the LXX translation of Numbers 12:8. While the Hebrew says that Moses saw the "likeness" or "form"[216] of the Lord, the LXX says he saw the "glory"[217] of the Lord. The LXX both affirms Moses'

212. Heb. מַרְאֶה.

213. Heb. מַרְאָה; cf. Exod. 38:8.

214. Michael Fishbane, "Through the Looking Glass: Reflections on Ezek. 43:3, Num. 12:8, and 1 Cor. 13:8 [*sic* 13:12]," *HAR* 10 (1986): 74.

215. Fishbane, "Through the Looking Glass," 74.

216. Heb. תְּמוּנָה.

217. Gk. δόξα.

face-to-face experience with the Lord and interprets it as a vision of his glory (cf. 2 Cor. 3:18).

Fishbane also hints that Paul's alteration of "mouth to mouth" in Numbers 12:8 LXX to "face to face" may reflect the influence of Deuteronomy 34:10, which refers to Moses as a prophet whom the Lord knew "face to face." Paul would not be the first to bring Numbers 12:8 and Deuteronomy 34:10 together. Philo did so in *Who Is the Heir?* 262. Deuteronomy 34:10 not only provides a closer parallel to Paul's wording for "face to face" but also provides another link to the motif of "knowing" and "being known"[218] which is prominent in this verse (cf. v. 8).

Paul's allusion to Numbers 12:8, then, is consistent with other early Jewish interpretations in understanding that in the age to come all God's people would have an experience similar to that which distinguished Moses from the other prophets. We already see the Lord as through a mirror (imperfectly) and know him as well as that experience allows (cf. 2 Cor. 3:18), but the day is coming when we will see him as Moses did, face to face, an experience of knowing him fully as we are already fully known by him.

Chrysostom emphasizes again that if even Paul's own experience can be compared to a "mirror" or a "riddle," imagine "how great a thing" it will be to see "God's open face."[219]

**13:13** Here Paul's praise of love reaches its climax or zenith. Not only is it greater than any spiritual gift, but it is also greater than any other virtue. *And now these three remain: faith, hope and love. But the greatest of these is love.* Great debate centers on the question of whether *now* is to be taken as a temporal transition or a logical one. That is, is Paul affirming the endurance of faith, hope, and love in this present life (they remain for now), or does "now" refer to his point in the argument ("So now [logical use] there remain, out of all the gifts and experiences compared and considered, faith, hope and love. *These are still on the table.* But the greatest of these [for reasons which include, among other things, its eschatological permanence] is love").[220] We will return to this question below after addressing the role of these virtues in the present life.

The preeminent place of these three cardinal virtues in this present life is recognized by all. Tying these three virtues together, Scott Hafemann points out that "[i]n the midst of the suffocating self-love of our modern and postmodern culture, the Bible is clear that our real hunger is to know the one true God revealed in its pages. Only in doing so will we satisfy our cravings for security (faith), find the purpose for which we exist (hope), and be able to live free from slavery to self (love)."[221] In his view many of us

218. Cf. also Num. 12:6 LXX: αὐτῷ γνωσθήσομαι.

219. *Homiliae in Epistulam i ad Corinthios* 34.2 (NPNF[1] 12:202).

220. Thiselton, 1071 (some emphasis removed).

221. S. J. Hafemann, *The God of Promise and the Life of Faith: Understanding the Heart of the Gospel* (Wheaton: Crossway, 2001), 17.

have substituted other things for the three cardinal virtues such that "instead of dependence on God for our lives ('faith'), we have substituted a mental assent to historical data that leads to making 'decisions' about God. Rather than trusting in God's promises for our future ('hope'), we have fallen back on a wishful thinking that is informed by our desires for heath and wealth. Hence, although called to consider the needs of others more important than our own needs ('love'), we seek money, sex, and emotional gratification at any cost."[222]

Horsley sees the threefold emphasis to be on

> (a) the *faith* that in the crucifixion and resurrection of Christ God has inaugurated the eschatological events leading to the new age, which enable the present and future life of the faithful; (b) the *hope* that enables the faithful to endure the sufferings and other problems of the continuing old age; and (c) the *love* that the faithful have for one another, which holds the community together in anticipation of the completion of God's fulfillment.[223]

Horsley highlights the relationship between eschatology and the role of these virtues even in this life. O'Donovan gives even greater emphasis to and clarification of the relationship between faith, hope, and love and eschatology. In his view, "whenever we take love seriously, even within the perfectly 'natural' perspective of the twofold command of love to God and neighbour, we stand under the shadow of the last things. The order of love, the created moral order, does not have eternity in itself, but looks forward to a new creation to fulfil it and make it wholly intelligible."[224] Christian love "is unintelligible except as a participation in the life of the one who reveals himself to us as Love, except, that is, as the entry of mankind and of the restored creation upon its supernatural end."[225]

O'Donovan provides a helpful explanation of the different relationships that faith and hope have to the future:

> Faith and hope each express our dependence upon the future: the present, in which we have to act, needs the future of God's kingdom to give it intelligibility, and so to give our acts a frame of meaning. . . . But the direction in which thought moves between the present and the future is different in either case. When we hope, we begin from the problematic character of the present, from its ambiguity and unsatisfying incompleteness, and turn gratefully to the future judgment of God which perfects the imperfections of the present and promises comple-

222. Hafemann, *The God of Promise*, 20.

223. Horsley, 179.

224. Oliver M. T. O'Donovan, *Resurrection and Moral Order: An Outline for Evangelical Ethics* (Leicester: Inter-Varsity Press; Grand Rapids: Eerdmans, 1986), 247.

225. O'Donovan, *Resurrection and Moral Order*, 246.

> tion.[226] In faith we move in the opposite direction. Beginning from the final judgment with its affirmation of man's created life and love, we turn gratefully back to the present, our appointed scene of action, to claim and enjoy that affirmation not simply as an object of hope but as an immediate reality.[227]

Thus, "[o]nly as the pilgrimage reaches the end which God has destined for it can the faith and hope of the church be validated and justified."[228]

Although the role of faith, hope, and love in this life has been readily acknowledged, we still need to address the question of whether or not Paul means to say that they endure into the life to come as well. A large number of interpreters takes *now* to refer to the temporal reign of the faith, hope, and love triumvirate over this present age.[229] These interpreters, such as Chrysostom, understand love to be the most excellent of the three because it is the only one of them to endure forever, whereas "faith indeed and hope, when the good things believed and hoped for have arrived, cease." He cites Hebrews 11:1 ("faith is being sure of what we hope for and certain of what we do not see") and Romans 8:24 ("hope that is seen is no hope at all. Who hopes for what they already have?"), while others cite 2 Corinthians 5:7 as well ("We live by faith, not by sight"), to the effect that faith and hope cease when they are turned to sight. It is yet "another encomium of love," exalting it exceedingly above the other two key virtues of the Christian life.[230]

Those following this approach seem to think that love is unique in that it alone survives the transition from this life to the next. O'Donovan, however, reminds us that even if "we can and should claim for love . . . a perdurance which cannot be attributed to faith and hope," it "would not be quite unique, for some such continuity is implied, too, in Paul's words about knowledge: 'now I know in part; but then shall I know even as also I am known' (1 Cor. 13:12, AV)."[231] We know, of course, that knowledge will be transformed in the transition from this age to the next, since that is Paul's point in vv. 8-12. Is the difference, then, that love suffers no significant transition while faith, hope, knowledge, and the like do? O'Donovan believes that such an idea "betrays a false conception: that in the perdurance of love we have to do with the reassuring permanence of something familiar to us and with which we are already at home."[232] Rather, we are

226. Elsewhere he argues that in hope, the future transformation that God has in store "is present to our minds by anticipation; it encourages us and sustains us by promising to our present experience, with all its ambiguity, a completion which will render it intelligible" (O'Donovan, *Resurrection and Moral Order,* 247).

227. O'Donovan, *Resurrection and Moral Order,* 253.

228. O'Donovan, *Resurrection and Moral Order,* 246.

229. For example, Calvin, 283; Hays, 230-31; Collins, 487; Witherington, 272.

230. *Homiliae in Epistulam i ad Corinthios* 34.5 (NPNF[1] 12:203). See also Spicq, *Agape in the New Testament,* 168-69.

231. O'Donovan, *Resurrection and Moral Order,* 246.

232. O'Donovan, *Resurrection and Moral Order,* 247. Furthermore, "[t]he life of love

> bound to speak of an opposition between love now and love hereafter, between labour and reward, between *desiderium* ["desiring"] and *delectatio* ["delighting"]. This is necessary, in the first place, because participation in the restored creation is by conformity to the death and resurrection of Christ. If the life of love is not in itself a burden, it does, nevertheless, involve us in burdens. No account of the Christian moral life can be adequate unless it is allowed to point forward to the resurrection.[233]

So even the love that will mark our lives in the resurrection will be somewhat different from the love we are commanded to manifest in this present life. In this life faith, hope, and love are all challenges which need support and which believers are exhorted to meet. If it were not so challenging to love people in this world, the Scriptures would not spend so much time commanding and exhorting us to love. In the life to come it will be a delight to love and not a challenge,[234] just as it will no longer be a challenge to trust God or to have hope. Then, our love will not be a love of people despite their shortcomings or our own. It will no longer be a love that goes against the grain, but one that delights in loving all those who coexist in the wonderful presence of the God who first loved us and who has fully transformed all that remains into that which is eminently lovable. It will also be a perfected love. "If the life of love to God and neighbour is a true participation in the restored order of creation, a responsive love to the divine love in which the divine mode of life becomes our own, what higher good can possibly be spoken of? Only a good that is essentially one with this good, a renewal and perfection of this good which we now have."[235]

If even the love we share with others in the age to come will be somewhat transformed due to the lack of challenges and the purity of the joy and delight with which it will flow, the fact that faith and hope would have to manifest themselves somewhat differently should not surprise us. Thiselton cites and supports Barrett's suggestion that "in the sense used when Paul asserts 'whatever is not of faith is sin' (Rom 14:23), 'the life of the age to come will rest on faith as completely as does the Christian life now.' Similarly, unless we conceive of heaven as a 'closed' or static state,

---

which we are given to live with God is a life that is from first to last oriented towards him as the original Love, from whom this love is given to us. Man's life of love can never pretend to curl up on itself like a furry animal and keep itself warm with the insulation of its own divinity" (248).

233. O'Donovan, *Resurrection and Moral Order,* 249. Thiselton, 1074, argues strongly against any eschatological change in love. In the process he cites Barth, who says that love is "the future eternal light shining in the present. It therefore needs no change of form" (Barth, *CD,* IV/2 [sect. 68], 840).

234. Witherington points out that love "is often best seen when the circumstances are not favorable or likely for its expression" (273).

235. O'Donovan, *Resurrection and Moral Order,* 248-49.

the openness of the heavenly life towards the future maintains the relevance of hope."[236]

We think that Horsley is correct to assert that *and now* has "a temporal as well as concluding logical force. The present tense 'abide' (which, together with 'love never ends' in v. 8, brackets vv. 8-13) connotes something present that continues into the future — that is, something that remains, endures, persists on into the kingdom of God."[237] This suggests a direct connection with the first clause of v. 8 ("Love never fails") and a contrast with all the things mentioned between that clause and this one, which things are all marks of one age or the other (partial knowledge is of this age, full knowledge is of the next). Unlike those other things, faith, hope, and love do not belong to one age as opposed to the other. They are the most important things humans can express in this life, and it is not a coincidence that they remain for the one to come as well. Unlike the previous verse with its twice-repeated "now . . . then" contrast, the *now* of this verse has no contrasting "then." This *now* remains.[238] "Paul contrasts the triad of prophecy, knowledge, and tongues, which are transitory, with the triad of faith, hope, and love, which last eternally."[239]

With the whole chapter revolving around the difference between love and spiritual gifts, it is natural to ask what led Paul to introduce references to faith and hope alongside love in this verse. These three virtues seem to have been commonly mentioned together by Paul and other early Christian preachers (cf. Rom. 5:1-5; Gal. 5:5-6; Eph. 4:2-5; Col. 1:4-5; 1 Thess. 1:3; 5:8; Titus 2:2; Heb. 6:10-12; 10:22-24; 1 Pet. 1:3-8).[240] Paul had made indirect

236. Thiselton, 1073.

237. Horsley, 179.

238. The words translated "now" are different (ἄρτι [2x] in v. 12 and νυνί in v. 13). The one used in v. 12 always has a temporal focus, while the one used in this verse is usually temporal but in many cases "the idea of time [is] weakened or entirely absent" (BDAG). Did Paul change his vocabulary because he had no temporal idea in mind, or because if he used the same vocabulary as in the previous verse the readers would have thought that faith, hope, and love were all (like those other things that are in effect "now" [ἄρτι]), limited to this present age (when it is agreed by all that at least love continues into the next)? In this context, filled with the language of "then" and "now," it seems unlikely that νυνί would be thought to have no temporal force whatsoever, even if it is weakened. Νυνὶ δέ, taken together, suggest that the following text is being developed by way of a temporal and/or logical contrast with what preceded (for examples in Paul see Rom. 3:21; 6:22; 7:6, 17; 15:23, 25; 1 Cor. 12:18; 13:13; 15:20; 2 Cor. 8:11, 22; Eph. 2:13; Col. 1:22; 3:8; Phlm. 9, 11). The interpretation we are setting out retains both a temporal component to νυνί and a contrastive force to Νυνὶ δέ, with the contrasting item between a present reality (or set of realities) that does not cease to be present or suffer a qualitative transformation "then." By qualitative transformation we mean that faith, hope, and love are not transformed into something significantly different. They are perfected and find that they are no longer operating in "hostile territory."

239. Garland, 626.

240. Fee, 650 n. 57, points out that A. M. Hunter (*Paul and His Predecessors* [2d ed.; London: SCM Press, 1961], 33-35) argued that the formula antedated Paul and suggested that "the words τὰ τρία ταῦτα might be translated 'the well-known three.'"

reference to faith and hope in the statement in v. 7 that love "always trusts" and "always hopes," suggesting that those two virtues are undergirded by, and particular manifestations of, love. Spicq believes that Paul "has just exalted [love] above all charisms [i.e., gifts], but he does not want to seem to discredit the two great virtues of faith and hope; hence, with pastoral and catechetical concern he says that on earth they are inseparable" from love.[241] Paul "explicitly sets down the hierarchy of values in the present economy of salvation."[242] Although of the three key virtues the Corinthians' greatest weakness was in the area of love, it is not the only virtue that Paul valued more highly than the spiritual gifts.[243] As Garland points out, "Paul probably added faith and hope to love here to allow the familiar combination to balance the triad of prophecy, knowledge and tongues. The inclusion of faith and hope also allows Paul to magnify love even more. Not only is love superior to spiritual gifts that are partial and will come to an end, but also it is superior to virtues that are absolutely essential to being a Christian."[244]

*But the greatest of these is love.* Those who believe that love is the only one of the cardinal virtues to continue on into the world to come usually believe that it is for that reason that it is the greatest[245] of them.[246] Thus, Spicq argues that love "is the greatest virtue, not so much here on earth where salvation, for example, is accomplished by faith, but rather in the light of its eternal duration. It will continue to exist in the next world where it will guarantee the definitive vision and communion with God. Its excellence is primarily eschatological."[247]

We find the view that it is only love which endures eternally unconvincing (see above), and are in agreement with those who find the superiority of love based not in the nature of love itself, but in the nature of God himself. Besides arguing from love's eternal endurance, Calvin also sees the superiority of love in that "each person derives personal blessing from

241. Spicq, *Agape in the New Testament,* 169.

242. Spicq, *Agape in the New Testament,* 169.

243. Collins, 485, points out that in 1 Thess. 1:3 and 5:8 hope "appears in the emphatic and final position" because it was "the reality that Paul needed to emphasize in writing to the Thessalonians who had been shaken by the death of some of their number. The needs of the Corinthians were different."

244. Garland, 625. Garland also points out that Paul progresses from three gifts in v. 8 to two in vv. 9-12a and one in v. 12b (623).

245. The adjective (Gk. μείζων) is technically in the comparative rather than superlative form. Since it is used in relation to a limited set of referents, its meaning is clear — it is greater than any of the others mentioned (and therefore it must be the greatest of the set). In English the superlative is required.

246. Cyprian seems to have held this view (cf. Bray, 101). See also the references to Calvin, Fee, Hays, Collins, and Witherington in n. 229.

247. Spicq, *Agape in the New Testament,* 170. The suggestion that love is not the greatest virtue on earth does not fit Paul's argument here at all, where it is precisely the importance of love in the earthly (and specifically Corinthian) context of the readers who are valuing other things more highly than love that he is stressing throughout this chapter.

his own faith and hope, whereas love is poured out for the good of others."[248] This already points to a more Christocentric or theocentric[249] answer to the question, which seems most fruitful.[250] Spicq (who argued above for love's superiority based on its eternal duration) wonders if it is not "enough that the Lord himself made it 'the first and greatest commandment.'"[251] Ambrosiaster said, "Love is the greatest because while faith is preached and hope pertains to the future life, love reigns. As 1 John [3:16] says: 'By this we know his love, that he laid down his life for us.' Love is therefore the greatest of the three, because by it the human race has been renewed."[252] Carson reminds us that while Scripture tells us "God is love" (1 John 4:16), "it is difficult to imagine how they could have said that God is faith, or that God is hope."[253] Garland points out that "[i]t is God's love revealed in Christ that creates the possibility of faith and hope" and that "[a]s an essential reflection of God's character, love can never end and is elevated to the highest good."[254] As was mentioned earlier, in placing this chapter on love in the center of his discussion of the proper worship of the one true God, Paul reflects (with no irony whatsoever) the modern maxim that "imitation is the sincerest form of flattery" and the idea that our worship is to take place within a community which is marked by this divine attribute and essential Christian virtue.

248. Calvin, 283. Spicq, *Agape in the New Testament*, 170, gives credit to Calvin for this idea.

249. Collins, 488, thinks that love is the greatest "because it is the very power of God at work." He points out that "[i]n some texts of late Judaism love is described as a gift of God's Spirit (*Testament of Gad* 4:7). It could be included among God's gifts to his people (1QS 5:4). Paul appears to be heir to this tradition, but he has given it a specific configuration insofar as he has made love the gift of God *par excellence*."

250. In keeping with his emphasis on the theocentric nature of love in this chapter, Söding points out that love's quality of enduring, both now and in the future, is a reflection of the fact that "God is the Eternal One, who has no beginning and no end (13:13; cf. Rom. 16:26)" (*Das Liebesgebot bei Paulus*, 131). Sirach 40:12 agrees that "faith" or "loyalty (to God)" will endure forever (Gk. πίστις; see Dennis R. Lindsay, *Josephus and Faith: Pistis and Pisteuein as Faith Terminology in the Writings of Flavius Josephus and in the New Testament* [AGJU 19; Leiden: E. J. Brill, 1993], 44-45). Other Old Testament and Jewish texts named qualities or things that were expected to endure forever (e.g., God's righteousness, Pss. 112:3, 9; 113:3; God's word, Isa. 40:8; his faithfulness, Ps. 117:2; his righteous regulations, Ps. 119:160; his name and renown, Ps. 135:13; his deeds, Eccl. 3:14; almsgiving, Sir. 40:7; goodness and justice, Sir. 40:17; truth, 1 Esdr. 4:38; the fear of the Lord, Ps. 19:9; truthful lips, Prov. 12:19). Of all the things said to endure forever, God's loyalty, steadfast love, or mercy (Heb. חֶסֶד) is mentioned most often (1 Chr. 16:34, 41; 2 Chr. 5:13; 7:3, 6; 20:21; Ezra 3:11; Pss. 100:5; 106:1; 107:1; 118:1-4, 29; 136:1-26; 138:8; Jer. 33:11).

251. Spicq, *Agape in the New Testament*, 171.

252. Cited in Bray, 101.

253. Carson, *Showing the Spirit*, 75 (see 74-75).

254. Garland, 626.

*c. Prophecy Is to Be More Highly Valued than Tongues in Worship Due to Its Edifying Power, 14:1-33*

As pointed out earlier, chapters 12–14 form a unit with a chiastic structure, with chapters 12 and 14 focusing especially on the spiritual gifts and the center chapter on love (with gifts mentioned at the beginning and end of ch. 13 as well), the key to the proper use of the spiritual gifts and to the Christian life in general. While chapter 12 introduced the theme of spiritual gifts and discussed their importance in more general terms, this chapter focuses on two gifts in particular, being almost completely dedicated to establishing the superior value of prophecy over tongues. The connection between chapters 12 and 14 is shown not only by the similar topic (spiritual gifts) but also by the relationship of the final verse of chapter 12 (12:31: "Now eagerly desire the greater gifts") with that of the first verse of this chapter (14:1: "eagerly desire spiritual gifts").[1] This chapter also includes some guidance on how to include prophecy and tongues in the church's public worship (and on the need to restrict some women's participation) in order to protect the orderly nature of the experience and not dishonor the God who is worshiped. It concludes with a warning to those tempted to reject Paul's guidance and a final word on the main subjects. Generally speaking, Paul "has two major concerns in this discussion: that Corinthian worship should manifest intelligibility (vv. 1-25) and that it should display order (vv. 26-40) so that all believers are built up and the unbeliever present in the assembly is challenged by the gospel, convicted, and converted (vv. 21-25)."[2]

This chapter not only continues the discussion of spiritual gifts that was begun in chapter 12 and remains in sight in chapter 13, but it is also bound to the discussion of prayer and prophecy in 11:2-16 (where the focus is on proper attire for men and women praying and prophesying during the meeting of the church). Since tongues is understood to be a special form of prayer, this passage also deals with prayer and prophecy in the church, and comes back to the issue of men and women in worship as it moves to its conclusion (vv. 34-35).

It appears that Paul has heard that there is a lot of speaking in tongues taking place in the church's gathered worship. It is (usually) not being interpreted, and those who are not speaking in tongues do not understand and are feeling alienated by the experience. Those speaking in

1. It is not quite appropriate to think of Paul as "[p]icking up where he had left off before his digression on love" (Collins, 489) since ch. 13, far from dropping all references to spiritual gifts, actually begins focusing our attention on the gifts of tongues and prophecy (13:1-2, 8-12), which end up being the subjects of the detailed discussion in this chapter. It is not really a digression, but a transition. Still, the only imperative in all of ch. 12 was in its last verse and, while ch. 13 lacks any imperatives, ch. 14 has twenty-one imperatives (all present imperatives). It is here that Paul provides the explicit instruction that is anticipated in 12:21 and is underwritten by his exposition of the theme of love in ch. 13.

2. Witherington, 276.

tongues evidently think that it is a wonderful experience and that it has strengthened their faith in God despite the fact that the rest of the church has not found it beneficial. Some wanted Paul to forbid people to speak in tongues (v. 39). Those speaking in tongues may be suggesting that tongues is a sign for establishing believers, that is, that it would be used to bring unbelievers to faith in Christ.

On the other hand, when some of the people prophesy, they go on and on and monopolize the meeting, not letting others have a word,[3] perhaps with the suggestion that they are under prophetic inspiration and thus cannot and should not stop until they have said all that they think God has put on their heart and in their mind.[4] Their exalted view of their own prophetic status may have hindered them from responding sensitively to the concerns of some other brothers and sisters in the church (vv. 36-38, 40).

It seems that some women are not only prophesying and ministering in the times of worship but also asking other people questions in a way that did not seem fitting and which diminished the orderliness of the worship experience (vv. 34-35, 40).

Paul responds by building on what he had written about love in the previous chapter, emphasizing the need to prioritize the edification, or building up, of the whole church. Back in 8:1 he had already made the point that building up others is what love does.[5] Along the way he quotes one Old Testament text (Isa. 28:11-12 in v. 21) that suggests that tongues further alienate those who are already alienated, and he alludes to others (Isa. 45:14 and Zech. 8:23 in v. 25) that speak of the salvation of the nations. He also appeals to God's nature as a warrant for maintaining orderly and peaceful worship gatherings (vv. 33, 40).

### *i. Introductory argument in favor of prophecy based on its edifying value, 14:1-5*

*[1]Follow the way of love and eagerly desire spiritual gifts, especially the gift of prophecy. [2]For those who speak in a tongue[6] do not speak to other peo-*

3. Witherington suggests that Christian worship at Corinth "involved rivalries and competition for 'air time' as each one has his or her own kind of speech" (14:26). "All were speaking simultaneously and few apparently were polite enough to listen to the other" (275).

4. As Craig S. Keener (*Paul, Women, and Wives: Marriage and Women's Ministry in the Letters of Paul* [Peabody, MA: Hendrickson, 1992], 78) points out, "1 Cor. 12:2-3 suggests that many of the Corinthians from pagan backgrounds had learned inappropriate forms of worship, forms which had carried over into their excesses [which are addressed] in chapter 14."

5. As Gorman (*Apostle of the Crucified Lord*, 275) puts it, "If cruciform love is the church's rule of life, that rule must be embodied when the church assembles for worship, as Paul has said already in 11:17-34 and as he says again in chapter 14. . . . The church gathers to worship God and to be edified, so its members must pursue gifts, and then exercise them publicly, in a way that is worshipful and edifying for others — that is, in love."

6. Or *in another language;* also in vv. 4, 13, 14, 19, 26, and 27.

*ple but to God. Indeed, no one understands them; they utter mysteries by the Spirit.* [3]*But those who prophesy speak to people for their strengthening, encouragement and comfort.* [4]*Those who speak in a tongue edify themselves, but those who prophesy edify the church.* [5]*I would like every one of you to speak in tongues,*[7] *but I would rather have you prophesy. Those who prophesy are greater than those who speak in tongues,*[8] *unless they interpret, so that the church may be edified.*

**14:1** The opening verse of the chapter introduces both the first paragraph (vv. 1-5) and the main section of the whole chapter (vv. 1-33), as well as reiterating the priorities that have already been suggested by Paul's discussion in chapters 12–13. Christians should make love their priority, and only then (in light of that priority) pursue gifts: *Follow the way of love and eagerly desire spiritual gifts, especially the gift of prophecy.* Chapter 12 indicated that of the gifts evidently present in Corinth prophecy (12:28) was to be the most highly valued (this is the point to be reinforced through most of this chapter). Chapter 13 established that love was to be valued more highly than any spiritual gift. In this chapter Paul will highlight prophecy as a spiritual gift whose exercise would be more naturally promoted by the principle of love than the gift of tongues since it more clearly serves to edify the church (which is what love seeks). The expression[9] translated *especially* means "*but rather, or rather,* or simply *rather,*" and "introduces an expr[ession] or thought that supplements and thereby corrects what has preceded."[10] The correction is that they should not seek just any gifts, but the gift of prophecy in particular, for the reasons to be explained in the rest of the chapter. That is not to say that the other gifts are without value, but that the Corinthians have been wrong to focus their pursuit on the gift of tongues when the gift of prophecy provides more of what the church desperately needs (edification) and is more consistent with the concern for others that is the mark of love. "What must be emphasized is that this imperative is now to be understood singularly in light of the exhortation to love that has preceded it. If the two imperatives are not kept together, the point of the entire succeeding argument is missed."[11]

The word for *spiritual gifts* here is the same one used in 12:1. Thiselton agrees that it "normally means *spiritual gifts* (i.e., gifts from, or characterized by, the Holy Spirit)" but thinks that "in this specific context it may well mean more specifically *spiritual utterances* or 'gifts of the Spirit for utter-

7. Or *in other languages;* also in vv. 6, 18, 22, 23, and 39.

8. Or *in other languages;* also in vv. 6, 18, 22, 23, and 39.

9. Gk. μᾶλλον δέ.

10. BDAG, "μᾶλλον," 3d. Thiselton, 1083, rightly points out that "[c]ompeting translations of the particle δέ offer greater difficulty, since *context* has to determine whether it means *and* or 'but'" (1083, bold font changed to single quotes), but he fails to consider μᾶλλον δέ as a set expression.

11. Fee, 655.

ance' within contexts of worship."[12] He admits that such a translation "assumes a greater degree of interpretative judgment than the Greek alone in strict terms explicitly bears"[13] and does not explain how the readers could possibly have discerned such a precise meaning without prior knowledge of a particular interpretation of the remainder of this chapter. Since the "normal" meaning of the word works just fine, it is not at all clear that the Corinthians would have been expected to apply some other meaning (or that we should). It is also not clear that Paul is particularly interested in promoting gifts of utterance over other gifts, as much as he is interested in helping the Corinthians to understand that of the gifts of utterance, prophecy is to be preferred over tongues. If Paul's reference to "the gifts of the Spirit" in 12:1 was a case of employing the preferred language of the Corinthians themselves, and their view of spiritual gifts was restricted to tongues and prophecy (or other speech gifts), by the time Paul finished 12:4-11 the Corinthians should have understood that in Paul's own view many gifts were given and distributed by the Spirit, including many that were not speech gifts. The term used in 12:1 is understood to apply to all of the gifts mentioned in that chapter. The Corinthians would not be expected to apply a more restricted sense at the beginning of this chapter.

**14:2** In vv. 2-3 Paul provides his most concise summaries of the natures of the gifts of prophecy and of tongues. Although speaking in tongues was not mentioned in the opening verse of the chapter, it does not take long for Paul to make it clear that he is not thinking simply about the value of prophecy compared to other gifts in general, but about the relative values of prophecy and tongues. The two gifts are contrasted in terms of the audience addressed by the speech involved and the comprehension of the other members of the congregation.

*For those who speak in a tongue do not speak to other people but to God.* Witherington thinks that the fact that Paul says that those who speak in a tongue *do not speak to other people but to God* is "a clear indication that glossolalia was seen as a prayer language or as a way to talk to God, not as a human language."[14] It does not indicate that it was not a human language, but that he did not expect that those gathered would normally know whatever language was spoken. It does suggest that speaking in tongues was understood as prayer, a view that is consistent with Paul's other comments on the subject. As a form of prayer, it is quite understandable that the Corinthians would think it a perfectly valid and natural component (perhaps even the most appropriate element) of worship. If Christian worship were just about the relationship between the individual worshipper and his or her God, that logic would be sound. A very important part, perhaps the

12. Thiselton, 1083 (italics his, bold font changed to single quotes). He cites Gillespie (*The First Theologians*, 129-30), who asserts that "[t]he 'greater gifts' are now specified as 'spiritual utterances' *(ta pneumatika)*, particularly prophesying."

13. Thiselton, 1083.

14. Witherington, 281.

most important part, of Paul's message in this chapter is that the public worship of God is at its heart a communal experience in which one honors God by keeping a clear focus on him and those others with whom one is engaged in worship.

Luke Timothy Johnson's assertion, mentioned above, that for Paul "tongues are an intrinsically noncommunicative form of utterance"[15] can hold only if we ignore Paul's assertion that people who speak in tongues are speaking to God. This is a remarkable statement, considering that the speech finds its origin in the Spirit. It is also speech which is "noncommunicative" (with respect to the human audience) only in cases where hearers are not provided with an interpretation. Collins points out that Paul uses the verb "to speak" twenty-four times in this chapter, suggesting "[t]he entire chapter is a discourse on speech."[16] Here, as he begins that discussion, he uses the verb three times, more than any other verse in the chapter.

*Indeed, no one understands them; they utter mysteries by the Spirit.* Witherington thinks that the word *mysteries* here "means 'unknown or secret things,' probably, that is, what is unintelligible."[17] In other words, he takes these two clauses to be essentially synonymous. This approach empties the word of its own content, perhaps to accommodate a prior understanding of the nature of speaking in tongues. Paul's statement indicates that the tongues speech has specific content, even if it is not understood by anyone other than God (and those with the gift of interpretation). As BDAG defines them, Paul's words suggest that the person "*utters secret truths in the Spirit* which the person alone shares w[ith] God, and which others, even Christians, do not understand."[18] The word *mysteries* was used in 13:2 in the description of the superlative hypothetical instantiation of the prophetic gift as the ability to understand "all mysteries and all knowledge." In marked contrast, those who speak in tongues are not given any special understanding of mysteries (at least not as part of that particular gift), but the ability to speak them to God. Although *no one understands them* (except God), Paul wants us to understand that they are not merely babbling. In fact, not only are they expressing content, but it is Spirit-inspired content of the type that a prophet could only dream of comprehending![19] The TNIV

15. Luke Timothy Johnson, "Tongues, Gift of," in *ABD* 6:597.

16. Collins, 490.

17. Witherington, 281.

18. BDAG, "μυστήριον," 1b.

19. Cf. Bockmuehl, *Revelation and Mystery in Ancient Judaism and Pauline Christianity*, 168-70. Fee, 656, thinks that the meaning of "mysteries" here could be similar to the meaning in 13:2 but "more likely it carries here the sense of that which lies outside the understanding, both for the speaker and the hearer. After all, 'mysteries' in 13:2 refers to the ways of God that are being revealed by the Spirit to his people; such 'mysteries' would scarcely need to be spoken back to God." Mysteries may well be a term that might be applied to the things that angels in heaven speak between themselves and/or to God himself. God is undoubtedly to be praised for the ways he works in heaven and on earth. These mysteries may

does well in capitalizing the word *Spirit* (along with the NRSV, ESV, NET, NJB, NLT, and CSB). We are, of course, in the middle of discussing gifts of the Spirit, and it would be understood that it is God's Spirit that reveals or allows his mysteries to be uttered.[20] Even apart from this context, in Paul's writing the word "[a]lmost always denotes the Holy Spirit, except in those specific contexts (14:14 and 32) where semantic contrasts clearly indicate otherwise."[21]

**14:3** Paul distinguishes the gift of prophecy from the gift of tongues primarily in terms of the person(s) addressed through each. *But those who prophesy speak to people for their strengthening, encouragement and comfort*. Carson points out that this verse does not provide a definition of the gift of prophecy, but describes its function in terms that could also be applied to other gifts such as teaching or even the interpretation of tongues, but which contrast with the function of uninterpreted tongues.[22] Still, the particular words chosen are undoubtedly significant for understanding the nature of prophetic ministry in the church.[23] The word translated *strengthening*[24] here is the same translated "building" in 3:9, and is the noun form of the verb which is translated "builds up" in 8:1 (see the comments there). On the Old Testament background to Paul's emphasis on building up the church, see the introductory comments on 8:1–11:1. The theme of edification or building up governs this chapter (14:3, 4, 5, 12, 17, 26). The gift of prophecy (properly used) results in people being stronger in their faith in and walk with Christ. The word translated *encouragement*[25] has to do with the "act of emboldening another in belief or course of action" (BDAG) and here reinforces the idea of the previous word. It may also mean essentially the same thing as the following word, translated *comfort*,[26] which has to do with "that which serves as encouragement to one who is depressed or in grief" (BDAG).

These three words strongly suggest that prophetic ministry, by its very nature, must flow out of a deep concern for the well-being of those who need to be strengthened, encouraged, and comforted. As Paul describes it, it is certainly not a ministry marked by a cold communication of theological or other truths, but one marked by commitment to and compassion for other members of the body.[27] The power of speech suggested here

---

perhaps be related to "the wonders of God" that were declared in Acts 2:11 or the "things that no one is permitted to tell" that Paul heard when caught up to the third heaven (2 Cor. 12:2-4).

20. See Fee, 656 n. 22. Translations that leave the word in lower case ("spirit") include the NIV, NAB, NASB, and KJV.

21. Thiselton, 1086 (emphasis removed).

22. Carson, *Showing the Spirit*, 102. Cf. Grudem, *Gift of Prophecy*, 181-84.

23. Witherington suggests that the gift "has a mainly parenetic quality, as was true of OT prophecy, though some theology would also be involved" (282).

24. Gk. οἰκοδομή: "process of building, *building, construction*" (BDAG).

25. Gk. παράκλησις.

26. Gk. παραμυθία.

27. Cf. Thiselton, 1088.

is remarkable, reminding one of what James 3:5-8 says about the power of the tongue, except that Paul speaks of its positive power for edification while James has in mind its destructive power. Paul literally says that "those who prophesy speak strengthening, encouragement and comfort to people." That is, the "strengthening, encouragement and comfort" are the direct objects of the verb *speak.* Thiselton describes these as "proleptic accusatives" pointing to what the speaker accomplishes or hopes to accomplish through the speaking.[28] The opportunity to bring strength, encouragement, and comfort to their brothers and sisters through our speech (as opposed to merely using our speech as an opportunity to express our thoughts or feelings) is to be highly valued and liberally employed. "The pastoral dimension is underlined not only by the contextual particularity which distinguishes prophesying from teaching (which may be more doctrinal or general)" but also by the impression that encouragement[29] "frequently rests on a personal relationship between the speaker and addressees."[30]

It is interesting to note that much Old Testament prophecy hardly would have been described as comforting, since much of it was dedicated to condemning disobedience and apostasy. Jeremiah describes two phases in his prophetic ministry, one during which he uproots things (namely, the corrupt form of God's community) and destroys them, and one during which he plants and builds up God's new community. It is normally God who does the tearing down and uprooting, the planting and building, but in Jeremiah 1:10 these activities are ascribed to Jeremiah's prophetic activity. It is because Paul is concerned about the edification of the church that he puts such a high value on the prophetic ministry, which, at this stage of salvation history, is primarily focused on building up God's eschatological community (while previously it was focused on uprooting the community that had rebelled against him). Those gifts and ministries that most effectively build up (i.e., strengthen) the community, such as prophecy, are those which Paul most highly values and would have us value.

**14:4** The two gifts are contrasted again — this time not in terms of who is addressed, but in terms of who is edified: *Those who speak in a tongue edify themselves, but those who prophesy edify the church.* The contrasts Paul makes between these two gifts in this and the prior verse may be diagrammed as follows:

| **Verses** | **Gift** | **Who is addressed** | **Who is edified** |
|---|---|---|---|
| **2, 4a** | *Tongues* | *God* | *The speaker* |
| **3, 4b** | *Prophecy* | *People* | *The church* |

28. Thiselton, 1087.

29. Gk. παρακαλέω.

30. Thiselton, 1088, referencing the arguments of C. J. Bjerkelund, *Parakalô: Form, Funktion und Sinn der parakalô-Sätze in den paulinischen Briefen* (Oslo: Universitetsforlaget, 1967), 188-90.

It is not a criticism of tongues that the gift edifies the speaker. Later in the chapter Paul will make clear that he speaks in tongues regularly, in private, and has no problem with people speaking in tongues alone with God — in fact, God has made such prayer possible through a gift of his Spirit. Thiselton gives some weight to the suggestion of Vielhauer and Schrage that Paul uses the term *edify* "as a double wordplay which may mean *self-sufficiency* or *self-affirmation* in some contexts and genuine building up of other people in other contexts," with the former being "firmly egoist and self-indulgent."[31] This seems to be reading too much contextual argumentation into the meaning of the word in different contexts. BDAG gives three definitions for the word, "to construct a building," "to construct in a transcendent sense" (as in the building up of the congregation), and "to help improve ability to function in living responsibly and effectively."[32] There is nothing in the word itself that would suggest to the Corinthians or us that to build oneself up is "egoist[ic] and self-indulgent." The following context will make it clear that it would be selfish to merely edify oneself when gathered as a church since in that context it is the edification of the church that ought to be the priority. The following verse, however, makes it clear that Paul has no problem with speaking in tongues per se, which would be a rather strange point to make if he just finished suggesting that those who spoke in tongues were self-indulgent.

When believers are gathered together, love calls for the exclusive use of gifts which will serve to build up the community. This principle may and should be applied beyond the very specific issue that Paul needed to address in Corinth. There are many other things that believers may find themselves interested in doing in worship which they find spiritually satisfying or beneficial for themselves, but which may not edify those gathered with them, or worse, which may serve as a distraction to others or otherwise detract from the edifying nature of the time spent together in worship. Love calls for all believers to exercise discernment in the use of our spiritual gifts, preferring those that will make the greatest contribution to the health of the body over ones that we might personally prefer to practice or that would seem to bring us greater respect or esteem (or power) in the community. As Witherington concludes, "Worship is mainly meant to be a group experience where one gives worship to God" and shares fellowship with others "so that all benefit."[33]

**14:5** Paul clarifies that his contrast between the two gifts is not to be taken as a criticism or condemnation of tongues per se. *I would like every one of you to speak in tongues, but I would rather have you prophesy.* That Paul would like them all to speak in tongues is qualified by the second half the

31. Thiselton, 1094, referring to Vielhauer, *Oikodomē,* 91-98, and Schrage, *Der erste Brief,* 3:388 (including nn. 62 and 63).

32. BDAG, "οἰκοδομέω."

33. Witherington, 282.

sentence where *but I would rather* reflects the same expression[34] that was translated "especially" in v. 1, and that "introduces an expr[ession] or thought that supplements and thereby corrects what has preceded."[35] Here the correction is not that he would be displeased if they could all speak in tongues, but that his greater wish would be for them all to be able to prophesy. The wish that they might all prophesy echoes Moses' own "wish that all the LORD's people were prophets and that the LORD would put his Spirit on them" (Num. 11:29), which seems to be in mind in Joel 2:28: "I will pour out my Spirit on all people. Your sons and daughters will prophesy."[36]

That Paul would be perfectly happy for them all to have one gift or another does not contradict his own awareness that no individual gift is actually shared by all members of the body (12:17-19, 29-30). That Paul could imagine *every one of you* either speaking in tongues or prophesying reflects a point that will be made more forcefully later in this chapter, that it was evidently both normal and expected that all those gathered in worship would participate in one way or another. It was mainly a question of which contributions would be most common or most highly regarded. In most churches throughout church history the majority of those participating in worship have done so by following a script written by those in leadership. The script calls for them to stand or sit to sing, pray, listen to a sermon, and so on. In some ways, Paul's description of a worship meeting has more in common with some Bible study or fellowship groups in which all who attend are expected to contribute in some individual way to the group conversation and/or fellowship experience (perhaps by providing food or music).

*Those who prophesy are greater than those who speak in tongues, unless they interpret, so that the church may be edified.* To be *greater* here has to do with "being relatively superior in importance" or "more prominent or outstanding because of certain advantages" (BDAG). That is, it is more important, more valuable, to prophesy in church than to speak in (uninterpreted) tongues, and greater prominence ought to be given to such people than to those who speak in tongues. Paul does not intend to establish a superior class or group of people (there are enough problems of that sort in Corinth),[37] but does mean to give greater prominence to the practice of some gifts (like prophecy) over others.

The TNIV agrees with the majority of English translations in understanding that Paul here is referring to interpretation *(unless they interpret)* on the part of the one who speaks in tongues (so also NIV, NET, NAB, NJB,

34. Gk. μᾶλλον δέ.

35. BDAG, "μᾶλλον," 3d.

36. See Kistemaker, 481.

37. The TNIV has transformed the singular verbs into plurals out of a preference for generic plurals over generic masculine forms. This would normally be reasonable since the singular forms in the Greek text serve to identify a kind or category of person (not a particular person), but in this case that translation choice could seem to underwrite the Corinthian penchant for divisiveness.

NASB, CSB). Some other translations think that Paul has another interpreter in mind and translate the same clause "unless someone interprets" (so NRSV, ESV, NLT). Collins points out that the verb in question "has an indeterminate subject, expressed only in the inflection of the verb." He recognizes that "in some cases" the interpreter would have been the same as the one who spoke in tongues and that "[g]rammatically that would seem to be the better reading of Paul's text." Still, in his view, "the principle of the allocation of gifts (12:4-11) implies that the interpreter would ordinarily be someone other than the one who speaks in tongues (cf. 14:27)."[38] The view that the interpreter would have been another person is explicitly reflected in several textual witnesses.[39] While those textual variants are to be rejected as interpretive clarifications and improvements, it may be that they reflect the correct interpretation of the more ambiguous text.[40]

Thiselton is right, however, to oppose that interpretation: "NRSV's 'unless someone interprets' is, in our view, disastrously misleading. The Greek does not mention any agent other than the one who speaks in tongues, who remains the subject of the verb. The insertion of 'someone' rests on a particular understanding of ['the interpretation of tongues'][41] (12:10) and the significance of ['to another'][42] in conjunction with this phrase in 12:10, as if a special agent was 'an interpreter' who 'interpreted' tongues."[43] It is not that the one who speaks in tongues would always be the interpreter, but that the only way in which the one who speaks in tongues turns out to be as important as the one who prophesies is if they themselves cause the church as a whole to be edified by providing an interpretation of what they said. If someone else provides the interpretation (which may have been more common, as Collins and others suspect), that third person makes a fine contribution to the edification of the church, but the same cannot be said for the one who spoke in tongues. The greater the edification of the church, the greater the contribution of the one exercising their spiritual gift(s).

This verse should not be taken to mean that interpreted tongues have the same nature as a prophetic message.[44] Paul says no such thing, and, in fact, already said quite the opposite in the previous verses. It is not that interpreted tongues take the form of prophecy, but that by being made intelli-

38. Collins, 494.

39. MSS 0243, 1505, 1739, 1881, *pc* read "unless someone interprets" (εἰ μή τις διερμηνεύει or εἰ μή τις διερμηνεύῃ), while F and G read "unless the interpreter is there" (εἰ μὴ ᾖ ὁ διερμηνεύων).

40. The simpler text, accepted by NA$^{27}$ and UBS$^{4}$, is εἰ μὴ διερμηνεύῃ, supported by 𝔓$^{46}$, א, A, B, D$^{2}$, K, P, 048, 0289$^{vid}$, 33, 365, 629, *al*, lat. A related variant (εἰ μὴ διερμηνεύει) is found in (Ψ) 𝔐.

41. Gk ἑρμηνεία γλωσσῶν.

42. Gk. ἄλλῳ δέ.

43. Thiselton, 1098 (emphases removed).

44. *Pace* Garland, 635, who, following Godet, says that through interpretation "glossolalia is transformed into prophecy."

gible they edify the rest of the church (as does prophecy). Such edification presumably takes place as people are ministered to by the content of the prayer or praise that is offered, just as they are when people offer prayer or praise to God (in normal voice or in song) apart from any form of tongues. Later in the chapter (vv. 18-19, 27-28) Paul will make it clear that he does not want any speaking in tongues to take place in the public worship of the church unless someone (the tongues-speaker or another member of the body with the gift of interpretation) can be counted on to interpret it.

The word translated *interpret*[45] was discussed above (see on 12:30). According to BDAG, the word meant either "to translate from one language to another" or "to clarify someth[ing] so as to make it understandable." This verse is placed under the second meaning, with the stated understanding that it is a matter of interpreting "ecstatic speech." The fact that the word is used in the context of speaking in *tongues* or "languages" (using the same terms as found in Isa. 19:18, Acts 2:4, 11[46]) would seem to suggest that the first category would be the more intuitive one in this case.[47]

### *ii. Arguments based on analogies from music and language, 14:6-12*

Having argued in favor of the superior value of prophecy in comparison with tongues for the edification of the church, Paul now focuses on the question of intelligibility as the key to edifying speech. As Fee suggests, in vv. 6-12 Paul offers a series of analogies that serve as arguments in favor of intelligibility.[48] Collins points out that this passage's references "to musical instruments and to the gifts of revelation, knowledge, and prophecy" recall the opening lines of chapter 13. The passage also reflects Paul's penchant (common to many ancient writers, including, e.g., the Gospel of Matthew) to offer a trio of illustrations. In this case, the flute and harp, the military trumpet, and (normally learned and spoken) foreign languages. These three illustrations work together "to demonstrate why it is that sounds must be sufficiently heard and properly distinguished if they are to be of benefit to people."[49]

Pastoral reflection on this theme must go well beyond the Corinthian issue of tongues versus prophecy to wider application of the relationship

45. Gk. διερμηνεύω.

46. Gk. λαλεῖν γλώσσαις.

47. Thiselton, 1098-99, gives examples of cases where the verb is used of people trying to put into words what existed only as an image or thought in the mind. None of those cases entail putting into words something that was already spoken (λαλέω) in a tongue/language (γλῶσσα), as in this case, as opposed to being merely seen with the eyes, thought with the mind, or felt with the heart.

48. Fee, 660.

49. Collins, 495.

between intelligibility and edification. Intelligibility may be lacking even when those ministering in other gifts do so in English, either through a lack of coherent thinking or argumentation or through the use of overly academic or theological vocabulary (or lingo) that goes over the heads of believers and/or unbelievers. In this sense, sensitivity toward "seekers" in the form of avoiding unnecessary or excessive "insider" language that would be unintelligible to those who have not learned to speak "Evangelicalese" is appropriate. Of course, Christians should learn some key theological terms and every community acquires its own terminology, but Christian leaders and churches must remain sensitive to Paul's point that clarity of communication is essential for both edification and evangelism.

### 1) Introduction of the Theme of Usefulness, 14:6

**14:6** Paul contrasts the usefulness of tongues with that of intelligible types of speech gifts. *Now, brothers and sisters, if I come to you and speak in tongues,*[50] *what good will I be to you, unless I bring you some revelation or knowledge or prophecy or word of instruction?*

Paul's use of another vocative, addressing the readers directly, *brothers and sisters,*[51] suggests that this verse begins a new unit. He speaks in the first person, applying to his own ministry the principle he wants the Corinthians to adopt. The question, *what good will I be to you?* is the one he would like every believer to ask as part of their evaluation of their use of their spiritual gifts and their other activities and/or behavior when gathered for worship. Here he asks the rhetorical question to make the point that if he were to spend a period of time with them in which he simply spoke in tongues and did not bring them a prophetic message or teaching they could comprehend, he would be of no use to them at all during that visit. The verb translated *what good will I be*[52] is the same one translated "I gain/profit" in 13:3. Putting the two verses together makes it clear that love entails seeking the gain/profit/good of those around us, and that only by living a Christian life that is dedicated to the benefit of others do we gain any eternal benefit ourselves. The same motif is found throughout chapters 8–10 and 12–14.

It may be that the Corinthians had questioned why Paul did not speak in tongues when he was among them, perhaps suggesting that he

50. In vv. 6, 7, 8, 9, 11, and 16 Paul employs third-class conditional structures (marked by the use of ἐάν with a subjunctive verb in the protasis). As pointed out previously, this structure "simply projects some action or event for hypothetical consideration" (Porter, *Idioms of the Greek New Testament*, 262). Paul wants the Corinthians to think through these hypothetical situations and draw the proper conclusions to guide them in their prioritizing of gifts and ministries and in the ways they spend their time in worship.

51. Gk. Νῦν δέ, ἀδελφοί. On the generic (brothers and sisters) meaning of ἀδελφοί, see above on 1:10.

52. Gk. ὠφελέω.

had not reached the spiritual heights that have now been achieved by some of them.[53] Some may have indicated that they would like to see Paul speak in tongues during his next visit to them.[54] If so, this response on Paul's part suggests that they should be more interested in benefiting from his prophetic and teaching ministry by helping them imagine what it would be like if they had to choose just one or the other (a visit marked purely by speaking in tongues vs. one in which he taught them and prophesied to them).

Several scholars have pointed out that the four terms mentioned (revelation, knowledge, prophecy, teaching) may be paired together on the understanding that the first two relate more directly to the perception of truth, while the last two relate more directly to the modes by which each of those kinds of truths are communicated to the congregation. In this understanding, something received by way of revelation is communicated in a prophecy and something that is perceived through knowledge is communicated in teaching.[55] This may well be the case, although Paul's use of the terminology is not consistent enough to be dogmatic. Fee comments that "as with the other lists in this argument, this one is also especially *ad hoc*" and that precisely what content Paul has in mind by revelation and "how it would differ from 'knowledge' or 'prophecy' is not at all clear." Furthermore, this verse, taken in conjunction with the list in v. 30, "suggests that there is a general lack of precision in Paul with regard to these various items."[56] Knowledge is sometimes associated with prophecy, and at other times seems to be distinguished from it (and here associated with teaching). One wonders whether Paul always has a clear distinction in mind between teaching and prophecy or whether he sometimes thinks of them as interrelated gifts or ministries, perhaps ones that have to do with the communication of (different kinds of) knowledge. Usage weighs against thinking that Paul uses the four words as technical terms. Hays is probably correct in suggesting that "the term 'prophecy' should be read throughout chapter 14 as synecdoche for all forms of intelligible speech gifts that edify the church."[57] This fits with our suggestion that in 11:4-5 prophecy and prayer serve as broad terms for virtually all discourse in worship, with prophecy being used in that case for all discourse addressed to the congregation and prayer for discourse directed to God.

53. Some commentators think that Paul is echoing the language of 2:1 ("When I came to you . . ."; Gk. ἐλθὼν πρὸς ὑμᾶς) and referring to his first arrival in Corinth. It is just as likely that he is referring to his upcoming visit and echoing his language in 4:21 ("Shall I come to you? . . ."; Gk. ἔλθω πρὸς ὑμᾶς; precisely as here).

54. Cf. Fee, 661.

55. See Grudem, *The Gift of Prophecy,* 138-39; Garland, 635; Conzelmann, 235 n. 20; Schrage 3:390.

56. Fee, 662-63.

57. Hays, 237.

### 2) Illustration: Musical Instruments That Do Not Give Distinct Messages Are Not Useful, 14:7-8

**14:7** It is unusual for Paul to refer to music or musical instruments. That he does so in a section dedicated to issues of worship may reflect the role of music in the worship of the ancient synagogue and early church, where "[t]he sounds of music appealed to the affect of those gathered and contributed to a holistic learning experience."[58] He writes: *Even in the case of lifeless things that make sounds, such as the pipe or harp, how will anyone know what tune is being played unless there is a distinction in the notes?* It was common to associate music with worship, and Philo speaks of heaven as "the original archetype of all musical instruments," which "was tuned with consummate skill for no other purpose than that the hymns sung in honour of the Universal Father may have a musical accompaniment."[59] Paul and the Corinthians are united in their desire to see believers' voices also used in praise of God (like the harp and the pipe), and Paul is especially concerned that they be used in public worship in ways that most effectively serve their ultimate purpose.

Just as Paul would not benefit the Corinthians if he simply spoke in tongues, a pipe or a harp would be useless as musical instruments (and aids to worship) if they were not capable of making a series of distinct (or consistent) *notes.* In *Antiquities* 7.306 Josephus refers to a harp that had or produced twelve different notes. Wisdom 19:18 says that "on a harp the notes vary the nature of the rhythm, while each note remains the same" (NRSV). How useless it would have been if the strings did not make different and distinct notes! Or if the notes which were supposed to stay the same kept varying! Certainly no one would be able to discern what tune someone was trying to play.[60] Such an instrument "serves no purpose but instead defeats its purpose."[61] The public speaking of tongues without interpretation makes no more sense than trying to play a pipe whose holes have been drilled in random places or a harp whose strings have never been tuned or even properly strung.[62] No recognizable music would be produced, and thus no useful purpose would be served. The flute, harp, and voice are beneficial only if they are effectively employed.

58. Collins, 495. On the early Christian usage of music Collins points us to 1 Cor. 14:15, 26; Matt. 26:30; Mark 14:26; Acts 16:25; Eph. 5:19; Col. 3:16. Collins, 496, also reminds us that the two particular instruments Paul mentions (flute and harp) were well known and associated not only with worship but also with joy (Matt. 11:17; Luke 7:32; Rev. 18:22; Philo, *On the Embassy to Gaius* 12) and even prophetic inspiration (1 Sam. 10:5; 2 Kgs. 3:15).

59. Philo, *On Dreams* 1:37 (LCL).

60. The Greek text includes a bit more parallelism which is lost when translated into less redundant forms in English (although see NET, NAB, NASB, CSB). Literally it reads: "Similarly with lifeless things that *produce* sound, whether a *flute* or a *harp,* if it does not *produce* a distinction in the notes, how will it be known what is being *fluted* or *harped*?"

61. Garland, 636.

62. Cf. Thiselton, 1103, "untuned strings or overblown wind produces mere noise."

**14:8** The point made in the previous verse (that communication must be intelligible to be useful) is now reinforced using a military analogy. *Again, if the trumpet does not sound a clear call, who will get ready for battle?* This illustration is distinguished from the one given in the previous verse in that it refers to "a signal instrument"[63] while the pipe and harp referred to musical instruments. Following the same line of thought as in the previous verse, Paul provides another illustration of energy wasted on an unintelligible act. That which is translated *trumpet*,[64] we might more commonly refer to as a bugle (so NRSV, ESV, NAB, NLT, NASB). Like the modern military bugle it did not have the valves which have been associated with modern trumpets since the nineteenth century. It was "a long, straight metal wind instrument with a bell and a mouthpiece" which was "capable of producing only a few natural tones that could be articulated loudly and distinctly."[65] Those "few tones" needed to be clearly and distinctly sounded in order to communicate any one of a series of particular signals so that the troops would know how to respond. The *War Scroll* describes military bugle calls signaling muster, alarm, ambush, pursuit, reassembly, enlistment, encampment, battle formation, funeral, retreat, and homecoming (1QM ii 16–iii 11; vii 13–ix 6; xvi 3-9; xvii 10-15). If the trumpeter (we would say "bugler")[66] does not know how to give the proper call to battle, or if the trumpet itself was incapable of giving such clear signals, no soldier would know whether they should be preparing for battle, setting up camp, or watching for an ambush. Garland suggests that some of the Corinthians who spoke in tongues may have thought of themselves as virtuoso worshipers worthy of being admired by the rest of the congregation. But Paul "puts their performance in a completely different light with the implication that the indistinct sounds made by the flute, harp, and bugle are made by inexpert players — mere novices."[67]

### 3) Application: Unintelligible Speech Is Not Useful, 14:9

**14:9** Just as a visit from Paul would be ineffective if spent communicating in tongues, and just as musical instruments or a military bugle

63. H. Lichtenberger, "σάλπιγξ," *EDNT* 3:225.

64. Gk. σάλπιγξ.

65. Lichtenberger, "σάλπιγξ," *EDNT* 3:225.

66. Collins, 496, thinks that "some suggestion to the effect that Paul's reflection has eschatological overtones might be gleaned from his reference to the trumpet" since "[i]t is an instrument he associates with the coming of the eschaton (15:52, where both the noun and the related verb appear, and 1 Thess 4:16; cf. Rev 1:10; 4:1; 8:2, 6, 13; 9:14)." Certainly the references to the trumpet in the *War Scroll* would support such an association as well. Although Paul does associate the trumpet with the eschaton in other contexts, it is not clear that such associations are to be understood to play a role in this present reference. Paul's comment here assumes that one cannot guess what the trumpet call might mean since it might be giving any one of several signals. His point is simply that if it does not give a clear signal, no one will know how to respond appropriately.

67. Garland, 636.

would be ineffective if they did not emit clear and distinct notes or signals, the Corinthians' behavior in worship reflects the same reality: *So it is with you.* The middle of this verse reflects a particularly close parallel with v. 7 (both have, literally, "unless [it/you] give, . . . how will anyone know what is being [fluted/said] . . .").[68]

*Unless you speak intelligible words with your tongue.* In contrast with every other usage of the word in this letter, the word *tongue* is here used of the physical organ used to speak rather than of the "tongues" (or languages) that are spoken by the glossolalist (12:10, 28, 30; 13:1, 8; 14:2, 4-6, 9, 13-14, 18-19, 22-23, 26-27, 39; cf. 14:21). Paul stresses the importance of using the *tongue* to *speak intelligible words* rather than using the tongue to speak in tongues. Garland thinks that "[t]he implication from this description of tongues as indistinct sounds is that the Corinthian tongues are not xenoglossolalia — speaking an unlearned foreign language — but the utterance of inarticulate noises and syllables."[69] But Paul's language[70] does not indicate that the speaker is not articulating words. It indicates that the words or speech being articulated is not "readily recognizable" (BDAG) or "easily understood" (Louw and Nida). It is not so much that "[n]o earthly lexicon could decipher their meaning"[71] but that the inner lexicons of the Corinthian believers could not decipher their meaning (without special assistance from the Spirit).

*how will anyone know what you are saying? You will just be speaking into the air.* The result of speaking in tongues (without interpretation) is that no one understands what is being said. To speak into the air was evidently a known figure of speech[72] meaning to utter words in vain.[73] Theodoret says that "the words melt into the air to no purpose."[74] In other words, you will be no more useful than the musical instruments and bugle of the illustrations in vv. 7-8.

### 4) Illustration: Normal Human Languages, When Not Understood, Are Not Useful, 14:10-11

**14:10-11** Paul compares the usefulness (or lack thereof) of the gift of speaking in tongues with that of the normal use of human languages when they are not understood. *Undoubtedly there are all sorts of languages in the*

68. 14:7 Gk. ἐὰν . . . μὴ δῷ, πῶς γνωσθήσεται τὸ αὐλούμενον.
14:9 Gk. ἐὰν μὴ . . . δῶτε, πῶς γνωσθήσεται τὸ λαλούμενον.

69. Garland, 636 (cf. Schrage, 3:394-96).

70. Gk. εὔσημος.

71. Garland, 636.

72. BDAG, "ἀήρ," 1. See Ovid, *Amores* 1.6.42, "dare verba in ventos"; Lucretius 4.931, "ventis verba profundam."

73. "In 9:16 Paul had used sparring in the air as a metaphor for futility; speaking in the air is of the same order" (Collins, 499). As Thiselton, 1105, puts it, "The speech-event is fruitless and pointless."

74. Theodoret, 220.

*world, yet none of them is without meaning.* [11]*If then I do not grasp the meaning of what someone is saying, I am a foreigner to the speaker, and the speaker is a foreigner to*[75] *me.* BDAG has, "There are probably ever so many different languages,"[76] or "There are numerous languages spoken in the world, with none devoid of meaning."[77] There are probably ever so many different kinds of speech in the world, with none devoid of meaning" seems to capture the idea. The word translated *languages*[78] usually means "sounds" or "voices," but v. 11 makes it clear that languages are in mind.[79] Theodoret's comment reflects the relationship between this verse and vv. 7-8: "What a harmonious rhythm is to a harp, and a call to battle to a trumpet, translation is to languages."[80]

That there are "ever so many different kinds" of languages would explain why it was so common for the tongues spoken in worship to be unknown to any of those who were gathered, without the special gift of interpretation.[81] The reference to the tremendous diversity of languages in the world (v. 10) and Paul's reference to a speaker being *a foreigner*[82] *to me* (v. 11) suggest that he already has Isaiah 28:11-12 in mind (see below on 1 Cor. 14:21-25). The Greek word for foreigner (related to our word "barbarian") is onomatopoetic, suggesting the sound of a foreign language to the ear of one who does not understand it. It calls to mind the "stumbling and stammering in speech" of "one who could not speak Greek properly."[83] Prior points to the Hellenistic hubris behind the term: "Greeks were very proud of the beauty of their language and regarded every other language as boorish and grating."[84] Thiselton thinks that "a further nuance of the irritating effect" may be seen in a comparison with the English expression "Blah-blah-blah."[85] Paul himself reflects greater cross-cultural awareness and sen-

75. This is a particularly clear case where Gk. ἐν means "to" (cf. BDF §220 [1]), given the parallel between the first part of the verse and the second (ἔσομαι τῷ λαλοῦντι . . . καὶ ὁ λαλῶν ἐν ἐμοί).

76. Under τυγχάνω.

77. Under ἄφωνος.

78. Gk. φωνή.

79. Most commentators point out that Paul uses a different word for languages here because he has used the most common one to refer to glossolalia (Conzelmann, 256; Fee, 665 n. 36; Thiselton, 1105; Garland, 637). Paul is also able to make a wordplay since the words translated "languages" and "without meaning" are based on the same root (essentially "all kinds of speech" and none is "speechless").

80. Theodoret, 220.

81. It is also possible that the frequency of this latter experience of someone speaking an unknown tongue contributed to Paul's thinking about the vast number of languages that must exist in the world.

82. Gk. βάρβαρος. BDAG defines the word as "pert[aining] to using a language that is unintelligible to outsiders, *foreign-speaking, of foreign tongue.*"

83. Collins, 497.

84. Prior, 245 (Collins, 497, uses the term "Hellenistic hybris").

85. Thiselton, 1106 (emphasis removed), pointing to a possible similarity between Gk. βάρ-βάρ and Eng. "Blah-blah-blah."

sitivity than most in that he recognizes that he himself (even as a speaker of Greek) would sound just as much like a foreigner or barbarian to those who speak different languages as they would to him. He will cite the text that deals with Israel's experience of not understanding the strange, unknown language of its foreign (Assyrian) invaders in v. 21.

Many interpreters have suggested that since Paul compares speaking in tongues with foreign (human) languages in this verse, he must not think that they are the same thing. The logic holds to a certain point. Speaking in tongues is not the same as simply speaking a foreign language. Those speaking and hearing the tongues are not actually foreigners to each other. The experience is similar (comparable) but not the same. One who speaks in tongues does not (usually) know what they are saying (unlike someone speaking a foreign language), they are not able to understand anything spoken to them in the same language, and so on. Even if the gift of tongues was understood to entail a Spirit-given ability to speak unknown human (and possibly angelic) languages to God (normally), as seems most likely, the closest thing to which some aspect of the experience could be compared would be that of engaging a foreigner where neither knows the language of the other. Such an experience, of course, is hardly conducive to clear or coherent communication, and the illustration is intended to associate speaking in tongues in public with a negative rather than a positive experience. How strange it would be for people who are not merely neighbors, but even brothers and sisters in Christ, to engage in an activity that turns them each into foreigners! This would not be a community-building experience but a community-alienating experience.[86]

### 5) Application: Seek to Exercise Gifts That Edify — Use Intelligible Words (14:12)

**14:12** The Corinthians (and we also) should apply the same logic Paul has demonstrated regarding the illustrations drawn from his own ministry, from musical instruments, from the military bugle, and from experience with foreign languages, all regarding the issue of usefulness or lack of usefulness, to their own practice of spiritual gifts, especially speaking in tongues: *So it is with you.*

Now Paul mentions the Corinthians' passion for spiritual things. In the following clause he will show that that passion should be more wisely directed. *Since you are eager for gifts of the Spirit.* In this case, *gifts of the Spirit* is literally "spirits" ("Since you are eager for spirits"). Oster thinks that Paul's way of phrasing this highlights "the pagan and idolatrous spiritual-

86. So also Garland (637): "Paul's critique of tongues implies that it does more than simply create frustration; it erects barriers of alienation — the sick feeling that one does not belong. What is worse, these feelings are awakened in a place where one is supposed to feel at home: the community of believers."

ity that was still misleading certain Corinthian believers in their understanding and practice of spiritual gifts. . . . Paul, in my judgment, is alluding to an animistic perspective that still has a hold on some of the Corinthian saints and which leads them to associate the supernatural spiritual gifts with the activity of various spirits."[87] If Paul had such a pagan perspective in mind, it hardly seems likely that he would have offered as mild a corrective as is found in the following clause (see also the comment by Thiselton below). Fee believes that it is "Paul's way of speaking about the Spirit manifesting himself through their individual 'spirits'" and that "[t]he clue lies in the usage in v. 32, where the 'spirits of the prophets' refers to the Holy Spirit's speaking prophetic utterances through the one who is prophesying."[88] The statement in v. 32 is revealing, but it appears that "spirits" there refers primarily to the prophets' own spirits through which the Holy Spirit works. It does not seem that that meaning works very well in this verse.[89] BDAG is probably on the right track in indicating that the plural here "is explained . . . by the varied nature of the Spirit's working." Along the same lines (and as though responding to Oster), Thiselton thinks it "unlikely that even the Corinthians sought inspiration from a plurality of spirits; rather, they sought a plurality of manifestations (as many as possible) from God's Holy Spirit." He prefers the translation "powers of the Spirit" to the more common "gifts of the Spirit" or "spiritual gifts" because the latter translations do not do justice to the unusual plural form of the word "s/Spirit."[90] Both his thinking and his sensitivity in translation strike us as being sound here. The term serves, on this reckoning, as an unusual way of referring to the gifts of the Spirit. The remainder of the verse, understood in light of the context, leaves no doubt that that is what Paul is talking about, since the building up of the church is understood to take place through the loving exercise of spiritual gifts.

Paul had earlier encouraged the Corinthians in their eager desire for spiritual gifts (12:31; 14:1; cf. 14:39), using a verb cognate to the noun he employs here;[91] it could literally be translated, "since you are zealots for powers of the Spirit." Here it becomes clear that the Corinthians were zealous or eager to experience spiritual gifts before Paul ever took up his pen to write them, and that his encouragement in that direction was rhetorically significant in terms of reinforcing what was a common value, but one that needed some modification and rethinking on the part of the Corinthians. Their eagerness for gifts (or powers) of the Spirit was not something Paul

87. Oster, 320.

88. Fee, 666.

89. Paul is clearly referring to his own spirit in vv. 14-15, and he could mean that the Corinthians are eager for the Sprit to manifest himself in various ways through their spirits. That this is a direct, albeit unusual, reference to the Holy Spirit seems more likely (as suggested by BDAG, "πνεῦμα," 6d).

90. Thiselton, 1107.

91. Gk. ζηλωτής; the earlier verb was ζηλόω.

was interested in squelching, but energy that he hoped to channel in more community-building, edifying directions.

This clause summarizes the main thrust of Paul's argument throughout this chapter so far: *try to excel in those that build up the church.* The word translated *try*[92] has been used three times in chapters 10 and 13 to refer to "seeking" one's own advantage or that of others (10:24, 33; 13:5). Here Paul uses it to exhort the Corinthians to seek gifts on the basis of the advantage of the church as a whole rather than of their own personal edification.

The word translated *excel* here usually has to do with exceeding in quantity or having an overabundance of something rather than excelling in quality or being particularly good at something.[93] If they are to have a superabundance of any gift, it should not be that of speaking in tongues, but of one that will serve to strengthen the church. The building up or strengthening of the church in its faith in and obedience to Christ is Paul's preeminent concern in this letter (3:9; 8:1; 10:23; 14:3-5, 12, 17, 26; see esp. the comments on 8:1, 14:4, and the introduction to this chapter). Thiselton reflects Paul's emphasis that "since the Spirit is also the Spirit of Christ, and since Christ gave himself *for others,* any claims about 'spirituality' or powers of the Spirit become problematic if they have more to do with self-enhancement than with the welfare and benefit of others."[94]

The communal or community concern has been apparent throughout. Paul is not concerned merely about the building up of individual Christians (although he is concerned that each believer be built up in their faith and walk in Christ), but about the growth and health of the community of Christ — the church. The word *church* (referring to "the totality of Christians living and meeting in a particular locality or larger geographical area, but not necessarily limited to one meeting place"; BDAG) is used twenty-two times in this letter. Of those occurrences, nine are found in this chapter, and thirteen are found in chapters 11–14. In this chapter Paul's attention is especially focused on what happens "in church" (i.e., in the gathering of the believers for worship and fellowship; vv. 19, 23, 28, 33, 34, 35) and for the edification of the church (vv. 4-5, 12).

Fee applies the heart of this verse to concerns within the charismatic and Pentecostal movements:

> In a time when charismatic utterances are experiencing something of a revival in the church, this paragraph is especially important to those in that renewal. The point of everything in corporate worship is not personal experience in the Spirit, but building up the church itself. Much that comes under the banner of charismatic or pentecostal worship

92. Gk. ζητέω. In this letter the word also appears in 1:22; 4:2; 7:27.

93. Gk. περισσεύω. BDAG gives two definitions: "to be in abundance" and "to cause someth[ing] to exist in abundance," although, inexplicably, it suggests the gloss "excel" for this verse. Similarly, Gerhard Schneider, "περισσεύω," *EDNT* 3:76.

94. Thiselton, 1107 (some emphasis removed).

seems very often to fail right at this point. However, it is not so much that what goes on is not understood by the others, but that it fails to have this final verse as its basic urgency. The building up of the community is the basic reason for corporate settings of worship; they should probably not be turned into a corporate gathering for a thousand individual experiences of worship.[95]

At the beginning of the twenty-first century the seeker-driven (and to a lesser extent the seeker-sensitive) movement may benefit from a different kind of critique on the basis of this same verse. The eagerness to communicate the message that the gospel of Christ meets the most profound needs of the human heart and provides divine guidance for more effective living seems to be drawing more and more people to churches in hope of gaining tangible benefits from the experience for their own lives. How many Christians gather for worship with the understanding that it is not about what they might gain from the experience but that their participation in worship should be focused on seeking to benefit and build up those who have gathered together with them? Even if that were the understanding, in many churches the opportunity to minister to others is typically given to a very small and select group who will lead us in song, prayer, and scriptural reflection. Larger churches tend to be strong on doing things in a fitting and orderly manner, but often at the expense of providing opportunities for most of the congregation to practice any spiritual gift and to walk away having played any significant role in building up the rest of the church.

*iii. Elaboration of the application given in verse 12, 14:13-19*

1 Corinthians 14:13-19 provides an amplification of the application given in v. 12 (seeking those gifts that will provide the greatest edification for the church), focused specifically on the issue of speaking in tongues. Prophecy, last explicitly mentioned in v. 6, will not be mentioned again until v. 22. Speaking in tongues is described as relating to such other speech-acts as prayer (vv. 14-15a), singing (v. 15b), praising/blessing God (v. 16a), and thanksgiving (vv. 16b-17).

In short, Paul argues that tongues should be used in the church only if they are interpreted and therefore provide edification for others (and greater edification for oneself as well). He will engage both his spirit and his mind (as well as other people's minds) in worship. He will continue to speak (pray and sing) in tongues, but in church he will be sure to pray and sing with his mind as well (presumably by offering interpretation of his tongues as well as by offering prayer and song that is not communicated through tongues). Verses 14-19 become quite self-referential, as Paul explains how he applies his thinking to his own use of the gift of tongues.

95. Fee, 667.

More precisely, Paul moves from the third person ("one") in v. 13 to the first person ("I") in vv. 14-15, to the second person ("you") in vv. 16-17, and back again to the first person in vv. 18-19. This is all intended to persuade the Corinthians to adopt a different *modus operandi,* of course, but it comes off in a much more gracious way by focusing on Paul's application of the teaching to himself than by constantly applying it to the readers in an overt and direct manner. That Paul's personal application is to be understood as an implicit appeal to the Corinthians to adopt the same approach is clear from the subtle transition from the first-person discussion in vv. 14-15 to the second-person explanation in vv. 16-17 (see the comments on v. 16).

### 1) Opening Appeal: Pray to Interpret Tongues, 14:13

**14:13** Paul exhorts the congregation: *For this reason those who speak in a tongue should pray that they may interpret what they say.* The *reason* someone who speaks in tongues should pray for the ability to interpret what they say is that just given in the preceding verse: that by interpreting the tongue they would contribute to the building up of the church while a failure to do so would be to contribute to an alienating experience for those observing it. That Paul thinks that the same person might have both the gift of tongues and the gift of interpreting tongues is made clear by this verse, although v. 28 suggests that they might also be aware of another person in the group with the gift of interpretation. It may be that Paul expected that the one who spoke in tongues would normally be given the interpretation, but the evidence is not clear. What is clear is that not everyone who spoke in tongues had the gift of interpretation. It is interesting that Paul does not simply say that they should pray that "someone" might be able to interpret what they say, or that they should pray "that it might be interpreted" (using a passive verb rather than the active verb he employed). It may be because the person providing the interpretation was seen as most directly effecting the building up of the church, and that was what each believer should hope to achieve for their brothers and sisters in Christ.

This verse gives us the clearest indication in the whole letter of at least one key element of what Paul had in mind when he encouraged the Corinthians to strive for the greater gifts (12:31). Part of striving for them, apparently, is praying that God would grant them to you. While other texts in this chapter indicate that praise, prayer, and thanksgiving were part of the worship of the church, this is the only verse that clearly refers to a specific request that might be made in prayer. It is not surprising that the request, while ostensibly being made on behalf of oneself, is actually a request that the one praying might be enabled to more effectively build up and bless the others gathered for worship. This suggests once again that our fundamental orientation in worship should not be that of seeking to receive something that will be good for us, but seeking to bring greater benefit and advantage to others.

### 2) Statement of a Dilemma: A Praying Spirit with an Unfruitful Mind, 14:14

**14:14** Paul speaks out of his own experience with tongues and with the difference between the participation of the spirit and that of the mind: *For if I pray in a tongue, my spirit prays, but my mind is unfruitful.* That the *spirit* here is Paul's own spirit is made explicit,[96] as is usual for those cases where Paul does not have the Holy Spirit in mind (which is one of the reasons why ambiguous references should almost always be taken to be references to the Holy Spirit).[97] Back in 2:16 Paul indicated that having the mind of the Lord (the mind of Christ) was one of the great blessings of being a Christian. Here he allows that it is a wonderful thing to pray with one's spirit, but that it is even better to pray with both the spirit and the mind. The contrast between spirit and mind "was well known in the Hellenistic world, where 'spirit' was considered to be a faculty superior to that of mind. In the Platonic view of inspiration the mind is somehow displaced or inactive, virtually asleep, when inspiration occurs. For Paul, unlike the Platonists, such inactivity is problematic." Paul wants to see "the spirit and the mind work together. His plea is for the complementarity of spirit and mind in prayer. Ultimately his anthropology is holistic."[98] Worshiping with an unproductive and unutilized mind would have been considered an unusual situation. Philo asserted that "it is in the heaven and in the mind that capacity resides to set forth in solemn strains hymns of praise and blessing in honour of the Father who is the author of our being."[99] Paul seems to agree with Philo that the mind is a remarkable gift that is to be employed in the praise and worship of God. Since Paul has a holistic view of worship, he sees it as undesirable to worship with only the mind or the spirit. He does not say whether or not his spirit is fruitful when he prays with his mind. One would presume that it is.

### 3) Autobiographical Response to the Dilemma: Praying and Singing with Both Spirit and Understanding, 14:15

**14:15** Paul asks and then resolves: *So what shall I do? I will pray with my spirit, but I will also pray with my understanding; I will sing with my spirit, but I will also sing with my understanding.* The question *what shall I do?*[100] is asked as

96. Through the addition of the pronoun μου (= my; τὸ πνεῦμά μου).

97. Fee, 670, thinks that Paul is referring simultaneously to the Holy Spirit and his own spirit: "my S/spirit prays." We do not doubt that the Holy Spirit was at work in Paul's spirit as he prayed, but there is no good reason to think Paul's expression means anything more than *my spirit prays.* The rest is understood from the context.

98. Collins, 501.

99. Philo, On *Dreams* 1:35.

100. The question (literally, "What, then, is it?") has the sense of "So what follows?" or "What does it mean?" (= "What are the implications?").

though Paul were thinking through what his most appropriate action would be. It serves as a less direct — although equally clear — way of helping the Corinthians understand the way he expects them to respond to his argument.[101] The word *understanding* represents (both times) the same word translated "mind" in the previous verse (and "intelligible" in v. 19). It has to do with that which is done through the engaged mind (and therefore is [presumably] intelligible and in accordance with the person's understanding).

Hays is right to point out that it is difficult to discern "[w]hether these two forms of prayer are meant to be simultaneous or sequential." In his view, "[i]f verses 14-15 are read as elaborations of verse 13, the latter is perhaps more likely: the worshiper prays in tongues ('with the spirit') and then, still under the guidance of the Spirit, offers an interpretation ('with the mind also')."[102] There is no reason to think, however, that Paul's prayers with understanding were limited to interpretations of his tongues, while it is clear that whether or not he prayed out loud in tongues in public prayer depended on whether or not he was confident that it would be interpreted. The thrust of the surrounding argument suggests that he rarely, if ever, spoke in tongues in public worship. His meaning could possibly be, *I will pray with my spirit* [in private], *but I will also pray with my understanding* [in church], although neither kind of prayer would have been completely restricted to one environment or the other. Given the following verse, Paul's point is either that he would pray only with understanding in the worship service, or that he would never pray in tongues in the worship service unless it would be followed up immediately by a translation.

Paul wants the spirit and the mind engaged in worship. Thiselton explains: "If only the mind is active, everything remains at a theoretical level; if only the heart is active, the door lies open to self-deception and credulity. If both are open to the Holy Spirit, the result can build up the community and bear the fruit (v. 14a) of love for the other."[103]

The references to singing, along with prayer, remind us again that we are in a section of his letter dedicated to the subject of worship. The thought of singing in tongues brings to mind the case of Job's daughters in the *Testament of Job*. For instance, when Hemera (one of Job's daughters) put on the sash she received from her father, "she spoke ecstatically in the angelic dialect, sending up a hymn to God in accord with the hymnic style of the angels" (*Testament of Job* 48:3).[104]

101. Paul uses four future indicative verbs (προσεύξομαι is used twice, followed by ψαλῶ, also used twice) to indicate his intended course of action, and (thereby) the course of action he hopes the Corinthians will adopt as well.

102. Hays, 237.

103. Thiselton, 1113.

104. The translation is that of R. P. Spittler, in *OTP* 1:866. The word translated "ecstatically" actually means to "speak out" (BDAG), to "chant hymns" (so LSJ for 1 Chr. [= 3 Kgdms.] 25:1 LXX), or to speak prophetically (see LEH). As Forbes points out (*Prophecy and Inspired Speech*, 183 n. 3), the translation "speak ecstatically" is tendentious.

Although Paul does seem to identify praying with one's spirit with glossolalia, he does not think normal prayer is any less spiritual or he would not prefer praying with the mind in public worship over praying with one's spirit. Paul does not explicitly say as much, but presumably he thinks that one's spirit is engaged even when one prays with the mind.

4) Anticipated Consequence of Rejecting Paul's Appeal and Example: Alienation versus Edification, 14:16-17

**14:16** Paul subtly shifts from the first person to the second person, from what he will do to what would happen if the Corinthians did not adopt his own strategy (advice): *Otherwise when you are praising God in the Spirit, how can the others, who are now put in the same situation as an inquirer, say "Amen" to your thanksgiving, since they do not know what you are saying?* Presumably the scenario he describes in this and the following verse is actually playing itself out on a regular basis during the church meetings in Corinth. The expression *in the Spirit* is translated "with the/your spirit" by virtually all English translations except the TNIV (e.g., NRSV, ESV, NIV, NET, NAB, NJB, NLT, NASB, KJV). Verse 14, with its reference to "my spirit," suggests that that may well be the spirit in mind in vv. 15 and 16 as well.

The next part of v. 16 is translated in quite an interpretive fashion by the TNIV: *the others, who are now put in the same situation as an inquirer.* The Greek being translated here more literally says, "the one occupying[105] the place of the outsider."[106] One assumes from the context that no one in the congregation would be in a position to say the "Amen" to the thanksgiving. On that basis, the decision of the TNIV to translate the word *inquirer*[107] applies to the

105. Gk. ἀναπληρόω. BDAG gives the meaning here as "to occupy a place" and says that "because of the ἰδ[ιώτης] of vss. 23f, [the verb] cannot mean 'the one who occupies the position' . . . of an 'outsider', i.e., in contrast to those speaking in tongues, one who is not so gifted. . . . Rather ἀ[ναπληροῦν] τὸν τόπον τινός means *take* or *fill someone's place* . . . , and τόπος here means a place actually occupied by an ἰδιώτης in the meeting (a view not shared by most Eng[lish] translators), but it is not necessary to assume that a section was reserved for catechumens. . . . On the other hand, [H. Lietzmann] asks whether baptized Christians would be better informed" (ellipses represent the omission of parentheses citing sources).

106. Gk. ὁ ἀναπληρῶν τὸν τόπον τοῦ ἰδιώτου. Interpretation is required for any translation, and the difficulty of understanding the phrase is reflected in the variety of translations: "anyone in the position of an outsider" (NRSV, ESV); "one who holds the place of the uninstructed" (NAB); "the one who fills the place of the ungifted" (NASB); "one who finds himself among those who do not understand" (NIV); "someone without the gift" (NET); "the uninitiated person" (NJB); "those who don't understand" (NLT); "the uninformed person" (CSB); "he that occupieth the room of the unlearned" (KJV).

107. ἰδιώτης. BDAG: "In 1 Cor 14:23f ἰδιῶται and ἄπιστοι together form a contrast to the Christian congregation. The ἰ[διῶται] are neither similar to the ἄπιστοι . . . , nor are they full-fledged Christians, but stand betw[een] the two groups, prob[ably] as prospects for membership and are therefore relatively outsiders." It is also a technical term of religious life: "In relig[ious] associations the term is used for nonmembers who may participate in the sacri-

rest of the congregation. Those other members have been socially alienated from their actual position as full members of the community by behavior that makes them seem like outsiders or mere visitors observing an experience which they are not equipped to interpret. The word Paul uses normally has to do with "one who is not knowledgeable about some particular group's experience" (BDAG). It seems to describe a person who is rather like an equivalent of the Jewish category of "God-fearers" (or the modern evangelical category of "seekers") — people from the local community who were curious about and interested in, and perhaps demonstrating significant commitment to the religion, but who had not yet taken the formal step of becoming a full member of the community.[108]

BDAG is adamant that the "place" or "position" mentioned here (see NRSV, ESV, NAB, NASB) refers not to a social position or situation but to an actual place in the room or facility where an inquirer might sit or stand.[109] The evidence suggests that Paul's expression does not actually have to do with one who typically held the place of an inquirer or outsider but that the key word means to "take or fill someone's place." That is, to take a place that someone else had filled or would normally fill. Paul is speaking of someone who takes a place or position which is not normal for them. In this case those who are full members of the congregation are taking the place of those who were merely inquirers. In such a case that must be taken metaphorically, suggesting that they are forced to assume the role of inquirers. The one "occupying the place of the outsider" has been placed in that very (social/religious) position precisely by the other person's act of praying (or "blessing") God in the Spirit (i.e., in tongues).[110] The fact that they are unable to say the "Amen" in this case confirms the outsider status that has been imposed on them.

Whoever Paul has in mind in this verse knows enough, it seems, to respond to a prayer by saying the "Amen." That implies that they are not complete strangers to the church since *Amen* is not a Greek word or response (and the practice of saying "the Amen" is not a Greek one), but a loanword from Hebrew which had been adopted by the church. This reference to the "Amen" provides a very rare insight into one aspect of early Christian (and, remarkably, Gentile!) worship: "The use of the liturgical term here to signify endorsement or solemn assent to the praise or prayer of another occurs in Num 5:22; Deut 27:15; 1 Chron 16:36; Neh 5:13; 8:6, and

---

fices." Furthermore, "[t]he closer relation which they, in contrast to the ἄπιστοι, held w[ith] the Christian group . . . is clearly shown by the fact that they had a special place in the room where the Christians assembled."

108. So also Oster, 325; Héring, 151.

109. This is despite offering evidence that the word could refer to a social or other "position." For τόπος meaning "position" BDAG directs us to "*T. Ab.* B 4 p. 108, 20 . . . ἕκαστος εἰς τὸν τόπον αὐτοῦ; Philo, Somn. 1, 238; Jos., Ant. 16, 190 ἀπολογουμένου τόπον λαμβάνων."

110. So also Hays, 237.

our verse reflects the appropriation of this use in the earliest Christian churches."[111] If the person knew enough to say "Amen," they might be expected to know what speaking in tongues was about as well. On the other hand, someone familiar with synagogue worship or with a church where people did not speak in tongues[112] in worship might know how to respond to prayer but not to speaking in tongues.

What was referred to as *praising God* (or "blessing" him) at the beginning of the verse is referred to as a *thanksgiving* at the end of the verse. Blessing God and giving thanks to him were interchangeable expressions (cf. Matt. 14:19; 15:36; 26:26, 27; Mark 6:41; 8:6, 7; 14:22, 23; Luke 22:17, 19; 24:30; John 6:11, 23; Acts 27:35; 1 Cor. 11:24).

**14:17** Paul writes simply and to the point: *You are giving thanks well enough, but the others are not edified.* Here, *the others* is literally "the other [person]" who "is not built up." The "other" is the whole category of people other than ourselves (thus the TNIV translation is appropriate). By this point in Paul's argument, that all those others are not edified (or "built up") is clearly understood as an indictment (8:1; 10:23; 14:3, 4, 5, 12; cf. v. 26).

As the saying goes, "It's not about you."[113] Worship is not even about "you and God." Jesus has shown us that it is always about "the other person." In some texts Paul emphasizes the importance of building up the community as a whole (the edification of the church body) and in others his focus is on building up each member of the body (the edification of each part). Here the focus is on the latter. Oster comments, "Paul acknowledges, though perhaps with some sarcasm, that the self-centered believers are doing a good job in their individualistic 'praise and thanksgiving' worship. They have, however, taken their eyes off the compass that always guides believers in the direction of serving and edifying the other person."[114]

### 5) Self-Presentation as an Example of One Preferring Intelligible Ministry over Tongues, 14:18-19

**14:18** Paul is thankful that he is extremely experienced in speaking in tongues[115] because it places him in a position to speak to the problem in

111. Thiselton, 1115. On the same page he also points out that the word "is also used more frequently in the NT at the end of the speaker's own ascription of praise or act of prayer (e.g., Rom 1:25; 11:36; 15:33; Gal 1:5; Eph 3:21; Phil 4:20; 2 Tim 4:18; 1 Pet 5:11; Rev 1:6)."

112. We do not know whether people spoke in tongues in any other apostolic church. The references to speaking in tongues in Acts do not seem to be regular worship experiences, but unusual occasions. No other book mentions the subject.

113. Popularized among Christians by Rick Warren, *The Purpose Driven Life* (Grand Rapids: Zondervan, 2002), 17.

114. Oster, 325. Similarly, Thiselton, 1116-17: "Paul trenchantly attacks the individualism and egocentric horizons which assume that corporate worship is simply about 'God and *me,' rather than 'God and all of us.'*"

115. Fee (674 n. 53) points out that Paul may be using hyperbole. It is not clear how he could possibly know if anyone in Corinth spoke in tongues more than he did.

Corinth with even greater authority: *I thank God*[116] *that*[117] *I speak in tongues more than all of you.* Fee is right to notice that "[w]ith this sentence he [Paul] outmaneuvers the Corinthians altogether. He herewith affirms their gift in the strongest of terms; but he does so in order to reorder their own thinking about what was going on in the assembly."[118] This sentence sets the Corinthians up for the one that follows, which will make it clear that even one who is highly committed to speaking in tongues should be committed to using gifts that are more effective at building up others when gathered with them for worship.

That Paul was extraordinarily proficient and experienced at speaking in tongues turned out to be valuable for his pastoral intervention with the Corinthians. It also comes as a revelation regarding his personal prayer life and spiritual experience that would be unknown to us were it not for the particular problem raised by the practice of speaking in tongues in Corinth (cf. 2 Cor. 12:1-7).

**14:19** In the context of the gathered church one's focus is to be on the *others* who are part of the same worshiping community: *But in the church I would rather speak five intelligible words to instruct others than ten thousand words in a tongue.* The expression *in the church* refers not to a place (such as a church building), but a context — the meeting of the church, and thus might be better translated "in church" (with NRSV, ESV) or "in a church meeting" (NLT; cf. NJB). The clause *to instruct others* is the key.[119] Since even *ten thousand words in a tongue* would not provide any edifying content for

116. A number of textual witnesses (K, L, 326, 614, 629, 945, *al*, [vg$^{cl}$], sa) add μου here, with the result that it reads "my God" in agreement with four out of the five other cases where Paul says, "I thank God" (Rom. 1:8; 1 Cor. 1:4; Phil. 1:3; Phlm. 4). The external support is not strong, and the addition is easily explained as an attempt to align this text with those other four examples.

117. While virtually all English translations have Paul saying that he thanks God *that* he speaks in tongues more than the Corinthians (rare exceptions include the NASB and the KJV), the best Greek texts lack any explicit "that" (Gk. ὅτι ["that"] is found in F, G, lat, Pelagius [all from the Western tradition], but that clearly reflects an attempt to improve the style and/or clarity of the verse). The two clauses of this verse, taken together, may mean simply that he speaks in tongues, giving thanks to God, more than all the Corinthians (or "I thank God in tongues more than all of you"). In Paul's writings (cf. Rom. 1:8; 1 Cor. 1:4, 14; Phil. 1:3; Phlm. 4), "I thank God" is usually followed by some subordinate clause introduced by "that" or a participial or prepositional clause in which he indicates the circumstances in which he gives thanks (e.g., "upon every memory"; the majority text [𝔐] has a participial form of the following verb ["I thank God, speaking in tongues more than all of you"], apparently reflecting a scribal attempt to make Paul's language fit his usual pattern). This may be another case where the following clause indicates the circumstance in which he gives the thanksgiving that he has in mind (although it is not introduced with a prepositional or participial phrase), but it seems much more likely that the majority of English translations are right in concluding that while *that* is not explicitly in the text, those witnesses which have added it have properly understood its meaning (cf. BDF §471[1]).

118. Fee, 675.

119. The verb Paul uses (Gk. κατηχέω) is related to the noun "catechesis" and was used in early Christian literature "only of instruction in theological matters" (BDAG).

the other worshipers, a mere *five intelligible words* would be preferable. The word *intelligible* here is literally "with my mind," picking up on the theme of vv. 14-15, where the antithetical terms were "spirit" and "mind." The contrast between "mind" and "tongue" here leaves no doubt regarding what Paul had in mind in those verses. That the five words would be spoken with the mind suggests that they would be spoken in accordance with the understanding (and in the language) of the speaker and therefore in a way that would be intelligible to the other worshipers. Paul's argument has consistently been in favor of intelligibility since that is the key to the edification of others.

The Greek word for *ten thousand*[120] is the source of our English word "myriad." It literally meant ten thousand, but BDAG notes that it is "used hyperbolically, as in Engl[ish] informal usage 'zillion', of an extremely large or incalculable number." "Countless" is another suggestion (cf. Louw and Nida; *EDNT*). It was indeed used that way in many texts. Perhaps a better English equivalent today would be a "billion" or a "trillion" — an incredibly large but real number (ten thousand was the largest category of number, similar to a trillion[121] in the vocabulary of most English-speaking adults).

Carson rightly sees that this verse, in conjunction with the previous one, provides an extremely strong defense of the private use of the gift of tongues: "If Paul speaks in tongues more than all the Corinthians, yet in the church prefers to speak five intelligible words rather than ten thousand words in a tongue (which is a way of saying that under virtually no circumstance will he ever speak in tongues in church, without quite ruling out the possibility), then where does he speak them?"[122] Clearly he did so in private. Paul's expression *ten thousand words*[123] *in a tongue* would seem to indicate that he understands the gift of tongues to entail the speaking of words rather than merely the uttering of inarticulate groans or longings of the human heart as suggested by some.

### *iv. Argument in favor of the superiority of prophecy to tongues based on biblical background and effect on unbelievers, 14:20-25*

In this section an introductory verse emphasizing the need for maturity (v. 20) is followed by several marked by biblical interpretation (vv. 21-25), focusing on ministries that do and do not elicit the desired response to

120. Gk. μύριοι.

121. There are much larger numbers in English (e.g., quadrillion, quintillion), but most people never use them.

122. Carson, *Showing the Spirit,* 105.

123. Gk. λόγους, from λόγος (the same word Paul uses for the five *words* spoken with his mind). Typically the word refers to a message or expression rather than to a single word. Either way, in this context one would not expect it to be used for a nonlinguistic entity.

God's appeal for repentance. In v. 21 the main text is cited from Isaiah 28:11-12. A conclusion is drawn concerning the function of tongues and prophecy in v. 22 (the part concerning prophecy anticipates the argumentation supporting it which is found in vv. 24-25), which is further clarified and supported in terms of the differing responses Paul would anticipate to church gatherings in which tongues (v. 23) or prophecy (vv. 24-25) are emphasized. While Isaiah 28:11-12 is explicitly cited in support of Paul's view of the public use of tongues, Isaiah 45:14 and Zechariah 8:23 are echoed in the final two verses regarding the prophetic ministry of the church. In Isaiah 28:11-12 the tongues of outsiders are used by God to appeal, futilely, to his disobedient people for repentance. In Isaiah 45:14 and Zechariah 8:23 the tongues of outsiders glorify God in the context of the redemption of his people. Understanding Paul's interpretation of Isaiah 28:11-12 is complicated by the fact that the principle he draws in v. 22 does not seem to cohere with the illustrations in vv. 23-25. If tongues are a sign for unbelievers (v. 22), why do they respond negatively to it (v. 23)? If prophecy is not a sign for unbelievers but for believers (v. 22), why does Paul describe its effect in terms of the conversion of unbelievers (vv. 24-25)? These are some of the issues that need to be addressed in our comments below.

1) Introduction, 14:20

**14:20** Recalling 3:1-2, Paul calls the Corinthians to spiritual maturity: *Brothers and sisters, stop thinking like children. In regard to evil be infants, but in your thinking be adults.*[124] Paul introduces this verse and the following argument, with the vocative *Brothers and sisters,*[125] which was last used in v. 6 and appears again in vv. 26 and 39. It often introduces a new step in the argument, and here it introduces his admonishment (in this verse) and the related biblical interpretation (vv. 21-25). In this case it also reinforces Paul's family solidarity with the readers in preparation for the chiding which they are about to receive for their childish thinking (and behavior). The rest of the verse is clearly intended to shock the Corinthians since those Paul has in mind evidently thought of themselves as being extraordinarily wise and spiritually advanced. The contrast is between those who are mature and those who are not.[126] Paul tells them that their thinking has been as

124. This verse has a chiastic structure:
Ἀδελφοί, (Brothers and sisters)
A μὴ <u>παιδία γίνεσθε</u> (do not be children)
B <u>ταῖς φρεσὶν</u> (with regard to your thinking)
C ἀλλὰ τῇ κακίᾳ νηπιάζετε, (but with regard to evil become like children)
B′ <u>ταῖς</u> δὲ <u>φρεσὶν</u> (but with regard to your thinking)
A′ <u>τέλειοι γίνεσθε</u> (be mature).

125. Gk. ἀδελφοί.

126. Thiselton, 1119, suggests that the word translated "children" by the TNIV and others (Gk. παιδίον) often denoted "very young infants of a few days old or newborn" and

immature as that of children. It is good to be childlike when it comes to innocence, but not when it comes to the critical thinking skills which are needed for mature Christian living for the health of a church!

In the following verse Paul will quote Isaiah 28:11-12. In the context of those verses the religious leaders complain that the prophet's message is too simple and naïve. They want to know what kind of people Isaiah thinks he will teach. They ask, "Who is it he is trying to teach? To whom is he explaining his message? To children weaned from their milk, to those just taken from the breast?" (28:9). Isaiah 28:10 may be intended to mimic the sounds of a child's introductory Hebrew class. The irony is that "[t]hose who are 'wise' and 'gifted' in their own eyes dismiss the plain message as 'childish,' when in reality it is the supposedly wise who think and act like children."[127] Paul's appeal to the Corinthians to reason as adults rather than children may echo Isaiah's encounter with childish people who thought they were too wise to hear his message.

2) Argument regarding the Negative Effect of Tongues, 14:21-23

a) Quotation from Isaiah, 14:21

**14:21** Paul finds guidance for this issue in the words of Isaiah: *In the Law it is written:*

*"With other tongues*
*and through the lips of foreigners*
*I will speak to this people,*
*but even then they will not listen to me,*
*says the Lord."*

Isaiah 28:1-29, in its original (Old Testament) context, consists of an oracle against the political and religious leadership of God's people (Samaria and Jerusalem). They had rejected God's counsel to rest and trust in him as being too naïve and had gone ahead in a policy marked by a drunken madness and formed other alliances. The leadership (rulers, priests, and prophets; cf. vv. 1, 3, 7, 14-15) refused to listen when God clearly and plainly explained to them what it meant to rest in him and to give rest to the weary (v. 12), so now God's voice of judgment will be heard in the barbarian language of their Assyrian invaders (v. 11). The verses immediately preceding our text evidently represent their mockery

concludes that "the English idiom 'children born yesterday' serves as a legitimate intensifier" (bold font changed to single quotes). But it is also used to refer to somewhat older children. We know only that it refers to very young infants when the context makes that clear (as it does not here).

127. Thiselton, 1121.

of Isaiah's message (vv. 9-10). Since the word used for "stammering"[128] usually means "derision" (*HALOT*), it may be that Isaiah intends a *double entendre* involving an ironic reversal: the "stammering" of the Assyrian invaders is God's punishment for the "mocking" perpetrated by the nation's leadership.[129] As Kwon has suggested, "the judgment of unintelligible speech serves as a metonymy for the experience of foreign invasion in general and, perhaps, the experience of exile in particular."[130] Such a metonymy would be based on the knowledge that one of the climactic covenant curses would be to suffer invasion "from a nation whose language you do not understand."[131]

Paul introduces his quotation by identifying it as something "written in the Law."[132] The expression *the Law,* when referring to the sacred texts of Israel, is sometimes used in a strict sense to refer to the Pentateuch, the first five books of the Old Testament attributed to Moses (Matt. 12:5; Luke 2:23; 24:44; John 8:5, 17; 1 Cor. 9:8-9; Gal. 3:10b; 4:21b; Heb. 9:19). It was also used in a wider sense, as here, to refer to Scripture as a whole (Matt. 5:18; Luke 10:26; 16:17; John 7:49; 10:34; 12:34; 15:25; Rom. 3:19). Here Paul uses it in the latter sense to refer to a passage from Isaiah. By referring to this text as something "written in the Law" (rather than in the prophets or Isaiah) Paul may be not only identifying it as a quotation from Scripture, but possibly also hinting that he locates its primary significance within the dispensation of the Mosaic covenant. His argument depends on a contrast between the situation of the Israelites and Jews under the law (in need of the redemption that has come in Christ) and the situation which already holds for those who have now experienced the redemption that was especially associated with part of the prophetic message.

Paul emphasizes the idea of "other" or "foreign" tongues and lips through repetition (literally, "other tongues . . . lips of others").[133] In Paul's case the issue is the use of strange languages in worship. While other early interpretations of the text could gloss over the text's reference to unknown languages[134] (and emphasize the idea of scornful or mocking words [e.g.,

128. Heb. לַעַג.

129. Duke L. Kwon, "Obfuscation and Restoration: Paul's Use of Isaiah in 1 Corinthians 14:20-25" (Th.M. thesis, Gordon-Conwell Theological Seminary, 2004), 8.

130. Kwon, "Obfuscation and Restoration," 9.

131. Deut. 28:49; cf. Jer. 5:15; cf. O. Palmer Robertson, "Tongues: Sign of Covenantal Curse and Blessing," *WTJ* 38 (1975), 47.

132. See our comments on the perfect tense "it is written (γέγραπται) on 1:19.

133. Or, "speakers of strange languages . . . lips of strangers"; Gk. ἑτερογλώσσοις καὶ ἐν χείλεσιν ἑτέρων.

134. In the *Isaiah Targum* and 1QH$^a$ (x [= ii] 19; xii [= iv] 16) the strange tongues and lips of Isa. 28:11-12 are those of God's rebellious people (false teachers according to Qumran, the people in general in the Targum) who reject his revelation and his true prophets. In the LXX it is not clear whether the message of v. 12 was spoken by the drunken prophets and priests or by the invading Assyrians (cf. B. C. Johanson, "Tongues, a Sign for Unbelievers? A Structural and Exegetical Study of I Corinthians XIV. 20-25," *NTS* 25 [1979],

1QH, *Isaiah Targum*]), Paul is interested in this text precisely because of its reference to God's use of unknown languages to communicate a message to his people.[135]

The different textual traditions (Hebrew, Aramaic, Greek) disagree about who spoke through the strange lips and tongues.[136] Paul agrees with the Hebrew texts in holding that it is the Lord who speaks through them. That is an important aspect of the text for him, and one that he emphasizes by adding the object pronoun *(to me)* and final quotation formula *(says the Lord).* Both Paul and the Corinthians understand that they are dealing with a phenomenon through which God himself communicates via unknown languages. Paul's particular way of presenting the text leaves no doubt about his view of the divine origin of the gift of speaking in tongues. If there is a problem with the gift or its employment, it is not because God does not speak through it.

---

182). Koch and Stanley argue that in the LXX "vv. 10-12 are mistakenly read as continuing the description of the disgraceful deeds of the 'priest and prophet' that begins in v. 7" (Stanley, *Paul and the Language of* Scripture, 201, following Koch, *Die Schrift als Zeuge des Evangeliums,* 64). Lanier thinks that the LXX has turned v. 12 into a call for endurance in the face of taunting invaders (whose words are found in v. 12; David E. Lanier, "With Stammering Lips and Another Tongue: 1 Cor. 14:20-22 and Isa. 28:11-12," *CTR* 5 [1991], 259-86). Each text (regardless of which words are attributed to which people) understands the passage to deal with a radical division between faithful and unfaithful Israelites. In some cases the stammering lips and foreign tongue are considered a cause for God's judgment, while in others they appear to be a sign of it.

135. The use of this verse may also suggest that Paul does indeed understand the gift of tongues to entail speaking human languages (as in Isaiah), although in this case they are not learned or expressed by normal means.

136. "Determining the precise relationship between the wording of 1 Cor 14.21 and the text of the LXX is one of the greatest challenges in the entire corpus of Pauline citations" due to "the distance of the Pauline wording from both the LXX and the Masoretic Hebrew textual traditions" (Stanley, *Paul and the Language of Scripture,* 198). Paul leaves out most of v. 12, evidently because he does not think that those clauses are relevant to his argument. His text appears to be an interpretive rendering, perhaps dependent upon an earlier Greek version that sought to conform more closely to the Hebrew text than the LXX (see Stanley). The Hebrew texts (MT and 1QIsa[a]) indicate that God would speak to his people "by stammering (or mocking) lips and by another tongue" because he had spoken to them before "but they were unwilling to hear." The LXX says that "because of the contempt of lips and through another tongue they will speak (λαλήσουσιν) to this people, . . . but they did not want to hear." Paul follows the Hebrew texts in understanding the speaker to be the Lord, but his text uses the first (λαλήσω; "I will speak") rather than the third person. It is not clear whether Paul's reading is based on an ambiguous form in v. 12b (cf. Stanley, *Paul and the Language of Scripture,* 201-2) or is Paul's adaptation. While both the Hebrew texts and the LXX represent the final clause as a historical observation, "they were not willing to listen," Paul's text transforms it into a shocking prediction (οὐδ' οὕτως εἰσακούσονταί — "*even then* they will not listen"). This seems to be his own modification, reflecting his interpretation of the significance of the strange language (in both Isaiah and the history of the nation). He also adds two other elements at the end that reinforce who the speaker is: the object pronoun "to *me*" (μου), followed by the formula "says the Lord" (λέγει κύριος). For more detailed examination of the textual issues see Stanley or Lanier.

Paul's greatest interpretive move related to the text form has to do with his perspective on the significance of foreign languages in the history of God's relationship with his people. Isaiah 28:11-12 indicates that God would speak to his people in judgment through a strange language because they did not listen to him earlier when he spoke in clear and simple terms. Paul surely knows that Israel's experience was due to its rejection of prior revelation in the common language of the people, but he understands (and he wants his readers to understand) that Israel's experience of hearing God speak in that unusual way (i.e., through the foreign languages of the invaders) did not have a spiritually transforming effect on them. This is most likely related to Paul's understanding that Israel (for the most part) continued to stand in need of conversion and redemption until his day (Rom. 3:9-20; 9:2-8; 27-33; 10:1-3; Gal. 3:10-13; 4:4-5, 25; 1 Thess. 2:14-16). Thus not even exile brought the nation of Israel back to God. As Kwon puts it, "Paul's textual purview appears to encompass a wider span of the historical narrative, namely, one that includes Israel's enduring unbelief even after their encounter with 'other tongues' in exile."[137] God not only spoke to his people through foreign invaders in the day or year of their fall, but he continued to speak to them through their experience of foreign domination over a period of decades and centuries.

### b) Conclusion drawn from quotation: Tongues confirm unbelievers in their unbelief, 14:22-23

The relationship between Paul's quotation of Isaiah 28:11-12 in v. 21, the conclusion drawn in v. 22, and the examples given in vv. 23-25 has proven to be extremely difficult to unravel.[138] Part of the solution probably comes in the relationship between Paul's quotation of Isaiah 28:11-12 in v. 21 and his allusion to Isaiah 45:14 and Zechariah 8:23 in v. 25. While v. 22 mentions both believers and unbelievers, the illustrations in vv. 23-25 focus exclusively on unbelievers and the way they respond to an encounter with a community that is speaking in tongues or one that is prophesying. The focus on unbelievers was signaled in the quotation's reference to Israel's unwillingness to listen to the Lord despite his attention-getting approach. In the Old Testament context the experience of the invading Assyrians was

137. Kwon, "Obfuscation and Restoration," 11.

138. See, besides the commentaries, Forbes, *Prophecy and Inspired Speech,* 175-82; Wayne A. Grudem, "1 Corinthians 14:20-25: Prophecy and Tongues as Signs of God's Attitude," *WTJ* 41 (1979), 381-96; Zane C. Hodges, "Symposium on the Tongues Movement: The Purpose of Tongues," *BSac* 120 (1963), 226-33; Johanson, "Tongues, a Sign for Unbelievers? A Structural and Exegetical Study of I Corinthians XIV.20-25," 180-203; Lanier, "With Stammering Lips and Another Tongue: 1 Cor. 14:20-22 and Isa. 28:11-12," 259-86; O. P. Robertson, "Tongues: Sign of Covenantal Curse and Blessing," 45-53; Karl O. Sandnes, "Prophecy — A Sign for Believers," *Bib* 77 (1996), 1-15; J. F. M. Smit, "Tongues and Prophecy: Deciphering 1 Cor. 14:22," *Bib* 75 (1994), 175-90; John P. M. Sweet, "Sign for Unbelievers: Paul's Attitude to Glossolalia," *NTS* 13 (1967), 240-57.

God's execution of the covenant curses on his unbelieving and unfaithful people.[139] In Paul's context it seems unlikely that the point of the gift of tongues was to signal Israel's continuing experience of God's covenant curses.[140] Just as the experience in Isaiah 28:11-12 did not result in the conversion of the hearers but expressed alienation between God and his people, Paul indicates that the use of the gift of tongues tends to result not in the conversion of unbelievers, but in their further alienation.

Paul's citation of Isaiah 28:11-12 highlights the fact that God could not even get his own people to respond to him, even when he spoke to them in an extreme, attention-grabbing manner (having tried more subtle approaches previously). His allusion to Isaiah 45:14 (in v. 25), on the other hand, relates to a later phase in God's relationship with his people, one when even Gentiles would come to recognize and worship the God of Israel for who he really is. The different responses in the two texts are related to the difference between those two consecutive phases in God's relationship with his people. Different modes of communication are associated with each of those two phases.

(1) Conclusion proper, 14:22

**14:22** Just as in 10:1ff. Paul drew a lesson for the church from the wilderness wanderings, here he wants the Corinthians to learn from the experience of Israel in exile: *Tongues, then, are a sign, not for believers but for unbelievers; prophecy, however, is not for unbelievers but for believers. Then*[141] links this verse to the previous one and indicates that a conclusion is being drawn from it. It has raised many eyebrows, since it has hardly been transparent to most readers that the citation from Isaiah establishes the points Paul makes here. Isaiah 28 is referring not to the spiritual gift of speaking in tongues, but to the foreign language(s) spoken by the Assyrian invaders which served as a sign of God's judgment executed against his people. Since the Assyrian speech served as a sign from God (and was described as a means by which God himself spoke to his stubborn people), it was not to be thought of as an ordinary case of hearing a foreign language. While Paul certainly understood the original context and nature of the tongues mentioned by Isaiah, he also knows that it was no accident that the Scriptures contained this reference to speaking in other tongues or languages and that the spiritual gift was at least analogous in that it was a special experience which God himself instigated. In Isaiah those who were confronted by the foreign tongues were disobedient and unbelieving Israelites (whose disobedience and unbelief had brought the situation upon them). While unin-

139. Cf. O. P. Robertson, "Tongues: Sign of Covenantal Curse and Blessing."

140. *Pace* O. P. Robertson there is no indication in the context that Israel's status was an issue in Corinth.

141. Gk. ὥστε.

telligible communication from God was a sign to his unbelieving people that the curses of the Mosaic covenant had fallen on them, the powerful prophetic ministry of the church is a sign that God's presence has been restored to his redeemed (and believing) people.

Hays points out that this verse "seems to stand in direct contradiction to the explanation that follows in verses 23-25, in which unbelievers are turned away by tongues and converted by prophecy."[142] Our surface reading of this verse might lead us to expect that tongues as a *sign . . . for unbelievers* would be especially effective in leading them to conversion (cf. Acts 2:4-41). Instead, Paul indicates that tongues were more likely to alienate unbelievers. Furthermore, one might expect Paul's statement that *prophecy is . . . for believers* to be illustrated by an example showing how effective the gift of prophecy is for building up believers. Instead, Paul says nothing about the impact of prophecy on believers but keeps his focus on the impact the gift is more likely to have on unbelievers.

Some have made an issue of the fact that Paul says that tongues are *a sign* but he does not use the word "sign" again with respect to prophecy: he merely says prophecy is not for unbelievers but for believers. But it was not necessary to repeat the word "sign" since the structure would lead the reader to understand the issue and to anticipate the use of ellipsis. Paul's language, *not for believers but for unbelievers,*[143] suggests that he is presenting a response to a view that tongues were, in fact, a sign for believers. It may well have been the Corinthians who introduced the language of "sign," suggesting that tongues were a sign given by God to believers which should be prominent in Christian worship. Paul's citation of Isaiah 28 seems intended to counter such a view.

Much study has been dedicated to discerning whether a sign would be expected to represent something positive or negative. Wayne Grudem has shown that the word could be used to refer to something positive or negative since it has to do with something that reveals God's attitude or intention, which would be positive or negative depending on the situation.[144] As Carson argues, "it is possible that verse 22 is commenting on the situation in *Isaiah's* day. The unbelievers faced judgment, and were addressed by God in the unintelligible language of foreigners; but there remained a godly remnant who benefited, not from tongues, but from prophecy — Isaiah's prophecy (see Isa. 8:16). In other words, the distinction as to whether a certain phenomenon served as a positive sign or a negative sign extends back into the context of Isaiah."[145] Paul clarifies in the context that a "sign for unbelievers," in this case, does not mean a sign benefiting unbelievers

142. Hays, 239.

143. Gk. οὐ τοῖς πιστεύουσιν ἀλλὰ τοῖς ἀπίστοις.

144. See Grudem, *The Gift of Prophecy*, 194-96.

145. Carson, *Showing the Spirit*, 115 (his emphasis), referencing Ralph P. Martin, *The Spirit and the Congregation: Studies in 1 Corinthians 12–15* (Grand Rapids: Eerdmans, 1984), 72-73.

but the sign normally reserved for unbelievers, which communicates God's judgment on them as such. The tongues of the Assyrians (and then Babylonians, Medes, and Persians) were a sign from God, a constant reminder to the Jews of their alienation from him and their need for forgiveness and restoration, a restoration that would bring salvation to the Gentiles as well.[146]

In 1 Corinthians 12–14 the theme of the Spirit brings the already-present aspect of God's saving and restoring (new creation) activity into the foreground, marking this as a time in which God is effectively communicating with his redeemed people. That very communication was expected, in keeping with Isaiah 45, to lead not only to the redemption of Israel but also to the conversion of those who witness God's work in and through his people. Paul's evaluation of tongues and prophecy in a public setting is governed by the distinction in Isaiah between a time of communication breakdown, alienation, and judgment and a time of restoration and restored communication which results in God's being glorified by those who witness his presence in the midst of his people.

Seen in this way, tongues are a sign to unbelievers in that the public experience of unintelligible communication from God highlights the sense and reality of alienation between the speaker(s) and those being spoken to. Such an experience was intended for God's people only while they were in a state of rebellion and unbelief and suffering the curses of the Mosaic covenant. Thiselton points out that "the experience of 'not belonging' to which Isa 28:11-12 witnesses as a sign of judgment . . . should not be illegitimately imposed upon believers who *do* belong and *should feel "at home"* in the worship of the Christian community."[147]

Prophecy was a sign for believers in that God would speak to and through them again in power only after they had been restored. If he was speaking prophetically through them again (speaking not in judgment but speaking "to people for their strengthening, encouragement and comfort"; 1 Cor. 14:3), it was a sign to them that the age of restoration and salvation had been inaugurated. The conversion of others through their prophetic ministry was further confirmation of that sign and a reminder to the Corinthians that they "are part of the fulfillment of God's plan to be worshipped among all the Gentiles, and it is Paul's ultimate purpose in writing to them to see them play their part in fulfilling this worldwide eschatological vision by glorifying God (see 6.20b and 10.31b)."[148]

146. See Roy Ciampa, "The History of Redemption," in *Central Themes in Biblical Theology: Mapping Unity in Diversity* (ed. Scott Hafemann and Paul House; Grand Rapids: Baker and Leicester, Eng.: Inter-Varsity Press, 2007), 254-308.

147. Thiselton, 1106.

148. Ciampa and Rosner, "The Structure and Argument of 1 Corinthians," 217. This is close to Forbes's suggestion (*Prophecy and Inspired Speech,* 179) that "the effect of prophecy on believers is, in Paul's view, a sign for believers in a quite specialized sense. The unbeliever's confession, 'God is truly among you', is strongly reminiscent of Isaiah 45:14 and

(2) Consequence of ignoring the conclusion, 14:23

**14:23** Earlier Paul pointed out that uninterpreted (i.e., untranslated) tongues are not useful to the church. Now he makes the point that they may even have an unintended negative impact on those who observe them and on the reputation of the church. *So if the whole church comes together and everyone speaks in tongues, and inquirers or unbelievers come in, will they not say that you are out of your mind?* The word translated *inquirers* here (and in the next verse) is the same word used in v. 16. Here, however, it is not referring to those who have been made to feel and respond like mere pre-Christian God-fearers or inquirers (by being exposed to unintelligible tongues in their own church), but to actual inquirers, people who have shown some interest in the Christian faith but who have not yet taken the step of expressing a clear faith commitment and joining the church through baptism. The unbelievers, if they are to be distinguished from the inquirers here (and it may well be that Paul is referring to the same people), would presumably be people who have not shown significant interest already but who have decided to attend the worship gathering and see what it is like, people who are possibly on the way to becoming inquirers. This says something about the openness of the early church and one of the approaches to evangelism or outreach that they learned and shared with the ancient synagogue.

Paul indicates that not everyone speaks in tongues or exercises the gift of prophecy (12:29-30), although the second possibility seems much more viable in his eyes. The idea of inclusive participation is highlighted in this verse and the next by the repetition of the word *everyone*/all (once here, three times in the following verse: "everyone speaks in tongues . . . everyone prophesies, they are convicted by all . . . judged by all"[149]). Those who do not know any better (visiting unbelievers or inexperienced inquirers) will think they *are out of* [their] *mind*. While the word used[150] often meant simply to be out of one's senses, it was also used in the context of religious experience to refer to a divinely induced altered mental state, such as was

Zechariah 8:23, where the realisation of the nations around about Israel that God is truly among his people is one of the signs of the fulfilment of God's promises to them. In this sense the unbeliever's confession, provoked by prophetic conviction of his sins, is a sign to believers of the eschatological presence of God among his people."

149. Gk. πάντες λαλῶσιν γλώσσαις . . . πάντες προφητεύωσιν, . . . ἐλέγχεται ὑπὸ πάντων, ἀνακρίνεται ὑπὸ πάντων. Oster thinks that "everyone" here means everyone who has the gift of speaking in tongues (Oster, 329). Thiselton is more likely correct in suggesting that these are "hypothetical clauses which paint an all-too-possible scenario" (1126) and that "[t]he buildup of clauses is deliberately impressionistic. In accordance with frequent uses of πάντες, *all*, Paul does not enumerate a statistical totality (explicitly denied in 12:30, μὴ πάντες γλώσσαις λαλοῦσιν; i.e., all do not speak with tongues, do they?) but uses the kind of impressionist description that we use when we say, "everyone was laughing" or "everyone was shouting . . ." (1127, emphasis removed).

150. Gk. μαίνομαι.

associated with Bacchic possession and inspiration.[151] Hays suggests that a "typical pagan Corinthian observing such a scene would say, 'Oh, this is just another group like the devotees of Dionysius or Cybele' — one more consumer option in a pluralistic religious market."[152]

Forbes thinks it "highly unlikely that unbelievers hearing the kind of glossolalia Paul is commending for the first time in a Christian context would recognize it as a familiar phenomenon."[153] He considers it "possible that the tumult of a large number of Corinthians speaking in tongues simultaneously would remind them of the frenzy of Hellenistic cult groups" but thinks it more likely to elicit "the thoroughly negative reaction 'you are all crazy.'"[154]

Whether the Corinthians would consider the experience very strange or somewhat comparable to other religious experiences with which they were familiar, Forbes is probably correct that Paul's basic point is that the reaction would be a negative one, in contrast with the reaction described in the following two verses. He believes that "Paul's understanding of part of the problem in Corinth (the observed fact that uninterpreted tongues in the presence of unbelievers leads them to reject what they see and hear) has consciously or unconsciously shaped his quotation of Isaiah, in order to make precisely that point: 'they (outsiders) will not listen to you, or to what you say about God.'"[155] It seems just as likely that Paul started not with the observed problem in Corinth (which he may never have personally observed) but with the quotation of Isaiah, which suggested to him that those addressed by tongues would not respond positively (a point which is found at the end of Isaiah 28:12 in both the LXX and HB and is strongly reflected in his own rendering). If this is correct, the conclusion *that you are out of your mind* represents a fundamental sense of repulsion in keeping with the expectation established by Paul's quotation in v. 21.[156] Chrysostom suggests that Paul is appealing to concerns regarding shame and honor, arguing that tongues "not only deprive of glory, but also bring shame upon those who have them in the eyes of the unbelievers," while "prophecy, on the contrary, is both free from reproach among the unbelievers, and has

151. "To be in ecstasy to the point of frenzy is a divine transposition from customary states" which "is a strongly affirmed religious phenomenon" (H. Preisker, "μαίνομαι," *TDNT* 4:360).

152. Hays, 238-39.

153. Forbes, *Prophecy and Inspired Speech,* 180 n. 68.

154. Forbes, *Prophecy and Inspired Speech,* 180 n. 68. Chrysostom (*Homiliae in Epistulam i ad Corinthios* 36.2 [NPNF[1] 12:216]) thinks that Paul's meaning is "that prophecy avails both among the unbelieving and among those who believe: as to the tongue, when heard by the unbelieving and inconsiderate, instead of profiting by it, they rather deride the utterers as madmen."

155. Forbes, *Prophecy and Inspired Speech,* 180.

156. H. Balz ("μαίνομαι," *EDNT* 2:375) points out that "[t]he 5 occurrences in the NT always express a negative judgment about people who appear with special authority or who report about experiences with the power of God."

very great credit and usefulness."[157] This seems all the more likely in light of the climax of the following two verses, where God receives glory from the conversion of unbelievers. If this is set up in contrast to that, it makes sense that Paul would highlight the potential loss of honor to those who speak in tongues with the implicit understanding that it would entail a loss of honor for their God as well.

### 3) Argument regarding the Positive Effect of Prophecy: Prophetic Ministry Leads to the Glorification of God on the Part of Converted Unbelievers, 14:24-25

**14:24-25** The superior value of prophecy over tongues may be seen in the potential positive impact of the former (in contrast with the potential negative impact of the latter which was suggested in v. 23). *But if an unbeliever or an inquirer comes in while everyone is prophesying, they are convicted of sin and are brought under judgment by all, as the secrets of their hearts are laid bare. So they will fall down and worship God, exclaiming, "God is really among you!"* The relationship between this text and the previous one is reinforced by the chiastic structure inquirer-unbeliever (v. 23)/unbeliever-inquirer (v. 24) as well as by the explicit contrast in the effects of the gifts. Paul does not expect everyone to prophesy, since not everyone has the gift of prophecy (12:28-29). But since all believers do have the Spirit and are real candidates to speak prophetically (see Joel 2:28), Paul encourages the Corinthians to pursue gifts such as prophecy and seems to think that any believer might try their hand and see if God might in fact use them to bring prophetic insight to the community. As in the previous verse, here he is describing a hypothetical situation (if everyone were to prophesy) and its potential impact on those who have yet to fully enter the Christian community. As pointed out in the comments on v. 23, the emphasis on inclusive participation is highlighted by the repetition of the word *everyone/all* three times in this verse: "everyone prophesies, they are convicted by all . . . judged by all").[158]

Paul's expectation that the prophetic ministry of the gathered community will lead to the conversion of visiting outsiders who will respond by bowing down and worshiping God and declaring "God is really here in your midst!" echoes Isaiah 45:14 and Zechariah 8:23.[159] Isaiah prophesies

157. *Homiliae in Epistulam i ad Corinthios* 36.3 (NPNF[1] 12:217-18).

158. Thiselton's suggestion that "it is more probable that ὑπὸ πάντων (grammatically either masculine or neuter plural) embraces 'all that is said' in the most inclusive sense (both prophets and the prophetic message) rather than exclusively the prophets only, especially since Paul's antecedent is not the noun *prophets* but the verb προφητεύωσιν (indefinite present subjunctive), 'everyone is using prophetic speech'" (1129, his italics, his bold font changed to single quotes), does not do justice to the anaphoric (back-referencing) relationship between the two occurrences of ὑπὸ πάντων (by all) and the earlier πάντες (everyone/all) or to the fact that the default expectation would be that ὑπό would introduce the (personal) subject of the passive verb, unless clear linguistic clues clearly suggested otherwise.

159. Possibly Dan. 2:46-47 as well. Cf. Richard B. Hays, "The Conversion of the Imag-

the conversion of Gentile nations in the time of the postexilic restoration of God's people. At that time, he says, the various peoples will become Israel's servants and will bow down to them and make supplication to them "since God is among you," and they will say "there is no god besides you, for you are God and we did not know it, the God of Israel, the Savior." Paul has changed the plural verb ("they will worship") to a singular ("he/she will worship")[160] since he is describing the conversion of an individual, and he has changed the pronoun from the singular ("in your [singular] midst") to the plural ("in your [plural] midst")[161] because he is describing the gathered community rather than the nation of Israel.[162] Paul expects Isaiah's script to be performed and his eschatological vision to be realized in the midst of the gathered community as it exercises its prophetic ministry.[163]

Hays points to the dramatic transformation in Paul's intertextual use in that in his scenario "it is the church — itself a predominately Gentile community — through which God will accomplish the eschatological conversion of outsiders," and the Corinthian believers have "stepped into the role originally assigned to Israel in Isaiah's eschatological drama."[164] This motif was signaled at the very beginning of the letter. In 1 Corinthians 1:2 Paul referred to the Corinthians as "those sanctified in Christ Jesus and called to be his holy people, together with all those everywhere who call on the name of our Lord Jesus Christ — their Lord and ours." We argued there that Paul was echoing Malachi 1:11 and the whole eschatological motif of the final universal worship of God which is to be brought about through Christ's work. The Corinthians have been reminded at key points throughout this letter that they are supposed to bring glory to God as Gentiles who have come to find true wisdom in Christ and his cross and who have learned to flee sexual immorality and idolatry and to give proper worship to the one true God. Their own encounter with Christ had kept them from being led away to idols to being led by the Spirit to confess "Jesus is Lord" (12:2-3) and worship God aright. Their conversion and worship are intended to lead others to do the same. In this way, the gift which has been promoted as the one most effective at building up the community is also now seen as most effective at bringing God glory through the conversion of the nations.

While those who speak in tongues "utter mysteries by the Spirit" which are unintelligible to others as the speakers worship individually (v. 2), the prophetic ministry, operating at an intelligible level, brings to light the secrets of the hearts of men and women and leads them to join in

---

ination: Scripture and Eschatology in 1 Corinthians," *NTS* 45 (1999), 391-93. For other texts anticipating the eschatological recognition of the God of Israel, see on 8:4.

160. From προσκυνήσουσιν to προσκυνήσει.

161. From ἐν σοὶ ὁ θεός ἐστιν to ὁ θεὸς ἐν ὑμῖν ἐστιν (Zech. 8:23 has ὁ θεὸς μεθ' ὑμῶν ἐστιν).

162. Cf. Hays, "Conversion," 393.

163. Hays, "Conversion," 393.

164. Hays, "Conversion," 394.

the worship of God's people. What does Paul have in mind in saying, *they are convicted of sin and are brought under judgment by all, as the secrets of their hearts are laid bare?* Are the particular and private sins of individual sinners brought into the open,[165] or does Paul have in mind the secrets which are found in the fallen hearts of all people? As Carson explains, while it may be "communication designed by the Spirit to expose the secrets of [the unbeliever's] own heart and thereby to convict him of sin, bringing him to repentance and worship," it may be stressed that the unbeliever "comes in and *overhears* what is going on in the *assembly,* and by that means is brought to recognition of need, and to repentance and worship."[166]

*v. Specific directions regarding the practical application of Paul's teaching in worship gatherings (general application to the church: Everyone ministers in an intelligible manner for the edification of the church), 14:26-33*

*26 What then shall we say, brothers and sisters? When you come together, each of you has a hymn, or a word of instruction, a revelation, a tongue or an interpretation. Everything must be done so that the church may be built up. 27 If anyone speaks in a tongue, two — or at the most three — should speak, one at a time, and someone must interpret. 28 If there is no interpreter, the speaker should keep quiet in the church; let them speak to themselves and to God.*

*29 Two or three prophets should speak, and the others should weigh carefully what is said. 30 And if a revelation comes to someone who is sitting down, the first speaker should stop.*

*31 For you can all prophesy in turn so that everyone may be instructed and encouraged. 32 The spirits of prophets are subject to the control of prophets. 33 For God is not a God of disorder but of peace — as in all the congregations of the Lord's people.*

Here Paul's focus moves from the preference for prophecy over tongues to specific guidance for worship in light of God's character as a God of peace rather than disorder (v. 33). Although Paul does not lose his focus on tongues and prophecy, he does introduce this section with some broader guidance about having everyone minister in an intelligible manner for the edification of the church (v. 26). In the central section he addresses the manner in which tongues (vv. 27-28) and prophecy (vv. 29-32) may be exercised in ways which are consistent with the peace and order which reflect God's character, the norm which governs the whole passage (v. 33).[167]

165. See Forbes, *Prophecy and Inspired Speech,* 181 n. 69.

166. Carson, *Showing the Spirit,* 116 (see also n. 22 on the same page).

167. The summary comments about everything being done "in a fitting and orderly way" (v. 33) also reinforce and summarize this part of the letter.

A concern for order and for submission, the latter resulting in the silencing of certain people in specific circumstances (a motif that will continue into the following passage), is clearly reflected throughout this passage. Peace and order are preserved by limiting the number of speakers with the gift of tongues and by their restraining themselves when an interpreter is not present (vv. 27-28). Peace and order are also preserved by limiting the number of speakers with the gift of prophecy and having them restrain themselves when something is revealed to a colleague (vv. 29-30).

#### 1) General Application: Everyone Should Worship in Intelligible and Edifying Ways, 14:26

**14:26** While *What then shall we say?* suggests that this verse may provide a conclusion to the previous paragraph, the vocative, *brothers and sisters,* suggests that it plays an introductory or, more likely, transitional role, introducing the next paragraph in a way which relates it to what went before: *What then shall we say, brothers and sisters? When you come together, each of you has a hymn, or a word of instruction, a revelation, a tongue or an interpretation. Everything must be done so that the church may be built up.* The clause, *When you come together,* reaffirms that Paul is continuing to discuss proper behavior in the context of the worship gathering. This is the last occurrence of this verb in this letter (see also 11:17, 18, 20, 33, 34; 14:23). The phrase *each of you* echoes the references to "everyone" and "all" in the previous verse and passage. As Conzelmann points out, *each of you* "must not be pressed to the effect that every single individual has one of the gifts mentioned, but means: one has this — another has that."[168]

The list of gifts or ministries here *(a hymn, or a word of instruction, a revelation, a tongue or an interpretation)* does not perfectly match any other. "Like all the former lists in these chapters, this final one is *ad hoc;* it is intended neither to give the 'order' of service nor to be exhaustive of what 'each one has' to offer by way of ministry."[169] Fee points out that the gifts listed "most likely . . . represent various types of verbal manifestations of the Spirit that should occur in their assembly."[170] This list clearly does focus on gifts that employ speech (gifts such as faith, healing, miracles, helping, and leadership [12:9-10, 28] are not mentioned). Fee asserts that "[s]ince the latter three are Spirit-inspired utterances, and are therefore spontaneous, it is likely that the first two are to be understood in that way as well, although that is not certain."[171] The assumption that any Spirit-inspired utterance must be spontaneous may owe more to modern charismatic/Pentecostal traditions and experience than to the biblical evidence. While it is clear from Acts that

168. Conzelmann, 244.
169. Fee, 690.
170. Fee, 690.
171. Fee, 690.

some people spoke in tongues spontaneously (Acts 2:4; 10:44-46; 19:6), it goes beyond the evidence to say that Spirit-inspired utterances are all spontaneous. A *hymn* could be a known composition or something fresh, but there is no reason to assume it was spontaneous (or to rule out that the Spirit might produce one spontaneously).[172] A *word of instruction* presumably reflects time in reflection and study. A *revelation* may be given during the time of worship, but there is no reason to assume that people would not bring to the service a revelation that they had received during the week.[173] Even a *tongue* (and possibly its *interpretation*) could have been given in advance of the meeting and repeated in the gathering.[174] The *interpretation* is, as clearly indicated earlier (12:10), an interpretation of something said through the gift of tongues. Spontaneity or the lack thereof does not seem to play any significant part in Paul's discussion of these gifts. That each one *has* one of those things seems to suggest that they bring them to the gathering rather than that they receive them during the meeting.

*Everything must be done so that the church may be built up.* This, of course, has been the overriding theme of this chapter, at least to this point. In fact, the point of this verse is not so much that everyone comes to the worship gathering with their own contribution to make (that is understood as the background to the main point), but that all those different contributions must be exercised in such a way that others, the church, are strengthened and helped by it.

### 2) Application regarding Tongues: Two to Three May Speak If There Is Interpretation, 14:27-28

#### a) Guidance on the use of tongues in worship, 14:27

**14:27** Tongues are not to be prohibited (see v. 39), but closely regulated for the sake of the health of the church. *If anyone speaks in a tongue, two — or at the most three — should speak, one at a time, and someone must interpret.* The difference between the beginning of this verse and the beginning of v. 29 is noteworthy. Given Paul's discouragement of the public speaking of tongues unless the speaker is certain there will be an interpretation, it is not surprising that he says, *if anyone speaks in a tongue.* He is not arguing in favor or against, but establishing the conditions that would permit it to take place in a fitting and orderly manner. Three is the largest number of tongue-speakers Paul would permit; he would be more comfortable with

172. Thiselton allows that it "may include extempore prayer or an 'interpretation' of tongues" but also speaks of "the strong possibility that, grounded in biblical tradition, the earliest hymns were probably from the Psalms of the OT" (1135).

173. As Thiselton notes (1135), the word "seems to suggest an act of divine disclosure on the spot" but "does not exclude the communication of what came to be revealed by God through some experience or through biblical reflection prior to the act of worship itself."

174. Despite Thiselton, 1135.

two, and even then an interpretation is required. If tongues will have a place in the church's worship, he does not want them to take up an inordinate amount of that worship time. If more than one person speaks in tongues, they should do it *one at a time;* thus "the scene imagined in verse 23 — a room full of babbling believers — is excluded."[175]

Depictions of ancient symposia (post-dinner parties where semiformal conversations often played a key role) often depict them as discussing a series of topics in which different members would share their viewpoint and engage the viewpoints of their companions one at a time. Here and in vv. 28-31 Paul's instructions promote a somewhat similar approach to establishing order and etiquette that would hopefully banish chaos from the worship meeting.

Paul's directives here lead us to understand, with Fee, that the Spirit "does not 'possess' or 'overpower' the speaker. . . . It is indeed the Spirit who speaks, but he speaks through the controlled instrumentality of the believer's own mind and tongue. In this regard it is no different from the inspired utterances of the OT prophets, which were spoken at the appropriate times and settings."[176]

Thiselton translates this verse and the next as, "If it is in a tongue that someone speaks, let only two or at the most three speak in turn, and let the one who speaks put it into words. However, if he or she cannot put it into words, let them remain silent in the assembled congregation, and address God privately."[177] This translation supports his contention that Paul expected any interpretation of tongues to be provided by the person who spoke in tongues in the first place. It depends upon Thiselton's long but ultimately unconvincing argument about the meaning and function of the Greek word translated *someone* by the TNIV, NIV, ESV, NET, NLT, and CSB and "one" by the NRSV, NAB, and NASB.[178] Paul may mean "someone

175. Hays, 241. "There seems to be no good reason" for the constraints imposed here unless they are "intended to be corrective. . . . Along with v. 23, the implication is that the Corinthians were doing otherwise. . . . The admonition in v. 32 is probably intended as much for this gift as for prophecy" (Fee, 692).

176. Fee, 692. Similarly, Carson, *Showing the Spirit*, 119, sees Paul pointing to "a remarkable and dynamic tension between the Spirit who is producing the gift and the individual who is its vehicle. Paul does not argue that after two or three have spoken, the Spirit will not grant the gift to anyone else; and therefore the fourth and subsequent tongues-speakers at any meeting must be fraudulent, or inspired by some spirit other than the Holy Spirit. Precisely the same dynamic tension operates in the gift of prophecy (vv. 29-30). The compulsion of the Spirit is not of the order where the prophet loses ability to hold his or her peace; and if a revelation comes to the fourth party, after three prophets have had their say, that does not provide warrant to the prophet to break the firm guidelines Paul is imposing on the church."

177. Thiselton, 1131.

178. Thiselton's argument is based on a misunderstanding of how εἷς ("one") functions when it serves as an indefinite article (not how it is functioning here in any case) and which part of εἷς τις ἐξ αὐτῶν ("a certain one of them") refers back to an antecedent (not εἷς ["one"], but αὐτῶν ["them"]).

should interpret" or "one person should interpret" or "one (of those mentioned previously) should interpret." He could hardly mean "each one should interpret" or "the one who speaks should interpret." There are several ways in which he could have said that, and this is not one of them.[179] Weight should not be placed on using v. 5 to interpret this verse, since different points are being made. Verse 5 does indeed mention the possibility that one who speaks in tongues might interpret their own speech (and thereby make as important a contribution as one who prophesies), but it hardly provides an interpretive key suggesting that all interpretations would be given by the same person who spoke in tongues. Paul is consistent in insisting that tongues be interpreted when used in public meetings. His various references indicate that that might happen in more than one way.

### b) Guidance for dealing with a lack of interpretation: Private prayer only, 14:28

**14:28** Paul allows tongues to be used in church only when it is clear that an interpretation will be given. *If there is no interpreter, the speaker should keep quiet in the church; let them speak to themselves and to God.* Although English translations seem to be unanimous in translating the opening clause as in the TNIV,[180] Thiselton and others would translate the opening clause "if he is not an interpreter" (or, in Thiselton's own wording, "if he or she (the speaker in tongues) cannot put it into words"[181]). According to this latter interpretation, only those who had both the gift of tongues and the gift of the interpretation of tongues would be free to speak in tongues in public. It would also mean that only those who had the gift of tongues could expect to receive the gift of interpretation. While both translations are theoretically possible,[182] Thiselton's depends on his unconvincing interpretation of the final clause of the previous verse to give it coherence, since the subject referred to in "he or she (the speaker in tongues) cannot put it into

179. For example, καὶ ἕκαστος αὐτῶν διερμηνευέτω ("and let each of them interpret") or καὶ διερμηνευέτωσαν ("and let them interpret"/"and they should interpret"). Thiselton's interpretation founders on the important difference between εἷς (one) and ἕκαστος (each).

180. For example, "if there is no one to interpret" (NRSV, ESV, RSV), "if there is no interpreter" (NIV, NET, NAB, NJB, NASB, CSB), and "if no one is present who can interpret" (NLT).

181. Thiselton, 1139 (emphasis removed).

182. Third-person forms of the verb εἰμι may have a subject which was previously referred to in the text, but they are also frequently used with indefinite subjects such as "there is . . ." or "there are. . . ." Matt. 10:13 has ἐὰν δὲ μὴ ᾖ ἀξία ("but if he is not worthy . . ."), while Num. 27:9 LXX has ἐὰν δὲ μὴ ᾖ θυγάτηρ ("but if there is no daughter . . ."; cf. Num. 27:11 LXX). The two other cases we have found where the verb is followed by a noun, as in this verse (rather than with an adjective as in Matt. 10:13), both mean "but if there is no . . ." (Num. 27:9, 11). For the meaning proposed by Thiselton, one might expect something like ἐὰν δὲ μὴ δύνηται διερμηνεύειν ("but if he is not able to interpret").

words" (Thiselton's translation) would presumably be the person just mentioned in the previous verse. But if the final clause of v. 27 means "one/someone should interpret" (rather than "the one who spoke should interpret"), it makes little sense to follow it up by saying, "but if he is not an interpreter," as though a definite or particular person were in mind. The English translations (like the TNIV) have it right.

The command that the speaker *keep quiet* when no interpreter is present represents the first appearance of a verb[183] which will appear again in vv. 30 and 34 (where the TNIV translates it "stop" and "remain silent," respectively), and which helps to provide coherence to this paragraph. In each case particular people are asked to restrain themselves from a particular sort of speech in order to preserve the orderly and peaceful flow of the worship meeting. In this case those who could speak in tongues should restrain themselves when they are not certain it would be interpreted, in order to spare the rest of the congregation from the alienating experience of uninterpreted tongues.

The statement that they should remain quiet *in the church* (meaning the church meeting, not a church building) seems strange at first, since the whole passage is about what should take place during the church meeting, making the expression seem superfluous. It is intended to evoke the contrast between what is appropriate at church versus what is appropriate at home (cf. 11:22), a contrast that underlies much of this paragraph and that rises to the surface, lexically, here and in vv. 19, 34-35. The distinction between the contexts of church and home helps us understand what Paul has in mind by the final clause of this verse.

Earlier Paul indicated that those who speak in tongues do not speak to people but to God. His direction here that they should *speak to themselves and to God* probably should be understood to mean that they should speak only loud enough,[184] or (more likely) only in such contexts (alone at home or elsewhere), that they would be heard only by themselves and by God (to whom the tongue is addressed). The prior reference to remaining quiet *in the church* suggests that the appropriate place to *speak to themselves and to God* would be at home.[185] The fact that the person feels enabled (by the Spirit, presumably) to speak in tongues during the service does not mean that God has authorized them to speak out to the congregation. The exercise of the gifts of the Spirit entails a mysterious relationship between the Spirit's enabling and human will and abilities. The fact that the gift is given by the Spirit does not mean that it cannot be used in places, times, and manners that are inappropriate and that would grieve the Spirit.

183. Gk. σιγάω.
184. So Oster, 335, and Witherington, 286, who say that it should be inaudible.
185. So also Fee, 693.

### 3) Application regarding Prophecies: Two or Three Should Speak and There Should Be Orderly Evaluation, 14:29-33

Here Paul turns from direct instructions regarding the use of tongues in worship to direct guidance regarding the use of the gift of prophecy. These verses follow the structure of the previous two (references to two-to-three speakers followed by the exercise of the companion gift; interpretation in the case of tongues, discernment in the case of prophecy). In this case, however, he elaborates a bit further in a way that reflects his high estimation of the value of prophecy for the life of the church (v. 31) and his recognition of the ability and need to exercise self-restraint for the benefit of the community as a whole (v. 32). He concludes the passage with a clarification of the theological basis for Paul's instructions (v. 33).

#### a) Presentation of general principle, 14:29

**14:29** As in his instructions regarding the use of tongues in the church, Paul's guidance regarding prophesying in church also mentions "two or three," but there are subtle and important differences: *Two or three prophets should speak, and the others should weigh carefully what is said.* Paul does not say "if someone prophesies," but *two or three prophets should speak.*[186] While tongues are not to be forbidden, prophecy is essential. Paul wants two or three prophets to speak and establishes guidelines that would keep a congregation from ever experiencing more tongue-speaking sessions than prophetic sessions. The three issues to be addressed include (1) whom Paul has in mind with reference to the *prophets,* (2) who *the others* are, and (3) the meaning of the verb translated *weigh carefully.*

While most interpreters understand Paul to limit prophetic messages to three per meeting, some think that he is limiting only the number of messages to be given by people who have been previously identified as *prophets* due to their consistent exercise of the prophetic gift, but leaves the door open for others who are not known as "prophets" to take the occasional opportunity to communicate a prophetic message. Much of this decision weighs on the relationship between this verse and v. 31a and the interpretation of Paul's statement that "you can all prophesy in turn" (see the comments on v. 31). It seems most likely that Paul has in mind three prophetic messages per meeting, whether the speakers were previously known as prophets or not. If he intended to leave the door open for other prophetic messages to be given (and weighed), he certainly could have been much clearer about it. It seems unlikely that various people might prophesy but only a subset of them would be included in Paul's statements about prophets.

186. As Thiselton, 1140, notes, "There is no reluctance about 'at most' three, but a positive and unqualified encouragement to speak."

Are *the others* who are to weigh the prophecies other prophets, or simply other members of the congregation? It would seem that various members of the church would be qualified to weigh prophetic messages, including especially prophets, those with the gift of discerning spirits, teachers, and the like. In v. 37 Paul invites "any [who] think they are prophets or otherwise gifted by the Spirit" to weigh the authority of his own teaching. In Acts 17:11 the whole church seems to be evaluating Paul's teaching, and it seems that the whole church is encouraged to test prophecies in 1 Thessalonians 5:19 (cf. 1 John 4:1), although it would not be surprising for certain members to be considered more qualified than others to engage in such work. So it appears that those recognized with the gift of prophecy would be the most common contributors of prophetic messages and those with the gifts of prophecy or discerning spirits would be the most frequent contributors of evaluations or weighing of those prophecies, but others would also be free to prophesy or to "weigh in" on the prophecies of others.

What does Paul mean by "weighing"[187] the prophecies? It has been suggested that Paul has in mind the interpretation of prophecies (with some delivering them and others explaining their meaning), but that has little to support it. BDAG has, "to evaluate by paying careful attention to, *evaluate, judge*" or, more specifically in this case, to "pass judgment on" them. Paul could mean the evaluation of the prophets themselves, but more likely he has in mind the evaluation of the messages given by them.

Paul seems to be picturing a gathering in which 0-3 prayers or songs in tongues are contributed (with someone interpreting any that are given), 2-3 prophetic messages are given and evaluated by the congregation, and others contribute, among other things, prayers, hymns, and words of instruction (cf. v. 26).

### b) Guidance on taking turns, 14:30-31

**14:30** Paul gives guidance to keep anyone from monopolizing the church's time in worship and to ensure that God's desire to minister through various people is not undermined. *And if a revelation comes to someone who is sitting down, the first speaker should stop.* Paul's wording reflects the assumption in the ancient church that the speaker would be standing so that *someone who is sitting down* refers to anyone other than the speaker. Perhaps the one who received the fresh revelation would indicate as much by standing up. If so, the first speaker was to recognize the next speaker by concluding and sitting down.

**14:31** Paul never loses sight of the purpose behind the gifts of the Spirit in the first place: the building up of the whole church through the Spirit-empowered ministry of the whole church. *For you can all prophesy in turn so that everyone may be instructed and encouraged.* See the comments on

187. Gk. διακρίνω.

v. 27 regarding the parallel between Paul's preference here and common approaches to structuring conversation at an ancient Greek or Roman symposium or banquet. Josephus (*Jewish War* 2.132) says that in their meetings the Essenes "allow each to speak in turn." In v. 29 Paul seemed to have limited the number of prophetic messages to three. When he says, *you can all prophesy in turn,* he evidently does not mean that every member of the congregation — or even every person with a prophetic gift and ability — could prophesy in any given meeting, but that any three might prophesy this time, and others would have their turn as well, presumably at future meetings.[188]

We have referred to Joel 2:28 and Numbers 11:29 at various points (see on 11:4-4; 14:5, 23-24) due to the relevance of those texts to any teaching about everyone (including men and women) prophesying in church. They bear mention again here as Paul uses language once more that points to the remarkable development that is reflected in the suggestion that the gift of prophecy is widely distributed among God's people.

Paul stresses again the function and purpose of the gift of prophecy: *so that everyone may be instructed and encouraged.* The reason Paul values intelligible speech gifts like prophecy is that they have the ability to strengthen the church through the members' ministry to one another. The verb used for *be . . . encouraged*[189] here is based on the same root as the noun used in v. 3, where Paul says, "those who prophesy speak to people for their strengthening, *encouragement* and comfort." It means "to urge strongly" in the sense of "urge, exhort, [or] encourage" (BDAG). Paul's use of the verb *be instructed*[190] is interesting. One would normally expect it to be paired with teaching.[191] Its usage here suggests that the prophetic ministry should not be radically distinguished from teaching, even if the two have different emphases.

The TNIV simplifies the text slightly by translating the repeated "all" in the Greek text just once. Literally it reads, "so that all may be instructed and all may be encouraged." Paul's repeated use of "all"[192] *(everyone)* gives it prominence. One might have thought that all could be encouraged and instructed even if only one person were to prophesy. Paul may recognize the need of even that one who spoke to encourage and instruct others to be encouraged and instructed by others as well. He may also recognize that a variety of speakers (with different styles, themes, and sensibilities) is more likely to succeed in ministering to the needs of all those gathered than any one individual message.[193]

188. So also Theodoret, 223.

189. Gk. παρακαλέω (the noun in v. 3 is παράκλησις).

190. Gk. μανθάνω: "to gain knowledge or skill by instruction" (BDAG).

191. See Deut. 4:10; Jer. 12:16; Rom. 16:17; Eph. 4:20-21; 1 Tim. 2:11-12; Wis. 6:9-10.

192. Gk. πάντες.

193. That *everyone* would be instructed by all those who prophesy raises interesting questions about the significance of the prophetic ministry of women to which Paul referred in 11:5.

c) Warrant for guidance based on the nature of the prophetic ministry, 14:32

**14:32** Christian prophets do not lose control in some ecstatic trance or as though possessed by some foreign spirit. *The spirits of prophets are subject to the control of prophets.* The use of spiritual gifts in the congregation is for the building up of the congregation as together they grow up into Christ and reflect God's renewed humanity. The use of spiritual gifts requires the engagement of the mind and/or spirit of the gifted individual and their ability to restrain, channel, and control their gift in a way that reflects their own progress in developing Christ-centered attitudes and priorities and in prioritizing that which will most benefit their brothers and sisters in Christ. Spiritual actions that can be wholly attributed to an external spiritual power would say little about and contribute little to the spiritual growth of the practitioner. No one is to use prophetic inspiration as an excuse for continuing on in contradiction to Paul's instructions.

d) Theological warrant for Paul's guidance on tongues and prophecy: God's nature, 14:33

**14:33** Paul insists that for worship to glorify God it must be done in a way which is fully consistent with and reflective of his nature and attributes: *For God is not a God of disorder but of peace — as in all the congregations of the Lord's people.* Debate continues over whether the second part of this verse belongs with the first part or with the following verses. Is God *a God . . . of peace . . . in all the congregations of the Lord's people* or is it that women should be silent *as in all the congregations of the Lord's people?* While a great many interpreters believe that the second part of this verse belongs more to what follows, a number of factors support the view that it goes with the first part of the verse. Chrysostom clearly thinks that the two parts of this verse go together.[194] He supplies the verb "I teach" so that the sentence reads, "God is not a God of disorder but of peace, as I teach in all the congregations of the Lord's people,"[195] suggesting, perhaps, that Paul simply elided the verb. The fact that some witnesses transpose vv. 34-35 (rather than vv. 33b-35 or vv. 33b-36) so that they come after v. 40 suggests that v. 33b was associated more directly with v. 33a than with v. 34.

There is a close relationship between this verse, which summarizes the theological basis for the teaching in this section, and v. 40, which plays a similar role. In fact, the point of v. 40 may be understood as the bridge between the two parts of this verse such that the thought is that *God is not a God of disorder but of peace,* [therefore everything should be done in a fitting and orderly way] *as in all the congregations of the Lord's people.* In other

194. So also Theodoret, 223.
195. Adding διδάσκω ("I teach") to the end of the text.

words, the point is not that God is the same in all the congregations, but that, as in all the congregations, worship should always be carried out in a way which is consistent with his character as a God of peace and order.

### *vi. Aside regarding the silence of women (another issue interfering with the fitting and orderly nature of the church's public worship), 14:34-35*

> [34]*Women should remain silent in the churches. They are not allowed to speak, but must be in submission, as the law says.* [35]*If they want to inquire about something, they should ask their own husbands at home; for it is disgraceful for a woman to speak in the church.*

Paul continues his discussion of proper worship in light of God's character as a God of peace rather than disorder (v. 33). As in the previous passage, the commitment to order and proper submission requires the silencing of certain people, in this case, distracting women. Peace and order are preserved by women when they restrain from asking questions in church that would be more appropriate to ask at home (vv. 34-35).

1) Statement of the Need to Remain in Submission, 14:34
2) Guidance for Dealing with Outstanding Questions on the Part of the Corinthians, 14:35

**14:34-35** Paul has already mentioned two contexts in which certain people should remain silent in the church: those who would speak in tongues when there is no interpreter (v. 28) and those who would go on prophesying were it not that someone else had signaled that they were ready to speak (v. 30). Now he adds a third situation where certain people should remain silent. *Women*[196] *should remain silent in the churches. They are not allowed to speak, but must be in submission, as the law says.* [35]*If they want to inquire about something, they should ask their own husbands at home; for it is disgraceful for a woman to speak in the church.*

These verses have created interpretive difficulties since they were first penned. Some witnesses[197] transpose these two verses so that they appear after v. 40, leading Fee, Hays, Schrage, and others to conclude that it is a non-Pauline interpolation. Such scholars think that this text began as a marginal note which was later introduced into the text at two different places (although mainly following v. 33). Ellis has suggested that it may have been written in the margin by Paul himself before sending the epistle

196. The Majority Text and a few other witnesses — (D F G) (ar b) sy; Cyp (Ambst) — support the more explicit reading "your wives/women" (αἱ γυναῖκες ὑμῶν) rather than simply "the women/wives" (αἱ γυναῖκες).

197. D, F, G, ar, b, vg$^{ms}$, Ambrosiaster.

on its way.[198] With thirty-six words it would be an extraordinarily long "marginal note"! One wonders how it could fit in the margin of an epistolary papyrus.

No witness lacks this text, and the arguments in favor of its authenticity are substantial.[199] The fact that the witnesses that transpose these verses to a later place in this chapter reflect a similar (Western) textual tradition has led most scholars to conclude that the transposition reflects an attempt "to find a more appropriate location in the context for Paul's directive concerning women."[200]

On first blush (and even on repeated readings!), the opening clause stating that *women should remain silent in the churches* seems to directly contradict Paul's teaching that women may pray or prophesy in worship as long as they maintain proper decorum (11:2-16).[201] A number of solutions to this seeming conundrum have been proposed. One that has found little support is that Paul's true feelings regarding the participation of women in the worship meeting are finally revealed here, leading the reader to conclude that the possibility raised in chapter 11 of having women pray or prophesy if appropriately attired was not one that Paul actually supported.[202]

Another solution has been to see these verses as an extended quotation from the letter the Corinthians sent to Paul and representing their views, to which Paul responds in v. 36.[203] Besides the perceived conflict

198. E. Earle Ellis, "The Silenced Wives of Corinth (1 Cor 14:34-35)," in *New Testament Textual Criticism and Its Significance for Exegesis: In Honour of Bruce Metzger* (ed. E. J. Epp and G. D. Fee; Oxford: Clarendon, 1981), 213-20. We might expect even greater discrepancies in the textual tradition if this were the case.

199. On the text see Curt Niccum, "The Voice of the Manuscripts on the Silence of Women: The External Evidence for 1 Cor. 14:34-35," *NTS* 43 (1997), 242-55, and Thiselton, 1148-50.

200. Metzger, *Textual Commentary*, 499.

201. Readers usually assume that the *women* Paul has in mind are Christian women, and this is almost certainly correct. One would expect him to give explicit indication if he had unbelieving wives in mind (e.g., γυναῖκες ἄπισται). It is likely, however, that there would have been some unconverted wives (married to believing husbands) in attendance at the Christian worship gathering, and it is just possible that Paul expected the Corinthians to understand (in light of his earlier references to women praying and prophesying) that the women he mentions here are those who are in attendance merely due to the fact that their husbands have joined themselves to this religious group. Such women might have been more likely to ask inappropriate questions.

202. Collins, 521, points out that "[u]nlike Paul's directives to prophets and those who have the gift of tongues no conditions are stipulated as to when silence is desired. The injunction appears to have a general import, underscored by the explanation that follows."

203. See Walter C. Kaiser, Jr., "Paul, Women, and the Church," *Worldwide Challenge* 3 (1976), 9-12; Neil M. Flanagan, "Did Paul Put Down Women in 1 Cor. 14:34-36?" *BTB* 11 (1981), 10-12; Gilbert Bilezekian, *Beyond Sex Roles: A Guide for the Study of Female Roles in the Bible* (Grand Rapids: Baker, 1985), 144-53; Gottfried Fitzer, *"Das Weib schweige in der Gemeinde": Über den unpaulinischen Charakter der Mulier-taceat-Verse in 1. Korinther 14* (Theologische Existenze Heute 10; Munich: Chr. Kaiser, 1963); J. Murphy-O'Connor, "Interpolations in 1 Corinthians," *CBQ* 48 (1986), 90-92.

with Paul's view as given in chapter 11, this position takes the masculine adjective in v. 36 (where "only" is masculine plural) as an indication that Paul is rebuking men in the church who have put forth the view reflected in vv. 34-35. Masculine plural forms are typically used to address mixed-gender groups (such as a church), and only clear evidence should lead someone to conclude that it is intended to address men in particular. Carson also points out that the other candidates for quotations from the Corinthian's letter to Paul seem to reflect a similar pattern, which this does not fit.[204] Of course, as Carson recognizes, those are "formal criteria for the *certain* quotations,"[205] and real life is not so neat and consistent that we can count on Paul always quoting from the source in the same way. Verse 36, however, would seem to be an insufficient response to the developed viewpoint in vv. 34-35. One would expect Paul to give more space to his own position than to that which he opposes, as would be the case if vv. 34-35 were a quotation from the Corinthians.

Most solutions to the perceived tension between these verses and Paul's position in chapter 11 have been based on understanding the silence or lack of speaking to entail refraining from a particular type of speaking. Indeed, the word translated *remain silent*[206] was already used twice before in this chapter. First, in v. 28, in reference to one with the gift of tongues remaining silent when no interpreter is available to translate the unknown tongue. Then, in v. 30, in reference to a prophet who is to stop speaking if someone else receives a revelation. The inclusion here of this discussion of the silence of women or wives is most likely explained by the fact that Paul had just finished discussing those two other situations that also called for silence on the part of certain participants in the church's worship.[207] In neither of those other cases, of course, are those people expected to remain silent at all times. Indeed, Paul is probably thinking of particular instances where different kinds of participants in the worship meeting should refrain from speaking.[208]

204. They "are short, they are usually followed by sustained qualification, and the Pauline response is unambiguous and does not require the addition of words or phrases to make sense of the text" (Carson, *Showing the Spirit*, 55).

205. Carson, *Showing the Spirit*, 128.

206. Gk. σιγάω.

207. Ellis, "'Spiritual' Gifts in the Pauline Community," in his *Prophecy and Hermeneutic in Early Christianity*, 27, n. 25, similarly suggests that the word translated "be silent" serves as "the catch-word connection between verses 28, 30, 34."

208. Witherington, 276, argues that the argument "is not gender specific" since "Paul requires respect, submission, and silence of any listener when any prophet is speaking (vv. 28-32), and his dealing with some women who are asking questions (vv. 34f.) is a specific implementation of principles already applied in general to everyone. One must assume that he singles these women out for comment because he had heard that some of them were notable violators of these principles. Throughout the chapter Paul is correcting abuses, and his words must be read in that context." Similarly, Oster, 340-41, argues that "one ought to remember that all three imperatives for 'silence' were in the setting of a correction of aberrant behavior, and therefore the silence desired was only in relationship to the point of abuse. . . . In the same manner, the conditions of 'silence' and 'not allowed to speak' can only contextu-

The word translated *to speak* was most recently used by Paul in reference to speaking in tongues and prophesying.[209] It has been suggested that Paul meant that women should not speak in tongues in church. In several previous verses that deal with appropriate speech "in church" Paul has emphasized his preference that tongues not be spoken there, although they would be quite acceptable at home (14:19, 23, 28). In that case, however, it is not clear why Paul would add these verses singling out the women since he has already addressed the question in a more general manner. It is also not clear how the Corinthians could have been expected to know that by "speaking" Paul had "speaking in tongues" in mind here, especially since the most recent use of the word was with respect to prophesying (v. 29).[210]

Despite the fact that the most recent reference to "speaking" had to do with prophesying, it does not seem possible that prophecy is the specific form of speech from which Paul is prohibiting female participation, given his discussion of it in chapter 11 (which indicates that women may prophesy as long as they do so with their heads covered).

A more popular solution has been to suggest that what women are prohibited from doing is participating in the weighing of the prophecies of others, which was mentioned as recently as v. 29b. Thiselton thinks that "it is likely that the contextually presupposed understanding which does not need to be explicated for the addressees is either a failure to stop speaking . . . , or more probably the disruptive sifting of prophetic speech (as in v. 29), which might involve (1) repetitive interruption with questioning; and (2) the possibility of wives cross-examining their husbands, especially if, as is developed in the *Didache,* issues of contextual lifestyle are part of the sifting."[211] He reaffirms this view, stating: "we believe that the speaking in question denotes the activity of sifting or weighing the words of prophets, especially by asking probing questions about the prophet's theology or even the prophet's lifestyle in public. This would become especially sensitive and problematic if wives were cross-examining their husbands about the speech and conduct which supported or undermined the authenticity of a claim to utter a prophetic message, and would readily introduce Paul's allusion to reserving questions of a certain kind for home."[212] In this he reflects a growing consensus, at least among conservative evangelical commentators.[213]

---

ally and consistently mean that the ban against the speech of these women (γυναῖκες, *gynaikes*) is in force only so long as they are in violation of the principles and regulations of 1 Cor 14:34-35. The principle that these particular women were violating is that of submission."

209. Gk. λαλέω; cf. 14:27-28, 29.

210. If, however, the Corinthians knew that Paul had been made aware that women were particularly at fault in the constant speaking of tongues in the church, they might be expected to recognize that here Paul is addressing that aspect of the problem in particular.

211. Thiselton, 1156.

212. Thiselton, 1158.

213. For example, Grudem, *The Gift of Prophecy,* 245-55; Carson, *Showing the Spirit,* 129-31; James B. Hurley, *Man and Woman in Biblical Perspective* (Grand Rapids: Zondervan,

Grudem, supporting this interpretation, suggests that v. 35 should be understood as follows: "Suppose that some women in Corinth had wanted to evade the force of Paul's directive. The easy way to do this would be to say, 'We'll do just what Paul says. We won't speak up and criticize prophecies. But surely no one would mind if we asked a few questions! We just want to learn more about what these prophets are saying.' Then such questioning could be used as a platform for expressing in a none-too-veiled form the very criticisms Paul forbids. Paul anticipates this possible evasion. . . ."[214] The level of deceptiveness and insincerity assumed in this speculation is remarkable.[215] It certainly would have been awkward in Paul's world to have a wife criticizing her husband's prophecy in public, and the assumption that such a situation would have been intolerable perhaps gives the greatest weight to the suggestion that it is what Paul has in mind here. There are several hints in this and the following verse that Paul is particularly concerned about behavior that would be offensive to a woman's husband. That they are to "be in submission" has been interpreted in a variety of ways (submission to Paul's instructions, to the law, to men in general) but in Paul's world (whether in Jewish, Greek, or Roman contexts) an unexplained reference to a woman's submission would normally be understood to refer to her submission to the authority of her husband. The following verse's statement that "they should ask their own husbands at home" also brings to mind a behavior inconsistent with this manner of respecting the husband and, as argued in the commentary on chapter 11, any "disgraceful" thing done by a woman would also reflect shame on her husband, as her head.[216]

There are a variety of ways, however, that a woman might have spoken in church in a way that would bring shame on her husband (and not properly reflect her submission to him). Two key possibilities have to do with two different approaches to Paul's statement that women with ques-

---

1981), 185-94. For a recent critique of this interpretation, see James Greenbury, "1 Corinthians 14:34-35: Evaluation of Prophecy Revisited," *JETS* 51 (2008), 721-31.

214. Grudem, *The Gift of Prophecy*, 253.

215. It is not clear why Grudem and others assume that the questions should be interpreted as thinly disguised critiques of their husbands. Such an assumption seems to say as much about one's views of women as it does about Paul's text here. It is a gratuitous reading of a text which merely mentions the asking of questions. It is not necessarily the case that they have been asking shameful questions, but that their speaking is shameful.

216. Grudem argues against the idea that only married women are restricted on the grounds that the proposal is guilty of "making Paul's command nonsensical. For it would allow very young and immature girls to speak in church while denying that privilege to all married women, even those who were much older and wiser and thereby much more qualified to speak" (*The Gift of Prophecy*, 248 n. 24). We will return to this question below, but note here that it is not at all clear that "very young and immature girls" would have been permitted to speak in church at all. The issue has to do with the circumstances under which *women* were, and were not, allowed to speak. The word used suggests "an adult female person" or "a married woman" (including possibly "a newly married woman" [BDAG]).

tions "should ask their own husbands at home." The problem could have been that they were asking their own husband questions (possibly embarrassing questions or ones that questioned the value of their prophecies) at church (in public) when they should have waited to ask them at home. It is more likely that the problem was that they were asking questions of other men during the church meeting rather than waiting to ask their own husbands at home. While it is possible that the questions the women were asking (whether they were asking them of their own husbands or of other men in the church) had to do with their own husband's prophecies (as suggested by Grudem, Thiselton, et al.), there is nothing in the text to suggest as much. That a woman should not interrogate or ask embarrassing questions of or regarding her own husband in public would have been intuitively known by anyone with any social sensitivity at all in Paul's world. It probably would have been so obvious that Paul would not feel the need to even address the subject or provide special rules to keep it from happening.[217] According to Thiselton, Paul also thinks that it is wrong "to speak thus in public worship"[218] but it is highly unlikely that it would have been considered appropriate for a wife to cross-examine her husband or to speak with him in a way that would "undermine the authenticity of a claim to utter a prophetic message" even at home! Paul admits, however, that whatever questions are asked are quite acceptable at home, even though they are shameful in the context of public worship.

Suggestions that the silence of women had something to do with tongues and prophecy (or the evaluation of prophecy) are supported by the emphasis on those subjects in the local context. But there is no clear support for any view that Paul was prohibiting women from speaking in tongues, prophesying, or taking part in the weighing of prophecies (and, again, we can assume that all would have recognized it to be outrageous to use such

217. Forbes, *Prophecy and Inspired Speech*, 273, argues that a problem with the view that Paul allows women to prophesy but prohibits them from participating in the weighing of prophecies is that it "makes a quite arbitrary distinction between the nature of the authority of prophecy and for discernment. On this view women may prophesy things which (we may presume) would occasionally override the authority of their husbands, yet they may not evaluate the prophetic utterances of their husbands, or other men." He also argues that "[i]f a wife's authority in prophecy is not her own, but the Spirit's, and that is why she may prophesy, then her husband's authority in prophecy is not his own either, and so having his prophecy evaluated by his wife is not an overturning of his authority. The same, of course, applies to their gifts of discernment." These are reasonable arguments, although it seems very unlikely that it would be seen as appropriate for a woman to prophesy things which would override the authority of their husbands (one might hope and expect that such prophetic messages would be given to someone other than a spouse) or to critique their prophetic messages either by making evaluative statements or by asking their husbands or other people awkward questions about such messages in public. The obvious need for tact and restraint would hardly require a rule prohibiting women from any participation in the (tactful) weighing of prophecies.

218. Thiselton, 1160, pointing out that "ἐν ἐκκλησίᾳ stands in semantic contrast to ἐν οἴκῳ."

opportunities to demean or criticize one's spouse). It may be, then, that having addressed two situations in which people needed to exercise restraint and hold their tongue, Paul went on to address a third such situation that was not directly related to the themes of tongues or prophecy but that did have to do with the related theme of maintaining decency, order, and peace in the worship service (vv. 33, 40).

Perhaps even more likely is the possibility that scholars have inadvertently assumed that the only speaking that took place in the context of the prophetic ministry was that of prophesying and weighing prophecies.[219] It is quite possible, even most likely, that the discourse had more components, such as opportunities to ask (nonevaluative) questions of prophets. This was, in fact, the most common mode of engaging prophets in the Hellenistic world. Boring contends that "Hellenistic prophecy could be the result of the spontaneous inspiration by the deity, but it was normally a response to inquiries in which human beings took the initiative and was subject to manipulation."[220] Furthermore, "[p]rophecy was generally directed to the needs and inquiries of individuals, revealing the will of the deity or future information concerning the personal lives of individuals."[221]

> The questions brought to oracles were both public and private in nature. . . . Delphi was distinctive because of its large proportion of public enquiries about how cities were to cope when confronted with natural catastrophes, divine prodigies or war; and how they were to sanction legislation, found colonies or please the gods. Naturally, Delphi also had its share of private queries typically, according to Plutarch, whether "one ought to marry, or to start on a voyage, or to make a loan." (Plutarch, *Moralia* 408C)[222]

This situation reflects the possibility, highlighted by Nadeau and recognized by Thiselton, that "a form of speech or timing of speech other than prayer or proclamation is involved which may generate more hellenistic than Jewish resonances."[223]

Witherington rightly sees that "it is very believable that these women assumed that Christian prophets or prophetesses functioned much like the oracle at Delphi, who only prophesied in response to questions, including

219. According to BDAG, this passage "refers to expression in a congregational assembly, which would engage not only in worship but in discussion of congregational affairs; the latter appears to be implied here, for it was contrary to custom for Hellenic women, in contrast to their privileges in certain cultic rites (cp. 1 Cor 11:5), to participate in public deliberations" (BDAG, "λαλεῖν," 2aβ).

220. M. Eugene Boring, "Prophecy: Early Christian Prophecy," in *ABD* 5:496.

221. Boring, "Prophecy: Early Christian Prophecy," in *ABD* 5:496-97.

222. J. R. C. Cousland, "Prophets and Prophecy," in *DNTB* 831-32. Cf. Witherington, 278.

223. Thiselton, 1158, citing D. J. Nadeau, "La problème des femmes en 1 Cor 14:33b-35," *ETR* 69 (1994), 63-65.

questions about purely personal matters. Paul argues that Christian prophecy is different: Prophets and prophetesses speak in response to the prompting of the Holy Spirit, without any human priming of the pump."[224] Perhaps some women were especially likely to treat their Christian prophets as they would other prophets in their world, by peppering them with questions such as "Will my child be a boy or a girl?" or "Should I employ this slave or that?" They may also be asking questions that are not part of the weighing of the prophecies but that are motivated by a desire to understand the content of the prophecies or the way in which the prophetic ministry works.

We should assume that unless there was a clear reference in the Corinthians' letter to Paul to a particular kind of women's speech in worship that was creating a problem in the church, the Corinthians would have found Paul's statement that women are not permitted "to speak in church" just as unclear as modern readers. Although it is stated without qualification, it clearly cannot be understood in any absolute manner. Verse 35 provides the clearest hint regarding the problem Paul was trying to address. There the emphasis is on the woman's desire to learn (TNIV, *inquire about*)[225] something. Paul says, *they should ask their own husbands at home.* Forbes follows this line: "Though it is possible that, in the context, the inquiries to which Paul is referring are actively a part of the evaluation of prophecy, the text does not require or naturally suggest that interpretation. Paul is not saying, 'if they have something to contribute, they should tell their husbands later' (when, of course, it might well be too late). He is saying that if they wish to learn . . . about anything they should ask . . . their own husbands later. Presumably the problem was that they were asking other people's husbands (or other people) on the spot."[226] Forbes and others have pointed out that in the Greco-Roman world it was considered scandalous for a married woman to carry on a conversation with another woman's husband: "There existed in the Graeco-Roman world in our period a strong prejudice against women speaking in public, and especially against their speaking to other women's husbands. In a society with strictly defined gender and social roles, and a strong view of the rights of a man over his wife, such behavior was treated as totally inappropriate."[227]

While there were opposing points of view, a traditional perspective is reflected in a number of remarkable texts. In his *Memorable Deeds and Sayings,* Valerius Maximus (from the early first century A.D.), speaking of the harsh treatment of some husbands toward their wives, mentions Quintus Antistius Vetus, who "divorced his wife because he had seen her in public

224. Witherington, 287.

225. Gk. μαθεῖν, from μανθάνω. It is translated "to know" (NRSV, RSV, NJB), "to learn" (ESV, NAB, NASB, CSB), "to inquire" (NIV), or "to find out about" (NET). The NLT translates the whole clause as "if they have any questions."

226. Forbes, *Prophecy and Inspired Speech,* 274 (ellipses represent the inclusion of the Greek terms).

227. Forbes, *Prophecy and Inspired Speech,* 274-75.

having a private conversation with a common freedwoman. For, moved not by an actual crime but, so to speak, by the birth and nourishment of one, he punished her before the crime could be committed, so that he might prevent the deed's being done at all, rather than punish it afterwards." According to this text, a wife should not be having a private conversation (where was her attendant?) with a stranger, certainly not a "common freedwoman" (and even more certainly not someone else's husband).

Plutarch tells us of a woman who accidentally exposed her arm when putting on her cloak: "Somebody exclaimed, 'A lovely arm.' 'But not for the public,' said she. Not only the arm of the virtuous woman, but *her speech as well, ought to be not for the public,* and she ought to be modest and guarded about saying anything in the hearing of outsiders, since *it is an exposure of herself;* for in her talk can be seen her feelings, character, and disposition. . . . For a woman ought to do her talking[228] either to her husband or through her husband, and she should not feel aggrieved if, like the flute-player, she makes a more impressive sound through a tongue not her own."[229] Plutarch implies that a woman's personal speech is as much an exposure of herself as nakedness.[230]

Even more remarkable is the language used by Marcus Porcius Cato (195 B.C.), who complained when women went out in public and spoke to men of influence, trying to convince them to overturn the Oppian Law, which restricted their use of luxurious goods: "Indeed, I blushed when, a short while ago, I walked through the midst of a band of women. Had not respect for the dignity and modesty of certain ones (not them all!) restrained me (so they would not be seen being scolded by a consul), I should have said, 'What kind of behaviour is this? Running around in public, blocking streets, and *speaking to other women's husbands! Could you not have asked your own husbands the same thing at home?* Are you more charming in public with others' husbands than at home with your own? And yet, it is not fitting even at home (if modesty were to keep married women within the bounds of their rights) for you to concern yourselves with what laws are passed or repealed here.'"[231]

228. Gk. λαλεῖν (as in vv. 34 and 35).

229. Plutarch, *Advice to Bride and Groom* 142C-D (Babbitt's translation [LCL], emphasis added).

230. Plutarch's concern about what is said in the hearing of "outsiders" is especially interesting given Paul's own reference to the presence of outsiders in the church's meeting (vv. 16, 24).

231. Livy, *History of Rome* 34.1 (cited in Mary R. Lefkowitz and Maureen B. Fant [eds.], *Women's Life in Greece and Rome: A Source Book in Translation* [2d ed.; Baltimore: The Johns Hopkins University Press, 1992], 143-44), emphasis added. In his speech Cato longs for the good-old-days: "Our ancestors did not want women to conduct any — not even private — business without a guardian; they wanted them to be under the authority of parents, brothers, or husbands; we (the gods help us!) even now let them snatch at the government and meddle in the Forum and our assemblies." He warned that "[a]s soon as they begin to be your equals, they will have become your superiors."

Jerome H. Neyrey suggests the view "that females should not speak to unrelated males, especially in public space" is the view held in "Rome as well as Greece, and for all periods of [ancient] history."[232]

Thus, the universal-sounding prohibition could be taken to mean that women were prohibited from nonliturgical forms of speech (i.e., they could speak as they participated in the use of gifts and in formal ways, but not in mundane, trivial, or merely ordinary conversation).[233] Even more likely is the suggestion that what was being prohibited was for women to approach and ask men in the congregation questions about things they were not understanding.

What does Paul have in mind when he says that wives should submit to their husbands, *as the law says?* If Paul intends to prohibit wives or women from participating in the judging/evaluation of the prophetic messages of others (cf. v. 29), Numbers 12:1-15 might be a candidate for his source since it deals with Miriam's criticism of her husband, (the prophet) Moses.[234] Paul alluded to Numbers 12:8 in 1 Corinthians 13:12. A more common interpretation[235] points to Genesis 3:16 and its statement to the woman that her husband will rule over her (cf. *4QInstruction* 2 iv 1-8). That text may be the one Paul has in mind. However, it seems to deal with a domination resulting from the curse of the fall. Thiselton is probably correct to follow Bruce in understanding Paul's reference to be to the creation narratives he usually points to when discussing relationships between men

232. Jerome H. Neyrey, "What's Wrong with This Picture? John 4, Cultural Stereotypes of Women, and Public and Private Space," *BTB* 24 (1994), 81. He points us to Plutarch's reference (*Lycurgus and Numa* 3.5) to women who "were too bold, putting on men's airs with their husbands even, to begin with, since they ruled their houses absolutely, and besides, on public occasions, taking part in debate and the freest speech on the most important subjects." Numa, however, "while carefully preserving to the matrons that dignified and honourable relation to their husbands which was bestowed on them by Romulus, . . . enjoined great modesty upon them, forbade them all busy intermeddling, taught them sobriety, and accustomed them to be silent; wine they were to refrain from entirely, and were not to speak, even on the most necessary of topics, unless their husbands were with them." He also points out the "flip side of this cultural prescription of female silence in public," which "is found in the stereotype of ancient females as gossips and busybodies," as in this example from Juvenal: "Better that your wife should be musical than that she would be rushing boldly about the entire city, attending men's meetings, talking with unflinching face and hard breasts to Generals in their military cloaks, with her husband looking on!" (Juvenal, *Satirae* 6.398-401, cited in Neyrey, "What's Wrong with This Picture?" 81).

233. Chrysostom thinks that Paul's point is that "if to them that have the gifts it is not permitted to speak inconsiderately, nor when they will, and this, though they be moved by the Spirit; much less to those women who prate idly and to no purpose. Therefore he represses their babbling with much authority" (*Homiliae in Epistulam i ad Corinthios* 37.1 [NPNF[1] 12:222]).

234. Cf. Walter Liefeld, "Women, Submission, and Ministry in 1 Corinthians," in *Women, Authority, and the Bible* (ed. A. Mickelsen; Downers Grove, IL: InterVarsity Press, 1986), 149-50.

235. Going back at least to Chrysostom (*Homiliae in Epistulam i ad Corinthios* 37.1 [NPNF[1] 12:222]) and Theodoret (223).

and women (cf. 11:3-12). In this case, the point would be that the law does not allow a wife to behave in an insubordinate way which brings shame on her and her husband, which is the kind of speech (in the worship gathering) Paul has in mind.[236]

As mentioned in the discussion above, v. 35 suggests that the problem had to do with inquiries that some women were making during the worship gathering: *If they want to inquire about something, they should ask their own husbands at home; for it is disgraceful for a woman to speak in the church.* Such inquiries in the course of the church meeting were deemed disgraceful (presumably both by Paul and by other members of the Corinthian church), and Paul counsels the women to follow the traditional approach that was much more broadly acceptable in that culture, which was for a woman to learn whatever she needed to learn through her own husband,[237] one of whose primary functions, according to ancient views of family roles, was to teach his wife.[238] Personal interaction between a married woman and other men was considered scandalous or, in Paul's words, disgraceful.[239]

236. 1 Peter 3:5-6 points to Sarah's obedience to Abraham (and the deference manifested when she called him "Lord" in Gen. 18:12) as the scriptural warrant for the submission of the wife.

237. Augustine reflects this view when he refers to this text and associates it with the idea of teaching a woman "through her husband" (*In Evangelium Joannis Tractatus* 15.8, commenting on John 4).

238. Hesiod, *Works and Days* (seventh century B.C.) counsels a man to "marry a young lady, so that you can teach her careful ways." Hesiod's counsel is quoted approvingly by Aristotle (fourth century B.C.), in his *Politics* 1344a. In his discussion *On Household Management*, 7.4-35, Xenophon (fifth-fourth century B.C.) discusses how to train and teach a wife. Philo (early first century A.D.), *On the Special Laws* 1:106-7, recommends marrying a woman who has not already experienced marriage since such women are most open to receiving the husband's instruction, "like perfectly smooth wax that receives the teachings which will be impressed on it." Pliny the Younger (late first century A.D.), *Letters* 1.16, upon learning of a wife who has become an accomplished writer, credits this fact to her husband "as the teacher who has made such a polished and learned lady of his wife." In Plutarch's view, the ideal was for a wife to praise her husband, saying, "My dear husband, you are my guide and philosopher, my teacher." He counseled husbands to teach their wives since if they do not learn from their husbands "they will, left to themselves, conceive a lot of ridiculous ideas" (*Moralia* 145). Later, the Babylonian Talmud came to affirm that "Before marriage a woman is a shapeless lump. It is her husband who transforms her into a useful vessel" (*b. Sanhedrin* 22b).

239. Philo agreed with many Greeks in arguing that "[m]arket places, and council chambers, and courts of justice, and large companies and assemblies of numerous crowds, and a life in the open air full of arguments and actions relating to war and peace, are suited to men; but taking care of the house and remaining at home are the proper duties of women; the virgins having their apartments in the centre of the house within the innermost doors, and the full-grown women not going beyond the vestibule and outer courts. . . . Therefore let no woman busy herself about those things which are beyond the province of household management, but let her cultivate solitude, and not be seen to be going about like a woman who walks the streets in the sight of other men, except when it is necessary for her to go to the temple, if she has any proper regard for herself; and even then let her not go at noon when the market is full, but after the greater part of the people have returned home" (*On the Special*

Paul's suggestion that the women ask *their own husbands at home* reflects that cultural context where a man could be expected to be better informed/educated than his wife and was understood to be the proper channel of information to the wife. Here, *at home* contrasts with *in the church* at the end of the verse, highlighting the private rather than public venue for the questions, in keeping with much ancient Greek thinking about the place of women in society.[240] In modern Western societies neither of those conditions normally hold. In many societies today women are no less prepared to ask appropriate questions than their husbands, and it is considered just as perfectly normal and appropriate for them to participate in public dialogues as it is for men. There is no longer any shame or disgrace associated with such engagement; rather, it would be considered shameful for a woman to be restricted from open participation in public conversations. The principles underlying Paul's counsel, that women (and men) not act disgracefully in public, or in ways which reflect a lack of respect for the dignity of their spouses, may well call for a different set of concrete behaviors in our churches than would have been expected in first-century Corinth.

Whether Paul has in mind participation in the critique of other prophets and their messages or disruptive (and shameful) chatter or conversations during the gathering, his main point seems to be that the women should show respect for order and for others (especially their husbands) in the worship setting. Just what that respect and order would look like would be indicated in part by the biblical principles Paul has in mind and in part by the social and marital context to which those principles are being applied.

Garland concludes that "Paul's instructions are conditioned by the social realities of his age and a desire to prevent a serious breach in decorum" and that he "may fear that the Christian community would be 'mistaken for one of the orgiastic, secret, oriental cults that undermined public order and decency.'"[241] In applying such a text to other contexts and cul-

*Laws* 3:169-71). Plutarch (late first century A.D.) argued that a woman's speech "ought to be not for the public, and she ought to be modest and guarded about saying anything in the hearing of outsiders, since it is an exposure of herself; for in her talk can be seen her feelings, character, and disposition. . . . For a woman ought to do her talking either to her husband or through her husband, and she should not feel aggrieved if, like the flute-player, she makes a more impressive sound through a tongue not her own" (*Moralia* 142C-D).

240. Gk. ἐν οἴκῳ versus ἐν ἐκκλησίᾳ. See Philo's exposition of this understanding, cited in the previous footnote.

241. Garland, 673, citing E. Schüssler Fiorenza, *In Memory of Her: A Feminist Theological Reconstruction of Christian Origins* (New York: Crossroad, 1984), 232. He also follows the suggestion that Paul "presents the practice of the Palestinian communities as a model to be imitated" (see D. J. Nadeau, "Le problème des femmes en 1 Cor 14:33b-35," *ETR* 69 [1994], 63-65). It may well be that the practice of the Palestinian communities served as the standard, although it also seems clear that Paul's guidance would have been particularly well fitted to minimize the offense to traditional Greek sensibilities regarding women in public places.

tures we must be aware of the extent to which Paul and other biblical authors are sensitive to the social norms of proper decorum in the places where they ministered. As mentioned above, in the modern (or postmodern) West it would be more scandalous to prohibit women from speaking with men than it is to allow men and women to speak freely with each other as long as our own sense of propriety is not offended. For a married man or woman to meet privately with a person of the opposite sex on a regular basis for prayer, study, and the like would be likely to raise questions. A married person who spends significant time discussing issues in private with a person of the opposite sex other than their spouse might raise some concerns. In some cultures and contexts one could still suggest that a wife should ask their questions of their own husbands at home (as was considered most appropriate in the Roman world) without blushing. In much of the world today such a recommendation would only discredit the person making such a statement, given the fact that the husband is hardly more likely to understand the issues better than his wife.[242]

*vii. Rebuke of spiritual arrogance among some Corinthians and call for them to acknowledge the divine authority behind Paul's message, 14:36-37*

36*Or did the word of God originate with you? Or are you the only people it has reached?* 37*If any think they are prophets or otherwise gifted by the Spirit, let them acknowledge that what I am writing to you is the Lord's command.*

These verses, coming on the heels of vv. 34-35, would make sense as a rebuke of women arrogating to themselves a prophetic ministry to which they were not entitled. That does not seem to be Paul's thought, however, since the "only" of "only people" mentioned in v. 36 is a masculine plural form, indicating that Paul has either men or a mixed-gender group in mind, and not women in particular.[243] These verses would fit perfectly after v. 32 or v. 33, which may well be why some Western textual witnesses moved vv. 34-35 to the end of the chapter, bringing these verses into direct

242. Carson thinks it implausible "that the women are silenced because they were uneducated; for again, we must ask why Paul does not silence uneducated *people,* not just women. And since Paul's rule operates in *all* the churches (vv. 33b-34), it would be necessary to hold that *all* first-century Christian women were uneducated — which is palpable nonsense" (*Showing the Spirit,* 126). But the logic of Paul's instruction ("ask their own husbands at home") requires that *as a general rule* the women in Corinth had husbands who were either better informed than they were or better able (given the cultural conditions) to find and provide answers to their questions than they themselves were.

243. This holds true unless the pronoun it follows was traditionally thought of as a masculine form and the adjective is masculine due to agreement. A search of the *TLG* database found no instances of ὑμᾶς μόνας (the same pronoun followed by a feminine accusative adjective) in any Greek document.

continuity with vv. 29-33 (see the comments on the text of vv. 34-35). This is probably a case where the text should stand as we have it (rejecting the transposition of those Western witnesses), but that the interpretation implied by the other textual variants may be correct — namely, that vv. 36-38 logically connect directly to vv. 29-33, not because vv. 34-35 do not come in between, but because those verses serve as a digression or parenthesis, dealing with another way in which worship was not being "done in a fitting and orderly way" (v. 40). Peace and order are preserved by the church as a whole when they submit themselves to the practice of all the churches and to Christ's authority reflected in Paul's guidance (vv. 36-38).

**14:36** Whom is Paul rebuking in this verse? Thiselton and Garland recognize a contrast between "only you" in this verse and the "all" in v. 33.[244] This would suggest a rebuke of those Corinthians who think they are free to go their own way, independent of any concern about what the rest of the churches do. Paul's argument is that the Corinthians' worship should "be in tune with the rest of God's churches."[245] We agree with this but also see in the verse a rebuke directed against those prophets who tended to monopolize the church's time, refusing to be silent long enough for others to have their own opportunities to speak to the congregation. Besides the contrast with the all in v. 33, there are also ties back to vv. 30-31. Verse 30 speaks of something being "revealed to another" (who should not be kept from speaking), while v. 31 says, "you can all prophesy." Thus, the word of God has not come to just those few who want to monopolize the meeting, but has come to others as well, who should also be allowed to speak. Such attitudes, and the associated behavior of dominating and monopolizing the church's time in worship, reflect neither the most excellent way of love nor the other-focused concern for edification which Paul has been stressing throughout this chapter.

Unfortunately, in most churches today the worship experience is structured in such a way that a very small group of people (in some cases only 1-3) does virtually all of the speaking and ministering to the rest of the congregation, which is often treated as an audience rather than as members of the body with gifts that should be used for the edification of the rest of the body.[246] This is not usually due to the kinds of attitudes that were present in Corinth, but may still result in treating a very small group of people as though they were the only ones who had been reached by God's grace and word.

Paul's questions in v. 36 open with a disjunctive particle[247] (translated "or") which indicates that the questions expect a negative answer[248] and

244. Thiselton, 1161, and Garland, 673.

245. Garland, 673. Cf. Fee, 698.

246. Of course, many churches attempt to accommodate greater "body life" in contexts other than the public worship service.

247. Gk. ἤ.

248. See R. Peppermüller, "ἤ," *EDNT* 2:111 (1c).

which reflects an argumentative tone. There is a sarcastic edge to the questions. *Or did the word of God originate with you?* could perhaps be paraphrased "Surely you don't think the word of God originated with you, do you?" and *Or are you the only people it has reached?* could similarly be paraphrased "Surely you don't think you're the only people it has reached, do you?" The two questions reflect opposite ends of a prophetic journey — a prophetic word's starting point ("originate") and end point ("reached"), its origin and ultimate destination.[249] Put together, they suggest the question "Do you think prophetic ministry begins and ends with you?" or "Do you think you are the be-all and end-all of prophetic ministry?" Paul hopes the Corinthians will instantly recall that the word of God did not originate with them, but came to them through Paul himself.[250] In 15:1-3 Paul will make the point that it is he who preached the word to them and that it is that word, which he had received and passed on to them, that was the basis for their very salvation. While Paul's role in bringing the word of God to the Corinthians is implied only subtly here, the following verses bring in Paul's spiritual authority in an explicit and very bold manner.

**14:37** Paul now brings in the full power of his apostolic authority in a remarkable way: *If any think they are prophets or otherwise gifted by the Spirit, let them acknowledge that what I am writing to you is the Lord's command.*[251] *Those who ignore this will themselves be ignored.*[252] Paul calls on members of the Corinthian church who perceive themselves to have a prophetic gift or other

249. The questions are, literally, "Was it from you [ἀφ' ὑμῶν] that the Word of God came?" and "Has it come to you [εἰς ὑμᾶς] only?"

250. Carson, *Showing the Spirit,* 131.

251. The word "command" is not found in D*, F, G, *(pc),* b, Ambrosiaster, leaving "is of/from the Lord" (κυρίου ἐστίν). There are two versions that have "is the Lord's command," one with "command" in the final position (κυρίου ἐστὶν ἐντολή, supported by ℵ*, 81$^{vid}$) and one with the verb in the final position (κυρίου ἐντολή ἐστιν, supported by 𝔓$^{46}$, ℵ$^{2}$, B, 048, 0243, 33, 1241$^{s}$, 1739*, *pc,* vg$^{ms}$). Yet others (D$^{2}$, ℵ, 𝔐, lat, sy, sa) have plural forms ("are the Lord's commands"; κυρίου εἰσὶν ἐντολαί), undoubtedly to agree with the plural relative pronoun that introduces the clause (literally, "the things I am writing you"). A few witnesses (A [1739$^{c}$, 1881]) have "God's command" instead of "Lord's command." Although the support for some version having "command(s) is quite strong," Barrett, 333, thinks that "it is much more likely that the short text was made more explicit by the addition of *command(s)* than *vice versa.*" Fee, 709 n. 3, responds that "in this case one has considerable difficulty explaining how a scribe would have created the singular ἐντολή as a 'clarifying addition.'" The reading with "command" seems to provide a slightly stronger explanation for the rise of the other variants (virtually all of which may be seen as attempts to either remove or improve upon the awkward appearance of the singular verb and noun in "these things . . . is the Lord's commandment").

252. Some witnesses (𝔓$^{46}$, ℵ$^{2}$, A$^{c}$, B, D$^{2}$, Ψ, 1881, 𝔐, sy) have an imperative rather than an indicative, as in ℵ*, A*$^{vid}$, D(*), (F, G), 048, 0243, 6, 33, 1739, *pc,* b, co. Metzger, *Textual Commentary,* 500, points out that "[t]he alteration between active and passive forms of the same verb accords with Paul's usage in 8.2-3, whereas the use of the imperative form may have been suggested by Re 22.11." The indicative is the more difficult reading, and therefore most likely the correct one (cf. Fee, 709 n. 4; Garland, 677). The TNIV translation seems to take the present to be futuristic.

special spiritual enablement to exercise that gift by confirming that Paul's instructions in the previous paragraphs were not simply the informed opinions of a Christian leader, but *the Lord's command,* that is, instruction given through the prophetic gift by which the Lord himself is guiding the church through the apostle. This suggests that what we might otherwise have mistaken for mere rational moral and theological argumentation was actually a prophetic message, and thus that we should beware of assuming that prophetic ministry will reflect some stereotypical form of speech which is clearly distinguishable from other forms (such as moral and theological argumentation). This may mean, as was mentioned earlier, that there is a lot more prophetic ministry going on in our churches than we often recognize.

Paul, of course, has no doubt whatsoever regarding the divine authority of his message, nor any doubt that anyone who is actually in tune with the Holy Spirit and who has a gift of prophecy or discernment will be able to recognize that his teaching is marked by the very authority of Christ himself. To deny the prophetic authority of Paul's teaching would not undermine Paul's authority but reveal that other person's lack of true prophetic or spiritual insight. Garland paraphrases: "If they do not recognize his instructions as valid, then they are invalidated as prophets and as spiritual persons."[253] As Thiselton puts it, "If a prophet's utterance contradicts *apostolic* utterances (let alone biblical tradition), does not that of itself disenfranchise the currency of the prophetic utterance?"[254] Carson notes how this verse ties together chapters 12–14. Here we find "a foundational test of the Spirit's presence, of 'spirituality' if you like: submission to the apostolic writings, not simply because they are the writings of an apostle, but because they are the *Lord's* command, and therefore tied irrevocably to the believer's confession, 'Jesus is Lord!' (12:1-3)."[255]

The expression *if any think* (literally, "if anyone thinks")[256] is precisely the same one that was used in 3:18 ("If anyone thinks they are wise") and 8:2 ("if anyone thinks they know something"). Fee points out that it "is probably no accident that the statement 'if anyone thinks that he/she is . . .' (3:18; 8:1; 14:37) is found in each of the three major sections of the letter (chaps. 1–4; 8–10; 12–14) and reflects these three crucial Corinthian terms ('wisdom,' 'knowledge,' and 'spiritual')."[257] This third usage of the expression brings in a third area of pride among some elite Corinthian believers, namely, a view of themselves as being especially endowed with the Spirit and prophetic gifts, along with Corinthian pretensions regarding wisdom and knowledge.[258]

How much material does Paul have in mind with his reference to *what I am writing you?* Smit thinks that Paul is concluding (and referring to)

253. Garland, 674.
254. Thiselton, 1163.
255. Carson, *Showing the Spirit,* 133.
256. Gk. εἴ τις δοκεῖ.
257. Fee, 11. Cf. Garland.
258. Cf. Garland.

all of chapters 12–14.[259] The fact that v. 39 summarizes the emphasis of chapter 14 may imply that he has that chapter in mind. Given the high density of imperatives[260] in the very specific instructions given in vv. 26-35, he may have those directives particularly in mind.[261]

### *viii. Threat to Those Tempted to Dismiss Paul's Authority, 14:38*

*[38]Those who ignore this will themselves be ignored.*

**14:38** Paul makes a play on words[262] which is open to various interpretations.[263] The verb[264] used twice in this verse is the same one Paul used in 12:1 (where it was translated "uninformed"). Although the word seems to be used with a different meaning (and context) here, Paul may have chosen it in part to serve as part of an inclusio echoing the language of the beginning of this unit on spiritual gifts. Barrett would translate it, "If anyone does not recognize this, he is not recognized," and thinks that Paul means, "he does not recognize the man in question as inspired in his opinion, not that he does not recognize him as a Christian."[265] Garland's view is more likely: "These words contain a far more serious threat" given that "[t]he implication of the passive voice is that such a person will not be acknowledged by God" and that Paul intends "a covert allusion to God's judgment," implying "the Lord will say to such persons, 'I do not know you' (Matt. 7:22-23)."[266] Thus it serves as Paul's "prophetic sentence of judgment" on anyone who would reject the authority of his teaching.[267]

259. J. F. M. Smit, "Argument and Genre of 1 Corinthians 12–14," in *Rhetoric and the New Testament: Essays from the 1992 Heidelberg Conference* (ed. S. E. Porter and T. H. Olbricht; JSNTSup 90; Sheffield: Sheffield Academic Press), 215-16, cited approvingly by Garland, 673-74. Smit thinks that vv. 37-40 are functioning as the rhetorical *peroratio* (the part of the speech which "closes the discussion on the subject and exerts pressure on the audience to take the intended decision") of chs. 12–14 (analyzed as a speech).

260. All ten are present imperatives, which, as BDF §335 points out, is the default tense for imperatives dealing with "general precepts (also to an individual) concerning attitudes and conduct."

261. Perhaps the similar use of πάντα ("everything") in both v. 26 and v. 40 also points in this direction.

262. Lang, 201. Hays, 244, points to similar scriptural statements "announcing God's eschatological punishment on those who reject the word of God" where the terms of judgment correspond to the original rejection of the person being judged, such as Mark 8:38 ("If any of you are ashamed of me and my words in this adulterous and sinful generation, the Son of Man will be ashamed of you when he comes in his Father's glory with the holy angels") and 1 Sam. 15:26 ("You have rejected the word of the LORD, and the LORD has rejected you as king over Israel!"). Cf. Fee, 712.

263. BDAG (ἀγνοέω 2) has, "anyone who disregards (it), is disregarded (by God)."

264. Gk. ἀγνοέω.

265. Barrett, 334.

266. Garland, 674.

267. Fee, 712.

### ix. Summarizing conclusion of the subjects of prophecy and tongues, 14:39-40

**14:39-40** Paul now provides a summarizing conclusion which applies the main point of this chapter: *Therefore, my brothers and sisters, be eager to prophesy, and do not forbid speaking in tongues.* If v. 38 suggested an inclusio with 12:1, this verse provides an inclusio with 14:1, wrapping up the more focused discussion on prophecy and tongues. Paul's arguments are not to be taken as an outright rejection of the gift of tongues, but as an attempt to help the Corinthians (and us) focus on what is really important in worship. It also serves as a corrective to some unedifying practices that were not consistent with the God-centered and other-centered approach to proper Christian worship. Paul's choice of terms is telling: one gift should be eagerly sought out while another is not to be forbidden. As he concludes this part of his discussion, Paul could hardly make it clearer which gift is to be more highly valued and more consistently practiced in the church's worship.

*But everything should be done in a fitting and orderly way.* Garland puts it beautifully: "The Spirit of ardor is also the Spirit of order." The Corinthians' "ardor for spiritual manifestations has destroyed the order of their assembly."[268] This verse echoes Paul's words in v. 26[269] and summarizes the emphasis found in vv. 26-39, although it applies not only to the material on tongues and prophecy but also to the material on the relationships between men and women in worship with which chapters 11–14 both open and close.

Paul does not idolize order. He "does not seek order for order's sake." Rather, it "is necessary only to constrain self-indulgent abuses and to create an atmosphere in which the gifts of all can work together to build up the community in love."[270] Paul has already pointed out that "God is not a God of disorder" (14:33), and if everything (public worship above all!) is to be done for the glory of God (10:31), it should reflect his orderly nature. "Paul has in mind both reverence and dignity appropriate to address to and from God."[271] Paul's instructions in this chapter have all been intended to guide the Corinthians to a more orderly and fitting approach to the use of spiritual gifts in worship so as to better reflect the glory of God. It is God's glory which is to be our preoccupation in worship, and that can be honored only when we maintain an atmosphere that does not distract people from his glory. Some Corinthians had manifested attitudes and behaviors which had drawn attention to themselves rather than to God, and which reflected a greater concern for self-edification than the edification of others.

268. Garland, 674.

269. This verse begins and ends with the same words as the last clause of v. 26: "Let everything be done . . ." (Gk. πάντα . . . γινέσθω).

270. Hays, 245.

271. Thiselton, 1167 (emphasis removed). He also suggests that Paul has in mind "a *missionary or evangelistic* rather than strictly aesthetic dimension."

## V. THE RESURRECTION AND CONSUMMATION, 15:1-58

Paul's first letter to the Corinthians is framed by Christ's crucifixion and resurrection. Paul stresses Christ's crucifixion in the opening chapters of the letter (esp. 1:13-22) and now brings the main body to a conclusion with an extended discussion of the resurrection. This chapter serves, in many ways, as the climax of the letter as a whole. In November of 1919 Karl Barth wrote a letter to Eduard Thurneysen in which he said, "Yesterday and today I sat over 1 Corinthians 15, but I came to a dead stop in the earliest stages as I started to work through it thoroughly. . . . The chapter is the key to the entire letter with its profound disclosures on this and that, which have their source in ultimate wisdom. Some of them have struck us recently like shocks from an electric eel."[1] This same perception has been affirmed in a variety of ways by different authors since then.

Some scholars have found in this chapter the ultimate evidence for the view that the Corinthians held to an overrealized eschatology reflected in its perceived emphasis on future eschatology. In fact, this chapter reflects a balance between realized and future eschatology. The gospel is summarized in terms of realized elements of eschatology. The Messiah has already died, and the resurrection of the dead has already begun with him (v. 4). The promise of the future resurrection of the dead is firmly established by the reality of the resurrection already realized in the person of Jesus Christ (vv. 12-23). Christ already reigns, but all things have not yet been put in complete submission to him (vv. 24-28). Paul's understanding of the nature of our future resurrection bodies is based primarily on the model of Christ's resurrection body (vv. 43-49).[2]

In the Introduction (21-28)[3] we touched on the way this chapter fits into a theological structure reflected elsewhere in Paul's thought in more concise forms.[4] In 1 Thessalonians 1:9-10 Paul reminds his readers how

1. "Barth is generally credited with being the first modern commentator to see that 1 Cor 15 provides the interpretative key to the epistle as a whole" (A. Katherine Grieb, "Last Things First: Karl Barth's Theological Exegesis of 1 Corinthians in *The Resurrection of the Dead*," *SJT* 56 [2003], 50, cited from Richard E. Burnett, *Karl Barth's Theological Exegesis: The Hermeneutical Principles of the Römerbrief Period* [Tübingen: Mohr Siebeck, 2001], p. 25 n. 59).

2. For this last point, see Brian S. Rosner, "'With What Kind of Body Do They Come?' (1 Corinthians 15:35b): Paul's Conception of Resurrection Bodies," in *The New Testament in Its First-Century Setting: Essays on Context and Background in Honour of B. W. Winter on His 65th Birthday* (ed. by P. J. Williams et al.; Grand Rapids: Eerdmans, 2004), 203-5.

3. See also Ciampa and Rosner, "The Structure and Argument of 1 Corinthians: A Biblical/Jewish Approach."

4. Our understanding is in radical contrast to that of Lietzmann, who introduced this chapter as follows: "Without internal or external connection with what has been said before, the treatment of a new theme follows." Our view is close to that of Karl Barth, who argued that this chapter "does not stand in so isolated a relation to the First Epistle to the Corinthians as at first glance might appear. It forms not only the close and crown of the whole Epistle, but also provides the clue to its meaning" (Barth, *The Resurrection of the Dead* [trans. H. J. Stenning; London: Hodder and Stoughton, 1933], 5-6).

they "turned to God from idols to serve the living and true God, and to wait for his Son from heaven, whom he raised from the dead." Paul's summary of the Thessalonians' narrative moves from the rejection of idolatry to the proper worship of the one true God and then to a combination of future and realized eschatology based on Christ's resurrection from the dead.[5] In this letter Paul now moves from the subject of turning from idols (chs. 8–10) and the worship of the living and true God (chs. 11–14) to that of the hope of the resurrection and the final establishment of Christ's kingdom (waiting for his Son from heaven, whom he raised from the dead). The connection between these subjects is reflected in Wright's comment: "If the road to true humanity is true worship, the end and goal of God's renewed humanity is of course resurrection."[6] It is through and at the resurrection that our transformation into God's renewed humanity, which has begun in this life and which is both reflected in and promoted by our worship of God (chs. 11–14), will be brought to its ultimate completion. Wright also points out that "[f]aith in the resurrection power of God, according to Paul, is the alternative to idolatry: it assigns to the creator God the power and glory which are properly his, the very things that idolatry characteristically denies, and, by denying, courts death."[7]

In one sense all of chapters 5–15 have to do with the body in one way or another. While chapters 5–7 focus primarily on the body's sexual purity (or lack thereof), and chapters 8–11 focus on eating and drinking, in chapters 12–14 the body serves as a metaphor for the healthy functioning of a church and its worship. While chapters 5–14 deal with the sanctification of the individual and corporate bodies of believers in this "time-between-the-times," chapter 15 looks forward to and relates all of that earlier material about what it means to be God's holy people in this present age to God's ultimate plans for the complete transformation of our bodies (= ourselves) and of our world and the final glorification of God in and through his creation.

This chapter provides tremendous resources for Christian theology and ethics. For Paul, the doctrine of the resurrection of the dead is at the heart of the gospel message (vv. 1-15), gives meaning to our life and service to Christ in this present age (vv. 16-19, 29-32), and serves as a fundamental basis for perseverance in Christ (v. 58). It also clarifies (as do some other New Testament texts) the relationship between protology and eschatology

5. While the thought structure of Rom. 1:21-25 relates directly to the first several sections of this letter (a lack of true wisdom results in sexual immorality and idolatry), Romans 8 and 15 make it clear that God's plan of redemption focuses its hope on the restoration of the proper worship of Jews and Gentiles and their participation in the resurrection and the restoration of the rest of creation.

6. N. T. Wright, *What Saint Paul Really Said*, 140. For an early and still very valuable account of Scripture's move from creation to redemption, climaxing in glorification, see Irenaeus, *Against Heresies* 4.38; 5.2 (brought to our attention by Sean McDonough).

7. N. T. Wright, *The Resurrection of the Son of God*, 735.

(the beginning and the end of the human story, vv. 24-28, 45-49) and the relationship between Christ's experience of resurrection and glory/reign and God's intentions for the rest of his people (vv. 20-28). The doctrine of the resurrection of the dead, more fully expounded here than in any other part of Scripture, makes it clear that God's purpose has never been simply that of "saving souls" for a disembodied existence in heaven, as though creation itself was of merely temporal usefulness and significance. Creation turns out to be not simply the context in which God is working out his redemptive work, but reflects instead the breadth of God's redemptive concern and plan. Physical, earthly, and bodily existence have to do with the nature of creation as God made it and, in a completely redeemed and transformed version, is part of the nature of the context and existence that God has in mind for us and the rest of creation throughout eternity. Our life in this world matters, in part, because it turns out to be not merely a waiting room in which we pass our time until being invited into the rest of the building where we will really live. Our life in this world establishes the starting chapters for a story that will continue and flourish in radically new ways (and not merely begin for the first time) upon the resurrection of the dead.

As Oliver O'Donovan has argued, "Christian ethics depends upon the resurrection of Jesus Christ from the dead":[8]

> In proclaiming the resurrection of Christ, the apostles proclaimed also the resurrection of mankind in Christ; and in proclaiming the resurrection of mankind, they proclaimed the renewal of all creation with him. The resurrection of Christ in isolation from mankind would not be a gospel message. The resurrection of mankind apart from creation would be a gospel of a sort, but of a purely Gnostic and world-denying sort which is far from the gospel that the apostles actually preached.[9]

O'Donovan also points out that "[t]he resurrection of Christ, upon which Christian ethics is founded, vindicates the created order in this double sense: it redeems it and it transforms it."[10] The proclamation of the res-

8. Oliver O'Donovan, *Resurrection and Moral Order: An Outline of Evangelical Ethics,* 13.

9. O'Donovan, *Resurrection and Moral Order,* 31. "The work of the Creator . . . is affirmed once and for all by this conclusion [i.e., the resurrection]. It might have been possible, we could say, before Christ rose from the dead, for someone to wonder whether creation was a lost cause. If the creature consistently acted to uncreate itself, and with itself to uncreate the rest of creation, did this not mean that God's handiwork was flawed beyond hope of repair? It might have been possible before Christ rose from the dead to answer in good faith, Yes. Before God raised Jesus from the dead, the hope that we call 'gnostic', the hope of redemption from creation rather than for the redemption of creation, might have appeared to be the only possible hope. 'But in fact Christ has been raised from the dead . . .' (15:20). That fact rules out those other possibilities, for in the second Adam the first is rescued. The deviance of his will, its fateful leaning towards death, has not been allowed to uncreate what God created" (*Resurrection and Moral Order,* 14).

10. O'Donovan, *Resurrection and Moral Order,* 56.

urrection of Christ "directs us forward to the end of history when that particular and representative fate is universalized in the resurrection of mankind from the dead. . . (15:23). The sign that God has stood by his created order implies that his order, with mankind in its proper place within it, is to be totally restored at the last."[11] This message gives meaning and significance to this present life, making it clear that our "life on earth is important to God; he has given it its order; it matters that it should conform to the order he has given it. Once we have grasped that, we can understand too how this order requires of us both a denial of all that threatens to become disordered and a progress towards a life which goes beyond this order without negating it."[12]

The most difficult exegetical problem faced in this chapter is the question of the meaning of "baptism for the dead" (v. 29) and how Paul expects his reference to it to advance his argument. More generally, 1 Corinthians 15 raises the issue of Paul's understanding of the nature of the resurrection body.

The historical situation which gave rise to Paul's writing this chapter is difficult to pinpoint with absolute certainty.[13] Common to all mirror readings of the chapter is the recognition, based on 15:12 ("some of you say there is no resurrection of the dead"), that some within the Corinthian congregation were skeptical about the concept of a future resurrection of believers. It is not that this group did not believe in any postmortem existence, since in 15:29 Paul speaks of a "baptism on behalf of the dead," which, though puzzling for us, was apparently quite acceptable to them. Rather, the notion of *bodily* resurrection seems to have been in dispute. If in 15:1-34 Paul contends that the resurrection of the dead is central to the gospel, in 15:35-58 he explains how the *bodily* resurrection of believers is neither unintelligible nor inconceivable. Indeed, the double question of 15:35, along with Paul's word of stern rebuke in 15:36, indicates that it was the very possibility of the body's involvement in the afterlife which some in Corinth denied. "With what kind of body do they come?" (15:35) is at the heart of the dispute, suggesting that some had philosophical or scientific objections to the idea of the resurrection of the body. It is not clear whether Paul has been made aware of this rejection of the resurrection through oral reports from Corinth or through some comment in their letter. Paul does not use the expression he has used elsewhere to introduce a subject raised by the Corinthians in their letter ("now concerning"),[14] implying that he probably is responding to some other report.

Unlike Greco-Roman philosophy, which expressed thoroughgoing

11. O'Donovan, *Resurrection and Moral Order,* 15.

12. O'Donovan, *Resurrection and Moral Order,* 14-15.

13. This and the following several paragraphs are slightly revised from our discussion in the *Commentary on the New Testament Use of the Old Testament* (ed. G. K. Beale and D. A. Carson; Grand Rapids: Baker Academic, 2007), 743-44.

14. Gk. περὶ δέ.

skepticism regarding any place for the body in the afterlife, Paul's Jewish inheritance affirms a sturdy belief in the resurrection of the body.[15] While explicit affirmation is reserved for certain Old Testament prophets, its foundations, as Richard Bauckham argues,[16] are firmly laid in the Old Testament portrayal of God as Sovereign Creator, Righteous Judge, and Divine Warrior.

Whereas some Old Testament texts use resurrection language to refer to national restoration (e.g., Ezek. 37:1-14), at least two declare a resurrection of the dead as a personal hope of life after death which is bodily in nature: Isaiah 26:19 promises a resurrection ("your dead shall live") which is explicitly corporeal ("their corpses shall rise"), and Daniel 12:1-3 speaks of the awakening of "many who sleep in the dust of the earth . . . some to everlasting life, and some to shame and everlasting contempt."[17]

Jewish intertestamental writings from almost every quarter include resurrection as central to their beliefs. Among apocalyptic texts, *1 Enoch* 51:1; 62:14-16; *4 Ezra* 7:32-33a; and *2 Baruch* 50:2, 4 describe resurrection in terms of the place where the dead are kept (variously in Sheol, hell, the earth, dust, and the chambers), "giving back" the deceased. In these texts those who rise eat, rest, and are clothed. *2 Baruch* 49:2 poses almost the same question as does Paul (1 Cor. 15:35b), framed in a prayer: "In what shape will those live who live in your day?" A prominent example of testamentary literature which reflects on the afterlife is the *Testaments of the Twelve Patriarchs.* For example, *Testament of Judah* 25:4-6 affirms the resurrection of those who have died in sorrow, poverty, or on account of the Lord, and *Testament of Benjamin* 10:6-10 mentions a resurrection in which "all are changed," with some to expect glory and others dishonor. As an example of historical literature, Josephus in the *Jewish War* speaks of "the revolution of the ages" in terms of a new habitation of a chaste body (3.374). In *Jewish War* and *Antiquities* he describes the belief of the Pharisees of a soul passing from one body to another (cf. 2 Macc. 7:10-13). A marked difference between Paul and this Jewish background is that from Paul's Christian perspective the general resurrection of the dead is preceded and indeed made possible by the resurrection of Christ: "For one man alone to be raised is a great surprise in the Jewish apocalyptic framework."[18]

Besides the general Old Testament and Jewish background regarding the resurrection of the dead, Paul shows dependence upon Genesis 1; 2:7; Psalm 8; 110:1; Isaiah 22:13; 25:8; and Hosea 13:14. He also cites the Greek poet Menander. His argument seems to be especially dependent upon the creation material (Genesis 1–2, Psalm 8) for its way of telegraphing what

15. Rosner, "'With What Kind of Body?'"; N. T. Wright, *The Resurrection of the Son of God.*

16. Richard Bauckham, *The Fate of the Dead* (Boston: Brill, 1998), 86.

17. Other texts, such as Job 14:14 and Pss. 16:10; 49:15; 73:24, also seem to imply belief in life after death, although the exegesis of such texts is more controversial.

18. Hays, 263.

God's original intentions were for humanity and, therefore, where the story of creation must be headed. As Wright puts it, "The argument is, in fact, an exposition of the future resurrection of all those who belong to the Messiah, set out as an argument about new creation. Genesis 1–3 forms a subtext for the whole chapter, and even when Paul appears to be merely offering illustrations of his point, these, too, are drawn from the creation stories."[19] He also points out that in both vv. 20-28 and vv. 42-49 "the place of Adam, and the reversal and undoing of Adam's fall and its results, is central" and that while in the former passage Paul quotes from Psalm 8 and its reference to creation, in the latter passage "he concludes triumphantly, as does the account of creation in Genesis 1, with humans bearing the 'image' — though now the image they bear, as in Romans 8.29, is the image of the truly human being, the Messiah."[20] He concludes that "there can be no doubt that Paul intends this entire chapter to be an exposition of the renewal of creation, and the renewal of humankind as its focal point."[21] Indeed, we should not be surprised that a chapter that expounds the relationship between the preaching of the good news of Christ and the resurrection of the body should do just that.

Like each of the earlier major sections of the letter (see 1:18–2:5 [neg.] and 2:6–3:4 [pos.]; 4:18–6:20 [neg.] and 7:1-40 [pos.]; 8:1–11:1 [neg.] and 11:2–14:40 [pos.]), this one is also marked by a negative argument followed by a positive one. The negative argument is found in vv. 12-19, where Paul deals with the negative consequences of denying the doctrine of the resurrection of the dead. That is followed in vv. 20-28 by a positive exposition of the consequences of admitting that Christ has been raised from the dead (and thus the reality of the resurrection). The structure of the argument as a whole may be outlined as follows:[22]

- V. The Resurrection and Consummation (15:1-58)
  - A. Affirmation of the Central Role of the Resurrection of Christ in the Gospel Message (15:1-11)
  - B. Explanation of the Consequences of Denying the Resurrection of the Dead (15:12-19)

19. N. T. Wright, *The Resurrection of the Son of God,* 313.
20. N. T. Wright, *The Resurrection of the Son of God,* 313.
21. N. T. Wright, *The Resurrection of the Son of God,* 313.
22. Witherington, 292, sees the chapter as a speech in miniature with an *exordium* (vv. 1-2), a *narratio* (vv. 3-11), a *propositio* (vv. 12-19), a thesis (v. 20), a *probatio* entailing a series of arguments (vv. 21-50), and a conclusion (vv. 51-58) which includes a *peroratio* (v. 58). Such a structure was never recognized, as far as we know, by any of the (rhetorically trained) Greek fathers (e.g., Chrysostom and Theodoret). Also, Witherington's thesis (v. 20) and his conclusion (vv. 51-58) make two different points and, rather than serving as the thesis for the whole chapter, v. 20 appears to be part of an argument in support of the broader thesis that the doctrine of the resurrection (especially our resurrection) is both true and essential to the gospel message (cf. vv. 12-13). Witherington's *probatio* is also too long and undifferentiated to be helpful.

C. Explanation of the Significance of Christ's Resurrection (15:20-28)
D. Exhortation in Light of Positive and Negative Responses to the Resurrection of the Dead (15:29-34)
E. Answers to Philosophical Objections to Belief in the Resurrection of the Body (15:35-49)
F. Explanation of the Necessity of the Resurrection for the Realization of God's Ultimate Victory (15:50-57)
G. Final Appeal in Light of the Affirmation of the Resurrection (15:58)

## A. Affirmation of the Central Role of the Resurrection of Christ in the Gospel Message, 15:1-11

*1 Now, brothers and sisters, I want to remind you of the gospel I preached to you, which you received and on which you have taken your stand. 2By this gospel you are saved, if you hold firmly to the word I preached to you. Otherwise, you have believed in vain.*

*3For what I received I passed on to you as of first importance:*[23] *that*
*Christ died for our sins according to the Scriptures, 4that he was buried, that*
*he was raised on the third day according to the Scriptures, 5and that he ap-*
*peared to Cephas,*[24] *and then to the Twelve. 6After that, he appeared to more*
*than five hundred of the brothers and sisters at the same time, most of whom*
*are still living, though some have fallen asleep. 7Then he appeared to James,*
*then to all the apostles, 8and last of all he appeared to me also, as to one ab-*
*normally born.*

*9For I am the least of the apostles and do not even deserve to be called an*
*apostle, because I persecuted the church of God. 10But by the grace of God I*
*am what I am, and his grace to me was not without effect. No, I worked*
*harder than all of them — yet not I, but the grace of God that was with me.*
*11Whether, then, it is I or they, this is what we preach, and this is what you*
*believed.*

Paul defends the central role of the resurrection in the gospel message primarily through the narration[25] of several episodes, including Christ's death, resurrection, and appearances (vv. 3b-8), his personal experience of Christ in his conversion and ministry (vv. 8-11a), and the Corinthians' own experience of the good news of Christ and his resurrection (vv. 1b-2, 11b).

23. Or *you at the first.*
24. That is, Peter.
25. These first eleven verses are constructed mainly out of a series of aorist indicative verbs, whose perfective aspect is commonly employed in narrating the mainline events in Greek narrative (see Campbell, *Basics of Verbal Aspect,* 38, 42, 84-85).

**15:1-2** In these two verses Paul is not only preparing to introduce the topic of the resurrection (through its crucial place in the gospel message itself) but is also reminding the Corinthians of the fact that their spiritual standing has been dependent upon Paul's ministry from the beginning, in part evoking the questions he asked in 14:36. *Now, brothers and sisters, I want to remind you of the gospel I preached to you, which you received and on which you have taken your stand. By this gospel you are saved, if you hold firmly to the word I preached to you. Otherwise, you have believed in vain.* The word of God did not originate with the Corinthians; it came to them through Paul's preaching. The word translated *remind*[26] (by the TNIV, NIV, ESV, NRSV, RSV, NLT) means "to cause information to become known: *make known, reveal*" (BDAG). BDAG indicates that the word is used here despite the fact that Paul is dealing with something "already known" because his instruction "evidently introduces someth[ing] new." As Conzelmann points out, the evidence of 1 Corinthians 12:3, Galatians 1:11, and 2 Corinthians 8:1 suggests that Paul uses the word "as a ceremonious introduction."[27] That is, the opening phrase "solemnly heralds the initial subject — the gospel Paul preached."[28] Robertson and Plummer may also be right in suggesting that "[t]here is a gentle reproach in the word. He has to begin again and teach them an elementary fact, which they had already accepted."[29]

Paul elaborates on *the gospel* through a series of four relative clauses[30] that combine to emphasize the crucial importance of the gospel (and, thus, of the resurrection) in the Corinthians' lives. The gospel (1) was preached to them by Paul; (2) they received it; (3) they stand[31] on it; and (4) they are being saved through it.[32] The four points seem to progress in chronological order, starting from their first experience with the gospel and moving to the process of salvation which they are presently experiencing and which God would bring to completion at the end (cf. Phil. 1:6).[33] They have had such a significant history and sufficient experience with the gospel that they should not really need to have Paul clarify its nature or implications for them. Paul will expand on the contents of the gospel he preached to them in vv. 3-8.

As discussed in the comments on 11:23, the language of "receiving" was used for the transmission of traditional material. Just as the Corinthians had received the tradition of the Lord's Supper from him, they had also received the gospel message and entered into their Christian identity

26. Gk. γνωρίζω.

27. Conzelmann, 250.

28. Garland, 682.

29. Robertson and Plummer, 331.

30. In breaking the two verses into separate sentences, the TNIV and other translations break up the series.

31. Paul uses the perfect tense of ἵστημι, referring to their current stance and status.

32. Cf. Findlay, 389-90.

33. Cf. Sampley, 975.

through Paul's ministry. "In both instances, the reminders of the tradition he passed on to them imply that they have veered off course."[34]

The Greek sentence becomes awkward at the end. The part translated *if you hold firmly to the word I preached to you. Otherwise, you have believed in vain* seems to be a qualifier Paul felt the need to add after having made such a strong statement about the Corinthians' assured benefits from the gospel. It contains "a caveat implicitly warning them not to deviate from"[35] the gospel.

*I preached to you* in v. 2 repeats the same line found in v. 1. In v. 1 Paul's line of thought followed a purely positive track leading to the Corinthians' salvation. Here Paul goes back to where he started in v. 1 to allow for the frightening possibility that they may *have believed in vain,* if they fail to *hold firmly to the word* (here *the word* refers to *the gospel* mentioned in v. 1) preached to them by Paul. Those who believe in the doctrine of the perseverance of the saints and those who reject that doctrine both agree that people who do not persevere in the gospel have no true claim on its promised blessings and benefits. Paul generally assumes that those who confess Christ will remain faithful to that confession (thus the positive tone of v. 1), but he also acknowledged the tragic truth that not all ended up doing so.

**15:3-8** Having introduced the gospel in terms of Paul's role in bringing it to the Corinthians and its fundamental importance as the key to their salvation, Paul now details the main points of its contents, giving special emphasis to the place of the resurrection in the gospel message: [3]*For what I received*[36] *I passed on to you as of first importance*[37]*: that Christ died for our sins according to the Scriptures,* [4]*that he was buried, that he was raised on the third day according to the Scriptures,* [5]*and that he appeared to Cephas, and then*[38] *to the Twelve.*[39] [6]*After that, he appeared to more than five hundred of the brothers and sisters at the same time, most of whom are still living, though some have fallen asleep.* [7]*Then he appeared to James, then to all the apostles,* [8]*and last of all he appeared to me also, as to one abnormally born.*

Christ is the subject of all the verbs from v. 3b to v. 8 except for the two in the relative clause of v. 6b (regarding the five hundred witnesses). In sev-

34. Garland, 682.

35. Garland, 682.

36. The words "what I received" are omitted by the Latin witnesses b, Irenaeus$^{Lat}$, and Ambrosiaster, an omission that was probably originally motivated by concern that they might contradict Paul's statement in Gal. 1:12.

37. TNIV translation note: Or *you at the first*

38. The Western witnesses D*, F, G, and lat have "and after these things" (Gk. και μετα ταυτα), probably to highlight the appearance to Peter as the climactic one (since "these things" would refer to everything up to the appearance to Peter).

39. Some witnesses (mainly Western, including D*, F, G, latt, sy$^{hmg}$) have changed "twelve" to "eleven," evidently failing to see that *Twelve* "is used here as an official designation" for the apostles (Metzger, *Textual Commentary,* 500). As Metzger suggests, the correction is a bit pedantic.

eral cases it was necessary to adopt passive constructions ("he was buried" rather than "they buried him," etc.) to maintain that consistency. Paul's recounting of the gospel message reflects the fact that it is first and foremost a message about Jesus Christ and what he has done for us, rather than being a message primarily about us and how we can be saved. It is Christ's story which gives meaning to our lives, not our story which gives meaning to Christ's life. Dietrich Bonhoeffer understood this and expounded it well in discussing our role as "participants in God's action in the sacred story" recounted in Scripture, "the history of the Christ on earth":

> It is not that God's help and presence must still be proved in our life; rather God's presence and help have been demonstrated for us in the life of Jesus Christ. It is in fact more important for us to know what God did to Israel and in God's Son Jesus Christ, than to discover what God intends for us today. The fact that Jesus Christ died is more important than the fact that I will die. And the fact that Jesus Christ was raised from the dead is the sole ground of my hope that I, too, will be raised on the day of judgment. Our salvation is "from outside ourselves." I find salvation not in my life story, but only in the story of Jesus Christ. Only those who allow themselves to be found in Jesus Christ — in the incarnation, cross, and resurrection — are with God and God with them.[40]

Paul had used the language of "receiving" and "passing on" traditions in 11:23 with respect to the Lord's Supper. The information about the gospel had been passed on as being *of first importance.* While the expression could mean "at first" (and Paul undoubtedly shared this with the Corinthians very early on in his ministry among them), the nearly unanimous preference of English translations (first in importance) is probably correct.[41]

The fact that he had *received* this information about Christ does not contradict his point in Galatians 1:12 that he received his gospel "by revelation from Jesus Christ." While the basic gospel message was received by revelation from the Lord, the formulation he used in preaching the gospel included elements that had been passed on to him by those who were Christians before him, perhaps including the fact that *Christ died for our sins* and that it was *according to the Scriptures,* that his resurrection took place *on the third day* and that that was also *according to the Scriptures,* and the information about the witnesses to Christ's resurrection.

Scholars are divided as to whether the main contents of vv. 3b-5 or 3b-7 originate from prior creedal material that Paul has adopted, or whether he himself is responsible for this particular formulation of the tradition. While Paul constantly mentions Christ's death and resurrection in his letters, various terms or expressions in these verses either do not appear else-

40. Dietrich Bonhoeffer, *Life Together* (Minneapolis: Fortress, 1996), 62.

41. Cf. BDAG, πρῶτος.2.a.α.

where in his writings, or only in other texts that many also perceive to be based on traditional material.[42] On balance, it seems likely that Paul has constructed this particular summary out of traditional pre-Pauline creedal material that would have been familiar to the Corinthians and other early Christians. Even if the expressions are not common expressions for Paul and if the material is constructed from previously existing traditional material, there is not even the slightest reason to suggest that it is anything other than what Paul himself takes to be a precise restatement of the key facts behind the gospel message.

Paul uses four key verbs to summarize the gospel: Christ died, was buried, was raised, and was seen (or appeared). The most prominent verbs are the first and third (died and was raised) — the two modified by "in accordance with the Scriptures." The second and third verbs (was buried and was seen) each seem to reinforce and confirm the verb that precedes. Christ's burial reinforces the fact that he truly died. The fact that Christ was seen by witnesses after his resurrection confirms the fact that he had truly been raised from the dead.[43]

Paul reminds the Corinthians that the death and resurrection of Christ, the central events of his gospel (v. 2), are *according to the Scriptures.*[44] The fact that Paul rarely refers to "the Scriptures" in the plural (1 Cor. 15:3-4; Rom. 1:2; 15:4; 16:26; cf. Gal. 3:10) suggests that the expression serves as a general reference to them here; normally when a specific text is in mind, it is referred to in the singular as "the Scripture." Barrett understands the point of vv. 3-4 to be: (1) that the cross is the climax of the events of salvation history as they are revealed in the Old Testament; and (2) that the message of the cross must be understood through the Old Testament categories of sacrifice, atone-

42. The syntactical sequence of vv. 3b-5a that reads "that . . . and that . . . and that . . . and that . . ." (Gk. ὅτι . . . καὶ ὅτι . . . καὶ ὅτι . . . καὶ ὅτι . . .) is not found elsewhere in Paul's letters. There are several references to Christ dying in Paul's letters (the exact phrase "Christ died" is found in Rom. 14:9, 15; 1 Cor. 8:11; 15:3), and Gal. 1:4 says that he gave himself "for our sins," but the precise expression "Christ died for our sins" is not found elsewhere. More surprising is the fact that the following precise expressions never appear elsewhere in Paul's letters: "according to the Scriptures" (repeated twice in these verses); "he was buried"; "on the third day." That "he was raised" appears only here and in the following argument of this letter (1 Cor. 15:4, 12, 13, 14, 16, 17, 20), although it also appears in Matt. 11:11 and Mark 6:14. That "he was seen" is repeated four times in vv. 5-8 and one other time in 1 Tim. 3:16, which many others perceive to be (pre-Pauline) traditional material.

43. Cf. G. Schneider, "θάπτω," *EDNT* 2:134: "The strictly symmetric arrangement of the formula indicates that "he *was buried*" (ἐτάφη) is coordinated with the reference to death (ἀπέθανεν). Like the fourth vb. (ὤφθη), ἐτάφη emphasizes the factual nature of the preceding statement, i.e., the death. . . . A correspondence, now antithetical, probably also exists between ἐτάφη and ὤφθη: The concealment of the one who was buried corresponds antithetically to the open proclamation of the resurrected one."

44. While much of the precise language used here is not found elsewhere in Paul, it often goes unnoticed that Paul usually discusses life and death not in that order but in the order death and then life, based on the pattern of Christ's own death and resurrection and our participation in his death and resurrection life.

ment, suffering, vindication, and so forth.[45] It is important to remember that *according to* does not have any connotation of doubt as it often does in English (as in, e.g., "according to Henry we're all fools"). The Greek preposition used serves as a "marker of norm of similarity or homogeneity" and could be translated (with that meaning in mind) as "according to, in accordance with, in conformity with" (BDAG). Here it introduces the Scriptures as the norm which governed Christ's death and resurrection.

Jesus had indicated that his followers should have known ahead of time, based on the Scriptures, that he, as the Messiah, would die and then be vindicated by being raised by God from the dead. Luke 18:31-33 says that Jesus told his disciples that "everything that is written by the prophets about the Son of Man will be fulfilled. He will be delivered over to the Gentiles. They will mock him, insult him and spit on him; they will flog him and kill him. On the third day he will rise again." After the resurrection Jesus told the disciples, "This is what I told you while I was still with you: Everything must be fulfilled that is written about me in the Law of Moses, the Prophets and the Psalms." Luke says that Jesus then "opened their minds so they could understand the Scriptures" and told them "This is what is written: The Messiah will suffer and rise from the dead on the third day, and repentance for the forgiveness of sins will be preached in his name to all nations, beginning at Jerusalem" (Luke 24:44-47).

A crucial part of the Old Testament background for understanding Christ's death and resurrection appears to be found in the ubiquitous prophetic tradition of Israel's own prophesied and then historical exile and (promised) restoration[46] and the early Christian understanding (originating with Christ himself) that the Messiah's destiny was bound up with that which God had appointed for Israel, the nation he led and represented. As Wright has pointed out, in the resurrection of Jesus, God has done for the Messiah, in the middle of history, what he had been expected to do for all his people at the end of history.[47]

Notwithstanding a general reference to the Old Testament, the statement that Christ's death was *for our sins* may be an allusion to, or echo of, the portrayal of the Suffering Servant in Isaiah 53:5-6, 11-12. Several psalms provided background via a prefiguring (at least) of the resurrection of Christ, especially those that praise God for delivering the righteous sufferer; see the use of Psalms 110 and 8 in 1 Corinthians 15:24-28 (cf. Ps. 16:9b-10 in Acts 2:24-31).[48]

45. Barrett, 338-39.

46. Ezekiel 37 and Hos. 6:1-2 describe Israel's exile and restoration in terms of the nation's death and resurrection.

47. N. T. Wright, *What Saint Paul Really Said*, 127. Wright provides a fine discussion of the Old Testament background to the New Testament teaching on the resurrection in *The Resurrection of the Son of God*, 108-28.

48. For discussion of the broader biblical background to the idea of God dealing with sin once and for all, see N. T. Wright, *The Resurrection of the Son of God*, 320-22.

As pointed out above, the statement that Christ was buried serves to reinforce the fact that he died.[49] As the gospels make clear, to be buried, in this and many other instances, does not mean to be placed in a grave and covered in dirt, but buried in the sense of being entombed, placed in a sepulcher as a final resting place (cf. Gen. 23:4-19; 50:5, 13). Wright points out that it also indicates "that when Paul speaks of resurrection in the next phrase it is to be assumed, as anyone telling or hearing a story of someone being raised from the dead would assume in either the pagan or the Jewish world, that this referred to the body being raised to new life, leaving an empty tomb behind it. The fact that the empty tomb itself, so prominent in the gospel accounts, does not appear to be specifically mentioned in this passage, is not significant; the mention here of 'buried, then raised' no more needs to be amplified in that way than one would need to amplify the statement 'I walked down the street' with the qualification 'on my feet.'"[50]

The rest of the chapter makes it clear that Paul's special interest in this exposition of the underlying facts of the gospel, for this present context, is found in the third verb: *he was raised.*[51] Paul is establishing the crucial importance of the resurrection for the heart of the Christian faith, the very gospel of our salvation. Without the resurrection Christ's death and burial would not be part of a story of good news and salvation. For the place of the resurrection in the broader theological argument of this letter and in the broadest conception of the redemption of fallen humanity and creation see our comments introducing this chapter.

The reference to *the third day* in v. 4 brings to mind Hosea 6:2 and Jonah 1:17. However, the phrase, "according to the Scriptures," may simply modify "was raised" and exclude the temporal reference (cf. similar syntax in 1 Macc. 7:16).

Just as the affirmation of Christ's death was followed by the reference to the confirmation of that event in his burial, the reference to Christ's resurrection is followed by a reference to the confirmation of that event through his series of appearances to his followers. Since the truth and importance of the resurrection is what is at issue in this chapter, it is not surprising that the section on the confirmation of the resurrection receives much fuller treatment by Paul than the previous ones. The fourth verb, *he appeared,* is the only one of the series that is repeated. In fact, it appears four

49. The verb used here (θάπτω) is not used elsewhere in the New Testament in reference to Christ.

50. N. T. Wright, *The Resurrection of the Son of God,* 321.

51. Paul uses the perfect indicative form here, as he also does in vv. 12-14, 16-17, and 20. The perfect normally expresses a state of affairs, and thus this would normally be taken to refer to Christ's risen state, to say that he "is risen." However, the temporal modifier, "on the third day," suggests that in this case the particular event of the resurrection is being stressed. If so, this could be a case of what is known as a historical perfect (frequently used with verbs that convey transition, in this case "raising") serving "to highlight the transition that is conveyed" (Campbell, *Basics of Verbal Aspect,* 107-8).

times in short order: once each in vv. 5-8 as Paul catalogues a series of key appearances made by Christ after his resurrection. Witherington points out that the term Paul uses "speaks to the objectivity of the appearances: Jesus 'appeared,' not 'they claimed to see him.'"[52]

Paul's selection of postresurrection appearances is unusual and calls for special comment. He indicates that he is listing the appearances in chronological order[53] but does not suggest that the list is complete. He seems to be exclusively interested in appearances to the apostles. Unless there were no apostles among the five hundred mentioned in v. 6 (and it would be difficult to imagine a group of that many followers of Christ gathered without apostolic representation in its midst at that point of the early church), Paul's select list of appearances is certainly limited to those entailing apostles.[54] There are only three individuals mentioned: the two most important leaders of the Jerusalem church (Peter and James) and Paul himself.

There seems to be a pattern in which Peter is followed by "the Twelve" and James by "all the apostles." In this way the chief of Christ's band of followers (Peter) is tied to the whole group of the earliest apostolic leaders *(the Twelve)* and then the subsequent leader of the Jerusalem church (cf. Acts 15) is related to the slightly enlarged group of apostles that seems to have included James and some others. As implied in the previous sentence, *the Twelve* refers not to the precise number of disciples since Judas was no longer among them, but to the name that had become attached to Christ's closest followers who originally were of that number. Acts 1:15-26 indicates that Matthias was added to the group after Christ's ascension.

In between the references to Cephas and the Twelve and to James and all the apostles Paul mentions Christ's extraordinary appearance to more than five hundred believers:[55] *then he appeared to more than five hundred of the brothers and sisters at the same time, most of whom are still living, though some have fallen asleep.* The fact that most of the five hundred *are still living* is probably mentioned because Paul is especially interested not just in listing apostles and groups with apostles who saw the risen Christ, but in a list of authoritative witnesses who were still living and able to confirm the testi-

52. Witherington, 301.

53. "Cephas, then . . . then . . . then . . . then . . . last of all . . . also to me . . ." (Gk. Κηφᾷ εἶτα . . . ἔπειτα . . . ἔπειτα . . . εἶτα ἔσχατον δὲ πάντων . . . κἀμοί).

54. The Gospels of Matthew and John both indicate that Jesus first appeared to women (esp. Mary Magdalene). John also mentions the disciples traveling to Emmaus. None of these fit the profile that most interested Paul.

55. The TNIV's *brothers and sisters* (so also NRSV; cf. NLT, "of his followers") translates the Gk. ἀδελφοῖς, which does not specify that there were sisters in attendance but tends to serve, in the plural, as a generic reference to a group of mixed gender (although it could also be used of a group of men). The TNIV translation reflects the fact that Paul probably does not expect his readers to imagine that there were five hundred men gathered in one place with no women present, although, as mentioned, it does make Paul explicitly mention women witnesses, which he does not.

mony.[56] Other than James, the son of Zebedee (one of the Twelve killed by Herod; Acts 12:2), and some of the five hundred who had since "fallen asleep," it seems likely that all those listed by Paul were still living and testifying to the resurrection when he wrote this letter.[57]

The James Paul mentions is undoubtedly the brother of the Lord, who became an important leader of the church in Jerusalem. James, the brother John and son of Zebedee, would have been included in the Twelve (we would expect "appeared again to James" if he were in mind). It is not clear who would have been included in "all the apostles," but presumably it included James and the remaining members of the Twelve. Among others who may have been included in the group we might mention Matthias, Barnabas (Acts 14:14; 15:2), Andronicus, and Junia (Rom. 16:7).

Paul places himself at the end of the list of Christ's appearances to apostles. Although neither Paul nor any other New Testament author ever suggested that Paul took Judas's place or became one of the Twelve, he clearly saw himself as an apostle as fully authorized as any other and of strategic importance similar to that of Peter himself (cf. Gal. 2:7-9). He is the only person listed who was not a believer at the moment of Christ's appearance. The list starts and ends with the two people who serve as God's apostolic "point men" for the ministry to Jews and Gentiles respectively (Cephas/Peter and Paul).[58] That it ends with Paul, to whom Christ appeared *last of all,* reminds the readers that the author of this letter, the founder of their church, is one of an extremely select group of people who were privileged to see the resurrected Lord, an experience that no one in their church could claim for themselves. "The Corinthians had had every kind of spiritual experience imaginable, as the previous chapters have made clear; but they had not seen the risen Jesus, nor did either they or Paul expect that they would do so."[59]

Paul says that Christ appeared to him *as to one abnormally born.* The word translated *abnormally born*[60] usually refers to an abortion or miscar-

56. For the contrary view that Paul's emphasis is on the fact that some have died, see Garland, 690. Since virtually everyone else on the list was still living, it seems more likely that Paul is pointing out an exception included in his list. Certainly the fact that some had died also highlighted the relevance of this discussion of the resurrection of the dead. Paul has already used the common euphemism of "falling asleep" twice before in this letter (7:39; 11:30), and he will use it repeatedly in ch. 15 (15:6, 18, 20, 51). In commenting on 7:39 we pointed out that it had been used as a polite euphemism among Greeks for centuries, but had come to serve as an allusion to the hope of the resurrection among Christians (cf. Eph. 5:14). In 15:54-55 Paul will show that it is based on the conviction that Christians face death as the last enemy, which has "lost its sting" because of Jesus Christ.

57. If Paul does not omit references to the appearances to the women because they were not apostles, it may be that he omits them because they were no longer living and able to serve as witnesses to the event.

58. Cf. Ciampa, "Galatians," *NDBT* 312; Ciampa, *The Presence and Function of Scripture in Galatians 1 and 2,* 145-47.

59. N. T. Wright, *The Resurrection of the Son of God,* 318.

60. Gk. ἔκτρωμα.

riage, although BDAG gives its meaning as "a birth that violates the normal period of gestation (whether induced as abortion, or natural premature birth or miscarriage . . . , or birth beyond term)" and proposes a gloss here of "untimely birth." Here the idea of a "birth beyond term" seems to be appropriate since the appearance to Paul was later than that of others *(last of all)* and came only after a period of opposition on Paul's part. It may conjure up the image of Paul as a grotesque infant whose birth experience was far from what might normally be expected. The "for" with which the next verse begins suggests that it provides the explanation for Paul's unusual simile here.[61]

**15:9** Paul explains what he had in mind in referring to himself in the previous verse as "one abnormally born:" *For I am the least of the apostles and do not even deserve to be called an apostle, because I persecuted the church of God.* In the very act of demonstrating his humility *(least of the apostles)* Paul simultaneously refers to his place of authority over the readers — after all, like the others listed, he is also *an apostle,* even if he does not feel deserving. It is not a question of whether he — or anyone else — thinks that he is deserving, but of what God has graciously chosen to do. Like the new birth (cf. John 1:13), the office of apostle (and Paul's "untimely birth") is not based on a human decision or human will, but is something given only by God himself. Paul clearly saw that the very thing that served as Paul's *bona fides* as a zealous, committed Jew (cf. Gal. 1:13-14; Phil. 3:4-7) made him the least qualified to be an apostle. Of all the people in his list of those who had seen the resurrected Lord, he is the only one that we know for certain[62] was not a believer at the moment of Christ's appearance. He was not merely an unbeliever, but a persecutor of the church. As the following verse makes clear, the fact that Paul does not deserve to be an apostle serves to highlight one of his constant themes: God's surprising and unreasonable grace, in this case that remarkable grace shown particularly to him in his apostolic calling.

**15:10** How could one who persecuted the church end up being so critical for the church's prosecution of its mission? The answer is obvious to Paul: the grace of God. *But by the grace of God I am what I am, and his grace to me was not without effect. No, I worked harder than all of them — yet not I, but the grace of God that was with me.* Paul is an apostle, and the apostle to the Gentiles in particular. It was not in cooperation with the grace of God, but *by the grace of God* that Paul is what he is (i.e., an apostle). Elsewhere Paul

61. For the suggestion that Paul may be alluding to Num. 12:12, where "Moses prays that Miriam, who has opposed him and been punished with leprosy, should not remain leprous, 'like one equal to a dead person, like a stillborn infant *(hōsei ektrōma)* that comes forth from its mother's womb with its flesh half consumed,'" see N. T. Wright, *The Resurrection of the Son of God,* 328-29.

62. We do not know when James saw the Lord or whether or not he was a believer when it happened. The others listed were part of the Christian community when they saw the Lord.

speaks at length on his calling to apostleship and gifting as a special manifestation of God's grace in his life (cf. Gal. 1:15-16; 2:7-9; Eph. 3:2, 7-9; Rom. 1:5; 12:3, 6; 15:15-19; 1 Cor. 3:10). The word translated *without effect* (others, "in vain")[63] appears four times in this chapter (here, twice in v. 14, and one last time in v. 58) and nowhere else in this letter. Here it has to do with something "being without purpose or result" (BDAG). Some translations, like the TNIV, translate it differently in each case, masking Paul's use of the word as a motif in this chapter. Verses 14 and 58 make it clear that in Paul's view everything turns out to be in vain if there is no resurrection. Paul's preaching, the Corinthians' faith, and all labor carried out in obedience to God are for naught if there is no resurrection of the dead. God's grace, of course, should not be expected to be to no purpose or result and was certainly not to no purpose or effect in Paul's life and ministry.

Paul's humble assertion in v. 9 that he was the least of the apostles finds a counterbalancing statement here in Paul's declaration that he *worked harder than all of them.* By *them* Paul means all the apostles listed in vv. 5-7, and he makes it clearer that that list was especially focused on apostolic witnesses to the resurrection. Luke 7:41-47 indicates that the greater the sense of forgiveness received, the greater the love and commitment of the forgiven toward the Lord who has forgiven them. Paul's sense of infinite debt to the God who had showed him such grace fueled a profound passion to spread the fame and glory of that gracious and forgiving God. No sooner has Paul strongly affirmed how hard he worked, however, than he corrected himself and pointed out that it was not to him that his untiring work should be attributed but to the grace of God. And Paul does not describe his hard work as a matter of cooperating with God's grace but entirely as an effect of God's grace. What was on display was not a manifestation of Paul's capabilities or efforts *but* of *the grace of God* that was with him.[64]

**15:11** Having spent a moment discussing God' grace in his own life and calling, Paul returns to his main point, the fact that early Christian leaders consistently placed the (cross and) resurrection at the heart of their gospel proclamation; thus it was at the heart of the message that led to the conversion of the Corinthians. *Whether, then, it is I or they, this is what we preach, and this is what you believed.* Paul brings together two different but related issues here. First, he has referred to the other apostles as witnesses to Christ's resurrection as a way of strongly confirming the historical reality of that event. He takes the opportunity here to point out that the gospel message he preached to the Corinthians was no different from that preached by all the other apostles he mentioned. They were witnesses to the resurrection event that was central to the gospel tradition passed on to

63. Gk. κενός.

64. For a discussion of the relationship between God's grace and Paul's apostolic effectiveness see Ciampa, *The Presence and Function of Scripture in Galatians 1 and 2*, 147-49.

and through Paul, and it played the same role in their proclamation that it did in his own. In saying *this is what we preach* Paul is making the point that all of the apostolic witnesses are on the same page and that the gospel message received and believed by the Corinthians would have had the same basic content regardless of which apostle had first preached it to them. To reject the message of the resurrection of the dead is not to reject some idiosyncratic pet theme of Paul's but to reject a core plank in the gospel message on which their salvation stood. The very fact that they are now members of the church in Corinth means that they had come to believe the gospel and that the resurrection was an essential part of that message. To walk away from that would be to walk away from the gospel itself. In the following passage Paul will clarify the consequences of a denial of the resurrection since some of the Corinthians have failed to perceive the magnitude of their theological and spiritual error.

## B. Explanation of the Consequences of Denying the Resurrection of the Dead, 15:12-19

> 12*But if it is preached that Christ has been raised from the dead, how can some of you say that there is no resurrection of the dead?* 13*If there is no resurrection of the dead, then not even Christ has been raised.* 14*And if Christ has not been raised, our preaching is useless and so is your faith.* 15*More than that, we are then found to be false witnesses about God, for we have testified about God that he raised Christ from the dead. But he did not raise him if in fact the dead are not raised.* 16*For if the dead are not raised, then Christ has not been raised either.* 17*And if Christ has not been raised, your faith is futile; you are still in your sins.* 18*Then those also who have fallen asleep in Christ are lost.* 19*If only for this life we have hope in Christ, we are to be pitied more than all others.*

We find a negative argument followed by a positive argument in this chapter just as we have in earlier sections of the letter. In vv. 12-19 Paul catalogues a series of negative consequences that would follow if in fact it were true that there is no resurrection of the dead. In short, the consequences would be that Christ never rose from the dead, Christian preaching and faith are for naught (and the Corinthians are still culpable for their sins), Paul and the rest of the apostles have given false testimony, Christians who have died are lost, and (in hyperbolic terms) Christians are the most pitiable people of all. While this is not exactly an example of *reductio ad absurdum,* Paul's enumeration of such drastic consequences is intended to show the untenability of the negative position. Verses 20-28 will take the positive side and explain the actual significance of the fact that Christ has indeed been raised from the dead (and thereby established and vindicated the doctrine of the resurrection of the dead). Corinthian skepticism concerning the place of the body in the afterlife is perfectly understandable in a Greco-Roman setting since his Gentile contemporaries had no notion of bodily resurrection.[65] As Wright puts it, "Christianity was born into a world where its central claim was known to be false. Many believed the dead were non-existent; outside Judaism, nobody believed in resurrection."[66] In the Roman world, "everybody knew dead people didn't and couldn't come back to bodily life."[67]

How does Paul's teaching on the resurrection body look against the backdrop of views in the ancient world? As we shall see, Paul's teaching on this subject is framed in sharp relief by such contrasting Greco-Roman views, sketched in outline from biblical and Jewish sources but given its distinctive hues from the palette of the risen Christ. To use a different metaphor, when it comes to conceiving of resurrection bodies, Paul swims against the tide of Greco-Roman teaching and with the flow of the Old Testament and its Jewish interpreters, but rides the wave created by the coming of Jesus.

**15:12-13** In the previous verses of this chapter Paul has established the essential role of the resurrection in the proclamation of the gospel. In these two verses he begins to point out that that fact raises a fundamental problem with any suggestion that there is no resurrection of the dead:
12*But if it is preached that Christ has been raised from the dead, how can some of you say that there is no resurrection of the dead?*
13*If there is no resurrection of the dead, then not even Christ has been raised.* Paul has already pointed out that it is in fact preached — by the numerous witnesses of the fact listed in vv. 5-8 — that *Christ has been raised from the dead.* The conditional[68] clause *(if it is preached)* does not suggest any doubt about the matter, but refers back to a reality that Paul has just established in the previous argument. Paul's argument here seems so clear that it hardly seems to merit comment on first reading but causes one to ask how the Corinthians could possibly have held to such a self-contradictory position. One can only assume that they had misunderstood Paul's preaching (and other early Christian teaching) about Christ's resurrection and its implications for Christians.[69]

Perhaps they assumed that the language of resurrection was used by Christians to refer to an improvement in one's spiritual status either in this

65. See Rosner, "'With What Kind of Body?'" 192-96.

66. N. T. Wright, *The Resurrection of the Son of God*, 35. Cf. Rosner, "'With What Kind of Body?'"; Peter G. Bolt, "Life, Death and the Afterlife in the Greco-Roman World," in *Life in the Face of Death* (ed. Richard N. Longenecker; Grand Rapids: Eerdmans, 1998).

67. N. T. Wright, *The Resurrection of the Son of God*, 316 (cf. 32-84, esp. 32-35).

68. The conditional εἰ used with an indicative verb in the protasis (the "if clause") reflects a "first class condition" which indicates "the assumption of truth for the sake of the argument" (Wallace, *Greek Grammar beyond the Basics*, 690). Here the context makes it clear that there is no doubt that *it is preached that Christ has been raised from the dead.*

69. Acts 17 suggests that pagan Romans responded to preaching about the resurrection with utter confusion (Acts 17:18) or mockery (Acts 17:32).

life or in a disembodied postmortem existence.[70] Pythagoreans held to a notion of "the soul being released from the body at death, with good souls flying to the upper realms."[71] Similarly, Plutarch saw the soul attaining the realm of the gods by freeing itself from the attachment to the senses and becoming "pure, fleshless, and undefiled" (*Romulus* 28.6).

It is also possible that the Corinthians thought that references to Christ's resurrection had to do with an improvement in his spiritual status similar to the apotheosis which the Roman emperors were believed to experience, being promoted to divine rank or stature after their death.[72] If so, they may have understood the Christian hope of resurrection to be a way of referring to an expectation that they would also be granted divine stature by God after they died. This was not the hope offered by Christ and the apostles, but only a shadowy parody of it. The gospel message was wrapped up in the bodily resurrection of Christ and its promise of the restoration and renewal of human life and creation, not an escape to some disembodied, ethereal world. (We refer the reader to our introduction to this chapter and to O'Donovan's comments on the relation between Christ's resurrection and the redemption and transformation of the created order which are found there.)

**15:14** Paul follows the two conditional clauses in the previous two verses with a third one in which draws out another consequence of denying the resurrection.[73] This one depends directly on the conclusion pointed to in v. 13b, which asserted that if there is really no resurrection, it would mean that Christ was never raised from the dead. *And if Christ has not been raised, our preaching is useless and so is your*[74] *faith.* Paul has no room for some "spiritualized" view of the resurrection and recognizes that any such message has nothing to do with what Christ himself and his apostolic representatives had claimed about his death and resurrection and its place in the redemption of humanity and creation. Perhaps there would be some other religious leader promoting a message along the lines of what the Corinthians had in mind, but it was not Christ or his disciples. Christian preaching and Christian faith are only as valid and credible as the resurrection message on which they are founded. The word translated *useless* is the same one translated "without effect" in v. 10 (where it was pointed out that it has

70. The word translated "resurrection" (Gk. ἀνάστασις) was also used for "a change for the better in status" (BDAG; for an example in the New Testament see Luke 2:34).

71. Bolt, "Life, Death and the Afterlife," 69.

72. Cf. Bolt, "Life, Death and the Afterlife," 70-71.

73. In Greek vv. 12, 13, and 14 all begin in precisely the same way, literally, "but/and if" (Gk. εἰ δέ). Paul will introduce v. 17 in the same way. In fact, the first five words of v. 17 are exactly the same as the first five of this verse: "And if Christ has not been raised" (Gk. εἰ δὲ Χριστὸς οὐκ ἐγήγερται).

74. A number of witnesses have "our" faith evidently due to "either itacism for ὑμῶν or mechanical assimilation to the previous ἡμῶν. In any case, the context seems to require 'your faith' as a correlative to 'our preaching'" (Metzger, *Textual Commentary*, 501; cf. Caragounis, *The Development of Greek*, 522).

to do with "being to no purpose or result"). It actually appears twice in this verse (literally, "our preaching is in vain [or for naught] and your faith is in vain [or for naught]"). The word will appear again in v. 58, where Paul guarantees that Christian labor is not in vain (or for naught). Wright draws out the implications that would follow if Christ had not been raised:

> The crucial point is not just that they are believing rubbish about the resurrection, and about Jesus, but that *the new age in which sins are left behind has not after all been inaugurated*. . . . For Paul the point of the resurrection is not simply that the creator god has done something remarkable for one solitary individual (as people today sometimes imagine is the supposed thrust of the Easter proclamation), but that, in and through the resurrection, 'the present evil age' has been invaded by the 'age to come', the time of restoration, return, covenant renewal, and forgiveness. An event has occurred as a result of which the world is a different place, and human beings have the new possibility to become a different kind of people.[75]

The resurrection gives meaning to Christian proclamation and faith, as it does to all work done in the Lord (v. 58), and it is the root of the Christian hope.

**15:15-16** It would be bad enough if Christian preaching and faith were simply mistaken and useless. Paul points out (assuming the readers accept the reality of the God of Israel) that there would also be even greater negative consequences: *More than that, we are then found to be false witnesses about God, for we have testified about God that he raised Christ from the dead. But he did not raise him if in fact the dead are not raised. For if the dead are not raised, then Christ has not been raised either.* As *false witnesses about God,* Paul and the other apostolic preachers of the gospel would stand under his judgment. Of course, to give false witness is an offense against the Ten Commandments (Exod. 20:16; Deut. 5:20), one which was cited by Christ himself (Mark 10:19; Matt. 19:18; Luke 18:20). According to Proverbs 19:5, "A false witness will not go unpunished, and whoever pours out lies will not go free." The first line is repeated four verses later: "A false witness will not go unpunished, and whoever pours out lies will perish" (v. 9). Given the seriousness of such an offense, God-fearing people like Paul and the other apostles could hardly be expected to knowingly give false testimony about God. Of course, Paul's statement also implies that if the apostles have not given false testimony about God (because he did raise Christ from the dead and the dead are raised), then those who say that there is no resurrection of the dead are guilty of being false witnesses against God and should not expect to go unpunished.

These verses also hold a subtle key to understanding Paul's language

75. N. T. Wright, *The Resurrection of the Son of God,* 332 (his emphasis).

throughout much of this chapter. Paul usually uses the passive voice when referring to the resurrection. That is, he speaks of the dead being raised or of the dead who are raised, as he does here of Christ having been raised. These passive verbs are used with the understanding that if they were reworded in the active voice, God would be named as the subject of the verb. This usage of the passive voice is usually called the "divine passive" because God's agency in the action is implied. There are three divine passives in these two verbs. *If in fact the dead are not raised* (= if God does not raise the dead); *if the dead are not raised* (again, = if God does not raise the dead); *Christ has not been raised either* (= God has not raised Christ either). This must be kept in mind as one reads this whole chapter since it would be a mistake to think that Paul or his readers would expect the dead to rise up on their own. In v. 15 Paul states explicitly what is implicit everywhere else. That it is *God* who *raised Christ from the dead.* What remains implicit but also understood in each of the dozens of references in this chapter to the dead being raised (passive voice) is that it is God who raises the rest of the dead, just as it is God who raised Christ.

**15:17** As Paul continues his listing of the negative consequences that would hold true if there were no resurrection of the dead, he reflects an Old Testament/Jewish view of the condition of Gentiles apart from Christ (which would apply to unbelieving Jews apart from Christ as well): *And if Christ has not been raised,*[76] *your faith is futile; you are still in your sins.* If there were no resurrection, it would mean that God would judge and condemn them for their sins. Paul had pointed out that Christ died "for our sins" in v. 3, but if God had not vindicated him by raising him from the dead, there would be no reason to believe that those sins had been dealt with. The Corinthians would be, as Ephesians 2:1-3, 2:11-12, and 4:17-19 describe their former life, "excluded from citizenship in Israel and foreigners to the covenants of the promise, without hope and without God" (Eph. 2:12). Paul's understanding of faith and its role in our justification is fully developed in other places in his letters (especially Galatians and Romans) but it is also clearly reflected in his verse. If faith were futile, believers would still be in their sins (culpable for them and standing under divine judgment). The clear implication is that since Christ has been raised, Christian faith is not futile but effective and believers no longer stand under God's judgment for their sins but have been forgiven, justified, and set free from their sins (cf. Acts 13:38-39; Rom. 6:7).

**15:18** Continuing his list of consequences, if there were no resurrection of the dead, Paul points out, *Then those also who have fallen asleep in Christ are lost.* Paul has already used the common euphemism of "falling asleep" several times in this letter (7:39; 11:30; 15:6, 18, 20, 51; cf. 1 Thess. 4:13-15), the most recent being in v. 6. In commenting on 7:39, we pointed

76. The opening clause of this verse is a repetition of the opening clause in v. 14 (Gk. εἰ δὲ Χριστὸς οὐκ ἐγήγερται).

out that it had been used as a polite euphemism among Greeks for centuries,[77] but had come to serve as an allusion to the hope of the resurrection among Christians (cf. Eph. 5:14, where a different Greek verb[78] is used for the same euphemism and where it is explicitly tied to the resurrection hope).[79] As 15:54-55 shows, it is based on the conviction that Christians face death as the last enemy, which has "lost its sting" because of Jesus Christ. In 1 Thessalonians 4:13-18 it is Christian confidence in the resurrection of the dead that serves to encourage believers in the face of those who have died ("fallen asleep") in Christ and which keeps them from grieving like people with no hope. The Christian hope is a hope tied up with the resurrection of the dead. If that were to turn out to be a false hope, there would be no reason to expect deceased believers to have any further existence. They would simply have perished.[80]

**15:19** Paul uses a bit of hyperbole as he considers the challenges of following Christ in light of the consequences that would follow (which he just outlined in the previous verses) if there were no resurrection of the dead: *If only for this life we have hope in Christ, we are to be pitied more than all others.* This is not to say that the Christian life does not have benefits besides the hope that goes beyond this life (joy, peace, purpose, forgiveness, meaning, etc.), but what ultimately underwrites our such blessings, especially in the face of the tremendous challenges and opposition that committed Christians have often found throughout history, is the knowledge of what God has in store for us in the resurrection. In other texts Paul refers to this as "the hope of glory" (Col. 1:27), or the full knowledge of Christ that includes experiencing both "the power of his resurrection and participation in his sufferings . . . , attaining to the resurrection from the dead" (Phil. 3:10-11). This is "the goal" of God's calling in Christ (Phil. 3:14). It is related to "the hope to which he has called [us], the riches of his glorious inheritance in his people, and his incomparably great power for us who believe" (Eph. 1:18-19). Earlier in this letter Paul referred to the time "when completeness

77. It was used as early as Homer's *Iliad* (11.241) and by other Greek authors after him. It was also commonly used in Greek epitaphs (see LSJ, BDAG).

78. Gk. καθεύδω.

79. See M. Völkel, "κοιμάομαι," *EDNT* 2:302: "The demarcation of the circle of those for whom κοιμάομαι is used is illuminating: It is in all instances, including 1 Cor 7:39, used consistently of Church members, David (Acts 13:36), or the ἅγιοι (Matt 27:52)." For Paul the term "is used primarily in connection with questions about the fate of Church members who die before the parousia (1 Thess 4:13ff.) or before the resurrection (1 Cor 15:12ff.)." While "the Pauline occurrences are not sufficient to justify the long-held view that expectation of the resurrection was inherent in κοιμάομαι," one may still affirm that it "is a term directly relevant to death and the associated Christian hope." It "not only emphasizes the fact of death and is also not merely used in the customary ancient euphemistic sense. Instead the ambiguity of the term makes possible an affirmation of both the fact of death and the Christian hope."

80. Cf. BDAG and *EDNT* on Gk. ἀπόλλυμι, which has to do with (one's final) destruction.

comes," when we shall see [God] face to face" and "know fully, even as [we are] fully known" (13:10-12).

The full logic behind this verse is most clearly seen in Romans 8 and in a later part of this very chapter. In Romans 8 Paul says that "our present sufferings are not worth comparing with the glory that will be revealed in us" (Rom. 8:18). Were it not for that future glory (which he identifies with our participation in the resurrection), our present sufferings would need to be interpreted through a very different calculus.[81] Similarly, in 2 Corinthians 4:17 Paul writes that "our light and momentary troubles are achieving for us an eternal glory that far outweighs them all." So again it is the eternal glory, not merely the present benefits of faith in Christ, which counterbalances the suffering that Christians may expect to endure in this life. The "light and momentary troubles" are seen as light and momentary only in the light of the eternal glory that awaits us (cf. Paul's description of them in 1 Cor. 4:9-13 and 2 Cor. 4:7-16; 6:3-10; 11:23-29). In the following verses in this chapter we find the same logic repeated. In vv. 30-32 Paul will ask, "why do we endanger ourselves every hour? I face death every day. . . . If I fought wild beasts in Ephesus with no more than human hopes, what have I gained?" The answer is given in vv. 51-53: "the trumpet will sound, the dead will be raised imperishable, and we will be changed. For the perishable must clothe itself with the imperishable, and the mortal with immortality." That is, a perishable, dishonored, and weak body is raised in glory and power as an imperishable spiritual body (vv. 42-44).

In 1 Thessalonians 1:9-10 Paul commends his readers since they had "turned to God from idols to serve the living and true God, and to wait for his Son from heaven, whom he raised from the dead — Jesus, who rescues us from the coming wrath." What they expected to take place when their wait for the resurrected Jesus was over is not made explicit there, but in Romans 8:23 Paul says that "we wait eagerly for our adoption, the redemption of our bodies." Evidently it is that message that led the Thessalonians to welcome the gospel message "in the midst of severe suffering with the joy given by the Holy Spirit" (1 Thess. 1:6).

Through most of this letter Paul has been pushing his readers to embrace the partial renewal of humanity which Christ and the Spirit are working within us even now, as we reject the world's false wisdom and the idolatry and immorality that flow from it and reflect Christ's wisdom and purity and the proper worship of the one true God in Christ. But all of this is just the first taste of our ultimate complete renewal to which the resurrection of Christ points us.

Looking back at the previous verses, we can reconstruct a positive version of Paul's soteriology out of his negative statements: Christians are not in a pitiable situation but a desirable and enviable one; they are not lost but saved; they are not in their sins but forgiven and justified; finally, they

81. Cf. Theodoret, 227.

do not merely have hope for this life, but look forward to the eternal glory that will accompany their resurrection from the dead.

## C. Explanation of the Significance of Christ's Resurrection, 15:20-28

*[20]But Christ has indeed been raised from the dead, the firstfruits of those who have fallen asleep. [21]For since death came through a human being, the resurrection of the dead comes also through a human being. [22]For as in Adam all die, so in Christ all will be made alive. [23]But in this order: Christ, the firstfruits; then, when he comes, those who belong to him. [24]Then the end will come, when he hands over the kingdom to God the Father after he has destroyed all dominion, authority and power. [25]For he must reign until he has put all his enemies under his feet. [26]The last enemy to be destroyed is death. [27]For he "has put everything under his feet." Now when it says that "everything" has been put under him, it is clear that this does not include God himself, who put everything under Christ. [28]When he has done this, then the Son himself will be made subject to him who put everything under him, so that God may be all in all.*

Having delineated the consequences which would follow if there were no resurrection of the dead (as some Corinthians had affirmed), Paul now moves from that negative argumentation to a positive exposition of the meaning and significance of the fact that Christ has indeed been raised from the dead. As Wright points out, this passage "takes the form of a small apocalyptic account of the coming of God's kingdom, establishing God's rule over the world and defeating all the enemies of his kingdom, much as Daniel 7, itself drawing on the creation account in Genesis 2 [*sic*, 1], in which the human race was set in authority over the beasts, envisages YHWH's kingdom as a new creation."[82] Paul's discussion reflects a contrasting typology in which Christ, the ideal human and final representative of the human race, reverses the corruption introduced by the first human and original representative of the human race and restores things to the way they were originally intended, with God's dominion perfectly expressed in the restored creation such that he is perfectly glorified as the one who is "all in all."

Thiselton points out that commentators tend to "emphasize the existential assurance of vv. 20-25: because Christ was raised, those in Christ will be raised, since he is the firstfruit of the whole harvest still to come." He acknowledges that the point is valid but perhaps misses Paul's main emphasis, since "vv. 20-25 prepare the way for vv. 26-28, which is about God and God's purposes, as is this whole chapter."[83]

82. N. T. Wright, *The Resurrection of the Son of God*, 313.
83. Thiselton, 1224 (emphases removed).

**15:20** Paul indicates[84] that he is now starting out on a contrasting line of thought, this time focusing on how things really are as opposed to how they would be if the Corinthians were right:[85] *But Christ has indeed been raised from the dead, the firstfruits of those who have fallen asleep.* That Christ has indeed been raised[86] from the dead was established in vv. 4-8, through the listing of apostolic eyewitnesses, most of whom still lived to confirm the fact.

*Firstfruits* is a metaphor "derived from the OT where it denotes the first portion of the crop (or flock) which is offered in Thanksgiving to God. As such, the term signifies the pledge of the remainder, and concomitantly, the assurance of a full harvest . . . the first installment of that part which includes, as by synecdoche, the whole."[87] By way of this metaphor Paul underlines the link between our fate and the fate of Christ; Christ's resurrection is not an isolated event but guarantees something even more stupendous. Theologically it suggests that our resurrection is not wholly separate from Christ's resurrection, but earlier and later parts of the same event, with the earlier part serving as a promise and guarantee of that which is yet to come. "[T]he whole point of Paul's argument . . . is that in the destiny of Jesus Christ, the one 'raised from the dead, the firstfruits of those who have fallen asleep' (1 Cor 15:20), is our destiny."[88]

There is also a cultic and representative logic at work in the firstfruits metaphor. The firstfruits were a part of the sacrificial vocabulary of the Old Testament.[89] It "has to do with the flawless firstfruits of natural products, the firstfruits of human beings, animals, and plants . . . , all of which are owed to Yahweh (or the sanctuary)."[90] The firstfruits is connected to the larger group (harvest, offspring, etc.) it represents so that what is done with it has implications for the status that the rest has before God.[91] "As a representation of the rest, the [firstfruits] were offered to the deity as the neces-

84. Gk. Νυνὶ δέ (literally, "but now").

85. BDAG points out that νυνί is often used, as here, to "introduc[e] the real situation after an unreal conditional clause or sentence"; e.g., 1 Cor. 12:18; 15:20; Heb. 8:6; 9:26; as well as variant readings of 1 Cor. 5:11 and Heb. 11:16.

86. Paul uses a perfect tense verb to stress the present reality of Christ's risen status. The perfect tense by itself does not indicate that something is permanent; it only references its present state (i.e., Christ presently finds himself in a resurrected state). The rest of what Paul says about the resurrection and Christ's defeat of death confirms that Christ is not merely living now but will live forevermore.

87. Martinus C. de Boer, *The Defeat of Death: Apocalyptic Eschatology in 1 Corinthians 15 and Romans 5* (JSNTSup 22; Sheffield: JSOT Press, 1988), 109. For a full discussion see Joel White, *Die Erstlingsgabe im Neuen Testament* (Texte und Arbeiten zum neutestamentlichen Zeitalter, 45; Tübingen: Francke, 2007).

88. Grieb, "Last Things First: Karl Barth's Theological Exegesis of 1 Corinthians in *The Resurrection of the Dead,*" 55.

89. See A. Sand, "ἀπαρχή," *EDNT* 1:116 (cf. Exod. 23:19; 25:2, 3; 36:6; Lev. 22:12; Deut. 12:6, 11, 17; 18:4; 26:2, 10; Ezek. 44:30).

90. Sand, "ἀπαρχή," *EDNT* 1:116.

91. Garland, 706, cites Parry to the effect that the word suggests the "first of a kind, involving the rest in its character or destiny."

sary consecration of the possessions before further use was allowed."[92] Paul's use of the metaphor suggests that "Jesus has been raised as the first and the representative of those who will be raised."[93]

As the Messiah, Christ is not only the King and Lord of his people, but also the ideal representative of his people, such that the destiny of his people is directly tied to his own destiny. In Romans 11:16 Paul alludes to Numbers 15:17-21 and seems to mix the metaphor of firstfruits with the concept of leaven to suggest that they have a similar kind of relationship. Just as the introduction of leaven into dough ends up changing (leavening) the rest of the dough (cf. 1 Cor. 5:6), what is done with the firstfruits also changes the status of the larger group that it represents: "If the part of the dough offered as firstfruits is holy, then the whole batch is holy." In a general sense the status of Christ's followers is changed by whatever their firstfruits undergoes, and in the specific case of the resurrection their resurrection is not merely parallel or similar to Christ's but is preauthorized, promised, guaranteed, and initiated by it. As Thiselton points out, with the firstfruits metaphor we have at least three interrelated ideas: "(1) prior temporality; (2) representation of the same quality or character; and (3) promise or pledge of more of the same kind to come."[94]

**15:21-22** In these two verses Paul unpacks some of the logic of his use of the firstfruits metaphor, showing the similarity and difference between Adam and Christ and how they functioned as representatives of the human race. Each verse begins with "for,"[95] implying that they provide a further explanation for Paul's statement in v. 20, and each maintains a strongly parallel syntax[96] which highlights the comparisons and contrasts they highlight: *For since death came through a human being, the resurrection of the dead comes also through a human being.* In v. 21 no particular people are named but we are told that two contrasting realities (death and resurrection) were both introduced "through a human being." That is what they have in common.[97] It goes un-

92. Joost Holleman, *Resurrection and Parousia: A Traditio-Historical Study of Paul's Eschatology in I Corinthians 15* (NovTSup 84; Leiden: E. J. Brill, 1996), 49-50.

93. Holleman, *Resurrection and Parousia,* 51. Holleman follows Wedderburn in suggesting that this is based on the ancient idea of corporate solidarity between a group of people and their representative or leader (175).

94. Thiselton, 1224.

95. Gk. γάρ.

96.

| | | |
|---|---|---|
| ἐπειδὴ γὰρ | δι᾿ ἀνθρώπου | θάνατος, |
| καὶ | δι᾿ ἀνθρώπου | ἀνάστασις νεκρῶν. |
| ὥσπερ γὰρ | ἐν τῷ Ἀδὰμ | πάντες ἀποθνῄσκουσιν, |
| οὕτως καὶ | ἐν τῷ Χριστῷ | πάντες ζῳοποιηθήσονται. |
| (for since | through a man | [came] death) |
| (also | through a man | [came] resurrection of the dead) |
| (for just as | in Adam | all die) |
| (so also | in Christ | all will be made alive.) |

97. Cf. Theodoret, 227: "it was right for [Paul] to call him a human being, though knowing him to be God as well, so that by bringing out the commonality of nature he might strengthen the point about the resurrection."

mentioned but is also understood that death and resurrection were brought to human beings by those representative human beings. Paul is presenting the most concise form of the story of redemption imaginable: the archetypal problem of sin finds its eschatological resolution through the climactic breakthrough of the resurrection accomplished by Christ.[98] As Wright puts it, "by asserting in verses 21-22 that Jesus is the true human and the Messiah, Paul explains both *that* his resurrection is the beginning of a larger harvest and *how* that harvest will be accomplished."[99]

Translations are divided as to whether the key term[100] should be translated *a human being,* as by the TNIV, NRSV, NAB, and NET alternative reading, or "a man" as in the NIV, CSB, ESV, NASB, NLT, and main text of the NET Bible. Of course, the persons being referred to were both men, as v. 22 makes clear. But while the term used is grammatically masculine, it does not refer to a man as opposed to a woman, but refers to a member or members of the human race. Where "man" is understood in a purely generic sense (as it used to be), it may be an acceptable translation. In many cases, however, it either sounds very gender specific or is even proposed to have a gender-specific significance and therefore may be misleading. The point here is not the gender of the people who serve as our representatives (Adam and Christ), but that they do in fact serve as members and representatives of the larger group of human beings who find their identity and their destiny in the one who represents them.

In v. 22 the particular human beings are named (Adam and Christ), and it is made explicit that they bring other human beings into the death and resurrection that they themselves experienced: *For as in Adam all die, so in Christ all will be made alive.* Paul has moved from metaphor to typology, clarifying the point made in v. 20. The fact that he introduces Adam into his argument without any clarifying explanation suggests that he assumes some knowledge of the biblical story found in Genesis 1–3. He may have taught it to them himself when he founded the church in Corinth. To be *in Adam* is to be part of the group which finds in Adam its representative and leader, which finds its identity and destiny in Adam and what he has brought about for his people. To be *in Christ* is to be part of the group which finds in Christ its representative and leader, which finds its identity and destiny in Christ and what he has brought about for his people. All humans who have not yet found redemption through faith in Christ remain *in Adam.* Those who have entered into the promise of new life, the life of Christ, are *in Christ,* and will find that their initial experience of the newness of life was but a foretaste of the ultimate restoration of life that awaits them in the resurrection. The expressions *in Adam* and *in Christ* reinforce

98. For a somewhat fuller presentation see Ciampa, "The History of Redemption."

99. N. T. Wright, *The Resurrection of the Son of God,* 334 (his emphasis; cf. his fuller discussion there).

100. Gk. ἄνθρωπος.

the idea of corporate solidarity that is found in the firstfruits metaphor as well. Paul's use of the future tense — *will be made alive* — stresses the future, as-yet-unfulfilled aspect of Christ's redeeming work, in keeping with where the argument is going in vv. 23-28, where we are brought right to the ultimate consummation in which the reign of sin and death is completely demolished. The following verse makes it clear that by "being made alive" Paul has in mind the resurrection since those who belong to him will be made alive (= resurrected) "when he comes."

As in Romans 5:12-21, Paul stresses the differences between Adam and Christ. The consequences of the resurrection of Christ (life for all) correspond antithetically to the consequences of Adam's sin (death for all). The former has broken the power of the latter. However, Paul is not teaching universalism (see 1 Cor. 1:18); the unqualified "all" of v. 22 who will be made alive is clarified by v. 23 with the phrase "those who belong to him."[101]

**15:23** Having affirmed in the previous verse that "in Christ all will be made alive," Paul now clarifies what he meant, including the timing, participants, and nature of the life to which he was referring: *But in this order: Christ, the firstfruits; then, when he comes, those who belong to him.* The first clause *(But in this order)* is literally "each one in its/his/their own class/group."[102] Paul's delineation of the two classes or groups who would participate in the resurrection to power and glory may have had a powerful impact on any Corinthian Christians who thought of themselves as important because they belonged to some high-status social group in the city of Corinth (and may have been tempted to be embarrassed by or look down upon members of the church of more humble means), as well as on any who may have thought of themselves as unimportant due to their lack of worldly power or influence (including, e.g., slaves). The two orders of priority are Christ himself and then *all who belong to him.* There is no further class distinction that is relevant to the order to or benefits of the resurrection.

Christ was already identified as *the firstfruits* in v. 20 (see our comments on the metaphor there). He was already made alive (resurrected) "on the third day" (v. 4), while his people will experience the same at the *parousia (when he comes).* The word used for *when he comes*[103] was used as a technical term in both religious (sacred) contexts and official administrative contexts. "It refers to both the epiphany of God or a god . . . and to the

101. Cf. Witherington, 304: "Paul does not discuss the fate of those outside Christ here. It is possible to read various ideas into his silence. It could be that he saw the nonbeliever's resurrection as separate from the Christian resurrection, but we cannot be sure. His point is to focus on what will happen to Christians, so the analogy is not perfect. There is a corporate solidarity in death and in new life in each case, but not all will be in Christ, and so not all will be affected by him in the way that all are affected by Adam."

102. Cf. BDAG on Gk. τάγμα.

103. Gk. παρουσία.

official visit of an emperor or some other high-ranking official to a provincial city."[104] When used in reference to Christ, it is "nearly always of his Messianic Advent in glory to judge the world at the end of this age" (BDAG). As Radl suggests, it is difficult to determine whether the usage of the term in early Christianity is influenced primarily by its prior use in official contexts (suggested by the Christian usage in relation to the coming of the "Lord") or sacred contexts (suggested by the Christian usage in relation to the coming of the "savior"): "Since, however, the emperor, too, could be received not just as a ruler, but also as a savior, official [*parousia*] terminology with its sacral elements probably stands closest to Christian usage."[105]

The fact that Christ, the firstfruits, has already been made alive clarifies that the new life of which Paul speaks is the resurrected life which has been the subject of this entire chapter. It also becomes evident that Paul is not concerned in this chapter with any resurrection of the unrighteous to judgment, but is fully focused on the question of the resurrection of the righteous, and of Christians in particular. *Those who belong to him* clarifies that not all the dead will enjoy the resurrection life Paul is describing here, but only those who are Christ's (presumably including the faithful people of God who died before Christ's first coming).[106] The expression also reinforces the idea of corporate solidarity that was already introduced with the firstfruits metaphor in v. 20 and reiterated in the concept of "in Adam" and "in Christ" in v. 22.

There is no suggestion that Christ would come to take his people away (as in dispensational eschatology); the idea is that believers (and creation) will experience their ultimate renewal and glorification upon Christ's return.

**15:24** The timing implied by this verse is ambiguous, but the main point remains clear: the story ends with all things in perfect submission to the Father. *Then the end will come, when he hands over the kingdom to God the Father after he has destroyed all dominion, authority and power.* There has been some disagreement over the timing implied by the first word of this verse. In v. 23 there is a time gap between the resurrection of Christ and that of those who belong to him. The word translated *then* in this verse is different from the one translated "then" in v. 23, but they both mean "being next in order of time."[107] Premillennialists (those who believe that Revelation 20 refers to an extended reign of Christ after his second coming) believe *then*

104. W. Radl, "παρουσία," *EDNT* 3:44.

105. W. Radl, "παρουσία," *EDNT* 3:44.

106. So also Theodoret, 227 (although he thinks that Paul's discussion includes the resurrection of both the lost and the redeemed). The resurrection Paul is describing in this chapter is the one that follows and participates in Christ's own resurrection to life and glory (vv. 20-23); people are not baptized on behalf of dead who will be raised to condemnation (v. 29), and the resurrection body described in vv. 40-57 is clearly that of those raised to life and glory.

107. See BDAG on ἔπειτα (v. 23) and εἶτα (v. 24).

here, as in v. 23, allows for a great expanse of time, so that the millennial reign of Christ may take place between the "then" of v. 23 and the "then" of v. 24 just as two thousand years have taken place between the resurrection of Christ and the "then" of v. 23. Amillennialist interpreters believe that Paul suggests here that the reign of Christ concludes when his people are raised from the dead and Christ immediately turns the kingdom over to the Father. The words used for "then" give no clue as to whether there is any delay between events. In the case of v. 23 the fact that there is a delay between the resurrection of Christ and that of his people is known through other means. It is not at all clear that Paul had any expectation that Christ would have a distinct millennial reign as opposed to an ongoing role reigning with his people forever.[108] Paul himself never gave a hint that he had all the details worked out on exactly how God's kingdom would unfold.

While Revelation 20 speaks of a thousand-year reign of Christ (often referred to as the millennium), the oldest and widest of biblical traditions indicate that the Messiah's reign will never end (cf. 2 Sam. 7:16; 1 Chr. 17:14; Isa. 9:7; Ps. 89:36-37; Dan. 7:14, 18; Heb. 1:8; Rev. 11:15; 22:3), and of course Genesis 1:26-28 shows that God's original intention was to have a human vice-regent reigning over all of creation in a perfect reflection of his own righteous authority.[109] We will grapple with this tension in our interpretation of the following verses. Theodoret (who is navigating the christological issues of his own day) was on the right track: "In handing over the kingdom to the God and Father he is not himself stripped of the kingdom; rather, he brings into subjection the tyrannical devil and his assistants, and forces all to do obeisance and acknowledge the God of all."[110] Similarly, Thiselton recognizes the importance of seeing that "since God and Christ as Lord are 'One,' this emphasis is not upon a 'discontinuation' of Christ's lordship as such, but upon its culmination within the terms of its purpose for this world and Christ's kingdom here."[111]

We must address the question of the identity of the *he* who *has destroyed all dominion, authority and power.* A strong scholarly consensus affirms that it must be Christ, since he is clearly the one who hands over the kingdom to the Father and the syntax gives no hint that the subject has changed. On the other hand, the fact that vv. 25-28 suggest that this verse reflects Paul's gloss or interpretation of Psalm 110:1 and Psalm 8:6[112] would point in a different direction. His more explicit interpretations of the references to putting enemies or everything under the king's feet in Psalms 110

108. This is not to prejudge the question of the interpretation of Revelation 20, but to point out that one's interpretation of that passage should be taken to complement what one might find in Paul, not dictate what one must find there.

109. See Ciampa, "The History of Redemption," esp. 257-58, 276-79.

110. Theodoret, 228.

111. Thiselton, 1231.

112. For an insightful discussion of a similar phenomenon in Rom. 1:17 see Francis Watson, *Paul and the Hermeneutics of Faith* (London: T&T Clark, 2006), 43-77.

and 8 in the following verses indicate that he understands those texts to say it is God who does that.[113] That this would mean God's placing everything under Christ's feet is here put in terms of his destruction of all (competing) dominion, authority, and power. The question of the relationship between this line and the allusions or citations of the Psalm texts becomes more critical once we understand that Paul does not merely cite them to support a view he derives from some other source, but rather that what Paul knows about this subject he knows based on what he has discovered in those texts.[114]

Things become more ambiguous, however, when we recognize that although the Psalms speak of God's putting his enemies (or all things) under the feet of his royal king, it was understood that in actual practice the king was expected to go out as the instrument through whom God would act and display his strength and power over enemies. That is, God would put the king's enemies under his feet by giving him victory over them in battle.[115] So, as Holleman says, "the idea that Jesus destroys every rule, authority, and power (v. 24c) is not necessarily in discord with the idea that God places the enemies under Jesus' feet (vv. 25b and 27). Paul certainly regards God as the subject of the subjection of the enemies under Jesus' feet (vv. 25b, 27)."[116] It is true that the syntax would lead one to think that Christ is still the subject of the final verb of the verse (destroyed), and Holleman is right that this is not "in discord with the idea that God places the enemies under Jesus' feet." The logical relationship between this verse and the biblical texts, however, suggests that the very idea of an "end" that comes with an ending of or transition in the Lord's reign (the handing over of the kingdom) *after* someone does something would lead us to look to Psalm 110 and find in the motif of reigning "until" God does something that he gives up that reign *after* God does that thing. Paul may have been perfectly happy to express himself in such a potentially ambiguous manner, given his understanding (consistent with the psalm) that God acts through Christ, and Christ is the agent of God's reign.

Verses 24-28 reflect the motif of a dominion gone astray and needing

113. That is, since it seems that to destroy all dominion, authority, and power is Paul's gloss interpreting what it means to put the Lord's enemies under his feet and Paul makes it clear in the following verses that God the Father is the one who puts the Lord's enemies under his feet, it would follow that the Father is the one who destroys all dominion, authority, and power.

114. See Watson, *Paul and the Hermeneutics of Faith* (e.g., 43, 47, 76, 422), for similar observations on other texts.

115. See the discussion in Holleman, *Resurrection and Parousia*, 59-60. He points out that "[t]he poet of Psalm 110(109) presents his 'lord' (the king) as remaining passive: he sits on his throne while God is defeating his enemies by making them into a footstool. Yet the idea behind the image is that the king and God are so closely related that, although the king is the actual ruler, it is God who exercises his power through the king. The king is the perfect servant of God so that through him God reigns over Israel" (60).

116. Holleman, *Resurrection and Parousia*, 59.

to be crushed so that the proper dominion might be restored. The general idea would have been familiar to anyone in the Roman Empire. Just as a Roman emperor would send out his leading general to put down seditious movements and rebellious vassal states and restore the emperor's authority throughout the empire, God has sent Christ to subdue all rebellion and opposition, to destroy all the enemies of God's kingdom, and to restore all of creation to its proper submission to the Father for his glory and the good of all creation.[117] As Wright points out, this description of Christ's role in reigning over all creation reminds us that Christ, "as the final Adam, the start of the renewed human race (compare Colossians 1.18b), is not only the model for the new type of humanity. He possesses the authority to bring it into being."[118]

Paul's description in this verse reflects the Old Testament and Jewish understanding of what would happen when God finally stepped in to put the world to rights again.[119] It seems likely that early Jewish and Christian conceptions of God's coming kingdom were shaped by Israel's and the church's knowledge and experience of world-dominating pagan suzerains.[120] The pretensions of pagan rulers were seen to parody the kind of sovereign rule that God himself is expected to exercise on behalf of his people one day, even as those same pagan reigns may well have informed Jewish and Christian understanding (by both comparison and contrast) of what such a reign might look like. To give an example of a similar pattern in the Old Testament, we note that the language of the submission of "peoples, languages, and nations" that is used in relation to the "one like a son of man" in Daniel 7:14 relates to the use of the same language with respect to Nebuchadnezzar in 3:4, 7, 29; 4:1, to Belshazzar in 5:19, and to Darius in 6:25.

Remarkably, the words translated *dominion* and *authority* in 1 Corinthians 15:24 are found in the ancient Greek version of Daniel 7:14, "and to him was given the dominion and the honor and the kingship, and all peoples, tribes, languages shall be subject to him. His authority is an everlasting authority, which will not pass away" (NETS translation of Theodotion's version). The words translated *dominion* and *authority* are found in both the Old Greek and Theodotion's version of the text. They also appear in both the Old Greek and Theodotion's version of the depiction of the end in

117. The wording here is deliberately chosen so that either the one being sent or the one doing the sending could be understood to be the one who puts down the rebellion (whether personally in the one case, or through his agent in the other).

118. N. T. Wright, *The Resurrection of the Son of God*, 342.

119. For a popular-level explanation of Christianity in terms of God's plan to "put the world to rights," see N. T. Wright, *Simply Christian: Why Christianity Makes Sense* (New York: HarperOne, 2006), passim.

120. This paragraph draws on Roy E. Ciampa, "Scriptural Language and Ideas," in *As It Is Written: Studying Paul's Use of Scripture* (ed. Stanley N. Porter and Christopher D. Stanley; Atlanta: Society of Biblical Literature, 2008), 53 n. 36.

terms of the termination of violent, wicked, and oppressive world powers and the establishment of God's kingdom in Daniel 7:27: "Then the sovereignty, power and greatness of all the kingdoms under heaven will be handed over to the holy people of the Most High. His kingdom will be an everlasting kingdom, and all rulers will worship and obey him" (TNIV). Earlier, in Daniel 2:44 we had learned that after a series of pagan world empires have had their day, "the God of heaven will set up a kingdom that will never be destroyed, nor will it be left to another people. It will crush all those kingdoms and bring them to an end, but it will itself endure forever."

Clearly, by *all dominion, authority and power* Paul means all the competing, corrupted, and perverted dominions, authorities, and powers that have been unleashed through Adam's idolatrous perversion of the reign given him by God in Genesis 1. An anti-imperial ideology is clearly at work here, as in the texts from Daniel cited above. As Witherington suggests, "Paul is trying to supplant the imperial eschatology which was clearly extant in Corinth and which looked to the emperor as the father and benefactor . . . with an eschatology that involves Christ and a truly divine Father."[121] The dominions which seemed to hold sway in the political, religious, and spiritual realms would all be destroyed in the face of the glorious appearance of the fullness of God's kingdom. This would also apply to the tendency in every human heart to assert one's own ultimate autonomy as a kingdom of one. No rebellious dominion, authority, or power may be allowed to stand if true peace, liberty, and righteousness are to reign. It is in this environment that God's oppressed and marginalized people may finally experience the freedom, righteousness, and peace for which they have hungered and thirsted. As Barth insists, "In the Resurrection of Jesus Christ man is once for all exalted, and appointed to discover with God his right against all his foes and thus set free to live a new life." That is, to live "the life for which God has set him free in the death of Jesus Christ."[122]

The two words from this verse that are found in the Greek versions of Daniel mentioned above also appear together several times in Pauline letters and suggest that for Paul the primary referents are spiritual or demonic powers. In Ephesians 1:20-21 Paul says that when God raised Christ from the dead, he seated him "at his right hand in the heavenly realms, far above all rule and authority, power and dominion." In Ephesians 6:12 Paul notes that "our struggle is not against flesh and blood, but against the rulers, against the authorities, against the powers of this dark world and against the spiritual forces of evil in the heavenly realms." And in Colossians 2:15 Paul adds that Christ "disarmed the powers and authorities" and "made a

121. Witherington, 305, also cited by Thiselton, 1232. See the excursus on Roman imperial eschatology in Witherington, 295-98 and the brief comments in N. T. Wright, *The Resurrection of the Son of God*, 337-38.

122. Karl Barth, *Dogmatics in Outline* (New York: Harper & Row, 1959), 121.

public spectacle of them, triumphing over them by the cross."[123] Even if the primary referents are rebellious spiritual powers, Paul's point must not be restricted to them. Psalms 8 and 110 refer to the submission of enemies (Ps. 110:1) or all things (Ps. 8:6) to the king. Paul's language should be understood in a similarly comprehensive manner, so that it includes "any kind of structural opposition to God, whether social, political, economic, ethical, spiritual," or other.[124]

Paul hints at the point that Adam, who was given dominion by God in Genesis 1:26-28, introduced a dominion of sin and death rather than the dominion of righteousness and life which would bring glory to God. This is more explicit in Romans. Romans 5:14 says, "death reigned from the time of Adam. . . ." Romans 5:17 states that "death reigned through that one man. . . ." The dominion of death is tied to that of sin. Romans 5:21 asserts that "sin reigned in death," Romans 6:12 warns that we are not to "let sin reign" in their mortal bodies, and 6:14 affirms that "sin shall no longer be your master." These texts, and especially 1 Corinthians 15:26, suggest that Paul has the dominions of death and sin particularly in mind, with sin and death personified such that they stand for all of the corrupt spiritual powers let loose in the world by Adam. The power of death and sin is to be utterly *destroyed*[125] as Christ brings the kingdom of God to its climactic consummation. As pointed out in our opening comments on this verse, this is Paul's interpretation of Christ's fulfillment of Psalms 110:1 and 8:6. Thus, "destroying" his enemies is Paul's interpretation of what is in mind when the Psalms say that God will put them under Christ's feet (note the alternation between "putting under his feet" and "destroying" again in vv. 25-27).[126] Their power and influence in the world are to be finally abolished.

Unfortunately, this portrayal of Christ's role in the world has too often served to underwrite violent and oppressive rule on the part of those who see themselves as agents of God's kingdom. While Christians may well have significant concerns about the ideological criticism of Scripture itself, they must always be prepared to engage in the ideological criticism of interpretations and applications of Scripture lest it continue to be used for evil in the guise of righteousness, oppressing the weak and powerless for the sake of the agendas of the powerful.[127] The validity of this theology and expression of political power is wholly dependent upon the infinite

123. The complete list of Pauline texts which combine the two words is as follows: 1 Cor. 15:24; Eph. 1:21; 3:10; 6:12; Col. 1:16; 2:10, 15; Tit. 3:1.

124. Thiselton, 1232.

125. Gk. καταργέω, here "to cause someth[ing] to come to an end or to be no longer in existence, *abolish, wipe out, set aside*" (BDAG).

126. In his interpretation of Psalm 110, G. A. F. Knight (*Psalms* [vol. 2; The Daily Study Bible; Louisville: Westminster John Knox, 1982], 180) suggests "annihilate all evil" as the meaning of "make your enemies your footstool."

127. Postcolonial criticism is particularly concerned about the kinds of issues raised by texts like this one and their reception history.

wisdom and righteousness of the one who destroys all other opposing powers and imposes his own kingdom on the world. When such a project is carried out (even on a lesser scale) by powerful (but not infinitely wise or righteous) human leaders and governments, whether under the Babylonian, Persian, Greek, Roman, or even modern empires, it is done in the name of righteousness and peace and often with a claim to divine (or natural) mandate. But it always ends up reflecting a parody of the perfect kingdom of righteousness and peace that could be established only by the infinitely wise and righteous King known for his self-sacrificial love for all his creatures, especially the weak and powerless. It is a sad irony that texts such as this one which speak of the ultimate condemnation of all empires but God's have nevertheless sometimes come to empower those who falsely perceive themselves to be following a divine model suited to their own ambitions.

**15:25** The *for*[128] at the beginning of this verse suggests that it is the basis for Paul's statement in the previous verse: *For he must reign until he has put all his enemies under his feet.* Paul's wording conflates the language of Psalm 110:1 with that of Psalm 8:6. Wright notes that "[t]his is not a mere 'appeal to scripture', as though Paul were mounting an argument about something else and needed to drag in a few proof-texts":

> He is thinking his way through a theology of creation and of humankind, and the biblical allusions indicate the narrative of which the resurrection of Jesus now forms the climax, helping the story to its intended goal. . . . [T]he failure of humankind ('Adam') to be the creator's wise, image-bearing steward over creation has not led the creator to rewrite the vocation, but rather to send the Messiah as the truly human being. The purpose is that in his renewed, resurrected human life he can be and do, for humankind and all creation, what neither humankind nor creation could do for themselves.[129]

*He must reign* reflects both "You . . . crowned him" and "made him ruler" from Psalm 8:5-6 and "sit at my right hand" (the position of a co- or vice-regent) in Psalm 110:1. Paul's reference to *all his enemies* reflects a conflation of "all things" from Psalm 8 and "your enemies" from Psalm 110. The reference to reigning *until* his enemies have been subdued comes from Psalm 110:1 ("Sit at my right hand until I make your enemies a footstool for your feet"). Psalm 8:6 contributes "put all . . . under his feet" (110:1 LXX has, "as a footstool for your feet"). Both 110:1 and 8:6 mention the king's feet.

The two texts clearly are dealing with a parallel thought and share parallel language (all things or enemies being submitted to the feet of the royal figure). Thus we are dealing with a type of *gezerah shawah* (a tradi-

128. Gk. γάρ.

129. N. T. Wright, *The Resurrection of the Son of God,* 334.

tional Jewish technique of interpreting two texts with shared terms or expressions [or sometimes merely shared themes] in light of each other), although it must be kept in mind that there is not just a lexical link between the two texts but a strong thematic connection as well. While Psalm 8 has Genesis 1 in mind and refers in the first place to the role for which God created humanity and Psalm 110:1 has the role of the Davidic king in mind, it would be a mistake to think the two texts are therefore unrelated. Psalm 110 states that God has in mind that the king will fulfill his original (and ultimate) intentions for humanity. The use of the Psalms suggests that the referent of *he has put* is God, and this is confirmed in vv. 27-28.[130] Hays comments that in 15:25-27 Paul "alludes to Ps 110:1 and Ps 8:6 as prophecies of Christ's enthronement at the right hand of God and ultimate authority over all creation. Thus Paul offers the earliest documentation of a christological exegesis of these psalms."[131] Together the psalms to which Paul alludes support his claim that all powers and authorities will be placed under Christ's feet and thus be subjected to God. In vv. 27-28 Paul's language follows Psalm 8 rather than 110, but both are clearly in mind here. Psalms 8 and 110 are also found together in Ephesians 1:20-22 and Hebrews 2:5-8.

In Psalm 110:1 YHWH promises to make the king's enemies a footstool for his feet. To "makes someone a footstool for someone else" means to "subject one pers[on] to another, so that the other can put a foot on the subject's neck."[132] The idea of defeated kings being treated like a footstool may be found in Joshua 10:24 (and less precisely, Isa. 51:23). As Allen indicates, "reflection of an ancient Near Eastern cultural pattern is evident: in the El Amarna letters vassals refer to themselves as the footstools of Pharaoh, while a similar promise features in an oracle from Marduk to the Assyrian king Esarhaddon."[133] What Psalm 110:1 has in mind by making the king's "enemies a footstool for [his] feet" is clarified in vv. 5-6 of the same psalm, which say, "The Lord is at your right hand; he [i.e., the Lord at the king's right hand] will crush kings on the day of his wrath. He will judge the nations, heaping up the dead and crushing the rulers of the whole earth." The Psalm's focus on crushing and judging kings, nations, and rulers is consistent with Paul's own reference to the destruction of all dominion, authority, and power in the previous verse.

The idea that this verse suggests that Christ's reign would come to an end was one that the Fathers regularly sought to correct. Jerome asks, "Will the Lord rule only until he has put all his enemies under his feet? Will he then stop ruling?" His answer? "Obviously it is only then that he will really begin to rule in the full sense of the word!"[134] Cyril of Jerusalem argues, "If

130. See Holleman, *Resurrection and Parousia,* 59-60.

131. Hays, *Echoes of Scripture,* 84.

132. See BDAG, "ὑποπόδιον."

133. Leslie C. Allen, *Psalms 101–150* (rev. ed.; WBC 21; Nashville: Thomas Nelson, 2002), 115.

134. *Against Helvidius* 6, cited in Bray, 161.

he is king before he has finally defeated his enemies, must he not be all the more king when he has completely mastered them?"[135] Theodoret supports the same view, arguing that "*until* here does not suggest time, but brings out that he will subject absolutely everyone"[136] (presumably in both the psalm and Paul's use of it). Gregory of Nazianzus also deals with the meaning of *until:*

> Must he cease to be king or be removed from heaven? Why, who shall make him cease, or for what cause? What a bold and very anarchical interpreter you are, and yet you have heard that of his kingdom there shall be no end. Your mistake arises from not understanding that "until" is not always exclusive of what comes after but asserts up to that time, without denying what comes after it. To take a single instance, how else would you understand "Lo, I am with you always, even unto the end of the world"? Does it mean that he will no longer be so afterward?[137]

While that may well be a stress that is easily missed, it seems the word "until" in Psalm 110:1 governs and accounts for much of the language of temporal sequence in 1 Corinthians 15:24-28, including "the end," "when he hands over the kingdom," and "after he has destroyed" in v. 24; "until he has put" in v. 25; and "when he has done this" in v. 28. The influence of the psalm on Paul's theology and wording should not be underestimated. For an attempt to do justice to the valid points made by the Fathers (and the biblical texts listed in the second paragraph of our comments on v. 24, which also guided the Fathers) as well as the fact that this passage suggests some transition in or end to Christ's reign once his enemies have been destroyed, see our comments on v. 28 and the quotations from Augustine found there.

**15:26** Paul brings his discussion of the destruction of God's enemies back to the theme of death which was introduced in v. 21. *The last enemy to be destroyed is death.* The word *enemy* comes from Paul's allusion to Psalm 110:1 in the previous verse, and the idea of a *last* enemy suggests reflection on Psalm 110 (and the point at which the "until" mentioned there would be reached) enhanced by Psalm 8 (that Psalm 110 had all the king's enemies in mind is understood to be implicit, while Psalm 8 more explicitly mentions "all things"). Paul's paraphrase in the previous verse mentioned "all his enemies," which prepared for this reference to the last of them. *Destroyed* comes from Paul's paraphrase of Psalm 8/110 in v. 24 (where "destroy" = "put under his feet"). The reference to and focus on *death* clarifies the rele-

135. *Catechetical Lectures* 15.29, cited in Bray, 161.

136. Theodoret, 228. So also Conzelmann, 272-73: "The purpose is not the temporal limitation of the sovereignty of Christ, but the fact that it is guaranteed by God and attains its goal."

137. *Theological Orations* 30, *On the Son* 4; cited in Bray, 161.

vance of this whole discussion of Christ's victory over enemies for the issue of the resurrection that governs this chapter. It is not just that Jesus reigns to bring in the fullness of the kingdom, but that his mission includes the destruction of death itself, and for death to be completely undone resurrection is required. A disembodied postmortem existence or the immortality of the soul would support an essentially Gnostic and quite limited victory over death, while resurrection bespeaks an absolute victory over and destruction of death. This will be Paul's point in vv. 54-55: "When the perishable has been clothed with the imperishable, and the mortal with immortality, then the saying that is written will come true: 'Death has been swallowed up in victory'" (v. 54). Then the victory taunt may be sung: "Where, O death, is your victory? Where, O death, is your sting?" (v. 55).

In Genesis 2:17 death was threatened as the consequence of the original sin against God and for his glory. In our comments on v. 24 we pointed out that in Romans 5:14 Paul says, "death reigned from the time of Adam," and that in Romans 5:17 he says, "death reigned through that one man." Romans 5:21 suggests that the dominion of death is tied to that of sin since "sin reigned in death." While sin brought death into the world, it may be argued that since sin first brought death into the world it has been the universal experience of spiritual death that has led to the flourishing and reign of the first sin in death.

**15:27** Paul has been interpreting Psalm 110:1 in light of Psalm 8, especially focusing on the former text's reference to the putting down of the king's enemies (see our comments on v. 25). Now he shifts his focus to the language of Psalm 8 in particular. The first sentence, *For he "has put everything under his feet,"* probably relates directly to v. 26. The *For* explains that even if the readers may not have intuitively thought of "death" as a dominion, authority, or power that would be put down (v. 24), Psalm 8, with its language of *everything* being placed in submission, means that we should think in the most comprehensive terms possible, that even death must be destroyed (thus the need for resurrection, as pointed out in our comments on v. 26). But once the idea of a comprehensive submission of everything to Christ is raised, it leads to the refinement Paul provides here. Will absolutely everything and everyone be made to submit to Christ? The answer is found in the psalm itself. There could only be one exception. If we are told that someone will place everything under Christ, presumably that someone is not included in the "everything": *Now when it says that "everything" has been put under him,*[138] *it is clear that this does not include God himself, who put everything under Christ.* The words *when it says* make it clear that Paul is citing Scripture (Ps. 8:6), as most English translations indicate with quotation marks around *"has put everything under his feet"* in the first part of the

138. Although his original quotation used the aorist indicative form (ὑπέταξεν), Paul's comment on it here employs the perfect indicative form (ὑποτέτακται), suggesting the state of subjection in which all things will be found once Christ's work is complete.

verse.[139] Paul has explained why death is to be destroyed (v. 26), or, more accurately, how human beings, through whom death came (v. 22), can exercise dominion over all things through their participation in resurrection along with Christ. If with Psalm 110 authority and dominion are considered in relation the enemies of God and his king, with Psalm 8 they are considered in relation to all of creation.

Psalm 8 is a psalm of descriptive praise for God's majestic work in creation. Verses 3-8 allude to Genesis 1:26-30 and comment specifically on the creation of humankind in the image of God and their function as God's vice-regent over the earth. The theme of the reign of God over all creation through his human vice-regent, and his glory displayed in that dominion, governs the psalm. That the king's reign is authorized by and serves as a reflection of God's reign is suggested in the psalm by the fact that it is God who does the crowning and gives the rule to the Adamic figure. The image is of a great king and suzerain who has the power and authority to grant other kings the right to reign over all or part(s) of his realm. It would be understood that the great king granting that right to reign would never be subject to the one to whom it is granted. Wright sees clearly that Paul is using the Psalms "to build a theology of new creation as the fulfilment of the intention for the old."[140]

The Adamic dominion motif from Genesis 1 also underwrites numerous Old Testament and Jewish texts about the idealized universal dominion to which the Davidic king was destined (e.g., Psalms 2, 65, 68, 72, 89, 98, 102, 138, and 148, Micah 7, Zechariah 9, and Daniel 7), although a messianic interpretation of Psalms 8 and 110 is not evident in the Jewish literature.[141]

As we pointed out in our comments on v. 25, Psalms 8 and 110 are linked by both *gezerah shawah* and an organic thematic connection. Paul deftly conjoins the two psalms. He had already incorporated the key word "all/everything" into his allusion to Psalm 110 in v. 25, and he had reduced "make a footstool for . . . feet" from Psalm 110 to "put under . . . feet" as in

139. Paul follows the LXX (which is in basic agreement with the MT) with just two differences. First, he changes the verb from a second-person to a third-person form so that "you have put" (ὑπέταξας) becomes "he has put" (ὑπέταξεν). The second-person form is present in three of the other four New Testament citations of the psalm: Phil. 3:21; Heb. 2:6-8; 1 Pet. 3:22 (cf. Eph. 1:22, which conforms to the wording found in 1 Cor. 15:27). This suggests that the change is due to literary contexts. While second-person verbs run through Psalm 8 in both the MT and the LXX, third-person verbs surround the quotation in 1 Corinthians 15. Paul uses the preposition ὑπό instead of the LXX's ὑποκάτω. There is no difference in meaning (they both mean "under"). It may simply be that Paul preferred the former, which is common in his letters, to the latter, which he never uses (and is used only infrequently in the New Testament).

140. N. T. Wright, *The Resurrection of the Son of God,* 335.

141. D.-A. Koch, *Die Schrift als Zeuge des Evangeliums,* 245. Jewish texts that refer to creation also carry the implication of God's dominion and authority over it (e.g., Sir. 16:17-20; *4 Ezra* 3:1-5; 6:38-59; Philo, *On the Creation of the World* 88; H. H. Drake Williams, "The Psalms in 1 and 2 Corinthians," in *The Psalms in the New Testament* [ed. Steve Moyise and Maarten J. J. Menken; Edinburgh: T&T Clark, 2004], 172).

Psalm 8. He interprets this psalm as applying to the Messiah as the one who brings to fulfillment God's intentions for humanity.[142] His point is that Christ as the last Adam retrieved the situation the first Adam lost. It is an explicitly christological use of the Old Testament, with the Old Testament notion of corporate representation as its presupposition; Christ represents his people (see 15:22-23).[143] The glorious destiny of humankind to be crowned and receive dominion, which we failed to grasp, is fulfilled for us through Jesus. The relationship between vv. 26 and 27 makes it clear that Paul "interprets 'all things' to include 'death.'"[144]

**15:28** Paul now brings us to the climax of the whole biblical narrative, where God's sovereign rule over all is perfectly reflected: *When he has done this, then the Son himself will be made subject to him who put everything under him, so that God may be all in all.* Paul continues to interpret Psalm 110:1 and Psalm 8:6 together (see the comments on vv. 24-27). *When he has done this* (literally, "when all things have been subjected to him") reflects the influence of the "until" in Psalm 110:1 (the king would reign until his enemies were in subjection or had been destroyed). That God *put everything under him* comes from Psalm 8:6. That the king in question would be God's son would be understood from the suzerain-vassal relationship implied by a great king granting another king authority to rule, as well as by the promise to David in 2 Samuel 7:14, reflected also in Psalm 2:7.

This verse must be interpreted with care to avoid a few possible misunderstandings. First, on a quick surface reading it could be taken to suggest that Christ is not subject to the Father at present — that he is somehow acting in an autonomous and even disobedient manner. Of course that is not what Paul means, and his meaning must inform what he said earlier about Christ reigning until everything was in submission to him. To understand Paul we will return to the analogy of a Roman emperor who sends out his top military general to quash a rebellion in the empire, raised in our comments on v. 24. While the general is out executing the war, he is surrounded by the symbols and instruments of power, and it is he who serves as the physical expression of the power of the empire in his battles against the rebels. Once he has accomplished his mission, however, he is expected to return to Rome, acknowledge that he is in submission to the emperor, and show that he does not intend to use the power of his armies to take over the empire by force. He does not cease to be a general or to have great power and influence, but the mission for which he was commissioned has been accomplished, and in a sense he becomes somewhat like a sword which has been returned to its sheath. As a general engaged against the enemies of the em-

142. Garland, 713, points out that "Paul interprets this psalm as applying to the Messiah, not to Adam or human beings in general." Paul indicates elsewhere that believers are also expected to reign (1 Cor. 4:8; Eph. 2:6; 2 Tim. 2:12); presumably Christ makes that possible through his own personal fulfillment of Psalm 8.

143. Heb. 2:5-8 is comparable in its use of Psalms 8 and 110.

144. Garland, 713.

pire, he exercised shock- and awe-inspiring power. Once the mission is accomplished, there is no need for him to continue to wield such power. It was, in theory at least, all about reasserting the authority, dominion, and glory of the empire and emperor, not about gaining power for himself.

As Augustine says, "It is necessary for Christ's kingdom to be manifested to such a degree until all his enemies confess that he does reign."[145] That is, "He reigns forever. However, in respect to the war waged under him against the devil, this conflict will obviously continue 'until he has put all his enemies under his feet.' But afterward there will be no conflict, since we shall enjoy an everlasting peace."[146] As pointed out above, Christ's reign was not a matter of simply holding the office of king for an extended period, but of reasserting God's kingly power against the disobedient and rebellious powers of this present age. The time will come when that particular form of or approach to reigning (the putting down of the enemies) will naturally come to an end. That time will be once the last enemy has been destroyed.

This verse was also problematical for the church fathers in that it was used by heretics to argue that since Christ would be made subject to the Father, he must not share the same divinity as the Father and must not be of the same essence as the Father. The standard response is summarized well by Augustine: "The rule of Catholic faith is this: when the Scriptures say of the Son that he is less than the Father the Scriptures mean in respect to the assumption of humanity. But when the Scriptures point out that he is equal, they are understood in respect to his deity."[147]

Modern commentators have suggested that Paul's concern was "to avert any mistaken impression that somehow God becomes subject to Christ or that Christ's reign infringes on God's absolute sovereignty."[148] Schweizer, for example, points out that "whenever 'the Son' is used absolutely, it calls to mind the contrast to 'the Father' and at the same time it describes a subordinate position in relation to the Father. In the same way, 1 Corinthians 15:28 uses this expression in an eschatological context to warn against the misunderstanding of Christ the Lord of the end-time as a second God alongside the Father."[149] Others have proposed that Paul's line of thought reflects either the fact that it was common in the Roman and Corinthian context for one to focus their worship on some personally preferred deity and to neglect "any serious reverence for a supreme, central

145. *Questions* 69.5, cited in Bray, 161.

146. *Questions* 69.8, cited in Bray, 161.

147. *Questions* 69.1, cited by Bray, 164. So also Chrysostom, *Homiliae in Epistulam i ad Corinthios* 39.7 (NPNF[1] 12:237-38) and Theodoret, 228-29. The challenge of respecting Christ's two natures "without confusion, without change, without division, without separation" (Definition of Chalcedon) will always be with us.

148. Garland, 713.

149. E. Schweizer, *The Good News according to Mark* (Richmond: John Knox, 1970), 283, cited by Garland, 813-14.

deity over the universe"[150] or that the Corinthian believers in particular (following such a tendency) were tempted to overplay the significance of Christ at the expense of recognizing the centrality of God the Father.[151]

Such mirror-readings are unnecessary and not supported by the evidence. It seems more likely that the focus on God's being all in all is a natural conclusion to Paul's own theological panorama. Richardson is certainly right in pointing out that the focus here on God the Father is "in line with Paul's theology elsewhere."[152] In Philippians 2 Paul starts with God's exaltation of Christ: "God exalted [Christ] to the highest place and gave him the name that is above every name, that at the name of Jesus every knee should bow, in heaven and on earth and under the earth, and every tongue acknowledge that Jesus Christ is Lord." But the story does not end there, for this glorification of Christ turns out to be "to the glory of God the Father" (Phil. 2:9-11; cf. Rom. 16:27; Gal. 1:3-5).

Since the language of "Father" and "Son" is covenantal language, it reminds us that the Son's role in the biblical and covenantal meta-narrative was always that of restoring and reflecting the glorious reign of the Father over all of his dominion. Paul simply takes us to the ultimate conclusion of the biblical narrative of redemption and restoration, which is that the creation which went astray and which the Son was commissioned to redeem and restore has come full circle to its complete submission to God — and beyond. But it was always about bringing creation to perfect submission to God. As Barth puts it, "To bring about the 'God who is all in all' *such* is the mission and significance of Christ."[153] This verse does not demean or marginalize Christ, but emphasizes that his mission will be fully and perfectly accomplished.

Our analysis of the structure of this letter has pointed out the programmatic structural role played by 1 Corinthians 6:20 and 10:31. As Paul approached the conclusion to the extended sections focusing on sexual immorality (chs. 5–6) and idolatry (chs. 8–10) and looked forward to the following sections in which a positive exposition would be given of principles of sexual purity (ch. 7) and instructions for the proper worship of the one true God (chs. 11–14), he introduced the glory of God as a fundamental warrant for the purity that should reflect our lives. At the point of transition in the discussion of sexual immorality and sexual purity Paul called on his readers to glorify God with their bodies (6:20). At the point of transition in the discussion of idolatry (esp. food offered to idols) and proper worship, Paul says, "whether you eat or drink or whatever you do, do it all for the glory of God" (10:31). While this verse does not explicitly use the language of glory, Paul's climactic statement that Christ's submission to the

150. Moffatt, 250, cited by Thiselton, 1237.

151. See Thiselton's discussion (1237) of Neil Richardson, *Paul's Language about God* (JSNTSup 99; Sheffield: Sheffield Academic Press, 1994), 114-15.

152. N. Richardson, *Paul's Language about God*, 114-15.

153. K. Barth, *Resurrection of the Dead*, 179 (his emphasis), cited by Thiselton, 1236.

Father after all of creation has been brought into full submission to him would be so that *God may be all in all* reflects a similar idea. The context suggests that for God to be all in all is for his reign to hold full sway, for his will to "be supreme in every quarter and in every way."[154] In other words, it is for God to be perfectly honored such that his glory is not diminished in any way but fully recognized and reflected in all creation.

Christ's resurrection and subjection or destruction of all his and God's enemies was and is essential to the realization of the renewed creation in which God is, as he ought to be, *all in all.* Augustine muses: "God will be the consummation of all our desiring — the object of our unending vision, of our unlessening love, of our unwearying praise. And in this gift of vision, the response of love, this paean of praise, all alike will share, as all will share in everlasting life."[155] Of course, if Christ does all that he does (including dying for our sins, v. 3) so that *God may be all in all,* certainly there is nothing in all the universe that ought to distract us from seeking to do the same. Sampley shows how critical the notion of Christ belonging to God is to the letter: "As he sketches the grandeur of God's culminating purposes, Paul's language drifts toward doxology: In the end, even Christ will be made subject to God, who is already in 3:23 credited as being the one to whom all else, including Christ, belongs and who in 8:6 is declared to be the one from whom are all things and for whom people exist (cf. 11:3)."[156]

## D. Exhortation in Light of Positive and Negative Responses to the Resurrection of the Dead, 15:29-34

> [29]*Now if there is no resurrection, what will those do who are baptized for the dead? If the dead are not raised at all, why are people baptized for them?*
> [30]*And as for us, why do we endanger ourselves every hour?* [31]*I face death every day — yes, just as surely as I boast about you in Christ Jesus our Lord.*[157]
> [32]*If I fought wild beasts in Ephesus with no more than human hopes, what have I gained? If the dead are not raised,*
>
> *"Let us eat and drink,*
> *for tomorrow we die."*
>
> [33]*Do not be misled: "Bad company corrupts good character."* [34]*Come back to your senses as you ought, and stop sinning; for there are some who are ignorant of God — I say this to your shame.*

154. Fee, 760. Cf. Barrett, 361; Garland, 714.

155. Augustine, *City of God* 22.30, cited by Bray, 165.

156. Sampley, 982.

157. A good number of witnesses (ℵ, A, B, K, P, 33, 81, 104, 365, 1175, 2464, lat, sy, co) include a vocative "brothers and sisters" (ἀδελφοί) in this verse, but the shorter reading, which omits it (supported by $\mathfrak{P}^{46}$, D, F, G, Ψ, 075, 0243, 1739, 1881, 𝔐, b, Ambrosiaster, Pelagius), is probably to be preferred (as reflected in most English translations).

Paul begins with a series of rhetorical questions (four in all) intended to show how absurd it would be to think that the resurrection is not at the heart of the Christian message. It is a key foundation for Christian baptism and for Paul's courageous and self-sacrificing work on behalf of the gospel. Paul is moving toward an even stronger use of the diatribal style in vv. 35-49, where he will introduce an imaginary or hypothetical interlocutor or debate partner whose viewpoint he will dismantle.

While the hypothetical situation, "if the dead are not raised," is behind this passage as it was behind vv. 12-19, here Paul does not focus on what the consequences would be if there is no resurrection. He focuses, rather, on the impossibility of explaining certain kinds of Christian behavior apart from their grounding in the resurrection teaching (vv. 29-32a) and on the need for the Corinthians to validate those same behaviors rather than adopting a position that would warrant corrupt living rather than the life of God's renewed humanity (vv. 32b-34). Along the way Paul cites Isaiah 22:13 (v. 32) and a line from the Greek dramatist Menander (v. 33). As he has done at numerous points throughout the letter (esp. in chs. 3–4 and 9) Paul uses himself as an example for the Corinthians once more here (vv. 30-32).

The first verse of this passage is undoubtedly the most difficult verse to interpret in the whole letter (with over forty different interpretations[158]). Understanding its relationship with the rest of this passage, and the role of this passage as a whole within the chapter, is also challenging. We will need to pay close attention to the contextual clues to provide an interpretation that is reasonable and convincing.

**15:29** Certain Christian behaviors, Paul argues, are inexplicable apart from their grounding in the resurrection of the dead. In a moment he will come to his own dangerous decisions (vv. 30-32). He begins, however, with an ambiguous reference to baptismal practice which has raised questions ever since: *if there is no resurrection, what will those do who are baptized for the dead? If the dead are not raised at all, why are people baptized for them?* Paul has already discussed the serious moral, theological, and existential implications that would follow *if there is no resurrection.* Here he raises the issue of the incongruence between such a view and the practice of people *who are baptized for the dead.*

The question *what will those do?* may be understood in a variety of ways, but Garland rightly points to the context for the clue to its meaning: "The parallel in 15:32, 'What does it profit me?' suggests that it implies, 'What good will it do them?' If there is no resurrection of the dead, nothing

158. For a thorough discussion of interpretative proposals see B. M. Foschini, "'Those Who Are Baptized for the Dead,' I Cor. 15:29, An Exegetical Historical Dissertation," *CBQ* 12 (1950), 260-76, 379-88; 13 (1951), 46-78, 172-98, 276-83; and Michael F. Hull, *Baptism on Account of the Dead (1 Cor:15:29): An Act of Faith in the Resurrection* (Atlanta: Society of Biblical Literature, 2005).

could possibly accrue from that rite."[159] Similarly, the NAB translates the phrase "what will people accomplish?"[160]

A quick and unreflective reading of the words *baptized for the dead* would seem to suggest that people are allowing themselves to be baptized in the place of and for the benefit of others who are already dead.[161] It has frequently enough been claimed that that is "the plain and necessary sense of the words."[162] Key arguments against this view include the fact that there is no biblical or historical evidence of any precedent or equivalent practice in the earliest church or in its pagan context.[163] References to vicarious baptism in the early Fathers are found in condemnations of Gnostic misunderstandings of this verse. That is, there is evidence that vicarious baptism may have been adopted by some heretical groups through the misinterpretation of this verse, but there is no evidence that anyone had ever thought of or practiced such a thing before Paul wrote this verse.[164] Such an interpretation is also so out of step with Paul's own understanding of baptism as it is reflected elsewhere in his writings that it is extremely difficult to believe that he would refer to such a practice without condemning it or at least distancing himself from it. It seems that whatever practice he is referring to here is one that reflects, like his own life-choices mentioned in vv. 30-32, an appropriate course of action given the fact that the dead will be raised.

Most other interpretations of the verse entail differing interpretations of one or more of the key terms: especially the word translated "for" and/or the word translated "the dead."[165] These interpretations usually

159. Garland, 716. One of the definitions of the key word (ποιέω) is "to undertake or do someth[ing] that brings about an event, state, or condition" (BDAG, which suggests "do, cause, bring about, accomplish, prepare, etc." as possible glosses).

160. The point is that those seeking some resolution to the problem of death by trusting in Christ and being baptized would have to look elsewhere for their solution, and there is nowhere else to look.

161. There are variations of this view. Some posit that the dead people were most likely converts (or seekers nearing conversion) who had somehow died before being baptized. Others believe that the dead people were family members of those being baptized in their place.

162. Parry, 228; A. Oepke, "βάπτω, βαπτίζω," *TDNT* 1:542 n. 63; H. Riesenfeld, "ὑπέρ," *TDNT* 8:512-13. Fee, 764, argues that "this reading is such a plain understanding of the Greek text that no one would ever have imagined the various alternatives were it not for the difficulties involved." He further affirms (764 n. 16) that "the plethora of opinions exists precisely because this is what it appears to say." This goes too far. Certainly, those who think that this is what the text appears to say on first reading are likely to look and propose alternative interpretations. However, the evidence of several early Fathers suggests that they did not think it appeared to say this at all (see Hull, *Baptism on Account of the Dead,* 40-43).

163. Witherington, 293, mentions "the famous *taurobolium,* baptism in bull's blood for the welfare of the emperor," but that is a later practice, dating from the second century A.D.

164. Again, see Hull, *Baptism on Account of the Dead,* 40-43.

165. Some scholars depend upon emendations of or different approaches to punctuating the texts, but these lack any support from the Greek Fathers and require unlikely breaks in the text. These approaches have not found much support (see Hull, *Baptism on Ac-*

understand baptism here to be the normal Christian baptism that people experience as part of their conversion experience. The expression the TNIV and other versions translate as *for the dead* is taken to refer to a motivating factor behind their baptism (i.e., behind their conversion). First, while the most common usage of the word translated *for*[166] is as "a marker indicating that an activity or event is in some entity's interest" (the first definition given by BDAG, with suggested glosses including "for, in behalf of, for the sake of someone/someth[ing]"[167]), it is also used as a "marker of the moving cause or reason" (the second definition given by BDAG, with suggested glosses including "because of, for the sake of, for").[168] Another gloss that has been proposed by scholars that is consistent with this definition is "on account of."

This second possible meaning opens up a host of interpretive possibilities, especially once various potential referents for *the dead* are considered. If "the dead" are not the dead in general, but particular Christians who had left their marks on others who later converted to the faith, the idea could be "people who are baptized (as part and parcel of their conversion) on account of the influence of believers who are now deceased." Some scholars have suggested that their parents or other beloved family members may have converted shortly before their death (whether from natural causes or by martyrdom), and now these young believers have also joined the body of believers via baptism out of love and admiration for their family members and a desire to see them again in the resurrection. Others have proposed that *the dead* here refers to other apostolic witnesses who have since passed away, suggesting a link between this verse, the reference to loyalties reflected in or based on one's baptism in 1:12-17, and the reference to some apostolic witnesses who have since gone to be with Christ in 15:6, so that it would be on account of the witness given by an apostolic witness or missionary who has since died that someone agreed to be baptized as a way of honoring them.[169]

Some interpretations hold that Paul uses the word translated "dead"[170] with two different referents (and meanings) in this same verse. O'Neill takes the first reference to mean "corpses" or "dead bodies" and the second to refer to people who are "completely dead," so that the mean-

---

*count of the Dead*, 21-28). Jerome Murphy-O'Connor has followed Godet, 2:389, in arguing for a metaphorical understanding of "being baptized" such that it means "those being destroyed" and takes the verse to be a Corinthian gibe aimed at Paul ("'Baptized for the Dead' (I Cor. XV, 29): A Corinthian Slogan," *RB* 88 [1981], 532-43). This approach has not gained a following.

166. Gk. ὑπέρ.

167. This is the meaning assumed in all interpretations entailing vicarious baptism.

168. See also Hull, *Baptism on Account of the Dead*, 100-102.

169. See James E. Patrick, "Living Rewards for Dead Apostles: 'Baptised for the Dead' in 1 Corinthians 15.29," *NTS* 52 (2006), 71-85.

170. Gk. νεκρός.

ing is: "What do those hope to achieve who are baptized for their dying bodies? If the completely dead are not raised, why then are they baptized for themselves as corpses?"[171] White's interpretation also depends on there being two different referents. He takes the first reference to *the dead* to be a metaphorical reference to the apostles who, while still living, are sometimes presented by Paul as "dead men walking" (to use a modern expression).[172] In his view, the second reference is to those who are truly dead. White then argues that the verse should be understood as follows. "Otherwise, what will those do who are being baptized on account of the dead (that is, the dead figuratively speaking; that is, the apostles)? For if truly dead persons are not raised, why at all are people being baptized on account of them (that is, the apostles)?"[173]

We think that the best approach is to translate the key phrase, "those who are baptized on account of the dead," and to understand the reference to the dead in light of the usage of the word throughout this chapter (see vv. 12 [2x], 13, 15, 16, 20, 21, 29 [2x], 32, 35, 42, 52). In every instance except the first usage in this verse the word "dead" either modifies "resurrection" (as in vv. 13, 21, 42), serves as the subject of the verb "are raised" (vv. 16, 29 [second appearance], 32, 35, 52), or refers to Christ being raised "from the dead" (vv. 12, 20). We note first that in every other instance in this letter "the dead" are people who have died. This is especially to be expected in a discussion of the bodily resurrection of the dead. Unless there are clear indications to the contrary, the reader should expect that a reference to "the dead" would be a reference to the dead who will be raised in the resurrection, the dead to which the resurrection is expected to apply. We also note that while the two verses in the last category are ambiguous, the other usages, and the discussion as a whole, make it quite clear that Paul is not interested in all dead people, but in those who will benefit from being raised to glory. That is, his references to "the dead" have the righteous dead (i.e., dead who will be raised to glory) in mind. Paul is concerned with the resur-

171. J. C. O'Neill, "1 Corinthians 15.29," *ExpTim* (1980), 310-11.

172. Joel R. White, "'Baptized on Account of the Dead': The Meaning of 1 Corinthians 15:29 in Its Context," *JBL* 116 (1997), 494. In 2 Cor. 4:10-12 Paul says, "We always carry around in our body the death of Jesus, so that the life of Jesus may also be revealed in our body. For we who are alive are always being given over to death for Jesus' sake, so that his life may also be revealed in our mortal body. So then, death is at work in us, but life is at work in you." In 2 Cor. 6:9 he says that he is dying and yet lives on. In Rom. 7:24 he asks, "What a wretched man I am! Who will rescue me from this body of death?" This motif already appeared in this letter in 4:9, where Paul says, "God has put us apostles on display at the end of the procession, like those condemned to die in the arena." Most remarkable is the fact that this motif undeniably appears in 15:30-32.

173. O'Neill's and White's interpretation (so also Murphy-O'Connor) both take the Greek word ὅλως to modify the second use of νεκρός, rendering the two together as "truly/completely dead" and thus distinguishing the referent of the second appearance of νεκρός ("the dead") from the first. Most interpreters understand ὅλως to modify the verb "raised" and mean "actually" or "in fact" or, when negated as here, "at all" ("if the dead are not raised *at all*"). On this see Hull, *Baptism on Account of the Dead,* 99-100.

rection of those "who have fallen asleep in Christ" (v. 18), those who "belong to" Christ and will be raised "when he comes" (v. 23). Those are the "all" who "will be made alive" (v. 22) that are his concern here. Paul is not concerned with the dead in general, but with the dead who will "bear the image of the heavenly man" (v. 49) and "inherit the kingdom of God" (v. 50), the ones who "will be raised imperishable" (v. 52). "The dead" Paul has in mind are those who will be "raised imperishable"; "raised in glory"; and "raised in power" (vv. 42-43). When he says that people are "baptized on account of the dead," we may assume that he means that they are baptized on account of the righteous dead, those who will be raised in power and glory. This, then, is more specific than dead people in general, but it does not suggest something as specific as living or deceased apostles or specific loved ones who have recently passed away.

We suggest that for believers to be baptized on account of the dead who will be raised in glory means that they have heard about these dead being raised up (to new life and glory) and that they want to be part of that group.[174] As Keener puts it, this may be Paul's "roundabout way of saying 'baptized so as to be able to participate in eternal life with Christians who have already died,' hence baptized in the light of their own mortality as well."[175] Of course, Paul strongly ties baptism to the hope of the resurrection of the dead in Romans 6:3-13 as well: "all of us who were baptized into Christ Jesus were baptized into his death? We were therefore buried with him through baptism into death in order that, just as Christ was raised from the dead through the glory of the Father, we too may live a new life. If we have been united with him in a death like his, we will certainly also be united with him in a resurrection like his" (vv. 3-5). Baptism itself is tied to the resurrection hope by way of its integral role in the conversion experience. It is not that baptism per se brings salvation, but baptism is understood to be the initial confirmation of faith and act of initiation into the body of Christ. Certainly this text echoes the theme of other baptism texts that indicate that baptism is part and parcel of the process of entering into Christian life and fellowship.

Thus we would paraphrase the verse as follows: "Now, if there is no resurrection, what will be accomplished by those who get baptized because

174. This seems to be similar to the interpretation we find in Theodoret, 231: "The baptized person, he is saying, is buried with the Lord so that, having shared death, they may also become sharers in the resurrection. But if the body is dead and does not rise, why on earth are they baptized?" Hull's note on this part of his translation of Theodoret's commentary (253 n. 26) is worth repeating: "Theodoret knows nothing of what is called 'some kind of vicarious baptism.' . . . Theodoret seems simply to be saying that if resurrection does not occur, the symbolism of death, burial and rising in the ritual of baptism is flawed and the rite futile."

175. Craig S. Keener, *The IVP Bible Background Commentary: New Testament* (Downers Grove, IL: InterVarsity Press, 1993), 486-87. We are reminded of the words of the gospel hymn traditionally used as a funeral march: "Lord, how I want to be in that number, When the saints go marching in."

of what they have heard about how our dead will be raised? If the dead are not raised at all, why are people undergoing baptism on account of them?"

Our proposal comes close to the suggestion that some others have made that Paul's text entails an ellipsis and that "baptism on account of the dead" means "baptism on account of the resurrection of the dead," but it is not quite the same thing.[176] We are not implying that there is an ellipsis or that the real subject is the resurrection (as others have held), but that while readers are tempted to think that the topic is simply the resurrection and "the dead" should merely play the role of a modifier, Paul's language suggests otherwise. In vv. 15, 16, 29, 32, 35, and 52 Paul uses the verb "are/will be raised" with "the dead" as the subject of the sentence. That is, at times Paul focuses precisely on "the dead" and what happens to them as his topic rather than merely reflecting a broad interest in the subject of the resurrection.[177]

It may be that Paul describes the people to whom he is referring in the third person rather than first- or second-person plural ("those who are baptized on account of the dead" rather than "you/we who were baptized for the dead") because different people find different things about the Christian message particularly appealing. If so, Paul has in mind those who were particularly concerned about the afterlife and whose primary motivation in responding to the gospel message was its promise that those who trust in Christ need not fear death, since the dead in Christ will be raised in glory and power. Paul has already demonstrated that the resurrection of the dead is at the heart of the Christian message. Fear of death and dying may have played a significant role in the conversion of many, who may have been impressed with the confident hope of Christian believers.[178] Paul indicated his own attitude toward death in Philippians 1:21: "For to me, to live is Christ and to die is gain." And in 2 Corinthians 5:2 he said that he longed "to be clothed with our heavenly dwelling."

176. Robertson and Plummer, 359, point out that "[t]he Greek expositors . . . explain the expression as referring to ordinary Christian baptism, ὑπὲρ τῶν νεκρῶν being taken as meaning 'with an interest in the resurrection of the dead,' *i.e.* in expectation of the resurrection. But is there any authority for this use of ὑπέρ? And is not the supposed ellipse of τῆς ἀναστάσεως very violent? If St Paul had wanted to abbreviate ὑπὲρ ἀναστάσεως τῶν νεκρῶν, he would have left out τῶν νεκρῶν, not τῆς ἀναστάσεως." But Paul almost never uses ἀνάστασις in an unqualified manner (the only exception appears to be 2 Tim. 2:18), and never does so in this letter. When he uses it in Rom. 6:5, it is usually understood as a reference to the likeness of Christ's resurrection, not a reference to the resurrection in general.

177. For an examination of evidence of preoccupation with the dead in Corinth, see Richard E. DeMaris, "Corinthian Religion and Baptism for the Dead (1 Cor 15:29): Insights from Archaeology and Anthropology," *JBL* 114 (1995), 661-82. See also the articles mentioned in the following note.

178. See Bolt, "Life, Death and the Afterlife in the Greco-Roman World," 51 (cf. 77-78): "Death was a grim reality in the first-century Greco-Roman world. In all sorts of ways, its shadow hung heavily over every aspect of human life and endeavor. The gospel of Jesus Christ, however, brought a message of life from the dead that had the potential to make an enormous impact on the lives of all who heard it." See also Rosner, "'With What Kind of Body?'" 192-97.

Hull highlights how this understanding relates to much else earlier in this chapter: "Paul presents the ongoing acceptance of baptism by one group within the Corinthian community as a praiseworthy example for the whole community. Baptism is an act of faith whereby they profess conviction in what Paul preached in Corinth, viz., Christ is raised from the dead and the dead in Christ are destined for resurrection." Hull thinks (tying in a reference to v. 34 at the end) that we "can almost hear Paul bellowing: 'Look at those eager baptismal candidates. Look at their faith. It was once yours. They believe all that I preached about Jesus. They do not doubt that many persons including myself have seen him alive after death. They do not doubt that those among us who have fallen asleep will rise on the last day. As a matter of fact, it is their firm faith in the resurrection of Christ and of his death that moves them to baptism. That is what they believe. That is what you once believed. Come back to your senses!'"[179]

The people of whom Paul speaks in this verse are like him in that their actions, like his own, amount to an act of faith in the resurrection: "[T]hose who are undergoing baptism on account of the dead affirm the resurrection by their actions. Just so, Paul affirms the resurrection by his actions. But the group in Corinth whom he addresses directly does not. The message is clear: the resurrection of the dead rightly motivates [those undergoing baptism on account of the dead] and Paul."[180] Of course Paul's calling led him to suffer tremendously for Christ (as we shall see in the following verses). We should not forget, however, that those undergoing Christian baptism in Paul's day were not entering into a socially dominant and respectable religion, but were identifying themselves with a religious movement that was known both for the suffering of its resurrected Lord and for the suffering and opposition that his disciples could expect to endure.[181]

**15:30-31** Having stated that those who affirm the resurrection do so through their commitment to being baptized, in vv. 30-32 Paul uses his own actions as another example[182] of behavior that affirms the resurrection and makes no sense apart from it: *And as for us, why do we endanger ourselves every hour? I face death every day — yes, just as surely as I boast about you*[183] *in*

179. Hull, *Baptism on Account of the Dead,* 235. Hull notes (231) that Paul is not reproving those who are being baptized on account of the dead; "he is reproving the Corinthians who deny the resurrection of the dead. Paul is not asking [those being baptized on account of the dead] to alter their actions; he is asking the Corinthians to alter theirs in terms of accepting what Paul preached to them. . . . Apparently, 'they' . . . are being offered as an example to the 'you.'"

180. Hull, *Baptism on Account of the Dead,* 232. The subtitle of Hull's book is "An Act of Faith in the Resurrection."

181. See 1 Thess. 2:14 and the motif of suffering in 2 Corinthians.

182. As Barrett, 364, and Thiselton argue, καὶ ἡμεῖς (TNIV, *And as for us*) "should be construed together as 'we, too' or 'we also'" since the καί "does not qualify the sentence as a whole but specifically 'we'" (Thiselton, 1249, his bold and italics changed to single quotes).

183. Witnesses to the text here are divided as to whether Paul includes an affectionate vocative reference to the readers as "brothers and sisters" (Gk. ἀδελφοί) at this point (𝔓[46], D,

*Christ Jesus our Lord.* Paul is employing "hardship talk, which Paul often employs as a sign of his endurance and trustworthiness, but here it is used to highlight the question: Why go to all this apostolic trouble if death has the final word? Paul's answer lies in his deep conviction that in sharing Christ's death believers become one with his suffering, and the powers of the old age vent their anger against the believers so that there is always . . . end-times suffering and tribulation."[184]

Paul uses a bit of hyperbole, speaking at first of being in danger *every hour* and then of (literally) "dying" *every day.* Christ himself had said in Luke 9:23-24 that whoever wanted to be his disciple must "deny themselves and take up their cross daily[185] and follow me. For whoever wants to save their life will lose it, but whoever loses their life for me will save it."

We know from the catalogs of his sufferings that he presented earlier in this letter (4:9-13) and those he will present elsewhere and that will figure prominently in 2 Corinthians (cf. 2 Cor. 1:8-10; 4:7-12; 6:4-10; 11:23-29; 12:10; Rom. 8:35) that Paul did indeed face constant danger and intense challenges due to his faith and apostolic calling. In 2 Corinthians 11:23 Paul says that he has been "often near death" (NRSV). One example is given in Acts 14:19, which says that Paul was stoned and then left for dead outside the city of Lystra. In Acts 9:16 the Lord told Ananias that he would show Paul "how much he must suffer for my name." Paul constantly exposed himself to danger because he knew that the dead are raised. He would remind the Corinthians of this in 2 Corinthians 1:8-9, where he said that he did not want them to be ignorant "about the troubles we experienced in the province of Asia. We were under great pressure, far beyond our ability to endure, so that we despaired of life itself. Indeed, we felt we had received the sentence of death. But this happened that we might not rely on ourselves but on God, who raises the dead."

Although Paul had not yet fully experienced death (despite "dying daily"), he lived as though he had already died and had nothing more to suffer from it (see our comments on "dead men walking" [v. 29]). That is, he faced death differently, and lived his life in a radically different manner, because he knew that he had already been baptized into Christ's death and was destined to be raised with Christ in the end. In this (only in a more radical way) he is similar to those baptized and committed to following Christ on the basis of the promise that the dead in Christ will rise again and of their desire to be among them when that happened. In pointing out that the

---

F, G, Ψ, 075, 0243, 1739, 1881, 𝔐, b, Ambrosiaster, and Pelagius omit the word, while א, A, B, K, P, 33, 81, 104, (326), 365, 1175, 1241, 2464, *pc,* lat, sy, and co include it). The fact that it is inexplicably missing from such strong witnesses suggests that it may have been added, but the supporting witnesses are also extremely strong (see Metzger, *A Textual Commentary,* 501; Thiselton, 1249). The NA$^{27}$ text includes the words within square brackets to show their great difficulty in deciding.

184. Sampley, 983.

185. Gk. καθ' ἡμέραν, as in 1 Cor. 15:31.

apostles are in constant danger from opponents of the gospel, Paul echoes the language of Psalms 44:22 and 119:109.

Paul reinforces his claim that he constantly exposes himself to grave dangers for the sake of his apostolic calling by invoking his boast in the Corinthians as a similar manifestation of Christ's empowering work in his ministry: *yes, just as surely as I boast about you in Christ Jesus our Lord.* The word translated *yes, just as surely as I*[186] is a "marker pointing to the basis on which someth[ing] is strongly affirmed," which is typically followed, as here, by a reference to the "pers[on] or thing by which one swears, affirms, or invokes sanction" (BDAG). Paul swears or invokes divine sanction by his boast[187] about the Corinthians in Christ the Lord. Fee points out that Paul's boast "probably does not so much refer to his telling others about the Corinthians as to their very existence as the result of his apostolic labors (cf. 9:2, 15-16)."[188] And it is, as Fee says, a very "telling oath": "To make sure that they understand the truth of his constant facing of death, he swears by that which is dearest to him, their own existence in Christ, which also came about by labors that had exposed him to such dangers."[189] Thiselton argues that people "swear or affirm only by divinity [or] by something of *ultimate importance* to them."[190] Following Fee's suggestion that the expression indicates what is most dear to the speaker, Thiselton incorporates the idea into his translation of the text: "Oh yes, by all the pride in you that I hold dear in Christ Jesus our Lord, I so affirm!"[191] He points out that Paul's unusual language here provides insight into his pastoral heart: "Here is a succinct pastoral theology of the *risks, fragility,* and *dearest, deepest concerns* of a pastor who is willing to sacrifice all for the gospel in the light of the gathering together of all at the resurrection."[192]

Paul's statement that his boasting about the Corinthians is *in Christ Jesus our Lord* clarifies that it "is not self-serving nor self-exalting. It rests completely on what Christ had done among them through his labors (cf. vv. 9-10). Thus they are his boast; but for Paul that ultimately means boasting in Christ."[193]

**15:32** Paul continues his discussion of how the hope of the resurrection has empowered him as he has repeatedly faced danger and death, now making a reference to a particularly harrowing experience in Ephesus: *If I fought wild beasts in Ephesus with no more than human hopes, what have I gained?*

186. Gk. νή (appearing only here in the New Testament and twice in the LXX — Gen. 42:15, 16), but often in oaths in other Greek literature.

187. Gk. καύχησις, "act of taking pride in someth[ing]" (BDAG, which gives the translation here as, *"as surely as I may boast of you"*).

188. Fee, ad loc.

189. Fee, ad loc.

190. Thiselton, 1251 (some emphasis removed).

191. Thiselton, 1222 (emphasis removed).

192. Thiselton, 1251.

193. Fee, 770.

This may be a different episode from the one he will mention in 2 Corinthians 1:8-9, where he refers to "the troubles we experienced in the province of Asia. We were under great pressure, far beyond our ability to endure, so that we despaired of life itself. Indeed, we felt we had received the sentence of death. But this happened that we might not rely on ourselves but on God, who raises the dead." The reference to Asia in that text may simply reflect that the struggles he faced in Ephesus (from where he is writing; 16:8) continued as he moved to other parts of Asia, so that the two texts may be referring to overlapping tribulations. While the near context has led some interpreters to think that Paul's reference to fighting wild beasts should be taken literally and as the climax of the list of the dangers he has faced, it is very unlikely that Paul, a Roman citizen, would have been forced to fight wild animals in an arena or other context. Balz agrees: "An actual *damnatio ad bestias* [case of being condemned to the beasts], which was decreed only with capital offenses against persons of lower status, would at any rate stand in conflict with Acts 22:25-29, according to which Paul is said to have stood on his rights as a Roman citizen. . . . Moreover, Paul would hardly have remained silent about such a condemnation in his catalogs of suffering."[194] It is possible to take the verb literally as "a contrary to fact (unreal) conditional sentence: 'if I had fought w[ith] wild animals'" (BDAG), but it seems unlikely that Paul would use a hypothetical case rather than one of his actual experiences of suffering as an example.

If the verb is to be taken metaphorically, as seems most likely, it would mean "to be in a position of having to contend with [formidable] adversaries" (BDAG). Beasts or wild animals were used repeatedly as symbols or metaphors for pagan rulers in Daniel 7. Philo uses it for pagan officials in *On the Life of Moses* 1:42. Later, Ignatius used it of the soldiers who held him captive in his *To the Romans* 5:1. Paul uses the metaphor of animalistic biting and devouring for destructive behavior between humans in Galatians 5:15. Fighting wild beasts is probably a euphemism for contending with dangerous, powerful political opponents or "bloodthirsty human antagonists who would eagerly tear him to pieces."[195] Garland points out that Paul's Roman citizenship "did not provide him protection from mob violence, but only the right to certain formal procedures."[196]

The phrase translated here as *with no more than human hopes*[197] is capable of being interpreted in various ways, as is reflected in the great diversity of English translations. The NRSV ("with merely human hopes") and CSB ("with only human hope") are similar to the TNIV. Others suggest "humanly speaking" (ESV), "so to speak" (NAB), "from human motives" (NASB), "from a human point of view" (NET), "for merely human reasons"

194. H. Balz, "θηριομαχέω," *EDNT* 2:148.

195. Garland, 721.

196. Garland, 721.

197. Gk. κατὰ ἄνθρωπον (see BDAG on ἄνθρωπος).

(NIV), "in a purely human perspective" (NJB), or "after the manner of men" (KJV). BDAG gives the meaning as "like an ordinary man" as opposed to "as a Christian sure of the resurrection." This same idea is reflected in Héring and Garland: "with a horizon limited by earthly humanity, that is, without hope of the resurrection."[198] This is almost certainly correct and is intended to stand in contrast with the actual background to Paul's willingness to expose himself to such dangers since he has made it clear that everything he does he does "in expectation of the future resurrection."[199] Paul's description of the scene entails both real and unreal elements. It is clear that he did grapple with extremely dangerous and fearsome opponents in Ephesus (metaphorically described as wild animals), but he did not do so with a horizon limited by earthly humanity, but as one whose life is founded on the hope of the resurrection.

The expression translated *what have I gained?* actually lacks a verb in Greek and is literally, "what to me the advantage/benefit/profit?" with the verb tense and mood to be determined by the reader in the context. The question is what would he have possibly hoped to gain from "sticking his neck out" for the cause of Christ — and the sake of those Ephesians who, like his Corinthian readers, came to Christ through him — if he believed death had the final word.[200] By God's grace he knew and acted in a way consistent with the fact that, thanks to Christ, life has the last word, not death.

Paul now follows through on the point that there is nothing to be gained from putting one's life in death-defying situations for the sake of the Christian gospel and its advancement if there is no resurrection: *If the dead are not raised, "Let us eat and drink, for tomorrow we die."* Paul cites Isaiah 22:13 (which also happens to reflect a motif in the Greco-Roman world) to point to the utter futility of a life without the direction and motivation given by the resurrection of Jesus Christ. It leads to a dissipated lifestyle. He already cited his own positive example of how one ought to live in the light of the resurrection in vv. 30-32a. Here he refers to the polar opposite. Isaiah 22:13 depicts the reaction of the inhabitants of Jerusalem while being besieged by Assyria and facing the grim prospect of their impending annihilation (22:12-14). Instead of repenting, they decide to "party like there is no tomorrow."[201] Paul uses Isaiah 22:13 to underscore the depravity of the human condition, "without hope and without God in the world" (Eph. 2:12). He uses the text as a way of summing up the logical entailment of denying or forgetting about resurrection. The Corinthians who doubt the resurrection are like the Jerusalemites who failed to live out of the resources of their own faith. The author of Hebrews points out that "without faith it is

198. Héring, 171, cited by Garland, 721 (similarly, Fee, 771, and Thiselton, 1251).
199. Garland, 720.
200. Cf. Thiselton, 1252.
201. Hays, 268.

impossible to please God, because anyone who comes to him must believe that he exists and that he rewards those who earnestly seek him" (Heb. 11:6). The reward Paul has in mind here is that which is ultimately dependent on the reality of the resurrection hope. Apart from that there is no sound basis for the moral life of the Christian.

Although Paul is citing an Old Testament text (albeit without a quotation formula to explicitly mark it as such), it is not necessarily important for his readers to recognize it as a scriptural quotation. The sentiment expressed in the line is widespread in both the Jewish and Greco-Roman worlds. As we pointed out in the comments on chapter 10, eating and drinking are often associated with idolatrous behavior in Old Testament and Jewish texts. In Luke 12:19 the rich fool says to himself, "You have plenty of grain laid up for many years. Take life easy; eat, drink and be merry." But God said to him, "You fool! This very night your life will be demanded from you. Then who will get what you have prepared for yourself?" (v. 20). Fee points out that "[i]n Plutarch's anti-Epicurean writings . . . the language of 'eating and drinking' was a formula for the dissolute life" and that that was in keeping with "contemporary anti-Epicurean sentiments, which (not altogether fairly) believed the Epicureans taught this very philosophy."[202] It is quite likely that the Corinthians Paul has in mind would be repulsed by the dissolute life popularly associated with and attributed to Epicurean philosophy. This letter suggests that they are more likely to be influenced by the more popular Stoic points of view. Paul's argument proposes a line of thought such as, "If you deny the resurrection, you might as well be an Epicurean!" with the expected repulsion at that thought serving Paul's rhetorical purpose. Paul had already criticized the Corinthians for moral and spiritual problems related to eating and drinking in the context of pagan dinners and temples in chapter 10 and of the Lord's Supper in chapter 11. This passage may have brought those criticisms to mind again at this point.

Paul effectively accuses the Corinthians who deny bodily resurrection of having a flawed basis for a lifestyle that pleases God, which will lead them to idolatrous and immoral behavior. Garland uses a beautiful turn of phrase: "Resurrection means endless hope, but no resurrection means a hopeless end — and hopelessness breeds dissipation."[203]

**15:33** Paul now moves from a biblical text with an anti-Epicurean thrust (v. 32b) to a quotation from the third- to fourth-century Athenian dramatist Menander: *Do not be misled: "Bad company corrupts good character."* The warning *Do not be misled*[204] is the same expression used in 6:9 and translated there as "Do not be deceived." It suggests that "they will be held ac-

202. Fee, 772.

203. Garland, 721.

204. Paul uses a present imperative, implying that it is a generally relevant exhortation. Here the generally relevant thing to learn is that *"Bad company corrupts good character."*

countable"[205] and therefore need to take the warning to heart. But, as Chrysostom indicates, Paul is also trying "to make some allowance to them for the past with a view to their return, and to remove from them and transfer to others the greater part of his charges, and so in this way also to allure them to repentance."[206] That is, he opens the possibility that some of the responsibility lay with anonymous others who have misled them.

The epigram from Menander's *Thais* was a popular one in Paul's day and would probably have been known to any educated Corinthian.[207] Thus, as others have pointed out, we cannot assume that Paul has read Menander "any more than one can assume that a person who cites a famous line from a Shakespeare play has read Shakespeare. It had become a cliché, perhaps even before Menander."[208] Paul's use of the quotation, rather than being a clue to the sources of his own thought, as Martin points out, indicates Paul's sense of where the ideas he is countering come from:

> The abrupt interjection of the saying in Paul's argument may indicate that he believes the Corinthians' skepticism to be due to influences from other sources — in fact to persons who have only "ignorance of God" (v. 34), a designation often used by Jews to refer to Gentiles. . . . All this suggests that Paul attributes the Corinthians' doubts [about bodily resurrection] to Greek philosophy.[209]

Witherington rightly points out that "[t]he rhetorical force of Paul's use of this proverb is powerful: These Gentile Corinthians are condemned out of the mouth of their own cultural heritage even apart from Scripture and apostolic tradition."[210]

The fact that Paul quotes an epigram dealing with the theme of corruption in a chapter dealing with resurrection, God's victory over corruption (see Acts 2:27, 31; 13:34-37), calls for attention.[211] In 15:42 Paul will assert that the human body is sown in corruption[212] and raised incorrupt-

205. Witherington, 292.

206. *Homiliae in Epistulam i ad Corinthios* 40.4 (NPNF[1] 12:247).

207. Cf. Conzelmann, 278 n. 139; Robertson and Plummer, 363, suggest that it "is uncertain whether Menander adopted a popular proverb, or the saying passed from the *Thais* into popular use. St Paul may have got the saying from either source." BDAG (ἦθος) points out that the proverb may go back as far as Euripides and that, according to Diodorus Siculus 12.12.[3] 4 (first century B.C.), "Charondas the lawgiver [5 B.C.] champions the principle that good men would easily have their characters ruined by association with evil men" and "it is said of a tyrant [in 16.54.4], . . . 'he corrupted people's morals through base speech.'" They note that similar ideas may be found "as early as Theognis" (sixth century B.C.).

208. Garland, 722.

209. D. B. Martin, *The Corinthian Body,* 275 n. 79.

210. Witherington, 292.

211. A point brought to our attention by Sean McDonough.

212. Here, and in the following texts of this paragraph, the key Greek word used is φθορά ("corruption"), the cognate noun to which the verb used here (φθείρω) is related.

ible. In Romans 8:21 Paul says that we are looking forward to the day when "the creation itself will be set free from its bondage to corruption and obtain the freedom of the glory of the children of God" (ESV). In Galatians 6:8 Paul says, "the one who sows to his own flesh will from the flesh reap corruption, but the one who sows to the Spirit will from the Spirit reap eternal life" (ESV). Christ came to undo all forms of corruption, including the corruption of creation, the corruption of the human body, and moral corruption. The gospel is to bring about the manifestation of God's renewed humanity, freed first from its addictions to false wisdom and to its corrupting influence in the forms of various vices, especially idolatry, sexual immorality, and greed, that flow from that false wisdom, and freed ultimately from even physical corruption at the resurrection from the dead. Any association with moral corruption is a clear sign that people are moving along the wrong trajectory.

In Witherington's view the *bad company* Paul is concerned about would have included "pagan friends at dinner parties in the temple and elsewhere."[213] According to Garland, Paul is presumably calling on the readers to "shun . . . those who deny the reality of death, who do not share the Christian hope of resurrection, and who behave disreputably."[214] But this raises the question of how the Corinthians, and we later readers, are expected to apply Paul's warning. Were the Corinthians (and are we) actually to shun or strictly avoid such people? Much of this letter has dealt with the question of how Christians are to navigate their various relationships as Christians living in the world but not being of it or becoming conformed to it. In 5:9-11 Paul said, "I wrote to you in my letter not to associate with sexually immoral people — not at all meaning the people of this world who are immoral, or the greedy and swindlers, or idolaters. In that case you would have to leave this world." He went on to say: "But now I am writing to you that you must not associate with any who claim to be fellow believers but are sexually immoral or greedy, idolaters or slanderers, drunkards or swindlers. With such persons do not even eat" (v. 11). If Paul has in mind here (in 15:33) people "who claim to be fellow believers but are sexually immoral or greedy, idolaters or slanderers, drunkards or swindlers" (5:11), then they are indeed expected to break fellowship with and strictly avoid them. But if he has in mind unbelievers with whom some Corinthians are spending too much time and who are having a negative influence on them, the application must be more nuanced. In 9:22 he gives himself as an example of one who has "become all things to all people so that by all possible means" he might save some. In 10:27 Paul makes it clear that believers are free to accept dinner invitations from unbelievers as long as they exercise careful judgment in how they engage with the people and food around them. And, of course, Christ himself was (in)famous for spending time

213. Witherington, 292.
214. Garland, 722.

with people who behaved disreputably. It is extremely unlikely, then, that Paul wants or expects the Corinthians to shun or strictly avoid unbelievers who deny the reality of death, who do not share the Christian hope of resurrection, or who behave disreputably. He has already indicated that that would be a misunderstanding.

What are we to make, then, of the warning, *"Bad company corrupts good character?"* As Thiselton points out, the word Paul uses for *company* "conveys the notion of a *clique*, a *group*, or a *'gang'* who regularly do things together and to which people 'belong.'"[215] And the word here is qualified as *bad* company, suggesting not all such groups are necessarily corrupting. The point is to be aware (and beware) of the corrupting influence that comes from extended intimate fellowship with others and to take steps to make sure that (1) we are spending sufficient time in extended intimate fellowship with people who know and love God and are known by him; and that (2) in our relationships with those who do not yet know Christ we are being a positive influence as salt and light (Matt. 5:13-16). It is of utmost importance to guard our hearts and the influences upon our moral compass. As we have argued throughout this commentary (as have others), some Corinthians were being overly influenced by the dominant values and thinking of the Corinthian city and of Roman culture and insufficiently influenced by their knowledge of Christ and of the basic moral and theological teachings of the Christian faith. They needed to learn how to be in the world without acting as people of the world. They needed to learn not to "conform to the pattern of this world, but be transformed" by the renewing of the mind and thus "be able to test and approve what God's will is" (Rom. 12:2). The clearest indication of what Paul had in mind is found in the following verse; as always, context is all important.

As things are, the Corinthians who deny the resurrection of the dead are themselves in danger of being *bad company* corrupting the good character of other believers who may more readily follow through with the moral implications of their denial of the resurrection.

**15:34** How are the Corinthians to respond to Paul's arguments about the resurrection and the quotations from Isaiah and Menander in particular (vv. 32-33)? As Fee puts it, "In typical diatribe style, the *argumentum ad absurdum* turns truly *ad hominem*, and becomes a word of exhortation for the Corinthians to mend their ways":[216] *Come back to your senses as you ought, and stop sinning; for there are some who are ignorant of God — I say this to your shame.* The word[217] translated *Come back to your senses* is used literally "of one recovering from a drunken revel, 'sober up'" (BDAG). Here it is being used figuratively, but it reminds the reader of v. 32b and suggests that if the Corinthians are not physically drunk, they still need to sober up spiritu-

215. Thiselton, 1254 (Gk. ὁμιλία).

216. Fee, 772.

217. Gk. ἐκνήφω.

ally. BDAG indicates that the whole first clause[218] should be translated "sober up for uprightness," while the NRSV has, "come to a sober and right mind." As Chrysostom puts it, Paul addresses them "[a]s if he were speaking to drunkards and madmen."[219]

The logical relationship between the first two verbs in this verse (*come back to your senses* and *stop sinning*)[220] is presumably that the readers Paul has in mind have been sinning due to the spiritual stupor they are in and that it is only when they sober up spiritually that they will stop their sinning. Sampley points out that the Corinthians were probably very surprised "that Paul should construe their actions as in any way representing sin."[221] What sins did Paul have in mind? A moment ago he mentioned "eating and drinking" as part of a dissolute lifestyle that failed to reflect the truth about God or about our life before him. This letter has already highlighted the vices of sexual immorality and idolatry, as well as greed, which had left their marks on the community. The relationship between chapters 1–4, chapters 5–7, and chapters 8–14 (as we argue in the Introduction, 21-25) suggest that a lack of true wisdom and a commitment to false wisdom lead to those and other vices. The near context points to an understanding of sin that further illuminates the source of the Corinthians' problems. The reason that the Corinthians need to come back to their senses and stop sinning is that *there are some who are ignorant of God.* On a first reading one may decide that the point is that the Corinthians have been lax in their evangelistic emphasis and that their bad behavior has made their faith noncontagious. But it seems more likely that something else, something more fundamental, is at stake here.

Chrysostom helpfully relates the failure to know God to the failure to believe in the resurrection, which makes sense given that that is the problem Paul has been addressing throughout this section. For a starter, Paul's reference to *some who are ignorant of God* is unlikely to be a reference to unbelievers. Of course there are unbelievers who do not know God! Rather, the *some* "picks up the resonance to the Greek ear of the 'some' of 15:12 who have, in effect, been the 'opponents' for the whole of the treatise from 15:1 up to this point."[222] Chrysostom thinks that this is Paul's way of deliber-

218. Gk. ἐκνήψατε δικαίως.

219. *Homiliae in Epistulam i ad Corinthios* 40.4 (NPNF[1] 12:247).

220. The first verb is an aorist imperative (ἐκνήψατε, from ἐκνήφω), and the second a present imperative (ἁμαρτάνετε, from ἁμαρτάνω). But *TLG* indicates that ἐκνήφω does not appear as a present active imperative in all of Greek literature (probably due to the relationship between verbal aspect and the verb's lexical aspect), suggesting that we should not make an issue of Paul's use of the aorist here. The (negated) second verb is usually translated, as here, "stop sinning." That may be the correct interpretation, given what we know from the context, but should not be based on the negated present imperative since that does not imply that the action was already ongoing (cf. Matt. 23:3; Mark 9:39; 13:11, 21; Luke 10:7; 1 Cor. 10:28; 14:39), nor should it be based on a contrast with the first verb in this case, given our comments above.

221. Sampley, 983.

222. Thiselton, 1256 ("some" changed from bold font to single quotes).

ately transferring some of the responsibility to others to save face for the Corinthians but that really their doubts about the resurrection reflect a lack of knowledge about God and his infinite power: "See how again he transfers his accusations to others. For he said not, 'You have no knowledge,' but, 'some have no knowledge.' Because disbelieving the resurrection is the temper of one not fully aware that the power of God is irresistible and sufficient for all things. For if out of the things which are not He made the things that are, much more will He be able to raise again those which have been dissolved."[223] In other words, "those who have no knowledge of God are those who do not believe in the resurrection of the dead."[224] If they knew God the way they should, their doubts about the resurrection would evaporate in the light of his glory and power. Jesus said as much in Mark 12:24 (and the parallel in Matt. 22:29): the Sadducees denied the resurrection, he said, because they did "not know the Scriptures or the power of God" and thus had gone astray.

Thiselton reminds us that "Paul regularly regards 'sin' less in terms (if at all) of *acts* (plural) of commission or omission than as an *attitude, stance, and state.*"[225] He has in mind "an *attitude, stance, and state* in which the human will is granted 'autonomy' to turn away from God and to seek self-gratification as the chief end of human life."[226] That is undoubtedly true, but we may also see the Corinthian sin as an attitude or stance with respect to God that fails to fully respect the extent of his sovereign power over all things.[227] Verse 28 serves as a kind of climax to the prior section in its bold assertion that all things will be made subject to God so that he "may be all in all." And as Paul goes on to discuss the foolishness of those who mockingly ask what kind of body the resurrection body will be, he points out that it is God who gives each thing its body, whichever kind it might have (vv. 35-38).

Some Corinthians are guilty of sexual immorality, idolatry, and/or greed; of a dissolute lifestyle. But those sins are a reflection of false wisdom and a reduced, sinful view of God and his power, the One who will destroy everything that is not submitted to him (6:13; 15:24-28). Much of this letter serves to provide a clearer picture of God and of his sovereign power exerted in and through Christ that is the ultimate solution to problem behavior.

223. *Homiliae in Epistulam i ad Corinthios* 40.4 (NPNF[1] 12:247).

224. Chrysostom, *Homiliae in Epistulam i ad Corinthios* 40.4, cited by Bray, 168.

225. Thiselton, 1256 (bold font changed to single quotes).

226. Thiselton, 1256.

227. There is also another way in which the Corinthians' sinning may relate to the relationship between God and the resurrection. In 15:15 Paul indicates that the apostles would be "found to be false witnesses about God" if he never raised Christ from the dead because they testified that he did. If there is a resurrection from the dead, i.e., if God has really raised Christ from the dead and will raise those who belong to him as well, it follows that some Corinthians may be found to be false witnesses about God because they have claimed otherwise.

Knowledge and ignorance (the lack of knowledge) are key themes throughout this letter. Some Corinthians evidently prided themselves on their vaunted knowledge. They claimed, "We all possess knowledge" (8:1), but Paul responded, "Those who think they know something do not yet know as they ought to know" (8:2). Evidently they thought that they were particularly strong in the area of knowledge about God, since they knew that "An idol is nothing at all in the world" and that "There is no God but one" (8:4). Paul's suggestion that those who doubted the resurrection (undoubtedly on the basis of intellectual problems they had with the idea) were not actually knowledgeable but rather lacked true or sufficient knowledge of God must have come as a shock to them.[228] His language would typically be used of pagans who had no real knowledge of God whatsoever.[229] The contrast between their self-perceived knowledge and Paul's claim that they lack knowledge of God is undoubtedly part of what Paul has in mind when he adds, *I say this to your shame.*[230] The whole verse reflects an extraordinary affront to the puffed-up Corinthians. They think that they are marked by intellectually superior knowledge and insight. Paul says that they need to wake up from their stupor and stop sinning since their unbelief in the resurrection reflects a lack of knowledge for which they should feel ashamed.

Sampley is sensitive to the rhetorical impact of the verse as a whole, suggesting that it all adds up to Paul "pushing the hearers to the limits" and "trying to shock them back to their (better) senses."[231]

> Why? Because he has come to the heart of the matter: Life in this world, immersed as it is in suffering and brokenness, and work in behalf of the gospel, can all be reduced to folly if there is no resurrection of the dead, if indeed death has the victory, and if indeed death has the last word. Human striving and achieving, even if inspired by the grace of God, is emptied of all its significance if death is the final verdict. How is one's work, indeed one's very essence, one's innermost being more than a whisper if it all ends in death? Paul posits that the resurrection of the dead, which is the logical and necessary outcome of the already-accomplished resurrection of Christ, gives life in the present its mean-

228. K. Barth suggests that these words "should be emblazoned on the pulpit steps and similar places so that pastors may be reminded every time . . . [that] not to have knowledge of God — makes everything vain, empty, and nugatory" (*The Resurrection of the Dead*, 181-82).

229. Cf. Thiselton, 1255 (citing Edwards, 430): "ἀγνωσίαν ἔχειν 'means more than ἀγνοεῖν' in Paul and in much biblical tradition. It is often synonymous, Edwards notes, with a darkened pre-Christian state (*1 Clement* 59). Since it often characterizes the Gentile mind, the thought seems to be, 'Some of you are cherishing that ignorance of God which belongs to the heathen.'" Cf. Wis. 13:1-2.

230. The expression he uses here is virtually identical to the one with which he begins 6:5.

231. Sampley, 983.

ing, allows and even demands that one enter struggles on behalf of the gospel, and assures that life's struggles and hardships have meaning, a meaning that is ensured by God and that will survive death's sting.[232]

### E. Answers to Philosophical Objections to Belief in the Resurrection of the Body, 15:35-49

35*But someone will ask, "How are the dead raised? With what kind of*
*body will they come?"* 36*How foolish! What you sow does not come to life un-*
*less it dies.* 37*When you sow, you do not plant the body that will be, but just a*
*seed, perhaps of wheat or of something else.* 38*But God gives it a body as he*
*has determined, and to each kind of seed he gives its own body.* 39*All flesh is*
*not the same: Human beings have one kind of flesh, animals have another,*
*birds another and fish another.* 40*There are also heavenly bodies and there are*
*earthly bodies; but the splendor of the heavenly bodies is one kind, and the*
*splendor of the earthly bodies is another.* 41*The sun has one kind of splendor,*
*the moon another and the stars another; and star differs from star in splen-*
*dor.*

42*So will it be with the resurrection of the dead. The body that is sown is*
*perishable, it is raised imperishable;* 43*it is sown in dishonor, it is raised in*
*glory; it is sown in weakness, it is raised in power;* 44*it is sown a natural*
*body, it is raised a spiritual body.*

*If there is a natural body, there is also a spiritual body.* 45*So it is written:*
*"The first Adam became a living being"; the last Adam, a life-giving spirit.*
46*The spiritual did not come first, but the natural, and after that the spiri-*
*tual.* 47*The first man was of the dust of the earth; the second man is of heaven.*
48*As was the earthly man, so are those who are of the earth; and as is the*
*heavenly man, so also are those who are of heaven.* 49*And just as we have*
*borne the image of the earthly man, so shall we*[233] *bear the image of the heav-*
*enly man.*

Paul moves into diatribe style, introducing a hypothetical or imaginary debate partner to represent a perspective he has undoubtedly encountered before (it would be a common one in the Greco-Roman world) and which he imagines has now found a home within the Corinthian church (vv. 35-36a). After explaining that the seed sown must be distinguished from that to which it gives birth and establishing the great diversity of types of bodies found in creation (vv. 36b-41), Paul answers the original question in a series of antithetical contrasts between the body sown in death and the one raised up by God (vv. 42-44a) and finishes with an explanation of how those two bodies reflect the image of the first (earthly) and

232. Sampley, 983.

233. Some early manuscripts have, *so let us.*

second (heavenly) Adams respectively (vv. 44b-49), so that the ultimate answer to the question is that it will have a body like Christ's. The passage as a whole reflects considerable reflection on Genesis 1–2, presupposing the idea that in protology (the study of creation's beginning) we find the keys to eschatology. It is understood that in many ways the last things will be like the first things, only even better.

**15:35** Paul adopts a diatribal form of teaching, introducing a hypothetical debate partner who undoubtedly represents a viewpoint he has actually encountered in other contexts and which may be shared by some of his readers.[234] It gives him an opportunity to provide a preemptive response to an objection that might have already been raised in Corinth or that might be likely to arise if not addressed here: *But someone will ask, "How are the dead raised? With what kind of body will they come?"* We pointed out in our comments on v. 12 that the idea of the resurrection of the dead was not a familiar one in the Greco-Roman world. Acts 17:18 depicts utter miscomprehension on the part of Epicurean and Stoic philosophers who mistook Paul's preaching of good news about "Jesus and the resurrection" as advocating "foreign gods" (note the plural). That Paul felt it necessary to explain at length, "With what kind of body will they come?" is explicable precisely because his Gentile contemporaries had no notion of bodily resurrection. Since Paul would certainly have encountered similar skepticism about the resurrection earlier in his ministry, it may be that his response to this question in the following verses is one that he had developed earlier in his ministry and which he has used on other occasions.

As Theodoret recognizes, Paul's question "is twofold, about the manner of the resurrection and about the future quality of the body."[235] And Theodoret's summary suggests that the question, *"How are the dead raised?"* is not asking, "How is it possible?" (to which the obvious answer would be that God does it miraculously). Rather, the word translated *how*[236] often has the idea "in what manner" or "in what way (exactly)?" so that (literally) "How do you read it?" (Luke 10:26) is not a question about how reading could happen but about the particular way the text is read (cf. Luke 10:26; John 9:10, 26; Rom. 4:10). So the question, "How are they raised?" is probably expecting an answer like "As reanimated corpses"; or "By the reassimilation of the disintegrated body parts." The second question, then, *"With what kind of body will they come?"* flows from the first and is related to it. It is a natural question that continues to be asked, perhaps even more skeptically, in the modern age. Dead bodies decompose and become part of the nutrients in the ground, and their molecules find their way into other living things. If those bodies have disintegrated and have been incorporated

234. See Stanley K. Stowers, "Diatribe," *ABD* 2:190-93; D. F. Watson, "Diatribe," *DPL* 213-14.

235. Theodoret, 232. See also N. T. Wright, *The Resurrection of the Son of God*, 343 (*pace* Hays, 269-70).

236. Gk. πῶς; see BDAG, LSJ, EDNT, and MM.

into other creatures, how can they be raised again? Will the dead *come* back in completely different and unrelated bodies? Or *will they come* in patched-up versions of their old bodies? As Ramsay MacMullen points out, "Resurrection in the flesh appeared a startling, distasteful idea, at odds with everything that passed for wisdom among the educated."[237]

Paul's response in the following verses does not answer scientific questions or explain all of the details (he never suggested that he knew or understood all of the details) but focuses on countering the crude and unimaginative perspective that is likely to underlie such a question by showing that the doctrine of the resurrection entails elements of both strong continuity and remarkable discontinuity between the dead and the resurrected body. The short answer to the *how* question is that the resurrection body will take place in a way similar to that in which a seed produces a plant or tree. The short answer to the question about the *kind of body* is that the resurrection body will be incorruptible, glorious, powerful, spiritual — that is, it will be like Christ's resurrected body.

Both questions are posed as asked not by someone who is genuinely interested in knowing what a resurrected body would be like or how it would be constituted or accomplished, but as a challenge from someone who thinks that the whole idea is ludicrous and is looking forward to seeing the speaker make a fool of himself as he tries to give a credible answer.[238] Paul is not embarrassed. For him it is clearly the questioner who is the foolish one.

**15:36** While the questions to which Paul will respond presume the foolishness of the resurrection hope, Paul intends to show the foolish arrogance that the questions themselves reflect:[239] *How foolish!* The term[240] translated *How foolish!* is the substantival use of the adjective "foolish" which was used many times in the LXX to address or refer to the "fool." Thus many translations translate it, "You fool!" (NASB, NAB, KJV; cf. ESV, "You foolish person!") or simply, "Fool!" (NET, NRSV). *How foolish!* (TNIV, NIV, NJB; cf. NLT, "What a foolish question!") seems to underplay the rhetorical impact somewhat. Paul's scornful rebuke, "Fool!" echoes Psalm 14:1[241] — a psalm from which Paul quotes in Rom. 3:11-12 — and evokes the whole Old Testament motif of the fool as one lacking spiritual and moral judgment. Whereas in the psalm the fool fails to acknowledge any accountability to God, here

237. Ramsay MacMullen, *Christianizing the Roman Empire,* A.D. 100-400 (New Haven: Yale University Press, 1984), 12.

238. Paul would not have responded as he does in v. 36 ("Fool!") if he thought the question might have reflected serious inquiry. As N. T. Wright points out (*The Resurrection of the Son of God,* 342), Paul's "sharp reaction" in the following verse suggests that he has framed the questions as posed by a dismissive skeptic.

239. As Garland puts it, "Placing a leading question in the mouth of a conjectural objector allows Paul to rebuke the questioner as a 'fool' . . . without directly insulting the Corinthians as foolish students" (727).

240. Gk. ἄφρων.

241. "The fool [LXX ἄφρων] says in his heart, 'There is no God'" (so also Ps. 53:1).

Paul's derision is occasioned by a failure to take account of the power of God in contemplating the possibility of a resurrected body.

*What you sow does not come to life unless it dies.* Paul's letters show that (unlike most modern and secular people) he usually thinks of life as that which will follow death rather than something that precedes it. So also here, the seed must die before it can really live. Paul's comment about life following death confronts the common Greco-Roman view that even if people do have some kind of postmortem existence, it is likely to be but a dark, colorless, and shadowy existence compared to the fullness of our experience in our bodies prior to death. Paul knows that the point of the resurrection of the dead is that for God's people the fullest life is yet to come. The afterlife to which Christians ultimately look forward is not like the experience of a leaf after it has died and fallen from a tree only to rot away, but more like the experience of a seed that germinates and then enters into a flourishing life of color and beauty to which its previous existence is hardly capable of being compared (cf. Rom. 8:18; 2 Cor. 4:16-17, etc.).

A specialist might point out that germination is not actually about a seed dying. Paul is not speaking as a horticulturist or agronomist, of course, but as one who, starting out from what he knows about death and resurrection, has found a helpful analogy in the relationship between a seed and what grows from the seed following germination. The fact that the seed is buried in the ground like a dead body but (like one resurrected from the grave) refuses to just lie there but rather sends life rising up from the ground[242] undoubtedly encouraged the analogy. Christ himself had used the same analogy to make a similar point. In John 12:24 he says, "unless a grain of wheat falls into the earth and dies, it remains just a single grain; but if it dies, it bears much fruit" (NRSV).

Much of the following discussion is clearly dependent upon Genesis 1–2, and Paul's interest in seeds as an analogy may also have grown out of his reading of Genesis 1 (see esp. Gen. 1:11, 12, 29). Jesus himself frequently used agricultural metaphors when discussing eschatological concepts (sowing and reaping, workmen, harvest, separating wheat from tares, etc.), and the early church seems to have followed suit. Paul will use the language of sowing repeatedly in the following discussion (see vv. 37 [2x], 42, 43 [2x], 44). He finds several parallels between the life of a seed and the resurrection of the dead. The fact that the more abundant life of a plant or tree emerges only after the apparent destruction of the surface integrity of its seed[243] is just the first of them.

**15:37** Paul points out that seeds are not just smaller or older versions of the things that grow from them, but are something quite different and seemingly less than what they will be, but full of potential: *When you sow,*

242. Cf. Theodoret, 232.

243. BDAG, commenting on *dies* (ἀποθνῄσκω), suggests that the idea is "decay" and that "w[ith] regard to what is being illustrated, this is called *dying*."

*you do not plant the body that will be, but just a seed, perhaps of wheat or of something else.* Paul mixes together language that is normally applied to seeds or plants with that which is applied to bodies and, in doing so, strengthens the conceptual relationship between the two ideas. "Now it was very appropriate for him to use different terms: he did not say, It does not sprout unless it dies; instead, he used our terms of the seeds to bring out from them our resurrection."[244] By *the body that will be* Paul means the plant or tree that will grow from the seed, but since he has in mind a resurrected body — the point of the discussion — he refers to the life/growth that emerges from the ground as *the body.* The point is that "bodies of plants . . . are different in kind fr[om] the 'body' of the seed which is planted."[245] The word *body* is also used in the general sense of *"any corporeal substance," "the body* or *whole* of a thing" or "generally, *the whole body* or *frame* of a thing" (LSJ).

Then when Paul refers to what is placed in the ground, he does not merely refer to a seed, but, literally, to "a naked seed" (TNIV, *just a seed*), once again taking language appropriate to a body and applying it to a seed.[246] Although it is planted as a "naked" seed (i.e., body), it will one day be clothed with incorruptibility and immortality, as Paul emphasizes in vv. 53-54. Since there is a clear parallel with 2 Corinthians 5:3-4, Wright makes the intriguing suggestion that "behind both passages stands the nakedness of the first humans in Genesis 2 (the passage which, quoted in verse 45, reveals itself as having been in Paul's mind for some while)."[247]

In saying that one does *not plant the body that will be* but only a naked *seed,* Paul draws our attention to the fact that the seed looks nothing like the body (plant or tree) that will come from it. Unless we have already seen what particular plants or trees grow from what particular seeds, we could not possibly be expected to guess what any particular seed would end up producing. While there is an organic relationship between the seed and the plant, there is also a tremendous discontinuity between the appearance and characteristics of the seed and the appearance and characteristics of the plant that grows from it.[248] Similarly, Paul would have us know, we would be foolish to look at a failing or decaying body and think that we could actually discern from its present appearance what it might look like in the resurrection. The difference between the two will be as dramatic as night and day or seed and flower.

244. Theodoret, 232.

245. BDAG, σῶμα. BDAG points out that Maximus of Tyre (second century A.D.) "makes a distinction betw[een] the σώματα [bodies] of the plants, which grow old and pass away, and their σπέρματα [seeds], which endure," and that the bodies of plants are also referred to in Apollonius Paradoxographus, *Mirabilia* 7.

246. BDAG notes that the adjective "naked" (Gk. γυμνός) here "is applied to a grain of wheat, when it properly belongs to the bodiless soul which is compared to it."

247. N. T. Wright, *The Resurrection of the Son of God,* 344.

248. This is what Murray Harris calls "identity with difference" (Murray J. Harris, *Raised Immortal: Resurrection and Immortality in the New Testament* [Grand Rapids: Eerdmans, 1985], 126).

Wright points out that Paul's distinction between the "naked" seed and *the body that will be* suggests that part of the answer to the question about what kind of body will be resurrected is that "the sort of body that it will involve is like the fully clothed version of something which at present is 'naked.'"[249]

**15:38** Now Paul explains what determines the kind of "body" any given seed will have and how they get those bodies: *But God gives it a body as he has determined, and to each kind of seed he gives its own body. It* here is the seed mentioned in the previous verse. God gives the seed that was sown a body. And he gives each seed *its own body.* There is an organic relationship between the seed and the thing that grows out of the seed, but it is *God* who *has determined* what kind of body it gets.

In Genesis 1:11-12 we are told that the reason there are "plants bearing seed according to their kinds and trees bearing fruit with seed in it according to their kinds" (v. 12) is that "God said" it should be that way (v. 11). We note, as it seems Paul did as well, that the text distinguishes between seeds that are found within the fruit to which it belongs and other kinds of seeds, and that "according to their kinds"[250] modifies both groups, so that there are varieties of both kinds and *each kind* has its own particular seed. For Paul this is another way of saying that each seed has *its own body* and that in each case it is *God* who *gives it [that] body,* who *has determined* what kind of body each will have. As Garland suggests, that God *determined* (or "willed")[251] what body each seed would have probably "refers to the apparent laws established for plants in creation."[252]

The expression *as he has determined* was already used with respect to the distribution of spiritual gifts within the body of Christ in 12:18 (where the TNIV translated it, "just as he wanted"). In both places Paul is emphasizing the theme of God's sovereign rule over creation, just as he does in other places using other language. That certainly has been a theme in the earlier part of this chapter, especially in vv. 24-28, where we are told that all things will be in full submission to God once Christ's redeeming and restoring work is fully accomplished. *God* is given slight emphasis by being fronted in the Greek text. As we pointed out in our final comments on vv. 15-16, God's role in the resurrection is indirectly intimated in the dozens of passive verbs referring to the dead who are raised (by God — "divine passives"). These will be highlighted again in vv. 42-44 and 51-52. God's central role in that is more clearly indicated in v. 57. Here, in the middle of his analogy based on seeds and bodies, Paul makes explicit that which he normally leaves implicit: it is *God* who *gives* each *a* resurrection *body.* That he does so *as he has determined* reinforces the theme of his sovereignty, par-

249. N. T. Wright, *The Resurrection of the Son of God,* 344.

250. In the LXX this is even more clearly emphasized, since it is mentioned four times (twice in each verse) as opposed to three times in the Hebrew text.

251. Gk. ἠθέλησεν (aorist indicative) from θέλω.

252. Garland, 729.

ticularly as it is reflected in his ultimate power over creation demonstrated both in the way nature works in this present creation (where each seed develops into whatever body God has determined) and in the way his ultimate power over creation will be demonstrated in the resurrection of the dead.

Paul's language stresses not only God's sovereignty but his sovereign grace in particular as the only sure ground of Christian hope, an appropriate climax to the epistle as a whole.[253] This theme was introduced with reference to Paul's own conversion and calling in 15:8-11 (where "grace" is repeated three times), and in this verse it is the ultimate explanation for how the dead are raised (cf. 15:35a): "*God gives* it a body" (which is not unlike the affirmation in 2 Cor. 5:1, "we have a building *from God*"). The notion of resurrection as a free gift is expressed in Romans 4, with ultimate reference to the resurrection of Jesus, where Abraham is said to have believed in God "who gives life to the dead" (4:17; cf. 4:25b). The need for the grace of God is nowhere more evident than in the case of resurrection, where the recipients self-evidently can contribute nothing whatsoever.

Paul has already seen Christ's resurrected body and probably spent some time thinking about why it shares the particular similarities with and differences from Christ's earthly body that it does. Clearly God had determined or willed just what a resurrected human body would be like, and that conclusion was manifest in the body Paul had been privileged to see for himself.

**15:39** In this verse and the following two, Paul's comments suggest that his thinking on this subject is shaped by his reading of the very first passage in Genesis: *All flesh is not the same: Human beings have one kind of flesh, animals have another, birds another and fish another.* The bodies mentioned in vv. 39-41 correspond to three of the days of creation in reverse order, the sixth and fifth in v. 39, and the fourth in vv. 40-41. His point is that there are various kinds of bodies and different levels of splendor for each (so it would be a mistake to think a human body would always have to be the same kind of human body, with the same level of splendor). He starts by pointing to different kinds of flesh (v. 39). Next he will distinguish earthly bodies from heavenly bodies (v. 40a), and then degrees of splendor or glory between the different bodies (vv. 40b-41). He will apply those distinctions to the resurrection in vv. 42-44. The opening clause, *All flesh is not the same,* is the key to everything else in vv. 39-41. The point is that since there are so many different kinds of bodies in the world, the skeptical Corinthian should not assume that a resurrected body is just like our present bodies. It may be quite different. Different creatures have different body compositions and characteristics. As anyone who enjoys a variety of foods would recognize, Paul might have mentioned the differences in, between,

253. See in particular the comments of K. Barth, Luther, and Calvin, carried forward in Thiselton, 1169-70. So also N. T. Wright, *The Resurrection of the Son of God,* 344.

or within the bodies (flesh or meat) of different kinds of animals (e.g., sheep, cattle, and pigs), birds (e.g., even the difference between dark and white meat within a chicken or turkey), and fish (e.g., oily and white fish). His thinking, however, is oriented by his reading of Genesis 1, and the fact that it describes God creating the world in terms of creatures designed to live and move in particular habitats: fish in the water and birds in the sky (both in Gen. 1:20-21, day 5), and animals on the ground (Gen. 1:24-25, day 6), and then humans also to live on the land (Gen. 1:26-28, also on day 6), but designed differently so as to have dominion over the others.

As we mentioned, Paul presents the bodies in the reverse order from that in which they are mentioned in Genesis. He begins with humans since the real issue is the nature of the human body (as it is at present and as it will be in resurrected form), and then he works backward through the other broad categories of creatures mentioned in Genesis 1 to make the point that it would be simplistic to think "a body is a body is a body."

**15:40** In this and the next verse Paul moves from days six and five of the creation narrative in Genesis 1 (the background to v. 39) to day four, introducing the idea of heavenly and earthly bodies and then the idea of various shades of splendor (or levels of glory) for various kinds of bodies, a point which will be useful when he gets to v. 43: *There are also heavenly bodies and there are earthly bodies; but the splendor of the heavenly bodies is one kind, and the splendor of the earthly bodies is another.* Dale Martin has asserted that Paul's use of earthly and heavenly terminology in this verse and the next reveals his indebtedness to a hierarchical conception of matter, as found in some Greco-Roman thought.[254] Thus, Paul begins at the lower end of the spectrum, with "earthly bodies," and moves on to higher "heavenly bodies." However, as we have already seen in vv. 38-39, Paul's comments reflect his reliance on the biblical tradition of creation, especially Genesis 1. Paul is walking backward through the various bodies mentioned in Genesis 1:14-28 (days 4, 5, and 6) and has now come to the lights that God placed in the sky "to give light on the earth" (1:15). We have already seen that day three of the creation narrative (Gen. 1:11-13) seems to have played a role in Paul's thinking in vv. 37-38. The following chart reflects the full set of relationships:

| 1 Corinthians 15 | Day of Creation | Element of Creation |
|---|---|---|
| vv. 36-38 | 3 (Genesis 1:11-13) | Seed-bearing plants and trees |
| v. 39a | 6 (Genesis 1:26-28) | Humans |
| v. 39b | 6 (Genesis 1:24-25) | Animals |
| v. 39c | 5 (Genesis 1:20b, 21b) | Birds |
| v. 39d | 5 (Genesis 1:20a, 21a) | Fish |
| vv. 40-41 | 4 (Genesis 1:14-19) | Heavenly lights (sun, moon, and stars) |

254. D. B. Martin, *The Corinthian Body,* 125-26.

Paul had been talking about earthly bodies; now he goes back to the heavenly bodies mentioned in Genesis 1:14-16, which were to provide light for those living on the earth. The fact that the heavenly bodies (which Paul will identify as the sun, moon, and stars in the following verse) provide light for those on earth (although to different degrees and in different ways,[255] as will be pointed out in the next verse) suggested that the former have greater splendor or glory than the latter.

Although BDAG gives the word *heavenly*[256] (used twice in this verse) two different meanings, either "pert[aining] to being in the sky or heavens as an astronomical phenomenon" or "pert[aining] to being associated with a locale for transcendent things and beings," this verse is the only evidence provided for the first definition. It will be clear when we get to vv. 48-49, where Paul uses the same word three more times, that he wants to exploit the fact that the Greek word for "heaven" may be used either for that part of creation which is distinguished from the earth, or for the dwelling place of God and those (angels, etc.) who live in his presence.[257] Here he has in mind not the uncreated original or primary "locus" of the divine presence but the created habitat of *heavenly* astronomical bodies,[258] but when he comes back to the idea of spiritual and heavenly bodies in vv. 44-49 it will be in the normal (divine) sense of *heavenly*, so that our bodies will be like Christ's heavenly body.[259]

Paul's use of the word *earthly* here differs in an important way from his use of the word in vv. 47-49, translated "of the earth" or "earthly" in those verses. As Wright points out, the word Paul uses here suggests "'upon-the-earth-ly', a word principally of location rather than composition," while the word used in vv. 47-49 is "'earthy', a word describing physical composition."[260] The heavenly/earthly dichotomy Paul finds in Genesis 1 and refers to here will be exploited in vv. 47-49 by transitioning to a slightly different kind of *earthly*-ness in contrast with what is *heavenly* in the divine sense.

Paul will also exploit two different meanings of the word translated *splendor*,[261] which appears four more times in the following verse (with the

255. Greek astronomers recognized well before Paul's day that the moon reflected light to the earth from the sun.

256. Gk. ἐπουράνιος.

257. Cf. BDAG on οὐρανός.

258. Paul's dependence on Scripture implies that he does not think of *heavenly bodies* as "spiritual beings clothed with light," as BDAG defines it. See N. T. Wright, *The Resurrection of the Son of God*, 346, and the discussion of spiritual bodies in v. 44.

259. "If Paul is aware of a shift in meaning between 'heavenly' as meaning 'the location of the sun, moon and stars', as in the present passage, and 'heavenly' as he uses it in verses 48-49, he does not indicate it, but leaves his readers to make the transition through his move . . . from metaphor and simile to explicit description" (N. T. Wright, *The Resurrection of the Son of God*, 346).

260. N. T. Wright, *The Resurrection of the Son of God*, 345.

261. Gk. δόξα.

same meaning as in this one)[262] and then will appear again in v. 43, but with a different meaning. It is the word more commonly translated "glory" (as the TNIV translates it in v. 43 [along with the NIV, CSB, NAB, and NJB], masking the relationship between the texts), which may mean either "the condition of being bright or shining" (with "brightness, splendor, radiance" as possible glosses for this meaning), as it does here and in the following verse, "a state of being magnificent" (with possible glosses being "greatness, splendor"), or "honor as enhancement or recognition of status or performance" (with potential glosses being "fame, recognition, renown, honor, prestige").[263] While BDAG places Paul's usage in v. 43 under the first definition as it does the usages in this verse and the next, its antithetical relationship with "dishonor" in that verse clearly indicates that glory in the sense of (majestic) honor is in mind, not luminescence, although it will certainly involve magnificent splendor as well.[264]

Paul's usage of the word for "glory" in this verse and the next and the distinction he makes here between the glory of earthly bodies and the glory of heavenly ones prepares the way for his introduction of the concept of the "image" of the earthly man and the heavenly man in v. 49. In 11:7 Paul tied together the concepts of "image" and "glory," as he also does in Romans 1:23 and in 2 Corinthians 3:18; 4:4. In the case of human beings, at least, a body's glory is directly related to the image it bears.

Bonneau and Garland have helpfully suggested that in vv. 39-41 Paul "highlights the distinction that exists between below and above. The 'below' is characterized by the use of the term 'flesh'; the 'above' is characterized by the use of the term 'glory.' This creates a hierarchy of opposites: 'earthly/below/lesser' and 'heavenly/above/greater.'"[265] This is essentially correct, although in this particular verse the term "glory" (or "splendor") may be applied in different degrees to both heavenly and earthly

262. N. T. Wright correctly points out that "[o]bjects on earth do not shine as do the sun, moon and stars; but they still have their own proper 'glory'. Here 'glory' seems to mean 'honour', 'reputation', 'proper dignity,'" and that "the word remains multivalent even in a passage where some of its uses seem to refer more or less directly to 'shining'" (*The Resurrection of the Son of God,* 345). The fact that in v. 41 Paul refers only to the difference in splendor or glory between the heavenly bodies and says nothing more about earthly ones suggests that the idea of splendor or luminosity is foremost in mind in here, but the fact that the earthly bodies have a different kind of δόξα ("glory"/"splendor") points to the different use of the word that Paul will make in v. 43.

263. All of these definitions and glosses are from BDAG.

264. Cf. H. Hegermann, "δόξα," *EDNT* 1:345: "The variety of usages corresponds to the different classifications of the meaning of the word. Δόξα is used synonymously with τιμή with the meaning *esteem, honor* (e.g., Rom 2:7, 10; 1 Tim 1:17; with ἔπαινος in Phil 1:11; 1 Pet 1:7). The opposite is ἀτιμία (2 Cor 6:8). Words connoting power are used to elaborate the idea of δόξα as *radiance of power:* δύναμις (Matt 24:30; Luke 21:27), ἐξουσία (Luke 4:6; 2 Thess 1:9), and κράτος (1 Pet 4:11; Rev 1:6)."

265. Garland, 731, referencing N. Bonneau, "The Logic of Paul's Argument on the Resurrection Body in 1 Cor 15:35-44a," *Science et esprit* 45 (1993), 85.

bodies since "the splendor of the heavenly bodies is one kind, and the splendor of the earthly bodies is another."[266]

Paul's exploitation of the differing meanings of the words translated *heavenly* and *splendor* or "glory" and the fact that his argument will move from one word for "earthly" to another with a somewhat different meaning reflect the fact that he is not proving his point from Genesis 1 but has found the ideas of heavenly lights versus less glorious earthly creations to provide a useful analogy which he hopes will also be useful to the Corinthians for grasping something of the difference(s) between our present bodies (or Christ's pre-resurrection body) and the resurrected bodies that await us (and the one that Christ already has). As Wright puts it, "Paul is careful not to imply that the analogies he is offering in [these verses] are actually analyses of how the resurrection itself will be. He is here setting up a network of metaphor and simile, not metonymy."[267]

**15:41** Paul has already referred to a distinction in splendor or glory between earthly and heavenly bodies. He reinforces his thought by pointing out the obvious difference in brightness between the sun, the moon, and the various stars. He continues to show the influence of Genesis 1, now the heavenly bodies or lights created on the fourth day of creation: "God made two great lights — the greater light to govern the day and the lesser light to govern the night. He also made the stars. God set them in the vault of the sky to give light on the earth" (Gen. 1:16-17). *The sun has one kind of splendor, the moon another and the stars another; and star differs from star in splendor.* The Genesis passage made a distinction in splendor or glory in referring to the sun and moon as "the greater light" and "the lesser light," with the stars being mentioned in a way that suggests lesser splendor than the first two. That the sun and stars have their own light and the moon has reflected light, if Paul even considered the distinction, is irrelevant to his argument. While Paul applied the word "flesh" first of all to various earthly bodies, he used the word *splendor* or "glory" primarily for heavenly bodies (see our comments on v. 40 on Paul's exploitation of the somewhat different meanings of the word translated *splendor* or "glory").

When Paul uses this material in vv. 42-43, it will be to point out that the resurrected body, a kind of heavenly body, is marked by glory (analogous, at least, to the sun, moon, and stars). Whether he is thinking of distinctions in glory between Christ and believers or between one believer's glory and that of another is not at all clear. The former idea at least may be in the back of his mind, but if it is, he does not develop the thought. He will make only the point that our new bodies will have glory that our present ones do not.

266. This holds despite the fact that the words "glory"/"splendor" are elided from the second clause (the word "bodies" is also elided from the two last clauses), so that it reads, "and that of the earthly ones [i.e., bodies] is another" (ἑτέρα δὲ ἡ τῶν ἐπιγείων).

267. N. T. Wright, *The Resurrection of the Son of God*, 345.

We will note in our comments on vv. 42-43 that the reference to luminescent bodies ("shine like the brightness of the heavens") and stars in the description of the resurrection in Daniel 12:2-3 may have encouraged or reinforced Paul's use of the references to heavenly bodies in Genesis 1 to explain the nature of the resurrection body in terms of shining heavenly bodies.

**15:42-44** Paul hasn't explicitly mentioned the resurrection since v. 35. Verses 36-41 were dedicated to developing an analogy based on distinctions within creation reflected in the Genesis 1 narrative. The points he made along the way include: God decided what each seed should become, and each seed undergoes radical transformation to become the plant or tree God designed it to grow into; even earthly bodies reflect different kinds of flesh (so it is not the case that "a body is a body is a body"); heavenly bodies have differing degrees of splendor or glory; and there is a radical difference between earthly and heavenly bodies (the former have different kinds of flesh, and the latter have different degrees of splendor or glory). Now the time has come to apply all of that to his explanation of the nature of the resurrection body: *So will it be with the resurrection of the dead.* The first clause of v. 42 (separated out as a sentence in most English translations) lacks a verb, and a form of the verb "to be" should be supplied. The TNIV and the NIV are virtually the only translations to supply the verb in the future tense *(it will be),* and that is probably a mistake. It would be better to go with something like the NRSV, "So it is with the resurrection of the dead," or the NET, "It is the same with the resurrection of the dead" (cf. NLT), which use the present tense, as do most translations. Throughout this chapter it has been clear that the future resurrection of the dead is organically tied to Christ's own resurrection and that the same principles apply.

What Paul says in these verses applies equally to Christ's resurrection and to the future resurrection of the dead. In fact, what Paul knows about the resurrection body he probably knows in large part due to his own personal exposure to Christ in glory, even if he and other Jews would have some prior expectations informed by the role the resurrection was expected to play in the broader scriptural narrative of the redemption of creation. That Paul's conception of the resurrection body of believers ultimately owes its origin to the resurrected Christ, "the life-giving spirit" (15:45), "the heavenly man" to whose "image" believers will conform (15:49), is strongly suggested by vv. 45-49. This would be natural, considering the impact Christ's appearance had on his life and ministry. Paul makes the same connection elsewhere: at the Parousia "the Lord Jesus Christ . . . will transform our lowly bodies so that they will be *like his glorious body*" (Phil. 3:20-21); for "we will certainly be united with him in a resurrection *like his*" (Rom. 6:5b; cf. 6:8b). Christ, the eschatological Adam, is the founder of a new and better humanity.[268] It is thus no coincidence that the words Paul uses to describe

268. As I. H. Marshall, *Jesus the Saviour* (London: SPCK, 1990), 173, points out, 1 Cor. 15:21-22, 45-49 show that Paul regards the heavenly Lord Jesus as still being human.

believers' resurrection are roughly the same as when he speaks of the resurrection of Christ.[269] As will be noticed in our comments below, some of Paul's key ideas about the resurrection body in 1 Corinthians 15 can be seen plausibly to derive from the prototypical resurrection of Jesus, specifically what he has to say about the power, glory, and spiritual nature of the resurrection body.

In the light of this, Paul's view of the resurrection body as encompassing both continuity with and transformation of the present body, what Murray Harris calls "identity with difference"[270] may well find its best precedent in the accounts of the resurrection appearances of the Jesus in the New Testament Gospels. Here Jesus is recognizable to his followers but clearly has a different mode of existence, to which adjectives like imperishable, powerful, glorious, and spiritual are appropriate.

Even if, like much else in vv. 36-41, Paul's distinction between earthly and heavenly bodies is dependent on Genesis 1, the tie between resurrection bodies and the lights in the heavens was probably also encouraged or inspired by the most explicit passage on bodily resurrection in the Old Testament, Daniel 12:2-3: "Multitudes who sleep in the dust of the earth will awake: some to everlasting life, others to shame and everlasting contempt. Those who are wise will shine like the brightness of the heavens, and those who lead many to righteousness, like the stars forever and ever." The Old Greek of v. 2 speaks of those who will "light up like the luminaries of heaven,"[271] while Theodotion's version has "shine like the splendor of the firmament"[272] in the same place (both translations from NETS). Both versions of the verse indicate that either the same or another group will shine like "the stars." The theme of the splendor or luminescence of the righteous in the resurrection is quite clear. Since Daniel's text is the clearest reference to the subject, one assumes that its influence on Jewish thinking on the matter would have been quite significant.

Throughout these verses Paul builds on his introduction of the agricultural motif of sowing seed which was last mentioned in vv. 36-37: *The body that is sown is perishable, it is raised imperishable; it is sown in dishonor, it is raised in glory; it is sown in weakness, it is raised in power; it is sown a natural body, it is raised a spiritual body. If there is a natural body, there is also a spiritual body.*

269. For a detailed chart see M. E. Dahl, *The Resurrection of the Body* (London: SCM, 1962). This is true of all of the main terms, including ἀνίστημι ("raise up"), ἐγείρω ("raise"), ἀνάστασις ("resurrection"), and ζάω ("to live"). Only the related compounds ἐξεγείρω ("raise up") and ἐξανάστασις ("resurrection"), which occur once in 1 Cor. 6:14 and Phil. 3:11 respectively with reference to the resurrection of believers, are not used of Christ's resurrection. The use of the συν- prefix in συζήσομεν ("we live with [him]"; Rom. 6:8; 2 Tim. 2:11), συνδοξασθῶμεν ("we may be glorified with [him]"; Rom. 8:17), συνεγείρω ("to rise up together"; Col. 2:12; 3:1), and συνεζωοποίησεν ("he made alive together with [him]"; Col. 2:13; Eph. 2:5) make the link between the two explicit at the lexical level.

270. Harris, *Raised Immortal,* 126.

271. Gk. φανοῦσιν ὡς φωστῆρες τοῦ οὐρανοῦ.

272. Gk. ἐκλάμψουσιν ὡς ἡ λαμπρότης τοῦ στερεώματος.

What, exactly, is it that *is sown*, and what does it mean to sow it? The Greek text has no explicit subject (literally, "it is sown perishable," etc.). Although some have suggested that what is *sown* is simply the dead corpse being buried in the ground,[273] it seems more likely that Paul has in mind the human being who experiences decay and death.[274] The subject of the verb should be understood to be a body, based on both vv. 37 and 44, which explicitly refer to the sowing of bodies. But Paul seems to be referring not to the body as a dead corpse (even if it is that), but identifying the body which is buried with the qualities which marked its existence prior to death. The body which is buried is that of one whose life was marked by perishability, dishonor, weakness, and the (very limited) animating power of the human soul (see on v. 44), qualities that are typically on greatest display as one passes from life to death.

The expression translated *perishable* is literally "in corruption/decay," and the expression[275] translated *imperishable* is literally "in incorruptibility/immortality." The literary parallelism between the first three antithetical statements reflects the repeated emphasis on the condition in which the body is sown or raised, and then the last antithetical parallelism (natural/spiritual) describes the basic orientation (as we shall see) of each body. The difference between *in* and *is* is unlikely to be crucial, but reflects the following antithetical parallelisms.

| | |
|---|---|
| The body is *sown in* . . . | The body is *raised in* . . . |
| • Corruptibility | • Incorruptibility |
| • Dishonor | • Honor/Glory |
| • Weakness | • Power |
| The body sown *is* . . . | The body raised *is* . . . |
| • Natural | • Spiritual |

As Wright's analysis suggests, the first antithesis deals with the nature of the bodies (as corruptible or incorruptible), and the last addresses the animating power of the bodies (*natural* human nature or God's Spirit). Those two frame the inner two antitheses which relate to issues of status and abilities of the bodies (honored/dishonored, powerful/weak). As we shall see, all four characteristics of the resurrection body reflect Paul's knowledge of Christ's own resurrection body based on both personal experience and scriptural reflection, and much of his description of the body

273. Theodoret, 233, argues for the first view. Garland, 732, points out, however, that "'[i]n dishonor' and 'in weakness' do not seem applicable descriptions of interment," that *weakness* "applies to a lack of power, not to its complete absence," and that it does not seem fitting "to refer to a corpse as 'animated by the soul'" (v. 44).

274. For other options, including the view that the sowing has to do with human procreation in general (see, e.g., Gen. 9:19; 4 Macc. 10:2) or the incarnation of Christ in particular, see Garland, 732.

275. Gk. ἐν ἀφθαρσίᾳ.

which is *sown* may also be based on reflection on Christ's experience and on his crucifixion in particular, as well as Paul's own experience of weakness and dishonor as one following in Christ's footsteps.[276]

The word translated *perishable* appears in Wisdom 14:12, which says that "the idea of making idols was the beginning of fornication [*porneia*], and the invention of them was the corruption of life." Here we have idolatry leading inexorably to *porneia* (sexual immorality) and corruption. Paul uses the same word in Romans 8:21 when he refers to creation's "bondage to decay." He uses the word in conjunction with the metaphor of sowing in Galatians 6:8 when he says that those who sow to the flesh "will reap corruption from the flesh" (NRSV). He will use the same word a few lines down in this same discussion when in v. 50 he declares, "the perishable [will not] inherit the imperishable." Corruption, or the condition of being perishable, is a result of the fall of humanity. In Genesis 3:19 God told Adam, "By the sweat of your brow you will eat your food until you return to the ground, since from it you were taken; for dust you are and to dust you will return." And the rest of creation has been subject to decay and corruption due to the same fall. A slightly different cognate word[277] for corruption plays a key role in Psalm 16:10 (15:10 LXX) and its use in relation to Christ's resurrection in the book of Acts (Acts 2:27, 31; 13:35, 37). The psalm has a promise that the Lord will not let his holy or faithful one see decay (or corruption). Peter says that the psalmist "spoke of the resurrection of the Messiah, that he was not abandoned to the realm of the dead, nor did his body see decay" (Acts 2:31). Paul quotes the same text in Acts 13:35 to point out that while David "was buried with his ancestors and his body decayed, . . . the one whom God raised from the dead did not see decay" (vv. 36-37). Although it was a corruptible body that was placed in Christ's tomb, it was not given the opportunity to experience corruption, but, as our bodies will also do (cf. vv. 53-54), it was clothed in incorruptibility. The undoing of the fall of humanity and of creation would be fully achieved only if corruption and decay were also completely overcome.

The word translated *imperishable* entails the negation of corruptibility[278] and as such was also a common word for immortality, although the more literal word for immortality[279] will feature along with this word in

276. Garland, 735, has suggested that the logic found in Paul's polarities is that, e.g., "[i]f there is a natural body . . . , then there must be a spiritual body." It seems more likely that just as Isaiah's encounter with God's display of his holiness made him fully conscious of his own uncleanness (Isa. 6:3-5), Paul's encounter with Christ in his incorruptible, glorious, powerful, and perfectly spiritual body made him fully cognizant of just how lacking our present bodies are of those qualities. If so, the logic would be, "I have encountered a wholly incorruptible, glorious, powerful, and spiritual body and now recognize just how perishable, dishonorable, weak, and unspiritual our present bodies are."

277. Gk. διαφθορά.

278. Gk. ἀφθαρσία; "the state of not being subject to decay/dissolution/interruption" (BDAG; the word is formed through the application of the "alpha privative" to the word for decay or corruption).

279. Gk. ἀθανασία.

the climactic vv. 53-54. Immortality in one form or another had become a religious ambition for many Jews and Gentiles as well (see 4 Macc. 9:22; 17:12; Wis. 2:23; 6:18-19).[280] Using the same word, Wisdom 2:23 states, "God created the human for immortality," and then the text explains how death and corruption came into the world. In Romans 2:7 Paul says that God gives eternal life to "those who by persistence in doing good seek glory, honor and immortality." 2 Timothy 2:10 notes that Jesus Christ "has destroyed death and has brought life and immortality to light through the gospel." The word will reappear in vv. 50, 53, and 54. In those verses Paul will affirm that the perishable cannot inherit the imperishable, but that "the dead will be raised imperishable, and we will be changed. For the perishable must clothe itself with the imperishable." As our comments on *perishable* or "corruptible" suggested, the book of Acts indicates that incorruptibility was a key feature of what it meant for Christ (or anyone else) to experience bodily resurrection. The resurrection completely swallows up the broadest and deepest effects of the fall of creation and humanity.

When Paul says that the body *is sown in dishonor,* one is reminded of what he said earlier in this letter about his own experience of being dishonored: "You are honored, we are dishonored! To this very hour we go hungry and thirsty, we are in rags, we are brutally treated, we are homeless. We work hard with our own hands. When we are cursed, we bless; when we are persecuted, we endure it; when we are slandered, we answer kindly. We have become the scum of the earth, the garbage of the world — right up to this moment" (4:10-13; cf. 2 Cor. 6:8). Of course Paul's personal experience followed the pattern established by Christ himself, whose passion consisted in large part of a series of events in which Christ was dishonored, whether by the religious or political authorities, by his own disciples, or by the others who were crucified beside him. Paul summarizes Christ's experience in Philippians 2:7-8 as one of taking on "the very nature of a servant" and "becoming obedient to death — even death on a cross!" Paul's catalogues of his sufferings (including the part just cited) suggest that he fully embraced the dishonor to which he was constantly exposed, knowing that it was the natural prologue to experiencing glory modeled after that into which Christ himself entered after his experience of dishonor (cf. Phil. 2:9-11). Of course the dishonor experienced by Christ, Paul, and every other human being is a result of Adam's sin and the dishonor that sin brought on the whole human race and which is being overcome through Christ's redemptive work.

After being sown in dishonor, the body *is raised in glory.* Genesis 1 suggested, as poetically expressed in Psalm 8, that God had "crowned [hu-

280. Immortality is a regular theme in Philo (*On the Creation of the World* 153; *On the Sacrifices of Abel and Cain* 5; *On Agriculture* 100; *On Drunkenness* 140, 212; *Who Is the Heir?* 35; *On Flight and Finding* 56, 59; *On the Change of Names* 210; *On Dreams* 1:181, 217, 218; 2:258; *On the Life of Abraham* 55; *On the Life of Moses* 2:61, 194; *On the Eternity of the World* 1, 27, 46, 47, 76, 150; *Questions and Answers on Genesis* 3:11; *Questions and Answers on Exodus* 15).

manity] with glory and honor" (Ps. 8:5). But humanity had lost most of its glory and would regain it again only in the resurrection.[281] Jung Hoon Kim has pointed out the association between garments of glory and the resurrection or eternal life in early Jewish literature.[282] *1 Enoch* 62:15-16 reads: "The righteous and elect ones shall rise from the earth and shall cease being of downcast face. They shall wear garments of glory. These garments of yours shall become the garments of life from the Lord of the Spirits." In *2 Enoch* 22:8 the Lord tells Michael to "Go and extract Enoch from his earthly clothing" and "anoint him with my delightful oil, and put him in the clothes of my glory." As a result he became "like one of the glorious ones" (22:10). This is the reverse of what happened at the fall. In the *Apocalypse of Moses* 20:1-5 Eve says that after she ate of the forbidden fruit, "my eyes were opened, and I knew that I was naked of the righteousness with which I had been clothed," and recognizes, "I have been estranged from my glory with which I was clothed" (cf. Rom. 3:23). Kim seems to overlook the possibility that this motif may have found its source in Psalm 8 and its description of humanity being crowned with glory and honor.

The word translated *glory* here is the same one that was translated "splendor" in vv. 40-41. As we pointed out in our comments on v. 40, BDAG mistakenly places the usage in this verse under the meaning "the condition of being bright or shining" (with "brightness, splendor, and radiance" as possible glosses for this meaning). The word's antithetical relationship with "dishonor" in this verse clearly indicates that glory in the sense of (majestic) honor is in mind, not luminescence, although it will certainly involve magnificent splendor as well.[283]

Although Paul and the rest of us must wait to experience this part of the story, Paul had already seen and experienced the glory of the resurrection body when Christ appeared to him (cf. v. 8). The themes of Christ's glory and the glory that awaits believers were important ones for Paul, and they grew out of his personal experience of Christ. As Paul approached Damascus, "a light from heaven flashed around him" (Acts 9:3; cf. Acts 22:6) and the Lord appeared to him. In fact, the light was so brilliant (Paul would describe it as "brighter than the sun" in Acts 26:13) that it blinded him (Acts 22:11).[284] In Romans 6:4 Paul says, "Christ was raised from the dead through the glory of the Father." Earlier in this very letter Paul spoke of

281. Cf. H. Hegermann, "δόξα," *EDNT* 1:345: "Participation in the divine δόξα is granted to the works of the Creator (Rom 1:21, 24), esp. mankind as that which God has created (1 Cor 11:7). But as mankind has been unfaithful to its appointed place and participation in the divine δόξα has been lost (Rom 3:23), δόξα takes on a central meaning in soteriological sayings."

282. See Jung Hoom Kim, *The Significance of Clothing Imagery in the Pauline Corpus* (JSNTSup 268; London and New York: T&T Clark, 2004), 30-57 (esp. 34-40).

283. See again H. Hegermann, "δόξα," *EDNT* 1:345.

284. Acts 22:11 refers to the splendor of the light (δόξης τοῦ φωτός), using the word that is used for splendor/glory in this chapter.

God's wisdom which he "destined for our glory before time began," and said that if the rulers of this age had understood it, "they would not have crucified the Lord of glory" (2:7-8). In 2 Corinthians 3:18 Paul says that we "contemplate the Lord's glory" and "are being transformed into his image with ever-increasing glory." In Colossians 1:27 Paul speaks of the mystery which is "Christ in you, the hope of glory." In Romans 8:18 he says that "our present sufferings are not worth comparing with the glory that will be revealed in us." In Romans 8:21 he declares that the creation itself will be "brought into the freedom and glory of the children of God." Christ, the firstfruits, has already entered into glory via the resurrection. His people can look forward to experiencing glory through the resurrection as well.

Paul's concern in these verses is with the consequences of rejecting the teaching of the resurrection, and not with divisions among the Corinthians. Still, it appears from the evidence of earlier chapters that some Corinthians may have been tempted to think of themselves as people of honor or glory and of others among them as people of dishonor (due to their social status and the kinds of tasks that were incumbent on them). If so, this verse would remind them that all (fallen) human life is marked by dishonor to one degree or another and that the ultimate distinction between dishonor and glory is not one of those which Corinthians made on a daily basis, distinguishing between various people in their city, but one that distinguishes between those who will know only the glory of this present world (which is itself marked by dishonor in comparison with the glory of the world to come) and those who know the divine glory in store for those who are known not by the important people in the city of Corinth, but by God himself (8:3).

Having highlighted the differences between our present earthly bodies and Christ's resurrection body (and our future resurrection bodies) in terms of the tremendous difference with respect to their relative (or absolute) (in)corruptibility and (dis)honor, Paul now points out that a similar contrast pertains to the immeasurable difference between the strengths of the body before and after its resurrection: *it is sown in weakness, it is raised in power.* While Paul sometimes makes different distinctions between the weak and the strong (e.g., the weak in conscience mentioned in 8:7-12), here he has in mind weakness as the common condition of human life in its fallen state. As he will make clearer in 2 Corinthians, Paul actually celebrates his human weaknesses (2 Cor. 11:30; 12:5, 9-10; 13:9), knowing that through them he identifies with Christ's own weakness, and that in both cases God makes his own power known through such human weakness. He also knows that, as in the case of Christ, one day his weaknesses will give way to a spectacular and definitive demonstration of God's power in him. Paul's thought here is nicely paralleled in 2 Corinthians 13:4, where he says that Christ himself "was crucified in weakness, yet he lives by God's power." Earlier in this letter Paul had said that "[b]y his power God raised the Lord from the dead, and he will raise us also" (6:14). Romans 1:4 asserts that Jesus Christ is declared to be or designated the Son of God "in power"[285] by his resurrection from the dead. In the same way, it is *in power* that believers will be raised from the dead on the last day. Psalm 110 had applied the Adamic dominion motif to the Davidic king in language that is worth recalling here, especially given its double usage of the key word *power,* found in this verse: "A rod of power the Lord will send out from Sion. And exercise dominion in the midst of your enemies! With you is rule on a day of your power among the splendors of the holy ones" (Psalm 109:2-3 LXX, NETS translation). The reign of the Davidic king is a demonstration of God's power through him. So also God destroys all competing powers and raises us up with the power that he has demonstrated in the defeat of those other awesome but ultimately much lesser powers. And the bodies he gives us in that resurrection are also marked by his power.

Some Corinthians had a mistaken understanding of strength and weakness, and in doubting the resurrection they showed a particularly grave underestimation of God's power. They may have thought of themselves as powerful people, but like the rest of us, they were infinitely weak in comparison with the power of those who will be raised up with Christ. A distinction between strong and weak people was common in the Roman world, but Paul reemploys the weak-powerful dichotomy so that it no longer reflects a line drawn through the middle of the church of Corinth, but is one in which both rich and poor, humble and elite find themselves on the same side both in this world and the next. Master and slave, the socially powerful and the socially powerless, were to recognize that even the greatest of human strength was weakness in comparison with the power to be displayed in each one of them (cf. 1:25). They have much more important things in common with each other than either group has in common with their unbelieving social peers in the city of Corinth and its environs.

The next antithesis Paul provides has been the cause of great confusion in the history of interpretation as the polarity of Paul's own theology has been interpreted through the prism of ontological polarities of later periods of history. Paul says that the human body *is sown a natural body, it is raised a spiritual body.* In the modern, post-Enlightenment context, the words *natural* and *spiritual*[286] are often taken, popularly at least, to suggest a distinction between the material and immaterial, or between the physical and the spiritual (so NRSV). But scholars have pointed out that the material/immaterial dichotomy is a modern one and that in Paul's world soul and spirit were not considered to be immaterial but of a lighter, thinner material than visible stuff.[287] Still, people thought of matter in terms of very different categories of physicality, in a way that approximated the modern

285. Gk. ἐν δυνάμει.

286. Gk. ψυχικός and πνευματικός respectively.

287. See D. B. Martin, *The Corinthian Body,* 126-29; N. T. Wright, *The Resurrection of the Son of God,* 148-51.

physical/spiritual dichotomy. But in such dichotomies both of the words Paul employs here would normally be used to refer to the thinner, invisible kinds of stuff.[288]

The word translated *natural* is the adjective form of the word "soul" or "life" (thus BDAG indicates that the adjective means "of the soul/life"). The scriptural basis for Paul's word choice here is given in the following verse when he quotes Genesis 2:7 in a modified form. There Adam is described as a "living being/soul." Paul contrasts "natural" or "soulish" people with "spiritual" people in 2:14-15, and, as Wright points out, he is certainly not dealing with a distinction between people who are physical and people who are not! Rather, Paul's usage suggests a distinction between people who "are living at the level of life common to all humankind" versus those who "are indwelt, guided and made wise by the creator's Spirit."[289] In this passage as well the distinction has to do with the difference between ordinary human life and life empowered by God's Spirit. The adjectives Paul uses describe "not what something is composed of, but what it is animated by. It is the difference between speaking of a ship made of steel or wood on the one hand and a ship driven by steam or wind on the other."[290] Wright follows Hays in pointing to the helpfulness of the Jerusalem Bible's translation of the verse: "When it is sown it embodies the soul, when it is raised it embodies the spirit. If the soul has its own embodiment, so does the spirit have its own embodiment."[291]

Elsewhere Paul's language reflects what is called inaugurated eschatology, including the idea that Christians have already begun to experience the blessings and realities of the last days, including the Spirit, such that they may be called "spiritual." Here, however, for the sake of the point he wants to make about the radical contrast between the two types of bodies, he describes a strict dichotomy between the life animated by the soul, or ordinary human life, and life fully animated by God's Spirit, which are two mutually exclusive experiences. To live in a resurrected body is to experience a new mode of existence, life directed and empowered by the Spirit, suitable to the age to come, in a body untainted by sin and death in any sense.

As Wright suggests, Paul's reference to a spiritual body appears to be "the most elegant way he can find of saying both that the new body is the

288. N. T. Wright points out that "if a reader of first-century Greek came upon a phrase containing the word *psychikos* [ψυχικός; "soulish"], contrasted with anything else, he or she might well expect that, if there was a physical/non-physical contrast in the offing, *psychikos* would refer to the non-physical side, and whatever was being contrasted with it would be seen as more firmly bodily, more substantial" (*The Resurrection of the Son of God,* 351).

289. N. T. Wright, *The Resurrection of the Son of God*, 350.

290. N. T. Wright, *The Resurrection of the Son of God,* 352 (cf. 348-55). See also Thiselton, 1276-77.

291. Cf. N. T. Wright, *The Resurrection of the Son of God*, 352; Hays, 272.

*result* of the Spirit's work (answering 'how does it come to be?') and that it is the appropriate *vessel for* the Spirit's life (answering 'what sort of a thing is it?')."[292]

In Romans 6 the "resurrection like his" which believers await (6:5) is not only one that guarantees mortal transformation but also moral transformation, that we "may live a new life" (v. 4), an existence that begins in the present. The fact that Paul tells us elsewhere that we have been sealed by the Spirit (cf. 2 Cor. 1:22; Eph. 1:13; 4:30) and that the Holy Spirit is the firstfruits (Rom. 8:23) and the "first installment, deposit, down payment"[293] (2 Cor. 1:22; 5:5; Eph. 1:14) on what we are to experience once our redemption has been fully consummated suggests that our resurrection experience could not be anything other than an existence in which the Spirit has full sway and through which the Spirit is fully manifest in and through us as it is in Christ himself. The contrast that Paul has in mind in this verse and the next is clarified in vv. 47-49, where Paul shifts to the contrast between the "earthly" and the "heavenly" man, implying a contrast between one who lives out of (merely) earthly power or resources and one who lives out of heavenly power and resources.

**15:45** Paul provides scriptural support for the distinction he made between a spiritual body and a natural body in v. 44 by referring once again to the creation narrative in Genesis. This time he refers to Genesis 2:7. Paul has already compared and contrasted Adam and Christ in vv. 21-22. Here he will do so again in order to explain how the poles of the earthly and heavenly are bridged through Christ: *So it is written: "The first Adam became a living being"; the last Adam, a life-giving spirit.* This is "one of the most controversial passages in the New Testament,"[294] and yet Paul's use of scripture here is relatively straightforward. Genesis 2:7 focuses on the creation of humankind. The verse says "the Lord God formed a man from the dust of the ground and breathed into his nostrils the breath of life, and the man became a living being." Paul's snippet quotation includes some subtle changes to the single clause he quotes, which would otherwise simply read, "and the man became a living being." First, he omits the initial "and,"[295] a typical omission to conform the quotation to its new context. Secondly, he adds "first"[296] to "the man," an addition which, as Stanley notes, "brings to formal expression the fundamental contrast between Adam and Christ as the first and last Adam (v. 45b) that forms the backbone of the ensuing argument."[297] Though the addition finds no textual support, it would not be out of place in the original text and could hardly

292. N. T. Wright, *The Resurrection of the Son of God,* 354 (his emphases).

293. Cf. BDAG, ἀρραβών.

294. J. R. Asher, *Polarity and Change in 1 Corinthians 15: A Study of Metaphysics, Rhetoric, and Resurrection* (HUT 42; Tübingen: Mohr, 2000), 110.

295. Gk. καί.

296. Gk. πρῶτος.

297. Stanley, *Paul and the Language of Scripture,* 208.

be considered objectionable in itself. Thirdly, Paul adds "Adam," so that his version now reads, "the *first* man *Adam* became a living being," where the LXX reads simply, "the man became a living being." While none of the LXX MSS have the word "Adam," both Theodotion and Symmachus have "the Adam man" (the reverse word order to Paul) at this point in their texts. The dual rendering in both these texts and in 1 Corinthians 15:45 is probably due to the ambiguous sense of Hebrew word used,[298] which can be a generic noun (human/man) or a proper name (Adam). On the other hand, the man who is referred to in the text is later called Adam so that the dual rendering of Paul's gloss serves as a simple reminder of the identity of that original man in Genesis 2:7.

The connection with the previous verse is not as clear in English translation as it is in Greek. The word translated *being*[299] is the noun usually translated "soul" or "life," which corresponds to the adjective "of the soul/ life" (natural) used in the previous verse. Adam became a living soul, a (normal) living human being, the archetypal example of a "natural" or ordinary human life and Paul's biblical proof that such is a category of existence.

Philo's exegesis of Genesis 2:7 (*Allegorical Interpretation* 1:31) has some interesting things in common with Paul's. In commenting on Genesis 2:7 Philo suggests that Genesis 1–2 describes both "the heavenly man" and "the earthly man." For him the heavenly man is the one described in Genesis 1:26-28 who is made in God's image (and not formed from the ground) and destined to have dominion over all creation, and the earthly man is the one described in Genesis 2:7 who is formed from the dust of the ground and shares in a "corruptible and earthly substance." The linguistic parallels are remarkable, but in the end the differences outweigh the similarities. Philo allegorizes the text, suggesting that it refers to two different kinds of people in the world. He takes Adam's becoming a living soul to mean that God breathed into his corruptible, earthlike mind the power of real life. For Paul, however, the earthly man is Adam and the heavenly is Christ. Of course, Paul's Christology seems to be particularly dependent upon those traditions that recognized in Genesis 1 God's intention that all of creation be ruled by a human vice-regent who would perfectly reflect God's own righteousness, truth, and glory. That is, the dominion motif of Genesis 1:26, 28 undergirds texts such as Psalms 2, 8, and 110, Daniel 7, and others. These very texts were evoked in vv. 24-28 of this chapter.

Interestingly, Philo states that "the divine Spirit had flowed into [the first man] in full current" (*On the Creation of the World* 144). Paul might have agreed with him. The great difference is that even if the Spirit flowed into the first Adam, Paul declares that it flowed out of the second Adam in life-giving ways since rather than being simply "a living being" he is "a life-giving spirit."

298. Heb. אדם *('ādām)*.
299. Gk. ψυχή.

What Paul knows about Adam being a "living being/soul" he knows from Genesis 2:7. How does he know that the second Adam became "a life-giving spirit"? The idea of a life-giving spirit comes from reading Genesis 2:7 in light of Ezekiel 37 (esp. vv. 6, 9, 10, 14). In Genesis 2:7 it is when God breathed into the man that he came to life. In Ezekiel 37: 6, 9, 10, 14 God repeatedly says, echoing Genesis 2, that it is by putting his breath or Spirit (the same word in both Hebrew and Greek[300]) in his people that they would be brought to life. Ezekiel 37 describes "a life-giving spirit" in the context of the resurrection of the dead, or the restoration of Israel described as a resurrection of the dead. As Garland recognizes, "'Giving life' is synonymous with raising the dead (Rom. 4:17; 8:11; 2 Cor. 3:6)."[301]

Jesus Christ is the true resurrection of the dead, the one whose Spirit brings the rest of us to resurrection life. Of course, Paul does not know this simply through his study of the Old Testament, but also through his own personal experience and the experience of other believers, all of whom experienced true life through Christ's own presence in them by the indwelling Spirit. Paul did not simply deduce that "an opposite presupposes its counterpart" and that "if there is a natural body, then there is also a spiritual one."[302] He had personally encountered Christ as the powerful, glorious, wholly spiritual, life-giving spirit and knew himself and other humans to be something other than and less than what he had encountered in Christ. Our perishable, weak, inglorious, and unspiritual condition becomes transparent in the light of Christ's imperishable, powerful, glorious, and wholly spiritual resurrection state.

This verse affirms the distinction Paul made in v. 44 between natural and spiritual bodies by pointing out that Adam was (merely) a living soul or being (with a natural body), as Genesis 2:7 attests, while Christ's resurrection body was (as Paul experienced it and the Old Testament background might lead one to expect) wholly spiritual. Adam received life as an embodied soul in a natural body (cf. Wis. 15:11); Christ gives life as a life-giving spirit. Paul uses Genesis 2:7 to set up one side of the contrast and to lead into the other. Paul's references to the first and last Adam will lead into the point he makes in vv. 46-47, namely, that there is an order to these things (cf. v. 23), and that the natural comes first and then the spiritual.

This verse serves as the opening shot in a complex argument stretching through vv. 45-49, in which Paul's allusion to Adam as "the first man" and "the man of dust" (both twice) and his use of Genesis 2:7 point to the significance of Jesus Christ, whose bearing is just as universal as that of our first ancestor. In the process Paul makes it clear how anthropology, Christology, and eschatology are all integrally and organically related, so that Christ is the one who brings about the consummation of the story of cre-

300. Heb. רוח; Gk. πνεῦμα.
301. Garland, 735.
302. Garland, 734.

ation by bringing humanity from the state in which it has found itself under Adam's leadership to the state that God has had in mind for it since the beginning. The contrasts that Paul will develop out of the contrast between Adam and Christ may be easily reflected in a chart:

| The first Adam was: | The last Adam was: |
|---|---|
| • Living being | • Life-giving spirit |
| • Natural ("soulish") | • Spiritual |
| • First man | • Second man |
| • Dust/of the earth | • Of heaven |
| • Earthly man | • Heavenly man |
| His people are those who are of the earth and bear his his image. | His people are those who are of heaven and shall bear his image. |

**15:46** As in v. 23, Paul points out that he is not discussing a static and eternal contrast, but that a particular chronological order has been reflected in the history of creation and new creation. As it turns out, that order is also reflected in the experience of all who come to know true life in Christ: *The spiritual did not come first, but the natural, and after that the spiritual.* The relationship with v. 45 makes it clear that by *the spiritual* Paul refers to Christ, the last Adam, and *the natural* refers to the first Adam. The language Paul uses here *(natural/spiritual)* goes back to v. 44. The flow of Paul's argument makes it clear that the difference between our present bodies and our resurrection bodies (v. 44a) parallels the difference between Adam's bodily existence and Christ's resurrected body (v. 45), the two figures that establish the very difference between a normal human body and a spiritual (resurrected) body (v. 44b). The order in which we experience the "natural body" and the "spiritual body" (v. 44) mirrors the order in which the two figures mentioned in v. 45 (Adam and Christ, the last Adam) appeared in human history. We do not know whether or not any Corinthians said that they had already entered into a wholly spiritual existence, but Paul's point is that (1) there are two very different kinds of bodily existence; (2) so far they have experienced only the one that is common to all of Adam's children; thus (3) they should look forward to the bodily existence that comes only after this first one (and is experienced only by God's own people).

**15:47** Having referred to a first and a last Adam in v. 45 and established their distinctive natures and reiterated the order of their appearance in v. 46, he now speaks of them in terms of a *first* and *second man* and highlights the distinctive origin of each: *The first man was of the dust of the earth; the second man*[303] *is of heaven.* Starting in this verse, Paul shifts from his ex-

303. There are a number of textual variants at this point, most of which seem to reflect attempts to clarify exactly who the second man is. "Man" is replaced by "the Lord" (ὁ κύριος) in 630 and Marcion (according to Adamantius), while "the Lord" follows "man"

tended contrast between the "spiritual" and the "natural" to an extended contrast between *earth* and *heaven* (v. 47), between the "earthly" and the "heavenly" (vv. 48-49). The second contrast helps clarify what Paul had in mind by the first, and builds on it by stressing the differing origins of the two men and the life that they brought/bring and that they represent. Paul had already distinguished between earthly and heavenly bodies, in a different sense, in v. 40. Now that distinction is being used to explain the difference between Adam's body and Christ's resurrection body. As Wright points out, here "Paul draws into the discussion the most fundamental aspect of creation, heaven and earth, as in Genesis 1.1, showing how the new creation represents, at last, the Jewish dream of the kingdom, embodied in the new humanity that, as in Philippians 3.20-21, comes 'from heaven.'"[304] The word translated *man*[305] (twice) is not gender specific but is used of "a person of either sex, w[ith] focus on participation in the human race, *a human being*" (BDAG). Of course, in this instance both people are known to be males, but Paul is interested in them not as two different examples of men (male human beings), but as two types of human being: the type coming from Adam's line and the type modeled after Christ's resurrection.

That Adam was *of the dust of the earth* refers once again to Genesis 2:7, which Paul had just cited in v. 45. Here and in the next two verses Paul uses a rare adjective based on the noun "dust" found in Genesis 2:7.[306] In fact, as Balz indicates, the word "might have been constructed directly (by Paul?) from ["dust"] (Gen 2:7 LXX). Thus it emphasizes that a person is made from dust and will return to dust, and thus lives only through the Spirit of God within (cf. in addition to Gen 2:7 also 3:19; Job 4:19; 8:19; 10:9; Eccl 3:20; 12:7; Pss 22:30; 104:29; 146:4; Dan 12:2)."[307] It underscores Adam's (and humanity's) perishability and earthy origin in contrast with the resurrected Christ's eternal nature and heavenly origin. Throughout vv. 45-47 Paul has worked through a series of polar oppositions (see the chart in our comments on v. 45) to draw stark lines of distinction between Adam and (the resurrected) Christ as two different kinds of human being. All of this leads up to vv. 48-49, where he will argue that human beings may share in both kinds of humanity. He will build on the Adam/Christ distinction to distinguish between what it means to participate in Adam's kind of humanity and what it means to participate in the new (renewed) humanity Christ has brought about through his resurrection from the dead.

---

(ἄνθρωπος ὁ κύριος) according to ℵ², A, D¹, Ψ, 075, 1739^mg, 1881, 𝔐, sy, and "spiritual" follows "man" according to 𝔓⁴⁶ (ἄνθρωπος πνευματικός). As Metzger (*Textual Commentary*, 501-2) suggests, it is the shorter reading (ἄνθρωπος) which "best accounts for the origin of the others." That reading is supported by ℵ*, B, C, D*, F, G, 0243, 6, 33, 1175, 1739*, *pc*, latt, bo.

304. N. T. Wright, *The Resurrection of the Son of God*, 313.

305. Gk. ἄνθρωπος.

306. The adjective is χοϊκός; the noun is χοῦς.

307. H. Balz, "χοϊκός," *EDNT* 3:469. *Sibylline Oracles* 8:445 uses the same word with reference to Gen. 2:7.

**15:48** In this verse and the next Paul now makes the link between the two kinds of humanity represented by Adam and by the resurrected Christ and raises the question of the nature of the resurrection bodies which believers will enjoy: *As was the earthly man, so are those who are of the earth; and as is the heavenly man, so also are those who are of heaven.* As pointed out in our comments on v. 47, Paul had already distinguished between earthly and heavenly bodies in a different sense in v. 40, and v. 47 suggests that such a distinction may also be applied to Adam and Christ (in his resurrection). Now Paul applies that same distinction to others based on their relationship with Adam and Christ. In context, *those who are of the earth* would be all humans in that they share an earthly origin and existence, while *those who are of heaven* would be those who receive their renewed bodies from God through the resurrection of the dead. Here *of heaven*[308] does not mean that they are originally from heaven or that they are headed to heaven (again, this is not about some ethereal heavenly existence but about the resurrection of the dead in the new creation). It has to do with "being associated with" heaven (BDAG). In this context Paul asserts that just as we have been marked by the earthly realm through our Adamic origin, thanks to Christ we will be marked by the heavenly realm through our resurrection from the dead. As Wright puts it, "The point is not . . . that the new humanity will exist in a place called 'heaven'. Rather it will originate there, where Jesus himself currently is in his own risen and life-giving body; and it will transform the life of those who are presently located on earth and earthy in character."[309]

Paul has already indicated in vv. 42-44 what it is to be like *the earthly man* or the heavenly man. To be like the former is to live a life marked by a lack of permanence, strength, glory, and unmitigated spirituality while to be like the latter is to enjoy all of those qualities in a resurrected body like Christ's own.

The Corinthians are to recognize themselves in the references to *those who are of heaven;* that is, the *we* who shall *bear the image of* Christ (v. 49), *the heavenly man,* includes all believers. This subtly reinforces the hope that all believers (including all Corinthian believers) share in common, a hope that separates them from all other peoples and groups of the world. If any Corinthian clique were tempted to think of themselves and their non-Christian friends as being somehow superior to their poorer and less powerful brothers and sisters in Christ (including the slaves) among them, this would be one more text reminding them that even their slaves will share a glorious future with Christ that their unbelieving social peers in the city could not dream of.

**15:49** Paul reinforces the point of v. 48 by bringing in the idea of two different images that we might bear: *And just as we have borne the image of the*

308. Gk. ἐπουράνιος.

309. N. T. Wright, *The Resurrection of the Son of God,* 355.

*earthly man, so shall we*[310] *bear the image of the heavenly man.* Like so much of what Paul says in vv. 38-49, the motif of the image also goes back to the opening chapter(s) of Genesis. While Genesis 1:26-27 (cf. Gen. 5:1) tells us that God "created human beings in his own image" (v. 27), Genesis 5:3 says that Adam had his children "in his own likeness, in his own image." This latter verse is surely the background for Paul's statement that *we have borne the image of the earthly man.* Genesis 5:3 does not suggest that Adam's descendants no longer reflected God's image. Genesis 9:6 indicates that humans continued to bear God's image, and in this very letter Paul has affirmed that man "is the image and glory of God" (11:7; see our comments there). The image of God has not been lost but merely tarnished or distorted. It does not need to be regained, but to be perfectly restored/renewed.

In 11:7 Paul tied together the ideas of God's image and glory (see also Rom. 1:23; 2 Cor. 3:18; 4:4), and in v. 48 he distinguished between the splendor or glory of heavenly and earthly bodies. In v. 43 he spoke of human bodies being sown in dishonor and raised in glory. The concepts of glory and *image* are probably linked throughout these texts such that we are to understand that *the image of the earthly man* lacks the glory with which it was previously created and is now an image of impermanence, weakness, ignobility, and of earthy humanness while *the image of the heavenly man* reflects God's glory in its incorruptible, powerful, honorable, and spiritual nature (cf. vv. 42-44). We spend these lives in bodies that reflect Adam's state after the fall; we will spend the rest of eternity in bodies that reflect Christ's state after his resurrection from the dead.

Paul's other references to the image we bear merit our attention for the light they may shed on Paul's point here. In 2 Corinthians 4:4 Paul says that the gospel "displays the glory of Christ, who is the image of God." Similarly, in Colossians 1:15 he declares that Christ "is the image of the invisible God." Paul tells the Colossians to "put on the new self, which is being renewed in knowledge in the image of its Creator" (Col. 3:10), and in 2 Corinthians 3:18 he states that as believers contemplate the Lord's glory we "are being transformed into his image with ever-increasing glory." In Romans 8:29 Paul affirms that God predestined believers "to be

310. There is a significant textual problem at this point in the letter. The vast majority of witnesses ($\mathfrak{P}^{46}$, ℵ, A, C, D, F, G, Ψ, 075, 0243, 33, 1739, 𝔐, latt, bo, Irenaeus [lat], Clement of Alexandria) read, "let us bear" (φορέσωμεν; aorist subjunctive) rather than "we shall bear" (φορέσομεν; future indicative; supported by B, I, 6, 630, 945, 1881, sa, and a number of later MSS). Most commentators agree with the editors of the NA$^{27}$ text in arguing that internal evidence is more significant than external evidence here (Metzger, *A Textual Commentary,* 502: "the context is didactic, not hortatory"). Fee, 787 n. 5, disagrees on the basis of the strong external evidence and the fact that the subjunctive is the more difficult reading. Garland, 738, is right that in this case "[i]nternal evidence must outweigh the external evidence," and Caragounis, *The Development of Greek and the New Testament,* 496-546, provides evidence that orthographical errors were so common in the ancient MSS that the argument regarding the more difficult reading is undermined and that in cases such as this one the reading which makes the best sense in the context (here, the indicative) is to be preferred.

conformed to the image of his Son." Putting these texts together, we can understand Paul's point in this verse against the more complete picture the combined texts provide. The *image of the heavenly man,* as one would expect from Genesis 1:27-28 (cf. Gen. 5:1; 1 Cor. 11:7), is the perfectly restored image of God, the image which we were intended to bear and which Christ bears without blemish (2 Cor. 4:4; Col. 1:15). God's plan of redemption entails, among other things, restoring the perfect reflection of his image in his people, now by conforming them to the image of his Son, Jesus Christ (Rom. 8:29). These points could be deduced from what Paul writes in these verses, but they are clarified by his other texts. Colossians 3:10 and 2 Corinthians 3:18 make it clear that the process of conforming us to Christ's image (the perfect and unblemished image of God) is one that begins as believers grow in Christ and are transformed by his presence in their lives even now. The process that begins in this life comes to its final consummation at the moment of the resurrection when our bodies experience their complete transformation and the rest of our ultimate transformation is also achieved (cf. Rom. 8:21-23).

Paul's argument in this chapter leaves out the initial phase of the transformation process — inaugurated eschatology — in order to reflect the starkness of the contrast between life under Adam's regime and life under Christ in the resurrection. Of course, part of the point of this chapter, as it relates to the first fourteen chapters of this letter, is that although we should already be reflecting God's renewed humanity as we learn true wisdom as it is found in Christ (chs. 1–4) and reject sexual immorality (chs. 5–6) and idolatry (chs. 8–10) in favor of glorifying God with our bodies and in our worship, and in all we do (chs. 7, 11–14), the complete and ultimate manifestation of God's renewed humanity in Christ will be fully realized only when God raises us from the dead, as he raised Christ, and makes us like him. While that process has begun, we "eagerly wait for our Lord Jesus Christ to be revealed" (1:7) because we know that that is when it will be brought to completion (cf. Phil. 1:6).

The word translated *bearing* means to wear apparel and is being used figuratively here, suggesting that believers wear the image of Adam or of Christ on our bodies as we would wear a robe, crown, or other external apparel.[311] The clothing motif goes back to v. 37, which spoke of a "naked" seed. The motif will be employed again in vv. 53-54, which speak of the perishable clothing itself with the imperishable and the mortal clothing itself with immortality. Kim thinks it "likely that this language of the wearing of the heavenly man's image reflects the concept of being clothed with garments of glory that is attested in Jewish apocalyptic literature (e.g. *1 Enoch* 62.15-16; *2 Enoch* 22.8-10). These documents use the imagery of clothing to describe the righteous and Enoch receiving a heavenly and immortal mode

311. Cf. BDAG; H. Balz, "φορέω," *EDNT* 3:436; Kim, *The Significance of Clothing Imagery,* 198.

of existence. Furthermore, it should be noticed that, like the preceding verses, verse 49 has been influenced by the Adam story in Genesis."[312] In our comments on v. 43 we noted that the poetic interpretation of Genesis 1 found in Psalm 8:5 may have encouraged the motif.[313]

We have all worn the (perishable and mortal) image of (fallen) Adam, but we will end up clothing ourselves with the (imperishable and immortal) image of Christ (the new Adam), in the resurrection from the dead. Gordon Hugenberger has pointed to evidence that the donning of clothing is a common part of an inheritance motif.[314] In the next verse (v. 50) Paul will talk about the possibility of inheriting the kingdom of God, inheriting the imperishable. The way that verse is tucked between references to clothing in this verse and vv. 53-54 raises the possibility that Paul is comparing our resurrection bodies to clothes given as evidence of our status as God's heirs. Certainly the motif of God's grace is involved in that it is God who changes us (v. 52) and who gives us the victory we need (v. 57). It is God who gives us the clothing of imperishability and immortality to wear.

## F. Explanation of the Necessity of the Resurrection for the Realization of God's Ultimate Victory, 15:50-57

> [50]*I declare to you, brothers and sisters, that flesh and blood cannot inherit*
> *the kingdom of God, nor does the perishable inherit the imperishable.*
> [51]*Listen, I tell you a mystery: We will not all sleep,*[315] *but we will all be*
> *changed —* [52]*in a flash, in the twinkling of an eye, at the last trumpet. For*
> *the trumpet will sound, the dead will be raised imperishable, and we will be*

312. Kim, *The Significance of Clothing Imagery,* 198.

313. The idea that Adam and Eve's nakedness entailed being stripped of the righteousness/glory with which they had previously been clothed (*Apocalypse of Moses* 20:1-5) also points in this direction.

314. Gordon P. Hugenberger, *Marriage as a Covenant: Biblical Law and Ethics as Developed from Malachi* (Biblical Studies Library Series; Grand Rapids: Baker, 1998), 199 n. 30. In private correspondence he has pointed out that Gal. 3:26-29 is another Pauline text that suggests a relationship between clothing and inheritance.

315. We find several variants in the MSS at this point, evidently all of which owe their origin to a sense of awkwardness about the text reading "we will not all sleep" after the passing of Paul and his whole generation. Thus some texts moved the negative from the first clause to the second, resulting in "we all will sleep, but we will not all be changed" (πάντες κοιμηθησόμεθα, οὐ πάντες δὲ ἀλλαγησόμεθα), which is found in ℵ, C, 0243*, 33, 1739). Some MSS (𝔓[46], A[c], [F, G]) conflated the two readings, so that they read, "we will not all sleep, but we will not all be changed" (πάντες οὐ κοιμηθησόμεθα, οὐ πάντες δὲ ἀλλαγησόμεθα). A few (Western) witnesses (D*, it, vg, Marcion, Tertullian, *al*) read, "we will all rise, but we will not all be changed." This reading avoids the original problem, but it may also have arisen "to counteract (gnostic?) denials of the general resurrection" (Metzger, *A Textual Commentary,* 502). The wording "we will not all sleep, but we will all be changed" (πάντες οὐ κοιμηθησόμεθα, πάντες δὲ ἀλλαγησόμεθα) best explains the origin of the others and has strong external support as well (B, D[2], Ψ, 075, 0243[c], 1881, 𝔐, sy, co, Jerome).

*changed.* [53]*For the perishable must clothe itself with the imperishable, and*
*the mortal with immortality.* [54]*When the perishable has been clothed with the*
*imperishable, and the mortal with immortality,*[316] *then the saying that is*
*written will come true: "Death has been swallowed up in victory."*

> [55]*"Where, O death, is your victory?*
> *Where, O death, is your sting?"*[317]

[56]*The sting of death is sin, and the power of sin is the law.* [57]*But thanks be*
*to God! He gives us the victory through our Lord Jesus Christ.*

In vv. 50-57 Paul explains how God's ultimate victory over his last enemy (v. 26) depends on the resurrection of the dead, and how that resurrection takes place. In our present state entrance into God's kingdom would be impossible. It is impossible for those characterized by perishability or mortality to experience it (v. 50). God must, and will, bring about such a dramatic change that mortal and perishable people gain immortality and imperishability (vv. 51-53). That is what the resurrection of the dead is all about. When God brings about that change, death is brought to its ultimate defeat and we enter into Christ's complete victory over death achieved through his cross and resurrection from the dead (vv. 54-57). In this passage Paul is dealing with the fundamental issue raised by those who doubt that the dead could be raised — their proper understanding that even if the bodies of dead people were brought back to life, they would not be capable of experiencing the everlasting, immortal life to which Christians aspire. Paul's argument up to this point has been dedicated to establishing that there are different kinds of bodies in the world. The Corinthians are correct to think that bodies such as we now have, perishable earthly bodies, are not the kind that could endure and enjoy the blessings Paul has in mind. Paul has made the point that it would be a heavenly body, a wholly spiritual body, like the one he knows Christ has, that would be necessary. In these

316. Some witnesses ($\mathfrak{P}^{46}$, ℵ*, C*, 088, 0121, 0243, 1175, 1739*, *pc,* lat, sa$^{ms}$, bo, Ir$^{lat}$, Ambrosiaster) omit most of the first half of the verse (leaving "When the mortal has been clothed with immortality"), and others (A, 326, sa$^{ms}$) put the second clause before the first (with other minor differences), leaving "When the mortal has been clothed with immortality, and the perishable has been clothed with the imperishable." A few (F, G, 614*, 1877*, it, cop) omit the entire verse. As Metzger explains, the shorter reading "probably arose accidentally through an oversight in copying, occasioned by homoeoarcton or homoeoteleuton," while the reading with the reversed order of the clauses apparently originated "when the oversight was noticed, but the omitted clause was restored in the wrong sequence," and the omission of the entire verse "is explained from homoeoteleuton with ver. 53" (*A Textual Commentary,* 502-3). The text as translated here is supported by ℵ$^{2}$, B, C$^{2vid}$, D, Ψ, 075, 1739$^{c(mg)}$, 1881, 𝔐, vg$^{mss}$, sy (with an added article in ℵ, A, 088, 33, *pc*).

317. Two variants arose in this verse due to the scribal tendency to assimilate New Testament quotations of the Old Testament to the text of the Septuagint. Two other MSS ($\mathfrak{P}^{46}$, B) mistakenly wrote "strife/dispute" (νεῖκος) because its pronunciation is similar to the word for "victory" (νῖκος; on both issues see Metzger, *A Textual Commentary,* 503).

verses Paul explains that it is only by a dramatic, God-given change (like the change a seed goes through to become a plant or a tree, vv. 37-38) that the kind of resurrection Paul and the other apostles have in mind can take place. God must transform our bodies from the kind that they are now to the kind that they need to be. It is that act of inconceivable power that makes the inconceivable conceivable.

Paul's discussion of the ultimate defeat of death will build on the motif of victory over death in Isaiah 25:8 and Hosea 13:14.

**15:50** Paul introduces both this verse and the next with a speech orienter, an introductory clause that highlights the importance of what is about to be said. The words *I declare to you* are, literally, "I say this,"[318] and the "this" points forward to what is about to be said. The expression adds nothing to the content of what Paul has to say, but it stresses the importance of what follows. The vocative, *brothers and sisters,*[319] also suggests a new start in the passage and adds extra stress.

So what is it that Paul wants to underscore by introducing it in this way? It turns out to be a point that may very well have been stressed by those Corinthians who found the idea of the resurrection of the dead incredible. He agrees with them *that flesh and blood cannot inherit the kingdom of God, nor does the perishable inherit the imperishable.* The combination *flesh and blood* is a Jewish idiom for a human being with a "strong emphasis on ephemeral character, shortsightedness, and moral weakness" or "in contrast to gods."[320] The two clauses seem to have a nearly synonymous relationship, suggesting that the ephemeral character of human life is foremost in mind in the reference to *flesh and blood.*[321] Taken together, the two clauses imply that *perishable* humanity *(flesh and blood)* cannot inherit the *imperishable kingdom of God.*

Paul's repeated use of the language of inheritance in this verse reflects a development in the Old Testament and Jewish theology of the land which had taken place in earlier Jewish thought and was confirmed by Jesus and the apostles. While the Old Testament speaks over and over again of inheriting the land,[322] Jews began to speak more and more of inheriting

318. Gk. Τοῦτο δέ φημι.

319. Gk. ἀδελφοί.

320. BDAG, "αἷμα."

321. The fact that such synonymous structures are so commonly used for the sake of clarification undermines any suggestion that Paul has different groups in mind in his references to *flesh and blood* and the *perishable* (see Garland's valuable discussion [740-42] of Jeremias's suggestion that the former refers to living believers at the time of Christ's coming and that the latter refers to the dead; see also the discussion in Kim, *The Significance of Clothing Imagery,* 201) or different destinies in mind in his references to the kingdom of God and imperishability.

322. The verb for inheriting (κληρονομέω) is found in conjunction with land (γῆ) in more than 86 verses of the LXX and New Testament (e.g., Gen. 15:7; 28:4; 47:27; Exod. 23:30; Lev. 20:24; Num. 14:24, 31; 18:20; 21:35; 26:53, 55; 33:54; 34:17; Deut. 1:8, 21; 2:9, 24, 31; 3:12; 4:1, 5, 14, 22, 26, 38, 47; 5:33; 6:1, 18; 7:1; 8:1; 9:4-6, 23; 10:11; 11:8, 10-11, 29, 31; 12:29; 16:20;

the earth[323] (same word but with a broader meaning), God's kingdom,[324] or eternal life.[325] It became clearer and clearer that God's intention was not simply to give Israel the Promised Land in the Middle East, but to bring his people into the new heavens and the new earth, to bring them into eternal life and an everlasting kingdom. Thus the promises about the land are swallowed up in the resurrection teaching so that all that was hoped for in terms of the restoration of Israel to the land and the restoration of the land (and all of creation) to an Edenic condition now finds its ultimate consummation in the resurrection of the dead and the complete renewal of creation that accompanies it. While some Corinthians assumed that the fact that the perishable cannot inherit the imperishable settled the question of the possibility of a resurrection of the dead in a negative way (even if they might have inconsistently held to the possibility that perishable people could inherit an imperishable, non-bodily existence), Paul understands that the objection is not insurmountable. In vv. 51-53 he explains how the human incapacity to enter into the imperishable kingdom of God is overcome.

**15:51-52** The previous verse began with a speech orienter highlighting Paul's agreement with a basic plank of the Corinthians' objection to the resurrection of the dead. Verse 51 also begins with a speech orienter: *Listen, I tell you a mystery.*[326] This time it introduces the explanation of how it is that the point made in v. 50 can be true and yet resurrection can still take place and should be affirmed. The key is change, and Paul indicates that the change involved is a *mystery* that was revealed. A *mystery* is something that is unknowable apart from divine revelation and which was therefore formerly unknown. But God has now revealed it to and through his prophets (and the apostles).[327] Evidence suggests that such revelation often came by way of inspired biblical interpretation.[328]

What is the *mystery*? *We will not all sleep, but we will all be changed — in a flash, in the twinkling of an eye, at the last trumpet.* On *sleep* as a euphemism for death, see our comments on 7:39; 11:30; 15:6, 18, 20. Paul's statement that we will not all sleep should not be taken as a promise that some would not die, but indicates that death was not inevitable for the Christian. Certainly Paul expects some believers to be living when Christ returns, so that

---

17:14; 20:16; 21:1; 23:21; 28:21, 63; 30:5, 16, 18; 31:13; 32:47; Josh. 1:15; 17:6; 18:3; 22:9; Judg. 11:21; 18:9; 1 Chr. 28:8; Ezra 9:11; Neh. 9:15, 22-23; Pss. 24:13; 36:9, 11, 22, 29; 43:4; Obad. 1:20; Isa. 14:21; 49:8; 57:13; 60:21; 61:7; Sir. 45:22; 1 Esdr. 8:80; Jdt. 5:15; Tob. 3:15; 4:12).

323. See Matt. 5:5.

324. See, e.g., Matt. 25:34; 1 Cor. 6:9-10; Gal. 5:21.

325. See, e.g., Matt. 19:29; Mark 10:17; Luke 10:25; 18:18.

326. It consists of ἰδού, the "demonstrative or presentative particle that draws attention to what follows" (BDAG, translated by the TNIV as *listen*), followed by *I tell you a mystery* (μυστήριον ὑμῖν λέγω).

327. See P. T. O'Brien, "Mystery," in *DPL* 621-23. He points out that "Paul normally employs the term with reference to its disclosure or its being revealed" (622).

328. Markus Bockmuehl, *Revelation and Mystery in Ancient Judaism and Pauline Christianity* (Grand Rapids: Eerdmans, 1990), 174-75, 225-27.

while it is possible that only some will die, all (believers) will certainly be changed.

Paul understands that in order for any human being to enter into God's imperishable kingdom, they must first *be changed.* Such a change will need to be experienced both by those who have died by the time Christ returns and also by those who are still living. That change will come suddenly. Paul uses two expressions to stress the suddenness of the event. The expression translated as *In a flash* by the TNIV and NIV ("in a moment" by NRSV, ESV, NASB, NET, NLT, CSB, and "in an instant" by NAB ["instantly" by NJB]) is one that refers to something that "cannot be cut, esp[ecially] because of smallness (e.g. particle of matter, uncompounded word)" (BDAG).[329] So the idea here is of the smallest unit of time, with the exact unit or measure being left to the reader's imagination. The word translated *twinkling* suggests "the shortest possible time necessary to 'cast' a glance."[330] Paul's language here is a particular way of reflecting an understanding that goes back to the Old Testament, that God's eschatological intervention to save and judge would happen suddenly (see esp. Isa. 29:5-6; 48:3 and Mal. 3:1; also Isa. 30:13; 47:11; Jer. 6:26; 15:8; 18:22; 49:19; 50:44; 51:8; Mark 13:36; Luke 21:34).

The *trumpet* as a sign of the day of the Lord in 15:52 recalls Isaiah 27:13, Joel 2:1, and Zephaniah 1:14-16 (cf. 2 Esdr. 6:23). In 1 Thessalonians 4:15-17 Paul indicates that his teaching about the relationship between the resurrection and the trumpet call is based on dominical teaching:

> [15]According to the Lord's word, we tell you that we who are still alive, who are left till the coming of the Lord, will certainly not precede those who have fallen asleep. [16]For the Lord himself will come down from heaven, with a loud command, with the voice of the archangel and with the trumpet call of God, and the dead in Christ will rise first. [17]After that, we who are still alive and are left will be caught up together with them in the clouds to meet the Lord in the air. And so we will be with the Lord forever.

The Lord's word that Paul has in mind is presumably similar to that recorded in Matthew 24:31, where Jesus says that at the time of the coming of the Son of Man "he will send his angels with a loud trumpet call, and they will gather his elect from the four winds, from one end of the heavens to the other." Matthew 24 and 1 Thessalonians 4 simply indicate that the trumpet call brings about the gathering of God's people at the end, without explicitly indicating how either dead or living people could enter into the new life initiated by that trumpet call. The last clause of v. 52 makes it clear that Paul understands that that trumpet call must bring about the radical change required for mortal human beings to enter into the immortal life of

329. Gk. ἄτομος.

330. G. Schneider, "ῥιπή," *EDNT* 3:212 (so also BDAG).

the resurrection: *For the trumpet will sound, the dead will be raised imperishable, and we will be changed*. The association between the trumpet call and the resurrection is traditional; Paul simply recognizes that the resurrection must entail a radical change in the nature of the resurrected body. Psalm 101:27 LXX may have played a role in Paul's thinking here. Speaking of the heavens and the earth, the psalmist says, "They will perish, but you will endure, and they will become old like a garment. Like clothing you will change them, and they will be changed" (NETS).[331] This passage is quoted in Hebrews 1:11-12. Kim holds that the idea is that "as a worn-out garment is replaced by a new garment, so the present cosmos when it is dissolved will be exchanged with a new one (cf. Isa. 65.17; 66.22)."[332] In Romans 8:19-23 Paul makes it clear that our resurrection is tied in with the restoration and renewal of the rest of creation. That may provide the key to Paul's understanding of what will happen to our bodies. If the old cosmos is to be exchanged for a new one as in putting on a new garment, it would be natural to assume that the same will take place with the bodies of the redeemed.

A trumpet blast was often a warning of danger or attack, but it could also signal any one of a number of different things, including attack. While the word used for victory in vv. 54-55, 57 could refer to victory in a contest or a war, the idea of victory over death suggests a victorious battle and the reference to a *trumpet* blast in this verse is then better understood to be the announcement of the Lord's arrival in battle, a battle that does not last more than a moment in time. It is the Lord's act of changing us from perishable to imperishable, of making us people over whom death has no power whatsoever, that constitutes death's defeat and our victory over it.

**15:53-54** Here Paul moves from the simple language of change that he used in vv. 51-51, to the metaphor of clothing oneself in a new and different set of qualities. These two verses reflect a close parallelism of language which is broken by the TNIV's decision to avoid the strict repetition. The first four lines literally read:

| | | | | |
|---|---|---|---|---|
| For | the perishable | must | clothe itself | with imperishability, |
| and | the mortal | [must] | clothe itself | with immortality. |
| When | the perishable | has been | clothed | with imperishability, |
| and | the mortal | has been | clothed | with immortality. . . . |

Perhaps Paul's high prose here is influenced by the fact that he is about to quote some poetic lines in vv. 54b-55.

Paul had already introduced the figurative use of the language of being *clothed* with the reference to the *naked* seed in v. 37. In v. 42 he had said

331. The Greek word for "change" that Paul uses in this verse in the LXX (ἀλλάσσω: "to make someth[ing] other or different" [BDAG]) appears twice in the final clause of the verse (καὶ ὡσεὶ περιβόλαιον ἀλλάξεις αὐτοὺς καὶ ἀλλαγήσονται).

332. Kim, *The Significance of Clothing Imagery*, 27 (cf. 28).

that in the resurrection the body is changed from being perishable to being imperishable; now he makes the same point by way of the figure of putting on a new set of clothing (cf. 2 Cor. 5:1-4): *For the perishable must clothe itself with the imperishable, and the mortal with immortality.* As Kim suggests, Paul's use of the imagery of clothing oneself with imperishability and immortality "shows a close affinity to the idea of the attirement of the righteous (who rise from the earth, that is, enter the heavenly order by escaping from the earthly order) with garments of glory or life (*1 Enoch* 62.15-16). The imagery also resembles the description of Enoch's transformation from an earthly to a heavenly mode of existence as the replacing of earthly with heavenly clothes (*2 Enoch* 22.8-10). These parallels suggest that the resurrection-clothing imagery in 1 Corinthians 15 is probably a product of Paul's recognition of the contemporary Jewish transformation idea, described by clothing symbolism."[333]

The perishable body *must clothe itself* with an imperishable one. This is the only way mortal and perishable human beings can inherit the imperishable kingdom of God (v. 50). Paul often uses the language of clothing or changing clothes figuratively for the transforming work of God through Christ in the lives of believers (besides vv. 53-54, see Rom. 13:12, 14; Gal. 3:27; Eph. 4:24; 6:11, 14; Col. 3:10, 12; 1 Thess. 5:8). We pointed out above that Hugenberger has suggested that the gift of special clothing is often associated with inheritance or the identification of a special heir in biblical and ancient Near Eastern thought.

Verse 54 explains (metaphorically) how the earthly body becomes fit for heavenly existence at the Parousia and how relates it to God's final victory over death: *When the perishable has been clothed with the imperishable, and the mortal with immortality, then the saying that is written will come true: "Death has been swallowed up in victory."* Death is vanquished by the resurrection. Paul supports this assertion with a quotation from Isaiah 25:8. The verse from which Paul quotes is part of an oracle of salvation (Isa. 25:6-10a) which envisions God's universal salvation of "all peoples" (25:6, 7; cf. "all nations" in 25:7) and the ultimate destruction of the power of death. The verse is frequently cited in rabbinic literature, where it is taken to be a divine promise that death would be no more in the age to come (*Mo'ed Qaṭan* 3:9; *Exodus Rabbah* 15:21; 30:3; *Deuteronomy Rabbah* 2:30; *Lamentations Rabbah* 1:41; *Ecclesiastes Rabbah* 1:7; *b. Pesaḥim* 68a; *b. Ketubbot* 30b).

Paul's *"Death has been swallowed up in victory"* differs markedly from the LXX, which reads literally, "death, being strong, swallowed (them) up" (the context suggests that the nations have been swallowed up by death). However, Aquila, Theodotion, and Symmachus have differing variants, some of which are quite close to Paul's citation.[334] Paul was probably following a preexisting Greek text (Rev. 21:4 cites the same tradition). Alterna-

333. Kim, *The Significance of Clothing Imagery,* 205.

334. See Stanley, *Paul and the Language of Scripture,* 210-11, for the details.

tively, as Hays indicates, Paul may have altered "punishment/penalty"[335] in Hosea 13:14 LXX to "victory"[336] and inserted it in his quotation of Isaiah 25:8 to create a word link with the next verse.[337] It is also possible that the Isaiah citation supplies the word "victory" to the Hosea text (see below).

The metaphor of "swallowing up" suggests the destructive power of an overwhelming force or creature.[338] Death may have its sting (vv. 55-56), but if it is *swallowed up* as prey it has more than met its match, like a mouse being swallowed up by a predator (1 Pet. 5:8 provides the image of "a roaring lion looking for someone to devour"). Once it is swallowed up, no trace of its existence is left behind. The victory over the swallowed victim is complete and uncontestable. In 2 Corinthians 5:4, in a similar context of discussing the overtaking of mortality by immortality, Paul expresses the desire "to be clothed with our heavenly dwelling, so that what is mortal may be swallowed up by life."

In Paul's mind, the final destruction of death requires the resurrection of the dead. In citing Isaiah's eschatological vision Paul ties God's triumph over death (and universal salvation) to the resurrection of the body. For Paul, resurrection is the necessary outcome of what God has done in Christ and what he intends to do for his people. Paul's personification of death, following the lead of both Isaiah 25:8 and Hosea 13:14, depicts it not as the inevitable and benign fate of all humans but as "an alien, inimical power,"[339] nothing less than a tragedy. In the words of Isaiah 25:7, death is "the shroud that is cast over all peoples, the sheet that is spread over all nations." Death for Paul is a power that casts its ominous shadow over us all and must be not just removed but defeated. A key emphasis of this whole chapter has been that what is required for complete victory over God's enemies includes the total defeat of death, "not a compromise in which death is allowed to have the body while some other aspect of the human being (the soul? the spirit?) goes marching on."[340]

**15:55-56** Paul's quotation from Isaiah 25:8 leads him to another Old Testament text about victory being taken from death as he celebrates God's final victory over death, both in the resurrection of Christ and in its implications for all his people. He quotes from Hosea 13:14 and then comments on that verse to show the relationship between victory over death and victory over sin (and its use of the law). Like the first four lines in vv. 53-54, the two lines of v. 55 reflect a tight parallelism:

335. Gk. δίκη.

336. Gk. νῖκος.

337. Hays, 276.

338. For examples of the usage of the word in the LXX see Gen. 41:7, 24; Exod. 7:12; 15:12; Num. 16:30, 32, 34; 26:10; Deut. 11:6; 2 Sam. 17:16; Pss. 34:25; 57:10; 68:16; 105:17; 106:27; 123:3; 140:6; Prov. 1:12; Job 8:18; Hos. 8:8; Hab. 1:13; Isa. 9:15; 16:8; 49:19; Jer. 28:34; Lam. 2:16.

339. De Boer, *The Defeat of Death*, 184.

340. N. T. Wright, *The Resurrection of the Son of God*, 358.

[55]*"Where, O death, is your victory?*
*Where, O death, is your sting?"*
[56]*The sting of death is sin, and the power of sin is the law.*

Hosea 13:14 is part of a prophecy of judgment upon Ephraim: "The guilt of Ephraim is stored up, his sins are kept on record" (Hos. 13:12). Verse 14 contains four rhetorical questions. The first two expect a negative answer: "Shall I ransom them from the power of Sheol? Shall I redeem them from death?" Paul quotes the last two, which act as a summons to personified Death and Sheol: "O Death, where are your plagues? O Sheol, where is your sting?" (ESV).[341] In the LXX the lines read, "Where is your punishment/penalty, O death? Where is your sting, O Hades?"

Paul's quotation of Hosea 13:14 raises the question of death's *sting*. In the psalm the sting seems to be in synonymous parallelism with "plagues" in the Hebrew text and "punishment/penalty" in the LXX. In Paul's citation "plagues/punishment" is transformed into "victory" so that there appears to be a synonymous parallelism between death's *victory* and its *sting*. Paul goes on to say that the sting of death is sin. If this is correct, it means that we should understand sin to be both death's victory and death's sting.

Con Campbell has argued that *the sting of death* would be better translated "the stinger of death" and that sin is not death's sting in the sense that it is the consequence of death, but rather, as Paul is usually understood to argue elsewhere, death is the result of sin. Death uses sin as a scorpion or bee might use its stinger to accomplish its purpose.[342] But BDAG points out, in commenting on the word for "sting" used here,[343] that Paul's use of the imagery is "transcultural: a friend of a teacher named Theodoros records in an epitaph that he felt a[n] . . . 'unceasing sting'[344] because of his death." This suggests that death's sting was thought of as the shadow of its lingering effects. Isaiah 25:8, quoted by Paul in v. 54, fits with this in that there the swallowing up of death is tied to the promise that the Lord "will wipe away the tears from all faces" and "remove his people's disgrace from all the earth."

341. The MT, LXX, and Paul's citation exhibit various differences. Hebrew: "Where, O Death, are your plagues? Where, O Sheol, is your destruction?" LXX: "Where, O Death, is your judgment? Where, O Hades, is your sting?" 1 Cor. 15:55: "Where, O Death, is your victory? Where, O Death, is your sting?" Leaving aside minor word order differences which may be explained on stylistic or rhetorical grounds, compared to the LXX, Paul has "victory" (νῖκος) instead of "judgment" (δίκη) and "Death" instead of "Hades." It is difficult to imagine why the LXX translated Heb. דֶּבֶר, ("plague") as "judgment" in the first place. We are left to conjecture. Stanley, *The Language of Scripture in the Letters of Paul*, 211-15, suggests that the LXX translators had a different non-Masoretic *Vorlage* (the LXX translation may reflect a reading of דברך ["your cause"] for MT's דבריך ["your plagues"]) and/or that Paul's Greek *Vorlage* itself had "victory." We should not rule out Paul's making the change to "victory" in order to link the present citation to the one in 1 Cor. 15:54.

342. Con Campbell, "The Stinger of Death," *The Briefing* 357 (June 2008), 14-15.

343. Gk. κέντρον.

344. Gk. κέντρον ἄπαυστον.

Thus it seems best to maintain the translation "sting of death" and recognize that Paul may alternate between seeing death's power behind sin's throne and seeing sin as the power behind death's throne. God will destroy death as well as even the shadow of its effects on us or creation. Paul's argument in this chapter starts with Christ paying the penalty for sin and moves to the destruction of all of God's enemies, including the presence and power of sin in our lives and death itself, the "last enemy," which is both a result of sin and the great promoter of sin. On the last day believers will find themselves both innocent of the guilt of sin and free of the power and presence of sin. This chapter is ultimately about the execution of God's plan, secured by Christ's death and resurrection and guaranteed by his continuing reign and ultimate destruction of his enemies, to bring about the complete renewal of humanity and creation. Not only will the ultimate enemy, death, be destroyed, but every trace of its causes and consequences, every one of its allies and partners will be removed.

Of course, for Paul, as in the teaching found in Ezekiel 36–37, it is spiritual death, manifest in the weakness of the flesh, that explains the human incapacity to resist sin's temptation. Romans 7–8 explicitly lays the responsibility for our death at the door of sin. Sin was even able to use the law/commandment, despite the fact that it is holy, righteous, and good (7:12). Sin "used what is good to bring about my death" (7:13). So clearly sin brings about death. But how did sin manage to use God's holy and spiritual law to bring about our death? It is not because sin is the ultimate evil power. It is due to the fact that "I am unspiritual, sold as a slave to sin" (7:14). It is "sin living in me" that causes me to sin (7:17, 20). There is something in me that is "waging war against the law of my mind and making me a prisoner of the law of sin at work within me" (7:23). The law was powerless "because it was weakened by the sinful nature" (Rom. 8:3). As Paul puts it in Ephesians 2:1-3, our sinful lives are grounded in the fact that we are "dead in [our] transgressions and sins." So in a very basic sense sin is the result of death just as death is (originally and ultimately) the result of sin. Paul had already said that "[t]he last enemy to be destroyed is death" (1 Cor. 15:26). Clearly for Paul it is death that uses sin for its purposes, and not the other way around.

Paul employs an eschatological hermeneutic in his use of Hosea 13:14, turning a text about judgment into one declaring salvation, for we are not under the law and the resurrection of Christ signals the beginning of the new age of redemption. "Paul projects an eschatological vision of a stingless death precisely because Jesus Christ has himself absorbed the sting on the basis of how his death and resurrection addresses the problem of human sin and the law."[345] Interpreting the passage from the perspective of the resurrection of Christ, Paul turns the summons to death into a taunt. The rhetorical questions now sneer defiantly at death's impotence in the

345. Thiselton, 1300.

face of God's powerful act of mercy and forgiveness in Christ. In Hosea death is called on to punish sin, but thanks to Christ such a role is no longer needed (1 Cor. 15:3, 17). Death's dominion over the whole earth has been ended, its "sting"[346] drained of potency.

Paul provides an extremely concise commentary on his quotation of Hosea 13:14 in v. 56. He suggests that the sting of death mentioned in Hosea 13:14b LXX has to do with sin, and points out that the law ended up reinforcing the power of sin and death over human lives. Paul's epigrammatic statements in v. 56 consist of two maxims, the second being built upon the first. The nexus between sin and death is prepared for by the allusions to the fall in 15:21-22. Vlachos argues convincingly that rather than originating from an issue in the Corinthian church, Paul's assertion that *the power of sin is the law* may also arise out of an edenic context. There is evidence that Paul found the triad of law, sin, and death present in the Garden of Eden. That law plays a catalytic role in Eden is implicit in the story depicted in Romans 7:7-11. There, as in Romans 5:12-14, the fall is the prototype for sins under the Mosaic law.[347]

Paul gives further evidence of his understanding of the relationship between sin and death in Romans 5:12, 21; 6:16, 23; 7:5, 13; 8:2. It seems that in Paul's thinking sin leads to spiritual death, and spiritual death is also, for everyone other than Adam, at the root of all post-Adamic sin.

**15:57** Having mentioned the power of sin and the sting of death in the previous verse, Paul switches back to the main theme — the fact that through the resurrection of the dead death has been robbed of victory and has been swallowed up by God's victory over it (and all enemies mentioned in vv. 25-26) through Christ: *But thanks be to God! He gives us the victory through our Lord Jesus Christ.* The motif of victory was introduced in vv. 54-55, where it was announced that rather than being able to claim victory death itself had been swallowed up in victory. Now Paul leaves no doubt whatsoever about where that inversion came from — how it is that victory has been stolen out of death's jaws and has swallowed up death itself. It is all *thanks . . . to God.*

The word translated "thanks"[348] is the word that is usually translated "grace" but which in contexts like this one serves as a "response to generosity or beneficence," is used "mostly of gratitude to God or Christ," and "refers to appropriate response to the Deity for benefits conferred" (BDAG). It is appropriately translated "thanks." As BDAG points out, in this usage it is common for the basis for the thanksgiving to be indicated in a participle

346. Gk. κέντρον (15:55, 56).

347. See Chris A. Vlachos, "Law, Sin, and Death, An Edenic Nexus? An Examination with Reference to 1 Corinthians 15:56," *JETS* 47 (2003), 277-98. See also Vlachos, *The Law and the Knowledge of Good and Evil: The Edenic Background of the Catalytic Operation of the Law in Paul* (Eugene, OR: Pickwick, 2009), 116-23. For key Pauline texts on the relationship between sin and the law see Rom. 3:20; 5:13, 20; 7:5, 7-9; 8:2.

348. Gk. χάρις.

agreeing with "to God" (e.g., 2 Cor. 2:14; 8:16; Josephus, *Antiquities* 6.145; Philo, *On Dreams* 2:213) such as is found in the Greek text here (in the TNIV the participial clause modifying "to God" is translated as a separate clause: *He gives us the victory through our Lord Jesus Christ*).

In v. 38 Paul pointed out that "God gives" the naked seed a body. That verse was already pointing forward to this one, where the idea is further unpacked. God's giving resurrection bodies to his people is part and parcel of what it means for him to give us the ultimate victory through Christ. Verses 20-28 made it clear that it is the resurrected Christ whose reign over all things brings God's enemies to their proper end and guarantees the ultimate conclusion in which God is "all in all." That is, Christ (more specifically, as here, the "*Lord* Jesus Christ") guarantees the Father's ultimate victory. Here Paul makes it clear that God's victory is also our victory. It is the victory that God *gives us . . . through our Lord Jesus Christ.* In a strange paradox, the Christian needs to learn that "it's not about me" but about Christ the Lord and his agenda. Once that has been properly grasped, one may go back and recognize that, as it turns out, God's agenda has been that of redeeming us (and the rest of his creation) and giving us the ultimate victory over the enemies of his righteous reign.

## G. Final Appeal in Light of the Affirmation of the Resurrection, 15:58

Paul introduces his conclusion to the chapter with a concluding conjunction and a vocative: *Therefore, my dear brothers and sisters. . . .*[349] This is followed up with a call to "be/become"[350] three things: "steadfast, immovable, always abounding in the work of the Lord." (The TNIV separates the three points into three distinct sentences with the final clause of the sentence seemingly modifying just the clause before it rather than the sentence as a whole: *Therefore . . . stand firm. Let nothing move you. Always give yourselves fully to the work of the Lord, because you know that your labor in the Lord is not in vain.*) The first two terms are synonyms, the first "pert[aining] to being firmly or solidly in place" and the second meaning "immovable."[351] The third part clarifies the precise manner or issue with which Paul would have the readers remain so steadfast and immovable, namely, in their constant involvement in the work of the Lord. The theme of constancy found in the first two terms is reflected in a slightly different way in the word "always" in "always abounding in the work of the Lord." To "abound" in the Lord's work, in context, is to be constantly giving oneself to that work (as

349. Gk. Ὥστε, ἀδελφοί μου ἀγαπητοί.

350. This is technically the only imperative in the verse (a present imperative). The other imperatives in English represent predicate adjectives and participles which detail the kinds of people the Corinthians should be.

351. BDAG on ἑδραῖος and ἀμετακίνητος (the second word is built out of the verb μετακινέω ["shift, change"] preceded by the "alpha privative").

suggested by the TNIV). To hesitate in, desist from, or carry out the Lord's work in a halfhearted manner would be to reflect a lack of firmness or steadfastness; it would be to be movable rather than immovable.

The logical relationship between the final clauses of the verse makes it clear that *the work of the Lord* here is the same as the readers' *labor in the Lord* in the final clause. What counts as the work of the Lord (or labor in the Lord) and what (if anything) does not? Paul refers to the work of or in the Lord in 1 Corinthians 3:13-15; 9:1; 16:10. He refers to things done out of service to Christ as labor in 1 Corinthians 3:8; 2 Corinthians 6:5; 10:15; 11:23, 27; Galatians 6:17; 1 Thessalonians 1:3; 2:9; 3:5; 2 Thessalonians 3:8. By *labor* is meant Christian ministry above all (see 3:8, where Paul uses the same word and speaks of reward for labor as he does in this verse), but probably also includes any activity that would be undertaken out of commitment to Christ, especially any "activity that is burdensome,"[352] that is, any activity that one would not naturally engage in were it not for their faith in Christ. Back in v. 19 Paul had said that "[i]f only for this life we have hope in Christ, we are to be pitied more than all others," presumably because we willingly engage in burdensome and/or dangerous activities for the sake of Christ or others that we might not be willing to do were it not for our resurrection-based faith.

The reason Paul gives at the end of the verse, *because you know that your labor in the Lord is not in vain*, applies to all of the exhortations at its beginning. It is because they know that their labor is not in vain that they should remain steadfast, unmovable, and always abounding in the work of the Lord. Paul uses the figure of litotes, a type of understatement in which an affirmative is expressed by negating its opposite. To say that our labor is not in vain is to say that our labor will be fully rewarded.

What Paul says about their labor here he already said would apply to their faith and his preaching (vv. 14, 17). He has already established that all of life is in vain if there is no resurrection. As it is, our life and labor are not in vain but have meaning, purpose, direction, and their proper final reward. The life of true wisdom which rejects sexual immorality, greed, and idolatry in favor of a life of integrity before the Lord who was raised from the dead and whose reign will consummate God's redemptive plan is the only life with ultimate meaning in that it reflects the continuity between God's renewed humanity both before and after the resurrection:

> The final verse of the chapter could be felt as an anticlimax, but only if we had allowed ourselves to forget the multiple ways in which this extensive discussion of the resurrection was linked to the rest of the letter. . . . [Paul] redirects [the readers'] gaze to the present time, to the tasks awaiting attention and the call to be "steadfast and immovable" in them. The point of it all has been that, despite the discontinuity be-

352. BDAG on κόπος.

> tween the present mode of corruptible physicality and the future world of non-corruptible physicality, there is an underlying continuity between present bodily life and future bodily life, and this gives meaning and direction to present Christian living.[353]

In 1 Corinthians 3:8-14 and 9:17-18 Paul spoke of God's reward for faithful service. The rewards to which Paul and his readers could look forward were mainly postmortem or post-resurrection rewards (as v. 19 made clear). This is in keeping with the model of Christ which Paul holds out in Philippians 2:5-11. We are to "have the same attitude of mind Christ Jesus had." He took "the very nature of a servant" and "humbled himself by becoming obedient to death — even death on a cross! Therefore God exalted him to the highest place and gave him the name that is above every name, that at the name of Jesus every knee should bow, in heaven and on earth and under the earth, and every tongue acknowledge that Jesus Christ is Lord, to the glory of God the Father." Christians do not expect to be given "the name that is above every name," but they do understand that as God has done with Christ he will also reward them for their own sacrificial and servant-like obedience to the gospel, and exalt them in the time of their own resurrection. In a similar vein the author of the Letter to the Hebrews exhorts us to fix our eyes on Jesus, "the pioneer and perfecter of faith": "For the joy set before him he endured the cross, scorning its shame, and sat down at the right hand of the throne of God. Consider him who endured such opposition from sinners, so that you will not grow weary and lose heart" (Heb. 12:2-3). This whole chapter serves as a call to faithful Christian service in the assurance that comes from the resurrection — the assurance that sacrifices made for Christ and his kingdom are not made in vain, but will be richly rewarded in the fullness of that kingdom.

## VI. LETTER CLOSING, 16:1-24

Paul has wrapped up the main theological and ethical points of his letter and will now close with some final bits of instruction, news, general exhortations,[1] and greetings. The cohesion of this final section is found in the rapid series of very concise pieces of instruction and information sharing, with a special focus on personal matters. It is also distinct in the density of its explicit references to particular Christian people or groups external to the Corinthian church (the Galatian churches, Jerusalem, Paul, Timothy, Apollos) and those who served as messengers of the church to others (Stephanas, Fortunatus, Achaicus). Most of this passage (vv. 1-12, 15-18) has to do with

353. N. T. Wright, *The Resurrection of the Son of God,* 359.

1. Between the instructions and the general exhortations there are twelve imperatives (vv. 1-2, 10-11, 13-14, 18, 20, 22) in the twenty-four verses of this chapter.

the plans of people who would or would not be traveling to Corinth and for whose visits the Corinthians should or should not have been preparing (Paul, Timothy, Apollos, Stephanas, Fortunatus, and Achaicus).[2]

The effectiveness of Paul's argument in chapters 1–15 is decisive for whether or not anything he says in this final chapter will matter. If the Corinthians failed to flee sexual immorality and idolatry and continued to allow Roman and Corinthian values and perspectives to guide their thinking and behavior, it would not bode well for the collection for the gift to those in Jerusalem or for the upcoming visits from Paul, Timothy, or Apollos. Of course, the evidence in 2 Corinthians (esp. chs. 2 and 7, not to mention chs. 10–13) suggests that there were indeed lingering issues that would complicate those things, but Paul concluded this letter with the hope that the Corinthians would respond positively to the main body of this letter and that he could go ahead with the plans outlined in these final lines.

## A. Instructions for the Collection for the Saints, 16:1-4

It seems that the Corinthians had asked Paul for further instructions regarding the gift he was collecting for the believers in Jerusalem. He is also clearly interested in making sure that the proper preparations are made so that it is ready to be sent on to Jerusalem once he arrives in Corinth. He introduces the topic (v. 1), explains what should be done in preparation for his arrival (v. 2), and how he will facilitate the delivery of the gift once he arrives in Corinth (vv. 3-4).

> [1]*Now about the collection for the Lord's people: Do what I told the Galatian churches to do.* [2]*On the first day of every week, each one of you should set aside a sum of money in keeping with your income, saving it up, so that when I come no collections will have to be made.* [3]*Then, when I arrive, I will give letters of introduction to the men you approve and send them with your gift to Jerusalem.* [4]*If it seems advisable for me to go also, they will accompany me.*

2. Jeffrey Weima argues that Paul's use of περὶ δέ ("now concerning") in 16:1, 12, shows that the letter closing can only begin with v. 13 (J. A. D. Weima, *Neglected Endings: The Significance of the Pauline Letter Closings* (JSNTSup 101; Sheffield, Eng.: JSOT Press, 1994), 201 (see his analysis of the structure of vv. 13-24 on p. 203). But while περὶ δέ clearly marks a new topic, there is no reason to conclude that the topic must be part of the main body of the letter. Unlike the material in previous sections, this material does not contain any developed theological or moral argument, but consists of information sharing and the most basic of procedural instructions. Also, within vv. 1-12, we find Paul's discussion of his and others' travel plans, a topic most commonly found in letter closings. The fact that this material regarding travel plans appears beside other materials that clearly belong to the letter closing strongly suggests that it too should be considered part of the letter closing. It may well be that the Corinthians touched on the subjects of the Jerusalem collection and a possible visit from Apollos in the closing of their own letter to Paul.

**16:1** Paul introduces vv. 1-4 with *Now about,* the way he introduced several of the new topics, starting with his reference to the letter from the Corinthians in 7:1.[3] It seems likely that the subject introduced this time, *the collection for the Lord's people,* was one about which the Corinthians had inquired in that letter, since the abrupt way in which he broaches the issue seems more consistent with the way a subject is brought up in a conversation when both parties know the topic is on the agenda. Presumably he deals with it at this point because the topic is directly related to his travel plans, a topic normally left for the closing of a letter. The word translated the *Lord's people*[4] is a challenge to translators. It has traditionally been translated "saints," although that word has gained different meanings over time and is not a particularly helpful translation in our day. The Greek term literally means "the holy ones," although not in the sense of morally or spiritually superior people but as a way of referring to God's people as those who have been especially consecrated to God (see our comments on 1:2, where the TNIV translates the term "his holy people"). Verse 3 makes it clear that in this context Paul is referring to the Christians in Jerusalem who were to be the recipients of a special gift from the churches founded by Paul around the northern Mediterranean. Paul mentions the gift being collected for the believers in Jerusalem not only here but also in 2 Corinthians 8–9 (following up on the instructions given here) and in Romans 15:25-32. It is also mentioned in Acts 24:17. More information on the circumstances behind the offering and the motivations for it may be found in those passages and commentaries on them.

Paul had apparently discussed this matter with the Corinthians before, either in person or in a letter, and did not feel the need to go into those matters again here. Later he would reinforce some points about the offering in 2 Corinthians 8–9.[5] It seems that the believers in Jerusalem had chronic economic problems, and Paul and other leaders encouraged the giving of material support from other churches to the mother church. As Jervis points out, most scholars have understood that for Paul the collection for the Jerusalem believers served as "a symbol of the unity of the Church. The collection was meant to represent, primarily to the Jewish Christians in Jerusalem, the unity of both gentile and Jew in Christ, and thereby to be a means of reconciling the Jewish and gentile branches of the Church."[6] It *may* also have had something to do with the Old Testament eschatological expectation that in the days of God's future redemption of Israel the Gentiles would make a pilgrimage to Jerusalem and the wealth of the nations would flow into that city.[7] While the word translated *collection* was "employed in epigraphical

3. Cf. 7:1, 25; 8:1; 12:1; 16:12.

4. Gk. ἅγιοι (plural of ἅγιος).

5. For earlier references to Paul's involvement with charitable gifts for the Jerusalem church, see Gal. 2:10 and Acts 11:27-30.

6. L. Ann Jervis, "Contribution for the Saints," *ABD* 1:1131.

7. See Isa. 60:3–61:6; 66:20 (esp. 60:5, 11; 61:6). Cf. Keith F. Nickle, *The Collection: A Study in Paul's Strategy* (Studies in Biblical Theology 48; London: SCM, 1966); Dieter Georgi,

and papyrological sources to denote collections of various sorts," it was used "chiefly of religious collections for a god, a temple, etc."[8]

At other points within this letter Paul has tried to reinforce the solidarity between this church and the other churches that had been founded. In 4:17 he spoke of "what I teach everywhere in every church," and in 7:17 of "the rule I lay down in all the churches." In 11:16 he said that "the churches of God" had no other practice but the one he enjoined the Corinthians to follow as well. In 14:33-34 he again wanted the practice in the Corinthian church to be consistent with what was done "in all the congregations of the Lord's people." Later on in this chapter he will bring greetings to the Corinthians from the churches in the province of Asia (16:19). Such notes testify to Paul's open agenda of contributing to the end-time universal worship of the one true God by Gentiles (see Introduction, 21-25) and recall the allusion to Malachi 1:11 in 1 Corinthians 1:2, where Paul refers to "all those who call upon the name of the Lord *in every place.*"

His statement in this verse that the Corinthians should *Do*[9] *what I told the Galatian churches to do* is consistent with this theme of biblical universalism. There was no reason for the Corinthians to handle this situation differently from other churches. The very project of a collection from the various predominantly Gentile churches spoke of participating in something larger than any one church and should have built a sense of common cause between the Gentile churches involved as well as between them and the intended recipients of the gift. There is much to be said for the benefits of like-minded churches putting their resources together to address a problem or meet a need that could not be effectively met by one or two churches on their own. In part Paul's project seems to have been intended to build a stronger sense of unity and solidarity among churches that may not have naturally tended to think of themselves as members of the very same family.

Of course the Corinthians cannot be expected to know what Paul told

---

*Remembering the Poor: The History of Paul's Collection for Jerusalem* (Nashville: Abingdon, 1992); F. F. Bruce, *Paul, Apostle of the Heart Set Free* (Grand Rapids: Eerdmans, 1977), 322-23, and the bibliography given in David J. Downs, *The Offering of the Gentiles* (Tübingen: Mohr Siebeck, 2008), 6 n. 18. While many have suspected or asserted that this serves as background for Paul's thinking on the subject, there is not sufficient evidence to clearly confirm or deny the association. Downs himself argues against it (*The Offering of the Gentiles*, 3-9).

8. Downs, *The Offering of the Gentiles*, 129 (the second is a quotation he provides from Adolf Deissmann, *Light from the Ancient East: The New Testament Illustrated by Recently Discovered Texts of the Graeco-Roman World* [trans. Lionel R. M. Strachan; New York: George H. Doran, 1927], 105). Downs (130 n. 34) points out that BDAG also indicates that the term (Gk. λογεία) was used especially of "a collection for sacred purposes."

9. Paul uses an aorist imperative in this verse but then a present imperative in v. 2. Either the aorist is used based on the summarizing force of its perfective aspect (see Campbell, *Verbal Aspect and Non-Indicative Verbs*, 86-88), or Paul is thinking here (in summary terms) of the project as a whole as a specific activity to be done (and in the following verse the present imperative reflects the fact that the instruction has to do not with one particular act but with an ongoing practice, perhaps one that will continue even after this particular collection has been completed).

the Galatians; his point in the second part of this verse is merely to point out that the directions he will give the Corinthians are the same as those given to other churches. He will spell out those directions in the next three verses.

**16:2** Having introduced the topic of the collection, Paul explains what preparations should be made for the collection before he comes to Corinth for his planned visit: *On the first day of every week, each one of you should set aside*[10] *a sum of money in keeping with your income, saving it up, so that when I come no collections will have to be made.* The first day of the week was, of course, the day on which Christ rose from the dead (Matt. 28:1; Mark 16:2; Luke 24:1; John 20:1). Christians began to gather together to celebrate on that day sometime soon after that (John 20:19; Acts 20:7). The mention of *the first day of every week* along with the purpose *that when I come no collections will have to be made* suggests that the setting aside of money would not be just the setting apart within one's own possessions but the setting aside of the money by presenting it to the leaders of the church (cf. Acts 4:34–5:2). Otherwise it would not matter which day a person chose to set money aside and collections would still need to be made upon Paul's arrival.[11] Paul's emphasis falls on the value of advanced planning and preparation rather than last-minute scrambling and the resultant pressure. While Paul's guidance here may well be applied to other financial commitments the members of a congregation take on (including commitments to a church's annual budget and other financial needs), it should be noted that Paul is not discussing giving toward a church's regular budget but the preparations to be taken for one particular and special project. Ralph Martin has pointed out that "what may have seemed to be a very mundane business — the duty of allocating a sum of cash from the weekly budget — is set in a noble frame by the reference to 'the first day of the week.'" As he argues, this clearly suggests that "there was, in his mind, no disparity between the 'secular' and the 'sacred', and no incongruity in the thought that the offering of money is an integral part of Christian worship. Money which had been honestly gained in the toil of the week is to be brought to the assembly of the Church and thus made part of the Sunday worship."[12]

The key word[13] in the phrase translated *in keeping with your income* has the sense "have things turn out well, *prosper, succeed*" (BDAG). Chrysostom emphasizes the passive voice of the verb: "He did not say, give 'this much,' or 'that much,' but 'as things have prospered for him,' whether much or lit-

10. On the present imperative here, see the previous footnote.

11. See S. R. Llewelyn, "The Use of Sunday for Meetings," *NovT* 43 (2001), 209-10, and Downs, *The Offering of the Gentiles*, 128-29, for linguistic and other evidence that Paul is referring to the "practice of donating monies to a common chest during weekly gatherings" and that this "would not have been unfamiliar to the believers in Corinth" (129).

12. Ralph P. Martin, *Worship in the Early Church* (Grand Rapids: Eerdmans, 1974), 79-80.

13. Gk. εὐοδόω.

tle. Nor did he say, 'what any one may have gained,' but, 'things have prospered for him,' signifying that the supply is from God.'"[14] This is probably reading in too much. The translation *in keeping with your income* may be read in a very modern way, as though each one's income would be consistent each week, while in Paul's world most people would be more likely to have good and bad weeks, weeks in which things turned out well financially and weeks in which they did not (weeks in which they were regularly employed and weeks in which they were not, or weeks in which they experienced greater or less benevolence on the part of others). The point is that those who made a lot of money in a given week would be expected to give more than those who did not. As Keener points out, Paul's instruction that each one should give as they have prospered is an application of Deuteronomy 15:13-14, where the Israelites are instructed to provide generously for their slaves who had gained their freedom after six years of service: "And when you release them, do not send them away empty-handed. Supply them liberally from your flock, your threshing floor and your winepress. Give to them as the LORD your God has blessed you."

**16:3-4** Paul now explains how he will facilitate the delivery of the gift once he arrives in Corinth: *Then, when I arrive, I will give letters of introduction to the men you approve and send them with your gift to Jerusalem.* Paul had already mentioned his plan to return to Corinth in 4:18-21, a plan the Corinthians clearly knew about before receiving this letter. He would make certain that the Corinthians' gift would be delivered in a way that would represent them well. The word Paul uses for the Corinthians's *gift* is the word usually translated "grace," but which is also used, as here, for a "practical application of goodwill, *(a sign of) favor, gracious deed/gift, benefaction*" (BDAG). The use of the word would still be a reminder that the gift was an extension of grace on the part of the Corinthians, just as the spiritual gifts they received from the Lord were an extension of his grace to them.

Their gift would be delivered by men who were especially approved by the congregation for the task. Those men would be authorized by both the Corinthian congregation and the apostle Paul himself, who would give them *letters of introduction* (literally, just "letters," but the TNIV translation is undoubtedly correct).

The men appointed by the Corinthians could go to Jerusalem without Paul, or he could accompany them: *If it seems advisable*[15] *for me to go also, they will accompany me.* Presumably by *If it seems advisable* Paul means, "If it seems advisable to you Corinthians," since he had stressed the approval of the Corinthians in v. 3. There could be various reasons why it would be ad-

14. *Homiliae in Epistulam i ad Corinthios* 43.4 (NPNF[1] 12:260).

15. Paul uses a third-class conditional structure (marked by ἐάν and a subjunctive verb in the apodosis) to indicate the tentativeness of this suggestion (see Porter, *Idioms of the Greek New Testament*, 261-62).

visable (or fitting, appropriate) for Paul to go along. No doubt he knew the people in Jerusalem and could make the proper introductions, while the appointed Corinthians would probably be newcomers to the city. Paul might also be better equipped to explain to the Jerusalem believers the background and intent of the broader project of which the Corinthian gift was a part than members of any one particular church. If Paul were to go, as the apostle to the Gentiles and the primary force behind the collection he would be the most prominent member of the group, so he says, *they will accompany me,* rather than, "I will accompany them."

## B. Travel Plans, 16:5-9

Paul provides the Corinthians with a tentative itinerary, mentioning the way by which he plans to come to Corinth on his next visit (v. 5), the plans he has for his time in Corinth (vv. 6-7), what he will be doing in the meantime, and why (vv. 8-9).

> [5]*After I go through Macedonia, I will come to you — for I will be going through Macedonia.* [6]*Perhaps I will stay with you for a while, or even spend the winter, so that you can help me on my journey, wherever I go.* [7]*For I do not want to see you now and make only a passing visit; I hope to spend some time with you, if the Lord permits.* [8]*But I will stay on at Ephesus until Pentecost,* [9]*because a great door for effective work has opened to me, and there are many who oppose me.*

**16:5** Paul plans to *go through Macedonia* on his way to Corinth.[16] This would normally mean traveling north by boat along the coast of Asia to Troas

16. His commitment is made clear through his use of a present tense verb (διέρχομαι) at the end of the verse for a future event (translated as *I will be going through*). This is one of the uses that Stanley Porter points to as evidence that indicative verbs do not have temporal significance. But as Georg Winer pointed out in 1863 (Winer, *A Grammar of the New Testament Diction: Intended as an Introduction to the Critical Study of the Greek New Testament* [Edinburgh: T&T Clark, 1863]), ancient Greek used the present tense "only in appearance for the Future, when, exactly as in Latin, German, English, etc., an action still future is mentioned as already present, either because it is unalterably determined, or is about to take place by some unchanging arrangement. . . ." It was sometimes "employed to denote what is just about to take place, — what one is intending to effect, and what he has already made the necessary preparations to do" (280-81). The same phenomenon is found in English, as pointed out by Georgia M. Green: "[T]he present tense can be used to refer to a future time as long as the event referred to is assumed to be prearranged, and there is an adverbial expression indicating a future time indicated explicitly or in ellipsis. . . . If the event is not (mutually) understood to be prearranged or scheduled," use of the present tense for the future might suggest that the speaker "had a firm belief in predestination, and believed that the speaker had an inside line on the Omnipotent's plans" (Georgia M. Green, "Some Interactions of Pragmatics and Grammar," in *The Handbook of Pragmatics* [ed. Laurence R. Horn and Gregory L. Ward; Blackwell Handbooks in Linguistics 16; Malden, MA: Blackwell, 2004], 411).

(perhaps taking coastal roads part of the way; cf. Acts 20:13-17), then traveling by sea over to Neapolis in Macedonia at the northern end of the Aegean Sea and following the Via Egnatia west at least until Thessalonica. From there he could have traveled down the eastern coast of Macedonia by land or sea into Achaia and to Athens and then on to Corinth (as he did on his first trip to that city; see Acts 17:13–18:1). David Gill points out, however, that the evidence of Romans 15:19 (where Paul says that he has preached the gospel "all the way around to Illyricum") suggests that he probably went through Macedonia from the east coast to the west coast, following the Via Egnatia to the Adriatic coast at Dyrrachium or Apollonia. From there he presumably went up the Adriatic coast to Illyricum and then back down the coast again to Achaia and Corinth.[17] It seems that Paul had in mind a longer, more thorough missionary experience this time, one in which he would carry the gospel through the heart of Macedonia. The Corinthians may have thought and hoped that he would take a direct route by sea straight from Ephesus. 2 Corinthians 1:15–2:11 and 7:2-16 give the impression that Paul ended up making an "unscheduled" visit before the extended visit mentioned here (possibly a direct visit from Ephesus by sea), a visit that did not go well and resulted in an unhappy letter to the Corinthians. The fact that he gives further directions regarding the collection for Jerusalem in 2 Corinthians 8–9 suggests that a key part of the agenda for Paul's next visit to Corinth, mentioned in vv. 1-4 of this chapter, had yet to be realized. There is something of a contrast between this verse and the following two in that while Paul will be simply passing through Macedonia (v. 5) he plans to spend some extended time with the Corinthians (vv. 6-7), a thought that should have reinforced to the Corinthians the special place they held in his heart.

**16:6-7** While in the previous verse Paul simply says that he will "come to" the Corinthians, he now makes it clear that he hopes to spend some extended time with them (unlike the Macedonians?): [6]*Perhaps I will stay with you for a while, or even spend the winter, so that you can help me on my journey, wherever I go.* [7]*For I do not want to see you now and make only a passing visit; I hope to spend some time with you, if the Lord permits.* Acts 18:11 indicates that Paul spent extended time (a year and a half) in Corinth during his "second missionary journey" and then extended time in Ephesus (2-3 years; 19:10; 20:31) during his "third missionary journey." Paul indicates in these verses that he wants to spend a block of time with them again during his next visit after having spent the extended time in Ephesus, to which Acts refers (see v. 8). Paul is very careful to fill his references to his plans with qualifiers to indicate that they are provisional: *Perhaps, I hope, if the Lord permits.*[18] Paul had already spoken of his plan to come to the Corinthi-

17. David W. J. Gill, "Macedonia," in *The Book of Acts in Its Graeco-Roman Setting* (ed. David W. J. Gill and Conrad H. Gempf; The Book of Acts in Its First-Century Setting 2; Grand Rapids: Eerdmans, 1994), 399.

18. *If the Lord permits* reflects another (see also the example in v. 4) third-class condi-

ans soon, "If the Lord permits," in 4:19. Paul knew what James taught his readers: we ought to say, "If it is the Lord's will, we will live and do this or that" (Jas. 4:15).

Paul's plans seem to be based on strategic advantage. Where would it make the greatest impact for him to spend his time? Paul's reference to winter reflects the fact that winter was not a good season for travel. Ship captains had to think about good places to leave their ships during the winter months, and travelers would also, then, have to think about where they would *spend the winter* (cf. Acts 27:12; 28:11). Paul could either spend some time in Corinth and then move on in time to spend the winter elsewhere, or he could decide to stay there longer and spend it in Corinth. This letter contains plenty of evidence that the Corinthian church would certainly benefit from an extended visit from an experienced Christian leader — and an apostle to the Gentiles no less — like the apostle Paul. One would expect it to help them do a better job of assimilating Christian teaching, values, and perspectives and of seeing how they engage and challenge so much of what the Corinthians had inherited of Roman and Corinthian values and perspectives. Paul knows the difference that personal engagement makes and that even the best of letters, full of the greatest wisdom and teaching, is a poor substitute for a leader who models the kind of Christian life and character they commend. Any Christian leader who thinks that the people with whom they minister only need more biblical, theological, and ethical teaching and content has failed to recognize that, to be properly taught, truth must be modeled.

One of the reasons Paul wanted to spend some extended time in Corinth was so that they could help him on his journey, wherever he goes (v. 6). The verb translated *help . . . on my journey* means "to assist someone in making a journey . . . with food, money, by arranging for companions, means of travel, etc."[19] He uses the same verb again in v. 11. Other examples may be found in Titus 3:13; 3 John 6; Acts 15:3; 2 Corinthians 1:16; Romans 15:24. Paul would be in need of such various kinds of assistance, and the preparations for his future travels would require time. They were to have set aside funds for the gift to Jerusalem before he arrived, but if they were going to provide Paul with support to go on and spread the gospel elsewhere (or even to go along with those bringing the gift to Jerusalem), they would need some time to put funds together and make other arrangements as well. Paul may have also hoped to spend some time recasting the vision for his work while among the Corinthians or possibly expanding his traveling ministry team with members from that church. Paul's relationship with the

---

tional structure (marked by ἐάν and a subjunctive verb in the apodosis), suggesting tentativeness (see Porter, *Idioms of the Greek New Testament*, 261-62). It is remarkable that in 2 Corinthians 1:15–2:1 Paul seems to be defending himself against accusations that he did not keep to his original plan.

19. BDAG, προπέμπω (emphasis removed).

Corinthians was not a one-way road. They needed his spiritual and ethical leadership and guidance, and he needed and received things from them.

**16:8-9** While Paul is eager to spend extended time with the Corinthians, his governing principle of advancing the gospel of Christ (expounded at length in ch. 9) made it clear to him that his visit to them must wait until after he had fully engaged the unusual ministry challenges and opportunities he had in Ephesus at that moment: *But I will stay on at Ephesus until Pentecost, because a great door for effective work has opened to me, and there are many who oppose me. Pentecost* was the Greek name for the Jewish Feast of Weeks (one of the three great Jewish festivals, the others being Passover and Booths/Tabernacles), which took place fifty days after Passover (see Deut. 16:9-12). It was an agricultural festival that came to be associated with promises of divine blessing and restoration. Christians came to associate it with the blessing of the Holy Spirit after the experience recorded in Acts 2:1-33.

Paul's reference to the approach of *Pentecost* (v. 8) may explain some of the biblical texts that have been on his mind as he writes this letter. Since Pentecost comes fifty days after Passover, he may have had passages related to either or both of those events on his mind. In 5:7-8 he mentions "Christ, our Passover lamb" who "has been sacrificed," and he calls on the Corinthians to "keep the Festival, not with the old bread leavened with malice and wickedness, but with the unleavened bread of sincerity and truth." Of course, the Passover provides the scriptural background to the Lord's Supper, described in chapter 11. Paul's references to "firstfruits" (15:20, 23; 16:15) may have been influenced by the offering of firstfruits during Passover (Lev. 23:10) or Pentecost (his reference to "the part of the dough offered as firstfruits" in Rom. 11:16 is certainly based on Lev. 23:10, 17 and Num. 15:18-21). Since both Passover and Pentecost were agricultural festivals, either or both could have inspired Paul's use of the language of sowing and reaping (9:10-11; 15:36-37, 42-44).[20] Our comments on men and women prophesying in 11:4-5 suggested that Joel 2:28-29 may have been in the back of Paul's mind, and Acts 2 suggests that the early Christians related that passage to the Pentecost immediately following Jesus' resurrection.

According to the book of Acts, Paul first arrived in *Ephesus* during what is known as his second missionary journey (Acts 18:19-21), but then he returned to Ephesus and made it his base of operations during his third missionary journey (Acts 19:1-20), staying there for two to three years (Acts 19:10; 20:31). The great city of Ephesus served as the capital of the Roman province of Asia. It competed with Smyrna for the title "First and Greatest Metropolis of Asia" and gave itself the title "First and Greatest Metropolis of Asia, Warden of Two Temples of the Emperor by decree of the Sacred

20. There may be a relationship between the language of "firstfruits" in 15:20, 23 and the language of sowing in 15:36-37, 42-44.

Senate, Temple-Warden of Artemis, Friend of Augustus, the City of the Ephesians."[21]

Paul uses the metaphor of an open *door* of opportunity for ministry in other places as well. In 2 Corinthians 2:12 he says that "the Lord had opened a door" for him to preach the gospel in Troas. In Colossians 4:3 he asks his readers to pray "that God may open a door for our message, so that we may proclaim the mystery of Christ." Here it is not merely a *door* but a *great* door of *effective work.* The word translated *effective work* suggests that Paul has in mind a door "the opening of which promises a rich field of labor."[22] The book of Acts gives us a glimpse of both the open door and the opposition that Paul found in Ephesus. We learn that Paul was able to use the synagogue as a hub of his teaching for three months (19:8) and then had daily discussions in a lecture hall for two years, "so that all the Jews and Greeks who lived in the province of Asia heard the word of the Lord" (19:10). God did miracles through Paul (19:11), and God moved in such a way that "the name of the Lord Jesus was held in high honor" (19:17) and "the word of the Lord spread widely and grew in power" (19:20). On the other hand, some became obstinate and publicly maligned the Christian message (19:9), and opposition to the gospel climaxed in a riot that endangered the lives of Paul and some of his co-workers (19:23-41). As Hays points out, Paul's statement, *and there are many who oppose me,* "recalls his earlier cryptic allusion to fighting with wild animals at Ephesus (15:32; cf. Acts 19:23-41) and prefigures his later — and equally vague — comments about a terrible affliction that he suffered in Asia (2 Cor. 1:8-11)."[23]

The book of Acts suggests that in several cases Paul moved on from certain towns or cities because of the severe opposition that was raised against him (Acts 13:50-51; 14:5-6, 19-20; 17:5-10, 13-14). Why would he mention opposition as one of the motivations for staying in Ephesus? Presumably he had to carefully discern the difference between situations where his presence roused such dangerous opposition that both he and the fledgling church had a greater chance of survival if he were to move on, thereby avoiding a crisis and allowing any new believers to "live peaceful and quiet lives in all godliness and holiness" (1 Tim. 2:2), and those where the opposition was not so severe and where his continuing presence could contribute to the strengthening of the fledgling church rather than to its destruction.

As Hays reminds us, "We who live in a time and place where the church is comfortably established should not underestimate the uncertainty and risk that attended Paul's missionary work. His description of his plans here shows that Christians may sometimes be called upon to stand

21. Maud W. Gleason, "Greek Cities under Roman Rule," in *A Companion to the Roman Empire* (ed. D. S. Potter; Blackwell Companions to the Ancient World; Malden, MA: Blackwell, 2006), 246.

22. BDAG, ἐνεργής.

23. Hays, 286.

and testify in dangerous circumstances, and that the place of greatest risk may also be the place of greatest opportunity for proclaiming the gospel."[24]

## C. Request on Behalf of Timothy, 16:10-11

> [10]*When Timothy comes, see to it that he has nothing to fear while he is with you, for he is carrying on the work of the Lord, just as I am.* [11]*No one, then, should treat him with contempt. Send him on his way in peace so that he may return to me. I am expecting him along with the brothers.*

**16:10** The word translated *when* by the TNIV (also the RSV and ESV) is usually translated "if" (as it is here by NET, NAB, NASB, NIV, NRSV, and NJB), but it is sometimes used in a way that "approaches closely" the meaning of the normal Greek term for "whenever" or "when."[25] The fact that Paul had already mentioned in 4:17 that he had sent Timothy to Corinth suggests that there was no serious doubt that he would be coming to Corinth. Fee and Garland are probably correct in suggesting "[t]he vagaries of travel in the ancient world may have caused Paul to express himself in this way, since he cannot predict the timing of his arrival."[26]

In 4:17 Paul described Timothy as "my son whom I love, who is faithful in the Lord," who would "remind you of my way of life in Christ Jesus, which agrees with what I teach everywhere in every church." Why does Paul find it necessary to warn the Corinthians to *see to it*[27] *that he has nothing to fear while he is with you*?[28] Paul knew what it was to minister in contexts

24. Hays, 286.

25. BDAG, ἐάν, 2. Evidence that it sometimes closely approximates the meaning of ὅταν (whenever, when) may be found in LXX Isa. 24:13; Amos 7:2; Tob. 6:17 as well as in John 12:32; 14:3 and Heb. 3:7.

26. Garland, 758; Fee, 821. So also Thiselton (1330) and others.

27. Paul uses a present active imperative (βλέπετε), which seems surprising at first since Timothy's reception appears to be a specific situation (which would normally be addressed with an aorist imperative). It could be argued that watching to make sure that Timothy was well received was not a particular act and that that motivated the use of the present imperative. It is probably more relevant to mention that according to *TLG* the second person plural aorist active imperative form of the verb (βλέψατε) does not appear in Greek literature until the fourth century, and that βλέπετε seems to have been the standard form for exhorting a group to take care in some way. Thus Paul's use of this particular form turns out to be unremarkable.

28. Christopher R. Hutson has argued that the clause translated *see to it that he has nothing to fear* by the TNIV should be translated "recognize that he is fearless" ("Was Timothy Timid? On the Rhetoric of Fearlessness (1 Cor. 16:10-11) and Cowardice (2 Tim 1:7)," *Biblical Research* 42 [1997], 65; cf. Garland, 759-60). Thus the clause "is not an exhortation for the Corinthians to 'look after' sensitive, inexperienced Timothy; rather, it is an admonition for them to 'recognize' the coming of an agent of the Lord" (Hutson, "Was Timothy Timid?" 64, cited in Garland, 759). While he is right to reject the common tendency to read certain texts in light of the assumption that Timothy was a weak and overly sensitive figure, the relation between

that were prone to incite fear. He just mentioned in v. 9 that there are many who oppose him in Ephesus. In 15:30-32 he says that he "fought wild beasts in Ephesus" (v. 32) and speaks of constantly being in mortal danger. Later he would write of "the troubles we experienced in the province of Asia" in terms of being "under great pressure, far beyond our ability to endure, so that we despaired of life itself" (2 Cor. 1:8). Paul knows that inasmuch as Timothy's ministry is an extension of his own, there is little he can do to guarantee a safe and peaceful ministry context and experience. In John 15:20 Jesus warns his own disciples, saying, "Remember what I told you: 'Servants are not greater than their master.' If they persecuted me, they will persecute you also." The same would apply to Paul and Timothy.

Unfortunately, it seems likely that Paul was not only concerned about how Timothy might be treated by unbelievers during his time in Corinth, but about how he would be treated even within the Corinthian church. Paul had addressed the fact that some Corinthian believers were treating some of their brothers and sisters shamefully in chapters 8–11 (esp. 8:11-12; 11:21-22), and v. 11 implies that he is concerned that they may treat Timothy with contempt as well if not warned in advance not to do so. Chrysostom helpfully suggests that 4:17 indicates that Timothy may have been intending "to rebuke them about the things concerning which Paul also had written" and that Paul feared that they might "attack him and spit upon him and plot against him, being grieved at the reproofs which came from him" or disrespect him as a matter of "revenge for the teacher's rebuke."[29] Paul wants them to respect Timothy as his trusted envoy, and he wants them to know that, as far as Paul is concerned, there is no great distinction between Timothy's ministry and his own since *he is carrying on the work of the Lord, just as I am.*

The *work of the Lord* was referred to in 15:58 as something to which the Corinthians should be fully dedicated, and, perhaps more importantly, in 9:1 Paul pointed out that the Corinthians themselves were "the result of my work in the Lord." It is Paul's work in the Lord to which the Corinthians owe their relationship with Christ, and Timothy is an extension of that work.[30] In v. 16 Paul will use a verb form related to the noun, *work,* in this verse in exhorting the Corinthians to "submit to . . . everyone who joins in the work and labors at it." There he is speaking on behalf of the household of Stephanas, but his words would clearly apply to Timothy as well.

**16:11** The *then,*[31] in *no one then,* suggests that the reason why *no one . . . should treat him with contempt* is that there is a close relationship or parity

---

βλέπετε and ἵνα (Hutson says that the ἵνα clause "is admittedly tricky") strongly indicates the meaning "see [to it] that . . ." not, "recognize that" (cf. Col. 4:17; 2 John 8).

29. *Homiliae in Epistulam i ad Corinthios* 44.1 ($NPNF^1$ 12:263).

30. Timothy may have been the one who carried this letter to the Corinthians, although it seems more likely that that role was undertaken by Stephanas, Fortunatus, and Achaicus (see on v. 17).

31. Gk. οὖν.

between Timothy's ministry and Paul's own ministry. To *treat . . . with contempt* is "to show by one's attitude or manner of treatment that an entity has no merit or worth."[32] As pointed out above, some Corinthians had already shown a penchant for treating other members of their congregation with contempt (see again 8:11-12; 11:21-22; cf. 2 Cor. 10:10).[33] Paul reinforces the connection between Timothy's ministry and his own in the rest of the verse, pointing out that Timothy will *return to* Paul, who is *expecting him.* Paul knew that Timothy, as his envoy, was likely to feel the brunt of any negative reaction to his letter to the Corinthians, and that that reaction might be expressed more strongly to the less highly respected and authoritative envoy than it would be to his own face, and he wanted to do what he could to preempt such a response. As Thiselton points out, "Paul's anxieties about Timothy's reception may have owed something to hopes and preferences in some quarters for a visit from Apollos instead."[34] Paul will break the news about Apollos's decision not to visit them at this time in the following verse.

Paul's instructions that the Corinthians are to *send*[35] Timothy *on his way in peace so that he may return to me* entails more than maintaining a cordial relationship with him at the time of his departure. The verb Paul uses is the same one translated "help . . . on my journey" in v. 6. As pointed out there, in a context like this, the verb translated *Send . . . on his way* means "to assist someone in making a journey . . . with food, money, by arranging for companions, means of travel, etc."[36] Timothy would need the Corinthians to provide him with a variety of things to make his return to Paul possible. The tasks of working together with Timothy to make the necessary preparations, gather the necessary resources, and then send him off on the journey would be unpleasant if there was no peace between them and him.

Paul has sent a team of believers to the Corinthians as his envoys (see v. 12), and they will be returning to him after completing the mission on which they were sent. Paul lets the Corinthians know that he expects them to take care of Timothy and provide for his return: *I am expecting him along with the brothers.* He should not be stranded due to a lack of help from the Corinthians. The Corinthians should make sure he is as well equipped and able to return to Paul as the rest of the brothers (who may, unlike Timothy,

32. BDAG, ἐξουθενέω. It is the opposite of a proper and healthy respect (see Prov. 1:7 LXX; 2 Macc. 1:27; Luke 18:9; 23:11; Rom. 14:3, 10; Gal. 4:14).

33. Rom. 14:3, 10 suggest that this may not have been an unusual problem in the early church.

34. Thiselton, 1332.

35. Paul employs an aorist imperative in exhorting the Corinthians to send Timothy back to him since the perfective aspect of the aorist imperative best serves the purpose of providing instruction relevant to a specific situation such as this. The aorist tense of the subjunctive translated *should treat him with contempt* earlier in the verse reflects the same role of verbal aspect.

36. BDAG, προπέμπω (emphasis removed). Cf. Rom. 15:24; 1 Cor. 16:6; 2 Cor. 1:16; Tit. 3:13; 3 John 6.

be men of means who are able to cover their own expenses). Of course, whenever Timothy did get back to Paul, he would be reporting on the treatment he received while among the Corinthians.

## D. Update regarding Apollos, 16:12

> [12]*Now about our brother Apollos: I strongly urged him to go to you with the brothers. He was quite unwilling to go now, but he will go when he has the opportunity.*

**16:12** Apollos was a topic of discussion (or mentioned as an example) already in 1:12; 3:4-6, 22; 4:6, and is mentioned elsewhere in the New Testament in Acts 18:24; 19:1; Tit. 3:13. See the commentary on 1:12. Paul has nothing critical to say about him. Rather, his reference to him as *our brother Apollos* communicates not simply that he recognizes Apollos as a legitimate member of the Christian community, but also the sense of family intimacy and closeness that is also intended in Paul's regular use of the same term in vocative references to his readers as "brothers and sisters" (most recently in 15:50, 58 and subsequently in 16:15). This use of the term "brother" is sandwiched between two references to "the brothers" (one in v. 11 and another in this verse), where the term refers to believers who were traveling and working in support of Paul's ministry. Paul's reference to Apollos as *our brother Apollos* may also reinforce not only their brotherly relationship in Christ but the cooperative relationship of their ministry as well.[37]

We have no way of knowing why Apollos was unwilling to go to Corinth at the time. The possible reasons would be limitless. We need to remember that travel was not a simple thing in those days and that it had to be carefully coordinated in light of weather or seasonal changes, work opportunities, family needs, present ministry challenges and opportunities, and more. He may have felt that the team that had already been put together (including Timothy and *the brothers*) was sufficient. Or it may have been that his life circumstances were not conducive to traveling at the time that the rest of the group would be heading off to Corinth.

It does seem remarkable, however, that Paul gives no indication that Apollos sent greetings to the Corinthians, unlike Aquila and Priscilla (cf. v. 19). This lends some support to the idea that he recognized that his oratorical gifts had created a personality cult, contributing to harmful divisions that should not be reinforced. As Thiselton indicates, "It may well be the case, as some have suggested, that Apollos's very reluctance to visit Corinth . . . arose from his disgust that some at Corinth had manipulated

37. E. E. Ellis, "Paul and His Coworkers" in *DPL* 183, helpfully describes Apollos as one of those long-term co-workers who "have a cooperative relationship with Paul but work in relative independence."

his name as a slogan to promote the claims of a so-called Apollos group."[38] If Apollos is unhappy with the church, Paul certainly does not come out and say so. Rather, he gives them hope that he will come to them eventually. Even if he is *unwilling to go now,* he *will go when he has the opportunity.* The language is sufficiently vague[39] to provide Apollos with the wiggle room to hold off on going until he thinks the right time had come.

## E. Exhortations, 16:13-14

Having prepared the Corinthians for his own coming as well as that of Timothy and informing them that Apollos would not be coming at this time, and before going on to commend those Corinthians who had served their church by coming to Paul and ministering to him, Paul provides a series of crisp exhortations[40] summarizing much of the message of the rest of the letter. Hortatory material appears in the closing sections of most of Paul's letters. It does not always have a clear relationship with the specific situation or themes of the body of the letter but it often does.[41] In this case the final exhortation of the series clearly reprises an important theme of the letter, while the ones preceding it provide a call for vigilance which would naturally be understood in light of the various challenges to the Corinthians' well-being that were described in earlier parts of the letter.

> [13]*Be on your guard; stand firm in the faith; be courageous; be strong.* [14]*Do everything in love.*

**16:13** The first four of Paul's five exhortations in a row all reflect the kinds of things a general might say to his troops before they enter into battle (although they would not add "in the faith" after "stand firm"): *Be on your guard; stand firm in the faith; be courageous; be strong.* What did the Corinthians need to be on guard about? The contents of this letter have suggested that they needed to be more vigilant about the negative leavening influence of certain Roman and Corinthian values and moral standards or expectations. They needed to guard themselves against the temptation to judge each other and treat each other on the basis of their secular social status rather than their shared status as brothers and sisters in Christ (chs. 1–4; 11:21-22). They needed to be on the alert for the corrupting influence of bad company and bad theology (5:1-7; 15:33). They needed to make sure that they did not continue in or fall into sexual morality (chs. 5–7) or become

38. Thiselton, 1332.

39. Gk. εὐκαιρέω: "to experience a favorable time or occasion for some activity" (BDAG).

40. All five of the imperatives in these two verses are present imperatives since their imperfective aspect is best suited to instruction of a generally relevant nature such as this.

41. Weima, *Neglected Endings,* 145-48.

complacent about the dangers of greed (6:1-11), idolatry, and self-centered religion (chs. 8–14). As Nützel suggests, Paul's "[e]xhortation to vigilance presupposes that Christians are always in danger of reducing their full commitment to God through Christ and of allowing themselves to be seized by things of lesser value."[42]

Paul exhorts the Corinthians to *stand firm in the faith.* To *stand firm* is to hold one's ground in a battle rather than to surrender or run away in the face of fearful opposition.[43] To *stand firm in the faith* is not merely to hold strongly to doctrinal convictions[44] but also, and perhaps especially, to persist in acting in a way that is consistent with faith in Christ. The Corinthians had shown some particular weaknesses in this area. They were prone to give in to the lax moral standards of their environment. Rather than "taking every thought captive to make it obedient to Christ" (2 Cor. 10:5), they were more likely to allow their thoughts (and actions) to be taken captive by Roman or Corinthian values and perspectives. Paradoxically, of course, standing firm sometimes requires fleeing (cf. 6:18; 10:14).

Paul's exhortation, *be courageous;*[45] *be strong,* reflects an Old Testament motif of a call to "be strong and courageous" under extremely challenging circumstances (Deut. 31:6-7, 23; Josh. 1:6, 9, 18; 10:25; 2 Sam. 10:12; 1 Chr. 22:13; 28:20; 2 Chr. 32:7; Pss. 26:14; 30:25).[46] Paul's own experience showed

42. J. M. Nützel, "γρηγορέω," *EDNT* 1:265.

43. The verb Paul uses (στήκω) is formed from ἵστημι, which in similar contexts means "to stand up against, resist," or "hold one's ground (Ps 35:13) in battle (X., An. 1, 10" (BDAG).

44. BDAG translates (στήκω) as "to be firmly committed in conviction or belief." It could perhaps be better defined as "refuse to relent in one's commitments (to convictions, beliefs, behaviors, etc.) in the face of serious opposition."

45. The word translated *be courageous* (Gk. ἀνδρίζομαι; "*conduct oneself in a courageous way*" [BDAG]) is based on the word for "man" (ἀνήρ), and is sometimes translated "play the man" or "act like a man." Some scholars have taken the etymology of the word as evidence for a high biblical view of the male gender, but the verb, like the related adjective (ἀνδρεῖος) and adverb (ἀνδρείως), is used of women as well as men (see BDAG, which points out under the entry for ἀνήρ that "[s]ome words with this prefix show erosion of emphasis on maleness"). In this verse as well the women in the church are undoubtedly expected to act courageously without abandoning their female identities. It seems likely that these terms are not being used to refer to being men as opposed to women, but of acting like mature (brave) adults rather than fearful children. In *On the Creation of the World* 105, Philo follows the traditional age distinctions given by Solon, the sixth- to seventh-century-B.C. Athenian lawmaker, in which being a man is the stage between being a youth and a middle-aged man (the stages are παιδίον, παῖς, μειράκιον, νεανίσκος, ἀνήρ, πρεσβύτης, γέρων). Paul himself suggested as much when in 13:7 he distinguished between the way he acted when he was a child (νήπιος) and the way he acts as a man (ἀνήρ). In any case, the fact that Paul uses a Greek word for "be courageous" that was built or based on the word for "man" is not a solid foundation for a theological point since usage of a Greek word does not imply support for ideology attributed to the Greek language itself.

46. There is a close linguistic parallel with Ps. 30:25 LXX (31:25 HB; 31:24 Eng.), with the same two verbs being used. It is made more interesting by the fact that the previous verse of the psalm calls on the readers to "Love the LORD" and reminds them that he "harshly punishes the arrogant" (NLT; cf. 1 Cor. 16:22).

why it would be necessary for faithful followers of Christ to be courageous. To be courageous is to faithfully carry out one's responsibilities even in the face of extreme danger and frightening circumstances. To be courageous is not to give in to fear or hopelessness or to let them interfere with one's duty (see LXX Deut. 31:6-7; Josh. 1:9; 10:25; 2 Sam. 13:28; 1 Chr. 22:13; 28:20; 2 Chr. 32:7; Dan. 10:19). In 4:10-14 Paul warned the Corinthians by highlighting the contrast between their attitude and experience and his own experience as a faithful disciple of Christ: "You are honored, we are dishonored! To this very hour we go hungry and thirsty, we are in rags, we are brutally treated, we are homeless. We work hard with our own hands. When we are cursed, we bless; when we are persecuted, we endure it; when we are slandered, we answer kindly. We have become the scum of the earth, the garbage of the world — right up to this moment." As pointed out above, he was experiencing opposition in Ephesus even as he wrote this letter (v. 9), and had already "fought wild beasts" in that city, constantly finding himself in mortal danger (15:30-32). Following Christ is not for cowards. And that was not only true in the first century. It appears that there were more Christian martyrs in the last century than in all of the previous centuries combined.[47]

**16:14** The final exhortation in Paul's punchy list reprises the key motif of love[48] which undergirds all of Paul's moral teaching in this letter. Love comes to the surface in 8:1 and reaches the heights of praise in the paean found in the center of chapters 12–14: *Do everything in love.* This was the point of 13:1-3 — that even the most wonderful acts, if not done out of love, are worthless in the eyes of God. Elsewhere in this letter Paul has said that all things are to be done for the glory of God (10:31). Furthermore, all things should be done for the sake of the building up of others (14:26), and they should be done "in a fitting and orderly way" (14:40). Ultimately all things will be subjected to Christ and God the Father "so that God may be all in all" (15:28). God is glorified when people act in love, when they put the welfare of others first and worship God in a way that is consistent with his own character. Self-sacrificing love is the model given to us by Christ and the key to the health and growth of his church and to the maturing of both individuals and the communities to which they belong. Christ-like love is a principal manifestation of God's renewed humanity, the sign that

47. See David B. Barrett, George Thomas Kurian, and Todd M. Johnson, eds., *World Christian Encyclopedia: A Comparative Survey of Churches and Religions in the Modern World* (2d ed.; Oxford: Oxford University Press, 2001), 11, which states that there were 45.4 million Christian martyrs in the twentieth century and 69.4 million in all of Christian history (which would mean that 65 percent of all Christians martyred were martyred in the twentieth century). For documentation, see Part 4 of *World Christian Trends, A.D. 30-A.D. 2200: Interpreting the Annual Christian Megacensus* (ed. David B. Barrett, Todd M. Johnson, Christopher R. Guidry, and Peter F. Crossing; Pasadena, CA: William Carey Library, 2001), where six hundred martyrdom situations in Christian history are listed, each with an estimate of the number of Christians killed.

48. Gk. ἀγάπη.

God's work in us — the work which will ultimately result in the resurrection of the dead and our complete renewal — has already begun to manifest itself. This, the fifth of five crisp exhortations in a row, is the clearest of them all and the one which most clearly reinforces the themes of the letter as a whole. It is not surprising that when Paul writes his own final greeting in his own hand, the final thought he will leave with the Corinthians is of his own love for them (v. 24).

## F. Commendation of Stephanas, 16:15-18

> [15]*You know that the household of Stephanas were the first converts in Achaia, and they have devoted themselves to the service of the Lord's people. I urge you, brothers and sisters,* [16]*to submit to such as these and to everyone who joins in the work and labors at it.* [17]*I was glad when Stephanas, Fortunatus and Achaicus arrived, because they have supplied what was lacking from you.* [18]*For they refreshed my spirit and yours also. Such men deserve recognition.*

**16:15-16** Paul gives a strong endorsement of the household of one of the brothers who had been sent from the church in Corinth to visit Paul on their behalf as people who model Christian service: *You know that the household of Stephanas were the first converts in Achaia, and they have devoted themselves to the service of the Lord's people. I urge you, brothers and sisters, to submit to such as these and to everyone who joins in the work and labors at it.* The TNIV has rearranged Paul's clauses to make them more orderly. He actually begins with *I urge you, brothers and sisters,* and then interjects the information about Stephanas and his household between that speech orienter and the actual statement of what he is urging them to do (namely, to submit to them and to people like them). Embedding the description of Stephanas's household in the very middle of the appeal to submit to them leaves no doubt about the basis of the appeal. It is precisely because they are people who *have devoted themselves to the service of the Lord's people.*

The word translated *first converts* is literally "firstfruits."[49] For the background to the firstfruits metaphor, see on 15:20. That background suggests not only that they were among the first converts in Achaia, but also that their conversion served as a promise of more to come and that they were an especially consecrated portion of the larger whole which God would bring to fruition in that region. That they were the firstfruits of *Achaia* suggests that Paul had his eye on the penetration of the gospel throughout that Roman province (of which Corinth was the capital), that is, that it was one of the fields from which he was hoping to reap a harvest, and Stephanas's household was the promise of more harvest to be had

49. Gk. ἀπαρχή.

from that field. Paul should not be taken to mean that Stephanas's household was the very first to be converted to Christ; rather, the term "first fruits derives its main significance not primarily from being first in a sequential sense, but first in the sense of constituting a sample, pledge, or promise of more to come." Paul evidently saw them "as those whose loyal work and witness holds promise of more believers to come, i.e., to be added to the Christian church in Achaia."[50]

We do not know who the members of that household were, besides Stephanas himself. It may have included his wife (if she was still living), slaves (if he owned any) or freedmen, and (adult) children. In fact, *Fortunatus and Achaicus* may very well have been part of that household (see on v. 17). Those Paul had in mind were old and mature enough to have *devoted themselves to the service of the Lord's people.*[51] Weiser points out that "[i]n the life of Paul's churches" *service* consisted above all of "charitable care for the needy, either in the respective churches themselves (Rom 12:7; 1 Cor 16:15) or for the Jerusalem Church in the form of a collection (Rom 15:25, 31; 2 Cor 8:4, 19f.; 9:1, 12). The word can, however, be used comprehensively for *all of the ministries* in the Church (1 Cor 12:5)."[52] As he suggests, Paul presumably has the care of the needy in mind in this verse. That is, they were a family known for practical expressions of love for those who were in need.

In light of the wonderful example set by Stephanas's household, Paul urges the Corinthians *to submit to such as these and to everyone who joins in the work and labors at it* (v. 16). Stephanas was being sent back to the Corinthians from Paul. The following verses indicate that he and his colleagues had proven themselves to be of great service to him, as he knew that they had already been to the church in Corinth. He must have been confident that whatever leadership Stephanas and the people of his household might be able to exercise back in Corinth could only contribute to the greater health and vitality of that church. Paul was so confident that that was the case that he urged them to submit to them and to people like them. The words *and to everyone who joins in the work and labors at it* points to a broader basis upon which to judge those whose leadership should be recognized. To join in the word and labor at it would include devoting oneself to the service of the Lord's people (as Stephanas's household had done), but would also include other kinds of Christian ministry, perhaps emphasizing those aspects that contributed to the missionary outreach of the church.

**16:17** As was not uncommon for Greek letter writers, Paul includes an expression of joy in the concluding lines of this letter (as he also

50. Thiselton, 1338 (emphasis removed).

51. The words translated *devoted themselves* usually have to do with structures of authority (cf. BDAG on Gk. τάσσω). As R. Bergmeier suggests, the line could also be translated "'they *have placed themselves* in the service of the saints,' in the sense of 'take on the responsibility/service'" (Bergmeier, "τάσσω," *EDNT* 3:337; his emphasis).

52. A. Weiser, "διακονία," *EDNT* 1:303 (his emphasis).

does in Phil. 4:10-20 and Rom. 16:19a).[53] He uses this expression of joy to highlight the effective ministry of the brothers who were sent by the Corinthians to meet his needs, and commends them as fine models of Christian service: *I was glad when Stephanas, Fortunatus and Achaicus arrived, because they have supplied what was lacking from you.* These three men may have served as the couriers for the Corinthians' letter. Clearly, they provided Paul with much more than just a letter. Paul's statement that these men *supplied what was lacking from you* should not be taken as a sort of criticism of the Corinthians, as though they had not done what they should have. As Garland suggests, "what he regards as 'lacking' is their physical presence" and thus "[t]he clause can be translated idiomatically as 'They make up for your absence.'"[54] The point is not a negative one, but the positive affirmation that thanks to their generosity, manifest in their willingness to send out these dear brothers to help Paul in his ministry, he lacks nothing from them.

We do not know anything about these men beyond what Paul tells us. Garland summarizes the little we can gather from their names: "Since Stephanas (short for Stephanophoros) bears a Greek name, he may have been an indigenous Greek or an immigrant. The mention of his household suggests that he was a man of means. Achaicus and Fortunatus may be slaves, freedmen, Stephanas's fellow artisans, or, less likely, his sons or brothers."[55] *Achaicus* has a Latin name meaning "man of Achaia," which must have been bestowed upon him somewhere outside of Achaia. Meeks thinks that he or his father "must have lived for a time in Italy, received the name there, and then returned to Corinth, probably as one of the freedmen colonists."[56] *Fortunatus* also has Latin name, meaning "fortunate," and he may also have been a freedman (his name was not unusual for a slave). Andrew Clarke thinks that Achaicus and Fortunatus were probably Stephanas's slaves or freedmen "and thus a part of his household."[57] This does seem likely. If so, they would be included among those to whom Paul says other believers should submit, due to their service to the church and the gospel.[58] For Paul,

53. See Weima, *Neglected Endings*, 149-50, for a discussion of the place of the "joy expression" in ancient Greco-Roman letters.

54. Garland, 769.

55. Garland, 770.

56. Meeks, *The First Urban Christians*, 56.

57. Andrew D. Clarke, "'Refresh the Hearts of the Saints': A Unique Pauline Context?" *TynBul* 47 (1996), 287.

58. "Thus we may have here people, including two of relatively low social standing, who are to be honoured for their 'serving' of the people, characterised in part by their refreshing of both Paul's spirit and that of others. The anomaly of 'servant' figures being 'respected' for their labouring is made all the more stark by Paul's insistence that these figures be submitted to (ὑποτάσσησθε) precisely because of their labour (1 Cor. 16:16). This verb implies the attribution of authority — an unexpected command in the wider Graeco-Roman context given the social status of the individuals concerned" (A. D. Clarke, "'Refresh the Hearts of the Saints,'" 288).

their standing in society was of less concern than their contributions to his life and to the life of the church.

**16:18** Paul suggests, by beginning this verse with *for*,[59] that it was by refreshing his spirit that those brothers had supplied what was lacking from the Corinthian church: *For they refreshed my spirit and yours also. Such men deserve recognition.* This is not to deny that they had brought Paul other kinds of valuable provisions and resources, but that his life and ministry had been replenished above all by the way in which they had ministered to his spirit or heart. In his careful study of the "refreshing of the spirit," Andrew Clarke has shown that it "relates to the feelings or emotions" of the person and "refers to the resulting effect of an action on one person's spirit by another person."[60] This was done, at least in part, no doubt, through the variety of ways in which they generously shared their lives and resources with Paul once they arrived.

Paul does not make a declarative (indicative) statement as the TNIV translates: *Such men deserve recognition*, but rather he gives an imperative based on the first part of the verse: "So give recognition to such persons" (NRSV).[61] As he argued in chapters 12–14 that gifts that edify or strengthen the church should be preferred, he points out here that people who give strength and encouragement to others, as Stephanas, Fortunatus, and Achaicus had done for both him and the Corinthians, should be given special recognition. Of course, to give them recognition is to hold them up as examples to be emulated by the rest of the church. Part of what Paul is doing is commending and (hopefully) strengthening the position of proven leaders loyal to him and his gospel, leaders he trusts to properly interpret and apply his teachings upon their return to Corinth.[62]

## G. Greetings from Others in Asia, 16:19-20

In vv. 19-20a Paul communicates greetings to the Corinthians from other churches and Christians with whom he has been ministering.

> [19]*The churches in the province of Asia send you greetings. Aquila and Priscilla greet you warmly in the Lord, and so does the church that meets at their house.* [20]*All the brothers and sisters here send you greetings. Greet one another with a holy kiss.*

59. Gk. γάρ.

60. A. D. Clarke, "'Refresh the Hearts of the Saints,'" 288.

61. Although the morphology (form) of the word (ἐπιγινώσκετε) could be imperative or indicative, the following οὖν ("so/therefore") leads virtually all interpreters to understand it as an imperative. A present imperative was called for (rather than an aorist imperative) since Paul is clearly making a generally relevant statement about the importance of recognizing these kinds of leaders and not merely calling for these particular ones to be properly recognized and respected.

62. Cf. Weima, *Neglected Endings*, 206.

**16:19** Paul has frequently mentioned other *churches* in this letter (7:17; 11:16; 14:33-34; 16:1), and has worked to encourage the Corinthians not to think of themselves as an independent group but as an organic part of a larger movement with some common traditions, values, and practices. They have been overly eager to find their own independent way in the world as a Christian community. The Corinthians' solidarity with other Christian churches is reinforced by the greeting Paul communicates from the *churches in the province of Asia* where he is when he writes them. Weima points out that "[t]he fact that Paul can speak for 'the church in Asia' (1 Cor. 16.19a) or for 'all the saints' (2 Cor. 13.12b) — or even more broadly yet for 'all the churches of Christ' (Rom. 16.16b) — reflects his own perception of his apostolic and authoritative status."[63] It would reinforce the Corinthians' perception of that status as well.

Acts 18:1-2 informs us of how it is that *Aquila and Priscilla*[64] were known to the Corinthians. They had been in Corinth before Paul arrived, and he had worked together with them. Their relationship grew to be so strong that when Paul left Corinth for Syria, Aquila and Priscilla went with him (Acts 18:18). Both Paul and Luke refer to Priscilla first and then Aquila in two out of three of their references,[65] presumably because she was a woman of unusual social stature and means and/or because of her unusual gifts and abilities as a Christian leader. Remarkably, the only two women mentioned by name in this letter are Chloe (1:11) and Priscilla, both of whom were of critical importance to the church (Chloe as the leader of a household, and Priscilla as a pillar of the church in Corinth).

Acts 18:24–19:1 informs us that it was Priscilla and Aquila who had given Apollos his more advanced instruction in Christian teaching and had sent him on to Achaia and Corinth. All those who considered themselves disciples of Apollos (1:12) might be presumed to also feel especially indebted to Priscilla and Aquila for the crucial role of their own ministry in his life. Although Apollos has not sent along greetings, Aquila and Priscilla have. In fact, they greet them *warmly*[66] *in the Lord*. That is, their greeting is an enthusiastic greeting reflecting the bond between those who share life in the Lord Jesus Christ.

It is not only Aquila and Priscilla who send warm greetings; *so does the church that meets at their house.* These highly admired Christians are the

63. Weima, *Neglected Endings*, 109.

64. Although many textual witnesses have *Priscilla* (Gk. Πρίσκιλλα), the diminutive form that appears in Acts (18:2, 18, 26), Prisca (Πρῖσκα; see BDAG), is the form Paul seems to have used (cf. Rom. 16:3; 2 Tim. 4:19). It is supported here by ($\hat{\imath}^{46}$), א, B, P, 0121, 0243, 33, 1175*, 1739, 1881*, *pc*, r, $vg^{st}$, sa, $bo^{pt}$.

65. See Acts 18:2, 18, 26; Rom. 16:3; 1 Cor. 16:19; 2 Tim. 4:19. This is Paul's one exception to that rule.

66. *Warmly* reflects the use of πολύς as an intensive adverb capable of suggesting various meanings (e.g., greatly, earnestly, strictly, loudly, often, etc. [so BDAG]), depending on the context. To greet someone in this way would be to greet them warmly or enthusiastically. On this usage in ancient letter greetings see Weima, *Neglected Endings*, 43-44, 110.

key leaders of another church, one which is presented as being eager to express its solidarity, its sense of common cause and common identity, with the Corinthian church. The more the Corinthian church came to understand themselves not as free agents or independent contractors but as part of a larger church, a larger community of followers of Christ committed to the same faith and the same fundamental values and to living them out in love and with grace, the better it would be for them. The fact that a church met in their house suggests that Aquila and Priscilla were people of significant means, with a home capable of hosting a number of guests. Paul's statement that *the church* sent warm greetings implies that it was a reasonably united church, at least in their attitude toward the church in Corinth. As Weima points out, "By sending greetings from 'the churches of Asia' (v. 19a), 'Aquila and Prisca' (v. 19b) and 'all the brothers' (v. 20), Paul . . . subtly increases his own authority and the weight of his letter by aligning himself with a former leading family in the Corinthian church (Aquila and Prisca) and with the churches from the whole province of Asia." He also "stresses that these converts at Corinth are not a group unto themselves but belong to a much larger family of believers to whom they are accountable" (cf. 1:2 and the development of this theme throughout the letter).[67]

**16:20** Greetings are also sent by *all the brothers and sisters* in Ephesus. As in most other cases, the one plural word traditionally translated "brethren" is properly understood to include both men and women (see also 1:10-11, 26; 2:1; 3:1; 4:6; 6:8; 7:24, 29; 8:12; 9:5; 10:1; 11:33; 12:1; 14:6, 20, 26, 39; 15:1, 6, 31, 50, 58; 16:15).[68] Here the addition of *all* makes it clear that Paul is bringing greetings from all of the believers in Ephesus and not merely from the church that meets in the home of Aquila and Priscilla. Even if there were some question about the use of the term itself, in this case the fact that both Aquila and Priscilla send greetings in v. 19 leaves no doubt that Paul does not have the greetings of just the men in mind.

Paul recognized the importance of reinforcing the social bonds uniting believers and churches with one another in Christ. In addition to sending special greetings from a couple who were probably among the most important influences within the Corinthian church (Aquila and Priscilla), Paul presents greetings from the Christians in a province (Asia) and one of its cities (Ephesus). As mentioned in the comments on v. 19, those greetings reinforce the Corinthian church's relationship with fellow believers in other parts of the empire, a relationship which has not been much of a concern to them, it seems. Relationships within the Corinthian

67. Weima, *Neglected Endings*, 206.

68. In 15:11-12 Paul has a small group of men or men and women in mind. The Corinthians presumably know which brothers (or brothers and sisters) he has in mind, but we do not, making translation difficult. It could be a group of men like Stephanas, Fortunatus, and Achaicus (v. 17) or a mixed group (e.g., we do not know whether Chloe's people included women or not, but we know that women (such as Priscilla) did travel as part of Paul's apostolic team.

congregation have not been well nourished or protected either. Paul's instruction to *Greet one another*[69] *with a holy kiss* is intended to reinforce the bond of love, peace, and respect within the congregation. The practice of kissing upon greeting (as well as departing and in other contexts) was the general custom in Paul's world.[70] The Old Testament and early Jewish literature are full of references to greetings including kisses, especially, but not exclusively, between family members.[71] It is the fact that Paul's command to greet each other with a kiss "reflects a widespread custom of the time . . . which explains why the command can be given in a rather simple and constant formulaic expression without any accompanying word of explanation."[72] Paul's reference to the kiss that should be given as a holy kiss probably reflects, as Weima again suggests, two concerns. First, there was "the importance of maintaining proper and holy motives"[73] while carrying out the greeting (cf. the comment on the need to relate to younger women in the church "with absolute purity" in 1 Tim. 5:2). The reference to a holy kiss probably has more to do, though, with a distinction being made between the standard greeting practiced by others and that practiced by the saints/ believers:

> For others, the greeting kiss "could be simply an expression of friendship and good will, but among Christians it assumed a deeper meaning; it symbolized the unity, the belonging together of Christians, in the church of Jesus Christ." The kiss expressed not merely friendship and love, but more specifically reconciliation and peace (see Gen. 33.4; 45.15; 2 Kgs 14.33 [LXX]; Lk. 15.20). In fact, the kiss exchanged between believers soon was referred to by early Christians as the *osculum pacis* ("the kiss of peace").[74]

Weima points out that "Paul's four closing exhortations to greet others with a holy kiss all occur in contexts where some degree of conflict exists within the congregation."[75] Paul's instruction to *Greet one another with a holy kiss* is a call for a regular concrete expression of the oneness that is ours in Christ.[76]

69. The use of the aorist imperative for greetings such as this was the norm since it was a particular greeting that was being delivered and not a general practice that was being addressed (see 3 John 15 for an exception).

70. See G. Stählin, "φιλέω," *TDNT* 9:119-24, 125-27, 138-46, as well as Weima, *Neglected Endings*, 112-13 and the bibliography he gives at 112 n. 2.

71. See the list of passages given in Weima, *Neglected Endings*, 112.

72. Weima, *Neglected Endings*, 113.

73. Weima, *Neglected Endings*, 113.

74. Weima, *Neglected Endings*, 113, who cites S. Benko, "The Kiss," in Benko, *Pagan Rome and the Early Christians* (Bloomington: Indiana University Press, 1984), 98.

75. Weima, *Neglected Endings*, 114.

76. See Weima's brief discussion of the suggestion that vv. 20-23 reflect an early Christian liturgical sequence and that "Paul deliberately shaped the closing of 1 Corinthians to serve as a transition from the public reading of the letter to the celebration of the eucha-

## H. Paul's Final Greeting and Farewell, 16:21-24

Paul's final words to the Corinthians, the greeting he wrote with his own hand, emphasize the themes of love and grace.

> [21]*I, Paul, write this greeting in my own hand.*
> [22]*If anyone does not love the Lord, let that person be cursed! Come, Lord!*
> [23]*The grace of the Lord Jesus be with you.*
> [24]*My love to all of you in Christ Jesus. Amen.*

**16:21** We do not know who served as the scribe for the rest of the letter, but Paul indicates that he has taken the reed pen in his own hand, signaling both the conclusion of the letter and his approval of the contents as written up by whoever served as his secretary in this case: *I, Paul, write this greeting in my own hand.* It was common for authors to use a scribe or amanuensis to take down their dictation.[77] The extent to which the wording of a document reflected a scribe's diction rather than that of the actual author may have varied, but it was likely to be minimal. In any case, "[a] concluding paragraph, normally brief, in the author's handwriting showed that he had checked the final draft and assumed responsibility."[78] That Paul refers to these final words as his "greeting,"[79] after communicating other greetings in the previous two verses, suggests that he wanted his act of taking up the pen to write these final words before sending off the letter to be interpreted as one more evidence of his personal love and respect for his Corinthian readers.

**16:22** It was pointed out in the introduction to the letter that the centrality of Jesus Christ and his lordship is a prominent theme throughout its contents. Each of the final three verses refers to Christ in one way or another. This verse makes it perfectly clear that one's attitude toward and relationship with the Lord is of ultimate significance. *If anyone does not love the Lord, let that person be cursed! Come, Lord!* Only those who *love the Lord* should expect to enjoy the tremendous blessings that result from his sovereign reign. We are reminded of Genesis 12:2-3, where God promised Abraham:

---

rist," and his proper conclusion that these verses should be understood in terms of their epistolary function rather than any hypothetical liturgical background (*Neglected Endings,* 85-86).

77. For the most detailed discussion see E. Randolph Richards, *The Secretary in the Letters of Paul* (WUNT 2.42; Tübingen: J. C. B. Mohr, 1991), 15-67. A more accessible and concise discussion may be found in E. Randolph Richards, *Paul and First-Century Letter Writing: Secretaries, Composition, and Collection* (Downers Grove, IL: InterVarsity Press, 2004), 59-93, or Jerome Murphy-O'Connor, *Paul the Letter Writer: His World, His Options, His Skills* (Collegeville, MN: Liturgical Press, 1995), 1-16.

78. Murphy-O'Connor, *Paul the Letter Writer,* 7.

79. Gk. ἀσπασμός.

"I will make you into a great nation,
  and I will bless you;
I will make your name great,
  and you will be a blessing.
I will bless those who bless you,
  and whoever curses you I will curse;
and all peoples on earth
  will be blessed through you."

The picture is that of a great suzerain king, one's relationship with whom determines whether one experiences blessing or curse. The same idea is developed in other Old Testament messianic texts. Psalm 2:1-12, for example, speaks of the Davidic king as one to whom are promised "the nations" as his inheritance and "the ends of the earth" as his possession (v. 8). His enemies are warned, "Kiss his son, or he will be angry and you and your ways will be destroyed, for his wrath can flare up in a moment. Blessed are all who take refuge in him" (v. 12). Jesus Christ, *the Lord,* is that promised king, and while he brings blessing to all who take refuge in him, those who refuse to give him the love and respect he is due fall under the curse of destruction that will come upon "all dominion, authority and power" which stands against him (1 Cor. 15:24).

Paul calls for a curse on anyone who does not love the Lord (v. 22). In the Old Testament such a curse formula was "used when the intention was to discourage someone from transgressing . . . a far-reaching legal or ethical demand. In this case the curse formula is the most severe means of separating the community from the evildoer."[80] Here the fundamental demand upon the Christian community — that which distinguishes it as a community — is to love the Lord. As Garland and others have pointed out, to love the Lord "is part of covenant loyalty. The covenant brings curses to those who do not love and obey and bestows blessings on those who do (cf. 1 Cor. 2:9). . . . The unstated premise is that God requires love (Deut. 6:4-6), and those who do not love the Lord can expect only condemnation."[81]

Paul moves right from the curse to the Aramaic expression *"Marana tha"* ("Our Lord, Come!"), which points to "the coming of the Lord in judgment to redress wrong and establish right."[82] The expectation that the Lord

80. J. Scharbert, "ארר," *TDOT* 1:409-10.

81. Garland, 774.

82. Colin Brown et al., "μαραναθά," *NIDNTT* 2:897. Depending on how the letters are divided, the expression could also mean "the Lord has come!" or "the Lord will (soon, surely) come," although the evidence favors the rendering given by the TNIV (as well as the NIV, NRSV, ESV, NET, and NLT). See Thiselton, 1347-52, for a full discussion and bibliography. Matthew Black suggests, "Perhaps the popularity of the formula was its ambiguity and hence flexibility: it could be fitted into different contexts, in the eucharist, as an imprecation, or as a confession ('the Lord has come')" ("The Maranatha Invocation and Jude 14, 15 [1 Enoch 1:9]," in *Christ and Spirit in the New Testament: Studies in Honour of Charles Francis Digby Moule* [ed. B. Lindars and S. S. Smalley; Cambridge: Cambridge University Press], 196).

would come to redress wrong and establish his righteousness in the earth grew out of Old Testament prophetic and apocalyptic texts (see 13:8-12 on the day of the Lord) and is found throughout early Judaism (e.g., *1 Enoch* 1:9) and the New Testament (e.g., Matt. 3:7; Luke 3:7; Eph. 5:6; Col. 3:6; 1 Thess. 1:10; 2:14-16; Jude 14-15; Rev. 6:17).

**16:23** While the first three verses of the letter lack any finite verb (having only participles), the final two verses lack any verb at all. Paul's grace benediction, *The grace of the Lord Jesus be with you,* is the "most common epistolary convention of a Pauline letter closing,"[83] appearing in every Pauline letter. It always includes three parts: the wish *(grace),* the divine source *(of the Lord Jesus),*[84] and the recipient *(with you).* English translations (like the TNIV here) normally supply the verb *be.* While it is undoubtedly some form of the verb "to be" that should be supplied, it is not clear whether the mood to be inferred is that of an optative (as is common for wishes, including most of Paul's benedictions or wishes elsewhere in his letters), "may it be . . . ," or an imperative (as suggested by parallels with other ancient Greco-Roman letters), "let it be. . . ." As Weima points out, there is not much difference between these two views. We are either dealing with an "imperatival optative" or an imperative expressing "the nuance of the optative": either way "it is a wish that the apostle confidently expects will be received and realized in the lives of his readers."[85] Weima indicates that Paul's grace benediction was framed in light of the fact that contemporary farewell wishes had developed in such a way that besides serving as a simple good-bye, they also "expressed concern for the physical welfare of the letter recipient," and Paul's adaptation may have been intended "not only to signal the end of the letter but also to express concern for the spiritual welfare of his readers."[86] In this way he also formed an inclusio with the salutation given in 1:3.[87] Grace gives meaning not only to Paul's life and ministry but to the very existence of every Christian. The openings and closings of Paul's letters make it clear that he recognized how utterly dependent he and his churches were on God's grace and that his desire was for that grace to be fully recognized and experienced in every Christian believer and church. In every Pauline letter except this letter and the one to the Romans, the grace benediction comes as the final line. In this case Paul provides a final, unusual, postscript in v. 24.

83. Weima, *Neglected Endings,* 78.

84. Many textual witnesses read "Lord Jesus Christ," but the shorter reading (supported by א*, B, 2, 33, 35, 226, 356, 442, 823, 1611, 1908, 2004, vg, goth, *al*) is to be preferred. Metzger (*Textual Commentary,* 503-4) points out that "[i]n view of the presence of the longer reading in other Pauline benedictions (Ro 16.24; 2 Cor 13.13; Ga 6.18; Php 4.23; 1 Th 5.28; 2 Th 3.18; Phm 25), as well as the natural proclivity of scribes to expand the sacred name, it is perhaps remarkable that any witnesses should have resisted such pressures."

85. Weima, *Neglected Endings,* 84.

86. Weima, *Neglected Endings,* 87.

87. Weima, *Neglected Endings,* 87.

**16:24** Paul had already highlighted his love for the Corinthians in 4:14, 10:14, and 15:58. The theme of love has been on the table at least since 8:1 and was revealed to be the marvelous key to much of the letter in chapter 13 as it is the eternally consistent mark of God's renewed humanity. While Paul usually closes his letters with a grace benediction, as he brings this letter to a close he comes back one more time to the crucial motif of love: *My love to all of you in Christ Jesus. Amen.*[88] Paul literally says, "My love [is/be] with all of you in Christ Jesus." It is more likely that the indicative is in mind in this case: He does not merely wish his love to be with them;[89] it *is* with them. It is another way of saying that he loves them, perhaps a more striking way to say it, since it is less common than his frequent reference to them as his "dear ones" or "beloved" (as in 4:14; 10:14; 15:58). His inclusion of *all* of the Corinthian believers in this expression of his love reflects Paul's own emphasis on the need for love to be expressed to and among all the members of the body and not just between factions or cliques within it. His final words reflect what he has said about love in the body of the letter and the fact that his concern is, as theirs should be, with the edification of the whole church, for the glory of God.

88. "Amen" is found in א, A, C, D, Ψ, 075, 1739[c], 𝔐, lat, sy[h], bo, and Pelagius (and in ESV, NASB, NIV, TNIV, RSV, KJV) but not in B, F, 0121, 0243, 33, 81, 630, 1739*, 1881, *pc*, sy[p], sa, bo[mss], and Ambrosiaster (or in CSB, NAB, NET, NJB, NLT, NRSV). It seems easier to explain its later inclusion as a liturgical conclusion to the letter than to explain why other witnesses would have omitted it if it were original.

89. The meaning could be that he wishes for his love to be fully recognized, received, and appreciated by the Corinthians.

# Index of Subjects

# Index of Authors

# Index of Scripture References

## OLD TESTAMENT

## NEW TESTAMENT

# Index of Extrabiblical Literature

## GRAECO-ROMAN LITERATURE